PUBLIC LIBRARY
Stoneham, MA

D0812069

ALSO BY STEPHEN WALSH

The Lieder of Schumann

Bartók Chamber Music

The Music of Stravinsky

Stravinsky: Oedipus Rex

STRAVINSKY:

A CREATIVE SPRING

STRAVINSKY

A CREATIVE SPRING

RUSSIA AND FRANCE, 1882–1934

STEPHEN WALSH

Alfred A. Knopf

New York

1999

THIS IS A BORZOI BOOK
PUBLISHED BY ALFRED A. KNOPF

Copyright © 1999 by Stephen Walsh
All rights reserved under International and Pan-American Copyright
Conventions. Published in the United States by Alfred A. Knopf, a division of Random
House, Inc., New York, and simultaneously in Canada by Random House of Canada Limited,
Toronto. Distributed by Random House, Inc., New York.

www.randomhouse.com

Published in Great Britain by Jonathan Cape Ltd., London.

Knopf, Borzoi Books, and the colophon are registered
trademarks of Random House, Inc.

Owing to a limitation of space, all permissions to reprint previously published material
may be found immediately following the index.

ISBN: 0-679-41484-3

Manufactured in the United States of America
First Edition

For Alexander, Becky, Izzy, and Leo

CONTENTS

Photographic inserts follow pages 172 and 364.

INTRODUCTION

AMONG THE VOLUMINOUS writings on Stravinsky by his friend and musical assistant Robert Craft are a pair of articles in which he discusses the problems and feasibility of writing the biography of his former employer. The earlier of the two, "Stravinsky—Relevance and Problems of Biography," starts by making it disconcertingly clear that "so far from condoning any 'personal' biography, if Stravinsky had allowed himself to think about it, he would surely have specified in his will that none be written," and he asks, "Does anyone have the moral right to use Stravinsky's own materials for a biography he would not have wanted?"[1] In the later article, written some years after the composer's death, Craft presents the problem in a somewhat different light. "A comprehensive biography," he suggests, "is still far from being a possibility, for the reason that the crucial information about Stravinsky's formative years through the period of *Firebird* is lacking." "We need," he adds, "a book similar to that of Bronislava Nijinska about her brother." And he laments the fact that while "the diary of Stravinsky's father, which covers Igor's life until age twenty in great, especially financial, detail, provides some but not all of the essential clues . . . the few Russian musicologists who have had access to the volume do not employ an even remotely psychoanalytical approach to the biographical material about the infant and the young child."[2]

I quote these somewhat terrifying observations not as an indication of the problems addressed by the present life, but as a kind of purge, knowing that the Stravinsky community will expect nothing less than an answer to Craft's questions, and knowing that I cannot and do not intend to provide it. Nobody acquainted with Craft or his writings will doubt that the questions themselves express, among other things, a certain anxiety about his own place in the biographical process; and perhaps they are even an obstacle erected quite consciously in order to convince himself and others that he himself cannot and should not attempt such a book. The various caveats certainly make perfect sense for him. After all, he was so close to Stravinsky and so intimately a part of his personal, domestic, and professional existence that almost anything he might write about the last quarter of his life would be not biography but autobiography. As for the other three-quarters, his view is blocked precisely by that closeness which it would be the first task of any serious biographer to evade. Craft, in fact (as he himself admits), is the very last person who should write a biography of Stravinsky; and the next last is anyone else who allows himself to be troubled by the anxieties Craft expresses.

Admittedly, if Stravinsky foresaw a "psychoanalytical" biography, it is not surprising that he feared it and did his best to make it unwritable, by (as Craft says) destroying papers and by (as Craft does not say) reinventing his own past in that wonderful series of conversation books which form such a bright flashing mirror in the eyes of anyone trying to glimpse the realities behind them. But to suggest that it might be "immoral" to write a simple life because its subject would not have wanted it done is no more than to suggest that only the official biography is morally acceptable, whereas historians know that the official biography is precisely the one that is historically (if not psychoanalytically) worthless. And history is surely crucial to our moral well-being. In any case, whatever else it may be, the present book—the first of two volumes on a huge and complex subject—is not official. Nor, by the way, is it psychoanalytical, though it inevitably contains remarks of a more or less psychological kind.

So much for what the book is not. I must now try to say what it is.

The need for a new biography of Stravinsky lies not in any need to illuminate his Freudian relationship with his parents, but in the much more basic need to establish the facts. There are complex reasons why this has never actually been done before. Until quite recently, Russianist musicologists spent most of their time on the nineteenth century, while twentieth-century composers like Stravinsky who left Russia in the emigration were studied by modern specialists who generally did not know Russian and had neither knowledge of nor interest in the particular artistic and social context in which such a composer had grown up. On these matters they turned to the master himself for information, and by and large the picture they formed was the one he wanted formed. Yet Stravinsky had turned against his Russian artistic origins in the twenties, and had begun to cultivate the image of the "synthetic" international master who owed little or nothing to provincial roots. And by the time he met Robert Craft in the United States after the Second World War, and particularly by the time Craft began to collect Stravinsky's reminiscences and table talk in the conversation books of the late fifties and early sixties, his Russian past was little more than a picturesque memory, a source of colorful anecdote, occasionally of special insight, but seldom of accurate record and almost never of proper psychological (never mind psychoanalytical) accounting.

When Stravinsky died in 1971, it was nevertheless Craft who was in a position to chronicle, publish, and annotate the hundred or more boxes of papers the composer left, before they were eventually sold in 1983 to Paul Sacher in Basle, where they now reside. Craft duly published a large and fascinating documentary biography, a diary, three volumes of letters, two "scrapbooks" of photographs and other documents, and a heavily foot-noted selection of diaries and letters of the composer's second wife, Vera, as well as a stream of articles and reviews, all of which established beyond question his unique authority as arbiter of what did and did not wash in Stravinsky biographical studies. In all this editorial work, Craft showed an encyclopedic grasp of contextual detail, a disconcerting but often highly stimulating penchant for lateral or associative thinking, an acute musical intelligence, and a mastery of English prose that is, alas, all too rare among those who write about music. What it did not show—and this must now be said—is a talent for factual or even textual accuracy. Admittedly the editing of Stravinsky's correspondence presented unusual problems. Not only was it as voluminous and wide-ranging as one might expect of a major artist who had had three nationalities and lived for nearly nine decades in four different countries, but it was in four main languages, not all of which the editor himself was able to read. For much of the actual translating, he was frankly dependent on others, some of whom—to judge from the results—were far from equal to the task. But how is one to account for much in these volumes that is purely editorial in character, the unexplained omis-sions, the wrong datings, the confused or reconstructed texts? These points need not be labored here, since they come up time and again in my own annotations of what follows. It only needs to be clearly stated that the body of critical English-language texts which are widely used and quoted as the most basic sources on Stravinsky's life and music are in fact textually and therefore materially unreliable to the point of being at times positively misleading in their presentation of the facts.

This is said with considerable reluctance, since I have no wish to belittle Craft's importance in Stravinsky's life or his crucial role as catalyst in the emergence of the composer's late style. To put it plainly, without Craft there probably would have been no *Agon,* no *Abraham and Isaac,* no *Requiem Canticles.* For me, this is quite sufficient to excuse any vagaries in his editorial work. Moreover, when I spent several days with him in Lon-don and Venice in 1995, recording conversations for a series of radio pro-grams, I began (or so I think) to understand better the complexity of the relationship between the two men and the extent of the personal sacrifice Craft had made—was in some respects still making—to the composer's muse, often in the face of relentless hostility from those who felt them-selves excluded by him or who saw in him an unscrupulous usurper of their family rights or intellectual influence. Detailed investigation of this topic belongs to the second volume of the present study. For the moment, I only want to make it absolutely clear that whatever criticisms may be made or implied in this first volume about Craft's editorial work are made in the context of a strong personal sympathy for the difficulty, verging at times on impossibility, of his role in Stravinsky's domestic and professional life, and an abiding gratitude to him for creating an intellectual environment within which Stravinsky could continue to produce new work, the best of which is equal to all but the very greatest he composed before Craft appeared on the scene.

Though Craft is to my mind wrong in thinking that Fyodor Stravinsky's account books afford "the essential clues" for a psychological study of his son, he is right that they are a major source of information about Igor's childhood, in that they provide a detailed material record of day-to-day activities which involved Fyodor in cash expenditure, whether the purchase of a comb or a pair of trousers, payments to priests or music teachers, or rail journeys to the country estates of his wife's relations. These account books remained unpublished until 1997, when Viktor Varunts included relevant extracts in the first volume of his *I. F. Stravinsky: Perepiska s russkimi korrespondentami*, a work mainly devoted to the comprehensive publication and annotation of Stravinsky's Russian-language correspondence. Thanks to Varunts's kindness, however, and that of Igor Stravinsky's great-niece Yelena Stravinskaya, who spent many hours at her St. Petersburg flat showing me the original account books and discussing their significance, and later supplied me with a draft of the Varunts extracts, I was able to incorporate the information in my biography from an early stage. In the same way, I was extremely fortunate that, precisely at the moment when I was starting research on the composer's early years, Varunts himself, with extraordinary generosity, put at my disposal his own transcripts of all the known surviving pre-1914 Russian-language manuscript materials (mainly letters) relating specifically to Igor Stravinsky. Although some of this material had previously been published, the bulk of it was unknown, much of it still scattered in Russian archives and difficult of access, not to mention legibility, to a foreign researcher like me. Working from Varunts's typescript, I was spared much of the agony of archival research in a Russia that, whatever the social and political changes of the past decade, remains in many essentials post-Soviet: bureaucratic, disorganized, and often (though by no means always) mindlessly obstructive. I love St. Petersburg and Moscow, but not even their best friends could claim that in the late 1990s they have been convenient places to live or work.

In one other respect to do with the Russian end of things I was fortunate at the outset. In 1996 Richard Taruskin brought out his brilliant and monumental *Stravinsky and the Russian Traditions,* and here once again I had an early sight of the text, partly through the author's generosity, partly through my own guile in making sure that the book's intending (and eventual) English publisher had my name well up his list of potential readers.

The importance of Taruskin's book to mine will be evident to anyone who reads both, and is in any case duly and I hope adequately acknowledged in my text and footnotes. Taruskin was the first writer to investigate and properly evaluate Stravinsky's musical background, including the Rimsky-Korsakov circle and its prehistory and the whole social and artistic context of the *Mir iskusstva* group, and his book, though not without its own distortions and exaggerations, is in the main a deeply convincing corrective to the "official" picture of the pre-*Firebird* years as a kind of inverted Nazarene childhood, "a period of waiting for the moment when I could send everyone and everything connected with it to hell."[3]

Apart from its actual text, Taruskin's book was important to me in drawing my attention to a large number of published Russian-language sources, including newspaper and journal articles, memoirs, and other such materials, nearly all of which had been ignored by previous writers on Stravinsky, including me. In most cases, I have consulted these materials for myself, and on occasion I have disagreed with Taruskin as to their interpretation. But this does not alter my indebtedness, which I hereby warmly acknowledge. It is perhaps fair to add that Taruskin does not deal, except cursorily, with Stravinsky's domestic life and is generally not much interested in its physical environment. These aspects of my book, whatever their virtues and defects, are, I think, new.

Also my own are the bulk of the English translations of Russian texts quoted, and this is equally the case with translations from other languages where I have had access to the originals. A specific problem arises over quotations from Craft's English translations of correspondence. As noted above, these translations are in general unreliable, and I have sought wherever possible to refer back to the original texts (published or otherwise) and have almost always preferred to retranslate, while still supplying reference to the published translation. The reason for this somewhat cumbersome procedure is that I do not wish to deny my debt to Craft even where I reject his versions. This debt extends well beyond the inevitably somewhat pragmatic use to which I have put his own writings. In some fourteen years of personal correspondence he has been constantly generous with advice, information, and what I might term biographical confidences. Moreover, it was from contact with him and his work that I first derived that feeling for the complications and contradictions in Stravinsky's personality which I hope informs the pages that follow. To the extent that this entails the blurring of those simple moral and psychological distinctions—the black-and-white juxtaposition of good and bad qualities—which have formed the basis of Stravinsky biographical small-talk ever since he himself began bullying concert agents and lying to journalists soon after the First World War, I owe the initial perception to Craft, though he will certainly not agree with all my conclusions on the subject. If, that is, my book breathes human sympathy for Stravinsky the man as well as the composer, I am indebted to Craft for reminding me that we love our friends not only for their virtues, and that it is the richest personalities who engage us most fully in the endless battle between reason and feeling, and between mammon and God.

A BOOK OF THIS KIND could not have been written without help from many quarters. I am indebted to several Russian friends for easing my path in Moscow, St. Petersburg, and elsewhere, especially Viktor Varunts and Mikhail Lobanov, who secured me introductions and accommodation, helped with materials, and have been unstinting in their friendship and support; Svetlana Savenko, who was my first Russian contact; Lyudmila Koryabelnikova, Galina Grigoreva, Valery Glivinsky, and Natalya Savkina, all of whom sacrificed their own precious research time to help me decipher Russian script; Yelena Ogneva, the Russian curator of the Volhynian Regional Museum in Lutsk, and an authority on Stravinsky's association with Ustilug, among other things; and Olga Rïbakova, the director of the Lomonosov (Oranienbaum) School of Music. Above all, I am deeply grateful to Yelena Stravinskaya, and her husband, Vsevolod Stepanov, for detailed information about the Stravinsky family, for the supply of materials, for guidance in recapturing the atmosphere of prerevolutionary Russia, and above all for their generous hospitality, to me and various members of my family.

One of the main pleasures of Stravinsky research today is that it entails frequent and extended visits to the Paul Sacher Stiftung in Basle, which has owned the Stravinsky Archive since 1983. The present study would have been inconceivable without the friendly, long-suffering, and efficient help of the Stiftung's archivists and musicologists, and I should like here formally to thank them all for putting up with me so often and for so long. In particular I am indebted to Ingrid Westen and to Ulrich Mosch and his predecessor Hans Jörg Jans for placing at my disposal their expert knowledge of the contents of the archive, for answering questions and supplying materials; to Lukas Handschin, Sabine Hänggi-Stampfli, Christina Dreier, Tina Kilvio Tüscher, and Johanna Blask for tireless practical backup; and to Felix Meyer, Robert Piencikowski, and Niklaus Röthlin for technical advice on various matters. I also received help from other visiting scholars, especially Margarita Mazo, Tom Gordon, and Angelo Cantoni.

On Polish matters I have been heavily dependent on outside assistance. Stefan Strawinski kindly supplied me with genealogies of the Polish branches of the composer's family and information on various related matters. Adam Zamoyski and Norman Davies answered questions on Polish history. Katherine Tylko-Hill and Alina Maciag translated essential Polish texts for me. Similar thanks are due to Karel Janovicky for information about Prague concert halls, and to Dominic Lieven for advice on Russian genealogy. On general historical questions I have been helped by Norman Stone, Mark Almond, and Robert Stradling; on matters of art history by Richard Dorment. Stewart Spencer tracked down Bayreuth performance dates. Oliver W. Neighbour provided detailed information on Stravinsky's *Khovanshchina* chorus and a photocopy of the sketches. Michael Nagy briefed me on the Abbado recording of that work. Noel Malcolm supplied information about Enesco's U.S. travels. Jeanice Brooks answered a stream of questions about Nadia Boulanger and the princesse de Polignac and put me in touch with the Polignac specialist, Sylvia Kahan, who was no less helpful. Joan Evans generously provided me with advance typescripts of several important articles by her on Stravinsky's relations with Germany in the twenties and thirties. Rex Lawson photocopied for me an entire file of documents relating to Stravinsky and Pleyel, and cleared up many problems to do with the Pianola and the reproducing piano. Annette Morreau took time out from her own research on Feuermann to chase up Stravinsky's American concert dates. Richard Buckle kindly answered questions on Diaghilev. Daniel Entin, of the Nicholas Roerich Museum in New York, dropped valuable hints about the origins of the *Rite of Spring* scenario. Luke Howard and Peter Faint shared with me their findings on Szymanowski and Jack Hylton, respectively. Philip Stuart put me right on a number of details to do with Stravinsky's recordings. Stephen Roe, of Sotheby's, was ever helpful and cooperative in allowing me sight of sale materials. Grateful thanks are also due to Patrick Dillon and Kevin Bourke for incisive editorial work, which spared me much error and inconsistency; and to Paul Griffiths and Colin Slim, for generously reading the text and making innumerable suggestions, on both factual and structural matters. Thanks to their sharp perceptions and critical sympathy, the book is appreciably better than it would otherwise have been. Finally, Chuck Elliott has been a crucial moral support and patient technical adviser throughout the book's protracted incubation.

From the start, I made contact with as many friends and acquaintances of Stravinsky as I could find, and, though I had one or two refusals, I found in general a gratifyingly high degree of willingness to give time reminiscing about this protean personality. I should like to express my sincere thanks—alas, in some cases posthumously—to the following for their kind cooperation. Elliott and Helen Carter; the late Vittorio Rieti; the late Paul Horgan; Edwin Allen; Claudio Spies; Betty Bean; Dominique Nabokov; Ivan Nabokov; the late Sir Stephen Spender and Lady Spender; the late Sir Isaiah Berlin; Henry Hardy; William T. Brown; Don Bachardy; Mae and Eve Babitz; Theodore Norman; Marilyn Stalvey; Miranda Levy; Brigitta Lieberson; Jean Stein; Madeleine Milhaud; John Andrewes; David Adams; Albi Rosenthal; Arthur Berger; Glenn Watkins; John Carewe; and David Drew. In general Stravinsky's own surviving family were, for a variety of perfectly understandable reasons, reluctant to talk to yet another potential nuisance; but his cousin Michel (Mikhail) Yelachich (who is also married to his granddaughter) treated me to a long, informative, and entertaining evening in Paris. Not all the material thus garnered has a place in this first volume of the composer's biography, and none of it has automatically been treated as authoritative. Nevertheless, such encounters provide an invaluable personal and anecdotal corrective to the tendency of library archives to stereotype and dehumanize their subject matter, and I learnt a great deal from them all.

I had much help from Stravinsky's various publishers and those who work for them: especially Tony Fell, Janis Susskind, Malcolm Smith, and Sylvia Goldstein (all of Boosey and Hawkes), James Rushton and the late Sheila McCrindle (of Chester Music Ltd), Eric Forder (of Schott/Universal), and Sally Cavender (of Faber Music). I am also indebted to the staffs of many libraries and archives in several different countries, but especially to John Shepard of the New York Public Library, J. Rigby Turner of the Pierpont Morgan Library, and Harry Joelson-Strohbach of the Stadtbibliothek in Winterthur. My own music department at Cardiff University has also been a fund of material and moral assistance, in both cash and infrastructural terms, and in the tricky matter of study leave. I should like to thank all my departmental colleagues for their support, tacit or otherwise. But in particular Timothy Taylor expended many hours of his own time, and much nervous energy, helping me combat that peculiar demon of modern life, the computer gremlin. Anthony Powers lent me books and kept me relatively sane by talking to me about Stravinsky's music. Finally, I wish to thank the staff of the department's music library, especially Gill Jones and Judith Hurford, for their unstinting help in locating sources and securing materials, often of an obscure and specialized character.

Work on the biography has been supported by funds from a variety of sources. A year of research in the Paul Sacher Stiftung soon after it opened in 1986 was made financially possible by a research award from the British Academy, who also subsequently paid for a three-month study leave under their Research Leave Scheme. The Leverhulme Trust gave me a substantial travel grant, without which a book entailing so much research in Russia, the Ukraine, France, Switzerland, Germany, Britain, and the United States would, at best, have had a very different character. I am deeply grateful to both these institutions.

As ever, the chief victims of all this have been my wife and children: but they have not remained passive. Alexander and Isobel, Russianists both, helped me in various ways in Moscow and St. Petersburg; Becky corrected my German and reorganized my filing system; Leo transcribed materials from the Paul Sacher Stiftung. My wife, Mary, has been an unfailing source of practical help and good advice. I am grateful to them all for enduring what has inevitably tended to become an obsession. Alas, their sufferings are by no means at an end. Volume 2 remains.

STRAVINSKY:

A CREATIVE SPRING

THE POLISH SINGER

THE SMALL TOWN of Oranienbaum lies on the southern shore of the Gulf of Finland, some fifty kilometers to the west of St. Petersburg. The ground rises gently from the sea to what remains today the main feature of the place, the great baroque palace of Peter the Great's corrupt favorite Prince Alexander Menshikov, with its rambling Dutch park—now, alas, somewhat forlorn—originally laid out in 1714. At one corner of the park a lake debouches into a stream by way of a modest waterfall surrounded by rocks and pine trees, a sufficiently Alpine setting, apparently, for the street which runs east from the park gate nearby to have been christened with the otherwise absurdly fanciful name Shveytsarskaya Ulitsa—Swiss Street.

But another, less imaginary thread links this provincial Russian street with the land of the cuckoo clock and the numbered bank account. For it was here, in the wooden dacha of one Khudïntsev—Oranienbaum house number 137—that Igor Fyodorovich Stravinsky was born at noon on 5/17 June 1882.* And while Switzerland may have left its faint mark on Oranienbaum, Oranienbaum was to leave an indelible imprint on Switzerland, a fact also recorded in a street name, no less incongruous—that of the rue Sacre du Printemps in the suburbs of Clarens, on the northern shore of Lake Geneva.

Like most provincial towns of what was once the Soviet Union, Oranienbaum is today a depressing epitaph to three-quarters of a century of bad management, bad economics, and bad architecture. The Soviets destroyed it by their own unique combination of neglect and vandalism. Menshikov's park, with its palaces and walks, was left to decay; but much of what otherwise remained from tsarist times, and survived the German bombardment of the early forties, was bulldozed and replaced by concrete and gray brick which, as usual, in turn soon crumbled and peeled. The town's name was changed from the too-German, too-Petrine "Orange Tree" to the harder-nosed Lomonosov, in honor of an eighteenth-century

---

*For an explanation of Old and New Style datings, see Appendix.

philologist from chilly Archangel. Shveytsarskaya Street became Ulitsa Vosstaniya—Revolution Street. The dacha Khudïntseva was heedlessly pulled down and replaced in 1934 by an electricity substation, itself now rusting and decrepit.[1] Of all the great birthplaces of Western art, this must surely be one of the most philistine and dispiriting.

More than seventy-five years later, Stravinsky told Robert Craft that "we never returned to Oranienbaum after my birth . . . and I have never seen it since."[2] But on this, as on countless other points of fact, his memory betrayed him. The Stravinskys went back to Oranienbaum at least twice, in the summers of 1884 and 1885, and Igor's younger brother, Gury, was born there too, on 30 July/11 August 1884, though in a different house.[3] The place was a fashionable summer resort for the Petersburg artistic-literary intelligentsia, and since Igor's father was a singer and a bibliophile, he was merely following a trend by summering there. Tolstoy, Nekrasov, and Fet, among writers, and—among painters—the realist *peredvizhniki* ("wanderers") Savrasov, Shishkin, and Repin, all stayed and worked in Oranienbaum.[4] Stravinsky apart, musicians remember it as the place where Musorgsky spent his last summer (1880), working on *Khovan-shchina* and *Sorochintsï Fair,* and quietly drinking himself to death.[5] In the second half of the nineteenth century a theatre was built in the station square, and Fyodor Stravinsky performed some of his best-known operatic roles there, including Varlaam in Musorgsky's *Boris Godunov,* Farlaf in Glinka's *Ruslan and Lyudmila,* and (a month or two after Gury's birth) Ramfis in Verdi's *Aida.*[6] Fyodor would transport his entire household to Oranienbaum in about the middle of May, and he himself would commute to and from St. Petersburg, Viborg, or even distant Moscow, according to the pattern of his performance schedule. It so happens that there was a family connection with Oranienbaum, since Fyodor's wife, Anna Kiril-lovna, had a first cousin, Ivan Ivanovich Kholodovsky, living there, and the account books record at least one subsequent visit by the Stravinsky children (in February 1892). Dyadya (Uncle) Vanya, as he was known to them, was an army general whose uniform braid Igor remembered sucking while he was being held up for a photograph.[7] We may picture Anna and her cousins walking in the Menshikov park in the high summer of 1884 with her four sons: Roman, aged eight, Yury, aged five, the two-year-old Igor, perhaps hand-in-hand with his stout German *nyanya* (nurse), Bertha Essert, and the tiny Gury, strapped to his wet nurse. Although no such actual photographs have survived from that age of studio portraiture, and although Igor Stravinsky remembered nothing of Oranienbaum itself, we can construct the rather stiff, well-behaved, Victorian family group, matri-archal and unsmiling, from the evidence of somewhat later family por-traits which do survive. Or was the reality, in Fyodor's occasional absence, more unruly?

As with every family event of the least importance, Fyodor Stravinsky recorded Igor's birth in painstaking calligraphic detail in his account book, together with the name of a young lady, Tatyana Yakovlev, who was to be his wet nurse for the first twelve months of his life; and he also kept the page of the calendar for that day, carefully inscribed with information about the birth, and with the name of the baby's personal saint—the Holy Martyr Prince Igor—pasted onto the page in addition to the official saints and martyrs listed for that day.[8] A mere six days earlier, Fyodor had been in Moscow singing Galitsky's aria from *Prince Igor* in a concert conducted by Anton Rubinstein, and Richard Taruskin argues that, while conventionally naming his son after a listed (if obscure) saint, the proud father really had in mind the less-than-saintly hero of Borodin's opera.[9] The implication that Fyodor had some special sense of his third son's musical destiny (since, after all, he apparently made no attempt at operatic names for the other three) might seem contradicted by Stravinsky's later recollection of his parents' disdain for his musical talent.[10] But as we shall see, the composer's memories of his family relations are no more to be trusted than his supposed reminiscences of his own baptism in the Nikolsky Cathedral, St. Petersburg, on 29 July/10 August 1882, which he describes in sensational detail, even down to his "intestinal reaction" at being immersed.[11] Of course, we are not really asked to believe that these are personal memories, merely a blend of family tradition with normal Orthodox observance. They do nevertheless draw attention to a contradiction between what Stravinsky tells us he felt about his childhood and what he actually felt about it if we believe surviving contemporary documents. Fyodor's "naming and honoring of the chosen one"—like the one in *The Rite of Spring*—may be a little too emblematic for real life, but it was nevertheless the prelude to a childhood of profound intensity and richness which Stravinsky never forgot and which colored his attitude, both to the world and to art, for the rest of his days.

Like all events and entities, every child is a zero point from which both the past and the future radiate outwards. But with Stravinsky the effect was magnified by war, revolution, and exile, and the sense of severance from the past is, with him, particularly acute. He himself expressed this (rather than any factual truth) when he told Craft that "the real answer to your questions about my childhood is that it was a period of waiting for the moment when I could send everyone and everything connected with it to hell."[12] But who exactly were the objects of this strange and surely retrospective Messianic venom?

The Stravinskys were, in the terms of late tsarist Russia, down-graded *dvoryane,* or minor nobility, though if we were to interpret that in modern Western terms, we should probably describe them as well-connected bourgeoisie, or perhaps urbanized gentry. Anna Kirillovna Stravinskaya, Igor's mother, came decidedly from the landowning, gov-erning classes of nineteenth-century Russia. Her maternal grandfather, Roman Fyodorovich Furman (1784–1851), had been a Privy Councillor *(taynïy sovetnik)* to Nicholas I and a finance minister on the governing council of the so-called Kingdom of Poland (actually by this time a fief of the Russian Empire), while Roman Furman's father, an agronomist origi-nally from Saxony, had attained the lesser, but nevertheless distinguished, rank of Court Councillor *(nadvornïy sovetnik).*[13] Moreover, Roman's mother, Yelizaveta Engel, belonged to another blue-blooded family of Privy Coun-cillors, while his aunt Anna Engel herself married into the aristocratic Litke family, and her children included two of the most famous admirals in modern Russian history, one of whom was incidentally also the great-grandfather of Sergey Diaghilev.[14]

Anna Kirillovna Stravinskaya was hardly less well connected on the paternal side. Her father, Kirill Grigorevich Kholodovsky (1806–1855), though he owned no land,[15] was a second- or third-generation nobleman who, like Furman, achieved high political rank under Nicholas I: he became a State Councillor, a member of the Council of Thirty, and Assis-tant Minister of State Properties. At the time of the birth of his youngest daughter in 1854, Kholodovsky was for some reason living in Kiev. Anna was the last of four daughters, and the only one who did not marry a landowner. Her widowed mother, Maria Romanovna, seems indeed to have opposed her marriage on these grounds, though Anna's youth (she was still only nineteen at the time of her wedding in May 1874 [OS]) and the fact that her intended was a musician were doubtless factors as well. Fyodor's letters of the time even had to be delivered covertly through a sympathetic Kholodovsky aunt. "It's terribly disagreeable for me, and even somewhat painful and distressing," he wrote from Odessa, "that Mamasha is so upset as to be actually growing thin and ill; I thought and think that the reason lies not simply in the idea of being separated from you, my dear, but in the fact that she perhaps regrets having agreed to our marriage at all; if so, then it will now be too painful for me to see her."[16]

For all Maria Romanovna's disapproval, Fyodor could point to quarter-ings no less impressive than his future wife's, even if he had a good deal less to show for it in material terms. The Stravinsky family, like the name, is Polish, a fact which needs to be stressed in view of recent and per-fectly understandable attempts by Kiev scholars to claim Stravinsky as a Ukrainian of Cossack lineage.[17] The so-called Soulima-Stravinskys are more accurately described as "Strawinscy Herbu Sulima," to adopt for the moment the old Polish spelling of the two names: that is, the Strawinscy family with the Sulima coat-of-arms. This simply means, for our purposes, that this branch of the Strawinscys claimed descent from the more ancient—probably German—house of Sulima. Stefan Strawinski traced the family tree back to the late sixteenth century, when the Strawinscys held high state office, in a kingdom where there were no hereditary titles and power was symbolized by honorific titles associated with purely ceremonial duties. For instance, there was a Strawinsky *Kasztelan* (castellan) of Minsk and Vitebsk, and another Strawinscy *Kasztelan* of Brest, who later became *Voyevoda*—that is, Governor—of the province of Minsk. These posts brought with them seats in the Polish Senate and royal lieutenancies; in other words, their holders were ceremonial grandees like modern British lords lieutenant, and inevitably they were large landowners. Gradually the family fortunes declined. In the next generation (the mid-seventeenth century), Strawinscys held honorary stewardships and magistracies; one Krzysztof Strawinscy was *czesnik oszmianski*—cupbearer at Oshmyany, a town between Vilnius and Minsk. But these were altogether more provincial appointments, conferring purely local authority. Of Fyodor's great-great-grandfather Stanislaw Strawinscy (who married in 1748) we otherwise know only that he inherited a village called Szokinie, in the Strava region, but, instead of leaving it to his eldest son, sold it to a nephew and, presumably, spent the money. A mere three generations later Fyodor's father, Ignaty Ignatyevich (1809–93), is no longer a freeholder at all, but a lease-holder and a working estate manager and agronomist, in the village of Novïy Dvor near Gomel in the southeastern corner of what is today Belarus, but was then in the Minsk province of tsarist Russia.[18]

While the genealogy depicts a gradual decay in the social and economic standing of the Szokinie Stravinskys (to revert, now, to a transliterated Russian spelling), the geography reveals a parallel southeasterly drift, but always within the borders of the ancient Grand Duchy of Lithuania—the eastern half of the pre-Napoleonic kingdom of Poland. To put this another way, Stravinsky territory was, very roughly, modern Belarus: that is, White Russian–speaking and Orthodox, as opposed to Polish and Roman Catholic. Nevertheless, according to the composer, Fyodor's father was still Catholic, while Fyodor was baptized Orthodox only because his Russian mother, Alexandra Ivanovna Skorokhodova (1817–98), was Orthodox, and under Imperial Russian law—relevant in the former Polish eastern territories after the partition of 1793—the children of a mixed marriage had to be Orthodox.[19] We can add, speculatively, that in wedding the daughter of a Russian Orthodox small-landowner in the remote southeast of those territories, Ignaty Stravinsky was marrying well beneath himself and his ancestry, but also that, in turning his children into Russians, he was opening to them new horizons and a new culture. Fyodor's somewhat rootless success as an opera singer might not have been possible without his first being *déclassé* and depolonized.

Ignaty Ignatyevich, Fyodor's father, seems in any case not to have taken kindly to his Orthodox wife, nor she to him. According to the composer, Ignaty was a womanizer; and according to the composer's niece Xenia, he was a bad businessman and a failure at estate management.[20] At all events the couple separated and soon divorced. Perhaps this was even as early as the 1840s, since Fyodor Stravinsky, who was born in 1843, was brought up in the house of his maternal grandfather at Bragin and later recalled sitting in the window of this house with his *nyanya*, watching the Cossacks ride home from the Hungarian war of 1848–49.[21] Ignaty went off to Poltava, in the Ukraine, where he again perhaps failed as an estate manager, since he ended his long life in Tiflis, in the house of his daughter Olga Dïmchevsky.

There is a bizarre footnote to this tale of Fyodor's ancestry. The maternal grandfather, Ivan Ivanovich Skorokhodov (1767–1879), is none other than the "old gentleman" of Stravinsky's *Dialogues,* who died at the age of III "as a result of a fall while trying to scale the garden fence on his way to a rendezvous."[22] This irresistible picture is both too good and too obviously apocryphal to be worth denying. But Skorokhodov seems to have been no philanderer like his son-in-law, but a sweet old man who put a roof over his daughter and her children and was still worrying about his grandchildren's welfare after they were married. A gentle, uncomplicated letter survives from him to Fyodor Stravinsky, among other things congratulating Fyodor's son Roman on his second birthday.[23] It is an awe-inspiring thought that if Roman had been Igor, or if Skorokhodov had survived three more years, composer and great-grandfather would between them have spanned two centuries of continuous life.

WHEN HE DECAMPED to Poltava, Ignaty Stravinsky left behind him four children, of whom Fyodor (1843–1902) was by some way the youngest. His two elder brothers, Alexander (1835–1916) and Konstantin (b. 1839), were both army officers, and his sister, Olga (b. 1837), also probably married a soldier (Dïmchevsky), since military service is the most likely reason for their having settled in the Caucasus. According to Craft, Fyodor was brought up apart from his sister and brothers,[24] which may, however, have been simply because his brothers had gone off to the army and his sister married by the time he was fourteen. Neither Uncle Konstantin nor Aunt Olga turns up in any connection with Igor Stravinsky, but he certainly knew his uncle Alexander Ignatyevich. A letter to his mother in St. Petersburg in the summer of 1903 refers to a bicycle accident in which Uncle Sasha had broken his leg while staying in the capital.[25]

Another explanation for Fyodor's separation from his older siblings may simply be that he was sent away to school, first at the Dvoryanskiy Uchilishche (School for Gentlemen) in Mozïr', some fifty miles from Bragin, then later at the gymnasia in Nezhin, away to the southeast of Chernigov, and (once more) Mozïr'. One of his Mozïr' teachers remembered him as "a tall, well-built, handsome young man [he was 18] distinguished by his good manners, who didn't have to be crammed but did his work with intelligence."[26] Perhaps Fyodor did work hard; after all, as a scholarship boy he was doomed to earn his living. But something more irresistible was already beginning to claim him. He had found his voice.

We do not know how or when music first came into Fyodor Stravinsky's life, but it may not have been much before Mozïr', since he never learnt a musical instrument, and there is no record of music playing a major part in the Stravinsky or Skorokhodov household.[27] At Mozïr', he joined the gymnasium choir and "was soon attracting the attention of the whole town" with his singing.[28] By his last year in the gymnasium (1864–65) he was taking roles in student operatic productions. But nothing seems to have been said about a musical career. Fyodor would study for the law: first at the New Russian University in Odessa; then, the next year, 1866, in the Faculty of Jurisprudence at the University of Kiev.

Naturally his abandoned mother was anxious on his account. She had two sons going to war, and perhaps a son-in-law as well. At least her youngest son would pass his exams, get onto the lowest rung of the civil service, and by this means—such was the Russian system—secure himself a position for life.[29] But there were two major snags. On the one hand, Alexandra Ivanovna's money was beginning to run out; and on the other, Fyodor's singing was starting to outstrip his enthusiasm for jurisprudence. It must have been almost the last straw when in 1868 he was forced by sheer penury to abandon his studies in Kiev and return to Nezhin, whose law school was more within the family means.[30] At any rate, his year in Nezhin seems to have been marked by concert giving at least as much as law studies. Nevertheless, he proceeded to St. Petersburg intending to take up a job in the Ministry of Justice, and only after he arrived there was he persuaded by friends to audition for a scholarship at the Conservatoire.[31]

These details of Fyodor Stravinsky's upbringing are unfamiliar to Western readers because, outside Russia, he has always been and is to this day known almost exclusively as the father of Igor Stravinsky, and the fact that he was a successful singer has been known, as it were, contingently, like the fact that Dvořák's father was a butcher. But in Russia things were quite different. From not very long after his debut on the stage of the Mariyinsky Theatre as Mephistopheles in Gounod's *Faust* in April 1876 until his final appearance, as Zuniga in Bizet's *Carmen*, on 3/16 February

1902, Stravinsky was almost unanimously regarded by his compatriots as one of the great operatic bass-baritones of his day. Unfortunately, as Richard Taruskin has observed,[32] not only did he never sing abroad—since he died just before the great Western "discovery" of Russian opera—but he also finished just too early for his voice to be commercially recorded; so his reputation remained local and, after his death, a matter of history. Unlike his great successor Chaliapin, we can judge him today only vicariously, through the opinions of his contemporaries, and through the parts he sang and especially those he created or that were written for him.

Stravinsky's twenty-six-year career coincided with what was undoubtedly a flowering of Russian opera, even though relatively few of the works in question ever entered the Western repertoire. This was the period of most of the operas of Tchaikovsky and Rimsky-Korsakov, the last two (unfinished) operas of Musorgsky, Borodin's *Prince Igor,* and a whole crop of lesser works by figures such as Cui, Taneyev, Rubinstein, and others whose very names are now barely remembered. The most famous of all Russian operas, Musorgsky's *Boris Godunov,* had already had its premiere by the time Fyodor arrived at the Mariyinsky, but he naturally sang in it (though never the title role), and his portrayal of Varlaam was one of the main factors in the opera's *succès d'estime* when it was revived for the first time in Rimsky-Korsakov's arrangement in 1896. His Farlaf in Glinka's *Ruslan and Lyudmila* was also famous, as was his Holofernes in Alexander Serov's *Judith*—a forgotten opera by a forgotten composer whose works were nevertheless repertory pieces in turn-of-the-century Russia. He created many roles, mainly character parts, including the Mayor in *May Night* and Grandfather Frost in *The Snow Maiden* (both by Rimsky-Korsakov), Skula in Borodin's *Prince Igor,* and, most famously, Mamïrov in Tchaikovsky's *Enchantress.*[33] And finally, of course, he dominated his field in the non-Russian character-bass repertory, singing Mozart (Leporello in *Don Giovanni*), Verdi (Sparafucile in *Rigoletto,* Ramfis in *Aida,* Pistol in *Falstaff*), Wagner (the Landgrave in *Tannhäuser,* Henry the Fowler in *Lohengrin,* Colonna in *Rienzi*), Weber (Kaspar in *Der Freischütz*), Meyerbeer (St. Bris in *Les Huguenots,* Don Diego in *L'Africaine*), and much else.

Although Chaliapin, when he came, was regarded as Stravinsky's successor (and was at first accused of imitating him),[34] it will already be apparent that the emphasis of their careers, and probably of their artistry too, was subtly different. Chaliapin finally conquered through an outsize voice, physical stature, and stage personality which he was willing to use to their limits regardless of inhibitions about taste or intellectual subtlety. Stravinsky, though his large repertoire included several major roles, was often content to show his mastery in relatively insignificant parts, which he studied exhaustively and with a painstaking approach to details of appearance and vocal inflection. About the quality of his voice, opinions differed.

Igor Stravinsky himself remembered it as beautiful though latterly in decline,[35] and referred in his autobiography to Fyodor's "beautiful voice and . . . amazing technique."[36] Fyodor's graduation report from the Conservatoire praised his "strong, sonorous and fresh bass, well honed, and of a very agreeable timbre . . . a voice which Mr. Stravinsky controls well, highly suitable for the stage."[37] The critic Edward Stark notes, on the other hand, that his voice was "not distinguished by beauty of timbre, [but] rather dry, and this dryness of timbre made itself particularly felt towards the end of his career."[38]

There were, however, no two opinions about his genius as a vocal actor. The period was one in which every medium of Russian art was dominated by the idea of realism, and though many operas of the time may now seem "realistic" only in the sense of a stereotyped, pasteboard verism, they still clearly offered opportunities for the delineation of individual character, particularly in minor roles, which did not have to carry the burden of heroism or romantic passion that lay at the core of most plots and of course dominated the music. Hence it may be significant that while Chaliapin is remembered in the overpowering but essentially "ham" part of Boris Godunov, Stravinsky was successful in the much smaller roles of the vagrant monk Varlaam and the Jesuit Rangoni, which could be portrayed in fine comic or villainous detail, like the marvellous but in some sense inessential "types" who roam the pages of Dostoyevsky or Tolstoy, or crowd around the edges of paintings by Repin or Surikov. We know how thoroughly Fyodor thought about the appearance of the characters he portrayed, because he drew a whole gallery of exquisitely detailed caricatures of himself in a wide variety of roles. He kept a detailed notebook in which he recorded ideas about these characters, and he used the huge library he began to collect in the early 1880s as a source for background information in the quest for still greater verisimilitude. Above all he evidently had a malleability of voice and a penetration of mind that were alike unusual among singers of his day, though we have perhaps grown more used to them in our own, which attaches so much importance to the integrated stage picture. We can assume, too, that Fyodor could rise to the vocal-dramatic stature of parts like Holofernes or Boito's Mefistofele, when occasion demanded.[39]

Fyodor graduated from the Petersburg Conservatoire in May 1873, and by August he was back in Kiev, making his professional stage debut there as Count Rodolfo in Bellini's *La sonnambula*. This is a big part for a debutant, but it seems that the Kiev intendant, Ferdinand Georgevich Berger, had heard Fyodor in a student *Barber of Seville* and knew what he was engaging.[40] The company was a newish one, established on a permanent footing only six years before, and perhaps that helped attract Fyodor back to what, after all, was by no means his native city. It did not, however, prevent him from following Berger when he left Kiev in the spring of 1874 to set up a south Ukrainian touring company based in Odessa. Fyodor was away from Kiev between April and August, with one brief return visit in May. But later in the year he signed up with the new Kiev intendant, Josef Yakevlevich Setov, and for the next two years the Ukrainian capital was to be his home.[41]

The May 1874 trip back to Kiev was an important one. It was in order to marry Anna Kirillovna Kholodovskaya. But though the Kholodovskys were a wealthy family, it was no society wedding. Perhaps it was Maria Romanovna's hostility which made Fyodor prefer to get married quietly "in some homely church . . . with an accommodating priest who would agree to read the banns in a single day,"[42] or perhaps it was just that he could only spare three days from his Odessa contract. In either event he wanted the arrangements made discreetly by his friend Gavriyil Trofimovich Nosenko, a Kiev doctor who also knew the Kholodovskys and may even have been responsible for introducing Anna and Fyodor in the first place.[43] In Odessa Fyodor was taking a new flat, quiet and well insulated, ready for Anna's arrival (had the neighbors complained about his practicing?). There is a hint of pampering and a desire to please at all costs in the way he offers her "as many servants as you like" (in a two-roomed flat). Maria Romanovna must have made it abundantly clear that she doubted Fyodor's ability to look after her daughter in the manner to which she was accustomed.

Anna, like Fyodor, was the youngest of four children who had lost their father, though in their case for a more remorseless reason. Kirill Kholodovsky had died of tuberculosis in 1855, when Anna was one year old, and since Anna's siblings were all sisters, we may perhaps with the confidence of hindsight detect the echoes of a maleless household in the intensity with which the nineteen-year-old girl clove to a man eleven years her senior in defiance of her mother's wishes. The fates accepted her decision as absolute, and she herself was to mother nothing but sons. Yet, if those sons and their children and grandchildren are to be believed, nothing ever displaced her love for Fyodor; or, if one love did come near to doing so, it was snatched from her when her eldest son, Roman, died at the age of twenty-one, five years before her husband. Fyodor reciprocated her utter devotion, and perhaps, too, he knew how to exact it, by his single-minded commitment to an art in which he was rapidly establishing supreme mastery. Anna was herself a musician. She could sing, play the piano, and (priceless talent in the wife of an opera singer) sight-read. But she was no Clara Schumann; there would be no conflict between her ambitions and his, no daylight between them, one could add. Later, as mother and grandmother, Anna Kirillovna laid herself open to criticism, and she suffered much (posthumously) at the hands of her famous son's selective and pitiless memory. But at the start we can trace everything to a tendency to love not wisely but too well. Adoring Fyodor as she did, there was not much love left for anyone else.

THE KHOLODOVSKYS were an attractive, well-to-do, well-educated upper-class Kiev family: a nest of marriageable girls. But at bottom they were provincial and conventional, and somewhat dull. Nothing here of that intellectual bohemianism which drove Sergey Diaghilev's remarkable aunt, Anna Pavlovna Filosofova, to lament the lack of spirit, as she saw it, in the artistic discussions and predilections of her son and nephew.[44] The atmosphere was just such as might produce a great creative artist, but hardly such as would comprehend him. Anna's sisters were all indeed already married, and all (probably) to landowners. The single doubt concerns Anna's eldest sister, Maria, who had wed a descendant of the Decembrist Pushchin about whom nothing else precise is known. The other two sisters had both, for some reason, married a pair of brothers, the sons of a Croat surgeon and professor of medicine in Kazan called Franz Leopold Yelachich, himself the descendant of a certain Franz Lukas Yelachich, who had arrived in Russia in the 1740s, it was said, as a Jesuit spy, had studied medicine, and had then gone, officially, as doctor on a series of botanical expeditions to China. Franz Leopold acquired vast estates to the east of the Volga, but fell out with his eldest son, Nikolay, and left all his property to Nikolay's brothers: Mikhail, who got the Kazan property itself; and Alexander, the youngest, who inherited a huge estate called Pavlovka in the Government of Samara, 150 miles to the southeast of Kazan.[45] It was Nikolay who, some time in the mid-1860s, married the second Kholodovsky daughter, Yekaterina, and bought an estate at Pechisky, near Proskurov, in the heart of western Ukraine some 170 miles southwest of Kiev.[46] And no doubt it was through them that Alexander Yelachich met and married Yekaterina's younger sister Soph'ya, in about 1871.

In 1876, a mere two years after Anna's marriage had completed the set of husbands, it was depleted once more by the death of Maria's husband, Nikolay Pushchin; and then the following year by the death of Yekaterina's, Nikolay Yelachich. For Yekaterina, bitterness was to pile upon bitterness. Her only son, Kirill, married Lyudmila Konstantinovna Pomazanskaya, a niece of the composer Lyadov, and the couple had two sons, Alexey and Alexander, after which Kirill Yelachich, too, died, aged only twenty-six, leaving his widow and her sons apparently completely dependent on her mother-in-law (meanwhile remarried to one Lazarenko). Once again, we have only Igor Stravinsky's vengeful reminiscences of the atmosphere at Pechisky in these years of his childhood. His aunt Yekaterina was an "orgulous and despotic woman who never managed to show me any kindness . . . though, to be just [sic], her supply was too alarmingly small to allow of any partition." Yekaterina, he continues, was busy ruining Lyudmila's life by "confiscating" her son Alexey, "a situation I would compare to that of Beethoven and his nephew but for the fact that Aunt Catherine [Yekaterina] was totally without musical talent." Yet the composer visited Pechisky effectively for the last time in 1901, when he was just nineteen.47

But then, as we shall see in due course, the young Igor had other reasons for detesting Pechisky.

Maria Pushchin had remarried, too, and we have already met her second husband. He was none other than Fyodor's friend the Kiev doctor Gavriyil Nosenko. Nosenko was to assume an overriding importance in Igor Stravinsky's life, and yet curiously the composer left no memoir of him. One senses a benign, reassuring presence. But Nosenko, too, was to endure a tragic and ominous loss, for, after giving birth to two daughters, his wife contracted tuberculosis like her father and died quickly, in early October 1882, aged only thirty-five.48 A certain mystery surrounds her death. At some moment in the 1880s Nosenko bought land in the far western Ukraine, in the village of Ustilug on the river Bug, purportedly for the benefit of his wife's health.49 But there is no record of the Stravinskys themselves visiting Ustilug until 1889, seven years after Maria Nosenko's death, whereas thereafter they visited the Nosenko estate often and sometimes for long periods. Did Gavriyil simply take a long time to restore the house, or did he buy it with his daughters', rather than his wife's, health in view? In either case, his fears were all too well founded.

ANNA AND FYODOR had no time for a honeymoon, but were soon back in Odessa, presumably in the well-insulated flat. It was the same in Kiev, when they returned there under Fyodor's Setov contract in the autumn. And it would be the same in St. Petersburg, where Fyodor joined the Imperial Theatres in August 1876. Always the remorseless grind of the repertory company, the same two or three roles week in, week out, the battle to keep old parts fresh while learning new ones: the umpteenth Mephistopheles and Kaspar alongside the new Sparafucile or Leporello. For Fyodor it would never be a case of selecting his roles and naming his fee, though a few years later it might well have been like that. In Kiev, his success was already so spectacular that Setov had to get the police to keep order outside the stage door when the performers were leaving the theatre.50 At his preliminary Mariyinsky Theatre debut in St. Petersburg in April 1876, as Gounod's Mephistopheles, both his arias had to be repeated.51 From August he was placed on contract at the more-than-respectable salary of 3,500 roubles for the eight months of the engagement.* But this committed him to a minimum of thirty-five perfor-mances, and the management could require him to sing more often if nec-essary.[52] The Imperial Theatres, protected by a state monopoly, did not yet see themselves as in serious competition with any rival company and did not fear that their artists would leave them in the lurch.

Anna meanwhile was fulfilling her own side of the contract. Her first son, Roman, was born in Kiev on 1/13 October 1875, and named after his Furman great-grandfather; Roman's brother Yury was born in St. Peters-burg on 28 November/10 December 1878. At that time the Stravinskys were living in a flat at 30 Ofitserskaya Ulitsa,[53] just along the street from the Mariyinsky Theatre. But in September 1881 they moved nearer to the Mariyinsky, to the flat (no. 66) at no. 8 Kryukov Canal which was to be Igor's home throughout his Petersburg childhood.

Two days after Igor's birth in Oranienbaum the following June, the director of the Imperial Theatres, Ivan Alexandrovich Vsevolozhsky, sent a telegram to the office of his management: "Report to the minister and draw his attention to Stravinsky's complete lack of voice." But the minis-ter, Count Vorontsov-Dashkov, saw through this backstage intrigue. His response was "to conclude an agreement [with Stravinsky] for three years at 8,000 roubles."[54] It was a good omen.

*For money exchanges and equivalents, see Appendix.

THE KRYUKOV CANAL ▬

KRYUKOV CANAL no. 66 was and remains a gloomy, warrenlike flat in a superior tenement block running much of the length of this section of the canal. You climb a cold, wide stone staircase to the second floor and, taking your courage in both hands, ring the bell on the heavy terra-cotta-red door of no. 66 itself. Outside, nothing much seems to have changed. It might be the same paintwork, the same door, the same canvas padding, the same old number plate as Igor saw every afternoon when he came home from school. Inside, a lobby leads into a central passageway, unfavored by natural light, which runs the full length of the flat—perhaps fifty feet. Doors open off both sides. On the left the kitchen looks out over a rear courtyard; to the right a series of larger rooms front onto the canal itself, a narrow but navigable waterway with streets on both sides and low bridges every few hundred yards, much as in other canal towns. Just along the street to the left, near the Mariyinsky, the former Ofitserskaya Ulitsa crosses the canal by the Bridge of Kisses (as Igor remembered it), which links the two sides of Kryukov. On the far side of the canal, in his day, was an elegant, late-eighteenth-century Italianate prison known as the Litovsky Zamok (Lithuanian Castle), originally in fact a church, and now replaced by a concrete apartment block of Soviet vintage.[1]

The Stravinsky flat was never turned into a *muzey kvartira*—an apartment museum—like Rimsky-Korsakov's or Dostoyevsky's Petersburg flats. For many years after the Revolution it was still lived in by the family, first by Anna herself (until her emigration to the West in 1922), then by her eldest surviving son, Yury, and his family. For a while, early on, it was even a state archive, with Fyodor's library as its core and Anna as archivist. In Stalinist times, when Igor Stravinsky was a nonperson and accommodation was at a premium, the flat was turned into a communal apartment, and so it remains to this day, with each room or pair of rooms occupied by a different tenant or tenants. As symbolic proof of St. Petersburg's failure to acknowledge her greatest composer, the commemorative plaque on the wall outside is actually on the wrong part of the block, forty yards from the Stravinskys' entrance.

Life in such a flat was crowded and claustrophobic during the long, dark Petersburg winter. After Gury was born in July 1884, the Stravinskys were a family of six, and the seven-room flat (plus kitchen) had also to accommodate as many as five or six servants. Apart from the children's *nyanya*, Bertha Essert, and one or another wet nurse, there were the factotum, Semyon Ivanovich Sokolov (who lived in what amounted to a cupboard in the entrance hall); the Finnish cook, Caroline; and at least two maids, who, however, perhaps did not live in.[2] What is more, the Stravinskys were probably out of the house much less than one might suppose. Fyodor, when not at rehearsal or performance, worked at home.[3] His study was a holy-of-holies, not just his workplace but his library—the home of one of the finest private collections of books in Russia. Moreover, the geography of the flat must have made it terribly hard to carry on normal life there without disturbing the great singer. Fyodor had an unpleasant temper and was feared not only by his children but by the assorted friends and cousins who sometimes visited the flat, as well as by the servants and anyone else in a menial capacity. One day in the late eighties Anna's young nephew Nikolay Yelachich called at Kryukov 66 and went first to the study to pay his respects to Uncle Fyodor. Suddenly, as he chatted with Fyodor, he became aware of strange shufflings and slappings in the next room, and when he investigated, he found Roman and Yury fighting tooth and nail but in almost total silence, so scared were they of their father.[4] Igor, who was admittedly not disposed to remember the agreeable sides of his parents' characters, recalled his father's uncontrollable rages and his capacity for making public scenes when his wishes were flouted.[5] There will be more to say about Fyodor's behavior towards his family. But with all allowance made, he cannot have been an easy man to share a second-floor flat with.

Yet the children, too, were much at home. Igor, or Gima, as he was known in the family, did not go to school until he was nearly eleven, and no doubt the same was true of his brothers. From early 1889, when he was six, he had a governess at home, which made one grown-up extra in the flat, and not necessarily of the most agreeable type. Igor's reminiscences of his governesses certainly portray them practically as a gang of sadistic perverts, a sort of composite of Kingsley's Mrs. Bedonebyasyoudid and a female version of Dickens's Mr. Wackforth Squeers. Perhaps they were, but the memory reads like a much later parental report. How else could he have known that the first, French governess was good-looking in the sense that might lead his mother to doubt her suitability, when he was only seven, or that the ugly Swiss spinster (perhaps the Agnes Richter of Fyodor's account book for 1889)[6] was dismissed when his parents found out that—among other unspecified proclivities—"she was rather too interested to see us boys into the bathtub?"[7] Perhaps the last governess, Pavla

Vasil'evna Vinogradova, who lasted at least till Igor went to school in 1893, was as obnoxious as Igor recalled, but there is something pathological in his memories of her which makes one wary of taking such reminiscences too literally. How vengeful is his story of being teased by his father one evening at dinner, in Vinogradova's presence, about his pronunciation of the word "pourquoi," vengeful even towards those—like Bertha and Semyon Ivanovich—whom elsewhere in his memoirs he treats as "safe" and loving.[8] Profound insecurity and a painful self-awareness are the real progenitors of such tales.

Igor was a tiny, fragile child who never lost his self-consciousness about his lack of inches. Quite early photographs with his younger brother show Gury already outstripping him.[9] But compared with both of them their older brother Roman was tall, dark, something of an Adonis. The composer's reminiscences of him, too, are hostile, but he admitted that he "thought [Roman] an exceedingly handsome brother and I was proud of him."[10] While Roman got his sultry good looks, no doubt, from the saturnine Fyodor and, perhaps, from his dark-skinned grandfather Kirill Kholodovsky, Igor was his mother's child. She too was minute in stature and fragile in build,[11] though of all the family her health seems to have been the most robust, apart from persistent and apparently chronic catarrh. Nevertheless, Igor's later obsession with his own and his family's health probably originated with her, or possibly with her mother, who had lost her husband early to tuberculosis. Igor himself believed that he was baptized so promptly out of fear for his survival, perhaps because he was so small.[12] But, for whatever reason, Anna and Fyodor were exceptionally nervous about their children's health. Tamara Karsavina recorded that when she and her brother went out in winter, her mother would issue routine wintry advice, "not to go on the ice, not to play with stray dogs, not to talk when out, and to breathe through the nose."[13] But Stravinsky remembered that "I was allowed out of doors only after my parents had put me through a medical examination, and I was considered too frail to participate in any sports or games when I *was* out."[14] This sounds like hyperbole. But family correspondence shows that it was not. Igor's many surviving letters of his childhood—mostly written in summer—are often obsessed with matters of health, both his own and that of his family. Sometimes it is nothing more than the usual tale of colds, mumps, warts, and boils that have always been normal epistolary topics for those who write out of duty rather than impulse. Igor will even report that there is nothing wrong with him. On arrival at the Rimsky-Korsakov holiday house at Krapachukha in 1903, he dispatched a brief postcard home announcing, "I arrived safely. I am not coughing and I haven't got a cold."[15] But sometimes it goes far beyond such minutiae. Once, during a Petersburg smallpox epidemic in August 1900, Igor devoted almost an entire letter to his parents in Pechisky to an account of his attempts to get vaccinated, excusing himself on the remark-able grounds that "I didn't go out yesterday [Tuesday], as I took a bath on Monday and the weather was disgusting."[16] At the age of twenty-five, and a married man, Igor was still writing to his mother in the language of the diagnostic clinic. "With us, thank heaven, everything is all right apart from minor ailments, such as general colds and mild stomach upsets. . . . Yesterday I had a tummy upset. I took some castor oil, went to the lavatory, and now I'm on a diet. We're all extremely careful, as we're scared of the spectre of cholera. . . ."[17]

These obsessions were not wholly without justification. Like their grandfather, both Igor and his brother Yury were consumptive, and though they both survived the disease, care was necessary. Igor's visits to the Yelachich estate at Pavlovka in 1903 and 1904 were mainly, if not exclu-sively, in order to pursue a strict regime of koumiss, the fermented mare's milk of the Tartars, which was regarded as a specific for chest complaints. Later, Yury was forced to live in Davos for two years with his wife and two small children. Igor recalled that his own tuberculosis had first showed itself after an attack of pleurisy when he was thirteen.[18] Bearing in mind that Roman Stravinsky died only two years after that, apparently from heart disease resulting from diphtheria when he was eleven, it is hardly surprising that Anna and Fyodor fussed about their other children's well-being.

Anna must have imposed on them the strict obligation to report on their health whenever they wrote. But when Igor recalls that he "felt only 'duties' " towards his mother,[19] we have to consider that such duties were the price of love as much as of tyranny. No doubt Anna was starchy and distant, as her granddaughters observed in later years.[20] In family photos with Fyodor she is stern, protective, the master-at-arms. But such, after all, was still part of the image of the bourgeois family in the nineties; and the posed photographs of the time are naturally much concerned with "images" in that sense. Nor do they necessarily lie, though theirs may not be the whole truth. Anna could certainly be difficult and at times oppres-sive. She disliked Yury's wife and did not forgive her for taking away her eldest surviving son barely a year after Fyodor's death.[21] She opposed Igor's musical ambitions to the point where he ran away to the home of the newly married Yury and would only go back after Yury had interceded with her. Doubtless she lectured Igor about his career, as she later ticked him off—undeterred by his world fame—for what she saw as his disre-spectful attitude to senior Russian composers like Glazunov and Scriabin.

The curious thing is the way Stravinsky himself remembered all this as an inexplicable series of phenomena, with neither rhyme nor reason to it, just as a child observes the strange, unmotivated behavior of grown-ups. Yet this is not how the actual child Igor responded to his mother. No doubt

Anna was egotistical, given to fits of emotionally induced illness, and intemperate when crossed. But there were reasons for such behavior, not all of them utterly disreputable. No need even to dwell on the circumstantial difficulties: the emotional crisis of marrying against her own mother's wishes; the hardships of life with an obsessively single-minded artist determined, perhaps, to avenge himself on those who did not believe in him; the cramped conditions of apartment life in a northern winter; the illnesses and bereavements. Enough simply to observe that Anna Kirillovna was a woman driven by love of a large family of gifted, egocentric men who did not themselves readily give back the love they probably felt but were incompetent to express.

The evidence for this is that as a child Igor hardly ever rebelled against the strict regimes to which he was subjected. Reading between the lines of his and Gury's letters home from Ustilug at the turn of the century, one senses a more casual attitude on the part of the youngest brother, while Igor's letters sometimes display a labored, self-immolating anxiety to please. Injunctions to report on his health, his expenditures, his activities, his cousins: all are honored beyond any possibility of censure. If this is what he meant when he referred to his mother's "torturing" him,[22] it was a torture to which he consented, for the simple reason that he wanted the love it implied, but in which he did not feel absolutely secure. His letters are affectionate, at times even ostentatiously so. Occasionally they break out into something like a *cri de coeur*. "I congratulate you, Mamochka, on your birthday. Don't take this badly . . . but as an expression of our pride that you exist with us, and [of our hope] that our family life together, which is beginning to break up, won't collapse any further and come to an end." "Alexander Franzevich has just brought a telegram from you, my darling. I embrace you so warmly, and thank you for it." "I knew, Musechka, that you were not in a state, my unhappy one, to be there alone without Papochka, with whom you were always together in Pechisky and never went there alone without him. I completely understand, and am worried sick on your account, since that journey upset you and reminded you with a new pang of the absence of our poor Papochka." "It was terribly hard, Musyulchik, that you were taken ill . . . particularly hard for me, as I was too anxious for you to come and selfish in my insistence on your coming, prompted, naturally, by a legitimate fear of being left alone. Write to me."[23] This last, written from Rome at the time of *Petrushka,* shows once and for all that the relationship between Igor and Anna, however painful—destructive, even—was mutual and expressive of a reciprocal need for love and support. In 1911, Igor no longer needed to be "tortured" by his mother, two thousand miles away in Petersburg. The fact is, he could hardly bear to be so far away from her at all.

Kryukov 66 was, withal, an ordered, unbending household, the kind of home where a lot that is done for the family good takes the form of restrictions and rituals and routines—the three Rs of the nineteenth-century bourgeoisie. This was surely Fyodor's kind of house. The child of a failed marriage and an unsuccessful father, he could take satisfaction in creating out of nothing a structured and dependable existence for his large family. How different from the Benois household just down the street, where the young Alexander Nikolayevich, Stravinsky's future collaborator in *Petrushka,* would "dash out of my nursery into the drawing-room and start prancing about and acting all sorts of things to the music" whenever his elder brother Albert sat down at the piano to improvise.[24] Here all was warmth and brilliance and shared enthusiasms. "If asked what was the special quality of this atmosphere [in our house]," Benois wrote,

> I would reply without hesitation: "It was artistic." It was artistic not only because our house was hung with many excellent pictures and contained some beautiful things in the way of furniture and *objets d'art,* and not only because my father was a professional artist and laid great store by everything artistic; nor again was it because most of my brothers and sisters drew or painted, and one sister married a famous sculptor; nor because most of our friends were interested in some form of art and were continually arranging amateur theatricals and concerts. It was because the very air of our house was saturated with art, so that there one breathed differently from the houses of other people.[25]

Here is Stravinsky's description of the Kryukov flat:

> Our flat was furnished in the usual Victorian manner—with the usual bad paintings, the usual mauve upholstery, etc., but with an unusual library and two grand pianos. To recall it gives me no pleasure, however. I do not like to remember my childhood, and the four walls of my and Goury's room represent my most abiding impression of home. Our room was like Petroushka's cell, and most of my time was spent there.[26]

Igor's reminiscence of his father as "not very *commode*"[27] was a view shared by Fyodor's own friends and colleagues. The great singing actor, of whom a diarist once grumbled that he "overacted as usual,"[28] could be chilly and uncommunicative to meet. But behind the cold, rational, self-disciplined exterior, Fyodor hid a nature that was sensitive, passionate, and easily wounded, the former being no doubt protective coloring for the latter.[29] Presumably the explosions of temper reflected the degree of control needed to keep order in such a personality. But Fyodor was usually able to let off steam in a more rational way. Day after day he kept a *raskhod-naya kniga*—an account book—in which he recorded not only cash expenditure, but family events and circumstances, bereavements, journeys and holidays, and a whole range of professional data to do with life at the Mariyinsky Theatre.[30] This kind of ordered *rapportage* seems to have been a deeply ingrained habit, which perhaps had its origins in his mother's straitened circumstances, and her insistence on strict accounting of even the most trivial expenditure. But the books, with their agonizing calligraphy, also reveal feelings which Fyodor seems to have been at pains to conceal from the prying world. When Roman dies in 1897, the thick black edging, the crucifixes and heavy expressions of woe, going on for many pages and months and recurring at annual intervals thereafter, are a curiously secretive and exclusive form of melodrama for a man accustomed to exaggerating the feelings of others for the benefit of a paying audience. Lesser family sorrows, particularly to do with health, are recorded more impassively. But their being recorded at all suggests something which might not have struck the casual visitor. Fyodor loved his family, worked for their well-being, and was grief-stricken by their misfortunes. His tragedy, and theirs, was that he could not always show them how much he minded about the things that happened to them.[31]

For such consolation, Igor and Gury would normally turn to the dependable Bertha Essert, the stout, homely German *nyanya* from Königsberg whom Anna had taken on in October 1881, before Igor was born, and who was to remain in the Stravinsky family—in charge first of Fyodor's children, then of Igor's—until her death at the Villa Rogivue in Morges in 1917.[32] In Igor's harsh reminiscences of his childhood, it is Bertha who takes his mother's place—Bertha who wakes him in the morning, Bertha who runs his bath, says his prayers with him at night, closes the curtains just enough to let in a crack of light from the street lamp by the canal. Aunt Bertochka, as she was Russianized, herself spoke no Russian, and through her Igor learnt a fluent German which essentially he never lost. Did Igor and Gury clamber all over her, as Igor's children were photographed doing at Morges twenty-five years later?[33] Perhaps not. Or if so, only in silence, like Roman fighting with Yury, or in the streets and parks of St. Petersburg, where the Victorian inhibitions of the somber second-floor apartment may have been temporarily, and within certain firm limits, relaxed.

THE ST. PETERSBURG into which young Igor and Gury stepped hand in hand with Aunt Bertochka was still in the 1880s, and even right up to 1914, the Petersburg of *Petrushka*, with its characteristic mingling of town and country, its vibrant street life, its glittering baroque exterior concealing a Dostoyevskian world of oppression and poverty. "My last Petersburg visit," the composer wrote in 1911 while at work on *Petrushka* itself, "seems to have done me a lot of good. The final act is turning out interestingly, continuous quick tempi and major keys somehow redolent of Russian food—cabbage soup maybe, bottle-boots, the *garmoshka* [concertina]— ecstasy! excitement! What's Monte Carlo? There you can't even smoke in the Salle de Jeu!"[34] Alexander Benois's later memory of the capital remains one of the most vivid:

> The well-to-do public walking on the main streets of St. Petersburg could be mistaken for those whom they strove to copy—that is, west-ern Europeans—because they dressed and behaved in conformity with them. But one had only to glance away from the pavement to the middle of the street and the western-European illusion disappeared entirely, for here was a surging stream of the most extraordinary vehicles—sleighs in winter, *droshkis* in summer, harnessed in a strange way and driven by bearded coachmen, all wearing wide great-coats and headgear of fantastic shape.[35]

Means of transport were also still close to the surface of Igor's memories of his native city fifty years after he left it, but, as befits a musician, more as a polyphony of noise than as a Repinesque tableau:

> The first such sounds to record themselves on my awareness were those of droshkies on cobblestone, or block-wood parquetry pave-ments. Only a few of these horse carriages had rubber tyres, and these few were doubly expensive; the whole city crackled with the iron-hooped wheels of the others. I also remember the sound of horse-drawn streetcars and, in particular, the rail-scraping noise they made as they turned the corner near our house and whipped up speed to cross the Krukov Canal Bridge.[36]

But these artistic responses to the city are rose-tinted compared with the reality. The Petersburg of the last two or three decades of the nineteenth century (and the first of the twentieth) was one of the most overcrowded and without rival the dirtiest, most diseased capital city in the whole of Europe. "Petersburg streets," wrote Andrei Bely in 1915, "possess one indubitable quality: they transform passersby into shadows."[37] This might have been intended as a memento mori. The mortality rate from epidemic and routine illness in the center of the city was frighteningly high, and when we consider that Roman Stravinsky had suffered from diphtheria in the mid-eighties, that Igor and Yury both had scarlet fever in 1886, that tuberculosis was endemic in the family until the Second World War and beyond, and that fear of cholera and smallpox is a constant refrain in family correspondence until Igor left Russia in 1914, we realize that the threat of death from infectious disease was by no means confined to the vagrant population. No wonder Anna and Fyodor worried about their children's health. Sanitary conditions were primitive and the water supply polluted, as it is again today but to a far less dangerous extent.

> Arrangements for the disposal of sewage . . . may be briefly referred to as a system of filthy cesspools in the back yards of all houses, with rough wooden carts to carry away the contents at night and pollute the atmosphere by the operation. At the same time, as though this were not enough, the citizens are supplied with water which nobody valuing his or her life dares to drink unboiled. St. Petersburg is probably the only city in Europe, or perhaps the world, where danger-signals in the form of placards with glaring red letters are posted up on house-fronts, inside tramcars and in most places of public resort, warning all and sundry against drinking raw water.[38]

Dirty and stinking, the Petersburg streets were also often excessively crowded. The influx of the rural population, which *Petrushka* documents as a phenomenon of the carnival season, was in fact an annual feature of winter in the capital. It brought color, vitality, country produce and smells, but it also brought poverty and homelessness, and it cluttered up the streets with a chaos of horse-drawn transport. Stravinsky later recalled the use of the Kryukov Canal by barges transporting scenery to the Mariyinsky Theatre, and Tamara Karsavina mentions the transport of logs by the same method, and describes how the street urchins would retrieve stray logs from the canal by hooking them with a nail on the end of a stump of wood.[39] But barge transport was only a small part of the commercial haulage within the capital, most of which was done by horse-drawn wagons, often conveying goods inefficiently from a port or railway station on one side of the capital to a factory on the other. It took years for the city's transport to become mechanized. Until 1907 the only public trams and buses were likewise horse-drawn, and in any case tram fares were mostly too high for the ordinary workers and peasantry to afford, so that the mass of the population continued to go on foot.

It was through such streets that Igor began his daily trudge to school in the spring of 1893, after his four years of home study with governesses, culminating in the entrance examination, which he took on 27 April 1893 OS.[40] His first school was the Second St. Petersburg Gymnasium, in the Kazanskaya, about twenty minutes' walk from home: past Zackar, the doorman ("a kindly old gentleman in an absurd Swiss beadle's uniform"),[41] out of the house, left along Ofitserskaya, right down the Fonarny Pere-ulok, then left along Kazanskaya.[42] There was an omnibus, but horse-drawn and so slow as to be not worth the five-kopek fare. So Igor got up at seven and walked.

Official secondary education in nineties Petersburg was, even by the Western standards of the time, a fusty and restrictive affair, designed at best to supply a basis of literacy, numeracy, and intellectual method for the university courses in such subjects as law and philosophy which in turn fed the state civil service. Mind broadening was definitely not on the syllabus. The state did not encourage independent thinking or educating the masses, and fees had been sharply increased six years earlier specifically to exclude "the children of coachmen, servants, cooks, washerwomen, small shopkeepers, and persons of a similar type, whose children, perhaps with the exception of those gifted with unusual abilities, should certainly not be brought out of the social environment to which they belong."[43] The curriculum was heavily biased towards the classics, supplemented by Bible studies and Slavonic, languages (German or French, and their literature), Russian language and literature, and basic mathematics. Neither science nor the practical arts subjects such as music were substantially taught in the "classical" gymnasia, though natural sciences figured in the so-called *real'noye uchilishche,* which were what we should call polytechnics providing purely vocational or technical education. Nevertheless, singing and elementary music theory were taught in the two lowest classes of the Second Gymnasium, and Igor will have had to study them.[44]

In his various memoirs, he recalled nothing of significance about his time at the gymnasium except that he detested it. But that may be partly because he lacked friends there, a confession he makes in his autobiography but modifies in *Expositions,* where he claims to have been "fond of two boys, both of them, though unrelated, with the name of Smirnov."[45] In any case, he was a poor pupil "who studied badly and behaved no better," as he told the music critic Grigory Timofeyev a few years later.[46] His surviving school grades confirm a low level of performance. When exams came up he was routinely crammed by university students hired for the purpose.[47] Admittedly, his brothers suffered the same indignity, which might suggest that Fyodor was disposed to put pressure on his sons to get good results. But Igor's reminiscence that at the private gymnasium he went on to at the age of sixteen "I was of course a very bad pupil" is partly borne out by a letter from the proprietor of the school, Y. G. Gurevich, to Fyodor grumbling about Igor's frequent absences from school and warning that he must "occupy himself this year less with music and more with science subjects, or else I foresee serious complications in the exams."[48] How did Fyodor, who was paying through the nose to get Igor into university, react to what looks horribly like truancy, or at least severe backsliding over schoolwork?

The fact that, by the age of eighteen, the budding composer was occupying himself "too much" with music is hardly surprising. But at what stage did this interest start to take over? We simply do not know. Stravinsky says in his autobiography and again in *Expositions* that his parents gave him his first piano teacher when he was nine, and he identifies her as a young Conservatoire pianist called Alexandra Petrovna Snetkova.[49] In fact the only music teaching of any kind recorded by Fyodor before September 1893 are a few casual lessons in May 1892 (when Igor was indeed still nine) given by a temporary governess called O. A. Petrova.[50] So the piano lessons with Snetkova cannot have started before the autumn of 1893, which might fit in with her young pupil's later memory that she told him "about the preparations at the Conservatory for Tchaikovsky's funeral" at the end of October (OS) 1893 (but not with his recollection that she taught him for about two years, since the account books show that their final lesson together was in April 1899).[51]

In any case the piano lessons acknowledged that Igor was musical and had a gift that needed encouraging. This is perfectly obvious from the Timofeyev letter, which states unequivocally that "my parents wanted to make a pianist of me and so, not stinting their means, gave me the opportunity to study with good teachers."[52] Even in his autobiography, written in the mid-1930s, Stravinsky is clear that his parents did their best to encourage his musical leanings, though he stops short of suggesting that they understood them, as indeed how could they?[53] His remark in *Memories* that they neither recognized his musical talent nor believed he had any is nothing less than a calumny against their memory, made at a time when he was nurturing the image of his early work as a "sport" with few if any antecedents.[54] It would have been more to the point to emphasize that at the time of his father's death in 1902, he (Igor) had composed nothing of the slightest significance, so that Fyodor would have had to be clairvoyant to "recognize his musical talent" to any specific or appropriate extent.

But Igor had been treated as a budding musician long before Snetkova came on the scene. When he was only five, Glinka's sister, Lyudmila Shestakova, sent him her portrait together with portraits of her brother and Borodin.[55] Perhaps this was no more than wishful thinking, but after all it was to Igor that she sent them, not to either of his older brothers. Igor had shown her a "little album" in which he had stuck pictures of other Russian composers—perhaps Tchaikovsky, Rimsky-Korsakov, and Musorgsky, all in varying measure old associates of his father. At the very least, Igor was glimpsing, and even being patted on the head by, some of the leading musicians of the day, who would visit his father to discuss productions or be entertained after performances. The mere fact of his meeting Shestakova, as Glinka's sister a kind of symbolic figurehead of the whole nationalist movement in Russian music, shows what a favored position he occupied as Fyodor's son.

Perhaps it was in the summer before or after the incident of the little album that there occurred the great feat of musical memory with which Igor impressed his parents by accurately singing back to them a folksong he had heard in the fields around the village of L'zy, where the family was spending the summer.[56] Igor tells us that it was in 1884, when he was two, and that "everyone was astonished and impressed at this recital, and I heard my father remark that I had a wonderful ear." But that must be wrong, and not only because of the Mozartian (un-Stravinskian) caliber of the performance itself. The Stravinskys were in Oranienbaum in 1884, and Gury was born there at the end of June. They did not summer in the forest village of L'zy, south of Luga, until 1889, though they were at nearby Vechasha in 1888, and at Skukov, still further south, near Pskov, in 1887. Oranienbaum would be an unlikely mise-en-scène for such an incident. But of course the location is unimportant anyway. What counts is that Igor performed a surprising musical feat of which his parents were proud.[57]

As he got older, Igor could "improvise" on the piano in the drawing room, which he found more amusing than listening to his father practicing "from the nursery to which my brothers and I were relegated."[58] And he could sight-read his way through his father's opera scores. He remembered getting to know Glinka's *Life for the Tsar* in this way, and since, like his mother, he was a good sight-reader, he probably learnt plenty of other Russian operas, including those of Tchaikovsky and Musorgsky, Rimsky-Korsakov, Serov, Borodin, and Dargomïzhsky, and the then-standard Western repertoire, to be discussed shortly. When, in the Ballets Russes period, he turned against opera, he was shamelessly biting the hand that had fed him. Probably, too, it was during these opera read-throughs that he acquired the habit of direct contact with the keyboard, and through that with the physical sound, which was such a vital part of his compositional routine.

But the real excitement was to be taken to the opera itself. How often or how soon this happened, we do not know, but by the age of ten at the latest Igor had been inducted into the mysteries of the Mariyinsky Theatre, with its exquisite blue-and-gold auditorium, its glittering chandeliers, and its grandly accoutred, richly perfumed clientele. "The spectacle of the theatre itself and of the audience bewildered me," he recalled, "and my mother said later that as I watched the stage, carried away by the sound of the orchestra . . . I asked her, as in Tolstoy: 'Which one is the theatre?' "[59]

But what was he actually taken to hear? His reminiscences are so contradictory on these matters that the biographer has to tread warily. Perhaps he saw *A Life for the Tsar* when he was seven or eight,[60] but if so, Fyodor was not singing, since his last appearance in that opera was at its fiftieth-anniversary gala in 1886, when little Igor was just four. Perhaps he was taken to Tchaikovsky's *Sleeping Beauty* in the winter of 1890, when he was seven,[61] and perhaps, too, he was, as he claims, already an experienced balletgoer, since ballet in St. Petersburg was generally regarded as the purview of the very young and the very old, and "the half-empty auditorium contained a special public—a mixture of children accompanied by their mothers or governesses, and old men with binoculars."[62] With the Mariyinsky a mere stone's throw from the Stravinsky flat, what more natural than that the boys should find themselves from time to time at a ballet matinee? And Igor in particular, with his musical leanings and his "little album," is unlikely to have missed such a treat, even though no one expected much of these afternoon ballet performances, which typically consisted of processions of short vignettes danced to mediocre music shoddily played—a far cry from either the symphonic flights of Tchaikovsky or the brilliance and flair of the as yet unborn Ballets Russes.

As for opera, the first production Igor definitely saw was of Glinka's *Ruslan and Lyudmila,* which had its fiftieth-anniversary gala performance on 27 November 1892 (OS), with Fyodor Stravinsky as Farlaf. Igor was ten and a half, and could hardly in his wildest dreams have expected to attend such a grown-up affair, with its overtones of a court ceremony and its heavy social connotations. But suddenly there he was in the carriage with his mother, trundling up the canal side and across Teatral'naya Ploshad'— Theatre Square—with the new Conservatoire building going up to the left on the site of the old Bolshoy Theatre. Igor remembered his loge seat and the lavish decoration and aroma of the theatre; he remembered watching the performance through his mother's lorgnette-binoculars; and he remembered stepping out of their box into the rear foyer at the interval and suddenly catching sight of Tchaikovsky, white-haired and corpulent though still only fifty-two.[63] But he remembered nothing about the music or the performance itself, which tells us no more than that Igor was a normal ten-year-old for whom visual impressions, pride, and excitement at being treated like a grown-up far outweighed detailed perceptions of a long and incomprehensible music-drama.

About other opera performances he may have attended in these early years we alas know little, beyond a hint that he saw one of Serov's operas— either *Judith* or *The Power of Evil*—that same winter season of 1892–93.[64] Fyodor Stravinsky's Holofernes and Yeryomka in these now forgotten works were alike famous. But gradually it must have become commoner and commoner for young Igor to take a seat in his father's box, to hear either some masterpiece of the Russian repertoire, such as Rimsky-Korsakov's *Christmas Eve* or Borodin's *Prince Igor* or Nápravník's *Dubrovsky,* or the latest sensation of European opera—perhaps Verdi's *Falstaff* or Massenet's *Werther.*[65] Smirnov tells us that he was "soon in the theatre five or six evenings a week. The Mariyinsky Theatre was for him almost a 'second home.' "[66] And some thirty years later Igor himself recalled that "I spent my childhood on the stage of the Opera."[67] In his reminiscences, he does not distinguish between operas played during his father's lifetime when he was still a schoolboy, and those he saw later when he had fallen under the influence of Rimsky-Korsakov. But the distinction is worth drawing, if only to attempt a picture of Igor's developing taste and experience—a picture which bears at best a very oblique relationship to the profoundly unreliable and tendentious account he gave more than half a century later in *Expositions and Developments.*

In the nineties the Mariyinsky repertoire was dominated by Russian works most of which were either never seen in the West or have long since disappeared from its boards, and by Italian and French opera. Glinka, Borodin, Tchaikovsky, and (spasmodically) Rimsky-Korsakov rubbed shoulders with Serov, Dargomïzhsky, and Rubinstein. But Musorgsky was not played. *Boris Godunov* had vanished from the Mariyinsky billings as long ago as 1882, and though Rimsky-Korsakov conducted his version in a series of four staged performances in the Great Hall of the new Conservatoire in 1896 (with Fyodor as Varlaam), the Mariyinsky only saw fit to revive the work as a vehicle for Chaliapin in 1904. *Khovanshchina* was largely unknown in Petersburg. Its first Mariyinsky staging was in 1911, a full thirty years after the composer's death, a fact that throws an ironic light on the bitter St. Petersburg reaction to Diaghilev's revival of this opera in Paris in 1913.[68] As for Western repertory, the staples were Meyerbeer, Rossini, Verdi *(Ernani, Rigoletto, Aida)*, early Wagner *(Rienzi, Tannhäuser, Lohengrin)*, Mozart *(Figaro* and *Don Giovanni)*, Weber's *Freischütz,* Nicolai's *Merry Wives of Windsor,* a few pieces by Donizetti and Bellini, Bizet's *Carmen,* and Gounod's *Faust.* The operas of Berlioz—"the great Hector," as Musorgsky had called him[69]—were ignored by the Mariyinsky as elsewhere, though *La Damnation de Faust* was regularly done there during the annual Lent closure, and his concert music was played "as much as it has ever been played anywhere in the world."[70] Wagner post-*Lohengrin* was no more than an occasional luxury before the turn of the century: *The Ring* had been toured by Angelo Neumann in 1889, but was not locally produced, even in part, until the early 1900s. *Tristan* and *Meistersinger* were first seen in St. Petersburg in 1898, but infrequently thereafter, though Stravinsky recalled hearing *Meistersinger* at the Mariyinsky with Rimsky-Korsakov and following the score.[71] *Parsifal,* however, was still embargoed. Of course, bleeding chunks figured in concert programs, and there were always the piano scores to bash one's way through. "I knew all Wagner's works from the piano scores," Stravinsky later recalled, "and when I was sixteen or seventeen, and at last had the money to buy them, from the orchestral scores."[72]

To modern ways of thinking, this was perhaps a limited and somewhat provincial repertoire, but it was formative for the young Igor. We too easily forget lost influences, and it is only recently, in the work of Richard

Taruskin, that the importance to Stravinsky of a now largely forgotten nineteenth-century Russian operatic tradition has been properly explored. He himself, needless to say, was not later always at pains to emphasize it, though he occasionally found it convenient to do so. Nor would one glean, from his own reminiscences, his serious-minded teenage contempt for Italian opera, as reported by the family friend Edward Stark: "I vividly remember the famous composer Igor Stravinsky, then still a gymnasium sixth-former, glancing at the newly issued Mariyinsky program, screwing up his nose dismissively, and remarking in a tone of inexpressible scorn: "The same old Verdicelli!"[73] How did Igor react, on the other hand, to the strong French element in the programs: the Gounod, the Bizet, the Massenet? The question raises the wider issue of intellectual influences on Stravinsky in his late teens, and will be deferred for the time being. We should merely note here that Mephistopheles in *Faust,* Zuniga in *Carmen,* and the Bailiff in *Werther* were regular parts of Fyodor's, and whether or not Igor saw him perform them, the scores will have been on his shelves.

As for Wagner, Igor's later, much publicized distaste for "the romantic orgiast" who was "certainly not a real musician," and whose endless melody "is the perpetual becoming of a music that never had any reason for starting, any more than it has any reason for ending," is far from foreshadowed by what we know of his attitude in his teens.[74] A notebook survives in the family archives labeled "Notebook of Igor Stravinsky: started writing from 1896, aged 13." It contains lists of composers' names (including Berlioz, Haydn, Bach, Mendelssohn, Glinka, Anton Rubinstein, Wagner, Tchaikovsky, Cui, Balakirev, Glazunov), and then, most strikingly, annotations on *Parsifal:* "1877—wrote text, 1879—composed the opera in rough, 1882—orchestrated the whole of *Parsifal.*" Igor then drew "Bayreuth" in the form of a castle and added information about the dates of composition of *Tristan und Isolde.*[75] That he was intrigued by these strange works he was unable to witness seems obvious. Wagner's picture is also prominent among a whole gallery of composers' photographs and reproductions on the wall of Igor's room at 66 Kryukov Canal—a photograph taken when he was about fifteen.[76] Nobody entering this room could possibly have doubted the direction of the boy's enthusiasm. Yet these were not merely pictures. Igor knew the music, too, even if he had never heard it, because he had played it for himself.

What else did Igor hear in his teens? The repertoire he lists in *Expositions* must have been that of the Russian Musical Society, whose concerts in the Assembly of the Nobles (the modern Philharmonia) were the staple orchestral programs for Petersburgers in the nineties.[77] The more adventurous Ziloti concerts were still in the future, as were the mixed chamber programs of the Evenings of Contemporary Music. But it is striking that Stravinsky seems to have forgotten about the Russian Symphony Concerts of Mitrofan Belyayev, a vital and unique phenomenon of St. Petersburg concert life which was to have a decisive effect on his early composition studies a few years later. Belyayev programmed only Russian music, and it was in his concerts that "Rimsky's *Antar* and Borodin's Second were played a dozen times for every performance of a symphony by Brahms or Bruckner."[78] Igor attended these concerts and here too heard a repertoire which, like the Mariyinsky operas, is now largely forgotten.[79] But this very raison d'être—to promote only Russian music—was to be his passport to a first full-blown professional performance of his own, something which might have been much longer coming in Berlin, Paris, or London.

Of such things, though, he as yet knew nothing. He lacked serious musical teaching, let alone a clear vocation. And music, as we shall see, was by no means his only artistic interest.

DEVOTEES OF RUSSIAN literature know about the great seasonal division in the domestic life of pre-Revolutionary St. Petersburg. Levin retreating to his estate after being refused by Kitty in *Anna Karenina;* Eugene Onegin vegetating as a country squire; Bazarov visiting, and undermining, the Kirsanovs in *Fathers and Sons;* Litvinov, the hero of Turgenev's *Smoke,* summering in Dresden and Baden-Baden. All in their different ways symbolize the Russian yearning for one or another oblivion from the heightened consciousness of the northern winter, with its diverse methods of combustion: its art, its society, or even, more prosaically, its good honest toil. For those who would assert, hyperbolically, that St. Petersburg literally empties in the summer, the statistics are disappointing. Only about a tenth of the population abandoned the capital every year from May or June to September before the turn of the century, and most of them were migrant peasant workers. But that tenth will also have included everyone you or I would admit to knowing: everyone, that is, of wealth, influence, and importance. It included the Stravinskys.

Going to the dacha has never implied a long journey. Petersburgers owned or rented country retreats—small or large—on the islands in the northern quarters of the capital itself. More ambitiously, they would take summer rentals in the wooded countryside a hundred miles to the southwest, or in the Valdye Hills to the southeast, or in the Finnish borderlands. But the expansion of the railway network in the second half of the nineteenth century made much longer journeys possible. Remote landowners could now also participate more readily in Petersburg life. Petersburg families could circulate around the distant estates of near relations. And well-to-do Russians as a whole could decamp alone or *en famille* to the spa towns (and casinos) of Germany and Bohemia, the Swiss mountains, or the Italian lakes, without necessarily first selling all their property or, like Onegin, vanishing to the world.

Fyodor Stravinsky never owned property. As the youngest of three sons, he cannot have inherited the Bragin house, and from his father there was nothing to inherit. A hardworking musician, he had neither the means nor the leisure to invest in real estate, and by the time he was prosperous enough to think of doing so, his health was failing. So he rented. He rented in Kiev and he rented in St. Petersburg. The Oranienbaum dachas were of course rented (1882, 1884, and 1885), and later Fyodor took houses at Skokov-Opochka, south of Pskov (1887), at Vechasha in the wooded lakeland to the south of Luga (1888), and at nearby L'zy (1889). Each year, as soon as school was done, he would install his family—complete with *nyanyas,* governesses, servants, and other indispensable hangers-on—in the house of his choice, and from May to August they would combine rural pursuits with various forms of self-improvement: reading, painting, music-making, or even—since it was a disadvantage of governesses that they were portable—schoolwork.

Igor's memories of these early holidays were understandably somewhat blurred, as we have seen in the case of L'zy. The dumb old peasant of the autobiography, with his bisyllabic chant which he accompanied with rhythmic "kissing" noises produced by squeezing his right hand into his left armpit, may have been a native of practically any of the above villages, just as the women of the well-remembered folk song may have been work-ing in any of the woods or fields of those regions.[1] The point about both stories, in any case, is that they are supposed to mark "the dawn of my con-sciousness of myself in the role of musician." They are not essentially reports of summer pleasures, but have an iconic significance whose Arca-dian setting merely emphasizes their pure, unwordly meaning.

But these holidays were, all the same, in their aimless and unhurried way, idyllic. The flight from the harsh and seemingly endless Petersburg winter to regions where it was always and eternally summer more than compensated for the monotonous and somewhat featureless reality of much of the Russian landscape. The resigned, somnolent world of Chek-hov comes irresistibly to mind. Nikolay Rimsky-Korsakov, who spent sev-eral summers at Vechasha from 1894 onwards, remembered it as "a charming spot: a wonderful large lake, Pesno, and a vast ancient orchard with century-old lindens, elms and so forth. The house was a heavy and clumsy structure, yet spacious and comfortable. The proprietress—an old woman—with her daughter, an overripe maiden, lived close by, in a tiny house, but did not interfere with us. The bathing was fine. At night the moon and the stars cast wonderful reflections on the lake. There was a multitude of birds. . . . We were all in love with Vechasha."[2] From Vasiliy Vasiliyevich Yastrebtsev, who visited Rimsky-Korsakov at Vechasha in 1894, we learn also that the garden had "magnificent allées bordered by lime-trees."[3]

As the children grew older and more able to endure long journeys, and as he himself perhaps felt increasingly secure professionally and more at liberty to absent himself from Petersburg for several months, Fyodor abandoned these rented holidays and preferred to spend the summer on the remote estates of his sisters-in-law. These involved journeys of monumental length and complexity, not always indeed simply by train. To get to the Pavlovka estate of Soph'ya Kirillovna Yelachich and her husband, you took a train from Petersburg to Tver, a journey of nine or ten hours. You then boarded one of the many steamboats which plied the navigable length of the Volga between Tver and Astrakhan, and for four days, apart from brief sightseeing stops in Rybinsk, Yaroslav, Nizhny-Novgorod, and Kazan, this well-appointed craft was your home; finally, at the small rye port of Chistopol on the river Kama, you abandoned ship and took to the road, in the form of a horse-drawn carriage, or (if you were unlucky) a springless tarantass, in which you bumped along the rough Bugul'ma road for another hundred miles to Pavlovka. Not surprisingly, stays at Pavlovka tended to be lengthy. Igor made this trip with his parents as early as 1883, for a stay of almost twelve weeks, and again for nine or ten weeks in 1886, which must have been the occasion when he mistook the portrait of the Tsar on the wall of the family cabin for that of a railway conductor.[4] Ten years later, in 1896, the Stravinskys were again at Pavlovka for the Yelachiches' silver wedding anniversary, and were photographed together on the front steps of the two-storey brick-built house.[5] Igor made his last visits to Pavlovka in 1903 and 1904.

These two- or three-month stays on the wheat-growing plateau of northern Samara must have severely tested the Russian capacity for suspended nervous animation. There is perhaps an echo of this in Igor's anxiety to leave with Vladimir Rimsky-Korsakov after a relatively short visit in 1904, instead of staying on for the good of his health.[6] Of course there was work to be done. On his later visits, Igor would spend part of the day composing. Earlier stays were probably dominated, like all the Stravinsky holidays in the nineties, by painting and drawing, for which Yury and Igor had both inherited their father's talent. As late as 1903, writing to his mother from Pavlovka, Igor asks for chrome yellow for his paint box, and this at a time when, as he explains in another letter, "I'm looking after my musical offspring most of all."[7] There were outings. In the hills around Pavlovka there were waterfalls and trout fishing; there were summits to climb. There were duck to shoot. Igor, less attached to game than his brothers, would take jars into the countryside to catch insects, a childhood enthusiasm which may have prompted his adult image of himself as an artist who could "wait [for ideas] as an insect can wait."[8] Perhaps there would even be the occasional trip to Bugul'ma, the main town of the region, eighteen miles away. About twice a week the post went, and there would be a scurry of eager or resigned letter-writing and anxious, sometimes competitive, sorting through the arriving post. "It's very annoying," Igor wrote to his mother from Pavlovka, "when with each post everybody gets letters, sometimes several, and I get nothing, yes nothing."[9]

Igor loved and respected his aunt Soph'ya as his mother's closest and most beloved sister. But he felt most attached to his uncle Alexander, who was open and friendly, easygoing in his attitudes, and above all a musician who took Igor seriously, shared many of his musical tastes, and loved talk about music, politics, philosophy, and religion (as he understood it). To put it plainly, Uncle Alexander was everything that Fyodor Stravinsky was not. We cannot go so far as to say that he was a father figure to Igor, not least because that would imply an inadequacy in Fyodor, where it would be fairer to understand an intricacy. But Alexander Yelachich was nevertheless a strong counterweight in the boy's emotional life, an opener of doors and windows, where Fyodor and Anna were cautious about intellectual ventilation. And yet there is no hint that Uncle Alexander was disapproved of or disliked as an influence on their son. The difference may have been more one of atmosphere than one of substance.

A lawyer by training,[10] Alexander Yelachich was by the time Igor knew him a pillar of the establishment: a high-ranking agronomist in the St. Petersburg civil service, as well as a huge and wealthy landowner beyond the Volga. But, like many of his class and generation, Yelachich held what we might now regard as "automatic" liberal views. Born in 1847, he was just too young to count as a true *shestidesyatnik*—a man of the sixties—but he was firmly of that intellectual tendency: broadly egalitarian, pro-emancipation (even though the Yelachiches must have suffered financially from the freeing of the serfs in 1861),[11] politically liberal— which meant left-wing, in the years before Bolshevism was known or understood by the Russian upper middle classes—interventionist, dogooding. Philosophically, Uncle Alexander seems to have been a positivist, but as an admirer of the French historian Ernest Renan, he will have found room for the "divine spark," while presumably sharing Marie-Jean Guyau's rejection of Renan's view that the great artist was rapidly being rendered obsolete by the development of science.[12] We can speculate further that Yelachich, like most Russian liberals of his time, more than half-sympathized with even the more drastic attempts in the eighties and nineties to bomb the Imperial establishment into a more open system of government, not foreseeing how quickly the violence would turn against established society in general.

Igor's later attitude to Alexander Yelachich in print was faintly condescending,[13] but at the time he was strongly under his uncle's influence. Nearly everything we know about his own sociopolitical views in the early 1900s confirms the debt, from his deprecatory ideas about property to his ironic reaction to an attempt on the life of a certain Admiral Dubasov.[14]

There is surely an echo of long evenings at Pavlovka, or the Yelachich Petersburg flat in Ivanovskaya, in the earnest discussions about national constitutions that kept Igor, his wife, and friends entertained in the early days at the Old Farm in Ustilug, and in the ardent Anglophilia which emerged from them: "[England—] what a country!—altogether marvellous!!!!!! Such political maturity and breeding. And all done by that 'Magna Carta of Liberties' and that amazing 'Habeas Corpus.' Enough! It makes me jealous, angry, and pained!!!!!!"[15]

Uncle Alya's musical tastes to some extent reflected his rationalist thinking. Admiration for Musorgsky, for instance, was more or less compulsory among true *shestidesyatniki*, because of the connection between his form of realism and the reformism of Chernishevsky, even though Musorgsky himself had been very doubtfully liberal in his own views. We can take it, in any case, that the mystical, Slavophile side of the folklorist movement—the side promoted by Vladimir Stasov—will not have appealed much to Uncle Alya, and if it is also true, as Stravinsky later alleged, that his uncle disliked Rimsky-Korsakov, that was probably as much due to Rimsky's increasing preoccupation with mystical Slav subject matter as to his having cast in his lot with the establishment as a professor at the Conservatoire and a guardian of academic rectitude.[16] Politically and intellectually, in fact, the Yelachich and Rimsky households were by no means far apart: rationalism, religious skepticism, and political liberalism they had in common. Only something in the tone—bohemian Hampstead versus bourgeois Putney—may have separated them.[17]

A committed taste for Beethoven still also carried with it the faintest hint of republicanism, just as you would expect a progressive thinker in the eighties and nineties to profess an admiration for Wagner. But Alexander Yelachich was a genuine musical enthusiast, not an intellectual opportunist. He was a good enough pianist "to accompany even the demanding Fyodor Stravinsky,"[18] and a "passionate musical amateur who would spend days at a time playing the piano."[19] Igor often played four-hands with him: Brahms piano quartets are mentioned, and Bruckner symphonies, as well as Beethoven, Wagner, and, by implication, the modern Russian symphonists, Tchaikovsky, Glazunov, Borodin, and (unexpectedly) Rimsky-Korsakov.[20] Uncle Alexander also took an interest in his nephew's music: Igor's early piano sonata was written at Pavlovka, and when his E-flat Symphony was part-performed in St. Petersburg in April 1907, his uncle gave him a medal in honor of the event.[21] On the rare occasions that the Pavlovka piano fell silent, there would be heated discussions about its music, which would

sometimes reach grandiose dimensions. Zhenya takes my side. Alexander Frantsevich, just as obviously, sometimes surrenders.

Yesterday, for example, we were talking about Rachmaninov. He doesn't want to get to know Rachmaninov, since it isn't worth it (he's a "piano composer"). So I told him he'd do better to hear and get to know Rachmaninov's piano concerto than my sonata. He said nothing, but it was obvious that he was placed in an awkward position: either to recognize my piece as superior to Rachmaninov's, which he doesn't know, or to abuse me, which he would never do. So obviously victory was on my side.[22]

The mood at Pavlovka was open; it was free and easy. Good. But the rough-and-tumble could also have its casualties. The Yelachiches, like the Stravinskys, had only sons, and the far from self-assured Igor may sometimes have found the bullish atmosphere, so different from the tight-lipped constraint of the Kryukov Canal, hard to take. Of the five Yelachich boys, three were significantly older than him. Nikolay, the oldest (born 1872), was already married (to a daughter of the poet Yakov Polonsky) by the time Igor went to Pavlovka as a teenager.[23] But the next two boys— Sergey and Mikhail, respectively eight and five years older than Igor— were more in evidence. Then there was Yevgeny (Zhenya), Igor's exact contemporary and his closest confederate at Pavlovka; and finally young Gavriyil, born only in 1894.

The Yelachich style was to tease. The two oldest brothers, especially, seem to have been prone to this unpleasant, because only covertly malicious, habit. And while it is Nikolay's teasing that has been immortalized in the memoirs of his famous victim,[24] it is Sergey who emerges from contemporary documents as the chief threat. "Sergey arrives tomorrow, which I'm not exactly overjoyed about, knowing his intolerable character and knowing how many unpleasant times he gave me in Ustilug. . . . Now that I'm a guest in their house he should surely treat me with more delicacy, but far from it; I'm certain he'll have no shame towards me, but will go on with his Ustilug behavior."[25] And so he did, in tandem with his younger brother Zhenya. Only, this time, Igor seems to have been himself shamed into a pretence of tolerance: "The usual Pavlovka teasings have started, which amuse them for some reason; they direct the teasing at me— teasing devoid of any nasty intention or character, just joking, though sometimes very witty."[26] This comes close to the Freudian syndrome of "identifying with the aggressor." But Igor was not the only observer of this Yelachich phenomenon. According to Gury Stravinsky, Sergey was a different man away from home: "not the Petersburg Sergey, nor the Pavlovka Sergey, nor in general the Sergey that everyone knows, but a happy, lively boy who is as naughty as a twelve-year-old."[27] The fact is that the Yelachiches were energetic, natural leaders, a dominant strain; but they were temperamental. Sergey was happy organizing the theatricals at Ustilug, but he did not always know how to behave when manners had to take precedence over the life force. Even Aunt Soph'ya was sometimes moody. "The chief pleasure," Igor told his mother in one of his Pavlovka letters, "is that Auntie has been in a good mood during these days, whereas most of the time she's in a bad one, and Alexander Frantsevich even told me that this mood nowadays seems chronic."[28] Yelachich life, to put it in a nutshell, demanded a robustness that Igor did not always possess. And yet he seems to have remembered Pavlovka with pleasure, and for that he could thank his uncle and aunt.

Very different were his memories of his aunt Yekaterina's estate at Pechisky. As we saw in chapter 1, the atmosphere here was poisoned for Igor by his aunt's overbearing and disagreeable behavior and by the invariable presence of the hated Vinogradova. But Pechisky was an ill-starred place for the Stravinskys, even without the help of aunts, governesses, and other such Dickensian horrors.

Pechisky was a large estate of almost three thousand acres, ten miles north of the regional Ukrainian capital of Proskurov (now Khmel'nitsky), on the edge of the wheat and sugarbeet region of central west Ukraine. Igor remembered it as "a dull place, but about thirty miles away was the city of Yarmolintsy which was lively and picturesque and renowned for its fairs."[29] One pictures Yarmolintsï, from the description in *Expositions and Developments,* amid a sea of wheat, vibrating with peasant dancing, the heel dance *(presyatka)* and the Cossack kicking dance (the *kazachok*), and with wonderful costumes in brilliant primary reds, blues, and yellows— the whole setting a kind of rural *Petrushka.* The reality was doubtless more squalid. As Stravinsky also recalled, Gypsies frequented the region, with their untidy habits and suspect morals, as they always have done fairs and fairgrounds. Poverty was everywhere. The peasants, when not in costume, were poorly clad and meanly housed. The rain would sometimes descend in torrents. Fyodor Stravinsky left a chilling description of this part of the Podolsky government during a wet summer:

> The crops rot where they lie, the as yet untied stooks sprout weeds, the not yet harvested corn is bent to the ground—and it rots too, sprouting grass and decaying to the roots. The beet which they plant in quantity in these regions for making into sugar has been shrivelled by some worm with the speed of a locust plague; the roads are impassable—awash with rainwater, the rivers have broken their banks. Total disaster. . . . And in the capital Petrograd [sic], they scribble away in the offices of the ministry of agriculture, gathering their statistics for this year's harvests, and they know nothing, understand nothing, and never have understood or will understand how the Rus-

sian people live and work in the Rus, in the provinces, where nobody knows about their departments or what they are for. They're certainly no use to the landlord or the tiller of the soil.[30]

Igor first set foot in Pechisky when he was not quite nine. But he then spent three consecutive summers there, and subsequently visited it several times before or after staying with the Nosenkos at Ustilug.[31] "My parents," he wrote in *Expositions and Developments*, "[there] openly showed their favouritism for my elder brother, Roman."[32] But the real meaning of Pechisky to Igor was something more complicated to do with Roman: the sense of rejection associated with his absence, and later with his death. After the first year in Pechisky (1891), Fyodor and Anna habitually used the place as a repository for whichever sons they did not want to take with them on the European trips they started making in 1892, and since (possibly excepting that first year) they always took Roman with them until Igor's first trip abroad in 1895—when it was Roman who stayed behind— it seems natural that Igor's distaste for Pechisky should have got mixed up with some sense of alienation from his eldest brother. One even feels that this systematic separation of two such different brothers may have reflected some definite hostility between them, as if their parents feared that the intense social contact of the long summer holidays would breed rancor and confrontation. In any case, Pechisky became, in his memory, Igor's punishment for not being Roman. So there was for him a horrible appropriateness in the fact that it was at Pechisky that Roman suddenly died, in June 1897, while Igor was away alone with his parents at the German spa of Bad Homburg; and that it was at Pechisky that they all bleakly reconvened.

Whether or not Fyodor and Anna had made a favorite of Roman in life, in death they did so. Fyodor's entries in his account book for that terrible summer and afterwards reveal only too starkly the intensity of the loss he and his wife felt at the premature death of their Adonis, and it is more than probable that they failed to conceal from their remaining sons that he— the departed one—had been their idol and their hope. How much easier, after all, for Fyodor to pour out his feelings for a son with whom he no longer had to communicate than he had ever found it to express his emotions towards the sons that he had before his eyes and within his four walls. How much easier, too, for Anna—the stern, unbending master-at-arms. Yet one may doubt whether, openly, they changed in any way except to become perhaps marginally sterner, marginally less communicative. Anna's laconic postscript to a letter of July 1899 from Pechisky to Fyodor in St. Petersburg (on quite other matters) may be read in this spirit: "Yesterday evening, that is at five o'clock, I drove to Roman, sat there till

six-forty-five, and, before sunset, went back home."[33] It may not be superfluous to observe, however, that failure to express feeling is not the same
as failure to feel.

You arrived at Pechisky by rail, getting out at Proskurov, "a dirty town of
23,000 inhabitants, including many Jews, [and with] extensive barracks."[34]
For some reason, the occupants of the barracks found their way quite often
to Pechisky itself, invariably no doubt on horseback. "I've already, yesterday, been for a ride on an officer's horse," eleven-year-old Igor wrote from
Pechisky. "Officers come every day and play cards; one of them taught
Alyosha to click his heels."[35] Soon Igor himself was playing soldiers with
his cousin Zhenya Yelachich and his brother Yury. But more dependable
fun was spider and insect hunting, Igor's future favorite Pavlovka pastime.

> Three days ago we went to catch tarantulas; we lowered a string with
> wax on it, and the tarantula at once grabbed it. I ran and fetched an
> axe to dig it out, and Zhenya dug a hole six inches deep and poked it
> with a knife; and suddenly the tarantula appeared, and so abruptly
> that we all yelled "Tarantula!" It seemed to take fright and started
> running off, but Zhenya put a glass over it so that it couldn't get out.
> We showed it to everyone. Then Zhenya put it back down its hole. As
> for lessons, I can tell you that we can't boast about our attentiveness
> and diligence.[36]

The final shaft, so seemingly beside the point, is not at all. What more poisonous spider than the unfortunate Vinogradova, the boys' governess?
And what better way of getting *her* under a glass than by exposing her failure to keep those boys' noses to the grindstone?

Igor, while remembering Pechisky as a place of correction, also remembered it—no doubt in compensation—as a place of discovery. Here, he
admitted in conversation with Robert Craft, he first met his future wife
Yekaterina Nosenko. "But I dislike talking about that now, since I am
afraid I might betray something sacred."[37] Pechisky had become a country
of the mind—terra incognita. Igor Stravinsky and Yekaterina Nosenko in
fact first met consciously at Ustilug in September 1890, before Igor had
set eyes on his aunt Yekaterina's house.[38]

Igor made the journey from Pechisky to Ustilug and back several times
in later years; but he more often travelled direct to Ustilug from Petersburg, or, later still, from the West via Berlin and Warsaw. It may seem prosaic to dwell on wheeled transport in the life of the composer of *The Rite of
Spring* and *Les Noces*. But travel was emblematic for nineteenth-century
Russians, as lovers of Tolstoy and Turgenev will not need reminding. Tolstoy's death at a railway station was no meaningless accident but the symbolic climax of a flight from reality—a death of Lear for the steam age. As

for Stravinsky, he spent months, perhaps years, of his life in railway trains. Nobody has yet seriously examined the effects of those incessant anapests of iron wheels over track connectors and points on the consciousness of the greatest rhythmic thinker since Beethoven; or the impact of those long, long days and nights in purposeful, powered motion through a slowly changing landscape. But only a fool (or an integral serialist) would suppose that they did not have any.

Even from Pechisky to Ustilug, a distance of 175 miles as the cranes fly, it was necessary to spend some eighteen hours in three different trains, ending with a six- or seven-hour, forty-mile journey with carriage and horses. From Proskurov you had to set off in the opposite direction (towards Odessa), in order to avoid crossing into the Austrian Empire at Volochisk, which would at best involve long delays for paperwork and the change of track gauge. You then changed at Zhmerinka and headed north towards Kazatin, on the main line, where you joined the overnight train to Kovel. At Kovel you rented horses and a tarantass with driver, and off you set southwards once again to Vladimir-Volïnsky and thence via a rough sand road to Ustilug.[39]

But this journey was the soul of brevity compared with the two and a half days' trip to Ustilug from St. Petersburg, with all that such a journey entailed for large Russian families: the interminable platform farewells, the mounds of luggage, the excited children and their various minders— the *nyanyas*, the governesses, the tutors—the porters to be tipped, the sleeping-car attendants to be buttonholed and if necessary bribed, the departure bells to be noticed and counted. These were in every sense spacious train journeys, remote from the cramped airline seats and inconvenient, understocked buffets of modern express travel. Not only were the compartments bigger, but the trains pottered along more slowly on their broader tracks, placing far less strain on nerve and sinew.[40] At mealtimes there would be lengthy stops at station restaurants along the way, where you would be served delicious, inexpensive food and drink by white-aproned Tartar waiters.[41]

The village of Ustilug, where Igor's uncle Gavriyil Nosenko had bought several thousand hectares of land at the end of the 1880s, was an old estate of the Polish Lubomirski family, who built a palace here, at the confluence of the river Bug and its eastern tributary the Luga, in the eighteenth century. In those days, Ustilug made money out of the northern grain trade. The grain was loaded on to barges, and shipped down the Bug and the Vistula to the port of Gdansk—the only North Sea outlet for Ukrainian corn. But the partition of Poland and the acquisition of the lower Vistula by Prussia in 1772 put paid to the grain exports and to Ustilug itself.[42] By the time Nosenko came here from Kiev, western Volhynia was in a depressed state, poorly connected by road or rail, its light industry at a low ebb. The region was in the so-called Pale of Settlement, that part of Imperial Russia in which the large number of Jews inherited from the former Polish territories were still compelled by law to reside (which accounts for the fact that ninety percent of the population of Ustilug was Jewish). Property prices were low, not least because the Poles to the west of the Bug were prohibited from acquiring property to the east of it. Whether because the particular line had died out, or because of routine confiscations by the Russian authorities, or even possibly because a member of the family had been imprisoned for subversive activities, the Lubomirskis had gone, the palace was a ruin, and the estate had reverted to the Imperial Exchequer, who sold it to Nosenko at auction.[43] For a time Nosenko lived in a surviving outhouse of the Lubomirski palace, before building a family house somewhat away from the two rivers, just off the main road to Vladimir-Volinsky. This house, single-storeyed but spacious and comfortable like Pechisky, was the Ustilug of Igor's childhood.[44]

If you drive today along the road from Vladimir to Ustilug, your overriding impression is one of neglect—but it is a very modern, subindustrial kind of neglect. Useless scraps of old, rusty metal litter the potholed highway; everything from the houses to the fields is poorly maintained. The impression is of a modern version of Turgenev's Oryol in *A Sportsman's Sketches*. But when Nosenko first arrived here the countryside must have had a markedly different appearance. Much of the woodland was cut in Soviet times for border surveillance,[45] but at the turn of the century there was a more generous feeling of woods and wheatfields. Above all, in its remote incommunicability, the region was profoundly, idyllically rural. The little Luga River, winding its way apparently aimlessly through flat, reed-fringed meadows and under steep wooded banks, seemed the very soul of antique rusticity—ever in motion, eternally at rest.

Although Nosenko's wife had died before he moved here, his Ustilug household had one charming feature which neither Pavlovka, Pechisky, nor indeed the Kryukov Canal could provide: it was warmly, pervasively feminine. Where Yelachiches and Stravinskys seemed only able to produce sons, Nosenkos could only manage daughters. Gavriyil had two of them: Lyudmila, born in 1879, and Yekaterina, born in January 1881, less than two years before her mother's death. Also usually at Ustilug in the summer were their cousins Olga, four years older than Igor, and Vera, the same age as him: the daughters of Gavriyil's nephew Dmitry Andreyevich Nosenko. Dmitry had an estate of his own at Omelno, twenty-five miles northeast of Lutsk. But after Gavriyil's death in 1897 he seems to have taken over the management of Ustilug on behalf of his two young cousins, who were still only in their teens. Meanwhile, their domestic needs continued to be catered for by their foster mother, the redoubtable Soph'ya

Dmitriyevna Vel'sovskaya, a distant and by now somewhat elderly relation of the Nosenkos, known to all and sundry as Baba Sonya.[46]

The Stravinskys first came to Ustilug as a family (though without Fyodor) in September 1890, arriving here from the Vel'sovskaya estate near Karkhov on their way home to Petersburg. Igor was eight, Yekaterina (Katya) nine. "From our first hour together," Stravinsky wrote seventy years later, "we both seemed to realize that we would one day marry—or so we told each other later. Perhaps we were always more like brother and sister. I was a deeply lonely child, and I wanted a sister of my own. Catherine, who was my first cousin, came into my life as a kind of long-wanted sister in my tenth [sic] year. We were from then until her death extremely close, and closer than lovers sometimes are, for mere lovers may be strangers though they live and love together all their lives."[47]

Nothing else in Stravinsky's memoirs rings so true. However much one may qualify the antagonism he later depicted between himself and his immediate family, it must already be clear that he suffered from an excess of masculinity in the family circle. The combination of male supremacy with male emotional reserve was stifling to an undersized boy of so highly strung and aesthetically sensitive a disposition, even if it was mildly tempered by the cozy warmth of Bertha Essert, who, whatever her other virtues, can have had no conception of the unusual gifts and temperament of her charge. And here he was, suddenly confronted by two attractive and intelligent female cousins, just slightly, tantalizingly his elders, but with no idea of bearing down on him or punishing him for having been born smaller and later than they. No Ustilug letters survive of this very early time. But chronology is of secondary importance here. Every time Ustilug is in question for the quarter-century during which Igor knew it, there is a suffusion of warmth and homecoming that is missing from other contexts, other communications. We know more about Ustilug, no doubt primarily because Igor and Gury wrote letters, and they wrote because their parents were not there but at Pechisky ("with" Roman), but also because the letters tell more, there being more to tell. And what they tell, no doubt unwittingly, is of a life substantially made by girls.

Thus: "We've already had a lot of beautiful days, so we've been able to ride and the girls (all of them), especially, to swim. Gury has been swimming too, and three of us, Katya, Olga Dmitriyevna and I, are drawing. . . . Olga Dmitriyevna says that my drawing is coming out well, and so says the most severe judge, Milusha [Lyudmila] (I'm as scared as fire of Milusha in this respect)."[48] Suddenly drawing and sketching, always a serious talent with the Stravinskys, have become the center of activity, surrounded by an arty mystique: "The grass is dark in places from the shade of the pines, in places there is no grass at all, and there appears the lilac-brown earth (or in places bright green—from the brilliant sunlight); the sun lights up the edges of the pines, revealing their brown-orange flowers; on the bottom of the trunks is the reflection of the light green grass, and above is the reflection of the blue sky."⁴⁹ . . . And so on. In another letter there is more drawing; there is wild-raspberry picking; there are preparations for that ubiquitous feature of the Russian country-house party, the open-air play; there is a tennis court to help build; there is study. In the evening there are piano playing and reading. There are special friends and innocent pairing off. "Gury's very fond of Vera Dmitriyevna; she always calls him her wonderful dear boy, and they're constantly off together in the britzka."⁵⁰ For that matter, Olga, Katya, and Igor do everything together and are teased about it, but it is teasing on an equal footing: "Vera Dmitriyevna calls all this sitting and drawing idiotic. So that's now our definition—to go and do something idiotic is to go and look at our drawings." When it comes time to leave, Milusha and Katya plead for the boys to stay: but "knowing that it doesn't depend on us, they beg it of you. God knows when we shall again get such a marvellous summer in Ustilug."⁵¹

The next summer, what were spontaneous groupings begin to assume more rigid outlines: "On the first or second day there was some small skirmish with Vera Dmitriyevna. But it wasn't my fault (as everyone acknowledged) and Vera Dmitriyevna changed her behavior after that. So now we're getting on famously—Vera Dmitriyevna even calls me 'dear Gima'—which is as good as I could hope for."⁵² The superficial rapport is even sealed by music: "I don't play now with Milochka, only with Kotik [Katya] and Vera."⁵³ Why Lyudmila is out of favor, we never learn. But Vera's fall from temporary grace, the summer following, is reported in malicious detail:

> When we meet, my dears, I'll tell you in detail all about this coquette—it frankly infuriates me. To my mind, the older one gets the more one should use one's head, but the older *she* gets, the more everything that's mean about her grows in size. It's hard to annoy such a delicate and gentle person as Safonov [a fellow guest], but she managed it. Yesterday we assembled to go to the wood to paint, and just before we set off she behaved in such a way towards him that he almost stayed at home—he was terribly cross.⁵⁴

Igor's eye, meanwhile, has lighted on "another new acquaintance—Lyudmila Fyodorovna Kuxina: the exact opposite of Vera Dmitriyevna. She's a remarkably sweet young lady, such a gentle, kind, and nice girl. She reminds me in many respects of Kotyula [Katya], and many others find this—although really they have little in common; she's very pretty and her figure is very graceful. It's very nice for Kotyula that I like her, as they're best friends."[55] Soon Igor is offering to accompany the best friend to the train at Kovel, "since she has still never travelled alone, either by rail or—more to the point—on horseback. She was terribly pleased and touched by it."[56] "It was a summer romance," Stravinsky remembered almost sixty years later, "forgotten in the first wind of winter and with disillusioning rapidity."[57] But he never forgot the young lady's name, and he did go with her to Kovel.

But what of Katya? "In Katen'ka I've found a great change: she has become significantly more serious. . . ."[58]

> You know, my dears, they've altered a lot this year, Katen'ka has become, to my mind, still more charming—but her constant and serious work has absolutely not changed. We get together a terrific amount—you know how when you see kindness in another person, you tend to become doubly attached to that person, you meet and understand them more easily, even if it is not the external aspect of their disposition. In Katen'ka I see this constantly, and she quite simply moves me.[59]

But is this the emotion of a young man in love? Not, at least, so far as *he* knows, since within days he is jogging along the Kovel road with his new friend Lyudmila Fyodorovna. The trouble is, cousins are *supposed* to love each other—blood being thicker than water—and how do you begin to tell when this kind of love is turning to Love? For Igor, though there are many gaps in our chronology, it seems that cousinly love was able to stretch a very long way before it broke free. "Please tell Katyusha," he wrote to his mother from Pavlovka fully two years later, "that I'd be unspeakably glad to get a letter from her. Please tell her that I too love her more than all her sisters and cousins and would be sincerely pleased to learn that she has remained as wonderful as she was before."[60]

No doubt Katya had told Anna that she was much fonder of Igor than of his brothers. But when would she tell him that she loved him in a way that made brothers irrelevant? We do not know, except that it was before August 1905, when they became engaged at the Nosenko estate of Omelno.[61]

LIKE ALL THE BEST Russian country houses, Ustilug was a melting pot—a microcosm of civilized life so concentrated that it sometimes seemed to breed new organisms.

Take the amateur theatricals. The resemblance between domestic theatre in nineteenth-century Russia[62] and the average game of charades or play reading at a modern English summer weekend is so slight that one needs to look elsewhere for a comparison: perhaps to the village play, long prepared, the focus of many people's lives for weeks and months on end, serious of purpose yet often terrible of effect, and above all inescapable. But even this hardly does justice to the high artistic seriousness and, more important still, high technical standards of Russian domestic drama at its best. Indeed, two of the most innovative theatrical enterprises in turn-of-the-century Moscow—Savva Mamontov's Private Opera Company and Stanislavsky's Moscow Art Theatre—actually began life as domestic entertainments. And there is a simple historical reason why this should have been so. Until 1882 public theatre was a state monopoly in Russia, so that unofficial, noncommercial, and above all innovative theatre had almost literally no professional outlet. It was forced back into the drawing room: it was a kind of theatrical *samizdat*.[63]

The Ustilug play dominated the holidays, and nobody was allowed to treat it lightly. It was performed outdoors on a stage roughly protected by a tarpaulin, and was frequently devastated by rain. Igor's letters of 1899 are full of the preparations: the rehearsals, the part learning, the setting up of the stage, the trips to Vladimir-Volïnsky to buy props and costumes, the ghastly weather, the cancelled performances. Two sets of plays were given: first they did Chekhov's *The Bear* (with Katya as the widow Popova, Gury as the servant Luke, and Igor as Smirnov), together with a Russian version of Hartmann's *Gleich und gleich gesellt sich gern*.[64] Later on, in August, there were three more short plays, by Karpinsky, Bilibin, and Potapenko, produced by Sergey Yelachich. Most or all of these were comedies, and there was clearly a certain amount of onstage hilarity. According to Gury: "At curtain up [in *The Bear*] . . . I found it so funny that I almost burst out laughing, as Kotyk screwed up her eyes in pain and began to sob." But "in the main," he reports, "everything went off well."[65] In his previous letter, however, this had not been exactly his expectation. As Anna Stravinsky reported from Pechisky to Fyodor in St. Petersburg: "[Gury] writes a few hours before their first performance . . . that they are all very nervous . . . and Igor, at the dress rehearsal the previous evening, was so nervous he made himself sick. 'What will he be like at the performance?'—asks Gury."[66] From Anna's report, we also learn about the audience for the Ustilug plays: "Thirteen of the so-called intelligentsia and a lot of ordinary folk will be their onlookers." The gentry, then, were risking making fools of themselves in front of their social inferiors. It was no mere after-dinner amusement.

Did these complicated arrangements give Igor some feeling for the theatre he would not otherwise have had: a feeling he could not have got from the Mariyinsky Theatre? It seems possible, but one cannot be confident.

He did later come to love the idea of the informal scaffolding stage, set up in the village square: *Renard* and *The Soldier's Tale* hinge on this type of ad hoc theatre. But neither their plots nor their rustic settings are exactly taken from the bourgeois repertoire which supplied the staple diet at Ustilug.[67] And although Igor certainly took the plays seriously, and sometimes had quite big parts in them, there is no particular evidence that his brain or aesthetic sense was strongly engaged in questions of genre or presentation, such as one might expect of the budding composer of *Petrushka*. Rather, as with many a seventeen-year-old, one senses a deep anxiety both to perform and to conform—to be, so to speak, inconspicuously conspicuous. And no doubt any other attitude would soon have had him in trouble with Dmitry Andreyevich, or, still worse, the dangerous Sergey Yelachich.

As for music, it still takes its place among the acceptable leisure-time activities—leisure, that is, from the play. "We play the piano endlessly,"[68] to be sure; but so they did everywhere in Russia in June, July, and August, just as they would take out their colors and paint the sunset or the edge of the wood, or take their copies of Tolstoy's *Resurrection* to the lime allée. There is as yet no hint that music is imposing itself, and above all no reference to composition as a summertime activity. Igor's creative aspirations are entirely concentrated on drawing and painting, a pastime at which, certainly, he was talented, but which also had the attraction that it was sociable and much cultivated by his girl cousins. Music meant performance: four-hand duets with Katya, or accompanying her and Vera as they sang. No doubt this was a real pleasure for them all, and perhaps it drew them closer together. But Igor's reports also make it clear that he was under orders: "I can say with my hand on my heart that I played until Dmitry Andr[eyevich] arrived. But now there's not a chance, since he's very busy and so tired that music irritates him, particularly learning things. Milochka and I don't play together now, only Kotik, Vera, and I sing a bit towards evening, and that's all the music."[69]

By now, as we shall see, he was having more serious piano lessons and his practice was under scrutiny. Back in St. Petersburg six weeks or so later he was assuring his parents that "I start playing the piano tomorrow (I mean exercises, scales, and suchlike finger stretchings)."[70] But of composition there is no mention in any letter of Igor's before 1903.[71] Indeed, if it were not for the survival of one fragmentary piano piece, a tarantella composed in October 1898, and a letter in which Igor states his intention of getting theory lessons from the Rimsky-Korsakov pupil Nikolay Tcherepnin, we might be tempted to doubt whether composition was even a speck on the horizon until after he left school in 1901.[72] No wonder Anna and Fyodor failed to recognize their son's creative talent.

The Ustilug which "was a haven for composing"[73] was still in the future: it was another house, in another century, and with a new owner.

THOUGH FYODOR STRAVINSKY never performed outside the Russian Empire, he did, in the last decade of his life, take his holidays there. He visited Germany, Austria, France, and Switzerland. In 1892 he went to Vienna, Prague, Dresden, and Berlin; and in 1893, after an even wider-ranging German tour, he, Anna, and Roman ranged as far afield as Paris, where—among the more routine sights—they attended Wagner's *Walküre* at the Opera.[74] But Igor's first trip abroad only came in 1895. With his parents and Yury, he went to the spa town of Bad Homburg, on the edge of the Taunus hills to the north of Frankfurt-am-Main, after which they all headed south for Switzerland, and the town of Interlaken, where Fyodor collected material and did some drawings for the role of Gessler in Rossini's *William Tell*.[75]

Bad Homburg, though much altered to meet the needs of a modern, motorized clientele, still preserves traces of a more stately time when it was a favorite resort of well-to-do Russian summer tourists, who came here to treat their real or imaginary intestinal disorders with the iron and sodium chloride waters in the springs of the Kurpark. The sodium-rich Elisabethenbrunnen, where on 2 July Igor and his parents were photographed in front of a carefully posed group of Kurpark visitors—the remnants, presumably, of the audience for the regular early-morning concert—is still in use, though the elegant wrought-iron colonnade behind the spring is, alas, gone.[76]

Perhaps the Russian visitors spent the rest of the day strolling in the Kurpark, visiting the castle or the deer park; perhaps they took the tram up to the huge Roman fort on the nearby Saalburg. Or perhaps they even ventured as far as Königstein, with its thirteenth-century castle, or the pretty town of Höchst, on the river Main just below Frankfurt. Homburg itself was a dullish place for a lively thirteen-year-old, but at least it was not just full of glum Russians. Rich Englishmen came here in some numbers, and Germans from Frankfurt, and the Stravinskys may even themselves have gone to Frankfurt and called on the elderly Clara Schumann, with Igor acting as interpreter.[77] Igor was intrigued by the foreigners, and especially by the English, whom he came across again at Interlaken, looking at the Jungfrau through their telescopes.[78] No doubt the starchy Fyodor and Anna steered clear of the casino; it would be hard to imagine anyone less like Dostoyevsky's Alexey Ivanovich in *The Gambler*—or indeed less like Dostoyevsky himself, who had been to Homburg years earlier and probably half-modelled his Roulettenburg on it. So it must surely have been on one of the Stravinskys' later visits, in 1897 or 1898, that Igor slipped into the casino and observed "the long rows of tables at which people played baccarat and bézique, roulca and faro as now, in the bowels of ocean liners, they play bingo."[79] Or it may have been in the tiny spa town of Bad Soden nearby, where the Stravinskys stayed for some weeks in 1898, in search of relief for Anna's catarrh from the town's hot carbonic springs. Certainly it was on this later visit that Igor drew the castle at Königstein, and the church and palace tower at Höchst on the Main, since the drawings are dated.[80]

Two years after this first visit abroad, in early June 1897, Igor again came to Homburg with his parents, this time alone. It must have been a proud moment. But it was to be all too brief. They had barely arrived at the spa when word came of the sudden death of Roman. In despair, they had to repack their bags and return to Pechisky with as much haste as the languid rail schedules of the time allowed. The atmosphere must have been appalling. Igor again recalled interpreting for his father at the railway station in Vienna; and he remembered the silent droshky journey from Proskurov to Pechisky.[81] But he recalled nothing of the ten dreadful weeks the family spent at Pechisky before the ritual return to St. Petersburg in late August: Anna and Fyodor in grim, inconsolable mourning for their son, the boys repressed and cheerless, hating Aunt Yekaterina even more than usual, hating Pechisky, hating summer holidays. It was not a good omen for foreign travel: everything arranged for the good of your health, and with what result? Early death.

But there was worse to come. Fyodor, for all these annual holiday "cures," had always enjoyed tolerably good health. But at some time in the spring of 1899 he fell awkwardly on his back during a Mariyinsky performance, and later began to suffer intense spinal pain, which in due course revealed itself as cancer.[82] By 1902 the case was hopeless. By June his wife was so afraid for him that she would not leave him alone in the house.[83] But somehow Fyodor dragged himself to Germany with the whole family, apparently for the newfangled X-ray treatment which alone held out the faintest hope of a cure. From Berlin, Igor wrote to a friend in Heidelberg:

> Dear Vladimir Nikolayevich! We've only now got to Berlin. I can say that we are having terrible luck. Father is sick the whole time. If it's not one illness, it's another. Not much fun. Early tomorrow morning we are going to Wildungen by the fast train. We'll be setting out with a half-invalid father. Write, my dear, to Wildungen, Poste restante, Herrn Igor von Strawinsky—that's important—here they call noblemen "von"—it's a general courtesy. So I'll await your news with impatience. Deep bows to all your worthy family—also from Papa and Mama.[84]

On 22 July the stricken family arrived at Bad Wildungen, in the wooded hills near Kassel, where Fyodor was to undergo treatment. As usual they stayed *en pension*, in the house of a family called Wilhelm. Igor dangled his legs out of the window and took photographs of the town, occasionally flashing a glance at his young landlady, who was holding him by the jacket. Fyodor was well enough to show her his gold watch, "a present from the Tsar." Gury cooked scrambled eggs and called Frau Wilhelm "Schwes-ter."[85] After three weeks of this sort of guest-house life, Igor must have been relieved to escape to his friends in Heidelberg. But: "In my absence Papa's illness (neuralgia) got worse, and he has now been in bed for some days in terrible pain. Today he's a little better, so we must hope that by the end of the week we shall get away from here, but where to—we're not yet very sure. In all probability we'll make first for Berlin, in order to consult with doctors about Papa's excruciating illness, and from Berlin we'll go wherever the doctors direct us."[86]

Adrift in the hospital towns of Germany, the twenty-year-old Igor might seem about to vanish without trace. What is he but the undersized, under-appreciated, undermotivated son of a famous but nearly extinguished father whose world was dying with him?

Did Igor himself know the answer to that question? Perhaps; or perhaps not. But at least he had by now consulted the oracle.

A POLYPHONY OF TEACHERS

IGOR'S VISIT TO USTILUG in 1899 was, by Russian standards, little more than an outing from Pechisky. On his parents' insistence, presumably, he went with them to Aunt Yekaterina's in early June, so that the family could be together at Roman's grave on the second anniversary of his death on the tenth. Later he and Gury were allowed to accept the invitation to Ustilug for a few weeks in July and early August, but they soon had to get back to Pechisky. Yury had gone off to Kiev to start his architectural office practice; Fyodor's "continual illness," as Igor wrote to Edward Stark, "is not wholly better, but is sometimes better, sometimes worse."[1] And, most tiresome of all, they had to be back in Petersburg early, in good time for Gury's start at Gurevich's gymnasium and Igor's entry into the seventh class there. By that time, literally a week of the curtailed summer holidays had been spent in railway trains.

Igor had already been at Gurevich's for a whole year. He had gained entry into the sixth class there with great ceremony at the end of May 1898, and Fyodor and Anna had given him a pocket watch "with a white patterned face," worth seventeen roubles, as a reward for "the industry he showed at the time of his exams."[2] But the start of the seventh class in the autumn of 1899 coincided with a new stage in his commitment to music. In due course, as we saw earlier, Gurevich would have cause to grumble at the way music was distracting the boy from his school subjects, and there is no reason to doubt the justice of the complaint. We know that by now Igor was an aficionado of the opera, had for years been collecting musical memorabilia, and was spending hours reading through opera scores at the piano. Now, soon after the start of the new school year, there was a fresh musical distraction: he had a new piano teacher.

At some stage earlier in 1899 the issue had come up of a proper musical training for Igor, and while Fyodor and Anna insisted on his going on to complete his university law training and qualify for the civil service, they must also have recognized the desirability and good sense of music teaching that responded to his talents and enthusiasm. Already there had been casual signs of a recognition on their part that Igor's music needed encouraging. In Germany the year before, Fyodor had even paid for a piano for his use at their lodgings in the Villa Dreikaiserhof at Bad Homburg, and had bought him a cherrywood conductor's baton in Berlin and some Wagner librettos in Frankfurt.[3] So now Snetkova had to go, after rather more than the two years Stravinsky later remembered having endured her teaching.[4] Her final lesson was in April. A few weeks later, he was writing to his school-friend Maximilian Osten-Saken about his intention to seek theory tuition from Tcherepnin,[5] and although there is no record of his actually receiving formal teaching in that subject for another two and a half years, he may have had some all the same, if we can trust his remark to Timofeyev, only six or seven years after leaving school, that his "shortage of theoretical knowledge . . . lasted until the final classes of the Gymnasium, when I began to take harmony lessons with [Fyodor] Akimenko."[6] Certainly the Timofeyev report rings true, and not just because the events it described were recent, but also because it was written before any significant measure of public success had begun to influence Stravinsky's view of his own past. So when Igor tells Timofeyev that his change of piano teacher was directly attributable to his parents' wish "to make a pianist of me," there seems no reason to doubt the literal truth of the statement, with its fairly heavy hint that being made into a pianist was not necessarily Igor's own most fervent wish:

> From childhood I was attracted by composition, and moreover took a lively interest in musical literature and sight-read a great deal, which brought me on a lot. But a lack of theoretical teaching gradually made itself felt. . . . I could improvise till the cows came home, and was quite carried away by it, but as I remember, in my younger days (in the first classes of the Gymnasium), I was unable to write down a single one of these improvisations, which I attribute to the aforementioned shortage of theoretical knowledge. In a word, I ripened in ignorance.[7]

So it looks as if the smart (and expensive) new piano teacher was a desperate attempt on Fyodor's part to turn Igor's dangerous leanings towards feckless creativity into a professional accomplishment which might at least earn him some money. If so, it is no wonder that Igor remembered the lady in question, Leokadiya Alexandrovna Kashperova, without much warmth but with a sense that, however competent in herself, she stood between him and what he actually wanted to do.

But Stravinsky's remarks about Kashperova[8] have, to some extent, to be interpreted. As a piano pupil of Anton Rubinstein, she was technically above reproach. But by this very token she imposed technical disciplines which the young composer, who had perhaps hitherto been rather softly taught and mainly treated the piano as a medium for private improvisation, found mildly irksome. For example, Kashperova's "idiosyncrasy" of forbidding the use of the sustaining pedal may have been a specific counter to the improviser's tendency to conceal uncertainty of harmony and texture by overpedaling. As such it was normal and sensible. As for her supposed limitations of repertoire, these again have a disciplinarian look, in pursuit of solid technique. She forbade him to play the Chopin he had been learning with Snetkova, a ban which may have made sense on technical grounds;[9] as for her disapproval of Wagner, that had nothing to do with pianism as such, of course, though it may have reflected Igor's piano *style* at the time. Kashperova herself played a much wider range of music than she allowed her pupil, which will not surprise good authorities today. She gave the first performances of Glazunov's E Minor Sonata (1902) and Balakirev's B-flat Minor Sonata (1905), so the allegation that her tastes got no further than Schumann is suspect.[10] In fact she herself was a composer of some ability, a pupil of Nikolay Solovyov, the composer of the opera *Kordeliya*, which had recently been revived at the Mariyinsky (with Fyodor Stravinsky in a leading role). Taruskin mentions a published symphony and "a piano concerto which she performed in St. Petersburg, Moscow and even Berlin."[11] It would be interesting to know whether she advised Igor on composition. Perhaps he played her his little tarantella, composed the year before. One would not expect her to have been impressed.

In any case, the late memoir of Kashperova fits a pattern which is to recur. Igor, with his lack of self-assurance, was much more likely to respect disciplined teaching at that stage than to rebel ostentatiously against it, even if it went against the grain. All the evidence of his relations with his father in his last years is that he loyally accepted a tight regime. For instance, the meticulous accounting for his movements and expenditure on the journey from Pechisky to Ustilug in July 1901 is almost comical in its imitation of Fyodor's own assiduous bookkeeping methods: no trace of rebellion there. Igor lists every item, including tips for porters and grooms, down to the last kopek. He also relates in detail an incident of a lost basket, with precise timings, locations, and the registration number of the porter concerned.[12] Something comparable will happen later with Rimsky-Korsakov, and (for a time) with Diaghilev, to look no further into the future. But the image of rebellion suited the aging Stravinsky, who wanted to distance himself from the narrow rules and petty preoccupations of provincial St. Petersburg, and from the insecure young man who accepted this village green as if it were the whole planet. He wanted rather to be thought of as a free spirit, a phenomenon without a history.

Kashperova, with her characteristic Russian strictness of method—that is, "her narrowness and her formulae"[13]—was only the first of several victims of this revisionist bent.

Another early victim was Gurevich and his gymnasium. Igor was an undistinguished pupil, but again not obviously a rebellious one. There is no hostility, only genuine concern, in Gurevich's complaint to Fyodor about his attendance. And Igor could work when he needed to, as the seventeen-rouble watch proved. The problem for a musician of his age was that just when his passion was maturing into a serious obsession, the Imperial schooling system offered it no outlet unless the talent was focused enough to support early entry into the Conservatoire. As we shall see, this was never an option for the young Stravinsky; his talent did not suggest it, and his parents would not permit it. So music was bound to get in the way of "work." In fact Gurevich's gymnasium was a good school— one of the best and smartest in Petersburg. "It was expensive and 'aristocratic,'" one old boy recalled. "Before and after school the corner of Ligovsky and Basseyna . . . was chockablock with private carriages, or sleighs in winter, which brought the pupils to and from school. . . . Our boys were poshly dressed, and the urchins yelled 'Swanks!' at us, and 'Ligovsky hussars!' But we worked hard."[14]

Later Gurevich, with his pince-nez and his long bushy sideburns, remained the butt of affectionate and nostalgic jokes among ex-pupils. But he was also the subject of less-than-sympathetic memoirs. "He was a kind man, devoted to the teaching profession and concerned about the fate of his pupils, but as a headmaster we disliked him at once. His intemperate yelling annoyed us boys . . . he didn't inspire respect, or love, or even fear."[15] Like most schoolmasters, he had his catchphrases, repeated in and out of season: the phrase *"shto bït ne mozhet"*—"which cannot be"— must have been a famous one, since Igor quoted it in letters a decade or more after he had left the school.[16] Perhaps it was occasionally uttered as a riposte to Igor's expressed intention to become a musician, which will hardly have endeared Gurevich to him. In his memoirs, Stravinsky's counterbalance to the school director was a bibulous mathematics teacher called Woolf, "an amateur musician [who] knew that I composed . . . [and] helped, protected and encouraged me."[17] But as he also recalled that the school itself was eight miles from home—more than double the actual figure—such memories need as usual to be treated with caution. He paints a delightful picture of himself (with no private carriage at his disposal) invariably missing the tram in the mornings and having instead to take a fiacre *(izvoshchik)* at forty or fifty kopeks a ride, then driving home along the Nevsky Prospect in a sleigh "protected by a net from the dirty snow kicked up by the horse."[18] But why did being late in the mornings necessitate a cab ride home? And how do you get two roubles a week (let alone four) out of a monthly allowance of four roubles,[19] even with a drunken maths teacher?

Whatever Igor actually felt about school, his main interests lay elsewhere. We can picture him rummaging through the music at Jurgenson's shop, where his father had an account and allowed him to buy approved scores such as necessary piano music or "worthy" items like Glazunov's *Cantata in Memory of Pushkin's One Hundredth Birthday;*[20] or at home practicing his "scales, exercises, and suchlike finger stretchings" for the demanding Kashperova;[21] or slipping into rehearsals at the Mariyinsky brandishing the free pass his father had obtained for him; or hurrying to the house of the feared composer-critic César Cui with an invitation to Fyodor's jubilee performance as Holofernes in Serov's *Judith.*[22] Perhaps, too, he is composing: small piano pieces or songs which we know about only because a year or so later, there they are, ready to be worked into a small portfolio to show to prospective composition teachers. Of such work there is not the slightest trace in letters or other documents of the time. It remains modest, hesitant, and apparently secret.

One other activity must have filled up any spaces in Igor's schedule. He was reading voraciously. He had always, in fact, had his head in a book, and his remark that "I read omnivorously as a child" is borne out by the list of adventure stories about explorers and shipwrecked sailors in an early letter from Pechisky,[23] as well as by the fact that Turgenev's *Sportsman's Sketches* had already been deemed a suitable tenth-birthday present the previous year.[24] By his own account his reading during his late school and early university years included a lot of standard texts; indeed, as we saw, his gymnasium courses included French and German as well as Russian literature. But oddly enough his own book list[25] mentions no work in French (though he read Guyau's *Problèmes de l'esthétique contemporaine* in Russian), and of modern German literature, only Hauptmann and the minor novelist Hermann Sudermann. His implication is that he read Goethe, Hoffmann, perhaps Schiller, but in Russian translation. Dickens, Scott, and Mark Twain are all referred to. He admired Gorky but, perhaps surprisingly, not Leonid Andreyev, whose novels might have been expected to appeal to a temperament attuned, as Stravinsky also claimed, to Dostoyevsky. "Dostoyevsky," he asserts, "was always my hero." But was he? In 1899 Igor, like the rest of educated Russia, was swooning over Tolstoy's *Resurrection* in the weekly review *(Niva)* in which it was appearing that very year.[26] It was Tolstoy's lucid social realism and moral didacticism, rather than Dostoyevsky's psychological obscurities and apocalyptic convolutions, that at that time struck the biggest chord with the thinking classes in St. Petersburg. In the nineties, by contrast, Dostoyevsky's reputation was going through one of those troughs which seem to have afflicted it in relatively stable times in prerevolutionary Russia,[27] which does not mean, of course, that Igor did not read him with enthusiasm, only that if he did so it may have chimed oddly with the somewhat conventional tone of the Kryukov Stravinskys. He remembered that his father had known Dostoyevsky, occasionally supplied him with concert tickets, and attended his readings, which he and Anna found "intolerably boring."[28] But there is not the faintest whiff of this in any family correspondence of the time, nor are any of the novels or novellas so much as mentioned.

Fyodor's library in any case gave Igor access to a variety of reading that went well beyond the standard classics, though it naturally contained them, often in fine or rare editions. Igor later recalled that he discovered Shakespeare, Dante, and the Greeks there.[29] But he is silent on other aspects of the collection. Like most bibliophiles Fyodor had his specialisms. He collected books that helped him research his operatic roles, and this led him into the byways of Russian, Ukrainian, and European history and folklore. But he was not essentially interested in a working library as such. He was a book lover who loved to be in the presence of books and enjoyed them for their rarity. This had some curious consequences. He collected first editions, certainly. But he also collected censored books; he had a complete collection of the revolutionary author Alexander Herzen in the Geneva-Lyons edition, and one of the (according to his own note) only twelve copies of the censored second volume of the Russian edition of Lecky's *Rise and Influence of Rationalism in Europe*.[30] What is hard to decide is whether the subject matter of these books was important to Fyodor, or only their rarity. Soviet sources are naturally inclined to draw attention to such elements in a tsarist library. They point out that Fyodor had no less than three different Russian editions of *Das Kapital* (which was not, curiously enough, banned), as well as a number of texts on Marx. But was Fyodor therefore a proto-Marxist? The idea is ludicrous. When Igor writes, "My parents were never liberals in any sense of the word," the implication is, of course, that they were conservative, not bomb-throwing anarchists.[31] But it seems more likely that they were passive liberal intellectuals, the sort who might quietly condone changes they would not necessarily promote. The section in Fyodor's library dealing with the legal systems and constitutions of other European countries, the Code Napoléon and Roman law, probably reflects his own early legal studies as much as an active interest in better systems of government; yet it has a curious echo in a letter his law-student son wrote to a friend a few years later: "We're constantly organizing group readings, in which my cousins Katya, Lyudmila, and her husband, the doctor, and his wife take part (they are Poles, and extraordinarily intelligent and well-educated). We read the constitutions of every country, and accounts (quite recently published) by excellent commentators (Zvezdich, Yuzhakov, Poshekhonov, and others). We've read about rotten Austria, we're reading about England."[32]

But what Igor chiefly took from his father's library was not so much specific intellectual influences as a love of reading and a fascination with books for themselves. This soon outgrew and long survived the impression left by any particular book he may carefully have taken down from his father's densely packed shelves in those early Petersburg winters.

AFTER THREE YEARS at Gurevich's, and despite (or perhaps because of) the dire prognostications of that pedagogue, Stravinsky at last matriculated into the University of St. Petersburg as a student in the Faculty of Law. His final diploma dates his admission to August 1901 (towards the end of that month, presumably, since he himself was in Ustilug or Pechisky for at least the first three weeks of it), and lists his courses: History of Roman Law, Foundations of Roman Law, History of Russian Law, State Law, Ecclesiastical Law, Police Law, Political Economy, Statistics, Civil Law and Process, Commercial Law and Process, Criminal Law and Process, Financial Law, International Law, Encyclopedia of Law, and History of the Philosophy of Law.[33] Soon afterwards he began for the first time to take private tuition in the theory of music.

It may not surprise us that Igor should take little interest in this battery of technical studies in law, a subject he had not the slightest intention of pursuing professionally. What may be more surprising is that he nevertheless went through with it at least sufficiently to qualify for a "half-course" diploma at the end of the five years. He was obviously under parental pressure. We do not know but can assume that Fyodor made registration for a law degree the condition of Igor's being allowed to pursue his private studies in piano and music theory. This is surely borne out by the fact that his official studies in theory with Fyodor Stepanovich Akimenko began in November 1901, only a month or two after the start of his law course. While Fyodor was alive, there was not the faintest possibility of Igor contravening his wishes in a matter of this kind, the more so, of course, as Fyodor's health declined during 1902. According to Igor himself, he attended few lectures and "had only a vague and uninterested memory of the University."[34] But it was not until after his father's death that there was any open revolt.

The weekly Akimenko lessons, which cost Fyodor one rouble fifty each, did not go well. For some reason, Igor found him "unsympathetic," and Akimenko was replaced, after only fourteen lessons, the following April.[35] His successor, Vasily Pavlovich Kalafati, proved more congenial, and though Igor portrays him as a pedant, he cannot conceal the fact that he learnt important lessons from this "small, black-faced Greek with huge black moustaches."[36] No doubt Kalafati, a Conservatoire graduate of 1899, was simply more understanding of the young man's primitive technique

than the newly graduated Akimenko, and the two became sufficiently intimate, after almost two years of work together, for Igor to address his
teacher as "Uncle Vasya," using the intimate *tï*.37

These two theory teachers were Igor's first contact with the pedagogic
school of Nikolay Rimsky-Korsakov, which was still completely dominant
at the Conservatoire and in St. Petersburg academic musical circles in general. Both were recent graduates of Rimsky's own class at the Conservatoire: formidable types, therefore, with a thorough command of harmonic
and contrapuntal method, able to turn a fugue as readily as most people
write a letter, well versed in techniques of musical form, and withal competent pianists or better. All this guaranteed nothing artistically, needless
to say. But for a young, largely untaught musician with ambitions but limited self-confidence, the initial impression must have been disconcerting.
Off he would go once or twice a week to the teacher's flat, or perhaps to
some gloomy upstairs room in the Conservatoire, whose corridors, then as
now, were awash with intense-looking student violinists displaying their
arpeggios to the atmosphere or composers with impressive scores under
their arms and self-important looks on their faces, hurrying off to classes
with Bach or Beethoven, or so they would have you think. Then would
come the presentation of the week's exercise; the anxious scanning of the
teacher's face for signs of approval (rare) or bafflement (usual); the shamefaced attempt to grasp the precise nature and extent of one's insufficiency.
The sheer apparatus of conservatory teaching has always been by its nature
intimidating, and there seems no reason to suppose that Igor Stravinsky
was more impervious to it than the next underqualified music student.

Perhaps Fyodor Akimenko, fresh graduate that he was, was a little too
inclined to turn up his nose at this callow youth who seemed not to realize
that the perfect fourth was a dissonance or that the *nota cambiata* resolved
inwards. Or this may be too facile a picture of Igor's problems with his first
teacher, since it is clear from his description of his lessons with Kalafati
that his second teacher was no less pernickety about technical precision,
though he may have been friendlier in the manner of his insistence.

Kalafati, like Akimenko, was engaged as a theory teacher. He taught
strict technique and made Igor do weekly exercises. There is no evidence
that he was in any sense a composition teacher looking over his pupil's
work-in-hand. According to Stravinsky,38 they covered chorale harmoniza-
tion, species counterpoint, writing in two and three parts, and fugue—a
systematic study rather akin to the graded study of drawing from perspective to life classes. Species counterpoint, for instance, requires the student
to combine new (vocal) melodies with a given melody according to a set of
tightly defined procedural rules which nevertheless leave scope for the
exercise of musical judgment. The two- and three-part invention copies
Bach's instrumental works in that genre and allows comparative freedom

within a well-defined set of prescriptions and prohibitions. Finally, the fugue transfers all these techniques to large-scale composition, introducing principles of form but without prescribing form as such. Behind this seemingly dry, academic structure lies, of course, the idea that discipline liberates: that the student who can write well-formed counterpoint according to the most demanding rules will not be restricted by technical limitations when it comes to writing in his own style. But at the same time, such a syllabus is not like the early study of law or medicine, where learning and experiment, respectively, largely supersede taste and expression. From the start, the student has to bring musical instinct to bear, and good writing—even at the simplest level—involves taste and feeling, beyond what rules can indicate. So when Stravinsky tells us that "Kalafaty taught me to appeal to my ear as the first and last test," we should not read this to mean that he was being encouraged to use strange harmonies or wayward counterpoints just because he liked the sound of them. Kalafati will simply have pointed out that, in the end, as between two "correct" pieces of writing, only the musical ear can judge which is better. This was doubtless an important and prophetic lesson for Igor, but, green as he was, it was very far from carte blanche.

What Kalafati thought of Igor's own compositions of the time, assuming he saw any, we can only guess. Of the two pieces which have survived, the little Scherzo for Piano, written at some time during 1902, is by any standards a clumsy piece of writing in the nineteenth-century Russian tradition of the scherzo-with-lyrical-trio, which would have been almost obliterated by the teacher's red ink if presented, as Taruskin supposes it to have been, as a weekly assignment.[39] The setting of Pushkin's "Tucha" (The Storm Cloud), which Igor wrote in January 1902 while still working with Akimenko, is a more successful but hardly less conventional exercise in romance style, with a fluent, orotund piano accompaniment, just enough harmonic variety, and accomplished word setting. But the point about these two pieces, as Taruskin observes, is that they are the mere chance survivors from the "first compositions, short piano pieces, 'andantes,' 'melodies' [i.e., songs], and so forth," which Stravinsky took to show Rimsky-Korsakov later in 1902.[40] To regard them as in any sense special, significant, or even intrinsically interesting would be a travesty of historical research.

On the seventh of December, seven weeks before composing his Pushkin setting, Igor had made his first public concert appearance as a pianist. He accompanied a choral suite for children's voices by Ivan Pokrovsky and/or an opera by a composer called Abta, at a concert in a school on the Sredniy Prospect on Vasil'yevsky Island, not far from the university.[41] Pokrovsky was already a friend of his, though not much is known of this friendship apart from what Stravinsky recalled in and after the 1930s. He remembered Pokrovsky as a Baudelairean counterbalance to what he called the "esprit belge" of his home life, and dated the friendship to the late 1890s, when "my life at home was . . . even more unbearable than usual."[42]

In fact Igor may have met Pokrovsky in 1900 or 1901, when the latter was a counterpoint student of Rimsky-Korsakov's at the Conservatoire[43] and Igor, still a gymnasium boy, was studying piano with Kashperova. Stravinsky recalled that Pokrovsky was in his final year at the university when their friendship was closest. But he later enjoyed modest success as a composer before his early death from tuberculosis in 1906.[44] He had songs, especially, published and performed, and was closely involved, as both composer and performer, with the Evenings of Contemporary Music, which were founded towards the end of 1901 and held their first public concert in March 1902. It was probably through Pokrovsky that Igor himself came into close contact with those concerts fairly early in their existence, and in this sense he can certainly be said to have been influenced by the older man.[45]

Apart from these actual or speculative facts, Pokrovsky is a misty, possibly emblematic figure in Igor's early life. He is supposed to have introduced Igor to French music in contradistinction to the prevailing orthodoxy of German-versus-Russian. But all we know about Pokrovsky's musical affiliations outside Stravinsky's memoirs is that he performed the supremely un-French Reger at two separate Evenings concerts in 1906, the year of his death.[46] As for likely French preferences in 1901, they included Gounod, Bizet, Delibes, and Chabrier, the names mentioned by Stravinsky in his autobiography,[47] plus Offenbach, Saint-Saëns, Chausson, perhaps Massenet, but hardly yet Debussy or Dukas and certainly not Ravel. But Stravinsky's suggestion that he was unfamiliar with those earlier composers even by 1897 is hard to take seriously. His father sang in Bizet's *Carmen* and Gounod's *Faust* and *Roméo et Juliette* as well as Massenet's *Werther*, and had their scores on his shelves. *Coppélia* Igor must surely have encountered at Mariyinsky matinees. Of course, it may well be that Pokrovsky inspired a taste for this music. But was that as significant at the time as the later Stravinsky, anxious to distance himself from the German classical and Russian nationalist traditions, liked to pretend? Gounod has always cut a rather odd figure in Stravinsky's pantheon of the thirties and after; Pokrovsky—as his John the Baptist—does so no less.[48]

The Evenings of Contemporary Music started a new epoch in Russian concert life, and one which soon began to ruffle the smooth orthodoxy of St. Petersburg music. Igor Stravinsky may or may not have attended the very first concert on 31 March 1902, though in view of his friendship with Pokrovsky and his (now discontinued) study with Kashperova, both of whom performed in the inaugural concert, it seems more than likely that he was there. But for the time being, his sights were set on a different target. Among his fellow law students at the university was Vladimir (Volodya) Rimsky-Korsakov, the composer's youngest son, and himself a competent violinist and viola player.[49] Although Igor had met Volodya's father formally more than four years earlier, at a rehearsal of his opera *Sadko* in the Conservatoire in February 1898,[50] and had been studying theory with former pupils of his, he seems not to have thought of approaching the Master for advice on his own compositions. The stimulus to do so probably came from Volodya. Stravinsky must have announced that his whole family were off to Germany for the summer, whereupon Volodya will have revealed that *his* family were also summering in Germany. They would be in Heidelberg so as to be near Volodya's older brother Andrey, a philosophy student who was spending a semester at Heidelberg University. Igor should try to arrange to visit them, and bring some music with him.

From Berlin and Bad Wildungen Igor wrote three times to Volodya, and at last, on 14 August, he set out from there to Heidelberg, a rail journey of some 150 miles. No doubt he had a recommendation from Fyodor in his pocket, as he told a newspaper interviewer in Geneva a quarter of a century later.[51] The Rimsky-Korsakovs had taken a house called the Villa Orotava at Handschuhsheim, on the northern outskirts of the town.[52] "We have a large and beautiful garden," Rimsky-Korsakov wrote to his publisher, Vasily Bessel. "Beyond the garden begins the climb up to Mount Heiligenberg, which offers superb walks through vineyards, chestnut and beech woods with marvellous views of the Neckar plain."[53] But there was no room in the house for Stravinsky, so he stayed in a hotel and simply spent the waking hours with his hosts. "They're all very pleased I've come," he wrote to Gury, on a picture postcard of the huge wine cask known as the Heidelberg Tun, "and in celebration we made a big outing to the Schloss, where this monster is to be found; the parents will tell you about the personal charms of this giant."[54]

Igor spent only about five days in Heidelberg before wending his way back to Wildungen. But they were to have momentous consequences for him and his work. Pooling Stravinsky's various later accounts of his session with Rimsky-Korsakov, we can form a fairly reliable picture of what took place.[55] Notoriously dry and matter-of-fact, Rimsky is most unlikely to have gushed over pieces like "Tucha" or the Piano Scherzo, which offer so little that is out of the ordinary for a composer already past his twentieth birthday. "He made me play some of my first attempts. Alas! the way in which he received them was far from what I had hoped."[56] Yet Rimsky must have sensed something out of the ordinary, something that caught his interest. Perhaps it was the very gaucheness of the writing, compared with the sheer technical fluency of so many of the students he saw day in, day out at the Conservatoire. Can he have been intrigued by the way in which the ineptitude of detailing in a piece like the Scherzo now and then seems almost to be forming itself into a definite musical idea: detailing like the curious and ineffectual "hocketing" or "hiccoughing" of the rhythm in the first two or three bars? Did he, at the same time, form a strong impression of Igor's musical personality from his playing and conversation? At least we can be reasonably sure that in failing to advise the young man to abandon the idea of becoming a composer, Rimsky-Korsakov was backing a musical instinct, not merely being nice to a close friend of his son's or even to the son of an admired—and dying—professional colleague, which would have been a response both superficial in itself and wholly out of character for him.

But Igor's technical shortcomings cried out in every bar: the poorly conceived, inert bass lines, the clumsy rhythms and square-cut phrases, all combined with a tendency to fall back on cliché, often misunderstood or misapplied. Obviously the young man would have to go on with his counterpoint lessons with Kalafati, since only by strictly supervised study would he be able to overcome these faults and write his own music properly, write it so that the ideas emerged in collaboration with the technique, not in defiance of it. Rimsky-Korsakov had complicated ideas on the teaching of composition. At the Conservatoire, composition students underwent a six-year course, of which the first three years were devoted mainly to the practical mastery of precisely those techniques that Igor had been studying privately with Akimenko and Kalafati, plus analysis and orchestration, and only in the final three years was the student let loose on extended free composition of his own, and then only in prescribed forms and genres.[57] But Rimsky-Korsakov was in favor of a flexible application of this scheme, and in certain cases he would even advise a student to avoid the Conservatoire course altogether. There was, he thought, too little emphasis on free composition in the first three years of the course, too much obsession with techniques and diplomas for their own sake.[58] The genuinely gifted student needed, rather, more individualized teaching and far more practical work, including experience at conducting, accompanying, and score reading; he needed to hear a great deal of music and base himself on good models; and he needed to work at counterpoint—the essential basis of all good composition—as an adjunct to his own writing, not just as a "pure" theoretical study, like algebra or trigonometry.

Igor Stravinsky was a prime candidate for this individualized method. Though an accomplished and intelligent musician, he was too untaught in the traditional techniques with which so many "natural" musicians grew up to be expected to master them, in the diploma sense, now. On the other hand, some of that teaching—the most basic and essential—he must nevertheless endure, for the sake of his own writing.

> Rimsky told me that before anything else I must continue my studies in harmony and counterpoint with [Kalafati] in order to acquire complete mastery in the schooling of craftsmanship, but at the same time he strongly advised me not to enter the Conservatoire. He considered that the atmosphere of that institution, in which he was himself a professor, was not suited to me, for I should be overwhelmed with work, as I had as well to go on with my University course. Moreover, as I was twenty he feared that I might find myself backward in comparison with my contemporaries, and that that might discourage me. He further considered it necessary that my work should be systematically supervised, and that that could only be achieved by private lessons. He finished by adding that I could always go to him for advice, and that he was quite willing to take me in hand when I had acquired the necessary foundation.[59]

That Igor was fortunate in this diagnosis goes without saying, and its value was to be reinforced time and again over the next six years of close personal and pedagogical contact with Rimsky-Korsakov and his circle. But more than that, he had struck up a set of friendships which were to be of vital importance to him during these years of slow artistic emergence. Volodya he already knew well. Exact coevals, they shared many instincts and interests, including a taste for a certain kind of silliness of the sort which can often inarticulately express a closeness where ordinary language may seem too bald and direct.[60] Their correspondence is for some years the most intimate in which Stravinsky engaged; it includes open discussion of artistic questions such as he seldom if ever risked later, and it touches on issues of personal feeling and interdependence which are almost totally absent otherwise. Volodya's brother Andrey, three years older, was not at first such a close friend, but was later, for a time, perhaps even closer. At the Heidelberg period Andrey was wavering between philosophy and music, and it seems possible that his growing preference for the latter was influenced by Igor's arrival on the scene.[61] These two, together with their parents and, somewhat less obviously, their younger sister, Nadezhda, were soon to constitute almost a second family for Igor.[62]

But meanwhile his first family still called. Returning to Wildungen, Igor found his father's condition significantly worse, and his sights set on the German capital as the last hope of effective treatment. By the end of August, Fyodor was installed in the Charlottenburg Sanatorium in Berlin. And there, unexpectedly, on the Unter den Linden, Igor again ran into his new friends. Nikolay Rimsky-Korsakov had returned to St. Petersburg with his two daughters, leaving his wife and sons to sightsee in Berlin. Together they all visited the National Gallery and the Deutsches Theater, went shopping, went to the zoo, spent nearly every day together. Igor's father, Nadezhda reported to her husband on 17 September, "is much worse, despite being examined, it appears, by all the professors in Berlin."[63] Ten days later, after the departure of the other Rimskys, Andrey and Igor went to *Der Freischütz* at the Westend-Theater. "I'm now sorry," Andrey wrote to his parents, "that I chanced to hear *Freischütz* for the first time in such a bad performance. The singers were pitiful. Stravinsky and I had a good laugh at the playing and the production. I felt absolutely as if I were in a provincial theatre."[64] The next day Andrey visited Fyodor and found him slightly better, in less pain, able to talk. But a month later the Stravinskys were back in St. Petersburg, and poor Fyodor's condition was hopeless. On 1 November Vladimir Stasov wrote to his brother Dmitry that he had just heard from Igor Stravinsky that Fyodor had only a week or ten days to live.[65]

The exaggeration was only slight. On 21 November 1902 (OS) Fyodor Stravinsky died in St. Petersburg, "on the couch in his study, saying, 'I feel so good, so very good.' His death," Igor wrote nearly sixty years later, "brought us close together."[66]

5

THE BELYAYEVTSÏ

IGOR, MEANWHILE, was already throwing himself with enthusiasm into the activities of his new circle of friends.

Outside the Conservatoire, Rimsky-Korsakov's tutelage was inextricably bound up with his social and musical life. Not only did he haul his pupils and associates off to the rehearsals of the Belyayev Russian Symphony Concerts, but he also held regular court in his own flat at 28 Zagorodnïy Prospect, which thus provided a focus for musical discussion, performance and play-through, and social gatherings for musicians in and on the fringes of the Rimsky-Korsakov circle.[1] When Igor first appeared on the scene, these meetings were apparently spasmodic and unplanned. Later they crystallized into a regular *jour fixe,* held roughly on alternate Wednesday evenings during the season. But the informal gatherings still went on, and remained the crucial melting pot for Rimsky-Korsakov's pupils and immediate associates. The actual "Wednesdays," which started up only in January 1905, were somewhat more formal, and tended to be relatively crowded.[2]

Such soirées, whether or not of the *jour fixe* variety, were part of the landscape of turn-of-the-century Petersburg. Mitrofan Belyayev himself had held a regular Friday at-home since the early 1880s, at which he had been able to indulge to the full his passion for chamber-music playing. But, like any Parisian salon, these get-togethers were also at once a source and an assertion of influence. Belyayev was a musically trained timber millionaire who had conceived a passion for the music of the youthful Glazunov, had sponsored its publication, and from there had gone on to set up a full-blown publishing house and, soon afterwards, an orchestral concert series, both devoted exclusively to the promotion and performance of music by Russian composers. At a stroke Belyayev had, in a naively patriotic, money-splashing way, institutionalized Russian music along lines that were inevitably conditioned by the time and the place. Glazunov was a pupil of Rimsky-Korsakov; Rimsky-Korsakov, though already (in 1882) long a professor of composition at the Conservatoire, was a former member—with Balakirev, Musorgsky, Borodin, and Cui—of the great anti-establishment school of Russian nationalists known as the *Moguchaya kuchka* (Mighty Handful, or simply the Five). Thus the supremely amateur, studiously maverick Balakirev circle of the sixties and seventies became overnight the official tendency in St. Petersburg music; to be published, to be performed, to be received by Mitrofan Belyayev was the goal of every aspirant composer, and, human nature being what it is, Belyayev naturally got the music he was paying for. The Belyayevtsï were born.[3]

Rimsky-Korsakov himself, as the professional musician most closely associated with Belyayev in the early days, acted as his adviser and quality controller. "Every young composer of the circle," he wrote, "usually first showed me his new composition and availed himself of my criticism and my advice."[4] The self-taught Conservatoire professor was bound to approve the professionalization of standards and increased, regulated productivity which the Belyayev apparatus entailed. "Thirty years have passed now," he wrote to Semyon Kruglikov in 1897, "since the time when Stasov would write that in eighteen sixty-something the Russian School displayed a lively activity: Lodïzhensky wrote a song, Borodin thought of something, Balakirev made up his mind to rework something, and so on. It is time to stop all that and travel a normal artistic path. I confess that I, at least, have changed greatly."[5] But by Stravinsky's time, even Rimsky-Korsakov was weary of the stereotyping and introversion, what Taruskin has precisely defined as the "guild" mentality, that resulted from so highly centralized a promotional mechanism. He had long been aware of the so-called New Russian School's tendency to reduce composition to a formula, where each new symphony, each new "fairy tale" tone poem was painstakingly modelled on some predecessor of proven excellence—very often by the dazzling but, at bottom, predictable Glazunov. One day, at a dinner at Glazunov's after a memorial concert for Belyayev in February 1904, Rimsky-Korsakov suddenly burst out to Vladimir Stasov:

> And do you know what it is that, amid all these festivities, toasts, congratulations and speeches, is secretly tormenting and tormenting me, deep down, relentlessly? Do you know? Today I'll tell you. Look over there—that one, sitting opposite us with his napkin tucked into his collar, and who is making all these wonderful, wise, pithy little speeches *(that was Glazunov himself)*—he is the last of us. With him Russian music, the whole New Russian period ends!!! It's horrible![6]

Rimsky-Korsakov's own at-homes therefore presented an at least implicitly more hybrid orthodoxy than Belyayev's. A Belyayevets phenomenon they undoubtedly were. Many of the regulars—people like the composers Lyadov, Glazunov, and Nikolay Tcherepnin, the conductor Felix

Blumenfeld, the singer Nadezhda Zabela-Vrubel—were more or less defining elements of the New Russian School. The automatic support for the Russian Symphony Concerts, the interminable discussions—often far into the night—of each latest Belyayevets masterpiece, the celebratory cantatas, the *de haut en bas* criticism of non-Russian music, especially if it displayed the slightest modernist tendency: all reflect a more or less "official" fusion of the self-protective attitudes of the original *kuchka* and the self-serving academicism of the New Russian School itself.

On the other hand, Rimsky-Korsakov was too well aware of the limitations of the New Russian School and too wise a teacher to exclude outside influences on principle or to suppress deviancy in whatever form. Just as he concealed a sensitive and considerate nature behind a dry, crusty manner, so he liked to deprecate any hint of catholicity or progressiveness of taste with a show of irritation embodied in a scabrous epithet, studiously recorded by the faithful Yastrebtsev. Thus Strauss's *Sinfonia domestica* was "vertical nonsense," Reger's C Major Violin Sonata was "horizontal nonsense," Mahler (on the strength of the Second Symphony, which he conducted in St. Petersburg in October 1907) was a "house painter" *(malyar)*, Scriabin and his ilk "all turn themselves inside out, and inside there's nothing but muck, a kind of Limburger cheese."[7] But significantly, while Debussy's *Pelléas et Mélisande* was regarded by the Rimsky-Korsakov circle as axiomatically "the music of retrogression, so to speak, and not of progress,"[8] and while the Master himself, when he at last actually heard the music in Paris in 1907, confessed to Louis Laloy that "he could not understand a note of it," he nevertheless "took the score away in order to study it at his leisure."[9] In other words, Rimsky-Korsakov was aware of the possible importance of such music, however much he might dislike—and, perhaps more to the point, fear—it himself.[10] The studious Yastrebtsev was perhaps not always aware of these hidden currents. There is neither humor nor irony in his report of Rimsky-Korsakov's Limburger cheese remark being followed by a performance of six of Scriabin's piano pieces. The famous Rimsky-Korsakov canard about not listening to Debussy for too long in case he end up liking it was probably a standard joke with him, to judge by the number of different versions of it which have come down to us. If so, it shows his own consciousness of an ambivalent and "dangerous" relationship with the new music of his time, an ambivalence which also colored his attitude to it in the context of teaching.[11] The fact is that praise as such did not come easily to Rimsky-Korsakov, and there are few recorded instances of his expressing unreserved enthusiasm for the work of another composer, except for minor Russian contemporaries, such as Glazunov, whose music presumably presented no psychological threat. As for the work of current pupils, Stravinsky's memory of his teacher's reluctance to praise is borne out by Maximilian Steinberg's more restrained memoir: "Nikolay Andreyevich was quite stingy with his praise and once explained this to us in the following way: '. . . If I occasionally praise you in class, that still doesn't mean that I'm so very pleased. But suddenly people will start asking whether it's true that I have such-and-such a pupil who shows every sign of being something approaching a genius.' "[12]

"A tall old man who wore his beard and his frock coat at right angles and with no curves apart from the two circles of his spectacles,"[13] Rimsky-Korsakov cut a decidedly stiff, authoritarian figure in the introverted, provincial world of St. Petersburg music. Stravinsky's later reminiscence that "he played his first composition to Rimsky-Korsakov, with the warning that should it fail to please, he would continue composing just the same,"[14] is hard to take seriously in view of the intimidating circumstances and Rimsky-Korsakov's notorious sharpness of tongue. It also conflicts with the sycophantic tone of the young man's subsequent letters to his teacher. The truth is that Rimsky-Korsakov exacted and was accorded the hierarchical niceties by all his junior colleagues. Any other attitude would have been unthinkable. The relationship was an essentially structured one, and reflected the Master's obsession with system and organization, and his genuine fear of disorder, in part a legacy of his desperate battle with his own technical deficiencies in his early years as a professor of composition. Every account of Rimsky-Korsakov's teaching stresses his insistence on a regular working method, and his distaste for any haphazard dependence on inspiration. His creative philosophy was purely that of the nineteenth-century bourgeois work ethic: he believed that idleness was a kind of sin, and that inspiration was the reward of persistence, rather than a fortuitous event without which there was no point in creative work. But he would have no traffic with revealed religion. Like Igor's uncle Alexander, he was a rationalist and a positivist, but of the Marie-Jean Guyau variety who believed that art revealed its beauty through function and order. In Nietzschean terms, he was an Apollonian; in Freudian terms, he was sexually repressed—his distaste for ballet, which was to affect Igor in an unforeseeable way, seems to have been above all a revulsion against the purely physical. Yet he adored Wagner, whose music is incomprehensible in purely Apollonian terms, and he himself wrote little but opera—hardly the rationalist's or the puritan's natural home—after the age of fifty.

These various attitudes, with all their contradictions and limitations, exerted a profound influence on Rimsky-Korsakov's pupils, and on none more than the young Stravinsky. A great deal of what Stravinsky later said or wrote about music—in his autobiography, in *The Poetics of Music*, in the conversations—can be traced back to Rimsky-Korsakov. It may even be that the very habit of self-contradiction, without which the mature Stravinsky would be inconceivable, had its essential origins in Rimsky-

Korsakov's deep-rooted tendency to cover his inspirational and emotional traces (and also incidentally explains Stravinsky's own profound ambivalence towards his teacher). Where the two composers differ, of course, is in the all-important matter of how these limitations and contradictions acted on their own music, though even here there is an unacknowledged, and by no means wholly negative, influence.

AFTER THE LONG, painful months of Fyodor Stravinsky's final illness, it must have been a relief for Igor to involve himself once again in purposeful activity, and one, moreover, which for the first time openly recognized his ambition to compose. Not that Fyodor's death brought any release from his law studies; Anna Stravinsky, with her photo of the encoffined Fyodor at her bedside, was all the more likely to insist on his wishes in such matters being met to the letter and with no chance of remission. But for the time being, the university could be treated with a certain sophomoric indolence, and Igor could get on with his counterpoint, playing, and concertgoing, and with the social life that went with them. His attendance at rehearsals, especially of the Russian Symphony Concerts, may have been facilitated by Rimsky-Korsakov, or he may have had free access as a university student. In any case, attend he did. It was probably at an RSC rehearsal on 28 February 1903 (OS) that he was first introduced to Rimsky-Korsakov's shadow, Yastrebtsev, who recorded inviting "a very nice and musical young man—Igor Fyodorovich Stravinsky, son of the well-known Russian opera singer"—to call on him.[15] Six days later, Igor was at Rimsky-Korsakov's fifty-ninth-birthday party at the Zagorodnïy flat—a momentous first visit, if such it was, since Igor had been commissioned by his mother, in accordance with Fyodor's own express wish, to present Rimsky-Korsakov with a portrait of her late husband as the Mayor in Rimsky's opera *May Night*.

Yastrebtsev's account of this party[16] provides a tantalizing glimpse of the young Igor's lively improvisatory talent. After Felix Blumenfeld—pianist, conductor, and composer—had played a series of piano pieces, Igor "presented some very charming and witty musical jests of his own"—presumably also for piano or for piano with voice. If these were written-down compositions, they have nevertheless not survived. Perhaps, as Taruskin speculates, they were comic pieces on texts by the imaginary nineteenth-century poet Koz'ma Prutkov, the fictitious bureaucrat whose literary ambitions had been used by Alexey Tolstoy and the Zhemchuzhnikov brothers as a pretext for a series of clever style parodies. A few years later Stravinsky was reporting having composed a number of Prutkov settings at this time.[17] In any case, to perform such pieces in such company, and on his first visit, showed courage on the twenty-year-old Igor's part, and perhaps even a degree of impudence, considering the audience, which included the aging Vladimir Stasov, the doyen of the old nationalist Slavophiles; Rimsky's most brilliant pupil, Alexander Glazunov; the music critic Alexander Ossovsky; one or two academic and literary figures, including the mythographer and librettist V. I. Belsky; Rimsky-Korsakov himself and his family; and some of Igor's fellow students, including the pianists Nikolay Richter and Stepan Mitusov—some twenty guests in all. But Stravinsky's performance was a success. "Clearly," Yastrebtsev gushed tautologically, "Igor Fyodorovich is a man of unmistakable talent."

Igor's contacts with the Rimsky-Korsakovs and their circle was not, of course, limited to soirées of this kind. He was already seeing a good deal of Volodya through their shared university life, and Berlin had cemented his friendship with the three-years-older Andrey, and also with Andrey's university contemporary Nikolay Richter, who seems to have turned up at some stage in Berlin, and to whom Igor felt close enough by January 1903 to dedicate his piano Scherzo to him.[18] Richter was one of many young Petersburg musicians who were studying at the university for the good of their career prospects while at the same time pursuing courses at the Conservatoire. Volodya Rimsky-Korsakov probably did the same. Another musician friend, Stepan Mitusov, had studied philology and law at the university, took Lyadov's harmony course at the Conservatoire, then for a time shared Igor's counterpoint lessons with Kalafati. Like Igor, he aspired to study composition with Rimsky-Korsakov; but, according to a late and very undependable memoir of Stravinsky's, he was refused.[19] Styopa Mitusov was in any case intimate with the Rimsky family. Like Richter, he was three or four years older than Igor, and had been an habitué of Rimsky-Korsakov soirées since 1899. He was a useful and enthusiastic singer, but his greatest talent was for impromptu theatricals. It was only at Zagorodnïy, he later announced, that he could "satisfy his thirst for tomfoolery," and this is borne out by Yastrebtsev, who variously depicts Styopa doing "a frenzied dance of a savage" to an accompaniment improvised by Glazunov, demonstrating a cakewalk with Stravinsky, or, again, giving "a very clever imitation of a French chansonette singing a fashionable 'cakewalk.' "[20] He was no less useful "backstage," and could turn his hand to doing the makeup for the Rimsky-Korsakovs' Christmas plays.[21]

Taken as a group, this was a much livelier and more cultivated set than you would normally encounter at 66 Kryukov Canal. "There were painters, young scientists, scholars, enlightened amateurs of the most advanced views," as Stravinsky later indulgently described them.[22] But the entertaining and open-minded Mitusov stood out even in this company. His interests ranged beyond music to literature, theatre, and painting, the last two of which Igor had previously explored as an amateur practitioner rather more, perhaps, than as an intelligent consumer. The Stravinskys quite often went to art exhibitions, but their tastes, like the pictures on their walls, were conventional. As for plays, Styopa "became a kind of literary and theatrical tutor to me at one of the greatest moments in the Russian theatre,"[23] and together they went to Chekhov and Ostrovsky, Gorky, Tolstoy and Griboyedov, as well as Molière, Shakespeare, and a variety of modern French plays. Needless to say, this list tells us at least as much about Igor's sheltered upbringing as it does about Styopa's enlightenment. How could the son of Russia's leading singing-actor have reached the age of twenty still unaware of the ferment in the theatre of Stanislavsky and his erstwhile associate Vsevolod Meyerhold?

But when it came to the visual arts, St. Petersburg offered much less challenging fare. In fact, the history of that city's, and Russia's, gradual awakening from an academicism closely parallel to that of contemporary Russian music is a history that directly concerns Stravinsky himself, even though he may as yet have had only a limited experience of it. Just as music was in the grip of an orthodoxy that had its origins in a radical, antinomian nationalism, so painting had been threatening to freeze into a sterile version of the realism which, back in the sixties and seventies, had itself been a secessionist idea—a kind of local equivalent of the Salon des Refusés. By the late 1890s, however, concrete evidence of a reaction against this realism, with all its historical and sociological baggage inherited from the time when (as in *Boris Godunov*) realism was associated with progressive thinking and a social conscience, had appeared in the form of the fortnightly art journal *Mir iskusstva* (The World of Art) under the editorship of a uniquely forceful, energetic, and single-minded young aesthete called Sergey Diaghilev. *Mir iskusstva* embodied what amounted to a radical conservatism in its attitude to art and design; it sought to restore the "old" ideal of beauty to its place at the very center of artistic consideration. It concerned itself exclusively with questions of design, color, and form, and had no truck with social or political goals, did not bother its head about the psychology of perception or the existentialist agony, and did not believe, with Musorgsky or Tolstoy, in the profound virtue of rural or peasant as opposed to urban culture, or that the world could be changed for the better by right-minded art. "Their mission," Taruskin writes of its founders, "was neither to explore the world nor to transfigure it, but to adorn it."[24] Insofar as the journal interested itself in peasant art—and it did to a considerable extent—it was in the purely aesthetic spirit of neonationalist movements everywhere at that time: for instance, in the spirit of the Arts and Crafts movement in England. Restoring and exploring the rich patterns and colors of rustic design, whether in embroidery, furniture, painting, or architecture, was a way of reinstating the pure aesthetic values which had been corrupted by the utilitarianism and functionalism of bourgeois urban commercial art. But unlike William Morris, or even their own onetime aristocratic patroness Princess Tenisheva, Diaghilev and his collaborators—Alexander Benois, Dima Filosofov, Lev Bakst, Walter Nouvel, and the others—were not, even in the remotest, most toffee-nosed, Fabian meaning of the word, socialists. Nor were they yet in any definite sense modernists. Theirs was an essentially reactionary, unyieldingly aristocratic, in modern jargon "elitist," view of art. It was art for art's sake, with no ulterior motive.[25]

Although *Mir iskusstva*, during its six years of existence from the end of 1898 to 1904, brought together many of the new tendencies which were to lead directly to the Ballets Russes, and thereby, only slightly less directly, to the great radical ballets of Stravinsky himself, there is no real evidence that he paid particular attention to the journal at that time or hankered after any association with its authors. "We took a passionate interest," he tells us, "in everything that went on in the intellectual and artistic life of the capital."[26] But if so, it was a consumer's interest, not a recognition of shared aims—as indeed how could it be when Igor was still quite newly attached to the Rimsky-Korsakov circle, with its unreconstructed, academicized sixties outlook: the musical equivalent of precisely that fossilized realism which *Mir iskusstva* was openly attacking in the visual arts? "I'm afraid I won't understand anything about it and it won't interest me," Rimsky-Korsakov would drily remark when asked if he intended to visit Diaghilev's great portrait exhibition in the Tauride Palace in the revolutionary spring of 1905. "For . . . I'm not at all erudite, and I don't take pleasure in looking at lots of people I don't know."[27] The question remained unspoken, yet plain: how could anyone concern himself with anything as obscure as portraiture when Russia was in the grip of a political upheaval which might well—and the sooner, the better—send all those gentry to perdition once and for all?

Stravinsky did, however—and despite Rimsky-Korsakov's general disapproval—get involved in the Evenings of Contemporary Music, which were an offshoot of the *miriskusstvan* spirit if only in the sense that their founders included two of the so-called Nevsky Pickwickians out of whose meetings and discussions *Mir iskusstva* had itself emerged. Igor had, as it happened, had several contacts with the Evenings at the time of their first concert in March 1902: his former piano teacher Leokadiya Kashperova was playing, and so was his close friend Ivan Pokrovsky. Whether or not Pokrovsky was also, as Stravinsky claims in his autobiography, one of the founders of the concerts seems more doubtful.[28] The official founding board, as listed by Taruskin, consisted of five men: the two Pickwickians, Walter Nouvel and Alfred Nurok; the music critic Vyacheslav Karatïgin; a piano-playing doctor-composer called Ivan Krïzhanovsky; and the pianist-composer Alexander Medem.[29] Stravinsky also claims that Nouvel and Nurok were already friends of his, and it is certainly just possible that he had met them through Mitusov, who according to Smirnov "had connections with the activities of *Mir iskusstva*."[30] Nouvel, who had been a school friend of Benois and Filosofov, and was to become a vital cog in Diaghilev's organizational wheel, was an instinctive dilettante with no strong artistic gift of his own: art lover, opera- and balletgoer, part-time pianist and composer, and with a taste for the new and marginal which sometimes led to quarrels within the World of Art group. Nouvel's trump card was his wide musical knowledge, fed—like Igor's—by a certain gift for piano playing at sight, and backed up by a dry, caustic intellectual snobbery and a dandyish self-assurance.[31] Nurok, too, was a musician more than a visual artist, and he always edited the musical articles in *Mir iskusstva*. According to Benois, Nurok "was a genuine and distinguished musician," but "suffered from a kind of paralysis of creative will, and was further handicapped by being a real dilettante. His lack of technique was a serious drawback to him when developing a good musical idea."[32] A baptized Jew, Nurok cultivated a satanic image which also largely defined his own literary and artistic tastes:

> He was . . . rather fond of posing as a cynic and even as a lover of refined depravity. Huysmans' *A Rebours*, which was in those days forbidden by the Russian censor, a collection of Verlaine's erotic poems and novels by the Marquis de Sade were Nourok's favourite books, and one of these volumes was usually to be seen peeping out of his pockets. . . . In reality, Nourok led a very quiet, decent and orderly life, worked as an official in the Naval Ministry, and took tender care of his old mother with whom he lived.[33]

Something of this kind of affectation can also be detected, with hindsight, in the early programs of the Evenings of Contemporary Music. Nurok's remark that the Evenings "fill their programs with nothing *but* novelties" and "wish to know nought else but what is new and 'unheard of,' and to complete their impudence . . . even try to seek out 'the new' in the old,"[34] was certainly a Huysmansesque fantasy in respect of the opening concert, which set uncontroversial new works by Rachmaninov and Glazunov beside Bach, Buxtehude, Saint-Saëns, and Brahms, with a leavening of smaller pieces by local "correspondents" such as Pokrovsky and Nouvel. Perhaps all new music organizations delude themselves in some such way. All the same, the idea of the Evenings was undoubtedly important in the St. Petersburg of 1902, in that they provided a platform for unconventional or small-scale works by composers not well enough known to figure on the mainstream programs of the St. Petersburg Chamber Music Society, and without the rigidity of planning which afflicted the orchestral concerts of the Russian Music Society and, even more, the

Russian Symphony Concerts. They also covered a wider spectrum of music from abroad. Stravinsky himself may have somewhat exaggerated the French ingredient in these programs, but only by emphasis: Debussy's Quartet and a few songs, the Piano Sonata of Dukas, works by Ravel and d'Indy *were* played, though not in the quantity he implies.[35] Of German composers, Reger was prominent, Wolf and Strauss only less so. But Strauss was already well known through his orchestral works. Early (pre-nineteenth century) music was also played, but again Stravinsky overstates its importance, according to Taruskin, by misattributing to the Evenings programs actually given under other auspices.[36]

We shall never know for sure, of course, how often Igor attended these approximately monthly concerts. But that they were regarded as essentially unmissable by young progressive musicians in St. Petersburg seems likely, and is borne out by the fact that Rimsky-Korsakov, who must have detested a lot of what was played, despised the amateurishness of the proceedings, and in particular disliked Nurok, having suffered from his *Mir iskusstva* reviews on several occasions, nevertheless supported the concerts by his presence, if only because music by his own pupils was being played. Stravinsky, however, was seldom among them. His only Evenings performance during Rimsky-Korsakov's lifetime—and the only one he himself ever attended—was in December 1907, when he accompanied Yelisaveta Petrenko in his Pastorale and one of the Gorodetsky songs, op. 6.[37] His F-sharp Minor Piano Sonata was not played, his own memory to the contrary notwithstanding.[38] As for his earlier appearance as piano accompanist to a cor anglais player,[39] Taruskin may be right that this was in the *Eclogue* by Igor's erstwhile counterpoint teacher, Akimenko; but the concert cannot have been, as he suggests, on 21 November 1902, which was the day Fyodor Stravinsky died.[40]

The point is that Stravinsky was no more than a fringe participant in these lively but probably rather seedy occasions—one of a large number of young Petersburg composers who had small pieces studiously performed, then as studiously forgotten. If anything, he was a member of the other, more official party: the Belyayevets youth, in attendance but inclined to view proceedings with a faintly supercilious air. If he spoke to Nurok or Nouvel, or chanced to meet Diaghilev or Benois, it had better be out of Rimsky-Korsakov's earshot. They were still the enemy. If, on the other hand, he met Nouvel's lover, the poet Mikhail Kuzmin, or such literary figures as Konstantin Balmont or Valeriy Bryusov or Alexander Blok, at the Evenings, he does not tell us so. Kuzmin he first met "with Diaghilev at Nouvel's St. Petersburg home,"[41] which cannot have been before 1909; Balmont and Blok, and presumably Bryusov, he never met at all, though he saw Balmont "at one of our concerts in St. Petersburg."[42] In other words his remark "The people I met at these concerts were also a great part of the interest. All the composers, the poets, and the artists of St. Petersburg were there . . ."43 needs decoding. Such people were to be *seen* there; and therein, perhaps, lay the interest.

AT THE START of June 1903, having received provisional student defer-ment of his military service44 and with two full years of university study now behind him, Igor set off for Pavlovka, making the long river journey with the Yelachich parents and various other fellow guests. It was hot and uncomfortable, the boat was overcrowded, and for a time it looked as if they would be stuck in Rybinsk, since there were no cabins available. But in the end all was well. Igor's friend Yevgeny Feierabend had to spend a night in the dining room, and there was a good deal of sleeping rough in second class. But that was all part of the fun. At Pavlovka, Igor spent much of his time drinking koumiss, and from the detailed accounts he rendered to his mother we can take it that, as usual, he was under orders: "3 June, three and a half glasses; 4 June, five glasses; 5 June, six and a half glasses; and already this morning a glass and a half."45 Koumiss was regarded as a specific for tuberculosis; but was Igor actually already a sufferer? By his own later testimony, he had had symptoms of the disease after an attack of pleurisy when he was thirteen. In none of his surviving health bulletins of the time is there any direct reference to it. Yet this was his first visit to Pavlovka for precisely seven years—that is, since he was just fourteen. The connection is irresistible: Pavlovka was a cure, whether or not for an ail-ment that a recently widowed mother was all too naturally inclined to exag-gerate. The following summer, Igor would again be packed off to the Yelachiches', and when he expressed the intention of leaving after only three weeks, heavy pressure would be put on him to stay for the good of his health.46

He had not yet had a lesson from Nikolay Rimsky-Korsakov, but he was composing, as he wrote to his mother three weeks after his arrival: "About myself I can tell you point by point in order of importance, as follows: (1) I'm drinking Koumiss in quantities of from five to five and a half bottles a day (I hope to increase it still more); (2) I'm playing, compos-ing, drawing, and painting, but I'm looking after my musical offspring most of all, and I'm indescribably happy since I feel that something is emerging."47

But what was he composing? If we trust his autobiography, he had already embarked on "a full-sized sonata for piano," that is, the Sonata in F-sharp Minor, though whether at Kalafati's or Rimsky-Korsakov's behest or on his own initiative, he does not tell us.48 In any case, the sense of joy in creation is already a foretaste of the Stravinsky to come, and there is no longer any hint that the music, the practice, the playing are being reported in fulfilment of a duty; nor, alternatively, is there any dissembling. Anna may have insisted that Igor continue his university course as Fyodor would have wished, but she has not imposed any corresponding embargo or limitation on his music. She seems even to have accepted the idea of his embarking on a conservatory course in tandem with his law studies, just like Richter and Volodya. The uncertainty was on his side: "You ask me, Mamochka, whether I intend to enter the Conservatoire this year—*I don't know*—that's the only answer I can give you. I shall come to Peter[sburg], and there we shall see."[49]

Igor stayed at Pavlovka a full two months, then left, but not for St. Petersburg. According to his deferment papers, he had to present evidence of his student status to the Conscription Office by 15 August, but on that very day he actually arrived at the village of Krapachukha, in the Valdye Hills near Okulovka, where the Rimsky-Korsakovs were summering. Probably Uncle Alexander had told him not to bother to present the documents in person, and had undertaken to write on his behalf.[50] Meanwhile, Mikhail Yelachich was returning to Petersburg via Moscow, and Igor had decided to go with him, "since I very much want to go to Moscow, even for the briefest time, the chance has arisen and I'll go, and I shall be very careful over expense."[51] Apart from short stops between trains (the last time in 1890 on the way to Kharkov, when they all took a carriage ride round the city), he had never even visited the ancient capital of Russia.[52]

The Krapachukha visit was made on the spur of the moment: there is no mention of it in any Pavlovka letter.[53] The fact was that the Piano Sonata was proving too much for his limited technique, and he wanted to consult the oracle.[54] He stayed with the Rimsky-Korsakovs for "about a fortnight" before continuing on his way to St. Petersburg, and during that time he must have had several three-hour sessions with the Master like the one he mentioned in a postcard home soon after his arrival.[55] To restrict the scale of the problem, Rimsky-Korsakov made him compose "the first part of a sonatina under his supervision, after having instructed me in the principles of the allegro of a sonata." There was also instruction in orchestration, and in the range of the instruments, and practical work in which "he would give me some pages of the piano score of a new opera he had just finished, which I was to orchestrate. When I had orchestrated a section, he would show me his own instrumentation of the same passage. I had to compare them, and then he would ask me to explain why he had done it differently. Whenever I was unable to do so, it was he who explained."[56]

Stravinsky himself tells us that Rimsky-Korsakov taught form and orchestration together "because in his view the more highly developed musical forms found their fullest expression in the complexity of the orchestra." But a more precise way of putting it might have been to refer to Rimsky's well-documented belief in the importance of practical work for advanced composition students, in which respect he opposed the too artificial and theoretical course structure at the Conservatoire.57 This concern for testing and implementation, so typical of Rimsky-Korsakov's hard-nosed and uncluttered approach to individual teaching, was to make an abiding impression on the young Igor and leave him with a real distaste for abstract theories of composition or writing according to classical (or any other) formulae. Admittedly, his teacher soon had him back at work on his own sonata, which was pre-eminently an exercise in modelling. But that was precisely a way of giving practical form to an academic discipline. At this late stage in his career, the conflict between empiricism and a dependence on formulae was coming to a head in Rimsky's own work. Stravinsky was able to extract from it the concepts of modelling and systematic, methodical work, combined with a readiness to experiment and accept unexpected outcomes. But as for the formulae, they would in due course be abandoned, or drastically reinterpreted.58

IGOR HAD DECIDED not to enter the Conservatoire, but to stick to his teacher's advice about private lessons. This may have been a cool-headed decision, or it may have been prompted by renewed tension at home. Yury was getting married, to his mother's intense displeasure; not only had Fyodor been dead less than a year, but Anna disliked her prospective daughter-in-law—the first woman who had ever come between her and her family—and no doubt she did her best to arouse a sense of guilt in her eldest surviving son. Yury had written to Igor in August describing the subterfuges he was having to employ in order to visit his intended's parents in Grodno. "I did it in secret," he explained, "because I didn't want to start a discussion just before Mama left [for Pechisky] and give her fresh cause for upset just when, so near her departure, she was not at her most human."[1] Yelena Nikolayevna Novoselova, whom Yury at last married in January 1904, just after the lapse of a year of mourning, was destined to remain Anna Kirillovna's only new female "rival." Igor would marry a beloved niece of hers. Gury would never marry at all.

Unlike his mother, Igor got on well with his sister-in-law from the first day, when, finding himself stuck at the wedding reception with no money for a tram, he hitched a lift home on the running board of Yury and Yelena's carriage.[2] "Yura and Lelya and the baby are here," he would write to Vladimir Rimsky-Korsakov from Ustilug a year and a half after the wedding, "which is very nice for me. For some time recently I've been somehow particularly close to Lelya and Yury, they're particularly dear to me."[3]

Yury Stravinsky had been working as an architectural engineer in Kiev, but after his marriage he took the post of assistant chief of track maintenance for the Imperial Railway in St. Petersburg, and moved into an official flat at the Nikolayevsky Station.[4] Meanwhile, tension mounted at 66 Kryukov Canal. Anna had now lost two of her four sons, and the third one needn't suppose that she would let him throw away his prospects for the privilege of starving in a garret, and her along with him. Knowing something of the personalities involved, we can imagine the scenes, in that tight-lipped, gloomy flat in the middle of a Petersburg winter. At last

Igor had had enough and fled. According to his own memoirs, he "sought refuge with a recently married Ielatchitch [sic] cousin, a man devoted to any form of revolution or protestation."[5] But his niece Xenia reports that he turned up at her newly married parents' flat, in a distraught and dishevelled state, and stayed with them for several days, until Yury at length took his courage in both hands and went to smooth things over at home.[6] Igor moved back into the Kryukov flat, and relations returned to their tense normality.

Meanwhile, the composition work begun under Rimsky-Korsakov's tutelage at Krapachukha continued in St. Petersburg. Whether this took the form of regular composition lessons is doubtful, in view of Stravinsky's statement to Timofeyev, a mere five years later, that his regular lessons only started in the autumn of 1905, after the end of his university course.[7] But he certainly went to the Master for help with the sonata, which was in any case essentially, as Taruskin has shown, a typical fourth-year composition portfolio project, and may well have been "set" by Rimsky-Korsakov back in the spring of 1903.[8] Of the Krapachukha sonatina there is no further trace. The scherzo second movement of the sonata is dated on the manuscript January–February 1904, so presumably the first movement—which would have, for academic reasons, to be got right before all else—belongs to the autumn of 1903. After finishing the scherzo, Igor must have put the work aside in order to compose the cantata for Rimsky-Korsakov's sixtieth birthday, in time for the actual celebration on 6 March. For reasons which are not known, but which may have had to do with his university work, the other two movements of the sonata were not composed until the summer.

The cantata, as Yastrebtsev calls it—though it was evidently little more than a ceremonial part-song with or without piano accompaniment—has not survived, and the only descriptions we have of it are a diary entry by Rimsky-Korsakov that it was *"neduren"*—not bad—and Yastrebtsev's faintly condescending *"premiluyu"*—very nice.[9] It was sung during supper at 28 Zagorodnïy by a little choir of Rimsky-Korsakovs and friends, including Stepan Mitusov, conducted by Stravinsky himself, and it had to be repeated by popular demand. One significant aspect of this occasion is that it shows Igor as by now sufficiently accepted as a member of the circle to be able to put himself forward as chief standard-bearer in praise of its leader. How much time he had spent at the Rimsky-Korsakovs since the previous summer is impossible to establish, but he must have been there often, for consultations, soirées, and social calls, particularly when relations at home were at their least agreeable, even if his later remark that "I was in [Rimsky's] home almost every day of 1903, 1904 and 1905"[10] has some considerable scent of hyperbole. He also attended the various rehearsals and performances which were always a feature of Rimsky-circle activities: he will, for instance, have been at the revival of Rimsky's own early kuchkist opera *The Maid of Pskov* (with Chaliapin as Ivan the Terrible) at the Mariyinsky on 28 October 1903; and he went with his teacher to the Russian Symphony Concerts, including the Belyayev memorial on 3 March 1904, at which Rimsky-Korsakov conducted his own prelude *At the Graveside*. We may picture him at rehearsals, earnestly following scores, with the Master pointing out felicities and infelicities; or at the Zagorodnïy flat, vigorously agreeing with Rimsky's pronouncements on the newest music, like his view of Debussy's *Estampes* as "to the last degree bad and inadequate; no technique, still less imagination. A cheeky decadent— ignoring everything written before him," or of *Pelléas* as music of retrogression.[11] Did Igor ever risk—or breathe silently—a "Perhaps this is also merely one point of view," as he claims to have done later when Rimsky-Korsakov ridiculed the idea of the afterlife?[12] It seems likely that he did not.

By the summer, in any case, the friendship with the Rimsky-Korsakovs had moved on to a new footing, and Igor invited Volodya to accompany him for a month's stay at Pavlovka, where he was again off to drink koumiss.[13] One senses something less than rapture at the thought of the four-day river journey (on his own this time) and the long empty weeks beyond the Volga. Volodya was to be both company for him and his pretext for an early departure, as we learn from a letter from Pavlovka to the Rimsky-Korsakovs at Vechasha:

> Igor originally planned to leave with me. That was decided some time before the trip. . . . Then after that, while we were getting our tickets, it turned out that his mother wanted him to stay in Pavlovka for at least six weeks for the good of his health. Igor said that he didn't need the good of his health and wouldn't stay in Pavlovka a day longer than me. So I was confident he would stick to his decision. When we got to Pavlovka, Igor at once announced that he would not be staying very long but would be leaving with me. Meanwhile, Anna Kirillovna wrote to Soph'ya Kirillovna begging her to somehow make Igor drink koumiss and stay at Pavlovka as long as possible. They all got at Igor so energetically that in the end he decided to stay.[14]

Igor and Volodya were hitting it off. On the Volga the weather was scorchingly hot, and it was like being on holiday. One smartly dressed, fat lady on the boat loudly threatened to unbutton her dress. At Nizhny-Novgorod, they took the funicular to the upper town; then, to save money, they bought a picnic and Igor made the boat steward bring him boiling water for the sausage by pretending he needed it for taking medicine. Farther on, at Liskovo—opposite the monastery of Makaryev—he warded off a mendicant nun by claiming to be a Catholic, and Volodya, who was trying hard to look like an American, broke down in helpless laughter.[15]

But after only two weeks—a mere weekend by Pavlovka standards—Volodya set off back to Vechasha alone, leaving Igor with the comfort of an invitation to join him there as soon as his koumiss level was up to scratch. Igor, meanwhile, dropped his mother a soothing letter with much description of healthy exercise, a detailed account of a hunting-cum-insect-collecting excursion with Gury and Zhenya Yelachich, a cursory health bulletin, and the usual grumbles about not receiving any letters—but not a word about the activity which was now uppermost in his mind, composition.[16] Information on this important subject he reserved for Volodya himself. "I'm getting on very well," he had already written a week before. "I've completed the finale and am writing the andante. I want to bring the whole sonata to you at Vechasha with the revised first movement."[17] A fortnight later, he has "already perfected the first movement, completed the finale and the andante, and also decided that the andante will be directly joined on to the finale, and that's all that remains—to compose this link. I can't tell you how pleased I am to have finished this piece; it's turned out large-scale but not, I think, tedious. I'd like to write Richter a letter about it, as it's dedicated to him."[18]

His self-satisfaction was justified, since, while the sonata is completely without noticeable individuality, it is a highly efficient exercise in prescribed forms and idioms, and a remarkable achievement, in purely compositional terms, for a student composer whose previous largest piece had scarcely exceeded five minutes in duration. The style and approach are unashamedly by the book. The basic four-movement form is that of countless late-romantic sonatas, not only Russian ones, though Taruskin is surely right to emphasize the indebtedness to models like Tchaikovsky's Grand Sonata in G, Scriabin's Third, and even the two three-movement sonatas of Glazunov.[19] As for practical matters like the treatment of harmony, rhythm, and thematic contrast, they are stereotyped—as they are, indeed, in some of the models. But the handling is seldom less than polished, and Stravinsky shows himself able to control a rich, post-Tchaikovsky palette and a big, quasi-orchestral keyboard manner, with barely a tremor. In its own terms, and forgetting who wrote it, the sonata is in its garrulous way effective, and still today merits the occasional performance.

As a piece of Stravinsky's, its most startling feature, beyond any question, is the advance it shows over his previous work. We shall encounter this quality again. It must also have impressed Rimsky-Korsakov, when Igor finally arrived at Vechasha in the second week of August with the fat manuscript under his arm. Was the Stravinsky of this dextrous A-major scherzo really the Stravinsky of that wretched little E-flat piece of only two years before? Was this grand first movement, with its majestic periods, really the work of a young man who a year ago had had to be told the difference between a second subject and a codetta?

Richard Taruskin argues that Rimsky was in fact so impressed that he agreed, on the spot, to take Igor as a private composition pupil. For Taruskin, the sonata was Stravinsky's *Probestück*.[20] We know, at any rate, that Rimsky-Korsakov at once enlisted Igor's assistance with the score of his latest opera, *The Legend of the Invisible City of Kitezh*. Yastrebtsev, who happened to turn up at Vechasha ten days after Igor, found master and pupil "occupied with the orchestration of *Kitezh* and also with writing the scenario into the orchestral score of scene 1, act 3, which was completed only yesterday."[21] Rimsky also, it is true, gave Igor orchestration assignments, including a rescoring of the brass-band opening of the polonaise in *Pan Voyevoda*.[22] But his readiness to treat Igor as even a menial collaborator was surely a greater sign of confidence. To read the proofs of *Kitezh* would a year or so later be the accolade of the unquestionably brilliant and talented Maximilian Steinberg.[23]

Igor perhaps continued working with the Master on his orchestral scores on their return to St. Petersburg in September. In any case he was certainly firmly in his Mariyinsky seat on 1 October for the premiere of *Pan Voyevoda*, an opera with which he must by this time have felt an intimate familiarity. In more ways than one it was an active autumn for Rimsky-Korsakov. His version of Musorgsky's *Boris Godunov* was at last staged at the Mariyinsky towards the end of November (with Chaliapin in the title role), ten days after Alexander Ziloti had conducted his Third Symphony, a work not previously programmed by anyone but Rimsky-Korsakov himself. It is inconceivable that Igor missed any of these performances. It may even be that the curious marching song for bass-baritone and piano which he wrote that December, to nonsense words about "how the mushrooms prepared for war" ("Kak gribï na voynu sobiralis"), was prompted by the sound of Chaliapin's voice, or by memories of the repetitive nonsense songs in Musorgsky's opera.[24]

It may equally be, of course, that this gentle satire on the reluctance of parasites to take up arms was suggested by a very different set of circumstances in Russia that autumn of 1904. The distant war with Japan, which had broken out with the Japanese attack on Port Arthur in February, and which the Russians, as a great power, should by the criteria of the time have been able to win, was dragging on with huge casualties on both sides. Physically, the war in Manchuria, at the far eastern end of the Russian Empire, presented no threat to the Russian lands themselves. But it was beginning to sap the authority of the state organization. The Imperial Baltic fleet was at sea, on a voyage that would take it more than six months and end with its almost total destruction in the Tsushima Straits in May 1905. Port Arthur had been under siege since August. Worst of all, the war meant that large elements of those forces whose peacetime role was to protect the state were heavily engaged, and moreover being badly depleted, in a theatre so distant that, for all practical purposes, they might as well have been on the moon. Russia was already a state riven by the threat of anarchy and revolution, in which there were almost daily attempts on the lives of state officials, including, sometimes, the Tsar himself or members of his entourage. The countryside was in more or less permanent crisis. In St. Petersburg, 1905 opened with a series of strikes and dismissals. The first great climax of these developments came on "Bloody Sunday," 9 January, when a peaceful deputation of workers and a crowd of bystanders were fired on in the Palace Square, and more than a hundred people were killed.[25]

The essentially apolitical Stravinskys were, if anything, quietly sympathetic to these popular movements. The summer of 1905 would find Igor and his cousin Katya enthusiastically reading up on the political constitutions of more democratic states,[26] and a year later Igor expressed the following impeccably redistributive sentiments in another letter to Volodya: "The tremendous revolution that is inevitably coming frightens me not at all, since I feel with all the strength of my soul that the money on which we privileged classes all live is not ours, particularly not mine, since I have so far produced not a single thing of value for public consumption. I shall be happy the day I can say I am living on money I have produced myself."[27] But it is hard to envisage him marching on the Winter Palace, or manning picket lines, or even, at this stage at least, putting his name to open letters. Nikolay Rimsky-Korsakov, the "confirmed Social Democrat,"[28] was a bird of quite a different feather. To Yastrebtsev, he confessed in mid-January that "of late he had become a 'vivid red,' but he asked me to stop talking about the shocking things that went on from the ninth January to the thirteenth, as all this upsets him terribly."[29] But within weeks he was to find himself willy-nilly at the center of a political imbroglio with the Conservatoire. Bloody Sunday was followed by a general strike in St. Petersburg, in which both university and Conservatoire students participated to the full. In the Conservatoire illegal meetings were held, attempts were made to expel the ringleaders, and finally the whole institution was closed down for two months. Following his unswerving instincts as a social democrat, and, one should add, as a teacher, Rimsky-Korsakov sided with the students. In early February he added his name to an open letter from a group of leading Moscow musicians (including Rachmaninov and Chaliapin) deploring state controls on art and freedom of speech, and in March—after a stormy meeting of the Conservatoire council—he published two open letters of his own objecting to the reopening of the Conservatoire under what amounted to police supervision, and calling for its emancipation from the control of the Imperial Russian Musical Society.[30] Within days, on 19 March, Rimsky-Korsakov was dismissed from his post of Conservatoire professor. But the matter by no means ended there. Overnight, he became "the martyr-hero of liberal and intellectual Russia,"[31] and on 27 March the Conservatoire students put on a hastily arranged concert in the Komissarzhevsky Theatre at which Rimsky's one-act opera *Kaschey the Immortal* was performed, interminable spoken tributes were delivered, and the proceedings were brought to an abrupt close when the police lowered the iron safety curtain, narrowly missing Rimsky-Korsakov's head as he stood on the platform receiving the adulation of the audience.[32]

Although the Conservatoire eventually reopened in the autumn, and Rimsky-Korsakov was reinstated along with several colleagues who had resigned, the reverberations of these events did not quickly die down. Throughout the autumn, the atmosphere in St. Petersburg remained tense. General strikes in October were accompanied by turbulent street demonstrations, which were usually suppressed with violence and bloodshed. Stravinsky remembered getting caught up in one of these one afternoon as he crossed the square in front of the Kazan Cathedral. "I was detained seven hours," he recalled, "but seventy years will not erase the memory of my fears."[33] Yet in general the reader of his autobiography and conversations is likely to be more than anything surprised and even disconcerted by the absence of any significant reference to the events of 1905, events which demonstrably affected his life at the time and ultimately changed it irrevocably. For example, Stravinsky nowhere mentions the student strike which drastically disrupted the university between January and August, even though it may have delayed his final exams by several months and his diploma by a year. It may even in the end have prevented him from taking a full degree.[34] Nor does he refer at all to his teacher's role in the Conservatoire affair, which must have been a source of ineffable pride to the majority of his students. His sole allusion to Rimsky-Korsakov's politics takes the form of a ludicrous pararaph on the supposed 1908 premiere of Rimsky's initially banned final opera, *The Golden Cockerel*, at which the composer is said to have been "too hopelessly in love with the soprano Zabela [-Vrubel] . . ." to take any interest in the politics of the affair.[35]

One, no doubt inadequate, reason for this lacuna may be that 1905 was in several respects a turning point in Igor's own life, and not because of anything to do with his university studies. It began auspiciously with his first significant premiere, that of the Piano Sonata, which Richter, its dedicatee, played at a Rimsky-Korsakov Wednesday on 9 February.[36] The work was greeted with admiration by the assembled Belyayevtsï, who included Glazunov, Belsky, Zabela-Vrubel, and assorted Rimsky-Korsakovs. "A very talented piece!" Yastrebtsev exclaimed in his journal.[37]

Having surmounted this hurdle, Igor's next task in the Rimsky curriculum was to compose a symphony, and this he set about with enthusiasm in the early summer at Ustilug, his first visit to the Nosenko estate since the year before his father's death.[38] "I think of you all the time," he wrote to Volodya from his cousins' house. "I'm living au naturel. I'm eating, sleeping, driving, riding. I'm zealously writing a symphony. The first movement is hatching. I'm finding utter satisfaction in the work of composition. I passionately want to play it to Nikolay Andreyevich and consult him about it. I'm longing to see you. I've got millions of things to tell you."[39] Suddenly music was pouring out of him. By mid-July the first two movements were already done, and by the start of August he had added the Largo, with its heavy echoes of Tchaikovsky's Queen of Spades.[40] The draft fair copy was completed on the fourth. But there was then an interruption, or at least a slowing down, and it was to be another seven weeks before he could claim a finished draft of the finale (it bears the date 24 September). But the delay was not merely a consequence of the well-known finale problem. In the second half of July, Anna and Gury arrived at Ustilug from Pechisky; Yury and Yelena were already there.[41] The Stravinsky family was together in the country for the first time since Fyodor's death. On 15 August, Igor took advantage of what may in any case have been a stage-managed gathering to announce his engagement to his first cousin, Yekaterina Gavrilovna Nosenko.[42]

This visit to Ustilug was probably the couple's first meeting for a long time, perhaps as much as four years—that is, since Igor's last stay there. The Nosenkos were and remained a Kiev family, and we do not hear of many visits to St. Petersburg. There was a Katya in the Pavlovka party in 1903, but it cannot have been *the* Katya, because less than two weeks after their arrival Igor was craving a letter from her, and in terms which make it clear that he had not seen her recently.[43] Katya Nosenko had been in Paris, at least in the spring of 1903 and probably for much of that year. She, Lyudmila, and their cousins Olga and Vera were photographed in the French capital in early April, and it must have been at that time that the four girls studied drawing together there.[44] Igor even recalled that Katya had lived and studied in Paris for a full three years before their marriage, from 1903 to 1906,[45] and while this may be an exaggeration, it suggests a specific memory of a long separation—not, of course, before the marriage, but before the engagement. Igor had meanwhile had his flings, or would-be flings. There had been a crush on a doctor's daughter called Lydia Walter, a "more sophisticated" brush with the half-sister of Stepan Mitusov, and a secret passion for the girlfriend of Ivan Pokrovsky's brother, as well as the "summer romance" with Katya's friend Lyudmila Kuxina.[46] No doubt there were other heartthrobs. But somehow Katya had existed above and apart from all this.

Was that summer at Ustilig essentially different from the old ones—the summers of Chekhov and wild raspberries, of riding and boating, and sketching in dappled birch woods? Perhaps not in outward appearance. But for Igor it was different, for one thing, because he was working, and working—as he seems ever afterwards to have done—with that joyous, vibrant energy which, in his music, transfigures toil and drudgery into buoyant movement, and movement into the divine grace of the dance. Different, too, because of Katya—no longer the beloved cousin but simply, openly, the beloved. From this whole summer we have only two letters from Igor, both to Volodya. But they both radiate happiness and, no less important, a measure of tranquillity and self-assurance that is new in our experience of this insecure, overregulated, underloved young man.

"Life flows on very peacefully," he announces: "I'm hard at work—all day long." In the evenings there are group readings, with Katya, Lyudmila and her husband, Grigory Belyankin, and a doctor and his wife: "They are Poles, and extraordinarily intelligent and well-educated."[47] "They all prided themselves on their liberalism," he later recalled of such circles, "extolled progress, and considered it the thing to profess so-called 'advanced' opinions in politics, art, and all branches of social life."[48] But while there *is* something curiously detached, even abstract, about these earnest rural discussions of Western systems of democratic government (which they studied, incredibly enough, in a book published quite openly in St. Petersburg the previous year),[49] not everyone at the Nosenkos' that summer was quite the woolly liberal of Stravinsky's memory. Stanislaw Bachnicki, the Polish doctor, was a friend and correspondent of Lenin's chief theorist, G. V. Plekhanov, had served a prison sentence in Lublin, evidently for political activities, and was living in Ustilug as an exile, forbidden by the authorities to live in any large town.[50] This fact gives sharper point to Stravinsky's observation that "despite living in the comparatively remote provinces, I hear and see a constant display of the most active, passionate interest in all current events," not to mention the anathema he hurls—somewhat rashly, perhaps, in view of the political situation—at "this damned empire of intellectual hooligans and obscurantists! The devil take them!"[51]

Struggling back to St. Petersburg that October, he found a city gripped by strikes and street demonstrations. He had fully intended to go by way of Vechasha, to show Rimsky-Korsakov his symphony and tell him about his engagement.[52] But travel was difficult, and this may have delayed him at Ustilug longer than he intended. Yastrebtsev does not record Igor's presence at 28 Zagorodnïy until 9 November, which was itself only Rimsky's second Wednesday of the autumn. The previous evening's revival of Rimsky's opera *The Snow Maiden* was discussed, and Igor and Nikolay Richter played Taneyev's Fourth Symphony four-hands, a work Taruskin believes to have served as a model for Stravinsky's own symphony.[53] Meanwhile, Rimsky-Korsakov continued to identify himself publicly with the workers and students. On 5 November, his new orchestral arrangement of the revolutionary song "Dubinushka" was included in a Ziloti concert, and a month later he personally organized a concert in the Tenishevsky School in aid of "the families of destitute working men."[54] A number of songs by Rimsky and others, with more or less relevant texts ("about freedom, prisoners and shackles"), were performed, and "at the end of the concert, the young people broke out into their famous workers' *Marseillaise* and *Warsczawianka*."[55]

Whether or not Igor participated in such manifestations, he forgot about them later on, for the understandable reason that his own work had assumed an overriding importance. He was now going to Rimsky-Korsakov for regular lessons, and they were painstakingly working through his symphony, marking in alterations and suggestions for revision.[56] There were also orchestration lessons, still consisting—we may assume—of exercises based on Rimsky-Korsakov's own recent work, perhaps including *The Legend of the Invisible City of Kitezh,* a vocal score of which the composer presented to his pupil after Christmas.[57] Yastrebtsev ran into Igor waiting for an orchestration lesson at Zagorodnïy in the late afternoon of the Monday before Christmas. After the lesson, they had dinner, exactly in the manner described by Stravinsky as routine after his lessons: "We drank vodka and ate *zakousky* together, then started the dinner. I would sit next to Rimsky and often continue to discuss some problem from my previous lesson."[58] On this occasion, the problem concerned Glazunov's Eighth Symphony in E-flat, which the forty-year-old composer had played for the first time at Zagorodnïy the previous Wednesday, and which Rimsky seems to have been treating as a model for the revisions to Igor's own symphony in that key.[59] Taruskin shows, for instance, that the crucial revision of the main first movement theme, which involved extending it and opening it out grammatically so as to imply development rather than closure, was a direct copy of Glazunov's own procedure. In any case, it is clear from the Paris manuscript that Rimsky was using Stravinsky's draft as a basis for thoroughgoing composition teaching based on good textbook practice but always with reference to the latest orthodox models. There is even something in the approach akin to his own work not so many years previously on Musorgsky's *Boris:* the same concern to smooth out, to convert into a musical "engine" that burnt the same fuel as the great works of the past, to render effective in some existing, well-known or well-remembered sense. Of course with Stravinsky there is no case for arguing that the work was already sui generis a masterpiece and should have been left alone. The revised version is in every significant way an improvement on what was, in its first form, a conventional work with warts—something even Rimsky-Korsakov would never have said of *Boris*.[60]

Katya may not have come with Igor to St. Petersburg in October, but by December she was there. Yastrebtsev reports her presence at the Zagorodnïy Wednesday on 14 December (when Glazunov played his new symphony), and she was there again on 4 January, at a big party in honor of Vladimir Stasov's eighty-second birthday.[61] By a nice coincidence, the main piece of music performed at the birthday party was the single completed act of Musorgsky's opera *The Marriage*, which Stasov, who was head of the art department of the St. Petersburg Public Library, had extracted from the archives of that institution, where it had been gathering dust since the composer's death in 1881. Among those singing was Gury Stravinsky, who had followed his brother into the law department of the university but had ambitions to emulate their father's career as a singer, and was now studying to that end.[62] Exactly a week later, on 11 January 1906, Katya Nosenko escaped the fate of Podkolesin's bartered bride in *The Marriage*, whom he abandons at the altar. But she was not, all the same, to be vouchsafed a ceremonial wedding. Forbidden, as first cousins, to wed, the couple went by open droshky to the northern St. Petersburg village of Novaya Derevnya, a journey of some five miles in the depths of the Petersburg winter, and there they were married, in the Church of the Annunciation, by

> a kind of Graham Greene bootleg priest—one who would marry us without asking for documents which would have exposed the relationship between us. . . . No relatives were present, and our only attendants were my best men, Andrei and Vladimir Rimsky-Korsakov, who knelt with us and held the gold and velvet wedding crown over our heads. When we reached home after the ceremony, Rimsky was waiting at the door. He blessed me, holding over my head an icon which he then gave me as a wedding present.[63]

It may perhaps be added that the absence of the bridegroom's mother (the only surviving parent on either side), and of all close relations need have had nothing specifically to do with the fact that the ceremony was illicit or in any sense disreputable. It was traditional in Russian weddings, and symbolized the abandonment of the family home, as in Stravinsky's own incomparable dramatization of the ritual, *Svadebka* (*Les Noces*), where the parents are represented at the church ceremony by proxies.

. . .

LATER THEY WENT to the Finland Station, and took a train to the little Finnish town of Imatra, with its great rapids down which the waters from Lake Saimaa tumbled towards Lake Ladoga and, eventually, the River Neva and Petersburg itself. "Imatra was frosty and white, and though the larger cascades still poured over the cliffs, the smallest were hibernating as icicles. We stayed in Imatra for two weeks, photographing the falls and sleigh-riding."[64] In fact they were in "wonderful Imatra," as Igor described it in a postcard to Andrey Rimsky-Korsakov, for exactly one week before continuing on to the Finnish capital, Helsingfors, from where on 19 January Igor sent Volodya a postcard depicting a "demonstration by the Finnish people on 6 November 1905."[65] Six days later, exactly two weeks after their droshky wedding, Igor was back at Rimsky-Korsakov's with his wife, playing Schubert's "Great" C Major Symphony and discussing Wagner's *Rheingold.*[66]

READERS OF THE PUBLISHED fragments of Katya Stravinsky's letters, together with Robert Craft's various commentaries on them, will form the impression of a pious, saintly, worn-out, self-abnegating woman, obsessed with the agony of ill health, and resigned—one could say, unnaturally so— to a vicarious, unregarded existence in the shadow of a celebrated and unfaithful husband.[1] This person may or may not have come into existence during the 1920s and 1930s. But she is not the Katya with whom Igor went to the Finland Station in January 1906, nor is she the Katya he had grown to love during the long summers at Ustilug. One might well ask why any vigorous or self-regarding young man would marry such a nunnish wife. The fact is, presumably, that he would not.

The best of the few surviving descriptions of Katya as a young woman is that of her niece and cousin Xenia Stravinsky, the younger daughter of Igor's brother Yury. Xenia knew Katya only as a tiny child, and her description is based on hearsay, from her parents, and from her sister, Tanya, who spent nearly a year with their uncle Igor's family in Nice in 1925–26. Xenia may also have remembered her grandmother Anna Stravinsky talking about Katya. The picture is therefore a family one, and has to be read in the light of the family's understandable resentment at the treatment to which Katya was later subjected. All the same, it rings true to the Katya who emerges, however dimly, from Igor's own letters of that earlier time. Katya, we learn, was

> a girl of rare spiritual beauty, this intelligent, profound and exceptionally warm-hearted woman with her quiet charm. We heard a lot about her from our parents, who loved her dearly. As a young girl, and even at the time of her marriage, Aunt Katya attached little importance to appearances, dressed modestly, and was very shy. She was mad about music (in her youth she studied singing seriously) and art. . . . But all this receded into the background when she became a mother of four and the wife of a great musician, and had to run a large household.[2]

But Katya's beauty was not just spiritual. Photographs of her at the time of her marriage and before show a beguiling tenderness of facial expression: soft, deep-set eyes, a generous but not sensuous mouth (in marked contrast to her more conventionally good-looking older sister), an air of calm inner poise. They only occasionally support the view that she was careless of her appearance, though her style is homely, or bourgeois Sunday-best, rather than *mondaine* or fashion-conscious. But there is little trace, at this or any other time, of the self-effacing "little woman." In photographs with Igor she does not recede, but looks directly and candidly at the viewer, to which one could add that Igor himself—though invariably unsmiling—seems to "belong" happily, even proudly, in the environment defined by his wife. This remains, always, a domesticated Russian environment (wherever it may be geographically), just as the life of Ustilug, which was for so long a part of everything Igor knew about Katya, was a rustic version of upper-middle-class Russian domesticity.

Nor was Katya, at nineteen and twenty, noticeably pious, any more than Igor himself. Indeed, the absence of any reference to churchgoing is a striking feature of Igor's letters from Ustilug, considering that he was as a rule assiduous in recording the fulfillment of duties for his parents' benefit. The assumption must be that church attendance was not specifically required. Igor later recalled that his parents were not regular churchgoers but insisted on attendance by their sons.[3] This may, though, have amounted to little more than Easter confession and communion, plus the *panikhida,* or requiem mass, in memory of Roman on his birthday, the first of October. In any case, by the time Igor left the gymnasium in 1901, he had, he says, completely given up going. At Ustilug, churchgoing would certainly have been easy enough, as there were two Orthodox churches in the village; but we do not hear that the Nosenkos attended, or that Katya's newfound seriousness, which impressed Igor in the summer of 1901, had any devotional coloring. This could, of course, be explained away (Fyodor and Anna might have been disturbed by actual piety). But a more straightforward conclusion would be that piety simply was not in question.

The Nosenkos were more associated in Ustilug with social welfare and "good works." Either during Gavriyil's time, or more probably after his death, the family had given money for the foundation of a free hospital, and it was there that the Polish doctor Bachnicki came to work in the early years of the century, presumably between 1901 and 1905.[4] The Nosenkos also gave ground for a public cemetery, and they built a fire station and a school.[5] However much or little of this was directly attributable to Katya, it helps define the somewhat Fabian character of the family's involvement in the life of a community which, after all, was almost entirely Jewish and, on the whole, poor. Bachnicki's daughter, Wanda, remembered Grigory and Lyudmila Belyankin as "progressive [and] exceptionally humanitarian in their thinking. Theirs was one of the few estates, if not the only one, whose workers did not go on strike in 1905, and whose owners (quite unbeliev- ably for the time) were addressed by the workers at their sugar refinery at Strzyzów thanking them for their humane treatment of their employees."[6] But a specifically religious tone was lacking.

Igor's first personal experience of Katya had been as simply one compo- nent of a feminine world that was itself delightfully new to him. But this world turned out to be not without its peculiar dangers. The girls could be factious; and who knows that Gury, if his point of view had come down to us, would not have had some teenage complaint to make about Katya, like those that Igor levels at her sister, Lyudmila, or her cousin Vera? But for Igor, it was Katya who had gradually assumed the burden of those unsatis- fied longings to which, at first, Ustilug as a whole had seemed to respond. She was the one who was sweet and affectionate to him when Milushka, three years his senior, started treating him with condescension, and when the sharp-tongued Vera was showing off and acting the coquette.[7] She was the one whose serious-mindedness resonated with his, whose love of music and painting echoed his, without (like the Yelachiches') threatening it with extinction. And perhaps she was the one person in Igor's first twenty years who recognized in him something exceptional and astonish- ing—even if she can hardly have guessed what it was. Above all, she gave him unqualified sympathy, which, for him, was always to be the pearl with- out price, and which was the single most vital omission of his home life. But she gave much more than that, and one should guard against accept- ing the implication that, in its physical and social aspects, her love left something to be desired. It was only later that it became necessary or con- venient to make such distinctions. In 1906 everything was surely one.

THE HONEYMOONERS were not entirely cut off from music. They had with them the vocal score of Rimsky-Korsakov's *Kitezh*, which the composer had given Igor before the wedding. "We still have your flowers in water and quite fresh," Igor wrote to Mrs. Rimsky-Korsakov from Imatra, "looking at them we remember you, and playing *Kitezh*, we think of dear Nikolay Andreyevich."[8] Igor was also contemplating a new work of his own, or so he informs us in his memoirs of half a century later: "The music of the *Faune et bergère* was growing in my head, and when we returned to St. Petersburg I began to write it down."[9] In fact there is no contemporary ref- erence to the new piece until early June, by which time the Stravinskys had been at Ustilug for at least three weeks. Igor writes from there to Volodya, in Vienna, that "I'm working hard. I've finished a song to verses by Pushkin ('Lila'), and composed a sketch for the orchestration. I've roughed out the march, on which there's still a lot to do, and I'm now busy scoring it (since I hadn't scored it to the end, you see, but only halfway). When I've finished that I'll get to work on the scherzo of the symphony."[10] But he had already written to Volodya, on 16 May, a long letter in which he makes no mention of any of this work.[11] So it looks as if the Pushkin song—which became "Pastushka" (The Shepherdess), the first of the three movements of *The Faun and the Shepherdess*—was a new piece of work, not known to Volodya, while the march, whatever it might be, was on the contrary a piece he was aware of.[12] The Russian editor of Igor's letters to Volodya takes it to be an early version of the third movement of the Pushkin cycle, but this is hard to square with the piece as we know it, which describes a frantic pursuit rather than a military exercise.[13] Another faint possibility is that the reference is to the first movement of the symphony, which might loosely be described as a march. Failing this, it must surely be a work that has not survived.

In any case, serious work on *The Faun and the Shepherdess* seems not to have begun until May—which does not mean, of course, that the music was not conceived, as the composer claimed, on honeymoon four months before. Early published editions bear a dedication to Katya. Whether or not that entitles us to interpret the work as a wedding present, it certainly is a somewhat bizarre epithalamium, with its voyeuristic account of the wet dreams of a delectable fifteen-year-old girl, followed, in the final song, by her pursuit and near-ravishment by a leering faun. The fact that the poems, written by Pushkin when he was himself only seventeen, are a literary conceit modelled on Parny's pseudo-Ovidian *Déguisements de Vénus* scarcely detracts from their essential tone of decorative erotic fantasy.[14] If Igor chose them as a suitable offering for his cousinly bride, then we may well need to adjust the usual view—encouraged in later years by the composer himself—of the couple's early relationship.

Igor's main activity on his return from Finland, however, was probably to continue prosaically his composition and orchestration lessons with Rimsky-Korsakov. Had they for some reason shelved work on the first movement and passed directly on to the Scherzo second? Or had Igor already revised the first movement during the autumn? All we know is that the symphony's partial performance a year later included the Scherzo and Largo but not the first movement, whose final revision was only completed in July 1907. Referring to his discussion of Glazunov's Eighth Symphony with Igor and Rimsky-Korsakov, Yastrebtsev mentions that "Rimsky-Korsakov and I share the same opinion of it—that the second movement [Scherzo] is the best and, after that, the first movement."[15] It is tempting to imagine that Rimsky was at the same time pressing Igor to revise the comparatively unproblematical Scherzo of his symphony, perhaps even envisaging a performance of a movement that represented a style of writing for which the young composer already had an evident flair.

Whatever the truth about this, we can take it that the symphony remained the focus of study. Not until he could get away to Ustilug would Igor be free even to write up the consequences of the spring's tuition, let alone to concentrate on something entirely new—even if, as Taruskin suggests, the new vocal work did fit into Rimsky's idea of syllabus progression and was very possibly begun at his prompting.[16]

Back from Imatra, Igor and Katya settled into 66 Kryukov Canal, which was by now occupied only by Anna and Gury along with the various family retainers. It might have seemed a recipe for disaster. But Anna was fond of Katya (or "Puti," as she was called within the close family), had always felt a responsibility for her and Milochka as orphan nieces, and got on well with her.[17] There were no scenes. Even so, life must have been as cramped as ever it was, with the young couple allocated a pair of gloomy back rooms—the former bedrooms of Roman and Yury—where, in the fullness of time, their first two children would be born and, presumably, accommodated; Bertha still occupied her end room; Gury, his and Igor's old front bedroom; while Fyodor's library was preserved by Anna as a shrine.[18] Nevertheless they put up with it, and indeed probably had little choice, since Igor still had no gainful employment and Katya's capital was tied up in the family property in Ustilug. Not until 1909, when Igor was starting to build up a modest income from publications and commissions, were they apparently in a position to rent a flat of their own, at 26 Angliyskiy Prospect, a few hundred yards out of town from the Kryukov Canal.[19]

Meanwhile, the gatherings at Zagorodniy Prospect continued as a rare fixed point in a rapidly exploding universe. On 26 January Rimsky-Korsakov stormed out of a meeting at the Conservatoire council, unable any longer to endure the insistent antipathy to the students and the open hostility to the new director, Glazunov, to whom Rimsky remained unshakably devoted and loyal. In fact it was only in response to Glazunov's pleas that he agreed to withdraw his resignation and stay on at the Conservatoire.[20] But the Conservatoire itself remained effectively at a standstill, and Rimsky continued to give his classes at home. Concert life staggered on, with only two Russian Symphony Concerts during the entire season, and the Russian Musical Society in a state of virtual collapse. The program for the second RSC on 2 March was symptomatic of the depths to which these concerts had sunk since the death of their founder, quite independently of recent political troubles: a staccato sequence of short works by Belyayevtsï, each more minor and ephemeral than the last, it made on Yastrebtsev "an unusually tedious impression."[21] The one encouragement was the acceptance of *Kitezh* for production at the Mariyinsky. But, though everyone at Zagorodniy was "overjoyed" at the news,[22] it took a full year for the staging to materialize.

Amid all the political turmoil, there is something touchingly abstracted about Yastrebtsev's levelheaded accounts of the musical comings and goings at the Rimsky Wednesdays. The fact was, as he confessed on that same 1 February, that "a new false progression or a fresh and original modulation is dearer to me than all your politics." And despite Rimsky's own heavy involvement in events at the Conservatoire and elsewhere,[23] many of his guests seem to have been closer to Yastrebtsev's view of things. "They talked about Wagner and Wagnerism," is his laconic remark about the gathering at that week's *jour fixe.* Two weeks later, Wagner again dominated proceedings, since "[Felix] Blumenfeld literally worships *Tristan.*"[24] But Yastrebtsev's political detachment and naiveté must have been a byword, since, at Belsky's a few days later, the librettist of Rimsky's more or less candidly republican last opera, *The Golden Cockerel,* assured the diarist that "the whole thing is going to take place in the land of the Naiads."[25]

Meanwhile, there were new faces at the Rimskys': not only such as Katya, who would occasionally appear with her husband—as she did, for instance, at Rimsky-Korsakov's sixty-second-birthday party on 6 March, when Igor played a Koz'ma Prutkov piece called *The Driver and the Tarantula.*[26] There were new pupils too, or rather old ones who, since the closure of the Conservatoire, had begun to appear at Zagorodnïy for their classes. Of these, the most interesting, and for Igor eventually the most important, was a young Jewish composer from the Polish-Lithuanian city of Vilna by the name of Maximilian Oseyevich Steinberg.[27]

Steinberg, though a year younger than Igor, had entered St. Petersburg University in the same year, 1901, but in the faculty of natural science. His real goal, however, was to become a composition pupil of Rimsky-Korsakov's, and to that end he enrolled at the Conservatoire as a member of Lyadov's harmony class. Like Stravinsky, Steinberg was theoretically backward, though a competent violinist. But because he presented himself as a Conservatoire candidate, rather than by direct introduction to Rimsky himself, he was forced to go through the theoretical mill at that institution, and it was only because he turned out to have an outstanding flair for such things that he came to the master's attention, probably during the 1903–4 session, when Rimsky praised him to Alexander Ossovsky for his taste, talent, and musical ear, and Glazunov reported to Rimsky that Steinberg had written the best piano accompaniment in the May end-of-year examinations, "confirming our expectations."[28] By the time Rimsky's classes moved from the Conservatoire to Zagorodnïy in the spring of 1905, Steinberg was his star pupil. That year his *Four Romances,* op. 1, were published by Belyayev at Rimsky's instigation, and within a few weeks of his first appearance at a Zagorodnïy *jour fixe* Rimsky had arranged for his orchestral Variations in G Major to be given a run-through performance by the Imperial Court Orchestra at one of their public morning sessions.[29] Steinberg was still a Conservatoire student.

Stravinsky and Steinberg had probably met before 1906, at rehearsals of the Russian Symphony Concerts. But their close friendship dates from that year. Stravinsky was a good deal less intimate with other favored Rimsky pupils, such as Nikolay Malko (the future conductor), Boris Asafyev (the composer, who also later wrote influential criticism under the pseudonym Igor Glebov), or the composer Mikhail Gnesin. Of these, only Gnesin figures in his memoirs. He was, says Stravinsky, "the liveliest and most openminded spirit of the Rimsky group . . . [and] was identified with radically antisectarian political and social views."[30] A Jew, like Steinberg, but from Rostov in southeastern Russia, Gnesin was for a time closer to the moving spirits of the Evenings of Contemporary Music and, beyond that, to symbolist poets like Ivanov, Balmont, and Sologub than he was to the calmer waters of the Zagorodnïy Prospect. But he was also, as Taruskin has skillfully shown, anxious to succeed with Rimsky-Korsakov—to be accepted, that is, as a correct, well-behaved Belyayevets.[31] His stock may possibly have risen with the democratic-spirited Rimsky during the 1905 troubles, in which Gnesin was an activist and was temporarily excluded from the Conservatoire for his pains. He still attended Rimsky's classes at Zagorodnïy during the closure.[32] But as for any more specific imprimatur, that did not come until March 1908, when Yastrebtsev, of all people, persuaded Rimsky-Korsakov to invite Gnesin to a soirée at the flat.

Ironically, Gnesin himself—like Steinberg—became a dull, respected Soviet composer and teacher. With Stravinsky, his relations remained always in the middle ground, but his antinomianism was clearly attractive and even important to Igor, not least because it leavened the stifling orthodoxy of the Rimsky circle and hinted at other avenues of exploration. The fact that it was eventually Stravinsky, and not Gnesin, who explored those avenues is merely one more anecdote in the history of spoilt youth and perfidious old age.

BY THE SECOND WEEK of May, after a brief visit to Kiev, Igor and Katya were once again installed at the Nosenko house in Ustilug, Igor having at last received his university diploma at the end of April.[33] As we have seen, he was now starting serious work on his Pushkin cycle, or "suite," as he called it, and he was at the same time planning the revision of the symphony's Scherzo. Ustilug, during those summer months of 1906, must have seemed an island of sanity and peace in a chaotic world. "Through our window," Igor wrote to Volodya, "I can see two hens sitting on the triangular roof. . . ."[34] But there are also echoes of outside reality in Igor's letters to Volodya, who had gone to Italy with his parents, and those to his own mother in Pechisky. Problems had arisen over Yury's health,[35] but the question of his taking the waters at Pyatigorsk, in the Russian Caucasus, was complicated by the political situation there, the local governor having decided not to lift martial law "since the loyal sick will come in any case to take the fatherland's waters, while troublemakers will be deterred."[36] Passionately, Igor pleaded with his mother to persuade Yury to go abroad instead. He and Katya had decided on similar grounds against a trip they had planned with Katya's foster mother, Baba Sonya Velsovskaya, to the Crimea,

> where the revolutionary ferment is at its most violent, with more or less daily strikes of ships' crews and mass meetings everywhere— and when you yourself are not taking part, alas (we're terrible egoists), any life in that wave of revolution is unthinkable, and in that kind of seething cauldron the only people who can thrive are those who are utterly indifferent to the life around them or who are ill-disposed towards the Great Russian Revolution. But we, as you know, are the exact opposite.[37]

The ambiguity of these remarks is almost their most striking feature. Igor shares the general repugnance of the educated classes for the tsarist government. He gloats over Prime Minister Goremïkin's resignation after the dissolution of the first Duma in July 1906;[38] he quotes the themes of vengeance and power from Rimsky-Korsakov's *Antar*;[39] he reads revolutionary newspapers.[40] He lectures Volodya on the scientific basis of socialism and urges him to study it in place of what he calls the "pseudo-science" of jurisprudence. But he trembles at the violence and perturbation, and is quick to dissociate himself from any active role:

> As a future public figure, I personally am a musician, not a politician. . . . [Yet] if I had plenty of time and weren't distracted by musical occupations, I would start studying scientific socialism in the most serious and thoroughgoing way. As it is I must needs make the best of merely superficial information. I'm glad all the same that music is the main thing for me. To get mixed up with politics is ruination for art. This I feel with all my being. And it strikes me that this age of universal politicization, in the sense of the powerful influence it had on art in the sixties, isn't in the least reflected in my works.[41]

This is a very remarkable statement for Stravinsky to have made in the year 1906, especially in the light of his friendship with the Polish doctor Bachnicki. The idea that scientific socialism, that hoary determinist obsession of the old left-wing intelligentsia, could somehow be persuaded to leave the arts out of its comprehensive account of society seems striking enough. But still more impressive is his choosing, at this "historic moment in Russian life," [42] to assert the autonomy of art, and to imply that in some way Russian art (including music) of the second half of the nineteenth century had been tainted by contact with political ideas: impressive not least because the remark contains no specific hint of aestheticism of the *Mir iskusstva* type, no defense of the decorative over the ideological, and certainly no trace of Yastrebtsev's bumbling, stick-to-my-last preference for modulation over revolution, but has instead the flavor of a robust, straightforward refusal to allow anything external to dictate the flow of his music.

Volodya had written Igor a particularly dispirited letter from Italy, "full of a gloom which to me is incomprehensible."[43] Probably the atmosphere in the Rimsky family as a whole was one of foreboding and unease,[44] and for a young man like Volodya, freshly graduated in a subject which—in all political likelihood—would soon be obsolete, the upheavals were something to view with apprehension. But Igor, by contrast, was still in a state of euphoria: in love with his wife, in love with his work. For him the revolution, a few practical annoyances apart, remained an interesting technical question. His feelings overflowed with generosity.

> I'm sure, Volodya, that our discussions on this issue won't be interrupted, and you will write often and candidly, as I am doing, loving you with all my soul. Volodya, my dear, I suppose you know and don't have to be told that I am not one of those people who in their good fortune forget their friends. Friends for me actually coincide with that word *always*. And I in my great happiness am devoting myself with all my heart to what is going on in the hearts of my friends.[45]

AFTER THE LONG, unbroken Volhynian summer, Igor and Katya returned once more to St. Petersburg with their quivers full. She, as Igor had told his mother in mid-July, was expecting their first baby. He probably had his Pushkin suite finished at least in draft, and a revised version of the symphony's Scherzo as well. There was talk of performance, something of which Igor still had no experience outside the four walls of 28 Zagorodnïy. But for the moment it was all Steinberg: Zabela-Vrubel sang his *Four Romances* at a *jour fixe* on 11 October, and seven weeks later (on 29 November) Steinberg and Stravinsky played his orchestral variations four-handed, by way of trailer for the performance at the Russian Symphony Concert the following week, and there were more songs. Rimsky-Korsakov was unstinting in his praise. "Very talented and moreover absolutely without 'snags,' " he said of the romances to Yastrebtsev, "which endears them to me very much."[46] Whether the Master's taste for clarity and polish was so much gratified by Stravinsky's Pushkin cycle we do not know. In all probability Yastrebtsev's later observation that "the voice part is not without awkwardness à la Musorgsky" and that "in places it is very beautiful, and above all young (though precisely for that reason also uneven)" reflects Rimsky-Korsakov's opinion.[47] But Stravinsky's own report that, after hearing the work performed, Rimsky "found the first song 'strange,' and my use of whole-tone progressions suspiciously 'Debussy-ist,' " is barely credible.[48] Whole-tone progressions were an absolute stock-in-trade of Russian music after Glinka. Moreover, Rimsky must have known the songs well from score by the time they reached the concert platform, whichever of the two early orchestral performances Stravinsky's memoir refers to. And they had probably already been sung, with piano, at a Rimsky Wednesday in February 1907.[49]

Was Stravinsky, in his euphoric mood of the summer, at all tested in his morale by the praise being heaped on the newcomer, Steinberg? We have too little information, but such contemporary evidence as we have suggests not. In 1906 they were still new friends, but the following year there begins a correspondence which is, more than cordial, intimate, and this is the start of a friendship which, as far as we can tell from surviving correspondence, photographs, and other stray documentation, lasted without hiccough at least until the early Russian performances of Stravinsky's first three ballet scores. In due course, the curious question of Stravinsky's poisonous later reminiscences of Steinberg will have to be faced.[50] But when Taruskin remarks that "it seems superfluous to ask how all this [praise of Steinberg] made Igor Stravinsky feel," he presumes too much. "How," he demands, "could Stravinsky not have deeply resented this usurper?" First, one might suggest, by not having a chip on his shoulder. Secondly, by dint of circumstances that Taruskin ignores. Stravinsky, recently married and evidently in a euphoric state, wrapped up in his work, in love with his wife and with a new baby son, is supposed to have become jealous of Steinberg for, among other reasons, getting engaged to their teacher's daughter, with whom Igor is incidentally assumed—on no better evidence than the survival of a few photographs of them together—to have enjoyed a "romantic attachment."[51] Equally, we are to suppose him embittered by Rimsky's candid favoritizing of Steinberg. But what do we know of this beyond a handful of diary records of passing remarks by Rimsky-Korsakov: interesting and suggestive in themselves, but not even a fraction of the whole story? Rimsky must have made literally thousands of remarks to both Stravinsky and Steinberg which will have given them a picture of which we, nearly a century on, catch no more than the echo of a sigh. Stravinsky will surely have known his standing with Rimsky at the time; but we, trying to measure his vulnerability to the standing of a supposed rival, do not know with any certainty what it was.

Or do we? Perhaps the most important of the many Stravinsky letters that, until recently, lay unpublished in Moscow and St. Petersburg archives bears directly on this question. It was written not by Stravinsky, nor to him, but by Rimsky-Korsakov's widow, Nadezhda, to their elder daughter, Sonya, in May 1910, two years after the Master's death, and only just over a month before the sensational Paris premiere of *The Firebird*. It puts paid once and for all to the idea that Stravinsky was seriously upstaged by Steinberg at 28 Zagorodnïy:

About Max, dear Sonya, you're deeply mistaken and jump to too hasty a conclusion. That he has talent is beyond doubt. . . . Papa, as well as Glazunov, always regarded him as outstandingly talented. He even placed him above Stravinsky, which I disputed in general, though in particular ways Max was undoubtedly more gifted musically than Igor. He has perfect pitch, which Igor hasn't, and he has astonishing sensitivity to beautiful harmony and fine voice-leading, which again Igor hasn't. Their direction is different. Igor is very intelligent, perhaps more so than Max, but Max is more versatile, has wide interests and knows a lot. . . . Igor strives for novelty at all costs, Max for beauty. The latter is to me more sympathetic, and in this Papa too valued him more than Igor. . . . As for Igor, I will say that, in spite of his likewise undoubted talent, intellect, and warm nature (more so, perhaps than Max's), his music does not make a strong impression, on me at least. I don't know a single one of his pieces about which I would say "Oh, how splendid!" or which I should want to play a lot. . . . I explain this by the fact that it doesn't have genuine musical beauty; his harmony is coarse and not graceful enough; melody, as you'd expect nowadays, is lacking; and there is a very noticeable intention to show off and startle with novelty. But at the same time his novelty is not actually all that new—he very much imitates the modern French, sometimes copies them, but since he passed through Papa's good schooling, his technique is much better than that of all those Ravels, Debussys, and co. He takes a lot of trouble to demonstrate that with him everything is logical and right, and as for its being beautiful—for him this is the last question, as long as it's new. I don't know what will come of this later on, but at present I don't at all like the direction he's taking. Papa somehow compared Igor and Max with Musorgsky and himself. This is partly true, but Musorgsky, with all his striving for novelty, undermining of authority, and occasional affectation, was head and shoulders above Igor in power and originality of gift. Musorgsky neither resembled anyone nor imitated anyone, but developed his own style. I don't think that Igor, even in the distant future, would do anything comparable. Of course, even Papa didn't equate him with Musorgsky, and only wanted by this comparison to point out a general characteristic—the striving for novelty and originality.[52]

The comparison is loaded and, at bottom, prejudiced. Nadya, like her late husband, was suspicious of modernism, and—perhaps less like him—was content with the safe haven of her schoolroom values. But she is also perceptive. In a sense, and by her own lights, her remarks are accurate and truthful. Indeed, their honesty is disconcerting. Steinberg was her son-in-law; and yet she admits that "in general" she would not place him above Stravinsky, while, if her husband did in fact do so, it was a close-run thing. Filter out the provincialism and the characteristically Russian lurchings to and fro and the portrait is not ungenerous. Stravinsky is outstandingly talented, intelligent, and warm-natured, sets logic above beauty, yet merits comparison with Musorgsky in the matter of individuality, if not stature. Of course, Nadya would not have placed Musorgsky above her late husband, as we automatically do, so that Steinberg comes out better than at first appears. But the point is that, in the mind of an essentially and (as we shall see) increasingly hostile witness like Nadezhda Rimsky-Korsakov, the comparison could still in all seriousness be made at all. It suggests that Stravinsky and Steinberg, so far from being deadly rivals, enjoyed comparable favor in Nikolay Rimsky-Korsakov's eyes too. And Stravinsky must have known this, which would help explain why his letters and general comportment do not, in the early years, show any sign of that griping envy which, in Taruskin's theory, he must actually have been feeling towards this upstart Vilna Jew. Later, things would begin to change. But for that, Nikolay Rimsky-Korsakov was not to blame.

8

FIRST AND LAST PERFORMANCES

FOR THE BELYAYEVTSÏ, the great event of the early spring of 1907 was the premiere of Rimsky-Korsakov's opera *The Legend of the Invisible City of Kitezh* at the Mariyinsky on 7 February. Igor, as we have seen, had intimate associations with this work. He had apparently helped Rimsky with the score of act 3, and he may well, as Taruskin argues, have had a hand also in the preparation of the vocal score.[1] At all events it was a copy of this vocal score that he and Katya had had with them at Imatra. That its music was close to him is evident from immediately subsequent works up to and including *The Firebird*. Its blend of pantheistic folk ritual with a kind of post-Wagnerian Christian mysticism, washed over by the sounds of nature and the ringing of heavenly bells, brought nearly fifty years of kuchkism to a glorious millennial climax in which, aptly or ironically, the city vanishes in a golden haze and is translated to paradise, where the lovers are at last reunited in a Parsifalian *Liebestod*.

Perhaps sensing that it might be the composer's swan song, the first-night audience greeted the work with rapture, despite poor choral singing and almost inaudible bells.[2] Following the local custom, wreaths were sent up on stage, including a special one in embroidered silk from Igor and Katya. But for Katya, at least, the perturbations may have been as much physical as spiritual, since her son Fyodor was born a mere ten days later, in the rear bedroom of the Kryukov Canal flat. Love had its reality as well as its fantasy for the composer of *The Faun and the Shepherdess*. Katya did not have enough milk to feed the new baby, and the proud father had to visit an employment agency, where he "was presented with several young women, drawn up in a row with their breasts bared. One after the other each of these squirted a few drops of her precious liquid into a little glass, which was handed to the young father for his appreciation. . . ."[3] But the wet nurse was a perfectly normal recourse for genteel Russians, not a particular clinical necessity. The old idea that sexual intercourse corrupted the mother's milk had long been overlaid by the actual institution, symbolized by the young women themselves, with their special costumes and hats.

Meanwhile the shepherdess, in eternal flight from her faun, was being coaxed onto the concert platform, in the shape of a run-through performance by Wahrlich's Court Orchestra. In the matter of string pulling, Rimsky-Korsakov had surpassed himself, having apparently persuaded Wahrlich to play not only the finished Pushkin suite, but also the as yet incomplete (in its revised form) Symphony in E-flat. The performances took place two days apart, on the mornings of 14 and 16 April, respectively, and—as usual with Court Orchestra run-throughs—they seem to have been confirmed only at a late stage, to judge from a note of the twelfth from Igor to Yastrebtsev, inviting him to attend.[4] On the Saturday, *The Faun and the Shepherdess* was sung by the mezzo-soprano Yelizaveta Petrenko, from the Mariyinsky. On the Monday, at the unmusical hour of ten in the morning, Wahrlich conducted the second and third movements of the symphony—the only two which yet existed in fully scored and revised form. These were not public performances, but "closed rehearsals for the benefit of the musical community." But at least some of Igor's family turned up. His uncle Alexander Yelachich attended both performances, and later, as we have seen, struck a medal in commemoration of the two events.[5] Stravinsky himself recalled that "the only bad omen was Glazunov, who came to me afterwards saying 'very nice, very nice.' "[6]

Bad omen? Not very much is known about Igor's personal relations with Alexander Glazunov, the most brilliant and—in his day—famous of Rimsky-Korsakov's pupils, a child prodigy of the 1880s, and by Stravinsky's day the acknowledged keeper of the Rimsky seal. Stravinsky's reminiscences of him are vitriolic,[7] but that is by the by. Some reconstruction is necessary.

For all his brilliance, Glazunov was profoundly conservative by temperament and wedded to the academic process still enshrined in the course teaching at the Conservatoire. He seems to have lacked his teacher's anxieties about the future of Russian music under such auspices, and certainly did not have Rimsky's grudging respect for new ideas and techniques. Among Rimsky's best younger pupils, Steinberg was Glazunov's type: fluent, correct, technically accomplished, modern only within decent limits.[8] Stravinsky was a different matter: a rapid and willing learner, but with a certain mystery factor due partly to his lack of intensive, systematic schooling, partly to his intellectual quickness and range—a combination which has always disturbed those whose brilliance is confined to method. Glazunov probably treated him with reserve, though surely not with open rudeness, and this will have intensified Igor's already well-developed feelings of insecurity. After Rimsky-Korsakov's death, Igor complained to his widow, Nadezhda, that "Glazunov . . . will not pay due attention to a letter from me or to my music, being somehow indifferent to me, which is why I am instinctively shy of approaching him."[9] Glazunov had indeed just given a newspaper interview, published two days after Rimsky-Korsakov's death, in which he had listed Rimsky's "brilliant galaxy of pupils" without mentioning Stravinsky, an omission that was presumably deliberate.[10] Later, he began to put it about that Stravinsky was nothing but an expert orchestrator. "*Petrushka* is not music," he told Telyakovsky in 1912, "but is excellently and skillfully orchestrated,"[11] a view which became routine in St. Petersburg. By 1912 Stravinsky, in turn, was certainly ready to write Glazunov off as a "pillar of academicism."[12] "To the devil with the Glazunovs, Kahns, and other 'great masters,' who have never moved an inch nor dared penetrate the mysteries of art. *Habileté* is fine in conjunction with genius, but without it art achieves only outward prettiness and a disagreeable (self-satisfied) fluency (finish). Creative work has no life for them—and their work ends up stillborn."[13]

Whatever Glazunov said about Stravinsky's symphony movements, he must have recognized at once the music's kinship with his own symphonic writing. This is partly because the work is a conscious imitation of an academic model of which Glazunov happened to be by far the most accomplished recent exponent: the solid, square-cut, four-movement symphony, with all its suitably contrasted themes in place, correct transitions and development sections with fragments of the themes treated in dialogue, a balanced and lucid key scheme, bright, effective orchestration, and so forth. But these are particularly attributes of the first movement, which, as we have seen, was being revised by Stravinsky under Rimsky-Korsakov's supervision, and was not yet ready for performance in April 1907. The Scherzo, which may or may not have preceded the Largo in Wahrlich's 1907 run-through, is also Glazunovan, but more effortlessly so—redolent of his ballet music as much as of his own symphonic scherzos. Stravinsky seems already to have had a flair for this kind of writing, a flair he tended to overexploit in his next few orchestral works, including the *Scherzo fantastique* and the rather bland Dance of the Princesses with the Golden Apples in *The Firebird*. But the model for the Largo, also much revised under Rimsky's eye, is neither Glazunov nor any other Belyayevets composer, but Tchaikovsky, long regarded by readers of the Stravinsky conversation books as Rimsky's bête noire, but in reality a good friend and a composer much admired in Belyayevets circles.[14] There is Tchaikovsky in the finale as well, in particular a flagrant borrowing from his own Fifth Symphony finale in Stravinsky's coda, alongside much that derives from Glazunov and his kuchkist predecessors. All in all, it is still very much student work.

The Pushkin suite is a different case since, although its models are no less respectable (indeed are in some cases the same), Stravinsky seems to have enjoyed more freedom in the way he handled them, and the result is both less "official"—to use Stravinsky's own word for the symphony—and at the same time fresher, "greener" in every sense. This is particularly true of the orchestration, which is lighter and more discriminating but not always more effective than in the symphony, and of the form—if only because it responds to the varying pace and imagery of the words. But while the word setting is polished, it hardly captures the self-conscious *volupté* of Pushkin's words, nor indeed their stylistic ironies. Stravinsky's own borrowings—whether or not they include Wagner and Debussy alongside the more obvious Musorgsky and Tchaikovsky, as he later claimed[15]—are simply what was available to an unformed writer at the time. The stylistic allusiveness and wizardry of *Mavra* or *The Fairy's Kiss* are still a long way below his horizon.

Two days after the second Wahrlich performance, Igor was at Zagorodnïy for a play-through by Steinberg of the first act of Rimsky-Korsakov's new opera *The Golden Cockerel,* and Rimsky presented him with the manuscript full score of the suite from his earlier Pushkin opera *The Tale of Tsar Saltan,* in honor of his first orchestral performances.[16] Soon Rimsky was off to Paris to take part in Diaghilev's season of Russian concerts the following month, and Max Steinberg went with him. But meanwhile, Igor had acquired a new protector, in the shape of the conductor and pianist Alexander Ziloti, a pupil of Liszt, and an influential figure in St. Petersburg music before the First World War on account of the regular series of orchestral concerts he had organized and conducted in the capital since 1903. Ziloti had married a daughter of the art patron Pavel Tretyakov, and his concerts were funded by Tretyakov money, which enabled him to hire the orchestra of the Mariyinsky Theatre and to engage international soloists and conductors. He also commissioned and performed new works, as well as importing major novelties from abroad. Not only were Ziloti's the best and most interesting concerts in St. Petersburg, but he himself was almost the only Petersburg musician who wielded significant influence abroad as well as at home. Both these factors were to prove important for Stravinsky.

Ziloti's first effort on his behalf was to approach the publisher Julius Zimmermann with the suggestion that he publish *The Faun and the Shepherdess,* whose performance by Wahrlich Ziloti had presumably heard. Zimmermann replied evasively, but the upshot of his effective refusal was that Rimsky-Korsakov, by now back from Paris, decided to use his influence with the Belyayev trustees to have the work published and performed under their banner.[17] Within a fortnight of Rimsky telling Steinberg that "we must try to remedy this matter somehow,"[18] everything was stitched up with Nikolay Artsïbushev, yet another Rimsky pupil and one of the trustees, and the work was slated for two further performances and for publication.[19] It would be hard to find a better illustration of the Gogolian workings of St. Petersburg musical life, or of the purely material benefits which came Stravinsky's way as a pupil of Rimsky-Korsakov.[20]

Meanwhile, at Ustilug Igor was working on two new pieces, as well as struggling to complete the revision of the remaining two movements of the symphony, all of which he dutifully reported to Rimsky-Korsakov in his long letter of 18 June. He has already, he says, written a song, "which I started in St. Petersburg and which I played you—the one with the bell chimes—and I'm thinking of writing another two on words by the same author." This was the first of the Gorodetsky settings, op. 6. The other new piece is an orchestral scherzo, based on Maeterlinck:

> I already had the idea of writing a scherzo in Peter[sburg], but I didn't yet have a subject. At a certain point, Katya and I read Maeterlinck's *Life of the Bees*, a half-philosophical, half-imaginative work which charmed me, as they say, head over heels. At first, for a program, I thought of selecting specific quotations from the book; but I see that this is impossible, since the scientific and artistic/literary languages are too closely fused, so I decided to follow an exact program but without having a quotation from the book as part of the title, which is simply *"The Bees* (after Maeterlinck). Fantastic Scherzo."[21]

No doubt Stravinsky was anxious to concentrate on this new project. But the symphony was still giving trouble. The revisions to the first movement were extensive, and would take until the end of June, he told Rimsky;[22] in fact, they took him another two weeks after that. And there was still the finale to do. When exactly Igor wrote finis to that is not known, but it may well not have been until the very end of the summer, or even the early autumn—by which time it must have felt a very dead project indeed.

Somehow, Igor managed to concentrate on work, despite upheavals around him which often demanded his attention. He and Katya had decided to build a new house, a few hundred yards from the one which Grigory and Lyudmila Belyankin had themselves been building for a year or two, on the ledge of land from which the ground falls away into the river Luga. Igor himself had made some designs, and must have spent a lot of time overseeing the early stages of construction. Ustilug boasted a brick factory owned by a Mr. Bernstein, a rich member of the local Jewish community who had made good in America, and from whom Igor bought the bricks for the new house.[23] Luckily, as he told Rimsky-Korsakov, the weather in June was atrocious, and there was scant temptation to go outside for pleasure.[24] For the first time we have an intimation of Ustilug as that "haven for composing" which it became for Igor especially when he moved into the new house the following year.[25] In the evenings, he and Katya played Beethoven four-hands, and he began to conceive "a lot of ideas about Beethoven, which I'll tell you in the winter, as it would take too long to expound them now."[26]

Whether Igor had yet devised daytime techniques for evading the noise and turmoil of a young family, in a house that was not his, may be doubted. The Nosenko house was as usual quite full enough, even though Anna Stravinsky was at Pechisky, Gury was in St. Petersburg singing the role of the Miller in Dargomïzhsky's *Rusalka* (presumably in a Conservatoire production), and Yury and his family had gone to Davos in search of treatment for his tuberculosis.[27] The Belyankins, it seems, were in residence, having not yet moved into their own new house. With their two children, assorted wet nurses, Baba Sonya (presumably), and perhaps also Anna Belyankin, Grigory's mother, who was a frequent Ustilug visitor during these years, the atmosphere must have been, to say the least, lively. It may also have been, where the children were concerned, somewhat competitive. Lyudmila's baby son, Gavriyil (or Ganya), was three months younger than Igor's Fyodor, and comparisons were inevitable. According to Igor—blissfully unaware of any bias—"Milochka tells us that Fyodor is more sympathetic than Ganya, that Ganya is much less friendly. . . . I am sorry for Milochka that she thinks this way. It probably upsets her a lot. But Katya and I also think that in general Milochka's children are not notable for calmness, probably because of the quality of her milk."[28] This might simply reflect the lingering envy of one sister who could not feed her baby for the other who could. But, whether or not because of the quality of his mother's milk, Ganya became a sickly epileptic, who was for a time apparently quite seriously ill. He remains a somewhat shadowy figure, unlike his older sister, Irina, at this time a pretty child of four, who was to remain close to Igor in his years of exile and to become a vital nexus not only between the Stravinskys and the Belyankins, but also between Igor and his life outside the immediate family.

By August, having completed the final revision of the first movement, Igor seems to have put the symphony on one side in order to work seriously on the Maeterlinck *Scherzo fantastique*. He had already had an intuition about its harmonic character: "The harmony of *The Bees*," he told his teacher, "will be harsh, like a toothache, but must at once be relieved, as with cocaine."[29] It may be that the idea of an abrasive harmonic coloring was prompted by the bees program, but the reverse is more likely, since nineteenth-century Russian music is well stocked with scherzo music depicting the weird or mysterious or magical, and in writing his piece Stravinsky must have been consciously aligning himself with that hallowed convention. From the music for the sorcerer Chernomor in Glinka's *Ruslan and Lyudmila*, through Musorgsky's *Night on the Bare Mountain*, Balakirev's *Tamara*, Lyadov's *Kikimora*, to the operas of Rimsky-Korsakov—and particularly the latest of them, *The Golden Cockerel*, whose first act Stravinsky had heard in a play-through at Zagorodnïy a mere two or three weeks before he left St. Petersburg for the summer—Russian composers had used wizardry as a trigger for unorthodox harmony, often of a more or less constructivist kind whose patterns involve deviating from the more fluid, language-like grammar of orthodox tonal music. All Stravinsky was doing in his scherzo was trying his hand at a kind of music that was all around him in the St. Petersburg repertoire and which called for a certain orchestral talent he had already shown himself to possess.

The program, with its buzzings and courtships and apiarian dancing, may well have emerged from specific musical ideas Stravinsky had for the work, or it may—as Taruskin has resourcefully argued[30]—have been primary and organic. More significant than the program, in any case, is this early (albeit conventional) connection in Stravinsky's mind between movement, orchestral color, and a "harsh" harmonic palette: the idea of a "modernistic" music which dances. Further than that one cannot go. In its actual music, the *Scherzo fantastique* remains wedded to a provincial tradition out of which it strays only to imitate another tradition—less provincial, but for that reason still more recognizable: the Wagner of *Parsifal*, which Stravinsky knew at that time not from performance (since it was still embargoed outside Bayreuth) but from the score. The contrast (the toothache/cocaine antithesis of Stravinsky's original idea) is abrupt and undigested, like much of the work's rather square-cut phraseology. But the orchestration is skillful and effective, and much lighter than in the symphony, even though the orchestra is numerically no smaller—it lacks only trombones and tuba, whose overuse, by Stravinsky's own later admission, was a specific complaint of Rimsky's about the symphony.[31] The particular discovery of the *Scherzo fantastique* is a way of making quite dense harmony transparent and very mobile. For the world at large this was not, perhaps, much of a discovery, but it was one Stravinsky needed to make for himself.

How much of the work Igor had composed by the time he returned to St. Petersburg in September or early October we do not know. Probably he drafted it out, then put it aside in order to revise the finale of the symphony, a task he had more or less completed by the time he left Ustilug, since the full score is dated "Summer 1907." But the full score of the *Scherzo fantastique*—a substantial piece of writing for some thirteen or fourteen minutes of quick or quickish music—took him until the following spring to compose: it was finished only on 30 March, by which time he had suddenly become a "figure" on the St. Petersburg musical scene, with a series of public performances which even Steinberg might have envied.

The very first of these—Stravinsky's public debut as a composer—was in an Evenings of Contemporary Music concert on 27 December, and consisted of a performance by Yelizaveta Petrenko of a pair of songs: the Gorodetsky setting "Vesna" (Spring)—"the one with the bell chimes,"[32] as Igor had told his teacher—and a vocalise, or song without words, which he called "Pastorale," and which may or may not have started out as one of the other Gorodetsky settings. Both songs had already had an airing at a Rimsky-Korsakov Wednesday on 31 October. Rimsky's daughter Nadezhda gave two performances of the "Pastorale," which Igor had composed only two days before and dedicated to her; and Igor "portrayed" the Gorodetsky song.[33] Nadezhda again sang the "Pastorale," as well as the Gorodetsky song, at a small gathering at Zagorodnïy on Christmas Day.[34]

These two pieces, different as they are from one another, puzzled Rimsky and his circle. The "Pastorale" was "an original song but not without strange harmonies," according to Yastrebtsev.[35] As for the Gorodetsky, Yastrebtsev was baffled by "the orgy of sounds" at the start of the song, while Rimsky-Korsakov frankly disapproved of the very conception of the piece. "I simply cannot understand," he told his faithful Boswell, "what pleasure anyone can derive from composing music to poems like Sergey Gorodetsky's 'Zvonï, stonï, perezvonï.' To me all this modern, decadent, impressionist lyricism with its wretched, empty, meaningless content and pseudo-Russian folk language is nothing but 'gloom and fog.' "[36] "The middle of the song," he added after the Evenings performance, "is very good and expressive in some places, but the beginning is frenetic and harmonically senseless."[37] Rimsky's dislike of this poem in which a lovelorn novice sings a lament for her abandoned lover, amid lurid descriptions of the "moaning" bells and cold, whitewashed convent walls, is easy to understand now, though at the time Gorodetsky enjoyed considerable prestige in neonationalist and symbolist literary circles in St. Petersburg.[38] But Rimsky's difficulty with the music had more to do with Stravinsky's gauche extension of the stock Musorgsky bell-tolling style, where the piano imitates the confused jangling of bells with harmonies which, by Rimsky's standards, must certainly have seemed hair-raising, whatever their graphic motivation. The Grieg-like middle section, where the novice sings her lament, presented no such musical challenge, even though the pseudo-folkery of the poem made Rimsky's flesh creep.

As for the innocent little "Pastorale," with its musette accompaniment and decorative melodic arabesques intertwining like the tendrils on a Romanesque arcade, its harmonies may well have struck Yastrebtsev as strange in their impassive simplicity and stillness, so unlike the normal "structured" harmonic grammar of the average Belyayevets song. Even the more open-minded Grigory Timofeyev, who reviewed the Evenings concert in *Rech'*, regretted what he saw as Stravinsky's "pursuit of novelty," which "led him into the sphere of the ugly, the unnatural, the apparently strained and self-conscious," while not denying the music "interesting and beautiful details of harmony."[39] But Timofeyev failed to distinguish between the markedly different styles of the two songs. Speculating on a possible source for the Attic restraint and transparency of the "Pastorale,"

Taruskin notes that 1907 was the year in which the great Polish harpsichord revivalist Wanda Landowska appeared for the first time in St. Petersburg. Her second concert, on 22 March, had included a suite from Francisque's *Le Trésor d'Orphée*, an early-seventeenth-century collection of lute pieces "which contains many rustic voltas with drone basses that conjure up a pastoral mood quite like that of Stravinsky's vocalise." The assumption that Stravinsky attended this recital is certainly not weakened by the fact that the program also included the Lanner *Styrische Tanz*, op. 165, which he later co-opted as the first of the ballerina's waltz tunes in the third tableau of *Petrushka*.[40]

Less than four weeks after the Evenings premiere of the songs came the promised second performance of *The Faun and the Shepherdess* by Wahrlich, Petrenko, and the Court Orchestra. This time, on 22 January, it was a proper public concert, in the orchestra's Musical Novelties series, and it also, remarkably enough, included the first complete performance of the symphony. Thus, not for the last time in his career, Stravinsky vaulted several rungs up the ladder of recognition in one go. The concert was quite widely reviewed, and although it was generally agreed that neither work showed individuality, the music was covered in detail and treated seriously as worthily representing the latest Belyayevets thinking. It must have been as a result of this concert that Timofeyev asked Stravinsky to supply biographical details for his encyclopedia entry, even though he himself again wrote somewhat guardedly in *Rech'*, finding the music too derivative (Schumann, Wagner, Borodin, and Glazunov are all mentioned), and the scoring of the symphony "rather heavy." Most reviewers found the Scherzo of the symphony most to their taste; most commented on Stravinsky's skill as an orchestrator; but many were critical of his setting of Pushkin, which, they tended to feel, he had taken too seriously and set monotonously. But one critic, Vyacheslav Karatïgin, remarked on "the cheerful, joyous turn of musical thought that is characteristic of Stravinsky in general, and that distinguishes him favorably from many of the newest composers, who are nearly all prone to stilted pathos, tortured lines, musical 'hysteria,' and other substitutes for profundity and substance. Stravinsky's ideas, too, are as clear and natural as their working-out."[41]

The second *Faun* was duly followed by a third, in a Russian Symphony Concert conducted by Felix Blumenfeld in the Great Hall of the Conservatoire on 16 February. Again the singer was Petrenko. And again the reviews noticed a lack of individuality, expressed once more in a failure to rise to the subtle challenge of the Pushkin text. A certain air of condescension prevails. One critic, noting that the work had been well received at its Court Orchestra performance, remarked that "such evenings have a 'family' character, and everything is applauded indiscriminately."[42] Another (anonymous) reviewer observed, more helpfully, that "the composition is very well worked out—we would even say too well, for in this five-star elaboration and polish one still senses the sweat of endeavor of the gifted student."[43] Indeed, this was all student work, which makes it unsurprising that it stuck to orthodox models. In any case, the performances were probably mediocre. The Court Orchestra concert was still based on the run-through principle, while the Blumenfeld concert, though doubtless properly rehearsed, seems all the same to have been an undistinguished affair. According to Yastrebtsev, pieces by Musorgsky and Rimsky-Korsakov went badly, and even the much-played First Symphony of Borodin was done only "acceptably."[44] Even so, as the twenty-five-year-old composer took his bow on the Conservatoire platform that February evening, he could well reflect that his late apprenticeship had come to its due fulfillment. He had shown that he could write, and write well. He had justified himself in the eyes of those conventional spirits, starting with his own family, who had doubted his vocation. He had established himself in musical circles as a man of talent. He had caught up with the naturals: the Steinbergs, the Tcherepnins, even the Glazunovs. He could choose his moment to overtake. His foot was poised on the accelerator. . . .

THE WEEKLY SUPERVISIONS with Rimsky-Korsakov continued nonetheless. Four days after the Conservatoire concert, Igor was at Zagorodnïy with the score of his new orchestral scherzo, no doubt taking advice on how to lighten the orchestration in comparison with the symphony.[45] Personally, the two seem to have drawn closer. In March and early April they attended the four evenings of Wagner's *Ring* together, sharing a Mariyinsky box. Yastrebtsev ran into them in the first interval of *Siegfried* on 29 March, both of them "in raptures over the opera's brilliant first act."[46] At *Götterdämmerung* six days later, when he again looked for them, they had gone out for a smoke. But Rimsky-Korsakov should not have been smoking within earshot of Valhalla, or anywhere else for that matter. At the end of December he had had a bad and prolonged attack of what Andrey records as bronchitis,[47] but which his father described as "some sort of asthma . . . I am now drinking lily of the valley."[48] By March, when he celebrated his sixty-fourth birthday, he was talking in fatalistic terms. He confided to Yastrebtsev that his heart had become weak and breathing difficult. "As you see," he said, "everything is proceeding normally; it's all moving towards a single end."[49] On 10 April, five days after *Götterdämmerung*, there was a sudden attack of angina pectoris, and six days later another attack, more severe. But in between, Rimsky was for a time well enough to receive guests; and on the twelfth there was a small gathering at which Max Steinberg, whose engagement to Nadya Rimsky-Korsakov had been announced a few weeks earlier, played from memory excerpts from

Igor's new scherzo, "The Bees," apparently by way of illustrating a discussion about the constructivist harmonies which that score shares with much of the later work of Rimsky himself.[50] But though Gury may have been present (he had called in the afternoon with a bunch of flowers for the ailing composer), Igor himself was not, having already set off for Ustilug, via Vilna, where he was visiting his aunt Matilda Stravinsky (the estranged wife of his father's brother Alexander), and from where he despatched a cheerful postcard to Max, whose birthplace it was.[51]

Somehow Igor knew that Max had been trying to phone him. But he was unaware of the reason. Then, in a newspaper, he read a notice of Rimsky-Korsakov's illness and at once dispatched a panic-stricken telegram to Zagorodnïy. Two days later he followed it up with a letter:

> Volodya, Andrey, my dears, I can't tell you what a stone lies on my heart, how sick I am in my heart. Minute by minute I think about my beloved Nikolay Andreyevich; how I should love to be nearby, to know all the details, as letters take such an agonizing length of time. . . . My dears, if you only knew how painful this is for me; write, as you would to a brother, for Nikolay Andreyevich is too dear to me. You know that.[52]

Meanwhile, he buried himself in new compositions. He wrote a piano study, finishing it on 1 May, then set to work on yet another orchestral scherzo, or "fantasy," as he had described it to Rimsky before leaving Petersburg, intending the piece as a wedding present for Max and Nadya. Late in May, the Rimsky-Korsakovs went to their country house at Lyubensk (hard by their old retreat of Vechasha), where they had spent the previous summer and which they were now in the process of buying. They had barely settled in when the Master had a further attack of angina. Again he seemed to recover. On 4 June Nadya and Max got married quietly in the local village church; the bride's father did not attend. Two more severe attacks followed, and in the early morning of Sunday 8 June there was a final attack, and he died. A thunderstorm had just been raging.

Igor downed tools at once and took the train to Plyussa, the station for Lyubensk, where he met the coffin, travelled with it back to St. Petersburg, and helped carry it from the railway station to the conservatory church.[53] Rimsky's funeral took place on the eleventh, a mere three days after his death, and Igor joined the huge cortege which followed the coffin to the Novodevichy Cemetery on the southern fringes of the city.[54] "It was," he later recalled, "one of the unhappiest days of my life." Gazing down into the open coffin, he wept, and Nadezhda Rimsky-Korsakov approached him—or so he later claimed—and inquired sardonically: "Why so unhappy? We still have Glazunov."[55] Curiously enough, it is from Glazunov himself that we learn that Nadezhda, like Anna Stravinsky before her, was the hardest hit of the whole family by her husband's death: "Her usual smile has not once appeared on her lips."⁵⁶ But though she was to prove herself a difficult and inflexible relict, there is nothing in her subsequent correspondence with Igor that supports such a cynical view on her part of his feelings for her late husband. Her long letter to her daughter Sonya, quoted in the last chapter, suggests that, less than two years after her husband's death, she bore Igor no personal ill will and was not noticeably disposed to discredit the relationship between him and her husband. The bitterness, when it did emerge, had specific causes, none of which yet existed.

Back at Ustilug, Igor at once composed an epitaph for his teacher, in the form of a Funeral Song (Pogrebal'naya pesn') for orchestra. The new orchestral fantasy—*Fireworks*, as it was now called—was already complete, and had been packed off to Lyubensk before the funeral. But Igor's story that the parcel came back to him "not delivered on account of death of addressee,"⁵⁷ if true, can only mean that it had arrived during the family's absence in St. Petersburg and been sent back by well-meaning retainers. At the funeral, Igor had told Andrey to expect it.⁵⁸ And, by whatever devious route, it was in the hands of its dedicatees, Max and Nadya, by 1 July, on which date Max wrote to Gnesin from Lyubensk describing the work: "I like it very much; the music is very typical of Igor, like *The Bees*. It's brilliantly scored, if only it proves playable, for it's incredibly hard."⁵⁹ As for the Funeral Song, it was complete and fully scored by the twenty-eighth, when Igor wrote to Mrs. Rimsky-Korsakov, apologizing for troubling her so soon after her bereavement. The fact was that he had written his work as a "tribute to the great memory of Nikolay Andreyevich—a tribute from his pupil, whom he loved," but "I do not know how to get it performed. This idea worries me terribly. It will be very painful for me if I do not manage to get it played in one or other of the memorial concerts for Nikolay Andreyevich. I have just written to Ziloti, asking his advice."⁶⁰ Igor had been prompted to write the piece by Volodya, to whom he wrote four days later, describing it as "the work you talked to me about when you saw me off in St. Petersburg."⁶¹ Volodya, no less depressed than two years before, had complained that he was "rotting alive" at Lyubensk.⁶² But Igor, bogged down with petty annoyances over the final stages of house building and possessed by the fear that he might not participate in the Rimsky tributes, had little time for his friend's miseries. Once more he wrote to Nadezhda. Ziloti had already within days of Rimsky's death commissioned Glazunov, and could not accommodate two funeral works. But perhaps Igor should try the Russian Symphony Concerts through Glazunov himself, or Count Sheremetev, whose private orchestra also gave concerts in St. Petersburg; or else he could try some provincial orchestra. The idea was anathema to Igor: a Rimsky tribute anywhere but in St. Petersburg was a second-class tribute. But perhaps Nadezhda could intercede with Glazunov?[63] Then suddenly, a week later, all his insecurities and self-doubts boiled over in an outburst of passionate anxiety to Nadezhda's youngest son:

> Today I received the newspaper *Novaya Rus'*, where I read about the Ziloti concert in memory of Nikolay Andreyevich, and it was distressing for me to think that I might really not participate in celebrating his memory, so great and dear to me. I envied Steinberg's flattering participation. All my hopes are in you and your mother—all I can say, or rather yell, to you in St. Petersburg—is this: please God, arrange it, Lord—I can't not take part, either in the Sheremetev or the Belyayev concert, but take part I must.
>
> Volodya my dear, I'm not myself, you can't imagine the effect this uncertainty has on me, to the point of dreading that I shall be too late, that the programmes are already made up and I shan't be there. Write to me, my dear, don't begrudge the time.[64]

One does not have to be a psychoanalyst to see that Igor was suffering from the loss of a father figure. Suddenly he was exposed, thrown into the cold world without the loving guidance and protection of a strong foster parent. The Rimsky family themselves, so recently bereaved, could not fill the gap, and perhaps they repelled any such suggestion. Igor's own family could hardly do so. The sense of rejection is almost tangible in his lament that "I do not want to appeal to Glazunov in writing—I suspect he will pay no attention and not answer."[65]

All he could do was wait, and compose. "The weather is disgusting," he told Volodya, "and I'm in a filthy mood. You ask if I'm writing the opera [The Nightingale]? Not yet. I'm composing some piano studies, and I've completed 'Rosyanka,' which I played you in its original form in St. Petersburg. You're right, Volodya, my work's going much quicker than before."[66]

9

THE IMPRESARIO AND
THE NIGHTINGALE

THE NEW HOUSE at Ustilug was almost finished. Igor himself had made the designs, based, for some reason, on the model of a Swiss chalet.[1] Despite its name—Staraya Mïza, the Old Farm—it would be a large, squat, white-stuccoed, bourgeois-looking house, quite different from Belyankin's modernistic edifice, which the locals said was designed like a ship, with a bridge on the roof, "from which Belyankin—like a ship's captain—gave orders through a speaking tube and oversaw work in the surrounding fields through field glasses."[2] The new Stravinsky house reminded a Polish traveller, Jerzy Stempowski, who visited Ustilug in 1939, of a gamekeeper's lodge:

> The interior seemed to me very unpractical and hardly suitable for the permanent home of a married couple with children. The better part of the ground floor was taken up by a spacious room with windows on both sides of the building. . . . The arrangement of the interior suggests that Stravinsky had no intention of living permanently in Ustilug, but it suits exactly the dual role—as a place of work and a summer retreat—which the house occupies in the composer's autobiography.[3]

It struck him that the large ground-floor room might have contained a grand piano and the composer's library. But, remembering Stravinsky's remark in his autobiography that "I have never been able to compose unless sure that no one could hear me,"[4] he looked for somewhere more private, and found an attic which as far as the Ustilugers could remember had been Stravinsky's workroom.

> It was reached by a wide, comfortable staircase which might have been made for Steinways and Pleyels. The staircase ended abruptly at the entrance to a low, dark corridor with a double bend, which led to a well-lit attic with two windows. This space was not exactly a room, but a long corridor with whitewashed walls, widening out at the

center. Even so the widest part did not exceed three meters. Here, one supposes, there will have been a piano and a table. The austere whiteness of the walls, the complete isolation and unusual shape of the recess were striking. . . . Because of its length, the attic was relatively airy and the shingle roof will not have warmed up quickly. Sitting by the piano or the table he will have had the windows behind him and the white wall in front, so that there was nothing to distract him. Finally, the isolation of the room from the rest of the house was complete.[5]

Unfortunately, the house has not survived in its original form, and Stempowski's impressions cannot now be checked, even to the extent of confirming that the house he visited was itself unaltered from Stravinsky's day. In September 1915 the *Russkaya muzïkal'naya gazeta* had reported that "the Ustilug estate of the composer Igor Stravinsky was devastated at the time of the Austro-German August offensive."[6] In the Second World War, after Stempowski's visit, the town was badly damaged by fire; but according to the composer's Polish biographer Ludwik Erhardt, Stravinsky's house only lost a chimney, knocked off by a stray missile.[7] What is certain is that the present house is very different from the house as the composer himself designed and knew it. Instead of the squat original, with its deep-pitched roof and attic dormers, there is now a stolid two-storey building, with a narrow staircase and a proper first floor where the attic described by Hostowiec used to be. The large, high main room has gone, and in its place is a low concert room with, presumably, small rooms above. And yet it is in a sense the same house. Photographs show that the asymmetrical ground-floor window plan is unchanged, but the roof has been raised and flattened, sovietized. Outside, the avenue of lime trees planted by the composer in 1907–08 has grown to maturity and is today home to an impressive colony of rooks and jackdaws, which would have pleased the composer of the three little *Recollections of Childhood* songs, "The Magpie," "The Crow," and "The Jackdaw."

Into this solid and agreeable edifice, the Stravinsky family moved some time in the late summer of 1908.[8] It was to be their summer home for five years, on and off—a short enough time in a long life, but for the history of music one of the longest of all times, nearly as long, perhaps, as Mozart's in Vienna or Wagner's in Zurich. Volodya was indeed right. Igor's work was going much quicker than before. But it was still far from earth-shattering. The second Gorodetsky song, "Rosyanka" ("Song of the Dew"), whose completion Igor announced in his letter to Volodya in mid-August, is like its companion an uncomfortable blend of salon folkery and high-flown mythologizing, this time in the context of an imaginary marriage-divination ceremony. Richard Taruskin, while pointing out

Rimsky-Korsakov's supposed detestation of pseudo-sectarianism of this kind, draws an intriguingly detailed comparison between the song and the vocal score of Rimsky's *Kitezh*, with which, as we have seen, Igor was intimately acquainted.9 But the Four Piano Studies, to which Igor returned after finishing the song, show that he was still as far as ever from a clear sense of musical direction. Here the plain influence is Scriabin, but not the contemporary, modernistic Scriabin of the *Poem of Ecstasy*, the Fifth Sonata, and the various satellite piano pieces, rather the ornate but harmonically traditional composer of the middle-period preludes and studies, which was the Scriabin still admired by the Belyayevets circle.10 The First, C minor, Study, already composed by the start of May, is shamelessly modelled on Scriabin's F-sharp Minor Study, op. 42, no. 2.11 Taruskin hints that this music was written for Rimsky's approval and to temper his dislike (real and presumably anticipated) of the songs.12 But if so Igor was still, in August, appeasing Rimsky's ghost, since the later studies, though drier in texture (with a preference for staccato left-hand figuring), are technically and harmonically similar and continue to copy Scriabin.13 In any case, Igor took trouble over the writing. The D major took another ten days after the letter to Volodya of 19 August, and the E minor a further ten days after that. The whole set was probably complete by 20 September, on which date Igor wrote once more to Volodya, asking him to transfer a cash sum of five hundred roubles to Belyankin in Ustilug.14 A few days later, the Stravinskys left Volhynia and, after a brief stay at the Nosenko flat in Kiev, returned to St. Petersburg.

The question of the Funeral Song was still unresolved. But the summer had not been a complete blank promotionally. At some time in April or May, Igor had shown his *Scherzo fantastique* to Ziloti, who was so enthusiastic about it that he at once wrote to the publisher Jurgenson with a strong recommendation: "Does your firm not wish to acquire the Scherzo for orchestra by Stravinsky (son of the famous S and last pupil of R-K), a superb piece which I'm performing next January? If you've no objection, then drop me two words and I'll send the score for you to look at; at last we've got some modern music!"15

Whether or not it was Ziloti who had proposed *The Faun* to Zimmermann the previous year, this time his influence was decisive. In less than a month Jurgenson had agreed to take Stravinsky's work, unable to resist the allure of remarks like "I'm convinced that he is second to none" and "It's very good that these people aren't stuck with old habits but are on a new road."16 All the same, Ziloti was more conservative about recommending an honorarium, and Igor had to make do with one hundred roubles rather than the two hundred he hoped for. The deal was signed on 31 July. "I'd have liked to add a little zero on the forms," Igor wrote to Volodya the next day, "but honesty didn't permit—the sum was filled in in words. One day I'll tell you (it would take too long to write) in what an odd way the negotiations with Jurgenson were conducted."[17] But Jurgenson was a major house, publisher of Tchaikovsky, and with an office in Leipzig set up in the 1890s with a view to exploiting Western copyrights, another prestigious factor, which in the long run would nevertheless spell trouble for Stravinsky. For now, he was lucky to have such a big piece accepted, and he must have known it. Jurgenson eventually brought the scherzo out in 1909—Stravinsky's first orchestral score to appear in print—by which time they already had the Gorodetsky songs and possibly also the Piano Studies in hand as well. Meanwhile Igor took a leaf out of Ziloti's book and wrote to Belyayev pressing them on the question of an honorarium for *The Faun and the Shepherdess*, the vocal score of which was expected out any day.[18] "In a few days," he had optimistically told Volodya soon after returning the second proofs some weeks earlier, "it should be possible to get it at Jurgenson's shop for six gold grivnas. . . . Now every cobbler will be humming my tunes."[19]

In view of Ziloti's high opinion of the *Scherzo fantastique*, and particularly his reasons for admiring it, it may seem odd that he should turn to the ultraconventional Glazunov for a Rimsky tribute only a few days later. But this was probably a diplomatic choice; and when Glazunov fell by the wayside, Ziloti may have preferred to accept Steinberg as substitute rather than include pieces by the still practically unknown Stravinsky in two separate concerts.[20] At all events, Steinberg's prelude duly acted as pallbearer at Ziloti's October concert, and an impressive one, by all accounts, with its respectful use of sketch material for an uncomposed drama by Rimsky-Korsakov himself—material which moreover includes an anticipation of the specific dissonant chord Stravinsky himself later used for the character of Petrushka.[21]

Exactly when or by whose agency Igor's own tribute at last found its niche in the Russian Symphony Concert conducted by Blumenfeld in the Great Hall of the Conservatoire on 17 January is by no means clear. But it must have been by early December at the latest, since on the thirtieth Igor wrote to Gruss with instructions for the recopying of the string parts, the originals having left no opportunity for page turning.[22] What happened to these parts afterwards is, alas, unknown, and since the score was for some reason never published, the music was lost.[23] We can reconstruct its character only from reviews and, very speculatively, by examining—as Taruskin has done—the convention to which the work belonged, and of which two immediate examples are to hand, in the shape of the memorial pieces by Glazunov and Steinberg.

One of the most intriguing things about the work, and the reason why its loss is so particularly frustrating, is that it was a Stravinsky lament at a time when his music was predominantly lively, ebullient, and extrovert.

Fireworks, its immediate predecessor and divided from it only by the event it commemorates, is a continuation of the strain of the *Scherzo fantastique:* sharper, more succinct, more spectacular perhaps, but essentially from the same drawer of Stravinsky's desk, as Steinberg told Gnesin. It uses its ideas more efficiently and effectively. But they are not, in themselves, markedly more individual, and in both works it is disconcerting that the slowest elements are the most derivative—though in *Fireworks* the incongruous Wagnerism of the *Scherzo fantastique* is replaced by a no less candid but at least more apt allusion to Dukas's *Sorcerer's Apprentice.*

The Funeral Song, by contrast, was "subjective music: the lament and moaning of a heart against the backdrop of a somber landscape. One seems to hear the sinister wail of a storm spreading its cheerless atmosphere, and in the midst of it is heard, at first pianissimo, then gradually increasing in volume, a beautiful theme of a somewhat Russian character."[24] Another review mentions a prominent theme for horn; yet another complains of Stravinsky "striving to assault the listener with every color in his musical palette."[25] One can try to accommodate these remarks to the composer's own memory of the basic idea, "which was that all the solo instruments of the orchestra filed past the tomb of the master in succession, each laying down its own melody as its wreath against a deep background of *tremolo* murmurings simulating the vibrations of bass voices singing in chorus."[26] Taruskin takes this description to mean that Stravinsky, like both Glazunov and Steinberg, quoted from the chant liturgy.[27] He also speculates on possible quotations from Rimsky himself. The reviews do not confirm this, though the quotations in the other two works *are* spotted[28]—which perhaps says only that they were more overt: Steinberg's, after all, are in the substance of the music, and may have been mentioned in the program. Several reviewers grumbled specifically about a lack of formal clarity, and some found the music artificial and even insincere ("Better keep silence," advised one, "if losing a friend and teacher leaves us cold");[29] few agreed with Timofeyev that the music struck a particularly soulful or expressive note. "More perspiration than inspiration" was a common verdict. One senses a slow, rambling piece of a somewhat amorphous character (though Timofeyev implies a ternary form, with a return of the Russian theme at the end) and an austere, somewhat neutral, rather than conventionally elegiac, tone. But the precise sound of this intriguing work continues to elude us.

IGOR'S FIRST AUTUMN in St. Petersburg since his teacher's death is the start of a period during which we know comparatively little of his movements. There were no more regular Wednesdays, though occasional gatherings continued at Zagorodnïy Prospect, at one of which Stravinsky,

Gnesin, and Steinberg played their music to Scriabin and received his somewhat condescending approval.³⁰ No more lessons; no Yastrebtsev. Katya was expecting her second child, and with Igor's career beginning to take a more promising turn, it was time to look for their own flat. Even so the baby, Lyudmila, was born, just before Christmas, at 66 Kryukov Canal, and only at some time in the new year did the family move to their apartment in the Angliyskiy Prospect.³¹ By that time Igor was at work on something new, the opera which he had mentioned to Volodya in August as not yet in hand.³² Volodya had specifically inquired about it, no doubt because it had already been talked about at Zagorodnïy in the spring. Perhaps Lyadov had first prompted the idea at Rimsky's last birthday party, when he

> started to talk about wanting terribly to write a small opera on some clever little Russian folk tale. But this he would do, he said, only if Belsky wrote the libretto with the beautiful, typically Russian expressions and turns of speech of which he . . . is such a master.
>
> "You'll laugh at me," continued Anatoly Konstantinovich, "but I'm in love with folksong refrains like 'Rozan, moy rozan, vinograd zelyonïy'—senseless but nevertheless moving."³³

Two days later, after the Russian Symphony Concert in which Steinberg's First Symphony had its premiere, there was another gathering at Rimsky's, and Stepan Mitusov proposed a toast thanking Nikolay Andreyevich for giving him "the chance to satisfy his thirst for tomfoolery."³⁴ The very next day Igor and Stepan were at Belsky's engaged in detailed discussions with the master librettist of Rimsky's *Golden Cockerel* about just such a small opera as Lyadov had dreamt of writing, but based, not on a Russian folk tale, but on Hans Andersen's well-known story "The Emperor and the Nightingale."

In his autobiography, Stravinsky says that he showed the preliminary sketches for *The Nightingale* to Rimsky-Korsakov, "and to this day I remember with pleasure his approval."³⁵ But he must have meant either the scenario which the three of them had drawn up at Belsky's that day in March (only a month before Igor's last meeting with Rimsky and departure for Ustilug), or else the sketches for *Fireworks*, which he implies in the conversations he showed to Rimsky that spring.³⁶ There is no evidence of any compositional work on the opera before the autumn, by which time Styopa had in all probability written the entire libretto for the first act. For one thing, Igor's time at Ustilug that summer is almost entirely accounted for by other work, and his only Mitusov contact was probably the dedication to him of the first of the Four Studies. For another thing, the earliest musical draft carries the starting date 16 November 1908.³⁷ Several other drafts followed by mid-January. But at this point there occurred the first of a series of interruptions which were to spell the end for many things in Igor's quiet St. Petersburg life, of which *The Nightingale,* whatever its seeming importance at the time, would eventually appear as little more than a passing symptom.

The winter season of 1909 was again a lively one for Igor. The Russian Symphony Concert with his Funeral Song was followed swiftly by Ziloti's first performance of the *Scherzo fantastique* in the Assembly of the Nobles on 24 January, an event whose significance must have been greatly enhanced by orchestral playing (from the orchestra of the Mariyinsky Theatre) of much higher quality than any previous Stravinsky work had enjoyed. No wonder Igor decided to dedicate the scherzo to "the great artist Alexander Ilyich Ziloti." Moreover, his name was beginning to be known outside the capital. Nine days after the Petersburg premiere, Emil Cooper conducted the scherzo in Moscow. But both performances received mixed reviews. "It's amazing," one critic remarked, "how all [Rimsky-Korsakov's] pupils without exception imitate him slavishly. . . . They've all adopted their professor's tricks, and all been impregnated with the idea that 'art equals technique.' "[38] The *Russkaya muzïkal'naya gazeta* critic, on the other hand, found it "a piece written with taste and imagination, orchestrated with artistry, not without diabolical humor in its rhythms and sonorities,"[39] while in Moscow, Vladimir Derzhanovsky concluded that it was "a curious, brilliant, and, in its way, masterly piece!"[40] Yet even these compliments were tempered by the feeling that noise, or at least sonority for its own sake, was beginning to take precedence over music in the usual sense of the word. Derzhanovsky actually called it "not much music and a lot of orchestra," expatiating on the special effects: "Everything in his scherzo (except for the trio) chirrs, whistles, buzzes, jingles, flutters." And the old kuchkist hack César Cui spoke for the whole of that section of Russian conservative opinion which would shortly disown Stravinsky altogether when he warned Maria Kerzina (the organizer of the Russian Music Lovers' Circle, which was putting on the Moscow concert) of "the same old bombastic lack of talent, absence of music, the pursuit of sonorities and orchestral effects, with various peculiar combinations of different instruments, the absence of logic and taste, frequent insincerity, and so on."[41] "In small doses and at first," he wrote a couple of weeks later, "this exclusive pursuit of sonority is quite diverting and amusing. But in big helpings it's monotonous and unbearable. These gentry are like a man who would drive away a good woman and get involved with God knows who, dyed and rouged, but heartless, yes and very likely mad too."[42]

Nevertheless, the piece went down well with the Petersburg audience, perhaps relieved by its vivacious good humor after the protracted solemnity of Elgar's First Symphony, which they were also hearing for the first time.[43] At all events, the composer was called out: "There were cries of 'Author!' after [the] performance, and Stravinsky appeared on stage walking very rapidly and holding his fur hat in his hand."[44]

One other member of the audience that night was sufficiently impressed by the *Scherzo fantastique* to seek closer acquaintance with its composer. Precisely when Sergey Diaghilev and Stravinsky met is hard to ascertain: whether at the actual concert or at some time afterwards. Richard Buckle assumes that Diaghilev introduced himself to the composer that very evening.[45] But Stravinsky later told quite a different story:

> I had been playing my *Fireworks* in the piano version at a concert in the Conservatory. Afterwards he sent round his card with a note, asking me to call the following day at 3.00 p.m. Of course I knew who he was, everyone did, so I went. . . . There was a small entrance hall, I sat and waited. Laughter could be heard from an inner room. Time passed. You know I was young, but already impatient. I grew restless. After twenty minutes I got up and moved to the street door. As I grasped the handle, a voice behind me said, "Stravinsky, pridite, pridite," come in. I went in. You know my dear, I've often wondered, if I'd opened that door, whether I would have written *Le Sacre du printemps*.[46]

Fireworks does seem to have been played at a private Conservatoire concert some time early in 1909, and perhaps more than once, since Craft refers to three private performances before the public premiere in January 1910.[47] At least one of these must have been orchestral, since, as we shall see, Stravinsky spent part of the following summer revising the work's scoring. Diaghilev's manager Sergey Grigoriev—normally a sober chronicler of his master's activities—notes that Diaghilev had heard *Fireworks* "at a concert at the Academy [i.e., Conservatoire] of Music" and had reported that "the composition made a great impression on me. . . . It is new and original, with a tonal quality that should surprise the public."[48] In any case it looks as if Diaghilev had indeed heard both the *Scherzo fantastique* and *Fireworks* when he decided that Stravinsky was an artist of whom he and his new ballet company could make use. But it was probably the scherzo, as conducted by Ziloti, that gave him his initial idea of commissioning some orchestrations from the young composer for the revival of Mikhail Fokine's *Chopiniana* which he was planning, under the new title *Les Sylphides*, for his forthcoming opera-ballet season in Paris that summer.

The task, though in a sense menial, must have excited Igor, not least because it meant that his work would be heard for the first time outside Russia. He knew all about Diaghilev, as he says. He had naturally heard from Steinberg and Rimsky-Korsakov about the brilliant season of Russian concerts in Paris in 1907, and from his friend the conductor Felix Blumenfeld about the sensational success of *Boris Godunov* in 1908. He must have sensed that it would stand him in good stead to make an effective job of the two transcriptions with which Diaghilev had entrusted him: the Nocturne in A-flat, op. 32, no. 2, which was to open the ballet, and the Grande Valse Brillante, op. 18, which was to close it. So he probably shelved *The Nightingale* more or less there and then and embraced what Buckle primly but perhaps rightly calls "the odious notion of orchestrating Chopin."49 Only the waltz has so far been published, and, still, neither arrangement is to be heard in modern performances of *Les Sylphides*. But the autograph score of the nocturne turned up in a Sotheby's sale in December 1992, and allowed us a glimpse of how the twenty-six-year-old composer was able to transfer an orchestral technique evolved mainly through showy scherzo music to an arabesque but essentially linear early-romantic piano idiom. The answer is that he transferred it very largely intact. Chopin's discreetly ornamental melody, which is accompanied in the piano piece by broken chords in an undeviating triplet rhythm, now acquires a whole repertoire of fluttering string embellishments, harp flourishes, and woodwind tremolos by no means remote in style from the decorative texture of the Fisherman's song in *The Nightingale*, which Igor had probably just been working on, and where a plain melody has similarly to pick its way through a tangled foliage of sonority. This in turn is no more than a refinement of the instrumental style of the *Scherzo fantastique*, and close to that of *Fireworks*, which still awaited a revision whose extent we do not know. The result may not have sounded much like Chopin, and Camille Bellaigue may well have been thinking of this piece, quite as much as the other orchestrations by Lyadov, Alexander Taneyev, Sokolov, and Tcherepnin (and Stravinsky's waltz), when he described the arrangements as "unspeakably vile."50 And yet, as a translation of Chopin into the language of art nouveau, it has a certain period fascination and may indeed have worked, "sounded," perfectly well aside from questions of style.51

In any event, the two arrangements must have impressed Ziloti when Igor showed them to him, as he surely did, since in early May Ziloti himself commissioned a pair of transcriptions from him. The conductor wanted orchestral arrangements of two settings of the "Song of the Flea" from *Faust* (the ones by Musorgsky and Beethoven) for a "Goethe in Music" concert he was planning for November. Somewhat to the distress of the bookkeeper in Igor, Ziloti overlooked the question of terms, and Igor, by now once again at Ustilug, found himself in some confusion writing for advice on the subject to Max Steinberg—who had arranged Bach's solo violin Chaconne for Ziloti.52 But Ziloti more than made up for the omission by once again taking up the cudgels on behalf of Igor's own music. This time it was *Fireworks*, the score of which the composer had sent him from Ustilug after reorchestrating it in May.⁵³ Ziloti decided to bypass Jurgenson, aware perhaps of a certain similarity of genre between the scherzo and the fantasy, and instead approached the Leipzig firm of Schott and Co., backing his recommendation by actually sending the score. "As you'll see if you examine it," he told Ludwig Strecker in his idiosyncratic German,

> it is a practical and very effective piece and in its "sharp-witted" fashion a masterpiece. It's also good from a purely *business* point of view, as it's short so won't cost too much. I shall be playing it in my series already next winter; in addition, I can guarantee that Mengelberg (Frankfurt am Main and Holland) and Mr. H. Wood (London) will also play it, and probably Nikisch and Mottl. It's a very good conductor's piece: not hard and lasts 5–6 minutes.⁵⁴

Strecker replied complaining that the number of strings needed to balance the wind was too many for an average orchestra, but offering nevertheless to publish if Stravinsky would forgo an honorarium.⁵⁵ This was too much for Ziloti, who insisted on—and got—200 marks (rather less than 100 roubles) for his young protégé: "not much," as Igor told Styopa Mitusov, "but it's flattering that they're printing it. The question of author's performance rights hasn't yet been sorted out. It looks as if they want to take it whole."⁵⁶ Meanwhile, Jurgenson had accepted the Gorodetsky songs, and in mid-May these proofs landed on Igor's by now somewhat cluttered desk. And there they sat for two months and more, while the composer cast about for a copy of the poems against which to check the punctuation. Then he remembered his willing librettist back in St. Petersburg. "Luckily I managed to find 'Vesna' in some collection or other," he told Styopa, "but 'Rosyanka' I haven't got. Maybe you can find this poem with precise indications of punctuation and send it to me."⁵⁷ But Styopa was away in the country, so instead Volodya got the job. However, as Styopa reported back to Igor, Volodya had "looked in all the bookshops but couldn't find it. Apparently it's sold out."⁵⁸ Thus did a lifetime of delegating stutter into motion.

Amid all these distractions, *The Nightingale* itself moved forward somewhat fitfully. Styopa, for all his wit and energy and lively cultivation, was a modest man with a low opinion of his own writing ability, and he inundated Igor with modified and remodified and re-remodified versions of apparently perfectly good verses, glossing them with asides like "But this is all bad," "The main defect in what I'm writing is that it's so pretentious," "I don't like this last couplet at all. I've got a few other variants, but they're weak too," or "Short and bad, isn't it? Don't despair, friend. If you dislike it very much, we shall write something else." Igor had to reassure him. "I like very, very much the start of the second act, or scene. I accept it. Please write the song of the nightingale soon."[59]

One of the problems was undoubtedly the extremely slender story—of the Chinese emperor who, in a fit of pique, promotes a mechanical rather than the real nightingale to be his singer-in-chief, but then finds that in his moment of direst need it is only the real bird that has the power to save him. This had to be fleshed out, not by dialogue of a more or less well-constructed kind, but by what amounted to fine poetic phrases of a vaguely symbolist import and character. Lyadov may have been joking when he expressed a wish to write an opera with senseless lines like "Rose-flower, my rose-flower, green vine,"[60] but if so the joke was precisely at the expense of the kind of obscure symbolism and imagery for which, to the despair of Rimsky-Korsakov's kuchkist sensibilities, Stravinsky had begun to display a predilection. Taruskin has shown how Belsky tried to smuggle an element of social protest into the text of the Fisherman's song—a line about "my bitter fate"—and how Mitusov (or Stravinsky) promptly deleted it.[61] The fact was that The Nightingale was not at all a kuchkist subject; it had no social or historical or ethnographic connotations, was not even Russian, and certainly did not, for Stravinsky, convey a political warning like that of the Cockerel in Rimsky's last opera. Its orientalism was decorative, almost abstract, like the curving foliage on a Japanese vase, or the sweep of a Beardsley dress, or the intricacy of a wooded landscape by Golovin. This was altogether closer to the world of Mir iskusstva, with its rejection of subject matter in the everyday sense, its cultivation of line and color, texture and pattern, its pursuit of beauty at the expense of "crude" meaning. There were operatic precedents: most notably Wagner—whole scenes of Tristan and Parsifal in particular—and, had they but known it, Debussy's Pelléas, where the beauty of inconsequence had become a positive obsession. But these were still very wordy dramas. In The Nightingale, words were for the most part needed only as transportation for the voice; as Stravinsky said later about the Balmont text of Zvezdolikiy, "Words were what I needed, not meanings."[62] But Balmont's text was already in existence. For The Nightingale, Styopa had somehow to provide it.

His method seems to have been to spin out more or less decorative lines, then make several versions, often reducing them as he did so. At the heart of each verse would be an idea like "The tears in your eyes are all the reward I need," and this might then be written up in several ways. As poetry, it has the weakness that its meaning, such as it is, precedes its language. But for musical setting this proved unimportant. Stravinsky needed only succinct embodiment in words of certain crucial ideas which, for him, already had a clear musical existence. Even the Nightingale's wordless "Ah" had meaning in this sense. "I've attached paramount importance to it," he told Styopa.

In general the first scene is full of the most vivid (don't be afraid) contrasts. On the one hand, the Nightingale* and the bosom of nature; on the other hand, the gang of semi-farcical Chinese nobility. Because of the latter the Nightingale comes still more into relief in all the beauty of its intimacy.

*The personification of soul (God! how opaque this word has become in our time!)[63]

"The personification of soul": well might poor Styopa puzzle over the kind of language such a being might speak, and indeed the kind of language others might speak in its presence. But he found effective answers to these questions: the idea, for instance, that the Emperor must be silent, merely nodding his head, until after the Nightingale has sung, and, later, the perception that Death must be laconic, were essentially his, though in some cases prompted by Andersen. Above all, he understood that for the opera composer, the librettist was nothing but a functionary. "Your fear of hurting my feelings," he told Igor later on in their collaboration, "is completely groundless, since everything I'm now writing, I'm writing for the glory of your talent; I don't count, and the question of the author's amour propre simply doesn't arise. Believe me, I'm happy that I can contribute a single brick to the erection of your building, and if this brick doesn't fit, I shall with double pleasure hasten to find another."[64]

This harmonious collaboration probably resumed in late March 1909, after the fulfillment of the Diaghilev commission; and by the time Igor went to Ustilug as usual, in May, he had written the orchestral introduction and was working on the Fisherman's song. But now there was another holdup, while he revised *Fireworks* and read the Gorodetsky proofs. Only in June could he again take up the opera.

He composed, as so often afterwards, in a mood of enthusiasm and joy. "Styopa my dear," he wrote, "how I should love to play you what I'm writing. I dare to think you would like it."[65] He explains in detail his plan for the Fisherman's song, with its recitative episodes, of which he enters a musical quotation. "The pizzicato is in the spirit of [Rimsky's] *Scheherazade*, I'm well aware, but the music is something different." (He must be thinking of the strumming pizzicatos which accompany the clarinet solos in the second movement of that work.) So far Styopa has written the text only for the first act; but Igor is keen to press on: "I'd urge you to hurry up, and if you get ahead a bit and write the Nightingale's song in the second act . . . then it would be a great joy if you could send it to me."

By late July, Igor has almost finished the first act, "composing with the orchestra [i.e., straight into the full score]—to my mind one should never do anything else."[66] And he even gives some modest technical information—a habit he decidedly did not continue.

With me a system of leitmotifs is almost wholly absent. In place of this reminder to the audience of what's going on, my music draws the listener into the mood and style of this or that person or topic. All this applies chiefly to the Nightingale and to nature. With the Chinese it's the contrary. The system of leitmotifs has been narrowed down to the point of caricature. The Chamberlain has a leitmotif made up of five notes. . . . The Bonze sings the same five notes, but in reverse.[67]

Just over three weeks later, the first act is complete. But then, instead of breaking off neatly at that point, he carries straight into the second act, the text of which Styopa has been writing. In mid-August his brother Gury, who is also at Ustilug, writes to Volodya: "Gimuchka does not leave his writing table and piano, and is composing *The Nightingale:* the first act is finished and already fully orchestrated. He is now on the next, but it will have to be interrupted by another essential task for Ziloti—orchestrating the 'Fleas'—ha, ha, ha, hee. You'll probably hear it and can judge for yourself—but I personally like this music *(Nightingale)* awfully."[68]

It was much as Gury said. Igor probably got almost nowhere with act 2 before deciding he had better get on with the Ziloti arrangements. Understandably he attacked the more congenial one first. The Musorgsky was finished on 3 September, and Igor no doubt at once set to work on the Beethoven. Meanwhile, on 4 September New Style (that is, 22 August Old Style, twelve days earlier), Diaghilev had sent a letter to Lyadov:

> You have told me, and I want to believe you, that you are not an enemy of my enterprise and that there is something in it that's to your liking. Moreover, you have told me that to order music from you requires a year's notice.
>
> Taking all this into consideration, I am sending you a proposal, or perhaps, to put it more modestly, a request to take on a piece of work with us. I need a *ballet* and a *Russian* one—the *first* Russian ballet, since there is no such thing—there is Russian opera, Russian symphony, Russian song, Russian dance, Russian rhythm—but no Russian ballet. And that is precisely what I need, to perform in May of the coming year in the Paris Grand Opéra and in the huge Royal Drury Lane Theatre in London.
>
> The ballet needn't be three-storeyed—and the libretto is ready—Fokine has it and it was cooked up by us all collectively. It's *The Firebird,* a ballet in one act and perhaps two scenes.[69]

10

BIRDS OF A FEATHER ▬▬

DIAGHILEV'S FIRST PARIS season of ballets in May and June 1909 may have been a spectacular artistic success, but it was achieved almost by accident, after the sudden death in February of his main Russian sponsor, Grand Duke Vladimir Alexandrovich, and the subsequent withdrawal of support by the grand duke's widow, had forced him to revise his original plan for a season of opera spiced with ballet in favor of a season of ballet with little more than a leavening of opera.

Perhaps ballet was, as Benois argued, the natural theatrical expression of the World of Art ideology, with its indifference to realism or representation, its love of the decorative, the exotic, the magical, above all its enthusiasm for a kind of Wagnerian *"Gesamtkunstwerk"* in which every element would contribute in equal measure to a completely rounded artistic impression.[1] But Diaghilev himself had certainly not been an instinctive balletomane. His professional entrée into the world of art had initially been through painting. But even that was to some extent opportunism, since he was not an artist himself and had never studied painting as a practical or technical discipline. Rather, his attitude to art in general had been formed in the atmosphere of broadly cultivated dilettantism which reigned in his grandfather's house in far-distant Perm, where his father and stepmother had gone to live in 1882 when he was ten. The house had soon become the cultural center of local life; there were concerts and domestic music making, books and literary evenings, and a general sense of tasteful well-being, and at school young Seriozha was able to cut an effortlessly urbane figure among the wide-eyed provincials, knowing things of which his schoolmates "had no notion, such as Russian and foreign literature, the theatre and music. French and German he also spoke fluently, and [he] could play the piano. Externally, too, he was very different. There was an elegance, a refinement, even a stateliness in his carriage. He was a perfect 'little gentleman' in comparison with us."[2]

But when he arrived in St. Petersburg as a law student at the university in 1890, it was his turn to find himself a provincial figure in the art-loving circles into which he was introduced by his cousin Dima Filosofov. Certainly he had charm, this "strong, handsome boy," as Walter Nouvel later described him, "young and in flourishing health, a trifle inclined to fatness, [with] an enormous head out of all proportion to the rest of his body . . . very beautiful large dark brown eyes, that were extraordinarily animated, and a small snub nose very ordinary in shape."³ But the two-years-older Benois, with his practical artistic background and intense love and knowledge of everything to do with the theatre, was irritated by Diaghilev's aspirations "to represent a real man about town and member of high society," while taking no more than a foppish interest in their "Society for Self-Improvement"—the Nevsky Pickwickians, as Benois called them—to whom Walter Nouvel would lecture on the history of opera, or Lev Rosenberg, alias Bakst, would discourse on Russian realist painters.⁴ Diaghilev, it was true, was knowledgeable about music; he could even sing respectably, and (with Nouvel) play the occasional piano duet. But to the cosmopolitan Benois, with his Franco-German father and Venetian mother, there was something embarrassing about this callow young Russian from the sticks ingratiating himself with the St. Petersburg beau monde and falling asleep at Pickwickian gatherings.

It was only gradually that Diaghilev's peculiar talent—not for the practice of art, but for its creative administration, his genius for imposing supreme taste and aesthetic knowledge on what the French call the "animation" of art and music—began to assert itself over this talented but still, in a sense, directionless group. The specific aesthetic tone—the "pure" cultivation of beauty, the utter detachment from social or political goals—was already set. But its realization in solid projects that would radiate beyond the four walls of Benois's drawing room would be Diaghilev's particular contribution. At its core, in the early years, was the World of Art review, *Mir iskusstva,* which for six years (1898–1904) served as a beacon for the revived interest in design for its own sake that challenged the long hegemony of the social realism of the sixties. *Mir iskusstva* was the first great product of Diaghilev's despised court-paying to the great and the good. It began with the support of the artist and collector Princess Tenisheva and the railway tycoon Savva Mamontov; then later, after their withdrawal, the greatest good of all, Tsar Nicholas II, guaranteed the review for five years. Meanwhile the director of the Imperial Theatres, Prince Sergey Volkonsky, another Diaghilev cultivar, had engaged him in 1899 as his junior assistant (an appointment which also entailed prestigious commissions for Benois, Bakst, and other members of the circle).

Even here, Diaghilev was not chiefly concerned with the stage. His main task was to edit the theatres' yearbook, and in fact his one brush with the stage, an ill-starred plan to put on Delibes's ballet *Sylvia* in 1901, led indirectly to his dismissal from the Imperial service. Much of his time since then had been taken up with *Mir iskusstva,* and with a series of journeys round Russia which eventually culminated in the great exhibition of Russian portraiture in the Tauride Palace in St. Petersburg in 1905. It was out of the spectacular success of this show that was born the idea of mounting a similar but broader-based exhibition of Russian art in the Grand Palais in Paris the following year. And it was from this venture, which at once caught a mood with chic Parisians, that Diaghilev—himself more a musician than a visual artist—conceived his 1907 season of concerts of "Russian Music Down the Ages," for which, as we have already seen, Rimsky-Korsakov travelled to Paris that May. The programs for these concerts were heavily loaded with operatic excerpts, including the final act of Musorgksy's *Khovanshchina* and Chaliapin singing all three bass roles in excerpts from *Boris Godunov.* So when the question arose of a third Paris season in 1908, a complete production of *Boris* with Chaliapin in the title role—the work's first-ever performance outside Russia—was a natural choice. Diaghilev might equally have thought of bringing Tchaikovsky's *Sleeping Beauty* to the West for the first time. But ballet was still far from his thoughts.

The real ballet lover of the group was Benois, and it was through his long-nurtured desire to create "a ballet of my own" that the first integrated World of Art stage work had come into being in the form of a one-act ballet, *Le Pavillon d'Armide,* based on a Théophile Gautier story in which the hero falls in love with a beautiful woman who comes to life from a Gobelin tapestry. *Armide* was a real collaborative enterprise. With music composed by Nikolay Tcherepnin to Benois's scenario, it eventually reached the Mariyinsky stage in November 1907, with designs by Benois, but in a much reduced and modified form in which there was a third and no less influential hand—that of the young dancer and choreographer Mikhail Fokine. It was Fokine, with ideas on ballet production strongly influenced by the free-movement, antimethod dancing of Isadora Duncan, who turned out to be the real catalyst through which the World of Art became the Ballets Russes.

Diaghilev saw *Armide* and was bowled over by the atmospheric richness and elegance of Benois's settings, the vitality of the dance movement, and perhaps even by Tcherepnin's sumptuous though shamelessly derivative score. "This must be shown to Europe," he told Benois.[5] And so it duly was, as the curtain raiser to his 1909 Paris season. The trouble was that it was as yet almost the only properly integrated ballet in the company's entire repertory, which otherwise consisted largely of what Nouvel called "salades russes":[6] compilations of party pieces choreographed to a miscellany of musical numbers from the orchestral, sometimes ballet or operatic, repertoire—like *Cléopâtre,* for which Tcherepnin cooked up a score at

Diaghilev's behest out of bits and pieces of Arensky and Taneyev, Rimsky-Korsakov, Glazunov, and Musorgsky;7 or *Le Festin,* a still more opportunistic mélange put together at the last minute when it became apparent that Diaghilev could not afford to mount the full-scale operas he had originally planned. Even *Les Sylphides,* though based on the work of a single composer and exquisitely coherent in its setting and choreography, remained musically a hotchpotch—the very orchestrations were by several different composers. The whole impression of the 1909 season was that music, and with it the *Gesamtkunstwerk,* had somehow got left behind in the quest for spectacle and visual poetry. "The young Russian composers," wrote Michel Calvocoressi, "need to get down to serious work in order to supply works of a more personal character fit to be shown to us; otherwise the presentations of Russian music abroad will be forced to preserve a retrospective character and will soon no longer interest anyone but historians."8

Diaghilev seems to have taken the hint that it was up to him to find these young composers and put them to work more or less at once. His first candidate, however, seems not to have been a Russian at all, but the Frenchman Ravel, with a Russian (or to be exact, a Ukrainian) only in second place. "We're deep in plans for future ballets," he wrote to Benois a week after the end of the Paris season:

> One is already ordered, *Daphnis and Chloe.* With the combined efforts of Bakst, Fokine, and Ravel, we've worked out a detailed program—and it's going like a dream. Now the question arises of a ballet for you and compiled by you, *The Ice House*—with music by Akimenko, who has arrived here from Dresden in answer to my call. . . . Akimenko strikes me as a very talented man, and I think this subject will suit him.9

But this was not the first time Diaghilev had thought of Stravinsky's one-time harmony teacher. Almost a year earlier Bakst had written to his wife that "Seryozha . . . wants to give Russian ballet in Paris next spring: *Armide* and *Giselle,* or something new written by one of the composers, most likely Akimenko, and the execution of the decor and costumes he's entrusting to Shura [Benois] and me."10

Too much should not be made of this unlikely enthusiasm of Diaghilev's for one of the most orthodox and straitlaced of the Belyayevtsï. Who else was there, after all? Petersburg music was effectively a choice between Conservatoire academics and the largely untried nonentities whose works bulked out the programs of the Evenings of Contemporary Music. No doubt Nouvel, himself more of an opera lover, pressed the claims of such figures from time to time. But the evidence is that Diaghilev was not yet ready to plunge into the mysterious question of what might constitute a dazzling musical equivalent of the decors of Bakst, Benois, or Serov, or the spectacular new choreography of Fokine. Taruskin makes precisely the point that Diaghilev's first Paris seasons were dominated by music whose old-fashioned kuchkism was the direct antithesis of everything that the World of Art stood for.[11] But he seems to have had little alternative. At least Rimsky-Korsakov, Musorgsky, and the rest had the virtue that their music was practically unknown in Paris and for some reason caught a mood: a sophisticated zest for the exotic and untamed. The improbable ferocity of Borodin's Polovtsian Dances or Glazunov's Bacchanale (in *Cléopâtre*) sent a tremor through the ostrich plumes of Proust's Paris. But it was a tremor which could not, Diaghilev must have known perfectly well, be rearoused indefinitely. Calvocoressi had a point; renewal was the necessary condition of such excitement.

Diaghilev soon saw through the wretched Akimenko. "On closer acquaintance," he told Benois, "we didn't take to Akimenko—bread and milk, silly and provincial."[12] Nothing more was heard of *The Ice House*. Instead, Diaghilev had Debussy in his sights, for a Venetian ballet called *Masques et bergamasques,* and he had approached Lyadov on the question of *The Firebird.*[13] But the charming vignettist of *Kikimora* and *The Enchanted Lake* was hardly first choice for a ballet to set fire to the Seine. And indeed there is plenty of evidence that Diaghilev had at first hoped that his "house" composer, Nikolay Tcherepnin, would write the new score. Tcherepnin's tone poem *The Enchanted Kingdom,* which had its first performance at a Russian Symphony Concert in March 1910, is openly based on a version of the Firebird story derived from Fokine's ballet scenario.[14] So it seems a reasonable assumption that its music started out as a direct setting of that scenario for dancing in the 1910 season. Why Tcherepnin did not in the end compose *The Firebird* remains a mystery. According to Benois, he was "prone to inexplicable changes of mood, and [his] attitude was in those days cooling towards ballet in general."[15] Taruskin suspects a tiff with the "notoriously difficult" Fokine.[16] But perhaps Tcherepnin was also put off by the drift of the Paris notices in 1909. Louis Laloy's dismissal of his score for *Le Pavillon d'Armide*—"the only extenuating circumstance one could invoke in favor of such insignificant music is that after five minutes one no longer hears it"[17]—was hardly encouraging for his chances of impressing the French with a new ballet written specially for them; nor, one might add, can it have raised Diaghilev's spirits on his composer's behalf. If Tcherepnin resigned voluntarily from the project, one can well imagine that Diaghilev did not waste much steam trying to dissuade him.

All this might suggest that the *Firebird* plan preceded the 1909 Paris season, rather than being a response to it. If, as Diaghilev told Lyadov, Fokine had a scenario ready in early September, it must have been worked out either the previous spring, or in Diaghilev's absence, since he was out of Russia between early May and early September. Benois's account is clear, however, that the *Firebird* discussions followed the 1909 season, and he does not include Diaghilev's name among the participants.[18] So it may be that the meetings he describes really did take place in July or August 1909, that they led to Tcherepnin's resignation, and that the invitation to Lyadov followed immediately thereafter. Diaghilev knew that the notoriously languid Lyadov would need pushing. "If you," he told Benois, "could work on him on your side, that would be splendid. At a pinch if Lyadov refuses it will be necessary to ask Glazunov, but how much nicer the former would be!"[19] Fokine recalls that Lyadov "arrived [at my house], read the script, and became very interested, taking the libretto with him when he left."[20] But that was that. Diaghilev must soon have realized that Lyadov was not going to produce. Did he sound out Glazunov? It seems not. Instead, bolstered by the advice of musicians like Tcherepnin and Boris Asafyev, he decided to take a chance.[21] He dispatched a telegram to Ustilug, asking his young Chopin arranger whether, if commissioned, he would be prepared to undertake what was by then rapidly becoming an urgent and formidable commission.[22]

Stravinsky had just made his Musorgsky arrangement for Ziloti and was faced with a dilemma: should he complete its Beethoven companion, then proceed with act 2 of *The Nightingale* while awaiting Diaghilev's firm commission, or should he embark straightaway on the ballet score, having regard to the shortness of time at his disposal, and risk his efforts being wasted? It may be that he decided there and then to return to St. Petersburg in order to find out more about the ballet and, perhaps above all, to try to see the scenario. The Beethoven song was certainly shelved, since the score is dated 3 November, less than four weeks before the concert on the twenty-eighth. But this fits in with Stravinsky's memory that he went to Lyubensk with Andrey Rimsky-Korsakov early in November, intending, he tells us, "a vacation in birch forests and snow-fresh air."[23] In the intervening weeks he must have had meetings with Fokine and the other members of the Ballets Russes team, and perhaps they included some of those sessions in which, according to Fokine's reminiscence, the choreographer mimed the action while Stravinsky improvised suitable piano accompaniments.[24] At Lyubensk, instead of holidaying, he went on tinkering with the ballet. The few sketches which survive for *The Firebird* may well date from this month in the country, at least to judge by their comparative remoteness from the music of the eventual ballet.[25] The composer himself recalls writing the first seven bars of the Introduction at Lyubensk,[26] plus some notations for later episodes, including, presumably, a fragment of the Khorovod that he presented to Steinberg, as a souvenir of a work "which, all the same, I think you regard as a series of curiosities and 'tricks.' "[27] By the end of the month he must have been back in St. Petersburg for the

Ziloti Goethe concert (on the twenty-eighth), at which his two song arrangements were performed by Chaliapin. The previous day his name had figured among the recipients of the Belyayev Glinka Prize, for his *Scherzo fantastique*. And it was at this precise stage that Diaghilev, having at last, presumably, divested himself of Lyadov, telephoned to confirm the commission which, in effect, would swiftly render Glinka awards of no account.[28]

This bizarre and complicated history reflects, of course, the still somewhat speculative, transitional character of Diaghilev's operation. But it also underlines the communal atmosphere which, at this early stage, Ballets Russes planning inherited from the days of *Mir iskusstva* and before. The famous World of Art tea parties, with Diaghilev's old *nyanya* presiding over the samovar, have their echo in the meetings described by Benois and Fokine at which the scenario of *The Firebird* was evolved. In true *Gesamtkunstwerk* fashion, the elements of the plot and its treatment had been thrashed out at conferences attended not only by writers like Remizov and the poet Pyotr Potyomkin, but also by painters like Golovin, Stelletsky, and Benois himself, by the choreographer Fokine, and of course by the composer Tcherepnin.[29] The whole idea answered Benois's own longcherished notion of a ballet based on authentic Slav mythology; but the way it evolved was highly artificial—a painstakingly reconstructed ethnology in the spirit of art nouveau and the work of neonationalist designers like Bilibin, Hartmann, and Polenova. The legendary figure of the Firebird was already a kind of insignia for the modern style in Russia: "Gorgeous yet enigmatic, a thing of preternatural, elemental freedom, she personified the indifference of beauty to the desires and cares of mankind. In this she was the very symbol of art for art's sake."[30] Now Benois, Fokine, and their fellow conspirators set about adapting this creature to the stage. To that end they combined elements from several published tales *(skazki)*, some about the Firebird, others about the demon Kashchey— whose "death" lives in an egg that must be broken in his presence if he is to be killed—and the archetypal Imperial Russian hero figure, Ivan Tsarevich.

Whoever was chiefly responsible for this synthesis—and there are various claimants[31]—the process must have been largely complete by the time the libretto came into Stravinsky's hands, whether in the early autumn of 1909 or after Diaghilev's phone call in December, even though the composer gives the impression that the scenario was still being worked out at meetings that he attended.[32] In one major respect he certainly did contribute. The final transformation and coronation scene were the composer's idea: a ceremonious replacement for Fokine's more conventional device of the final divertissement, and one which already suggests a feeling for the ritual aspects of dance drama. Significantly, Fokine by his own admission yielded reluctantly to the change.[33] But in essence, the scenario was, for Stravinsky, a fait accompli.

How did the twenty-seven-year-old composer respond to having to write to order in this way? His later remark about having been "less than eager to fulfill the commission" can certainly be taken with a pinch of salt, and so can his observation that "*The Firebird* did not attract me as a subject."[34] The evidence is that he applied himself to it diligently, and without protest. Not only did he manage to compose three-quarters of an hour of sumptuously orchestrated music in less than six months—which was quick by any standards and a much higher rate of production than would later be normal with him—but he accepted a collaborative element in the writing which would have been dust and ashes for him later on. According to Fokine,

> Stravinsky visited me with his first sketches and basic ideas, he played them for me, I demonstrated the scenes to him. . . . [He] played, and I interpreted the role of the Tsarevich, the piano substituting for the wall. I climbed over it, jumped down from it, and crawled, fear-struck, looking around—my living room. Stravinsky, watching, accompanied me with patches of the Tsarevich melodies, playing mysterious tremolos as background to depict the garden of the sinister Immortal Kostchei. Later on I played the role of the Tsarevna (Princess) and hesitantly took the golden apple from the hands of the imaginary Tsarevich. Then I became Kostchei, his evil entourage—and so on.[35]

The composer's own less colorful and somewhat dismissive memoir nevertheless tends to confirm the working method: "To speak of my own collaboration with Fokine means nothing more than to say that we studied the libretto together, episode by episode, until I knew the exact measurements required of the music."[36] But presumably it was only the narrative episodes that were worked out in this fashion, and even so we obviously cannot be sure that the music Stravinsky wrote down was what he had improvised for Fokine. On the other hand, the set dances must have been composed in the normal way, with no more than a specification or a dance title to hand. One of the surviving sketch pages has a list of such headings written down by Fokine for the composer's benefit—albeit not yet correct as to the final version.[37]

Stravinsky later grumbled that the work "demanded descriptive music of a kind I did not want to write," and he referred to "music as literal as an opera."[38] These are, in effect, the Fokine episodes—what Stravinsky accused Fokine of calling "*my* 'musical accompaniment' to *his* 'choreographic poem' "—and it is true that not only is there no such music in *The*

Nightingale, but it also plays a sharply decreasing role in the next few ballets. Yet, curiously enough, these "recitative" passages, as one might call them, contain some of the work's most imaginative and original writing: for instance, the extraordinary Carillon féerique and the ensuing dialogue between Kashchey and Ivan Tsarevich, neither of which figures in any of the published suites. By contrast the set-piece dances are conventionally brilliant in the Russian manner, and often very candid in their models; Scriabin in the Dance of the Firebird, Rimsky-Korsakov in the Supplication, Glazunov in the Dance of the Princesses, a whole lineage of kuchkist folklorists in the Khorovod and the coronation music. The individuality of this music lies in its glittering orchestration, though even in this respect Stravinsky was not always the innovator he later thought himself.39 What *was* new about *The Firebird* was the astonishing mastery of resource and technique on the part of a composer of such limited experience. Of course, the work is conventional: "What do you expect," as Debussy said later, "one has to start somewhere."40 But it does a number of very difficult things with extraordinary expertise: the operatic device of transition, which Stravinsky practically abandoned in subsequent stage works, is handled like a master. The impulse and sense of interior movement in the dances, particularly those of the Firebird and Kashchey and his retinue, are extraordinary for a first dance work, even if the music is metrically rigid, like so much earlier work by Russian composers. Finally, the score hardly ever seems overloaded, despite the huge orchestra and extremely complex instrumental tracery. Much of Stravinsky's Rimsky-Korsakov training had been in the field of orchestration. All the same, it is hard to explain the sheer precision of sonority in most of *The Firebird* except in terms of an instinctive grasp of the properties of instrumental sound, an almost infallible inner ear.

While Stravinsky was hard at work on the Diaghilev commission, Ziloti's promised performance of *Fireworks,* postponed from October, at last materialized in a concert on 9 January (OS). For those in the know about the Diaghilev commission, it might well have come as a trailer: brief, dazzling, harmonically sophisticated, and with an orchestral wizardry that would have encouraged the best possible expectations of the ballet. For some reason, though, it made little impact on its first (documented) audience. Perhaps the performance was inadequate. It may have been on this occasion that Fokine heard Stravinsky grumbling about the Mariyinsky orchestra's playing of his work: "The composer complained that they treated his music with utter contempt, as if they were ridiculing it."41 Or perhaps, as one reviewer put it, the piece was simply "too short and not vivid enough for the audience to be able to attune to it as they should";42 one might equally suspect it of being too subtle. For the first, but by no means last, time, a Russian public simply could not follow what Stravinsky was on about. But the press notices were more hopeful. Diaghilev's old associate Alfred Nurok, reviewing the concert in *Apollon*, made the perceptive and prescient observation that "without going beyond witty hints at the reproduction in sound of a sensational explosion of sky-rockets, it captures truly startlingly in its musical essence that peculiar psychic elation aroused by the spectacle of fiery entertainments. And such an impression is achieved in music only through its richness of substance, however bejewelled."[43] It would be precisely in his ability to make sonority into substance that one of Stravinsky's greatest artistic achievements would lie. And despite any temptation to onomatopoeia, this was in essence a miriskusstvan achievement, a fascination with color and design and a rejection of subject matter in, at any rate, the narrative or "realist" sense. That, as Taruskin points out, is no doubt why Nurok liked it.[44] And that, if at all, is why at this very moment Stravinsky might *not* have chosen to write the "descriptive" music in the Fokine episodes of *The Firebird*.

Nevertheless, write it he did. Throughout January, February, and most of March he sat at his desk in the Angliyskiy Prospect, toiling away at the piano score. He finished it on 21 March. But by then he must have long since begun orchestrating, since by the start of April he had scored nearly half the work, whereas the remainder took him more than another month.[45] No doubt Diaghilev had told him, as he had previously told Lyadov, that the full score would be needed for part copying by mid-March.[46] So Stravinsky must have been desperately writing up the score as he went, folio by folio, and handing the pages to the copyist, long before he had finished composing. Matters were not made any easier by another commission from Diaghilev, for an orchestration of a Grieg piano piece, "Kobold" (op. 71, no. 3) for a charity ball being sponsored by the magazine *Satyricon* on 20 February. It seems incredible that Diaghilev should have disrupted his young aspirant's tight schedule with so seemingly trivial a task. But there was a reason. Something crisp was needed for Diaghilev's brilliant young prodigy, the twenty-one-year-old Vaslav Nijinsky, to dance at the ball. And perhaps the impresario had again had a refusal from Tcherepnin, who may well have been even more urgently busy with the score of his *Enchanted Kingdom* for the Belyayev concert on 12 March. Stravinsky's arrangement was in any case duly danced; and it was effective enough to find its way into a new "salade russe" divertissement, *Les Orientales*, which Diaghilev was planning for the Ballets Russes Paris repertoire in June.[47]

There was one other interruption during the final stages of composition, perhaps in early March. Stravinsky's own account of this unexpected visitation has entered the folklore of twentieth-century music:

One day, when I was finishing the last pages of *L'Oiseau de Feu* in St. Petersburg, I had a fleeting vision which came to me as a complete surprise, my mind at the moment being full of other things. I saw in imagination a solemn pagan rite: sage elders, seated in a circle, watched a young girl dance herself to death. They were sacrificing her to propitiate the god of spring.[48]

The composer goes on to relate how he described his vision to his friend the painter and ethnographer Nikolay Roerich, who "welcomed my inspiration with enthusiasm, and became my collaborator in this creation." The story may be true. The autobiography is hardly to be trusted on points of authorship, but the factual substance of the claim—that Stravinsky had the idea for *The Rite of Spring* in the spring of 1910—is already found in a letter to the editor of the *Russkaya muzïkal'naya gazeta*, Nikolay Findeyzen, written less than three years afterwards and still before the work's first performance.[49] Roerich himself, however, denied the story on various occasions. He claimed, for instance, that he had discussed future work on a ballet with Stravinsky as early as 1909, when the two had presumably met at Diaghilev's. On one occasion he recalled offering Stravinsky two possible subjects, one based on the idea of a chess game, the other on "the Great Sacrifice," as the work was for a long time to have been called.[50] Early newspaper reports of the collaboration attributed the subject to Roerich, and though Stravinsky subsequently referred to these reports, he did not deny them.[51] There will be more to say about all this in due course. But it does seem clear that Stravinsky was already thinking about a neonationalist fertility rite while still finishing off his picture-book fairy tale, a work which, as Taruskin has observed, is not without a vernal symbolism of its own.[52]

No sooner was the piano score of *The Firebird* ready than Diaghilev began to set up sneak previews designed to secure favorable advance coverage in the press. The French critic Robert Brussel, who seems to have spent several months in St. Petersburg at least partly as a contact for Diaghilev's Paris associate Gabriel Astruc, attended one such play-through at Diaghilev's flat in the Zamyatin Pere-ulok. His much later account has to be understood, though, as well informed by hindsight:

The composer, young, slim and uncommunicative, with vague meditative eyes, and lips set firm in an energetic looking face, was at the piano. But the moment he began to play, the modest and dimly lit dwelling glowed with a dazzling radiance. By the end of the first scene I was conquered: by the last, I was lost in admiration. The manuscript on the music-rest, scored over with fine pencilings, revealed a masterpiece.[53]

At about the same time, Diaghilev arranged for Stravinsky to play excerpts at the offices of the journal *Apollon,* presumably though the influence of the paper's music critic, Diaghilev's friend Alfred Nurok. This particular soirée took place on 10 April, and Nurok himself reported it, rather matter-of-factly, in the pages of *Apollon.*54 Meanwhile, rehearsals had got under way, in the Yekaterinsky Hall, to which the company had been banished the year before from its original home in the Hermitage Theatre. Stravinsky attended every rehearsal, sometimes helping out at the piano, in music which—though it now strikes us as quite conventional—was already difficult for dancers "brought up . . . on easy rhythms and obvious tunes."55 "He was particularly exacting about the rhythms," Grigoriev recalled, "and used to hammer them out with considerable violence, humming loudly and scarcely caring whether he struck the right notes."56 Afterwards, Diaghilev, Nijinsky and Stravinsky "generally ended the day with a fine dinner, washed down with good claret."57 Or perhaps they would go by boat to one of the various nightclubs or restaurants on the wooded islands to the north of the city.58

Suddenly, another Stravinsky—the bon vivant—has appeared alongside the family man and the severe, dedicated artist; and we can hardly doubt that it is Diaghilev, specifically, who has inducted him into an aspect of St. Petersburg that already feels a world away from the Kryukov Canal, or the Zagorodnïy or Angliyskiy Prospects, though physically a mere steamer ride. It is Paris—a somewhat provincial Paris, no doubt—*avant la lettre.* Yet another sub-Parisian aspect of the dying capital—the seedy, arty Bohemian world of literary nightclubs such as the Stray Dog, which opened a year or so later in a damp cellar off the Mikhailovsky Square—probably did not claim their attention. Had it done so, Igor might have encountered much earlier a number of artists who would later be important—and more than important—to him.

But St. Petersburg was about to move into inferior conjunction. When Diaghilev and his dancers left Russia for Berlin and Paris at the start of May, Stravinsky rapidly scored up the final pages of his ballet and set off with Katya, their two tiny children, and Anna Stravinsky to Ustilug.59 It seems unlikely that he had any inkling of how very little he would ever again see of the city of his childhood.

THE PUPPETEERS

By the time Stravinsky arrived in Paris from Ustilug at the end of the first week of June,[1] the company's season was already in full swing, having opened on the fourth with a typical triple bill of *Carnaval* (Schumann's piano work turned into a *salade russe*), a new Fokine ballet to the music of Rimsky-Korsakov's *Scheherazade,* and a curtain raiser made up of bits and pieces from the previous season's *Le Festin* and the *Polovtsian Dances.* Musically this gallimaufry was at best no improvement on the previous season; even *Scheherazade* was done incomplete, without its lyrical slow movement, and to an orgiastic scenario by Fokine that made mincemeat of Rimsky's carefully plotted tales of Sinbad the Sailor, the Kalendar Prince, and the rest. From the grave, Rimsky might still have been heard protesting: "How chagrined I should be if I learned that Miss [Isadora] Duncan dances and mimetically explains, for example, my *Scheherazade, Antar,* or *Easter Overture!* . . . When [miming] foists itself unbidden upon music, it only harms the latter by diverting attention from it."[2] But what ears did the Paris of the duchesse de Guermantes (alias Countess Greffuhle) or Princesse Yourbeletieff (Misia Edwards) have for such dreary lamentations? Fokine's frenzied choreography and Lev Bakst's voluptuous designs were a sensation, and the travel-poster Russian orientalism they represented was already the rage as Stravinsky stepped off the train, for the first time in his life, at the Gare du Nord that June day just before his twenty-eighth birthday.

So far as we know, the composer did not faint away with anticipation on the arrival platform, as the ballerina Lydia Lopukhova had done a week or so earlier.[3] "My excitement on arriving in the city," he tells us with perhaps studied ambiguity, "could hardly have been greater."[4] In any case it was under control. Soon he was in the thick of rehearsals. Although the genre was new to him, he seems to have had a profound sense of the composer's importance in rehearsing a new work, as if there were already stirring in him that fear of the performer which later grew into a whole artistic creed about the dangers of "interpretation." Tamara Karsavina, who was to dance in place of the originally designated Firebird, Anna Pavlova, recalled that "often he came early to the theatre before a rehearsal began in order to play for me over and over again some specially difficult passage.... It was," she continued, "interesting to watch him at the piano. His body seemed to vibrate with his own rhythm; punctuating staccatos with his head, he made the pattern of his music forcibly clear to me, more so than the counting of bars would have done."[5] These piano practices and run-throughs took place at first in the Green Room of the Opéra, where the company was appearing that season. In the final week before the first performance, Stravinsky also attended the orchestral rehearsals of the conductor, Gabriel Pierné, and, as Grigoriev recalls, "endeavored to explain the music; but energetically though the musicians attacked it, they found it no less bewildering than did the dancers." Diaghilev's levelheaded regisseur adds that "rehearsals on the stage were absolutely vital; and so were at least two dress rehearsals, on account of the complicated sets and lighting and, above all, of the music, which sounded quite different when played by the orchestra from what it had sounded like when played on a piano."[6] Bronislava Nijinska, who was dancing one of the enchanted princesses, records that at the first orchestral rehearsal, the sonorities were so unexpected that "many dancers missed their entrances."[7]

For the first, but by no means last, time Stravinsky experienced Diaghilev's genius for brinkmanship, for controlled disorganization, for the last-minute surmounting of insuperable obstacles. The management of the Opéra was obstructive, "as it didn't want to give up the theatre to Russian shows."[8] But the Russians could be their own worst enemies. At the rehearsal on the day before the premiere, Fokine suddenly produced a whole crew of extras for the coronation scene, none of whom, naturally enough, had anything to wear. Diaghilev had to ransack Bilibin's wardrobe for the *Boris Godunov* of two years before in order to clothe them, thereby no doubt enhancing the *Gesamtkunstwerk* feeling of the Ballets Russes' first newly commissioned ballet. One may imagine the confusion in the wings, with this milling throng of amateur thespians getting in the way of the dancers and scene shifters, and trying to avoid the horses that Diaghilev had lined up as mounts for the symbolic horsemen of Night and Day.[9] The chaos is unlikely to have been much alleviated by Diaghilev's decision to direct the complex lighting scenario personally. But it probably had the effect of raising the general temperature, and word soon got around among *le tout Paris,* as well as in Russian émigré circles, that *The Firebird* would be a momentous occasion, too exciting to miss. "I'm staying till the Sunday," the sculptor Stelletsky wrote to the ballet's designer, Alexander Golovine, on 16 June. "I want to see *The Firebird*.... Serov has also put off his departure for this ballet."[10] When the first night came—Saturday the twenty-fifth—the theatre must have glittered with diamonds and tiaras even more than the Mariyinsky on a gala night, while smelling strongly of perfume, as the composer made a point of recording.[11] But the audience, though a typical Diaghilev Almanach de Gotha, did not only consist of the *gratin*—the Paris upper crust. Many leading musicians and artists were also present, intrigued to know what would be Diaghilev's musical equivalent of Fokine, Bakst, and Benois, and attracted by rumors of a notable unveiling. "Mark him well," Diaghilev told his dancers during rehearsals, indicating Stravinsky, "he is a man on the eve of celebrity."[12] And he will have been careful to make sure the word spread. Stravinsky claims to have met Proust, Saint-John Perse, Claudel, Sarah Bernhardt, and, on the stage after the final curtain call, Debussy, who made some kind remarks and invited him to dinner.[13] He may also have met—or have already met—the twenty-one-year-old Jean Cocteau (already a Diaghilev groupie), the composers Ravel, Satie, Falla, Maurice Delage, Florent Schmitt, and Proust's former lover Reynaldo Hahn, the writers André Gide and Gabriele d'Annunzio, as well as Diaghilev's aristocratic patronage committee, headed by Countess Greffuhle, and more informal backers such as Misia Edwards (née Godebski), Charles Ephrussi (one of the models for Proust's Swann), and the sewing-machine heiress the princesse de Polignac (Winnaretta Singer). Perhaps he came close to being mobbed on stage, as Karsavina and Nijinsky had been on the memorable first night of the 1909 season.[14]

No wonder the performance itself remained a blur. Probably it lacked polish in a number of respects, both orchestrally and on the stage. Golovine's sets, according to Benois (who missed the early performances), were enchanting as gouache drawings but essentially untheatrical:

> The artist had depicted Köstchei's gardens in the early morning, just before daybreak, when everything is steeped in a transparent greyness. A group of poisonous toadstools, not unlike Hindu pagodas, symbolized Köstchei's residence; beneath were layers and outlines of different colours, suggesting overgrowths and thickets that were soft, green, damp and close. But although this sketch of Golovine's was indeed a masterpiece, it was absolutely unsuitable as a décor. The greatest experts in stage planning could not have made head or tail of that maze of approximation. It seemed like a huge, chequered carpet, blazing with colour but devoid of any depth.[15]

But Fokine liked the designs: "The garden was like a Persian carpet interwoven with most fantastic vegetation. And the castle was of the most unbelievably sinister-looking architecture. All the scenery was in dark tones, with the golden apples shining eerily."[16]

What struck the Parisian reviewers—perhaps predictably, in view of their earlier demands for a music to match the other elements of the company's work—was the integration of music, dance, and design, into what

Henri Ghéon, writing in the *Nouvelle Revue française,* called "the most exquisite marvel of equilibrium that we have ever imagined between sounds, movements and forms," a "danced symphony" quite unlike the usual type of ballet in which the dance merely illustrated the music.[17] Ghéon thought Stravinsky a "delicious musician." Most of his colleagues praised Stravinsky on the understanding that he was merely the latest—if also the most gifted—in a long line of Russian colorists in the nationalist tradition. In other words he was absorbed, with honors, into the existing picture of the exotic Ballets Russes, the only composer, perhaps, with an originality equal to that of Bakst or Fokine: "the only one who has achieved more than mere attempts to promote Russia's true musical spirit and style."[18]

The sheer brilliance of the music—its dazzling execution and skillful absorption of various elements which could be bundled up and labelled "For Russian Export"—was certainly one reason why nobody seriously commented on its derivativeness or noticed that it hardly satisfied the World of Art ideal of a nationalism purified of old-fashioned ethnic anecdotalism. Today it is easier to hear it as a hotchpotch of kuchkist-type folk-song setting à la Borodin, the "sparkling" academic ballet style of Glazunov, and a few exoticisms from Rimsky-Korsakov and Scriabin—all handled with a flair and expertise that far outdistanced most of its models. Benois might argue that the ballet was disappointing as a total artwork or as a serious treatment of its mythic subject matter, but even he had nothing but praise for the music. "If *L'Oiseau de feu* did not turn out to be exactly what I had dreamed of, the fault does not lie with Stravinsky, for the score is undoubtedly one of his finest creations."[19] But, allowing for that exaggeration about the music, this is a professional view. For the lay public, and even for much of the press, *The Firebird* marked the arrival of the integrated Russian ballet "product." And even for the participants it provided a launching pad for subsequent works which really would justify that kind of description.

In any case the work's triumph was so great that Diaghilev quickly announced a short run of supplementary performances, including two of Stravinsky's ballet to add to the original three. This was the chance for the composer's Russian circle to catch up with music whose success had taken them all, it seems, quite by surprise. Andrey Rimsky-Korsakov and the pianist Nikolay Richter hurried off to Paris to hear for themselves, and Andrey wrote to his mother (and, separately, to Volodya) that he was enchanted by *The Firebird*—music and orchestration—but enraged by *Scheherazade* and the butchery to which it subjected his father's score.[20] Igor, too, seized the opportunity to return to Ustilug, grab his wife, mother, and younger brother, and haul them back to Paris—with, naturally, the two children and their retinue—in time for the final performance on 7 July. He was at Ustilug no more than two days. But he and Katya must there and then have had a major talk, the outcome of which was that they decided not to go home to St. Petersburg but to winter in Switzerland and France. The whole plan is mapped out in his letter to Roerich begun at Ustilug on the second (NS):[21] after Paris they would go to Brittany for the rest of the summer, then to Lausanne, and finally, in November, to Beaulieu-sur-Mer, in the south of France near Nice. But this plan was Igor's alone, not Katya's. It is already outlined in a letter he had dashed off to Nadezhda Rimsky-Korsakov from Berlin, on his way back to Ustilug two days earlier,[22] and it seems inconceivable that there could have been any previous family discussion on the subject.

Why this sudden urge to hibernate? Was it somehow connected with the big Paris success, "which has naturally encouraged Diaghilev in the idea of further collaborations"?[23] Was it a matter of health, the old tubercular bugbear, or simply because Katya was again pregnant and might benefit from sophisticated Western treatment? There is only casual, circumstantial support for these possibilities. Katya's illness did emerge after childbirth, but not for another three and a half years; and there is no specific evidence of ill health in 1910. Katya had had babies fairly happily in St. Petersburg.[24] Health was always an issue, of course, but no more now than at any other time. As for the Diaghilev project, that would have argued for Russia, since Igor was already planning a work with Roerich, who lived in St. Petersburg but was summering at Haapsal in Estonia. Much the most likely explanation is that to live abroad was a "grand plan"—a *grandiozniy plan*," as the composer described it to Roerich—that went with Parisian fame while fulfilling some deep-seated Russian urge to escape from the icy grip of the northern winter. "Igor," Andrey wrote to his mother, "is floating on air at the success of his ballet, and at the praise which has been and still is being showered on him. He's in raptures over the French, and says that only here do you find real taste and art, etc. He's even talking of emigrating completely. All this makes reasonable people very much shake their heads."[25]

Had Igor's own head been ever so slightly turned by his success, as Max Steinberg—who must have been listening to Andrey—told Gnesin?[26] It would have needed a stiff neck to prevent it, certainly. But some Petersburgers would probably have expected it, hoped for it, detected it anyway, like Ziloti's wife, Vera Pavlovna, who told her sister that "Stravinsky has been here . . . puffed up and behaving like a genius being modest."[27] Theodore Stravinsky was later convinced that the move was due to "my mother's delicate health," and Igor himself told Volodya: "[The cost] doesn't matter if it's for the good of the children. Meanwhile it's hard to judge about Katya, since she's in that condition where one always feels well [i.e., pregnant]. How much good the trip will do her—time will tell."[28]

The Stravinskys—including Anna, Gury, Baba Sonya, Bertha Essert, and, it seems, the entire Belyankin family—were in Paris for no more than three days before taking the train to La Baule, at the southern end of the Breton coast, where they settled down in the Villa Mauricette, "a chocolate-coloured chalet in a pinewood."²⁹ La Baule, Igor told Roerich, "is a very modest place, overcrowded with children of all ages."³⁰ Theodore, who was three at the time, later recalled "the cry of the waffle-seller on the beach— *'Arrivez papas, arrivez mamans, faites plaisir à vos enfants'* "—and he remembered his first taste of salt water, which may also, incidentally, have been his father's.³¹ There was constant walking, Igor told Roerich; but bathing is not mentioned, despite (or perhaps because of) his unceasing preoccupation with his family's health.³² His real desire was to get on with his new ballet, *The Great Sacrifice.* But he had lost the piece of paper on which he had scribbled down the scenario he and Roerich had discussed in the spring, and at the end of July—still without a reply from his collaborator—he remained creatively becalmed, unable to do more than sketch ideas for the new score. Meanwhile Diaghilev, having wheedled out of him the existence (if not the details) of the new project, was putting pressure on him to go back to Paris to discuss it; but Stravinsky, short of funds and growing more reticent about his work, refused. Perhaps it was at this moment, among the children of La Baule, that the first ideas for a very different kind of work, about puppets, entered his head.

To fill in time, he spent part of July writing a pair of songs for his brother Gury to sing with piano accompaniment, settings of two well-known Verlaine poems: "Un grand sommeil noir" (from *Sagesse*) and "La lune blanche" (from *La Bonne Chanson*). It was the first time he had set any language but Russian, and perhaps he only did so now because nothing else was to hand.³³ The *Two Poems of Verlaine* are musical siblings: in the same key, and similar in pace, mood, and texture. And though their French declamation is odd, their world is nevertheless studiedly Gallic; Taruskin finds in them echoes of Debussy's *Pelléas*, which Stravinsky tells us he went to see in Paris as the composer's guest.³⁴ There is equally some flavor of Erik Satie. Written for Gury at a time when he was just embarking on his professional career, they are our only material record of the character of his voice, which must have been a dark, lyrical bass-baritone, very even in quality, and somewhat higher in range, as Igor notes, than that of their father.³⁵ But though the composer never heard Gury sing his songs in public, sing them he did, on at least two occasions: with piano, at another St. Petersburg Evenings concert in February 1914, and, perhaps more interestingly, with orchestra at a Moscow concert conducted by Nikolay Malko the following 4 July (OS), on which occasion he sang the songs, as a pair, in Russian, then encored one of them (we do not know which) in French. By a tragic irony, Igor Stravinsky had left Russian territory for good a mere three or four days before. He did not see or hear Gury, and in fact he never saw or heard him again.

Towards the end of August 1910, the family caravan left La Baule and headed via Paris for Switzerland, as Katya's baby was due in September and the plan was for her to have it in a Lausanne clinic. Stravinsky told Craft that they stayed first at Chardonne-Jongny, which is not actually a place but the name of a station serving two villages on the rack-and-pinion railway from Vevey up Mont Pélerin, deep among vineyards on the north shore of Lake Geneva.[36] By the first week of September, in any case, they were firmly ensconced in Lausanne itself, the capital of the French-speaking Canton de Vaud. A long and rambling letter to Volodya, written soon after their arrival, describes the geography of the town and, more helpfully perhaps, the geography of their accommodation in it. Anna, Gury, Baba Sonya, Bertha, and the two children were settled into a pension directly opposite the clinic; Katya and Igor lived in the clinic itself, while Igor also had a small attic room in the pension, where he could compose in peace. And what is he composing? The Verlaine songs, he tells Volodya, he has "already sold to Jurgenson. I'm now working on some larger pieces, after which I shall then start (in due order) the ballet about which you probably know from the papers."[37] These larger pieces were a pair of movements for piano and orchestra, "a sort of Konzertstück" based on "a distinct picture of a puppet, suddenly endowed with life, exasperating the patience of the orchestra with diabolical cascades of arpeggi."[38] Stravinsky must already have seen this in a folk context, since he asks Volodya to send him folk-song collections from Jurgenson's music shop: "such collections as they have, except for the two parts of Nikolay Andreyevich's collection and the first part of Balakirev, which I've got." Something—whether his initial trouble retrieving the Roerich scenario, or political intricacies to do with Diaghilev, or an inability to get down to so daunting a work amid such an unsettled lifestyle—had prompted him temporarily to shelve The Great Sacrifice. On the twenty-third he was present at the birth of his third child, Sviatoslav.[39] By the end of the month the caravan had moved on to the small suburban town of Clarens, between Vevey and Montreux at the eastern end of the lake, a place much favored in the past by writers and musicians (Tchaikovsky had lived here for a time after his disastrous marriage in the winter of 1877–78). They stayed briefly at the Hôtel-Pension du Châtelard, next to the railway, before moving into rooms in a house called Les Tilleuls (The Limes) a few hundred yards up the hill.[40] But the puppet-pianist was still in need of its own midwife, who duly arrived at Clarens a few days later, in the stately and reassuring form of the great impresario himself.

Diaghilev, as we have seen, already knew about The Great Sacrifice. But its very existence raised problems for this profoundly manipulative and political man. He also knew that Fokine had already been involved in discussions with Stravinsky and Roerich about the new ballet,[41] and this did not please him. Fokine, he let it subtly be known, was played out. He, Diaghilev, was tired of this naturalistic genre style of choreographic production, even if, in pure dance terms, it did amount to a revolutionary advance on the rigid old idiom of the Imperial Ballet. In reality, he was jealous of Fokine's independence and, like everyone else who worked with him, resented his overpowering vanity and conceit. Stravinsky had told Roerich that he thought Diaghilev was relieved that Benois was not involved, since Diaghilev and Benois had also rowed (over the visa issue and Diaghilev's misattribution to Bakst of the scenario of *Scheherazade*). But by late July that *froideur* was already thawing, thanks to a diplomatic mission to Lugano by Diaghilev and Nijinsky. On the other hand, Diaghilev did entertain doubts about Roerich and his new scenario.[42] Above all, he detested the idea of a major work being hatched without his involvement, and it was surely this strain of his personality that prompted him to try to divert the young composer into working with his new ally (as he thought) Benois.

That he had already begun this campaign before arriving in Clarens seems certain. As early as 27 July Bakst had reported to his wife that Diaghilev had an idea for a ballet based on Poe's *Masque of the Red Death*, with music commissioned from Stravinsky.[43] But by this time Bakst knew all about *The Great Sacrifice*, having been with Diaghilev when the matter was discussed.[44] Later, on the very day that Stravinsky wrote to Volodya, he also sent a note to Benois assuring him of his intention to collaborate with him after *The Great Sacrifice*, but at the same time pointedly thanking him for having written to Roerich approving of that project.[45] Yet in June Benois had stormed off to Lugano determined to have nothing more to do with the Ballets Russes. So what had changed his mind? Naturally, Diaghilev's visit to Lugano. We can imagine the scene: the master manipulator wooing his injured designer with the possibility of a collaboration with the new star composer, but warning him not to lose the fish by getting his line tangled with Roerich's.[46] Diaghilev knew perfectly well that *The Great Sacrifice* was close to Stravinsky's heart, and that simply to oppose it would be to risk losing him altogether. Lurking in the wings was his bitter enemy Vladimir Telyakovsky, director of the Russian Imperial Theatres. "Has Diaghilev made it up with Fokine?" Stravinsky asked Benois innocently two months later. "This question is very important, since if the answer is yes, then *The Great Sacrifice* will be Diaghilev's, but if no, then it will be for Telyakovsky, which is by no means so good!"[47] Whether or not Fokine was the real issue, it was plain that Diaghilev could not count on Stravinsky at whatever cost.

So when, on his arrival at Clarens, he found Stravinsky at work not on the Roerich project but on a concert piece about a puppet, he seized the opportunity to propose converting it into a stage work with Benois as scenarist and designer. "Yesterday," he wrote to Benois from Clarens, "I heard the music of the Russian Dance and Petrushka's Shrieks which he has just composed. It is a work of such genius that one cannot contemplate anything beyond it. You alone can do it."[48] This letter supports Stravinsky's claim, in his autobiography, that he had already thought of the title—and ipso facto the subject matter—before Diaghilev's appearance,[49] even if his first image, as he told a Paris interviewer in 1928, had been "a long-haired man in a dinner jacket: the musician or poet of romantic tradition [who] sat at the piano and rolled diverse objects over the keyboard while the orchestra burst out in vehement protests, sonic fisticuffs."[50] A more reliable confirmation is a chance remark in a letter to Benois written only a few months after Diaghilev's visit, that "when I was composing *Petrushka* but didn't yet know that this little section would grow into three tableaux, I imagined him giving his performance on the Marsovoye Pole."[51] In any case, the Petrushka subject played straight into Diaghilev's hands. Benois, he knew, was a devotee of the traditional Russian Shrovetide fairground, with its puppet booths and its ice slides, its brass bands and Turkish drums, and its "strong smell of cooking pancakes and 'Berlin' doughnuts, as it mixed with the rising vapours of vodka."[52] He would never be able to resist such a collaboration. "How annoying," Diaghilev slyly wrote to Roerich from Paris a few days later, "that Stravinsky will not have the ballet [i.e., *The Great Sacrifice*] ready for the spring, but *ce qui est remis n'est pas perdu*."[53] Roerich, meanwhile, could, if he liked, design part of Rimsky's *Sadko* for the 1911 season. (He apparently did not like.) Of *Petrushka* there was no mention.

Meanwhile, Benois, by now back in St. Petersburg, was being elusive once again. A long letter from Stravinsky in early November still failed to rouse him from his inertia, and even when, at Igor's request, Gury dropped him a reminder from 66 Kryukov Canal,[54] it took him another month to write, "imploring you to excuse my long, unseemly, and tactless failure to reply to your kind, interesting and in every respect touching letter. But you yourself already know the reason for this distressing state of affairs and why I do not go into the details thereof. Today at last some of the fogs have dispersed. The director has arrived. . . ."[55] Diaghilev, in other words, was being uncommunicative, and Benois, with recent troubles in mind and touchy about his role in the impresario's scheme of things, was not prepared to be neglected. But this delay had the inconvenient result that more music came into being without discussion, a state of affairs very different from what had happened with *The Firebird*. By early November Stravinsky had, he told Benois, written the entire first tableau (of four) apart from the *fokus*—the conjuring trick (whereby the puppets come to life)—as well as the second tableau, the music for which was the original "Petrushka's Shriek." And still there was no detailed scenario. Not until the middle of December 1910 (OS), when Igor would at last wend his way back to his home city for the first time since leaving it in May, would the two finally meet and work out a detailed plan for the new ballet.

But while this new collaboration hung fire, storm clouds were beginning to gather round his oldest and closest St. Petersburg friendships. Already there had been signs—faint but threatening—in Igor's letter to Volodya of early September, a letter full of elaborate self-exonerations for not having written, which barely conceal resentments at not having been written to. An old insecurity, but with new twists. Igor expected some response from his friends to his Paris success (which had been witnessed, after all, by Andrey Rimsky-Korsakov and reported to his family in detail). But he must have sensed a difficulty. It was one thing for him to be among Nikolay Andreyevich's star pupils, but quite another matter for him to shoot off to Paris, of all places, and rocket to stardom in that notoriously frivolous capital without the slightest authority of the best Petersburg judges: those who knew his strengths and weaknesses and could be counted on to sponsor his career in the manner best suited to his talents. Did they really think this way, the Rimskys and the Steinbergs, the Glazunovs and the Gnesins? There is some evidence that they did, or soon would, and plenty of evidence that Igor suspected it of them. Perhaps he even partly deserved it. "Igor is intoxicated with the French," Steinberg had told Gnesin.[56] But how stupid! What the French really liked was mindless ballet dancers prancing around in tights and tutus (or less) to messed-up versions of great Russian music. Look what they had done to *Scheherazade*. Nadezhda Rimsky-Korsakov had let the world know in no uncertain terms what serious musicians thought of such goings-on in a letter to the newspaper *Rech'*, protesting at the butchery of her late husband's work.[57] And what was the result? Diaghilev himself, who everybody knew had been actually rejected as a composition pupil by Rimsky-Korsakov, had the nerve to reply invoking a whole list of French composers as witnesses in his defense—composers like Debussy and Ravel, whose own work flouted the most elementary rules of good compositional practice as taught at the St. Petersburg Conservatoire.[58]

Anyway, St. Petersburg would soon have its chance to pass definitive judgment on Stravinsky's new masterpiece, since Ziloti was including it in his concert on 23 October (OS), and Igor was planning to be there in person to receive the bouquets or the brickbats. He would be going via Moscow (for talks with Jurgenson), he told Andrey, then on to St. Petersburg, where he would see them all and they could talk about the events of the winter.[59] Did he finally lose his nerve, or was he genuinely unable to go for lack of the money to pay his fare?[60] Money certainly was a worry for him. He was supporting a large household in pension accommodation, and his income remained uncertain, despite a five-year contract which he had struck with Diaghilev for performances of *The Firebird*. "You can't imagine," he wrote to Volodya, "what living costs us and what it will go on costing."[61] The seemingly endless moves can hardly have helped. In mid-November, only a week or so after the St. Petersburg concert which Igor had decided not to attend, they were off again, from Clarens to Beaulieu-sur-Mer, a few kilometers from Nice. Here they settled into a first-floor apartment over "a confectioner's where we ate sugared violets and sugared mimosa-blossoms."[62] "It's terribly interesting what this trip has given him," Katya wrote to her mother-in-law (now back in St. Petersburg) after some ten days in Beaulieu, "but I'm afraid that all the same without Benois it will be hard to work everything out properly, as indeed without a ballet master. And for Gimura [Igor] it's difficult to get on with that sort of work."[63]

So it seemed. On the twenty-third he went off on a quick visit to Paris to see Diaghilev, who was shortly going to St. Petersburg. On the twenty-fifth he attended a rehearsal of his *Fireworks* for a concert under Louis Hassl-emans in the Salle Gaveau, and "for the first time I heard my piece in a really good performance. All difficulties were overcome, all my intentions came out, everything shone like gold. I was moved."[64] But he could not stay for the actual concert, having already booked his rail ticket back to Beaulieu. Perhaps that was just as well, since Florent Schmitt reported in *La France* that "a remarkable work by M. Igor Stravinsky went almost unheard thanks to the turbulent indifference of the Parisian judges and jury, most of whom care very little . . . for what we call music."[65]

As for the Ziloti *Firebird*—not the complete ballet, but the original concert suite, ending with the Infernal Dance—all he could do was read the Russian papers and wait for news. Disregarding as far as possible the routine abuse of the daily press ("horrifying poverty of melodic invention," "a lot of notes but not much 'music,' " "risks losing his way . . . in Kashchey's magic garden"),[66] and its grotesque ignorance and stupidity (one critic thought it had been premiered at La Scala, Milan, and was likely to provoke a diplomatic incident between Italy and Russia), he may well have been dismayed to learn from one of the more perceptive and sympathetic Petersburg reviewers that "the loyalist section of our public was incensed by the last item on the program. Many deserted the Assembly of the Nobles during the performance of this suite. I don't doubt," the writer continued, with studied elaborateness, "that for those who have not heard Stravinsky's music, this will be an insufficient argument in its favor, but unfortunately I have no means of giving even the most approximate 'pen portrait' of *The Firebird*."[67] And what about that word "loyalist"? Loyal to what? The answer will have been only too obvious from the review by the older ex-Rimsky pupil Jazeps Vitols, in the German-language *Sankt-Petersburger Zeitung:*

> Stravinsky, it seems, has forgotten the concept of pleasure in sound. His *Scherzo [Fantastique]* and his *Fireworks* already show the path the composer intends to follow; in his ballet *The Firebird* he has covered a fair portion of that journey. We hear about the unusual success which Stravinsky's work had in Paris during the Diaghilev ballet season. Even the envious could not deny the virtuoso handling of the orchestra in the symphonic suite from the work—we've heard nothing like it. . . . All the same, for the most reasonable listener the suite can prompt only recognition together with astonishment, from where, as is well known, it is quite a distance to admiration. Hand in hand with the utmost refinement of instrumental technique on the part of this author goes a clearly marked contempt for the triad and for consonance in general. . . . However, Stravinsky's dissonances unfortunately quickly become wearying, because there are no ideas hidden behind them.

"Where Mr. Stravinsky can go after this music," Vitols went on, "how he can further reinforce his effects—probably only he himself knows; one almost wants to say: 'So young and already so . . . knowing.' One thing Mr. Stravinsky has not yet given us: a theme, an idea, something true and serious, a concept from deep down. Perhaps we don't have the right to demand this from everyone."[68]

"Everyone here," Igor told Andrey, "is amazed and highly indignant at how, judging from the papers, my suite was received."[69] But still there was no personal communication on the subject. "I'm puzzled not to have heard from you," he had written to Andrey less than a week before.

> After the performance of my *Firebird* Suite, mother wrote to me that you would write in detail. I've waited and waited—and have lost patience. Apart from the general wild abuse in the papers, I know nothing. Even Ziloti has not written. I take it very seriously to heart. Not a word from anyone. To tell the truth, I had a right to expect a letter from you. I have received a very short postcard from Steinberg, from whom I also had had no news—except that Ziloti for some reason wanted to cut the Khorovod from the suite and Steinberg defended it, for which I am very grateful to him. But about their own impressions, or the impression made on the Russian musical establishment by my new piece, nobody writes a word, from which I conclude that on all of you, as on the public, my *Firebird* made either a small or a negative impression. It's hard, sometimes even

unbearable, particularly when such a distance separates us and one gets no news.[70]

It was apparently true that Max had dissuaded Ziloti from making this bizarre and senseless cut. Gury, who had travelled home with Anna, had written after a rehearsal on the day before the performance describing Steinberg's "keen participation in the performance." Igor wrote quickly back to Max that

> once again I've had evidence not only of your brilliant memory but also of your truly friendly attitude, which has touched me. Gury writes that you do not approve of the scherzo [the Dance of the Princesses with the Golden Apples] and adagio [Pas de deux]. As regards the former you have a case (to my mind) on grounds of musical style, but as for the latter—this saddens me as I find that it works pretty well and is extremely fantastic.[71]

But Max seems not to have responded to Igor's urgings to write more about his impressions. The failure is hard to account for except on grounds of simple reticence; unable to enthuse wholeheartedly, he could not bring himself to prevaricate, and preferred silence and a principled stand on the point of cuts: an honest but not particularly generous attitude. As for his Rimsky-Korsakov in-laws, the absence of any spontaneous expression of pleasure at their friend's success looks horribly like mean-minded family solidarity. They might have forgiven Igor his success in Paris. But that it should so signally outstrip anything their own father had achieved there, and, what was worse, be associated with equally successful piratings of their father's work—that was more than flesh and blood could stand.

By a supreme irony, *The Firebird* is dedicated to Andrey Rimsky-Korsakov. It might as well have been dedicated to his memory. "Why is it necessary," Igor wrote to him a couple of months later, "to approach my music with a conservative yardstick? Probably so as to beat me on the head with it. Let them beat! If only they would beat! Soon you'll be saying the same. I began with your health, and end with your burial. I'm sorry."[72]

THE RIGHT MAN IN
THE RIGHT PLACE

FOR HIS FIRST BALLET, Stravinsky had had to make do with a ready-made scenario on a given and immutable subject. His second was quite the reverse. Here the idea for the subject was his—even if he had not at first thought of making a stage work out of it—and considerable portions of the music were written before the story was fleshed out to any significant extent. Exactly how far this process had gone by the time Benois became fully involved is hard to decide. Stravinsky later played down Benois's contribution. But that was because he had talked himself into resenting the one-sixth royalty that Benois took from concert performances of the ballet.[1] On the other hand, one has to guard against the opposite tendency. Just because Stravinsky tried to deny Benois's role, it does not follow that that role was either more or less substantial. In fact we know that Benois contributed much detail, a great deal of atmosphere, and an immense reservoir of enthusiasm to this stage treatment of a subject which reminded him of some of the richest and most formative theatrical experiences of his childhood.[2] His designs for the Paris production were unforgettably brilliant and vivid. What is much less clear, however, is how much he contributed initially to the basic elements of the treatment, the various characters and their relationships, the plot, and above all the scenic method, with its different levels of action, its pageantry and intimacy, its theatrical modernism.

Benois's first inkling of the new ballet must have been Diaghilev's coaxing letter from Clarens, a week or so into October. Stravinsky, as we saw, intended to go to St. Petersburg at the start of November for the *Firebird* concert, and for discussions with Benois and Diaghilev about the new ballet. But on 3 November he wrote to Benois that he could not come to Russia, but that, under pressure from Diaghilev, he now planned firmly to compose *Petrushka* before *The Great Sacrifice*.[3] At this stage Benois's participation is far from certain. "If you have been booked to write the ballet with me," Stravinsky writes, "I can't possibly reject the idea." Benois seems not to have replied until just before New Style Christmas, when he at last expressed his readiness "to combine with you in lawful wedlock for bringing our offspring into the world on the boards of the Monte Carlo theatre."⁴

But Stravinsky's letter already assumes a lot of narrative detail. Here is Petrushka, a kind of Punch equivalent, a remote fairground descendant of the commedia dell'arte with its stock tales about Harlequin, Columbine, Pulcinella, Tartaglia, and the rest. Petrushka likewise has his standard plots and routines. He is violent, quarrelsome, deceitful, always in trouble with the law, but of course indestructible, which is why the children love him and identify with his unquenchable anti-authoritarian naughtiness. "Tell Gury," Igor wrote to his mother a few days later, "that my Petrushka is turning out each day completely new and there are new disagreeable traits in his character, but that he delights me because he is absolutely devoid of hypocrisy."⁵ Here too are the black man, the Moor, a minor figure in the original but now promoted into Petrushka's main antagonist and eventually (very uncanonically) his murderer; the Ballerina, a Ballets Russes transmogrification of Columbine, pretty, flirtatious, shallow, but irresistible; and the showman Magician, "who, after the Moor has killed Petrushka, would come on stage, grab all three [puppets], and leave with an elegant and affected bow."⁶ What is hard to establish is how much of this detail had been worked out in collaboration with Benois. In his autobiography, Stravinsky claimed that he and Diaghilev planned it all at Clarens.⁷ However, as we saw, that book is suspect where relations with Benois are concerned. But if Benois had been involved, the question remains: how? No correspondence survives between him and Stravinsky for October 1910, and they almost certainly did not meet, though it is conceivable, if unlikely, that Diaghilev went to Lugano again after Clarens.⁸ Stravinsky assumed, in his early-November letter to Benois, that Diaghilev was by then in St. Petersburg; but he probably was not, and even if he had been, it would not explain how Stravinsky already knew about plot details which are supposed to have originated with Benois.⁹ Nevertheless, Benois claims unequivocally in his own reminiscences to have invented all the essential elements of the scenario himself, including the Blackamoor, the device of bringing the puppets to life, and with it the fundamental contrast between the real world of the fairground and the artificial life of the puppets in their boxes and booths.¹⁰ But in his letter of 9 December, he refers to "your (so far) mysterious account of the ballet [by which] I was again won over. . . . Everything you promise for it pleases me completely." Then only three days later he wrote again, lamenting the difficulty of collaborating at such a distance. Diaghilev had vetted some of his detailed suggestions (in his letter of the ninth) and declared them unworkable in conjunction with the music Stravinsky had already written but which Benois, of course, did not know. "The sorest place," Benois wrote, "is the link between the scenes. In your version the first scene ends with a frenzied dance for the three main characters, and the second begins with Petrushka emoting alone. Then the scene with 'Columbine' ends with a blackout, the Moor kills Petrushka, not Petrushka the Moor. . . ."[11]

In these two letters, Benois offers a mass of intricate scenographic detail which shows, among other things, that he is all the time thinking in terms of the stage design and how it will control or reflect the action. For instance, he invents a positively Feydeauesque scheme of to-ing and fro-ing between the two little houses the Magician has built "by magic" for Petrushka and the Moor. But not much of this found its way into the final scenario. On the other hand, there is still no clear elaboration of the crowd scenes which became such a striking and essential feature of the ballet. At this stage the fairground crowd is still merely part of the setting, like the chorus in an Italian opera. By the time of his November letter Stravinsky has composed the opening carnival music,[12] which would presumably involve the corps de ballet. In *his* letters Benois elaborates the role of the crowd in the final scene, ending with "a general dance with illuminations, a quadrille for the officers and ladies, and lastly a general final dance with crashings and janglings."[13] But this ending was soon rejected, leaving a vacuum which it took the composer another four months to fill. Meanwhile, Benois's workings are essentially in the spirit of the old-fashioned *ballet d'action*, of the kind that Fokine could be relied on to embody in his new kind of flexible, psychologically precise choreography.

The missing element was the main subject of discussion when Stravinsky at last arrived in St. Petersburg at about Christmas (OS).[14] With Diaghilev's return, the familiar daily World of Art meetings at his flat had started up again, just as in previous years, with Diaghilev's old *nyanya* serving tea and *bubliki*. Now Stravinsky could play them his music. "What I now heard," Benois later wrote, "surpassed my expectations."[15] And perhaps it also transformed his mental picture of the stage. Did he, as he listened to what Diaghilev had described to him in advance as the "parade of Russian music" in the Russkaya, or Russian Dance, suddenly glimpse the wonderful procession of peasant and proletarian characters—the wet nurses and coachmen, the peasant with his bear, the Gypsies and the dashing young merchant[16]—who dominate the final tableau and set the scene for its dénouement? These types presumably at any rate emerged from the discussions, along with the idea of the "masked revellers," which, Benois tells us, was the composer's own contribution.[17] We can catch something of this whole imaginative picture in Stravinsky's own account of the trip to Andrey: "My last Petersburg visit seems to have done me a lot of good. The final act is turning out interestingly, continuous quick tempi and major keys somehow redolent of Russian food—cabbage soup maybe, bottleboots, the *garmoshka* [concertina]—ecstasy! excitement! What's Monte Carlo? There you can't even smoke in the Salle de Jeu!"[18]

Within little more than a fortnight of returning from St. Petersburg to Beaulieu Stravinsky had composed most of the music for this new sequence of dances, as he told Benois, "so that there remains only the end of the fourth scene—the 'masks,' the 'drama,' the 'cripples,' and the 'revelry.' "[19] And during that time he also rewrote the barrel-organ scene in the first tableau, substituting a music box for the second organ grinder, who had been meant to appear on the opposite side of the stage to the first one.[20] In both cases, the composer himself was also responsible for the scenic detail, questions of musical substance being on each occasion woven into the action. In the organ-grinding scene, instead of giving the second organ grinder and his dancer exactly the same pair of tunes as the first, he gives the sequence twice to the same musician and dancer but with the music box playing a kind of quodlibet against them, rather in the manner of the minuet in Mozart's *Don Giovanni*. For the final tableau, Benois gets a blow-by-blow account of the dancing bear and the scene with the merchant, complete with timings. Here again there is music on stage:

> Gradually a carousel starts to warm up and play, for a time dies right down, starts up again, and to it, or rather in spite of it (because the merchant actually doesn't dance to the carousel, but crawls out of the tavern independently) . . . he dances to some kind of music which emerges with the steam of the cabbage soup from the inn. After that he squeezes his *garmoshka,* then again dances to the accompaniment of the inn, then again the *garmoshka,* then the carousel starts up, and our merchant passes on, as at the start, with his theme.[21]

But Stravinsky had actually anticipated Benois's enthusiasm for the sounds and smells of old St. Petersburg. He had even solicited Andrey's help with certain popular tunes he intended to incorporate in the work. A week or two before his St. Petersburg trip (and before he knew he would be making it), he got Andrey to send a pair of street songs he had once heard him and Volodya singing.[22] (He later recalled that Andrey "did send the music, but with words of his own fitted to it, facetious in intent, but in fact questioning my right to use such 'trash.' ")[23] Then one day in January at Beaulieu he and Maurice Delage, who was staying with him, overheard a hurdy-gurdy in the street below the first-floor window, playing a tune that struck him as suitable for the organ-grinder scene in the first tableau— and perhaps even suggested it, since this part of the score had otherwise already been written. The first barrel-organ tune and the music box were Andrey's, but the second barrel-organ tune is the Beaulieu *trouvaille,* "Elle avait un' jambe en bois," which to Stravinsky's chagrin turned out to be in copyright, and was therefore to cost him a significant percentage of his *Petrushka* royalties for the rest of his life.[24] More to the point musically, this tawdry little tune is very similar in general character to the Russian street tunes with which it keeps company in the ballet; and it was precisely that gimcrack quality—the cheapness of urban rather than rustic popular music—to which the Rimsky-Korsakovs, with their academy-biased view of folk song, objected.

What the Rimskys could not see was what Stravinsky was going to do with this kind of material, how he would enliven it in a completely new way. They apparently discussed such questions while Igor was in St. Petersburg. "All these arguments of Gnesin's about this current work of mine's supposed 'reflex' reaction against Russian music are sheer nonsense," he told Andrey:

> Gnesin is a clever and subtle man, but he's *spoiled*. His opinions suffer from the same one-sidedness—pernicious one-sidedness—as those well-known views about the Russian style of Roerich, Bilibin, Stelletsky, as compared with the Repins, the Perovs, the Pryanishnikovs, the Ryabushkins, and the rest. I value these latter very highly, but does that mean that Roerich, Bilibin, and Stelletsky are any less Russian for me?[25]

In other words, why regard the neonationalists (Roerich and company) as in some way traitors to Russian art just because they looked at Russianism in a different way from the old *peredvizhniki* realists? For the academics of the New Russian School the question itself was heretical. And not surprisingly this position was seized on by Andrey and Volodya as part of their defense of their father's standing. All the less would they admit the virtue of Stravinsky's earthy and untheoretical bundling together of different kinds of popular music into a sort of musical *lubok,* or colored peasant print,[26] for the fact was that it seemed to them to challenge the continuity of the Rimsky school, while at the same time threatening to relegate it to the status of a mere provincial irrelevance. Stravinsky, of course, knew what they were thinking. "What's wrong with you, my friend, that you don't write?" he asks Andrey, knowing full well. But in fact the troubles between them were only just beginning.

The staging of *Petrushka,* of course, would have to reflect the musical idiom, but above all it would be conditioned by the changing levels of the action. The Petersburg stage had already witnessed a number of experiments based on the stylization in puppet shows and various ideas lifted from the ancient theatre of masks—from Greek drama to the commedia dell'arte. Vsevolod Meyerhold's production of Blok's symbolist play *Balaganchik* (The Fairground Booth) in December 1906—one of many stage works of the time that drew on the characters of the commedia—had played in an artificial box set which could be lifted bodily into the flies in full view of the audience. Benois himself had recently been involved in staging a Petrushka play by Pyotr Potyomkin in which masked actors had performed "with their heads over the edge of a curtain and little wooden legs dangling below"—an effect, he recalled, "more pitiful than funny."[27] In any case, a device like that obviously would not do for dancers. In the ballet, the crucial element would be the contrast of aspect between the wide-angle effect of the crowd scenes and the close-ups of the puppets in their boxes. In his reminiscences, Benois claims that "I suddenly *saw* how this ballet ought to be presented."[28] But the evidence of the correspondence is that the "virtual" aspect of the stage handling only developed gradually out of the idea of bringing the puppets to life. In a January letter which has not survived, Benois suggested using ceremonious devices such as drumrolls, whistles, or gong strokes as markers for the different incidents—especially, one might suppose, for the different *levels* of incident.[29] There was already a musical precedent, since Stravinsky, perhaps at Benois's suggestion, had composed a timpani and side-drum tattoo by way of introduction to the conjuring trick episode, in which the Magician brings the three puppets to life. But at this point Stravinsky raised an objection which shows that he was still thinking in a somewhat literal way about the work's dramaturgy. He pointed out that it would be a mistake to use the same tattoo idea as a signal to the stage crowd (as in the trick) and as a link between scenes, which would be a signal to the theatre audience.[30] Oddly enough, Benois seems to have accepted the objection, since Stravinsky's next letter deals with the physical consequences of omitting the drumroll link between the different tableaux. Either Petrushka will have no chance to catch his breath after the hectic Russian Dance, or Stravinsky, already short of time, will have to compose another whole minute of linking music.[31] Finally the drumroll link was retained, in the distance, without timpani, but with interpolated woodwind figures: a somewhat belated recognition of the fact that in the theatre of masks and puppets it is precisely such devices, blurring the distinction between stage and auditorium, that help give the drama its special magic.

Stravinsky worked hard at Beaulieu throughout January and February. On 25 January he was able to send Diaghilev the completed four-hand piano score of the first tableau. By early March the first three tableaux were ready in piano score, the first tableau was fully scored, and Stravinsky was expressing optimism about a rapid completion of the whole work.[32] At this point he suddenly fell inconveniently ill, with what "was diagnosed as intercostal neuralgia caused by nicotine poisoning."[33] In his autobiography he claimed to have been "at the point of death, this illness causing a month of enforced idleness."[34] But there is no mention of it in a letter of 7 March to Andrey Rimsky-Korsakov, although the letter includes a health bulletin (his children have whooping cough, and he himself has a cough and a cold),[35] while by the twenty-sixth he could write to Andrey's mother, in reply to what was presumably a get-well telegram, that "I am now better. I've already started working, but I've given up smoking for a while. My strength is gradually coming back."[36] Even a two-week illness, though, was more than he could afford in the circumstances, and by 6 April, when the Ballets Russes opened their first Riviera season in the ornate Théâtre de Monte-Carlo, the problem of the work's ending was still unresolved.

The problem was dramaturgical as much as musical. Writing in mid-March to Alexander Ossovsky, the St. Petersburg manager of Sergey Koussevitzky's new Rossiyskoye muzïkal'noye izdatel'stvo (Russian Music Edition, known early on as Russische Musikverlag, or RMV, since it was based in Berlin), the composer outlines a scenario which, in the fourth tableau, still preserves the final bacchanalian dance that was Benois's original idea for the ending, after the Magician has picked up Petrushka's corpse and revealed it to be full of sawdust.[37] But Stravinsky does not, of course, tell Ossovsky, a potential publisher, that the ending is causing difficulties. On the contrary, he shows himself already able to negotiate with a shrewd sense of his own advantage. He lets Ossovsky know that he is second in the queue for the new work. He coolly prevaricates about the terms of his *Firebird* agreement with Jurgenson—"2,000 roubles honorarium and printing of full score and parts"—whereas he had told Andrey Rimsky-Korsakov that "our *Firebird* has been sold to Jurgenson on quite favorable terms. He is printing everything—score, parts, piano score—for 1,500 gold roubles!"[38] But there seems little doubt that he was keen for an agreement with Koussevitzky's prestigious and well-funded enterprise. For some reason he seems to have had doubts about Jurgenson; and though Jurgenson was at this moment bringing out several of his works in print, Stravinsky went on resisting all his proposals for a long-term contract.[39] Meanwhile, by the end of April an informal agreement had been struck with RMV, and the printing of the still incomplete *Petrushka* materials, by this time a matter of considerable urgency, had been put in hand.

With Diaghilev and his company established in April in Monte Carlo, Stravinsky frequently made the seven-mile journey from Beaulieu, either to the disused Palais du Soleil theatre, where the company was rehearsing, or to the Riviera-Palace hotel at Beausoleil, above the town, where Diaghilev and his premier danseur, Vaslav Nijinsky, were staying. He probably went to the opening performance, of *Giselle* and *Scheherazade*, on the ninth, and he was almost certainly at *The Underwater Kingdom*, a ballet based on the second act of Rimsky-Korsakov's opera *Sadko*, on the nineteenth, and the new Tcherepnin ballet, *Narcisse*, on the twenty-sixth, after which he wrote to Andrey that it was "a superb piece—his best composition. Delightful dances."[40] About the *Sadko* ballet he was naturally silent to

Andrey, though he certainly saw it, either in Monte Carlo or in Paris in June, since the following month he wrote to Volodya defending the concept but attacking Fokine's choreography.[41] Both Benois and, of course, Fokine himself were in Monte Carlo, and they will doubtless have discussed *Petrushka*—the staging in general and perhaps the still unresolved ending in particular. But no preliminary rehearsals seem to have taken place, since Fokine was too busy working on the new Monte Carlo repertoire, which also included the Weber ballet *Le Spectre de la rose*.[42] Between Monte Carlo and Paris Diaghilev had arranged a two-week season at the Teatro Costanzi in Rome, as part of the World Exhibition of Art, and it was in the Italian capital that Stravinsky would have willy-nilly to compose the final pages of the ballet, and Fokine invent and rehearse his choreography from scratch.

The Stravinskys left Beaulieu for good on 6 May. They travelled together as far as Genoa, where they separated, Igor continuing on to Rome while Katya and the rest of the family set off via Basle and Berlin for the summer at Ustilug. "I'm terribly worried about their move," he wrote to his mother (and Gury) from Rome, "but I couldn't possibly go with them as I had barely enough time."[43] In his hotel, the Albergo d'Italia, near the Piazza Barberini, he worked away feverishly on the ending of the ballet, while Vera Nosenko, who was in Rome studying medicine, read the proofs of the first three tableaux and looked after him "very diligently. She orders me to take powders, valerian, and in general everything that can still be done mechanically . . . ruling me with a rod of iron—all thanks to her, dear soul."[44] Clearly, relations with Katya's Nosenko cousins had improved since the early Ustilug days. Benois and the painter Valentin Serov and his wife were staying in the same hotel: "We sit next to them at the *table d'hôte*," Igor told Anna. "Very nice." The composer had a piano moved into his hotel room, and there at last he worked out the wonderful, enigmatic ending of the ballet: the brief pursuit, the murder, the Magician's revelation that Petrushka is only a puppet, the apparition of Petrushka's ghost, and the Magician's frightened exit. From his own room every morning Benois overheard "a confused tangle of sounds, interrupted from time to time by long pauses . . . the maturing of the last bars of the fourth act."

> When everything was ready, *Petrouchka* was played to Diaghilev and me from beginning to end. Diaghilev was no less delighted with it than I; the only thing he argued about was the "note of interrogation" with which the ballet score ended. For a long time he would not agree to it, but demanded a more traditional solution—a curious proof of how strongly influenced Diaghilev was by "academic prejudice" even in 1911![45]

Oddly enough, Benois never directly claimed credit for this ending, though it is consistent with an idea he had had early on of "the weary, jealously coquettish Petrushka who finally loses patience and thanks to this frees himself from the depraved spell of the Magician,"[46] except that for Benois Petrushka's freedom had depended on his killing rather than being killed by the Moor. The Hoffmannesque idea of the living spirit instilled in him by the Magician actually escaping to freedom at the very moment of the puppet's "death" does seem to have been Stravinsky's, as he later claimed. As for the music, with its subtle transformation of the accordion-like carousel theme, its deliciously pungent scoring for oboes, horns, and trumpets, and the quizzical, tonally ambiguous pizzicato ending which so puzzled Diaghilev, no wonder the composer was, and remained, "more proud of these last pages than of anything else in the score."[47] Their only-apparent simplicity was symptomatic of the sheer moral effort of discarding precisely the conventional, bacchanalian finale which Diaghilev wanted and which had always also been Benois's idea of the actual ending.

It took Stravinsky nearly three weeks in Rome to finish his score, and meanwhile, rehearsals began which demanded his participation. He attended program-planning meetings with Benois, Tcherepnin, Fokine, Grigoriev, and presumably Diaghilev himself.[48] And he and Benois still found time for sightseeing with the Serovs and Tamara Karsavina and her husband, and for excursions to Albano and Tivoli, each an hour or so away by train. In the evenings, starting on the fourteenth, they went to the company's performances, which included the Benois-Tcherepnin *Pavillon d'Armide* but not Stravinsky's *Firebird*.

The rehearsals for *Petrushka* took place in a basement canteen of the Teatro Costanzi, "to the accompaniment of noises not dissimilar to a boiler factory and the thud of machinery."[49] After a spell of wet weather early on, it became hot and suffocatingly oppressive in that cellar full of dancers working flat out to prepare a complicated and innovatory ballet in insufficient time. Benois drew Stravinsky at the piano in his waistcoat, "his only concession to the heat and fatigue, [and then only] after a proper apology for appearing in shirtsleeves."[50] A marginal note on the drawing records the fact that "Fokine can make *nothing* of the rhythms of the Coachmen's dance!"[51] But for Fokine "the Dance of the Coachmen [was] the most pleasing to me," and it was Nijinsky, as Petrushka, who "was not too strong musically and [for whom] counting was a problem." Nor was Nijinsky alone, Fokine says: "I worked quickly and pleasantly, but I must admit that with Stravinsky's music, composition cannot progress so rapidly as with Chopin or Schumann. It was necessary to explain the musical counts to the dancers. At times it was especially difficult to remember the rapid changes of the counts. . . . It was necessary to stop continually and make excursions into mathematics."[52] Fokine ends by blaming Stravinsky for unnecessary rhythmic complication; in the masquerade section of the finale, for instance, "I believe that Stravinsky could have achieved the same musical result with a more natural rhythm for this dance."[53] He then claims the main credit for turning Stravinsky's (and Benois's) "tediously static crowd on stage" into "a gay and merry one." But the truth is evidently that Fokine, now officially Diaghilev's choreographic director, was finding it harder and harder to accept the modernistic tendencies in Stravinsky's work; moreover, he was in a state of nerves at the shortage of time and the quantity of work to be done. Karsavina, who was dancing the Ballerina, recalled him "ruffling his hair, enervated, hysterical; reprimands and tears and general tension electrifying the atmosphere."[54] Fokine tormented Nijinksy, Igor told Gury, "to the point where it was impossible to speak to him."[55] "If you only knew," Igor wrote to Volodya two months after the event, "what improbable efforts and what unpleasantness the production of *Petrushka* cost Benois and me because of Fokine's capriciousness and despotism and, at the same time, lack of sensitivity."[56] The collaboration hardly promised well for the future.

From Rome, the dancers went to Paris at the start of June, only a few days before the opening of the season at the Théâtre du Châtelet, their first in Paris as a permanent company. *Petrushka* was to open on the thirteenth, but still it was far from ready. There was trouble with the orchestra, who, according to Prince Peter Lieven, burst out laughing when they first saw their music.[57] There was trouble with the sets, which had arrived from Russia in a damaged state; and there were technical difficulties over the sheer number of props the work demanded, which meant that the ballet always had to be first on the bill.[58] Finally there was the now seemingly inevitable row between Diaghilev and Benois, who was incensed at Bakst's retouching of the damaged portrait of the Magician which glowered down on Petrushka in the second tableau. Grigoriev, as ever Diaghilev's calm center, paints a picture of almost overwhelming chaos at the dress rehearsal, with Stravinsky and Fokine still arguing about tempi, the dancers complaining of lack of room to dance, and the lighting—as in *The Firebird*—in complete disarray.[59] The stage rehearsal on the eleventh had gone on till past midnight, Katya Stravinsky reported from Paris to her mother-in-law, while Diaghilev tinkered with the lighting.[60] Even as the curtain was due to go up on the first performance, there was a twenty-minute delay while Misia Edwards found four thousand francs to enable Diaghilev to pay off his costumier.[61]

Yet once again the success was overwhelming. The transformation was partly due to Nijinsky, who, after seeming lackluster and even uncomprehending during rehearsals, was suddenly transfigured "when he put on his costume and covered his face with make-up."[62] But Karsavina as the brainless Ballerina, Alexander Orlov as the Blackamoor, and the old Mariyinsky ballet master Enrico Cecchetti as the Magician were all excellent, and the production, with its precisely observed and calculated detail, suddenly showed the Parisian audience—used to equating Russianism with the fantastic, the sensuous, or the barbaric—a cooler, more oblique, artistically more truthful kind of theatrical folklorism. As for the music, under the thirty-six-year-old French conductor Pierre Monteux, "in many respects [it] surpassed *Firebird*," Igor reported to Volodya; "its success was colossal and increasing. [But] you're wrong to think that the press was bought off by Diaghilev. From this I can see that you're not au courant. This year the press took absolutely no interest, and all those who have got into the way of hurling abuse at the time of the Russian Season hurled abuse."[63]

In fact this was not strictly true. *Petrushka* was both widely and on the whole appreciatively noticed, and the negative comments of more conservative critics like Pierre Lalo and Gaston Carraud were more or less candidly associated with disgruntlement at the late cancellation of Dukas's *La Péri*, which they took as a direct snub to the Ballets Russes' French hosts. No "buying off" there. On the other hand, Alfred Bruneau, reviewing the rehearsal of the twelfth, was in seventh heaven over the new work's

> prodigious intensity of movement and color. It conveys equally well the amusing hubbub of the public festivities and the poignant anguish of the hero. It is at once burlesque and pathetic. Its rhythms have a vigor, an inexhaustible verve. The sounds of the piano, mixed with those of the orchestra, give it a quite new character. Its orchestration, amusing, subtle, flavorsome, has an extraordinary sonic richness. Its form possesses complete freedom. I do not conceal my joy at having heard it. . . .[64]

"*Petrushka*," Louis Vuillemin enthused in the arts daily *Comoedia*, "is a marvel. . . . It is quite simply astonishing. . . . There is not an indifferent bar. And what boldness in the orchestral layout! What fluency! What life! What youth!" And he noted with awe that "even the rehearsal received an ovation."[65] But perhaps the shrewdest criticism of all was uttered in private, by Katya in a second letter to Anna Stravinsky:

> I had to listen to a mass of banal compliments from a lot of people, whose opinions were pretty indifferent and scarcely sincere. . . . All the same we were quite dissatisfied with the performance in places, and, strange as it may seem, the coachmen and wet nurses went mostly better than we expected, while the scene with the Blackamoor was quite indifferent. Nijinsky proved a real artist and did Petrushka

superlatively, moving, and with deep feeling. And after all there was nothing easy for him, none of his leaps, no display, it was completely new for him and he made of it something utterly beautiful. Karsavina was charming. Benois's costumes and decors were marvellous. I only find that there's not enough room for the crowds. . . . At the actual performance there was the same success, a lot of applause, Gima was called out, and again praise and enthusiasm, sincere and insincere.[66]

On French musicians, many of them (like Ravel, Delage, and Schmitt) already at least passive admirers of *The Firebird*, the new work made a powerful impression. Six months later the forty-nine-year-old Debussy, who had got to know Stravinsky during the previous Paris season, wrote to his friend the Swiss musicologist Robert Godet:

Do you realize that near you at Clarens is a young Russian musician: Igor Stravinsky, who has an instinctive genius for color and rhythm? I am sure that he and his music will give you infinite pleasure. . . . And then it doesn't "show off"! It's made of real orchestral stuff, directly, in a way which concerns itself only with the events of its own emotion. There is neither caution nor pretension. It's childlike and untamed. Yet the execution is extremely delicate. If you get a chance to meet him, don't hesitate.[67]

Later, Debussy praised *Petrushka* to its composer: "I do not know many things as good as the passage you call the Conjuring Trick. There is in it a kind of sonorous magic, a sort of mysterious transformation of mechanical souls, which become human by a spell of which, until now, you seem to be the sole inventor. Finally there are orchestral certainties that I have found only in *Parsifal*. I'm sure you will understand what I mean."[68] Debussy was not afraid to pay Stravinsky the even sincerer flattery of at least discreet imitation. Many things in his later piano music, but also in the as yet unwritten parts of the orchestral *Images*, and even the Diaghilev ballet *Jeux*, seem distinctly affected by *Petrushka*, though such things have to be understood in the light of the existing strong Russian influence on the French master.

As for the Russians themselves, they had to wait more than a year and a half before hearing a note of *Petrushka*. The first fragments were played at a St. Petersburg concert conducted by Koussevitzky, whose RMV had by that time published the score, on 23 January 1913 (OS), and a week later in Moscow. This, and all subsequent pre–First World War performances in Russia, consisted of the same three movements, which coincided with the movements the composer subsequently turned into a concert piece for piano solo: that is, the original Russian Dance and second tableau ("Petrushka's Shriek"), plus the final tableau with concert ending. So the generally uncomprehending reaction in the public prints, which often included the view that the work was illustrative theatre music that could not succeed in concert form, was entirely based on performances which omitted the opening carnival scene up to and including the conjuring trick, as well as the whole third tableau and the—admittedly strange—final pages of the fourth. Even Max Steinberg succumbed to this view and made bold to tell Stravinsky so.[69] But not all Russian musicians and critics were impervious to the fascination and vitality of the music, heard for itself. The young Moscow composer Nikolay Myaskovsky, reviewing the work from the proof score and without having heard a note of it or seen a step of the ballet, echoed Vuillemin in describing the music as "life itself."

> All its music is full of such ardor, freshness, wit, such healthy, incorruptible gaiety, such reckless daring, that all those deliberate vulgarities, trivialities, that constant accordion background, not only do not repel but, on the contrary, entice all the more. . . . The music of this extraordinary ballet is so integrated, suffused from first note to last with such an all-consuming ardor and inexhaustible humor, that you completely lose the desire to embark on a more detailed scrutiny—it would be like dissecting a living organism.[70]

After the Petersburg premiere, Myaskovsky wrote to the twenty-one-year-old Sergey Prokofiev that the music had "turned out still more enchanting than in the score."[71] But Prokofiev's opinion was much more grudging. After making the usual point about illustrative music, and offering a word of praise for the orchestration, he asks:

> Is there any music in the ballet or not? Yes and no—no and yes. No doubt there's many a place in the ballet where the music is out and out good, but a huge part of it is modernist padding. However, in what circumstances does he bring in padding? When, in general, is padding permissible (if it is in general permissible)? It seems to me, at the official or boring places, prompted by an unsuccessful scenario. And Stravinsky? He writes at the most interesting moments, at the liveliest points of the staging, not music but something that might brilliantly illustrate the moment. And this something is nothing but padding. But if he can't write music for the most crucial parts, but fills them up with any old thing, then he's musically bankrupt. And if we can agree that Stravinsky makes a hole in a new door, it's a small hole, made with a very sharp topical little knife, and not with a big axe, which would give him the right to be called a titan.[72]

For Russians, it should be emphasized, *Petrushka* presented a special challenge of which foreign audiences and musicians have always been largely unaware. The borrowed tunes—the urban popular songs, the rural folk songs, the tradesmen's cries—were so well known to ordinary Russians that it was genuinely hard for them to hear the work as in the fullest sense an original product, rather than just a brilliantly assembled, stunningly orchestrated medley stitched together with a few pages of bizarre, no doubt clever, but ultimately insubstantial mood music: "modernist padding," as Prokofiev called it. Stravinsky, he probably meant to imply, had thrown out of the window all the solid precepts of good Petersburg composition teaching in favor of a few harmonic tricks pinched from Debussy, Ravel, and company, and, having no ideas of his own, had simply raided the common pool of more or less vulgar melodies, which Parisians did not know and would not judge at their true worth. The fact that Paris had fallen for it hook, line, and sinker was naturally galling to a conservatory-taught Petersburg composer like Prokofiev, however modernist in his own tastes. For those numerous musicians and critics who lacked Prokofiev's stomach for modernism the work's foreign success was even harder to take. For Stravinsky's own closest friends and associates, the family and fellow pupils of Nikolay Rimsky-Korsakov, it was hardest of all, since it so clearly tended to marginalize everything that guaranteed their own status, and threw a sharp and penetrating light into their provincial little fishpond. Many—though not quite all—of them duly reacted like blinking fish.

Petrushka itself, of course, easily outlived such anxieties, and never lost a shred of its early popularity. But what precisely was its deeper artistic significance at the time? For Benois and other artists of the Diaghilev circle, it was quite simply the perfect manifestation of the World of Art spirit on the stage. For one thing, it was a proper *Gesamtkunstwerk:* despite the purely musical origin of the concept, in the final product music, scenario, stage design, and dance seemed to have been invented all of a piece out of the spirit of Russian popular art and with complete disregard for the clichés and conventions of those various disciplines. Just as the whole style of the music seemed to have emerged from the character of its ideas, so Fokine had found a completely new dance idiom for the puppets and the *lubok* "types" of the final tableau, free of almost all (except ironic) reference to classical routines; and Benois, in his scenario and designs, had brilliantly hit off the special character of Russian life, not through a Repinesque, Ryabushkinesque heightened realism, but through a gallery of colorful stylizations which actually caught a deeper symbolic reality by filtering out the individualities, the private agonies, the rights and wrongs which—in the World of Art view—had come between the old realist art and the pictorial essence of its subject matter.

Stravinsky, as we saw, was slow to grasp this symbolic aspect of the staging. But his music sensed it from the start. His Russian Dance, one of the two concert pieces that antedated the ballet project, is based on a pair of folk tunes from published collections,[73] but it certainly is not a setting of them in any sense that Musorgsky or Borodin would have understood. Stravinsky simply takes figures from the tunes and plays with them in a semi-improvisatory way, varying the rhythms, allowing the accents to fall in different places, teasing the melodic design into subtly different shapes, while accompanying the whole thing, not with textbook harmonies like the ones Rimsky-Korsakov and others used in their collections, but with mechanical patterns—drone figures, repeated or parallel chords such as one might play on a piano or an accordion with an absolutely rigid hand, or little fragments of melody played over and over but with slight hiccoughs (as if a needle had jumped across a groove on a gramophone record).

This fractured realism—while brilliantly apt for a trio of mechanical dolls in the process of coming to life—is something inherently stylized and pattern-based, and much concerned with the motif as an abstract entity, certainly not with the folk song as a pickled version of peasant life as such. In this it clearly resembles the work of neonationalist painters and designers like Bilibin. But the comparison should not be pressed too far. Because music is what it is—and, one has to add, because Stravinsky was what he was—the treatment of rhythmic and melodic pattern and of orchestral color in Petrushka was to have consequences far beyond the comparatively limited resonances of neonationalist design or the World of Art. It heralded a complete change in the way musicians, and in particular creative musicians, thought about music. It freed rhythm once and for all from the old regularities, the old four-bar schemes, and allowed it to react directly to variations in the melodic phrase. In the same way, harmony, instead of obeying textbook grammatical rules, became simply a matter of sonority allied to melody—a sort of "field," like the din of a crowd before the ear has had time to (or if it has decided not to) pick out individual voices. The consequences of such freedoms would soon be very apparent in Stravinsky's own work. The fact that, for the time being, he was able to present them in so highly palatable a form, at a time when modern music was increasingly taking refuge in private worlds of agonized expression and opaque language, is not the least achievement of this dazzling score. Such things cannot be explained historically. They depend exclusively on the right man being in the right place at the right time.

RUE SACRE DU PRINTEMPS

IN ALL, FOUR PERFORMANCES of *Petrushka* were given, in rapid succession, before the season ended on 17 June. The next day the company set off for their first appearance in London. But as neither Stravinsky ballet was on the program (owing to Diaghilev's theory that the English public was not yet ready for such advanced work), Igor and Katya left that same day to rejoin the rest of their family at Ustilug in time for the Ukrainian summer "with its juicy fruit and the white strawberries smelling of pineapple."[1]

But the young parents had no plans for an idle summer. Katya would be kept busy by her three small children and supervising their supervisors, running a household of ten or more, and managing the kitchen gardens, orchards, and plantations which had been laid out round the new house four years before. But hers was also the strain of worrying helplessly about Igor's work and absences. "Today," she wrote to her mother-in-law after he had gone off to Karlsbad to see Diaghilev in August, "I'm particularly sad and depressed without Gimura; he's so far from me! In general I'm specially longing for his return this time. When he went to Smolensk, it wasn't so gloomy, since you were here and it was for less long and not so far. And it still bothers me that Gimochka hasn't written at all."[2]

For Igor himself, *The Great Sacrifice* was looming, and he was also faced with the tiresome and time-consuming task of proofreading the as yet unpublished full score of *The Firebird,* and all the materials for *Petrushka,* which were being prepared simultaneously by different publishers. He would in effect be dealing with all three of these drastically different works at once. As it happened, things worked out otherwise. Still plagued by the lack of a definitive scenario, he made up his mind to delay starting on the new ballet until the end of the summer, and meanwhile wrote to Roerich urging on him a meeting at the estate of Princess Tenisheva at Talashkino, near Smolensk, where Roerich was working on the interior painting of the estate's new neonationalist church.[3] But Roerich was not expected at Talashkino until mid-July. In the meantime, Igor hatched two smaller works, revived plans for an old, larger one, fussed about his itinerary for the next year, and set about mending (or at least locating) fences with his

Russian friends, from whom he had been so suddenly and dramatically cut off by geography and art the previous year.

Volodya Rimsky-Korsakov had written to Gury, expressing curiosity about *Petrushka* but attacking Diaghilev for continuing to stage excerpted versions of his father's music in ballet form. He seems also to have inquired about Igor's plans for the coming year, and to have asked Gury, not without a certain sly incredulity, about his brother's real standing in the eyes of competent Parisian musicians.[4] The Rimsky-Korsakovs really did suppose Igor's success to be a seven-day wonder, probably achieved by buying off the press. So Gury had to point out that his brother was also being lionized in the more discriminating salons, and indeed had made his mark so firmly among connoisseurs of music and the arts, and felt such an affinity with them, that he had made up his mind to settle in Paris for the year: "very sad for us, another year's separation, which for us, with our close-knit friendship, will be a very sensitive time."[5] But Gury was out of date, for on the very same day Igor wrote to Benois that "at first I had a plan to live in Paris, but circumstances have now changed owing to the children's poor health, and we've decided to spend at least part of the winter (until January, that is) at Clarens."[6] The Rimskys would have to swallow their pride: Paris was ruled out only by health, whereas St. Petersburg was simply ruled out—it was not just too cold but too provincial and, to read between the lines of both brothers' letters, frankly insufferable. "You know, my dear," Igor would tell Andrey a few weeks later, "that it's better [at Clarens] not only for the family but also for me. It's necessary for me to get spiritually stronger. At home I become a real neurasthenic."[7] Why? Because, Gury told Volodya, "he is now working hard, and can only manage when he doesn't have to expend such a large part of his temper, nerves and health on battles as he would undoubtedly have to, and with particular force, in St. Petersburg."[8]

What these battles might have been like emerges with blinding clarity from Igor's letters to Volodya this summer. His defense of Diaghilev is lucid, energetic, and goes well beyond the simple expression of loyalty to his good angel. Volodya has attacked the whole idea of transferring concert works or operatic scenes to the ballet stage, questioning Diaghilev's integrity in doing so. But then it turns out that what he really despises above all else is ballet itself, in which respect he is merely reiterating the standard Petersburg intellectual prejudice against an art form which had long been the purview of children, governesses, and dirty old men.[9] For Volodya ballet is simply "the lowest form of art." But Igor, while admitting his distaste for the *salade russe* aspect of Diaghilev's work and, more specifically, regretting the omission of the third movement of *Scheherazade*, will not allow that choreographing concert works is inherently inartistic.

"In principle, I'm just in favor of beautiful (and complete) scores being staged with good choreography." And he goes on:

> It's clear to me that you simply *do not like* and are not interested in ballet, and attach no great significance to it. I can only tell you that I, on the contrary, love and am interested in ballet most of all, and this is no empty enthusiasm, but a serious and profound delight in theatrical spectacle—as living visual art. And I'm simply perplexed that you, who so loved the plastic arts and were so keenly interested in painting and sculpture . . . can pay so little attention to choreography— the third type of plastic art [and consider ballet the lowest form compared with opera].[10]

If Michelangelo were living today, he suggests, ballet is the one theatrical expression he would recognize, "the one form of theatre which sets itself the basic goal of beauty and nothing more . . . just as Michelangelo's sole aim was the beauty of the visible." As for opera, how can Volodya be in favor of that but against ballet, since both are compound art forms with their own value—neither lower nor higher, but simply different? Opera, too, is often banal, or downright bad, but Volodya favors it out of sheer bias against Diaghilev, due—Igor implies without quite stating—to his "misuse" of Volodya's father's music. But "I think that if you were to go often to the ballet (well done, of course), you would see that this 'lowest form' would give you immeasurably greater artistic pleasure than any operatic performance . . . a pleasure which I have already experienced for many years, and which I so terribly want to infect you with and share with you."

Igor's growing preference for ballet, which would soon develop into an open hostility towards opera, was partly, as he admitted, due to the influence of Benois. But other factors were also at work. Just as Benois's ideas about staging ballet—and specifically *Petrushka*—had been stimulated by recent experimental productions by Potyomkin and Meyerhold, with their use of masks, puppetry, and stylized movement, so Stravinsky himself was becoming aware of a new mentality in the theatre, tilted away from the drama as a figurative image of real life (as in Stanislavsky) and towards the concept of the stage as a self-contained world with its own symbolic laws conditioned by factors such as space and movement, illusion, and the character of the human body as an expressive instrument in its own right. He was reading on the subject. He was impressed by a recent, somewhat Nietzschean essay on dance by the German stage director and theatrical reformer Georg Fuchs, which attacked what it called "literary theatre" and the whole classical tradition of abstract intellectualism, and called for a new approach to theatre in which dance and the cult of the body played a pre-eminent role alongside music. Fuchs derided polite modern expressions of the dance impulse: ballroom dancing, the classical ballet, even the work of Isadora Duncan, which to him was nothing but a series of statuesque poses linked by more or less irrelevant music. He wanted dance to reassert its fundamental role in primitive societies: that of a sacred, ritualistic expression of the whole community. "I shall not rest," the co-author of *The Great Sacrifice* told Andrey Rimsky-Korsakov two months later, "until you have read this article and given me your opinion in writing, with your signature attached, confirmed by the local police."[11]

Nevertheless, while held up on his own new ballet, Stravinsky toyed with the possibility of dusting off his unfinished opera, *The Nightingale*, and completing it in some as yet undefined collaboration with Benois. "This is admittedly an opera, something towards which we have both equally cooled," he told Benois, "but work with you may rehabilitate matters, and I shall in any case take up what I began on it. It's devilishly amusing to compose such chinoiserie. Don't you think so, my dear?"[12] With *The Great Sacrifice* booked for the 1912 season, the Andersen opera would be for 1913; but he could still be writing the second act of *Nightingale* during the two months before he planned to get down to the ballet. For some reason (perhaps a refusal from Benois) he soon abandoned this idea, and the next we hear of the opera is seven months later, when he informed Mitusov of his decision not to complete the work but to leave it, and publish it, as it stood—a single, integrated "scene from Andersen's tale." "A lot of water has flowed under the bridge," he wrote, "and I'm already not what I was when I composed *The Nightingale*."[13] His current work on the Roerich ballet must have made him acutely aware of the difficulty he would have reviving the style of the earlier work. But there was the other reason too: the fact that he had now come to detest opera, "that lie masquerading as truth," as he was to call it in a newspaper interview a few months later, whereas "I need a lie masquerading as a lie."[14] Perhaps he was also swayed by the consideration that the existing act was a potential source of income, just when he had learnt that the production of the new Roerich ballet—and the associated earnings—would be delayed for a year. Certainly money would be a major factor in his decision, a year later, to complete the opera after all.

Meanwhile, he had to find something else to write—something small which would not distract him for long but keep the spirit alive amid the aggravating correspondence with Volodya and the arduous proofreading and publication plans. As he had done the previous summer, he turned to word setting; but this time his eye fell on a contemporary Russian poet, the symbolist Konstantin Balmont. During late June and July he made settings for high voice and piano of two exquisite Balmont poems, "The Forget-me-not" ("Nezabudochka-tsvetochek") and "The Dove" ("Golub"). And when these were done, he turned to a much more obscure poem called "Zvezdolikiy" ("The King of the Stars") and set about making it into a short work for male-voice chorus and orchestra. On 20 July, after a month in Ustilug, he wrote to Florent Schmitt that "I've begun another piece (for choir and orchestra) which has got to be either strong or nothing—and I must finish it. I'm playing only French music—yours, Debussy, Ravel—it does me good, you know, a great consolation in our Russian desert. Only Scriabin attracts my attention. Try to get to know him."[15] But this, too, was soon interrupted by the visit to Roerich at Talashkino, and by subsequent necessary travels. Stravinsky managed more or less to complete the piano score before at last starting *The Great Sacrifice* in September. The full score had to wait until the following year.

All three Balmont poems come from a single collection called *Zelyoniy vertograd* (The Green Garden) which was published in book form in 1909; but all had previously appeared as part of a smaller selection in the journal *Vesi* in 1907, at the period when Stravinsky was setting verse by another symbolist, Sergey Gorodetsky.[16] Balmont, like Gorodetsky, cultivated a strain of pseudo-archaism which at times assumed the guise of a highly colored theurgical mysticism similar in tone to certain contemporary works of Scriabin, particularly *Prometheus,* the piano piece "Vers la flamme," and the unfinished *Acte préalable.* At other times the modelling on old sectarian verse is more discreet and refined, and suggests, as Taruskin points out, a neonationalist type of stylization. Stravinsky set both types. The two songs have an almost porcelain quality of nature imagery— the forget-me-not, the dove, the rose—which barely conceals an erotic symbolism that was originally, it seems, religious in its connotations. But it is the porcelain quality that mainly interested Stravinsky, and the songs are essentially abstract studies in line, texture, harmony, and formal patterning of a kind which, in *Petrushka* and still more *The Rite of Spring*, take on a more specific, not to say drastic, narrative significance.

He might well have said of these two poems, as he said of "Zvezdolikiy," that their "words are good, and words were what I needed, not meanings."[17] But where the songs do have a cool, decorative quality, the setting of "Zvezdolikiy" undoubtedly picks up the mystic grandeur of the poem, with its echoes of Nietzsche in stanzas like the following:

> *"I reign," he said, "and alone!"*
> *Thunder roared in echoes.*
> *"Now is the hour!" he said in his glory.*
> *"The harvest is waiting, Amen!"*

The music, with its quality of heightened choral plainchant accompanied by a series of theatrical gestures in the orchestra, is perhaps the closest Stravinsky ever came to the rhetoric of Scriabin—though its apparent

Fyodor Stravinsky
in 1885

Fyodor and Anna
Stravinsky with (right)
Alexander and Soph'ya
Yelachich, Kiev, 1890

Kryukov Canal, with the Mariyinsky
Theatre behind. The Stravinsky flat
was on the second floor.

Khudïntsev's dacha in Oranienbaum,
where Igor Stravinsky was born in 1882
(drawing by Fyodor Stravinsky)

Igor at fifteen
months, Kiev,
September 1883

The Stravinsky family at tea, St. Peters-
burg, c. 1892; (clockwise from left): Igor,
Roman, Anna, the servant Semyon
Sokolov, Fyodor, Yury, Gury

The Nosenko girls with
Gavriyil Nosenko at
Ustilug, c. 1895. Katya
holds the whip.

The Stravinsky and Yelachich families at Pavlovka,
1896. Igor Stravinsky is sitting on the steps
between his older cousins Mikhail and Nikolay
Yelachich, with Gury Stravinsky to Mikhail's right.

The Gostiny Dvor, Nevsky
Prospect, St. Petersburg, 1898

Igor and Gury
Stravinsky with
their mother in
Ustilug, 1904

Igor Stravinsky's house
at Ustilug, c. 1910

Igor and Katya Stravinsky at Zagorod-nïy Prospect 28 with Rimsky-Korsakov, his daughter Nadya and her fiancé Maximilian Steinberg, 1908

Mikhail Fokine directing a rehearsal of *The Firebird* with the composer at the piano and Tamara Karsavina (center), 1910

Fokine and
Karsavina in *The
Firebird*, 1910

Igor and Katya Stravinsky,
St. Petersburg, 1906

Igor Stravinsky with Vaslav Nijinsky
in his Petrushka costume, 1911

remoteness from the ballets of the period is certainly exaggerated by its lack of any strong rhythmic impulse or metric shape. The actual harmonies, with their recurrent patterns of interference and discord, have plenty of equivalents in *The Rite of Spring*. But they seem to have presented insuperable difficulties for choirs at that time, even after the composer had simplified the chorus from six-part down to four-part when he was orchestrating it in the summer of 1912.[18] At least two early performances—one planned for Moscow in August 1912, the other for Paris in May 1913—fell through apparently because of the music's technical difficulty, and neither of Stravinsky's publishers—RMV or Jurgenson—wanted to publish,[19] though Boris Jurgenson eventually did so in 1913 after digging his heels in on the question of honorarium.[20] But the work was not performed in public until 1939.

In the second week of July Igor at last set off for Talashkino, leaving Katya and the three children at Ustilug with Gury and his mother. *The Great Sacrifice* had by now lain dormant for more than a year. But Talashkino was a good environment for reanimating it. Here Princess Maria Tenisheva, whose husband had secured a monopoly on those river steamers which Igor knew so well from his Volga trips to Pavlovka, had set up an Arts and Crafts community which served both as a center for the work of leading easel artists like Vrubel, Golovin, and Serebryakova and as a workshop for the design and manufacture of folk-art reproductions and a museum for the princess's growing collection of genuine peasant artifacts. Roerich was an old friend of hers, and his work and enthusiasms embodied many of the different aspects of the Talashkino enterprise: painter and ethnographer, archaeologist and mythologist, he summed up that curious mixture of practicality and mysticism, of functional design and high art, of sociology and religion, which motivated so many Arts and Crafts communities of the time. *The Great Sacrifice*, with its stylized but carefully planned rituals, its ethnographic detail, and its art-for-art's-sake purity, was a real Talashkino sort of work, not least because the princess was herself a musician, a singer manqué, and an enthusiast for the Russian folk music which she may faintly have discerned behind the violent rhythms and harsh dissonances of the new ballet, when she eventually heard it.

Stravinsky's visit was a planning trip, and he does not seem to have written any music at Talashkino, beyond taking down a few folk songs performed for them by a singer and gusli player called Sergey Kolosov, who was in Smolensk to collect material on Glinka.[21] The main task was to agree a scenario with enough detail to provide a compositional framework, in place of the presumably somewhat general forms of the libretto which Stravinsky and Roerich, and later the two of them with Fokine, had worked out in the spring and summer of 1910.[22] In any case it seems likely that these early scenarios, if such they were, differed in important details from the plan Stravinsky took away from Talashkino after a few days there. Roerich had told the *Peterburgskaya gazeta* that "the new ballet will give a series of images of a holy night among the ancient Slavs. The action begins with a summer night and finishes immediately before the sunrise when the first rays begin to show."[23] So even the time of year, perhaps the single most famous thing about the ballet, was different in the original concept. These and other details were thrashed out in the princess's brightly painted guest house. Roerich recalled that "Princess Tenisheff asked us to write on the beams of this multicolored house some excerpts from *Sacre* as a memento. Probably even now some fragments of Stravinsky's inscriptions remain there still."[24] "The Princess Tenishev," Stravinsky recalled, "gave me a guest house attended by servants in handsome white uniforms with red belts and black boots. . . . In a few days the plan of action and the titles of the dances were composed. Roerich also sketched his famous Polovtsian-type backdrops while we were there, and designed costumes after real costumes in the Princess's collection."[25] "The artist N. K. Roerich and the composer I. F. Stravinsky have converted their one-act ballet into two acts," reported the *Peterburgskaya gazeta* a few weeks later, "and given it a new name: *Festival of Spring* [*Prazdnik vesnïy*]."[26]

It must have been on the journey home to Ustilug that the composer, having missed his connection at Brest-Litovsk, bribed a goods-train guard to let him ride in a cattle truck, which turned out to be occupied by a bull, "leashed by a single not-very-reassuring rope, and as he glowered and slavered I began to barricade myself behind my one small suitcase. I must have looked an odd sight in Smolensk [probably Kovel] as I stepped from that *corrida* carrying my expensive (or, at least, not tramp-like) bag and brushing my clothes and hat, but I must also have looked relieved."[27] Chastened—or fortified—by this authentically Scythian experience, he continued work, not on the new ballet, but on the choral piece, *Zvezdolikiy.* Strange though it may seem, he was working to a timetable. He had always planned to start the ballet in the autumn and finish it in the spring, which is what had happened with both previous ballets.[28] There was *The Nightingale* nagging at his conscience. And in any case he still planned to leave at the end of August for his winter quarters in Clarens, perhaps even calling on Benois at Lugano on the way to discuss the opera. As it turned out, there was a change of plan. Instead of Clarens, he went to the Bohemian spa of Karlsbad to meet Diaghilev, apparently in response to an SOS from the director, since Diaghilev—on his way from Venice to St. Petersburg—actually put up the money for his fare.[29] From Warsaw he wrote to Andrey Rimsky-Korsakov on 21 August, having received a letter from Andrey just as he was leaving Ustilug, which seems at last to have reacted, perhaps equivocally, to *The Firebird,* but to have said nothing at all about

Petrushka.³⁰ By the twenty-third Igor was in Karlsbad, where he learnt that Diaghilev had invited him, not in order to discuss the Roerich ballet, but still with the old intention of wooing him away from this project—of which Diaghilev remained acutely suspicious—in favor of some unspecified collaboration with Bakst (presumably *The Masque of the Red Death*). But this time Igor, surer of himself after *Petrushka*, stuck to his guns, and Diaghilev had to content himself with querying a few details of the scenario, advising Igor to consult Benois in Lugano, and proposing a council of war with Roerich in Warsaw or Moscow—which last the composer successfully evaded. It seems likely that Diaghilev was not really unhappy about *Festival of Spring*, as it was now being called, but simply could not come to terms with its apparent utter lack of artistic dependence on him. At any rate he formally commissioned the ballet in Karlsbad, for a total fee of four thousand roubles, thereby at least ensuring its material dependence.³¹

Igor left Karlsbad for Lugano on the twenty-fifth, and was there, at the Benois house—Casa Camuzzi—in Montagnola, for four or five days, presumably discussing the distant *Nightingale*, though perhaps the matter of the Roerich ballet was also raised for form's sake. But by the end of the month he was back in Berlin, where he discussed terms for the new ballet with RMV's Berlin director, Nikolay Struve, and sold him the Balmont songs for two hundred roubles.³² He thus got back to Ustilug, on 2 September, "in an excellent humor," Katya observed, "and dreaming a lot about our life at Clarens,"³³ but still faced with the task of proofreading both *Petrushka* and the full score of *The Firebird*, for which he was being pressed by Jurgenson with a view to Emil Cooper's Moscow premiere of the suite the following March.

Was it such chores, or simply the need for respite from travel, that kept him now at Ustilug for a whole month beyond his original intention? He had long since marked out the "*Sacres du printemps*—a sort of cult of the Slavic Old Believers," as he very misleadingly called it in a September letter to Florent Schmitt, as a work he would compose at Clarens: "I'm madly impatient to get to Clarens so that I can at last *work*, since here I can hardly organize my jobs in a properly relaxed way—there are too many little things to do before we leave."³⁴ Meanwhile, he worked away on the short score of *Zvezdolikiy*, eventually completing it on 1 October (NS), by which time he had already lost patience and started work on the ballet, even though, as he told Roerich,

> we're all in terrible disorder here and everything is packed up. . . . I've already started composing: I've "sketched" (as they say) the prelude ("Dudki") and I've gone on and also "sketched" the "Divination with twigs"; I'm terribly excited!

The music is coming out fresh. The image of the old woman in squirrel skins has not left my mind the whole time that I've been composing the "Divination," but she stands before me running in front of everyone, only stopping every so often, interrupting the smooth flow of the general "trot." . . . For the first time I've connected the appearance of the "painted women" from the river with the "Divination with twigs"—this has come out very smoothly and I'm pleased with it.[35]

Already we glimpse the ethnographic detail—the pipes *(dudki)* and divinations and animal skins—which was Roerich's great contribution from Talashkino and before.

A few days later the extended family set off on their three-day journey to Switzerland. On the seventh they were in Warsaw, from where Igor at last managed to reply to Andrey's letter of nearly two months earlier. "What could be better or more pleasing," he asked,

than the development of the established art forms? Surely only one thing—the development of new forms. As I see you, you stick to the former, but since I don't see you, I can't be sure what you subscribe to, and perhaps, who knows, you have subscribed to the latter, not in words or with the brain, of which not everyone has as much as he needs, but with the feelings, of which everyone has as much as he needs. Yes or no? Probably yes. Don't stop yourself feeling.[36]

One wonders what Andrey, defending his family honor and his own limitations, made of this friendly hint that he really did like *The Firebird* and would like *Petrushka,* if only he would surrender to his true feelings. Alas, he seems not to have replied.

At Clarens, the Stravinskys settled once more into Les Tilleuls, and here, in a small ground-floor room below the family's first-floor flat, composition began in earnest on a work so much postponed, so much incubated.[37] The neutrality of the environment seems to have suited him, or at any rate not to have disturbed him. Outside, street traffic was little and still frequently horse-drawn. Every morning, work "was interrupted . . . by a train [which] he used to anticipate . . . with hatred and baited nerves."[38] The emphasis was on routine. We know nothing external about Stravinsky's life for the next month or more, as he grappled with concentrated intensity with the music of the first part of *The Rite of Spring.* Even the details of his progress escape us. We know only that by mid-November, when he went to Paris "by my own wish as a rest from urgent composition,"[39] there was enough music written for him to play it to Diaghilev at Misia Edwards's flat. The impresario had come to Paris from London specifically to hear the excerpts, as well as to pay Stravinsky the first installment of his commission fee.⁴⁰ He also arranged a hearing of *Firebird* and *Petrushka* at Gabriel Astruc's apartment, for the benefit of his new English patroness the marchioness of Ripon, who, Stravinsky told Benois, "was very interested by them and would like them to go to London." As for the *Sacre* excerpts, "everybody liked them awfully."⁴¹ But we can only speculate exactly what they were: the Introduction and Augurs of Spring presumably, plus no doubt the Spring Rounds and the Games of the Rival Tribes, which were the next movements to be drafted in the sketchbook.⁴²

Stravinsky stayed in Paris with Maurice Delage at 3 rue de Civry, in the sixteenth arrondissement, a house which had already served him as a hideout during the exhausting days of the *Petrushka* performances in June. Delage rented a small cottage or "pavilion" next door to his house, and here there met regularly a group of musicians—composers, performers, critics—who had adopted the name "Apaches" from the epithet hurled at them by a news vendor they had jostled in the street one day as they came out of a concert.⁴³ These "Apaches," or "hooligans," were artistically in fact a fairly sedate, middle-aged company: Delage himself, a late starter as a composer, was now in his early thirties; Ravel, the most prominent member (and himself at work on a Diaghilev commission), was thirty-six, as was the pianist Ricardo Viñes; Florent Schmitt was forty; and of the critics in the group, Michel Calvocoressi and Emile Vuillermoz were both well into their thirties. They were nevertheless progressive in their tastes, and they all adored Stravinsky. Indeed, Calvocoressi, a polyglot who numbered Russian and English among his languages, had recently published in the *Musical Times* one of the first general articles about his music to appear anywhere.⁴⁴ Though Stravinsky never became intimate with any one Apache—was never on *tutoyer* terms with them—they were to give him consistent friendship and support, which he, in his way, did his best to reciprocate in kind, at any rate for as long as it remained unquestioning. He may or may not, at this stage, have played Delage and his friends something from the new ballet. Probably Schmitt played, or at least talked about, the new concert version of his own ballet *La Tragédie de Salomé*, and perhaps raised with Stravinsky the possibility of Diaghilev staging it in this form. Stravinsky did at least mention the work to Diaghilev and even acted as go-between on practical questions concerning it. But it must be said that his gushingly expressed desire to "play it endlessly and madly from start to finish" does not ring entirely true.⁴⁵

Back in Clarens, he worked on steadily at the first part of the score, and by the fourth week of January he was able to tell Benois that "I've been working a great deal lately and have almost completely finished the first scene, not only the music but the orchestration as well, and have only the actual ending (Dance of the Earth) to write. If you see Roerich give him my best wishes and tell him that I seem to have composed well."[46] He and Katya took a few days off "so that my powers don't dry right up," and celebrated their sixth wedding anniversary in Italy: perhaps Genoa, certainly Milan, from where Igor wrote Benois a detailed account of his reactions to the Brera Gallery, and its "ever better and better reproductions of 'masterpieces,'" which drove him to "the conclusion that the stronger the impression you get from a work of art, the more jealously you have to guard this first impression from every attempt by 'art' reproductions to stand in for the genuine article."[47] But it seems unlikely that he went to Berlin for the Ballets Russes performances there in January, for all his detailed memoir of the visit.[48] Stravinsky's letter to Schmitt of 2 February states unequivocally that he had had no news of Diaghilev since November, and it also shows that he was still unaware of the threat to the company's planned season in St. Petersburg caused by the destruction of the Narodny Dom theatre in a fire on 20 January: "I don't even know," he told Schmitt, "if Diaghilev intends to play my ballets in his St. Petersburg season which is supposed to be happening in February." In fact he only learnt of the cancellation of the Russian season from his mother nearly two weeks later.[49]

Stravinsky spent February in Clarens, finishing off the first part of *Sacre*. The conclusive dating is provided by a letter to Roerich, for whose benefit Stravinsky certainly had no motive for inventing any delay. "I completely finished the first scene a week ago," he wrote on 6 March, "that is not just the actual music, but also the orchestral score."[50] In fact he sought to allay Roerich's anxiety about the work's being ready in time for its Paris opening in the summer: "Although both our acts are identical in length, the first scene still represents a good three-quarters of the whole in terms of work, since the tempi are all frenzied, which means there's a mass of writing." It seems clear that at this stage the composer still assumed that the work would be given that spring—probably, as he optimistically told Andrey, at the end of the Paris season. "My God," he enthused, "what a joy it will be for me to hear it. Come, my dear—just come! It's unnecessary even to talk, but just hear it. It seems I've indulged in some self-advertisement. But if you hear it you'll understand what we have to talk about. It's as if twenty years, not two, have passed since the composition of *Firebird*."[51] Only when Diaghilev and Nijinsky arrived in Monte Carlo from Vienna in mid-March did he pay them a visit and at last discover that the new ballet would have to be postponed, as he informed Benois,

since Fokine turns out to be overloaded with the production of [Ravel's] *Daphnis*, [Reynaldo Hahn's] *Le Dieu bleu*, the revival of *Firebird*, and rehearsals of *Petrushka*, a work he hates. But not a word of this to anyone, since none of it is public knowledge until Serge has discussed it with Fokine. I personally—and Serge too—do not want

Fokine to produce it, since he will understand absolutely nothing about this entire piece.⁵²

There was another factor, too. Diaghilev was angling for the work to be choreographed by Nijinsky, but first Fokine had to be got rid of, and Nijinsky had to cut his teeth on Debussy's *Après-midi d'un faune* that coming May. Stravinsky may have known something of all this, but if so, he kept his counsel. He, too, had had enough of Fokine, as he told his mother in a long diatribe against the choreographer's *"habileté,"* which, rather significantly, he compared with Glazunov's—and received a flea in his ear from Anna for his pains.⁵³ But whether he would have thought the inexperienced Nijinsky a suitable substitute, in a work of such complexity, is quite another matter.

Meanwhile, he played Diaghilev and Nijinsky the first half of his score. "He and Nijinsky are wild about it," he reported to Anna; and to Benois, more ambiguously: "It seems that Diaghilev is stunned by my 'Sacrifical' inspirations."⁵⁴ By this time a substantial chunk of the Introduction and Cercles mystérieux in the second part had been drafted too, as well as some notations for the Glorification. But once back from Monte Carlo, he laid the work aside and instead took up the more mundane task of proofreading the four-hand piano reduction of *Petrushka*, as well as combing through the full score and parts, which were on the point of publication, for mistakes to go on an errata sheet. This seems to have occupied much of his working time during the three weeks he was in Clarens. "I'm desperately busy," he told Max Steinberg, in an attempt to persuade his old friend to visit him in Clarens on his way to Paris early in April.⁵⁵ And we may well believe him. What with proofs and correspondence, grumbling to Struve about misprints in *Petrushka*, worrying Jurgenson for the orchestral parts in time for the Monte Carlo revival of *Firebird*, corresponding with the conductor Pierre Sechiari about a projected performance of *Zvezdolikiy* in Paris in May, pestering Benois to get him a painting by the Lithuanian artist-composer Čiurlionis, and to give him one of the original costume designs for *Petrushka*, to say nothing of more personal correspondence with his mother, with Andrey, with Steinberg—it is a wonder that he found time for composition at all, even allowing for Katya's no doubt tireless and uncomplaining clerical help. Yet it does seem likely that he wrote some more pages of *Sacre*, unless he was fibbing—in that fulsome way he was beginning to find socially convenient—when he told Calvocoressi that "the *Sacre* will soon be finished. I shall have the pleasure of playing it to my friends, of whom you are one of the first."⁵⁶ Perhaps, when he left Clarens on 13 April to go to Monte Carlo in time for the rehearsals of *Petrushka*, the whole second part was indeed at least mapped out. But much detailed composition still remained, and much must still have been unclear to him. It would be many weeks before he could again calmly address these questions.

For him, composition was always impossible amid the ferment of rehearsal and performance, and Monte Carlo was no exception. He was there, curiously enough, for more than a fortnight, and though his participation in the rehearsals for *Petrushka* and, afterwards, *Firebird* was no doubt valuable and energetic, his only progress on current creative work during that time was to play through what he had so far composed of *Sacre* to Diaghilev and the young Monteux, now the company's regular conductor, and the obvious choice to conduct this difficult new ballet after his success with *Petrushka*. Monteux was summoned to a tiny rehearsal room in the Théâtre du Casino, and there, he recalled,

> Stravinsky sat down to play a piano reduction of the entire score. Before he got very far I was convinced he was raving mad. Heard this way, without the color of the orchestra which is one of its greatest distinctions, the crudity of the rhythm was emphasized, its stark primitiveness underlined. The very walls resounded as Stravinsky pounded away, occasionally stamping his feet and jumping up and down to accentuate the force of the music. Not that it needed much emphasis.
>
> I was more astounded by Stravinsky's performance than shocked by the score itself. My only comment at the end was that such music would surely cause a scandal.[57]

Something else happened during the company's Monte Carlo season that was to have consequences for the new ballet: Fokine and Diaghilev, relations between whom had been difficult for almost two years, agreed to part company at the end of the coming Paris season, which would effectively leave the Ballets Russes without an experienced choreographer. Nijinsky, meanwhile, had been working on a statuesque choreography for Debussy's *Faune*, partly influenced by a visit he and Diaghilev had recently paid to Emile Jaques-Dalcroze's School of Eurhythmics at Hellerau.[58] But nobody could be sure that the approach would succeed; and above all nobody could say with confidence whether the great dancer would be able to cope with the vastly more complex demands of *Sacre*, in which, moreover, he himself would not be dancing. The prospect may well have disturbed Stravinsky. But did he really, as the painter Konstantin Somov himself claimed, propose to Somov that he participate in *Sacre* "as coproducer and, of course, scenery and costume designer,"[59] or did Somov simply misunderstand a casual or even jocular invitation to help Nijinsky with certain details of staging?

From Monte Carlo, Stravinsky followed the company to Paris via

Clarens in the middle of May. In Paris he again stayed with Delage. On the twenty-ninth, he was at the Châtelet for the premiere of *Faune*, with Nijinsky's notorious masturbatory gesture with the scarf; and he took part in the crisis meetings Diaghilev called the following day, in order, presumably, to consider whether any changes were necessary before the next performance. It was the first time, according to Buckle, that a Diaghilev ballet had ever been booed.[60] Ten days later, after various tactical delays on Diaghilev's part, Fokine's production of Ravel's *Daphnis and Chloe*, designed by Bakst, had its premiere with, by a nice irony, Nijinsky in the male title role. Stravinsky, of course, was present, sharing a box with Ravel, Schmitt, and Delage,[61] having previously, he tells us in his autobiography, heard a piano run-through by Ravel, presumably at an Apaches get-together.[62] The following afternoon, as in Monte Carlo, he himself gave a play-through of the completed parts of *Sacre*. "I still preserve the memory," Debussy wrote to him a few months later, "of the performance of your *Sacre du printemps* at Laloy's. . . . It haunts me like a beautiful nightmare and I try in vain to retrieve the terrifying impression it made. For which reason I look forward to its production like a greedy child who has been promised sweets."[63]

For all this vigorous sociomusical existence, which was to remain for Stravinsky one of the great attractions of Paris and was eventually to leave its stamp on his entire life, he left France for Ustilug in the second week of June 1912 in a tense and nervous state. He did not go to London with the company, and so did not witness the considerable success there of *Firebird*, the first music of his to be heard in the English-speaking world. The Ballets Russes was like a hothouse. The season was too long, he told Benois, there was too much second-rate music, too much "Greek" ballet with designs by Bakst, too many quarrels fomented by Fokine.[64] He was expending a lot of energy on negotiations over royalties, percentages, and copyright. He was "penniless and completely up to my eyes in debt." He had even got entangled in a lawsuit with a pianist called Miquel Alzieu, to whom he had lent money for a concert tour.[65]

"What does next year have in store for us?" he inquired rhetorically and more than a shade apprehensively of Benois. There were some encouraging signs. *Faune* had been a success, despite unsuitable designs by Bakst: "a cross between Gauguin and Munch—not particularly nice, and besides they didn't fit the music or Nijinsky's astonishing invention." And Stravinsky had enjoyed discussions with Diaghilev's friend and patron the Russian diplomat and antiquarian prince Argutinsky-Dolgurokov, about "that fantastic porcelain (Chinese) eighteenth century," but also about "that region of the Veneto [Benois was in Venice] with its patriarchal life, its landscapes and threshing barns, its corn stooks and yellow sun. . . . Dreams pursue me towards some big undertaking, and that's why it's simply vital for me to see you."[66] Vital, apparently, because of *The Nightingale*—no longer as dead as it had seemed when he wrote to Mitusov less than five months before—but vital for other reasons too. No serious Venetian project with Benois ever materialized, and the mere suggestion now strikes a jarring note (though Benois had his own Venetian dream at this time: a "Veronese ballet" to the music of Debussy's *Fêtes*).[67] But that, of course, is because we know what came next. For Stravinsky this important question was as yet without an answer.

"The *Sacre* [sic] is still not completely finished. I shall finish it now."[68] Stravinsky was at Ustilug for two months from mid-June to mid-August, but he did not manage to complete the ballet. No doubt there was more still to write than he was openly admitting. But he was also plagued by other tasks. A letter had come from Vladimir Derzhanovsky, one of the organizers of the Moscow Evenings of Contemporary Music, inquiring about repertoire for an all-Stravinsky program being planned for a Temperance Society concert by his Moscow Evenings colleague Konstantin Saradzhev.[69] In particular, Saradzhev was keen to include *Petrushka,* not a note of which had yet been heard in Russia. But, though the score was out, the parts were still in proof, and—it soon became clear—unlikely to be ready in time. Derzhanovsky also asked about the symphony; but in this case, although Stravinsky had the (manuscript) parts, he had given the score to Rimsky-Korsakov, it was still in Nadezhda's possession, and "it seems to me for various reasons not completely appropriate for me to approach [the family] personally."[70] As for *The Faun and the Shepherdess,* the parts were still with the Belyayev committee, whom Stravinsky had been pressing on the matter of publication. What about doing a whole vocal group, including the recent songs? Who would sing them? Then there was the new choral piece, *Zvezdolikiy,* which he was orchestrating now: "But I warn you that the piece is very difficult and very short."

Stravinsky was quite prepared to involve himself in such matters of planning. But he was powerless to resolve all the difficulties. In the end *Petrushka* could not be done, because RMV, perhaps working to instructions from Koussevitzky, found it impossible to release the parts in time, while Diaghilev's materials were out of reach in London, where the company had recently completed a highly successful season at Covent Garden.[71] Meanwhile, the composer managed to complete the orchestration (and revision) of *Zvezdolikiy* for dispatch to Derzhanovsky on 8 August.[72] But the work was not performed, presumably—as Stravinsky had half-predicted—because of its unusual difficulty in proportion to its size and duration. As for the symphony, he did eventually summon the moral courage to remind Max, at Lyubensk, of Saradzhev's need for the score, but could not resist grumbling about Volodya's and Andrey's uncommunicativeness or pointing out that if Max wanted to see him at the time of the

Moscow concert, it would be as easy for him to come to Moscow as for Igor to go to Lyubensk. "Before Moscow," he remarked with studied lack of tact, "I have to go abroad to several other places on business, and for that reason I shall lose a lot of work time."73

He lost, in fact, almost a month. Diaghilev again wanted a conference, and this time his chosen meeting place was the Wagner festival at Bayreuth. Stravinsky set off on about 16 August, travelling via Berlin, where he probably made a last-ditch attempt to cadge some *Petrushka* parts from Struve, and two days later arrived in Nuremberg, from where he scribbled Steinberg a postcard: they were off to Bayreuth the next day to hear *Parsifal*.74 Bayreuth was two hours from Nuremberg by train. Did they, at the last minute, decide after all to go in time to catch Hans Richter's last-ever Bayreuth *Meistersinger* that same day, the nineteenth, as Stravinsky later recalled?75 It seems likely. As for *Parsifal* on the twentieth, the quasi-religious atmosphere of the proceedings may well have tortured him as much as he reports in his autobiography, with its comical description of himself as a hapless intruder in the whole Wagner experience.76 But it would be dangerous to take this as an authentic indication of his reaction to the music itself. Less than six months later, as it happened, he heard *Parsifal* again, at a private performance in Monte Carlo, and this time we have his immediate report, in a letter to Steinberg written only a week after the event:

> I was in Monte Carlo for *Parsifal,* but didn't see a thing as I sat in a side box (Raoul Guinsbourg's), which I didn't mind, since I could appreciate the great art of Wagner from the direct source of that greatness and not through the medium of pygmies swarming around the stage—they get terribly in the way, even when you don't see them (I recognize that part of the blame is Wagner's in this particular work). This was the second private performance (of three)—tickets were distributed by invitation, though at a cost of twenty francs, and they called it a rehearsal of *Parsifal*—what nonsense, thought up merely to avoid infringing the will! I saw Cosima [Wagner] in the front row—a right old piece of junk and a skinflint into the bargain.77

Evidently the "Wagnerian musician," who at the age of thirteen had drawn Bayreuth in the form of a castle and painstakingly catalogued the dates of *Tristan* and *Parsifal*,78 had not changed as much in the intervening years as he would later have liked us to believe.

From Bayreuth, Stravinsky and Diaghilev proceeded to Lugano for a conference with Benois. They were joined there by Nijinsky, who had been dancing with the company in Deauville. Presumably ideas for a Venetian ballet were still being canvassed, and Diaghilev may also have been plotting a Maeterlinck ballet to Stravinsky's *Scherzo fantastique*—to judge, at least, from his barrage of telegrams about Maeterlinck to the composer in Ustilug later on, in September.[79] But Benois records only his thoughts on *Sacre*, of which Stravinsky once again played what he had so far written.[80] According to Buckle, Diaghilev soon returned to Paris by way of an excursion with his two fellow-travellers to Lake Maggiore and the Isola Bella. But Stravinsky went back to Lugano and stayed on for a further week, as we know from the survival of another letter to Steinberg written from there on 1 September. Max had written reproaching him for no longer wanting to see his old friends, to which Igor replied that he was now so busy that he could not even come to Saradzhev's concert and had in fact just wired Moscow to that effect. In two days he was off to Venice for a week.[81] In Venice he was joined once again by Diaghilev, with Nijinsky and, it seems, Misia Edwards with her future third husband, the painter José-Maria Sert; and here, in a ground-floor salon of the Grand Hotel, opposite Santa Maria della Salute on the Grand Canal, he again played *Sacre*, and Diaghilev—who had by now heard some of this music at least three times before and all of it at least once—is supposed to have asked the composer, "Will it last a very long time this way?" to which Stravinsky is supposed to have replied, "Till the end, my dear!"[82]

After his week's holiday in Venice, Igor was back in Ustilug by 11 September (NS). He at once wrote to Derzhanovsky asking him to return the score of *Zvezdolikiy*, and within a week he was again at work on its orchestration,[83] having presumably become dissatisfied with a task carried out in a certain amount of haste five or six weeks earlier. No doubt he divided his time between this relatively mechanical process and the more demanding creative work on the final scenes of *Sacre*, which Craft is probably right in saying was still complete only as far as Mysterious Circles.[84] Meanwhile, he set about mending fences with Max. "I'm very, very pleased," he wrote on the twenty-sixth,

> that you've been delivered of a new offspring, whose character greatly interests me. I shall be heartily glad to see you and make the acquaintance of *Metamorphoses*, which I think is worthy of a better fate, entre nous, than a Ziloti concert. I've got a great deal to discuss with you about this, and, for all our apparent differences, you and I are arriving at certain general conclusions (which will reconcile our muses—which, by the way, haven't quarrelled).[85]

He was now definitely coming to St. Petersburg for a few days. "Try to free yourself from all commitments," he pleaded. "I want very, very much to see you." Max's new ballet certainly gave Igor a timely opportunity to condescend to his supposed erstwhile rival; or was it simply a chance to make a generous gesture? No doubt both motives were present in his subsequent, clearly genuine, but only partially successful attempts to persuade Diaghilev to stage the work. What we cannot tell—because there are no references to the work in his surviving correspondence with third parties—is what he really thought of it as a piece of music.

The visit to his home city, which was destined to be his last for half a century, finally materialized at the start of October. He was there from about the fourth to the seventh (NS), purely, he told reporters, to see his family and friends. Rumors of discussions with Telyakovsky about possible production of his ballets at the Mariyinsky were premature, he said: "My agreement with Diaghilev prevents me giving anyone else the right to stage them," he told Mikhail Dvinsky of the *Stock Exchange Gazette*.[86] He visited Max Steinberg, who played him *Metamorphoses* and was treated in return to excerpts from *Sacre*, which left him bewildered and unhappy.[87] And he called on Nadezhda Rimsky-Korsakov at Zagorodnïy Prospect and asked her if she would lend Jurgenson her manuscript score of his symphony for engraving (she was extremely reluctant to do so, and a correspondence ensued, at the end of which she agreed to lend the score only to have a hand copy made of it). He saw Andrey and possibly, though not certainly, Volodya, with whom relations had distinctly cooled since the disagreement over Diaghilev, and who was these days much closer to Gury. He called on Benois and briefly discussed the apportionment of *Petrushka* royalties.[88] He was photographed for the last time in old St. Petersburg, leaning coolly, dandyishly, on the mantelpiece.[89]

Then, on 7 October 1912 (NS), he quietly took a train back to Ustilug and prepared for the annual move to Switzerland.

PETRUSHKA MEETS PIERROT

THE FAMILY WERE probably to have left immediately (on 9 or 10 October), but at the crucial moment little Lyudmila went down with a cold, and for the second year running they all had to exist for several days surrounded by boxes and suitcases.[1] No doubt the precious *Sacre* manuscript was packed up with the rest. So in desperation, and longing for creative work, Igor had to write something else. It was perhaps at this moment that he began a setting of Sergey Klichkov's poem "Vsya ona ubrana" (All has been cleared away), a fragment of which survives in one of his sketchbooks of the time.[2] But if so, it was soon abandoned. His eye had fallen on a volume of Japanese poetry in Russian translation, and he now set about the composition of the first of three lyrics taken from this volume: a verse by the Japanese poet Akahito. On the fourteenth he wrote to Maurice Delage an uncharacteristically sentimental letter reminiscing about "that little pavilion which silently guards the memories of our compatible life of a year ago . . . that little pavilion with its little rooms which I so wish to see again."[3] The point was that the "little pavilion," where the Apaches met in the rue de Civry, was Delage's Japanese retreat, decorated in the fashionable oriental style and cluttered with objects and prints which the composer had picked up in the Far East on business trips with his father. Stravinsky himself had succumbed to this taste, perhaps under the influence of his Parisian friends, though orientalism was by that time so widespread that it seems pointless to try to identify a single source. On his walls at this period, whether in Ustilug or Clarens, "the place of honour was reserved for Japanese prints,"[4] some of them perhaps even acquired for him by Maurice himself.[5] No wonder he dedicated "Akahito"—named, like its two companions, after the author of the original poem—to Delage.

At last the Stravinsky caravan set off for Clarens, travelling as usual via Warsaw and Berlin, where they spent the day between trains, shopping, visiting the Tiergarten, and finally being seen off at the Anhalt Bahnhof by the entire staff of RMV, which "meant a grand distribution of Berlin sweets among us children,"[6] Theodore recalled. At Clarens, the family settled this time into the Hôtel du Châtelard, just below the railway station—

abandoning the less expensive, less central Les Tilleuls after two winters. But it surely made no great difference, since the Stravinskys had a way of transporting their environment with them, transforming their often no doubt somewhat dingy, run-down pension apartments into fragments of bourgeois Russia, with hangings and drapes, prints, ornaments, clocks, family photographs, and even small items of furniture, to say nothing of household equipment and, above all, the paraphernalia of the composer's trade—the pens, pencils, and rubbers, the music paper, the rastra he used to draw his own stave lines, the sketchbooks, and of course the piano. "Every time," Theodore recalled, "that we moved house for a few weeks my father always managed to give an air of permanence to what was in fact very temporary. . . . All his life, wherever he might be, he always surrounded himself with his own atmosphere."[7] It was a gift that would stand him and his family in good stead in the coming years.

For a month at the Châtelard, having finished "Akahito" in its voice-and-piano version on 19 October, and with one short break for a trip to Paris in the first half of November, Stravinsky could at last immerse himself once again in the closing sections of *Sacre*. The sketchbook suggests a powerful concentration of effort, from the Glorification of the Chosen One (or Wild Dance of Glorification, as the first composition draft calls it), through the Evocation of the Ancestors and the "Action of the Old Ones"—to the Sacrificial Dance, a movement he must have had in his mind for many months but which this seems to have been his first attempt to compose out in detail. What the sketchbook does not indicate, though, is how much of this music had already been sketched at Ustilug. Perhaps, as he implies in the conversations, everything had been thought out up to the Sacrificial Dance, "which I could play, but did not, at first, know how to write."[8] But if so, the sketches reveal little trace of this problem. As usual with Stravinsky, the music appears on the page—albeit in draft form—like an object plucked out of the air, exactly as the composer seems to have wanted to suggest when he described himself sententiously as "the vessel through which *Le Sacre* passed."[9] But these notations were actually the end product of a laborious process of sonic experimentation, carried out always at the keyboard, and involving much trial and error, much sounding and resounding—a process which, long before his actual music became experimental, had led his brothers to dub him "the piano tuner."

A kind of end—though not *the* end—came suddenly and impatiently one Sunday in mid-November, three days before he had rashly committed himself to joining the Ballets Russes for their autumn season in Berlin. Bang in the middle of the Sacrificial Dance, and with the crucial final episode still undrafted, an alfresco Russian scrawl in blue and red crayon announces "Today 4/17.XI.1912 Sunday with an unbearable toothache I finished the music of the Sacre. I. Strav. Clarens, Châtelard Hotel." Much other detail remained to be settled, including the instrumentation of at least the final dance itself. But in its essential elements, he must have felt that the work was in some sense complete. A week before, in Paris, he had given a piano run-through to his Apache friends in Auteuil, an event which Florent Schmitt reported ecstatically in the columns of La France, speaking of the music's "unheard-of beauty and truly the revelation, albeit private, of this new proof of the genius of the young Russian composer."[10] Stravinsky also called on Debussy and heard his new ballet, which Stravinsky had wanted him to call Le Parc but which Debussy insisted on calling Jeux, as expressing "in a convenient way the 'horrors' which take place between these three characters."[11] But Stravinsky was impressed by the work itself, which, he told Steinberg, was "a marvellous piece. I must admit I didn't expect from the Debussy of today such a youthful upsurge."[12] To Derzhanovsky, soon afterwards, he described it as "Debussy's freshest, most youthful work of recent years."[13] He was back in Clarens on the twelfth, and a week later one of Diaghilev's old patrons, Princesse Edmonde de Polignac, wrote to him in Clarens inviting him to write her a short work by the following April for between thirty and thirty-six players for a fee of three thousand francs.[14] By early December, the idea had crystallized into a fifteen-minute concerto. But not a note of any such work seems to have been written, and by early April, when the princess wrote to Stravinsky asking him how he was getting on, another, still more lucrative project had pushed it firmly into the background.[15]

Stravinsky arrived in Berlin in time for the first night at the Kroll Theatre on 21 November. Firebird opened the proceedings, and Richard Strauss was in the audience. To the young Russian in person he was affable enough by his lights, advising him that "you make a mistake in beginning your piece pianissimo; the public will not listen. You should astonish them by a sudden crash at the start. After that they will follow you and you can do whatever you like."[16] But he told the press "it's always interesting for one to hear one's imitators [Nachfolger]," a condescension which Stravinsky reported to Benois as a remark made in conversation about Petrushka.[17] The fact is that Stravinsky detested Berlin on this visit: "It's simply shit—real Russian, that is to say German, shit. There's not a thing there. Intolerable boredom." The comparison with Russia went further. Strauss was "king of Berlin, like Glazunov and Lyadov," a touchy point for Stravinsky, whose recent visit to St. Petersburg had been a disagreeable reminder of the provinciality of his home city. Even the Kroll itself—the Neues Opern-Theater, as it was at that time known—was "old and bad." The fact was that since his father's death he had never spent so long in one city except St. Petersburg and Paris, and it came as a shock—an unpleasant taste of the suitcase life of the travelling theatre company in midwinter. Having told Andrey that he planned to stay a month, he barely survived three weeks, wiring Roerich that he did not "reckon to stay any longer in this terrible dump Berlin."[18]

Yet the visit was neither artistically nor socially without its positive aspects. Diaghilev had hired Thomas Beecham's orchestra from London for the Berlin season, and it covered itself with glory under Monteux's baton. "These Englishmen," wrote one critic, "play with a sovereign authority all too rare nowadays anywhere."[19] Stravinsky himself was in raptures. "It's enough to say," he told Derzhanovsky, "that the orchestra's entire string section amounts to a whole museum of old Italian instruments!!! I've never heard such marvellous sounds anywhere as this amazing orchestra revealed in my scores. Also their attitude to me and my works was highly considerate and artistic. Oh, if only Russian audiences could hear my music played by them!"[20] Even *Petrushka,* which the London orchestra had not played before, was superb. It seems that Diaghilev had to take a deep breath before risking this work with the notoriously stuffy Berlin audience.[21] When at last he did so, on 4 December, practically a fortnight into the season, he not only enjoyed a success equal to if not greater than in Paris,[22] but he brought about one of the great musical meetings of the twentieth century by inviting Arnold Schoenberg and his wife, Mathilde, to the performance and introducing the two composers. Schoenberg, who had been living in Berlin for more than a year, returned the compliment by inviting Stravinsky and Diaghilev to the final matinée performance of his *Pierrot Lunaire,* in the Choralionsaal in Bellevuestrasse (off the Potsdamerplatz). Schoenberg himself was conducting, and Stravinsky followed in a score given him beforehand by the composer, paying much less attention to the *diseuse,* Albertine Zehme, in her Pierrot costume. By Stravinsky's account he met Schoenberg several times in the week that remained of his Berlin stay after *Petrushka.* But he did not meet either Webern or Berg, for all Eduard Steuermann's supposed memory of a dinner at Schoenberg's Zehlendorf house with all four composers.[23] Webern was in Stettin, suffering from severe nervous illness and insomnia, and Berg was far away in Vienna, as his correspondence with Schoenberg proves.[24] A week after the final *Pierrot* Schoenberg, too, left Berlin for a trip to St. Petersburg, where he conducted his *Pelleas und Melisande* and was photographed in the courtyard of the Assembly of the Nobles in an enormous fur coat lent him by Ziloti.

Whatever the two composers talked about, we know they were impressed by each other's music. "I really liked *Petrushka,*" Schoenberg wrote in a jotted note fifteen years later, "parts of it very much indeed."[25] As for Stravinsky, his admiration for *Pierrot,* which fluctuated in after years with the musical politics of the moment, is attested by several letters and newspaper interviews of the time. Soon after his Berlin visit, he wrote to the music critic Karatïgin in St. Petersburg:

I've just read your review of the Ziloti concert in which Schoenberg conducted his *Pelleas*. I saw from what you wrote that you really like and understand the essence of Schoenberg—that truly outstanding artist of our time, and I therefore think you would not be uninterested to know his latest work, wherein is most intensively displayed the whole extraordinary stamp of his creative genius. I'm talking about his [*Pierrot Lunaire*], which I recently heard in Berlin. Here's something you "Contemporaries" ought to play![26]

To Schmitt he wrote that "Schoenberg is a remarkable artist—I feel it!"[27] And a week or two later he told the *Daily Mail* in London that "Schoenberg is one of the greatest creative spirits of our era."[28]

One looks inevitably for signs of this enthusiasm in Stravinsky's own music. A week after returning to Clarens, on 18 December, he added a second Japanese lyric, "Mazatsumi," to the first, and immediately scored up the accompaniment for two flutes (with piccolo), two clarinets (with bass clarinet), piano, and string quartet—an ensemble which looks, and sometimes sounds, very like Schoenberg's flute (doubling piccolo), clarinet (doubling bass clarinet), piano, violin (doubling viola), and cello. Stravinsky had in fact already projected an instrumentation for "Akahito" of piccolo, flute, piano, two violins, two violas, and cello, so the change after hearing *Pierrot* was no more than to drop one viola and add two clarinets.[29] But to compare the actual writing for clarinet in "Mazatsumi," and especially its manner of dialoguing with the flute and other instruments, is to feel immediately the faint but distinct imprint of what Stravinsky later called "the instrumental substance of *Pierrot Lunaire* . . . not simply the instrumentation of this music but the whole contrapuntal and polyphonic structure."[30] The same can hardly be said of "Akahito," or of the third lyric, "Tsaraiuki," which Stravinsky added on 22 January. Here the instrumental and melodic patterns are entirely consistent with the art-nouveau treatment of color and line in *The Rite of Spring*. Nor is it easy to pursue a Schoenbergian thread in Stravinsky's immediately subsequent works, where the inexorable stripping down of manner and method leads to a simplicity that is mysterious but not arcane, and above all not elliptical, like the stifled complexities of Schoenberg's and Webern's great miniatures of the time. It would be almost three years later that Debussy would speak of Stravinsky "leaning dangerously in the Schoenberg direction."[31] But by then the "danger" would be long past.

In one other important respect, Berlin was a frustration for Stravinsky. He had "finished" *The Rite* before leaving Clarens; he had worked on the orchestration on the Berlin train.[32] He had presumably discussed the music with Monteux. But rehearsals with the dancers had not begun, because, as Grigoriev wrote to Stravinsky after his departure for Clarens,

Nijinsky "is waiting for the costume designs."[33] Roerich had in fact sent them, but to Clarens, so that Stravinsky had to forward them to the company in Berlin. Nijinsky, he told Roerich in some irritation, "was supposed to start staging *The Rite* yesterday, Friday [the 13th], and begged me to stay, but I couldn't possibly, and it was decided that if it were difficult for him to cope without me, then he would wire me to come. . . . Lord! If only Nijinsky could succeed in staging it, but it's so complicated."[34] Meanwhile, Diaghilev and Nijinsky had paid a second visit to Hellerau, pursuing their (evidently collective) instinct that Dalcroze's Eurhythmics held clues to the choreography of the complicated meters of *The Rite,* and had brought back a young Polish-Russian dancer called Miriam Ramberg, who seemed to them enough of a performer to help them interpret the new ballet in Dalcrozian terms.[35] Miraculously transformed into Marie Rambert, she was to exert a strong controlling influence on Nijinsky's choreography. But still more than a month would pass after she joined the company before Nijinsky could at last report that rehearsals were under way.

Back in Clarens Stravinsky was as ever inundated with correspondence. Jurgenson, from Moscow, was putting heavy pressure on him to enter into a permanent contract in return for publishing unsaleable white elephants like *Zvezdolikiy*.[36] But Stravinsky had no intention of binding himself to a provincial Russian publisher who could not secure for him copyright on internationally successful scores like *Petrushka,* as RMV, with its Berlin office and influential conductor-proprietor, could apparently do. His tortuous correspondence with Benois over registration with the French copyright agency SACEM shows that he was already well aware of the importance of establishing copyright through publication in countries that were signatories to the Berne International Copyright Convention, which neither Russia nor the United States was; and there is something almost pathetic in Jurgenson's vain attempts to convert his early support for Stravinsky into a continuing interest in his growing international reputation, while being left to deal with the slippery and usually insolvent Diaghilev over the one lucrative work, *Firebird,* which—apart from the impresario's five-year exclusivity—the Moscow firm did more or less own. The Benois letters already present Stravinsky as a hard-nosed customer in business matters. And they also reveal another, more frankly unpleasant, side to his character, which we can assume to have developed under the influence of his right-wing World of Art friends, with perhaps some gentle assistance from an Apache or two. At least, there is no significant anti-Semitism in his early family correspondence, or in any of his documented dealings with the Rimsky-Korsakov circle. Such a thing would not, indeed, have been in keeping with the essentially liberal tendency of those groups. But with Benois and Diaghilev, whose art specifically rejected political regeneracy even if it did not actually require racial exclusivity, there was no such inhibition. Benois's and Stravinsky's remarks about their Paris agent Léon Bernstein are typically gratuitous in that they are in no sense part of any complaint about his effectiveness, but merely gentile privilege bought with his five percent. What's all this about the Jew Bernstein, Stravinsky asks, "he of the bulbous nose, the shady brow, the frizzy hair and the unbearable, stinking breath? . . . If you get tired of the yid, let me know."[37] The only faintly redeeming feature of such ribaldries is that, with Stravinsky, they seem always to have been confined to private letters (and, presumably, conversation). There is no evidence that he ever behaved equivocally or worse towards any Jewish friend or associate, or allowed anti-Semitism to color public statements or actions. On the contrary, his outspoken praise of Schoenberg might seem to argue that at this stage anti-Semitism was for him a kind of inverted shibboleth—a private mutual reassurance between exiles of a certain caste. Whether or not it remained that way will have to be considered in due course.

As for his closest Jewish friend, Max Steinberg, Stravinsky was performing acts of supererogation on his behalf. In Berlin, he had worked on Diaghilev to the point where the impresario, cool though he was towards *Metamorphoses*, had agreed to stage it at some future date. Bakst had been won over to the piece when Steinberg had played it to him and Diaghilev, and had since been delighted by the orchestral excerpts conducted by Ziloti at the end of October (OS); but Diaghilev, he told Stravinsky, had "muttered some acid pomposity" and later "swore at me about my 'idea of music.' "[38] Bakst, however, had not been in Berlin, and it had been left to Stravinsky to keep up the pressure. His report to Steinberg from the German capital has an unmistakably patronizing air, while falling well short of triumphalism. He had "discussed it with Diaghilev all day long and persuaded him to accept your splendid work," despite its being yet another "Greek" ballet (on top of *Daphnis, Faune,* Tcherepnin's *Narcisse,* and Roger-Ducasse's *Orphée*). "In any case it would be too sad for us to reject the idea of putting on your piece, so it was decided to let you know it's accepted, and that's what I've done." "*Firebird* went very well," he adds modestly. "The press was magnificent. Today is the first night of *Petrushka*."[39] Whatever Steinberg may privately have thought of his friend's tone, he took no open exception to it, but answered with due, if morose, gratitude.[40] He must have felt helpless and out of it. He could run errands for Igor: ask on his behalf at Zimmermann's about small kettledrums and piccolo trumpets for the new Roerich ballet, or brief the publisher Bessel on the existence of Igor's Musorgsky arrangement, which Bessel wanted to print. But for his own music he was trapped in the local Belyayev-Ziloti routine, unless Diaghilev came to his rescue; and for that he could only sit and wait, since, even when in St. Petersburg, Diaghilev was notoriously uncommunicative unless he wanted something from you, and it was far from certain that he genuinely wanted *Metamorphoses.*

One other trouble was that life in Russia itself was starting to assume a more disagreeable aspect politically and economically. Fear of war, Katya's brother-in-law Grigory Belyankin wrote to her from Ustilug, had led to a crisis of business confidence and the threat of banking collapse. He strongly advised her to transfer all her capital forthwith from the local bank into branches of one or other of the major national banks.[41] Yet the same letter contains detailed instructions about the Stravinskys' purchase and lease of a vodka distillery in the Ukrainian town of Rovno, a hundred miles or so to the east of Ustilug, which suggests that not only did the composer see his own future as tied indefinitely to his wife's Volhynian estate, but neither he nor his advisers foresaw that, even in the event of the war they already feared, this might be an unsound investment. There is no sharper reminder of the "feudal social background against which the modern-spirited artist was composing his masterpieces,"[42] and no clearer indication of how little that incongruity—so obvious to us in the light of subsequent events—was apparent to the denizens of that strange temporal borderland of the years just before 1914. A stab of pain felt in Clarens on the seventeenth and recorded in Ustilug on the twentieth is like an electric current arcing across centuries. "Although I gather from your letter," Belyankin grumbles to his sister-in-law a few days after the alfresco blue and red crayons in the *Rite of Spring* sketchbook, "that Gima is very busy, I am certain that he finds time to write to Diaghilev on business, and despite the very painful toothache. I am no less busy. . . ."[43]

From Berlin, the company had gone on via Breslau to Budapest, arriving there just before Christmas. Still there were no *Rite* rehearsals, and at last Diaghilev cabled Stravinsky in exasperation: "If you do not come here immediately for two weeks *Sacre* will not happen."[44] So off poor Igor had to set once again, abandoning Delage—who had arrived in Clarens four days before to translate the Japanese lyrics into French and to compose his own Hindu songs—to the tender care of Katya and the children. A new city, a new hotel (the Hungaria), but the same problems. Clutching his draft score of *The Rite,*[45] he reached Budapest on 4 January in a bad mood, went straight to *Firebird* in the Royal Opera House, and afterwards vented his spleen on Monteux for the poor playing of the orchestra.[46] Two days later the company moved on to Vienna. Here there was more orchestral trouble in store. As usual, Diaghilev delayed programming *Petrushka* until he had the measure of his audience. But he seems to have reckoned without the orchestra. According to Stravinsky, this was not the regular Hofoper orchestra "complete and unaltered, but the ballet band, which was full of conceit and as a result couldn't play a thing."[47] The trouble began at the first rehearsal when the composer, dissatisfied with the orchestral sound, demanded an increase in the number of players, whereupon the string players threw down their bows, pronounced the music *"schmutzig"* (dirty) and *"Schweinerei"* (obscenity), and refused to go on playing. Diaghilev made a little speech and seemed to have smoothed things over, but at the performance on the fifteenth, again according to the composer, the players quite simply "sabotaged" the music.[48] Stravinsky fled, probably taking the overnight train back to Switzerland that same evening, and there consoling himself by composing the third and last Japanese lyric, "Tsaraiuki," and swapping letters with Schmitt, who was full of the idea of a chamber concert built round *Pierrot Lunaire* and Bartók's First String Quartet. "As for my *Japanese Lyrics,*" Stravinsky wrote, "all three are at your disposal . . . if you would like them. Perhaps I can come on my return from London, and even, *horribile dictu,* play the piano part (because there is a piano, a grand naturally) in this huge orchestra."[49]

After a weekend spent with Katya and her sister at Beaulieu and Monte Carlo, where he attended *Parsifal* and glimpsed Wagner's widow, Cosima, he was soon off again in hot pursuit of the Ballets Russes, who were opening in London with *Petrushka* on 4 February. As before, Stravinsky arrived just in time for the opening. But this time there were no problems with the orchestra. In fact, the composer told the *Daily Mail,* even this same Beecham orchestra had never played it better.[50] A week later he gave the paper a more swashbuckling interview, dismissing Bach and Beethoven, attacking the Viennese as "barbarians" who "could not play my *Petrushka*" and who had "chased Schoenberg away to Berlin," and expressing his distaste for opera in the now immortal metaphor that "music can be married to gesture or to words—not to both without bigamy." "In any case," he added, "opera is a backwater. What operas have been written since *Parsifal*? Only two that count—*Electra* and Debussy's *Pelléas.*"[51] After his Berlin encounter with Strauss, the first of these exceptions might seem unexpected. But Stravinsky had just seen *Elektra* at Covent Garden and had been bowled over. "I went twice," he told Max, "and with total delight. It's his best work. Let them go on about Strauss's constant vulgarisms—to that I can only say, first, that if you go deeper into German works of art, you find they all suffer from this, and secondly time can smooth over the shocking contemporary tastelessness and present the work as it really is. Strauss's *Elektra* is a wonderful piece."[52]

Stravinsky, the great admirer of the Magna Carta and habeas corpus, also offered fulsome praise of his hosts, who disported themselves with such decorum and expressed themselves so politely about his music. "Personally," he told the *London Budget,* "I find more inspiration in the grey beauties of London than in any other city. . . . I think the English are amazingly intelligent. Not that they plume themselves on it, but in their quiet, dignified way, very little escapes their notice."[53]

Whom had he met? The cultured ladies of Mayfair and Bloomsbury: Lady Ripon and her daughter, Lady Juliet Duff; the tall, theatrical Lady Ottoline Morrell, whose invitation to Nijinsky and Bakst to tea and tennis in Bedford Square the summer before may indirectly have given birth to *Jeux*;[54] Queen Alexandra, who "looked like a birthday cake . . . smiled at me but said nothing; as she was quite deaf, however, and as this affliction of hers was universally known, any compliment about my music would not have been in order."[55] One wonders how the young Russian managed to connect such figures with the glories of the English political system. Perhaps it was easier in the case of the Lancashire pill millionaire Sir Joseph Beecham, who was backing Diaghilev's London seasons, or his conductor son, Thomas, whose orchestra had impressed Igor with its workmanlike, unstuffy attitude in Berlin; or the bluff, Falstaffian music critic Edwin Evans and his friend the composer Cyril Scott, with both of whom Stravinsky dined and whom Delage, who had himself met Evans in London, synthesized neatly if unintentionally into a single, omnicompetent "Scott Evans."[56]

At least these musicians' candid enthusiasm for Stravinsky's latest music must at that moment have been a welcome relief from the printed opinions of their St. Petersburg opposite numbers, which had somehow reached Stravinsky in London after the Russian premiere of *Petrushka* (the concert excerpts) on 5 February. "I see the [Petersburg] newspapers are now all comparing my work with the 'smashing of crockery,' " he told the *Daily Mail*.[57] In fact the press for Koussevitzky's performance was by no means universally negative, though Stravinsky may well have tired of being told—by even sympathetic critics who had not seen his ballet and had only heard half of the score—that the work needed the stage to make an impact, that, as Alexander Koptyayev put it, "Mr. Stravinsky detests mere music, and on the whole gives his music only an insignificant role in the general impression. . . . This music longs for a hundred stamping feet on the stage."[58] But what must in particular have stuck in his craw was a single review by the critic of the *Russkaya molva*, who stated paradoxically that "if it weren't for the great gifts of Benois and Stravinsky, this piece with its vulgar motives would be a monstrous crime. Yet who knows, might not *Petrushka* be the prelude to its own kind of musical futurism? If so, then perhaps it would be better if it had never seen the light!"[59] Even here there was no smashing crockery, only "glittering scraps and the clatter of bells." But no wonder such images became twisted in Stravinsky's mind, when their author was his erstwhile dearest friend, Andrey Rimsky-Korsakov.

That there was personal animus in Andrey's review was apparent not only to its victim. Four days after it appeared Vladimir Derzhanovsky, in Moscow, wrote to the composer Nikolay Myaskovsky, the author of a long and admiring article on Stravinsky's symphony in Derzhanovsky's journal *Muzïka* the previous August: "I was distressed to read A. Rimsky-Korsakov's views on *Petrushka* in no. 75 of *Russkaya molva*. They're somehow not very well-meaning."[60] Derzhanovsky offers no explanation for this hostile bias, though there was an immediate and perfectly public context of which he must have been aware. Less than two weeks before the Petersburg *Petrushka*, a notice in the *Russkoye slovo* had announced that Diaghilev, "having familiarized himself with the manuscripts of Musorgsky's opera . . . disagreed with many of Rimsky-Korsakov's ideas . . . and has decided to commission the well-known young composer Stravinsky to 'put together' a new *Khovanshchina*."[61] Diaghilev had in fact been plotting a production of Musorgsky's unfinished opera—about the clash between the old and the new Russia on the accession of Peter the Great—at least since 1910, before it had even been professionally staged by a St. Petersburg company. But this was the first public announcement of a firm intention to modify Nikolay Rimsky-Korsakov's performing version with its various omissions, reconstructions, and touchings-up, even though Diaghilev had previously hinted at some such idea during his controversy with Rimsky's widow over the ballet versions of *Scheherazade* and *Sadko* in the autumn of 1910.[62] It says a great deal about the tight provincialism of St. Petersburg musical life that such an announcement should have caused consternation. One newspaper, the *Birzhevïye vedomosti*, even conducted a straw poll among "leading musical figures" as to the rights and wrongs of revamping Rimsky-Korsakov's revamp.[63] A certain touchiness colored the whole discussion. "It would seem," wrote Mikhail Dvinsky, the author of the article, "the Rimsky-Korsakov who edited and orchestrated *Khovanshchina* is now rejected as defective. He has been judged not good enough 'for the West,' and must be rectified." For many, it was the last straw that such rectification should be in the hands of a Rimsky pupil, and one, moreover, who was already the object of local jealousy. "Would Stravinsky really lift his hand to correct his own teacher?" asked César Cui rhetorically, in his contribution to the poll.[64] At Zagorodnïy Prospect, eyebrows must have been at double altitude. A few days after the straw poll, Max Steinberg wrote to Igor asking him to supply a written explanation for insertion in Andrey's paper, the *Russkaya molva*, in whose columns Igor had just witnessed his best work being damned to the rafters. "I personally give no credence at all," Max added, "to these nonsensical rumors that you have been commissioned to 'correct' Nikolay Andreyevich's orchestration."[65] In fact Igor could with a fairly clear conscience have denied the "rumors," since the commission was essentially to orchestrate passages that Rimsky had cut out, though it did involve one small act of rescoring (of Shaklovity's aria in act 3), and one crucial act of recomposition: the replacement of Rimsky's final chorus with a new one based on the same Schismatic chant that Musorgsky had himself indicated as the intended basis for the finale he never wrote. But by the time Igor got back to Clarens from London and read Max's card, Diaghilev had already effectively answered it for him in a letter to the editor of the *Birzhevïye vedomosti*.[66] Between Stravinsky and Steinberg the matter was not mentioned again. But it sealed the fate of Stravinsky's friendship with Andrey.

While St. Petersburg tore its hair over *Khovanshchina*, Stravinsky, still in London, was more preoccupied with his new ballet. Just before London, Nijinsky had written to him from Leipzig that rehearsals were at last under way, despite the strain of travel and hotel rooms and his own dancing. For Nijinsky the work aroused apocalyptic visions: "I know the effect 'Spring Festivals' *[Rite of Spring]* will create, once it's the way we want it. A new and stunning impact on the ordinary spectator; and for some it will open out new horizons. Wider horizons, flooded with a new kind of sunlight. They will glimpse new colors, new lives. Everything different—new, beautiful."[67]

But technical problems remained when rehearsals continued in London. Stravinsky had provided Nijinsky with a detailed movement plan together with rhythmic abstracts which attempted to show how the dance accents were supposed to work in counterpoint with the musical accents.[68] But this scheme did not go well with the Dalcrozian method that Nijinsky and Marie Rambert—Rithmichka, as the dancers nicknamed her—were trying to apply, which was essentially a system of translating rhythm and meter into bodily movement,[69] and had a built-in preference for working with, rather than against, the metric accents in the music. Moreover, on the practical level, Nijinsky was a poor communicator and tended, Buckle suggests, "to treat his interpreters as puppets."[70] Meanwhile, the music gradually got slower and slower. At the first rehearsal the composer attended, in the Aldwych Theatre, he "flew into a rage because the tempi were so slow. He yelled, banged his fists on the piano cover; he was appalled at the way rehearsals were going. Nijinsky was made very nervous by Stravinsky. There was a dreadful scene at a rehearsal—which was stopped."[71]

Returning to Clarens on 25 February—perhaps by way of Paris, where Paule de Lestang sang the Balmont songs on the twentieth[72]—Stravinsky still had the full score to complete, as well as the introduction to the second part, some of which was not yet even satisfactorily drafted. By 8 March the Sacrificial Dance was at last fully scored, on the nineteenth he solved the problem of the part 2 introduction by adding what are now its opening pages (up to figure 86), and on the twenty-ninth he wrote finis to the orchestral score of this addition—the last music of the whole work to be composed.[73] But all this delay meant that there was little time left for the work on *Khovanshchina*, and at some stage reinforcements were called up in the shape of Maurice Ravel—yet another Apache, the dedicatee of

Stravinsky's "Tsaraiuki," and a known admirer of Russian music and orchestration. Because Stravinsky had the necessary Musorgsky materials with him in Switzerland—including a copy of the published Rimsky edition fully marked up with Diaghilev's instructions—Mohammed had to come to the mountain; so Ravel duly turned up in Clarens with his mother on 17 March, and put up at the Hôtel des Crêtes, just across the railway line from the Châtelard. He was observed by the six-year-old Theodore. "I can still see leaning by my father's side on the wrought-iron balcony outside our windows . . . a little man, perfectly turned out, with glowing eyes, tufted eyebrows and a fine head of slightly silvering hair. I can still hear them whistling a short phrase five, ten, fifteen times to the blackbirds in the garden who, to my childish delight, ended by whistling the same phrase back to them."[74] Ravel worked on the new orchestrations for the opera while Stravinsky added the finishing touches to the ballet, and only then drafted his powerful, neo-Russian setting of Musorgsky's old Russian chant.[75] Stravinsky showed Ravel his Japanese lyrics and discussed Schoenberg's *Pierrot Lunaire* with him and a Clarens neighbor called Ernest Ansermet, a conductor and former mathematics professor at Lausanne University, who had taken over as director of the Kursaal orchestra at Montreux at the start of the previous season. They were intrigued by Schoenberg's way of combining major and minor chords, which Ravel thought perfectly acceptable "provided the minor third is at the top and the major at the bottom." "But if you can do it that way round," Stravinsky said, "I don't see why you can't do the reverse; and *if I want to, I can*."[76] He may have mentioned—may even have demonstrated—how he had already combined major and minor in the same register in *Zvezdolikiy* and *The Rite of Spring*, the harshest possible version of this color clash. The *Japanese Lyrics*, however, confine themselves to Ravel's approved layout.

The immediate upshot of these discussions was that Ravel began to compose his *Trois Poèmes de Mallarmé* (for the same forces as Stravinsky's *Lyrics*), and to hatch "an admirable plan for a [Paris] Concert to stir up a Row," which would include all three works.[77] On 4 April Diaghilev wired from St. Petersburg for Stravinsky to meet him in Monte Carlo the following Tuesday (the eighth). But the chorus was almost certainly not ready and Stravinsky did not go. Two weeks later Diaghilev, now in Monte Carlo for the Ballets Russes season, still had not received Stravinsky's *Khovanshchina* material. This time the composer dispatched it by post, at the same time no doubt responding to Monteux's request—also from Monte Carlo—for the corrected autograph full score of *The Rite*.[78]

Curiously enough, Stravinsky seems to have had no plans to go to the Riviera for the ballet season, even though one might suppose him desperate not only to discuss the problematical aspects of his score with the conductor, but also to see how the hapless Nijinsky was surviving the attentions of Rithmichka and the muttering discontent of his fellow dancers. If he did go, the visit or visits were brief. "I shall probably be here all the time until Paris," he told one correspondent in March, while still adding the final touches to *The Rite of Spring* in Clarens.[79] The *Khovanshchina* work, in effect a five-and-a-half-minute composition plus some arranging, probably took him until mid-April, after which there was a trip to Lake Maggiore and Varese with Ravel before the latter's return to Paris towards the end of the month. Meanwhile, the telegrams and letters from Monte Carlo flowed in, indicating that Stravinsky was elsewhere. Diaghilev wired on the nineteenth, twenty-first, and twenty-seventh, and Monteux wrote on the fifteenth, the day before *Petrushka* opened. By the end of April the company was on its way to Paris.

Hardly less surprising is that Stravinsky seems to have been in no hurry to get to Paris himself, and arrived there only on 13 May, nearly a fortnight after the dancers and only slightly more than that before the premiere of his ballet on the twenty-ninth. He was under constant pressure from Jurgenson over proofs: those of the symphony, because the autograph score borrowed from Mrs. Rimsky-Korsakov had to be returned; and those of *Zvezdolikiy*, because it was still supposed to be slated for performance in Paris at the end of May, though the composer himself had known since the autumn that Sechiari could not find the singers to sing it.[80] Then, just at the crucial moment, the children went down with tonsils and adenoids and had to be operated on one by one; even Igor had to have his nose cauterized for adenoids, as he informed Max dispassionately from his hospital bed in Lausanne.[81]

There are, it seems, many rites of spring: the purgative, but also the re-creative. On the very day that Stravinsky crossed the last *t* of his ballet, 29 March, the Moscow journal *Muzïka* announced, apparently out of the blue, that his next work would be another ballet, *Svadebka* (The Little Wedding). One might wonder who was Derzhanovsky's informant, since there is no trace in his correspondence with the composer. It was probably Alexander Sanin, a former stage director at the Mariyinsky and well known in the West as Diaghilev's stage director for *Boris Godunov* in Paris in 1908. Sanin had written to Stravinsky in early March with a request that he compose a work for a new Moscow venture called the Free Theatre, of which Sanin had been appointed "organizer, stage director—effectively the animator." Sanin had a specific work in mind, which Stravinsky had mentioned to him when they had met in Paris: "You told me about your *Svadba*. . . . We should like to know in greater detail what this *Svadba* is."[82]

Stravinsky himself probably did not yet know. In any case, he ignored the "Wedding" bait, and instead offered Sanin the existing eighteen-minute *Scene from Andersen's "Nightingale"*—a fairly grotesque piece of opportunism considering that Sanin had asked for "a three-act full-evening work."[83] On the one hand, he plainly saw the chance to make use of a performable score without further creative effort on his part; on the other hand, he must have been wary of putting too much faith in Sanin and his enthusiastic idealism, his "many hopes and dreams," his bottomless budget. Yet the commission *had* come at an opportune moment. In Russia the Stravinskys' income was prey to the economic instabilities about which his brother-in-law had already warned them; in the West it was in the hands of the brilliant, evasive Diaghilev, whose own funds were in permanent crisis, who insisted on exclusivity for all Stravinsky's ballets, and who would soon begin to claim that he was not obliged to pay for them at all if, like the *Firebird,* they were not protected under the Berne Convention.[84] Now here was an invitation to name his own project and his own fee. But with the Polignac concerto still unwritten, it was small wonder that he turned hopefully to an existing score that was lying idle; and no wonder that, after mechanically rejecting Sanin's suggestion that he add a second scene to round off the Andersen tale, he then at once sent a second telegram and letter agreeing after all to compose *two* further scenes, in return for a sumptuous fee of ten thousand roubles, which would enable him to postpone the three-thousand-franc (about twelve-hundred-rouble) Polignac commission, but which made even the gushing Sanin and his expansive boss, Konstantin Mardzhanov, turn pale and conspiratorial.[85] In accepting the fee, Sanin tried vainly to hedge it round with limitations: delayed installments, no performance rights charges, absolute secrecy, a long Russian exclusivity, no publishers' hire fees. But Stravinsky had his man, and he knew it; Sanin had given too much, too early; his effusions had been too impassioned, too urgent. He would not withdraw now. Stravinsky's response was ruthless and intransigent: "You make impossible conditions. Struve cannot enter into an agreement with me. It's your business to make an arrangement with the publishers. Stravinsky."[86] Mardzhanov himself made one last vain attempt to lower the fee to seven thousand five hundred roubles. But there was nothing doing. "Concessions possible," Stravinsky cabled back, "only as regards installment payments because faced with dilemma of writing either opera [for you] or ballet for Diaghilev."[87] *Alea jacta est,* as Sanin himself had declared at the start of his very first letter. The die was cast.

FISTICUFFS AND A BAD OYSTER

AFTER THREE (out of four) Paris seasons at the Châtelet, the Ballets Russes were in new premises for their spring season of 1913. The Théâtre des Champs-Elysées, in the avenue Montaigne a few yards up from the place de l'Alma and the river Seine, was a dazzling expression of Gabriel Astruc's confidence in art as an expression of the contemporary spirit. Today its bold concrete-and-marble façade, smoothly articulated by Emile Antoine Bourdelle's low-relief friezes, seems as much as anything a prelude to the great age of the cinema. But Astruc intended to put into it live operas and ballets on the largest scale, played to an audience that would combine a variety of moneyed elements: the Parisian *gratin,* the well-heeled tourists who were starting to invade the French capital each spring, the bourgeois art snobs, the ragged aesthetes who, then as now, imagined that dressing like an "artist" was a painless way of being one. The theatre combined extreme comfort with an exceptionally open auditorium which not only gave uniformly excellent sightlines and clear, even acoustics, but did away with many of the old insignia of class division while at the same time separating the entire audience—king and commoner alike—from the proscenium frame, exactly as in a cinema. Jean Cocteau suggested that so prosaically luxurious a theatre was hardly conducive to a lively response to new art.[1] But the reverse seems to have been the case, and it was the unusual freedom and fluidity of the auditorium which, during that first season, helped generate a response that was at times perhaps a shade too lively.[2]

The theatre had opened in early April with, among other things, a production of Berlioz's *Benvenuto Cellini*—its first in Paris since the original staging of 1838. "Rest assured," Ravel wrote cuttingly to Stravinsky in Clarens, "the acoustics of the Théâtre des Champs-Elysées are so perfect that you can even hear the refinement of Berlioz's harmonies."[3] Ravel lived not far away, in the avenue Carnot (just off the place de l'Etoile), and had found the Stravinskys and their three children accommodation in the comfortable Hotel Splendide nearby—two rooms and a bathroom for twenty-five francs a night. Arriving on the thirteenth, Igor plunged at once into piano rehearsals for *The Rite of Spring*, even though Nijinsky must have been on tenterhooks about the premiere of Debussy's *Jeux*, which he was both choreographing and dancing, only two nights later. On the fifteenth Debussy's exquisite ballet, with its white-clad trio of tennis flirts—Karsavina, Nijinsky, Lyudmila Schollar—left Diaghilev's first-night audience mystified, and eventually mirthful, at its association of such subtly nuanced music with a choreography of swinging arms and angular poses, a music which, as Debussy told Robert Godet, "was content with opposing its light arabesques to so many ungainly feet—which don't even beg pardon." "This man," he wrote of Nijinsky,

> counts quaver triplets with his feet, checks them on his arms, then, suddenly struck down with hemiplegia, watches the music go by with a cross look. This is apparently called the "stylization of gesture." . . . It's hideous! It's even Dalcrozian, since I regard Mr. Dalcroze as one of the worst enemies of music! And you can imagine what havoc his method can wreak in the soul of this young Nijinsky savage![4]

Since *The Rite of Spring* was an ensemble ballet, while *Jeux* involved only the three solo dancers, Nijinsky had left the Debussy to the last minute, whereas the Stravinsky was ready, choreographically, by the time the company reached Paris. But Diaghilev had superstitiously delayed the Stravinsky premiere until the anniversary of Nijinsky's *Après-midi d'un faune*, 29 May—ironic confirmation of the greater importance he attached to *The Rite* than to the new, purpose-built Debussy. All the same, there may have been a point of caution as well, since if the dancers were ready, the orchestra certainly was not. Monteux had managed two full orchestral as well as some sectional rehearsals of part 1 of the ballet in Paris at the end of March; but he had of course been unable to rehearse the Paris musicians, who were mostly members of the Orchestre des Concerts Colonne,[5] during the season in Monte Carlo, and with the composer arriving so comparatively late, and with other new ballets as well as the usual repertoire to rehearse, time was getting short. Somehow Monteux fitted no fewer than seventeen orchestral rehearsals into those last two weeks, as well as five stage rehearsals with the dancers. "The musicians," he recalled later, "thought it absolutely crazy, but as they were well paid, their discipline was not too bad! When at last I put the whole thing together, it seemed chaotic but Stravinsky was behind me pointing out little phrases he wished heard."[6] "Everybody was confused," Henri Girard, one of the double-bass players, told Truman C. Bullard, by the complicated rhythms, atrocious dissonances, and strange sounds to which our ears were not accustomed. Musicians started to stop Monteux, asking if the parts were correctly printed, wanting to know, for example, if "my B natural is correct as my neighbor is playing B flat." This went on for a certain time until Monteux said angrily, "Do not stop me asking if you have a mistake. If you have one, I will let you know." Monteux was gifted with an extraordinarily accurate ear, besides being a fantastic reader. . . .

There is an incident I remember well. When we came to a place where all the brass instruments, in a gigantic fortissimo, produced such an offending conglomeration that the whole orchestra broke down in a spontaneous nervous laugh and stopped playing. But Stravinsky jumped out of his seat, furious, running to the piano and saying, "Gentlemen, you do not have to laugh. I know what I wrote," and he started to play the awful passage, reestablishing order.[7]

By the time of the open dress rehearsal on the twenty-eighth, such problems may have been resolved, but there remained a sense of unease, due partly to the sheer complexity of the score, partly to a feeling that Nijinsky and his dancers were not wholly at one with the music or each other, partly perhaps to Diaghilev's own instinct that trouble was in the air. The fact that the dress rehearsal nevertheless passed off quietly (unlike that of Debussy's *Pelléas et Mélisande* eleven years earlier) gives some indication of the reasons for the uproar which broke out within minutes of the start of the official premiere the following night. The audience for the twenty-eighth was largely a specialist one with a society element, as Stravinsky himself described it in his autobiography:[8] an audience of music critics (disgruntled, perhaps, at not having been invited to the premiere), musicians, artists, art lovers, and others whose interest in the event, as we may suppose, was essentially pure-minded, since they did not—like the first-night audience—get a full program of ballets or a notable social cachet. The twenty-ninth, on the other hand, was a subscription evening with a full program *(Les Sylphides, Rite of Spring, Spectre de la rose, Prince Igor)*, attended by the whole range of Astruc's clientele, most of whom, moreover, would already have seen and sniggered at *Jeux* two Thursdays before.[9] Some of the more philistine elements may well have come prepared for some fun at Nijinsky's expense. Word had got about after the final rehearsals that the new ballet was difficult, violent, incomprehensible;[10] what better response to these disturbing qualities than laughter and ridicule? "These so-called 'society' people," as Florent Schmitt described them, "unable to see, hear and feel for themselves, these grown-up children . . . could only respond to these splendors, so immeasurably remote from their feeble understanding, with the stupid hilarity of infants."[11]

But Schmitt himself, and others among Stravinsky's admirers, made matters worse in true Gallic fashion by responding to the remarks in kind, which naturally ensured their continuation. The various individual exchanges—Schmitt hurling abuse at the *"garces du seizième,"* Carl Van Vechten being pommelled on the head by the man behind him, the calls for a dentist at the sight of Maria Piltz with her head resting on her clenched hands at the start of the Sacrificial Dance—are now so much a part of the folklore of the occasion that it seems as pointless to deny them as to repeat them. What seems certain is that the trouble started before the curtain rose, and then got worse partly as a result of the bizarre spectacle of the Young Maidens—the so-called *Shchegolikhi,* or tarted-up girls—in their squawlike costumes, toes turned inwards, knees bent, their heads tilted onto their hands, in utter contradiction of what the ordinary man understood by the term "ballet"; partly as a result of the combative nature of the work's supporters. "It was only," wrote one privileged critic who had got into the premiere, "by straining our ears amid an indescribable racket that we could, painfully, get some rough idea of the new work, prevented from hearing it as much by its defenders as by its attackers."[12] Here and there actual fighting broke out.[13] If the music was heard at all, it can only have been as a component of the uproar, to which it must appreciably have contributed.

After only a few minutes of this, Stravinsky left his seat in the fourth row of the stalls and hurried backstage, slamming the door uselessly as he went. "I have never again been that angry. The music was so familiar to me; I loved it, and I could not understand why people who had not yet heard it wanted to protest in advance."[14] In the wings he found Diaghilev, flicking the house lights in the hope of calming the worst of the din, and Nijinsky standing on a chair yelling out numbers at the dancers.[15] When the curtain fell on the first scene, Girard told Bullard, Astruc went out and spoke to the audience, pleading with them not to interrupt the second part.[16] But it made no difference. Somehow the dancers held ranks, despite the fact that "by the time the curtain went up we were pretty scared" and that "the uproar in the audience made it hard to hear even this music";[17] somehow Monteux piloted the orchestra to the end; somehow Maria Piltz, who had replaced Bronislava Nijinska as the Chosen Virgin after Bronislava had revealed that she was pregnant, not only danced her ferocious solo but, if Romola Nijinsky is to be believed, danced it beautifully.[18] "I recall Maria Piltz," Andrey Levinson wrote,

facing calmly a hooting audience whose violence completely drowned out the orchestra. She seemed to dream, her knees turned inward, the heels pointing out—inert. A sudden spasm shook her body out of its corpse-like rigor. At the fierce onward thrust of the rhythm she trembled in ecstatic, irregular jerks. This primitive hysteria, terribly burlesque as it was, completely caught and overwhelmed the spectator.[19]

Even when the curtain at last came down, the battle continued. Amid competing applause and protests, Stravinsky, Nijinsky, and the dancers took several calls (Monteux presumably waiting for the end of the whole bill).[20] Almost unbelievably, Nijinsky, who must have felt mentally and physically quite drained, was back onstage within twenty minutes or so, as the Spirit of the Rose in *Le Spectre de la rose*.

The press, the next morning and in the ensuing days, reflected the audience's polarization of response. Inevitably there were some critics who, whether they had heard the dress rehearsal or merely witnessed the premiere, felt affronted by the primitive violence and discordance of the proceedings and were disposed to ridicule what Henri Quittard, in *Le Figaro*, called their "laborious and puerile barbarism."[21] "It seems," wrote another hostile reviewer,

> that in the quest for a primitive, prehistoric *effect*, [the composer] has worked at *bringing his music close to noise*. To that end, he has concentrated on destroying all sense of tonality. One would like to follow in the score (which I didn't receive) this eminently *amusical* labor. I can give you an idea which corresponds to my impression: play on two pianos, or four hands on one, transposing one part but not the other by a tone: so, for example, when you have C-E-G on the one hand, you will have D-F-A [sic] on the other, *and at the same time*. Or if you prefer to mistune by a semitone, don't be afraid. The point is to avoid nearly always any of those ignoble chords which used to be thought of as consonant.[22]

But by no means all the dissenting voices were candidly hostile or acerbic. There were critics who, much as they might dislike the asperities of the new Stravinsky and the remorseless stampings of Nijinsky's post-Dalcrozian dance, could not bring themselves to dismiss out of hand the composer and premier danseur of *Petrushka*. For some the new score might be a regrettable lapse of judgment, for others an as yet impenetrable effusion by a composer whose previous ballets "asserted a mastery so incontestable that it would be rash to set oneself up as censor of a work by the same composer before studying it closely, with the attention and respect it deserves."[23] Meanwhile the forces of progress were more than ready with their heavy guns and their extravagant battle cries. The apostolic Florent Schmitt—his own premiere only just over the horizon—was quick to proclaim Stravinsky as "the Messiah we've been waiting for since Wagner, and for whom Musorgsky and Claude Debussy, as well as Richard Strauss and Arnold Schoenberg, seem to have prepared the way."[24] The arts daily *Comoedia* carried no fewer than four notices, all broadly sympathetic, in two consecutive issues, and then dispatched their critic Gustave Linor to all four subsequent performances, presumably to report on the continuing antics of the public as much as on the increasingly (if never entirely) audible music. The coverage on the thirty-first included strong and substantial pieces by Louis Vuillemin and, most strikingly, by the paper's editor-in-chief, Gustave de Pawlowski, who launched into a spectacular assault on the first-night audience, which "summed up all the astonishment one must feel in noting the stupid, reasoned malice of what is conventionally known as the Parisian élite in the presence of any enterprise that is genuinely new and daring."[25]

Specialist critics saw at once the epoch-making side of this newsworthy theatrical incident. For Igor's friend Michel Calvocoressi, fresh from translating the messianic text of *Zvezdolikiy, The Rite* marked "the beginning of a new stage in Mr. Stravinsky's activity, and permits us to recognize very clearly in him not just the grandson of Glinka and Borodin . . . but the man of his time and perhaps its prophet."[26] The young critic of the short-lived, (theoretically) bimonthly journal *Montjoie!*, a composer who wrote under the name Roland-Manuel, went still further:

> In order to communicate to his work the somewhat hard brilliance, the enormous power of these primitive rites, much older than the Dionysiac outbursts . . . the musician—like the choreographer—had to break the hallowed canons, had deliberately to change the color of *his* music and *all* music. Igor Stravinsky has achieved this marvel with a simplicity which it doesn't seem an exaggeration to call that of a genius: the musical material is superbly new, new like that burst of sap which it glorifies.[27]

Both these writers showed an awareness of the two aspects of *The Rite of Spring:* the narrative and ethnic tradition to which, in conception, it belonged; and, on the other hand, that apparent break with every tradition, which was what made it so disturbing an experience for the sophisticated, supposedly unshockable Parisians. A few months later, the novelist and literary critic Jacques Rivière would be able in all earnestness to devote a long and penetrating article to both the music and the choreography, with hardly a single reference to their ritual subject, but concentrating entirely on internal process and actually arguing the music's complete avoidance of the picturesque and descriptive—an approach which must have astonished those readers and critics who had heard the insistent patterns of repetition as a kind of impressionism of the primitive: what Cocteau later called the "Georgics of prehistory."[28]

BUT WAS STRAVINSKY himself ready to abandon the sources of *The Rite* in favor of its possible musical consequences? Ever since the first discussions with Roerich in 1910 and the visit to Talashkino in 1911, the "idea" of the work had been closely bound up with its ethnographic subject matter, starting with the mental "image of the old woman in squirrel skins . . . running in front of everyone, [and] stopping every so often."[29] More than a year later, and with the score virtually complete, he told Nikolay Findeyzen that "throughout the work I use lapidary rhythms to give listeners the feeling of the closeness of men to the earth, the community of their lives with the soil."[30] Actual folk song remained a crucial musical source, as the sketches prove, even if Stravinsky never actually went collecting in person.[31] The whole suggestion is of a stylized re-creation of peasant myths and idioms, exactly as in the paintings and graphic designs of Roerich, including, of course, his exquisite set designs and studies for *The Rite of Spring* itself.

As late as the week before the first performance, Stravinsky gave an interview to Ricciotto Canudo, the editor of *Montjoie!*, which came out on the day of the premiere in the form of an article that still gave prominence to the graphic, narrative elements of the music's inspiration. It was called "Ce que j'ai voulu exprimer dans *Le Sacre du Printemps*" (What I wished to express in *The Rite of Spring*).[32] The composer later strenuously disavowed this article. But, while he probably did not physically write it, there seems little doubt that it accurately reflected his thoughts, which were—to generalize from the article—that the specific, neonationalist ritual presented in *The Rite* was expressive of that universal terror which seizes the whole of nature when confronted with the force of its own renewal. There is in fact little in this somewhat Nietzschean program to embarrass the composer of *Zvezdolikiy.* The train of events is nevertheless confused. The idea for some kind of article had come from Canudo (whom Stravinsky had met through Schmitt the previous summer, but whose writings on music he had certainly encountered before that).[33] An undated note from Canudo, probably of 19 May, invites Stravinsky to the *Montjoie!* office in the Chaussée d'Antin to discuss it, and later notes remind the composer that proofs are waiting to be read.[34] Was Stravinsky really surprised by the text as it appeared in print? According to Craft, he sent a note by hand to *Montjoie!* on 5 June disowning the article, to which Canudo replied as one grieved at a betrayal, breaking off relations (which, however, in fact continued). But no such note from Stravinsky has resurfaced, and Canudo's wounded reply was actually written in response to a notice the composer inserted in *Excelsior* in early July, disclaiming a rumored collaboration with Canudo.[35] Stravinsky later sent a copy of the article to Derzhanovsky, who duly published it in Russian in *Muzïka*.[36] This time Stravinsky did protest, vehemently, repeatedly, and, it may be thought, somewhat extravagantly, complaining that the translation distorted his ideas, though never once suggesting that the original article had done so.[37] In fact a comparison of the two texts shows only quite minor verbal discrepancies. Of any significant distortion, there is little or no trace.

The *Montjoie!* article had amounted to a stylistic summary of both Stravinsky's and Roerich's contribution to the ballet. The apocalyptic tone of "the total, panic-stricken rising of the universal sap" and "the obscure and immense sensation that all things experience at the moment when Nature renews its forms" was associated with Roerich, and it seems that—after the "obscure and immense sensation" of the first performance—Stravinsky was at last beginning to have had enough of it.[38] On the other hand, the article also suggests new lines of musical development which, with hindsight, we can see as prophetic. Stravinsky told his readers that

> the whole prelude is based on a constant and equal mezzo-forte. The melody there develops along a horizontal line which swells or contracts only according to the volume of instruments—the intense dynamism of the orchestra rather than the melodic line itself. From this melody I have consequently excluded the *strings*, with their crescendos and diminuendos—much too evocative and representative of the human voice—and I have placed in the foreground the *woodwind*, drier, cleaner, less prone to facile expressiveness, and by that very token still more moving to my taste.[39]

Suddenly there emerges from the whole art-nouveau apparatus—the pseudo-ritual, the Talashkino costume designs, the stamping rhythms, the folk-song patterns intertwining like the peasant motifs on a Bilibin title page—a specifically new and hypermodern approach to materials which is essentially independent of style.

In its origins *The Rite of Spring* had stayed broadly faithful to the World of Art nationalism of *Petrushka*. It was an artificial re-creation of some folk reality: not meant to be accurate or realistic as Stasov or Musorgsky would have understood those terms, and certainly not conveying a Stasovian social message, but still by intention profoundly true to the spirit of the culture from which it derived its subject matter and materials. In other words, it was still a work of Russian nationalism, kuchkist in a sense, much indebted to Rimsky-Korsakov's ideas of a properly researched use of ethnic materials, while plainly rejecting the academic pedantries with which Rimsky had fenced his own and his pupils' work. At the same time, it absorbed a lot from the theurgic wing of nationalist art. Behind it lay Gorodetsky's Yarilo, the sun god, the star-faced one of *Zvezdolikiy*, and all those other epicene pantocrators of millennial late tsarism. Its violence was not only primitive; it was modern, protorevolutionary, destructive as well as recreative, oppressive as well as liberating. Above all, it was excessive; it lacked restraint and moderation, it preached self-annihilation through the senses, just as much as it observed it through the window of Roerich's imaginative archaeology. It was romantic self-absorption gone mad.[40]

How much of this was conscious, on either Roerich's or Stravinsky's part, is of relatively little consequence. Insofar as it was in the work, Stravinsky became aware of it, and rejected it. But the way the music was written—its internal mechanisms—intrigued him more and more. Sitting at his upright piano in Les Tilleuls, picturing to himself the little old woman in her squirrel skins, or the young girls with their painted faces, or the Chosen One dancing herself into the frozen earth, he did not simply crash around on the keyboard like an angry child looking for the most repellent cacophony he could find, as some critics chose to imagine. His work was painstaking, and the results systematic. This is not to say that the violence of the concept, its sheer animal force, had no bearing on the musical technique. On the contrary; he looked for types of chords which could convey the human terror of the action. But having found them, in a particular kind of transparent dissonance—transparent in the sense that one can perfectly well hear the simple elements it consists of—he then used that type of chord as a binding motif, one which could be varied in many different ways, while keeping its essential character intact. He found that he could combine melodies in the same way: not smoothly (as in a round or a Bach fugue), but harshly according to certain regular patterns. And later he noticed that he could combine them in and out of phase, so that the harmony fluctuated within predictable but not necessarily pre-planned limits. As for the rhythm, that, too, could work transparently, by varying basic patterns in a simple additive or subtractive way which kept the patterns clear while disrupting their even flow.

The "automatic" aspects of such writing, which Stravinsky hints at in the *Montjoie!* article, depended to some extent on a flat style of performance. You could not have musicians "expressing" their individual tunes in a way that might obscure the patterning. For the same reason, Stravinsky found himself preferring instruments which articulated well, like the woodwind and trumpets, or sometimes whole groups of such instruments, each playing a particular, generic music: flute music, oboe music, and so forth. These groupings can literally be seen in the printed score; they form strips of particular densities across the page—densities which in themselves may not alter significantly for a minute or more in performance. Writing in this way, Stravinsky was indulging a particularly Russian love of pure sonority, a love he shared with Glinka and Tchaikovsky, and perhaps derived from them. What was new was his implication that such instrumentation was self-structuring, and provided all the gradations of loud and soft, all the expressive intensity, that the music called for, without any need for balancing or interpreting or "expressing" by the performer. It was these details which constituted the real modernism—revolutionary or otherwise—of *The Rite of Spring*. As for the noise and violence, the musical blood and guts, the physical excess, perhaps they were no more than a signal to history, a symbolic enactment of the death and rebirth of the musical language; but they certainly were not its substance.

INCLUDING THE DRESS REHEARSAL, the inaudible first night, and the semiaudible second night on 2 June, Stravinsky may have attended as many as three performances of *The Rite*. Late on the third he was admitted to a nursing home called Villa Borghese in the quiet suburb of Neuilly-sur-Seine, suffering from acute enteritis, apparently the result of eating a bad oyster at dinner. At first there was no clear diagnosis. Then suddenly, on the seventh, his temperature began to rise alarmingly, up and up till it reached 106 degrees.[41] The doctor now diagnosed typhoid fever and prescribed cold baths, a drastic treatment which induced an "agonizing" reaction, as Katya told Stepan Mitusov, "but really gives a good result and every time lowers his temperature by a degree."[42] Recovery was painfully and frustratingly slow. Anna Stravinsky came from St. Petersburg, and Katya lived in the Villa Borghese with her husband and (presumably) children, and such correspondence as could not be avoided, she handled. She kept in touch with Sanin and with Mitusov, urging them to come to Ustilug for discussions about *The Nightingale* as soon as Igor was back home, and giving Styopa elaborate travel instructions which today read like Baedeker at his best, full of practical advice about itinerary, hotels, where to rest and for how long, and how to name-drop the Belyankins ("the owners of Ustilug") in order to get the best treatment in nearby towns like Kovel and Vladimir-Volïnsky.[43] She held Jurgenson at bay on the question of proofs, and she answered Max's anguished inquiries about the need or otherwise for him to meet Diaghilev and Bakst in London for discussions about the *Metamorphoses* ballet.[44]

Igor's Paris friends—Delage (who "was with me constantly"), Schmitt, Ravel, Debussy, Manuel de Falla, Alfredo Casella—brought him news of the outside world.[45] Debussy had been at the first night with Misia Edwards and had turned to her at one point and whispered, "It's terrifying—I don't understand it"—a perhaps surprising reaction for someone who a few days before had calmly sight-read the four-hand score with its composer.[46] But to his friend André Caplet, Debussy wrote that "I am saving up for you a read-through of *The Rite of Spring*, which cannot leave you indifferent,"[47] and he and his wife tried hard to invite the Stravinskys to dine in the days after the premiere, unaware that Stravinsky had been taken ill.[48] From Delage, perhaps, Igor learnt that the last three Paris performances of *The Rite* (on 4, 6, and 13 June) had all gone off at least less violently than the premiere, while *Khovanshchina*, on the fifth, had been a brilliant success, thanks not least to sensational choral singing by the Russian Pokhitonov Choir and a spectacular staging by Sanin.[49] But this had owed nothing to Stravinsky's contribution, which was not even performed. At the last minute Diaghilev substituted the original Rimsky ending, possibly because he had spotted Andrey Rimsky-Korsakov in the audience for *The Rite of Spring* the previous evening and decided to hold his fire in the simmering controversy over the reworking of the Rimsky version. Eventually, Stravinsky's closing scene was announced for the third performance, on the ninth, but Gustave Linor, reviewing the performance for *Comoedia*, seems to have suspected a trap, and remarked pointedly that he had heard only the second act and part of the third (Musorgsky's acts 3 and 4). His instincts did not betray him. The chorus was not sung, and once again its first performance was announced, for the sixteenth, the date now usually given in the Stravinsky literature.

In fact the first date on which we can be reasonably certain that it was performed is the eighteenth—the fifth performance in the run of six—to judge from a brief, unsigned notice in *Comoedia* the next morning, informing readers that "the final chorus, recomposed by M. Igor Stravinsky on four themes by Musorgsky, produced a great effect."[50] No doubt this was a notice placed by Diaghilev. But they were not his sentiments. In his production notes, he recorded that

> [Stravinsky's] finale wasn't much better done [i.e., composed] than Rimsky-Korsakov's. Moreover, in the theatre, during the performances, Stravinsky's very gentle music (especially at the start) was completely crushed by the noise of the machines for distributing the smoke round the pyres on which the sectarians were to burn. . . . Alas, the last act wiped out the impression made by *Khovanshchina* on the public, and the opera ended disappointingly. Puccini, who was

in my box for the premiere, summed up his opinion in an unexpected phrase: "A lot here," he said, touching his forehead, "and nothing here," touching his heart.[51]

Two months later Stravinsky wrote to Derzhanovsky that the chorus "was done with great success three times in Paris," which would support the sixteenth for the date of the premiere. But he adds that "the critics, who attended the opera's premiere *in corpore* and supposed that my chorus was being played (in fact Rimsky-Korsakov's was played) tore it completely to pieces."[52]

None of this reached Stravinsky from Diaghilev himself. In his autobiography, the composer remembered that "Diaghilev called in nearly every day, though he never came into my room, so great was his fear of contagion."[53] But Katya told Steinberg that Igor was "hardly seeing Diaghilev, since Sergey Pavlovich and the whole company are scared of the typhoid and don't visit him."[54] And according to Stravinsky's later recollection, "Diaghilev never did visit me, but he paid my hospital bill."[55] Perhaps this last, important point is the meaning of the composer's remark to Benois that at Neuilly "I became convinced of the good brotherly feelings of Seryozha . . . and I satisfied myself about the complete indifference of all his ballet and opera collaborators."[56] They, certainly, did not visit, whether out of fear or sheer overwork—in a Paris season which lasted more than five weeks without break and was then at once followed by a three-week London season starting on 24 June. While Igor was recovering from his unpleasant illness sufficiently to be able to write his own letters and proofread the slow movement of his E-flat Symphony—"walking like a fly on two feet," as he told Max[57]—his "ballet and opera collaborators" were dancing and singing his latest works to an audience very different in perception and excitability from Astruc's subscribers in the avenue Montaigne.

After the Paris experience, Diaghilev approached the London premiere of *The Rite* on 11 July at the Theatre Royal in Drury Lane with some trepidation. How would the starchy English, with their austere sense of propriety, react to this explosive music and its novel, unballetic choreography? Perhaps cuts should be made. It seems to have been Delage, now also in London, who alerted Stravinsky to this threat—one which, with memories of Diaghilev's unscrupulous attitude to the works he had adapted for the ballet, he was bound to take seriously. Either in a careless moment, or with deliberate intent, he let slip to José-Maria Sert that he felt unable to trust Diaghilev in such matters. Sert at once wired Diaghilev to that effect. Meanwhile, Stravinsky fired off a letter to Monteux expressly forbidding him to accept cuts. According to Misia Edwards, who described the scene to Stravinsky in a long and emotional letter a few days later, Monteux confronted Diaghilev on the very day of the premiere, announcing in front of Nijinsky and the entire corps de ballet . . . "I am the representative of M. Stravinsky, who has written me: 'M. D[iaghilev] has the audacity to want to make cuts in my work. I make you responsible, etc. etc.' " and he added, "You can ask for my resignation and send me back." Serge replied that indeed he could envisage a lawsuit based on the grounds that he, Monteux, in the name of the French musicians, was acting against him. But most serious of all, this incident completely undermined his authority. The dancers refused to rehearse and Nijinsky spoke to [Diaghilev] as if he were a dog.[58]

Did it happen in quite this way? If so, it seems curious that Monteux had already written to Stravinsky four days before, reassuring him on the question of cuts.[59] But Misia, a Russian-born Pole who had been one of Diaghilev's first Paris backers and his most loyal supporter and friend in the capital, was in any case an instinctive manipulator who thought always in terms of grand alliances, driving wedges, and all those other hallowed devices of the social tactician. Knowing Stravinsky's supreme importance to the Ballets Russes, she feared his hostility to Diaghilev, and made up her mind to shame him into a reconciliation. She pictured Diaghilev alone and abandoned in a foreign city: "The unhappy man left the theatre alone and spent the whole day in the park. I was astonished that he hadn't come for me as he always does; I didn't see him until quite late. I won't go on, dear friend, about the pain you've caused him, but you can be sure that I spoke to him the way you yourself would have done."[60] But of course Stravinsky was not himself to blame for these miseries. They were the fault of "that shabby, jealous little group that has surrounded you with pettiness"— Delage, Casella, Schmitt, and the rest. Stravinsky, Misia had written from London a few days earlier, should not let a Frenchman like Delage destroy his Russian blood-brotherhood.

> Serge has always protected your interests, which are his own. . . . At this moment *Le Sacre* is the vindication of his life. You must understand that he would prefer to do anything rather than sacrifice it. Because he's risking a great deal in giving it here, he is all the more determined. . . .
>
> As for me, I believe that only you can *save* him, and I also think that I prefer the worst Russian thing to any French work, no matter how inspired.
>
> After several years, that's the conclusion I've come to. Be Russian! Remain Russian! Diaghilev can only be the soul of Russianness. . . . I regret *very much* that you are unable to come; you would have been a great help to your friend and would quickly have sifted out the truth from all the petty cliques' gossip and meaningless drivel.[61]

It is a remarkable fact that throughout the several pages of these two letters, Misia never once denies that Diaghilev had intended to cut Igor's score. And yet she succeeds in presenting the impresario as the wronged party, and the composer—who rarely forgave violence to his music, whether by word or deed—as misguided and unreasonable. After the performance on the eleventh, which had been preceded—somewhat bizarrely—by a talk before the curtain by the music critic Edwin Evans, Misia had cabled Stravinsky in Berlin, on his way home at last to Ustilug: "Complete success *Sacre* spoiled by your letter Monteux unjustly wounding Serge." Stravinsky must already have received Misia's first (London) letter, but he had not yet learnt the full horror of Diaghilev's public humiliation and his day in the park. Perhaps he was simply relieved that things had gone well and by his confidence that Monteux had protected his interests. At all events he could afford to be conciliatory. Chastened, he cabled Diaghilev on the twelfth:

"Sorry to have caused trouble but did not understand your diplomatic position."[62]

THE NIGHTINGALE AND
NOT THE LARK

DEPRESSED AS HE WAS by the debacle in Paris, and still in some measure convalescent from his typhoid, Igor could not take the rest he certainly needed when he got to Ustilug in the middle of July. His contract with the Free Theatre stipulated delivery by 20 September. And while it must have been clear to him that his illness had put such a deadline out of reach—and Mardzhanov accepted this too, wiring, "Don't worry about work. Do it when well"[1]—he was nonetheless desperate to complete the opera in good time, both because the revised contract delayed payment of four-fifths of the fee until after the work's completion and (we can assume) because when all was said and done *Nightingale* remained an interruption, almost an irrelevance, as compared with the quite different sort of work that was stirring in his thoughts. So Styopa Mitusov had been placed under strict orders to set off for Ustilug the minute he got Stravinsky's signal.[2] Although, as the composer had told Sanin, a complete scenario existed from the first stage of the collaboration, before *Firebird,* much of the libretto for the second and third acts had still to be thrashed out.[3] Until the text was in order, composition could not properly begin.

Styopa duly arrived at Ustilug, and a few days were spent drafting the libretto of the second act, some of which he had already written four years before, and agreeing on a framework for the third, of which nothing yet existed beyond the scenario.[4] Back in St. Petersburg, he took up his old procedure of composition by letter, trying out different variants of a single idea, invariably working towards the most succinct version possible, almost as if the composer were there before his eyes shaking his head at the sheer wordiness of this or that attempt. "Don't be afraid to curse or reject," Styopa pleads at one point, "I need to have a completely clear conscience." And a few days later: "Of course, as you know, I'm worried that the whole thing is bad, worried sick."[5] All of a sudden, after buying a copy of the *Japanese Lyrics* at Koussevitzky's music shop, he becomes aware of a plagiarism: "Oh God! Quite unintentionally it turned out I'd cribbed from the Japanese. How it happened I have absolutely no idea. In any case, it was unconscious. You, of course, will have noticed at once. I've redone it as follows."[6] In the Nightingale's song to the Emperor at the start of act 3, Styopa had unwittingly adapted the central idea of "Akahito"—the poet's inability to distinguish between snowflakes and white roses—to a slightly more elaborate conceit about white roses and twinkling stars. But the theft was trivial. "With my usual delicacy," Igor replied, "I didn't want to tell you you had pinched from 'Akahito'; but it doesn't mean a thing, and I assure you anyway that I like the first version better than the second. Keep it, for God's sake."[7] With his growing distaste for opera and its tendency to encourage an overblown style and "ham" acting, he naturally preferred the precision and conciseness of the original thought, a preference of which Styopa was perfectly well aware. "Do you know," he observes,

> I really don't like the Emperor's phrase: "odnako, shto eto takoye" [But whatever is this?]—there's something vulgar about it, inconsistent with an emperor's dignity. Wouldn't it be better to change it, for example to "eto-shto?" [what's this?]? It may be less clear, but accompanied by a suitable gesture and musical expression these two words can be much more significant and express better the feeling of surprise for which even words are inadequate.[8]

The composer's response is no less revealing.

> I *greatly* approve of what you've written of the Nightingale's song in the third act—it's wonderfully unexaggerated, and the approach . . . is excellent, beautiful! I also agree to changing "odnako, shto eto takoye" to "eto-shto?," though I didn't mind the previous version. Don't be upset, my friend—it's typical of you, as I'm well aware—you can never under any circumstances settle on anything. But what you've written is already superb and coalesces with the music in a single integrated rhythmic block.[9]

For Igor, the overriding question must have been whether he could accommodate his post-*Rite* style to the pre-*Firebird* idiom of the opera's first act. Perhaps he never did wholly manage this. But at least he covered his tracks, with a neatly ironic treatment of the porcelain world of the Emperor's palace after the decorative tapestry of the forest and the Fisherman in the fading moonlight. Moreover, he was soon composing at a steady rate, and with characteristic absorption. Max Steinberg had written from Lyubensk to inquire whether it was true that "you are going to finish *Nightingale*? I'll be very glad, as I've sincerely regretted up to now that this marvellous piece has remained unfinished."[10] Now Igor could write back that he was "completely submerged in work. I am composing *Nightingale*, and reading endless proofs."[11] And José-Maria Sert he told, rather gushingly: "I work, I eat, I sleep, and I never think of anything but *Rossignol* [*Nightingale*], Serge [Diaghilev], our theatre, Misia and you. . . ."[12]

By mid-August (NS) much of act 2 was written: everything up to the Chinese March, but possibly not yet the march itself, plus the scene of the Japanese envoys and the "song" of the mechanical nightingale.[13] Presumably the march—that incomparable piece of sardonic chinoiserie—was composed next, followed by the song of the real nightingale, which was ready in draft by 24 August, and then finally the closing scene of the act, in which the Emperor, finding that the real nightingale has flown away, angrily banishes it and appoints its mechanical rival Chief Singer of the Imperial Left-Hand Bedside Table. At the same time Mitusov peppered Ustilug with ever more refined drafts of the act 3 text. But these Stravinsky seems to have placed on one side. His first task was to produce a finished piano reduction of acts 1 and 2 so that RMV could get on with printing this vital tool of any work involving singers. Then he would have to prepare full scores of those same acts, incorporating various revisions he intended to make to the original score of the first act. And only then could he comfortably work on the final act.

At the very outset of discussions, Sanin had proposed Benois to design the new opera. As a Ballets Russes stage director, he was well aware of the close understanding between the co-authors of the company's most successful ballet, and perhaps it was an open secret that Stravinsky had already sounded Benois out about the possibility of collaborating on a completion of this very work. That would also explain why, in proposing the opera's completion, Sanin had apparently understood its character. But the Benois idea misfired. Under contract to the Moscow Arts Theatre, he was unavailable to work for the rival institution, and although Sanin ("the demonic Alexander Aximovich," as Benois called him) did his best to tempt him "to commit an extreme folly and quit the Arts Theatre for the obscurity known as the Free Theatre," something about the new venture— an overambitiousness doing service for clear artistic aims—made him step back from the brink, even though "in so doing I had to take my leave of any dream of *The Nightingale.*"[14]

Benois was not in Paris for the Diaghilev season that year. "It may seem strange," he told Stravinsky, "but . . . Astruc puts me off. I'm so dreadfully tired and in need of a rest, that the thought of seeing that nose, that beard, that top hat, and hearing that (beautiful) accent . . . is simply intolerable."[15] Stravinsky might well have hoped to see Benois, discuss *Nightingale* with him, perhaps persuade him to change his mind. But then came the twenty-ninth of May, hotly pursued by the bad oyster. From his bed of physical and mental pain, the composer cast around for a designer who, as he later explained to Benois, "was persona grata [with the Free Theatre], would see all of them sooner than I would, and say some warm words about me." What more natural than to turn to his fellow veteran of the battle of the Champs-Elysées, Nikolay Roerich? "So I got talking to him about *Nightingale*, and saw that he flared up strongly and undoubtedly wanted to design it. I pressed him on it. Perhaps that was all very fine, but after some time I began to have my doubts, and I'm still doubting. . . ."16 They were doubts which Benois, who had been played off against Roerich once before, was perfectly ready to share. "I'm confident," he told Stravinsky unblinkingly, "that Roerich will do it marvellously. But there are a few things he probably will not manage, and these would interest me extremely."17 The obvious solution to the dilemma would be for Diaghilev to produce the opera in Paris; but Sanin had (probably naively rather than disingenuously) given Benois to understand that Stravinsky's agreement with the Free Theatre precluded this, although in fact the Free Theatre had bought a three-year exclusivity only for Moscow and St. Petersburg and had, almost unbelievably, omitted to insist even on the world premiere. Stravinsky, of course, knew this perfectly well. But he knew also that the real problem with Diaghilev was his pathological dislike of works commissioned by other people, especially when they interfered with work destined for his own company, as was the case with *Nightingale*.18 In any event, Igor was having serious misgivings about Diaghilev's attitude to his latest work.

> He even said . . . that [*The Rite*] should have been "laid down" after composition, since the public isn't yet ready for it—but why did he never suggest any such thing before, neither at the time of *Mir iskusstva* nor later? . . . I've come to the conclusion that he is not encouraging me in that direction—that is, I'm without the one real support in promoting my artistic ideas—and you'll agree this completely flattens me, since I cannot, you understand, cannot compose what he wants—that is, repeat myself—I'll repeat anything you like but not myself, because that's how people write themselves out.19

But by this time Diaghilev's troubles had gone beyond the purely artistic. His distaste for *The Rite of Spring*, if distaste it was, had become personal.

On 15 August, the Ballets Russes dancers had embarked at Southampton at the start of their first South American tour, and Nijinsky, who had been in Germany with Diaghilev, Nouvel, and Benois discussing a project for a rococo ballet to music by Bach, joined the ship at Cherbourg the next day. But Diaghilev did not sail. Perhaps he really was, as rumor had it, too frightened of the sea, or perhaps he simply did not dare leave Europe with the following season still unplanned, and with important irons in the fire, including the Bach project (which involved Ravel), a Strauss commission, the possible Steinberg ballet, and perhaps even a sniff of a new work by Stravinsky. So instead the tour was in the charge of Diaghilev's business associate and financial genie Baron Dmitri de Gunzburg. Whether or not Gunzburg engineered, connived at, or merely suffered the emotional transformation which ended with Nijinsky's marriage to the young Hungarian dancer Romola de Pulszky in a Buenos Aires church on 10 September will probably never be known. Diaghilev heard the news in a Venice hotel. In high spirits, the superstitious impresario had just seized Misia Edwards's parasol and opened it when the telegram arrived announcing the wedding. Diaghilev was "overcome with a sort of hysteria, ready to go to any extreme, [and] sobbing and shouting, gathered everybody around— Sert, Bakst, etc. . . . We immediately took Diaghilev, drunk with grief and rage, to Naples, where he launched himself on a frantic bacchanalia. But he was beyond consolation."[20] Small wonder that when Stravinsky next saw Diaghilev, two or three weeks later in Montreux, he found that *The Rite* had become a scapegoat for the betrayal which now obsessed Diaghilev to the virtual exclusion of all else. Nijinsky was finished, the Ballets Russes were finished, *The Rite* was finished, and, as Stravinsky put it coolly to Benois, "the possibility has gone for some time of seeing anything valuable in the field of dance and, still more important, of again seeing this offspring of mine, which cost such unbelievable efforts to choreograph."[21]

The Stravinskys had returned from Ustilug only a few days earlier, with the usual stops in Warsaw, where Igor and Styopa Mitusov met to discuss progress on *Nightingale*, and Berlin, where Igor saw Struve and bought music, including pieces by Myaskovsky and the Sixth and Seventh Sonatas of Scriabin.[22] As chance would have it, Scriabin himself was en route from Berlin to Lausanne, where his father was Russian consul, and the two composers travelled together, discussed each other's music, and swapped invitations. Although, as Stravinsky later reported to Derzhanovsky, Scriabin "knows nothing about my works and talks about them by hearsay, using other people's words,"[23] whereas Stravinsky was familiar with and genuinely admired the older man's music, the two composers seem to have hit it off to a surprising extent for such self-absorbed personalities. Perhaps that was because Stravinsky was as yet far from being the overdefensive, overprotesting scourge of historical rivals that his conversation books suggest he became in later life. Still quite newly famous himself, he retained the undogmatic curiosity which Benois had remarked in the fresh young composer of *The Firebird* a mere four years before.[24] In his bag he had the two sonatas he had bought, and he frankly told their composer how much he liked the Seventh especially.[25] He pressed Scriabin to visit him at the Hôtel Châtelard, and when Scriabin later wired that he could not come, Stravinsky called on him instead and spent a long afternoon at the Lausanne lakeside suburb of Ouchy, there were more "very interesting discussions," and Scriabin played his two most recent sonatas, nos. 9 and 10, which Stravinsky "liked incomparably more than his immediately post-*Prometheus* works."[26]

No sooner were the Stravinskys back in Clarens than Diaghilev himself turned up at the Hôtel Beau Rivage in Ouchy, on his way from Venice to Paris. This was on 30 September. Igor still knew nothing of Nijinsky's marriage,[27] and it must have been in relating the whole treacherous, ghastly train of events the following day, in the stately surroundings of the Palace Hotel in Montreux, that Diaghilev turned "into a madman who begged me and my wife not to leave him alone."[28] But Stravinsky, though delighted to see Diaghilev, "as I'm very devoted to him and love him very much,"[29] hardly seems to have noticed the impresario's distress, so upset was he by the jinx on *The Rite of Spring* and Nijinsky's "incomparable" choreography,[30] as well as by Diaghilev's sudden capitulation (as it seemed) to his enraged public. The trouble was that any possible damage to Stravinsky's existing ballets was in danger of being compounded by a new threat, with more immediately disastrous implications for the family budget: the Free Theatre was rumored—less than three weeks before it was due to open—to be in financial difficulties.

Exactly when and how Stravinsky first got wind of the new venture's problems, we do not know. Perhaps it was from his brother Gury, who had been singing in the Narodnïy Dom in St. Petersburg, but must have had contacts in the Moscow theatre and may even originally have hoped to join the Free Theatre.[31] Benois now reported a situation that was partly disturbing, partly reassuring. Some said that all was well—there was money, the shows were promising to be lively and well sold—but some said the money was running out, the shows were tasteless and extravagant, Mardzhanov was impossible to work with, etc. Benois himself thought that the theatre would survive for a while, that *Nightingale* would be staged, and that otherwise the company would "alternate interesting things with impossible and unbearable shit and monstrous vulgarities. But Muscovites gobble up the best with the worst, since today in general everything is swallowed in the same way, and all standards have gone out of the window."[32] What Benois was not yet in a position to judge was the role of music in the Free Theatre's scheme of priorities. When the theatre at last opened its doors on 8 October (OS), with an adaptation of Musorgsky's unfinished opera *Sorochintsï Fair*, it became evident that all was far from well in that quarter. Max Steinberg, who had visited Moscow in October, wrote that "the new theatre seems very suspect to me; at least in *Sorochintsï Fair* the music was on the lowest level."[33] Derzhanovsky was more specific:

> It's an interesting venture, but for a musician barely acceptable, since music there is completely disregarded, and the voice and

wishes of the only musician there, [Konstantin] Saradzhev, are drowned in the dilettantism of the rest of the management. . . . The situation gets still worse, in that the company is very weak in its personnel. Even assuming that *Nightingale* is *three times* simpler and more basic than the Japanese songs, it will still be inaccessible to the singers there . . . they're little more than students, and with doubtful *purely musical* training. With such singers God help them cope with Tchaikovsky's harmonies, and even those of [Rimsky-Korsakov's] *Kashchey* they're hardly in a state to sing.[34]

By threatening to resign, Saradzhev managed to secure greater autonomy for the musical side of things. "All the same," Derzhanovsky wrote, "despite a highly gifted conductor and a good (if small) orchestra, there remains a significant defect in view of the disgusting acoustics, which give no compactness to the orchestral sound, so that each section, while individually managing a clear, incisive sound, is unfortunately unable to fuse this sound into any kind of unity."[35]

No wonder Stravinsky was pleased, as he told Sanin, when Diaghilev changed his mind about *Nightingale* and decided after all to stage it in Paris the following spring.[36] And no wonder no one paid much attention to Sanin's amiable protest that Russia must come first.[37] Diaghilev had already descended on Struve in Berlin and taken away with him a firm contract for the performances in Paris and London, together with a set of proofs of the piano score of act I. But when Struve sent these same proofs to the Free Theatre early in December with a contract for the Moscow production, Mardzhanov—nervous, presumably, about the commitment of funds—"swerved away from concluding the agreement."[38] By that time the contract with Diaghilev was signed and sealed, though admittedly not yet paid for.

The music itself, of course, had still to be completed—a worry that no doubt influenced Mardzhanov too. After the concentrated work in the summer at Ustilug, Stravinsky had again got bogged down in proofreading and in irritable correspondence over sometimes trivial matters. There was the dispute over the *Montjoie!* translation in *Muzïka*. Meanwhile, Derzhanovsky had opened up another avenue of friction. Anxious to print up-to-date reviews of Stravinsky's latest music, he asked him discreetly to supply Myaskovsky with early proofs of each new work. Stravinsky promptly sent Myaskovsky (on loan) an autograph copy of the first part of *The Rite of Spring*, a work already published in four-hand piano transcription but still held up in full score.[39] But the contact seems to have given him another idea: that Myaskovsky might also be willing to help him with his backlog of proofreading. Some time early in August he sent his Petersburg colleague a telegram. But the reaction was unexpected, at least to the self-preoccupied genius. Myaskovsky was furious, offended, wounded to the quick that Stravinsky should overlook the importance of his—Myaskovsky's—creative work and treat him like a mere office boy, a publisher's reader, a proofreading hack. "Why do I have to consider myself less busy than Stravinsky?" he testily asked Derzhanovsky. "This whole business with him sickens me. . . . He obviously simply doesn't know how to proofread; last time it was done for him by Steinberg, now he wants to foist it on to me while he swans around abroad—well, let him stay at home."[40] To Derzhanovsky fell the complicated task of excusing Mya-skovsky to a colleague who was too useful and important to alienate, and to arrange for an alternative proofreader in the shape of one Boris Vasilevich Karagichev, another *Muzïka* contributor.

Stravinsky may have been losing touch with his motherland, but he certainly had not yet, in his heart, abandoned her. His efforts on Derzha-novsky's behalf—his willingness to supply materials, to persuade busy French musicians like Ravel and Schmitt to write for *Muzïka,* or to act as go-between in Derzhanovsky's efforts to persuade Debussy to attend an Evenings concert in Moscow during his forthcoming Russian visit— reflect a real concern to cultivate a sympathetic Russian environment for his own music. They are not simply an example of what Taruskin has cyni-cally called "Stravinsky's precocious mastery of the art of *faire réclame.*"[41] Obviously the Rimsky-Korsakovs and the Sabaneyevs were a lost cause. Andrey had published a predictably poisonous notice of the Paris *Rite,* as an accompaniment to his diatribe against Diaghilev's *Khovanshchina,* in the *Russkaya molva;* Sabaneyev had launched a viciously prejudiced and ill-informed attack on the ballet score, based purely on a "study" of the four-hand reduction, in the so-called *Voice of Moscow—Golos Moskvi.*[42] But such things no longer damaged Stravinsky very greatly with intelligent musi-cians, since their ulterior motives were transparent. Sabaneyev, at least, did not surprise Derzhanovsky, "since [for him] the one God is Scria-bin and Sabaneyev is his prophet . . . [but] I don't understand [Rimsky-Korsakov] since there is some personal animus noticeable in what he writes, which in itself is quite superficial and essentially gives very little towards a negative evaluation of *The Rite of Spring.*"[43] But a perceptive and sympathetic musician like Myaskovsky, or indeed like the composer-critic Boris Asafyev, whom Stravinsky met in Paris a few months later at the time of the *Nightingale* premiere, was another matter. To judge from what such critics wrote, or from what he heard about their opinions, they might be thought to represent the true voice of progressive Russia, Petersburg equivalents of Schmitt or Delage, friendly associates for such time as Stravinsky might find himself once again based in the Russian capital. But it was just as well that he did not know what they said to each other about him and his music. Myaskovsky in fact blew hot and cold on *The Rite of Spring*, resisting it with his symphonic brain even while he responded to it with his musical ear: "simply rather poor in invention, faintly barmy, but in places not wholly bad," he called it in a letter to Prokofiev.44 Nor was Myaskovsky far behind the Rimsky-Korsakovs in his resentment of Stravinsky's foreign success. "As for his health," he railed to Derzhanovsky, "so now it isn't only the poor who get ill, and in any case I don't suppose he's been living in Clarens in any less comfort than in his dukedom [Ustilug]. Above all I think that when some commission falls through and he has to stop being in such a hurry, it'll do him nothing but good— he'll get down to some real work."45 Finally, when Lyadov died a year or so later, Myaskovsky shamelessly told Asafyev that he could have wished it had been Tcherepnin, Steinberg, "or even Stravinsky."46 If Stravinsky had gone to Moscow or back to St. Petersburg expecting a hero's welcome from a band of well-disposed progressive fellow musicians, he might well have been cruelly disabused. But fate spared him that experience.

In spite of these various distractions, the second act of *Nightingale* was finished, in full score, by the start of November.47 While writing it up during October, Stravinsky had also found time to compose a set of three children's songs, based on tunes he had written (he later claimed) in 1906, though White is surely correct in saying that the piano parts of the Three Little Songs (*Souvenirs de mon enfance*), with their crisp harmonic displacements, must have been done in 1913.48 The three songs, which were issued very promptly by RMV, are dedicated to the Stravinskys' three children, in reverse order: Svetik, Milusha (Lyudmila), and Fedik (Theodore). So perhaps a certain sentimental uxoriousness was involved, since Katya was once again pregnant, and Igor was in the middle of the longest unbroken period with her and the children since the time of *The Firebird* and her previous pregnancy. Throughout the autumn he stayed at the Châtelard, working away, presumably, on the third act of *The Nightingale*. The only absence we know about was a trip to Zurich in mid-December to hear Mahler's Eighth Symphony, "this German *Kolossal Werk*," as he described it to Delage. "I find that the only quality in this symphony is the inflexibility of utter barefaced platitude. . . . Fancy that for two hours you are made to understand that two times two is four, to the accompaniment of E-flat major performed *fffff* by 800 people."49 He was acquiring a circle of local friends and acquaintances, including the French composer Henri Duparc, who was living in retirement at Vevey, and the conductor Ernest Ansermet, who had a house called La Pervenche next door to Les Tilleuls. It was with Ansermet that Stravinsky went to hear the Mahler in Zurich. Now the Swiss conductor wanted to program Stravinsky's symphony and asked him to approach Jurgenson for the materials.50

For some reason the third act proceeded slowly or not at all. Stravinsky may have been discouraged by the flow of pessimistic rumors about the

Free Theatre, and particularly by Struve's report that Mardzhanov was procrastinating over the contract. After all, Free Theatre money had been his overriding motive for agreeing to complete the work in the first place, and there was no question of a compensatory payment from Diaghilev. In any case, it was obviously proving difficult for him to form a mental picture of the work on the stage. Previously he had always worked closely with a designer and/or a choreographer. But this time there was no choreography, and the intended designer, Roerich, had gone silent, as Sanin reported in his last surviving letter to the composer.[51] Then, two weeks later, Diaghilev broke the logjam by announcing that his production, at any rate, would be designed by Benois.[52] Suddenly the work came into focus visually. Some time before Christmas, the composer sent Benois a list of the characters and settings with, presumably, an account of the stage action and suggestions for colorings, all of which Benois promptly lost. "I wanted to start on the production right away," Benois wrote back,

> and now this hold-up comes. I beg you to send a second set at once and also a more detailed libretto. I implore you not to insist on the colours—since I have other ideas of my own and I think it will be good. The hall in the palace will be pink with blue and black. But Lord, what about the main thing—the music?! Is it possible that I shall have to work without this chief source of inspiration and without your personal prompting?! How to arrange a meeting.[53]

But no meeting could be arranged, and by the time Benois's letter reached Clarens there had been a devastating change in the Stravinskys' family life. Katya had her baby, a little girl called Milène, in the Clinique Mont Riant in Lausanne on 15 January. But after an apparently perfect delivery, complications suddenly developed in the form of a recurrence of Katya's childhood tuberculosis in her right lung. Because of his wife's confinement, Stravinsky was unable to attend the Paris premiere of his *Three Japanese Lyrics* on the fourteenth. But he at last got away to Paris for a few days on the nineteenth, and it was only after his return to Lausanne on the twenty-fifth that the first symptoms of her illness appeared. "The poor thing," he told Benois, "had to wait for a fall in her temperature before moving to a sanatorium in the mountains. This we have now done."[54] The sanatorium was at Leysin, almost five thousand feet up in the Alps to the east of the Rhone valley. A steep rack-and-pinion railway took visitors from Aigle to the very top of the village of Leysin, above which loomed the grim, turreted Grand Hotel—in reality a sanatorium—which was to be Igor's and Katya's home for the next three months. "The doctors think the illness insignificant, thank God, but bearing in mind the general weakness of the organism after giving birth, they find it prudent to take an unhurried treatment, complete physical rest—which is thoroughly possible here—and *suralimentation* [feeding up]."55 Meanwhile, the children (including, presumably, Milène and her wet nurse) stayed in Clarens with their grandmother, who had just arrived from St. Petersburg.56

About the premiere of the Japanese songs, in the Société Musicale Indépendente concert organized by Ravel in the Salle Erard, Igor received mixed reports. Delage wrote that there had been "some hissing," but Calvocoressi noted "the triumphant success of your songs" and alleged that there had been "calls for an encore" which were ignored because of the length of the program—a slightly improbable claim in view of the brevity of the songs and the fact that Delage's much longer *Quatre Poèmes hindous* were repeated.57 "One might strongly wish," wrote Florent Schmitt in *La France,* "that the SMI would soon reprogram these songs, which were poorly heard and whose too fleeting charms left behind them nothing but a wake of respectful and admiring astonishment."58 But the critic of the SIM *Revue musicale,* Jean Poueigh, though sympathetic to the program as a whole, was unimpressed by Stravinsky's use of the ensemble which he shared with Ravel's *Trois Poèmes de Mallarmé* and the Delage cycle in the same program: "As a rule fresh, dreamy, lively, or disturbing," he wrote, "these timbres only served in M. Igor Stravinsky's songs to produce noise. Well, after all, that's a result."59 But everyone agreed that Lyubov Nikitina had performed the songs beautifully. She sang them again two nights later, with piano (Alfredo Casella), in illustration of a lecture by Calvocoressi, and this time "Tsaraiuki," at least, was encored.60

Stravinsky's own visit to the capital a few days later was a hectic round even by his standards. He spent a day with Delage, and dined with Debussy, who "was somewhat pale and wasted, and seemed to have something unpleasant on his mind."61 He had a meeting with Monteux about the conductor's plans to include *Petrushka* and *The Rite of Spring* in his new concert series in the Casino de Paris. He discussed *The Nightingale* over dinner with Diaghilev, Misia, and Bakst, heard about the mending of fences with Fokine, and no doubt endured long diatribes against Nijinsky, whom Diaghilev had peremptorily dismissed from his company but not, we may be sure, from his thoughts. One wonders whether Igor let on that he had received a long and bewildered letter from the great dancer begging him to intercede with Diaghilev.62 After all, he himself had a vested interest in Nijinsky's reinstatement, at least as a choreographer, though he must also have known—or sensed—Diaghilev's dangerous intractability on a subject of such pain and humiliation to him. Later he played through the two completed acts of *The Nightingale* at Misia's apartment in the avenue Kléber. It was Misia who drew attention to the stylistic inconsistency between the acts, while Seryozha was more preoccupied with scenic detail: for instance, did the "Draughts" scene at the start of act 2 really have to be played with the curtain down, as Igor insisted because he had some idea of a Chinese shadowplay?[63] Jean Cocteau was at this run-through, and it was either here or in the offices of the *Nouvelle Revue française,* where Stravinsky again played the work a night or two later to a musico-literary audience including Ravel, Monteux, André Gide, and Jacques Rivière, that Cocteau broached his idea for a ballet called *David,* which would (improbably) blend the paraphernalia of the fairground with ritual elements from the Old Testament. Cocteau introduced the composer to the actor and stage director Jacques Copeau, a member of the editorial board of the *NRF* and founder of a new experimental theatre company called the Vieux-Colombier. Copeau promptly invited Stravinsky to compose a suite of dances for the new company.[64] But before long this scheme seems to have become subsumed in the *David* project, and within days of Stravinsky's return to Lausanne Cocteau was enthusiastically plotting a working trip to the shores of Lake Geneva.

Ever since the Russians had exploded onto the stage of the Châtelet in 1909 and the twenty-year-old Cocteau had engineered a meeting with Diaghilev at Misia Edwards's salon in the rue de Rivoli, the Russian ballet had been the focus of his creative ambitions. He longed to contribute, whether as designer, scenarist, or pure *animateur.* His was the classic response of the brilliant but childlike dilettante to the bewilderingly integrated display of varied professionalisms that lay at the heart of the early Russian seasons. Diaghilev quickly sensed this disconcerting inadequacy in Cocteau's genius. His notorious injunction to the young Frenchman to "astonish me" clearly hinted that Cocteau had more to offer the Ballets Russes as a purveyor of camp or risqué ideas than as an out-and-out artist-craftsman in the Benois-Karsavina-Stravinsky mold. And it was true that, with his studiously effeminate turnout (usually including rouge and lipstick) and his exhaustingly witty conversation, Cocteau did make a shocking, paradoxical impression that was all too easily revealed as manner masquerading as matter. Yet it was also true that the shocks and paradoxes, the wit and the teasing, could, under the right circumstances, point the way to new and substantial work. They needed, though, to catch a mood, or else to present themselves in a form that invited a certain elevation or hardening of tone, a measured rejection of boulevardism in favor of proper artistic coherence. In due course this would come to pass, and in a context that even Diaghilev could not deny. But for the seeming incongruities and associationism of *David,* the time was not, as it turned out, ripe.

"Remember that I must finish *Nightingale* first," the composer warned his would-be collaborator after Lausanne had become Leysin and the prospect loomed of completing this fairy-tale conquest of Death in the immediate vicinity of a Swiss sanatorium in midwinter.[65] But he did not at first tell Cocteau how much work remained to be done on this short but recalcitrant ending. To Benois he was more candid. As late as 9 March, by which time Cocteau was actually installed at Leysin with his lover and collaborator the painter and Dalcrozian Paul Thévenaz, Igor was telling his designer that "I'm rather scared of this act, since it can't be short (which would be desirable in view of the lack of action) because of its slow tempos."[66] Struve, by now in a state of considerable anxiety, made the composer promise to deliver the third act by the thirtieth; yet by the following Saturday (4 April), the manuscript was still not in the publisher's hands, even though Stravinsky had in fact completed the vocal score eight days before.[67] Small wonder if Cocteau found Stravinsky's commitment to the *David* project enigmatic, to say the least. But he had his own ways of concealing from those who expected most of him that, in fact, hardly anything was happening.

Is it true, as Cocteau's biographer Francis Steegmuller suggests, that Stravinsky did his best to dissuade his "cher petit Jean" from coming to Switzerland at all?[68] The fact is that, considering the pressure he was under, Stravinsky was remarkably encouraging and let pass several pretexts for keeping the pernickety, hypochondriacal Cocteau away from the chilly, germ-laden heights of Leysin. He was in no position, after all, to refuse work. *Svadebka* might be in the pipeline for Diaghilev, but Diaghilev was both a tyrant and an elusive payer, and it was as well not to be completely dependent on him. If the Vieux-Colombier could commission *David*, then *Svadebka* would have to wait. On 15 February Stravinsky wrote to Cocteau from Leysin, proposing a formal commission and a fee of six thousand francs in return for a two-year exclusivity for Copeau's theatre.[69] But Cocteau's reply, explaining sorrowfully that the Vieux-Colombier was more or less destitute and "was only hoping to revive some old work of yours and mine, or three short dances, which you could write like three songs for a concert,"[70] made it clear that he had quite misjudged that situation. Cocteau may well have been using the Vieux-Colombier as a bait while in reality fully intending to offer the work to Diaghilev, as Stravinsky later told Steegmuller.[71] But if so he kept this to himself. In mid-March 1914, Stravinsky was still treating it as a Vieux-Colombier project and making arrangements to meet Copeau in Paris, despite the unsatisfactory financial aspect.[72] In any case he would have known that Diaghilev would not buy *David* until *Nightingale* was ready, if then. So it seems either that he was at least mildly attracted by *David* in itself or that he liked Cocteau and wanted the diversion of his presence amid the ice and fog of Leysin.

But *The Nightingale* would not go away. Struve had been keeping Igor informed on the Free Theatre's continuing evasiveness over the contract.

But now another knight entered the Russian lists, in the shape of the conductor Ziloti, acting on behalf of Telyakovsky at the Mariyinsky. Here was a possible escape from the clutches of the failing Moscow theatre. Struve set out the conditions on which they could consider rescinding their agreement with Mardzhanov, and Stravinsky wrote directly to Ziloti explaining the situation, describing the work and above all imploring him not to let Telyakovsky try to judge the music until he himself could play it to him,

> since if it's played without me . . . at best nobody will be able to stand it, and they'll say "nonsense pianissimo," as the late Nikolay Andreyevich [Rimsky-Korsakov] used to say about Debussy (in contradistinction to "nonsense fortissimo," which he said about Strauss). Better if I play it myself. . . . Maybe it could be arranged like this. If we could meet, I could play it to you, and then you could yourself present my work to Telyakovsky.[73]

With all this on his mind, Stravinsky did now suggest a postponement to Cocteau, and a few days later, on 1 March, he hurried off for four days to Berlin for discussions with Ziloti and Struve, and to play Ziloti the first two and a half acts. But by this time there was no dissuading Cocteau, and he duly arrived in Leysin with Thévenaz on the seventh, apparently to a somewhat frosty welcome, to judge from Cocteau's "don't cold-shoulder me for having come" in a note sent by hand to the Grand Hotel that same day.[74]

Cocteau was at Leysin for more than a fortnight, but it seems doubtful that any significant collaborating took place. While Stravinsky went on composing Nightingale in his quarters in the annex to the Grand Hotel, Cocteau finished off his surreal book Le Potomak—a curious blend of cartoon strip, social satire, and literary posturing which he always claimed was inspired by The Rite of Spring (and which is in fact dedicated to Stravinsky). At the same time he wrote daily letters to his mother and friends enthusing about their imaginary progress on David. At first the letters are more or less factual. "Igor is composing prolifically," he tells Comte Etienne de Beaumont. "Is there much snow in your garden? Here, a meter, and the result is the most utter silence. . . . it snows and snows and snows. The lights keep going out. One overeats . . . and a consumptive lady is expressing herself badly by playing Chopin. Ah David! . . . The Rite sounds marvellous in the hotel lobby, played by a lady patient and Thévenaz."[75]

But soon, an element of wishful thinking starts to creep in. Mme Cocteau learns that "I am enthused by Igor's idea for David,"[76] while for André Gide the picture is one of "intensive work. Igor Stravinsky is a dynamo. Thévenaz is amazing. I think that David is going to be something extraordinary."[77] A few days later, Cocteau tells his mother that "Thévenaz is working with Igor in the annex," and then, remarkably, "Stravinsky played something of the future *David*. Impossible to say how beautiful it was. . . . *David* will be *short* (twenty minutes) but as Igor says it's a drop to poison a five-act elephant," and finally, "*David* will be *prodigious*. But what work! (Albeit short—the whole thing will last twelve minutes.) . . . Nothing remains of my original text."[78] Thévenaz left on the twentieth, and on the twenty-third Cocteau sent his mother the most truthful of his Leysin letters: "Diaghilev sends Igor telegram after telegram. No doubt he's going to put a spoke in our wheels."[79] Then he himself went sadly off down the mountain.

Did Diaghilev make trouble over *David*? It seems likely that he did. He distrusted and perhaps even disliked Cocteau, and was in any case understandably anxious about *Nightingale* and paranoid about Stravinsky's Russian contacts. He was jealously protective of *Svadebka* and had already effectively warned Sanin off that project.[80] At one point, Cocteau solicited Misia's support against Diaghilev's jealousy and his instinctive taste for the spectacular and grandiose, whereas "the whole idea of *David*, its brevity, its orchestra, its molding, its lack of ornament, demands a very small stage."[81] Whether or not Misia lent her support is, naturally, quite another matter. Cocteau eventually decided she had not. By the time of the *Nightingale* premiere, in May, Serge had grown "suffocating. Misia, too, under his thumb, is becoming offensive."[82] Misia's biographers consider that "Cocteau was apt to feel that Misia was a troublemaker when her schemes to help him failed, and an enchanting friend when they succeeded."[83] But this may, of course, have been a perfectly sound judgment on his part.

Nevertheless, to suppose, as some do, that Stravinsky would have abandoned a project that interested him artistically because of Diaghilev's opposition is somewhat naive. There is little hard evidence that he was ever deeply interested in *David*. He certainly did intend to write a set of three dances for Copeau,[84] and it may be that these became identified in his mind with the three dances of David—around the head of Goliath, before Saul, and around the Ark—as Cocteau described them in his letter to Misia. It may even be that these three dances are directly connected with the Three Pieces for String Quartet, the first of which Stravinsky started composing at Leysin less than a month after Cocteau's departure, but which had probably already been discussed in Paris with Misia in January.[85] Cocteau, after all, thought of David's dances as "the acrobatics of a fairground gymnast. . . . The three dances, their performance and the three poems, it's all a kind of *music hall, three numbers* for acrobats."[86] And the string quartet pieces, too, have a music-hall connection, since the second piece is a portrait of the English clown Little Tich. But none of this proves—if anything, it rather disproves—that Stravinsky was ever engaged by the idea of *David* as a theatre piece, which, as far as Cocteau was concerned, was the whole point.[87]

Two days after Cocteau's arrival at Leysin, Stravinsky wrote to Benois a letter which puts *David* into perspective. "I'm thirsty to see your sketches," he writes. "I'm convinced that this is a masterpiece, for even from a distance I can sense your passion, I can sense that you are in love. Under these conditions (I'm sure) you will do something enchanting. I'm delighted to be working with you. I'm working indefatigably."[88]

Benois's vivid stage picture for *The Nightingale*, which Stravinsky called "scenically . . . the most beautiful of all my early Diaghilev works,"[89] can already be glimpsed in his letters: the extraordinary idea of defining an action in terms of color; the witty ceremony of the processions, including the idea, which Stravinsky seized on with rapture, of the Emperor walking on behind the elaborate palanquin that is supposed to carry him; the sense of a choreographed dramaturgy which was part and parcel of Benois's idea of staging opera with the singers invisible in the pit and the stage action presented by dancers. As Stravinsky may or may not have learnt from Diaghilev, Rimsky-Korsakov's *Golden Cockerel* was already being planned in this way; and *Nightingale*, with its tightly compressed libretto, its bird heroine, and its statuesque action, would be its pair, in a double bill of disembodied, balleticized operas such as might have been calculated to turn Andrey Rimsky-Korsakov's hair gray.

In spite of the inevitable break in musical style between the first act and the other two—and whatever its standing among Stravinsky's theatre works as a whole—*The Nightingale*, as staged in Paris in May 1914, was a classic of the World of Art approach to theatre: beauty of color and decoration rather than logic or plausibility of action; a tight integration between music, text, and design ("The fact is," Benois told the Moscow conductor Emil Cooper, "that I can't get on with designing the staging until I know at least something of the music");[90] an overriding element of fantasy; and an insistence on motif and pattern—what Benois called a "Chinoiserie *de ma façon*, far from accurate by pedantic standards and even, in a sense, hybrid, but undoubtedly appropriate to Stravinsky's music" (which had also reduced chinoiserie to a set of stereotypes, treated, however, with great wit and decorative refinement).[91] Design and choreography (by the young Boris Romanov) were no mere adjunct, but an integral part of the drama. So it may seem ironic that at this precise moment, the two great ballets which had preceded *Nightingale* were embarking on what was to prove at least as durable a career as concert works. Benois himself had attended the concert premiere of *The Rite of Spring*, conducted by Sergey Koussevitzky in Moscow on 5/18 February (the performance was repeated a week later in

St. Petersburg, where Benois heard it again). "I don't know," he told Stravinsky,

> if Koussevitzky conducted it right, as I haven't heard an authoritative performance, but I received the required impression. The success, alas!, was rather great, despite the fact that after part 1 about a hundred people left the hall. I say "alas" since, naturally, they applauded wildly just to cock a snook at Paris; and indeed it is sickening to succeed with a public which, for a joke, stands to applaud Bach, Beethoven, Wagner, Scriabin, you, Rachmaninov. . . . But I'm glad that Nurok liked it, and that there were loud boos from the Rimsky-Korsakov clan. That's comforting.[92]

It seems likely, in fact, that the performance was very poor. Derzhanovsky thought it "well done, but with too many squeaks among the bangs,"[93] but Myaskovsky heard that "Koussevitzky played the *Rite* twenty times worse for you than for us—and it wasn't up to much here, though they say that all the critics left the performance in raptures. It seems that the misanthrope disagrees with the other experts, but I am on his side, for after all I know the work a bit, and I didn't recognize too much of it."[94]

Monteux, meanwhile, programmed *Petrushka* twice in his Casino de Paris series, on 1 and 15 March, playing the complete ballet score for the first time in the concert hall.[95] In Russia, only the three-movement version had so far been played. Yet Monteux's impression contradicted that of Steinberg and many of the Russian critics. "You cannot have any idea," he wrote to the composer, "how much this music gains by being played in concert! Every detail is heard and carries throughout the hall, and musicians who have heard it in the theatre find that they have never heard it so well! For you it has been a really considerable success."[96] Still battling with *The Nightingale*, Stravinsky could not accept Monteux's invitation to play the piano part, or even attend the performance. But towards the end of the month, with the opera out of the way, he could once again interest himself in performances of his music. On the thirtieth he attended Ansermet's morning rehearsal of his Symphony in E-flat in the Kursaal at Montreux, and seems to have taken up the baton (for the first time, so far as is known) and conducted at least one of the movements. But by the same afternoon he was on a train for Paris, and he did not attend the actual Montreux concert on 2 April—the first performance of the symphony outside Russia. On the fourth he went to Monteux's rehearsal of *The Rite* in the Casino de Paris (near the Trinité), and he was at the performance on the afternoon of the fifth, which Craft wrongly but in a sense truthfully describes as "the *first* complete performance that Stravinsky had heard."[97]

From a musical point of view, the concert was as brilliant a success as the ballet premiere had been a catastrophic failure. The orchestra played superbly, and the music was heard, as Louis Laloy reported, "in the most respectful silence, and was endlessly acclaimed."[98] Several critics at once recognized the work as a masterpiece. Pierre Lalo, by no means an instinctive lover of the modern, found the music

> no more barbarous than it is ugly. From start to finish it is the work of an extremely refined musician, refined in sensibility and taste, and in possession of all the resources of his art, none of which he sacrifices to some unknown idea of primitive savagery. . . . There is no feeling of effort or artifice; everything is natural, everything is spontaneous; everything bursts forth with an abundance, a richness, a force of impulse and movement by which one is rapidly seduced, transported, conquered; everything serves to reveal a work given birth without concern for theory or doctrine, a work created in joy, the joy of a musician who, quite simply, enjoys making music.[99]

Paris had made amends. "At the last chord," wrote Emile Vuillermoz, "delirium takes hold of those present; a fever of adoration sweeps through the audience. They yell the name of the composer, and rush to look for him. An unprecedented exaltation reigns in the hall. The applause goes on to the point of vertigo."[100] When they found him, they hoisted him onto their shoulders and carried him out of the hall and into the place de la Trinité. In the street "a policeman pushed his way to my side in an effort to protect me, and it was this guardian of the law Diaghilev later fixed on in his accounts of the story: 'Our little Igor now requires police escorts out of his concerts, like a prize fighter.' "[101]

Stravinsky was soon back at Leysin, working on a new piece, superficially as unlike The Rite, or for that matter The Nightingale, as it would be possible to imagine. The dry little miniature that became the first of the Three Pieces for String Quartet was initially composed in April as a movement for piano duet, perhaps, as we saw, envisaged as one of the dances for Cocteau's David or else simply inspired by the fairground aspects of that project. Although Stravinsky made a fair copy of the piece, its nature is experimental.[102] It toys with the possibilities of a musical "machine," in which three or four different, very simple, motives are set to run simultaneously but each with its own controlling rhythmic pattern not geared to that of the others: a merry dance for clockwork musicians. There are in fact precedents for this kind of writing in Petrushka as well as The Rite of Spring, but nothing where the mechanism itself is so much in the foreground. Stravinsky was literally as well as figuratively marking time. In order to write Svadebka, as he now conceived it, he needed materials from

Russia. But his circumstances made it hard for him to go there. His symphony had been so successful in Montreux that the Scherzo was repeated by popular demand on 16 April, and Stravinsky himself went along to the Kursaal to conduct it, his first public appearance on the rostrum.[103] Ten days later he was in Paris again for Monteux's second Casino *Rite*. But although he told his Parisian friends that he was off to Kiev, there is no other sign that he went.[104] Instead he moved with Katya—now seemingly much restored—back to Clarens, and then, in the middle of May, came word that the Moscow Free Theatre, of which so much and so little had been expected, had closed down after only one season, a mere seven months, of active existence. By a worrying coincidence, Astruc's Champs-Elysées venture, which had collapsed at the beginning of November, had lasted almost exactly the same length of time.

Soon afterwards Igor set off for Paris, to hear and see the piece for which Mardzhanov's theatre, though he never put it on, is today best remembered. As the previous year, the composer arrived at a comparatively late stage of rehearsals for a production that had hung in the balance for several months, only partly because of the late appearance of the work's final act. Astruc's failure had left Diaghilev without significant financial backing, and it was only in March that the company's old London patron Sir Joseph Beecham agreed to advance the money necessary to ensure that the 1914 season would take place. Meanwhile, Benois had been ill, the complicated sets for *Nightingale* were not being built nor the sumptuous costumes made, and there was no sign of early musical rehearsal, possibly because the conductorship was being divided, between André Messager (for Paris) and Emil Cooper (for London), and Cooper himself was tied up in Moscow with the Imperial Opera, whose musical director he was.[105]

Notwithstanding these troubles, the season went ahead more or less as planned, and the production of *Nightingale* achieved a visual perfection which remained in the minds of many who saw it as one of the pinnacles of the prewar Ballets Russes seasons. Benois himself recalled the staging in ecstatic terms: "for the first time in my life," he wrote, "I felt genuinely moved by my own creation."[106] But reactions to the opera itself were a good deal more equivocal, even though the music had distinguished admirers, particularly among those with a bent for the decorative, such as Reynaldo Hahn, who doubted whether "a more fascinating quality of illusion or a more perfect accord between music and staging has ever been achieved in the theatre. . . . The music of *The Nightingale* is of a perfect logic, and adapted to the subject with a truly extraordinary delicacy and discernment."[107] Emile Vuillermoz, while admitting that the music was "a miracle of Far Eastern art, not only in its characteristic sonorities and melodic intervals, but in its feeling," was perturbed by the break in style:

An evolution so radical and so abrupt is an exceptional phenomenon. Half a century of music seems contained between this opening—where it is easy to note influences and collect amusing quotations—and this ending where we see that the technique of *The Rite of Spring* was not a gauntlet thrown down on behalf of prehistory but a progressive step towards that extreme division of sound which our senses demand when their curiosity has been frustrated.[108]

Several reviewers found that the music was upstaged by the decor. And a sufficient number commented on the poor orchestral playing to make it likely that Stravinsky's open letter to Monteux praising the orchestral playing was more exculpation than refutation. The performance had been shaky—one reads between the lines—but the musicians were not to blame.[109] Monteux had taken over from Messager less than two weeks before the premiere, and most critics who noted the weakness routinely exonerated the conductor. Behind much of this, needless to say, was a certain disappointment that *The Nightingale* had failed to reawaken the aggressions of the previous May. Far from drowning the music, the audience barely even called out the composer, who managed a third curtain only by dint of reappearing with somewhat indecent haste after the second. Succès de scandale was very plainly replaced by succès d'estime.

Perhaps it was that kind of season. Certainly the other new works made little impact. Strauss's *Josephslegende*, conducted by the master himself less than a month before his fiftieth birthday, was a pale echo of his operatic collaboration with Hugo von Hofmannsthal—which did not stop it taking up the lion's share of the orchestral rehearsal time. Its most notable attribute was a handsome new premier danseur called Leonid Myasin (Massine), whom Diaghilev had picked up in Moscow. As for *Midas*, Diaghilev's grudging fulfillment of his longstanding promise to stage Max Steinberg's *Metamorphoses*, the best that anyone could say for it was that it was "far from a work of genius, but nevertheless . . . pleasant and the performance was charming and in excellent taste."[110] Only one of Steinberg's three symphonic movements was used; Fokine choreographed it without his usual spirit; and instead of the hoped-for Bakst, who had been so enthusiastic about the music when Steinberg played it through in St. Petersburg, the ballet was designed by the less spectacular Mstislav Dobuzhinsky. Max was in Paris for a good fortnight before *Midas* opened on 2 June, and he spent much of the time with Igor. He dutifully attended the rehearsals of *The Nightingale*, and even helped out (in some unspecified capacity) when it became a matter of all-hands-on-deck to get the singers up to standard in time. He sat in cafés with Igor, Benois, Edwin Evans, and Delage, or walked the boulevards with them far into the night, discussing the works that were being rehearsed, or ballet and music in general. He was terribly nervous, he admitted to Nadya, but Igor was being sweet and friendly, and was so convincing in argument that Max was all but won over to his artistic views.[111]

Then something went wrong. After the *Nightingale* premiere, Igor retreated to Delage's, and suddenly started making himself disagreeable to his Russian colleague. "Igor," said Max, "is being rather a pig." Two or three days before *Midas*, Stravinsky dropped in and began lecturing him about something or other, startling Max by his pomposity. All at once the atmosphere between them was sour, and Max abruptly abandoned an intention he had formed to visit the Stravinskys in Clarens between the Paris and London seasons. Obviously Igor was upset by the performance of *The Nightingale* and by its reception. But why take it out on an old friend? Perhaps because he knew that Max, while professing admiration for the first act, detested acts 2 and 3 of this Janus-faced work, and so he decided to cast him as scapegoat for its comparative failure. Max had been telling his wife that "I understand nothing of this rubbish," and that "either it's nonsense or *Midas* is untalented trash," and some flavor of that attitude, if not its actual expression, must have come out in their "bitter discussions about music"—as Max described them to Nadya. Perhaps the discussions had included the long talk about *The Rite of Spring*, which Max had threatened in his last postcard.[112] Or perhaps they discussed the rights and wrongs of staging *The Golden Cockerel* as a ballet, a subject on which Max remained a Rimsky-Korsakov through and through. Whatever it was they talked about, so vigorously and in the end so acrimoniously, it effectively put an end to their friendship.

A few days later Igor was back in Switzerland. The decision had already been taken in February not to go to Russia that summer, mountain air being regarded as imperative for Katya's health.[113] So instead, from Clarens, the extended family now moved to the tiny upland town of Salvan, a resort of larchwood houses, set on a plateau above Martigny in the Valais. Stravinsky later described the Villa Bel-Air as "a chalet . . . rented from peasants."[114] But in fact the house was yet another large *hôtel-pension*, or boardinghouse, just outside the main village, with a big field opposite that Theodore recalled the Swiss army using as a shooting range during the tense days of late June 1914.[115] His father went back to work on the instrumental sketches which ended up as the Three Pieces for String Quartet. But he was not to be left in peace for very long. Within a week, a telegram from Diaghilev summoned him to the London rehearsals of *Nightingale*, which was being conducted for the first time by Emil Cooper. So off he dutifully set.

He was in London for just over a week, and it was to be an unexpectedly productive visit, in what might at the time have seemed quite trivial ways. *Nightingale* itself was received no more than politely on 18 June by "the clustered, nodding tiaras and the white kid gloves" of Diaghilev's society audience.[116] But on his first night in London, the fifteenth, Stravinsky went to a futurist concert at the Coliseum, and for the first time encountered the "buzzers, whistlers, rattlers, exploders, murmurers, cracklers, thunderers, gurglers, and roarers" of Luigi Russolo's noise menagerie, and heard the poet Emilio Marinetti hold forth on the subject of "The Art of Noises."[117] To say that Stravinsky was influenced by these amiable Italian eccentrics would be grossly to misunderstand the true nature of his own interest in "noise," though it was natural enough that a manifesto-writing nonmusician like Marinetti should have seen in the composer of *Petrushka* and *The Rite of Spring* artistic support for his theories about the abolition of the past in favor of an age of machines and proto-fascist violence. But Stravinsky became sincerely fond of the group, not so much liking their politics (perhaps) as amused by antics which, when all was said and done, posed no artistic threat while being touchingly fueled by a genuine admiration for his own work. "The Futurists were absurd," he wrote later, "but sympathetically so, and they were infinitely less pretentious than some of the later groups that borrowed from them. . . . [They] were not the aeroplanes they wanted to be but they were at any rate a pack of very nice, noisy Vespas."[118] Diaghilev was interested as well, and saw collaborative possibilities.

It may or may not have been on the same bill that Stravinsky first saw the clown Little Tich, with his long flat shoes which could turn into stilts, his jerky, balletic movements, his balance and elevation—all of which also fascinated Nijinsky. Did the composer suddenly identify this talented dwarf with the fairground aspect of Cocteau's *David*, or simply notice a connection between these movements, viewed with detachment, and the chamber music he had been sketching? Or was he, as he himself later recalled, directly inspired by the clown to compose the music which became the second of the Three Pieces for String Quartet? The exact chronology is elusive.[119] What seems clear is that he was wide open to influences at this juncture when the past of *The Nightingale* had at last been cleared away and the future was bright with new concepts. From this London visit, at all events, date several musical impressions which found their way into his sketchbooks of the time or into subsequent pieces. With Edwin Evans, he attended a demonstration of the Pianola put on by the Orchestrelle Company at its Aeolian Hall headquarters, and may have heard a pre-publication performance of a set of rolls of his Four Studies, op. 7, which came out later in 1914.[120] Then "one Sunday afternoon," Evans wrote,

> Stravinsky and I took a taxi and, roaming through the deserted City of London, came upon St. Paul's just as the bells were pealing.

Stravinsky stopped the cab, and listened intently to the "changes," taking occasional notes on the back of an envelope. He was most enthusiastic about the inexhaustible variety of the sequences in which he claimed to hear the most wonderful music. There is something about *Les Noces,* and particularly about its strange concluding pages, which makes me wonder whether, in all essentials, the substance of the music, or at least the percussive element which animates it, was not born in London on that Sunday afternoon a few weeks before the outbreak of the first world war.[121]

Perhaps. But in Stravinsky's sketchbooks the bell notations figure alongside a fragment of melody which also, he tells us, "came to my ear in London, in July *[sic]* 1914," and which provided the second tune for the opening song of his next work, *Pribaoutki.*[122]

As he wended his way back to Salvan later that week, he may have known perfectly well that, amid all these new beginnings, he was leaving behind something that was approaching its end. Andrey Rimsky-Korsakov had been in London to report on Diaghilev's balleticization of *The Golden Cockerel,* and the two men had had a long talk, perhaps the "calm, friendly, and frank conversation" for which Andrey had confessed himself ready in his last letter, in January,[123] but certainly not without its tensions, as Andrey wrote to his mother the day after the meeting. With more than a trace of self-satisfaction, he reported that he had "told Igor a lot of things he hadn't chanced to hear for a long time." *Khovanshchina* proved, he said, that Igor's tributes to his teacher's memory were nothing more than empty words.[124] But neither was it in Stravinsky's nature to gloss over past offences against his own work. He too, he had written barely four months before,

> would like our friendship not to become, as you put it, an illusion. I only fear one thing, that it might happen without our knowledge by virtue of the differences in our outlook in matters of art, and as a result of my increasingly sparse and remote meetings with you. In any case, after your letter (whose sincerity I have no reason to doubt), neither your poisonous fulminations against my compositions nor your protests against my "anti-artistic" conduct must alter our fine and friendly relations.[125]

There was no going back. Such a letter, followed by such a meeting, would surely have ended things with the Rimsky-Korsakovs even if events had not carried them off, still fighting as the waters broke over them.

FRAGMENTS OF OLD RUSSIA

ON THE DAY that Gavrilo Princip fired his fatal pair of bullets in Sarajevo, Sunday 28 June 1914, Igor Stravinsky was working at Salvan on the tiny piece for string quartet he was modelling on the disjointed movements of Little Tich.

Returning from London a few days earlier, he had found waiting for him a letter from Alfred Pochon, second violinist in the Flonzaley Quartet, asking if he would consider supplying a work for the quartet's forthcoming European and American tour.[1] Whether or not the first of the eventual pieces was already in quartet form, the suggestion obviously chimed with his working interests of the moment, as long as it was understood (and Pochon did seem to understand) that the result would not remotely be a string quartet in the conventional sense of the term. He had in fact been tinkering with a set of fragmentary ideas which lent themselves, not to extension or development, but to a kind of loose sequence, or to different sorts of multiple repetition with slight variations in the figure or with phased combinations of instruments. He had tried them out with piano, and also with a small mixed ensemble of strings, piano, and winds; he referred to them later, in a letter to his publisher, as "chamber music," and he told Struve's colleague Erich Zingel that there would be five of them in all.[2] Other kinds of short pieces were boiling up in his mind, and he must have expected that some of them would be for instruments. But Pochon needed the pieces by mid-August, and by then only three were ready, and Stravinsky's work was already taking a somewhat different turn.

It is almost as if the quartet pieces were a surrogate response to some deeper impulse which, for various circumstantial reasons, could not yet be satisfied. *Svadebka*, in particular, simply could not be written, because certain necessary texts and melodies were not to hand. Of course, Igor could ask his remaining Russian friends to send them, or his mother, who was or would soon be on her way back to St. Petersburg. But this was too precise a method for a composer who probably did not yet know exactly what it was that he wanted. What he really needed was to rummage: to go through his own and his father's libraries, to browse round a few shops, fill a suitcase or two. He had planned just such a trip to Kiev in the spring, but had apparently been forced to call it off. This time he must at all costs go, and not just for the books. His finances were becoming precarious. Diaghilev, as usual, was procrastinating over payments for *The Nightingale,* the lucrative Free Theatre deal had fallen through, and the Mariyinsky, even if they eventually took the opera, would be unlikely to pay an equivalent fee.[3] Now there was talk of an Austrian war with Serbia, which would mean with Russia, and it was already two years since his brother-in-law had warned him that his Ukrainian bank deposits and mortgages were at risk from the political situation. It was high time—it might even be the last chance for some while—to investigate these dangers on the ground. Moreover, Grigory Belyankin, who had power of attorney over the Stravinskys' Ustilug affairs but was always grumbling at how little time they were able to devote to them, was pressing Igor to come before the end of June Old Style.

He finished the quartet piece about Little Tich on 2 July, and that day or the next he set off for Kiev. He was away ten days—truly a flying visit, considering that at least four of them will have been spent in railway trains. He went to Ustilug and discussed the latest plantings with the gardener Kozlovsky, met Zhuchky the dog's new puppy, walked the orchards and borders, wandered through the house he had designed and watched being built—the house born with his marriage. The lime trees he and Gury had planted seven years ago were starting to make some height. Perhaps he stood in the avenue and reflected on the past and the future, watched the Luga winding below the house, the horses grazing peacefully on the other side of the river, the line of poplars beyond; or perhaps he simply made businesslike arrangements with Kozlovsky, checked the house, collected a few books and manuscripts, and departed—by car these days—along the sandy road towards the train at Vladimir-Volïnsky.

In Kiev he presumably had meetings with Katya's cousin Dmitry Andreyevich Nosenko, to whom he and Katya had lent the remarkable sum of eighty thousand roubles. At any rate he appointed a lawyer with power of attorney to deal in future with the Dmitry debt, part of which seems subsequently to have been discharged by an (ultimately) worthless transfer of land.[4] He then probably went shopping. He was looking for books: collections of Russian folk poetry and song, books on language, dictionaries, anything that would open the door into that virtual world of the Slavic past which he had already glimpsed beyond the showy art nouveau of the Russian ballet. Some of these things he had found in his own library at Ustilug; others he bought. His eye was taken by artifacts: he purchased a couple of dozen shawls from Muscovy ("My God, what shawls!" he told Benois later, "not inferior to yours in *Petrushka*—forgive me").[5] Everything was suffused in a creative radiance, perhaps like Wordsworth's "higher power than Fancy" giving assurance of "some work of glory there forth-with to be begun."[6] On the train back to Switzerland, surrounded by the prewar tensions of Poland and Germany, he pulled out a volume of poems and plays by Koz'ma Prutkov and began to read about the poet and the oak tree, the north wind and the southern gale, and the affinity of all the forces of the universe. "Ah, Shura, my dear! the things I've found there!" he wrote to Benois. "God himself is indicating that we should work together. For God's sake look at it and read it soon—it's only a few pages—the last thing in the book: it's called 'The Affinity of Universal Forces'—a mystery in eleven scenes. . . . From this moment I can find no peace. I think only of this, I dream about it. My dear, have compassion!!!"[7]

Wrapped up with the letter was the book. Benois, like all educated Russians, knew his Koz'ma Prutkov but he could not think of these old satires—the affectations of an imaginary bureaucrat "with romantic impulses and a prosaic mind"[8]—as material for theatrical comedy in 1914, which needed to be "something else: either funnier or more terrible."[9] Nevertheless he reread the book, waited a few days, then took a deep breath and wrote back. Meanwhile, Stravinsky, beside himself with impatience, had written again: "Total silence! What a bore. Do answer, friend, if only on a postcard, how I long for your first opinion, at least, about 'The Affinity of Universal Forces.' "[10] Meanwhile, he was reading Remizov's novel *Judas, Prince of Iscariot* with almost as much excitement as Prutkov. But a letter, and the book, were already on their way from St.-Jean-de-Luz, where Benois was spending the summer.

> I really, not exactly dislike "Kozma Prutkov," but simply fail to under-stand the huge importance it has assumed in Russian literature and the whole of Russian life. Well, it's funny, lovable, silly, in places really talented, but genuine power of humor and authentic artistic laughter (which Gogol and Dostoyevsky gave us in such measure) I fail to see in this overlong and (in the bad sense) rather naive parody salad. In a word, in my opinion it isn't worth bothering with "Prutkov."[11]

Duly chastened, Stravinsky made a few sketches for Prutkov—"music very different from that of his other works of the time," according to Robert Craft[12]—then laid it aside for good. Did he have some vision for this rather ponderous satire on the Great Poet who is rescued for posterity when the southern gale uproots the oak on which he is in the process of hanging himself? Years later he described his idea as "a comic piece for the theatre, a kind of *Renard*."[13] But the mock heroics and pseudo-symbolism of *Prutkov* are precisely not in the spirit of the authentic folk impulse which animates not just *Renard* but the other, much smaller, Russian settings that surround it, to say nothing of the great ceremonial expression of that impulse, *Svadebka*. Stravinsky was simply having trouble containing his excitement. And he may have been mistaken in supposing—out of sheer habit—that he needed a collaborator.

Now, in the peace and quiet of Salvan, he began to sort out his impressions. He had picked up several major nineteenth-century collections of Russian folk verses and tales: Afanasyev; Sakharov; the collected ritual songs of Kireyevsky; Sheyn's *Songs, Customs and Beliefs;* and Dahl's *Explanatory Dictionary.* He had folk-song collections—Istomin, Linyova—and he had his own ideas. He was looking at all this material in quite a new way: not like a well-bred kuchkist setting the "right" tune, intact, to the "right" words in the "right" situation, but instead as if he could somehow enter into the actual spirit that first gave these songs and poems life and reinvent it, through them, in an entirely modern image—an image which just happened to be coarse and ebullient, antisophisticated, innocent of rules, richly simple, intelligent and subtle, as they in their way had been. It is tempting to see this sudden fit of ethnicity as an instant pan-Slavic response to the Austro-German threat, and indeed there was, as we shall shortly discover, an element of that, though it can hardly have been part of the original idea, which in the case of *Svadebka* went back almost two years. But Stravinsky himself was at first just as inclined to feel alienated from everything to do with the Western world and its art. While Diaghilev, who had adored the idea of *Svadebka* from the moment he first heard of it, bombarded its composer with telegrams from London asking him how the ballet was going and whether he could yet come to Salvan to hear any of it, Stravinsky was fulminating to Benois about "this elderly director with his monocle and his Myasin boy":

> God, I'm sick of them! How much better to stay here and breathe. Here there's sun, limpid dark-green grass, real-life, slow-moving people—all of them old, but even the small children talk so that you can't understand a word—mostly inarticulate, ventriloquistic noises—"thi" instead of "they." Terrific! . . . Oh! how I feel this [Diaghilev] business isn't for me. Precisely because its artistic life is over, and is now pure commerce—which is the one thing that stops me (since I survive on it) from breaking with this international soldiers' club. Does Seryozha realize that or not? I think not. If he does, then there's no way out, he's dead and rotten. He now stinks to high heaven, and it's a familiar stink, old and stagnant.[14]

Diaghilev had admittedly brought this diatribe on himself by his reluctance to settle his debts—a reluctance which was by now becoming chronic, as Stravinsky's publishers were also finding out to their cost. But even if Diaghilev had been paying up, the composer would certainly, in his new mood, have resented his dependence on "pure commerce" at a time when his writing was experimental and inherently hard to market, and while the rich pickings of his early ballets were soaking away through unsound Russian investments and intractable Western copyright conventions. In the end, the main reason for writing the quartet pieces—the last of which he completed on 25 July—may well have been that Pochon offered a series of performances, though no commission fee. This gave Stravinsky leverage to demand from Struve the steep honorarium of two hundred roubles for each of these tiny pieces, which he shamelessly totalled up to a thousand for five pieces, even though he had only written three.[15] He then wasted further time writing up an orchestral arrangement of the accompaniment to his Verlaine songs and trying to sell it to Jurgenson, who coolly declined to pay on the grounds that it was commercially worthless and that in any case he owned it already by the original contract for the songs.[16] And he let himself in for a reduced orchestration of the finale of *Firebird* to go with the Lullaby as a popular piece for provincial orchestras. Stravinsky planned to conduct this piece himself at the Queen's Hall in London the following April.[17] But again the motive was commercial: he would obviously hope to copyright the arrangement more securely than the wretched original ballet, which, having been published in Russia (a nonsignatory), was not covered by the Berne Convention.

Meanwhile, his experiments with the Russian folk texts were starting to bear fruit. He was making preliminary drafts for the scenario of *Svadebka*, basing himself on Kireyevsky and on the second volume of Tereshchenko's *Manners and Customs of the Russian People*, with its exhaustive survey of wedding rites in Russia in the 1840s. And in August he composed three tiny songs, for male voice with a small instrumental ensemble, on nonsense poems taken from the third volume of Afanasyev's *Skazki* (Tales), calling them *Pribaoutki*—a type of song in which logical, linear sense is abandoned in favor of wordplays, assonances, and internal rhymes: an earthier, and often saltier, Russian prototype of "Hey Diddle Diddle" or "Goosey-Goosey Gander."[18] Technically, in the way they miniaturize the rhythmic and harmonic language of *The Rite of Spring*, these songs might be seen as an ethnic equivalent of the quartet pieces. They even have some of the same constructivist leanings, and a similar coarse wit. But why then is it that they seem so much richer and more momentous, in spite of their exiguous dimensions? For one thing, Stravinsky had hit on a hitherto unknown sonority, a noise that might be made by an octet of peasant virtuosos who happen to have learnt the entire corpus of Western music and then forgotten it. Their sounds—harsh, vibrant, absolute: each one like an object you want to steal and put on your mantelpiece—belong in some ethnographic heaven to which only composers, musicians, and their wide-eared listeners (certainly not ethnographers) are admitted. In the vocal part—apparently so rudimentary, with its few notes and blunt repetitions—the vital new element is the way rhythm is enlivened by a curious treatment of word accent. Looking through his Kiev booty, Stravinsky had suddenly realized that in these Russian folk poems the stress often fell in different places on the same word, or simply on the wrong syllable. "The recognition of the musical possibilities inherent in this fact," Stravinsky told Robert Craft, "was one of the most rejoicing discoveries of my life; I was like a man who suddenly finds that his finger can be bent from the second joint as well as from the first."[19]

Probably the recognition was more than just observation, since his ballets had already made exciting use of thrown rhythmic accents and variable meters in a purely orchestral context. The words simply added one more dimension. But it was a particularly suggestive one, since words have meanings as well as sounds, and if you play around with the sounds you imply that the meanings, too, might be playthings. In fact, Stravinsky was probably more interested in the way the wrong accents could work against the right ones to make a highly subtle and complex rhythmic music. To get the full point, the listener (or at least the singer) has to know what is "right" even as he sings what is "wrong." So, for non–Russian speakers, these marvellous little songs have never been without their esoteric side.

In the next few months, Stravinsky wrote more pieces along the same or similar lines. At the end of September he added a fourth *pribaoutka*, "The Old Man and the Hare," rounding the song off with a tiny recapitulatory epilogue—the only instance of formal repetition in the whole collection. Next, in December, he wrote a choral setting for unaccompanied women's voices of a poem about a pike ("Shchuka"), which he had come across in Sakharov's *Legends of the Russian People* complete with a prosodic analysis showing how the accents in the poem cut across the normal pronunciation.[20] This was to be the first of four "divination" choruses, based on poems connected with a kind of "Tinker, Tailor" ritual in which trinkets belonging to the unmarried local girls were drawn out of a dish one by one while poems were chanted foretelling the prospects of each.[21] The connection with the pagan-Christian wedding rituals in *Svadebka* is obvious enough. And in fact Stravinsky had by this time at last begun to compose the ballet, little suspecting how much else he would have to compose before it was completed and performed. In January there would be another chorus ("Puzishche"), and then, during 1915, a series of lullabies for contralto and a wonderfully unlikely trio of clarinets (in E-flat, A, and bass clarinet in B-flat): the so-called *Berceuses du chat*, which reduce the new idiom to its most wittily and imaginatively condensed form. None of this music helped Stravinsky's finances, or can have hoped to. Even if the

Russo-German operations of RMV had not been curtailed by the outbreak of war, one can imagine the enthusiasm with which Struve would have greeted this jumble of miniatures for no known ensemble and lasting barely longer than an orchestra takes to tune up. As Jurgenson had said of the orchestration of the Verlaine songs, they would simply have been outlay without income. The much-touted idea that Stravinsky's wartime pieces for small mixed ensemble were in some way written as an economy would have raised a caustic laugh in Moscow and Berlin.

EARLY IN SEPTEMBER, the Stravinskys moved back down to Clarens and took up residence in La Pervenche as sublessees of Ansermet (whose Montreux orchestra had folded because of mobilization at the end of August). Anna Stravinsky had gone back to Petersburg to be with Gury, who was now a member of the Imperial Theatre company and singing at the Mariyinsky. Baba Sonya had also gone back with the Belyankins, and Katya, still somewhat frail, needed help with the children. So Bertha Essert was summoned from Russia as an elderly, almost seventy-year-old *nyanya* for this next generation of Stravinskys.[22] Her arrival was also, in a small way, the first acknowledgment by Igor and Katya that their own return to Russia could no longer be counted on as imminent. The war had gone badly for Russia in August; in the West the situation had quickly become attritional; and by September few believed that peace would return within a matter of weeks, as had been widely supposed at the start of hostilities. Not surprisingly, Stravinsky's lurking prejudice against Germans quickly turned to a hatred which grew "by the hour," as he told Bakst.[23] A few days later he went to see the French musicologist and novelist Romain Rolland at the Hotel Mooser in Vevey, in order to hand him a letter supporting Rolland's protest against the destruction of Louvain and the bombardment of Rheims Cathedral. The letter itself is a conventional enough diatribe, except that it significantly denies the Germans even the title of "barbarian," since a barbarian "is the bringer of a conception of culture other than our own [while] modern Germany cannot be considered as bringing a new culture." Much more revealing is the long conversation between the two artists, the gist of which the pacifist Rolland recorded in his journal:

> Stravinsky is about thirty; he is small, sickly looking, ugly, yellow-faced, thin and tired, with a narrow brow, thin, receding hair, his eyes screwed up behind a pince-nez, a fleshy nose, big lips, a disproportionately long face in relation to his forehead. He is very intelligent and simple in his manners; he speaks easily, though sometimes searching for the French words; and everything he says is personal and thought-out (true or false). The first part of our conversation was

about politics. Stravinsky states that Germany is not a barbarous country, but decrepit and degenerate. He claims for Russia the role of beautiful and healthy barbarism, bursting with new seeds that will impregnate the world's thought. He reckons that after the war a revolution, already in preparation, will overturn the dynasty and found a United Slav States. Moreover, he partly attributes the cruelties of tsarism to German elements incorporated into Russia, which have gained control of the main wheels of government or the administration. The attitude of German intellectuals inspires in him a boundless mistrust. Hauptmann and Strauss, he says, have the souls of lackeys. He sings the praises of the old Russian civilization, unknown in the West, the artistic and literary monuments of the cities of the north and east.[24]

They had talked next about music, and Stravinsky had expressed in somewhat different terms his newfound distaste for the showier aspects of the Russian ballet. Clearly with Benois's *Nightingale* in mind, he had complained about the way theatrical design was tending to limit music by making its expression too specific. He had attacked the Wagnerian idea of the *Gesamtkunstwerk,* so dear to his World of Art collaborators. Music must be sovereign. "Suppress color! Color is too powerful. . . . We should just keep lighting . . . gestures and rhythms." He had talked about his new songs— "dicts," he had called them:

> The amusement for him is to get brusquely in music from one image to another that is quite different and unexpected. He has, he says, to write every day, with or without inspiration. Nothing equals the joy of the first conception, when the idea emerges still living from his consciousness. "It's an almost sadistic pleasure," he says. Once it begins to be expressed, the joy is already diminishing. And when the work is complete, it no longer exists for the composer. It then begins a life in which the whole public, listeners or readers, participate, recreating it in their turn; it continues to evolve often for centuries; and from nobody is it more remote than from its original creator.

But though Stravinsky might feel distant from his old ballets and former colleagues, the colleagues had by no means abandoned him. Even before he had moved back down to Clarens, Diaghilev had wired from neutral Italy pressing him to come with Katya for a few days to Florence, where he and Massine had rented a villa.[25] Diaghilev wanted, of course, to discuss a project, one which had emerged from his summer sightseeing tour of northern Italy with his new young dancer friend. They had been studying religious art and had conceived the idea of a ballet built round a sequence of the conventional religious subjects of Byzantine and Renaissance painting and sculpture, a work which came to be known as *Liturgie*.[26] But, whether out of genuine poverty or because of the issue of *Nightingale* payments, Stravinsky refused to go to Florence unless Diaghilev paid his fare. Eventually, at the end of September, Diaghilev wired money, and the composer perhaps went. But the meeting, if it happened, was inconclusive. Diaghilev soon returned to the charge, and even performed the—for him—rare act of writing letters. The Croat sculptor Ivan Mestrovic (who was living in Rome) was involved; and there was question of a contract in connection with a supposed 1915 American tour. Diaghilev was perfectly aware, of course, that Stravinsky might be enticed by money. He even raised the possibility of a concert which Stravinsky would conduct at the Accademia di Santa Cecilia in Rome in January 1915. This scheme swiftly fell through,[27] and when January came Diaghilev was still peppering the reluctant and supposedly indigent composer with telegrams trying to lure him (back) to Italy.

Diaghilev described *Liturgie* to Stravinsky as "a sacred spectacle, an ecstatic Mass, in six or seven short scenes. The period is roughly Byzantine; of course, Mestrovic will treat it in his own way. The music is a series of a cappella choruses, purely religious, perhaps inspired by Gregorian chant."[28] Did Stravinsky ever seriously consider collaborating in this aesthetes' fantasy, whose musical and artistic prescriptions seem so far from his clearly defined preoccupations of the time? It seems that he did. No identifiable sketches survive. But as late as August 1915 his Clarens neighbor the American journalist Stanley Wise, of whom he saw a good deal during his time at La Pervenche, reported that Massine and Stravinsky were collaborating in

> a sort of modern Passion Play. It is to consist of a complete series of moving tableaux—one cannot call them ballets—giving the life of our Lord beginning with the Annunciation. The scenes will be separated from one another by vocal entr'actes (no orchestra) all of course liturgic in character which occasionally overlap the scenes. There will be something like 25 tableaux. They expect to produce this (as also *Svadebka*) in Paris next May—if war permits of performances there. I said to Strawinsky that I feared such a work might not be permitted in England . . . & he said—"I don't know about that but I am *sure* they will not allow it in Russia." . . . None of the music of the *Liturgie* has been written yet.[29]

Wise can only have got this information from the composer himself. Massine later claimed to have witnessed a contract for *Liturgie* and *Svadebka* between Stravinsky and Diaghilev, which bears out Stravinsky's remark that "I refused to do the ballet . . . because Diaghilev wanted me to compose it and *Les Noces* [*Svadebka*] for the same price."[30] But the composer told Ansermet in 1919, somewhat ambiguously, that "I long ago gave up the idea of doing the music for *Liturgie*—it doesn't interest me,"[31] which certainly seems to imply that it once had.

Perhaps in any case it was this protracted bombardment from "the elderly director with his monocle" that prompted a minor diversion from the visionary Russia of *Svadebka* and the *Pribaoutki,* in the form of a little satirical Polka for piano duet which Stravinsky penned on 15 November, the very date that he wrote to Diaghilev in Rome accepting the idea of conducting there in January. At any rate, he later claimed that the piece was "a caricature of Diaghilev, whom I saw as a circus animal-trainer cracking a long whip."[32] It was one of a series of "easy pieces" which he began to write at about this time, designed as duets with one easy part suitable to be played by his older children. There was a "Valse des fleurs," written a few days before the Polka, then a March (based on a tune called "The Blacksmith and His Son" in a collection of old Irish folk songs Stravinsky had bought in London in January 1913), and another Waltz—the last three being the ones later published as the Three Easy Pieces.[33] The music, perhaps inspired by the piano music of Satie, is very slight, but the synthetic idea—the idea of modelling on a stereotype something which strongly suggests but does not in fact belong to that stereotype—is of moment, since it is possible to regard it as the first faint glimmer of neoclassicism in Stravinsky. The most striking point is that the pieces are in some sense "composed" like the Russian songs; there is the same oblique angle on simple material, the same use of elementary, quasi-mechanical patterns, the same wit and economy of texture—almost as if a substitution of material had taken place while the composer's back was turned. But the music remains trivial, in a way that the songs never are.

Katya's health was still giving occasional grounds for concern, so at the beginning of January 1915 (probably just before Russian Christmas on the seventh) the whole family decamped once again to the mountains, this time settling in the small town of Château d'Oex, in the Pays d'Enhaut behind Montreux. They installed themselves in a large *hôtel-pension* called the Hôtel Victoria, on the road out towards Saanen. Igor had planned to spend a few days in Paris at or just after Western Christmas, but had to abandon the trip, as he told Ravel, because of shortage of funds.[34] He did manage, during January, to get as far as Geneva, where Ansermet was now conducting the subscription concerts in the Théâtre de la Ville de Genève. On the twenty-third he heard his friend conduct *Petrushka* (excerpts only) for the first time, and at the rehearsal (on the twenty-second) again met Rolland, who referred in his journal to the "dislocated, furious, burlesque hysteria of [the music of] Stravinsky, [which] seems to go very well with the great madness of the present time. The aesthetic value of this Russian music is not to be doubted. . . . But one finds in it not a single moral value, no force of reason, order, peace, harmonious and humane action."[35] It was perhaps also during this visit that Stravinsky went with Ansermet to a bar in Geneva where a Hungarian cimbalomist called Aladár Rácz was playing, and he was so excited by Rácz's performance of a Serbian *kolo* that he "leapt to the cimbalom [struggling] with his sleeve to try to pull out the cuff, on which he wanted to write down the music he was hearing. I was a little too sure of myself as a young man," Rácz recalled, "and I sized him up from head to foot, thinking, 'You won't be able to write down what I'm playing!' And indeed he soon stopped taking notes."[36]

A day or so later Stravinsky, with Rácz's help (but without revealing his identity), bought a battered old Schunda cimbalom from a Gypsy in the city and left it with Rácz to be repaired. The Swiss art historian Adrien Bovy wrote to Stravinsky that he had been asked

> to call at Maxim's [bar] to remind the cimbalomist of your order and give him your address. I saw him yesterday evening. The work is done. I asked him his terms: "I don't know," he said; "this gentleman, is he a musician?"—"Yes, he's a musician." "Well, what do you think I should ask?" I began to write: M. Igor Stravinsky; I showed him the name. His colleagues didn't believe it. And he added: "If I'd known *beforehand*, I wouldn't have dared play. . . ." So you'll be getting his delivery at Château d'Oex and you owe him nothing. But he has scruples, since he says that this music is impossible to write down.[37]

The cimbalom duly arrived at Château d'Oex; Stravinsky himself cleaned it up and, with Rácz's help, learnt to play it; and for almost five years the twangy sonority and essentially melodic-rhythmic technique of this large peasant dulcimer were to take on a dominant role in his instrumental thinking.

Meanwhile, Diaghilev was again deluging him with telegrams from Rome, insisting on his immediate presence for discussions with Mestrovic about *Liturgie*. Diaghilev's tactic was to fabricate a four-month trip to Africa from mid-January in order to bully the composer into swift compliance. But Stravinsky would not budge until after the fifteenth (Milène's first birthday), and when the fifteenth came he refused to leave Switzerland for fear of the aftershocks of the huge earthquake at Avezzano in the Abruzzi two days before. Though furious, Diaghilev could do nothing except "postpone" Africa and try to keep up the pressure on the uncooperative composer. At last Stravinsky gave way and went to Rome in the second week of February, probably on the eighth, two days after Ansermet's repeat concert performance of the *Petrushka* excerpts. About the meetings with Mestrovic we know nothing, but there was more energetic socializing with the futurists. At least some of them were among the very select audience at a tea-reception thrown by Diaghilev in the Grand Hotel on the thirteenth, when Stravinsky and Casella played the Three Pieces for String Quartet four-hands, and excerpts from *The Firebird* and *The Rite of Spring*, and Stravinsky accompanied Marya Freund in a group of his songs. Then, when Casella conducted the Italian premiere of *Petrushka* at a concert in the Augusteo the following day, mild audience protests were abruptly countered by Marinetti yelling provocatively, "Abasso Wagner! Viva Stravinsky!"[38] Other reports, though, suggest that there was an ovation. Stravinsky wrote to his mother that "I had to take a large number of bows from my box. . . . After this there were continued lengthy demonstrations in the corridors. All the Italian futurists were present and saluted me noisily. Marinetti came specially from Milan."[39] According to the futurist sculptor Umberto Boccioni, Stravinsky had specifically invited him to the Grand Hotel because "he wants to meet me and do something with futurist . . . color, dance, and costume."[40] But the only eventual collaboration—to call it that—was in 1917 with the painter Giacomo Balla, from whom Diaghilev commissioned an elaborate, nonchoreographic light show to accompany a performance of Stravinsky's *Fireworks*.

Stravinsky had brought with him to Italy his draft score for the first scene or so of *Les Noces*, and at some stage of the Rome visit he gave Diaghilev a private preview, presumably crooning and groaning the vocal parts. But however questionable the actual sound, Diaghilev was smitten. "Finish *Svadebka* quickly," he wrote a few weeks later, "I'm in love with it."[41] It seems likely also that he played Diaghilev the little Polka he had written for, and about, him, as well as perhaps the March (but hardly the Waltz, which was not composed until the following month).[42]

By 19 February, Stravinsky was back at Château d'Oex, in a physical and emotional world unbelievably remote from the hubbub of Rome and the intellectual fisticuffs of the futurists, Diaghilev, and the Russian emigration, to say nothing of the daily battles between the pro- and anti-interventionists on the Italian political scene. To some extent this division had been a part of his life since he first came to Paris in 1910. But the outbreak of war, and his own increasing preoccupation with a kind of virtual Russian ethnography, emphasized it to the point almost of caricature. Outside his work, and however purely Russian the atmosphere in the home he and Katya carried round with them, he never adopted the rustic manners or peasant dress of the classic Tolstoyan rural idealist; nor was he ever the shabby litterateur, with frayed cuffs and baggy-kneed trousers, beloved of twentieth-century artistic lore. In his life and in his music, the watchword was order. If in his dress, such correctness was emboldened by a certain dandyish ostentation, that was surely as much from a fear of provincialism as out of any specific enthusiasm for fashion. It was occasionally overdone. Rácz's description of the composer in his monocle, his red tie and green waistcoat, fidgeting in a tight jacket from which he could scarcely extract his shirt cuff, is detectably, if not openly, satirical.[43] Stravinsky's primary colors, the reds, greens, and yellows, the checks of his trousers even, became a byword, and they must have absorbed an appreciable amount of the money of which he claimed to be so short. But the neatness of his studio, like the calligraphy of his scores, however obsessive, was an absolute necessity for his work, and inseparable from it. "Stravinsky's writing desk," one of his closest Swiss friends wrote,

> resembled a surgeon's instrument tray; now the order which the surgeon there sets out is one last chance he gives himself in his struggle against death. The artist too (in his way) is engaged in a struggle with death. These bottles of different-colored inks, each in its hierarchical place, play small part in a grand affirmation of a superior order. They keep company with different sorts and shapes of rubber and every kind of glinting steel object: rulers, scrapers, knives, pens, not to mention that particular wheeled instrument which Stravinsky himself had invented for the drawing of staves. One may recall St. Thomas's definition: beauty is the splendor of order.[44]

Whether or not he saw himself as engaged in a struggle with death, such order, for Stravinsky, was the single greatest purpose of domestic life. From it he could safely stray, and to it confidently return, re-entering it like the portal to his own music, whose patterns and routines it metaphorically shared. This may seem a one-sided view of home, and one that failed to allow for the vagaries of family life and the needs of children and their minders. But it was evidently accepted by Katya, at least for as long as she had reason to suppose that her husband's demands were his way of loving her and their children exclusively. After that, her attitude naturally became more complicated.

By now the general form and character of Stravinsky's *Les Noces* were coming into focus. The idea of "a choral work on the subject of a Russian peasant wedding"[45] had been there from the very start, in 1912. Either at Salvan or soon after moving into La Pervenche, he had outlined a three-act scenario that painstakingly followed the protracted rubric from the first arrival of the *svat*, or matchmaker, at the bride's house to the wedding feast and ceremonial bedding of the new couple.[46] But it took him much longer to find the severe ritual structure—largely eschewing anecdote or pantomime—which is such a powerful feature of the finished work. By

March this character was emerging, but the structure was not yet firm. In Milan at the very start of April he met Prokofiev and let slip a barrage of detailed information which the younger composer promptly relayed to Derzhanovsky in Moscow, who no less promptly published it in a long and exhaustive article in *Muzïka* at the start of May.[47] The ballet now has its four tableaux, though not exactly in their eventual form or order, and it has the character of "an *act*, the contents of which unfold before the hearer and viewer in the plain and shapely form of folk festivities." Prokofiev has understood, or been told, that the *Pribaoutki* which Stravinsky wrote in the autumn were "born in the first instance, perhaps, as splinters off the *Svadebka* score." As for the orchestration, this has plainly arrived at the broad composition it will preserve till the work's completion in draft in 1917: that is, a kind of glorified peasant band of some forty players, with solo strings and a sizable body of winds and percussion. There is as yet no word about the imitation gusli (the Russian folk psaltery) which Stravinsky compiled out of harp, harpsichord, and cimbalom and which replaced the piano, harp, and pizzicato strings of the earliest drafts at about this time. But already it is clear that Stravinsky's later memory of having "completed the first tableau for an orchestra of the size of *Le Sacre du printemps*" was a serious distortion. The *Noces* band was always "an orchestra of soloists."[48]

These spring months of 1915 were productive ones for Stravinsky. In mid-August he could tell Stanley Wise that the work was two-thirds composed, presumably in its "1917" orchestration.[49] He also wrote the little four-hand Waltz to go with the Polka and the March, and arranged at least the Waltz and the March for an ensemble of a dozen or so instruments. There were other *Noces* "splinters": a pair of the (eventually) four *Berceuses du chat* (nos. 2 and 3 as published), the "Puzishche" chorus, and other unused sketches which would in due course provide the starting point for a new stage work, *Baika* (*Renard*). The Hôtel Victoria, unlike the Châtelard or Les Tilleuls, was unable to meet his need for complete sound insulation when composing. So he rented a room in the village, installed a piano, and there, amid the relative comforts of Western European middle-class life, worked away at these bucolic expressions of the urge to renounce those comforts and the materialist ethic that had given them birth.[50]

But this mountain idyll was, as usual with the Stravinskys, short-lived. Probably the damp spring weather forced them back down to Clarens—much later, all the same, than envisaged at the New Year, when Igor had told Ravel that they planned to go for January, "the best winter month," and Schmitt that they would stay "for as long as the weather is good."[51] Their return seems to have coincided with Igor's second Italian trip. But no sooner was he back from Milan than he and Katya decided they should try to find a family home in the vicinity, having finally wearied, one assumes, of the interminable caravan of pension life and short-term rentals. The new address, wherever it might turn out to be, would be their sixth in less than a year and a half.

Diaghilev had by no means given up on *Liturgie*. His latest idea was that the original plan to perform the dances in silence and with music only for the interludes would not work, since "absolute silence is death and there is not and cannot be absolute silence in any air space."[52] Instead he wanted Igor to come to Milan to hear Russolo's noise machines, with a view to collaborating on some kind of atmospheric background score to replace that unattainable silence. The soirée, one of the minor pinnacles of the futurist movement, took place in early April in Marinetti's cluttered flat, in which Oriental knickknacks and heavy carpets and tapestries clashed violently with vibrant futurist paintings. Massine was there with Diaghilev, "a vertical hippopotamus" (in Francesco Cangiullo's memorable description), "eccentrically rouged, with an enormous chrysanthemum in his buttonhole," and Stravinsky, "as ever, tiny, light-haired, myopic, but with, by way of compensation, a nose of massive caliber supporting the bicycle of his glasses."

> For the moment, dear Marinetti, the center of attraction was Russolo with his thirty intonarumori [noise intoners]. Stravinsky wanted to get an exact idea of these bizarre new instruments, and possibly insert two or three of them into the already diabolical scores of his ballets. A *crepitatore* crackled with a thousand sparks, like a torrent of fire. Stravinsky let out a whistle of insane joy and leapt from the sofa like one of its springs. A *frusciatore* rustled like silk petticoats in winter, like new leaves in April, like a wind-torn sea in summer. The composer hurled himself in a frenzy at the piano, trying to find that miraculous onomatopoeia, but he tested every semitone with his avid fingers in vain, while the dancer [Massine] waggled his legs professionally.[53]

Despite this marvellous evening, there was no collaboration, Stravinsky never used any of Russolo's instruments, and *Liturgie* never got its score. Prokofiev, in his letters to Myaskovsky, never even mentions the futurists, though he was at Marinetti's that night. The encounter with Stravinsky meant more to him: they had "made good friends and we're in mutual creative sympathy and so forth. His new *Pribaoutki* with orchestra [sic] is superb. He and Diaghilev are very interested in you and want to get to know your works, but they curse Petrograd to the devil."[54] How Diaghilev could combine an enthusiasm for Russolo with an interest in the postromantic symphonist Myaskovsky is hard to imagine. But perhaps, deep down, he was never so very much interested in either.

As for his greatest current love, *Les Noces,* he heard it again in Milan, and then yet again at Clarens at the end of April. In March he had still hoped to have it for whatever and wherever his next ballet season would be. "Expect us about March 20," he had written at the beginning of the month, "and have a big ballet ready—or I shall be very angry."55 But by the time he and his newly re-forming company took up what was to be an eight-month residence at the Villa Bellerive in the Lausanne lakeside suburb of Ouchy in May, he must have realized that, with the war dragging on, the one event was as unpredictable as the other.

The Stravinskys themselves, meanwhile, were house-hunting. With Diaghilev at Lausanne and Ansermet far away in Geneva at the other end of the lake, they had decided to leave Clarens altogether and settle instead in the small town of Morges, much nearer to Lausanne on the Geneva side. Their—or at least Igor's—first landfall, in June, was the Villa des Sapins, which was presumably a pension chosen as a base for on-the-spot research. But by September, the whole family had moved into a house near the lake called the Villa Rogivue, "with a turret and a slate roof," which became in effect their first family home.56 Here at last they could behave not as the eternal unloved guests of the *hôtel-pension*, but as hosts and homemakers themselves. Visitors, instead of entering purely on business, could become, in Theodore's phrase, "real people . . . whom my parents were always delighted to welcome to their house and table."57 In place of the masterly transformation of the drab boardinghouse atmosphere into a three- or four-roomed enclave of concentrated Russianism, there was now a sense of profound and overriding Russian domesticity compounded of a deep-rooted style of life lived in an environment, and among objects, that were themselves by no means exclusively Slav but may have been acquired in Switzerland or Italy or Paris.

There were bicycles for exploring the countryside around Morges and along the lake. Igor would cycle over to Ouchy, ten miles away, to see Diaghilev and the other inmates of his dance colony. "Imagine a large house on the edge of the lake set in a park," Misia Edwards reported to Cocteau in July, "with Serge as master of the house and, as mistress, a young Russian, the wife of an embassy councilor in Rome, who fell madly in love with them all in Rome this winter and who for the past two months has been here keeping house for him. Some painters, the Stravinskys, Massine, make up an extraordinary group that never stops working."58 The housekeeper was Ruzhena Khvoshchinskaya, the wife of Vasily Khvoshchinsky, an attaché in the Russian embassy in Rome, who was a close friend of both Diaghilev and Stravinsky. Massine was still dreaming of *Liturgie* and working on its choreography with the dancers. But it was no longer a live project, and "as more and more dancers arrived and our prospects improved, *Liturgie* was abandoned and we started work in earnest."59 Misia, on the other hand, had intended to sound Stravinsky out on the old *David* project. But when she went to Morges and heard him play through the first half of *Les Noces,* she knew at once that there was no hope. "Imagine the most beautiful work of our greatest musician, with the quality of *Petrushka* as seen through *Le Sacre.* . . . He has opened yet another door, and there everything is permitted, everything is sonorous, joyous, and each note takes you by surprise, just as you would wish—and overwhelms you."[60] Also at Ouchy were two leading painters of the Muscovite avant-garde, Natalya Goncharova and Mikhail Laryonov. Goncharova, a namesake and descendant of Pushkin's wife, had designed *The Golden Cockerel* for Diaghilev the previous year. But her work was remote from the exotic neonationalism of the prewar Ballets Russes, and instead cultivated an austere, angular folklorism recognizably akin to the "virtual" Russianism of *Les Noces.* She and Laryonov, who lived together but married only much later, were to be a major determinant of the new direction in Ballets Russes design after the war.

Not long before the Stravinskys moved into the Villa Rogivue, the combined Austro-German armies had launched a major push across the river Bug into Volhynia. "I very much fear," Myaskovsky wrote to Prokofiev, "for the summer (or is it winter?) retreat of our famous Igor Stravinsky, since things are happening in those parts."[61] A few weeks later, the *Russkaya muzïkal'naya gazeta* reported that Stravinsky's Ustilug estate had been devastated in the August offensive.[62] How much damage the house itself suffered we can only surmise. Grigory Belyankin had done his best to save Igor's and Katya's belongings. He had loaded everything onto a train at Vladimir-Volïnsky and fled with it eastwards to the home of his wife's Velsovsky relations beyond Poltava, where it quickly sank without trace.[63] At Ustilug, the heady smell of alcohol hung in the air for days as Grigory piped the contents of the distillery into the river to stop it from falling into the hands of the Austrian soldiers.[64] The precious liquid—such of it as was not promptly scooped out and drunk in ever greater dilution by the thirsty Volhynian peasantry—flowed down the Bug into the Vistula, down the Vistula and out into the Baltic, where it mingled with the dying waters from the Neva, far to the northeast.

18

A FOX AMONG THE VINES

THE MOVE FROM CLARENS to Morges took the Stravinskys closer to the heart of that Switzerland which, for five years, they had known only as visitors, as birds of passage. It paralleled the move Ernest Ansermet had made the year before in quitting Montreux for Lausanne, before passing on to the modernity and relative cosmopolitanism of Geneva. In Morges there lived the Vaudois writer René Morax and his brother, Jean, who was a painter. And halfway between Montreux and Lausanne, in the tiny lakeside hamlet of Treytorrens, the novelist C. F. Ramuz had settled on his return from Paris at about the time of Ansermet's move, in one wing of a house belonging to a local vineyard owner. Ramuz was already the dominant figure in a cultural revival centered on a new publication called the *Cahiers vaudois,* a monthly review designed to feed on the roots of French-Swiss identity, but defined as something specifically not French, and certainly not Parisian: "a review at once modern and Vaudois, works that were neither academic, nor provincial, but audaciously original and candidly unrefined." Several years before, Ramuz, who was powerfully under the influence of Cézanne, "had discovered our mountains and our Nature, that is, the elements of that art that is at once universal and local, the essential components of that rude 'climate' . . . which sought to renew the spiritual atmosphere of our land."[1] The first *Cahiers* of 1914 reflected in their physical character the plain, earthy directness and high moral purpose that had prompted the original idea, by the writer and critic Paul Budry, one winter evening at Ansermet's house, La Pervenche, in Clarens. Printed on handmade paper, rough-trimmed, and illustrated with the angular woodcuts of Henry Bischoff, they proclaimed that same rustic integrity and slightly knowing simplicity that we might associate with the work of the English stonecarver and typographer Eric Gill. They were modern yet antimodern, earthy yet intellectual, national yet supranational: "without patois, without costume or custom, without folklore, without the academic Felibrige of a Mistral. We must be Vaudois only to the extent that we are universal."[2]

Through Ansermet or otherwise, Stravinsky had already met several members of this circle: he knew the art historian Adrien Bovy and the painter Alexandre Cingria and his poet brother Charles-Albert, two Catholic artists who stood out against the Helvetic—Protestant, noninterventionist, "little Switzerland"—tendencies that were strong, then as now, in the cantons. He may already have met the Morax brothers, and the playwright Fernand Chavannes, and Edmond Gilliard, the co-founder of the *Cahiers* and its principal organizing spirit. But he did not meet Ramuz until he arrived in Morges. According to Ramuz himself, they met in the autumn of 1915, at the time of the wine harvest. "Ansermet brought him to me from Montreux, where he—Ansermet—was at that time conducting the Kursaal orchestra."[3] But Ansermet no longer conducted at Montreux, and if they arrived by train, at Epesses (as Ramuz recalls), they must have come from the other direction, from Lausanne. Another story, told by Bovy, is that he and Alexandre Cingria brought the composer to Treytorrens by car from Geneva—or perhaps they came from Geneva and picked Stravinsky up in Morges.[4] The month was probably July, since the earliest surviving communication is a letter from Ramuz of 9 August. For Ramuz the wine harvest was emblematic: it was that aspect of the Vaud which, direct from the soil, yielded something fine, clear, and subtle. Through the *vendange,* the Vaudois writer took possession of the Russian composer and made of him, in his own eyes at least, a Vaudois:

> A strange encounter, ours; it seemed that everything must separate us. You were a musician, I not; you were Russian and from far away, I was already where I am still, where I was born; we did not speak even the same language. The things which surrounded us, you could and should have seen in one light, I in another; you in your light, I in my light; they should have come between us. How then did it happen nevertheless to be by way of them, through them, that we so quickly and completely made contact; still more, that you confirmed me in the love I bore them?[5]

The question asked cannot be answered with confidence, but the question begged can. That the two artists quickly became intimate—though this side of *tutoiement*—is beyond doubt, despite Stravinsky's later equivocal attitude and the somewhat hostile documentation assembled by Robert Craft after the composer's death.[6] They were soon meeting, if not every day, at least very often, as is shown by the inconsequential tone of Ramuz's letters and the frequency with which he announces that he cannot come today or tomorrow, or refers to some commission from yesterday. When they could not meet, they spoke on the telephone, an instrument to which Stravinsky was by now inured, though Ramuz, with his antimodern, antitechnological Vaudois bias, was not. Ramuz had no phone at Treytorrens. But when he moved, early in 1916, to the Lausanne suburb of Cour, a mere dozen kilometers from Morges, he found "an Olde Worlde 'lodge' set in a large garden but with all the amenities . . . [and] in the neighborhood, the chimney pipes of a laundry and various altogether Seine-et-Oise aspects which are particularly precious to me these days."[7] The telephone was at the laundry, a mild inconvenience which, as Ramuz implies, enabled him to reconcile a certain affectation of bohemianism with the solution of practicalities such as "questions of housekeeping, of milk, eggs, and potatoes, which, once they take on a certain importance, end up by being decisive." "I live," he told Delhorbe, "as I suppose I would live at Jouy-en-Josas"—that is, agreeably placed in rural suburbia but well within reach of modern life when necessary.[8] The point is—though you can read Ramuz's letters for a long time without discovering the fact—that he was married. He had a young daughter, conceived out of wedlock, whom he loved sufficiently to put himself out when she was ill. But his wife, Cécile (née Cellier), he seems never to have forgiven for the more permanent embarrassment of their forced marriage. "Ramuz," Stravinsky said, "was the kindest of men (except to his wife, whom he . . . continued to call mademoiselle, in a strict, hard voice, in front of his friends)."[9] In his letters, Ramuz's domestic pronoun is nearly always the first person singular.

Stravinsky's own family, loving and integrated as it was, also had to endure a great assumption of independence on his part. Certainly, if he entertained at the Villa Rogivue, his guests would enjoy the richer comforts of home life. "At about five o'clock," Ramuz related of the period of their working collaboration,

> we would be brought a snack of very strong coffee, fresh bread, and jam. . . . We certainly earned the nice dinners cooked for us by the old *nyanya,* and which, having started late . . . went on until the last train; with vodka (to start) then blinis, and shchi . . . minced meat, soft pastries sprinkled with hot butter; with combinations of soup and meat as well, and those dark-red beetroot soups which made me think of the mythical times of Russian history when they tell of conquerors drinking, from skulls (we had bowls), the blood of their enemies.[10]

But just as often, there would be cafes or restaurants, and the company would be exclusively male. Géa Augsbourg drew Stravinsky and Ramuz on the balcony of a lakeside restaurant near Lausanne with Ansermet, Budry, and Edmond Gilliard, over the caption "The *Cahiers vaudois* at Grandvaux," giving the group the air of a routine, even somewhat weary, conviviality.[11] The year, though, was 1915, a time when, in neutral Switzerland, "passions stayed hidden in the depths of hearts."[12] The *Cahiers* talked about that neutrality, and argued—even perhaps passionately—for alignment with

France and for rejecting the supposed Berne (that is, Swiss-German) image of "a land whose poverty-stricken features can now be unmasked, a land which is depersonalizing and internationalizing itself, where anxiety is becoming sterile, a land which repels every truthful form and truthful art, which is bogged down in a vague idealism and the pursuit of a tight-lipped material progress, a land of hoteliers and schoolteachers."[13] One can picture Stravinsky warming to the idea that the future might be secured by cleaving to regional values, even if he was less impressed by the idea of a Vaudois Afanasyev or even Koz'ma Prutkov than Ramuz implied when he remarked of *The Soldier's Tale* that "I was Russian: the subject would be Russian; Stravinsky was Vaudois (at that time): the music would be Vaudois."[14] He could share his new friends' disgust with materialism. What was it he had said to Benois? "How much better to stay here and breathe. Here there's sun, limpid dark-green grass, real-life, slow-moving people."[15] Admittedly that was partly because he had caught Diaghilev cashing in at his expense. But the idea of a new art based on the oldest of truths—that of the soil and man's marriage to it—that was genuine enough. And he would prove it in the only way that mattered—by creating that art out of the new Russian seeds which, as he had told Romain Rolland, were going to impregnate the world's thought.

Exactly when he put *Les Noces* to one side and started to compose the work that came to be known in Russian as *Baika pro lisu, petukha, kota da barana*—The Tale About the Fox, the Cock, the Tomcat, and the Ram—but is universally known in the West as *Renard,* is difficult to establish; it was probably in the late summer of 1915, soon after the move to the Villa Rogivue. Stravinsky had been seeing a good deal of Diaghilev at Ouchy and was well aware of the obstacles in the way of a Paris premiere for *Les Noces* so long as the war continued, even though he told Stanley Wise in mid-August that he was still hopeful of a production the following May.[16] The first sketches for *Renard* in fact go back a whole year, but only in the sense that Stravinsky incorporated various *pribaoutka* notations into the larger work, which thus became a kind of glorified stage enactment of such songs. Even comparatively late in 1915, where the sketches show Stravinsky working towards the twenty-minute "merry performance with singing and music" that we know, the performance itself had evidently still not taken shape in his mind, and the sketchbook is simply labelled "Children's Songs."[17] Taruskin shows how Stravinsky apparently began by setting two of the songs in Afanasyev's tale "The Cat, the Cock, and the Fox," and only then made up his mind to set the actual story, which gradually emerged as an imaginary quasi-improvised performance by strolling players, rather as if modern street actors were to make up a play about the Three Little Pigs out of a string of nursery rhymes to do with pigs and wolves.[18]

Like the early versions of *Les Noces, Renard* would be played by an idealized, if outsize, peasant band, with a whole spectrum of (mainly solo) winds and strings, a noisy percussion section, and—to bind the sound into a suitably clangorous whole—Stravinsky's pride and joy, his Schunda cimbalom, now firmly installed in the blue-painted turret room which he used as a studio at the Villa Rogivue. Ramuz, from the laundry telephone, had pictured him "solidly wedged into an armchair, smoking a cigarette down to the butt, taking a swig of strong coffee or Armagnac between phrases, [and] utterly determined, at whatever inconvenience to me, not to interrupt a conversation in which he was getting excited about a cimbalom . . . or about a little Hungarian who played it."[19] Now the cimbalom was in action, and Stravinsky was actually composing " 'on' it (as I normally compose 'on' a piano), with two sticks in my hand, writing down as I composed,"[20] though the sketches suggest that only the actual cimbalom part, at most, was written in that way. The four male singers would be part of the ensemble, not part of the action, like a team of narrators taking over the various roles as necessary, but sometimes joining in as a group. Once it became apparent that a stage performance would be involved, mimes or dancers seem to have been assumed. But it is not clear that the idea of duplication was present from the start.

Of all the vocal works in this neo-Russian phase, *Renard* is perhaps the purest, considering its size. *Les Noces* remained pure in concept, but would eventually be somewhat hybridized in execution; *The Soldier's Tale* would be hybrid from the outset. *Renard* is sheer, unadulterated Russian folk art as reimagined by an unwilling exile who had persuaded himself that the future of music, if not the world, depended on tapping down to the deepest roots of a culture which, as a matter of fact, he himself did not know at first hand and which perhaps had never even actually existed. Certainly no such vibrantly, ebulliently, richly uncouth musical idiom ever had. Meanwhile, he was still chipping tiny fragments off the same block. Two *Berceuses du chat* had already been composed in the spring; he now added two more to complete the cycle of these astonishing little songs for medium voice and three clarinets, which that other master of the compressed miniature, Anton Webern, later found "so indescribably touching. How those three clarinets sound! And *Pribaoutki*. Ah, my dear friend, it is something really glorious. This realism leads us to the metaphysical."[21] He also wrote what is musically the simplest of all these songs, the "Pesenka Medvedya," or "Song of the Bear," a bedtime story about an old man and woman who get eaten by a bear with a limewood paw, which eventually became one of the *Tri Detskiye pesenki*, or *Three Children's Tales*.[22]

You could hardly guess from any of these works that a terrible war was being fought not a hundred miles from the composer closeted in his turret overlooking the untroubled Lake Geneva. They are like messages from inside the whale, in Orwell's memorable phrase.[23] In no normal sense are they "relevant." On one single occasion, Stravinsky deigned to write a piece of war music, a piano piece called *Souvenir d'une marche boche,* which the novelist Edith Wharton had requested in August for a volume of manuscripts she intended to sell for the benefit of homeless Belgian children, the *Livre des Sans-Foyer.* And this, according to Soulima (who was admittedly not quite five at the time), he wrote "on the spur of the moment."[24]

Yet the fighting did also nevertheless leave its mark on *Renard.* It was precisely the isolation that the war imposed on Stravinsky that enabled him to work out this whole bizarre notion of inventing a new, hyper-modern style out of the fragmented elements of an antique folk music, without immediate regard for any likely performance—something he had not considered doing with a theatre piece since before *The Firebird.* True, there was a financial motive. *Les Noces* was a Diaghilev work. But the Ballets Russes were blocked in Europe by the war, and nobody would now dare to predict for how long, though there was an American tour planned for early 1916. Meanwhile, Stravinsky was losing income, both because his works were no longer being played and because his publishers were effectively out of action: Jurgenson, cut off in Russia by sheer distance and the problems of communication in wartime, and RMV, because their main office was in Berlin, the capital of belligerent Germany. Stravinsky spent a good part of 1915 negotiating with Ziloti in St. Petersburg (or Petrograd, as it was officially known after August 1914) over the plan to stage *The Nightingale* at the Mariyinsky, and another plan to present *Petrushka,* which was still known in Russia only from the concert suite. But the correspondence was arduous and spasmodic, and though Stravinsky did receive six thousand roubles for *The Nightingale* early in 1916, neither work was played till after the Revolution.[25] As for publication, if works like *Pribaoutki* or the *Berceuses du chat* might have presented difficulties in peacetime, in wartime their prospects were grim indeed.

Renard, on the other hand, might be saleable, if not to a publisher or impresario, then perhaps to one of those rich Paris ladies who had backed Diaghilev and at least one of whom had already tried to commission work from Stravinsky himself. The trouble was that he had not been to Paris since war broke out, and there is no sign that he was prepared to reopen so sensitive a discussion with the princesse de Polignac by letter. These days his center of gravity was Geneva, where Ansermet was still presenting regular subscription concerts in the municipal theatre. Early in December Stravinsky heard his friend conduct the Swiss premiere of the *Firebird* Suite, and just over two weeks later, on the twentieth, he himself stepped onto the rostrum of the city's Grand Théâtre to direct the same work for the first time, as an entr'acte during a gala matinée which Diaghilev was putting on to help prepare his dancers for their American tour.[26] For one eight-year-old Russian boy, history repeated itself that afternoon:

How surprised, overjoyed and bursting with pride I felt when my parents told me that they would take me with them! . . . When the hall was dark and the stage lit by the footlights, I saw my mother sitting next to me in our stage-box looking very pretty in her pale blue dress. And then from the orchestra pit, a great black hole full of little lights, there suddenly rose the dim figure of my father, light and supple, to be greeted with a burst of applause. He reached the conductor's desk in a single bound, bowed to the audience, turned round and quietly proceeded to break his conductor's baton. I held my breath . . . but he simply found it inconveniently long![27]

The danced part of the program, which included Massine's own first ballet, *Soleil de nuit,* was conducted by Ansermet, who was booked for the American tour and was appearing with the Ballets Russes for the first time. Diaghilev had arranged a second gala matinée at the Paris Opéra nine days later in aid of the British Red Cross, and this time Stravinsky was to conduct the complete *Firebird,* with dancers. On the twenty-fourth, just as he was leaving Morges, Ansermet wired from Paris that the orchestra, which he was rehearsing for the gala though he himself would by then be on the high seas, was mediocre and that there were too few rehearsals: "situation difficile pour vous," he noted encouragingly.[28] But the performance, on the twenty-ninth, seems to have passed off without hitch; Stravinsky himself even later boasted to Ziloti that "I conducted the Paris performance of my ballet *The Firebird* . . . with colossal success."[29] But the question in everyone's mind was whether it was any longer possible to take this sumptuous, glittering, fairy-tale art seriously at all. Jacques-Emile Blanche overheard the young editor of a progressive arts paper tell Astruc:"*Mon cher maître,* you got out just in time! This art is finished—*Schéhérazade* has grown wrinkles. Let's put cubism on the stage. My colleagues and I at *L'Envol* will have some ideas for you after the war. . . . You wait!" And the "modern, ugly colourless audience," Blanche recorded, "left the Opéra as if it were Good Friday and they had just heard Bach's [St. Matthew] Passion."[30]

Stravinsky, of course, was not waiting until the end of the war to explore an art whose austerity might have struck Blanche's young editor as more in the spirit of the times. On Christmas Day, at the quai Voltaire flat Misia now rented with her ex-husband Alfred Edwards's money, he had again played part of *Les Noces,* nervously, from the full score (which was much more complicated than the later published version), and with Massine somewhat ineptly turning the pages.[31] And he also at last saw the princesse de Polignac, previewed *Les Noces* for her too, and contracted to compose *Renard* by mid-July for a fee of 10,000 francs.[32] There was a final meeting with Diaghilev at the Hôtel Edward VII, at which payments were agreed for his continuing exclusivity over *Firebird*, which Stravinsky had renewed the previous spring for three years, over Jurgenson's head. Diaghilev handed over 3,500 francs on the spot, on account of a total retainer of 16,000 for the year 1916.[33] But while the meeting was amicable, and Stravinsky subsequently defended Diaghilev staunchly with Jurgenson in justifying what was blatantly a deal for siphoning royalties directly into his own pocket without having to share them with a publisher,[34] it was the start of new and protracted quarrels over money which were to echo through their correspondence of the next few months and eventually lead to something like a candid breach between them. The curious thing—and it is a profoundly Russian trait—is that even at the height of mutual recriminations, the deep artistic sympathy and warm personal affection somehow remained intact, and the epistolary embraces and endearments continued unabated until nearly the end, when it became for the first time possible for the two men to meet on a railway train and not communicate.

Stravinsky returned to Switzerland and his Alpine friends, as Diaghilev called them, in time for Russian Christmas on 7 January. Such occasions were assuming ever greater importance for the Stravinskys, whether because of the condition of exile, or because of Katya's illness, or simply because of their growing family and the fact that they were now for the first time in a home of their own. When the princesse de Polignac, who was staying at Ouchy as she had been in 1912, dined at Morges one evening early in February, she was struck by the festive appearance of the house,

> all brilliantly lit up and decorated in the warm colors that the Russian Ballet had brought to Paris. . . . I can never forget the delight of that evening at Morges: the table brilliantly lit with colored candles, and covered with fruit, flowers and desserts of every hue. The supper was a wonderful example of Russian cuisine, carefully prepared by Madame Stravinsky and composed of every form of zakousky, then bortsch, tender sterlets covered with delicious transparent jelly and served with a perfect sauce, various dishes of fowls and every sort of sweet, making it a feast to be always remembered.[35]

While the princess was in Switzerland, it was agreed that Laryonov would design *Renard*, just as his partner, Natalya Goncharova, was already at work on *Les Noces*, though neither work, as it turned out, would face an audience for several years.[36]

Not long after her departure, there were more guests at the Villa Rogivue, and this time the implications for the composer were more disturbing. Vaslav Nijinsky, his wife, Romola, and their little daughter, Kyra, had arrived in Lausanne, via Berne, after what can only be described as a concerted international campaign to secure them passage from Budapest (where they had spent the first year of the war under virtual house arrest) to the United States, where Diaghilev, whose rage against his former lover and premier danseur had by now given way to the realization that the Ballets Russes were a great deal less marketable without him, had unilaterally contracted him to appear with the company. According to Romola, Stravinsky came to see them in Lausanne, took them round the city, made friends with Kyra, and invited them to visit him at Morges.[37] There was a delay over French visas, which were being arranged in Paris by the countess Greffuhle. Meanwhile, Diaghilev urged Stravinsky by telegram to talk Nijinsky into a frame of mind favorable to the Ballets Russes, and then, when Nijinsky still lingered in Switzerland while it appeared (from Cleveland, Ohio) that he was free to travel, Diaghilev reproached Stravinsky bitterly for—as he had learnt from Nijinsky's transatlantic escort, Henry Russell—dissuading him from setting out. Russell himself certainly believed that Stravinsky was responsible, though it is hard to see how, with presumably limited Russian and no more than a casual acquaintance with the personalities involved, he can have been so sure. Stravinsky heatedly denied the charge, and alleged that Nijinsky had refused to leave Switzerland until formally exempted from service by the Russian military authorities.[38]

On the face of it, he had no motive for obstructing Nijinsky's passage, unless temporary irritation with Diaghilev over his late payment of the third *Firebird* installment be regarded as one.[39] But the composer later admitted that he had himself hoped for a booking with the company in New York, "and in my ingenuousness even begged Nijinsky to make his own participation in the performances depend upon my engagement."[40] Did he actually put pressure on the dancer not to leave Switzerland without some guarantee on this point? Romola wrote that Stravinsky spent much of their visit railing against Diaghilev for breaking his promise to secure him an official invitation to join the company in New York.[41] But, curiously enough, there is no contemporary evidence of any such understanding between Stravinsky and Diaghilev: no sign of it in their own correspondence, or in Ansermet's American letters to the composer, which would be an expected channel for negotiations of that kind. Moreover, Romola's account of their Lausanne visit is in general so gratuitously hostile to Stravinsky, whom she portrays as insufferably vain and self-centered, and so inaccurate in certain matters of provable fact, as to taint everything she says of a more personal nature. She was, when all is said and done, herself the wife of a genius—a wife who must repeatedly have been made to feel responsible for destroying her husband's career by (as she says) putting personal feelings before the development of art. Did Stravinsky, however courteously, also make her feel an intruder? She claims that he did. As for Nijinsky, he found fault with Stravinsky on quite a different count, if we can trust the childlike montage of his diaries: that of declining to look after Kyra while he and Romola were in America (a request Romola does not mention). But the diaries are more interesting for their shrewdly paradoxical image of Stravinsky the paterfamilias, especially their portrait of him as "an emperor, and his children, his wife and his servants [as] soldiers. Stravinsky reminds me of Tsar Paul, but he will not be strangled because he is more intelligent than Tsar Paul."[42] Even if the choice of comparison recalls that Nijinsky was himself on the brink of insanity, the actual charge against Stravinsky, of domestic autocracy at times bordering on tyranny, cannot wholly be rebutted.

Stravinsky was kept intermittently in touch with events in America by Ansermet. After a muted opening in New York, *Firebird* and *Petrushka* had enjoyed such a "colossal success" in Boston that Ansermet had the idea of approaching American publishers on the subject of the "easy" piano pieces, little guessing that Stravinsky's gratitude for this intervention would come in the form of a demand for twenty-five thousand Swiss francs as a fee for a package deal including an arrangement for instrumental ensemble as well as the four-hand and two-hand keyboard versions.[43] Later, Ansermet explained that it had been essentially a succès d'estime. Americans were curious about this new Russian composer, particularly since the Flonzaley performances of the quartet pieces during the autumn and the publication of Carl Van Vechten's prophetically titled book *Music After the Great War,* with its graphic firsthand account of the *Rite of Spring* premiere.[44] But he doubted that the ballets had been properly understood as music, despite (in New York) an orchestra that was "frankly worth any number of Lamoureux or Colonnes," with "the best tuba player in the world. If you heard him in *Petrushka,* you would weep for joy." America, he told the composer,

> is a lout heap (more or less boche or Jewish in character). All dominated by German or Italian taste (in music!). Yet there is at the bottom of this immense country a forgotten or lost soul which has found its way into the *incredible music* you hear in cafes!! And the absence of traditions has forced this people—in their towns, their bridges, their machines—to improvise splendidly and with genius. These two elements are very close to us; they are precisely what we like, and what your work has revealed in Europe. To free this country from the boche imprint, reveal it to itself, and teach it that it belongs with us—and at the same time to take on this wonderful field of activity—would be a fine dream.[45]

The tour lasted through April, with Nijinsky making a belated debut in New York on the twelfth in *Le Spectre de la rose* and *Petrushka.* Meanwhile, the Ballets Russes had been invited by King Alfonso XIII to perform in Madrid, and as soon as they landed at Cadiz, on 17 May, Diaghilev wired Stravinsky, in Morges, to join them. Despite the difficulties of wartime travel, Stravinsky set off two days later on his first-ever trip to Spain (travelling via Paris, where he saw Misia and discussed with her the possibility of linking *Renard* in a double bill with a new Satie-Cocteau ballet, successor to *David*).[46] Like many Russian musicians before him, he sensed a spiritual attachment to that—for Russians—most remote corner of Europe. "This is not mere curiosity appeal," he wrote a few years later.

> Between the popular music of Spain, above all the music of Andalusia, and that of Russia I perceive a deep affinity which attaches doubtless to their common origins in the East. Certain Andalusian songs remind me of the melodies of our Russian country regions, awaken in me atavistic memories. The Andalusians have nothing Latin in their music. They owe their feeling for rhythm to their Oriental heredity.[47]

Arriving in distant, neutral Spain at the height of a war which had cut him off from his homeland and threatened his whole livelihood, he perhaps had some feeling of liberation, a sense of entering a zone outside time where actions did not have inexorable consequences. "When I reached Madrid at nine o'clock in the morning I found the whole town still fast asleep, and I was received at my hotel by the night-watchman with lantern in hand. Yet it was spring. The people rose late, and life was in full swing after midnight."[48] Craft, presumably quoting the master himself, called it "one of the most exciting months of his life."[49] He was acclaimed at successive performances of *The Firebird* and (starting on 6 June) *Petrushka,* and was several times received by the balletomane king and queen. He met leading Spanish musicians, and cemented his friendship with Manuel de Falla, the composer of *El amor brujo,* who heard him play *Les Noces* for the umpteenth time. He went to bullfights, at one of which he saw Paco Madrid gored. He went to Toledo and the Escorial, and was struck by the "mystic fervour" of Spanish Catholicism, "so closely akin in its essentials to the religious feeling and spirit of Russia."[50] And he heard Spanish folk dances and songs and even bought gramophone records of this music in which, he told Romain Rolland a few weeks later, he saw "the ideal of music, spontaneous and 'useless,' music which has no wish to express anything, which pours from the soul, a music that is different for every different soul."[51]

According to Craft, there was a romance with Lydia Lopukhova, the young dancer who had fainted with excitement on first arriving at the Gare du Nord in 1910.[52] Even before that she had been the first Paris

Columbine in Fokine's *Carnaval,* and Taruskin suggests plausibly that the Ballerina in *Petrushka* was modelled on her doll-like, *ingénue* virtuosity in that role.[53] She had rejoined the company in America and was now with them in Madrid. Whatever the precise significance of that discreet term "romance," it was Stravinsky's first recorded infidelity. Lopukhova had danced the Firebird ("très mal," according to Ansermet)[54] and the Ballerina ("très bien") in America, and at the end of the tour had got married to Diaghilev's new financial manager, Randolfo Barocchi. But Barocchi was apparently not in Spain, having stayed in America to organize the company's coming winter tour.[55] On 26 May, his wife again took the part of the Firebird on the company's opening bill in Madrid, and she played the Ballerina in the two performances of *Petrushka* at the end of the two-week season. After the final performance on 9 June the dancers were given two months' holiday. But Stravinsky did not leave Spain until the twentieth, nor does he seem to have gone with Massine and Diaghilev on their trip to Catalonia. Did he spend this time with his new prima ballerina? If so, it was not the last time Barocchi failed to hold on to her. Three summers later she eloped from London with a young Russian general,[56] and eventually, after a brief rapprochement with Barocchi, abandoned him for good in favor of the economist John Maynard Keynes.

Renard, contracted for July, was still unfinished, though enough of it existed for Stravinsky to be able to play it through in Madrid to, at least, Diaghilev, Massine, and their new friend Eugenia Errazuriz, whom the composer had met for the first time at one of the *Firebird* evenings. Mme Errazuriz was a Chilean silver-mining heiress, a fiftyish beauty, rich, chic, and already patroness of Picasso, to whom she had been introduced by Cocteau the previous year, and to whom she in turn introduced Diaghilev in Paris on a quick visit during May 1916.[57] She now began to cultivate Stravinsky, too, evidently seeing in him some artistic resemblance to the great Spaniard: "what a genius!" she told the composer: "as great as you, *cher maître.*"[58] She sent him postcards from Spain, and was soon paying him a monthly subvention of one thousand francs, interspersing it with letters complaining about her health: "I cannot travel—I am alone and humanity seems nasty to me," she wrote in one letter which had begun with regrets at an illness of his.[59]

From Morges at the end of June, Stravinsky had written to the princesse de Polignac asking for the remaining four thousand francs of his commission fee for *Renard,* conveniently overlooking the fact—of which she was polite but firm in reminding him—that the money was due only on delivery.[60] Apologizing for not having had the contract to hand, he nevertheless assured her (11 July) that the work was finished and that he was now writing up the full score. But this may have been a face-saving "completion," since the actual autograph vocal score is dated only 1 August and still lacks the opening and closing march for the instruments.[61] Not until the beginning of September was the princess able to acknowledge receipt of the full score manuscript and, with a clear conscience, have the balance of the fee credited to the composer's bank.[62] Meanwhile, since it was her intention to perform *Renard* at her mansion in the avenue Henri Martin, a French singing translation was needed, and for this she had agreed to pay Stravinsky's friend Ramuz a fee of three hundred francs. Neither she nor, at first, Stravinsky can have had a clear idea of what the work would entail. But Ramuz was more circumspect. In mid-July he wrote to Stravinsky asking him for the money in advance, since a medical treatment for weak nerves was "my only plan on earth for the summer; this will mean travel, and that will incur expenses."[63] When the composer at last sent Mme de Polignac the finished translation, early in October, he made no bones about the difficulties Ramuz had had to surmount and candidly asked her to increase the fee to five hundred.[64]

"We met almost every day," Ramuz wrote later,

> in the blue room overlooking the garden; we were among the drums, the timpani, the bass drums, every kind of bashing instrument (or percussion, to use the official term), to which had recently been added the cimbalom I mentioned before. . . . I had a sheet of paper, a pencil. Stravinsky read me the Russian text verse by verse, taking care each time to count the number of syllables in each verse, which I would write down in the margin of my paper; then we made the translation, that is, Stravinsky translated the text for me word for word. It was a word-for-word so literal as to be often quite incomprehensible, but with an inspired (nonlogical) imagery, meetings of sounds whose freshness was all the greater for lacking any (logical) sense. . . . I wrote down my word-for-word; then came the question of lengths (of longs and shorts), also the question of vowels (this note was composed to an *o*, that one to an *a*, that one to an *i*); finally, and most important of all, the famous and insoluble question of tonic accent and its coincidence or noncoincidence with the musical accent. . . . A kind of intimate, initial accord presided. It had been very quickly understood that there would be no rules, that there could be no rules, that there should be none. It had been very quickly understood that there would only be special cases. Each one entailed its own solution, and solution is not the word, for each one assumed the intervention much rather of taste than of understanding in the discursive, analytical sense. We were making soup. When you make soup, you taste it, adding water or salt.[65]

By this time Diaghilev was in northern Spain, at San Sebastián, where the company was mounting a short season, including a new Massine ballet to Fauré's Pavane. There was the usual flow of telegrams, almost exclusively about money and contracts, and it may have been partly weariness at Diaghilev's incessant procrastination on these subjects that made Stravinsky suddenly blurt out to Misia:

> It's becoming increasingly difficult for me to come to an understanding with D.
>
> I feel that we are rapidly growing apart. Art in itself no longer interests him. He is tired of it.
>
> And besides it's very tiresome always to hear the same talk about "the young" and "the old"—one must be young, Diaghilev says—that's stupid and untrue and tragic at the same time. He no longer gets any pleasure from his work. His life is burned out and I think of all this very often, with profound bitterness.
>
> There, my dear, my latest impression of your Serge.[66]

It was true enough that Diaghilev was obsessed with youth, both in the flesh and as a concept. But Stravinsky probably had reason to take a more skeptical view of the great man's attitudes. Diaghilev had heard *Renard* in Madrid, but he had obviously expressed himself coolly about the intangible beauty of its new language simply because it was being written for someone else. Ansermet seemed to suggest as much when he relayed from Madrid Diaghilev's guarded remark that "I've always thought the 'Cock' [*Renard*] a splendid thing and the one thing I reproach Igor for is having used up there the best of what he could have kept for *Les Noces*,"[67] which might be a tactful version of Stravinsky's own Diaghilevism that "this *Renard* is some old scraps [Igor] found in his dresser drawer."[68] The truth is, Igor told Misia, that "in Madrid that work left him completely indifferent (naturally, as does everything I write that is not for him)."[69] But then Stravinsky's sensibilities had scarcely been flattered by Misia herself, since the letter to which he was replying had contained a scathing and uninhibited attack on his string quartet pieces, which Misia had just heard in Paris. "I detest the second piece, you understand," she had written, "I *detest* it with a passion, yes, yes! Why do you write such things?"[70] No wonder he had temporarily had enough of Parisian neophiliacs.

Yet everything as usual blew over, and within a few weeks he was back in Spain with the company, travelling this time to San Sebastián and on to Bordeaux, where he, Diaghilev, and Massine waved the dancers off on their second United States tour on 8 September, "a wild and stormy night," as one of them recorded in her memoirs.[71] Why did he repeat the tiresome wartime journey, presumably interrupting his work with Ramuz, and on what pretext? It may well have been in order to see his Lopushka, with whom he was photographed in Bordeaux before the boat sailed. But it may just as well have been to discuss new projects with Diaghilev while living for a few days at his expense. At least one new project *was* discussed on this trip. Stravinsky wrote to his mother from Bordeaux, announcing that Diaghilev "is spending the winter in Rome, and we'll be preparing a new piece."[72] But this cannot have been *Renard,* since, quite apart from Diaghilev's equivocal feelings about that work, the princesse de Polignac's contract gave her exclusive rights in it for five years.[73] Probably Diaghilev had already had the idea of turning *The Nightingale* into a ballet, and the composer had not been back in Switzerland many weeks before he was again under pressure to wait on his Seryozha, this time in Rome; as usual "the matter [was] very urgent."[74]

Obediently, he set off for Rome on 7 November. He was there for a week, and the *Nightingale* ballet was certainly discussed in some detail, including no doubt the question of confining the arrangement to those two acts which Stravinsky had composed in 1913–14, as was in fact done. The voices were now to be removed, the orchestra slightly reduced, and various cuts and reorderings made in the musical sequence. Diaghilev was no sleeping partner in these processes, as is shown by a remarkably decisive letter he wrote to Stravinsky listing the necessary revisions. "In both the Nightingale's songs," he insisted, "you must at least reduce the number of bars (that is, individual bars), since [otherwise] they will come out as boring places in the choreography. And don't come grumbling to me about it! I'm a man of the theatre, and not yet, thank God, a composer."[75] Stravinsky did not come grumbling to him, but in nearly every case did as he was told, which is all the more remarkable since their parting in Rome seems to have been soured by a row over the expenses for Igor's trip: "I, too, am very sorry that I didn't say goodbye properly to you and Massine, but left in terrible turmoil and confusion and much affected, I must admit, by our difficult financial accountings. I would honestly like to avoid such conversations in future, and for this reason I shall let you know my terms for coming, and you can always accept or reject."[76]

Perhaps this trouble with his old friend was the indirect cause of a distasteful incident at the Russian embassy when Stravinsky went there for his exit visa and to arrange for his sketches and music manuscripts to be sent back to Switzerland in the diplomatic bag—presumably because he had had difficulties with these highly suspicious documents at the Swiss-Italian border on the outward journey. Stravinsky's hostility to Germans had, if anything, intensified, and his manner had become at times, as Rolland had noticed when they met on a Thünersee steamer in July, "superficial and violent, in his judgments as in his music. Intelligent and lively as well; but within his own lighthouse beam: a piercing ray of light, and all around—utter darkness."[77] At the embassy he inquired—jokingly, he afterwards claimed—whether there was anyone there with a good Russian name apart from his friend Vasily Khvoshchinsky.[78] Afterwards, Khvoshchinsky wrote him a furious letter pointing out that he had only received his accreditation

by courtesy of the first secretary, Vasily Nikolayevich *Strandtmann;*

I can assure you that if in his place there had been someone else with a hypothetical *Russian name* you would never have got your papers. And if you get anything of the sort at the Paris embassy, that will also be by courtesy of the first secretary there, Baron Ungern-Sternberg. I'm very much afraid that if you want exclusive services at the Rome embassy you will have to wait until all its members are to your taste; perhaps that will coincide with the moment when you part with the German *bonna* [nursery nurse] who brought you up and who is still bringing up your children?[79]

Stravinsky sent the letter on to Diaghilev, who had witnessed the incident, with the comment "I think he's gone mad";[80] and it was true that Khvoshchinsky was becoming quarrelsome and rowed openly with Diaghilev a few days after the embassy incident at a concert at which Toscanini conducted the Funeral March from *Götterdämmerung* amid shouts of protest, and Khvoshchinsky "loudly defended the performance of Wagner."[81] Was this also a case, as Craft suggests, of *cherchez la femme?* Madame Khvoshchinskaya, who had been so attentive to the dancers at Ouchy, was a beautiful woman who, to Diaghilev's annoyance, had caught Massine's eye, and whose letters to Stravinsky have an eager warmth that might, with encouragement, have spilt over into passion.[82]

Or was it nothing more than the frayed nerves of wartime and impending revolution: fisticuffs in the lifeboats of a sinking ship?

19

NEVER MORE GO HOME

STRAVINSKY RETURNED to Morges on about 14 November, but set off almost at once for Paris, where he had an appointment with the director of the Paris Opéra, Jacques Rouché. He went to a Colonne Concerts rehearsal of Ravel's *Rapsodie espagnole* and Debussy's *Martyre de Saint-Sébastien* and saw both composers, the latter "feeling much better," despite the rectal cancer which was slowly killing him.[1] On the sixteenth Stravinsky attended a soirée at the house of Princesse Eugène Murat and played *Petrushka* to an audience that included Bakst, Cocteau, Satie, Milhaud, Mme Errazuriz's friend Countess Jacqueline Rehbinder (wife of the first secretary at the Russian embassy—yet another Khvoshchinsky German), and the cabinet attaché at the French foreign ministry, Paul Morand. Morand scrutinized Stravinsky critically, much as Rácz had done: "very much the dandy, mustard trousers, black jacket, blue shirt and collar, yellow boots, clean shaven, slicked-down blond hair, bad teeth, myopia, thick lips."[2] He probably also played the four-hand piano version of his quartet pieces, as well as excerpts from *Renard*. At any rate Bakst sent a note the next day that "Violette Murat is in such raptures over your quartet that she asked me to let you know that she 'will have the score engraved.' "[3] Stravinsky must have followed Bakst's suggestion that he telephone the princess to discuss her idea, since within days of his return to Morges he drafted—with Ramuz's help—a detailed proposal for publication of several of his recent works, though not the quartet pieces, since "circumstances . . . do not permit me to have the quartet engraved in Europe." He suggested instead the *Berceuses du chat* and *Pribaoutki*, a suite of Easy Pieces for piano four-hands, and "finally my latest work, of which I think you already know some parts that I played you when I had the pleasure of making your acquaintance: *Renard*, 'pièce burlesque' (piano score only)." He had discovered that all this music could be printed for four thousand francs. Moreover, he told Mme Murat, the four works were all "from the same period and all in the same spirit, which is why I should be happy for them not to be published separately and, very likely, at long intervals." The dedications, he regretted, were all allocated, but he could offer her the actual manuscripts "as a feeble but very sincere proof of the lively gratitude I feel towards you."[4]

Soon he was involved in negotiations with a Geneva concert agent and theatrical publisher called Adolphe Henn: a dangerous name, one might feel, for a publisher of a work about a predatory fox, except that Henn acted purely as an agent between the paymistress and the printer, and took no financial risk himself.[5] To what extent the princesse de Polignac was kept informed about these plans to publish "her" work is far from clear, but the omission of the full score—which was her property—suggests that she was not directly consulted. There could well have been trouble, since the great Parisian patronesses were as jealous as tigresses. At one point, Mme Murat told Stravinsky that "since September I have not been speaking to the princesse de Polignac," hinting that she did not want any *ennuis* with her about the publication.[6] But there are no echoes of this in the composer's correspondence with Mme de Polignac. She had been casting herself as go-between with Rouché, who wanted to stage Stravinsky's *Scherzo fantastique* as a ballet about bees. Whose idea that was we do not know, but it seems to have originated when the composer was in Paris at the start of 1916, since by February the princess was already writing to Morges asking after the performance materials on Rouché's behalf.[7] Later, for help on the question of staging, Rouché himself approached Stravinsky, who pointed out that "we can't do it by letter. I need to meet the choreographer. A piano reduction needs to be made (for rehearsal). I can come to Paris for all this if someone pays."[8] Someone did pay—presumably the princess, who had already once tactfully offered to act as his host from the moment of his departure from Morges;[9] and the ballet was duly staged at the Opéra, under the title *Les Abeilles*, on 10 January, with choreography by Léo Staats. But Stravinsky had been taken ill and was unable to conduct, as he had intended. Instead, the baton was taken by Gabriel Grovlez.

He was in no financial position to refuse this adaptation—any more than that of *The Nightingale* or, a few months later, *Fireworks*—even if it had crossed his mind to do so.[10] But it invited trouble. The notoriously litigious Maurice Maeterlinck, author of the book *La Vie des abeilles*, on which Stravinsky had based the scherzo in the first place and which was recognizably if not explicitly the source of Staats's choreography, wrote claiming authorship of the scenario and threatening legal action. Stravinsky managed to fend him off, but only by pretending that the work's apiarian inspiration was general in character and derived from more than one source, and by reminding the author that in any case he had been privy to Diaghilev's old 1912 plan for a *Scherzo fantastique* ballet.[11] Remarkably, this disclaimer later turned into a flat denial of any connection with bees, even though the Schott score to this day begins with a brief program note on exactly that subject. Stravinsky labelled his Maeterlinck envelope "Letter from M. Maeterlinck and his ridiculous statements about *Abeilles*, a classical ballet without subject fitted to the music of my *Scherzo fantastique*,"[12] and he told Craft that "*Les Abeilles* was unauthorized by me and, of course, I had not seen it. . . . The bees were a choreographer's idea. . . . I have never attempted to evoke them in my work (as, indeed, what pupil of the composer of the *Flight of the Bumble Bee* would?)."[13] Did he himself believe these fictions? The trouble is that, in order to acquit him of dishonesty, one has to discredit his memory—which, for a memoirist, is a very qualified salvation.

At least *Les Abeilles* did not involve his compositional energies, unlike the *Nightingale* adaptation, which still stood between him and a clear run at the final tableau of *Les Noces*. But in any case, within a month of his return to Morges after the November Paris trip he went down with a violent bout of intercostal neuralgia which incapacitated him, at least partly, over (Western) Christmas and into the New Year. "There were moments," he tells us, "when I could scarcely breathe. . . . My legs were almost paralysed . . . and I could not move without assistance. I shudder even now at the thought of what I had to endure."[14] Katya again took up her pen and corresponded on his behalf. "My first impulse when I got your letter," Diaghilev quickly replied from Rome,

> was to get on a train and come to you. Unfortunately, my American affairs demand my constant presence here for a while longer. . . . Of course, a change of air would be very good. If you and Igor intended to come to Italy together, I promise to fix you comfortable accommodation and an agreeable stay. Igor likes ballet, rehearsals, talks, walks, and, finally, tireless sightseeing of divine Italy. If it's really a question of nerves, then, God knows, one needs to get away for a time from that damp, gray lake. Here there's not a day without sun, and the spirit can rest.[15]

Tell Igor not to worry about *Nightingale,* Seryozha added.

But Igor was not altogether out of action. On 22 December he drafted another Russian chorus, "U Spasa v Chigisakh," to add to the two he had written at Clarens and Château d'Oex, and on New Year's Day he composed a fourth, "Ovsen": they became nos. 1 and 2 of the published set of *Four Russian Peasant Songs,* or "Dish-Divination Songs," to borrow Taruskin's translation of the Russian title, *Podblyudnïye.* The new pieces are as brilliant and fresh as their older companions. But they are also plainly studies for *Les Noces,* and they prove that he was now once more thinking about the ballet. Not yet exclusively, though. He was also planning a further set of easy piano duets for the Henn publication, and the first of these—the mysterious little Andante which opens what became the

Five Easy Pieces—was written down on 4 January.[16] Three more pieces followed in February: Balalaika, Galop, and Napolitana; and the final piece, Española, was written down on 3 April, just before Stravinsky set off once more for Italy, though it is tempting to link it directly with his Spanish trips of the previous summer. The Napolitana, on the other hand, was written before, not after, his first visit to Naples. And although he accuses Ravel of mistaking the Galop for a can-can, it does in fact incorporate material that he himself labelled "Cancan" in a series of sketches from 1914 and 1915 belonging unmistakably to the "music-hall, café-concert atmosphere" in which, as he had told Ansermet, the earlier Three Easy Pieces had been conceived.[17]

The somewhat intermittent composition of these little pieces is striking. Each one can hardly have been more than a day or two in the writing, but the February pieces were finished on the sixth, twenty-first, and twenty-eighth, respectively. The strong implication is that Stravinsky was now preoccupied mainly, not with the creative problems of Les Noces, but with the demanding but more mechanical work of adapting and rescoring The Nightingale. Some time in mid-January, Diaghilev probably stopped at Morges on his way from Paris back to Rome, as promised in his letter to Katya. Stravinsky was well enough, perhaps, to attend rehearsals for Ansermet's Geneva concert performance of Petrushka on the twenty-seventh, and he was certainly at the concert itself, taking a curtain call which was abruptly curtailed when "he saw a group of admirers approaching with a Petrushka doll, heard the demonstration of approval increase," and turned tail.[18]

By a curious coincidence, the Russian premiere of the complete score of Petrushka (as opposed to the three-piece suite always previously played) was given at a concert in the Petrograd Conservatoire under Nikolai Malko on the very same day. This first encounter with the magical, life-bestowing music of the Tour de passe-passe and its reciprocal, the ending in which the hitherto enslaved puppet mocks his tormentor from the roof of his former prison, may well have assumed an unintended emblematic significance in the audience's mind. Less than a month before, Rasputin—that sinister embodiment of the charlatan-animator idea—had been murdered in the Yusupov Palace and his body dumped unceremoniously in the Moyka Canal. Petrograd was more than ever a powder keg. On 9/22 January, there had been mass strikes in memory of the Palace Square massacre of 1905. Somehow the regime hung on, like the shell of a gutted building, waiting for the first strong wind to send it crashing to the ground. That wind at last blew in March, the last week of February Old Style. On the eighth, there were more demonstrations and strikes. In the next few days several army regiments mutinied, and on the fifteenth, after trying unsuccessfully to reach Petrograd by rail, the Tsar abdicated at Pskov in favor of his brother Mikhail, who, however, declined the crown. Petrushka's cry had been heard at last.

Stravinsky was in Lausanne the day the news broke, and saw Ramuz that day as on so many others.

> We were climbing the Petit-Chêne; we were going from south to north and this great wind from north to south. We were going against this north wind; it blew with such violence as to prevent the women from advancing, making their skirts (which they still wore long) flap and twine round their legs. It took our breath away. Stravinsky talked to me about Russia. . . . It all seemed newly begun for her, in effect, in this new beginning of the season. This great north wind was blowing: it was as if Russia came on it to us, breaking her own winter, which she drove before her, creating these blasts of air, frozen but shot through with a radiant sunlight. . . . He had already decided to go back. He was making his travel plans. His place was "back there," now that this back there was also going to be his home.[19]

It went without saying that this new Russia would restore the spirit of the old, as Stravinsky had told Rolland—the true Russia of Pushkin and Gogol and Musorgsky, of Tolstoy even,

> the holy Russia of the Orthodox, a Russia stripped of its parasitic vegetation; its bureaucracy from Germany, a certain strain of English liberalism much in fashion with the nobility, its scientism (alas!), its "intellectuals," their inane and bookish faith in progress;—the Russia of before Peter the Great and before Europeanism . . . a peasant, but above all Christian, Russia, and truly the only Christian land in Europe, the one which laughs and cries (laughs and cries both at once without always really knowing which is which) in *Les Noces,* the one we see awaken to herself confusedly, and magnificently full of impurities, in *The Rite of Spring.*[20]

How far off those earnest talks at Pavlovka and Ustilug about democratic constitutions and habeas corpus must now have seemed; and how inane and bookish, compared to the reality which now spoke to him—not, certainly, from the soil of Russia herself, but from the Russia of his creative imagination—"our dear, liberated Russia," as he called it in a jubilant telegram to his mother in Petrograd.[21]

But another familiar and all too real voice could be heard calling him in the opposite direction. The main corps of the Ballets Russes was not yet back from its winter tour of the United States, but meanwhile Diaghilev had gathered round him in Rome not only Massine and his small quorum of dancers, but a motley of other artists, including Picasso and Cocteau, Bakst, and—somewhat later—Ansermet, plus, a shade incongruously, an old Petersburg music critic called Mikhail Semyonov. Diaghilev had rented a flat with Massine on the Corso Umberto, and the two of them had spent part of the winter rummaging in libraries for old music to turn into ballets and old dance manuals on which to base their choreography. Massine had made a ballet of Scarlatti sonatas, orchestrated by Vincenzo Tommasini, called *The Good-Humored Ladies:* "a small masterpiece," Diaghilev had told Katya, "all merriment and liveliness from beginning to end."[22] And he was now working with Cocteau and Picasso (but in the absence of its composer, Erik Satie) on their new fairground ballet, *Parade.* During (probably) the second week of March, while Nicholas II's world was tumbling in ruins, Diaghilev took Massine, Cocteau, and Picasso on a sightseeing trip to Naples. But Stravinsky was not with them, not yet having left Switzerland. Diaghilev now wired a proposal that he conduct concerts in Rome, Naples, and Milan in mid-April.[23] But Stravinsky wanted to finish *The Song of the Nightingale,* as it would be called, before moving again. Only when this was practically done, on 2 April, did he go to Berne to arrange his visa through the Italian embassy. The next day he completed the Five Easy Pieces to go in the batch of Murat works for Henn; on the fourth he wrote finis to the *Nightingale* ballet; and by the fifth he was in Rome.

As before, he found himself in a whirlpool of artistic enthusiasm and excitement. He at last met Picasso. Diaghilev had mobilized the futurists to work on both *Nightingale* and a short "spectacle" based on *Fireworks.* Fortunato Depero was designing *Nightingale* in the dehumanized spirit of Marinetti, with "rigid, geometrized space suits that concealed not only the body, but the hands and face, while geometric protuberances indicated whiskers, eyes, and mouths."[24] A photograph, of what Lynn Garafola takes to be "the completed set, reveals a stylized futurist garden, with fronds, flowers, and shrubs rendered as freestanding cones, arc segments, and discs. Varnish and enamel were used to enhance the brightness of the colors."[25] In the end, Diaghilev withdrew the production, apparently on financial grounds, and the model for the futurist garden was dismantled and sold to pay Depero's rent.[26] But Balla's *Fireworks,* which entailed neither dancers nor costumes, but merely "a light show played on a setting of geometrical solids," was duly presented in the Teatro Costanzi on 12 April.[27] This "gala" evening had been preceded by one on the ninth, and by an afternoon concert on the eleventh at which Stravinsky presumably conducted *Fireworks, Firebird,* and a suite from *Petrushka,* and canvases by Picasso, Braque, Natalya Goncharova, and the futurists were exhibited in the theatre foyer.

After the events of mid-March in Russia, Diaghilev had received "a telegram signed by many of the most prominent names in Russian art, Gorky, Chaliapin, Benois, Bilibin, etc., asking him to go to Petrograd 'to take in hand the management of the Arts.' "[28] Though sympathetic to what he, like Stravinsky, believed to be the purport of the new regime, he seems wisely to have hesitated to take on so vague and grandiose a portfolio. "I think," Ansermet confided to Stravinsky, "that he's mainly afraid of the journey." But at the same time the question arose of what national anthem to play at the gala now that there was no longer a Tsar for God to save. Stravinsky recalled that "the idea of opening the performance with a Russian folk-song suggested itself to Diaghilev, who chose the famous *Volga Boat Song*."[29] But Taruskin has shown that the idea almost certainly came direct from Petrograd, perhaps in the dispatch from the prominent names, and had actually been proposed by Andrey Rimsky-Korsakov in an article in his own paper, *Muzïkal'nïy sovremennik,* a week or two after the abdication.[30] Whether a Stravinsky commission as such came from Petrograd is much more doubtful. Probably Diaghilev was simply instructed what the new national anthem would be, and—either lacking or disliking the existing arrangement by Glazunov—persuaded Stravinsky to make a new one at the last minute. The composer relates how he sat up all night in his friend the diplomat-composer Gerald Tyrwhitt's apartment dictating the arrangement, "chord by chord, note by note, to Ansermet, who wrote it down."[31] And not surprisingly, his strident antiphonies, for wind and percussion without strings, evoked the old Russia of Ramuz's north wind, "in incongruously archaic terms that ill accorded with the liberal constitutional republic the Provisional Government was trying to establish."[32]

Stravinsky seems to have hit it off with Picasso from the start. On the sixteenth the artist made the first of his three famous portrait sketches of the composer, the austere, vertical, monocled one (though Stravinsky told Craft that the monocle was in fact one half of a broken pair of spectacles). And in Naples, whither they proceeded with the entire company the next day, the two great men did all their sightseeing together, but under leaden skies which somewhat belied Ansermet's lyrical description of "Napoli the insane. Yellow on a blue sea, mechanical pianos. Balconied bordellos on the street with girls taking foot baths. A cow in the courtyard. Odor of Spain. Smoke in the sky and burning lava in the body."[33] They were "both much impressed with the Commedia dell'Arte, which we saw in a crowded little room reeking of garlic."[34] They visited the aquarium, went to puppet shows, and combed the back-street shops for watercolors; and they were arrested, in best Quartier-Latin style, for urinating against a wall, then released when the policeman heard them addressed as "maestri." But such stories pursued Stravinsky. "A certain anecdote about a Madrid urinal enchants me and Picasso," Cocteau had written to him the previous summer: "a perfect image of the illicit, rococo shamelessness and luxury, but reported to us as a scandal and to make us laugh."[35] The actual ancedote, alas, has not survived.

The company played twice at the Teatro San Carlo but made little impact, and although Stravinsky remembered a fortnight's stay in Naples, he was there in reality no more than four or five days before returning to Rome, where he spent two days with Tyrwhitt and then set off back to Morges on the twenty-fourth.[36] His visit to the amenable Englishman left a trail of debris in its wake. Tyrwhitt had to send on a packet of letters that the composer had left behind; and then, in May, a large box of cigarettes mysteriously turned up on his Rome doorstep with no addressee, but obviously, in Tyrwhitt's view, meant for Stravinsky, who had set up a private international grid for the supply of tobacco during the war years. Stravinsky had already had to employ Tyrwhitt's good offices to get the Picasso portrait sent to him in Switzerland in the diplomatic bag, after the Italian border police had insisted on regarding it as "a plan of fortifications," when the composer tried to export it in person.[37] "I hope," wrote the long-suffering diplomat, "that you have now received all your other things (the music I gave to Diaghilev, the dolls, etc.)." He had even undertaken to get for Stravinsky recordings of Spanish music through a friend in Madrid.[38] The great delegator was in top form.

Within days of the return to Morges, "one fine spring afternoon," the old family nurse, Bertha Essert, died suddenly of a hemorrhage. "For the first time," Theodore wrote, "I saw my mother and father in tears and their close friends being strangely gentle and protective towards them. . . . The Villa Rogivue became a very sad place." "I mourned her," Stravinsky told Craft, "more than I did, later, my mother."[39]

But Bertha's death may well have got caught up with his sense of separation from the land of his childhood, both real and metaphorical. Or if it did not at once do so, it was soon destined to. The first sign that all was not going smoothly in Petrograd came in connection with the still active plan to produce The Nightingale there. At the end of May a wire came from Ziloti announcing that he had been appointed manager of the Mariyinsky and inviting Stravinsky to select a designer, "as per the author's rights." But after Stravinsky had nominated Benois, Ziloti wrote to say that the choice had caused trouble, since there was no such author's right after all, and Telyakovsky had already booked Golovin.[40] "You imagine that we are in the kingdom of freedom here, and are even showered with every kind of 'excess,' " Benois wrote a few weeks later, "whereas in fact we are in the kingdom of excess and nonsense without freedom, or at least without the sense of freedom. Dear friend, it's very bad and uncomfortable here, and we more than occasionally envy you for being too far away to see this nightmare."[41]

Already the Petit-Chêne and its north wind were receding into a world

of dreams. The reality remained lakeside Swiss, and in its way comparatively idyllic, despite the Bertha sadness. There was already a new *nyanya*,
a gentle, affectionate girl from Neuchâtel called Mina Svitalski, a name
which, as pronounced by the six-year-old Svetik, came out as, and remained,
Madubo. And Stravinsky could continue work—how concentratedly we do
not know—on *Les Noces*, a concept nearly as old as Svetik himself. There
were more chips off the old block, in the form of two children's songs—
"Tilim-bom" and "Gusi-Lebedi" ("The ducks, the swans, the geese . . .")—
to add to the song about the bear of eighteen months earlier.[42] And there
were the by now routine plays-through of the unfinished ballet. One of
these took place—somehow—on an excursion to Rolle, along the lake,
with Charles-Albert Cingria and the Russian choral conductor Vasily Kibalchich, "with his brick-shaped head and admirable gold spectacles. He was
the chorus, not an individual, but a race: the whole of sacerdotal and
administrative Russia." And Katya, sitting very straight at one end of the
piano and saying, " 'That's good,' like the wife of a great chef, pointed and
comfortable, like a tent with a winter brazier."[43] Stravinsky was seeing
more of Cingria, a keen cyclist, classical scholar, literary fantasist, and
enthusiastic drinker. They would bicycle about the countryside together: to
Lausanne to see Ramuz, or to Yverdon, on the Lac de Neuchâtel, where
they would drink the local *vin ouvert* and totter on—if Stravinsky can be
believed in this—all the way to Neuchâtel itself.[44] "Cingria was nearly
always drunk," Stravinsky reflected, "and he was passionate only about
neumes, but he was also the most amusing and affectionate companion
in the world."[45] He had the added advantage—over, for example, Ramuz—
that he never collaborated with Stravinsky on any significant work and
therefore never claimed any share in his royalties or his glory.

But Stravinsky could not settle down at the Villa Rogivue after Bertha's
death, and decided instead to move once again to the mountains. That
would in any case be good for Katya's lungs, and, alas, also for little eight-
year-old Mika's, which had apparently come out in sympathy with her
mother's.[46] They found a house just outside the village of Les Diablerets,
eight miles east of Leysin: Les Fougères, a timber-topped chalet rented
from a carpenter, with an attached workshop where the composer could
settle down to finishing the last tableau of his ballet. The beau monde was
again putting other temptations in his way. Ida Rubinstein wanted him to
write incidental music for Shakespeare's *Antony and Cleopatra*, which she
planned to put on in Paris in the spring in a new adaptation by André
Gide. And although Stravinsky was hesitating over the exact character of
the intended production, fearing a Rubinstein blockbuster in the manner
of Debussy's *Martyre de Saint-Sébastien*, he was sorely tempted by his
perennial need of money and frustrated by the difficulties of arranging a
meeting with his prospective collaborators. With Bakst, who would be the

designer, he refused point blank to discuss anything by letter. His need for precision, for detail, for practical collaboration, was never more in evidence, and it was this, almost as much as their inability to see eye to eye about production style (an inability which reflected Bakst's growing alienation from the modernist tendencies of Stravinsky's new Russianism), that would in due course put paid to the project.[47]

In the midst of all this, on 14 July, the Stravinsky caravan set off for Les Diablerets. "In the traditional Russian fashion," Theodore tells us, "the whole household moved. . . . Leading the procession went the piano; then came suitcases and packages; our dog Mouche and a complete farmyard of animals in wicker cages; followed by the cook, the housemaid, the governess, Madubo, papa, mamma and us four children." The piano presumably went into the carpenter's workshop, and "on the astonished walls of this unusual work-room there immediately appeared photographs of the extraordinary 'sandwich-men' that Picasso had designed for *Parade*. . . . Stravinsky worked that whole summer at the joiner's workbench on the last scene of *Les Noces*."[48]

But of course there were interruptions. Within days, Diaghilev arrived, fresh from his first Paris season since before the war and from yet another Spanish tour, at the end of which he had packed off the whole company to South America, under Grigoriev's management, and with Nijinsky as premier danseur and Ansermet as conductor.[49] Naturally, he wanted to know how his favorite ballet project was getting on. But he also wanted to talk money. His *Petrushka* exclusivity needed renewing; and knowing that *Les Noces* was nearing completion, he wanted at last to settle terms for that, too. It must have been a brief visit, since the paperwork was still incomplete when he had to leave on the twenty-fifth, and Stravinsky went with him in the train down to Aigle so as to finalize the details before they parted.[50] The next day, Tyrwhitt arrived, bearing cigarettes. A little later, in the second week of August, André Gide came, with the seventeen-year-old Marc Allégret (the future film director) and his elder brother, André, to discuss *Antony and Cleopatra*. They met at a student chalet called Revenandray, above Les Diablerets, drank a lot of punch, showed off in front of the assembled students, and drew up a list of movements for the incidental music.[51] Later, Stravinsky invited Gide and his "nephews" to dine at a nearby restaurant.[52] At the end of his stay, the novelist turned up at Les Fougères. Theodore saw the would-be collaborators playing cards in the garden, then saw Gide leave—furious at having continually lost at the game, as Igor told the children when he got back from the station.[53] But was there perhaps some more professional reason for a bad atmosphere, which the composer felt it necessary to explain away?

One day the family came home from an afternoon picking raspberries in the woods near Les Diablerets, to be met by the telegraph boy with a wire announcing that Gury Stravinsky had died in Rumania—not in battle, but ignominiously of typhoid fever, Igor's oyster sickness—at Iasi, on the Moldavian border. Like Igor, he had been exempted from military service, but had actually thrown up his singing career early in the war and volunteered for the support services (provisioning and medical supplies) on the southwestern front near Lvov. It seemed that, apparently unbeknownst to his mother or brothers, he had gone down with typhoid quite early on, had recovered, but—his constitution weakened by unremitting work and poor living conditions—had fallen victim to a second attack on 3 August.[54]

Igor was distraught at this second loss in just over three months. "I can't suppress the grief which has descended on us," he wrote to Anna. "I have lost something infinitely dear, infinitely close to me, someone to whom I feel an unrepayable debt—I know how much he loved me, how much he loved Katya and the children. . . . Musechka, I feel so wretched and orphaned. My Musechka, why am I not with you, so as not to have to express in words and characters what can't in any case be expressed?"[55] "Unrepayable debt"? We still know curiously little about Gury Stravinsky, but we do know that he had been Igor's closest companion in childhood, as the composer himself always afterwards maintained, and a vital moral support at difficult times for his nervy and insecure older brother: at Pavlovka, at Ustilug, at Pechisky, even at 66 Kryukov Canal. But above all, Gury was an artist like Igor, and the only one of his immediate family with whom he could discuss his music. Gury is the sole member of Igor's family about whom one asks: Would things have been different for the composer had he lived? Would he, for instance, have considered returning to Russia if Gury had still been there in the twenties? The question, like all of its kind, is idle. But it refuses to go away.

THEY STAYED at Les Diablerets for seven weeks. Stravinsky worked away at the final tableau of *Les Noces* at his carpenter's bench, and meanwhile, down in the valley, Ramuz—having completed his translations of *Renard* and the various songs—was starting work on the ballet text. He even planned to come up to Les Diablerets, but nobody could find anywhere affordable for him to stay. All the same, he probably did eventually come, and, among other things, an agreement was worked out on the author's rights for his translation of *Les Noces*. Ramuz was on thin ice here; and when he asked the composer to agree not to let the French text be published apart from the music except with his permission, Stravinsky seems to have taken this as an attempt to dictate terms on publication of the libretto. There was an irritable exchange of notes, and though Stravinsky's letter has not surfaced, it is easy enough to read its contents in the light sarcasm of Ramuz's "Thank you for giving me precise details on my rights in the event that you relinquish yours lock, stock, and barrel. . . . You are much better at these things than I am."[56] But the olive branch was not far behind. "I think you are very angry, so I reach for my nicest paper and best envelopes to write to you. I wanted to come and see you this afternoon, as they'll have told you, but I'm still scarcely on my feet. Throat, head, everything. And to cap it all, daughter and wife look like wanting to follow my example. No one is sleeping anymore. Pity us."[57]

As well as the text, Stravinsky was thinking about the instrumentation, and while still working with his overgrown peasant orchestra (forty players or so) was toying with a completely new idea involving that strange mechanical instrument the pianola, which played, more or less automatically, by means of paper rolls perforated with "instructions" to the piano mechanism. The year after his London visit of June 1914, he had been in touch with the Orchestrelle Company about the possibility of making piano rolls of his early ballets, and by June 1917 his Geneva lawyer, Philippe Dunant, was doing battle with Orchestrelle over the bizarre British law of mechanical copyright, which allowed (at a fixed royalty) unprotected arrangement for such instruments of any music that had appeared in print. Now, in August, he wrote separately to Orchestrelle, via the ever-willing Tyrwhitt, to ask about the possible use of piano rolls for *Les Noces*—not, presumably, for a commercial transcription, but as a part of the orchestra.[58] At the same time, he composed a completely new work for Pianola, a kind of mad study based on "the whimsicalities of the unexpected melodies of the mechanical pianos and rattletrap orchestrinas of the Madrid streets and the little night taverns."[59]

The precise motive behind this study is hard to establish, since it certainly was not commissioned.[60] Undoubtedly he was attracted by the mechanical character of the instrument and by its remarkable powers of bravura: its ability, as it were, to emulate a pianist with sixteen arms and no feelings. Perhaps, more practically, he saw a completely original piece as a way round the copyright law, though his subsequent attempt to reserve the arrangement rights suggests that he had failed to understand that no roll publisher would buy a work which he did not control absolutely, since the later appearance of any version in print would destroy his exclusivity. It was left to Edwin Evans in London, to whom Stravinsky sent his study at the end of October, to explain these refinements, and to try to restrain the composer's optimism about the commercial possibilities of a medium hitherto associated almost exclusively with arrangements of popular tunes.[61] The trouble was that Evans was by no means a disinterested party, as Stravinsky was quick to notice. Desperate for gainful employment, the English music critic had the bright idea of getting Orchestrelle (or Aeolian, as they soon became) to commission from other composers, including Casella and Tyrwhitt, and of then building a series of lectures about the pianola round the new works, to which, meanwhile, he would effectively retain exclusive rights. Stravinsky was understandably somewhat piqued by this kidnapping of his work, and remained ever after-wards mildly suspicious of "this splendid (naive and not very intelligent) Evans."[62] But it must quickly have become apparent that nobody stood to gain or lose a great deal by such pieces. So the hurt was not very deep.

Early in September the caravan lumbered back down to Morges, where Stravinsky made a brief detour to visit the painter René Auberjonois at the Hôtel du Mont-Blanc. The purpose of this visit seems to have been mainly financial, and while Auberjonois sketched his guest, he heard a tale of woe, about how events in Russia had deprived Stravinsky of the income from his Volhynian property while royalties in the West were unpaid and there was little immediate prospect of earnings from new work.[63] Stravin-sky had met Auberjonois through Ramuz a year or so before and had planned to visit him at Sierre in February, but for some reason had not kept the rendezvous.[64] He now wanted Auberjonois to use his contacts with art collectors in German Switzerland to help sell the manuscript full score of *The Firebird*. But he may well have broached another practical mat-ter at the same time. The Villa Rogivue was being sold and the Stravinskys would have to move. Did Auberjonois know of a suitable house or flat to let? As it happened, Auberjonois did; in fact his wife had found a beautiful apartment in a large late-eighteenth-century house called the Maison Bor-nand, almost in the center of Morges. "Her mistake," as their son Fernand wrote later, "was to show it to Igor who said it was exactly what he had been looking for and who moved in soon afterwards."[65]

Within a month of returning to Morges, the Stravinskys moved into the Maison Bornand, taking possession of the entire second floor—a huge, well-laid-out apartment which easily absorbed their growing stock of furni-ture and bric-à-brac. There was also "an additional room which he had had fitted out as a study and which you reached only by what was practically a secret staircase, doubly, triply barricaded with doors of which you could not very well decide (this was the amusing thing about them) whether they were more to protect the musician from his household or the household from his music. I should incline rather to the latter alternative."[66] There was a lovely garden and a "view of the lake between a church and a tall sequoia."[67] Ramuz could now work on the translation of *Les Noces*, as he had previously worked on *Renard*, in collaboration with the composer. The sketch score itself was at long last finished on 11 October, a few days after the move, but the "wedding cart" still trundled onto the stage each day, "rolling noisily across the pine floor" as the occasionally bawdy Russian text was converted into a slightly more presentable French equivalent. Ramuz remembered the scoring as "fortissimo from beginning to end" and as "having even been conceived on the assumption of a mechanical reproduction,"[68] which suggests that Stravinsky may already have been talking about his pianola idea, even though the 1917 sketch score is firmly for a thirty-nine-piece orchestra, including such diverse elements as harpsichord, cimbalom, and harmonium. But in any case he was not yet working on a new version. Instead he had a completely new work in hand, a "ragtime" for a smaller group of instruments gathered round the now inevitable cimbalom.

Like most café haunters of wartime and even prewar Paris, Stravinsky was perfectly well acquainted with the kind of rag and pseudo-rag music which jangled through the music halls and the American bars of the French capital.[69] By 1918 this so-called jazz was an established part of the chic Parisian scene, and the claim that at that time "my knowledge of jazz was derived exclusively from copies of sheet music, and . . . I had never actually heard any of the music performed" may be taken as one of Stravinsky's more implausible reminiscences of this period.[70] Craft himself had already previously noted that Stravinsky started collecting gramophone records of American "popular" music (whatever that might mean) as early as 1914,[71] and by the end of 1915 the composer was telling Stanley Wise that "I know little about American music except that of the music halls, but I consider that unrivalled. It is veritable art and I can never get enough of it to satisfy me."[72] No doubt this "American jazz" (or ragtime) was a production-line commodity compared with the "incredible music" (presumably the early stirrings of Dixieland, with its much wider syncopations and strident polyphonies) which Ansermet reported hearing in New York cafes during his United States tour with the Ballets Russes early in 1916, and of which he brought back sheet copies and possibly even recordings for Stravinsky.[73] But in any case, Stravinsky knew something about ragtime and had a fair idea of its sound by 1916, and even talked about writing such a piece himself.[74] There was certainly nothing particularly novel about the basic rag ingredients, the syncopations, swung melody, and dotted rhythms, when Stravinsky eventually composed his own *Ragtime* in the autumn and winter of 1917–18.

The piece itself is a relatively modest tribute to the idiom, only a little more ambitious—and even a little less adventurous—than the style parodies in the Easy Pieces. After all, when he started it Stravinsky was still expecting to compose *Antony and Cleopatra*. At the end of October, he wrote to Bakst setting out his terms for Ida Rubinstein, and asking when the music had to be completed;[75] and the few sketches were probably made in the first half of November. But meanwhile, Bakst had replied arguing passionately against what he described as "your idea for a modernist interpretation of the staging" and suggesting provocatively that "it is better to call off the production if you adopt a selfish attitude to it," in spite of which the composer still clearly envisaged going ahead with the music, since he wrote two or three times before Christmas to Ida's agent in a vain attempt to agree a contract.[76] But his terms, too steep even for the expansive Ida, clearly reflected a no more than qualified artistic commitment. In December he probably returned to *Ragtime,* as well as jotting down a tiny little vocal Berceuse for Mika, with tributes to the dog Mouche and the children's governess, Madame Reymond.[77] Then suddenly he went down with what the doctor thought was pleurisy, followed in February by a heavy bout of flu, and even such casual work had to be postponed. The draft completion of *Ragtime* was held up till early March, and the only other work he seems to have managed during these weeks was a transcription of certain passages in *Petrushka* to serve as a basis for the Pianola arrangement that was being made by the Aeolian operatives in London.[78] By March, when Gide wrote to ask what was happening about *Antony,* the collaboration was for Stravinsky little more than a memory of a failed business project.[79]

While he had been unobtrusively sketching *Ragtime* in Morges, on the night of 7 and 8 November 1917 (NS), the Bolsheviks took over almost as unobtrusively from the well-named Provisional Government in Petrograd.[80] Unlike the "February" revolution, its successor passed almost without comment in the Stravinsky household, which must long since have given Kerensky's government up for dead. Then, almost as the draft of *Ragtime* was being completed, on 3 March 1918, Lenin signed the infamous Treaty of Brest-Litovsk, which took Russia out of the war at the humiliating cost of large parts of her European territories, including Poland and Volhynia. The composer's better-documented memory of finishing the fair-copy score of *Ragtime* on the morning of the Armistice, 11 November 1918, shows only how the monumental can persistently cling to the insignificant.[81] It was not with a bang but with a whimper that Stravinsky's Russia came to an end.

Even so, the Revolution and its aftermath left him anxious and, in his own eyes at least, virtually destitute. His home and income were gone, his family scattered, his future apparently at the mercy of politicians and immigration officials. Diaghilev, he told Misia in despair, owed him thirty thousand francs and had paid him nothing for six months; Mme Errazuriz had sent nothing for four. When Misia tactfully posted him an anonymous check for two thousand francs, he naturally saw through the subterfuge but could not refuse the loan. "I cannot tell when I shall be in a position to return this sum to you," he wrote back, "and that embarrasses me horribly."[82] Misia had also enclosed a check from Mme Errazuriz. And meanwhile, other friends were active on his behalf. Ansermet wrote to Manuel de Falla in Madrid mentioning Stravinsky's plight;[83] Falla approached the pianist Artur Rubinstein, who was himself based in Spain, and Rubinstein promptly sent five thousand francs to the composer in Switzerland. Whether or not Rubinstein "tactfully disguised the gift by inviting Stravinsky to compose something for him" is hard now to establish.[84] But the composer certainly took it in that spirit, and at once offered to write "an important piano piece this summer, specially for him."[85] The earliest notations for the *Piano Rag Music* were duly made soon after the completion of *Ragtime* in March. But by that time another, more urgent and absorbing project had come up, and the piano piece had to be shelved.

It was just in these gloomy early months of 1918 that he and Ramuz had their idea for a travelling theatre-piece about a soldier who barters with the Devil his whole past life (in the form of a violin) for easy wealth and a spectacular marriage. Stravinsky later claimed that he had thought of the work a year before, and that he himself drafted a plot outline from the Afanasyev original, which he then translated for Ramuz to turn into a fully fledged libretto. But one is mildly suspicious of this claim, and not only because Stravinsky's account of the genesis is so riddled with demonstrable errors of fact.[86] The first surviving reference to any such piece is by Ramuz in a letter of the end of February 1918: "I'm thinking a lot about the tale which, I hope, will 'ripen,' and with you too."[87] In any case the treatment itself is so unlike any previous Stravinsky theatre piece that it is hard to believe he had given it any formative thought before handing the project to Ramuz. Ramuz's own account is that one day, they started discussing the possibility of "writing a piece which could do without a big hall, a huge public; a piece with, for example, music for only a few instruments and only two or three characters. . . . All that remained was to leaf together through one of the volumes of the enormous compilation of a distinguished Russian folklorist whose name I forget."[88] And there it was, Afanasyev's tale of "The Deserter and the Devil," ready for Ramuzification in the form of a story with action ("to be read, played, and danced," as the eventual title page puts it), the author himself being, as he admitted, not a man of the theatre, and wanting to show Stravinsky that "the theatre could be conceived in a much wider sense than usual, and that it lent itself perfectly . . . to what might be called the narrative style."[89]

From the start *The Soldier's Tale* had a *Cahiers vaudois* ring to it. Its Russian roots were firmly replanted in the Vaud soil, where they at once sprouted wider connotations, exactly as in Ramuz's original ideas about the *Cahiers*. The troupe would go from town to town, village to village, taking its theatre with it in the form of a trestle stage with portable sets designed by Auberjonois, and its music in the form of a tiny instrumental ensemble directed by Ansermet. Two or three actor-dancers would mime out the action recounted by a narrator (Ramuz). But, exactly as in a mystery play, the meaning would be universalized: the Soldier, the violin, the Devil, the King, and the Princess—the symbolic apparatus of a world where old values and certainties were rapidly disintegrating in the face of war, exile, and heartless materialism. This was much more Ramuz's literary world than Stravinsky's, however much it might seem to take Stravinsky's actual circumstances as subject matter. Ramuz had written novels *(Aimé Pache, La Vie de Samuel Belet)* about the clash between modern life and rural values, whereas Stravinsky had never been remotely interested in social or psychological questions of that kind; and *The Soldier's Tale* itself always preserved the character of a musicalized novel, even in the much-curtailed later versions of the text, still furnished as they are with anecdotal details, lengthy verbal descriptions, genre portraiture, and all those other impedimenta of realist narrative which Stravinsky had been at such pains to expunge from his latest texted dance works.

Although the *Tale* may have been devised as a moneymaking project, it was quickly apparent that it could not go ahead at all without financial backing. Within a day or two of Ramuz's first written communication about the work, a letter had been drafted and sent to Werner Reinhart, a music-loving, art-collecting tea importer whom René Morax knew in Winterthur, asking for his support. Reinhart was more sympathetic than they could have dared hope, thanks largely, it seems, to a genuine enthusiasm for Stravinsky's music. He at once put cash at their disposal.[90] But the idea of broader sponsorship fell on stonier ground. The authors found themselves circularizing an assortment of bankers, industrialists, and local dignitaries, and even entertaining them in their homes, but with apparently only limited success. Meanwhile, the expenses mounted. Neither Ramuz nor Stravinsky seems to have foreseen the administrative complications of putting on their own show: the problems of casting and coaching, of locating musicians good enough to play difficult modern music in wartime Switzerland, and of getting them all often enough into one place for adequate rehearsal. A string of would-be actors—at first mainly students[91]—were roped in, rehearsed, and in one or two cases paid off, before a proper working cast was assembled, a problem aggravated by the fact that the work itself was all the time evolving, the text being revised, and the music significantly expanded from its modest beginnings.

As a collaboration, *The Soldier's Tale* was considerably looser than Stravinsky's previous joint projects. The writer wrote and the composer composed, but the play and the music remained essentially distinct concepts, each developing in its own way and according to its own time scale. Because of the sheer quantity of spoken text, particularly in the first part of the work, Ramuz could revise it radically (which he did several times before the first performance) without forcing the composer to alter his score. At one stage, a whole character (the King) was removed from the play, possibly in order to save a performer's fee and expenses.[92] But this seems to have had no effect on the music, which had evolved from the start as a series of separate movements, in accordance with the intention that it should be "completely independent of the text and constitute a 'suite' which could be performed in concert."[93] Only where lines of text were to be recited rhythmically over the music, as in the opening Soldier's March, the Little Concerto (which the Soldier plays after winning his violin back), and the Devil's Song, was closer collusion necessary, and it is significant that apart from the march, these were among the last pieces to be composed.

The idea of the opening march itself already figured in the early discussions, and in composing it, Stravinsky used material from his *Antony and Cleopatra* sketches of the autumn.[94] So Craft must be wrong when he says that the original intention was to use only a solo violin, which would have made both dramatic and musical nonsense in such a piece. Other early sketches, for the Waltz and the Tango perhaps, support the violin idea, but here of course the story calls for a big solo on that instrument (in the coda of the Tango, written on 16 March, Stravinsky used a theme which he later said he had dreamt being played by a young Gypsy fiddler).[95] It does seem, though, that the eventual ensemble of seven players, usually regarded as a concession to wartime stringencies, was bigger than at first envisaged and certainly bigger than Ramuz wanted.

> The violin alone wasn't enough; the piano had been excluded at once as too cumbersome and not rustic enough. But Ramuz had imagined it would suffice to add an accordion or guitar to the violin—why not a mouth organ? . . . After Stravinsky had explained that he needed a bass with his violin . . . that he needed to fill the gap between the violin and the bass with two woodwinds—clarinet and bassoon . . . and when later he announced he would also need a trumpet and trombone—always a pair—Ramuz opened terrified eyes and looked flabbergasted, though you never knew if his astonishments were real or feigned. To round things off, Stravinsky declared triumphantly that he would make do with a single percussionist, but he didn't mention that this player would have at his disposal a whole shopful of instruments.[96]

Stravinsky tells us that he bought his own percussion in Lausanne and learnt to play it as he composed,[97] though Ramuz had pictured him surrounded by "instruments de choc" back at the Villa Rogivue.[98] When Stravinsky turned up in Geneva one (probably) August afternoon to coach Lyudmila Pitoëff in the part of the Princess, he was preceded by a percussionist wearing a belt of drums "like strange fruits cut in half, and quiet because it suited them but precisely provocative in their menacing silence."[99] The description is apt, because the drums in *The Soldier's Tale* are as much the Devil's music as the violin is the Soldier's, and no less so when they accompany the violin discreetly, as they do in the Princess's Tango.

While the music was being written, Stravinsky was relatively insulated from the practical organization of the travelling theatre. On 25 April, he met Reinhart for the first time at Auberjonois's flat in Lausanne (three days after a concert at the Lausanne Conservatoire in which Ansermet and Nino Rossi had given what was billed as the first performance of the two sets of Easy Pieces),[100] and he also entertained Reinhart at Morges, played him some of his recent music, and talked to him about art. But in the early stages it was Ramuz who bore the brunt of the day-to-day planning, wrote letter after letter to collaborators and sponsors, and auditioned the cast, all of which he did with every appearance of calm good humor. Not so the designer, Auberjonois, who grumbled furiously to his Basle friend Hans Graber at having mortgaged his entire summer

> to a work which is, in sum, not mine. . . . Reinhart is coming next Thursday, and I should like, without quite daring, to make him understand what an ill-chosen moment this is for throwing oneself into an affair of such importance. Stravinsky desires the performance so badly that he will enthuse Reinhart, I'm afraid. If you see Reinhart, won't you tell him that this production isn't urgent—but strictly between ourselves, I implore you.[101]

The problem for Auberjonois was that as a design project, the piece was complicated, and involved designing, to precise measurements, a stage-within-a-stage, several sets and elaborate drop curtains, costumes and (for the Devil) a number of masks, to accompany a work that was not yet written in theatres that had not yet been booked with a cast that had not yet been chosen. He had never designed for the stage before. Stravinsky, by contrast, could write his music without apparently worrying who was going to play it. By early July, Auberjonois had (on Ramuz's instructions) bought all the cloth for the sets and was pressing Reinhart for the exact dimensions of the theatres in which the work was to play.[102] But it was another month before any firm steps were taken to fix the instrumentalists, since, as Ramuz told the composer, there was no point in approaching Reinhart for the extra money until they knew exactly where they stood.[103] As late as 13 August, with the premiere a mere six or seven weeks away, Ansermet was still considering breaking off negotiations with his fixer, the Zurich clarinettist Edmond Allegra, over his estimates for the musicians' fees and expenses.[104]

The fact is that, until August, when he started keeping a daily account of his out-of-pocket expenses, Stravinsky left much of the planning of the performances to his collaborators.[105] He and Ramuz continued to meet regularly, and probably spoke very often on the phone. He may have attended auditions—for instance, on 13 July, when Ramuz met the actor Gabriel Rosset, a young classics student and painter called Steven-Paul Robert, and other aspirants at the Salle Rouilly in Lausanne; and he probably went with Auberjonois to Geneva on the twenty-second to meet Lyudmila Pitoëff and her actor husband, George.[106] But it was in August, by which time most of the music was complete, that he became heavily involved in rehearsals and auditions, and in intensive discussions about the performance and production. There were frequent visits to Geneva, to see Ansermet, who was by now engaged in recruitment for the new Orchestre de la Suisse Romande; Fernand Closset, its future leader and the intended violinist in *The Soldier's Tale;* the Pitoëffs; or his publisher Henn. He would often catch the lake steamer, which was much slower than the train but also cheaper and, as Auberjonois pronounced it, more restful.[107] Or he would take the boat from Morges to Ouchy, the landing for Lausanne, where Ramuz would meet him and carry him off for pre-rehearsal discussions, or to visit Auberjonois working half-naked in his oven of a studio ("like the hold of a battleship during a battle"),[108] or to rehearse with the new Devil, Jean Villard, or the "brilliant cross-eyed Narrator," Elie Gagnebin, a young paleontologist from the university.[109] They had to work hard on their actors. Rosset was originally to have played the Devil, with Robert as the Soldier ("this pallid sketch of the part," as Ramuz described his efforts to Auberjonois).[110] Then the role of the Devil had been split between Rosset and Villard, presumably because Rosset could not dance.[111] Later the authors decided that Robert was unsatisfactory, and Rosset took over as the Soldier. At one point, Stravinsky even proposed dancing the final scene himself, much to Ramuz's delight: "You will live it rhythmically and save everything"—which at least indicates the difficulty the young actors were experiencing with the music's complex and unforgiving rhythmic language.[112] But the idea was surely no more than exasperated fantasy amid the confusion of last-minute casting and recasting. In the end Villard played the Devil, but George Pitoëff performed the Dance of Triumph, while Lyudmila—who was no ballerina and could not dance on pointe—evolved a particular style of "movement" for the Princess which, to judge from Auberjonois's drawing of her in rehearsal with the composer, may have owed something to Isadora Duncan.[113] No doubt the Russian in her and her husband could respond to Stravinsky's incredible physicality in contact with the stuff of his own music. "You had to see him at the piano," Villard recalled, "unrestrained, hammering the keys with nervous hands and sustaining his dynamism with an improbable number of kirschs, gulping them down one after the other, then correcting their sometimes too drastic effects with a no less enormous intake of aspirin."[114]

For their Swiss colleagues, this may all have seemed a mere caricature of "theatre" as they understood it. Even Ramuz was sometimes at odds with Stravinsky's direct, almost physiological relationship with his art. There was a row about the Devil's masks, which Ramuz wanted abstract but which Stravinsky preferred straightforward and obvious, in the childlike style of a magic lantern. "I've had quite lively altercations with Stravinsky," Ramuz told Auberjonois, adding optimistically that "they always end well, and are merely evidence of the degree of passion in the imagination."[115] But the composer's annotations on Ramuz's letters suggest that he was not always so sure of his co-author's imagination, or its practical effects.[116] In particular, Ramuz's love of anecdotal complication and his somewhat Gallic taste for a free interplay of words and music probably fell foul of Stravinsky's insistence on clarity, simplicity, and control. Nearly all the many revisions in the text, both before and after the first performance, were concessions to the composer in these respects.[117]

The idea of a trestle stage set up in village squares had long since been abandoned, no doubt because the mounting costs of the operation meant that theatre seats had to be sold in quantity and at high prices in order to recoup. So they were to play in municipal theatres in Lausanne, Winterthur, Zurich, Geneva, Basle, and perhaps St. Gall, and for the Zurich Lesezirkel (reading circle). Almost until the first performance, at the Théâtre Municipal in Lausanne on 28 September, there were anxieties about the audience. Ramuz tried to sweeten the ticket prices by admitting ticket holders to the dress rehearsal on the twenty-seventh. A few boxes were sold to sponsors. But, according to Stravinsky, it was only when he himself approached the grand duchess Helen, the ex-Tsar's first cousin, who was living in exile at Ouchy, and persuaded her to support the performance, that it became "a very *mondaine* affair," with full attendance de rigueur for the local Russian emigration and the diplomatic corps in Berne.[118] The house on the twenty-eighth was duly packed. But it was hardly the public they had envisaged, and Ramuz later reported to Stravinsky that the well-to-do section of the audience had been annoyed by the piece, and he feared the same would happen in Geneva, where they were to play on 16 October.[119] The voyeuristic idea of rustic performance observed by a cultured audience of intellectuals had not yet become the stuff of music theatre. *Renard* and *Les Noces* were as yet unperformed. Stravinsky's music since *Petrushka* was generally unknown in Switzerland. The teasing simplicity of the new work's musical ingredients, its curious blend of Russian folksiness and a gallery of borrowed styles—waltzes, ragtimes, even a somewhat crumpled Lutheran chorale—put together in the thinnest, most abrasive scoring imaginable: this kind of sophisticated hypermodernism was as yet without context for a Swiss audience, to say nothing of the Swiss press, who reacted, in the main, in a spirit of well-disposed bafflement. In any case, it had been hard to follow the words, especially Pitoëff's couplets. The president of the Zurich Lesezirkel, where the work was slated for performance at the end of October, wrote to Ramuz in some alarm at its "incomprehensibility."[120]

Neither of them need have worried. Zurich did not see *The Soldier's Tale*, nor did Geneva or any of the other intended venues, and there was no second performance in Lausanne. Already, before the premiere, a killer more potent than anything the opposing armies had thrown at each other at the Somme or Verdun was attacking civilian and military, neutral and combatant alike. By the start of October, the Spanish influenza epidemic was in full swing in Switzerland as elsewhere, taking its toll of a population debilitated by four years of physical and mental privation. Stravinsky, Ramuz, Auberjonois, and Ansermet were all struck down, though in the Stravinsky household the attack cannot have been of the most severe, since the flu was commonly fatal to the already sickly. Nevertheless, Theodore remembered, "everyone had to take to their beds, and I can still see Father buried under piles of blankets, his teeth chattering, a big beret pulled down over his eyes and in a very bad temper, while my mother staggered round in her dressing-gown handing out medicines, infusions and linctuses to the whole family."[121]

According to the composer, the epidemic struck Lausanne the day after the performance, and all public halls were closed by law.[122] But the later cancellations were as much due to individual illness as to local regulation. The Geneva performance of 16 October was still on on the fifteenth, but had to be cancelled because two of the instrumentalists went sick;[123] and for the same kind of reason, Ramuz had to go alone to Zurich on the twenty-eighth and read his text to the assembled Lesezirkel.[124] By then, Ansermet was preoccupied with the debut concert of the OSR in Geneva at the end of November and refused to go to Zurich or Winterthur (on the thirtieth), so those performances could hardly have taken place even without the flu.[125] Stravinsky was predictably annoyed at what he saw as a breach of faith, since it had always been understood that the work would go on tour. Perhaps, in the end, he was mollified by Ansermet's remark that the theatres were in any case playing to empty houses because of the fear of illness.[126] Certainly the financial disaster was greater than the artistic, since the loss of performances robbed them of their chance to recoup on what had proved a heavy outlay on planning and design. The two authors probably shared less than two thousand francs for their seven months of concentrated work, while the score had at least (narrowly) avoided landing on the growing pile of Stravinsky's unperformed wartime masterpieces.

Reinhart himself underwrote the production and secured the authors against actual loss. He also, supposedly, commissioned the work itself; but if so, we do not know how much he paid.[127] Was there also a commission for the Three Pieces for Solo Clarinet which Stravinsky said that he wrote for the clarinet-playing Reinhart (in October and November) as a thank-you for his support for *The Soldier's Tale*?[128] At all events Reinhart received the manuscripts of both works, which still reside in the Stadtbibliothek at Winterthur. But the other participants were left to lick their wounds. Ramuz had hardly enough money to pay his winter fuel bill. Pitoëff had to beg an advance from Stravinsky, while assuring him that "the Germans will surrender soon and the war will end, after which the Bolsheviks will be cleaned out."[129]

Auberjonois found solace in the fact that "if my costumes were not perfect, I had the satisfaction of seeing the ensemble of my little theatre with its curtain, and some of my backcloths. I had all the material difficulties—old pieced-together cloth, lack of colors, etc. In spite of that, the result wasn't bad."[130] But his later memory was harsher:

> Thanks to Stravinsky, the work's guiding hand, the company didn't make too bad a job of it. Ramuz puffed along behind and Gagnebin copied Ramuz. Yet the faults multiplied! The roles sat heavily on the too realistic portrayals, with their hesitant buffooneries . . . not in the music, certainly, but in the Ramuz style. We should have had more dancing, with the Soldier in ballet pumps. . . . [But] the whole company had fun, and that's really what saved the piece.[131]

WHO OWES THE PIPER
CALLS THE TUNE

THE WAR ENDED. But it made little immediate difference to the Stravinskys' circumstances. Perhaps they shared the exhilaration as everyone stood in the square at Morges listening to the distant buzz of guns on the Franco-Swiss border, celebrating the Armistice.[1] But their own troubles were far from over. Travel remained difficult, and especially so for White Russians, effectively stateless since the Treaty of Brest-Litovsk in March. In any case Stravinsky's financial position remained parlous. Diaghilev's exclusivity in *Firebird* had expired in June 1918, and in *Petrushka* a year before that. But both works had gone on figuring prominently in Ballets Russes programs, in America, Spain, Portugal, and now London, without a franc paid to their composer, and it was cold comfort to him that Diaghilev was within his legal rights, since *Firebird* was in the public domain anyway, while royalties on *Petrushka*, a work copyrighted from Koussevitzky's Berlin office, were frozen for the duration of hostilities.

Stravinsky had made various efforts to find himself a contract publisher in place of Henn, who had merely acted as a paid agent and had bought nothing from him. Since 1916 he had been in correspondence with Otto Kling, of J. & W. Chester, who had acquired the London agency for all Stravinsky's Russian publishers, but was unable to exploit it, since everything was either unprotected or alien.[2] Kling managed, just as the war was ending, to get Stravinsky six hundred francs for three performances of the unpublished Three Pieces by the London Philharmonic Quartet, but only by renting them manuscript parts which Stravinsky had had copied for the purpose in Geneva. A whole year would pass before the composer drew significant money from Chester by assigning to them his published works, and actually selling them his unpublished ones. The piano score of *Ragtime*, with the famous line drawing by Picasso on its cover, was being published by Editions de la Sirène, an arty Parisian house founded in 1918 by the Swiss-born poet and novelist Blaise Cendrars with a view to publishing what Cendrars, in his first approach to Stravinsky in April 1918, had called "the authentic works of our generation."[3] Cendrars had lost an arm in the war fighting for the French, and looked, to Jean Hugo, like "some northern mariner, whaler or pirate, who had knocked about the seven seas and was full of tales of what he had seen at the four corners of the globe."[4] He was a close friend of Eugenia Errazuriz, and kept a room in her Paris apartment—an arrangement which did not prevent La Sirène from printing *Ragtime,* late in 1919, with her name misspelt in the dedication, so that the whole issue had to be instantly withdrawn. Stravinsky managed to touch Cendrars' business partners for one thousand Swiss francs for this five-minute piece. But it was hardly an association with a great future.

But if the peace made little immediate difference to Stravinsky's income, it soon began to play havoc with his expenditure. Just over a week after the Armistice there arrived at the Hotel Bayerische Hof in Lindau, on Lake Constance, one of those straggling Russian families that were to become a familiar sight in postrevolutionary Europe: the large, bearded patriarch with his handsome wife, well dressed, both of them, in a travel-weary kind of way; their pretty fifteen-year-old daughter and her sickly, retarded brother of eleven, together with the patriarch's widowed mother and the inevitable *nyanya,* all surrounded by the usual suitcases, hatboxes, baskets, porte-plaids, and the rest of the migrant paraphernalia of the Russian aristocracy. These were the Belyankins, newly arrived from Odessa, where they had spent the last three years since being forced by the invading Austro-German armies to abandon Ustilug and even the family apartment in Kiev for Poltava in the East, before seeking permanent escape by way of the Black Sea. They arrived stateless and without prospects, unable even to enter Switzerland for lack of papers and future means of subsistence. To the Ukrainian Legation in Berne, such arrivals at such a time were a nuisance or worse, and in the end Igor had to go to the Swiss capital in mid-December and take personal responsibility for his in-laws, depositing a bond in gold francs, and agreeing to put them up at his home in Morges.[5]

It was to be no short-lived arrangement. The Belyankins stayed at the Maison Bornand until the Stravinskys themselves left it a year and a half later, when the entire extended family emigrated with one accord to France. Ansermet's little daughter, Anne, would visit Morges with her father and be dazzled by the sprawling household with its "cousins and uncles who, curiously, kissed you on the mouth" and the "large, comfortable table spread with unexpected dishes and surrounded by grown-ups."[6] Grigory Belyankin, a marine architect by training and a practical landowner by inclination and aptitude, was hardly in his element in a small-town apartment in Switzerland, and he probably remained unemployed for as long as they stayed there. His brother-in-law endured the situation with surprising good grace considering his own straitened circumstances. No doubt he felt grateful to Grigory for having been such a conscientious caretaker at Ustilug. But he was also sincerely fond of this bluff ex-sailor and his wife, Igor's cousin as well as Katya's sister, and seems to have supported them out of genuine affection and respect for the ties of blood. His own mother was still trapped in Petrograd; his brother Yury and his wife and daughters were heaven knew where; the other Nosenkos and Yelachiches might be scattered or scattering to the four corners of the globe. But here at least, in this little Vaudois town, they could re-create a distillation of the old Russia, an island of family warmth and solidarity in the ocean of war and revolution and social disintegration. It was something which Igor had always craved, something he needed for his work, and something to which he would go on returning, no matter what the lures of fame and the world, until the tide at last broke over the island and this particular corner of old Russia sank finally into lamented, irretrievable oblivion.

Meanwhile, he needed desperately to earn money for the island economy. While the war lasted he had had, in effect, to improvise. He had eventually found a buyer for the full score of *The Firebird*, in the shape of Jean Bartholoni, a Genevan oil millionaire, composer, and grandson of the founder of the Geneva Conservatoire, who some time in late 1917 or 1918 paid him eight thousand francs for the manuscript.[7] He had come by individual payments or loans, from Artur Rubinstein, Misia Edwards, Thomas Beecham, the princesse de Polignac, as well as the monthly stipend from Mme Errazuriz.[8] But of any regular, dependable income from his music there remained no sign. One recourse might be to convert existing scores from which he was earning nothing into more practical works for concert use. *The Soldier's Tale* was a particularly sore point. He and Ramuz had worked hard on it for months only to see the performance run destroyed by epidemic. Yet the music was essentially distinct from the play. So it was logical to extract a concert suite and arrange it for a simplified ensemble, featuring the crucial violin with piano and, by way of variety, clarinet—unless he added that instrument in the hope of a commission from Reinhart.[9]

The next idea was for a new concert suite from *The Firebird*. Here the issue was not simply technical feasibility, since even for orchestras which could muster the quadruple woodwind and large percussion and string sections called for by the existing suite, the performance material was out of reach with Jurgenson in Moscow and (though Stravinsky did not yet know this) with Jurgenson's Leipzig agent, Robert Forberg. What infuriated Stravinsky was that thanks to Diaghilev's (unpaid-for) exclusivity, the political situation, and the punitive copyright laws, he could earn nothing from what was by far his most popular work. But if he made a new suite, out of different movements and for a reduced orchestra, it could be published as a new work in a Berne Convention country like Britain, and if necessary defended in law on the grounds that property rights no longer existed in Russia after 1917. In this spirit he started negotiations with Kling, who was understandably wary of the situation, insisted that the composer indemnify him against future claims, and even took counsel's opinion on Stravinsky's copyright status as a Russian émigré. Nevertheless, Kling did in due course publish the new suite, unaware that Jurgenson had shrewdly assigned rights in the work to Forberg. The stage was set for the first of many legal and moral bloodlettings over the rights to Stravinsky's early ballets.

He himself usually emerged badly from these lawsuits in the material sense, and he has been judged severely for them by posterity in the moral sense. But few have taken the trouble to understand his actual circumstances, or the full extent of his vulnerability—and particularly his *sense* of vulnerability—in the Europe of his day. A Russian artist, it seemed, had no rights, no protection, effectively did not exist except as a producer of glittering objects for the delectation and profit of others. To this day, artists who negotiate contracts or haggle over percentages are routinely regarded as mercenary even by those whose business it is to make money out of their work. But Stravinsky not only had no control over his most successful compositions; he was at the same time regarded as a natural refuge by fellow exiles—family and others—who took it for granted that he was raking in millions and living in the lap of luxury in his Lake Geneva hideaway. Even Robert Craft, with the entire Stravinsky archive at his disposal, made the mistake of assuming that the composer had far greater earning power in 1918 than he was prepared to admit.[10] That Stravinsky had been "careful" about money even before the war cannot be denied; it was a legacy of his father's meticulous bookkeeping and the requirement Fyodor placed on his children to account rigorously for every kopek. But it was only in the terrible insecurity and instability of 1917–18, when Igor had growing dependants and little or no dependable income, that he developed that aggressive and intransigent manner which Craft found so shocking in his business correspondence of the twenties and thirties.[11] The letters to Kling are the first (though not the worst) of the kind: severe, demanding, candidly price-conscious, as if every advance, every percentage, might be the last the composer would ever earn, and worse, as if every counterproposal concealed a trap that must be either exposed or evaded. It was a style which could easily become a habit. But it was born genuinely of desperate worry.

Stravinsky later told Kling that he had worked on the new *Firebird* Suite for six months, from October 1918 to March 1919.[12] But this was a legal fiction to support his claim that it was technically a new work. As late as Christmas 1918, the full score was not even in his possession, having been sold to Bartholoni and lodged with the Conservatoire library, from where— Ansermet told him—it had since been borrowed by Vasily Kibalchich.[13] In any case the reduced version of the Berceuse and finale already existed (the Berceuse had been conducted by Florent Schmitt in Bordeaux as long ago as February 1914). The remaining movements were reorchestrated in February and March 1919, in time for Ansermet's Geneva concert with the OSR on 12 April, when the whole suite had its first performance.[14]

Meanwhile, just after Christmas, Stravinsky had embarked on yet another series of Russian songs with piano, experimental pieces which in fact show traces of having been written with cimbalom accompaniment in mind. He had heard and met a gifted Croat soprano called Maja Strozzi-Pecic, and wrote the songs at her request. Her husband, Béla Pecic, appeared with the composer in a performance of the Easy Pieces for piano duet in Lausanne on 5 March. But soon afterwards, the Pecics left Switzerland, and Maja—though the songs are dedicated to her—seems never to have sung them.

These curious and arresting pieces are, among other things, evidence that Stravinsky was again brooding on *Les Noces,* just as the earlier bursts of Russian song had tended to coincide with work on that score. In particular, the cimbalom quality in the accompaniment—a concentration on line, glissando, and repeated-note figures—seems to hint at a new idea for the ballet's instrumentation, even though the first surviving reference to the new version (with its scoring for two cimbaloms, pianola, harmonium, and percussion) came only in June.[15] But the retreat into Russianism, after *The Soldier's Tale* and in the midst of work on *The Firebird,* was not entirely a positive sign, however fascinating the product. Rather it is evidence of a (for Stravinsky) rare uncertainty in creative aim. The sketchbooks of these months are a glorious muddle of random ideas, a medley of inspirations with little consistency of plan and, as it turned out, many eventual destinations. For instance, there are sketches for two of the Russian songs, "The Drake" and "Sektantskaya," alongside fragments clearly identifiable with the Symphonies of Wind Instruments, a work almost certainly not yet envisaged as such. Not far away are notations that belong to the *Piano Rag Music,* a piece Stravinsky had been planning since March 1918 in response to the donation from Artur Rubinstein, but which he finally wrote up only in June 1919. In another book, again mixed up with *Piano Rag* material, are more ideas that went variously into the wind symphonies and the Concertino for string quartet, some of them scored for harmonium—a fact which again links them to *Les Noces.*

Stravinsky probably tinkered with the ballet during April and May. He had a harmonium in his study, and jotted down registrations on the back of a copy of a telegram sent to Ansermet on 11 May. At this stage, there was no question of a string quartet, the commission for which came only in August, and it was surely *Les Noces* that still dominated his thoughts. But one can readily imagine the anxiety with which he contemplated his "work in progress" as spring faded into summer and still there appeared no prospect of any settled livelihood for himself and his seemingly endless family of the helpless and the infirm. As if an epileptic nephew and a consumptive wife were not enough, his daughter Mika continued to show an alarming tendency towards the same condition as her mother, and in February she had fallen quite seriously ill.[16] But what could he, the provider, offer for their future support? A piano piece in return for money long since spent; a ballet suite that might prove legally unsalable; and a new-old ballet which, as Diaghilev grumbled to Ansermet, "leaves idle the musicians I've got, and asks me for only four, one of whom, however, I have to get from Honolulu, another from Budapest, and the others from God knows where."[17]

By this time Kling was negotiating London performances of Stravinsky's music (including a production of *The Nightingale* by Beecham), but he still fought shy of undertaking to publish it, partly, he said, because there were no music engravers available.[18] There was also the nagging difficulty over rights, since Stravinsky could hardly assign to Chester rights he himself did not own. Eventually Kling took over all the works Henn had published during the war (with the help of a donation from Bartholoni, since Henn was still owed money). But not till the end of the year was there a proper contract for the unpublished works, including *The Soldier's Tale* and *Les Noces*. Meanwhile, Stravinsky had tracked Struve down in Copenhagen, and wrote him a wildly optimistic letter about new works and new honoraria, to which Struve replied that he was himself as indigent as the composer and that RMV, nationalized in Moscow, was for the time being practically defunct abroad.[19]

All this generated a lot of correspondence but little if any cash. Struve was off to New York to explore possibilities there. But in June he wrote glumly that Russians had little protection for their work in the United States—another Berne nonsignatory—and that Stravinsky's only hope from that source was to cross the Atlantic himself and write film music, a suggestion Stravinsky seems to have ignored.[20] He had his own opinion of the rapacity of American impresarios. He had been infuriated by a production of *Petrushka* at the New York Metropolitan in December 1918, conducted by Monteux and with choreography by the former Diaghilev dancer Adolph Bolm. Needless to say, he would not be receiving any royalties. In a rage of embittered frustration he fired off a letter to Otto Kahn, the chairman of the Met, questioning Kahn's moral right to present his work without payment while he, the composer, was unable to feed his children. However, the letter was sent, not direct, but via an unknown American acquaintance (possibly Mrs. Daniel Gregory Mason), to whom Stravinsky relieved his feelings with even greater warmth. "Writing to you as a *true* American," he confided:

We in Russia also have our Trotskys (Braunsteins), and I myself should be highly annoyed if anyone were to take them for authentic Russians. . . . I don't go on about the décors and costumes which I discovered in *Vogue,* and whose Judeo-boche taste can't be denied to be contrary to my intentions and to my personal tastes. I suppose that the rest of the show, including the dances (M. Bolm is a Jew), displays the same influences.[21]

As for Kahn, his response was unexpected. Claiming that he had not previously known Stravinsky's address, he sent him 1,245 francs for the five performances. Then, being (as Stravinsky remarked cynically to Ansermet) an astute Jew, "he placed himself at the head of a committee which had been formed to come to my assistance."[22] In fact, the composer's dire circumstances had already been reported in America, and a support committee set up under the patronage of various philanthropic New York ladies, including Mrs. Mason and Mrs. Marie Brooks. Between May and September, Stravinsky received some fifteen thousand francs from this committee, a sum which relieved him of immediate anxieties during that period. He also had an offer from Maurice Guest, the manager of the Century Theater in New York, to go at Guest's expense and write a work for him there. Later Struve came close to negotiating a highly paid U.S. concert tour for him. But Stravinsky, heavily committed (as he felt) in Europe and candidly nervous of the journey, made difficulties and then apparently backed off altogether. A tense exchange before Christmas over his plan to sell the manuscript of *The Rite of Spring* to a New York dealer, over the head of its publisher and (therefore) owner, is his last surviving direct communication with this most sympathetic of his early publishing managers.[23] Less than a year later, Struve was killed in an accident in a Paris lift.

Stravinsky's own hopes of an improvement in his finances were still firmly fixed on the elusive Diaghilev. The two had not met since parting at Aigle station in July 1917 after agreeing on a contract worth, in theory at least, twenty-seven thousand francs to the hard-pressed composer, though the fact that twenty thousand of them were for a two-year exclusivity in *Les Noces*—a work which still did not exist in a performable state—may partly explain why Stravinsky seems to have left Diaghilev in peace on that subject. The first sign that he meant to go back on the warpath came in mid-April 1919 in a letter to Misia Edwards requesting a loan and grumbling about Diaghilev's protracted silence.[24] Stravinsky knew, of course, that the Ballets Russes had been trapped in Spain and Portugal for nearly a year after returning from their South American tour in the autumn of 1917. But he also knew that since then they had been having a more productive winter season in London; and in any case he was now composing *Les Noces*

again. Only a week or two earlier he had described it to Struve as "a cantata, or oratorio, or what have you, with dance, for four soloists, choir, and
an ensemble that I am in too much of a hurry to describe."[25] So it was natural that his thoughts should fly back to that Diablerets contract; and perhaps it was also natural that he should commission Ansermet, who was on
his way to London to conduct Diaghilev's spring season at the Alhambra,
as his negotiator, debt collector, and general go-between with the errant
impresario.

The Alhambra season opened on 30 April, with a program that included
Petrushka. The next day Ansermet wired that Diaghilev had promised to
pay the royalty arrears and also an advance on *Les Noces*.[26] He seemed well
off, Ansermet thought, after a successful winter, though "much aged and
shrunken in every dimension"; and he was full of plans for an autumn season in Paris, with the premiere of *Les Noces* and perhaps even *The Soldier's
Tale*—"if only one could do without Ramuz," he had tactlessly mused to
the Swiss novelist's closest friend.[27] But any thought that Diaghilev might
be coming to heel was soon dashed by Ansermet's next letter. Diaghilev
was now grumbling about the choir in *Les Noces* and claiming that in any
case the exclusivity payment had been meant to include *Liturgie* as well. As
for the existing ballets, he was again retreating behind copyright law,
under which no royalties were owed, while offering, nevertheless, to make
ex gratia payments for friendship's sake.[28] In a fury of righteous indignation, Stravinsky rejected all question of accepting as a gift what he
regarded as his due, and instead sent Ansermet a detailed account of the
contractual position—a document which, incidentally, accords with what
we know from earlier correspondence. Diaghilev's so-called "moral solidarity," he complained,

> has no great value, when you think of the monstrosity of asserting
> that "since *Petrushka* was published in Germany and *Firebird* in Rus-
> sia" he had the right to pay nothing, but that since after all he is good
> and kind he would pay me, for these two works which he has already
> performed a *great* number of times, a *very small* sum of money. . . . I
> was physically ill when I learnt all this, not at the actual recourse to
> "legal" rights, but at the fact of alluding to those rights (however
> imaginary) at a time when a friend is in a very difficult position.
> Strange idea of friendship![29]

In Morges, Ramuz had to endure what he called "one or two fairly tragic
afternoons" with Igor on the subject.[30] It grated particularly that Diaghilev
was now taking cover behind a legality which he himself had never
observed. For years he had failed to make rental payments to Jurgenson
and RMV for precisely the works which he now claimed entitlement to

perform without payment. Yet he could not have gone on performing them at all if Stravinsky had not sold him an exclusivity, over his publishers' heads and at least partly on the grounds that he, Diaghilev, was the only significant promoter of Russian music abroad. And Stravinsky had been perfectly right in this. Had he denied Diaghilev his exclusivities and assigned all rights to his publishers, he would now be left without even his virtuous anger, since—with or without performances—no royalties would have been payable, or presumably paid, for wartime rights. That was why he continued to negotiate with Diaghilev over *Les Noces,* and even give him first refusal on it, "out of moral solidarity," as he told Ansermet, only half-sarcastically (since of course he still had hopes of the twenty thousand francs).[31] He knew perfectly well that Diaghilev was desperate to stage *Les Noces.* Even *The Song of the Nightingale,* which was already paid for and which Diaghilev was thinking of putting on with designs by Matisse, was hardly on the same level of interest. And most of his other projects were mere "*amusettes:* Rossini-Derain or Pergolesi-Picasso salads," as Ansermet himself so aptly described them a few days after the Alhambra premiere of Massine's Rossini ballet, *La Boutique fantasque,* arranged by Respighi and designed by Derain.[32] Even *The Soldier's Tale,* for all Diaghilev's interest in it, was not really his sort of piece: it was too literary, and too intimate for the kind of season he was planning for the Apollo in Paris. "He would turn it upside down," Ansermet told Ramuz—meaning, of course, get rid of the text.[33] It was *Les Noces* that he needed in order to recapture his Parisian stardom, however much he might grumble about the chorus or the bizarre new instrumentation. But Stravinsky would withhold this new masterpiece until Diaghilev settled his debts, as he told Misia, knowing that she too desired *Les Noces* more than anything else and that her influence could well be decisive.[34]

Stravinsky was surely right to resent Diaghilev's attitude. And yet the impresario was not without genuine financial anxieties of his own. "Before the war," he explained to Ansermet,

> I could lose 120,000 francs a season in London. I knew I would always find resources in Russia. Some merchant would be ennobled, and I would get the consideration, out of which I could create art. Now there are no Excellencies or Grand Dukes left; a year ago I had debts of a million; London has saved me; but I'm not rich; I've only been able to pay my debts; and as I've now only myself to count on, if I want to survive I must be careful.[35]

He knew from firsthand reports that Russia was, for the time being at least, finished as a source of succor. Albert Coates, a Petersburg-born

Englishman who had been chief conductor at the Mariyinsky throughout the war years and had conducted the Russian premiere of *The Nightingale* in May 1918, had arrived in London with terrible news of postwar conditions in Petrograd. ("He told me," Ansermet reported to Stravinsky, "that he left your mother in good health, only anxious at the lack of money.")[36] Soon afterwards, a letter of positively devastating import reached Diaghilev, via Bakst, from Walter Nouvel, who had been forced to abandon his own mother in Petrograd and flee to Helsingfors to avoid being interned as a Finnish citizen. The last winter in the Russian capital had been a nightmare. Benois had had to sell all his pictures to survive at all, but now faced ruin and starvation, since there were no longer any buyers. Nurok had died, after spending the whole winter bedridden. Bakst's wife, and the other Botkine sisters, were living in indigence in Moscow.[37] Diaghilev had told Ansermet that he would probably soon transfer the Ballets Russes to a syndicate and either stay on as director or take over a theatre in Russia. But this was obviously at least half fantasy. "My impression," Ansermet told Stravinsky, "is that he is in the process of making himself a small fortune to secure his own future."[38] And who could blame him? In some ways, Diaghilev's future was blacker than anyone else's, since his very livelihood only began with the generosity of people who, for the most part, no longer had money to give.

In the end it was almost certainly Misia who found the way out of this impasse. She herself had arrived in London towards the end of June with Mme Errazuriz, and there was a tense interview with Ansermet, who convinced them that Diaghilev's account of the rights situation was mendacious. Misia had insisted that the Ballets Russes' success in Paris depended on new work of greater substance than *La Boutique fantasque;* she wanted *Les Noces* and a revival of *The Rite of Spring*.[39] Soon afterwards, Diaghilev himself had gone off to Paris. But by 12 July he was back in London, talking about a Paris season at the Opéra or the smaller Gheusi vaudeville theatre, asking after *The Soldier's Tale,* and grumbling promisingly about the choir and orchestration of *Les Noces.* When Ansermet raised the question of money, he simply said, "Oh! That's understood, Misia spoke to me about it, and I'm going to settle it as quickly as possible." And when Massine protested against the text in *The Soldier's Tale,* Diaghilev now took the line that "Stravinsky is a man who knows what he's doing, and if we take his work we must take it as it is."[40] These reports were quickly followed by a firm cash offer of ten thousand francs a year for nonexclusive rights in the two early ballets, an offer Stravinsky accepted after haggling briefly over the terms of the agreement. Diaghilev wanted an April start (to include the London season just ending); Stravinsky wanted August, to keep the London rights separate. Stravinsky wanted a three-year term, but

Diaghilev—"very depressed and tired, and weeping a good deal"—had told Ansermet frankly that he doubted whether the Ballets Russes would last more than another year. This time Stravinsky had to give way. His financial situation had improved, thanks to the American funds, and in any case there was a real danger that if he did not accept, Diaghilev would go to court, lose, and be forced to pay arrears on *Petrushka*, none of which, however, would ever reach Stravinsky himself, thanks to the regulations on payments to aliens, which stayed in force until late July 1919. On the other hand, if he accepted, there could then be discussions on *Les Noces*, *The Song of the Nightingale*, possibly *The Rite of Spring*, *The Soldier's Tale*, even *Renard*, to say nothing of new work.

By the start of August, he and Ramuz were busy revising *The Soldier's Tale*, shortening the text and redistributing the speech, music, and dance, specifically with a view to production in Paris, and clearly with Diaghilev's preferences in mind.[41] The new version of *Les Noces* was already half finished. The composer was at first skeptical about staging it at the Opéra. He saw it as a divertissement rather than a ballet, and envisaged not only the dancers but also the choir, instruments, and conductor all together on the stage, so that it was absurd to think of sets, which would not represent anything but merely be there for the sake of decoration.[42] But two weeks later Ansermet was able to reassure Diaghilev that Stravinsky had come round to the Opéra idea, partly thanks to the influence of Ravel, who was on a visit to Geneva, and who was himself writing for the Opéra what Ansermet called a "ballet nègre" (presumably in fact *La Valse*).[43] What Stravinsky feared, Ansermet explained, was a folkloristic setting in Goncharova's angular neonationalist style. The new instrumentation suggested a more mechanistic, posthumanist context for the determinist ritual of the wedding itself—a context which would be actually visible on the stage. How far the latest bizarre instrumentation had been suggested or at least accompanied by the idea that these weird contraptions—the harmonium, pianola, cimbaloms, and assorted drums and bells—would form part of the set, is difficult to decide. In any case the concept was never destined to be put to the test. Stravinsky persevered with the pianola idea, but in the end yielded to the practical difficulties they presented and abandoned the whole idea. As for the score, he seems to have got no farther than the second tableau, which was already more or less complete by early August 1919.[44]

Meanwhile, the three-month Alhambra season had ended on 30 July; Ansermet returned to Geneva, and Diaghilev set off with Massine for Venice, rather studiously avoiding Morges on the way. Instead it was Ansermet who handed the composer Diaghilev's check, through the window of a train at Morges station on 8 August. Yet curiously, amid all the bitterness and rage, the two great prizefighters could not wait to see each other again. Diaghilev seems to have pressed Stravinsky to join him in Venice; Stravinsky may first have responded rather sharply, but then, after a ticking off from Ansermet, wired in more measured terms that he could not get a passport but hoped Diaghilev would visit him in Switzerland.[45] In the end it would be Paris after all. "We have urgent matters to discuss," Diaghilev cabled on the twenty-eighth. Craft suggests that this refers to the deal over the early ballets; but that was the one and only issue that had actually been settled already, and obviously what Diaghilev in fact wanted to talk about was new ballets for his Paris season—dear old *Les Noces* and the rest, and he hoped to persuade Igor to compose a completely new work he had in mind.

As Stravinsky travelled to Paris—for the first time in nearly three years—at the end of the first week in September, he may again have reflected somewhat ruefully on the state of his current work.[46] Except for the single *Soldier's Tale* performance, he had had no substantial premiere since *The Nightingale* in May 1914. Apart from *Renard,* a whole drawerful of smaller pieces still awaited performance, many of them radically new in style. *Les Noces,* on the other hand, was still incomplete. Otherwise, all he had to show for the year's work was a string of arrangements, a three-minute piano solo (the *Piano Rag Music,* completed at the end of June), a few songs, and some rather indeterminate sketches. Naturally there was curiosity about his work. Both the Chicago Opera and the New York Metropolitan had expressed interest in *Les Noces;* Hamilton Harty wanted *The Song of the Nightingale* for the Hallé in Manchester; and Arnold Schoenberg had written from Vienna asking for a new piece for his Society for Private Performance.[47] But in the event none of this opened up new work. The one productive approach had come in August from Alfred Pochon, offering Stravinsky five hundred dollars for a new string quartet.[48] The commission had given him an idea of how he might use up some of his unused sketches from the spring and early summer. One batch of these, written probably in July while he was still working on *Les Noces,* had made prominent play with a harmonium. But that instrument now began to give way to strings, not always in the conventional quartet arrangement.[49] In fact so much was sketched for strings that it looks as if Stravinsky may have intended a much bigger work than the brief Concertino which he eventually hatched a year or so later. But not for several months did he glimpse the more brilliant and radical score for wind instruments to which the rest of these ideas would lead.

Meanwhile, he was in a receptive frame of mind for Diaghilev's idea that he should compose the music for a ballet devised by Massine round the Neapolitan commedia dell'arte character Pulcinella. Diaghilev had decided that the right music for this subject was by Pergolesi, for which he needed an arranger, orchestrator, and general enabler—very much as

Tommasini had been for Scarlatti in *The Good-Humored Ladies* and Respighi for Rossini in *La Boutique fantasque*. Unsurprisingly, he had not at once thought of Stravinsky for this essentially menial task. Back in May, when the project had first been mooted, he had approached Falla. But Falla was spending the summer in Madrid with his shutters closed, working away on a three-act operetta based on themes by Chopin, and he could not be tempted even by the prospect of working with his fellow Andalusian Picasso.[50] So Diaghilev seems to have made up his mind to use the idea as a device for winning Stravinsky back as a collaborator, in spite of their recent contractual squabbles, until such time as the next masterpiece, *Les Noces,* should be firmly ready for production. "I know you are much taken with your Alpine colleagues," he remarked sardonically to Stravinsky when they met in Paris, "but I have an idea that I think will amuse you more than anything they can propose."[51]

Perhaps more remarkable than the offer was its acceptance. Stravinsky was no longer in the habit of taking on other people's projects; and *Pulcinella* was a concept which, whatever he may have said later, came to him straight off the peg. The actual subject had been inspired by Massine's researches into the commedia dell'arte in the Royal Palace Library in Naples, probably in 1916 and 1917, while the choreography would be based on notations in a set of seventeenth- and eighteenth-century dance manuals which he had bought at a Paris auction in 1916. As for the Pergolesi connection, that was probably Diaghilev's own idea. He and Massine had visited the Naples Conservatory and selected what Massine called "fifteen hitherto unpublished instrumental pieces" from "the original Pergolesi manuscripts there."[52] A few months after receiving the commission, Stravinsky told a Paris reporter that *he* and Diaghilev had ransacked the libraries of Italy for Pergolesi material.[53] But that was pure fantasy. Until September there had never been any suggestion of Pergolesi-Stravinsky. "When he said that the composer was Pergolesi," Stravinsky recorded of the Paris meeting with Diaghilev, "I thought he must be deranged. I knew Pergolesi only by the *Stabat Mater* and *La Serva padrona,* and though I had just [sic] seen a production of the latter in Barcelona, Diaghilev knew I wasn't in the least excited by it."[54] He agreed, all the same, to look at the material Diaghilev handed him—material consisting of manuscript copies which Diaghilev had had made or acquired, in Naples and London, of music by no means all of which was in fact by Pergolesi.[55] "I looked," he says, "and I fell in love." Within a week he had arranged the Tarantella, working directly onto the copyist's manuscript, and by the time he returned to Morges on the sixteenth the ballet had been agreed on in principle and Picasso had made the little promissory drawing of Pierrot and Harlequin which Stravinsky reproduced in his autobiography.[56]

He was in Paris for a fortnight, catching up on past life but also enjoying his first taste of postwar Parisian gaiety, already subtly different from its aristocratic prewar equivalent. The musical atmosphere, too, had changed. Debussy was dead, and the whole world of so-called impressionism, the sumptuous neoromantic musical canvases of *Daphnis and Chloe*, *The Nightingale*, Schmitt's *Salomé*, and the effete Orientalism of Delage's little pavilion and Misia Edwards's Chinese salon, must now have seemed almost unimaginably remote. Stravinsky did not even look Schmitt or Ravel up.[57] But he went and played his new *Piano Rag Music* in the Palais-Royal apartment of the painter Jean Hugo, to an audience that included Diaghilev, Massine, and Picasso, but also two of Cocteau's young protégés, Georges Auric and Francis Poulenc, both of whom he was meeting for the first time.[58] According to Hugo, Stravinsky was drunk by the time he sat down at the keyboard; but what effect this had on his rendition of the notoriously awkward *Piano Rag* is, naturally enough, not recorded.

Like cartoon Russians, Stravinsky and Diaghilev could hug and get drunk together by night and still wrangle bitterly over money and contracts by day. The main bone of contention was now *Les Noces*. Diaghilev had put off any idea of presenting it in his coming winter season in Paris and was instead planning a London premiere the following autumn; and he now wanted a three-year exclusivity starting then. But Stravinsky was determined to hold him to the May starting date they had evidently agreed on in Paris, and when Diaghilev sent a four-thousand-franc advance on the assumption of a postponement, Stravinsky (who had in any case gone off the three-year idea, as he was hoping to sell the ballet to America) stuck his nose in the air and simply refused to accept it.[59] But all this was mere shadowboxing anyway, since *Les Noces* still did not exist in a performable state, and its composer was now hard at work on something else. *Pulcinella*, which had started out as an arrangement worked onto a set of copyists' manuscripts, was rapidly becoming a composition in its own right, and when Diaghilev tried through Kling to get Stravinsky to send his score page by page ("so that he could make changes to it if he felt the need," as Kling put it), Stravinsky answered in his loftiest I'm-no-Tommasini mode that "Diaghilev gave me all the necessary indications in Paris. If he's made changes since then, it's too late, as my work on Pergolesi's music is organic—I'm rewriting each piece and making a whole through timbre and modulation (tonality)."[60] Diaghilev, of course, had assumed that the work would become his property once Stravinsky had finished with it, which is probably the real reason why "he went about for a long time with a look that suggested The Offended Eighteenth Century" after the work was finished.[61] The type of score *Pulcinella* had turned out to be had become another item in their contractual quarrel.

Organic or not, *Pulcinella* was having to be put together in somewhat piecemeal fashion, amid a series of interruptions—some agreeable, some less so. On 8 November, the composer probably took part in a concert of his works in the Lausanne Conservatoire, playing the eight Easy Pieces with the Spanish pianist José Iturbi, who had settled in Geneva and was teaching at the conservatory there. Iturbi also gave the public premiere of the *Piano Rag Music* and—with José Porta and Edmond Allegra—the trio suite from *The Soldier's Tale;* Allegra played the Three Pieces for Solo Clarinet; and Tatyana Tatyanova sang the *Pribaoutki* and the *Berceuses du chat,* with piano accompaniment by Iturbi.[62] At least, Stravinsky's participation in this concert was announced. But if he did take part, it may well have been with a migraine which he said he had had for a week when he wrote to Kling on the fourteenth.[63] Moreover, Katya was ill again too. She spent more than a fortnight in a Lausanne clinic in mid-November, and by his own admission her absence made Igor tense and irritable. Plans for a Brussels production of *The Soldier's Tale* had just fallen through, supposedly because of Stravinsky's and Ramuz's exorbitant cash demands—a charge against which the composer tetchily defended himself with the observation that "I too always work at music with an artistic aim, but no one can blame me for wanting this work to earn me my living."[64] And it was true that very little of the four thousand or so francs for the Brussels production was destined to end up in his pocket. Nevertheless, Otto Kling, who was already trying to balance the possible commercial advantage of expensively purchasing the new *Firebird* Suite against the likelihood that Stravinsky had no business selling it to him,[65] and who was on the brink of signing an exclusive contract with the composer for a total down payment of sixty-seven thousand francs,[66] and who probably knew, moreover, that Stravinsky was about to sign a contract with Diaghilev for a three-year exclusivity in *Pulcinella* (a glorified set of arrangements) and *Les Noces* (an apparently unperformable ballet) for a further twenty-five thousand francs on top of the ten thousand a year he was already getting for *Firebird* and *Petrushka,*[67] must have found it a little hard to swallow in practice what was no doubt a blameless sentiment in theory. And perhaps that was why, when the Brussels organizers wrote Stravinsky a sharp letter care of Kling, the publisher—to Stravinsky's intense indignation—sent it on without comment, as if endorsing its tone.[68]

Then, on 6 December, came the concert premiere of *The Song of the Nightingale* in one of Ansermet's subscription concerts with the Suisse Romande in Geneva—Stravinsky's first major orchestral premiere since the first night of *The Nightingale* itself, five and a half years before. It was followed four days later by a repeat performance in Lausanne. Ansermet took trouble over what was a symbolically important event for him as well. He allocated six full rehearsals to the twenty-minute score, even though the program also included Berlioz's long and difficult *Symphonie fantas-tique;* and Stravinsky, who attended several if not all of them, seems to have been pleased with the result. "Ansermet worked wonders," he told Kling. But the public reaction was by no means so unambiguous. "Big tumult in the Victoria Hall after the performance," he reported, "with booing and catcalls (pre-planned, unfortunately) on the one hand, warm applause and counter-protests on the other."[69] There were whistles and shouts of "dada," and the press reviews were elaborately and expansively hostile, per-haps partly—as Craft suggests—because *The Rite of Spring* had not yet been heard in Switzerland, and the audience was unprepared for the ener-getic modernism of a symphonic poem entirely based on the post-*Rite* sections of the original opera.[70] But the connection with dada—an alien movement that had nevertheless been born in Switzerland—suggests also a political impulse, in the form of a postwar reaction against foreign revo-lution on the part of the neutral and (as the *Cahiers vaudois* would have said) inward-looking Genevois. After all, *The Soldier's Tale* had played in Lausanne—admittedly to a more cosmopolitan audience—without protest. And *The Song of the Nightingale,* too, seems to have pleased Lausanne at least marginally better than Geneva.[71] Perhaps it was a factor that Stravin-sky had associated himself with a dada congress which Tristan Tzara had organized in Geneva at the time of the OSR concert, and had even pre-sented a talk in which he explained "with ceremonious gestures that the dada musician has to assume the posture of a Moravian wet nurse in the pursuit of her trade and modify the resulting notes with the greatest possi-ble use of street noises."[72]

Worn out by all this activity and by Katya's illness, Igor took her off at the end of December for a few days' holiday in Locarno before hurrying back to Morges and his piecework on *Pulcinella.* But within three weeks or so he was on the way back to Paris for rehearsals of the Ballets Russes pro-duction of *The Song of the Nightingale,* which was at last reaching the stage at the Opéra on 2 February. Much had changed since Depero had planned his dehumanized, geometric staging in Rome three years before. The futurist idea had been replaced by a porcelain modernism designed by Matisse, with clear, brilliant colors and an air of what Charles Tenroc described unkindly as "snob-funereal export chinoiserie."[73] Massine felt that the ballet was "one of my most successful efforts at collaboration with a designer."[74] And yet, as a whole, it was not a success, perhaps because Massine "had followed the principle of imposing a rhythm on the dance steps that was independent of the musical rhythm," with the result that "although the company had worked desperately hard for weeks, the ballet gave the impression of having been poorly rehearsed."[75]

Stravinsky's music, nevertheless, pleased the connoisseurs, pleased those who remembered the original opera with nostalgia, and displeased only conservative critics who had had no opportunity to vent their spleen on the great iconoclast during almost six long years of war and its aftermath. Tenroc pronounced anathema in the *Courrier musical* on this "arthritic music [which] is the negation of dance, and drives it to suicide."[76] But Roland-Manuel, the critic of *L'Eclair*, remembered *The Nightingale* as "without doubt M. Stravinsky's most accomplished work to date" and praised the revision for its clarity and anti-impressionism,[77] while for Louis Laloy—one of the earliest prophets of *The Rite of Spring*, and a profound admirer, too, of *The Nightingale*—the revised score had "achieved the solidity of a symphony."[78] Laloy, indeed, praised music, design, and choreography almost without reserve. But for all that, the work had only a handful of performances, and was then not revived until 1925, by which time everyone had forgotten Massine's choreography and the ballet had to be restaged by Balanchine.

Diaghilev must nevertheless have been quietly relieved to have reestablished working contact with Stravinsky, and on the very stage of their inaugural triumph a decade before. He now wanted to set up a series of new Stravinsky ballets—a kind of postwar retrospective, which would include not only *Pulcinella* and *Les Noces,* but also *The Soldier's Tale* and the long-awaited revival of *The Rite of Spring. Pulcinella* itself was well in hand. Picasso had done a series of drawings at the start of February, presumably in the light of discussions with Diaghilev and Stravinsky, which may or may not have included the famous scene in which Diaghilev threw Picasso's initial "Offenbach period" drawings on the floor and stamped on them before storming out of the room.[79] It was now only a matter of Stravinsky completing the score when he went back to Morges.

The other projects, however, were less secure. Whatever his supposed jealousy of the composer's Alpine colleagues, Diaghilev seems to have genuinely wanted to stage *The Soldier's Tale;* no contract was ever signed, but one certainly existed as late as March 1920,[80] and the subject must have been on the agenda in Paris. One of the main bones of contention was Ramuz's collaboration. Whatever Misia may have persuaded him to tell Massine, Diaghilev certainly had little interest in the text as such, but wanted a dance work based on the original story, with Stravinsky's music, designs by Picasso, and as little actual Ramuz as he could get away with. Alas for any such ballet (and for all the built-in "suite" character),[81] Stravinsky had omitted to establish clearly with Ramuz an entitlement to excerpt his music and reuse it in whatever way he might choose, while Ramuz himself was understandably reluctant to allow his literary contribution to be discarded and his story and title exploited in the theatre in ways over which he had no control. So when Stravinsky reappeared from Paris in mid-February and broached the possibility of a *Soldier's Tale* ballet, Ramuz stipulated his own participation as the price for free use of the title and subject matter, and offered on these terms to devise a new scenario for the choreographic version of the tale.[82] What became of this proposal is uncertain. It seems likely that it did not suit Diaghilev (who was choosy about his collaborators). But perhaps Stravinsky held it against Ramuz that he had stood in the way of a lucrative and artistically fruitful collaboration. At all events, Stravinsky's resentment when Ramuz's libretto was printed that summer by the *Cahiers vaudois* with no mention of the composer on its title page (and with mistakes in the list of instruments) has all the flavor of a tu quoque. "Simply the program of the *Soldat* premiere," he grumbled, "in place of this defective page, would have been enough to evoke in the reader the spirit of the intimate collaboration between *you and me* in *our Soldat.* I mind enormously about this, my dear Ramuz, and it would upset me a lot if it were you who had composed this unfortunate page quite consciously and for some reason. . . ."[83] Later, Stravinsky would portray himself as having prevented Diaghilev from turning the work into a ballet, in which "the dancers were to go about wearing advertisements, American sidewalk walking-advertisements, 'sandwich men,' as they are called, or pickets."[84] And perhaps he did veto that particular production idea. But the final reasons for abandoning the *Soldat* ballet altogether seem to have been that Massine had too much else on his plate, Picasso lost interest, and Rouché, the director of the Opéra, continued to oppose putting so intimate a piece into so huge a house.[85]

For some time Ramuz and Stravinsky had been renewing their pre-*Soldat* collaboration on the texts of the Russian songs, and there was talk of further creative work together—though we know no details, only tantalizing hints in Ramuz's letters of the time. But in any case nothing came of them. Instead, Stravinsky spent much of the next two months composing the rest of *Pulcinella* and trying to persuade Chester to publish the new *Firebird* Suite, in the teeth of Kling's realization that his ownership of the work might be successfully challenged in court by Jurgenson or his heirs in title. Eventually, in mid-March, Kling agreed to pay ten thousand francs for the suite, in return for the indemnity, which Stravinsky duly supplied.[86] But this was really no more than an explanation of Jurgenson's position as the composer understood it, and for Kling the suite would in due course prove to be a poisoned chalice.

Pulcinella was at last finished on 24 April, its completion having perhaps been interrupted the previous week by a flying visit to Monte Carlo, where the Ballets Russes were presenting a brief spring season—their first visit to their old headquarters since 1914.[87] But meanwhile, Stravinsky was probably already dusting down his old 1919 sketches with a view to working them into the string quartet Pochon had commissioned the previous

August. He even wrote to Pochon, late in February, assuring him that he was sketching the work and expecting to compose it in the summer—though his actual motive for writing was to beg Pochon to pay him the five hundred dollars in advance, excusing himself on the grounds of the Belyankins and their utter dependence on him.[88] But when it came to writing the piece, sketches which had in many cases looked like string music began to assume a more hybrid appearance; and by the time he was forced to down tools and set off for Paris for the *Pulcinella* rehearsals on 7 May, he seems to have been no closer to a distinct picture of a string quartet than he had been the previous summer, when string sketches had been mixed up with ideas for a piece with harmonium.

The ballet's premiere was on the fifteenth, again at the Opéra. Massine himself danced the title role, Karsavina was Pimpinella, and Ansermet conducted. That morning, *Comoedia* had run a front-page interview in which Stravinsky again claimed to have personally found the "unpublished" originals in Naples, but in which he also, more importantly, offered his first considered thoughts on the aesthetic basis of the whole conception. Anyone tempted to think of *Pulcinella* as another glossy transcription in the *Good-Humored Ladies* tradition was in for a surprise. "This," Stravinsky announced,

> is a new kind of music, a simple music with an orchestral conception different from my other works. And this novelty resides in the following: Musical "effects" are usually obtained by the juxtaposition of nuances; a *piano* following a *forte* produces an "effect." But that is the conventional, accepted thing.
>
> I have tried to achieve an equal dynamism by juxtaposing the timbres of the instruments which are the very foundation of the sound material. A color only has value in relation to the other colors which are placed next to it. Red has no value in itself. It only acquires it through its proximity to another red or a green, for example. And that is what I have wanted to do in music, and what I look for first of all is the quality of the sound.
>
> I also look for truth in a disequilibrium of instruments, which is the opposite of the thing done in what is known as chamber music, whose whole basis is an agreed balance between the various instruments.
>
> And this is quite new; nobody has ever tried it in music. There are some innovations which cause surprise. But the ear becomes bit by bit sensitive to those effects which are at first shocking. There is a whole musical education to be undertaken.[89]

It was to prove a prophetic manifesto, however disappointed Stravinsky may have been by the ease with which the best critics came to terms with this latest revolution of his. Louis Laloy found the music "classical" in its sources and in the scale of its orchestration, but "thoroughly modern or, rather, thoroughly personal in its disposition of these two elements." He asked, Had Stravinsky the right to use his material in this way?, and answered: "Without any doubt, since his work is charming. In art, the sole principle is that of results, and a masterpiece achieved at the cost of a sacrilege would be none the less admirable for that."[90] Even the conservative Reynaldo Hahn thought *Pulcinella* a "graceful, strange, and seductive paraphrase." And he raised a distinction which the composer himself was to find useful in later years:

> As I was permitting myself to be astonished that M. Stravinsky should have modified Pergolesi's little melodies in a Stravinskian sense and orchestrated them with those inspired diableries of which he alone is capable, an eminent and charming woman reproached me for "respecting" old things instead of "loving" them, and my friend Diaghileff retorted that without this *Pulcinella* all the pages of Pergolesi of which M. Stravinsky has made use would have remained unknown. I could have answered the former that it was a singular way of "loving" old things to change their appearance, and the latter that the first requirement for revealing unknown pages was not to present them back to front.

But then, he concluded, art and logic hardly belong together. "Having made this point, I hasten to say that M. Stravinsky has never given proof of greater talent than in *Pulcinella,* nor of a surer taste in audacity."[91]

By whatever means, Stravinsky had at a stroke reestablished himself with Parisians as the most chic and brilliant modernist—the supreme genius of the unexpected, in that age of the artist as illusionist and magician. Moreover, *Pulcinella* had brought together two such geniuses, in another of those dazzlingly integrated shows which proved that the World of Art spirit was still in command at the Ballets Russes, however much the rest of the world might have turned towards the utilitarian and functional. Picasso's moonlit cubist Naples and masked harlequinade not only fitted the music like a glove but were in themselves, in Buckle's simple description, "one of the most beautiful stage settings ever made." What better way of celebrating this marriage of styles and talents than to climb into one of a convoy of motorcars after the show and drive out with Diaghilev and his entourage to an illegal "dancing" at the suburban mansion of an ex-convict called René de Amouretti; to drink oneself into a state of schoolboy insouciance, and round the night off in a wild mattress fight with one's artistic confrères and one's former and future patrons—the Murats, the Misias, the Etienne de Beaumonts?[92] Truly, Paris had never been quite like Lausanne or Geneva; and now, with all pretense gone of a French ruling class that was somehow in control of events, it was even less so.

It was only a matter of time before he would have to choose between them.

CHERCHEZ LA FEMME

STRAVINSKY STAYED on for at least ten days[1]—long enough, perhaps, to run across Diaghilev's old *Salomé* designer, Sergey Sudeykin, who arrived in Paris with his wife, Vera, at the end of a tortuous journey from the Crimea a few days after the *Pulcinella* premiere. But Paris was not yet the focus of his immediate plans. Since early in the year he had had his sights set on Rome as a future base, and had been mobilizing his Italian contacts to find him an apartment there, including the composer Gian Francesco Malipiero, Count San Martino, and possibly the long-suffering Tyrwhitt, now Lord Berners, who, though no longer in the diplomatic service, still kept a house in Rome. By late May, however, it had become clear that Rome was a poor option. San Martino had found nothing; postwar living conditions were hard; and when all was said and done, Italy was far from the center of operations for a Francophone Russian composer with an English publisher.[2] All the same, he seems to have planned to spend the summer in Positano. But then at some stage this plan, too, was changed, and instead the Stravinskys decided to head northwest, bypass Paris itself, and settle for the summer in Carantec, a village on the north coast of Brittany. On 8 June they set out from Morges for the last time: the Stravinskys and the Belyankins with their retinue, more than a dozen travellers in all, taking the night train to Paris from Geneva, where Marguérite Ansermet saw them off, the children drank grenadine, and Igor solemnly poured his thirteen-year-old son, Theodore, his "first *real glass of beer.*"[3]

Seaside Brittany was a curious choice for a family that for a decade had been inured to lakeside Switzerland, however much it may have appealed to the mariner in Grigory Belyankin. Its chief virtues were that it would occupy the six children and their minders, benefit Katya's lungs, and perhaps give Igor the peace and quiet he needed for composition. But Carantec was at least as far as Morges from Paris, and hence (the visa problem apart) at least as inconvenient for house hunting, which—with Rome out of the reckoning—had now become a matter of urgency. In any case the weather was bad, and their fellow inhabitants were less peaceable than they may have hoped. "Admittedly the peasants are all right," he told Ramuz,

> but peasants are all right everywhere—even in Bocheland! After all why shouldn't they be? I'm tired of the picturesque and they're having a flower festival in this seaside village—the people who come here are conventional little Frenchmen who can't afford Deauville—not in the least amusing—people who start singing unnecessarily loudly in the street under our windows at bedtime because they think holidays are an excuse for letting off steam.[4]

It can hardly have improved matters that the Stravinskys were there just as much because they too could not afford Deauville—at least metaphorically speaking. As usual, the two families stayed *en pension,* and after less than a fortnight (even of Carantec) Igor was vainly pressing Kling for a double payment on the monthly three-thousand-franc installments by which Chester was discharging their contract debt of sixty-seven thousand.[5] In London his *Pulcinella* had opened on 10 June. Ansermet, while conducting for Diaghilev, was also planning a Stravinsky program in the Wigmore Hall in mid-July, with the first concert performance of the *Soldier's Tale* music, a whole series of Russian songs, and the three quartet pieces. But the composer, stranded at the farthest opposite corner of the English Channel, was condemned to follow these important events by letter.

The problem was by no means purely financial. In fact, Ansermet issued Stravinsky a firm invitation to attend the Wigmore Hall concert all expenses paid. But he declined, for reasons at which we can only guess, since his letter of refusal is lost.[6] No doubt he was anxious about Paris accommodation in the autumn, and he did in fact go to Paris with Katya and her sister for ten days at the start of August. But meanwhile he was also deep into a new composition, one for which many sketches existed but which he was only now recognizing for what it was. The impulse had come from a quite unexpected quarter. At some time during the spring—probably during the Paris trip in May (since no written commission survives)—he had been asked by Henry Prunières to write a short piano piece for the supplement to a commemorative issue of his newly founded journal, the *Revue musicale.* It must have struck the composer almost at once that he had the material for such a piece, something in the manner of a solemn chorale, among the previous summer's string and harmonium sketches with which he had been tinkering with Pochon's quartet commission in mind. He probably even asked Prunières if an ensemble piece would be acceptable, since the editor wrote to him on 20 June telling him not to bother to make a piano reduction. But Stravinsky had by that time changed his mind, and on the very same day, working at a piano sent at his request to his Carantec pension by the Paris firm of Pleyel, he wrote the chorale out as a piano piece (albeit one for a large pair of hands).[7]

By now he must already have decided on a work for winds, since as soon as the chorale was finished he began to tack sections onto the front of it with instrumental indications which make it obvious that only winds were now in question. In this way he rapidly compiled the nine-minute score of the Symphonies of Wind Instruments from back to front, completing the whole work in short score—very nearly in its final form—on 2 July. Nothing could be farther from the popular conception of musical composition as a process of starting with a tune, contrasting it with other tunes, developing them, repeating them, coming to a climax, then finishing. Stravinsky had been messing around with these ideas for the best part of a year with no clear idea what sort of work they would make. Now, having been forced to write a two-and-a-half-minute ending, he surveys his sketchbooks, pastes ideas together, inserts other ideas, adds inserts to the inserts, then assembles the whole thing in an order and an architecture which seem to bear not the slightest relation to a coherent or organic plan. No wonder the resulting work is in formal terms one of the most radical even he had ever written. It might seem surprising that it hangs together at all.[8]

There was no time to produce a detailed score of the new piece, as the Pochon string quartet—already long since paid for—had at last to be composed, and there were revisions to the *Soldier's Tale* music which Ansermet needed for his concert on the twentieth. Ansermet was making encouraging noises about the brilliance of his London players (including the Hungarian violinist Jelly d'Arányi, a niece of Joachim's and friend of Bartók's), but extremely discouraging ones about the financial arrangements: "Everyone is abandoning me," he moaned, "and I think I'll be ruined."[9] But it was all right on the night; the hall was full, the performances good, the press lively, and the finances—thanks to last-minute support from Eugenia Errazuriz, Margot Asquith, Lady Colefax, and others—substantially in profit. People were turned away. An elderly gentleman stormed out in a fury. Diaghilev, who came with Massine and Nouvel, "looked as if he had a tummy ache," but the next day, on seeing the reviews, was much more enthusiastic and pronounced the press excellent. "I must say," Ansermet chortled with some complacency "that not a single one of our ballet premieres has created so much stir." The *Daily Mail* even ran a leading article "which concluded that, whatever one may think of the music in this concert, it's the start of a new era in music, and a blow struck against all the fashionable music of the last hundred years."[10] And to cap it all, the music had made a hit with the players: "The trumpeter Barr . . . played the *Soldier's Tale* part like a clarinet, and told [Edward] Clark: 'Nobody has ever written so well for trumpet and cornet as Stravinsky, which is why I love playing his works. It's ten years since I touched my cornet, but it's a real pleasure to pick it up again since [the music] is so well written for this instrument."[11]

Stravinsky had been pressing Ansermet to visit him in Carantec on his way back to Geneva. But Ansermet insisted on going straight home in order to mollify his wife, who, he remarked innocently, was "at the end of her patience,"[12] and if the two friends met at all, it was between trains at the Gare du Nord on the thirty-first, by which time the composer may have been apartment-hunting with *his* more patient helpmeet and her sister.[13] Those ten days in Paris were to prove a decisive interlude in the pseudo-idyll of Carantec. They had no luck finding anywhere permanent to live. But they ran into an acquaintance of Igor's, the fashion designer Gabrielle "Coco" Chanel, whom he had first met through Misia Edwards and Diaghilev, probably during rehearsals for *Pulcinella* in May. Misia, after living with José-Maria Sert for twelve years, had at last married him on 2 August, and perhaps the Stravinskys went to the wedding that Monday in the gloomy church of Saint-Roch, rue Saint-Honoré. They will have seen the scrawny, gamine Coco there. She and Misia had been inseparable since the death of Coco's English lover Boy Capell in a car crash in December 1919. The following March she had moved into a large art-nouveau villa called Bel Respiro in the wealthy Paris suburb of Garches.

> She had had her villa stuccoed in beige and its shutters lacquered in black—two hues which made the entire neighbourhood frown. . . . Bel Respiro opened a dubious parenthesis in the series of bourgeois residences—luxury cottages and rich men's bungalows that were like little temples to matrimony, displaying their half-timbering like so many proofs of social success. Whereas those black shutters . . . The occasional passerby would stop and stare between the branches at this villa that looked like nothing on earth. What could he make of it? The house resembled a painted canvas, trompe-l'oeil in 1920s colours, a stage setting turned to the future.[14]

Coco now proposed that the Stravinskys and (presumably) the Belyankins should come and share her shuttered splendor for as long as it took them to find somewhere of their own to live.

Bel Respiro was a large house, and it needed to be. Either at about the time the Stravinskys moved in, in the second week of September, or soon afterwards, Coco imported a new lover in the notable form of the twenty-nine-year-old grand duke Dmitry Pavlovich, a nephew of Tsar Alexander III, and widely notorious as one of the murderers of Rasputin.[15] Or so Chanel's biographer, Edmonde Charles-Roux, assures us. Robert Craft tells a somewhat different tale. According to his account, the affair with Dmitry Pavlovich did not start until January or February 1921,[16] and meanwhile, she had been carrying on a more or less covert affair with . . . Igor Stravinsky. There is evidence to support this story. Towards the end of her life, Chanel told Paul Morand that she and Stravinsky had been lovers.[17] Craft accepts that there was an affair, but contradicts himself by saying, first, that Stravinsky moved his family to Biarritz so that he could pursue it, then, secondly (on the same page), that the move was to enable him to be with Vera Sudeykina. There is in fact little doubt that by the time the Stravinskys moved to Biarritz, in late May 1921, the affair with Chanel was over. But, as we shall see, it probably lasted long enough, with or without the grand duke, to have prompted the move, which was already in the composer's mind in mid-March.

How, before that, did Stravinsky manage to carry on a liaison with his landlady under the eyes not only of his wife and children, but also possibly of his sister-in-law and her family, to say nothing of the Bel Respiro servants? Presumably the affair was pursued, not in suburban Garches, but at Coco's apartment in the Ritz, a subterfuge—if such it was—facilitated by Igor's frequent absences in central Paris. At the villa, the even tenor of family life was undisturbed. The butler's daughter Suzanne remembered being given watercolors by Mika and playing with Milène "in a huge room which did service as a nursery," but apparently recalled nothing about an affair that would certainly have dominated gossip below stairs?[18] She also remembered the villa "resounding with the echoes of the piano. . . . But Milène and I would go right close to the door, and at times this music was so powerful that it scared us." Stravinsky had at last finished his string-quartet piece for Pochon, a four-minute, single-movement work which he called Concertino, and he was now mainly at work on the full score of the Symphonies of Wind Instruments.[19] This was no mechanical task, such as in later years he would perform while being read to by his wife or assistant. It may only have been at this stage, at Garches in late September and October, that he could begin to work out the special problems presented by an orchestra of twenty-four wind instruments; and the task of laying out this strange progression of seemingly arbitrary, unrelated dissonances and incantations may well have entailed a great deal of experimentation at the piano, testing out of spacings and balancing of registers.

But the two little girls may have overheard something even more terrifying. *The Rite of Spring* was emerging from its six-and-a-half-year hibernation. Diaghilev's plan to revive the ballet in a new choreography by Massine was well advanced, and RMV were talking seriously of issuing the score, which had lain in proof in Berlin since the first year of the war.[20] By October 1920 a copy of these proofs was in Stravinsky's possession, and it seems highly likely that at some time during the early autumn he looked them over, played through the score, perhaps even dusted off the published piano-duet arrangement and tried it out with one or other of his pianist friends. At any rate, Coco Chanel must surely have heard something of the music that autumn, since she suddenly, and apparently spontaneously, turned up at Diaghilev's hotel one day and handed him "a cheque exceeding his wildest hopes" to enable him to go ahead with a ballet whose orchestral requirements alone could well have bankrupted him in his current financial circumstances.[21]

During the summer, Massine had visited Stravinsky to discuss the ballet, and the composer had admitted "that he had not been entirely satisfied with the original choreography [and that] the result had not been a satisfactory synthesis of music and movement. He also thought that Nijinsky had made a mistake in following too closely the rhythms of the score."[22] Massine's version would be more abstracted, and would follow literally only the music's sectional design, not its rhythmic or metrical detail. Stravinsky explained their intentions to Michel Georges-Michel of *Comoedia*. Massine, never having seen the work danced,

> at once noticed that my music, far from being descriptive, was an "objective construction." Every musical work comes by way of impressions which crystallize in the brain, in the ear, and, bit by bit, though mathematically, concretize into notes and meters. The choreographer's task, in his turn, was to crystallize his impression and realize it, no longer for the ear but for the eye. . . . As we needed a pretext for the scenic realization, we by common consent chose my original evocation, that of pagan Russia. . . . But I shall never insist too much on this: we have suppressed all anecdotal, symbolic, etc. detail which might weigh down or obscure a work of purely musical construction that needs to be accompanied by a realization of correspondingly pure choreographic construction.[23]

The ideas, to say nothing of the language, look forward very clearly to the composer's various later neoclassical manifestos which stress the importance of architecture over expression and picturesque imagery; and they show that Stravinsky was already trying hard to shake the Russian mud off his boots and break with the old travel-poster associations of the Ballets Russes. Cocteau's *rappel à l'ordre*—recall to order—had sounded. But for Stravinsky, unlike for Cocteau, it would always sound a warning against the figurative and the regional, as well as against emotional excess and romantic self-indulgence, even though there was no logical reason to extend it in those directions. In fact such pronouncements are much closer to the ideas of the Russian formalists and their obsession with language and structure as against superficial content, even though Stravinsky had had no contact with such recent aesthetic movements in Russia, and would not do so for another two years. Perhaps, in some remote way, they hark back to the World of Art, with its aesthetic purity and its distaste for so-called realism, though almost every paragraph of the correspondence with Benois over *Petrushka* questions this distaste; or perhaps it was just that, after a decade of tracing the thread of modernism through a highly individualized version of Russian folklore, Stravinsky was tired of all the cats and the hares, the nonsense rhymes and the counting songs. Perhaps, even, urban, cosmopolitan Paris had simply replaced sleepy semirural Morges in his mental topography.

In any case, this particular meeting of minds hardly made life much easier for the dancers, and certainly not for Lydia Sokolova, who danced the Chosen One in the Paris season which opened, back in the Théâtre des Champs-Elysées, on 15 December. Sokolova had been terrified at rehearsal by the sight of the composer "wearing an expression which would have frightened a hundred Chosen Virgins, [prancing] up and down the centre aisle of the Champs-Elysées, while Ansermet practised difficult passages of music with the orchestra."[24] Now, at the performance, she had not only to dance Pimpinella in the first work on the bill, *Pulcinella,* but then, when it came to *The Rite,* she had to stand stock still with her feet turned inwards and one arm raised across her body for twelve minutes before starting her dance, then perform what reads—at least for a nondancer—like a miracle of sustained, coordinated athleticism before collapsing in perfect synchrony with the final chord and the fall of the curtain.[25]

For the first time, a Paris theatre audience had heard *The Rite of Spring* through without interruption, and at the end it gave the work—and especially its sacrificial victim—an ovation of which she, in her exhaustion, was scarcely conscious. Stravinsky went on stage, took her hand, and kissed it. And in the press, the music was widely discussed as an accepted classic. Roland-Manuel spoke of "this prodigious *Rite of Spring* which marks a date in the annals of music."[26] And he praised the new choreography, preferring its "purity and profound musicality" to the "archaism" of the old Nijinsky version. But not all the work's admirers were willing to take Stravinsky's revisionist interpretation lying down. Why, Emile Vuillermoz enquired, was it necessary to rewrite history in order to justify a new approach? He reminded his readers of the composer's original "explanation" of *The Rite,* in his *Montjoie!* article, with its rich anecdotal and picturesque coloring, and protested that

> today we are invited to treat all these beautiful details as null and void! Nijinsky understood nothing; it is Massine who has grasped the music of *The Rite* better than the composer himself and who has at

last stripped it of all symbolism and all anecdote. New injustice and new error! . . . Massine's realization is not basically different, for all the more ambitious claims, from the original conception. It is quite simply less new and less personal.

In any case, what did the choreography matter? "The whole of the Dance of the Earth is in the orchestra. But we would regard it as a wicked act not to render today due homage to the memory of the first producer of The Rite, now erased from the land of the living."[27] But if Nijinsky, as everyone now knew, had entered the dark world of the schizophrenic, Vuillermoz seems also to have sensed that Massine's days were numbered as Diaghilev's chief choreographer and premier danseur: "sole guardian," he called him, "of the house aesthetic—at least for the time being." Almost as the Vuillermoz article came off the press, Diaghilev's faithful régisseur, Grigoriev, was handing the young dancer his marching orders in the Teatro Costanzi in Rome, where Massine had arrived as usual to rehearse the company for its evening performance. The writing had been on the wall at least since the Paris Rite, when—at the first-night party—Massine had enacted a clumsy and ostentatious charade about eloping with Sokolova. In fact, the true object of his intentions, as Diaghilev was quick to find out, was a young English dancer called Vera Savina (née Clarke). In Rome, where the company had arrived on New Year's Eve, Diaghilev had had Massine followed by private detectives. And when Massine left, Savina left with him. Three months later, the couple were married in London.[28]

As the new year dawned, Stravinsky's own domestic arrangements were also in a state of uncertainty. Since August he had been trying to secure a visa for his mother to leave Russia, and had written to Soviet officials on the subject, as yet without result.[29] He had failed to find a suitable apartment in Paris, and his thoughts were turning increasingly to the idea of renting a studio and (presumably) taking a family house outside the capital—an idea which may well, as Craft claims,[30] have been prompted by the complications of his emotional life, but which might surely have occurred to him in any case, given his profound need for a peaceful working environment. Coco, among her other benefactions, had offered to pay for a Salle Gaveau concert which Stravinsky would conduct of his works. But Garches itself clearly could not last, and in fact Stravinsky managed little serious composition there. He had put together the Concertino, orchestrated the Symphonies, perhaps revised The Rite; now, in January and early February, he composed a set of eight tiny piano pieces, The Five Fingers, presumably in response to a vague commission Pochon had elicited from the New York music publisher Schirmer.[31] Then, when Diaghilev returned mournfully from Rome on 18 February, he found himself yet again confronted with the eternal problem of *Les Noces,* which Diaghilev had firmly decided to present in his Paris season in May or June.

At least he had by now found himself a studio. Pleyel's director Gustave Lyon, so accommodating the previous summer in rushing a piano to Carantec, now offered him an attic in their office-cum-factory in the rue de Rochechouart, and there he installed himself at some time during the following weeks.[32] The immediate need was to work on the pianola part he still intended to provide for *Les Noces,* but he also had had the bizarre notion of pianolizing its cimbalom parts, and to that end Pleyel had actually taken his instrument away in order to convert it to play perforated rolls. Admittedly, this was only partly due to his growing obsession with the mechanical principle as such. Cimbalom players were about as easy to find in Paris as cheap apartments, and since both Ansermet and Stravinsky himself were also plotting to conduct the as yet unperformed *Renard,* it made sense to have a mechanical virtuoso rather than be kept waiting by the not invariably obliging Aladár Rácz. The composer had pictured himself hiring Rácz as a "kind of secretary to work with me on copying and help me in all kinds of ways in my musical work and play the cimbalom in *Les Noces* if they don't manage to mechanize that instrument."[33] But Rácz was making difficulties, Ansermet reported, and had recommended a Romanian cimbalomist in Paris by way of substitute.[34]

Meanwhile the pianolized cimbalom was soon dropped, and instead the composer, licking his lips at the thought of his new studio, was now envisaging a whole quartet of pianolas alongside the harmonium and percussion; or so at least Otto Kling understood from Ansermet.[35] Perhaps Stravinsky thought that, with less than three months to go till the premiere, this hypermechanization would in some way simplify matters. But Kling was aghast. Not only was there far too little time to engrave the chorus material and extract such instrumental parts as would still be needed, but the whole question of rental would need renegotiating, since the piano rolls would be manufactured by Pleyel but still belong to Chester, a problem quite unforeseen at the time of the original agreement with Diaghilev. There is more than a note of despair in the publisher's letter. But he need not have worried. The long agony of *Les Noces* was still far from over; there would be no production in 1921, and within weeks, the entire mechanization had been abandoned in favor of a new, and no less ephemeral, combination of wind instruments and percussion. "I think," the composer remarked innocently, "that this new ensemble will suit you better for exploiting the work than the old version with its mechanical instruments, which could have given you all kinds of difficulties. . . ."[36]

To what extent these difficulties included problems of synchronization, as the composer later claimed, is far from certain.[37] The Pleyela, like the Aeolian-Orchestrelle Pianola, was a "player piano" which allowed the operator to manipulate secondary features such as dynamics, tempo, and even nuances of rhythm and phrasing, through a mechanism of pedal and manual controls. The actual rolls were normally cut by hand, by a technician working from either a music manuscript or a pencil draft (unlike the reproducing-piano system, in which the rolls were cut direct from the pianist's playing and were meant to reflect his performance exactly). So a measure of flexibility was at least theoretically possible. But normal practice at Pleyel seems to have been to fix everything to do with tempo and rhythm on the roll, leaving only dynamic nuance to the operator. And while, as Rex Lawson points out, this will have fitted in well enough with Stravinsky's increasingly severe views on interpretation in general, it may well have ruled out any idea of synchronizing one or more Pleyelas with other instruments and voices, or indeed with each other.[38]

On the evening of the day Stravinsky wrote to Kling about his studio, 19 February, he went with Diaghilev, Sergey Sudeykin, and his wife, Vera, to see a new show at the Théâtre Femina, in the Champs-Elysées. The show was a Russian revue called the Théâtre de la Chauve-Souris (the Bat Theatre), a transplant of a cabaret founded in Moscow in 1908 by a supporting actor at the Moscow Art Theatre called Nikita Baliyev. This Chauve-Souris was an automatic attraction for Russians in Paris that year, since not only was the show a reminder of the Moscow and Petersburg they had known, but the acts it presented—the playlets and parodies, the sketches and sentimental songs—remained themselves essentially Russian even where Baliyev had expunged or modified the verbal content for the benefit of his growing non-Russian audience.[39] As it happened, though, there was a more direct connection for Diaghilev and Stravinsky, since Sudeykin was Baliyev's designer and Mme Sudeykina, herself a painter, costume designer, and former actress, had helped make the costumes. After the performance, the party repaired to an Italian restaurant in Montmartre. "Igor is moody today," Diaghilev confided to Vera, "so please be nice to him."[40]

What did they talk about that evening? Did the Sudeykins describe their life together in St. Petersburg, whither they had eloped from Moscow in 1916? Did they talk about friends and acquaintances in the old tsarist capital, their fellow artists and poets at the Stray Dog nightclub, for which Sudeykin had famously painted the décor, or the "za-um" ("supra-rational") music performed there by the composer Arthur Lourié—whose name Igor knew as that of the director of music at the Commissariat of Popular Education, the addressee of his request the previous summer for help with his mother's exit visa? Did they reminisce about their (probably bigamous) wedding in Yalta in February 1918; their friendship there with Osip Mandelstam, Sorin, Bilibin, and other writers and artists of the Russian Silver Age; their year in a basement flat in Tiflis? Did Igor possibly even ask after his brother Yury and his artist wife, Yelena, last heard of in Yalta, where Yury had settled for his health in 1910? Or did they talk simply about the theatre and the Chauve-Souris, swap anecdotes about Parisian life, grumble about the cost of living and the philistinism of the world at large as they sipped their Barolo and picked at their prosciutto di Parma? Whatever the topic, Igor was not moody but lively. Vera thought him "the wittiest, most amusing man I had ever met"; and she took out a pack of cards—"all that remained her of this world, and for the next," as Tom Rakewell might later have said—and told his fortune.[41]

The cards, if she read them correctly, will have warned her of more than a mere emotional attachment. Except where it already touched on the Ballets Russes, the Sudeykins' world was in many ways remote from Stravinsky's. The bohemian tracks left by the Kuzmins and the Burlyuks, the Akhmatovas and the Mayakovskys, in the snow of the Mikhailovsky Square, along the damp, reeking courtyard and down the steps into the cramped Stray Dog cellar, would hardly have tempted the Stravinsky or even the Diaghilev of 1912 to extend his itinerary by two or three hundred yards from the Hotel Europa or the Assembly of the Nobles, along the edge of that same square. The literary and artistic cliques of Petrograd—the Formalists and Hylaeans and Acmeists and Vorticists—would have seemed thousands of miles from the Russian ethno-paradise of Stravinsky's *Les Noces*. Had not Lourié himself told Benedikt Livshits—admittedly on the basis of *Petrushka* and *The Rite of Spring*—that Stravinsky was "already old hat"?[42] And the young experimenter in microtones would hardly at that time have found unexpected salvation in the bucolic pages of *Renard*, any more than the futurist-minded Mayakovsky—who visited Stravinsky in Paris late in 1922—could see beyond his ironical view of Stravinsky as a "pillar of European art . . . an innovator and at the same time the reviver of the baroque!"[43]

But meanwhile, Stravinsky's first visit to the Chauve-Souris had brought him into contact with yet another province of Russian art that shared few if any borders with his own recent work. Cabaret remained in 1921 a subculture, not of demotic art, but of bourgeois literature, music, and dance, a risqué half-world in which fragments of Pushkin, played or recited more or less straight, rubbed shoulders with colorful "living doll" tableaux, old Gypsy ballads, soulful romantic duets, marching songs, and saucy musical song-and-dance sketches attached to more or less exiguous plots. The Chauve-Souris, as John Bowlt has pointed out, was a less arty, less intellectual affair than St. Petersburg cabarets like the Stray Dog. It pandered unashamedly to émigré sentimentality and clichéd foreign ideas about "the expansive Russian soul."[44] One of the Baliyev sketches, which went by the name "Katinka (Old Polka from the 1860s)," concerned "the too-modern daughter of old-fashioned Russian merchants. To her parents' displeasure she has learned to dance the polka at boarding school, and angers them furthermore by announcing her intention to marry an officer. They refuse to give their consent to such a marriage. Katinka then pretends to be dying, and the frightened parents yield to her wishes. She then expresses her happiness in an ecstatic dance."[45] According to Artur Rubinstein, who went subsequently to the Chauve-Souris both with and without Stravinsky, the polka itself was "played on an accordion by a bearded comic and danced by the most voluptuous blonde imaginable. A Rubens but with curves that were anything but flabby, she would appear showing most of her charms and would leave the audience agape."[46]

The most immediate effect of the Chauve-Souris on Stravinsky was that he fell head over heels in love with the voluptuous blonde, whose name was Zhenya Nikitina. Whether or not we believe Rubinstein's highly colored account of the composer coming to him in despair at his supposed impotence in the ultimate presence of this mock-exotic creature, it seems certain that there was an affair. Rubinstein tells of subsequent dinners at Fouquet's with the lovely Zhenya, the Sudeykins, and presumably Stravinsky. Later she asked the composer to write something for her, and the result was the orchestration of the little four-hand piano polka in the Three Easy Pieces—originally a portrait of Diaghilev as a circus master, but now transformed into a Chauve-Souris dance complete with Katinka's own theme added by way of a brief coda on flute and trombone.[47] Even in this form the music was too much for Baliyev, who seems to have watered it down, changed the scoring, and no doubt softened the harmony. "One must never risk entrusting honest work to that sort of establishment," Stravinsky later remarked sagely, conveniently forgetting the finer details of the circumstances.[48]

One Sunday morning a week or so after the Montmartre dinner, a handsome boy of seventeen tapped unannounced on the door of Diaghilev's room at the Hôtel Continental. Diaghilev seems to have been expecting a visitor, and the boy was admitted. But though he had seen Diaghilev before, Diaghilev did not know him. "How I would like to meet him," Boris Kochno had told his friend Vera Sudeykina. "I saw him once in the foyer in the Théâtre des Champs-Elysées and almost fainted. Such an appearance!"[49] Boris was not a dancer, nor even a musician, but a poet. Like the Sudeykins, whom he had known in the Crimea, he had fled from civil-war-torn Russia the previous year. He had talked to Vera about his love affairs "and said that he was free at present and looking for a 'higher attachment.'" Now that higher attachment was—if not in the fullest sense—to become a reality. Boris began to appear in Diaghilev's company, to make himself—as Diaghilev told him a good secretary should—

indispensable. One day the Polish composer Karol Szymanowski, waiting for Diaghilev with Artur Rubinstein in the lobby of the Hôtel Continental, was shattered to see a boy he had loved in Kiev coming down the stairs behind the great man.[50]

Boris's first secretarial duty for Diaghilev was to accompany him to Madrid for the Ballets Russes' season in March and April. Perhaps as a respite from the emotional complications in his own life, Stravinsky decided to go with them, and it was at this moment, it seems, that he laid his plans for a family move to Biarritz, breaking his journey to look for a house in the Basque village of Anglet, between Biarritz proper and Bayonne.[51] He was in a deeply miserable state. He was still in love with Coco and may have rowed with Misia on her account. Chanel herself told Morand that Misia had been furious with her for usurping her role as the composer's patroness, and she pictured Misia's new husband, the bearded José-Maria Sert, warning Stravinsky off,

> until one day I said to Ansermet: "This is idiotic, the Serts are mad. Everyone's talking. Picasso is making jokes. Let Igor come back and be friends." Stravinsky came back. He came back every day, and taught me music; the little I know about it, I owe to him. He talked to me about Wagner, about Beethoven, his bête noire, about Russia. Then one day: "The ballet is off to Spain," Stravinsky said to me. "Come with us." "I'll come and join you" [I said].

Alone in Paris, Coco dined with Grand Duke Dmitry Pavlovich (who—in her account—had only just turned up in the French capital, for the first time since 1914), and decided to go with him to Monte Carlo. "Misia was on the lookout. She at once wired to Stravinsky in Spain: 'Coco is a shopgirl who prefers grand dukes to artists.' Stravinsky nearly died. Diaghilev wired me: 'Don't come, he means to kill you.' "[52]

Robert Craft understandably dismisses these details as an old woman's bragging. Can we really believe that the affair "transformed [Stravinsky] from an unassuming, timid man into a hard, monocled man; from vanquished into victor"? Is it credible that, as Misia is supposed to have told Coco, "Stravinsky is in the next room, wringing his hands, and wanting to know if you will marry him or not"?[53] Perhaps not. But it hardly needs saying that sexual humiliation is not the exclusive fate of the naturally humble, nor do those who inflict it necessarily see their victims in quite the same light as other people. At least two old friends observed the composer's turmoil and anxiously awaited the outcome. "I hope your stay in Spain will have gone well," Ansermet wrote from Geneva at the end of March,

But what's going on? Have you made peace with the Serts? And with yourself? I keep turning this question over. What are they doing at Garches, and at the rue Cambon [Chanel's working premises]? I've talked the whole thing over with Ramuz, since a telegram from you raised the question. He was quite upset by it all, but doesn't judge quite as I do. Not people's feelings. But the consequences. As rigorous as you know him, he leaps to extreme solutions; but it seems to me an abstract logic, the same as paralyzes him, I think, in his life. He told me he wouldn't write to you (I'm to tell you) since, not being with you, and unable, for lack of money, to be with you, he doesn't feel he has the right to say to you, from a distance and without doing anything, what he would like to say to you.

Now, dearest Igor, courage. I'm with you with all my heart in your pain. . . .[54]

The Ballet Russes' visit to Madrid straddled Easter, which fell that year on 27 March. The week before Easter itself, Diaghilev, Stravinsky, and Kochno headed south to Seville for the Holy Week processions, and they stayed on for the feria, the Easter fair with its bullfights and flamenco and its pulsating nightlife. Diaghilev's professional motive for going to Seville was to engage flamenco dancers, and for a time he even seems to have enthused Stravinsky with the idea of a flamenco opera based on *The Barber of Seville*, with a libretto by Boris and incorporating guitar improvisations like those of the Seville cabarets.[55] "Almost nightly," relates the impresario Charles Cochran, who was with them in Seville, "we gathered together some of the best singers and guitarists, and arranged our own Quadra Flamenco [sic]."[56] For all the excitement and color of these long Sevillian nights, it was the formal precision and severity of the music which fascinated Stravinsky. "Nothing in any of this," he wrote in his *Comoedia* article "Les Espagnols aux Ballets Russes" a few weeks later, "of the impassioned improvisation which we get, for example, from the whirling dervishes. No improvisation at all: an art that is very much worked out, very meticulous, very logical in its way and coldly calculated. I would almost call it a classical art, whose rules, though different from our school, are no less rigorous. In a word, an art of composition."[57]

Diaghilev had another, quite different, project up his sleeve. He had in Seville with him a four-hand score of Tchaikovsky's ballet *The Sleeping Beauty*, which he had decided to put on the following season as the ultimate tribute to the vanished glories of imperial Russia. But he needed Stravinsky's help with the music, which was both too long and too short: too long to be played complete to audiences unused to symphonic ballet on that scale; too short in that the only available orchestral score lacked certain items which had been cut before the St. Petersburg premiere in 1890.

They sat at an upright piano in the hall of the Hotel Alfonso XIII in Seville, clattering their way through the sumptuous music, deciding what to leave out and (perhaps) what to put in, savoring the riches of a score which was still largely unknown outside Russia, even perhaps laughing at the thought of the Parisian reaction to music so remote from the tenets of chic modernism. This was their contribution to the feria, from the far corner of Europe: *les russes aux ballets espagnols.* Back in Madrid, the two-week session went ahead, with Stravinsky himself conducting *Petrushka* for the first time. He saw Falla and was painted by Robert Delaunay. By 14 April, after an absence of four weeks, he was back in Paris and its sea of disturbing emotions.[58]

He had presumably already fixed on his new house by the beach at Anglet, and at the end of May, after the short Ballets Russes season, he and his family moved out of Bel Respiro and dragged themselves wearily another five hundred miles to the far southwestern corner of France— their second such move in less than a year. The Belyankins remained for the time being in Paris. The Cottage l'Argenté, as the Anglet house was called, was small and cheap, and there was an adjoining studio where Stravinsky could compose, because—as he told Ramuz—"it goes without saying that I cannot live and work fruitfully in Paris."[59] Nevertheless, he now had his studio in the rue Rochechouart, and this soon became a pied-à-terre as well as an office. "I also slept in this Pleyel studio," he told Craft, "and even entertained socially there, so it must count as one of my 'residences.' "[60] That is putting it mildly. Pleyel would sometimes be his base for weeks on end, and despite his disclaimer to Ramuz, he did compose there as well as work on his Pleyel rolls. But the move to Biarritz established a division in his life which was spiritual as well as emotional and practical. Before the war Empress Eugénie's favorite resort had also attracted Russian visitors in substantial numbers; a large Orthodox church had been built there, and there was a sense of Russian community which intensified with the final exodus of Whites after the victory of the Bolsheviks in the civil war late in 1920. For Katya, as her illness slowly advanced, such a spiritual "home" seems to have been increasingly necessary, and although the domestic atmosphere was probably not yet as intensely sacramental as it became a few years later in Nice, the feeling of Russia-in-exile must have been strong. For Igor, such an atmosphere was to become not less but more important for his work, not only because it created a haven of peace and security from a more and more intrusive world, but because the social-religious frameworks of old Russia reflected certain newfound aesthetic preoccupations which were gradually invading the very subject matter of his music. Order, authority, the medieval idea of the artist as a humble, anonymous artisan erecting his cathedrals to the greater glory of God: such images were already in his subconscious mind, whether or not he had yet read Jacques Maritain's *Art et scolastique,* the key text of neo-Thomist aesthetic theory, which had come out the previous December. The fact that this old hieratic Russia had been replaced in reality by a Soviet hierarchy of commissars and apparatchiks only served to enhance its appeal. If Orthodoxy was dead at home, it must be the more zealously guarded abroad, and the Stravinsky house would be among the first to offer it shelter.

Nevertheless, within days of settling them all in at Anglet, the composer was back in Paris, and by 7 June he had travelled on to London for the Ballets Russes season, which had already opened a week or two earlier. It was his first visit to England since 1914, and it was destined to bring him into conflict with a press which, on his previous visits and through Ansermet's recent reports, he had by and large found sympathetic and amenable.

He arrived just in time to hear the twenty-eight-year-old Eugene Goossens (himself a composer) conduct *The Rite of Spring* in a concert in the Queen's Hall. Goossens was still little known as a conductor, and had conceived his enthusiasm for Stravinsky as a violinist under Henry Wood in 1912 and in Beecham's orchestra for *The Nightingale* in 1914. In his memoirs he claims that the impulse to conduct *The Rite* himself came from hearing an inadequate performance under Ansermet, which can only have been in the Paris run the previous winter.[61] He got together his own hand-picked orchestra, and arranged private finance, which—like Ansermet's the previous summer—nearly failed him at the last minute. Yet the performance seems to have been remarkably good. Stravinsky himself, who had reached his seat (with Diaghilev and Kochno) just as Goossens was raising his baton and who at the end took several platform calls, told Edwin Evans that "his music had never sounded so well before."[62] Another critic wrote that the performance "made the reputation of Mr. Eugene Goossens as a conductor":

> We knew that [the work] would benefit by the interpretation of a creative mind in full sympathy with the musical developments in which it is a landmark, but we were hardly prepared for the extraordinary command of the conductor's craft which enabled Mr. Goossens to carry out with brilliant certainty and powerful energy the conception which was essentially a composer's conception of a fellow-composer's work.[63]

Alas, by the time these and other more or less appreciative reviews reached the newsstands, Stravinsky had had to endure a considerably less cogent performance of another of his works in the same hall, as well as its aftermath in the press. Three days after the Goossens concert, Serge Koussevitzky—the proprietor of the RMV and veteran of the Russian premieres of *Petrushka* and *The Rite of Spring*—conducted the London Symphony Orchestra in the world premiere of the Symphonies of Wind Instruments. Stravinsky had heard Koussevitzky play solo double-bass in St. Petersburg, but this was his first encounter with the great man's conducting, and it was not an edifying experience. Ernest Newman reported that "many people in the audience could not keep from laughing at the music, and at the end there was more hissing than I have ever heard in an English concert-room."[64] But the composer was in no doubt where the blame lay. In fact, he told the *Weekly Dispatch,*

> The audience did not hiss enough. They should have been much angrier. I make no reproach against the splendid musicians, but the score of my music was not crafted, and I myself did not know it as my own work. Will you allow me to say that there is no intention of jesting in it? On the contrary it is a composition which represents my most serious reflections and aims at the present time.
>
> The radical misunderstanding was that an attempt was made to impose an external pathos on the music. The title should not have been "Symphony" but "Symphonies," and the point of the music lies in the juxtaposition of three different symphonies.
>
> Far from reproaching my London audience, I would say that the wonderful reception of *The Right of Spring* [sic] on Tuesday was compensation for a long period of neglect and discouragement.[65]

But in his irritation, the composer succeeded only in stirring up a hornet's nest. Ever pedantic and theoretical, Newman (who had not read the *Dispatch* interview and was dependent on hearsay) nevertheless accused the composer of indiscretion: "The performance was under Mr. Kussevitsky; the orchestra was the London Symphony. However rapidly the work may have been rehearsed, we can surely assume that at any rate the notes were right. An inadequate performance of a piece of music may fail to reveal all the innermost soul of it, but if the notes are right the music will at least talk sense if there is any sense in it."[66] Did Newman seriously believe this rigmarole? His hostility to the Russian visitors in general and to Stravinsky in particular was barely concealed, so much so that Diaghilev wrote to the *Daily Telegraph* (for some reason), protesting about Newman's review of *Petrushka* and Prokofiev's *Chout,* and the generally uncomprehending notices of the latter ballet.[67] Nine days later, on the twenty-seventh, *The Rite of Spring* itself opened in the Massine production at the Prince's Theatre—its third London performance that month, since Goossens had repeated his concert version on the twenty-third. Afterwards Stravinsky received a laurel wreath. "The intention," Newman wrote the following Sunday, "was to put a halo round Stravinsky's work; the effect was to lay a wreath on its coffin. . . . So ends," he added, "the history of the most farcical imposture in the music of our time."[68] But a week later he managed an appendix on the Symphonies. He recalled that Stravinsky had

> publicly found fault with Mr. Kussevitsky a few weeks ago: the impression was sought to be conveyed that the wind-instrument symphony in memory of Debussy sounded so ridiculous because the conductor had tried to make it expressive! . . . Very good; by all means let a composer write in that style if he wants to. All we ask is that he shall write well in that style. Our complaint is simply that Stravinsky cannot do what he sets out to do.[69]

Now Koussevitzky himself entered the lists for the first time. He had not so far thought it proper, he announced, to comment on Stravinsky's remarks about his performance; "but now, 'as the chicken is dead, and everyone knows it,' it is surely permissible for me also to say a few plain words." He had only played the Symphonies, he claimed, because of "the personal and persistent requests of Mr. Stravinsky himself," who "brought me personally the whole material of the symphony just before the rehearsal, and was present at both of these." Far from introducing "expression," he had had no time to do anything but "play what was written in the partition quite automatically." His own opinion of Stravinsky's music was high, but there was nothing new in either the scoring or the musical content of the Symphonies, "except some false and not convincing harmonies. . . . In my opinion, [it] represents a stage of decline in Mr. Stravinsky's art." And he concluded: "Even the greatest composers have sometimes weak moments in their art, [but] that does not give them any right to attribute their own mistakes to other people."[70]

Had Koussevitsky confined his letter to an explanation of the circumstances, there could have been little complaint. But the judicial tone was insufferable. "I am sending you a piece by one of your Jewish friends," Diaghilev wrote to Stravinsky, now back in Anglet:

> As your *sincere* friend, I advise you to beware of the services of all these musical Jews, since you are *beginning* to see what this friendship is worth. I shook with rage as I read the piece by this swine. To my way of thinking, Russians abroad, especially now, don't have the right to settle scores among themselves—for which reason he must be held responsible for his *criminal* letter. One can't reply to *him*, but I shall stand up for you in my next letter to the English public.[71]

Stravinsky replied by return of post, agreeing that for him to answer Koussevitzky was impossible, while hoping that one of his English friends would do so. "But any answer, clearly, should be not to the malicious idio-cies and banalities of Koussevitzky, but to what comprises the essence of that whole Jewish (as you say) German mentality."[72] There was, as far as is known, no answer, and Stravinsky was still brooding on the affair more than six weeks later, when he asked Ansermet to "see what can be done in the English press against Koussevitzky's letter." Ansermet had his own quarrel with the Russian conductor, who was using his money to hijack the Paris concert season, and was even—Ansermet alleged—"intriguing to replace Monteux in Boston."[73] But nothing could be done; and Kousse-vitzky was to prove too useful to Stravinsky for there to be any question of a public vendetta, however suspicious he might remain of him in private.

That June in London, Stravinsky recalled, was hot and socially demand-ing, "one continuous round of lunches, teas, receptions, and week-ends which left me no time to myself."[74] Naturally, this is an oversimplification. For one thing, he came and went; at some time in mid-June he went back to Anglet, returning to London just in time for *The Rite of Spring* on the twenty-seventh.[75] For another thing, there was work to do. *The Sleeping Beauty* had to be planned in detail, with the defective full score now to hand. Moreover, Diaghilev was nervous about the work's reception, and at some point came up with the idea of preceding it with an operatic curtain raiser. "We looked," he later told *Comoedia*, "among the works of Mozart for a piece that could be played with *The Sleeping Beauty*. But our search was in vain, and M. Stravinsky offered to compose the necessary score."[76] Diaghilev had recently bought an 1833 edition of an anthology of Russian poems and prose called *Novoselye* (The Housewarming), which included the first publication of Pushkin's verse story "Domik v Kolomne" (The Lit-tle House at Kolomna). Pushkin himself figured prominently among the writers portrayed at table in the book's frontispiece.[77] Something about this witty but unassuming poem, whose tale of a suburban maiden who brings her soldier-lover into the house disguised as the new cook is pref-aced by an ironic disquisition on the neglect of classical meter, appealed to Stravinsky, who promptly invited Boris Kochno to turn it into an opera libretto.

Whether or not memories of "Katinka" and the Chauve-Souris went into the inspiration for *Mavra*, as Taruskin brilliantly and persuasively argues, the voluptuous Zhenya herself was by now no longer first in Stravinsky's thoughts. Perhaps, in London, he pursued a brief flirtation with Juanita Gandarillas, the wife of an Argentinian diplomat called Anto-nio Gandarillas, nephew of Eugenia Errazuriz.[78] But in Paris on his way home, something much more serious happened. He fell passionately in love with Vera Sudeykina.[79]

GUISES AND DISGUISES

TWO WOMEN more contrasted than Vera Sudeykina and Katya Stravinskaya would be hard to imagine attracting the same man. The daughter of a provincial Ukrainian doctor and landowner, Katya still carried with her the educated homeliness and leisured seriousness of remote Russian summers, with their emphasis on family life, intellectual and moral self-improvement, and a certain spiritual serenity which, with her illness, had matured into a piety bordering, as time passed, on sanctity. Warm, naturally unsophisticated, and quietly intelligent, she never wholly adapted even to her wartime Vaudois environment, let alone to the social ecology of twenties Paris, Biarritz, or Nice, and the homes she created in those and other places were always in some sense outposts of old Russia, comfortable but cluttered, with heavy wallpapers, brocades, kilims, family photographs, and (later) icons prominent among the bric-à-brac of emigrant life, and an authoritarian, patriarchal atmosphere which was only partly a reflection of her husband's real need for silence and tranquillity.

Vera de Bosset had also been brought up in provincial Russia, but her parents were not themselves Russian (her father was French, her mother Swedish), and for her there seems never to have been any danger of finding herself imprisoned in a vanishing culture. Born on Christmas Day 1888 (OS) in St. Petersburg, she was an only child, and photographs suggest that she was pampered (rather than sheltered or spoilt), and spared the self-annihilating rough-and-tumble of life in a large rural family.[1] Her father owned a factory for the processing of coal for industrial use at Kudinovo, to the north of Moscow, and Vera was educated by governesses at home, on the family estate at Gorki (Novgorod Province), and at Kudinovo itself, until she was thirteen. She then went to a Moscow boarding school, but not—by her own account—a very tight-lipped one, since it permitted the girls to attend the theatre and even encouraged their own theatrical aspirations by giving them drama classes. She also studied music and, for a time, dancing. When she was nineteen (in 1908) her father enrolled her in the University of Berlin, as a student initially of science and philosophy, later of art history.[2]

Vera de Bosset's education was therefore liberal by the standards of the day, and she emerged from it with an unusual degree of independence for a well-brought-up young lady who was not evidently bothered by the fashionable issue of female emancipation. She seems to have been emancipated without having had to think about it. Tall, dark-eyed, and extrovert, she charmed everyone she met. She received the attentions of stage and film directors, was engaged by the Kamerny Theatre in Moscow, and even appeared in films, including as Hélène in Yakov Protazanov's *War and Peace*. "Remember," she told a London glossy magazine in 1979, "it was shocking to be an actress then."[3] By the time she was twenty-three—according to Craft, who presumably had the information from her—she had married twice, and by the following year she had run away from her second husband (a compulsive gambler aptly called Robert Shilling) and taken up with the artist Sergey Sudeykin, who was himself already married to a cabaret dancer and actress called Olga Glebova. Through the bisexual Sudeykin, Vera entered a world of pure moral bohemianism, in the orbit of the Petersburg literary nightclub Brodyachaya Sobaka—the Stray Dog. In 1913, the year the couple are said to have eloped, Olga Glebova-Sudeykina was the unwitting cause of the suicide of the bisexual poet Vsevolod Knyazev, who (like Sudeykin) had been Mikhail Kuzmin's lover but turned his attentions to Olga just as she was taking advantage of her husband's departure to have an affair with Alexander Blok.[4] Anna Akhmatova, Olga's flatmate (to put it no more strongly) and herself a former lover of Sudeykin, had an early intimation of the moral turmoil behind this louche existence, in a poem written in 1912:

> *All of us here are revellers, whores,*
> *How joyless our life together. . . .*[5]

Vera herself was later close to Kuzmin; and in Alushta (Yalta) in 1917 she knew Osip Mandelstam, and was even the inspiration of one of his most exquisite poems:

> *The stream of golden honey flowed from the bottle*
> *So long and slow that our hostess had time to say:*
> *Here in sad Tauris, whither fate has carried us,*
> *We are never bored—and she glanced over her shoulder. . . .*
>
> *But in the white room, the silence stands like a spinning-wheel,*
> *Smelling of vinegar, paint, and cool wine from the cellar.*

Do you remember, in the Grecian house: the wife everyone loved—
Not Helen, the other—how long she embroidered. . . .[6]

By the time she and her husband reached Paris in May 1920, she was certainly no stranger to the rootless existence of itinerant artists, and seems to have thrown herself without a qualm into the *mondaine* Parisian art and theatre world. The thirty-two-year-old woman whom Igor Stravinsky met at the Chauve-Souris that February evening was well aware of her power over artistic and intelligent men, and although Craft describes her as immune to the fault of affectation, photographs of the time suggest to the unbiased eye that she at least knew how to pose for the camera. Clothes-conscious and herself a gifted designer, she would soon open a fashion and theatre-accessories boutique in the rue de la Boëtie—later rue Euler—from where she made the costumes for various Paris stage productions, including *The Soldier's Tale* (1924) and *The Firebird* (1926). All her life, she would prefer to live within walking distance of small boutiques of the Parisian kind.

The friendship probably became an affair in the second week of July, when Stravinsky was in Paris for several days on his way back to Anglet. Ever afterwards he marked the fourteenth as their anniversary.[7] Later that month Vera wrote to him at the Cottage l'Argenté, relaying her husband's opinion that "it is time for you to return to Paris and to rest from your rest."[8] Her letters of the time are carefully noncommittal, always associating Sudeykin with her endearments, presumably because, living in a Paris flat, she could not be sure of concealing them from him, or that they would not be read by Katya in distant Biarritz. But the contents are obviously coded. Behind all the harmless-looking pluralities—"both of us love you," "[Sergey] loves you [and] misses you," "we kiss you tenderly," "I kiss you tenderly [and] S. kisses you also"[9]—is a private intimacy barely disguised as loving friendship. Vera's effortless spontaneity must have come to her aid in this difficulty. She of all people could make an effusion of feeling towards a fellow exile seem as natural and innocent as the Paris weather. But her "most heartfelt greetings to Ekaterina Gavrilovna" would hardly be misunderstood by a lover who could end a letter of his own with an uninhibited "I embrace you with love and longing. I miss you."[10]

While Igor "rested" in Anglet, Vera made herself useful to him in Paris. It was her way of being with him. "Please give me errands," she pleaded, "even every day; I will be glad to do them." She ordered him a new pair of trousers; she offered to act as a surrogate parent by advertising for a tutor for his children and interviewing respondents; and she even served as his agent in a proposed collaboration with the dada artist Francis Picabia, who wanted Stravinsky to write music for his play *Les Yeux chauds.* "Tell me whether this interests you and what you would like me to do about it," she wrote, adding shrewdly: "If you are not interested, please do not blame me, since in that case I would hesitate to propose anything again."[11] But she was not above asking favors in return. She hoped he might get Pleyel to lease her a piano at cut price. He sent her his photograph and asked for hers in exchange. "You look perky," she told him, "and not at all angry, as you seem to be in some of your other photographs."[12]

Igor's "rest" consisted, of course, of starting work on the Pushkin opera, his first significant new score since leaving Switzerland. He must already have had part of the libretto with him, since on about 20 July he sent a postcard to Diaghilev in London announcing that he had started work on *Domik,* as he called it, and imploring Kochno to reduce the amount of recitative in the remaining part.[13] Diaghilev had wired his intention to visit Anglet for further discussions, and on the thirtieth Stravinsky telegraphed back with an unexpected proposal for a hotel booking: "Should I reserve you two admirable ground-floor rooms with bath at Belyankin's Château Basque hotel food unmatched anywhere full board for two 250 francs."[14]

Did the great man take up this suggestion? He was probably unaware of Belyankin's vocation for the catering trade, and may well have suspected some complicated *Mavra*-esque practical joke involving the bearded ex-mariner (alias Pushkin's hussar, whose cover is blown when he is caught shaving by Parasha's mother) and his exquisite eighteen-year-old daughter, alias Parasha herself. But it was true. The country cousins had indeed soon followed the Stravinskys south, and Grigory, in desperation at his seemingly unquenchable indebtedness to his brother-in-law, had conceived the notion of a restaurant serving the large émigré Russian community in Biarritz. According to Artur Rubinstein, who arrived in Biarritz at about this time, Belyankin found the backing he needed among the richer elements of that community;[15] but it seems likely, from subsequent events, that the actual premises were provided, if not paid for, by Coco Chanel, whose fashion business had a major outlet in Biarritz. For a time all went well. There were accordionists and balalaika players, and in due course a dance floor, and Grigory really was—it seems—a talented chef. But Belyankin's debts ("above all to us, who are once more in a rather 'too exact' situation," as Stravinsky told Ramuz)[16] were so great that most of the takings went on servicing them, and when after less than six months Chanel decided to reclaim her premises as a "maison de couture,"[17] the unlucky family were once more cast onto that great ocean from which, it seemed, only their famous relative could ever rescue them.

Mavra, though, was going well. What had started out as a curtain raiser, a pièce d'occasion, was beginning to take on a novel and suggestive aspect, prompted by the mock-didactic element in Pushkin's tale. As a story, "Domik" is trivial, certainly, but its triviality is ironic, the first nine verses (out of forty) being a mock disquisition on metrics, combined with a mock lament at the neglect of classical idioms. "Our tabor," Pushkin complains, "we have transported from the classical heights to the flea market." While discussing the staging of *The Sleeping Beauty*, the collaborators must surely have found themselves weighing up the merits of the unfashionable Tchaikovsky against those of the *kuchka*, on the one hand, and those of the modern movement in Paris, on the other; and from there it would have been only natural for Stravinsky, who had already turned his back on the graphic and anecdotal elements in the ultramodern *Rite of Spring*, to cultivate a musical disquisition equivalent to Pushkin's—to use this silly story about a cook caught shaving as a vehicle for a kind of style-polemic in favor of what he had now decided was the "classical" Russian tradition.

Probably this polemical idea began with Tchaikovsky. But it must soon have migrated back in time to a composer who was not only a contemporary of Pushkin (and of the "Domik" story), but who also happened to be universally revered as the father figure of all Russian music since: Mikhail Glinka. No doubt it amused and stimulated Stravinsky that the composer of *A Life for the Tsar* was almost completely disregarded in the West. In fact, when he wrote to his Berlin publisher asking for scores by Glinka, the reply came back that the music was unobtainable.[18] Undaunted, Stravinsky was already writing Parasha's opening song in the style of the popular romances of Glinka's day—a style Glinka cultivated in his own drawing-room songs, and one that is as remote as possible from the folk-song-based "realism" of the *kuchka* or the vibrant ethnic modernism of *Renard* and *Les Noces*. As Taruskin points out, this kind of song was also the staple diet of the Chauve-Souris. But Stravinsky's version somehow filters out all the sentimentality and coarseness of the original, while preserving—in an oblique, modernized, and above all sublimated form—all the essential ingredients of the ham cabaret number. It is at this precise moment that Stravinskian neoclassicism, both as an act of allusion and synthesis and as a style with its own tics and mannerisms, makes its debut.

From the start, Stravinsky loved writing the music. It was going well, he told Ramuz in August;[19] and a few weeks later he confided to Ansermet that "the opera is taking shape well, even very well—*you'll like it*—it's very different from what I've been doing."[20] But there were interruptions. Rubinstein's arrival in Biarritz came as a reminder that, earlier in the year, Stravinsky had promised to write him "a sonata made of the material of *Petrushka*."[21] According to Rubinstein, there had been an angry scene in the Pleyel studio after he had annoyed Stravinsky by describing the *Piano Rag Music* as "written for percussion rather than my kind of piano," and Stravinsky had in turn irritated the great pianist by asserting that "the piano is nothing but a utility instrument and it sounds right only as percussion." But the argument had been defused by Rubinstein demonstrating certain effects of half-pedalling in *Petrushka,* and Stravinsky had at once offered to make the transcription. Now the pianist had turned up in southwest France and the promise had to be redeemed. This was a new experience for the composer; he had worked with dancers and choreographers, with writers, even with conductors, but he had never before worked directly with a virtuoso instrumentalist. The Three Movements from Petrushka clearly show the effects of such a collaboration. They were to remain the only piano music Stravinsky ever wrote that he himself could not readily play, and indeed their exploration of the bravura and coloristic possibilities of the piano was such that even Rubinstein found them "very difficult to perform."

The two men worked, Rubinstein says, in the afternoons.[22] Either Rubinstein would go to Anglet, or Stravinsky would come to Rubinstein's hotel, the Palais, overlooking the Grande Plage, and show him "pieces of *Mavra,* or his progress with *Petrushka.*" Occasionally they would attend bullfights. Stravinsky remembered a corrida in Bayonne at which "a bull dislodged a *bandillera* and sent it through the air and into the heart of the Consul-General of Guatemala, who was standing by the railing, and who died instantly."[23] By the second week in September, the transcription was complete, and this time Rubinstein did take the work into his repertoire, though "played my own way, making it sound as I heard it by the orchestra more than as a piano piece."[24] But he never recorded it, "because I knew my Igor. In a bad mood he might announce: 'Rubinstein betrays my work when he performs it.' "[25] In fact, Stravinsky never even mentioned Rubinstein and the *Petrushka* movements in the same breath, except to record that the pianist paid him five thousand francs for the transcription.[26] But the visit left a deep impression on Rubinstein. After quitting Biarritz at the end of September, he wrote to Stravinsky that "I simply have to tell you how much happiness I owe you during this recent time. In the end *nothing* mattered beside that. . . . it all made me realize with added force how fine it is to live close to such a being as you."[27]

The *Petrushka* transcription was by no means the only distraction during these weeks of late summer. Stravinsky also managed to finish off the orchestrations which became the Suite no. 2 for small orchestra, and he had to cope with proofs of the vocal score of *Les Noces,* which Kling was pressing ahead with on the assumption that, whatever still had to be done to the orchestration, the substance of the piece was now complete. Somehow, *Mavra* seems to have survived all this competition from what was in effect an "old" and different Stravinsky. But when, on 20 September, Diaghilev and Kochno again turned up in Biarritz, it was probably as much to discuss *The Sleeping Beauty,* whose planned London opening was now a mere five weeks away. Diaghilev's main worry over the summer had been casting, since his regular dancers were out of touch with the classical style of Tchaikovsky's most Imperial ballet; and moreover, since his aim was to run the show night after night—in the manner of long-running popular hits like *Chu Chin Chow*—double or even triple casting was needed. But it was now becoming a matter of urgency to resolve certain musical issues, among them the question of added numbers, which had probably been discussed but never settled in Madrid and London. Only now, it seems, did Diaghilev firmly commission Stravinsky to orchestrate the two items he wanted to reinstate, the Variation d'Aurore from act 2, which was to be turned into a variation for the Lilac Fairy herself and danced by Lopukhova, and the entr'acte for concertante violin, which he needed to cover a scene-change later in the same act.[28]

The composer must have viewed the task with somewhat mixed feelings. In theory, he was all in favor of the revival and more than ready to promote Tchaikovsky's ballet as "the most authentic expression of that period in our Russian life which we call the 'Petersburg Period.' "[29] But in practice it was a nuisance. *Mavra* was going well, but would now be interrupted for a month or more. On the other hand, work on the ballet supplied a reason—or a pretext—for a visit to Paris; at least, Stravinsky did go there, either with Diaghilev or, more probably, a week or so later. He was in Paris when he completed his orchestration of the Lilac Fairy's Variation— as it was now to be—on 10 October, which suggests that Diaghilev had not been able or willing to bring all the materials he needed for the purpose (the defective Mariyinsky full score and the Ziloti piano reduction) with him to Biarritz. And it was on the tenth in Paris that he penned, or at least signed, his open letter to Diaghilev defending Tchaikovsky's music, in advance, against the expected criticisms: that it was vulgar, emotional, self-indulgent, and all the rest. "I have just read again the score of this ballet," he wrote. "I have spent some days of intense pleasure in finding therein again and again the same feeling of freshness, inventiveness, ingenuity and vigour. And I warmly desire that your audiences of all countries may feel this work as it is felt by me, a Russian musician."[30]

One scans the letters and documents of these weeks in vain for any sign of the mental and emotional turmoil which Igor must surely have been experiencing as he shuttled to and fro between the more and more mutually exclusive halves of his life. At home in Anglet, the Stravinsky family were packing up for yet another move—a short one for once, to a house called the Villa des Rochers, in the rue de la Frégate in Biarritz itself, behind the Grande Plage, next to the Russian church. Much absent in the past months, he could regard his wife and children with a certain objectivity but no sense of alienation. He found them all, he had told Ramuz, in good health:

my wife looking well and in good spirits, the children all bigger—
Theodore very lanky (taller than me, which admittedly isn't very difficult), doing magnificent murals in a huge room in the house of an
old friend of mine who adores Theodore and his painting—he's a
very happy boy—much changed—and now always very cheerful.
Nini [Svetik] is growing into a nice-looking boy but still the same—
doesn't draw anymore, does nothing but play the piano and keeps
restarting the same waltz that he composed at Garches. . . . Mika
[Lyudmila] thinks of nothing but setting up a house and farm with
chickens, cows, etc. when she gets married; while Milène, having as
yet no very clear desires of her own, makes do with desiring the same
things as Mika.[31]

Of course, this kind of letter is inseparable from its addressee, and we may
imagine that Stravinsky was no longer favoring Ramuz with emotional
confidences after the episode of the *Soldier's Tale* libretto and his reported
remarks about the Chanel affair. That part of his life was over and done
with, and the shores of Lake Geneva seemed as far away now as Petrograd or Ustilug. By October Ramuz was fussing over a proposed staging
of *The Soldier's Tale* by the Paris impresario Jacques Hébertot, but its composer had other fish to fry and was interested in the Hébertot scheme
mainly as a source of income. "I must tell you, *mon vieux*, that I shall have
absolutely no time to spend on this business—the whole season being
stuffed as full as my trunk when I'm off on a trip."[32] But meanwhile Ansermet, whose own marriage lay in ruins as the result of an affair in London
during the summer, planned to conduct the Symphonies of Wind Instruments in Geneva at the end of November, and schizophrenically bombarded Stravinsky with a mixture of technical inquiries and personal
confessions which drew a sympathetic response but not a word of emotional reciprocation.

  Though barely a year old, the Symphonies must have begun to seem
like a voice from the past, just as Igor's Swiss friends had lost the proximity and shared intimacy of former times. The future was *Mavra*, Tchaikovsky, Vera, and Paris. And little by little these things were getting
entangled. *Mavra*, with its stylistic coquetries and in-jokes, was a distinctly
Parisian concoction, even if Paris knew little and cared less about its actual
ingredients. Then suddenly Vera and Tchaikovsky got mixed up with one
another. "I would love to go to the premiere of *The Sleeping Beauty*," Vera
had written to Igor Fyodorovich in mid-September, "but I do not know
whether I can manage it."[33] She managed it, in the end, by the simple expedient of taking part in the performance. Diaghilev wanted a tall, handsome
actress with good carriage for the mimed part of the Queen, and Vera
Sudeykina was the obvious solution—though one inevitably wonders

whether her casting had an ulterior motive, since it must have followed quite soon upon the visit by Diaghilev and Kochno to Anglet. Sudeykin was a fiercely possessive husband, and needed some persuasion to allow his wife to absent herself in London for what might turn out to be many weeks.[34] On the other hand, Kochno was close to the Sudeykins—at least he was beholden to them—and might have seemed unlikely to lend himself to a stratagem whose probable consequence would be to drive a wedge between them. But here, too, as we shall see, appearances may have been deceptive.

Time was short for so complicated a stage production. In the space of two months, Bakst grumbled to Diaghilev, "I've had to make, with my own hands, more than two hundred maquettes, costumes and sets, not to mention the accessories, the wigs, the shoes, the jewelry," whereas "at the Imperial Theatres they allocated a year and a half to staging a ballet."[35] Stravinsky, he claimed, was in similar case. This was an exaggeration, since the composer was orchestrating only some six minutes of music. Still, his arrangement of the violin entr'acte was ready only a few days before the scheduled opening, which, however, was two or three times postponed because of production problems. When on 2 November the Alhambra Theatre curtain at last went up on this spectacular and expensive extravaganza (renamed *The Sleeping Princess* to avoid confusion with the pantomime *The Sleeping Beauty*), the performance was so plagued with accidents that afterwards Diaghilev "sobbed like a child and all of us around him had difficulty calming him."[36] Several important pieces of machinery had failed to work. The enchanted forest had not risen and the mists had not descended. The critics, though, did not fail to condescend, studiously ignoring the point that the show's apparent old-fashionedness was its most modern feature: as the *Times* reviewer put it, "M. Stravinsky has told us that we may, nay, must enjoy this melody, so those of us who enjoy a frank and unaffected tune are sure of being in fashion for once,"[37] which was not quite what Stravinsky meant when he claimed Tchaikovsky as a model of directness and good taste "at a time when so many people, who are neither simple, nor naïve, nor spontaneous, seek in their art simplicity, 'poverty,' and spontaneity."[38]

Stravinsky had arrived in London a week before and attended the final rehearsals in the unheated Alhambra Theatre.[39] Goossens, who was conducting the ballet, was at the same time embarking on what Ansermet had grudgingly described to the composer as "a splendid season of four concerts with enormous publicity,"[40] the first of which, on 27 October, included the British premiere of *The Song of the Nightingale*. Presumably, Stravinsky was there. Was he impressed, and if so, what can he later have made of Ansermet's griping criticisms of Goossens's rehearsal of the Symphonies of Wind Instruments for the third concert in the series some six weeks later, by which time the composer was again safely tucked up in Biarritz? "It's very disagreeable," Ansermet wrote,

> for me to talk about the impression I received at his rehearsal on the eve of the concert. But I must tell you it frankly. I had the feeling that G. hadn't looked at your score. There was simply no tempo for me to call wrong; it was a matter of whim, and even worse than K[ousse-vitzky]. . . . After the rehearsal, I pressed him a good deal on the *Symphonies,* since it pained me to think that this work was once again to be sacrificed to London. I told him *everything* I should. I think it will have been better the next day, but I'm not sure and can't check. Diaghilev and Nouvel told me they understood nothing.[41]

But that earlier week in London, Stravinsky had other things on his mind. Vera was there, for once apparently without her husband,[42] and an affair which had been smoldering half-hidden behind suggestive dedications and epistolary formulae suddenly burst out with full physical and emotional force. Within the Ballets Russes company, it must soon have been fairly common knowledge. There is only light irony in an enigmatic poem that Kochno penned for Vera on Igor's second day in London:

> *Dear Friends of my childhood*
> *What is new in the company?*
> *What about Lyda, Lyda Lopokova?*
> *And Igor—the old friends?*
> *But I find things out by chance*
> *I was blessed with a gift of omniscience.*
> *And, for you, what could be nicer than a family of*
> *Friends, like Vera, from childhood.*[43]

So something had happened to supplant an old affair—one, moreover, which had recently shown signs of life, perhaps that very spring in Paris, when Lopushka had returned to the company for the first time since her elopement two years before. But was the seventeen-year-old Boris also issuing a delicate warning, and if so, what exactly was its purport? The young poet had a romantic fondness for obliquely autobiographical versification. A few months later he wrote a poem for Vera's husband, referring to the time in 1921 when Sudeykin had been painting his portrait, and implying that a distant and hopeless passion of that period when *Mavra* was in "her" infancy had now, in February 1922, at last been requited.[44] For Boris—unless his poem is a more than usually deceptive fiction—was himself in love with Sudeykin, and therefore had his own reasons for encouraging or discouraging the "friendships" on which he laid such euphemistic stress. Perhaps his closeness to Vera was already that of a collusion in a common aim—or perhaps he merely hoped to make it so. Intrigue is a lively substitute for blighted love. And it was an activity that went well enough with Boris's "omniscience."

At all events, he was only too willing to act as Pandarus in an affair that was itself rapidly assuming Shakespearean proportions. By the time he left London a few days after the Tchaikovsky opening, Stravinsky had firmly appointed Boris as his messenger boy. But Boris was at first slow to communicate. "Astonished a week without news," Stravinsky wired him from Biarritz on the fifteenth.[45] But the next day a letter did arrive, followed at last on the seventeenth by one from Vera, forwarded poste restante by Boris. Stravinsky wrote back at once:

> Verochka, I've at last got the letter from you that I've been so anxiously expecting. I too didn't realize I was so much in love. I've been simply beside myself going a whole week without any letters from you. Every day I've been chained to the post office—the postmen now know me intimately—and there hasn't been a thing. I've gone home along the hot streets of Biarritz in an evil and discontented frame of mind, which I've had to conceal in this street.[46]

A few days earlier he had had a visit from Sudeykin, who had arrived at Biarritz in a jealous fury, muttering threats against his wife. And although, Igor told Vera, "we parted in harmony and peace and he seemed quite reconciled, this display of mad jealously is obviously not an isolated instance. He told me straight, 'I cannot be responsible for my actions, I could kill her' and I assure you Verochka that if he is in the same frame of mind as I saw him on Thursday I think he would be capable of it."[47]

Sudeykin's anger and torment preyed on the composer's mind, and two days later he replied to a second letter from Vera that "I think it is inescapable, that it is important and has to be that you must return to him. . . . I agree with you that one cannot build one's happiness on the grief of another."[48] But this too left him dissatisfied, and that same day he wrote again:

> My Verochka, I've just sent you a letter, since I wanted to take advantage of the fact that there is no one in the house and I have enough peace and quiet, which is so nice; but in the feverish haste and agitation of my first letter today, I failed to answer one of your questions, my Verochka. And this question is so dear to me, so longed-for and loving, that I've now been going around with the letter and its question for twenty-four hours and rereading it and carrying it in my left-hand pocket, afraid of being parted from it. You want to know *one*

thing only, will I love you whatever happens? Ah, Verochka, can I answer you in any other way than you *now* answer the same question that I put to you?49

While this correspondence was passing through Boris's letterbox at the Savoy Hotel, Sudeykin, fresh from his meeting with Stravinsky, was turning his fire on Diaghilev. Vera's absence, he said, was upsetting his mental balance, and had given him a fit, which Igor had actually witnessed during their "working" breakfast in Biarritz. Igor agreed with him that Vera ought to return to Paris. And he appealed to Diaghilev's better nature as he understood it: "I've given you Boris (if he bores you, I'll take him back with pleasure), as well as Vera Arturovna. In this, I showed my love for you."50 Diaghilev may well have chuckled up his sleeve at this bizarre piece of moral blackmail. But he did think about a replacement Queen for the Tchaikovsky. And when Sudeykin wrote again in even more anguished terms, mentioning the poor state of his heart "owing to continuous worry," referring to his doctor, and signing himself querulously, "Your Sergey (who has not had much good from you)," Diaghilev agreed to release Vera from the contract which her husband had signed on her behalf two months before.51 By Christmas she was back in Paris.

It is easy to believe that Stravinsky had been shaken by his recognition of Sudeykin's emotional vulnerability, and perhaps he really did for a time intend to give Vera up. But it was probably also in his mind that Sudeykin was in a position—and desperate enough—to create a scandal that could upset the foundations of his whole creative and domestic life. The artist might even carry out his threat and kill Vera. She herself may have thought it possible: "He really didn't send for me out of caprice," she wrote to Diaghilev after Christmas.52 But when she had told Igor that "one cannot build one's happiness on the grief of another," she must have been thinking at least as much of Katya, a very different kind of victim from the fickle denizens of the Stray Dog or the Silver Age in exile. Yet if Igor was unwilling to abandon his family and unable to abandon Vera, what was the solution? As their letters flowed back and forth, almost daily, during November and early December, an image of his future double life began to take shape in Igor's mind, and he fought against her attempt to persuade herself "that separation from you is inevitable, that our love will not be eternal and that it is already necessary to begin to calm down." Such remarks, he told her, plunged him "into the most frightful terror." He could not think of ending their affair. "You must believe in my love," he insisted, "but remember that everything depends on you. We love each other too much and I WANT IT TO BE LIKE THIS AND LIKE THIS IT WILL BE."53 Thus, obliquely, he defined the terms of their life together for the next two decades.

Somehow, amid all this turmoil and deception, he got on with *Mavra*.

His ability to dissociate his creative work from the circumstances of his life had never stood him in better stead, and while the account of his passions during these months may resemble a romantic novella, his own operetta on the subject of illicit passion maintains a sure ironic touch at the expense, precisely, of cheap emotion. At its center was a musical version of Pushkin's idea of a trivial narrative tricked out with ludicrously self-important digressions on general moral questions and matters of poetic technique. Like his great compatriot, Stravinsky was—in Taruskin's phrase—"more interested in his telling than in his tale."[54] But whereas Pushkin had poked Byronic fun at the posturings of self-absorbed romantic poets, Stravinsky was more interested in the "poetic" models themselves: more occupied, that is, with the possibilities of a style based on a gestural language which might itself be out of date but which could be deconstructed and reassembled to provide a symbolic basis for a new language with its roots in history. So *Mavra* is both a skit—a sidelong glance at the "old Russia" of the Chauve-Souris—and, on another level, a vigorous invention in which style itself functions on several interacting, interlocking planes. On yet another, third, level, it is a polemic in favor of a particular kind of Russian art and against another kind which, Stravinsky had decided, was no longer viable, at least for him in the situation in which he found himself. Russian he could not avoid being. But he could at least be Russian in a way that, as Pushkin, Glinka, and Tchaikovsky had found, opened broader vistas and refused to be "merely" Slav. Here surely, rather than in *Pulcinella*, was "the epiphany through which the whole of my late work became possible."[55]

All this was intensely invigorating and absorbing, and the work went well. "For three weeks I've seen nobody," he told Ansermet early in December (without telling him who it was he had last seen: the raging Sudeykin). "I'm not moving, but am working without respite at my opera, which has every appearance of turning into a 'masterpiece'!"[56] And a few weeks later he assured Diaghilev that "*Mavra* seems to be the best thing I've done."[57] "The work on *Mavra* alone gives me a lot of strength . . . and faith in myself," he told Boris: "The quartet is the best [music] I have written so far in *Mavra*. I have managed to achieve such a clarity and simplicity as I have not been able to do before."[58] By early February the work was four-fifths complete. "I am now working ten hours a day," he wrote to Boris, "and orchestrating what I have composed."[59] No wonder he was so quick in later years to defend *Mavra* against its detractors; not only did it have hidden emotional significance, but it was a work of creative resolution. But still, his earlier music came back to haunt, or at least distract, him. Ansermet had described the "respectful but disconcerted" reception of the Symphonies of Wind Instruments in Geneva at the end of November.[60] Now, in February, Chester bombarded him with proofs of the vocal score of *Les Noces,* and—not always politely—demanded a full score for production in time for Diaghilev's Paris season in May. Incredibly, Stravinsky was still able to contemplate a completely new instrumentation of this ancient and mildewed score. Gone now were the mechanized instruments and the winds and percussion of the various 1921 versions, and in their place was a "perfectly homogeneous, perfectly impersonal, and perfectly mechanical" orchestra of four conventional pianos with percussion,[61] a scoring which finally transported the bucolic prewar conception into the bright, classical world that was rapidly becoming home to the musicians of postwar Paris.

But the world was still not quite ready to receive *Les Noces.* In London Diaghilev's Tchaikovsky run had ended in early February in financial disaster, and he was now faced with the task of mounting a Paris season with no money, an incomplete company, and no possibility even of translating the spectacular white elephant of *The Sleeping Beauty* to the stage of the Opéra, since the London impresario Oswald Stoll had sequestered the sets and costumes as security against the massive debt. Diaghilev's latest idea for *Les Noces* was that it should be choreographed by Nijinsky's sister, Bronislava, who had arrived in London from Kiev in the autumn in time to prepare some of the dances for the Tchaikovsky ballet. Fresh from the life-and-death atmosphere of reconstruction in the new Soviet Union, the serious-minded Bronya had been bemused by the faded magnificence of *The Sleeping Beauty,* but was thrilled at the thought of work on Stravinsky's ballet, with its solemn and austere re-creation of what was in effect a Russian rural ceremony of rebirth. One day in March, Diaghilev took her to Stravinsky's Pleyel studio, and for the first time she heard the composer play this music which he had first played for Diaghilev almost seven years before. Later they called on Goncharova, who had been designing and redesigning *Les Noces,* in styles as varied as the work's changing orchestrations, ever since 1915. In the current sketches, according to Bronya,

> both men and women wore heavy costumes, the long robes of the women trailing on the ground, heads decorated with high kokochnoks, the men with beards, all shod in heavy footwear. The body, the instrument of the dancer, attired in such a costume, its movements concealed, is like a violin enclosed in its case. The sketches of Gontcharova seemed to me to be diametrically opposed to the music of Stravinsky and also to my conception of the choreography of the ballet.[62]

Bronya did not conceal her distaste from Diaghilev, who, however, was not ready to abandon Goncharova's neonationalist concept without at least a show of autocracy, and coldly informed the young woman that in that case she would not be choreographing the ballet at all.[63]

This was almost certainly a bluff, since apart from Bronya Diaghilev did not have a choreographer to whom he could entrust so important a work.[64] She was a gift from heaven, and he knew it. How soon he went back to her we do not know. But he certainly told Stravinsky almost at once that she would be his choice, since only a month later he was wiring the composer in Monte Carlo asking him if her work on *Les Noces* (and his) could be ready in time for the Paris season in May. Stravinsky's reply ("Am certain that Bronya will never put *Noces* on in a month") suggests, however, that she had as yet done little or nothing towards the production, and conceivably did not yet even know that she was again in line to do it.[65]

But then what had taken Stravinsky to Monte Carlo? Diaghilev had planned a four-week season there at the last minute as a stopgap before Paris, and he was also already envisaging a grander autumn season on the Riviera, possibly including the premiere of *Les Noces* if it should prove impossible to have it ready for the spring. But also constantly in his mind was the question of cost. *Les Noces,* with its chorus and four tableaux and technical complexity, was a relatively expensive work to put on. If it were to be postponed, perhaps Raoul Guinsbourg, the manager at Monte Carlo, could be offered the *Mavra* premiere in compensation—a cheaper work, with only four singers and a single set—and that in turn would reduce Paris costs. But then what about Diaghilev's contract with Jacques Rouché at the Opéra, which stipulated a season including both of the new Stravinsky works? Rouché was already losing the big Tchaikovsky spectacular (in favor of a single act of excerpts called *Aurora's Wedding*). If *Les Noces* were also to be ruled out, some substitute would have to be found. Luckily, such a work was ready to hand, unperformed, and available to Diaghilev at no greater cost than the swallowing of a modest dose of pride. He could present *Renard,* the old Polignac commission from 1916. Rouché would accept this in lieu, Bronya could choreograph it in her own way, and *Mavra* would have to be retained as well to fulfill the contract. This may have been decided before Stravinsky went to Monte Carlo, where Bronya was already at work on *Renard.* Diaghilev had not given up all hope of *Les Noces,* but Stravinsky's telegram effectively laid it to rest for another year.[66]

In the event the Paris season opened on 18 May with the Tchaikovsky and *Renard* (paid for, magnanimously, by the princesse de Polignac,[67] conducted by Ansermet, and sung in French), together with *Carnaval* and the *Polovtsian Dances. Mavra* would come later. Diaghilev had at first somewhat quixotically approached Sudeykin to design *Renard,* but Sudeykin—hardly surprisingly—made such absurd conditions that Diaghilev quickly abandoned him in favor of the more amenable as well as artistically more suitable Laryonov.[68] It must have been a brilliant and unexpected production for an audience whose last Stravinsky premieres had been *Pulcinella* and *Le Chant du rossignol*. Nothing quite like Stravinsky's raucous, ebullient music had ever been heard on a French stage, and it was superbly backed up by the spirited buffoonery of Nijinska's choreography (with Bronya herself as the Fox), and by Laryonov's spiky animal costumes, in his wittiest neonationalist idiom. But this twenty-minute re-creation of a rustic performance by medieval strolling players, with its fifteen-piece band, four male singers, and four mimes on the stage, cut a bizarre figure in the stately surroundings of the Palais Garnier. And it baffled the press, including even the sympathetically disposed Vuillermoz, who found it "heavy clownery, obscure and indiscreetly drawn out,"[69] and maintained that Stravinsky's talents as an entertainer were not on the level of his musical genius—though a few days later, in the *Revue musicale*, he admitted that "this special humor is perhaps not very effective in a theatre like the Opéra."[70] Only Louis Laloy came close to grasping the spirit of the piece. "*Renard*," he insisted,

> is a small-scale work in which musical and scenic energy reaches its maximum concentration. It is a music without thickening, comparable to a painting without chiaroscuro. What power of sound and rhythm there is in it has to be heard to be believed. From the first notes, that flourish on the brass marking the entrance of the characters, one is gripped as if by the throat, or even bodily, with an urge to join in the dance and never let up. But this magic dance is also a joyous dance, for M. Stravinsky is a born musician. This devil of a man could, if he wished, draw music from a box of matches or a hatbox.[71]

But *Renard* may well also have puzzled those who had read yet another open letter by its composer in defense of Tchaikovsky, on the front page of that very morning's *Figaro*. There, Stravinsky had once again played down the importance of the *kuchka* and their picturesque nationalism, in favor of the more aristocratic and cosmopolitan tradition of the composer of *The Sleeping Beauty*—alias *Le Mariage de la Belle au bois dormant*. "I feel much closer," he wrote,

> to a tradition that might be traced back to Glinka, Dargomïzhsky, and Tchaikovsky.
>
> For the Russianism of the Five came out above all as opposition to the conventional Italianism that reigned in Russia at that time, and found expression in a picturesqueness which readily struck the imagination of foreign audiences. But that day is gone: opposition to

Italianism no longer has any purpose, and we find quite a new flavor in works whose Russian nature is revealed outside this need to oppose and without the aid of that picturesqueness which itself today seems to me perfectly conventional.[72]

Though meant as another apologia for Tchaikovsky, this could easily have been decoded by the sharp-eared into a repudiation of much of Stravinsky's own previous music, including *Renard*, the most radically anti-Italian, most hermetically Russian work of his that Parisians had yet heard. And perhaps it was some such perception which lured Marcel Proust, at a party in the Hôtel Majestic after the performance, into risking an effusion about late Beethoven which Stravinsky rudely and perhaps unexpectedly rejected with an irritable "I detest Beethoven."[73]

What was not yet apparent was the direct connection between the open letter and the other new Stravinsky work in the season, *Mavra*. Diaghilev had kept the little opera back for a fortnight, apparently because of the delay in finalizing the program in late April. Once the work was firmly slated for Paris, however, he was faced with the question of design. He was nominally committed to Bakst as a result of their *Sleeping Beauty* deal, but had probably always intended to renege on that commitment, which had been extracted from him by force.[74] When Bakst now discovered that Diaghilev planned to commission designs from a young Russian cubist called Leopold Survage, he saw red for the last time in his long association with the Ballets Russes. "I shan't work for you any more," he wrote petulantly to his old friend, adding, "show this letter to Stravinsky."[75] But Stravinsky—who had just been in Monte Carlo while Diaghilev was still in Paris—probably had nothing to do with the decision. Certainly he felt no particular loyalty to Survage, whose *Mavra* sets he dismissed only a year or so later as "Galeries Lafayette cubism."[76] Bakst, though, was confident in his resentment. "I'm not surprised," he wrote spitefully to Diaghilev after the premiere, "to learn of the failure of the new work by Yankel Stravinsky." And he advised Kochno: "Beware of instructions from Stravinsky. He's a great musician but a *small* brain."[77] Bakst had only another two and a half years to live, and neither quarrel was made up.

Five days before the stage premiere, Diaghilev tried the twenty-five-minute opera out in a "private" concert preview with piano in the Hôtel Continental, as part of a program pointedly entitled "Russian Music Apart from the Five" and also including pieces by Glinka, Dargomïzhsky, and Tchaikovsky.[78] Katya Stravinsky, though in Paris, did not attend. Just before the concert Stravinsky, who was playing the piano, scribbled her a note describing the scene: "We're all terribly nervous. All of us . . . will be on the stage—it's in the bordeaux and gold room where we dined last autumn—but they've built a platform."[79] According to Craft, Vera

Sudeykina was also absent, having been warned off by her husband.[80] But no doubt Stravinsky was expecting her. And perhaps, after all, she did go: at any rate her diary for that day, 29 May, records cryptically: "In the evening: Diaghilev," while the actual premiere, on 3 June, is marked by a large heart-shaped flower.[81] Sudeykin's interdict was in any case decisive, and within the next few days she left him.

For the premiere on the third (conducted, like the preview, by Gregor Fitelberg), Diaghilev sandwiched *Mavra* between *Petrushka* and *The Rite of Spring,* perhaps in the hope of hiding it between his two strongest Stravinsky works, which happened, moreover, to represent in full force precisely those tendencies that *Mavra* was supposed to refute.[82] But Diaghilev himself was no polemicist, and if—as Stravinsky later recalled—he was anxious about *Mavra,* it can only have been because he doubted its qualities as music theatre.[83] His fears were justified, and the opera was—as Bakst noted with more accuracy than generosity—a failure, despite excellent singing from a cast that included the young Oda Slobodskaya as Parasha. Stravinsky claimed that there was discord between Diaghilev and Bronya Nijinska, who staged the piece and whom Diaghilev could not forgive for looking like what she in a sense was, a female version of her brother.[84] But to the Parisian mentality, which was only just getting used to the rebarbative Stravinsky of *The Rite of Spring,* not to mention *Renard,* this new, tonal, songlike (if not tuneful), quasi-Italian but this time Russian-language Stravinsky was intrinsically baffling, as is shown even by the majority of those reviews that were comparatively favorable, like Laloy's in *Comoedia* (which gets the plot wrong and says hardly anything specific about the music), while to the unsympathetic the work was nothing more than "recondite nonsense" enacted by a cast of featureless dramatis personae.[85]

Among French critics, the notable exception to this blank incomprehension of Stravinsky's latest volte-face was Roland-Manuel in *L'Eclair.* A composer himself, Roland-Manuel was firmly in the Stravinsky-can-do-no-wrong camp. But while his description of *Mavra* is a brilliant point-by-point map of neoclassicism (though not yet so-called)—with its airs, duos, and ensembles, its Italianate melodies, its revived sense of key, and its disconcerting mixture of styles—even he wonders, with due deference and with every expectation of being proved wrong, whether a "pastiche" of this kind is a wholly legitimate artistic endeavor: "I owe it to the truth to say that I am not entirely convinced."[86] But the recently appointed music critic of the *Nouvelle Revue française,* Boris de Schloezer, was less inhibited. Himself a White Russian who, like the Sudeykins, had reached Paris via the Crimea the year before, he was the only critic of *Mavra* who to some extent shared Stravinsky's background and who therefore perhaps knew too much about the work's sources.[87] He could trace the music's ancestry back to what he called the Russo-Italian style that had originated with Alyabyev,

Verstovsky, Glinka, and Dargomïzhsky, and that had had "a greater or lesser effect on nearly all Russian composers, including even those, like Musorgsky, who considered that they were drawing exclusively on national folk sources."[88] The Stravinsky of *Renard* had remained free of this tendency, in cultivating what de Schloezer called a "Negro-Russian" style, influenced by the syncopated, percussive rhythms and brutal harmonies of so-called primitive music. But *Mavra* raised questions about this whole stylistic development.

> For the moment we can leave on one side the explanation Stravinsky has given in print. A work of art speaks for itself, and for now we are dealing purely with *Mavra* and that is what we have to judge. It seems to us that this synthesis of Italo-Russian and Negro-Russian elements which Stravinsky has tried to realize is not possible. Perhaps we are wrong, and *Mavra* is no more than a passing failure. For the time being, though, the composer has not proved the point, and we may doubt the value and vitality of this style, which combines with Russian and Gypsy romances the sounds and rhythms of a jazz band. Stravinsky has not achieved unity; the constituent elements of his work are at odds and fight among themselves.[89]

Probably the attempt to view *Mavra* historically at that time, and to judge it fairly on that basis, was doomed to failure. De Schloezer's attempted history was organic. But Stravinsky's was polemical and ultimately the product of elective enthusiasms. As he wrote to Roland-Manuel, in uncharacteristically benign response to his admittedly muted criticism:

> I derived much pleasure from reading your article on *Mavra,* and I am not at all bothered by its concluding reservations; on the contrary, since if you were one day to experience what you call the legitimacy of my intentions, new joys would perhaps be awaiting you, and then I hope that you would experience, as well, an enthusiasm for certain types of music our differing appreciation of which divides us somewhat from one another.[90]

But de Schloezer's criticisms provoked a more defensive response, perhaps specifically because he knew too much about the "certain types of music" and could place the work within a broader tradition than suited Stravinsky's polemical intention. Like Roland-Manuel, de Schloezer had tried to footnote his remarks with an "It is entirely possible that I am wrong . . . but if, after a year, I see that I *was* wrong, I want to be the first to admit it"—the qualification had, he claimed, been cut. But this time Stravinsky was unmoved. "Why after a year," he inquired, why not after two or even five years? And, more generally, if you allow the possibility of a mistake in your evaluation of *Mavra,* then you should have waited before writing your review, or at any rate refrained from such categorical statements as "*Mavra* is Stravinsky's first failure. . . ." Unless this phrase was distorted by the editor, it would seem to me that the phrase that *was* cut would not have changed the sense at all; on the contrary, had it been printed, *it* would have made no sense.[91]

Thus, hand in hand with the conscious rejection of an aspect of his past went a rejection of those who criticized him in terms of it. It was the start of a war which, in his lifetime, never really ended.

FOUR PIANOS AND A WEDDING

SOMEHOW, IN THE WEEKS that followed *Mavra*, Stravinsky managed with sovereign detachment to concentrate on new work. He had in mind some kind of piano concerto with wind and timpani. But as he surveyed the existing sketches, the piano and timpani dropped out, and he was left with a small mixed ensemble of woodwinds and brass—a combination he later claimed to have dreamt (though since he also says that the dream ensemble preceded any of the musical ideas, a claim contradicted by the sketches as well as in his autobiography, we should treat the story with caution).[1] In any case, the octet ensemble was settled by the time he completed a draft of the first movement on 16 August. But soon afterwards, having begun to plan the variation second movement round two earlier sketches (variations C and E respectively), he was interrupted by external events, and the Octet was shelved for—as it turned out—fully three months.

The cool objectivity of this music, which Stravinsky described soon afterwards as "not an 'emotive' work but a musical composition based on objective elements which are sufficient in themselves,"[2] might be construed either as compensation for the turmoil in his life at the time or simply as further evidence of his ability to cordon his creative work off from the outside world. But in either case the contrast is striking. Perhaps the anguished passions of the previous November had cooled measurably. But the perturbations of an uncertain future cannot have been greatly stilled. Vera had left her husband at the end of May, by which time—according to Robert Craft—Igor had told Katya about the affair and provoked "a tearful, 'Dostoyevskyan scene.' "[3] In mid-August (on the nineteenth) Sudeykin set sail for the United States with a bundle of sketches and paintings, and from that moment their marriage was effectively at an end, even though Vera sent a notably affectionate postcard winging after him ("You are now approaching New York and can see the Statue of Liberty. May she bring you victory"),[4] and even though nearly three years later a Philadelphia gossip page took advantage of the simultaneous presence of Sudeykin and Stravinsky in New York to report the painter's alleged view that Vera had only left him because he was less successful than Stravinsky, and Vera's alleged confession (presumably extracted from her by transatlantic telephone or thought waves) that she would consider going back to him if he could ever offer her "the aesthetic companionship and fling at fame which I crave."[5]

The composer's home life was about to be further complicated by the arrival of his mother from Petrograd. In June he had secured French permission for her visit, and it was now merely a question of Anna acquiring a Soviet exit visa. But however desired emotionally, her coming was both a challenge to her son's domesticity and one more charge on his exchequer, and he can hardly have regarded it with absolute equanimity. The Belyankins were still, or again, more or less dependent on him, and their only remote hope of repaying their growing debt was through restitution on their Ustilug property, which was now—unhelpfully for Russians—in Poland. Not surprisingly, money worries once again invaded Stravinsky's correspondence. His latest idea, he told Ansermet in July, was to take out French naturalization in order to protect his copyright as an inducement to potential publishers.[6] He had been back in Paris for meetings with an American publisher called Richard Hammond, and the naturalization idea seems to have been Hammond's (though he must have known that French nationality would not have protected Stravinsky's music in the United States).[7] The trouble was that other publishers were still proving wary of his latest works, with their awkward, unconventional instrumentations and lack of obvious salability. Kling had turned *Mavra* down long before its first performance.[8] Wilhelm Hansen in Copenhagen later for some reason accepted the tiny Concertino but nothing else. Nobody was much interested in the Symphonies of Wind Instruments. RMV were in the process of opening a Paris office; but they had been thrown into disarray by Nikolay Struve's sudden and violent death in a lift accident in October 1920. By early 1922 their only new Stravinsky score was *The Rite of Spring*, which at last landed on the composer's doormat in February; *The Song of the Nightingale* and Three Pieces for String Quartet would soon follow, but there was still no contract for any new work. Then, in July, as an unwanted reminder of the whole uncertainty of postwar music publication, a letter arrived from Boris Jurgenson in Moscow, imploring Stravinsky to intercede with Diaghilev for desperately needed back royalty payments on *The Firebird*. "The other day," he added, "I received a letter from Chester in London, informing me, in passing, that they have got some new *Firebird* suite from you. Isn't there some misunderstanding here?"[9]

One way and another, Stravinsky was plagued by old works. The printing of *The Rite of Spring* by no means laid that complex score to rest, since the edition turned out to be riddled with mistakes and would even have been held up, if the composer had had his way, while he and Ansermet prepared an extensive foreword and three-page errata.[10] Ansermet, who was planning to conduct the work in Berlin in November, was understandably anxious to have reliable orchestral parts available for that performance. But while correcting the printed material, he had a bright idea. Why not extract a concert version of the prelude to part 2, with slightly reduced wind sections, and the closing bars sutured somehow into a concert ending? Incredible as it now seems, Stravinsky not only agreed to this bizarre idea without demur, but actually sent the new ending by return of post.[11] Whether or not Ansermet ever conducted the piece separately in this form, he undoubtedly used it in his first-ever Geneva performance, the following February, where—pressed for time and unsure of his orchestral extras—he did "the first part complete, followed at once by the introduction to part 2 in the new arrangement."[12] The composer's reaction is not recorded, but nor is there any record of Ansermet ever again playing the work in this truncated form.

By August 1922, Stravinsky was on tenterhooks about his mother's arrival in Berlin. The German authorities were insisting on his being on the quayside at Stettin when she docked there, but it was impossible to tell how soon her Soviet visa would be issued or how quickly thereafter she could get the necessary German and Belgian transit visas. On the twenty-eighth he set off again for Paris to await firm news,[13] no doubt glad enough of a pretext to spend time with Vera now that her husband was definitively out of the way. But after more than a fortnight during which he seems to have done little else, except correct proofs of the three quartet pieces and stitch up the *Rite of Spring* prelude for Ansermet, he went back to Biarritz and promptly took to his bed with flu. "Impossible to concentrate," he had told Poulenc, promising him a long letter "when I am calmer."[14] Exactly when he finally left for Berlin is hard to establish, but there is at least negative evidence that he gave up waiting for confirmation of Anna's visa (which was finally stamped on 12 October), since there is a gap in his correspondence after 18 September. If so, he may have spent as many as seven weeks kicking his heels in the German capital before Anna's ship at last steamed into Stettin, the main Baltic port for Berlin, on 10 November.[15] They had not seen each other for eight years.

In Berlin, too, Igor was hardly able to work. Craft tells us that he wrote a concert ending for the Nightingale's song in his opera, presumably at the behest of Struve's successor, Ernest Oeberg, whom he saw often and got to know well during these weeks.[16] Berlin at that time was something of a center for the growing Russian emigration, since Stettin was the first convenient Western port for ships descending the Baltic, not all of which carried voluntary or ostensibly temporary exiles like Anna Stravinsky. The philosopher Nicolas Berdyayev, exiled for his opposition to the Soviet policy of atheism, arrived in Berlin by the same route only a month or so before her:

> There were twenty-five of us [exiles], and, together with our families, about seventy-five. The boat *(Oberbuergermeister Haken)* for the voyage from Petersburg to Stettin was entirely occupied by our party. When we left Soviet waters behind us many had a feeling of being out of danger: until then no one was certain that we would not be sent back at the last minute. A new life was opening before us. We felt free; yet in me the sense of freedom was transfused by a sense of intense pain at parting, perhaps irrevocably, with my native land. The voyage across the Baltic was wonderful; the sea was calm and smooth; the sun beat down from an unclouded sky, and the nights were mild and starry. On arrival in Berlin we were met with courtesy and kindness by representatives of various German organisations. . . . No Russian *émigrés* came to meet us.[17]

Stravinsky may or may not have met Berdyayev in Berlin. But he did certainly meet another, younger Russian thinker of not wholly dissimilar views, who had recently arrived in Berlin via Turkey and Bulgaria. Pierre Souvtchinsky (Pyotr Suvchinsky) was a rich, cultivated amateur musician and litterateur with aspirations as a singer, who had been for a time involved with Andrey Rimsky-Korsakov's journal, *Muzïkal'nïy sovremennik,* and subsequently with Boris Asafyev as co-editor and financial backer of a short-lived new-music journal called *Melos.* No doubt Souvtchinsky was quick to explain to Stravinsky that he and Asafyev had broken with Rimsky-Korsakov (early in 1917) over his refusal to publish an article by Asafyev "that foresaw the importance of Stravinsky, Prokofiev, and Myaskovsky."[18] After leaving Russia in 1920, Souvtchinsky had become involved with the nascent Eurasian movement in Sofia, and had co-published two books that effectively set out its agenda, Prince Trubetskoy's *Yevropa i chelovechestvo* (Europe and Humanity) and a set of essays called *Iskhod k Vostoku* (Exodus to the East), two of which Souvtchinsky himself had written.

Many aspects of Eurasianism must have sounded echoes for Stravinsky of his own wartime attitudes as expounded to Romain Rolland that distant afternoon at Vevey in 1914, attitudes which were presumably common currency among the nervy and unwilling exiles of the first month or two of war. Stravinsky's image of Russia as the storehouse of "a beautiful and healthy barbarism, bursting with new seeds that will impregnate the world's thought," reads uncannily (and with due allowance for the events of the intervening years) like the obverse of Pyotr Savitsky's millennial description of the post-Revolutionary Russian spirit: "In immeasurable sufferings and deprivations, in the midst of hunger, in blood and sweat Russia took upon herself the burden of searching for truth, on behalf of all and for the benefit of all. Russia in sin and godlessness, Russia in loath-someness and filth. But Russia in search and struggle, in a bid for a city not of this world."[19]

But one element of Eurasianism had had no place in the composer's Vevey outburst, and it was precisely this gap which Souvtchinsky had set out to fill in his own pair of essays: the idea, that is, that the great Russian renewal would come about specifically through the revival of the Orthodox Church, under whose "one great and all-resolving dome . . . a wise and calm people and an intelligentsia that has recovered its sight will peace-fully unite."

> The world was entering a new age, the Age of Faith; a new deep, organic, truly integral structure was to replace the apartness, the end-less splitting, the rationalism, and the sterility characteristic of the dying world of the past.[20]

Souvtchinsky saw the chief expression of these new currents of thought "in music, the highest of the arts, and drama, the two being, of course, closely related." One can well imagine that he put such ideas with a certain urgency, and that the impressionable Stravinsky absorbed them in his own way, however resistant he (like Berdyayev) may have been to the foggy insularity and the bitter factiousness which actually characterized émigré life, whatever its philosophers may have tried to insist about organic struc-tures and peaceful unity.

It certainly seems doubtful whether the composer any longer expected much of the millennial Russian spirit. That, for him, had suffered its political demise after the failure of the great postwar Revolution, which, he had prophesied to Rolland, would "overturn the [Romanov] dynasty and found the United Slav States."[21] Recently he had been taking much more interest in the United States of America, which he imagined as a land of progressive artists and thinkers who would at once see the value of his work and be prepared to pay him good money to conduct it for them. Back in France, there had been much talk of American tours with Diaghilev and Ansermet, though nothing had yet come of it. Now, suddenly, at the recep-tion desk of the Hotel Russischer Hof in Berlin, he found himself being addressed by a young man who described himself as "an American com-poser" and spun him a tale about the "young, enterprising, new-spirited composers" of that country, all of whom, it seemed, were rabid Stravinskians, and all of whom wrote music "not at all like contemporary German, English or Italian music" but exceedingly like Stravinsky's own not-quite-latest, late-Russian manner.[22] The twenty-two-year-old George Antheil had correctly divined that his Americanness was his largest single claim on the attentions of his idol, and he was forward enough to draw full value from that perception. By his own implication they had lunch together ("and also, more often than not, breakfast, dinner and supper") practically every day of Stravinsky's stay in Berlin. Stravinsky was doubtless struck by the young man's vitality and enthusiasm and by his knowledge of modern music. But above all he seems to have been impressed by Antheil's pianism. In any event he told Antheil that "you play my music exactly as I wish it to be played,"[23] and he even offered to set up a concert for him in Paris as well as putting him in touch with Ansermet with the idea of a Swiss tour.[24]

Stravinsky's ulterior motive, which does not figure in Antheil's self-advertising memoir, is that he wanted to use Antheil's agent, Martin Hanson, to set up an American tour for himself and Ansermet and transatlantic publication of his works. Souvtchinsky had wired him from Berlin in mid-December, apparently to the effect that Antheil was not to be counted on. "What you write me about Antheil," Stravinsky replied, "I already knew, but I'm not relying on him, only on the people who stand behind him and who will set everything in motion for me."[25] To this end, it seems, he was prepared to endure continual petty irritations from the flighty and self-absorbed Antheil, who (like some American reincarnation of Diaghilev) rarely answered a letter or left a forwarding address. It was only when Hanson at last turned up in Geneva in mid-March (without Antheil) and made it clear to Ansermet that he would help organize a concert tour so far as was consistent with his primary commitment to his young client, but would under no circumstances involve himself in matters of publication, that Stravinsky seems to have realized that he was wasting his time.[26] Perhaps there was some residual annoyance at this failure in his abrupt cold-shouldering of Antheil when they next met in Paris in June, an incident which Antheil—with disarming candor—explains as the result of Stravinsky's having discovered that he was a "four-flusher": a bluffer who had been bragging to all and sundry about his intimacy with the great man.[27]

Antheil's is the only memoir we have of Anna Stravinsky's arrival in Berlin on 10 November 1922. She brought with her a pile of Stravinsky's "earliest attempts at composition," but also "a faint but typical Soviet Russian contempt for his present 'mercurial' (as she considered it) reputation in Paris."

One evening, while I was sitting with both of them, I heard Mrs. Stravinsky and her son break into a heated prolonged argument. She would not give in and finally Stravinsky almost broke into tears, so wrathful did he become.

At last he turned to me and translated: he, Stravinsky, no longer able to stand his mother's inordinate admiration for Scriabine (when, after all, she had a son destined to become more famous than Scriabine would ever become!), admonished her, criticizing her taste, and finally admitting to hating Scriabine. Whereupon she had answered, "Now, now, Igor! You have not changed one bit all these years. You were always like that—always contemptuous of *your betters!*"[28]

Antheil could not know that the Petersburg contempt for Stravinsky's Paris reputation was long pre-Soviet. But in every other respect the story rings true. Anna had not changed either, and for a moment Igor must have felt as if he were back at 66 Kryukov Canal, sitting at table with his parents, stern and unbending, or at Pechisky, enduring the guilt of having survived his in every way handsomer, more talented eldest brother.

It was twenty years, to the month, since his father's death.

IGOR SURELY HEAVED a sigh of relief as he and Anna set off on the return journey to Paris on 13 November, and he was probably no more than mildly sorry to miss Ansermet's Berlin *Rite of Spring* a week later. Souvtchinsky wrote him a detailed report the same evening. A hostile section of the packed audience had equipped themselves with penny whistles—a very unspontaneous way, Souvtchinsky thought, of showing disapproval. But in any case the whistling was drowned by the applause and shouting. Having thus, he hoped, pleased the composer, Souvtchinsky risked a criticism of the work's ending, which he thought weakened by the softening effect of the strings; instead it would be better "to *harden* the sound and make it like stone right to the end—like a cast-iron machine. . . . I'm convinced that the *divisi* strings work against the realization of your timbre-rhythmic concept."[29] That Souvtchinsky wrote in this way at all suggests that he had already struck up a close rapport with the composer, who was as a rule positively uninterested in adverse criticism of his music. But it also suggests that textual details had been discussed in Berlin, perhaps with Ansermet, who had previously written Stravinsky a long letter regretting, among other things, the abandonment of the original idea of alternate bowed and plucked strings in this ending. But Stravinsky's marginal note on Ansermet's letter shows that he felt himself to be up against the shortcomings of orchestral players: "As orchestras will never contain anyone but fools, I feel bound to stick to the complete removal of the pizzi[cati] in the Sacrificial Dance."[30]

Mother and son seem to have stayed in Paris together until almost the end of November, which must have severely if not completely curtailed Igor's freedom of movement where Vera was concerned, since it went without saying that, however brutally candid he might be with Katya about his affair, his mother had to be kept in the dark. This might be fairly easy in distant Biarritz, but was much harder in Paris, where the situation was openly acknowledged—at least as far as was consistent with the social code of the Faubourg-Saint-Germain. But Igor could not leave at once, since he had been booked to conduct three of his own works—*Fireworks*, some excerpts from *The Nightingale*, and the *Firebird* Suite—at a concert at the Gaumont-Palace in Montmartre on the twenty-fifth.[31] So he settled briefly back into his Pleyel studio routine, working on the second movement of the Octet. There he was visited by the poet Mayakovsky, who left a vividly futurist impression of the factory:

> Interestingly, what you first encounter in this factory is not "the divine sound," but modern music production, all mixed up—from the musician to the commander of the baggage train. Outside is the factory block. In the yard there are enormous trucks with pianolas ready for dispatch. Further on—the howling, singing and rumbling of the three-storey building. On the first floor is an enormous room gleaming with pianola cases. In odd corners virtuous Parisian couples listen pensively to demonstrations of every conceivable musical gadget. On the second floor is the concert room—the best, most favored in Paris. It's inconceivable not to play or sit here to the end of the working day. The heart-rending wail of pianolas being tested penetrates even through closed doors. Here, bustling and panting in sheer dignity, is the factory owner, M. Lyon, sporting his order of the Légion d'honneur. And finally, at the top, the tiny room of the musician, cluttered with pianos and pianolas. Here he creates his symphonies, hands them in to the factory, and, finally, corrects his music at the pianola. He talks enthusiastically about the pianola, "writing for eight, for sixteen, for twenty-two hands!"[32]

Stravinsky played some *Nightingale* excerpts, the study for pianola, and fragments of *Les Noces* and *Mavra*. But Mayakovsky (whose understanding of music, Stravinsky later remarked, was "wholly imaginary") was unimpressed. As for the composer, he saw before him "a somewhat burly youth . . . who drank more than he should have and who was deplorably dirty, like many of the poets I have known."[33]

Like Stravinsky on his most recent trip, Mayakovsky had reached Paris from Berlin. They seem not to have met there. But Mayakovsky had run across Diaghilev, who (seeing him as a possible collaborator) had apparently helped with his French visa;[34] and he had also picked up with an old Stray Dog friend, the composer Arthur Lourié, who—for reasons that are still uncertain—had defected from the Soviet Union in 1921, while on an official visit to Berlin in his capacity as head of music in the Commissariat of Popular Education. Lourié and Mayakovsky travelled to Paris together in November 1922,[35] and one might suppose that Mayakovsky would have introduced his companion to Stravinsky, considering that Lourié also had connections with Anna Stravinsky and had almost certainly met her in St. Petersburg in 1920 at the time of Igor's first inquiries about her visa. But Lourié had heard or suspected that Stravinsky was for some reason prejudiced against him—no doubt because of his Bolshevik associations—and he did not seek a meeting,[36] even though, unlike Mayakovsky, he remained in Paris for more than a year until he was secretly denounced to the French Foreign Ministry as an unreconstructed Communist and forced to leave the country.

Eventually, at the end of the month, Stravinsky took his mother to Biarritz, and settled her in at the Villa des Rochers with the family of which he had recently seen so little. Nor did he stay for as much as a full month this time, but returned to Paris—probably in Christmas week—in time for a Jean Wiéner concert of his works in the Théâtre des Champs-Elysées on the twenty-sixth.[37] Wiéner was a pianist and composer in his mid-twenties who combined a passion for jazz with an active enthusiasm for all kinds of new music, which he promoted in what became the most dependable and by a long way the most enterprising concert series in twenties Paris. At the first Festival of the International Society for Contemporary Music in Salzburg the previous August, when the trio suite from *The Soldier's Tale* had been withdrawn for lack of rehearsal time, leaving Stravinsky unrepresented in what was supposed to be the most prestigious festival of new music, Wiéner had insisted on playing the *Piano Rag Music,* with "enormous success," as Poulenc reported to the composer.[38] Now Wiéner had well-founded plans for his Christmas Stravinsky concert, backed by money from the princesse de Polignac (enough at least to attract other sponsors in the modish world of Parisian arts patronage). Such disinterested support was comforting to the composer; he found it all very "chic," he told Ansermet.[39] But the Salzburg rebuff was another matter. It fed all his old insecurities, and even poisoned his attitude to his own friends. "Here I am," he protested,

> at the "head of modern music," as they say and as I'm willing to believe now that I've reached the age of forty, and here I am being ignored in the big time at the "grand international congress" of

Salzburg—capital of Mozart, who for me is what Raphael was for Ingres and is for Picasso. Does it all make sense? It's true that the committee reserved important places in the program for Darius Milhaud, Ernest Bloch, Richard Strauss (probably Corngold [sic], Casella, Varèse too)—all musicians of "international" standing. One shouldn't begrudge it them too much—the poor things go to a lot of trouble. . . . What's to be done (as Ramuz asks)?—Nothing, nothing to be done. It's quite true, and that's what's hard. Ah! the bastards! The only satisfaction is that it hardens one and . . . that's what bastards deserve! All they deserve![40]

What grated with him was surely that word "international," effectively banishing Paris and its modish flippancies to a provincial backwater. In any case, it wasn't as if his music had enjoyed unqualified success even there. Look what had happened to his beloved *Mavra*. *Renard* had been only a degree or two better; and before that, there had been the massacre of his Symphonies of Wind Instruments in London. And meanwhile, publishers were falling over each other to avoid buying his works. No wonder he set store by the Wiéner retrospective, which was to include no works more than four years old, and at least two Paris premieres—the Three Movements from *Petrushka*, played by Wiéner himself, and the Symphonies, conducted by Ansermet. The Pro Arte Quartet were playing the little Concertino, and there was also the *Pulcinella* suite and a concert performance of *Mavra*.

Although Georges Auric reported a "very great success . . . for the admirable *Mavra*,"[41] it seems that something went badly wrong. "I left the theatre utterly disgusted and in despair," Stravinsky wrote to Auric's friend Poulenc, "Ansermet too. The rehearsal actually promised us a good performance of *Mavra*. And you saw how the singers buggered me up. . . . I'm in a very bad temper, and I have reason to be."[42] Ansermet's morale was badly undermined by the concert. "I got home from Paris very affected by the bad performance of *Mavra*; it has pursued me, and at every moment I re-experience the agony of this or that passage; obviously if the singers had held firm, nothing would have stopped; but I'm perfectly aware that I myself was reduced, tired, incapable of making the effort that I could have done at other times to make things work at all costs."[43] Did the performance almost or actually break down? It seems that it did.

Once again Stravinsky was in Biarritz for barely a week before boarding the train for Paris, and this time—whatever he may have told Katya, and especially his mother—the overriding motive for the trip was to spend time with Vera. He was away for most of January and February. Vera's diary records trips to the theatre and cinema, an outing to Rouen, a weary round of lunches, teas, and dinners.[44] They went to the Grand Guignol and, early in February, with Diaghilev and presumably Kochno, to the Trianon Lyrique in Montmartre, where Louis Masson was conducting Cimarosa's *Matrimonio segreto* and Gounod's *Philémon et Baucis* ("a musical marvel," Stravinsky told Ansermet).[45] Gounod's decorative mythology, especially, appealed to what was left of the World of Art in Diaghilev, while for Stravinsky, it had the attraction that it was charming, well crafted, economical, and above all unpretentious, in which respect it chimed with his own creative preoccupations of the moment, as well as with the virtues of taste and refinement he had been arguing in his preferred Russian lineage of Glinka and Tchaikovsky.[46]

Vera had made friends with Igor's niece Irina Belyankin, now a beautiful girl of nineteen who had come to work for Chanel in Paris and had simplified her name to Ira Belline. Thus a trace family element entered into Igor's alternative life; but it was a disaffected one, since Ira can have felt little but distaste for the scraping dependency of her parents' existence in Biarritz, and must have set herself from the start to eradicate such dependency from her own life. To what extent this distaste yet included that measured contempt for her Stravinsky cousins which comes out in her much later correspondence with Vera is impossible to tell.[47] But it should not be assumed, since Ira certainly remained on affectionate terms with her own family. What is clear, though, is that in Paris, Ira, with her physical advantages, assumed a lifestyle which rapidly distanced her from her recent provincial émigré background and aligned her with the *mondaine* world to which her uncle was already inured. It was a world which her cousins, for reasons beyond their control, could never enter.

These weeks in Paris perhaps had a certain honeymoon character. Successive entries in Vera's diaries speak for themselves, if not always quite in the sense one might suspect from their published text: "[January] 20— Thunder and lightning over Rouen Cathedral; Rouen duck 45 francs— divine, divine!"[48] But Igor was also working, as ever. The Octet still lacked its finale, and meanwhile he was coming under what was by now his annual pressure, from both Diaghilev and Kling, to complete *Les Noces* for the ballet's spring season. Trying to ward off this pressure on his friend's behalf, Ansermet instead incurred his wrath for letting slip to Diaghilev that the Octet existed and that he, Ansermet, had heard some of it—a claim Stravinsky made no bones about denying to Diaghilev in his turn, thus turning himself, he grumbled to his Swiss friend, into "an unintentional liar" as well as representing Ansermet as a conscious one. But for the conductor what was painful was "that you could have thought I was betraying you. . . . As for appearing a liar to D., that can only send me up in his esteem; it's the only thing he likes."[49]

But Diaghilev was now firmly programming *Les Noces* for May or June,

Stravinsky with
Alexander Benois at
Tivoli, 1911

Claude Debussy and
Stravinsky, photographed
by Erik Satie at Debussy's
home, probably 1912

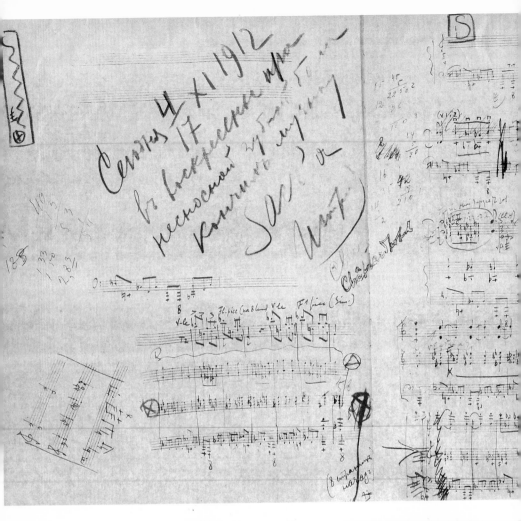

A page from the *Rite of Spring* sketchbook. The inscription reads "Today Sunday 4/17 XI 1912 with an unbearable toothache I finished the music of Sacre. I Strav Clarens Chatelard Hotel."

Leonid Massine, Natalya Goncharova, Mikhail Laryonov, Stravinsky, and Lev Bakst at Ouchy, August 1915

With C. F. Ramuz (right) and the family of the painter Albert Muret at Lens (Valais), 1918

Ernest Ansermet, Sergey Diaghilev, Stravinsky, and Sergey Prokofiev, London, 1921

With Lydia Lopukhova
at Anglet, 1921

Katya Stravinsky
with her children
Milène and
Theodore,
Morges, 1919

Stravinsky with
his two daughters,
Morges, 1919

Vera Sudeykina at
the Royal Gaillac,
Paris, 1923

Tanya Stravinsky, Nice, 1925

With Pierre Monteux,
Barcelona, 1928

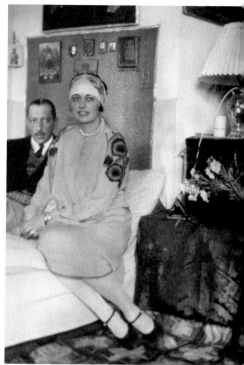

With Vera in her Paris
flat, 1926

Stravinsky conduct-
ing, c. 1928

With his mother at
Echarvines, 1929

Arthur
Lourié, 1928

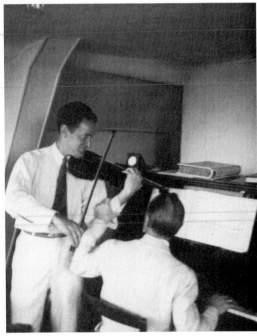

Rehearsing with Samuel
Dushkin at Voreppe,
September 1931

At dinner with Gavriyil
Païchadze, c. 1930

Svetik (Soulima) and Igor
Stravinsky with Dushkin,
c. 1933

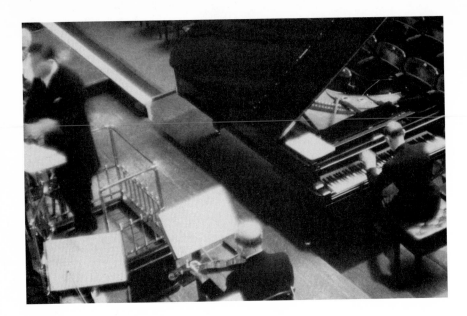

Rehearsing his Capric-
cio under Eugen Pabst,
Hamburg, January 1933

Coaching Svetik in
the mid-thirties

and meanwhile there was the continuing project of making piano rolls of his existing works. So at some stage the Octet was again shelved. At Pleyel, Stravinsky had been "Pleyelizing" *Petrushka*, the Five Easy Pieces, and *The Song of the Nightingale*, which actually figured—in this form—in a Wiéner concert on 23 February.[50] Garafola suggests that Diaghilev's final decision to stage *Les Noces* that spring was prompted by a visit to a performance by Alexander Tairov's Kamerny Theatre, with its echoes of Soviet modernism.[51] Certainly by mid-March, now back in Biarritz, Stravinsky was "working on *Les Noces* and finishing the Octet—this piece which dots the *i*'s."[52] But the *i*'s were to remain undotted for another two months. Instead he spent a week on the ballet, went back to Paris for a week, returned once more to Biarritz for the four or five days of Easter, then immediately catapulted off, via Paris, to Monte Carlo, where Nijinska needed his help rehearsing the ballet and where—no less to the point—he could again be with Vera.[53] Here the score of *Les Noces* was at long last finished, on 6 April. Yet four weeks later Chester had still received only the first fifty-two pages of the manuscript full score and were being threatened by Diaghilev with legal action for nondelivery of the orchestral material. Only on 6 May was Stravinsky, still in Monaco, able to confirm the dispatch of the remaining pages to the copyist in Paris. Two weeks later, himself back in Paris, he completed the finale of the Octet.

Bronya had got her way with Diaghilev over the production style of *Les Noces*, which would completely reject the picturesque, neonationalist Russianism of Goncharova's costumes. "There should not be any colorful ostentation in a country peasant wedding," she told him. "I see the costumes as being of the utmost simplicity and all alike."[54] Her thinking was decidedly early-Soviet in its inspiration: "There would not be any leading parts. . . . The action of the separate characters would be expressed, not by each one individually but, rather, by the action of the whole ensemble." At the same time, the group movements were highly geometric, like a constructivist stage design. But no doubt she knew that Stravinsky had devised his score precisely so that even the solo voices would not coincide with the characters on stage but would act, so to say, as individual expressions of a group feeling; and this had been a feature of the score since 1915. What she may well not have known was the extent to which her ideas also chimed with Stravinsky's recent musical thinking, his growing preference for an art of clear linear relationships and expressive forms, an art untainted by the sentimental preconceptions of the individual performer: the art, indeed, of the Octet. In fact the astonishing thing about Nijinska's choreography is that it might have been born at the very moment that Stravinsky decided to limit his orchestra to four pianists and six percussionists, and yet—like that scoring—it seems to reflect essences that were part of the work from the beginning.

The first night of *Les Noces*, at the Théâtre de la Gaîté Lyrique on 13 June (conducted by Ansermet and with the Russian choir of Stravinsky's old friend from the Swiss days, Vasily Kibalchich) was preceded by a private preview at the princesse de Polignac's house in Passy and a gala *répétition générale* of almost prewar splendor, as perhaps befitted a work that had first been publicly announced in imperial Russia more than a decade before and that in a sense directly fulfilled the promise of Stravinsky's last prewar ballet that same year. And certainly *Les Noces* was the nearest thing since *The Rite* to the kind of work Diaghilev's patrons had been expecting of his leading composer. Here was another pagan, or quasi-pagan, peasant ritual, expressed through vibrant rhythms and harsh, incantatory fragments of folk melody. Of course, *Les Noces* was more severe, less picturesque than its great predecessor. Goncharova's uniformly brown and white costumes and rudimentary set, with painted-on windows or (in the final scene) painted bed visible through an open door, accorded perfectly with what Boris de Schloezer called "the 'choral' or 'round-dance' spirit of the production," in which all individualism was suppressed in the interests of social groupings.[55] Oddly enough, the one perverse, "boulevardier" element, Diaghilev's idea of placing the four pianos (or, to be exact, two double Pleyels, played by Georges Auric, Edouard Flament, Hélène Léon, and Marcelle Meyer) on the front sides of the stage in full view of the audience—and thus implicitly a part of the set—seems not to have been found disruptive. Perhaps it was felt to express the organic unity between the sung music and the scenic action.[56]

Les Noces was welcomed by Paris with enthusiasm and a certain sense of relief that *Mavra* could now be seen as an aberration and perhaps quietly forgotten. Emile Vuillermoz, for instance, while perfectly well aware (as his *Excelsior* review shows) that *Les Noces* was the earlier work, talked elsewhere of *Mavra* as a "futile gesture" which had been in some sense corrected by the "new" ballet.[57] Even the more sophisticated de Schloezer evaded the worrying question of sequence by suggesting the specious metaphor of the zigzag for Stravinsky's development, while formulating an assessment of *Les Noces* which in effect saw it as a 1920s "recall to order" sort of piece: "If *Noces* is the most moving, most deeply felt of Stravinsky's works, if it shakes us to the point of tears, it is because it is his most rigorously constructed, stylistically most pure, the one which is worked out entirely, and however far one pushes analysis, in formal elements."[58] This conveniently overlooked the fact that *Les Noces* had originally been conceived before the completion of *The Rite of Spring*, and that almost every note of it belonged to a time when Stravinsky was inventing an unfettered, bucolic modernism out of folk ingredients: an art as bibulous and unkempt in its way as the drunken cavortings in the final tableau of the ballet. It was all very well to talk, as de Schloezer had recently done, about the "purely formal beauty" of the Symphonies of Wind Instruments—a later, essentially more statuesque work in the same general vein.[59] But the emotion of *Les Noces* must surely begin, not with its form, but with its subject matter, and with what H. G. Wells so perceptively called the "gravity . . . deliberate and simple-minded intricacy . . . deep undercurrents of excitement [and] richly humorous solemnity" of "the peasant soul."[60] In his heart, de Schloezer knew this as well as the next man. "Actually," he told his Russian readers, "what is particularly striking on first acquaintance with *Les Noces* is its emotional meaning; it disturbs and affects one. . . . I would call it the most human of all Stravinsky's works; it's his greatest achievement—one of the summits of post-Wagnerian art."[61]

STRAVINSKY STAYED ON in Paris for nearly a month after the premiere, but this time there were professional as well as socioemotional reasons for not hurrying back to Biarritz. Above all, the possibility of solving his financial problems through a lucrative United States tour had become something of an obsession with him. During May he had had meetings with several American concert agents in Paris, including Alexander Kahn and A. F. Adams of the Wolfsohn Bureau in New York, with a view to a trip the following winter. In particular there had been a plan for a concert tour with the Philadelphia Orchestra and its conductor, Leopold Stokowski. In the end the only practical outcome of all this had been an agreement for Stokowski to conduct the United States premiere of the Symphonies of Wind Instruments. But now Stokowski was expected back in Paris at the end of June, and no doubt Stravinsky was anxious to see him in order to explore ways of reactivating the Philadelphia plan. Nothing much is known of their meeting, but the composer must have taken the opportunity to acquaint Stokowski with his money worries, since little more than a week later Stokowski sent him a check for one thousand dollars, explaining that it was the first of six half-yearly donations from an anonymous admirer in Philadelphia whom he identified simply as "Madame." Robert Craft has argued persuasively, if not conclusively, that "Madame" was a cover for Stokowski himself.[62] But in any case Stokowski was energetically promoting Stravinsky's music in the United States. In October 1923 he conducted *The Song of the Nightingale*, in November the American premiere of the Symphonies, and in December that of *Renard*. He told Stravinsky that "I have had the most profound musical pleasure in studying and conducting your works this season, and although the public is extremely hostile, I shall continue to present them."[63] There was, however, still no sign of a firm agreement for the composer to go and perform it himself.

Meanwhile, Stravinsky had asked Ansermet to approach Werner Reinhart on his behalf, either for direct financial support or, more likely, about the possibility of performances of his music in Switzerland.[64] Ansermet wrote to Reinhart early in June. Stravinsky's financial situation, he said, was parlous in the extreme; his American plans had come to nothing; his old contract with Diaghilev over Les Noces meant that he was drawing no new income from the Paris performances.[65] He might have added that Stravinsky's Russian nationality was still standing in the way of performances of his work, not to mention payment for them. At a meeting of the ISCM in Zurich in April, Ansermet had been forced to withdraw The Soldier's Tale (the full suite, this time) from the forthcoming Salzburg Festival because the lack of a Russian section had meant that there were no section funds to pay for rehearsals; instead, the Pro Arte Quartet were going to play the Three Pieces and the Concertino.[66] But as it happened, Reinhart had just written to Stravinsky about a planned production of The Soldier's Tale, in German translation, in Frankfurt in late June, under a young conductor called Hermann Scherchen. Would Stravinsky authorize the performance?[67] It looks as if this was a plan hastily cooked up by Reinhart, Scherchen, and Ansermet at the Zurich ISCM jury. As yet, there was no German translation of the text (it was done in late May by Reinhart and his brother Hans); Reinhart's request for permission was sent less than four weeks before the performance on 20 June; and the piece could only be staged at all by borrowing Auberjonois's existing sets and costumes and in the hope that the Pitoëffs, now in Paris, would be able to help with the production (they were not). Scherchen had wanted Ansermet to conduct, but he would be in Paris on the day in question, conducting for Diaghilev.[68] So Scherchen, who had for some time been toying with the idea of presenting the work in Berlin, had to learn it rapidly himself.

Hopeful as he was of more direct succor from his Zurich patron, Stravinsky deemed it politic not only to approve the production in principle, but also to waive his royalty.[69] Reinhart did not disappoint him. With his letter of 6 June he enclosed a check, along with the gentlest of hints that "another small score that you judge me worthy to possess" would be a welcome companion to the manuscript score of The Soldier's Tale which he already owned. On the thirteenth Stravinsky duly sent him the sketches for Les Noces, "in lively regret at his absence from the premiere today."[70]

For all his well-publicized indigence, Stravinsky did not spend his Paris weeks in a garret or a soup kitchen. Instead he dined often and no doubt well: at the princesse de Polignac's, at Prince Argutinsky's. He was guest of honor at a famous party on a Seine barge thrown in honor of the Noces premiere by Gerald and Sara Murphy, a rich American artist couple in the penumbra of the Ballets Russes (and the partial models for Dick and Nicole Diver in F. Scott Fitzgerald's Tender Is the Night).[71] He went on

25 June to the private premiere chez Polignac of his friend Manuel de Falla's puppet opera *El retablo de Maese Pedro,* in which Wanda Landowska played the harpsichord part, and which was followed by a banquet.[72] He was at Astruc's "Fête Merveilleuse" at Versailles on the thirtieth, at which Diaghilev's company danced *Aurora's Wedding* in a specially decked-out Hall of Mirrors, Boris Kochno appeared as a Roman herald in a Louis XIV tableau, and a new young aspirant, Serge Lifar, began to insinuate himself into Diaghilev's favors.[73] And he attended Darius and Madeleine Milhaud's flat-warming party in the boulevard de Clichy on 5 July. There were excursions with Vera to the châteaux at Pierrefonds and Chantilly. Returning to Biarritz (on 9 July) may have been an unhappy reminder of his straitened means and misdirected feelings. But he may also have been glad of the rest.

This time he was in Biarritz for exactly a month, before setting off yet again, for Paris and Weimar, where Scherchen was repeating the Frankfurt *Soldier's Tale.* In order to cross France by train, then as now, one was more or less forced to go via Paris. But, as usual, this was no more than a pretext in Stravinsky's case, since not only had Vera been charged with arranging his visa at the German consulate, but for the first time she would be travelling with him. The Weimar performance was on the nineteenth. They left Paris on the fifteenth, and shortly before eleven that evening they arrived at the station at Griesheim, on the far edge of the occupied Rhineland and still some twenty miles from Frankfurt:

> In Paris I could not get a through ticket. All I could obtain was a ticket to the station where the zone of occupation began, a little way from Frankfort. It was quite late when I reached the little station, which was occupied by African soldiers with fixed bayonets. I was told that at that hour there was no means of communication with Frankfort, and that I must wait till daylight, contenting myself till then with the bench in the waiting-room, which was, moreover, already crowded to overflowing. I wanted at first to look for a bed in the village, but was warned that it would be risky to go out in the dark because of the vigilance of the sentries, who might mistake me for a vagrant. It was so dark that I had to abandon the idea and stay at the station, counting the hours till dawn. It was not till 7 a.m. that, guided by a child, and after a tramp of half an hour along rain-soaked roads, I finally reached the shelter of the tram which took me to the central station of Frankfort, where I found a train to Weimar.[74]

Fate could hardly have arranged a less auspicious first night for the two illicit travellers, and one inevitably wonders whether they felt or expressed any misgivings. Of course, nothing of the kind emerges from the blandly

diplomatic pages of the autobiography. But they must have been prepared for difficulties and discomfort in the Germany of 1923. Not only
was the political situation tense after the French reoccupation of the Ruhr
and Rhineland in January, but the country was wracked by hyperinflation which badly affected services and supplies. "I can see no end to
it," Ferruccio Busoni had written from Berlin to Isidor Philipp in Paris
less than a fortnight before. "My dear wife has a daily struggle to find
butter at 300,000 Marks a pound! (Everything else in proportion.) Often
enough there is none to be had. . . . How unpleasant this all is! Wicked!
Inhuman! The masks are falling. They reveal nothing but the deformities
which had been so shamefacedly concealed. . . . How that resounds into
contemporary art! The oxen on the roof and the swine in the cellar."75
Busoni, though in failing health, was himself going to Weimar, where
Egon Petri was playing in a concert including some piano pieces of his and
Hindemith's song cycle *Das Marienleben*. Vera and Igor went to this concert (on the eighteenth), and they sat next to Ferruccio and Gerda Busoni at
The Soldier's Tale in the Nationaltheater the next evening. Busoni was
deeply affected. He and Gerda "wept hot tears," Stravinsky reported to
Ansermet, "so moved were they by the tale."76 "One had become a child
again," Busoni said; "one forgot music and literature, one was simply
moved. *There's* something which achieved its aim! But let us take care not
to imitate it!"77

For Stravinsky these few days in Weimar were a revealing contact with
modern art in general. The musical events took place within the framework of the week-long Bauhaus Exhibition, and the concerts were attended
by some of the great figures of the modern movement, including Paul Klee
and Vasily Kandinsky, as well as probably Walter Gropius, and perhaps
László Moholy-Nagy.78 Whether or not they saw in *The Soldier's Tale* some
reflection of their own concern with functional simplicity and economy,
Stravinsky himself came away with a more confused idea of the cross-
fertilization between modern music and the visual arts. "I saw with my
own eyes," he told Ansermet, "the gigantic abyss which separates me from
this country and from the inhabitants of Central Europe as a whole.
KUBISMUS is stronger than ever, and the most ridiculous thing is that it
goes arm in arm with the IMPRESSIONISMUS of Schoenberg."79 Apparently there was no Schoenberg on the Weimar programs Stravinsky heard,
and in fact he had probably not heard any since 1912. But he may have had
in mind something Ansermet had once said to him about Hindemith
being "a sort of boche Prokofiev infinitely more sympathetic than all the
other sub-Schoenbergs,"80 because his next remark was a denunciation of
Hindemith's songs, "which bored me to tears—it's a kind of H[ugo] Wolf!
A pity, I was expecting otherwise." The only new music he admitted to liking were the Busoni piano pieces (the first three of the *Fünf kurze Stücke*

zur Pflege des polyphonen Spiels and the *Prélude et étude en arpèges*).[81] But he was impressed with Scherchen's conducting of his own work, and with the cast (including Carl Ebert as Narrator), apart from "a young Frankfurt idiot miming the role of the Princess [and] striking *oriental* (sic) attitudes in a gauze costume!" Above all, it was a relief—amid all the Bauhaus right angles and steel tubes—to re-encounter Auberjonois's pretty 1918 décors, even if they were "set against a horrible background, a very vulgar blue, a little in the tone of Laryonov's *Snow Maiden*."

That same night they were in the train for Wiesbaden—apparently with no repetition of Griesheim—and by the twenty-first they were back in Paris, where Stravinsky again lingered for over a week, making further excursions with Vera: to see Argutinsky at Magny-en-Vexin, and to visit the spa at Enghien-les-Bains, in the northern suburbs, where Vera was apparently thinking of taking a cure.[82] Benois had arrived in Paris on a visit from Petrograd, where he had been made director of the Hermitage. He went on the Magny trip, and there were lengthy discussions about possible collaborations. Stravinsky envisaged *Mavra* and a revival of *The Nightingale*, but knew very well that Diaghilev would not want them, being content with Survage and the Matisse *Song of the Nightingale*. He also sensed that Benois was jealous of Picasso, and that this would lead to friction with Diaghilev once the pretty-pretty Gounod which he was at present designing for the company's winter season in Monte Carlo was succeeded by anything more modern or prestigious. And it was true that Benois did not approve of Diaghilev's postwar direction, in which he detected a "pervading *snobisme* . . . the veneer of passing fashion, a veneer that gives a work of art a temporary success, but makes it fade quickly. . . . I was ready to undertake experiments even more risky than those which now occupied Diaghilev, but genuine artistic impulse was still for me the mainspring of creative activity; the wish to perplex or to produce a sensation made me as indignant as ever."[83] After the Gounod season, Benois never again designed for the Ballets Russes. But his association with Stravinsky—"who was still one of my favourite composers!"—was not yet at an end.

In Biarritz, at the start of September, Stravinsky had a visit from another old associate. His last known direct contact with Koussevitzky had been their very public tiff over the London premiere of the Symphonies of Wind Instruments two years earlier. "That Stravinsky ever forgave Koussevitzky," Craft has written, "is a wonder."[84] The explanation can probably be found in a card the composer wrote to Diaghilev at the time of the quarrel: "If you still think it necessary to answer in this or that form, bear in mind that *la bête est venimeuse*. He can do a great deal of harm to you and me. The whole Russian world is in his hands (this wasn't the case before). . . . Don't write, don't stir the shit. It seems to me he'd be very pleased if you were to answer. It's necessary to go quietly."[85] Behind the reconciliation lay the composer's material insecurity. He needed Koussevitzky as a conductor, and he needed him as a publisher. It surely was no coincidence that Ernest Oeberg came to Biarritz a week or so after his chairman, and that Stravinsky's contract with the new Paris-based Edition Russe de Musique (ERM) was signed (for *Mavra*, the Octet, and the much-abused Symphonies of Wind Instruments) on 21 September.[86] Stravinsky had meanwhile been discussing with Koussevitzky's secretary, Vladimir Zederbaum, a plan to perform the Octet under the auspices of a new Paris chamber-music organization called Dixtuor, which Koussevitzky was setting up; and now Koussevitzky was pressing him to direct the work himself in October, once again in the vast spaces of the Opéra, and in a program otherwise devoted to orchestral works—including Prokofiev's D Major Violin Concerto and Beethoven's Eroica Symphony, both of which Koussevitzky would himself conduct.[87] This may possibly have encountered the difficulty that Stravinsky had already agreed to conduct the Octet in a Wiéner concert in early November, on the firm understanding that it would be the premiere.[88] But, as the composer wearily informed Ansermet, Koussevitzky was offering "a fee too big for me to refuse."[89]

Koussevitzky's eye also fell on a new work for which Stravinsky had made a few sketches in July, and which resurrected his original idea for what had become the Octet, of a piece for solo piano, winds, and timpani. Presumably, the conductor remarked, Stravinsky was writing the piano part for his own use.[90] Apparently, this rather obvious idea had not occurred to him before. But on reflection it had considerable appeal, not least because it would enable him to establish a correct style of performance (as he perhaps told Koussevitzky with a glint in his eye). He needed to brush up his technique by practicing Czerny exercises. But the essential idea of an authoritative reading was merely an extension of his work at Pleyel, where he and his assistants were, so to speak, playing into a machine his concept of the score as living sound. He might even slap an embargo on the new work, thus making sure not only that nobody else could "interpret" it in his or her own way, but also that anyone who wanted to hear it would have to book him, Stravinsky, as soloist, with financial advantages that he was not slow to calculate. By November his negotiations for a United States tour had sprouted no less than twenty-five dates as soloist in the Piano Concerto, at a thousand dollars a shot.[91] He had learnt from his conductor-guest how to, as he himself had remarked unpleasantly to Diaghilev, "en tirer le profit de juif."[92]

Meanwhile, the Octet performance on 18 October, with the eight players framed by acoustic screening on the huge Opéra stage, can hardly be said to have launched his career as a conductor. It was his only appearance on the program, and he suffered bad stage fright, he later recalled, because it was the first time he had conducted a premiere of one of his works.[93] Perhaps he was also a shade overawed by the surroundings—the very theatre in which, thirteen years before, *The Firebird* had taken wing amid so much glitter. The incongruity of listening to the somewhat dry, minutely calculated Octet in such sumptuous surroundings certainly struck some members of his audience. Jean Cocteau saw "the back of an astronomer [engaged in] solving this magnificent instrumental arithmetic with its figures of silver."[94] Darius Milhaud noted that "the audience smiled, as they often do with wind instruments, but they applauded warmly at the end."[95] And surely among the smilers was Boris de Schloezer, who "kept thinking of a Rossini who could think polyphonically and for whom syncopated and polymorphic rhythms were no longer a mystery."[96] But de Schloezer also had a more significant point to make, with a hint of an "amende honorable." The Octet, he wrote, "bears witness once again to the extraordinary capacity for renewal of this powerful and lucid nature, [and] what, in *Mavra*, seemed to us no more than an experiment, an attempt, is in the Octet brought off fully and decisively."

Soon after the concert, Stravinsky made a gramophone recording of the Octet in the studio of a firm called Bernard Roux, in the Maison Pleyel—his first venture in this particular technology. It was still the era of acoustic recording, and capturing a piece for eight wind instruments was fraught with problems, added to which the engineer miscalculated the length of the finale and ran out of wax before the end. If a commercial release had been intended, this defect must have put paid to it, and though Stravinsky received test pressings of his own, they seem not to have survived, and no other copies are known to have been distributed.[97]

The Wiéner concert in the Salle des Agriculteurs on 7 November marked Stravinsky's first-ever appearance as sole conductor, and it seems to have gone well. He himself reported to Ansermet "a very great success as much for my works as for my conducting—I hope this last point won't make you jealous";[98] and de Schloezer remarked that "the performance was excellent and the composer's baton picked out the meters with great precision, a little 'à l'Ansermet.' "[99] The Octet was repeated, and there were excerpts from *Mavra* alongside the *Berceuses du chat.* But the main item was the "grand suite" (as Stravinsky called it to distinguish it from the suite for trio) from *The Soldier's Tale,* apparently the first time the music had been heard in Paris in any form.

Vera had attended the Octet premiere, and they seem to have gone together to the two framing Koussevitzky concerts (on 11 and 25 October), in the second of which the maestro conducted *The Rite of Spring.* But for the Wiéner concert Katya came to Paris, a fact Stravinsky was careful to mention in his letter to Ansermet. How long she stayed is a matter of conjecture. Igor himself did not return to Biarritz until the twenty-fourth, but Katya had probably left by the fifteenth, since Igor lunched with Vera,

Cocteau, and Tristan Tzara in Saint-Cloud the following day. Perhaps her visit explains—or is explained by—a note inserted on a separate sheet in Vera's diary for 22 October: "Igor writes constantly now about Ekaterina Gavrilovna's jealousy. He is trying to protect her in every way. If we go to Spain, those two weeks will be unbearable for her, since she imagines us together all the time. I wonder whether he shouldn't tell her that he will come later. There is no need to worry about my feelings."[100]

It seems not to have occurred to her that the best answer to her scruples might have been not to go at all.

WORDS SPEAK LOUD,
ACTIONS LOUDER

AT SOME POINT in the autumn of 1923, Stravinsky for the first time put on paper a set of observations about one of his own works, in the form of a short article called "Some Ideas About My Octuor." In true Parisian style, the piece is neither a program note nor an analysis, but a position paper: a miniature artistic manifesto. Yet for some reason the article appeared not in Paris, nor even in French, but in English in a Brooklyn monthly called *The Arts*, where it seems to have been placed by Gabrielle Picabia in her capacity as Paris agent for the New York Foreign Press Service.[1] It must have made bizarre reading for the magazine's American subscribers, who had as yet had no opportunity to hear a note of the Octet, and for whom European aesthetic politics probably at most conjured up the romantic image of Roderick Hudson or Isabel Archer in the novels of Henry James. "My Octuor," Stravinsky announced, "is a musical object." And he then proceeded to explain how his new work was governed by purely formal considerations; how wind instruments had been chosen "to render a certain rigidity of the form I had in mind . . . because the difference of the volume of these instruments renders more evident the musical architecture"; how all expressive nuance had been ruthlessly excluded in favor of these frozen volumetrics and strict tempo relations, which in turn articulated the music's main formal process—counterpoint; and how all questions of expressive meaning and interpretation came back to the music itself in its purely formal realization. "This sort of music," he concluded, "has no other aim than to be sufficient in itself. In general, I consider that music is only able to solve musical problems; and nothing else, neither the literary nor the picturesque, can be in music of any real interest. The play of musical elements is the thing."

This curious article, with its stodgy, officious, and sometimes opaque prose, was not Stravinsky's first assertion of a formalist basis for his music, but it was his first attempt at a systematic exposition. As long ago as 1913, at the time of *The Rite of Spring*, he had remarked in his *Montjoie!* interview that he had excluded strings from that work's prelude as being "too evocative of the human voice, with their crescendos and diminuendos," and had preferred the "drier, cleaner, less expressively facile woodwinds"; and by 1920 he had been claiming that the whole action of the ballet was no more than an emanation of the music, rather in the manner of Wagner's "deeds of music made visual":

> The work's embryo is a theme that came to me after I had finished *The Firebird*. As this theme and what followed from it was conceived in a brutal and forthright manner, I took as developmental pretext what that music actually evoked, that is, prehistoric Russia as I, being myself Russian, conceive it. But bear in mind that this idea comes from the music, not the music from the idea. I have written an architectonic work, not an anecdotal one.[2]

Such blatant revisionism raises a number of distinct issues. One can hardly overlook the fact that, with Stravinsky, denying the status of a collaboration had financial implications of which he was perfectly well aware. For some time, for example, he had in effect been obstructing stage performances of *The Soldier's Tale* because of a grievance over the mutual dependence of music and text, whose significance, for him, was that it entailed shared royalties. How else are we to interpret the fact that when he at last agreed to the Paris production in April 1924, it was only on condition that his share of the royalty be augmented by a secret cachet of ten thousand francs?[3] On the other hand, his music since *The Soldier's Tale*, at the latest, had undeniably moved towards abstraction; the final *Noces* scoring had stressed the ritual at the expense of the picturesque (the architectonic at the expense of the anecdotal), and even *Mavra* was obviously "about" something less factual than the servant problem in 1830s Petersburg. Above all, the Symphonies of Wind Instruments had distilled the ethnic style into a kind of pure formal essence, of which it really did seem to be true to say that "the play of musical elements is the thing." But at the same time, there is something about Stravinsky's manifesto formalism which gives it a particular place in the history of such writings, as much as in the history of his own creative work.

In one sense the formalism of "Some Ideas" is no more than an extreme version of the art-for-art's-sake doctrine of *Mir iskusstva*. The idea that beauty is more important than social realism is the first and most important step towards the idea that form is more important than content—or, to be exact, that form is the only aesthetic definition of content, a view with a long history going back to Hanslick and beyond. But Stravinsky's image of a music that ruthlessly excludes anecdote and nuance, a music which, so to speak, proves the primacy of form by refusing to admit anything not demonstrably (and in the most primitive sense of the word) "formal," is a specifically modern, postwar manifestation of the old purism. To what extent he was aware of or influenced by contemporary formalism in Russian art and criticism is hard to establish, but the answer is probably not much. He had met Mayakovsky, and perhaps talked about the Russian futurist notion that "genuine novelty in literature does not depend upon content. . . . A new light thrown on the old world may produce a very interesting interplay. . . . If there is a new form, there must also exist a new content. . . . It is form that determines content."[4] But Stravinsky's appeal to a conventional definition of form itself is at odds with the futurist desire to strip words of their meanings and concoct a language that would be "beyond meaning" *(za-um)*. He may have heard about this concept from Vera, and would doubtless have discussed it in greater philosophical and technical detail with Lourié, if Lourié had yet chosen to present himself. But *za-um* is precisely not the spirit of the formalism in "Some Ideas," which argues "meaninglessness" not as a desirable but as an innate property of musical sounds.

This is not an irrational but an essentially rational concept, and its spirit is French. It strongly recalls the antiromantic atmosphere of the *NRF,* particularly as expressed in the reviews of the early ballets by Jacques Rivière, for whom

> the great novelty of *The Rite of Spring* is its renunciation of "sauce." Here is a work that is absolutely pure. Bitter and harsh, if you like; but one which has no juice to dull its brilliance, no cookery to rearrange or spoil its contours. It is not a "work of art," with all the usual palaver. Nothing blurred, nothing reduced by shadows; no veils or poetic softenings; no trace of atmosphere. The work is whole and untreated; its parts remain quite raw; they are served up to us without anything to prepare the digestion; everything here is plain, intact, limpid and unrefined. . . . *The Rite of Spring* is the first masterpiece that we can set against those of Impressionism.[5]

Rivière's attack on Debussy (who is later named) was part of a movement to reinstate the "classical" virtues of French art: the virtues of clarity, restraint, and precision. Restraint may not have been the most obvious attribute of the early Stravinsky, but it could be detected in a certain quality of containment. "The sounds die," Rivière insisted, "without having trespassed beyond the space they occupied as they were born. . . . Never has one heard a music so magnificently limited."

By 1923 this "recall to order" was sounding through much serious criticism and an increasing amount of the work criticized. One of its first significant expressions in the field of music had been a brilliant article on Stravinsky by no less an authority than Ernest Ansermet himself, published in 1921, and asserting the primacy of form over anecdotal content in terms so obviously prophetic of "Some Ideas" as to make it evident that the subject had been discussed between them. "A work by Stravinsky," Ansermet remarks, "neither describes nor relates things, but manifests them." And he already insists on the primacy of counterpoint, and on the question of style as an objective choice: "not 'What to do?' but 'How to do it?' "[6] Two years later, Boris de Schloezer is referring implicitly to the "neoclassicism" of the Symphonies of Wind Instruments (on account of its stark economy of means),[7] and can even, as we saw in the last chapter, call *Les Noces* Stravinsky's most rigorously constructed, stylistically purest work, "the one which is worked out entirely . . . in formal elements."[8] Cocteau's own description of Stravinsky directing the Octet—the astronomer solving an arithmetic of instruments—might well have been suggested by the composer's own thinking, but it actually harks back to the very first phrase of Cocteau's own artistic manifesto, *Le Coq et l'Arlequin:* "Art is Science made flesh." Whether or not the biblical allusion—to "the Word made flesh" in St. John's Gospel—was anything but chic wordsmithery in 1918, it was to assume prophetic significance in the shadow of a tragedy which afflicted Cocteau personally, and French literature in general, as 1923 drew to its close.

By that autumn, Stravinsky must also have come across a little book of what might be called moral aesthetics entitled *Art et scolastique,* written at the end of the war by Jacques Maritain, a philosophy lecturer at the Institut Catholique in Paris, and published in 1920. Maritain, a Catholic convert from Protestantism, and by this time a professional philosopher in the central Thomist tradition of the Roman Church, had set himself the task of extracting a "philosophy of art," as he himself called it, from scattered references and suggestions in the writings of the medieval scholasts. Just as neo-Thomist theology sought to apply Aquinas's thinking in the context of modern faith, so Maritain sought there an aesthetics relevant to the situation of modern art, at a time, he wrote, "when everyone feels the necessity of escaping from the immense intellectual disarray inherited from the nineteenth century, and of rediscovering the spiritual conditions of a labor that is *honest.*"[9]

To what extent Maritain was privy to the fluctuating movements and countermovements in the arts just before, during, and after the First World War is not wholly clear. No doubt there appeared a certain parallel between art and theology at a time when modernism was as controversial an issue in the Vatican as it was in the Théâtre des Champs-Elysées. But in any case, Maritain hit several nails squarely on the head, at least so far as any artist with antiromantic leanings was concerned. In developing from Bergson a view of art as an activity of the humble "maker" *(homo faber)*, he was aligning himself with the many artists of the time who rejected the posturings and melodramatics of the late romantics; and in describing art as an autonomous intellectual "virtue" and divorcing it from concepts of social meaning or morality, he came close to the formalism which Stravinsky was to express so starkly in his own essay three years later. In fact *Art et scolastique* is a kind of primer of artisan modernism in its art-for-art's-sake as opposed to its machine-for-living mode. The composer (for example) is a humble provider who must nevertheless insist on the integrity of his work and its freedom from outside moral and emotional pressures. Stravinsky in Biarritz must have read with a thrill of recognition Maritain's observation that "the tedium of living and willing stops at the door of every studio"; that "from the moment that the Artist works well . . . 'it matters little whether he be in a good or bad temper.' If he is cross or jealous, he sins as a man, he does not sin as an artist"; and that "art does not at all mind whether the artist himself act well as a man, it is more concerned that the work produced should itself, if possible, make perfect use of his activity in its own way."[10]

Reading *Art et scolastique* in 1920 or 1921, Stravinsky will have understood it mainly as an aesthetic treatise with a bearing on his own work. It seems unlikely that Maritain's religious or spiritual affiliations will have absorbed his attention at that time. There is no particular sign of his yet having read Bergson, or Maritain's *La Philosophie bergsonienne* of 1914. He will have noted—perhaps with mild disapproval (for reasons which will shortly emerge)—that in *Art et scolastique* Maritain here and there quotes Cocteau's *Le Coq et l'Arlequin*. Any suggestion that a personal association between Maritain and Cocteau would in due course change and enrich his own response to these ideas would probably have met with his irritated incredulity.

ON 12 DECEMBER 1923, Raymond Radiguet, the twenty-year-old author of *Le Bal du comte d'Orgel* and the most brilliant prodigy in French writing since Rimbaud, died of typhoid caught—like Stravinsky's a decade earlier—from eating a bad oyster. Ever since he was just sixteen, Radiguet had been under Cocteau's "protection," and his death shattered his thirty-four-year-old lover, not least, perhaps, because Radiguet had recently taken what Cocteau himself called a "fiancée" (Bronya Perlmutter), not wishing, he had told Georges Auric, "to become a forty-year-old-man called 'Madame Jean Cocteau.' "[11] Stravinsky knew Radiguet through Cocteau, and probably went to his funeral with Vera at Saint-Honoré-d'Eylau.

During the war—himself rarely in Paris—he had tended to lose touch with Cocteau, who was in any case away for long periods on war service. Then in 1918 came *Le Coq et l'Arlequin*, an extended pamphlet which elevated Satie into the musical apostle of the new generation, while respectfully dismissing Stravinsky as "an octopus which you'd do well to flee or it will eat you": "When I wrote *Le Potomak*, I was blinded by my own difficulties; Stravinsky helped me out of them as a box of cheddite releases the ore. Now emerged from my blackness, I see him as one of the rest."[12] It seems unlikely, in any case, that the central message of *Le Coq*—that music needed to become simpler, more mundane, more frivolous—would have appealed deeply to Stravinsky, whatever its superficial resemblance to *NRF* classicism. But the idea that he might be obstructing that process will certainly have irritated him, and the specific disloyalty of the accusation must have been positively wounding. As recently as 1917, Cocteau had reminded him "that *Le Potomak* opens and closes with a letter to you, [and] that the Eugènes were born mysteriously from the music of *The Rite*."[13] Now, that ballet was "a masterpiece, but I find in the atmosphere surrounding its performance a religious complicity among adepts, that hypnotism of Bayreuth." And while "Wagner wanted the theatre, Stravinsky was dragged there by circumstances. . . . Isn't this just the kind of music one listens to head in hands?"[14]

By August 1922, nevertheless, the wound had healed. He and Cocteau, Stravinsky told Ansermet, were "now 'friends.' Anyway, it must be said that their (the whole Cocteau set's) attitude is a lot more chic than that of the gang of sophomores [*normaliens*] on the *Nouvelle Revue française* and the poor Jew [Henry] Prunières (who feels completely lost)."[15]

Behind this outburst lay his beloved *Mavra*. The *NRF* had aroused his fury by appointing Boris de Schloezer—whose dissection of *Mavra* he had just been reading in *Posledniya novosti*—as its music critic. Prunières's crime was equal but opposite; his *Revue musicale* had ignored *Mavra* altogether (apart from quoting an extract from de Schloezer's *NRF* notice in its press roundup), but had run a cool review of *Renard* by Emile Vuillermoz, formerly one of the composer's most dependable allies, but the author now also of a vicious attack on *Mavra* in the columns of *Excelsior*.[16] Moreover, de Schloezer was also serving as editorial assistant on the *Revue musicale*. Cocteau, on the other hand, was well disposed towards *Mavra*, and was about to publish a vigorous defense in the unlikely pages of *Vanity Fair*, where he excoriated the professional press for not giving a great composer the benefit of the doubt: "It would be simple to say to oneself, 'He is stronger than I. His instinct is surer. He must be right. It would be wise to follow him!' No. Everybody thinks, 'He is mistaken and I—clever fellow—am the only person who knows it.' "[17]

Meanwhile, among the Cocteau "set," the youthful Francis Poulenc had recently endeared himself to Stravinsky with an article in *Les Feuilles libres,* taking the Paris critics sharply to task for their benighted attitude to "that marvellous work."[18] It was Poulenc who alerted him to the existence of de Schloezer's *NRF* review; and Poulenc who fed him the choice epithet *"normaliens"* (applied to *"musicographes"*), which he promptly regurgitated in his letter to Ansermet.[19] In general, the Cocteau composers of Les Six loved *Mavra* for its apparent homage to the Satiesque ideals of *Le Coq et l'Arlequin,* even though—as Taruskin has shown—Poulenc's own great admiration was also based on a broader technical and stylistic perception that had little to do with the captious polemics of that dangerously seductive pamphlet.[20] Cocteau, Poulenc, and also Auric, in a later article in the *Nouvelles littéraires,* all referred specifically to Satie. Satie himself had not seen *Mavra,* but he could sympathize about its treatment by the Fourth Estate. "I do not permit myself to judge you," he wrote, "for I am not a 'pawn' like those I would rather not mention: they are too stupid, the poor things. Besides, this is not surprising, and on top of this, they are idiots."[21]

Whatever Stravinsky may have thought of being suddenly cast in a double act with the composer of *Parade,* it was comforting to be officially back on terms with so influential and ubiquitous a group of artists. In December, he saw and liked Cocteau's cut-down modern French translation of Sophocles's *Antigone.*[22] And in general it seems that the more time he spent in Paris in 1922 and 1923, the more at home he found himself, once again, with Cocteau's perverse and coquettish brilliance, with his genius for inhabiting the world as if it were a vast surrealist painting. "I enjoyed the bird party," Jean writes in July 1923, recalling the Milhaud housewarming, where the entertainment had included performing birds, "but I was sorry to say goodbye to you. Here [in the Gironde fishing village of Le Piqueÿ] Auric turns his back on the sea and typewrites: Radiguet is dictating his novel to him." Later he sends Stravinsky a drawing of a fellow holiday-maker whose parrot is supposed to have attacked Auric and Radiguet, with the caption: "This is the gentleman who owns the enormous parrot that bit the typists."[23]

But after Radiguet's death, the surreal and the supra-real invaded Cocteau's life in more drastic and material forms. At Monte Carlo with the Ballets Russes in January, he took to heavy opium-smoking in company with Auric, Poulenc, and Louis Laloy. But it was Auric who, with whatever precise intention, showed him a possible alternative therapy, by taking him, one day in July 1924, to the Paris suburb of Meudon and introducing him to Jacques Maritain and his Russian wife, Raïssa, a convert like her husband. Raïssa recorded the visit in her journal: "For the first time Auric brings Jean Cocteau to us. Distraught—despairing almost—since the death of Radiguet, he comes to Jacques having been told that he could help him find peace, and God, once again. After this first visit, God gives me, as I pray for Cocteau, a joyful assurance of his conversion."[24]

STRAVINSKY SPENT the autumn of 1923 in Biarritz, working on his Piano Concerto, and planning a series of conducting engagements which, he must have hoped, would provide the desperately needed financial security his compositions seemingly could not. He was still involved in negotiations for an American tour. But a much more definite project was for him to conduct a concert of his works in Antwerp in January. This had been proposed, apparently out of the blue, by the London concert agent Ibbs and Tillett the previous January, in response to an inquiry from the Antwerp Société des Nouveaux Concerts. It was his first full-scale engagement as a conductor; but by the time it took place, there was also a booking for Spain in March. And suddenly Stravinsky, who before November 1923 had never conducted more than single items on programs, was a serious international concert performer with a network of agents and a daily business correspondence which was soon threatening to swallow up what was left of his free composition time. It may or may not be coincidence that 1924 was also the year in which the confusion of old and new scores dispersed and Stravinsky at last achieved the mature status of a one-work-at-a-time composer whose works were premiered in the order in which they were written. The Octet article, with its sharp statement of aims, is symptomatic of this change. Stravinsky borrowed its tone—severe, matter-of-fact, a shade robotic—for his business letters, which from the start make few concessions to what might be called the expressive needs of ordinary human intercourse, and sometimes go so far as to overlook the elementary fact that agents, as Alexander Kahn was soon forced to remind him, were also entitled to payment.[25] He even visited this new hard-nosed manner on his in-laws—if, as one assumes, it was at his behest that on New Year's Day 1924 the Belyankins, who were reactivating their Château Basque project with the help of Stravinsky money, signed a formal IOU for their debt to him and Katya, which had now grown to forty-three thousand francs, a formidable sum equal to more than ten of Igor's hefty concert fees of the time.[26]

For his Antwerp concert on 7 January, Stravinsky had proposed *The Firebird* and *Pulcinella* suites, *Fireworks,* and some fragments of *The Nightingale* to be sung by the young Brazilian soprano Vera Janacopoulos. This was rather short, even if, as is likely, he was doing an extended form of the original *Firebird* Suite (with the Berceuse and Finale tacked on to the end). So he at first had the idea of orchestrating some early songs; then, short of time, he suggested to Janacopoulos that she sing *The Faun and the Shepherdess* instead; then—when she declined to learn a biggish new work which (she doubtless reflected) would seldom if ever be required of her again—they settled on the orchestrations: of "Tilimbom" from the *Three Tales* (in a much extended form) and the early "Pastorale," with its accompaniment arranged for woodwind quartet.[27] Stravinsky clearly respected the young soprano, who when still only twenty-two had sung the American premiere of *Pribaoutki*: "a very talented singer," Prokofiev—who was present—had called her. "She treated [the songs] affectionately, and sang them excellently, except, perhaps, 'Kornila' ['Uncle Armand'], which is too low for her voice."[28] She must, nevertheless, have been a versatile performer with strength in all registers and a certain robustness of delivery if she could sing both the Nightingale and *Pribaoutki* with success—music of quite different tessitura and vocal technique.

Stravinsky was in Belgium for a fortnight, travelling—as he coyly forewarned a Brussels acquaintance—not with his wife but with "a friend from Paris."[29] Ansermet was also to have conducted a Stravinsky program in Brussels, but had withdrawn at a week's notice because of "overwork and a bad cold";[30] so Stravinsky undertook to deputize for him. There was much to-ing and fro-ing between Brussels and Antwerp, thirty miles away. On 5 January, in Brussels, they heard Arthur Prévost conduct the Symphonies of Wind Instruments with the wind band of the Régiment de Guides ("a bit flabby," said Stravinsky);[31] the next day there was a public rehearsal for the Antwerp concert. Then it was back to Brussels to rehearse for the Ansermet date on the fourteenth, then to Antwerp again for the concert on the seventh. It added up to nothing less than a Stravinsky festival, with lavish wining and dining, the inevitable press conferences, and no doubt some heavy VIP treatment. At times the hospitality may have become oppressive. They were a good deal with the musicologist Paul Collaer, who had founded the Brussels Pro Arte Concerts with Arthur Prévost two years before, and who had recently published an article on *The Rite of Spring* of which Stravinsky approved. They spent a day with Collaer at his house in Malines, and sat up half the night while Igor dictated his life story for Collaer to include in a book he was now planning at Stravinsky's own suggestion.[32] Yet oddly enough, the composer continued to fret about money, and even dispatched Vera back to Paris for the express purpose of borrowing some. As is the way with the superior poverty, she was greeted on her return to Brussels on the eleventh "with champagne."[33]

The Brussels program, originally planned by Ansermet, was a mixed affair, built mainly round wind or wind-based music: the Octet, *Mavra*, and the "Song of the Volga Boatmen," but leavened with strings in *Pribaoutki*, the two string-quartet works played by the Pro Arte, and finally *Pulcinella*, confusingly billed as the "Third Suite for Small Orchestra," and done, perhaps, with solo strings (as in *Mavra*). The concert was a huge success, and the critics, both here and in Antwerp, treated the composer with respect—"One can no longer in good faith," wrote one, "regard Stravinsky as a simple humorist"—and his conducting was admired as being first cousin to the music itself: "It was enough to watch him, to observe his brusque jerkings, to understand the animating role played by rhythm in this music."[34] Stravinsky's claim, in *L'Etoile belge* on the morning of the Brussels concert, that "I am a musician of my country, but I don't deal in folklore," must nevertheless have puzzled the audience for *Pribaoutki* that evening. They were not to know that the rejection of folk music was part of the new formalist aesthetic and had nothing in particular to do with reality.

At the morning rehearsal, Vera had run into a slice of her past in the person of Arthur Lourié, and she promptly hauled him off to lunch with Stravinsky: "Lourié," she recorded in her diary, "is so pleased to be present and to be talking to Stravinsky that he blushes."[35] Was this their first actual meeting? It seems possible, notwithstanding Craft's claim—for which there is no accessible evidence—that Lourié had accompanied Vera and Igor to Brussels. Five weeks later, Lourié wrote from Paris to Stravinsky (in Biarritz) about "the results of work on my commission"—by which he meant proofreading the score and parts of the Octet. But this could easily be a task Stravinsky delegated to him in Brussels. Two months after that, Lourié was writing from Wiesbaden, having been expelled from France as an unreconstructed Bolshevik.[36]

Whether or not Stravinsky had—as Lourié feared—been hearing "evil things" about him, he was obviously impressed by his enthusiasm for his music and, probably, by his knowledge and grasp of it. Lourié, too, had started writing about Stravinsky. But he was more interested in Stravinsky's scores than in his biography, and was positively eager to read proofs and make piano reductions, since it gave him an opportunity for close textual study. He had, he told the composer in his February letter, already asked Oeberg for the unpublished scores of *Mavra* and the Symphonies of Wind Instruments. As for Stravinsky, it was typical of him to be more interested in the Jewish Lourié's practical value as an office boy and, perhaps, as an articulator of ideas than in tales like Prokofiev's about "that scum you so politely refer to as Artur Sergeyevich" who "failed to issue Asafyev with the right documents for the removal of my manuscripts into storage, as a result of which the people who were quartered in my flat used my [second piano] concerto as fuel for the stove."[37] No doubt every emigrant composer had or knew of some such complaint against the former Petrograd commissar. And Lourié made things no easier for himself by his refusal expressly to reject or attack the Soviet Union, even though he had long since converted to Catholicism and was now much more interested in Ignatius Loyola than in Karl Marx.[38] Reading the *Spiritual Exercises*, he found them "almost like Stravinsky in theology, with the same dry heat."[39] Such flattery was well aimed at a composer who was already seeing and describing his work in terms of intellectual disciplines, whether or not he was yet conscious of them as specifically religious in character or impulse.

The Belgian concerts were a triumph: so Stravinsky assured Falla, and so the Pro Arte confirmed to Ansermet;[40] he could look forward to his March concerts in Barcelona with equanimity. But meanwhile he had to finish the Piano Concerto, and—what was perhaps more nerve-wracking—he had to learn to play it. Towards the end of February, barely a week before his departure for Spain, only the slow movement was finished; the first movement was complete apart from the orchestration. But the finale was still not written, there was a piano reduction to be made and proofs to check, and he had to prepare his Barcelona concerts. "It's enough to drive you mad," he grumbled to Ansermet.[41] And now there was a proposal that he extend his Spanish tour to three full weeks and conduct also in Madrid.[42] Why did he accept? We have to assume that, as ever, his financial circumstances—real or imaginary—made the offer unrefusable. He was caught in the poverty trap of the man who, unwilling or unable to adjust his needs to his means, had no other choice than to adjust his means to his needs. Of course, he was lucky to have that choice, denied to most of us. But if we try to calculate the number of additional works he might have written had he not condemned himself to spend a sizable proportion of each year on concert tours, the bargain seems much less good, even if we accept his own argument that by conducting and playing his own works he was laying down a tradition of how they should be performed. In any case that argument is suspect. By 1924 there were several conductors—Ansermet, Monteux, Stokowski, Goossens, Vladimir Golschmann, among others—with a perfectly adequate grasp of his music and much better baton technique than he had or would ever acquire. The other side of the equation—the music he wrote specifically for his own use—is only partial recompense. After all, he could have written it anyway, and a good deal else besides.

The irony is that it was often these very conductors who prepared the ground for Stravinsky himself. In the United States, just as he was planning his own first concerts in Belgium and Spain, his music was making huge advances in Boston and New York. At the end of January, Monteux gave the first performances of *The Rite of Spring* in those cities, with, he told the composer, huge success in both.[43] A few days later, Stokowski gave the New York premiere of the Symphonies of Wind Instruments. "There was," he told Stravinsky, "a great deal of hissing, and a great deal of applause. But, although the reception was only half good, I feel that your music is gaining in understanding in America."[44] Robert Lyon, son of the director of Pleyel, Gustave Lyon, was in the United States and attended both the New York concerts.

First I heard Monteux's *Rite—remarkable* performance, and the sort I think you like. Precision! and a big success as well. Then the symphony [sic] under Stokowski also had some success, though at Philadelphia it had raised storms. . . . I have the impression that in winter [19]25–26 you will have enormous standing here, but as yet it's embryonic and the public is only just beginning to open its eyes— things are moving fast.[45]

Two weeks later, Lyon wrote still more encouragingly: "You're making considerable advances and I have the impression that next winter [i.e., 1924–25] will be a time of triumph for you. I'm seeing [Arthur] Judson [manager of both the New York Philharmonic and the Philadelphia Orchestra] on Tuesday, and since I can't get a reply from our friend Stokowski I propose to draft out a contract with Judson which I can explain to you in person."[46] But this proved too sanguine, and by March Stravinsky was still getting offers from Judson "which I consider even less advantageous than his first one. I really don't understand the people over there— the more my name becomes known to the American public, the less they offer me."[47]

The Spanish concerts (three in Barcelona and one in Madrid) had been no less successful than the Belgian ones—partly, no doubt, because audiences were being given their first glimpse of the great wild man of modern music, partly because his actual programs were conservative and included no recent work except the undaunting *Pulcinella*. They contained, in fact, no fewer than three pre-*Firebird* works, including at last *The Faun and the Shepherdess* ("not at all a bad piece," the composer assured Ansermet),[48] and nothing else essentially later than 1914 except "Tilimbom." There had briefly been talk of the first part of *The Rite of Spring;* but in the end the extra players could not be found.[49] Igor and Vera spent a fortnight in Barcelona, having drowned their scruples and travelled together from Paris in a wagon-lit. They went to Gypsy cabarets and at least one bullfight; they went to the opera and, perhaps in penance for *Pulcinella*, saw Pergolesi's *Serva padrona*.[50] And on their last day there was a chamber concert including the Three Pieces for String Quartet, followed, in the evening, by a ministerial banquet at the Ritz. When they set off for Madrid on the twenty-first, Vera records, there were "flowers and applause," and of course everywhere there were photographers and interviewers. In Madrid Stravinsky for the first time explicitly denounced the music of his teacher, Rimsky-Korsakov, something he had been doing implicitly since his Tchaikovsky propaganda of 1921. "He was my teacher in the Petrograd Conservatoire," he told one reporter, not quite truthfully, "and I felt a real admiration for him; but now I realize the artificiality of his Russianism and orientalism."[51] While the distant past fed his latest music, his own past was receding rapidly towards the vanishing point.

AFTER WHAT MUST have seemed like years of negotiation and pressure, there was at last to be a production of *The Soldier's Tale* in Paris. Having given up with Jacques Hébertot in Paris, Ramuz had been hoping to set up a Swiss run, but was finding it impossible to cast the work from Lausanne, where he was as usual imprisoned by lack of funds. Surely Stravinsky, so much in Paris, could do it better. But the composer was still unwilling to give up precious time to what amounted to the promotion of Ramuz's interests, not least because—as a man of the theatrical world—he knew, as Ramuz was slow to realize, that casting and stage presentation were not the author's province but the impresario's, whatever may have been the case in wartime Switzerland. Still, if Ramuz wanted the Pitoëffs, why not offer "that dangerous pederast" Hébertot, to whom they were contracted, the Auberjonois sets free for a January or February Paris staging in return for the release of the Russian pair for Switzerland?[52] It might have worked; but Ramuz, at sea in the world of commerce, had already offered Hébertot stiffer terms, which led eventually to a blank refusal to release the Pitoëffs. For the hapless Ramuz, typically, this was the end of the world. But the more practical-minded Ansermet, who in any case could not make the Paris dates, simply set up rehearsals for a postponed German-language production in Zurich in April with a local cast.[53]

Meanwhile *The Soldier's Tale* had once again become a tactical weapon in Parisian theatre politics. Stravinsky seems to have started it, in January, by hinting on the phone to Gabrielle Picabia that a production might be a good business proposition. She soon came back with two proposals: one from a wealthy ex–prima donna called Marguérite Bériza, and one from Count Etienne de Beaumont, the original of Radiguet's Comte d'Orgel and wartime organizer of the ambulance unit in which Cocteau had also served. Beaumont was now running an organization called Les Soirées de Paris. He wanted to stage *The Soldier's Tale* in a two-month season of what Gabrielle called "an arty program" which Beaumont hoped might also include a plastic realization of Stravinsky's Octet, with designs by Picasso and choreography prepared and danced by Massine and Lopukhova.[54] Stravinsky at once turned down the Octet idea on the grounds that the music was still too little known in its concert version for a *forme plastique* to be appropriate. But it may also be true that, as Buckle suggests, he was wary of antagonizing Diaghilev by associating his work with Massine.[55] That Diaghilev was nervous about these *Soldier's Tale* projects is beyond doubt. Ansermet, who had been using Gaby's plans (with some idea that they would involve Jacques Copeau) as a bargaining counter with Diaghilev for the Ballets Russes season that spring, was rung up in Geneva by Nouvel, who wanted to know whether he was working for Bériza, Beaumont, or Massine and promptly made him an offer for the coming ballet season which ruled *The Soldier's Tale* out, since the dates would clash.[56]

Mme Bériza had no such elaborate ideas as Beaumont's, but was content to stage the piece in Auberjonois's original sets and costumes and with the full (revised) Ramuz text, whereas Beaumont had plans for a pantomimic version, presumably much as originally conceived by Diaghilev and Massine back in 1920, and with the text greatly reduced. Gabrielle preferred the Beaumont scheme, partly no doubt on artistic grounds but also hoping that Ramuz would accept a one-third royalty for the reduced text, and she wanted Bériza bought off with *Mavra*. But Ramuz dug in his heels about his fifty percent, refused to have his play altered by anyone else, and poor Gaby was suddenly learning at first hand why Paris had had to wait almost six years for any sort of production of this seemingly harmless little work. "I shall drop out," she threatened, "unless I get more support."[57] The less ambitious Bériza version it had in any case to be, a mere three performances in the Théâtre des Champs-Elysées in late April, with designs adapted from the originals by Auberjonois himself, Ansermet conducting (because Stravinsky refused point-blank to interrupt his concerto preparations), and the Pitoëffs: George as Narrator and Lyudmila as the Princess. But Gaby at least got her (or rather Stravinsky's) way over the allocation of cash, by the simple expedient of a separate, secret deal which gave him an extra ten thousand francs plus two thousand as appearance money.[58]

Both Ramuz and Auberjonois were anxious to avoid what Ramuz, in a letter to George Pitoëff, had called "outmoded aestheticism."[59] Auberjonois wrote to Stravinsky that he had been to see Cocteau's *Antigone*, and "among things that were great and strong, I was struck by some very tawdry details," whereas for their piece freshness and simplicity were all-important.[60] But in 1924 Paris the rustic and natural were not at all the wear. Nor, it turned out, were they aspects of George Pitoëff's acting technique. He seems to have delivered the narration in the heightened tones of a grand tragedian—described by Gabriel Marcel as "pathos of the most forced variety."[61] "You wouldn't believe it," Auberjonois wrote to Ramuz (who had been in Paris for rehearsals but missed the performances), "but Pitoëff doesn't understand, for all his goodwill—he speaks tragically or overplays and sometimes swamps a pair of plainly inadequate supporting actors."[62] The press, nevertheless, did not spare Ramuz. Marcel thought the text "obscure, grimacing, puerile," and André George found that "despite the excellent efforts of artists like the Pitoëffs, the total nullity of the text spread its lamentable grayness over the whole affair. Truly the leap from Ramuz to Stravinsky is too great: the engine stalls."[63]

Stravinsky had at last finished his Piano Concerto (on 21 April), and he must have given a private run-through in Paris, since Ansermet was soon informing Reinhart that "I've just heard Stravinsky's Piano Concerto, admirably played by the composer. It's a very important work . . . in the line of the Octet but in a more monumental style and à la Bach!"[64] Ansermet was eager to book the composer to play the concerto in Geneva and Winterthur, not least because Stravinsky had no doubt told him that he intended to keep it for his own exclusive use for the next five years.[65] And there were already tentative bookings from Scherchen (who was at that moment conducting the Swiss performances of *The Soldier's Tale*) for Berlin, and from Prévost for Brussels. So the Czerny studies, and the lessons he had been having in Paris with Isidore Philipp,[66] were already paying off even before a note had been struck in anger—and even though neither the Berlin nor the Brussels performance actually happened. Meanwhile, the princesse de Polignac was organizing a preview at her house a week before the public premiere on 22 May. By then, a mere fortnight or so after the Bériza season, Stravinsky would have to be note perfect.

The Polignac preview duly took place on the fourteenth, with Jean Wiéner playing the orchestral part on a second piano, and with the whole performance (including an introductory talk given, presumably, by the composer himself) repeated the following afternoon in the Salle Gaveau.[67] At the Koussevitzky concert in the Opéra the following week, Stravinsky seems to have suffered another attack of stage fright; aggravated by the fear of memory lapse. "You cannot imagine," he told Ramuz, "the pleasure you gave me with your letter, which arrived just as I was taking a taxi at the stand to march to the scaffold."[68] But his famous story of having been unable to remember how the slow movement started until the conductor hummed him the opening notes was probably an anecdotal recollection of some general anxiety, since it is not borne out in detail by contemporary reports. Prokofiev told Myaskovsky that "Stravinsky played himself, and not at all badly; he was scared stiff and had the score beside him on the stool. But there were no incidents."[69] But the piece, though highly successful in performance, was more or less routinely disliked by the press (apart from de Schloezer, who took his colleagues to task in the *Revue musicale*),[70] and tended to divide musicians. Berners wrote to Stravinsky, after attending one of the previews, that "the Concerto made such a strong impression on me that I feel enthusiasm every time I think of it."[71] But the hard-to-please Prokofiev disliked its Bach-Handel elements, while admitting that they were livened up by "the modern dance-syncopations" and that the concerto was generally well made. Boris Asafyev later adjudicated this question neatly:

My first impression of the work was that its composer had lost his way and become becalmed in a sea of stylization. But after having given closer attention to the style of Handel and other Italian sources which might have served as models for Stravinsky, I became persuaded that the initial impression was in fact false. Though there is, of course, a superficial similarity of intonations, rhythms, and general procedure, Stravinsky's syntax and rhetoric are deeply contemporary.[72]

For Stravinsky himself the concerto was to prove one of his most important works, for the simple reason that for the next five years he played it almost wherever he went, so that it was the one genuinely modern score of his that became widely known in the twenties.

Four days later, he was back on the rostrum, conducting a gala revival of Les Noces for Diaghilev at the Théâtre des Champs-Elysées. Ansermet had finally decided, only a month before, not to appear with the Ballets Russes that season, but to go instead to Argentina to conduct at the Teatro Colón. Diaghilev had booked the elderly André Messager to take over the French repertory, but he was still without a conductor for Les Noces, Petrushka, and The Rite of Spring, when he happened to run into Monteux in a taxi in the Champs-Elysées and there and then persuaded him to step into the breach. At the theatre, Stravinsky was rehearsing Les Noces. "I sat in the stalls with my score at the first rehearsal," Monteux later recalled, "following every note. I had studied it thoroughly and I at once noticed that no one came in on time, chorus or soloists (Stravinsky at that time was not the conductor he is today, having little or no experience with ensembles). The performance went through, and was a huge success with the Paris public, who always adored Stravinsky." Monteux persuaded Diaghilev to give him a rehearsal of his own. "I worked with the chorus, who knew their parts perfectly; it sufficed to give them their cues at the right places. As for the soloists, they sang in any key and anywhere. They had to learn their parts. A few days after that rehearsal I had my first performance of Les Noces. It went perfectly and I was satisfied, but it had not the success as when conducted by the composer. C'est la vie! Ha ha!"[73]

Diaghilev had commissioned from Picasso a sensational new front drop curtain for the 1924 season, in celebration of the Olympic Games, which were being held in Paris a few weeks later: or to be exact, he had commissioned the curtain from Alexander Shervashidze, who made a hugely enlarged copy of a Picasso gouache of two giantesses running on a seashore.[74] This megalithic novelty was offset on the first night, not only by the austere geometry of Nijinska's Les Noces, but also, in quite a different way, by the fluttering sexual ambiguities of Poulenc's Les Biches, which had its first Paris showing on the same bill, following its Monte Carlo premiere in January. Whatever may have been his later opinion of Poulenc's music, Stravinsky seems genuinely to have admired *Les Biches*. Not only did he tell Poulenc (before he had seen the ballet) that he thought its score very beautiful,[75] but he also praised it to Prokofiev, who told Myaskovsky that he could not understand "why Stravinsky admires it so much, and even took offense when I accused him of insincerity."[76] Prokofiev himself thought the work rubbish; but perhaps he felt that Stravinsky's good opinion was not unconnected with Poulenc's praise of *Mavra* the previous year. What Stravinsky thought of Auric's *Les Fâcheux*, which had its Paris premiere on 4 June, is not directly recorded, but he ought—on the Prokofiev principle—to have liked it as much as *Les Biches*, since Auric, too, had praised *Mavra* in print.

Diaghilev had just found a new young Russian composer who had arrived in Paris from St. Petersburg via New York, and whom he wanted to commission to write a new ballet with Kochno. Vladimir Dukelsky dined with Stravinsky, Diaghilev, Misia Sert, and assorted hangers-on at the Pré Catalan in the Bois de Boulogne after the *Fâcheux* opening, and was taken soon afterwards by Auric and Poulenc to see Stravinsky in his Pleyel studio, bearing a piano concerto he had written for Artur Rubinstein. Rather improbably, it may seem, Dukelsky records that Stravinsky praised the concerto for its Petersburg proficiency. "There is nothing like Russian conservatory training," he is supposed to have said, "and your young French friends [Auric and Poulenc] would have been better off had they studied with Taneiev, Glazunov or their pupils."[77] Stravinsky, of course, had not done so either. But there is no real reason to doubt the remark. Twelve years earlier he had been fierce in his condemnation of Glazunov, "who has never moved an inch nor dared to penetrate the mysteries of art"; but when ticked off by his mother, he had insisted that, while rejecting Glazunov's creative work, he did not at all deny his contribution to the academic life of his time—and this is still, more or less, the tone of his autobiography of the mid-thirties.[78] The relentless personal and professional hostility to Glazunov is the product of a later time.

Dukelsky also describes, with a certain drooling relish, the company at dinner in the Pré Catalan that June evening: the regal Misia, with her disconcerting habit of talking with "intonations so intimate and a vocabulary so special, that the monologue was unintelligible to all but the person addressed"; Jean Cocteau "of the fallen-angel face . . . and the fanciful, if not always intelligible, line of gab"; Coco Chanel, "looking like a jockey in drag"; Stravinsky, in tails, "not unlike an emaciated Pickwick"; Diaghilev himself—his palate "so jaded that he had to pour virtually a whole shaker of salt and another of pepper on whatever he ate, and then cover the dish with a thick layer of Savora, his favorite condiment, in order to taste anything at all."[79] Dukelsky would probably have been astonished to catch a glimpse of a letter Stravinsky wrote less than a fortnight later from Paris to Ramuz in Lausanne:

> Here in the evenings Vera and I go sometimes to the Ballets Russes, sometimes to the "Cigale" ("Beaumont Palace")—and everywhere one sees nothing but the snobbery and nastiness of horrible people who flutter about, and who (happily) play no part in your life, princesses who do nothing but ask you to lunch, honest bourgeois who listen to *L'Education manquée* as if it were *The Rite of Spring*—because they are at the Ballets Russes performance where Chabrier's piece is being done between *The Rite* and Auric's *Fâcheux.* . . . Is there something funny about that? Yes, but in the long run one is seized with disgust and could easily become a pessimist, which is what I most fear in the world.[80]

Was this purely for the benefit of the high-minded and profoundly un-*mondain* author of *The Soldier's Tale*? No doubt to some extent. But, after all, such ambivalence towards material things is commonplace enough, not least among Russians, real and fictional, and it may well have been intensified in Stravinsky just then by the logjam of concert engagements in his diary for the next nine months. The American tour, he told Ramuz, was now firmly fixed for January to March 1925 (though no contracts were signed until late August), and in between were a trip to Copenhagen in July and tours of Holland, Switzerland, and Germany later in the year. All this would bring in the extra money he needed to keep his complex life afloat, but whether that was a good or a bad thing, he found it hard to say. In any case—the unspoken thought—composition would have to wait.

Weary of the winter gales on the Atlantic coast,[81] he and Katya had decided to move from Biarritz to Nice, at the other end of the Midi, and planned a house-hunting trip at the end of July. Meanwhile there was Copenhagen: a single concert in the Tivoli.[82] With Vera he took the train through Belgium, lunching with the Collaers in Brussels on the way. It was his first-ever visit to Denmark, and his second ever performance of the Piano Concerto with an orchestra; but for neither the first nor the last time there were visa problems on the way, and in the end they had to hire a car in France and cross the Belgian frontier at a different point. "I beg you, my dear," he implored Ramuz when he got back to Paris—and thinking of his autumn visit to Switzerland—

> to take steps, I no longer know through whom, for me to be given a visa for several months (two would be enough) by your consulate in Paris. . . . Look around, my friend, for someone who could fix this up

for me, as it is absolutely intolerable to lose whole days in consulates (as has just happened with my trip to Copenhagen), filling in forms answering stupid questions (color of my mother's and father's hair, etc.), when I'm having to skip from town to town and country to country! The Germans have given me this kind of visa for half a year; admittedly the pigs have made me pay through the nose—200 francs!! But who cares about that, so long as I avoid the irritations and waste of time.[83]

He and Katya had found a house in Nice, the Villa des Roses in the boulevard Carnot, but "at what a price!!!" he grumbled to Ramuz. "I do not even dare to type it."[84] Before moving, he managed a peaceful August in Biarritz, during which he composed the first movement of a new solo piano sonata and at last signed a contract for his American tour;[85] and a turbulent first half of September in Paris, arranging visas, and engaging in an irritable correspondence with his Berlin concert agent, who had taken the liberty of interpreting "Germany" as including Poland and Czechoslovakia, and had booked concerts in Warsaw and Prague as well as various German cities. "Why Warsaw?" Stravinsky moaned, still perhaps thinking of it as a tsarist city, or as one where Russians were none too welcome.[86] As late as mid-October he was still wriggling on the hook. The visas were not coming through, the advance had not been deposited, etc., etc. It seems not yet to have struck him that since Volhynia was now in Poland, Warsaw was the very city that held the key to the Belyankins' (as well as his own wife's) hopes of land restitution. And this was now as urgent as ever for the Belyankins, since the Stravinskys' move to Nice had almost literally cast them and their new Château Basque adrift on the Atlantic gales, which in a bad winter could smash the mirrors and plate-glass windows of the harborside restaurant and threaten the whole tottering enterprise with irretrievable bankruptcy.[87] But perhaps in any case the Belyankins and their troubles were for the moment far from his thoughts. Soon after the move to Nice, and as if stricken by another of the plagues of Egypt, all four Stravinsky children went down with diphtheria, a disease so menacing to adolescents of uncertain health and weak respiration that one Sunday the seventeen-year-old Theodore almost suffocated, and was only saved, Stravinsky told Ansermet, by last-minute vaccination. The entire household—maids, governesses, and all—were lined up and vaccinated on the spot, and soon afterwards the house itself had to be systematically disinfected.

"A good start! Eh?" Stravinsky remarked drily as he put the finishing touches to his piano sonata, and departed on what was to be an almost unbroken five-month absence from his new home.[88]

"O MY AMERICA! MY NEW-FOUND LAND"

THE TRAIN FROM PARIS to Warsaw took Stravinsky back for the first time since 1914 to any part of prewar tsarist Russia. Poland, then an imperial *guberniya,* was now once again an independent state; and moreover, its territory had since 1921 officially included Volhynia and the whole of the former Nosenko latifundia at Ustilug. So the Belyankins had naturally cast their eyes towards Warsaw in the hope of a land restitution which might solve their business problems in Biarritz. But their case was fraught with difficulties. The land and the surviving buildings at Ustilug would long since have been occupied by small local farmers, whose claims naturally carried more weight with authorities overwhelmed by problems of land shortage and the threat of ethnic minorities than did the unenforceable rights of a group of absentee Russian landowners. All the same, Belyankin had optimistically retained Warsaw lawyers, and the claim was actually due to be heard in the week of Stravinsky's visit. Lyudmila briefed him on the calls he should pay and reminded him of the publicity value of the newspaper interviews he would inevitably be giving. She instructed him to "complain that your land is being taken away because you do not maintain your home in Poland, yet at the same time you are not allowed to live there."[1] After all, her sister, Katya, was also a land claimant at Ustilug, while Igor was still in theory a mortgagee in Rovno.

He gave several interviews; but if he raised the land question, no one saw fit to report his remarks. Insofar as anyone was interested in his visit to the Polish capital, it was purely in his capacity as a composer, the greatest living, as Karol Szymanowski assured the readers of the *Warszawianka.*[2] Politically he was more likely to be an embarrassment. It was rumored (falsely) that he intended to seek Polish citizenship; but whether or not, as Erhardt suggests, the Polish National Democratic Party "purported to smell Bolshevism in his music," the real (official) difficulty may have been that he was a White Russian, to whom any restitution of rights could have infringed Polish agreements with the Soviet Union under the Treaty of Riga (1921). Certainly, Stravinsky did not go out of his way to establish republican credentials. In between his two concerts on

4 and 6 November he and Vera attended a thunderous dinner of the old Polish aristocracy, and on the seventh, his last day in Warsaw, he proudly displayed to a reporter from the *Wiadomosci Literackie* a Soulima heraldic seal with which he had been presented by a certain Jan Strawinski, a distant cousin from the formerly powerful Mirowszczyzna branch of his father's family. "He is as delighted as a child with it," the interviewer noted, "and talks about his noble origins and the signet ring which his father gave his eldest brother." After hesitating for a time where to put the seal, he at last fetched a red morocco case containing a gold watch given to his father by Tsar Alexander III, and put the seal in it. " 'A Soulima coat of arms and an Alexander III watch—they somehow don't go together,' someone remarks. 'With me everything goes together,' Stravinsky replies."[3]

The reporter, Jaroslaw Iwaszkiewicz, had come to the composer's room in the Hotel Bristol expecting a conventional interview. But instead, the business with the coat of arms was followed by a different kind of aristocratic demonstration, a performance of the new Piano Sonata—perhaps its very first—to an audience of (probably) six, including Vera Sudeykina, the pianist Alexander Borovsky, and Gregor Fitelberg, who had conducted the orchestra in the Piano Concerto in the two public concerts.[4] "You see," Stravinsky remarked when the performance was over,

> "this is how I compose; from color I proceed to drawing. Now I wrestle with drawing to the detriment of color. . . . The main thing is to know how to eliminate. . . . The hardest thing is to finish. It was necessary to make it 'clipped,' as you sometimes see the crupper on a horse, short and powerful. How difficult I found this ending!" . . . "Why do you change rhythm so often?" somebody asks the composer. "Often?"—he is astonished. "I change it only when it is absolutely necessary."[5]

He was getting used to outlining his aesthetic philosophy to newspaper reporters, and the Polish interviews give the most rounded portrait so far, much more so than "Some Ideas About My Octuor," which is too doctrinaire, too fatally limited by coherence and consistency. He tells one Warsaw interviewer that "even when the music"—he goes on to mention *The Firebird* and *Petrushka*—"is at first glance attached to a literary or pictorial basis, in my artistic conception it preserves all the traits of absolute music," but then proceeds to suggest, more candidly, that "the time is past when I tried to enrich music. Today I should like to construct it. I no longer strive to expand the sphere of musical expression. I strive for the very essence of music." In the same interview, he elucidates the somewhat arcane idea of counterpoint set out in the Octet article.

Even in my earlier works I took an interest in the problems of counterpoint. Suffice it to mention, for instance, the polytonal counterpoints in *Petrushka* (F-sharp and C), the Russian Dance, and a series of pages in *The Rite of Spring*. Today counterpoint has become the starting point of that stage in the creative process which we call "composition." This idea of pure counterpoint has given my most recent works a new and particular style which I intend to propagandize in person in the world's main musical centers.[6]

The new style was quintessentially that of his last three instrumental works, the Octet, the Piano Concerto, and the Piano Sonata, with their uncompromising dependence on the hard brilliance of wind instruments and piano. They were "dry, cold, and transparent, like an 'extra dry' champagne, which gives no sensation of sweetness, and does not enervate, like other varieties of that drink, but burns."[7] As for the "appeal to eighteenth-century music," as he called it, "the reason is that I am running away from romanticism. . . . [But] what I have got from ancient music is Stravinsky and only Stravinsky."[8] And then, in a remark of supreme insouciance, he draws the veil wide: "Counterpoint is necessary, since it's a school. You have to go through it like a smallpox jab. But you also have to achieve independence here. For my part I treat harmony like a woman I invite to dance. What really attracts me just now is the element of mathematics in polyphony."[9]

Such remarks draw attention to a quality in these instrumental works that tended to be obscured by the schoolmasterly posturings of articles like "Some Ideas." It was the same Stravinsky as before: irresistibly physical, the supreme master of rhythm and movement, to which he was now adding a clarity and directness of line and an economy of workmanship that excited the admiration of every contemporary musician who understood that the "recall to order" could not be reduced to a simple matter of *musique d'ameublement*—music as furniture. "Clean work," he himself commented when he played the sonata to Joseph Szigeti and two colleagues at Blüthner's piano shop in Leipzig the following month; and Szigeti understood at once that the "work" was as important as the "clean": "Needless to say he was referring not to his playing but to the intensely 'worked out' contrapuntal texture."[10] But Boris Asafyev, writing a year or so later for a dwindling Soviet readership, saw it as a "flawless monolith of intensely concentrated energy," and he also understood it as transitional, since "the artistic asceticism is so extreme, the dynamics and kinetics of the piano are locked into such a narrow frame, there is such scrupulous avoidance of any emotional tone to the material."[11] It was as if the purity and economy needed a spiritual outlet of which Stravinsky himself was not yet quite aware.

After a week in Warsaw, he and Vera went on to Prague. They heard Weber's *Freischütz* in the Neues Deutsches Theater, under Alexander Zemlinsky, and on the thirteenth Stravinsky conducted a concert of his chamber works—including the *Soldier's Tale* Suite, the *Japanese Lyrics*, and excerpts from *The Nightingale* (with the composer at the piano)—in front of a huge audience in the vastly unsuitable Great Lucerna Hall, by Wenceslas Square. The atmosphere, one critic reported, was lively:

> During *The Soldier's Tale*, part of the audience burst out laughing, which prompted a protest from the other part, who were taking the concert perfectly seriously. . . . At the end of the concert, half the hall applauded warmly and called the composer out, while the other half hissed their disapproval no less sharply. There were even, interestingly, listeners who hissed and applauded at the same time. Igor Stravinsky took hisses and applause alike with stoical seriousness, and bowed solemnly.[12]

The Prague newspapers, like their Warsaw counterparts, wanted to know his opinion of his contemporaries. But his answers must have puzzled anybody who read more than one paper. He told one reporter that he had heard nothing by Schoenberg since *Pierrot Lunaire* (1912),[13] but another that he recognized Schoenberg as "a great inventor, a harmonist who marks out new paths in that field; I respect all the achievements he has pioneered in today's music, though I travel an absolutely different route. But for me Schoenbergian rationalism and his aesthetic principles are unbearable. He reminds me, in contemporary music, of an Oscar Wilde or a romantic German . . . a dolled-up Brahms."[14] He added that "I actually haven't the time to keep up with European musical movements: I'm too busy composing and performing my own works." Yet a few weeks later he told the Berlin Russian-language paper *Rul'* that "I'm very interested in contemporary tendencies in the young German music and keep up with everything that goes on in this area."[15] A decided wariness, bordering on insecurity, is apparent in these remarks. Obviously he did not know Schoenberg's recent serial or proto-serial music (of which the Serenade and the Wind Quintet had both recently been premiered), had heard that it embodied an important constructivist tendency but had no idea what that tendency was—as the Wilde (in more ways than one) comparison shows. Unfortunately, his interviews were sometimes syndicated abroad, so that his remarks were more widely circulated than he may have imagined, and in more accessible languages than Polish or Russian. It was this sometimes inconvenient fact about modern newspapers that was soon to result in a crucial, and as it turned out decisive, confrontation between the two masters of modernism.

From Prague, meanwhile, it was on to Holland and a series of four concerts, including two under Mengelberg ("one of the greatest conductors," Stravinsky told *Rul'* three months later).[16] At this point, Vera struck off back to Paris, partly to relieve her business partner, Tula Danilova, who telegraphed that she had broken her leg, but partly because in any case she could not accompany Stravinsky on the next stage of his tour, to Switzerland, because Katya was coming from Nice to visit her cousin Olga Nosenko in Lausanne. For both Igor and Katya it was the first visit to Switzerland since moving to France in 1920, and the composer seems to have decided at an early stage that to confront his Vaudois friends—and especially his Winterthur patron Reinhart—with his Paris mistress would not be politic. The plan for Katya to come to Switzerland is already mentioned in Stravinsky's letter to Ramuz of 12 September.[17] Craft implies that Vera went to Winterthur and Geneva, but not to Lausanne, for fear of Olga.[18] But Katya was almost certainly with him in Winterthur, where he played his Piano Concerto (on an unsuitable Pleyel instrument)[19] under Volkmar Andreae and they stayed with Reinhart; and in Geneva, where he played the concerto under Ansermet and conducted the Octet. Perhaps Katya had made a scene. Or perhaps even Vera had; after all, both were faced with a three-month separation from him. And while Katya might briefly enjoy her new status as the wife of a touring virtuoso, Vera was for once reduced to marking off his concerts in her diary, on the basis of his daily telegrams.[20] It was a situation that could hardly be expected to last. America would force some kind of an accommodation.

From Geneva, Katya went back to the Villa des Roses, and her husband continued on his way to Leipzig, where Vera again awaited him. They lunched with Furtwängler, and Stravinsky played his concerto in the Gewandhaus under the great man on 4 December, a performance that was repeated in Berlin four days later. "He conducted it wretchedly," the composer recalled in his declining years, "even worse than Kussevitsky at the première."[21] But the Berlin papers, hearing Stravinsky perform his music for the first time, were sufficiently impressed by the new concerto. He was, they agreed, "no mere fantastic shocker, no mere Charlie Chaplin of music, no mere trapeze artist."[22] And in the Blüthnersaal he enjoyed what one discriminating listener called "a strong and undisputed success" conducting a chamber concert that included the *Soldier's Tale* Suite (without its Triumphal March, since the percussion part had too many page turns), the Octet, and the *Japanese Lyrics*.[23]

Two weeks later, on 27 December, Stravinsky sailed from Le Havre for New York on the SS *Paris*, after what cannot have been more than a few days in Nice, and a concert with Pierre Sechiari in Marseilles (on the twenty-first). Vera and Robert Lyon went to see him off, and after the boat sailed, Vera wrote to Katya—apparently with her consent but almost certainly at Igor's wish—describing his departure. "It is difficult," she wrote, "to talk about all those moments that trouble or touch us and that also give meaning to everything. But you will understand, since we have a common language. To whom, if not to you, should I write about what is dear to me? And from whom but you can I receive news that is dear to me?" Igor's cabin was "the best one, in the exact center, and with all conveniences," including a piano, installed on Lyon's instructions; Igor's valet, Alexis Sabline—specially hired for the trip—had come from third class to help him unpack. The weather was stormy, and when they went on board there had been music playing, and the bar and restaurant had opened, "all of this so that the passengers would not think of the stormy night and of the possible dangers awaiting them." When visitors were asked to leave, Igor had stayed below in his cabin. "He must have felt depressed. The experience of leaving like that can only be balanced by the joy of returning. Robert Lyon left with the night train, but I spent the night in Le Havre, listening for the whistles in order to hear when Igor's boat left, but I could not distinguish them from the whistles of other boats."[24]

Whether such picturesque embroideries were truly likely to calm Katya's anxiety or simply exacerbate her jealousy is an unanswerable question, in the absence of letters on her side. But it is hard to imagine her tearing open Vera's envelope in a placid or acquiescent spirit, or, as she read it, missing its faint but unmistakable tone of condescension—the actual lover comforting the half-abandoned wife. As for her feelings when, two months later and again apparently on her husband's insistence, she received a visit from Vera at the Villa des Roses and had to allow her name to be appended to a joint telegram to Detroit ("We are together today and embrace you"), they can only be guessed at. It seems unlikely, though, that the situation is adequately described by Robert Craft's observation that "the two women instantly understood each other."[25]

THE CROSSING took eight days, and it was stormy and bleak: "not so much sun as a twenty-franc piece," Stravinsky told reporters in his apartment at the Hotel Langdon on East Fifty-sixth Street on the day after his arrival late on 4 January. In New York there was deep snow. The composer remembered being met by the violinist Paul Kochanski, "stamping his frozen feet on the jetty."[26] And he may have had more opportunity than he bargained for to examine the skyscrapers—even in that pre–Chrysler Building, pre–Empire State Building age—as his cabs picked their way through the plowed snow and the abandoned cars. That morning he was already rehearsing the New York Philharmonic for their first Carnegie Hall concert on the eighth. In the afternoon he faced the Fourth Estate. And in the evening, according to the next day's New York Times, he went out "to dine and to hear on its native heath the dance music that the Old World has called American jazz."[27]

From the start, Stravinsky was lionized by the wide-eyed Manhattan press, so hard-bitten on its own ground, so easily impressed on other people's. A dozen of them crowded into his hotel room, and hung on every paradox, every bon mot, apparently untroubled by his lack of English—what one of them called his "Gatling-gun volley of alternate French and German." "Mr. Stravinsky," H. O. Osgood assured his readers,

> is the interviewer's delight. A question to him is merely the first tiny snowball, which he proceeds to roll down hill, making it grow larger and larger at every step until it has developed into a whole paragraph, or even a chapter. The trouble of interviewing Mr. Stravinsky is not to know what to write, but to know what to be able to leave out. It all deserves inclusion, for the composer has a mentality that is on the qui vive every moment of the time, and one bright, witty, quaint expression follows another so quickly it is hard to recall them.[28]

When the archmodernist let slip that "I detest modern music," "the interviewers fairly whooped with joy. There was the headline." Monocled, and sporting a sweater that was either orange and gray or brown and rose (depending on which paper you read), Stravinsky leant on the grand piano and insisted that "my music is not modern music nor is it music of the future. It is the music of today." And when pressed to name the actual modernists, he smiled. "I shan't mention any names . . . but they are the gentlemen who work with formulas instead of ideas."[29]

The program of his first concert with the New York Philharmonic, in Carnegie Hall on the eighth, though in fact conditioned by practicalities, may well have seemed deliberately chosen to distance him from the most straightforward idea of modernism. Alongside the *Firebird* Suite, he conducted two earlier works, the *Scherzo fantastique* and *Fireworks,* and of his recent music, only *Pulcinella;* the only remotely "difficult" piece was *The Song of the Nightingale.* The concert opened with the "Volga Boatmen" arrangement, which Stravinsky was still defiantly using as a national anthem. The program's blandness must have worried Clarence Mackay, the orchestra's president, since he wrote to Stravinsky asking him to add *The Rite of Spring* for the third concert on the Saturday evening, the tenth. But the composer understandably sidestepped what would have been for him a frighteningly underprepared debut, and the only difference on Saturday was that a suite from *Petrushka* was substituted for the *Firebird* music.[30]

Apart from the *Scherzo fantastique,* all these works had been heard before in Manhattan, "and to be strictly honest . . . all have had better performances than that of Thursday evening."[31] Even *The Rite of Spring* was becoming familiar territory to New Yorkers. Monteux had conducted it, amid popular and critical acclaim, almost a year before; and Monteux's Boston successor, Koussevitzky, had included it in a Carnegie Hall concert less than a week before the composer's arrival. The coincidence prompted Lawrence Gilman, the *Herald Tribune* critic, to a lengthy disquisition on "the swift changes that have occurred in Stravinsky from year to year (we had almost said from month to month, and from work to work)" and on "the inescapable fact that in each of his significant incarnations he has displayed authentic genius."[32] But it also, of course, drew attention to the relative dullness of the early *Scherzo,* in which Gilman found "historical interest, but little of any other kind," and which his *Times* colleague Olin Downes saw as no more than "a piece of brilliant instrumentation by a student mastering his business with precocious rapidity."[33]

Although, apart from a few details, Stravinsky the composer still commanded an admiring press in New York, and although his three Carnegie Hall concerts were greeted with ecstasy by a huge audience which crowded round the platform at the end clapping and cheering until he appeared in his hat and coat, "plainly showing that another engagement claimed him,"[34] Stravinsky the conductor was more coolly appraised by the critics. They found his directing dull and somewhat cautious; and while Gilman praised its vitality and rhythmic force, he noted that "in finesse and clarity, in tonal balance, in nuance, [it] left something to be desired." To some extent, no doubt, this was—as Gilman also remarked—an aesthetic objection to Stravinsky's conscious antiexpressiveness. But after all, as Downes smugly concluded, "few composers are good interpreters of their own productions," so it was hardly surprising that "one of the least eloquent interpreters of Stravinsky is Stravinsky."

For the first month of his visit, Stravinsky was based in New York. He must have spent a lot of time trying out the eighteen different pianos which, he later told his family, Steinway had put at his disposal for his concerto appearances. On 11 January he was guest of honor at a dinner in the old Steinway Hall, at the end of which he was presented with a large chocolate cake in the shape of a grand piano with a score, inscribed with his name, open on the desk.[35] This was no mere Steinway office party. The 120 or so guests included Rachmaninov, Nikolay Medtner, Fritz Kreisler, Josef Hofmann, Furtwängler, and another figure from Stravinsky's Petersburg past, the conductor Alexander Ziloti, now a professor at the Juilliard School. Four days later, Stravinsky directed a charity concert at Vincent Astor's house on Fifth Avenue, and this time the program, devoted to chamber and vocal works, could genuinely reflect an at least comparatively forbidding Stravinsky. The soprano Greta Torpadie sang the *Berceuses du chat* and two of the *Three Tales,* as well as the early *Faun and Shepherdess,* the "Pastorale," and the Gorodetsky songs (all with the composer at the piano); and there was a performance of the trio suite from *The Soldier's Tale*. The picture was filled out by a more substantial, prestigious, and presumably, for the composer, lucrative "Evening of Chamber Music with Igor Stravinsky," given by a group of New York Philharmonic players in the Aeolian Hall on the twenty-fifth, which added the United States premieres of the ensemble *Ragtime* and the Octet to a concert performance of *Renard*, which Stokowski had conducted just over a year earlier. This was America's first encounter with the neoclassical Stravinsky in musical—as opposed to theoretical—form, and she was not at all sure she liked it. The hall was by no means full, the applause no more than polite, and Lawrence Gilman, with almost sadistic disloyalty to an admired master, called the Octet

> a dreary little piece, imaginatively sterile, feeble in invention and of a peculiar, oppressive dullness even in its "tempo giusto" Finale. Its counterpoint is not so much reckless as unresourceful; and the whole work has an astoundingly infantile character, a vacuous naïveté which is not unlikely to cause you to rush to your shelf of scores when you get home in order to assure yourself that the name of the composer of the Octuor is the name that appears on the title page of the *Sacre du Printemps*. It seems incredible.[36]

As for *Ragtime*, done with harpsichord instead of cimbalom, it positively invited condescension in the land of Scott Joplin, which tended to hear it as a joke. "Evidently," Olin Downes wrote, "to many, it was funny. Others found it merely poor ragtime, often vulgar and farcically obvious, now and again malicious, but without the saving grace of humanity, laughter and invention, which redeem malice and make it the fitting sauce of comedy."[37] For Gilman the best music in the concert was the *Nightingale* excerpts (all from the pre-*Firebird* part of that opera): a strange and ominous change of heart by a critic who, not three weeks before, had been studiously analyzing Stravinsky's vertiginous development and astonishedly claiming that "every one of his chief phases has produced a masterpiece."[38]

Stravinsky had arrived late for the afternoon rehearsal in the Aeolian Hall, having spent three days in Boston, where he had given the first two United States performances of his Piano Concerto with Koussevitzky on the twenty-third and twenty-fourth. No doubt Koussevitzky had seen to it (by way of Edition Russe) that these performances preceded the New York premiere; and he had taken steps to ensure a success for his visitor by devising an all-Stravinsky program, with the concerto framed by suites from the two early ballets, *The Firebird* (the original 1912 suite) and *Petrushka*. One wonders whether Stravinsky rose early enough on the Saturday to witness the brilliant total eclipse of the sun visible in clear skies over Boston that breakfast time.[39] Oddly enough, there is no mention of this rare and unforgettable phenomenon in any interview, letter, or subsequent account of the visit. Perhaps he felt about it as he later claimed to feel about mountains: "they tell me nothing." Or perhaps he was simply wary of any inclination to interpret such experiences as in some way the source of musical inspiration. As he assured Paul Rosenfeld, who interviewed him back at the Aeolian Hall rehearsal in New York: "If I went out and narrowly escaped being run over by a trolley car, I would not immediately rush for some music paper and try to make something out of the emotion I had just felt."[40]

As well as prompting such topical shafts of antiexpressionism and a mild sideswipe at Schoenberg ("really a romantic at heart who would like to get away from romanticism"), Rosenfeld gives the first detailed account of Stravinsky in rehearsal, and of his intensely physical, mimetic style of conducting.

> If he had been late, there was no laggardliness in his mind at all. Never a doubt as to exactly what it was he wanted and the means to arrive at his end! He himself might not be able to play all the instruments assembled before him; still he could tell the musicians how to get the effects wanted. . . . In passages of complicated rhythm, he stopped the orchestra, sang the measure very quietly, and then left the musicians to play it after him. Once there was a dispute. He stuck his nose into the score, read a few bars carefully, then said to the instrumentalist, "You must make it this way," and sang the notes.
> . . . The man was abrupt, impatient, energetic, but never ironic either of himself or of his interlocutors; most exemplary in his relations with the players. It was apparent they were working out a little problem together, and Stravinsky had some suggestions which might enable them all to solve it. A kind of interest radiated from him to the musicians, who began entering into the spirit of the animal comedy [in Renard], and kindling him in return. . . . His arms at all times mimed the rhythmic starts and jerks, till one could actually perceive where his music came from.[41]

Robert Lyon had negotiated a contract between Stravinsky and the Aeolian Company of New York whereby Aeolian acquired the non-French rights to the composer's pianola rolls and which also involved his cutting four new rolls a year for the Aeolian Duo-Art system. At some time during this first month on the East Coast, he accordingly went to the Aeolian studios and recorded the first movement of his Piano Concerto and all three movements of the sonata, a piece which still awaited its first public performance.[42] Perhaps he also went to Carnegie Hall to hear a young Polish-American violinist called Samuel Dushkin, or to Town Hall to hear his Paris colleague Nadia Boulanger lecture on "Modern Music and its Evolution."[43] He renewed acquaintance with Paul Kochanski (whom he had known in Europe, through Rubinstein, since before the war) and promised him a work for violin and piano.[44] There must have been many such reunions in the melting pot of postwar New York. But there were also heavy social duties of an essentially local character, of which perhaps none was more bizarre than the tea-reception by the Women's Committee of the Philadelphia Orchestra after his matinee concert in the Academy of Music in that city at the end of January, at which

> two thousand elderly ladies . . . had me sit on a throne and then pro-
> ceeded to parade in front of me, each one kissing my hand. When the
> eight-hundredth one passed, I could not bear any more of it. I
> excused myself as best I could and told them not to come looking for
> me because, by the time I got to Europe, my hand would be utterly
> wasted and I would not be able to conduct concerts. Worst of all, I
> had to tell them all of this over a loudspeaker so that they could
> hear me.[45]

The *Philadelphia Inquirer* the next morning respectfully listed the ladies of the committee, "who took turns introducing the composer and pouring tea for the guests."

He conducted twice in Philadelphia, then returned to New York for his last Manhattan engagement before setting off into the hinterland. With Mengelberg and the New York Philharmonic, he gave two performances of the Piano Concerto.[46] As in Boston, the new work went down well; the Carnegie Hall subscribers were "stirred," in Olin Downes's opinion, by "its rhythm alone, and the magnificent virtuosity of Mr. Stravinsky's performance—he seemed to have endless speed, power, precision at command, and was in fact himself a complete rival orchestra." But Downes himself was torn on the rack of his evident distaste for music which he could nevertheless not bring himself to deny was the work of a master. In his agonizing equivocations, there is much that is perceptive. He found in the work "no emotion, but ruthless, driving energy, and a spirit that is imperious and sardonic," and inquired:

> Is there really any such thing as music which has no echo of the pas-
> sions of the human heart? Perhaps. If so, then Stravinsky may really
> be on the track of a new music, abstract, classic in its conception, a
> music that derives its existence and its vital force simply by the con-
> flict of opposing melodic lines and the propulsion of conflicting

rhythms. But as the expression of an extraordinary brain and a certain phase of modern temperament this piano concerto is without a parallel.[47]

In the month that followed, Stravinsky had ample opportunity to compare rail travel in the United States with his prewar experiences in the Russian Empire. From New York he headed for Cleveland—a journey of some fourteen hours. Then, after conducting the Cleveland Orchestra on the twelfth and fourteenth, he hurried back to Philadelphia, where he was due to play the concerto under Fritz Reiner on the fifteenth. In his autobiography, Stravinsky describes how Reiner (at that time conductor of the Cincinnati Symphony Orchestra) achieved an immaculate performance with the Philadelphians on a mere half-hour rehearsal, something that "could never have occurred, notwithstanding the prodigious technique of the conductor and the high quality of the orchestra, if Reiner had not acquired a perfect knowledge of my score, which he had procured some time before."[48]

At supper after the concert, Stravinsky found himself next to George Enescu, who had been playing the violin at the Chamber Music Association that evening. It seems to have been their first meeting. Enescu had himself recently come from Cleveland, where he had conducted the Theban Dances from his as yet unperformed opera *Oedipe,* and it is an intriguing thought that he may have mentioned the work, and even perhaps described his treatment of Sophocles. Ever since conceiving the idea of an Oedipus opera long before the war, Enescu had been obsessed with a setting that would enhance and intensify the play as he had seen it performed with Mounet-Sully in the title role at the Comédie-Française in 1909. This concept of an enriched but essentially faithful and comprehensive narrative is so remote—in both theory and practice—from the work which Stravinsky and Cocteau began to discuss a few months after the Philadelphia meeting (and which Enescu himself in after years described as "insolent cubism") that one can almost sense an open, if no doubt amicable, disagreement between the two composers at that time. Or it may be that Stravinsky listened to Enescu but held his peace; or it may of course be that the subject was not even mentioned.[49]

From Philadelphia, Stravinsky once again headed west, this time for Chicago, and here he spent nearly a fortnight—his longest stay in any city on the tour except New York. As usual, he conducted two concerts, this time sharing rehearsals with the local conductor, Frederick Stock, another undemonstrative performer who made an abiding impression on him.[50] He also, with Greta Torpadie, repeated his Astor program of six weeks before, as *digestif* to a dinner given in his honor by the Chicago Arts Club. The composer John Alden Carpenter, husband of the Arts Club president, took him on a tour of the famous stockyards. Towards the end of the month he went on to Detroit, where he promptly picked up a heavy cold that prevented his accepting an invitation from Henry Ford to visit his car factory but did not prevent his both playing the Piano Concerto (under Victor Kolar) and conducting the other items in his concert with the local symphony orchestra—a combination he was making for the first time and against his own preferences, according to a preview in the *Detroit News*.[51] By the next day, in Cincinnati, he was so unwell that he took to his bed in the Hotel Gibson and Reiner had to step into the breach and rehearse the orchestra. On the fifth he still felt groggy, and Reiner stood by at rehearsal holding a medicine bottle.

> But as soon as the music started Stravinsky forgot all about his cold. He became enthused, inspired, and led the men through his difficult pages at a fast pace. His overcoat was thrown across the railing of the conductor's stand. Soon he became so warmed up that he peeled off his coat, too. The last time he did this there was disclosed a pink sweater. This time it was a white woollen sweater cut short, like a vest. In ten minutes more Stravinsky was bathed in perspiration, wrapped a towel round his neck and repeatedly wiped his forehead with it.[52]

By the day of the first concert, the sixth, all such anxieties were quite forgotten. "No concert within memory," reported one critic, "has equalled this one for sheer thrill. Before the concert was over the audience had been transformed into a seething, applauding mob, while the men in the orchestra became howling dervishes."[53]

Three days later, Stravinsky was back in New York and preparing to fulfill his final American contract, to make a series of gramophone records for Brunswick Records. His Brunswick contract, which had been under negotiation since the autumn, is dated 14 March. But by then he had already cut the four 78 rpm sides (per annum) stipulated by the contract. He recorded seven of the eight *Five Fingers* pieces, the Waltz, Polka, and Andante from the two sets of Easy Pieces, and the *Valse pour les enfants* on the eleventh and twelfth in the company's Broadway studio.[54] These were still, unfortunately, acoustic recordings, with the piano pointed at a large loudspeaker horn, which transmitted the vibrations directly by way of a diaphragm and a needle to a blank wax disc. So it is scarcely surprising that they were never published, since the first, vastly superior, electrical (microphone) recordings were actually being made that same week at the Victor studios in Philadelphia; and in any case the choice of repertoire—which was limited by Stravinsky's piano-roll contract with Pleyel—was hardly such as to excite great enthusiasm in a market where the recording of modern music was still an experimental concept.[55] It was presumably to help remedy this problem that he soon set about composing a more solid piano work that would give him something to record in the second year of the contract. Meanwhile, on his last full day in New York he went to see *Petrushka* at the Met, and it was on this occasion, during the curtain calls, that he encountered the production's designer, Sergey Sudeykin, bowed curtly to the audience, and turned rapidly on his heels.[56] But Lawrence Gilman, who was at the performance, seems to have noticed nothing untoward, unless his final shaft is a hint to the contrary. Stravinsky, he wrote, "was thoughtfully supplied with a wreath the size of a cartwheel. He looked well in spite of his winter in Boeotia, and seemed unaffectedly happy—though one never can tell."[57]

Stravinsky sailed away the next day, taking with him an understandably confused set of impressions of his ten-week visit. "I have fallen in love with America," he had told a reporter in Cincinnati, "you can quote me as saying just the nicest imaginable things about this country."[58] He had certainly been lionized in a way that must have taken him back to his early years in Paris. And though the society was more provincial, duller, and less glamorous, it was also more vital and energetic, and by no means less affluent or less anxious to support music which it might not like or understand but which it was perfectly ready to accept as important if Europe said it was. More than a year later, he was still telling reporters that "America, with its gigantic growth, inspires me . . . there is no premium on laziness in America. Everybody works. The possession of huge wealth does not exempt the owner from work, if he desires to retain the respect of the people. The tempo of America is greater than the rest of the world. It moves at a wonderfully swift pace. It all appeals to me."[59] America reciprocated. "His appearance," the *Detroit News* had announced, "whether the public likes his music or not, is the outstanding event of the season." And to prove it, Stravinsky was taking home with him something in the region of twenty-five thousand dollars—the equivalent of nearly half a million dollars today. By any outward material or artistic criterion, the tour had been a smashing success.

And yet it may have crossed his mind that the popular acclaim he had been accorded had been, in essence, that of a circus star, the musical equivalent of the bearded lady or the dog with two heads. "The American public," one Chicago critic noted, "has thought of him as a weird figure, reared from the cradle on a diet of discord, preaching an evangel of ugliness, racking our nerves to create a sensation."[60] Everywhere, the press had commented on his surprising physical ordinariness. "Not from any outward appearance," said the *Boston Post* critic, might this be the man from whom has come such devastating music. . . . There is in Mr. Stravinsky's aspect and manner, in his extraordinarily rapid, almost mechanical motions, in his slight body and his eyes that seem just to have left off peering in a microscope, more to suggest the entomologist than the musician. That he is an intellect, an enormously developed mental machine, seems the most obvious conclusion.[61]

"A slight, nervous, baldescent, goggled, pleasantly homely figure," Gilman had thought, "looking somewhat like one of Mr. Wells's great-orbed Martians":[62] in more modern language, an alien disguised as a human being, or even—could it be?—the devil with a butterfly net.

Like a circus freak, he had to some extent been held—or had held himself—at arm's length. He seems not to have met any important American "classical" composers, such as they were: certainly not the still barely known Charles Ives, not Henry Cowell, and above all not the expatriate Frenchman Edgard Varèse, whose *Intégrales* had its first performance in New York while Stravinsky was in Detroit, but who, according to Craft, was conspicuously absent from Stravinsky's own concerts.[63] Nor does Aaron Copland, who had met Stravinsky at Nadia Boulanger's in Paris and who was in New York at the time, mention having attended any of Stravinsky's Carnegie or Aeolian Hall concerts.[64] No doubt some of these composers did attend. But there is no feeling that Stravinsky sought personal or intellectual contact with the new American music, or interested himself in its tendencies. He may slightly have feared having to defend, or even modify, his sweeping strictures against the "music of the future"; may indeed have felt a certain insecurity at the idea of a modernism not his own. For whatever reason, the only American music in which he expressed, and displayed, interest was jazz: a music which, whatever its novelty, posed no intellectual (or one might add professional) threat.

The most remarkable thing of all is that after adding up his American experiences—to say nothing of his American earnings—he seems to have pronounced a purely negative judgment within the four walls of his own home. "He disliked America and the Americans," his niece reported in a letter to her parents, "and says he's never seen such a dull and dreary race."[65] Whether this was the condescension of the Old World towards the New, or merely a reflection of the America to which the touring artist, immured in his luxury hotel or smothered by the lavish embrace of uptown society, is in the end inevitably confined, is a matter for conjecture. But it remains a curious, and in some ways disconcerting, spectacle.

THE GIRL FROM LENINGRAD

STRAVINSKY WAS DUE to conduct in Barcelona on 28 March. So, when the *Aquitania* docked in Cherbourg on the twentieth, instead of going back to his family in Nice, he went to Paris, and from there—two or three days later—with Vera straight to Spain. In Barcelona he conducted two concerts and, in a third, played the Piano Concerto under Monteux, and only then, nearly three weeks after his arrival from New York, did he at last return to the Villa des Roses. His wife and children had been there for more than six months, he for barely six weeks.

While he was mid-Atlantic, a handsome Russian girl of twenty arrived in Paris from the newly renamed Leningrad. She spent three days in the capital, called twice at her uncle Igor's flat, and telephoned him, without success. She must have missed him by scarcely a day, since she left Paris for Nice on the very Saturday that he arrived there from Cherbourg. Tatyana Stravinsky was the older of Yury and Yelena Stravinsky's two daughters, and like her father she was consumptive, which seems to have been the main reason why her parents had proposed her for an extended visit to her uncle's Mediterranean home, though her sister, Xenya, also talks vaguely of "motives of a personal order."[1] Yury had come back to Petrograd from the Crimea with his family in 1923, but there was little or no work for an architect in the former capital, and he would have been less than human if it had not struck him that his daughters'—and perhaps his own—best prospects lay in re-establishing contact with the famous and presumably wealthy brother to whom he had been so close in the years immediately before their separation. Such hopes did not stop short of open requests for financial or quasi-financial help. While Tanya was in Nice, Yury suggested that she persuade Igor to send him copies of his published scores, and later he mentioned money directly to his younger brother, at least to judge by Tanya's remark, in a letter home, that "Uncle Igor would very much like to help you, but his finances are at present hanging by a thread, and with all his family expenses he's not in a position to do it just now."[2] Another idea was to put emotional pressure on Igor to accept invitations to conduct in Russia, something he had consistently declined, ostensibly because he was too busy, but in fact clearly for reasons of a more complicated kind. Yury's natural desire to lure the prodigal home encountered an equally natural resistance to that painful and alien attraction, with its threat to reopen wounds which had still, as we shall see, barely healed.

Tanya, in any case, would be able to improve herself in France. Not that there was any specific plan for her to study (the Leningrad Stravinskys could hardly have afforded anything of the kind). The idea of a typing course, paid for by Uncle Igor, came later, and it was suggested, not by her parents, but by the Stravinsky children's music teacher in Nice, Alexander Nápravník (a son of the composer-conductor).[3] But she would get to know her cousins, learn to speak French, and—who knows?—make herself some useful contacts. What in fact happened is that she rapidly conceived an adoration verging on a definite crush for her dazzling and sometimes flirtatious uncle, which gradually matured into a more serious love for her oldest cousin, Theodore, two years her junior. But since their cousinhood was double—they were first cousins through Theodore's father, and second cousins through his mother—the mere possibility of marriage raised specters of inbreeding for a family already ravaged by hereditary illness. So Tanya had sadly to leave. "It all happened so suddenly," she told her parents early in February 1926, "that I couldn't even write to you in time. I'm already writing from Paris. Nothing bad took place. . . . I told Auntie everything, for her to pass on to Uncle. I understood that it was impossible for me to stay."[4]

Tanya's letters home during her eleven-month stay at the Villa des Roses are a wide-eyed diary of life in the Stravinsky household. She pictures the villa itself, "in the best part of town . . . in the depths of a wonderful garden." And she describes its inhabitants:

> Aunt Katya is very young-looking. She's well-dressed, and wears a little lipstick. The girls are dressed in the English style, and very sweet. Milochka [Milène] is simply charming and very like Xenya, while Mika is not very pretty, but beautifully proportioned and sturdy. . . . In general the children are delightful, but they are still more or less children, including Fedya [Theodore] (who's a whole head taller than me). . . . Fedya, Mika, and Svetik speak Russian quite well, but they sometimes express themselves in an awfully funny way. . . . I like Svetik best. He's the warmest. Usually I spend the day with the boys, as Milène is ill and Mika is studying hard. . . . Fedya has given up music lessons, as he's taking painting so seriously. But he understands music very well; he's musically educated, and he seems to me very talented.[5]

But after a week or two these impressions are subtly revised. Fedya now "is much older in maturity than his years. He's completely grown-up, in both cast of mind and appearance. . . . I can talk seriously only with Fedya, the others are definitely small children. . . . Svetik is a charming boy with a face like a peach and soft fluffy hair. . . . Milène's a strange girl, reserved, still very much a child, very gifted at music and generally good at everything. Mika is quite unremarkable, just a nice, affectionate girl."6 Tanya found the grandmother she had not seen since before the war somewhat distant, much aged, and quite a hypochondriac; but "she puts up with the most terrible racket and yelling from which *you* would have fled long ago."7

The apartment was huge: on two upper floors, with an internal staircase. Apart from the family there were three servants and the governess, Madubo; so when Uncle Igor at last came home on 7 April there were eleven of them, and it must have been as crowded and noisy as the old days in the Kryukov Canal flat from which Tanya had recently come, but which these days echoed only to the noise of a vanished age. Perhaps not surprisingly, Katya disliked visitors, and rarely had guests for dinner: only Nápravník, who always stayed to supper on his teaching days. "She complains all the time about their huge expenses and the amount of money that goes out. They economize on trifles, but of course never alter their lifestyle."8 Once, in August, when Cocteau came to dinner and talked so brilliantly that Tanya was driven to compare his wit with Fedya's (of all people), she observed that for her aunt it was "torture . . . to be a hostess. She gets so tired that she can hardly speak. God—how happy I'd be in her place. . . . I certainly wouldn't avoid Uncle's friends and I'd go everywhere with him."9

Tanya saw Uncle Igor for a whole week in April, before he was off again to Rome, this time taking Katya and Fedya with him. He treated her

> very affectionately, but I've only seen him at table and for a few minutes each evening. He was working all the time upstairs in his room. I was at once struck by his being so very short, but extremely smart. He wears silk shirts, a monocle, etc. Instead of a waistcoat, he has multicolored knitted blouses, which he changes nearly every day. He told us masses of interesting things about his travels. He's unbelievably lively, bursting with sheer vitality and energy. At table, to Granny's horror, he started "spoiling" me. He gave me liqueurs which are put out only for him, began teaching me to smoke, and kept saying improper things during the conversation. But he made sure I wasn't embarrassed before he said anything.10

Though Tanya is unlikely to have known it, Igor had started writing a piano work as repertoire for future Brunswick recordings (with each movement of a length to fill one side of a ten-inch disc);[11] and meanwhile, an actual gramophone ("the latest system") had arrived in the house from America, together with the incomplete Roux pressings of the Octet and records of dance music. They would open the large doors between the drawing room and the nursery and "have a proper ball with the three men, Uncle, Fedya, and Svetik."[12] One August evening when Vera Nosenko was staying, Igor and Fedya had been out for dinner.

> We were standing in the hall on our way to bed, when suddenly in came Uncle and Fedya in their dinner jackets, all gleaming, perfumed and gay. Uncle grabbed Vera by the arm, Fedya me, and Svetik Mika, and they began rushing round the room with us. It was a real "Rape of the Sabine Women." Granny almost fainted. Finally, Uncle seized me by the arm and took me to my room, saying that it was children's bedtime. But I ran back of course, and we went on romping for a long time.[13]

Pleyel had also sent the latest model of pianola, with a set of Stravinsky rolls and more dance music. "We've learnt to operate the machine," Tanya is soon informing her parents,

> but we can't control all the nuances. When Uncle controls his pieces himself, nothing remains obscure and everything is so beautiful that no even faintly sympathetic listener can fail to like them. I've only now seen how his works are made: it's sheer genius. . . . If you were to hear Uncle's works, and not understand or like them, it would all be the performer's fault, since there couldn't be any other reason. I myself am no fine judge, but all the same I now understand everything.[14]

And Yury and Yelena, themselves artists of rather advanced tastes, are left in no doubt that not everyone at the Villa des Roses appreciates Uncle Igor as well as their Tanya. She had sent them a photo of her portrait painted by Fedya, with the observation that "you won't mind about his having elongated my face, since that's his style. He didn't one bit want me to send you this photograph, but I persuaded him that you aren't like Granny, who can only do with photographic likenesses."[15] Alas, Yury did not like the portrait any more than his mother had done. But Tanya had her explanation ready. "Actually," she wrote back, "it's very difficult to judge from such a small photograph, but I'm certain that you would like the actual portrait. You probably have no understanding of the new trends in painting. The greatest master of this tendency is Picasso. And Picasso these days has nothing in common with the old things that you know."[16] This was probably enough to elongate the faces at number 66 Kryukov Canal as well.

Even Igor must have felt uncomfortable about leaving Nice yet again so soon after his return from a three-month absence, and no doubt the idea of Katya going with him was his. Why Fedya should have gone too is a matter for speculation. Perhaps it was an eighteenth-birthday treat; or perhaps it was felt that he should not be left unsupervised with his charming cousin. In any case they went, a stately Russian family party, and destined to return in still greater state, since in Rome poor Katya went down with influenza, which turned rapidly to pleurisy; an operation was performed, two liters of fluid were pumped from her ailing lungs, and she returned to Nice at the start of May on a stretcher. Tanya was horrified at "how pale and exhausted she looked. She can't speak and can't sleep at night for constant terrible headaches. Depression reigns in the apartment. Everyone upstairs talks in whispers and tiptoes about. Granny is up and down the stairs all the time, her own dizziness forgotten."[17]

Igor was thrown into a state of perturbation by Katya's illness. His own Rome concerts had gone quite well: a Piano Concerto under Bernardino Molinari in the Augusteum, and a chamber concert in the Accademia di Santa Cecilia at which the Octet, the *Soldier's Tale* Suite, the *Japanese Lyrics*, *Pribaoutki*, and *Ragtime* had been greeted with an ovation punctuated by whistling.[18] But Scherchen, who was in Rome to conduct the new Pirandello production of *The Soldier's Tale*, found his conducting "stiff and of little merit," while in himself the composer was "the whole time extremely nervous and bad-tempered." Scherchen had implored him to attend the Pirandello rehearsals, to no avail. But at the performance, Stravinsky grumbled about everything, commiserated with Scherchen at having to work with "such poor material," and complained to him about lighting effects which, Scherchen told Reinhart, were simply following the new Chester score, "overseen, and in some respects altered, by Stravinsky *himself*! When I told him that I had particularly requested the new edition, he directed his insults at Ramuz. . . . No, that was very disagreeable (and I regret this last impression of mine extremely, even if my personal relations with Stravinsky oughtn't to be affected by it and in fact naturally on my side have not been)."[19] The point is that while Scherchen may have disliked Stravinsky's disloyalty to his co-author, he by no means disagreed with his opinion of Ramuz, who "has truly broken up into the symbolic-dramatic, romantic-yearning, what with Stravinsky was simply a play of unlimited riches."[20] The view was widely held among cognoscenti, and of course that did not help reconcile the composer to the hybrid character of the work itself. As for Scherchen, after his contretemps with Stravinsky he vowed never again to conduct a staged performance of the *Tale*.

After Rome, Stravinsky had intended to go soon to Paris once again. But with Katya ill, he could not leave Nice. According to Tanya, he managed only a two-day trip to Toulon in the second week of May. She gives no reason for the expedition, and would probably have been astonished to learn that it was made in company with Vera Sudeykina—though no doubt Katya knew, and perhaps poor Theodore did too, since Stravinsky had chosen Rome, of all places and times, to inform his son of the situation between himself and Vera.[21] Tanya would also perhaps have been intrigued by such tangible mementos of the Toulon trip as the nude photograph of her uncle taken by Vera at Le Lavandou.[22] Yet somehow even she was made aware of a certain quality of narcissism in this small but well-formed genius. In the hot weather of mid-May, she discovered that "Uncle looks after himself a good deal and is so well developed that he is completely covered with muscles. He's very strong, and can easily lift one and a half times his own weight with one hand. He and Auntie have a bath every morning, then do gymnastics."[23] He played them his new sonata, as well as parts of the Piano Concerto and *Mavra,* and told Tanya that "when he goes to the piano [to compose], he tries to forget all existing forms of composition, all devices, so that his work should be created in the literal sense of the word. . . . This uses up all his strength, and after two or three hours of work, he feels completely washed out."[24]

Ten days later, having completed the fair copy of the Cadenza-Finale of the new piano work, he did finally leave for Paris, once more taking Theodore, who had a commission "finishing off the dining-room in some chateau or other."[25] This was to be another long absence, of fully eight weeks. Igor had told his niece to tell her father that he could not spare time from composition for a Russian tour, so he presumably also told her about the studio where he continued to compose and make piano rolls when he was in Paris. All the same, there is not much evidence that he spent time on creative work during these two summer months of 1925. The Serenade, as he called the piano work, was shelved till August; the little orchestral suite he had made out of the Three Easy Pieces plus the Galop from the Five Easy Pieces was already in proof and being checked by Arthur Lourié, now himself firmly back in Paris;[26] and the violin-piano work he had promised Paul Kochanski, an arrangement of five movements from *Pulcinella,* seems also to have been written in August. He may conceivably have worked on the piano rolls of *The Firebird,* the mechanical rights to which were ceded to Pleyel by Jurgenson's European representative, Robert Forberg, at the end of May.[27] But his main musical activity was to do with performance. On 6 June he went to the premiere under Koussevitzky of Prokofiev's noisy Second Symphony and—according to its composer—"understood not a note of it."[28] A week later he himself took part in a "Stravinsky Festival" conducted by Koussevitzky at the Opéra, playing his

Piano Concerto and taking the baton in *Ragtime*—the Paris premiere of the full instrumental version.

He also played his Piano Sonata on 9 June at a soirée given by the princesse de Polignac—to whom the work is dedicated.[29] A few weeks later Prokofiev told Myaskovsky that "Stravinsky has completed a frightful piano sonata, which he himself plays, not without chic. But as music it's a sort of pockmarked Bach."[30] By that time the sonata had also been performed in public, at the Donaueschingen Chamber Music Festival in July, but not by Stravinsky. In Rome he had played it to Scherchen, who had promptly recommended it to Heinrich Burkard at Donaueschingen. But Stravinsky could not—or would not—accept Burkard's invitation to perform; and the sonata was given instead by the composer-pianist Felix Petyrek, "practically at the eleventh hour," as Reinhart told the Berlin music critic Adolf Weissmann.[31] "Igor Stravinsky's Piano Sonata," the *Revue musicale* reported, "astonished by its learned sobriety, without however displaying the usual rhythmic riches"—a description, perhaps, of the performance rather than the music.[32]

Besides these various concerts, there was the usual Ballets Russes season, reduced this year to a week, but still with two Stravinsky pieces: *Pulcinella* and *Le Chant du Rossignol*. The Pergolesi ballet, on the opening night (15 June) was a routine revival, but for *Rossignol*, on the seventeenth, Diaghilev had commissioned a new choreography from a young Georgian dancer from Petrograd called George Balanchivadze, who had turned up in Paris with a small troupe of dancers the previous November. Balanchine, as Diaghilev decided to call him, had no great experience as a formal choreographer, though he had—oddly enough—been preparing *Pulcinella* with his troupe in the season before they left Russia.[33] But he was quick on the uptake. And, moreover, he knew the music of *The Nightingale* from the time when he had taken part in Meyerhold's rehearsals for the opera in Petrograd in 1918.[34]

Though still only twenty-one, Balanchine was brimming with self-confidence and far from overawed at working with the famous Ballets Russes, whose dancing, as a matter of fact, he found mediocre.[35] It may not even have crossed his mind that his choreography was replacing that of Diaghilev's fallen favorite Massine (who had however been hauled back onboard to stage Dukelsky's *Zéphyr et Flore* and Auric's *Les Matelots*). Unlike Diaghilev's other protégés past, present, and future, the new choreographer was exclusively and—as Diaghilev would have put it—"morbidly" heterosexual; in fact, he was already married, to a beautiful eighteen-year-old member of his Petrograd troupe called Tamara Geva. It was at Balanchine's suggestion that the fourteen-year-old Alice Marks was engaged, as Alicia Markova, to dance the Nightingale itself: a child so slim and undeveloped that Matisse had to design, and Vera Sudeykina to make, a completely new costume for her. Whether or not Balanchine consulted Stravinsky about the actual choreography is not recorded. There are no firm grounds for calling this their first collaboration.

Stravinsky was naturally more likely to be "consulted" in Paris by long-lost relations or visiting Russian musicians than by expatriate dancers. One such visitor to the green room after his Koussevitzky concert on the thirteenth was his cousin Georgiy Yelachich, the younger son of Nikolay Yelachich, Stravinsky's eldest Pavlovka cousin. Georgiy was a violinist, now living, in some indigence, in Paris, and not unreasonably hopeful of trading modestly on his relationship with the most famous composer of the day. Unluckily for him, Stravinsky had already developed an allergy to such approaches and, according to Tanya, only vouchsafed his young cousin "two words" before passing on to the next nuisance. To his doting niece, such perfunctory behavior was entirely natural. "You can't imagine," she assured her parents, "how nagged he gets, even though he only receives the most unavoidable visitors."[36] But there was nevertheless something behind Stravinsky's attitude, something that wide-eyed Tanya could hardly have seen or understood, even though she did see and recount many of its symptoms. A month or so earlier, while her uncle was still in Nice, a letter from her father must have mentioned casually that Nikolay Yelachich was practicing Igor's new Piano Concerto. It was too much for the unforgiving composer. "Please don't tell Aunt Sonya," Tanya begged Yury, "but Uncle simply doesn't want Uncle Nikolay to have his concerto or any of his other works. Uncle Igor loves him very much, but he knows his playing too well, and he doesn't want him to play his works."[37]

Igor did love his Russian past, more than he later cared to admit, and he went on loving the things in it that he had loved when he had been part of it. He went on loving his mother, and he went on loving his brother. Above all, he loved Dyadya Alya—Uncle Alexander, Nikolay's father, who had understood him so much better than anyone except Katya. Uncle Alexander had been dead for nine years. Until Georgiy, Igor had not set eyes on a Yelachich face for thirteen. But with blood as thick as that, what difference did a few years make? Only, when it came to music—that was another matter. When Igor thought of music and Russia, he saw nothing but incomprehension and bitter reproach. He must have shuddered at the thought of those Rimsky-Korsakovs, howling abuse at his *Rite of Spring;* Max Steinberg, whose friendship could not run to even a general expression of enthusiasm for the music that it was so exciting Igor to create; Sabaneyev and Vitols and the rest, with their rambling, never-ending denunciations; even friendly voices like Karatïgin or Myaskovsky, who finally could not forgive him his foreign acclaim. How could he ever again face such a gang? How could he look them in the eye and imagine that he saw anything but glazed-over distaste and envy, the hatred of those who believe that the inadequacies of the child they once knew entitle them to despise the adult they now fear? Perhaps Igor himself feared that knowledge. There is some evidence that he did.[38]

And now, to cap it all, Steinberg himself turned up in Paris and, having left a note at Pleyel, ran into Igor in person at the Prokofiev premiere. To his amazement his old friend not only greeted him coldly, but showed no interest in a meeting. At the "Festival Stravinsky," poor Max did not even bother to present himself at the green room; Igor, he wrote spitefully to Nadya, "looked like a performing monkey on the rostrum, and *Ragtime* was sheer filth." All the same, he swallowed his pride and dropped Igor a note requesting tickets for *Pulcinella* and *The Song of the Nightingale*, being, he confessed, in no position to pay for them himself. The tickets duly appeared; and at *Nightingale* Max saw Igor again, thanked him, and heard him say that "he very much wanted to meet, but was terribly busy and not a free agent." Max was so upset that he could not bring himself to stump up the twenty-franc admission tax on his "free" ticket for *Pulcinella*. Instead, he stayed at home, and the two composers, once the twin great-white-hopes of the Belyayevtsï, never set eyes on each other again.[39]

Thirty years later Stravinsky told Craft that "after hearing the [piano] concerto [Steinberg] wanted to lecture me about the whole of my mistaken career,"[40] which might suggest that Max had mentioned that work in his first letter, perhaps in the same tone as he had adopted years before over *The Rite of Spring*. Of course, Stravinsky's memoirs are quite untrustworthy on such points. Steinberg, who by this time was notorious with his Leningrad pupils for his pedantic attitudes and stuffy tastes, probably did detest the Piano Concerto.[41] Yet Stravinsky's behavior was undeniably extreme, and even tinged with paranoia. Tanya gathered that Steinberg had written several times, and went on writing even after being warned off, which is clearly an exaggeration. Uncle Igor had talked about being "bothered" by this unwanted acquaintance, and went so far as to advise his brother in Leningrad to have nothing to do with Steinberg, who had recently written to him in Nice offering to take back messages.[42] A few weeks later, Max did ring Yury and express his astonishment at Igor's attitude, an astonishment Yury transmitted to Tanya, who as usual defended her uncle.[43] And that was that.

Igor clearly could not face old Petersburg anymore. But he was just as clearly afraid of the new Russia. When interviewers asked him if he planned to go to Russia, he answered evasively: in fact he would tell them, as he had told Steinberg and as he told his German agents Wolff and Sachs, that he did not have time.[44] Yet his music was performed there, and the invitations to him were perfectly genuine. As late as 1928, Ansermet would conduct *The Rite of Spring* and the Symphonies of Wind Instruments in Leningrad, to ecstatic applause. Moreover, Stravinsky had recently had a letter from Stepan Mitusov, asking him questions with a view to a performance of *Pribaoutki*. True, Styopa's letter had an air of heroic determination in the face of difficulties. "Life is hardship," it said,

> many trials. Yet despite the years, ill health, malnutrition and other misfortunes, I, Igor, have so far not darkened my spirit, either by grumbling about my fate or by feeling indifference towards the realities of life. Believe me, Igor, I work all day and all that time is not enough. There are days when I sit at the piano from eleven in the morning till twelve at night, almost without getting up.[45]

Though Stravinsky did not fear work, the "realities of life," in Mitusov's sense, were not exactly his cup of tea. Effectively nothing of his old life remained in Russia. He knew this from Yury and Tanya. Did he fear that if he set foot there he would not be permitted to leave, that he would be absorbed willy-nilly into the gray drudgery and wretchedness of daily life under a regime which, in principle, hated him and all his kind, whatever they might for the time being protest about his music? No doubt that was an exaggerated fear at the time. But if it is what his instincts told him, we can hardly say they were fundamentally wrong. It is only quite striking that they should have spoken to him so clearly, so comparatively early.

He had more and more to lose in the West. His American tour had left him richer than ever before, and even though Belyankin promptly touched him for a ten-thousand-franc loan (to tide him over until the fat profits he confidently predicted from the coming Biarritz season started rolling in),[46] there was plenty left for him to buy his first car, a Renault, and drive it back to Nice. He, Theodore, Vera, and, presumably, a driver (Tanya mentions "an experienced person") set out from Paris on 17 July. The six-hundred-mile trip took them almost four days, and it was an epic adventure. They were held up by a thunderstorm in the Alpes Maritimes, and nearly drove over a precipice. They arrived in Nice with a mud guard missing. Two telegrams a day were dispatched to the Villa des Roses, and even so Katya was so scared by the whole affair that when the travellers arrived she made a scene and, as Tanya tactfully reports, "nearly upset Uncle."[47] But Katya's edginess may well have had as much to do with Vera as with precipices.

As soon as he got to Nice, Stravinsky hired a regular chauffeur, and the whole family except Anna and Milène drove off to Monte Carlo: four of them crowded on the backseat, with Katya practically on Igor's knee, Tanya on Fedya's, and Mika and Svetik in front with the chauffeur. Later, in August, a more sedate party—without Tanya and Svetik—drove to Marseilles and Aix, stayed away two nights, and came home raving about the delights of motoring.[48] Stravinsky also found it amusing to contemplate his new employee. "Every day," he wrote to Ramuz, "Theodore and I go out in my car with my chauffeur. For I have a chauffeur who, for the time being, is very nice, costs me a lot, and introduces me at every moment to his chauffeur friends: one became the proprietor of a bistro, the other a bicycle seller, etc. He presents me by saying: 'This is my new boss.' "49 He even suggested keeping Tanya on as a secretary once she had finished her typing course.50 But perhaps Yury vetoed this idea, since nothing more is heard of it.

He was soon back at his desk, working on the Serenade and, in due course, the violin suite for Kochanski. "I work regularly every morning on composition," he told Ramuz, "bathe in the sea every morning (before work), and in the afternoon I write letters, prepare my next 'season,' and also play the piano so as not to lose the technique acquired this past year."51 A year or so before, he had told an interviewer in Madrid that "to economize on effort, I do the more difficult part of composing in the morning; in the afternoon and evening, I transcribe, copy, correct proofs, etc. I get up at about eight, do physical exercises, then work without a break from nine till one."52 Always a creature of routine, he was finding it increasingly necessary to organize his time, since so much of each year would have to be lost to concert tours, and so much of each day to the correspondence they entailed. Moreover, the Serenade, which he had started writing in the spring to satisfy a purely practical need, was threatening to come between him and larger projects. He finished the eventual first movement, Hymne, with its curious whiff of Chopin, on 3 August; but the Rondoletto, begun ten days later and interrupted soon afterwards by the violin suite, lay on his piano until late September, and the whole twelve-minute work was only finally completed on 9 October. At the same time, he admitted to Reinhart that he was planning a symphony—the culmination, no doubt, of his recent series of "classical" instrumental pieces (and a curious echo of his graded work with Rimsky-Korsakov twenty years before).53 No wonder he at first resisted Alfredo Casella's invitation to come and play his sonata at the ISCM Festival in Venice in early September, and only changed his mind when Reinhart—his most important patron at that moment—interceded.54

But it was not only routine correspondence that disturbed his days that August. A few weeks before, his American tour secretary and interpreter, Alexis Sabline, had written a curious, two-edged letter hinting at some question to do with Stravinsky's New York financial guarantees, about which he had himself supposedly been approached by an unknown American called Weisman. Blackmail announces itself as much by its tone as by its substance, and Sabline's intentions must have been clear at once, even though it was a month or more before he made overt threats of publicity or legal action. Embittered by the composer's failure to pay him a salary for his services in the United States, Sabline threatened to make public the contents of a series of telephone conversations he had overheard in which Stravinsky had imputed financial double-dealing to the orchestra manager Arthur Judson. Sabline actually installed himself in Nice, and there were meetings between him, Igor, and Katya, during one of which the composer evidently lost his temper and rushed out of the room. Later Sabline retained a lawyer to press home his intention to seek some form of public redress if his demands were not met. But this was a desperate shot for a man who probably did not have contractual evidence of his claims, and in general Sabline's attempts at blackmail look like a rotten advertisement for his secretarial services. Stravinsky easily saw him off by engaging lawyers of his own. The question remains: how could he have judged so poorly as to engage such an assistant in the first place? If, as one half suspects, Sabline's appeal lay precisely in his willingness to work without formal payment, it is tempting to conclude that the composer got no less than he deserved.[55]

In spite of the demands on his time, he had no qualms about extending what need only have been a three-day trip to Venice into a fortnight's Italian holiday with Vera. His sole commitment was to play the sonata in a mixed chamber-music program at the Fenice Theatre on the eighth, and even this performance nearly had to be cancelled because of a painful abscess under his right index fingernail which disappeared—miraculously, he always afterwards insisted—at the moment when, having craved the audience's indulgence, he removed the bandage and sat down to play.[56] But, as we shall see, Stravinsky was in the mood for miracles. On the way home from an excursion to Florence after the Venice concert, he stayed in Genoa and there chanced on "a life of Francis of Assisi which I bought and, that night, read."[57] This copy of Johannes Joergensen's biography was to lead directly, he claimed, to his next stage work, the idea for which quickly pushed the symphony he had been planning to the back of his mind. It was another of those sudden revelations—like the waking dream of The Rite of Spring or the sleeping dreams of The Soldier's Tale and the Octet—which helped explain his creativity as a sort of apostolic vision, a spontaneous phenomenon without a history.

A cynic might argue that the five thousand francs Stravinsky had negotiated through Reinhart for his ten-minute appearance on the Fenice stage was a powerful inducement to the most recalcitrant abscess to make itself scarce, even if—as he lied to Casella—it was no more than half his usual fee.[58] But as Reinhart (who was meeting Stravinsky's regular travelling companion for the first time) had told Casella: "You know as well as I do that he has a large family to support."[59] And after all, Schoenberg, who was also appearing at the festival as conductor of his own Serenade, was receiving a comparable fee, albeit for a somewhat longer and more demanding visit which involved rehearsals of that novel and difficult work. Stravinsky was already in Venice on 7 September, the day of Schoenberg's concert. But there is no evidence that he attended it, nor that the two composers renewed their acquaintance of thirteen years before. Nevertheless, Schoenberg did go to hear Stravinsky play his sonata the next day, and, according to the ISCM's chairman, Edward Dent, walked out.[60] Soon afterwards, Anton Webern relayed to Alban Berg Schoenberg's description of the music and its composer. "He told me about the disaster of 'modern music,' including Stravinsky, of whom he said that he had had his hair cropped close; he 'bachelts' (Bach Imitation)."[61] This can only refer to the sonata.

The allusion to "modern music" may have been a conscious reference to Stravinsky's own satirical use of that phrase at his New York press conferences. As recently as July, an article had been syndicated in a number of German newspapers, purporting to be an interview with Stravinsky conducted in Carnegie Hall by a certain N. Roerig. In fact the article is clearly a paste-up of the various printed New York interviews.[62] But in any case, we know that Schoenberg read it, because he kept a cutting, to which he later added a commentary, and later still a series of marginalia.[63] For instance, opposite the remark "Apart from jazz, I detest all modern music. I myself don't compose modern music at all, nor do I write music of the future, I write for today," Schoenberg scribbled: "He himself doesn't compose modern music at all—therefore he doesn't detest it. He writes unmodern music 'for today.' " But that was in 1932. His more immediate response was a creative one. In the months after Venice he composed the *Three Satires* for chorus, the second of which is an attack on Stravinsky no more disguised than Stravinsky's own New York references to Schoenberg:

> *Why who could be drumming away there?*
> *If it isn't little Modernsky!*
> *He's had his pigtails cut.*[64]

The brief setting is an elaborate canon, surely intended to mock Stravinsky's claims to have written "a contrapuntal chorus" in *Les Noces*: "a contrapuntal chorus," Schoenberg scrawled on his newspaper cutting: "what the little Modernsky imagines to be counterpoint." And in the much longer third satire he makes fun of "the new classicism":

> *No longer shall I stay Romantic,*
> *I hate Romantic;*
> *From tomorrow on I'm writing*
> *Only the purest Classical!*

But there is no reason to suppose that Stravinsky had any inkling of this work of his not-yet-official rival until many years later. Meanwhile, he had been pushed into a quasi-official antagonism by his own friends, and on quite different grounds.

Back from Italy, in the fourth week of September, he finished off the Rondoletto of the Serenade and composed the Romanza, apparently still intending to write two further movements.[65] He was also planning his autumn concert tour of Switzerland and Germany. As before, Reinhart oiled the wheels. Stravinsky had told him that since (possibly to Reinhart's surprise) his Swiss—like his Venetian—fee was only half what he normally charged, he had to insist on a minimum of four concerts to justify the trip. Reinhart, having secured him only two dates (in Zurich and Basle), now proposed to top them up with a private recital in Winterthur for a double fee, which Stravinsky accepted "above all since I am this time bringing with me my elder son as well as my wife—a pleasure I could not refuse him."[66] Did Reinhart, who by now was surely aware of the composer's domestic complications, pause over the idea that he might be subsidizing his conscience? His correspondence betrays no flicker of any such innuendo. But then Stravinsky was at pains to offer quids pro quo, by accepting Venice "only because you are the intermediary," and by agreeing to Reinhart's request to allow his protégée, the young Australian violinist Alma Moodie, to play the violin suite in Europe, leaving the American exclusivity to Kochanski (a concession that soon benefited Stravinsky himself, by providing him with repertoire and an instant duo partnership).[67]

Amid all this planning and correspondence, the new "St. Francis" project was starting to take shape, in discussion with, of all people, Cocteau. For the second year running, Cocteau was summering at Villefranche, a mere two kilometers from the Villa des Roses on the other side of Mont Boron, in a smart, sleazy harborside hotel called the Welcome. But whereas in 1924 Villefranche had meant an opium-drenched refuge from tortured memories of Radiguet, this year the atmosphere had changed and complicated dramatically. Cocteau had spent six weeks in the spring drying out at a private hospital in the eighth arrondissement of Paris. Then suddenly, in June, he had experienced the religious "conversion" secretly predicted a year before by Raïssa Maritain. At Meudon he had by chance encountered a former disciple of Maritain's named Father Charles Henrion, now a missionary in the Sahara, "a tall, tanned figure in a white burnous."[68] Within forty-eight hours, Cocteau had talked with Henrion and made his confession, and the day after that he took communion. Now, in Villefranche in August and September, he worked on his *Lettre à Jacques Maritain,* a pamphlet designed to advertise the change that he wished it to be thought had come over his life, and on two related literary works, a poem called *L'Ange Heurtebise* and a play about Orpheus.

For Cocteau it was perfectly natural to turn such an event into theatre—more natural, indeed, than to live it in detail. While writing to Maritain that "opium resembles religion to the extent that an illusionist resembles Jesus," he was again smoking opium.[69] When he dined with the Stravinskys in mid-August, he can hardly have failed to discourse on the whole experience, touching on the handsome Father Charles, and perhaps recounting the strange, drug-induced incident in Picasso's elevator in which, prompted by a mysterious voice, he had read the name "Heurtebise" on the maker's nameplate. He may even have gone so far as to explain that the Angel Heurtebise was in fact Radiguet, who would return as the angel of death in *Orphée*. Stravinsky liked the idea of the angelic elevator maker who was "also a glazier who carries wing-shaped slats of glass."[70] But what can such boulevardier witticisms have offered him for a theatrical work of his own? And what can Cocteau's stagy, smoke-girt religiosity have suggested for the austere classical drama that was already stirring in his own mind?

Cocteau had completed *Orphée* by early September, and probably read it to Stravinsky on his return from Italy. The composer, he told Valentine Gross, "is kindly helping me with the musical side."[71] But Stravinsky had views of his own about the form their collaboration would take. He proposed, he said, to entrust Cocteau with "the verbal realization of the idea which has pursued me for some time of composing an opera in Latin based on a tragedy of the ancient world that everyone would know."[72] That idea may have been influenced by Cocteau's sophisticated updating of the Orpheus legend; but it seems unlikely that Stravinsky, his thoughts fixed on a large-scale tragic drama, saw any role for the stage trickery and trompe l'oeil cleverness of *Orphée*. He may have had in mind Cocteau's translation of Sophocles's *Antigone*, which was a straightforward speech-by-speech precis, modern but restrained: a classic reclassicized in the twenties manner. Such at least seems to have been the playwright's own assumption, since his first text for *Oedipus Rex* was just such an adaptation. But to his chagrin, Stravinsky rejected it. Cocteau was sent firmly back to the drawing board, with instructions to produce a "conventional" operatic libretto, with arias and recitatives: a "still life," Stravinsky later called it, rather than an "action drama."[73] Meanwhile, Stravinsky himself set off, via Paris, on his autumn tour.

In Switzerland, where he was joined by Katya and the two oldest children, he played the concerto under Volkmar Andreae in Zurich and under Hermann Suter in Basle. And in between he went to Winterthur, stayed with Reinhart, and played the sonata, the violin suite with Alma Moodie, and possibly also the Serenade, completed five weeks before.[74] It was a miniature festival of neoclassicism, a summing-up of his latest phase. Then it was Germany and Vera. In Wiesbaden he played for the first time under Otto Klemperer, already one of his keenest admirers among German conductors. The Piano Concerto, Klemperer told Peter Heyworth, made a great impression on me. But at the beginning in rehearsal we had a little misunderstanding. I did the orchestral introduction a little too romantically and Stravinsky said, "No, no. You must think of Savonarola." Then I understood. I conducted *Pulcinella* after the concerto, and I began with two Bach chorales, orchestrated by Schoenberg. I remember that Stravinsky said, "Good, good. These two things of Schoenberg are very good."[75]

Four days later in Berlin, Stravinsky and Moodie played the violin suite for the first time in public, amid grumbles about the arrangements, which, in one critic's view, deprived the ballet music of its most effective attribute, its orchestration; "and the otherwise excellent violinist Alma Moodie played it, what's more, with notable lack of security."[76] The suite figured again in a Stravinsky festival put on by Scherchen in Frankfurt the following week; Stravinsky also gave the public premiere of the Serenade, and the next night Scherchen conducted the first performance of the little suite for small orchestra (later published as no. 2), while Stravinsky played the concerto and conducted *Mavra*—only the second time he had ever agreed to play and conduct in the same concert.[77]

The tour ended at its northernmost point, Copenhagen, where he conducted a chamber-orchestral program including the new suite and was photographed after the concert at a reception in the Restaurant Nimb, sitting next to the sixty-year-old Danish symphonist Carl Nielsen.[78] In that polished company, Nielsen looks as if he would rather be at home finishing his Sixth Symphony, which was still not ready and was due for performance a mere nine days later. Curiously enough, the composer of that austere and eccentric masterpiece later complained of *The Soldier's Tale* that "the human body is equally unattractive to me when it is too fat and when the skeleton is too clearly visible."[79] What Stravinsky thought of Nielsen's music, if he ever heard any, is not recorded. He might have attended Nielsen's first rehearsal, but probably did not, if only because the Royal Danish Ballet had buttonholed him to conduct their *Petrushka*, revived by no less a ballet master than Fokine, the next day. By the following day, 7 December, he was on his way back to Paris.

The next night he dined with Ernest Oeberg, who had become a trusted friend since taking over the post of ERM's Paris representative after Struve's death in 1920, and who had recently been with him in Berlin and Frankfurt. During the meal, Oeberg suddenly collapsed with appendicitis. He was rushed to hospital, but the appendix burst, peritonitis ensued, and within three days he was dead, with Stravinsky still at his side. Greatly shocked, the composer wrote to Ansermet—on the train back to Nice—that "I feel orphaned without him,"[80] and this was no exaggeration, for Stravinsky did depend on his Russian publishers for all kinds of supererogatory services and advice (including financial), and he seems to have felt professionally exposed without their personal succor. But it had been altogether a bad twelve days in Paris. His friend Count Guy de Matharel had been pawed by a lion through the bars of its cage at the Cirque de Paris on the day after Oeberg's death and was still in hospital. Poulenc had suffered an accident to his hand. Igor arrived back in Nice to find the children all convalescing from flu and his mother recovering from a hernia operation.[81]

"I pray God," he told Ansermet with understandable warmth, "that the new year will begin better than this old one has ended."[82]

THE PRIEST AND THE ORACLE

IT MIGHT ALMOST have been superstition about dates that made him delay starting *Oedipus Rex* until 1926 had actually dawned, and meanwhile fill the intervening days by orchestrating the remaining Easy Pieces into a second suite for small orchestra.[1] But there was a practical reason as well. Cocteau's French libretto, revised at the composer's behest, was being translated into Latin by a young Sorbonne theology student called Jean Daniélou, and the translation was not yet in Stravinsky's hands. Cocteau himself appeared at Villefranche on New Year's Day, and brought with him at least the text of the opening, since within a few days Stravinsky was already sketching the main part of the chorus (after figure 2), to various arrangements of the words "E peste serva nos qua Theba moritur." Yet on the eighth Cocteau wrote to Daniélou that "I await—we await—your first text with the greatest impatience."[2] And on the nineteenth he told his mother that "for the third time [Igor] has obliged me to begin my work all over again. . . . I must rewrite the ending and correct the beginning."[3] Meanwhile, Stravinsky had drafted Oedipus's first arioso, "Liberi, vos liberabo," and had sketched his way backwards, via the "E peste" chorus, to the very opening, with its Verdian image of the people imploring Oedipus to deliver them from the plague.

Although this was a new kind of music for him—his first vocal writing of any kind for four years, and his first for chorus for nine—he seems as usual to have had an absolutely clear idea of the style needed. The chorus itself is in all essentials an extension of certain rhythmic and melodic ideas in the first movement of the Serenade, but somehow transmogrified into a monumental chorus in the manner of Gluck. Oedipus himself, on the other hand, at once adopts a florid bel canto style which matches (and, as the work proceeds, diminishes with) his conceit and self-assurance. This is the "golden, curling, twisting, beringed music" which glowed in Cocteau's ears as he walked back late at night to Villefranche after his working sessions with Stravinsky.[4]

But nobody seems to have been nearly so sure about the theatrical idiom appropriate to such a work—an opera with a static dramaturgy and a text in a dead language. Cocteau's rewritings had finally produced a narrative in the form of a series of tableaux, delineated in each case by the entrance and exit of a single defining personage, but otherwise immobile apart from gestures of hand, arm, and head. This may well have been just what Stravinsky had always envisaged. But Cocteau wanted to dramatize, or at least spell out, the way in which the audience would relate to so austere a spectacle, and this would be the task of the Speaker, surely Cocteau's own invention (as Stravinsky later maintained), and a role that from the first he intended for himself.⁵ The Speaker would only pretend to explain the story, doing so, in fact, in a deliberately confusing and elliptical fashion. His real function would be to articulate the space between the modern audience and the ancient drama, and to act as a kind of visual acknowledgment of the plurality of styles in which it was clothed, musically and scenically.⁶

In some respects the Speaker was a refugee from Cocteau's *Orphée* of the previous year, a play in which Eurydice dies after licking a poisoned envelope and Orpheus's severed head, interrogated by a music-hall policeman, gives his name as "Jean Cocteau." Cocteau resisted the temptation—or perhaps did not dare—to import such postprandial witticisms into *Oedipus Rex*. But one important technical device, as well as some scenic details, did eventually come, indirectly, from the play. When the curtain descends at the end of act I (after Jocasta's entrance and the "Gloria" chorus), then immediately goes up again on the same scene and a repeat of the chorus, the opera seems to be echoing the pivotal moment in *Orphée* when the hero descends to Hades, and the curtain falls, then rises on an exact repeat of the same scene as Orpheus reappears on stage. The scenic parallels are even more striking. A diagram of the stage set in the published text of *Orphée* shows, for instance, that the mirror through which Death enters and exits is in exactly the same place as the fountain from which Tiresias appears in the equivalent diagram in the score of *Oedipus*. There are also suggestive parallels between Cocteau's ideas for entrances and exits covered by trick lighting in *Orphée* and the use in *Oedipus* of curtains and trapdoors to show the characters arriving and departing without their own volition.

The *Oedipus* drawing is credited in the score to Theodore Stravinsky. He may well have drawn it. But the conception was unquestionably Cocteau's. It was in early February that Tanya fled to Paris, and Igor took Theodore, with Cocteau, for a trip to Marseilles to distract him from his misery. Cocteau remembered "a wonderful trip to the mountains. February had covered them with rosy trees. Stravinsky had brought his son Theodore. Our chauffeur spoke in oracles, one finger pointed upwards. We called him Tiresias."⁷ No doubt the idea of having the not quite nineteen-year-old Theodore work on the designs for *Oedipus* was another stratagem to take his mind off his cousin, and Cocteau's letters of February and March studiously attribute ideas to the young designer, as if anxious to reassure the father that his plan is working: "*I am delighted with Theodore,* whose progress is enormous and his correcting (which is the best measure of value) of a perfect intelligence. He is beginning to see the detail without losing sight of our groupings. His King's daughters are exquisite, and he had the idea *on his own* of the treacherous hand on the shoulder, which is a first-rate find."[8]

The Marseilles excursion was only one—and not even the first—of several interruptions to early work on *Oedipus.* Two weeks before Tanya's abrupt departure, Igor had himself made a brief trip to Paris, perhaps for a meeting with Oeberg's successor, Gavriyil Païchadze. He and Vera dined with Lourié on 21 January, and the next day he quixotically presented Vera with a new car—a Renault, which, according to her diary, she sold again at the end of May. They may also have gone to hear Nadia Boulanger lecture on Igor's music and Wiéner play the Piano Sonata in the Ecole de Mangeot.[9] But Stravinsky did not stay to hear Youra Guller play the sonata and the *Petrushka* movements in a Salle Gaveau Stravinsky concert, which may have spared him a painful experience, since Lourié reported that Guller had played poorly and left out the third *Petrushka* piece (repeating the second instead), and that the conductor Vladimir Golschmann had made a mess of the Octet.[10]

A more serious interruption loomed in the shape of a five-week concert tour of Holland, Budapest, Vienna, and Zagreb in late February and March, a trip which cast a long shadow backwards, since Stravinsky had promised Mengelberg to conduct *The Rite of Spring* for the first time in Amsterdam, and was already nervously examining the score for ways of simplifying its metric difficulties, especially in the Danse sacrale. He spent several days in late January and early February revising the barring and orchestration "so as to clarify the bass and fix the accentuation and dialectical cut of the music's phrase."[11] At the same time he rescored the Evocation des ancêtres. Meanwhile, *Oedipus Rex* got no farther than the end of "Liberi, vos liberabo," Oedipus's first solo, before Stravinsky had yet again to set off for Paris—as ever his first base on conducting tours.

In Holland he played the Piano Concerto under Mengelberg in Rotterdam and Amsterdam. On 28 February, he conducted *The Rite of Spring* for the first time, in a packed Concertgebouw. And two days later, in Haarlem, he conducted the two little orchestral suites (packaged as one under the title *Huit Pièces enfantines*).[12] Then it was back to Paris for a week, before he and Vera again set out for Budapest and the Piano Concerto under Emil Telmányi—his first visit to the Hungarian capital since the prewar, pre-Trianon days of 1913. In Vienna he again played the concerto, this time under Dirk Fock in the Musikverein. He arrived in mid-rehearsal and at once caused a stir, according to one reporter, "by reaching for his glass cigarette holder and lighting a cigarette. Herr Bottstieber, the general manager, turns pale, since it is the first time that anyone has ever smoked in the hall." In the concerto, Stravinsky's fingers fly over the keyboard "like a group of dancers on a stage. He leaps from the keyboard to the conductor's podium and back to the piano with the agility of a dancer, and, at the end, stepping down in youthful waltzlike movement, lights another cigarette."[13] There was a reception for the president of the ISCM, Julius Bittner, in the Hotel Imperial, and since Berg and Webern were among the guests, Stravinsky surely met them.[14] Unfortunately there is no word about any such meeting in Webern's or Berg's published letters or, for that matter, in Stravinsky's own correspondence or reminiscences. Vera's diary is full of lunches and dinners with Dutch and French ministers of state, and even refers to a performance of *Die Fledermaus*, but says not a word about modern Austrian composers.[15] Stravinsky told reporters "those who regard my work as atonal don't know me. They're inspired proponents, but they don't understand me so well, perhaps, as Schoenberg, whose work *can* be thought of as atonal."[16]

From Zagreb, they headed for Nice by way of Milan, where Arturo Toscanini was planning to conduct *Petrushka* and *The Nightingale* at La Scala in May. Six months before, Stravinsky had seen Toscanini in Venice and discussed these concerts with him and the possibility of his acquiring the manuscript score of *The Nightingale*.[17] But now the Italian maestro was able to demonstrate his enthusiasm in the most practical way. Stravinsky was impressed. He sat at the piano for a choral rehearsal and was struck by Toscanini's intimate knowledge of the score and his methodical, self-effacing attitude to the music. Then, a month or so after his return to Nice, a telegram announced that Toscanini had been taken ill and invited the composer to take his place on the podium.[18] This time he was in Milan for a week and a half in mid-May, conducting the two works both separately and as a double bill. Thirty years later he still recalled Toscanini's efficient preparation, even though by that time he otherwise had hardly a good word to say for the Italian maestro.[19]

His account of this whole episode in his autobiography is one of the blandest and most poker-faced passages in that often bland and poker-faced book. He can hardly have been unaware that at the time of their March meeting, Toscanini was already at work preparing the first performance of Puccini's final opera, *Turandot;* or that his illness after the opening on 25 April was the more or less diplomatic outcome of a succession of clashes with Mussolini culminating in Toscanini's flat refusal to play the Fascist hymn "La Giovinezza" at the premiere, and Mussolini's consequent absence from the first night. "During the interval," the *Corriere della sera* had unblinkingly reported, "the audience awaited Mussolini's previously announced arrival. But the prime minister did not wish to attend, and explained the reason behind his sensitive gesture: he did not want his presence in any way to distract the public, whose attention had to be entirely devoted to Puccini and his last work. Mussolini will attend a later performance of *Turandot*."[20] Toscanini was thus able to fall ill and avoid further confrontation once the prestigious premiere was out of the way. Stravinsky must have known this story, if not from Toscanini himself, then from his own compatriot Boris Romanov (the original choreographer of *The Nightingale*), who had staged the Milan *Petrushka*, was in the swim at La Scala, and dined with Igor and Vera more than once during their May visit. And however vague Stravinsky's information on Mussolini at that precise moment, he was soon to learn what the Fascists were made of when he heard from Charles-Albert Cingria how his brother, Alexandre, had been deliberately jostled in a Milan art gallery, arrested as a pickpocket, then held in jail on the grounds that the blade of his pocket knife exceeded the permitted length. The arrest was an error. Alexandre had been mistaken for Charles-Albert, who had made no secret of his antifascist views, and who was himself arrested in Rome later that same year and imprisoned for two months without trial.[21] But it would have been hard for the Stravinsky of 1935, the time of the autobiography, to report such matters objectively, since by then he had been received by Mussolini and had spoken admiringly about him to the Roman press.[22]

He is silent, too, on whether he heard *Turandot* at so early a stage in the composition of his own opera. But he almost certainly did. He had grown fond of Italian opera. He had become an unashamed admirer of Verdi, whom he described as "immense, an imagination of genius, and especially great as a dramatic composer" (while adding pointedly that he liked Verdi less "when he tries to be a sort of Italian Wagner. In my opinion his best opera is *Rigoletto*").[23] There was certainly no longer any question of the *"verdicelli"* of his Petersburg days. Instead Italian opera, so despised by Parisian culture vultures, had become an important counter in the great aesthetic game of the twenties. As for Puccini, he had treated Stravinsky with respect, had called on him in his sickroom at the Villa Borghese after *The Rite of Spring*, and later invited him to stay at (presumably) Viareggio, an invitation Stravinsky recalled with pride in after years, though Puccini had died before he could take it up.[24] Stravinsky arrived in Milan in May 1926 with a firm desire to hear *Turandot*, "expressing his regret at the death of its composer, whom he had known and who had so appreciated *Petrushka*."[25] It is inconceivable that his hosts would have failed to invite this accommodating and politically useful genius to at least one of the three or four *Turandot* performances conducted by Ettore Panizza, Toscanini's deputy, while he was in the city.

Vera came back with him to Nice at the end of March, though whether or not she was a houseguest at the Villa des Roses is not recorded. She hung around, in any case, for a week. She and Igor went to Cannes together, and they may have visited Picasso and his Russian wife, Olga, at Juan-les-Pins. But by the time she left for Paris at the start of April, Stravinsky was once again immersed in *Oedipus*, having already finished off the opening chorus and arioso (up to Creon's entrance). On the day of her departure, he started Creon's aria, "Respondit deus"—"The god replies."

Perhaps some oracular, still small voice spoke to him, too, that Russian Holy Week. On the Tuesday he wrote to Diaghilev, who was in Monte Carlo with the Ballets Russes, a letter which astonished and moved the hard-nosed but soft-hearted impresario:

> I have not observed the fast for twenty years, and it is out of extreme mental and spiritual need that I do so now—in a few days I shall go to confession and before confession I shall ask forgiveness of everyone I can. I ask you too, dear Seryozha, with whom I have worked so much during these past years without repentance before God, to forgive me my transgressions as sincerely and cordially as I ask it of you.[26]

"I read your letter in tears," Diaghilev replied, "since I have never, not for a minute, ceased to regard you as a brother."[27] He himself was not a communicant, though he had for years been fascinated by the rituals of the Orthodox Church, as his *Liturgie* had shown. But there had been no particular sign that Stravinsky was very occupied with such things, nor is there evidence that he had been a churchgoer since leaving Russia in 1910, even though in Biarritz he had lived practically next door to the Russian church. He wore a crucifix under his shirt, but he did not refer in interviews to God and the saints. Until 1926 he had never composed a single note of church music. Yet for all that, his reconversion, or (to use Péguy's term) *approfondissement,* was not entirely without its history.

Cocteau's return to the sacraments the previous summer, though typically theatrical and self-advertising, was in many ways a symptomatic event for mid-twenties Paris. For forty years Catholic renewal in France had meant a reconciliation between individual sensibility and the idea of a collective faith, as against the institutional Catholicism represented—until its condemnation in 1926—by the ultraconservative, highly politicized Action française. In practice the renewal embraced a multitude of intellectual and aesthetic positions. In its early stages its associations were romantic, existential, and mystical. "We conceived at that time," Paul Valéry wrote later, "the feeling that a kind of religion might be born, whose essence would be poetic emotion."[28] But after the First World War, the tide turned sharply against the idea of aesthetics as arbiter of spiritual values, and instead the link between spirit and sensibility shifted towards a concept of utility and order, much as with the modernist view of art itself. In *Art et scolastique* Maritain encapsulated one aspect of this tendency, in his notion of art as an "honest labor," and his rejection of the intellectual confusion of the nineteenth century. The new image of the artist as a reincarnation of the anonymous craftsman from the era of St. Thomas Aquinas finds, as we have seen, many an echo in the pronouncements of contemporary artists, not excluding Cocteau's plea for "a music for every day . . . a music I can live in like a house."[29] The fact that Cocteau was able to square his newfound spiritual and aesthetic austerity with the continued smoking of opium and a social existence that was neither humble nor abstemious was perhaps beside the point. The attraction of neo-Thomism lay not in the fact that (like any worthwhile religion) it imposed sometimes inconvenient moral constraints, but in that it provided a spiritual correlative for an aesthetic need that was widely felt as itself in some sense "moral."

As we saw, Stravinsky probably read *Art et scolastique* in the early twenties, to judge from the Maritainisms in "Some Ideas About My Octuor."[30] This was also the time of his reconciliation with Cocteau, after the early performances of *Mavra*. He was back in close touch with Cocteau during 1923 and 1924, and much in his company in the late summer of 1925, immediately after the episode with Henrion and at the time of the *Lettre à Jacques Maritain*. But though Stravinsky must have heard a great deal about Maritain, they did not meet until 10 June 1926, when he, Vera, and Lourié dined at Meudon.[31]

Lourié, though he had been back in Paris since the end of 1924, had also apparently not met Maritain before, though he had known his wife, Raïssa, in Russia, and it is by no means easy to pin down the extent of the philosopher's influence on him up to this time. An article he wrote on Stravinsky's Piano Sonata in 1925 might reflect Maritain in its rejection of the "decadent evolution" of romanticism, but it as yet lacks the specific ethical slant of Thomism.[32] By contrast, the Stravinsky survey he wrote for the new Eurasian Russian-language journal, *Vyorstï*, a few months later (it was completed in March 1926) suggests a more direct reading, particularly in its observation that the first quarter of the twentieth century has been a process of recovery from the confusion of the nineteenth, and its relating of the newfound classicism to a spiritual or "theocentric" consciousness.[33] But this is still little more than a detail. In any case, the whole question of Lourié's influence on Stravinsky at this period remains a vexed one. Lourié was fond of elaborating abstract and highly tendentious doctrines of history in a way that strikes one as alien to Stravinsky's supposed distaste for a priori theorizing.[34] Yet some such pseudohistoricism is already apparent in the composer's own remarks about Tchaikovsky and the *kuchka* in his open letters at the time of *Mavra*, long before he had met Lourié or, for that matter, come across Souvtchinsky and his Eurasian brand of historicism. It was left to Lourié to turn these ideas into an intellectually presentable "system." But there is no particular reason to believe that the ideas were specifically his.35

In one important respect Lourié may have felt instinctively drawn to Maritain. They were both prewar Catholic converts, Maritain from Protestantism, Lourié from Judaism.36 For Stravinsky, by contrast, Russian Orthodoxy remained the natural way; not only his upbringing, but his entire creative preoccupation before 1920, had kept his imagination firmly within the Orthodox world, and this attachment can only have been cemented by his meeting with Souvtchinsky, who must have insisted that "Orthodoxy is the main value for the Christian Eurasian."37 But there were conflicting pressures in twenties Paris, where the big émigré community preserved its old Orthodoxy in the teeth of the powerful philosophical and literary presence of French Catholicism. On the one hand, the intelligentsia flocked to the Orthodox Church as a bastion of those ancient Russian values which were being so brutally undermined by the Soviet Union. On the other hand, cultivated, Western-looking Russians like Stravinsky could not but be impressed by the lofty tradition of Catholic thought, so much richer and more broadly based than anything Orthodoxy had to offer. Small wonder that he was for a time, as he told his Swiss Catholic friend Charles-Albert Cingria, attracted by the ecumenical movement then being promoted in Paris by Nikolay Berdyayev, who had been holding regular discussions with Catholic intellectuals, including Maritain, since arriving in Paris from Berlin in 1924.38 On the other hand, it seems significant that Stravinsky should have mentioned this to Cingria so soon after his own first meeting with Maritain. It suggests quite forcibly that under all the circumstances—Lourié's influence, Cocteau's conversion, the visit to Meudon, where conversion had become almost a way of life—he himself had no immediate idea of switching his allegiance.

But then Paris was by no means Stravinsky's spiritual center, however important it may have been for his heart and brain. The core of his existence, after all, was his music, and this he wrote, for the most part, at home in Nice, in an atmosphere undisturbed by intellectual or doctrinal disputation. Precisely when this atmosphere began to assume a specifically religious character is impossible to say. Craft asserts that the "new religiosity" was a consequence of Stravinsky's complicated emotional life: in effect a reaction of guilt. He notes that it was in Biarritz that the composer began to develop the habit of dating his manuscripts by church festivals: an early sketch for the Piano Concerto is said to be dated "Tuesday, 17 July [1923]: St. Alexis's Day" (though in fact the sketch is merely written on a blank diary page for that date, which is perhaps not quite the same thing).39 Stravinsky himself says that "for some years before my actual 'conversion,' a mood of acceptance had been cultivated in me by a reading of the Gospels and by other religious literature," but he adds that "perhaps the strongest factor in my decision to re-enter the Russian Church rather than convert to the Roman was linguistic. The Slavonic language of the Russian liturgy has always been the language of prayer for me,"[40] which may be literally true, but probably refers to a more general atavism behind his loyalty to the routine religion of his childhood. Certainly one of his first creative acts as a communicant was to compose a simple liturgical setting in Slavonic of the Lord's Prayer, for use in the Russian church in Nice.[41] Soon afterwards an Orthodox priest, Father Nikolay Podosenov, came to live with the Stravinskys, and they gave him a private apartment at the Villa des Roses, and even planned a purpose-built chapel for his and their use.[42]

However directly or indirectly Lourié may have influenced these developments, he was well aware of them and shared the mood they evoked. His letters, which had occasionally referred to religious literature in passing, suddenly become pious and confiding. Describing his holiday by the sea that August, he mentions "a little church where I heard Mass every day. I fasted twice during my stay. In fact, as the Uspensky [Assumption] fast has just finished, it occurred to me that you too might be fasting, and my thoughts were with you throughout that time."[43] Meanwhile, his wife, Tamara (née Persitz, a rich ex-publisher, and, like him, Jewish), was being converted to Christianity by Maritain. "I haven't put pressure on her," Lourié reports, "only prayed." But two rambling letters to Stravinsky on the subject of prayer and personal affliction tell us much about the devotional atmosphere that had invaded their relationship in the past few months. They also suggest that Stravinsky's decision to remain Orthodox may not have gone without at least discreet protest from Lourié. Tamara herself wanted to convert to Orthodoxy, and although it was an issue between them, Arthur had decided to submit to her decision. A month later he quotes St. Paul: " 'We compel every human thought to surrender in obedience to Christ': what inspiring words—enough for a lifetime."[44] He too had changed a lot since the carefree days of the Stray Dog.

But there was little sign of any such surrender on Stravinsky's part. He was so distracted in the months after Easter that he scarcely even touched Oedipus again until August. He had practically reached the end of the scene with Creon—the point at which Oedipus promises to scour Thebes for Laius's murderer and drive him out of the city—when the invitation came from Milan to conduct in Toscanini's place. From Milan he went straight to Paris with Vera. There then ensued a summer for which he could only appease Katya—or salve his conscience where she was concerned—by taking her to Italy, in her turn, for the second half of June: showing her Milan (where he played his concerto under Scherchen) and spending the next fortnight with her visiting Florence, Rome, Naples, and the island of Capri, then depositing her in Nice and hurrying back to Paris. As for the rest of his family, they scarcely set eyes on him for three months.

In Paris, work consisted mainly of cutting piano rolls of *The Firebird*. Tanya was still in Paris, finishing her typing course and living in a cheap hotel in the Latin Quarter, near her "aunt" Irochka (her mother's first cousin). The Ballets Russes season had opened in the Théâtre Sarah Bernhardt on 18 May, the day Uncle Igor arrived in Paris from Milan, and she and her paternal cousin Ira Belline had complimentary passes and went night after night, sometimes with Igor and Vera. Tanya was in ecstasies over Parisian life. There were wild drives in the country, one of which ended only at two in the morning after a burst tire and a breakdown. After that her parents seem to have tut-tutted at her extravagant lifestyle, since in her next letter she hastened to assure them that she could not wait to get back to Leningrad and that "these delights are all very well, but . . . the rest of the time I see around me such hardship that any pleasure disappears."[45] Perhaps she was thinking of what Ira had told her about her parents in Biarritz, about her mother's declining health, and the terrible difficulties they were having to make ends meet. Igor had recently made them another huge loan of twelve thousand francs to tide them over while (as they fondly hoped) the Château Basque was sold, bringing the total debt to nearly forty-five thousand.[46] The Belyankins had invited Tanya to visit them in Biarritz, but—perhaps frightened at what she might find—she never went. She contented herself with her glamorous cousin. One night at the ballet, she reported, Ira and Vera Sudeykina looked so beautiful that the entire theatre turned to stare at them, "and if I'd been a major coquette, I wouldn't have gone with them."[47] The Château Basque predictably failed to sell, and the Belyankins were left to struggle on for another season.

Early in June the ballet moved on from Paris for a six-week season in London, opening at His Majesty's Theatre on the fourteenth with a program that included the British premiere of *Les Noces*. Diaghilev had had the bright idea of fielding a team of composers in the four piano parts: Auric, Poulenc, Rieti, and Dukelsky. But the audience and the critics were not mollified. "The noise," Dukelsky recalled, "was deafening—boos, hisses and catcalls mingling with cheers and thunderous applause."[48] As for the press, it was almost uniformly either abusive or supercilious. "We read," said the *Daily Telegraph*, "that if one of the immense number of accents 'synthetic and contradictory' (whatever that may mean) were displaced, the meaning of a whole episode would be changed. Does it not suggest, somehow, a dreadnought kept together with safety pins? . . . Anyhow, the music suggested grave reasons for the melancholy of both bride and bridegroom."[49] In the *Sunday Times*, Ernest Newman was in his element:

> The totality of the various noises is mostly hideous. From the score, however, one can see that it is simply late Stravinsky with all his well-known characteristics and all his obvious shortcomings,—the scrappy, repetitive Russian tunes, the helpless reiteration of tiny accompaniment figures . . . and the nonsensical changes of time signature that look so wonderful on paper but really amount to nothing in performance. . . . Some of the tunes have the usual Russian piquancy, but musical Europe is already more than a little tired of the moujik and his half-baked brain.[50]

Some reviewers gave full vent to their satirical powers in describing the stage setting. "The bride," wrote the *Times* critic, "lives in a house with one tiny window in it, the bridegroom in one with two windows. That and the nature of the calisthenics is the only difference between scenes one and two. We return to the one tiny window for the departure of the bride, and then are transported to an equally drab scene, with the bridal bed piled with pillows inside a rabbit hutch, for the scene of the barmecidal love feast."[51] It must have been such relentless trivializations that goaded H. G. Wells into penning his famous open letter to the press:

> Writing as an old-fashioned popular writer, not at all of the highbrow sect, I feel bound to bear my witness on the other side. I do not know of any other ballet so interesting, so amusing, so fresh or nearly so exciting as *Les Noces*. I want to see it again and again, and because I want to do so I protest against this conspiracy of wilful stupidity that may succeed in driving it out of the programme.
>
> How wilful the stupidity is, the efforts of one of our professional guides of taste to consider the four grand pianos on the stage as part of the scene, bear witness.
>
> Another of these guardians of culture treats the amusing plainness of the backcloth, with its single window to indicate one house and its two windows for the other, as imaginative poverty—even he could have thought of a stove and a table;—and they all cling to the suggestion that Stravinsky has tried to make marriage "attractive" and failed in the attempt. Of course they make jokes about the mothers-in-law; that was unavoidable. It will be an extraordinary loss to the London public if this deliberate dullness of its advisers robs it of *Les Noces*.
>
> That ballet is a rendering in sound and vision of the peasant soul, in its gravity, in its deliberate and simple-minded intricacy, in its sub-

tly varied rhythms, in its deep undercurrents of excitement, that will astonish and delight every intelligent man or woman who goes to see it. The silly pretty-pretty tradition of Watteau and Fragonard is flung aside. Instead of fancy dress peasants we have peasants in plain black and white, and the smirking flirtatiousness of Daphnis and Chloe gives place to a richly humorous solemnity. It was an amazing experience to come out from this delightful display with the warp and woof of music and vision still running and interweaving in one's mind, and find a little group of critics flushed with resentment and ransacking the stores of their minds for cheap trite depreciation of the freshest and strongest thing that they had had a chance to praise for a long time.[52]

Newman's review, meanwhile, had stung Diaghilev into retaliation. The four pianists had reluctantly to draw lots, and the winner—Dukelsky—was detailed to go to Newman's seat at the next performance and pull his nose.[53] Luckily, Newman was not in his seat, no noses were pulled, and Diaghilev had to content himself with barring the great man from subsequent performances.

Stravinsky himself witnessed none of these excitements, being due in Milan three days after the London opening (for the same reason he probably missed the opening of Cocteau's *Orphée* at the Théâtre des Arts on the fifteenth, though he and Vera went to the final rehearsal earlier that day). But when he got back to Paris, he decided to make the trip to England; and instead of the wearisome and sometimes nauseous sea crossing, he booked himself on to a commercial flight from Le Bourget to Croydon—a hardly less nerve-wracking but considerably less protracted (as well as considerably more expensive) journey, which took about three hours. "I enjoyed it immensely," he told reporters at Croydon, though he later told his son Theodore that he had been "very frightened."[54] He was in London for three days, attended *Les Noces*, dropped a hint to Diaghilev about the "homage" he and Cocteau were preparing for his twentieth anniversary season,[55] then went back to Paris, presumably by the same mode of transport, on the eleventh. But there was no sign as yet of his returning to Nice, even though he had recently put his name to a contract with Edition Russe for the completion of *Oedipus* by the new year.[56] Instead he lingered in Paris for another three weeks, seeing a good deal of Lourié and Souvtchinsky (who had moved to Paris from Berlin the previous year), Cocteau, and his closest nonprofessional friend of the moment, Guy de Matharel, making expeditions with the Arthur Honeggers and others, and going to the cinema with Vera. Not until the end of July did he and Vera at last set off for Nice by car, accompanied by Cocteau and Matharel. By 6 August, Vera was back in Paris, Cocteau was ensconced at the Welcome, and Stravinsky was once again in Thebes, grappling with Oedipus's "Sphynga solvi" and the seer Tiresias.

Considering the novelty and originality of the concept, there is astonishingly little sign of creative struggle or uncertainty in the composition of *Oedipus Rex*. He seems to have known, with the sureness of second sight, exactly what kind of dramatic work it was possible to build on the stylistic foundations of *Mavra* and the Octet. And he apparently had no fear of the dangers of erecting so grand a structure on what is to the conventional ear so unstable a base. As usual, the sketches give little idea of what might have gone into their evolution, the hours of experimental singing and playing in his upstairs studio at the Villa des Roses. All we know is that, on the same day that he composed Oedipus's angry accusation of bribery, "Stipendiarius es, Tiresia" (1 September), he wrote to Païchadze at ERM that he had decided to divide the opera into two parts—which suggests that in beginning to imagine the "Gloria" chorus, he had also pictured the device of the falling curtain immediately after Jocasta's entrance (like that of Catherine the Great in the second act of Tchaikovsky's *Queen of Spades*) and the exact repetition of the chorus, like the parallel scene in *Orphée*.[57] For the rest he worked steadily and with few hitches, as if to a set routine. While writing the Piano Concerto he had told Ansermet that "I do gymnastics every morning, and sunbathe from twelve till one,"[58] and this routine had altered only slightly when he told a Madrid interviewer that he got up at eight, exercised, then worked till one.[59] No doubt things were much the same now. He would write roughly the same amount of music each day, and in the six weeks up to mid-September he composed in short score the whole work from "Sphynga solvi" (fig. 56) to the end of the first section of Jocasta's aria (fig. 100)—some eleven minutes of music, not counting the "Gloria" reprise. The sketches and drafts on loose sheets were apparently worked into the increasingly formal short score as he went along, so that, for example, the date at fig. 100—16 September—tallies with the earlier and more numerous dates in the loose sketches, and was obviously entered on that day. He then broke off work, spent the weekend (one devoutly hopes) with his family, and on the Monday set off once again for Paris.

This time the main reason for the trip seems to have been to help see Vera into a new apartment (or "little house," as she calls it in her diary—perhaps thinking of the *domik* in *Mavra*), at 22 rue du Ranelagh, in the sixteenth arrondissement. But he may also have been curious to inspect the costumes she was making to Natalya Goncharova's designs for the London revival of *The Firebird* at the end of November. The feature of the revival was to be two spectacular new décors, including a brilliant montage of domes, churches, and towers as backcloth to the final scene. As for the costumes, some would be brand-new, others would be adapted from the old and by now somewhat shabby Golovin wardrobe—a particular talent of Vera's. She told Buckle that she "bought yards of common old lace curtains, painted them gold, and cut them out into patterns to stick on top of Golovine's old costumes for the boyars in the wedding scene."[60] But while Vera was patching up the costumes, Stravinsky was having to think about patching up his old *Firebird* contract with Diaghilev, which had effectively lapsed since the last revival in 1922. Then, just when he and Païchadze were starting to consider how to extract a performance royalty from the canny impresario, the whole question of ownership of this most popular of all his works suddenly became an issue involving lawyers and tribunals—an issue which seriously threatened his ability to earn anything from it at all.

The first sign of trouble came at the end of October in the form of a telegram from the German publisher Robert Forberg, claiming title to Jurgenson's copyrights and challenging the composer's right to exploit *The Firebird* through another publisher.[61] Stravinsky had known, of course, that he was on doubtful ground selling Chester the 1919 suite (since the *Firebird* music belonged automatically either to Jurgenson or—if it was unprotected—to the world). But, desperately short of money as he was in 1920 and assuming, not unreasonably, that Jurgenson was permanently out of action at least as regards foreign promotion, he asserted what he thought of as a moral right, while protecting his legal position through a formal letter to Chester making clear Jurgenson's original interest but hinting that the recent suite, which had supposedly taken six months to compose, was effectively a new work for copyright purposes.[62] Both morally and legally, this position might have been stronger had he taken any trouble to establish Jurgenson's situation first. But he did not. In 1922, Ernest Oeberg made the disagreeable discovery that the Moscow publisher had transferred his foreign rights to Forberg, who was now busy reprinting the 1912 *Firebird* Suite;[63] and a few weeks later Jurgenson himself wrote to Stravinsky indicating his intention to collect back royalties from Diaghilev and querying the agreement with Chester.[64]

The ERM position was complicated by the fact that Forberg had appointed them his representative for London and Paris. The obvious solution would be for Jurgenson to sell his interest back to the composer. How much, Forberg politely inquired, would Stravinsky think of offering?[65] We do not know how he replied, but it seems safe to assume that Forberg was far too well aware of the value of the asset for any likely offer to have been halfway acceptable. In the end they appear to have decided to let Jurgenson do his worst, reasoning that he would hardly take legal action over so doubtful a matter as foreign rights in a work first published in a country that had never signed the Berne copyright convention. So it came as an unpleasant surprise when, a week after the *Firebird* revival opened in London, Forberg filed a formal complaint in Leipzig against Chesters; their German representative, Schott; and Stravinsky himself, claiming that the work had in fact been first published in Germany, and entering as evidence a transfer of rights from Jurgenson backdated to August 1918.[66]

It seems highly unlikely that Jurgenson had ever properly established foreign rights (for which it was technically necessary for a Russian publisher to print his scores in a Berne Convention country such as Germany, France, or Great Britain). But the Leipzig court, perhaps naturally biased in favor of a German publisher against a British one, and in favor of a Soviet house against an opportunist White Russian composer, quickly decided that he had done so, and ordered Chester and Schott to stop selling the 1919 material or renting it out, and to compensate Forberg for past royalties. The judgment was to have tiresome consequences for Stravinsky's relations with Chester, who not unnaturally accused him of selling them a pig in a poke, and tried hard to recover from him a proportion of their losses. Otto Kling had died in 1924, and since then contacts with his abrasive son Henry had in any case grown somewhat stiff and ill-tempered. The Forberg defeat was simply the last straw. But the real irony was that even if the court had found for Chester, it would scarcely have helped Stravinsky, since the implication that the work had always been in the public domain outside Russia would have left it generally unprotected in the West. His real interest lay with Forberg, who in securing the copyright would necessarily have to pay the composer due royalties. For neither the first nor the last time, he had expended a lot of time and energy, in correspondence with Kling, with Ludwig Strecker at Schott, with Païchadze, and no doubt worked himself into a fury at the importunities of publishers and the villainy of lawyers, and all in the end on the wrong side as far as his own interests were concerned.

On the day Forberg's first menacing telegram arrived (29 October), Stravinsky was drafting the chorus's muttered "trivium"s in *Oedipus*—the word of doom which triggers his memory of the old man he had killed at the junction of the roads to Daulis and Delphi. One wonders whether Stravinsky, with his tendency to paranoia, drew any parallel for his wife's benefit. "Suddenly I'm afraid, Jocasta, suddenly I'm very afraid. Jocasta, listen. . . ." Money matters crop up even more than usual in his November correspondence. And at the end of the month, with *Oedipus* still barely three-quarters composed, he again set off for Paris, probably with the double intention of discussing the Forberg affair with Païchadze and ways of financing the new opera with the princesse de Polignac. But the trip was a frustrating one.[67] He did not see the princess, and instead the question of *Oedipus* was broached with her by Cocteau. Stravinsky had gone back to Nice on 18 December with incipient flu and a temperature of 102. A few days later Cocteau wrote that he had seen the princess and described the work to her, and she had said, "It is the principal event in the music of our time, so we shall succeed and put it on, but not without knife-blows,"—a combined prospect which "was rejuvenating her and putting a glint in her eye."[68]

Within a fortnight, Stravinsky had finished the scene with the Messenger and the Shepherd, and was drafting the passage which relates "how the queen had hanged herself and Oedipus had put out his own eyes with her golden clasp."

A VERY MACABRE PRESENT

STRAVINSKY HAD ALL the time intended *Oedipus* for Diaghilev's 1927 Paris season. But he was also adamant about keeping its character secret from him, and since the production had nevertheless to be planned and paid for, the result was a comedy of confusion and intrigue which in the end nearly scuppered the performance altogether.

The secrecy at times verged on the pathological. "I'm astonished," Stravinsky wrote to Cocteau in February, "that you raise the question of silence. But naturally, *parbleu*! Do you not feel the need for it yourself?"[1] Yet Cocteau did not so much question it as revel in it. He was like a child who has found the cupboardful of Christmas presents and goes around with an "I'm not letting on that I've found the presents" look on his face. Diaghilev had long since found out about the collaboration, and Cocteau's disclaimers had an extremely hollow ring. "Serge asked me," he had written, "if I was writing a religious work with you. I assumed my most candid air and said no. I asked Igor, he said; Igor said no, but I thought that perhaps he wanted to keep the surprise. Reply quickly what you think of this interrogation. Until further orders I shall continue to deny tenaciously."[2] But nobody was even supposed to have told Diaghilev that the composer had a collaborator, let alone who it was. "In questioning you about the subject of the work," Stravinsky replied suspiciously, "he seems to know that it is precisely with you that I am collaborating. Unless that's pure provocation, and I hope that you have not allowed yourself to be taken in."[3] Meanwhile, Ansermet had been staying at the Villa des Roses, and Stravinsky had let him in on the secret, no doubt partly because he might be needing the conductor's help in preparing the performance. But this led to fresh recriminations. "I'm very upset," Ansermet wrote, "by what you tell me. I don't know any Nabokov and I haven't seen any Russian musicians since I saw you. I haven't mentioned Oedipus, Theodore, Cocteau, or anything which could give away the slightest detail about your new work to anyone. But I didn't realize that I even had to pretend not to know anything. And yet I haven't sought to boast that you've shown it me."[4]

Stravinsky had never been the kind of composer who talked much about work in progress, but even so such obsessive reticence was new. After all, he had shown Diaghilev the *Petrushka* pieces, and had played him portions of *The Rite of Spring* and *Les Noces* as they went along. Admittedly, *Oedipus* differed from those works in involving a collaborator throughout—one, moreover, who was a notorious chatterbox. But why should Stravinsky not want Cocteau even to let on to Diaghilev that they were working together? Was he nervous of the impresario's reaction to a work so unlike anything he had written before, a work not just devoid of dancing, but virtually devoid of all movement? Was there not in fact something almost deliberately anti-Diaghilev about the whole opera, as if the old tyrant had been cast in Stravinsky's mind as Laius himself, murdered at the parting of the ways and usurped by his own composer "son"?

That Stravinsky feared Diaghilev's opinion can hardly be doubted. But the issue was more complicated than that. For ten years, they had fought over contracts and money, and the bitterness had at times reached the point at which direct communication between them might have become almost inconceivable. And yet in 1919, after their worst and most protracted quarrel, Diaghilev had commissioned *Pulcinella* in an atmosphere apparently without recrimination. Now there was tension in the air over the new *Firebird* deal, aggravated no doubt by the Forberg affair. Yet if they argued, as Diaghilev might have said, it was like brothers jostling for a seat at table, and never for a minute forgetting that they shared their meals. That very January Katya had had her appendix removed, an operation which—in her debilitated condition—necessitated a fortnight in hospital. As so often in the past it was Diaghilev, of all Stravinsky's friends, who expressed most concern and best understood the perturbation Katya's illnesses caused him. "I know," Stravinsky wrote to Diaghilev in Monte Carlo, when Katya was about to be discharged, "how much you have taken to heart my anxiety over her operation, and I sincerely thank you, my dear, for your sympathy."[5] But the minute contracts were mentioned, Diaghilev went quiet. "Tell him," Stravinsky instructed Cocteau sharply a few days later, "that he would do much better to answer the letters people write him instead of trying to discover the surprise behind my back."[6] But the trouble was that his letter to Monte Carlo had gone on to request settlement for the recent Milan *Firebird*.

But if Diaghilev was to be kept in the dark about *Oedipus*, then someone else would have to take on the organization and in particular the fundraising. Stravinsky and Cocteau were already in touch with the princesse de Polignac, who had promised support but in terms which ominously foresaw the political ramifications of such an unusual project. Now in mid-February, with the final chorus still incomplete, the composer again broke off work to go to Paris. On the nineteenth he and Vera lunched with Eugenia Errazuriz and Princesse Violette Murat—a lunch at which the new work must have been discussed but from which nothing significant seems to have emerged. Probably he also saw Misia. But Misia was in the throes of a painful divorce and had other things on her mind. A few days later, Igor and Vera set off by car for a week's tour of eastern France—Nancy, Strasbourg, Lunéville.7 Not until the second week of March did he return to Nice and, on the fourteenth, complete the draft score of the opera. And not till then did he at last put his mind unreservedly to the question of how this difficult and unprecedented work was to be got onto the stage in time for a premiere in May or June.

A concert agency called Zerbason, whose director was one of the innumerable Georgian princes and princesses who swarmed around Paris in the twenties, had been engaged to book the performers;8 and this prince, Alexis Zereteli, estimated that the best part of a hundred thousand francs would be needed to cover the cost. Mme de Polignac, however, had done some sums of her own, and she calculated that a fifth of that amount would pay for the solo singers, chorus, and orchestra. At the same time, she could secure for herself the role of fairy godmother to the work by throwing in an additional fifteen hundred dollars—expressed pointedly in the stable currency of international banking—as a fee to the composer, who in return would supervise a private avant-premiere at her house.9 Any other money would have to be found elsewhere. Cocteau had indeed led her to understand that he had other irons in the fire. But his main target, Coco Chanel, was proving elusive, and by the time Cocteau managed to buttonhole her, at the start of April, she had already heard about the project from Misia, who had with well-measured venom conveyed to her the princess's remark that "they're waiting for you, my dear, you're the moneybags."10

"You can well imagine," Cocteau added naively to Stravinsky, "that Mme de Polignac did not say such a thing." But one can better imagine that she did. Knowing that Chanel was in the offing, she had purposely arranged her own contribution so that Coco would have to give a larger sum for the less prestigious function of paying for the stage performance. At the same time she did her best to prevent that performance taking place by the neat and businesslike device of refusing to release any money of her own until the whole production was assured, on the grounds that if in the end no performance were to take place, the performers would still have to be indemnified. "I do not know," she told Stravinsky, with triumphant and withering contempt, "if Cocteau found among his friends the necessary support for which he was hoping."11 In other words, Coco Chanel could jolly well pick up the tab, as befitted a self-made businesswoman who was barely so much as received in the Faubourg-Saint-Germain.

Chanel was willing neither to be frog-marched by a sociocultural rival into this expensive sponsorship, nor to be remembered as the woman who refused to support *Oedipus Rex*. She wanted to help Stravinsky, to whom she had been devoted, and Cocteau, to whom she was still. But she would not, could not, do Winnaretta Polignac's bidding. So she did the only other thing possible, and went to Spain for ten days. Stravinsky, who had been inclined to agree with Cocteau that Chanel was the victim of poisonous gossip,[12] quickly changed his mind. He had wired Chanel at her hotel in Cannes, but received no reply. "So you misunderstood her," he told Cocteau: "She was in no hurry at all to take decisions that were of extreme urgency for us. To tell the truth, I have nothing more to write to her now, except to thank her for having been willing to interest herself in the realization of *Oedipus,* but that, given the shortage of time for taking decisions, I have had to give up my involvement and have handed the matter to Diaghilev."[13] Cocteau could not bring himself to think ill of Coco, on whom he had become dependent for the money that paid for his opium cures, though it did eventually dawn on him that it was the princesse de Polignac rather than Misia who was behind the gossip at her expense.[14] But Chanel had after all held her own politically. By the time she got back from Spain on 17 April and offered the additional eighty thousand francs needed for the stage production, Stravinsky had indeed handed the whole enterprise over to Diaghilev himself, who had quickly decided against risking staging so unusual a work at such short notice, amid all the other preparations for the spring ballet season.[15] So Chanel neither refused nor paid, and the first presentation of *Oedipus Rex* was in concert form, with an avant-premiere in the avenue Henri Martin, and under the sole patronage of the princesse de Polignac, who—as soon as she learnt that it would be a concert performance and that she was the only patron—promptly upped her support by a cool sixty-five thousand francs.[16]

Part of the original idea for *Oedipus* had been that Cocteau (as the Speaker) and Stravinsky (as conductor) would give their services free of charge.[17] Mme de Polignac's initial offer had superseded that idea, and later Stravinsky even thought of backing down so that his fee could go towards the staging.[18] Eventually he did conduct. But Cocteau was not Diaghilev's choice as Speaker, and instead the part was taken by the twenty-three-year-old actor Pierre Brasseur, "a very handsome, very young man [who] was deliberately chosen . . . to spite Cocteau."[19] Diaghilev may not have disliked Cocteau as much as is often said, but he certainly distrusted him, socially as well as sexually. Cocteau was a butterfly and a gossip, and often childishly, transparently disingenuous in a way that could make him an irritating enemy and a dangerous ally. His attempted revenge against Diaghilev over the Speaker casting was typical. At the time that a staged version was still on the cards, Stravinsky had written that Diaghilev planned to "take Theodore's décor and realize the piece as it was conceived."[20] But once the staging had been abandoned, Cocteau wrote back ingratiatingly that "I find Theodore's sketches admirable and Serge's victory annoying, as he does not want them at any price," adding in a postscript the suggestion that Stravinsky "insist that Theodore's maquettes be shown and you will poison Serge and justice will be done."[21] Cocteau's true motive, however, was blatant: "the entire balance depends on the Speaker. Make sure that I can rehearse the actor at the same time that you rehearse the orchestra. In his desire that the work fail while having the appearance of a cantata in his honor, Diaghilev is capable of anything." But Stravinsky, who was not given to intrigue, replied candidly that Cocteau's remarks about Diaghilev and Theodore "must be supposition on your part, since on the contrary Diaghilev spent the whole evening with Theodore examining his sets, finding them very good and giving him advice for the next production."[22] Cocteau could only bluster a self-justification that struck close to home indeed: "I am happy to know that Serge has understood the beauty and novelty of Theodore's work, which will enrage those imbeciles who live in Paris and spread false news."[23]

Stravinsky spent Russian Easter (24 April) at home, working on the orchestral score of *Oedipus,* and organizing "a small distribution of charity through our Father Nikolay to people who are barely alive from sickness," as he informed Diaghilev, adding that "if you yourself want to give at least something small and collect from those around you, you will be doing a charitable deed."[24] But the score was still incomplete when he left for Paris on 3 May, and it was only finished a week later, early in the morning of the eleventh, at Vera's rue de Ranelagh flat. On the twenty-ninth, after a morning rehearsal, came the avant-premiere in the two-hundred-seat grand salon of the Polignac mansion. There was no orchestra, and the composer himself accompanied the singers—five soloists and a male chorus—on the piano.[25] Even so, the work's monumentality must have chimed oddly with the elegant Empire revivalism of the princess's music room, though perhaps not as oddly as the uncouth *Renard* would have done if it had ever entered these portals, as originally intended.[26] The official premiere of *Oedipus,* conducted by Stravinsky, was the next night at the Théâtre Sarah Bernhardt, with the male chorus on stage in front of a drop curtain, but the soloists—including Stéphane Belina-Skupievsky as Oedipus and Hélène Sadoven (the original Neighbor in *Mavra*) as Jocasta—enigmatically tucked away with the orchestra in the meager and notoriously dead-sounding pit—"mon pissoir," as Diaghilev called it.[27] The new work formed half of a plain double bill, with *The Firebird* in the new Goncharova designs.

Not surprisingly, the reception by the ballet audience was cool if not openly hostile. Even at the Polignac soirée a certain restiveness had been noticeable.[28] In the theatre, the bizarre geography of the performance and the absence of any visual stimulus combined all too effectively with the relentless formality of music and text to provoke a certain impatience and irritability. On top of everything the composer's conducting was by no means wholly secure, a fact which the music's stylistic transparency may well have made obvious even to the inattentive ear. At rehearsal, Klemperer recalled, "there was a passage he simply couldn't get right." Then "at the performance I sat next to Jean Cocteau, who was very musical. At one moment it was *comme ci, comma ça,* and Cocteau whispered, 'He can't do it. This is impossible.' "[29] After the performance, Stravinsky was in a foul temper; and such newspaper reviews as troubled themselves with the danceless new work were hardly calculated to improve his mood. "It seems to me quite pointless," wrote one, "to expatiate on a certain *Oedipus Rex* by M. Stravinsky, performed by—sorry! at—the Ballets Russes. This is not a dance parody of Sophocles' masterpiece, but a soporific oratorio with people singing in evening dress and in Latin. The patrons of the dance festivities were not amused!"[30]

Not for the first time, it was left to Boris de Schloezer to grasp the epoch-making significance of a work which so brilliantly returned Stravinsky, in his latest manner, to the theatre, where he belonged. Almost alone among the Paris reviewers, de Schloezer saw the connection between the old Stravinsky and the new, and sensed the dramatic and musical power locked up in the highly formalized concept of the opera-oratorio. He understood the function of the Handelian and Italian-opera elements in the music. At first, he admitted, the listener suspected a mere pastiche. But this idea could not survive close examination. "Stravinsky, it is true, makes use of the opera-oratorio framework modelled on Handel; but into this frame the composer introduces heterogeneous elements which he manages to amalgamate, by I do not know what miracle, and on which he imposes that specific character which belongs only to his art." What was really involved, de Schloezer sensed, was a completely new concept of artistic creativity and individuality. Here was a composer who seemed "to want to renounce absolutely what is known as inspiration, fantasy, all artistic spontaneity, accident, personal choice, in order to resolve . . . problems of pure form." In fact it was precisely in its anti-individualism that *Oedipus Rex* was most revolutionary. It recalled an article of Jacques Rivière's on the crisis in the very idea of freedom, a crisis which de Schloezer saw particularly at work in modern music. Stravinsky, he asserted,

> is the only composer who pursues his goal in full consciousness and with a systematic rigor which for anyone else would end extremely dangerously. There are plenty who have a presentiment of this tendency; but even if they go with the current when it carries them along, they do not initiate it and they act, one might say, without conscious judgment. While the author of *Oedipus Rex* knows what he wants and is even not afraid to go against some of his most personal

inspirations: for when you see so forceful and violent a personality as Stravinsky's strain all his considerable powers to achieve the "banal" (in the real, original sense of the word), you cannot help feeling that this effort sometimes costs him dear.[31]

Characteristically, de Schloezer disliked only the Cocteau elements: particularly the so-called Speaker, of whom "one has but a single desire: that he shut up at the earliest possible moment, this puppeteer with the pretentious title." Ironically, in view of Stravinsky's usual response to de Schloezer, this was exactly his own later view. "I detest the speaker device, and I do not much like the speeches themselves," he told Craft, going on to denounce the snobbery and obscurity of lines like "Now you will hear the famous monologue" and "The witness of the murder emerges from the shadow."[32] At the time, he seems not to have expressed any such opinion in public, but it can be deduced from the absence of almost any reference to Cocteau or the Speaker in contemporary interviews, and especially the pointed avoidance of any such mention in Arthur Lourié's long *Revue musicale* article on *Oedipus,* which came out two or three months after the premiere.[33]

Of course, the role's dramatic point is bound to remain obscure in a concert performance. Some in the first Paris audiences may even have thought it a compromise dreamt up on the spur of the moment to cover the lack of staging. Diaghilev simply disliked the whole work, which was a specific denial of everything he had always aimed at in the theatre: the alliance between music, movement, color, and gesture, the expressive vigor and sensuality of the human body, the manipulation of three-dimensional space. One has only to look at the other ballets in the 1927 season to see how remote Stravinsky's "austere vocal concert"[34] was from Diaghilev's preoccupations of that or any other moment: Sauguet's *La Chatte,* with its glittering constructivist set by Naum Gabo, and its exiguous plot, "which served mainly as an excuse for a series of movements in which a number of lightly-clad, bronzed young men, led by Lifar, then in the flower of his youth, executed a series of movements reminiscent of a gymnastic display";[35] or Prokofiev's *Le Pas d'acier,* with its provocative images of revolutionary industry; or Satie's *Mercure,* with designs by Picasso (revived from Beaumont's 1924 season at the Cigale), which Diaghilev added to the *Oedipus* bill for its second performance on 2 June; or indeed *The Firebird* itself, in its new scenic dress, but otherwise a scarcely faded reminder of the balletic genius of the young Igor. No wonder Diaghilev called *Oedipus* "un cadeau très macabre" (a very macabre present)[36]—and made no attempt, in his two remaining seasons, to bring it to the stage in proper form.

The Paris season ended on 11 June, and the company headed for a London opening at His Majesty's Theatre on the thirteenth. Stravinsky, who had a BBC studio date the following week, lingered in Paris, and on the fourteenth took part in a "Mechanical Music Gala" in the Théâtre des Champs-Elysées, playing works of his own on the Pleyela, while Jean Wiéner demonstrated the all-electric Brunswick gramophone, the Panatrope, through which—as a note in the program confidently predicted—the music "will make itself heard in all parts of the hall as well as a powerful orchestra."

Stravinsky had also submitted to being interviewed by the most antagonistic of his old Russian critics, Leonid Sabaneyev. Sabaneyev was keen to find out what the great iconoclast now thought of Russian music past and present, and Stravinsky—knowing that his remarks would get back to some of their targets—was happy to oblige. "Scriabin isn't a musician at all," he told Scriabin's greatest admirer, adding mendaciously that "I never liked him as a composer, and don't see that a musician can possibly like him." Prokofiev? "There's something unstable in his cultural makeup, something about his musical talent. And this is precisely what's now bringing him success in Russia." New music in Russia? "What I know of it is totally alien to me. Myaskovsky's a gifted musician, but his line of development is to me quite foreign." The past? The *kuchka* he declared utterly second-rate except for Musorgsky: "The typical kuchkists are Balakirev and Rimsky-Korsakov, and they are hopelessly old-fashioned. . . . Tchaikovsky understood Glinka more correctly and seems a more legitimate heir." But his own *Oedipus* was also in the Glinka line: "It's my most important work, the one in which I've achieved the greatest simplicity of style and the nearest approach to that ideal style which Glinka realized in his *Life for the Tsar*." But he disliked talking about his work. Composition was like praying, and "when you pray, you only have to think about the words you are praying with, and all prayerfulness vanishes."[37]

Finally, Stravinsky told Sabaneyev that he was too busy to visit the Soviet Union, and besides, "there is at present much on the purely musical side in Russia that is not yet ready for me." This one phrase irritated Myaskovsky, when he read the interview, more than all the sideswipes at Russian composers, including himself. "He's right," he told Prokofiev:

> we still have too many musicians who know the literature, and we're not yet such barbarians as the European public, who don't want to know anything, least of all anything Russian, and can't judge the sources of his inspiration; unfortunately all this is for the time being absurdly obvious, and all his Glinkaism is mostly almost unrecognizable mock-antique, old friends distorted—Musorgsky, Tchaikovsky, and, alas, Rachmaninov. Jocasta, Oedipus—Rangoni (in *B[oris]*), the Scribe *(Khov[anshchina])*, Mazeppa, the Pretender—some Korsakov hereabouts ("From Homer"), and the basic chorus is the same as

Rachmaninov's *Fate*. But, taking it for all in all, as they say—if you can get through the tedium of the first act, it's strong and even good.[38]

Some of Myaskovsky's comparisons now seem bizarre, and what his remarks chiefly illustrate is the annoyance felt by even well-disposed musicians in Russia at Stravinsky's apparently inexplicable success abroad. In any case, as de Schloezer saw at once, the fact that Stravinsky drew on a wide variety of sources was obvious, and an important aspect of his formalist, anti-individualist stance; recognition of the actual sources was beside the point. It was the way he fused them "by I do not know what miracle" into an entity of such severe structural purity that gave the music its unique power, even without the theatrical dimension. Prokofiev was soon spreading round Paris Myaskovsky's theory that Stravinsky was avoiding Russia because his sources were too well known there. But he contradicted it a year later when he identified the material of *Apollo* as "picked from the most shameful pockets: Gounod, Delibes, Wagner, even Minkus . . . all treated with the utmost skill and mastery."[39] Whatever else might be said of these allusions (and whether or not one agreed what they were), it could hardly be suggested that they were unknown to Paris audiences.

In London, Stravinsky played and conducted in his first-ever broadcast concert—an hour-long program transmitted live on 19 June. It was, in fact, he told reporters, his first encounter with a microphone.[40] Alas, no reports have surfaced of what might now be seen as a momentous debut. A few days later there was another, when he took the baton for the first time in public in London and directed a Diaghilev triple-bill of *Petrushka*, *Pulcinella*, and *The Firebird* (with King Alfonso of Spain in the audience). This time the hacks were present, and showed themselves ready to praise Stravinsky's conducting so long as he confined himself to those ballets that did not disturb their *idées reçues*. The fact was that the dancers had not been at their best that season. At the first night, Herbert Hughes reported, everything had been done "in a dull and slovenly fashion, and with so little address that a ballerina [Alexandra Danilova] slipped on a loose strip of carpet and landed on a place where a ballerina ought never to land." But with the composer at the helm, things changed. "It was as though father himself had paid a purposeful visit to the nursery. Every dancer from A to Z was on the tiptoe of form."[41] "Mr. Stravinsky," the *Times* agreed, "proved to be a first-rate conductor of his own works. He knows exactly what he wants, gives a decisive beat and does not fuss the orchestra. The result was clean and lively playing, with plenty of rhythm, on which so much of this music relies for its effect."[42]

He conducted only the one performance, then went back to Paris, not

even staying for the evening most dreaded by Diaghilev: the British premiere of *Le Pas d'acier*, with its apparent glorification of everything most
detested by Tory London society. According to Goossens, who was conducting, Diaghilev took a revolver to the performance (on the fourth of
July, itself hardly a date to cheer bulldog hearts) and threatened to fire it in
the air at the first sign of a demonstration.[43] But by then Stravinsky was
back in Paris with Vera, treating himself instead to a Buster Keaton film
(presumably *The General*). By mid-July he was in Nice, starting work on a
new ballet that would be as far removed as anyone could imagine from the
world of dancing factory workers and gun-toting impresarios.

Apollon musagète, as it would long be called, was Stravinsky's first
entirely new work since *The Firebird* whose character was to some extent
determined by outside money. Or so it appears. Possibly some such idea
had been mooted or even discussed during his 1925 American tour. But
the firm commission, for what Robert Lyon called a "pantomime of your
choice,"[44] had arrived only in April 1927 from Carl Engel, the head of
the Music Division of the Library of Congress, and it was hedged about
with stipulations which suggest that Engel—or his paymistress, Elizabeth
Sprague Coolidge—may have had in mind some such work as *Renard* or
The Soldier's Tale (which still awaited its United States stage premiere).[45]
The Music Room endowed by Mrs. Coolidge in the library had hitherto
been used almost exclusively for chamber music, and specifically for an
annual chamber festival held in April. Now the idea for 1928 was to adapt
the room as a miniature theatre and play a program of small-scale ballets
of which Stravinsky's new work would be the centerpiece. There would be
a small pit, Engel told Stravinsky, with room for about twenty musicians
and, on the wingless stage, not more than three or four dancers, including
Adolph Bolm, who would also be choreographing the work.[46] Engel sent a
photograph of the room with its fixed stage setting, and it seems clear that
the artistic character of the ballet Stravinsky composed—for a medium-
sized string orchestra—was to some considerable extent controlled by
these limitations.

Nothing was said about subject matter, but Stravinsky quickly developed an idea of his own for the opening scene, in which Leto gives birth to
Apollo by flinging her arms round a palm tree and resting her knees on
the tender sward. The description, which Stravinsky wrote on one of his
first sketches in mid-July, is so expressive of the prevailing Attic radiance
of the whole ballet that one readily believes his claim that the idea for a
classical ballet based on Greek mythology had been with him for some
time.[47] Such a ballet, indeed, was the most natural companion imaginable
to the posed, statuesque drama of *Oedipus:* a paradox of immobility rendered mobile. What no critic of that or any other time—not even the
admirable de Schloezer—could possibly have deduced from *Oedipus* was

the tone of the music on which Stravinsky had already settled for his first new ballet for eight years, a tone which completely renounced the violence, abrasiveness, and even ebullience of everything that typified the concept "Stravinskian."

A visit to the Villa des Roses in July 1927 would hardly have betrayed this new serenity. Stravinsky himself, he told Païchadze on the day before he sat down to *Apollo*, was feeling "pretty ill from the nervous point of view."[48] It had been a bad year. The annoyances of the Forberg case had been aggravated by the failure of *Oedipus Rex;* and he was now getting letters from Henry Kling at Chester demanding an indemnity for having, as Kling put it, "sold our company the copyright for a work that no longer belonged to you."[49] Worst of all, within days of his return from Paris, Katya went down with pleurisy and retired to her bed in the stifling heat of the Riviera midsummer. In this oppressive atmosphere, Igor somehow preserved the cool air and fresh light of the opening tableau of *Apollon musagète,* in which the god of formal perfection is conducted by his attendant goddesses to the chilly heights of Mount Olympus. Then, taking the hint from his work, the composer himself conducted his ailing wife by train to the less forbidding hills around the Lac d'Annecy, installing the entire family for six weeks in a house (probably a pension) in the tiny village of Echarvines, a mile or two from Talloires (to complete the symbolism, they probably made the trip on the fifteenth of August, the Feast of the Assumption of Our Lady). Here he finished off the Variation d'Apollo and composed the Pas d'action, with its sublimely intricate four-part canon. By the time the family descended once more to Nice towards the end of September, the ballet was almost half composed, its mood apparently quite untouched by the anxieties and (one can scarcely doubt) recriminations of the sublunary world.

As soon as he got back home, Stravinsky wired Diaghilev in Monte Carlo, and the next morning Diaghilev called on him at the Villa des Roses.[50] It was already common knowledge that Stravinsky was at work on a ballet. For instance, a few days before, Prokofiev, who was on the west coast of France at Saint-Palais and had not seen Stravinsky since June, had told Myaskovsky that Stravinsky was writing a new ballet for Diaghilev.[51] Perhaps this was merely his assumption; or perhaps Lifar had been gossiping about Stravinsky's delight over his dancing in *La Chatte* and his promise to write a new ballet specially for him, even though he was "working overtime on a commission for America!" "How fragile is human memory, and how little to be relied on," Lifar laments in his book on Diaghilev, referring to Stravinsky's assertion in his autobiography that the American commission and *Apollon musagète* were one and the same.[52] But for once Stravinsky's memory was more correct than his conduct. At least Diaghilev seems for a time to have believed that *Apollo* was being devised for Lifar—unless he knew about the Washington commission but chose to conceal it from the young dancer. "There is a short, fast movement in your first variation—there are to be two for you," the impresario told Lifar, "and the opening is danced to an unaccompanied violin solo. Very remarkable! . . . I embraced [Igor] and he said: 'It's for you to produce it properly for me: I want Lifar to have all sorts of flourishes.' "⁵³

Stravinsky knew perfectly well that Diaghilev's jealousy of commissions not his own was quite likely to turn him against a work for years, if not for good. Look what had happened with *Renard* and especially *The Soldier's Tale*. But by linking *Apollo* to Diaghilev's young paramour, he could use the impresario's sentimental and sexual attachment as an insurance for the ballet's future. Of course, it would soon come out about the American contract. But when it did, Diaghilev would grumble, then submit, rather than sacrifice this prize showcase for Lifar's charms. And so it proved. "This American woman is completely deaf," he is supposed to have assured Stravinsky, who replied that "she's deaf but she pays."⁵⁴ There was a brief skirmish in the public prints. Diaghilev disingenuously told the *Excelsior* columnist Michel Georges-Michel that Stravinsky had refused to compose a new ballet for his twentieth season in 1927 "because ballet is 'the anathema of Christ' "; he then proceeded to offer an account of *Apollo* so garbled as to be plainly a deliberate distortion. "Life today is a conflict of workers, motor traffic, or wireless waves. So Stravinsky's melody, instead of touching the moon, instead of taking inspiration from the song of the nightingale, will talk about the machine, will be inspired, not by vague murmurings, but by the mechanism of a factory strike, I suppose."⁵⁵ "This is what I get for being so frank with him," Stravinsky wrote gloomily to Ansermet, enclosing the Diaghilev interview and a cutting of a corrective interview he himself had given to *L'Intransigeant*.⁵⁶ Outlining the scenario and the circumstances of the commission—"a musical work (ballet or pantomime) to be played to a restricted, very select audience—the inner circle of the White House, for example"—he had carefully implied in the interview that he was writing without fee and in return for the manuscript, "which remark," he had added, "I address to those who try to represent me as a musician who works exclusively for big money." As for the music's atmosphere, "I should like it to remain in the aural memory as a pure fresco in the manner of Poussin."⁵⁷

Apollo had been interrupted for the whole of October, half of which Stravinsky spent in London with Vera, adapting his Pleyel rolls of *The Firebird* and *Petrushka* for the Aeolian Company's Duo-Art reproducing piano, and writing lengthy introductory articles and analytical notes to go on the rolls—the only such things he ever produced.⁵⁸ This bizarre trip seems actually to have been undertaken at the behest of Pleyel, who were by this time effectively (though not, until June 1928, contractually) Stravinsky's agent for all mechanical rights—whether to do with piano rolls or gramophone recordings. Gustave Lyon, the firm's director, had long been planning a new Paris concert hall with scientifically designed acoustics, and on 18 October the new Salle Pleyel was duly opened with a grand gala concert including the 1919 *Firebird* Suite conducted by Stravinsky and *La Valse* conducted by Ravel. The three-thousand-seat reinforced-concrete hall was a spatial embodiment of the needs of music like Stravinsky's more recent work. Corners had been rounded, moldings eliminated, and the ceiling constructed in the form of what one reviewer called "a huge inverted flight of stairs,"[59] in an effort to eliminate the crudities and echoes which the modern orchestra seemed to provoke in even the most amenable of the old-fashioned halls. The balance and clarity of the sound were excellent; solo lines retained their intimacy in the huge space; sight and hearing were good from every seat. Yet there was, it seems, room for improvement, and when (as happens curiously often with new concert halls) the magnificent edifice was gutted by fire a mere eight months after it opened, Robert Lyon's first comment to Stravinsky was that "we'll make it better," which the composer at first took to mean "less ugly," but which actually referred, it transpired, to the acoustics.[60]

Stravinsky again drove to Nice with Vera at the end of the month. But she was soon on her way back to Paris. Then for nearly three months he scarcely stirred from the Villa des Roses, apart from a single flying visit to Paris at the end of November, ostensibly for the sole purpose of issuing his *Apollo* corrective in the columns of *L'Intransigeant*.[61] The fact was that the ballet had to be finished in good time for its Washington premiere at the end of April, and from February onwards he would be almost permanently tied up with concert tours of one kind or another until well into the summer. It was one of those moments when the sheer professionalism he had imbibed from Rimsky-Korsakov rescued him from lurking disaster. Like his teacher, he knew how to work regularly and produce at a steady rate, whatever the difficulties of mood or inspiration. But more than Rimsky, he had the ability to enter and re-enter the unique world of a particular composition, without any loss of concentration or quality of thought. Where Rimsky had insisted on composing, however poorly, Stravinsky insisted on composing well. Thus the variations for the three muses, which were fully composed during November, took up the tone of the preceding music exactly as if Apollo and his muses had been waiting, frozen on Olympus, for Dr. Coppélius to return and throw the switch that would restore them to life and movement. And so it was too in December with the Variation of Apollo and the Pas de deux, originally sketched in reverse order. So well did composition go during these weeks, in fact, that by 9 January, two days after Orthodox Christmas, Stravinsky had finished the draft score in solving the final problem of how to link his Coda music, by way of the Apotheosis, to the recapitulation of the main opening theme.[62] Even Prokofiev, who affected to detest the work's "pitiful" material and "shameful" supposed derivations, confessed his admiration for this ending. "In one place, on the very last page of the work," he told Myaskovsky, "he has shone and managed to make even his disgusting main theme sound convincing."[63]

Two weeks later Stravinsky played the entire score to Diaghilev and Balanchine, who came over from Monte Carlo to hear it.[64] Balanchine was to choreograph the work for the Ballets Russes production, his first Stravinsky premiere, and the composer repeatedly called out the tempi for his benefit as he played.[65] Already it seemed that the Washington production, which none of them would see and the composer could not supervise, was being ignored as in any sense decisive for the work. The real premiere, with the real Apollo—Lifar—and the composer conducting, would be in Paris.

A MONTH OR SO BEFORE the completion of *Apollo*, Arnold Schoenberg had been in Paris, and two concerts of his music had been given in the Salle Pleyel, including the world premiere of his Suite, op. 29, and two performances of *Pierrot lunaire*.[1] Lourié wrote to Stravinsky and described the first concert, which *Le Figaro* had provocatively advertised as "the most important event in Parisian musical life in recent years." He mocked what he called the "tense, worked-up atmosphere," and the music itself, which had made a terrible impression on him. Henry Prunières, the director of the *Revue musicale*, had thrown a reception after the concert, "but of course I did not attend this pagan ritual." Lourié in fact spends more time describing, and is more sympathetic to, a recent concert by the Russian composer Lev Theremin with the electronic instrument he had invented and to which he had given his name. Though bored by the music, Lourié was impressed by the technology, which took him back to his own experimental days in St. Petersburg, when he had come across Theremin and heard a demonstration.[2]

Such letters—and there are several of the same general type—force the question of Lourié's exact role in Stravinsky's life and thinking during these years when, according to Robert Craft, he was as close to the composer as Craft himself was later, or when—to use Richard Taruskin's phrase—he was "a virtual member of Stravinsky's household."[3] That such a view is an exaggeration the reader will already suspect. But the question is greatly complicated by the partis pris of those who speak with the most authority. Craft, for instance, has his own perfectly honorable reasons for playing up Lourié's importance. He makes no secret of the fact that he himself has suffered doubts about his entitlement and qualifications to exert on the aging Stravinsky the influence that he undoubtedly did exert. For Craft, Lourié is a precedent, a kind of historical excuse, a proof of the conditions which justified his own role—namely, that Stravinsky was somebody who took color from his surroundings and who positively "*wanted* to be influenced."[4] On the other hand, when Lourié's biographer questions Nicolas Nabokov's description of Lourié as "Stravinsky's shadow," we have to bear in mind that for Gojowy one of the main tasks is to establish Lourié's importance as a personality, composer, and thinker in his own right and that the highly publicized association with Stravinsky is an obstacle to that goal.[5]

From 1924, when Lourié was at last permitted by the French authorities to live in Paris, he was automatically drawn close to Stravinsky by his old friendship with Vera Sudeykina. This was not quite a conventional platonic relationship. Some nine years earlier, when Sudeykin had brought Vera back to Petrograd from Moscow, he had installed her in his spacious marital apartment on the Fontanka, where his then wife, Olga, was already conducting an unconcealed affair with Lourié, and the four of them had proceeded to cohabit, if not actually in a state of free love, at least in a free and easy intimacy of a sort more or less commonplace among artists in the ambit of the Stray Dog. Tall, myopic, nail-biting, and prematurely balding, but with intense eyes and thick, sensual lips, Lourié never seems to have had any difficulty attracting women of an intellectual cast but a physical nature. When he first reached Paris, via Berlin, late in 1922, he had with him his wife, Tamara.[6] But this was not a love match; rather, Lourié seems to have been caught on the rebound from an intense but for some reason unsatisfactory affair in Petrograd with Anna Akhmatova. And although he had converted to Catholicism at least as long ago as 1913, the pious, faintly sanctimonious air which hangs round his later correspondence with Stravinsky was apparently new at that time. It may have come partly from Maritain. But then Maritain specialized in transformations of this kind, and the combination of piety and a dubious past (or in some cases present) was entirely normal at Meudon.

Lourié saw much more of Vera in Paris than he did of Igor. When Stravinsky was around they would often dine together. But Arthur and Vera would also dine quite often when Igor was at home in Nice or away on tour for any reason without her. Arthur and Igor both used her flat in the rue de Ranelagh as a letter box, and Arthur would even write his letters there, ready to hand straight to Vera when they were finished. This, in fact, was the "household" of which he was virtually a member. His one recorded stay at the Villa des Roses (in the spring of 1926) was followed by a gushing letter of thanks,[7] but though he befriended Stravinsky's sons in Paris in 1930, his letters only ever included greetings to Katya after the whole Stravinsky family moved to Paris in 1934. The letters are in fact among other things a constant record of Lourié's attempts to recover with Igor an intimacy that he never had any difficulty preserving with the easygoing Vera but that Stravinsky increasingly withheld, for reasons which—so far as it is still possible to understand them—will emerge in due course.

This is not to deny that, for a time, the two men were close. In Paris in the late twenties, they were on instant telephonic terms, something that was as yet far from normal. As Arthur himself later grumbled: "Before, when you were in Paris, I only had to telephone in order to see you. Now it's hard to get you on the phone. One has to make a plan through others, and this spaces out our meetings indefinitely."[8] But Lourié was more and more a victim of Stravinsky's overpowering need for lieutenants rather than comrades and his readiness to make the most extravagant demands on their loyalty. Lourié was, after all, a serious and committed composer in his own right. In the Petrograd days, he had shone as one of the most versatile musicians in that shadowland of artistic experiment; and in Germany and Paris he continued to write music of an unusual and independent cast of mind, even though he had little immediate hope of either performance or publication. Yet after meeting Stravinsky in 1924, he gave up hours of his time to the performance of menial musical tasks for him like correcting proofs for the Octet and the orchestral suites, and making piano reductions of the Octet and the Symphonies of Wind Instruments. He may even have planned a monograph on Stravinsky's music, which was certainly not intended to be a rush job but would, if it had ever been written, have involved detailed study of all the works, including the very latest, as well as long conversations and protracted correspondence about the ideas behind them. Up to a point, of course, these were all ways of making, if not much, at least some money—the first desperate necessity for any émigré. But in the process, Lourié was subjugating himself more and more to Stravinsky's mind and personality, a predicament from which, as it turned out, there was no painless escape.

The chief product of this involvement was a series of articles which, taken as a whole, amount to not so much a perceptive or particularly illuminating view of Stravinsky's music as a studiedly extreme assertion of its aesthetic meaning in the specialized and doctrinaire intellectual atmosphere of 1920s Paris. The first article was a short study of the Piano Sonata, which came out in Prunières's Revue musicale in 1925, and this was followed in fairly rapid succession by articles on Oedipus Rex (1927, also in the RM) and Apollo, a shorter piece which appeared in the Pleyel house journal, Musique, in 1928, in the form of an open letter to Robert Lyon. In between, Lourié contributed two major articles in Russian to Souvtchinsky's new Eurasian journal Vyorstï; and he capped the whole series with what turned out to be in some respects a seminal article—in English—on the whole issue of modernism, which appeared under the provocative title "Neogothic and Neoclassic" in the American journal Modern Music in the spring of 1928.[9]

Disentangling what is Stravinsky and what Lourié in these articles is quite hard. Lourié was by nature a systematic thinker, while Stravinsky, though of a sharply analytical turn of mind, tended to formulate ideas as he went along to explain his artistic convolutions in a way that seemed to confer on them a measure of historical legitimacy. For instance, his attacks on opera in the early days were simply a roundabout way of defending the seriousness of ballet, a medium that was routinely despised by musicians and intellectuals before Diaghilev came on the scene. Later, when he wanted to write operas, the specific arguments about words and music were quietly forgotten. *Mavra* came out as an opera partly because of its polemical idea, partly perhaps because Stravinsky had fallen under the influence of old-fashioned Russian cabaret. But meanwhile, *The Rite of Spring* had to be historically reinvented as an "objective construct" in order to distance it from the kuchkist tradition to which it palpably belonged but which Stravinsky had by 1920 decided to abandon. In a sense the Octet article of 1924 marked a new phase in this tendency, since it raised general issues about the nature of music, and the relationship between method and product, form and content, which in practice no composer as busy or focused as Stravinsky could have had the time or inclination to pursue in relation to each subsequent composition.

This was where Lourié came in. As an ex-commissar, he cannot have been without experience in the craft of tendentious exegesis, and as a former habitué of the Stray Dog, he was well versed in the polemics of modern manifesto art. He knew (had slept with) Acmeists, had arrived in Paris with a Futurist, had had close dealings with Symbolists and Formalists. He, like Stravinsky, had read Maritain's *Art et scolastique* just at a moment when he was susceptible to the influence of an anti-individualist theory of art with its roots in Catholic thought. When he and Stravinsky met in Amsterdam in January 1924, they may well have discussed Maritain, and the composer probably showed Lourié his Octet article, with its already somewhat Thomist ideas about form and beauty. A few months later Stravinsky was expressing himself spontaneously in similar, if more amenable, terms to Polish journalists. "The music of my latest works," he had told one, "is already from beginning to end absolute music. . . . The time has passed when I tried to enrich music. Today I should like to construct it."[10] "Does my appeal to the eighteenth century surprise you?" he had asked another. "The reason lies in the fact that I am running away from romanticism. But . . . what I've got from old music is Stravinsky, and only Stravinsky."[11]

Lourié's own first Stravinsky article, on the Piano Sonata, already begins to assemble these ideas into something like a theory, if sometimes expressed in the language of the commissariat. At its center is the Maritainesque view of the nineteenth century as a time of corruption and disarray:

The romantic sonata, as it continues to evolve, sheds its organic activity and its instrumental dialectic. It replaces them with an inorganic schema in which it realizes itself through a false adaptation of song to instruments. . . . Stravinsky's Sonata deliberately abandons the way of this decadent evolution. It addresses anew the question of instrumental thought and that of the organic form of the sonata. Such is the nature of this return to the original tradition of the eighteenth century. It determines logically the birth of a formal type.[12]

The leading decadents for Lourié, in relation to the sonata, are Scriabin and Debussy. But a year later, in his *Vyorstï* survey, he developed the antithesis into a more active and dangerous polarity.

Among those who create the living experience of our day, *a pathos of feeling is clearly giving way to a pathos of consciousness.* In the collision of these two forces a new style is being born. On the one hand, neo-Gothic: by which I do not at all mean anything medieval, but a striving for expressiveness, as an *ens in se*, emerging in invidualism, subjectivism, chance and the exceptional. . . . On the other hand, *geometric* (purely musical) *thinking*, the true expression of which is *plastic realism*. To be precise: the neoromantic (that is, revolutionary) *sensation* is overcome by the classical or religious *consciousness*.[13]

Later in the piece Lourié suggests Schoenberg as the antithesis of Stravinsky (with Scriabin and Debussy now similarly treated as counterpoles): "the same opposition between [on the one hand] elements of individualism and subjective, extramusical expression, and [on the other hand] a suprapersonal principle, bringing with it equilibrium and unity."[14] But the point is not developed, and instead Lourié spends much of the article elaborating the main idea behind *Mavra*: namely, Stravinsky's impulse to distance himself from the fashionable Russianisms of his youth—kuchkism, symbolism, Scriabinism, even miriskusstvism—and reassert his descent from "the pure sources of Russian music," Glinka and Tchaikovsky. He suggests that the "objective method" has been a virtue of Russian music ever since Glinka, and that this objectivism was "a tie which bound all Russian musicians into one family . . . regardless of personal artistic aspirations, and despite differences of temperament, individual taste, etc."[15] There are hints of a specifically Eurasian line of argument. *The Rite of Spring* freed Russian music from its old dependence on the West and asserted "the Asian spirit of Russia." But then, "if underlying the Symphonies of Wind Instruments there is a chorale not of a Western type but close to the Orthodox practice, *Pulcinella* is already entirely built on a revived classicism. . . . In the Octet, the Piano Concerto, the Sonata and Serenade, revived classical formal types are finally crystallized."[16]

Much of this shows Lourié as an intellectual opportunist (not to say a profoundly inaccurate historian and highly tendentious reasoner). The Eurasian idea, so far as it goes, is developed only in his two Russian-language articles in Souvtchinsky's paper. The French pieces are preoccupied with the classical sources and different types of formalism. But this is also true of the *Oedipus Rex* part of his "Dve Operï" article in *Vyorstï*, which was published separately in French and German. In his heart of hearts, Lourié—a Catholic Jew—was closer to the internationalism of Stravinsky's recent works than to any supposed Eurasianism in the earlier ballets. Maritain meant more to him than Trubetskoy; and it is hard to reconcile anti-individualist observations like the one about Stravinsky returning us "to the long lost joys of a time when the genius of handicraft was the basis of art"[17] with the candid particularism—almost nationalism—of the Eurasians. But then this also reflected Stravinsky's own leanings in the twenties, and was almost certainly a result of conversations between them. How far Stravinsky went along with Lourié's more specious lines of reasoning—like his idea that *Oedipus Rex* was modelled on Handel "not because of any taste or personal sympathy for that composer . . . but because [his] formulae continue to possess a certain practical value"[18]—is hard to tell. There is no record of his objecting to them. But he may have accepted them because, in a sense, they flattered him by treating his models as a convenience rather than a controlling artistic precedent.

Lourié was in any case a born systematizer, and in the end his pigeon-holing mentality did harm. After the Schoenberg concerts of 1927, he came back to his idea of a division between the "neogothic" and the "neo-classic" in modern music and, on the basis of this division, drove a wedge between Schoenberg and Stravinsky which was to remain as a barrier—in Stravinsky's mind at least—for almost a quarter of a century. "To treat the matter dialectically," he suggested innocently,

> Schönberg may be considered the *Thesis* and Stravinsky the *Antithesis*. Schönberg's thesis is an egocentric conception dominated by personal and esthetic elements which assume the significance of a fetich. Here esthetic experience takes the place of the religious, art becomes a kind of substitute for religion. Stravinsky's whole aim, on the other hand, is to overcome the temptations of fetichism in art, as well as the individualistic conception of a self-imposed esthetic principle. From this point of view, art is the normal function and projection of experience. The principle here affirmed is the limitation of

the ego and its subordination to superior and eternal values. The two movements, characteristic of the modern artistic world, divide it into two camps, each of which, though possessing many variants, follows on the whole one or other of these banners.[19]

"Stravinsky's art," Lourié continued, "is a reaction against Schönberg's esthetics and all conceptions belonging to that order." This was scarcely true, since Stravinsky knew little about Schoenberg's aesthetics and virtually none of his music. Yet Stravinsky himself, in his pragmatic way, had formulated a not dissimilar idea in one of his Prague interviews, in comparing Schoenbergian rationalism and aesthetics with the work of Oscar Wilde.[20] What rationalism has to do with Wilde, the reader is not told. But Lourié does his best to pin it down. "Atonality," he explains,

> leads to the creation of a new principle of musical construction which, in seeking to control the element of emotion and evoke a purified and obedient material, becomes itself subject to this element—a phenomenon not recognized until recently. The further we are from the period in which works deriving from this principle are composed, the more they appear in their true light; they reveal their essential nature as subjective and determined by a psychological element which is, above all, extra-musical.[21]

Thus serialism is merely the latest manifestation of the individualism to which Lourié has objected all along. But he is too clever to overlook the obvious riposte that neoclassicism has also tried to "control the element of emotion and evoke a purified and obedient material." The neoclassic, no less than the neogothic, is now seen as outworn and outmoded; "most of its adherents are already falling into formalisms and imitations of the classic. . . . The truly classical is not there." But Stravinsky is "polymethodic" and already "no longer even a neoclassicist." Writing about *Oedipus Rex,* Lourié had dwelt at painful length on its supposed models. But in his short piece on *Apollo* he talks only in general terms about the music's "algebraic" precision, its quest for "purification" and "catharsis," and its "struggle against the charm and temptation of aesthetic fetishism." The conquest of the individual has now led Stravinsky "towards the *spiritual,* aiming thereby at the long-lost unity of the moral and the aesthetic."[22]

IN THE WEEK in which he completed the draft score of the new ballet, Stravinsky was also busy settling the terms for his next work, which Ida Rubinstein was commissioning for a new ballet company she was setting up in Paris. It was the second time that Ida had tried to interest him in one of those hybrid stage spectacles which had been her trademark ever since she had staged and starred in d'Annunzio's *Le Martyre de Saint-Sébastien,* with music commissioned from Debussy, at the Châtelet in May 1911. The *Antony and Cleopatra* proposal had never really appealed to him. But something about the new project had caught his imagination; and it was Benois, with his sharp musical antennae and his intimate knowledge of Stravinsky's mind and taste, who had hit on the formula that the composer of *Mavra* found hard to resist. Benois's idea was for a ballet with a score based on music by Tchaikovsky; but not his ballet music, nor his symphonies, whose rigid form "might prevent the creation of something organic and integrated. It would be another matter if we were to assemble certain piano pieces which could be organized under the banner of some well-known subject, or still better for which a subject could then be chosen, since they would already be bound together by purely musical affinities."[23] Benois even listed several pieces that struck him as suitable; and just as with *Pulcinella,* for which Diaghilev had presented him with the idea and the material, so with *The Fairy's Kiss:* Stravinsky accepted the package more or less as it was handed to him, even if what he did with it was no more predictable in the one case than in the other.

But there was no question of an immediate start on the Tchaikovsky material; in fact there was scant prospect of settled work for the next six months—a worrying state of affairs, since Ida wanted the score by the end of the summer in time for an autumn premiere. Stravinsky was due in Paris to conduct a pair of concerts on 10 and 18 February in the new Salle Pleyel, including *The Rite of Spring* (the first time he had conducted it in Paris) and the French premiere of the *Huit Pièces faciles,* as the two small orchestral suites were still commonly known. In various contrasting ways, he seems to have impressed his old friends the Parisian critics. "It remains an accepted fact," André Schaeffner wrote, "that Igor is a bad conductor; but perhaps there is a kind of bad conducting which is better than the good." But André Coeuroy had a more imaginative explanation for this syndrome. Stravinsky, he wrote, "does not conduct; he lives. Rhythm is made flesh in the form of a little man who bends his legs like a fencer taking guard, who splays his thighs like a horseman, who snaps his elbows back like a boxer on the attack, who looks alternately, or all at once, like a bird, an engineer, a Kobold, and a surgeon."[24]

From Paris, Stravinsky went with Vera to Berlin, where Klemperer was staging *Oedipus Rex* in a triple bill with *Petrushka* and *Mavra* at the recently reconstituted Kroll Opera. As it turned out, this was not quite the stage premiere, which took place at the Staatsoper in Vienna under Franz Schalk on 23 February, two nights before the Kroll opening. But the Berlin production occupies a particular place in the Stravinsky annals, not just because the composer attended the final rehearsals and the first performance, but because the staging was the first of a new work by Klemperer's company and to some extent set the modernist tone of this notable if short-lived enterprise. Whereas Alfred Roller's designs for the Vienna production were (according to an unnamed friend of Stravinsky's) "a mélange of Louis-Quinze and Hubert Robert,"[25] the Kroll performances were given in a relentlessly abstract, rectilinear set by the company's resident producer, Ewald Dülberg.[26] And whereas in Vienna the choir sang from the pit while the stage chorus mimed, in Berlin everything was essentially as in the stage directions except for the Speaker, who appeared in what Adolf Diesterweg called a "timeless costume" because, he suggested, Klemperer was afraid that this "Baedeker of the stage" would arouse merriment if he came on in modern evening dress.[27] There is in fact some evidence that this change was made only after the dress rehearsal, since Theodor Adorno, who reviewed the rehearsal some weeks later but apparently did not attend the premiere, borrows Diesterweg's phrase—"zeitlose Kostüm"—to describe the Speaker's outfit with the clear implication that it was not what he himself saw.[28]

Stravinsky later claimed that "I wince when I recall the [Kroll] performances," though he admitted obliquely that they were musically good (using the ambiguous epithet "well prepared").[29] But at the time he told reporters that "the production of *Oedipus Rex* satisfied me completely," and a few years later in his autobiography he recorded that "the execution of *Oedipus* . . . was of the highest order."[30] Admittedly he also told Mengelberg's secretary, Sam Bottenheim, that he disliked the Tiresias (Emanuel List), and he presumably agreed with ERM's Berlin director F. V. Weber that Caspar Koch was a poor Oedipus, to judge from the tone of Weber's account of the second performance, in which he wrote, "Koch again sang Oedipus! And as badly as at the premiere; he again fell down at precisely the same places."[31] None of this seems to have dampened the enthusiasm of an audience which, at the first night, was largely made up of delegates at a Berlin trade conference. Loud applause was leavened by some mild hissing. But the press was in large measure favorable, both to the work and to the production, and the music was disliked only by writers and musicians who were already taking up positions of hostility to neoclassicism, like Adorno, who described the work as "a pre-Handelian oratorio stripped of its flesh, its skeleton blown to bits, the fragments reassembled in the shape of the skeleton, then filled up and held together with concrete";[32] and Arnold Schoenberg, who, after hearing the dress rehearsal, made a diary note that

the orchestra sounds like a Stravinsky imitation by Krenek.

I do not know what I am supposed to like in *Oedipus*. At least, it is all negative: unusual theatre, unusual setting, unusual resolution of the action, unusual vocal writing, unusual acting, unusual melody, unusual harmony, unusual counterpoint, unusual instrumentation—all this is "un," without *being* anything in particular.

I could say that all Stravinsky has composed is the dislike his music is meant to inspire.33

Once again it seems that Stravinsky did not meet Schoenberg in Berlin. He may have encountered Adorno, his future scourge, at the dress rehearsal. But he certainly did, at least, run across the Marxist utopian philosopher Ernst Bloch, who was at the premiere, attended the production party after the show, and was seen dancing a minuet with the composer.34 However, the carefree atmosphere soon evaporated after Stravinsky's departure. At the end of the second performance, Klemperer made a scene backstage, prevented the unfortunate Koch from taking a curtain call, and refused to do so himself. Later, according to Païchadze, he was summoned by the minister of fine arts and asked to explain the poor quality of the singing at the Kroll.35 The third performance was cancelled, and Klemperer went off on what Païchadze called "diplomatic sick leave," though it seems clear that the conductor, a clinical manic-depressive, was in a genuinely disturbed condition and in serious need of rest.36 Païchadze was in any case swayed by this incident against a casual promise he had made to Klemperer to give him the European premiere of *Apollon musagète,* which Stravinsky had played to the conductor in Berlin. It was suddenly apparent to Païchadze that this crystalline score was not suited to the hyperintense Klemperer style (though Stravinsky might not have agreed; when he heard Klemperer rehearse *Apollo* in June 1929, he complained about the muddy textures, but blamed the size of the orchestra rather than the conductor; with the strings suitably reduced, "everything became sharp and clear").37

To get him out of his promise to Klemperer, Païchadze urged Stravinsky to dream up an exclusivity in respect of stage performances, either for Diaghilev or for Ida Rubinstein—unusual advice from a publisher, especially in view of Diaghilev's notorious reluctance to pay his dues. There was never any serious question of Rubinstein. The new ballet had had Diaghilev's name on it ever since the first partial play-through in the autumn, and after the meeting with Balanchine Stravinsky was more than ever keen to ensure that the Ballets Russes could produce the work on reasonable terms. "All the same," he told Païchadze, "I should like some guarantee, which is why I proposed to Diaghilev . . . very easy and modest terms. I feel that if these are too much for him, then we have to give up the idea of exclusive rights and simply switch to per-performance payments, which I don't much want with Diaghilev, since he's a very unreliable payer."38

Nobody was giving much attention to the approaching production on the far side of the Atlantic. But for Washington the performance on 27 April was a major event, nothing less than the first-ever American world premiere of a ballet by a major international composer. The little Music Room of the Library of Congress had been adapted into a theatre—which one reviewer described, rather fancifully, as modelled on "the fundamental constructive principles of Baireuth [sic]."[39] Twenty-five string players (plus the conductor, Hans Kindler) squeezed into the pit—nine fewer than the number to which Stravinsky would reduce the Kroll orchestra the following year—and on the stage the four dancers (Adolph Bolm, Ruth Page, Elise Reiman, and Berenice Holmes) performed a restricted choreography by Bolm, "their faces wreathed in properly lyric smiles [and] counting diligently as they executed enchainments originally devised for eight-bar phrases in two-four time, to measures that varied from three to nine beats and phrases that ended whenever the composer chose."[40] There were sets by Nicolas Remisoff: a pile of rocks and some ruined Corinthian columns, and, between them, Apollo "clad in gold sandals, pink tights and a gold tunic decorated with red festoons. Upon his long golden curls he wears a helmet from whose crest burst many fulsome plumes. In his hand is his lyre." Presumably out of consideration for the finer feelings of Mrs. Coolidge and the other Washington ladies, Apollo's birth was not presented, and instead a thurifer appeared in front of the curtain and placed a censor on a tripod in the middle of the stage. The sacred flame ascended and the curtains parted.

According to Olin Downes, the new ballet (under its full title, *Apollon musagète*) was coolly received, and there was more enthusiasm for the other items on the program: danced versions of Ravel's *Pavane pour une infante défunte* and Beethoven's Eleven Mödlinger Dances and a harlequinade to music by Mondonville. But the *Washington Post* dutifully noted (in its news columns) that "much applause greeted the close of the new ballet," and its reporter's sole complaint was that "at times the orchestration seemed a trifle too loud."[41] Nobody appeared very comfortable with the music's style. Downes, while admiring its polish and expertise, questioned its inspiration and sincerity and grumbled about its harking back to old genres. His *Times* colleague referred helplessly to "those who claim to understand Stravinsky," and reserved his sympathy for Bolm and the other dancers: "Superficially, here was ballet music of the most conventional sort; but to the ear of the choreographer this pseudo-lyricism proved to be little more than a candy coating for the most vicious contrary rhythms and the most persistent irregularities of time, which bore no more relation to the conventional ballet than to Bellini, under whose style they were so neatly tucked away."[42] The trouble was that the American critics—quite apart from any individual shortcomings of technique or perception—were having particular difficulty keeping up with Stravinsky's manner. *Oedipus Rex* had recently been heard in Boston, but not yet in New York;[43] *The Soldier's Tale* had had its full New York premiere only a month before *Apollon musagète; Les Noces* and even *The Rite of Spring* were both still relative newcomers. The press did not like having its authority—its ability to point the route for a less informed readership—undermined in this way, and its response was to combine a knowing, *de haut en bas* tone with confusions of praise and blame, and sometimes even a willing admission of incompetence in what, after all, was not quite honest music. In their defense, one can only say that even a fellow composer like Nicolas Nabokov confessed to a similar difficulty with *Apollon musagète* when he first heard it. "For even by comparison with Stravinsky's preceding compositions it seemed to me too artificially restrained and stylistically 'quotational.' "[44]

Nabokov, moreover, had on the face of it been in a good position to observe and absorb Stravinsky's latest work in its preparatory stages, since his own ballet *Ode* was in rehearsal at Monte Carlo at exactly the same time as Balanchine and Lifar were at work on *Apollo* (as Diaghilev, to Stravinsky's irritation, was trying to call it).[45] *Ode* was if anything still more indebted to eighteenth- and nineteenth-century models—to the world of the divertissement and the antique image of sweetness and simplicity. In fact, when Nabokov had played his score through to Stravinsky the previous October, Stravinsky himself had cheerfully remarked to Diaghilev: "You know what it's like? It's as if it were written by a predecessor of Glinka, someone like Gurilyov or Alyabyev." And to Nabokov: "From where do you know all this Russian salon music of the 1830s? It is unmistakably and naïvely Russian."[46] But once *Ode* was in rehearsal at Monte Carlo, Diaghilev had for some reason taken against it; and by the time the ballet (as choreographed by Massine and with Ira Belline miming the part of Nature) had struggled past its first night at the Théâtre Sarah Bernhardt on 6 June, Nabokov was in no state to appreciate the stylistic complexities of anybody else's music. *Apollo,* by contrast, had gone smoothly in rehearsal—largely in the absence of its composer, who was away from Nice for all but a few days at the beginning of March and the beginning of April. He and Balanchine had no doubt talked about the work and its staging, and Stravinsky probably commuted to Monte Carlo while he was in Nice.[47] But in essence the collaboration which Stravinsky later called "among the most satisfying in my artistic life" was one of the least close in terms of personal or epistolary contact.[48] Balanchine was able to evolve his notions of an abstract, nonanecdotal choreography—notions which formed the whole basis of his subsequent working intimacy with Stravinsky—free in large measure from his influence or interference.

The Diaghilev *Apollon musagète* opened on 12 June, Paris's first new Stravinsky ballet for five years. The composer himself conducted, and the designs were by André Bauchant, a painter of neoprimitive peasant canvases, rather incongruously recruited to supply a physical context for a work which seemed so little to require one.[49] But while Bauchant's Olympus (a "furrowed sugar-loaf," as one critic described it)[50] may have seemed too mundane and tangible an image for the home of the gods, his costumes—the three muses in white ballet skirts of different lengths, Apollo in a simple red and gold tunic—caught nicely the convention of sentimentalized classicism (the classicism of Delibes and Minkus as much as of Rameau) which is never far beneath the surface of Stravinsky's music. For Stravinsky himself these designs were neither severe nor conventionalized enough. He praised the choreography as "the first attempt to revive academic dancing in a work actually composed for the purpose."[51] But there is something overaustere, a hint of Lourié scholasticism, about this compliment, where Balanchine's choreography (at least in its modern revivals) is no more rigidly dependent on classical models—one might say no less ironically so—than Stravinsky's music. It is precisely the point of this marvellous score that it frequently and wittily defies the conventions to which it initially lays claim—in which respect it satisfies the vital needs, as opposed to the textual theories, of any worthwhile neoclassicism. And the same can be said of Balanchine's contribution.

"The success," according to Apollo himself, "was *fantastic,* and my own reward an enormous ovation."[52] Even allowing for Lifar's impenetrable vanity, this seems to have been no less than the truth. Stravinsky, who came to detest Lifar, was still ready to admit that "the success of *Apollo* as a ballet must be attributed to the dancing of Serge Lifar and to the beauty of Balanchine's choreography."[53] Diaghilev was so moved that he bent down and ceremoniously kissed the dancer's leg, telling him: "Remember it, Seriozha, for the rest of your days. I am kissing a dancer's leg for the second time in my life, the last was Nijinsky's after *Le Spectre de la rose!*"[54] The critics, less impressionable, could not fault the music, but neither could they find great enthusiasm for its "thoroughly academic moderation. Nothing picturesque. No invention. No abandon. Melodies of a facile verve, almost without development or ingenious modulation. A practically total submission to the doctrines of the seventeenth, eighteenth, and first half of the nineteenth centuries."[55] The *Figaro* reviewer, Pierre-Barthélemy Gheusi, thought he detected on Stravinsky's face, as he conducted, "the smile of a worldly faun. He seemed highly amused, as if humming to himself: 'Yes, it's really me, the destroyer, the revolutionary, the inventor of discords, the setter of multicolored baroque gems, the irreverent juggler of harmonies, it's I who have decided to write this noble Greek imposition, in praise of everything I have burnt!' "[56]

As might be expected, the periodical reviewers were less easily distracted by the issue of style. In the *Revue musicale,* Henry Prunières called

Apollon musagète a faultless masterpiece and observed that Stravinsky's classicism "is no longer, as of late, an attitude; one feels him to be responding to an intimate need of the mind and the heart," adding that "I should very much like to know the name of the composer who would be capable of writing the finale of this ballet."[57] Boris de Schloezer, writing in the *NRF,* was if anything even more impressed by *Apollo* than by *Oedipus Rex.* He dwelt on "Stravinsky's faculty for renewal, the veritable heroism with which he refuses to exploit past successes by reducing them to formulae," and compared the new ballet with Mozart's *Magic Flute,* recently conducted in Paris by Bruno Walter, suggesting that while

> Mozart possessed [divine] 'Grace,' which so to speak came quite naturally to him, Stravinsky has conquered it: this serenity, this purity, the author of *Apollo* has only achieved at the cost of painful efforts and struggles. . . . Whatever may have been the circumstances which led to the birth of *Apollo,* the work reveals to us its author's secret, his thirst for renunciation, his need for purity and serenity. . . . From this point of view *Apollo* contains not only the aesthetic lesson that every masterpiece teaches us, but also a moral lesson, I shall even say: religious. What will be Stravinsky's next work? On what route has he yet to embark? It seems very daring to indulge in predictions of this kind; however, I shall risk saying that after *Apollo,* in all logic (but is our logic that of the artist), Stravinsky can no longer give us anything but a Mass.[58]

BALANCHINE TOLD Richard Buckle that Diaghilev, finding Terpsichore's variation musically too similar to Calliope's, had cut it at subsequent performances.[59] It seems almost incredible that he did anything of the kind, not because the music would not bear it (Diaghilev was unscrupulous in such matters), but because the form of the ballet itself would hardly do so. In any case, the cut was certainly not made in Paris in 1928 or at the London premiere on 25 June, since these performances were all conducted by the composer. A paragraph in *Figaro* two days after the opening reports that Stravinsky was so pleased with the music's performance and reception that he had decided to conduct the entire run himself.[60] He knew perfectly well, of course, that he had written one of his finest works. And Diaghilev—whether or not he still resented the Washington premiere—surely knew it too.

DEATH OF A SHOWMAN

As FAR AS CONDUCTING went, the *Apollon musagète* performances were little more than an incident in a crowded spring. In March Stravinsky had spent ten days in Barcelona, being fêted, interviewed, and photographed, and preparing and conducting two concerts featuring *The Rite of Spring*. Early in April he went to Rome with Katya for a week and conducted *The Nightingale* at the Teatro Reale, in two double bills, one with Casella's ballet *La Giara* and the other with Bellini's opera *La sonnambula*.[1] Then, after a mere two or three days in Nice, it was on to Amsterdam via Paris, this time once again with Vera. Perhaps curious about his reaction to a work he had first (and possibly last) encountered in St. Petersburg, he went to hear Mengelberg conduct Strauss's *Ein Heldenleben* in the Concertgebouw. "What a piece of music!" he exclaimed to Ansermet. "And how much care and security of performance Mengelberg brought to it!"[2] On the twenty-fourth he himself conducted a concert performance of *Oedipus Rex*, his first since the Paris premiere.

Ansermet, whom Stravinsky saw again in Paris at the end of the month, was just back from his first trip to Russia, where he had conducted *The Rite of Spring*, the Symphonies of Wind Instruments, and excerpts from *Mavra* in Leningrad and Moscow, had seen Yury and his family, and had lost his heart "to your compatriots, not as Bolsheviks, but as Russians."[3] He had met Boris Asafyev, had shown him the scores of *Mavra* and the Symphonies (which Asafyev knew only in Lourié's published piano reduction), and praised him more than was wholly agreeable to Stravinsky, whose last news of Asafyev may have been that he had written for Andrey Rimsky-Korsakov's *Muzïkal'nïy sovremennik* during the war. He read Ansermet's letter "with an avidity that you can guess." But he added:

> I'm astonished at the enthusiasm you bring back for Boris Asafyev. I don't know him personally, but I've often had occasion to read what he writes about music—and if you read that, you would perhaps change your opinion. I read what he wrote about Rimsky and Tchaikovsky and was very surprised to note his membership rather

of the Andrey Rimsky and Steinberg clan than of the clan opposed to that nest of old wasps, since Asafyev had often been mentioned to me as the only one who really counts in Russia today.4

Had he known that Asafyev was at that very moment in the closing stages of a profound and detailed monograph about his music, he might have expressed himself still more forcibly. As it is, the caustic marginalia in his copy of *Kniga o Stravinskom* (Book About Stravinsky)5 bear silent witness to the insecurity and irritation he often felt in the presence of those few critics who showed a serious understanding of his music. Like Myaskovsky, Asafyev was uncomfortably well briefed on those sources of his work which Stravinsky had been in the process of putting behind him: not so much the plagiarisms (real or imaginary) as the folk ingredients in works like *Les Noces* and *Renard* and the popular and vaudeville background to *Mavra*. He also had a taste for anthropological-cum-sociological interpretation that was deeply uncongenial to the author of "Some Ideas." "One must not forget," he writes, "that *Noces* is the embodiment of the ancient cult of the family and of reproduction."6 "Better forget it," growls Stravinsky, "since that really has nothing to do with it." And when Asafyev asserts his "firm belief that everything is reducible to simplicity and clarity . . . that life is a mechanism . . . that reflexes determine our whole behavior in the material world; and that economic and industrial considerations condition all our creative work" the composer inquires acidly: "Is this irony or a bow to the Communists?"7 But touchy though he was about any search for meanings—and above all, sociopolitical meanings—in his work, there is fear as much of the past as of the present in these ill-tempered marginalia. "How well I know these Russian intellectuals and their discussions," he notes on one page, "and how little they've changed in the twenty years since I left Russia."8

Early in May he went from Paris to London, where he conducted *Oedipus*—its first airing in Britain—for the BBC on the twelfth and the thirteenth. These were, of course, live radio performances, transmitted direct. There was no staging and no audience, which did not deter Ernest Newman from reviewing the work in considerable detail off the air two Sundays running, through the modest radio loudspeakers of the day and with the help only of the published vocal score, and coming to the conclusion that, on the whole, and with all due allowance for Stravinsky's incorrigible indecisiveness in the matter of style, his inability to see (as was so clear to Newman) that the greatest music had always been and always would be couched in the simplest, most "diatonic" language, "with the familiar vocabulary and in the familiar grammar of music (or such expansion of these as normally goes on in every generation)": with due allowance for all this, *Oedipus Rex* suggested that "Stravinsky now looks like becoming once more the interesting composer he was in his earlier days. . . . *Oedipus Rex* has revived our almost moribund hopes for the composer of *Petrouchka* and the *Sacre du Printemps*. He shows signs of becoming again what he has not been since *L'Oiseau de Feu* and parts of *Le Rossignol*—a humanist."9

But the master was spared this homily in a language of which he was still blissfully ignorant. By the time it appeared in print he was back in Paris, where, the previous evening, he had played his Piano Concerto in the Salle Pleyel under Bruno Walter, in a program that also included Mahler's Fourth Symphony. To his surprise, Walter ("this *Romantiker* from another era") proved a lively and dependable accompanist, who "followed me as nimbly as anyone with whom I ever played the piece."10 But if the concert was an unexpectedly happy experience, its aftermath was not. Stravinsky had contracted with an impresario called Firmin Gémier to give the Salle Pleyel performance in association with what turned out to be a fake charity called the Union française de la Société universelle du théâtre. When his fee failed to materialize, he sued Gémier and his agent Georges Caurier. But although judgment was eventually (after nearly four years) given in the composer's favor, and Gémier was ordered to pay his costs and Caurier his fee, no money ever changed hands, for the good reason, as Stravinsky's lawyer Louis Gallié wearily informed him, that both Caurier and the self-styled Société were to all intents and purposes bankrupt. For Stravinsky it always seemed as if, in the words of George Eliot's Mr. Tulliver, the law was "made to take care o' raskills."11

Three days after the Paris premiere of *Apollon*, Stravinsky signed a contract with Columbia Records which was to prove a good deal more fruitful. He undertook to record—and Columbia to issue—twelve 78 rpm record sides per year for the next six years. Less than a fortnight later, in London, he recorded the first six of these, in the form of an abridged version of *Petrushka* (of the whole ballet, that is, not the by then usual concert suite starting with the Tour de passe-passe); and before the end of the year, in Paris, he had added a further eight sides of *Firebird* music, made up of the published 1912 suite plus the Berceuse and Finale.12 Despite his Brunswick contract of three years earlier, these were his first electrical recordings, and he was sufficiently impressed by the whole process to tell an interviewer from *Les Nouvelles littéraires* that

> the gramophone is at present the best medium for transmitting the thought of the masters of modern music. . . .
>
> If I was eager to conduct the recordings of *Firebird* and *Petrushka* for Columbia, it's because I wanted, by this perhaps still inadequate yet already satisfying means, to try to inscribe my traditions, my will, and to show in what spirit I want to see my works played. If there

exists a certain difference between any of my performances on the rostrum and at the microphone, I still have to say that I find greater truth in the latter than when the baton is entrusted to a [professional] conductor, however intelligent or respectful of my work.

The gramophone was an improvement on the mechanical piano, not least because with the Pleyela the transmission process was not direct: there was an intermediary, in the form of a paper roll, cut by an assistant. But the new medium also had its disadvantages, some of which (including the short playing time per record side) it shared with the old acoustic process, while others were built into the whole idea of the perfectable document which, in theory, was what attracted Stravinsky to the medium.

> To get the best performance, you have to repeat a piece tirelessly, that is, pile fatigue on fatigue, and yet at the moment when the nerves are at the end of their tether, when the violinists' arms are failing, when the mind is deadened by the monotony of the task, precisely then you have to be perfect: it's this version that they record. . . . The exact pitch on the gramophone is determined by the speed at which you play the work. Under these circumstances I had to gain three seconds out of three minutes fifty, and begin recording this piece three times over, at the same speed, measured on a stopwatch, like a sporting record.[13]

The *Petrushka* sessions lasted two days, after which Stravinsky went straight back to Paris, and thence, after renewing his contract with Pleyel, and after a farewell dinner with Nouvel, Diaghilev's cousin Pavel Koribut-Kubitovich, Païchadze, Ira Belline, and Vera (who had not gone with him to London), home to Nice.[14] He had been away almost eleven weeks.

The family lingered only a few days in the midsummer heat of the Côte d'Azur, and were soon on their way to Echarvines, the hamlet they had stayed in the summer before, just above the Lac d'Annecy village of Talloires. The Chalet des Echarvines, where they put up, was a small boardinghouse which offered Igor none of the privacy or isolation he needed for composition. So instead he optimistically, and as it turned out vainly, took a room in a nearby stonemason's cottage, installed a piano, and worked away at his Tchaikovsky ballet, based on Andersen's story about the child marked out from infancy by the fatal kiss of the Ice Maiden. From the adjacent room a disgusting smell of garlic and rancid oil wafted into his studio, pursued every lunchtime by the terrified cries of the mason's wife and child, as their violent breadwinner returned home from his morning's labors. In the afternoons, the composer retreated to the boardinghouse and did what he calls "work for which I did not require a piano."[15] This was mainly orchestration. Early on, before there was enough ballet music to score up, he worked on an orchestral version of the little pianola study he had composed for Mme Errazuriz in 1917. Later, he orchestrated what he had composed of the ballet. It was not his normal working method. But then the circumstances themselves were far from normal, since he had promised to deliver three-quarters of the ballet in piano score by the beginning of September:[16] it was already early July, the premiere was in November, and he had so far written nothing.

Stravinsky had a sound practical instinct where his own work was concerned, and he was not usually incautious about deadlines. He may at first have envisaged a work that was much more substantially an arrangement of Tchaikovsky songs and piano pieces than what he eventually composed; or he may simply have intended a shorter ballet. The half-hour-long *Apollo*, with its strings-only scoring, had taken fully five months to compose. *The Fairy's Kiss*, for full orchestra, ended up half as long again, and there were barely four months in which to write it, allowing for a trip to the Dutch resort of Scheveningen, where Stravinsky was booked to play his Piano Concerto in early September. No wonder he told his friends he was too busy to entertain them. "I'm working from ten in the morning to eleven at night," he informed Païchadze. "I've never wanted a little walk so badly."[17] His only break had been a flying visit with his children to see Koussevitzky and Païchadze at Combloux, followed by an excursion to "that sad casino" at Thonon-les-Bains, on the southern shore of Lake Geneva—a trip that had been planned as a grand reunion with Stravinsky's old Lausanne collaborators Ramuz, Ansermet, Auberjonois, and Elie Gagnebin, but which, in the event, only Auberjonois could make.[18] As for Koussevitzky, the composer told Ansermet spitefully, "he has the whole summer off, and in this respect I shall be in spiritual communion with him for at least two days."[19]

Perhaps Combloux itself was the real spiritual attraction. The outing took Stravinsky from the green hills around the Lac d'Annecy through the more dramatic Alpine scenery of Upper Savoy. There were views of Mont Blanc; and Stravinsky might briefly imagine himself amid the mountains of the Bernese Oberland around Interlaken, where Andersen's "Ice Maiden" is set. By now, early August, the lengthy tale had been reduced to a mere carcass—Stravinsky told Benois—and he had dropped Andersen's title in favor of the more suitably abstract, allegorical *Fairy's Kiss*.[20] Nevertheless, there remained a much sharper sense of locale than in *Apollo*, which had neither peasants nor weddings, neither grieving mothers nor abandoned brides. Admittedly, Stravinsky wanted the work done classically, just like its predecessor. "I pictured all the fantastic roles as danced in white ballet-skirts"; but the rustic scenes were to take place "in a Swiss landscape, with some of the performers dressed in the manner of early tourists and mingling with the friendly villagers in the good old theatrical tradition."²¹ Meanwhile, Tchaikovsky's music was also being subjected to a process of transformation and abstraction more subtle and far-reaching than anything Benois can have envisaged when he had first made the suggestion seven or eight months before.

Stravinsky himself seems only to have made up his mind exactly how to compose the work at a remarkably late stage. Most of the first scene is based on ideas from Tchaikovsky's *Children's Songs*, op. 54. But Stravinsky wrote to Païchadze as late as 16 July, nearly a week after getting to Echarvines, asking him to send a copy of the songs. Of course, he must have known them already, and doubtless had the relevant themes in his head, since although the songs finally arrived only on the twenty-third or twenty-fourth,²² the scene was complete in piano score by the twenty-fifth. All the same, it is a feature of this opening tableau that it uses fewer themes than the two which follow, and generally in a less altered state, almost as if Stravinsky arrived by experiment at the synthetic technique which largely distinguishes the Tchaikovsky treatments in *The Fairy's Kiss* from the Pergolesi arrangements in *Pulcinella*. From the outset the second tableau, begun on 29 July, is freer and more deconstructive in its handling of the original material.

Despite its unexpectedly intricate method, the ballet was duly three-parts written by the time Stravinsky left for Scheveningen at the end of August. Up to that point, Nijinska had been choreographing on the basis of individual sections the composer dispatched from Echarvines.²³ Now, in Paris on the way to Holland, he met her at the Edition Russe.²⁴ It must, though, have been almost the only collaborative meeting before the final rehearsals. Back in Nice after Scheveningen, the composer seems to have run into difficulties with the ending of the third tableau and with the short but highly original fourth. Not until mid-October (a month late, according to his publisher)²⁵ did he at last complete the work in piano score. Finishing the orchestration took another fortnight. It was not a moment too soon. Less than a week later he was due to play his Piano Concerto in Zurich, after which he had a month of Paris recordings (*Firebird* and *Pulcinella*) and concerts (with the new Orchestre Symphonique de Paris), culminating in the Rubinstein premiere itself at the Opéra on the twenty-seventh.

Not since *Petrushka* in Rome, 1911, had the completion of a Stravinsky score caused such gnashing of teeth. Ida all but wept down Païchadze's telephone.²⁶ Benois, so close to Stravinsky during work on *Petrushka* and *The Nightingale*, complained to Svetik, who was acting as his father's secretary, that he could not finish his design for the final tableau without hearing the music ("Ridiculous," Svetik was instructed to say: "how has he managed the first three without hearing any?").²⁷ At first, Stravinsky had no intention of letting Ida, Bronislava, or Benois hear a note until he could play it to them himself. "Nijinskaya will howl, of course," he told Païchadze, "but pay no attention."[28] Then only three days later he realized that there was no chance of this happening, so he authorized Païchadze to give the score to a pianist and insist on strict observance of metronome marks.[29] A mere four days before the premiere, he was spending so much time correcting errors in the parts that he had to refuse admission to rehearsals even for close associates like Souvtchinsky and Lourié.[30]

The Rubinstein season included a string of new ballets, including, most notably, Ravel's *Bolero* (premiered on the twenty-second). Milhaud's *La Bien-aimée* was an arrangement of pieces by Schubert and Liszt; there was a Bach pastiche by Honegger. And then there was *The Fairy's Kiss*, neither strictly original, like the Ravel, nor strictly pastiche, like the Milhaud, but a somewhat uncomfortable blend of the two. Writing in the *Revue musicale*, Henry Prunières found it incomprehensible that Stravinsky should waste his time composing Tchaikovsky, even if he did it better than Tchaikovsky himself.[31] Diaghilev, who had come over from England to spy on the opposition, found it "tiresome, lachrymose, ill-chosen Tchaikovsky, supposedly orchestrated by Igor in masterly fashion. I say 'supposedly,' because it sounded drab, and the whole arrangement lacked vitality. But what went on on the stage," he continued,

> it is impossible to describe. Bronya showed not the least gleam of invention, not one single movement that was decently thought out. As for Benois's décor, it was like the sets at the Monte Carlo Opera House: these Swiss landscapes were worse than anything by Bocharov or Lambin (Grigoriev will be sure to remember them). The theatre was full, but as for success—it was like a drawing-room in which someone has suddenly made a bad smell. No one pretended to notice, and Stravinsky was twice called to the curtain.[32]

Diaghilev admittedly had his own agenda where Ida Rubinstein was concerned. By nature intensely jealous of rivals, he could be particularly sour where rival work by former associates of the Ballets Russes was concerned: and the *Fairy's Kiss* team were entirely what he would have regarded as "inventions" of his own company (possibly excepting Benois, whom he might have accepted as a co-founder). "What's this I hear," he had written to Stravinsky back in August, "about your offering *Apollo* to Ida Rubinstein?"[33] And it was true that Païchadze had been negotiating with Ida for a production of that work, as Stravinsky admitted. But this was normal business: "I myself never offer my works to anyone, either directly or through the agency of others," he insisted.[34] Probably Diaghilev's edginess on the subject was aggravated by the disagreeable symptoms of his diabetes (not yet diagnosed), which were being treated with varying degrees of hopelessness in the face of the patient's stubborn refusal to moderate his lifestyle. But there was another factor as well. In the last few years, Diaghilev's overpowering enthusiasm had been, not for the ballet at all, but for books. He had even, for the first time, taken an apartment in Paris, solely to house the collection he had been building up on the company's tours. As it happened, this collecting mania was a point of contact with Stravinsky, who was himself collecting religious objects and books, which he lent to the Russian church in Nice. "When do you leave for Mount Athos?" the composer had enquired only this last August.

> I must say that I am very envious of you, all the more because what draws me to this holy place is something quite different from you; what I ask you to do for me is bring me a number of icons (oleographs) and a wooden cross, having them blessed there on the spot. Since I know that you are going to Mount Athos for books, I should be grateful if you could bring me a catalogue of everything they have currently on sale in Russian and old Slavonic.[35]

Preoccupied with his books, Diaghilev was becoming more and more disillusioned with the ballet. He now

> avoided talking about the world of his ballet company, peopled with unconscious and rebellious subjects whom, in the last years of his life, he ruled wearily and, it seemed, out of obligation. The perilous administration of this world which the glare of the footlights rendered unreal and magical, but which in the gloom of the wings became once more colorless and basic, incoherent and tumultuous, began to weigh heavily on his shoulders, and any allusion to his theatre, the dancers' names and the titles of the ballets, was to him simply an unwelcome reminder of his duties.[36]

That *The Fairy's Kiss* was the sole reason for the coolness which descended on relations between Stravinsky and Diaghilev at about this time may therefore be doubted. Diaghilev was simply feeling negative about ballet in general. When the Paris Russian-language paper *Vozrozhdeniya* published an interview in which he ridiculed "poor Rubinstein's hunchbacked figure with its helpless bent knees [and] the utter confusion of her attempts at classicism," Stravinsky was upset on her account but could not deny the accuracy of the appraisal.[37] "There is no one in the artistic world," he admitted, "who seems to me so mysteriously stupid as this woman."[38] Then again, Diaghilev's latest love, the sixteen-year-old Igor Markevitch, who had come to see him at the Grand Hôtel in Paris in November, was neither a dancer nor a choreographer but a budding composer, a pupil of Nadia Boulanger. Meanwhile, Diaghilev began to treat his own ballets and their composers in an increasingly high-handed and irrational way. The cut in *Apollo,* which was probably first introduced on the 1928 autumn tour, suggests a careless but perhaps also slightly vengeful attitude to this concise and beautifully proportioned work. Such treatment of his music would normally have been quite enough to explain any cooling of feelings on Stravinsky's side. Yet even when the issue of the cut had reached the point where Païchadze threatened to deprive Diaghilev of *Apollo* altogether,[39] the composer still professed himself baffled by Diaghilev's unfriendly behavior, claiming that "he has for some time avoided meeting me for reasons which are clear only to him."[40] And it was perfectly true that, even at their bitterest, professional quarrels between the two had never in the past led to a severing of personal ties.

For Paris music lovers in general, the great event of autumn 1928 was not the Rubinstein season, nor even the Diaghilev season which followed in December, but the inauguration of a major new orchestra, the Orchestre Symphonique de Paris. This had been founded under the auspices of Pleyel, and was designed to herald the new era of the Nouvelle Salle Pleyel, though the fire in July meant that the first concerts would in fact have to take place in the Théâtre des Champs-Elysées.

The OSP was not just a gesture towards the new Salle Pleyel. It was itself a new broom. It was specifically constituted to improve the players' conditions, and hence the quality of their playing. The musicians were mostly young; they were salaried, deputies were forbidden, and there were daily three-hour rehearsals to back up the eighty concerts the orchestra was to give each year, a density of work which—in theory at least—guaranteed the kind of consistency and discipline Parisian orchestras had hitherto conspicuously lacked. Finally, there was no grand conductor-in-chief. The orchestra was run by a triumvirate of Alfred Cortot, Ernest Ansermet, and Louis Fourestier, who themselves conducted a majority of the concerts. For Ansermet, who had never had a conducting base in Paris outside the Ballets Russes, it was a huge opportunity, but also a huge frustration, as he found himself having for the first time to cope directly with the internal politics, the maneuverings and vacillations which for Parisians, then as now, were the stuff of artistic life. Even before the first concert, he was grumbling to Stravinsky that, with only a quarter of the concerts at his disposal, and with his colleagues much less interested in innovation, the programs would not have the emphasis he wanted.[41] Rightly, as it turned out, he distrusted Robert Lyon's "mania for the unstable."[42] Stravinsky, too, soon ran up against the kind of fatuous bureaucracy which can also seem a Parisian speciality, when the OSP's administrator, Etienne Pellier, took issue with him over his insistence that the orchestra meet all hire charges as well as paying him what Pellier deemed a "quite high fee."[43] The composer, increasingly on edge in his dealings with agents, impresarios, and other necessary intermediaries, detonated in a controlled explosion of injured contractual rectitude, and the unfortunate M. Pellier retreated in confusion.[44]

Stravinsky's debut concerts with the orchestra (on 16 and 17 November) were superficially a strong indication of Ansermet's commitment to modernist programming. Few commercial orchestras would have risked consecutive evenings of unadulterated Stravinsky, even with the prize-fight element of the composer himself as conductor. But the programs themselves were plainly to some extent designed to take the *b* out of this boldness. Apart from the far-from-abrasive *Apollo,* which figured in both concerts, there was nothing musically later than the brief pianola study of 1917, given for the first time (as "Etude") in its new orchestral dress. On the other hand, the Friday concert was half taken up with the early Symphony in E-flat, its Paris premiere, and the first time Stravinsky himself had ever conducted it complete. On the Saturday, the *Scherzo fantastique* was paired with the early suites from *Firebird* and *Petrushka.* Apart from the study, the post-*Rite* Stravinsky was represented only by the two Suites for small orchestra and the "Song of the Volga Boatmen." Of the "difficult," revolutionary Stravinsky, there was little trace.

It was left to Ansermet himself to fill this gap with *The Rite of Spring* in one of the orchestra's early concerts in the reopened Salle Pleyel on 28 December, this time as part of a program which allowed two-thirds of the rehearsal time to be devoted to this one work.[45] Typically, Ansermet took immense pains preparing the performance, and in the process reopened the old problem of metric notation in the Danse sacrale, as well as the vexed question of string pizzicati in this same dance, many of which had been deleted in the first published edition of 1921.[46] The discussion seems to have borne fruit in Stravinsky's own first recording of *The Rite* the following May. But by that time, ironically, the Swiss Ansermet had been maneuvered off the OSP committee in favor of the Frenchman Pierre Monteux, who was currently working as Mengelberg's deputy with the Concertgebouw and whom Cortot went to see on the OSP's behalf in Amsterdam early in 1929. Ansermet certainly considered himself to have been the victim of simple chauvinism.[47] But it seems clear that the Pleyel board had decided after all that a star conductor was needed, and that the fifty-three-year-old Monteux, with his international reputation and deep roots in Parisian musical life, fitted the bill. For the French, Ansermet was a comparatively provincial, as well as artistically disconcerting, figure: a modern specialist whose conducting of the classical and romantic reper-

toire could seem clinical and unemotional and if anything apt to exaggerate the defects in an inexperienced orchestra as yet unable to match the
precision implied by such a style. There was also a danger, as Boris de
Schloezer had been quick to point out, in the idea of the "committee of
three," each of whom would have his own approach that would cut across
the work of the other two and prevent the orchestra from establishing a
settled manner of its own.[48] Of course, for Stravinsky Ansermet's "textual-
ity" and lack of emotionalism were huge virtues, whereas he detested star
conductors, not least (perhaps) because they were much harder to control.
But he would soon—at least in his opinion—have other, more specific,
grounds for distrusting Monteux.

Stravinsky was not in Paris for the Ansermet *Rite*, and he had also
missed Klemperer's Paris début with the OSP a week earlier. But his spies
were active. Vera gave him a dazzling account of *The Rite of Spring*, which
bore out Ansermet's own claim that "it sounded as clean as on the Pleyela."[49] As for Klemperer, Lourié reported that he had conducted *Pulcinella*
accurately and well and had generally made an excellent impression, both
as a conductor and as a person; but then, Lourié added defensively, "you
always say I am mistaken in my judgments about people."[50] In fact,
Stravinsky will have concurred with this one. He admired Klemperer, and
liked his respectful and painstaking attitude to new music, in contrast to
the lordly conservatism of most German conductors. When, a month later,
he went to Dresden to direct a concert performance of *Oedipus Rex*, he and
Vera met Fritz Busch and heard him conduct *The Queen of Spades* and also
Strauss's latest opera, *Die ägyptische Helena*. But while impressed with
Busch as "an excellent musician and conductor," he was pained by a mentality so "hostile to any new tendency."[51] Klemperer, on the other hand, was
in the thick of the new music. His Paris concerts had included recent
works by Hindemith and Krenek, and he was again planning to get
Stravinsky to Berlin to play his concerto, an intention that had fallen
through at the time of the Kroll *Oedipus*. It was typical of Klemperer that
when this idea at last came to fruition in June 1929, he programmed the
concerto uncompromisingly with two other major works by Stravinsky,
Apollo and *Les Noces,* and conducted them with such conviction that audience and press were virtually unanimous in their enthusiasm.[52]

Stravinsky himself, though, may have been wearying of the concerto,
while perhaps also recognizing that his exclusivity in so effective and well-
thought-of a piece was costing him royalties. One Berlin critic complained
that he played the work "like a Phonola, so metronomically [*regelmässig*],
so soullessly. Klemperer seems to have been of the same opinion, since on
one occasion he cast a furious glance at his pianist."[53] In Nice that Christmas he embarked on a new and very different work for piano and orchestra, apparently inspired by the bravura elegance of Weber, a composer he

had always been prepared to single out from the Teutonic heavyweights ever since telling Romain Rolland, back at the start of the war, that Weber was the only "pure" German composer he liked.[54] At the same time he made an orchestration of the second of the three string quartet pieces from 1914, perhaps already with a view to grouping the three of them with the pianola study as an orchestral suite. But the piano work, like the Andersen ballet the year before, probably did not get very far before Stravinsky had to set out for Dresden, and then, at the end of February, Paris, for a Salle Pleyel concert on 5 March.[55] Thereafter the picture was all too familiar. The *Rite of Spring* recording sessions in May (the seventh to the tenth) were followed by a three-day trip to London for more Aeolian recordings, and then—in Paris again—rehearsals with Lifar for *Renard,* which was opening on the twenty-first.

Diaghilev had decided to revive the piece in the original Laryonov designs but with new choreography by Lifar—his first venture in that particular arena. Lifar himself, in a highly colored account of his work on this short ballet, claimed to have invented what became the most famous idea in the new staging, the use of four acrobats to double the four dancers (in addition to the four singers, who, as before, would be in the pit with the band).[56] But Buckle accepts Kochno's assertion that the idea was Diaghilev's and that its object was precisely to paper over gaps in Lifar's own choreographic invention.[57] For Lifar, of course, it was important to establish ex post facto his status as guardian of the Diaghilev tradition: hence also his heavy playing down of Balanchine's role as choreographer of the main new work that opening night, Prokofiev's *Prodigal Son,* which—according to Lifar—enjoyed a clamorous success exclusively because he took the last-minute decision to ignore Balanchine's choreography and dance the title role as if he were playing himself. After *Renard,* which preceded the new ballet, he is supposed to have refused to take a bow with Stravinsky, who is supposed to have cried, "If you do not come now, I swear you'll make an enemy of me for life." Quite why Stravinsky (who certainly was unremittingly hostile to Lifar in after years) should have minded so much not being upstaged by a neophyte choreographer is hard to imagine. As for Balanchine, his genius was happily proof against the machinations of even this most resourceful of his early dancers, and *The Prodigal Son* has come down to us as—with *Apollo*—the greatest of his early ballets.

Stravinsky was in Paris for just over three weeks. He seems, rather pointedly, to have avoided Monteux's "Stravinsky Festival" of the three prewar ballets, with what was by that time "his" (Monteux's) orchestra, at the end of the month. He nevertheless soon became aware of a French Gramophone Company advertisement in the Salle Pleyel program for that concert, which puffed Monteux's new recording of *The Rite of Spring* by declaring

(1) That the interpretation of the *Sacre* created by M. Monteux in the course of the memorable premieres of 1913 has been approved and sanctioned by the composer.
(2) That without the perseverance of M. Monteux, who repeated it in concert in 1914, the *Sacre* would today perhaps be forgotten.
(3) That M. Monteux's interpretation is today considered classic, the sole model on which all conductors base themselves for their performances.[58]

He did go a few days later to hear an even older colleague, Alexander Glazunov, conduct the OSP in his own best-known ballet, *The Seasons*. Stravinsky recalled that in the green room after the performance Glazunov greeted him surlily.[59] But this is not borne out by Glazunov's own account of the meeting, in a letter to Steinberg written soon after the event. "Stravinsky unexpectedly appeared," he reported, "and asked me whether I remembered him. Of course I recognized him immediately. He expressed his pleasure in the music of my ballet, and perhaps sincerely at that, since once long ago he asked me to give him the score to examine and didn't return it for a long time."[60] But Stravinsky's sincerity can hardly have been much more than skin-deep, all the same; his real opinion of Glazunov was surely closer to that of Lourié, who, on hearing a year or two later that Rimsky's star pupil was taking a job in Berlin, inquired: "What can Glazunov teach them there? Perhaps the forgotten art of composing by tuning fork."[61]

The Ballets Russes season ended on 12 June, and from Paris the company proceeded to Berlin for a short season in the Charlottenburg which included *Apollo* and *The Rite of Spring*, with Lydia Sokolova as the Chosen One. Stravinsky had followed on to Berlin from London, where he had played the Piano Concerto in the Queen's Hall under Goossens. However, his visit had nothing to do with the ballet, but was in fulfillment of his engagement to play the concerto with Klemperer at the Kroll on the seventeenth. Ansermet was conducting the ballet performances, and the two certainly met. But Stravinsky and Diaghilev avoided one another, as they had apparently also managed to do in Paris. The trouble over the *Apollo* cut had come to a head towards the end of the Paris season, aggravated in Stravinsky's mind by the fact that Diaghilev was vindictively getting his own back on Païchadze by suing him and Prokofiev for having published *The Prodigal Son* without a credit for Kochno, the author of the scenario. "This is what it means," he remarked bitterly to Ansermet, "to have dealings with these nice people from the Ballets Russes."[62] A few days later he asked Ansermet to warn Diaghilev that in London, whither they were both once more bound, he and Vera had taken a flat in Albermarle Court, the block where Diaghilev habitually stayed.[63] This time, Stravinsky had a BBC concert on the twenty-seventh (with *Apollo* and *The Fairy's Kiss*), and did not wait for the ballet opening on 1 July. But Diaghilev had come early from Berlin with Kochno and Igor Markevitch, and the five of them travelled on the same train from the Gare du Nord.

The exact details of their last meeting will never be known. According to Stravinsky, there was a brief and embarrassed conversation on the platform, after which they went to their different compartments and exchanged no further words.[64] In London, almost incredibly, they did not meet, even though (according to Vera) they occupied adjacent flats and could hear each other's voices through the wall.[65] Stravinsky was rehearsing hard; and on the day after the concert he left for Paris. By 3 July he was in Nice, and a week later the family was back at Echarvines. Soon after their arrival, they heard from St. Petersburg that Igor's and Katya's aunt Soph'ya Yelachich (the widow of his favorite uncle, Alexander) had died at the age of seventy-six.[66] Exactly a month later, on 11 August, Anna Stravinsky—Soph'ya's only surviving sister—would celebrate her seventy-fifth birthday. On the nineteenth, Igor went with Theodore and Svetik to visit Prokofiev, who was spending the summer at Culoz, some twenty miles to the west of Talloires. Their return must have evoked memories of Les Diablerets twelve years before, when they had come home from a picnic and been met by the postboy with news of Gury's death. Katya had sat up late for them. Diaghilev had died that morning in Venice, in his room at the Grand Hôtel des Bains de Mer on the Lido. Misia Sert, Boris Kochno, and Serge Lifar were with him.

As ever, the quarrels and petty jealousies evaporated in the face of what amounted to a family bereavement. To Nouvel, he wrote of "that sharp pain which I bear within myself from the sudden disappearance of my passionately beloved Seriozha," adding that "I found relief in the knowledge that apart from me there are other people whom he loved and who now mourn him bitterly in their hearts."[67] "We are sharing the same sorrow," Nouvel wrote back.

> I am bereft of a man to whom I was tied by a friendship of forty years. But I am happy today that I never failed to be faithful to this friendship. Many things united us and many things separated us. Often I suffered from him, often I was revolted by him, but now that he is in the grave all is forgotten and all is forgiven. And I understand now that no ordinary measure of the conduct of human relations could be applied to so exceptional a man. He lived and died "one of the favoured of God." But he was a heathen, and a Dionysian heathen, not an Apollonian. . . . His death, a pagan's death, was beautiful. He

died in love and beauty and under the smiles of those two gods he swore by, and served his whole life, with such passion. Such a man must be loved by Christ.[68]

Diaghilev, on his side, had never wavered in his artistic loyalty to Stravinsky. On the very day that he and Stravinsky had scarcely spoken on the platform of the Gare du Nord, he had told Lev Bernstein: "Stravinsky is the living embodiment of a true enthusiasm for, a true love of art; the personification of eternal striving. . . . He is constantly on the move, seeking out at every step how to deny the very thing that he has been in his previous works."[69] A month before his death he wrote from London to his "little" Igor, Markevitch: "*The Rite of Spring* had a real triumph yesterday. These imbeciles have come to appreciate it. The *Times* says that *The Rite* is for the twentieth century what Beethoven's Ninth was for the nineteenth! In the end, one must have patience and be a little philosophical in life in order to see from above the obstacles that the small and limited put in the way of every effort that escapes the ordinary."[70]

A PASSAGE OF RIGHTS

THAT THIRD SUMMER at Echarvines Stravinsky did not return to the mason's cottage, but instead rented a prefabricated summer house where he continued work on his new piano concerto. As before, the family stayed *en pension* in the village. One day Prokofiev came with Ansermet and Souvtchinsky, and Stravinsky played them what he had written of the concerto and explained to them the Weber connection. Prokofiev, who had been extremely sour about *Apollo* and no more than grudgingly appreciative of *The Fairy's Kiss* ("Here at least there's some material, even if it's rented"), liked the new piece, which he told Myaskovsky was going to be titled so as to avoid the criticism of insufficient virtuosity that had been levelled at the earlier concerto.[1] Stravinsky had thought of calling it a divertimento until (Prokofiev claimed) he heard that both Prokofiev and Myaskovsky were planning such works. The eventual title, Capriccio, appears for the first time only in a letter to Stravinsky's Viennese agent in late September, by which time the work was more than two-thirds written.[2]

Whatever the reason for not calling it a concerto, the style and sonority of the Capriccio are notably unlike those of its predecessor. Since his last solo piano work, the Serenade, Stravinsky had included the instrument only in *Oedipus Rex*, where much of the keyboard writing is purely linear and articulative. The Capriccio picks up and extends this way of writing, to the point of working up actual musical ideas from the opera (such as the ostinato theme from the opening chorus) into concerto material. There are even times when Stravinsky seems to be thinking of the piano as a mechanized cimbalom—an instrument played with two sticks and therefore unable to play thick chords or dense counterpoint, but good at flourishes and repeated notes. Perhaps it is no coincidence that he had just been conducting *Renard*—with its important cimbalom part—for the first time, even though, musically, there may be few points of contact between the ethno-fantasies of the earlier work and the suave, *grazioso* cosmopolitanism of the later.

Stravinsky was being reminded of the whole *Renard* context not just by the Paris performances, but also by Ramuz's *Souvenirs sur Igor Strawinsky*, which Ramuz had sent him in the form of a series of pamphlets during the second half of 1928, and which was eventually published as a book in the autumn of 1929.[3] It may be that the nostalgic, "où êtes-vous maintenant" tone of the *Souvenirs* irritated Stravinsky, and certainly his guarded reply to Ramuz's request for a written contribution to the book edition in the form of annotations and correspondence barely conceals a certain annoyance at this one-sided exploitation of an association he himself valued as a purely personal memory.[4] But Stravinsky was more susceptible to nostalgia than he chose to admit. When he told Ramuz that "these *Souvenirs* have touched me deeply,"[5] he probably meant it, however much he may have regretted Ramuz's taste for the public expression of such private sentiment. Nevertheless, behind these veiled reproaches and repressed feelings there were practical considerations which could never be ignored in any dealings with Stravinsky, especially in the twenties and thirties. And 1929 was a particularly awkward year for former collaborators of his.

In the *mondain* Parisian half of his existence, Igor had been a constant and enthusiastic cinemagoer. But for obvious reasons silent films had never had any direct professional significance for him. With the advent of the soundtrack in 1927, this changed. The first talkies, not unnaturally, were musicals, and it was not long before the more serious-minded movie producers, too, started to turn their attention to music as subject matter for film. At a gala evening at the Théâtre des Champs-Elysées in December 1928, Columbia Records showed a film of Stravinsky—"mécanicien en sweater"—conducting (probably) one of his *Firebird* recording sessions, with the sound synchronized from the recording itself.[6] Such film projects, and possibly others, raised the quite new question of musical copyright in relation to the cinema; and the question was not only what royalty would be paid, but to whom.

In March 1929, Stravinsky wrote to Païchadze, in response to a verbal request, asserting his sole authorship of the text of *Les Noces* and his role in the collective composition of the scenario of *The Firebird* (implicitly refuting Fokine's claim to authorship, which had always previously been accepted in allocating royalties).[7] Exactly why Païchadze wanted this particular letter at this particular moment is not clear. But the likelihood is that Stravinsky had been approached about the filming of his ballets, and Païchadze was anxious to establish bargaining positions and legal documentation before signing any contract. Three months later another question arose about filming *Petrushka,* and Stravinsky wrote a similar letter, in which he claimed that Benois's role had been limited to designing the sets and costumes and to advising Fokine on the production and choreography. Benois had been called co-author, Stravinsky asserted, merely as the simplest way of getting him a royalty under the rules of the Société des Auteurs et Compositeurs Dramatiques, and he could not lay claim to any rights beyond what he collected from the SACD itself.[8] This was untrue, of course. But more to the point, it was patently factitious, and Païchadze's legal counsel dismissed it out of hand, observing that in strict law Stravinsky was obliged to consult all collaborators, however minor, before disposing of a work by contract. The best thing, he advised, was to invite Benois's consent and collaboration, and sue him for abuse of right if he refused.[9]

Although the immediate *Petrushka* problem soon blew over, merely thinking about his collaborators' claims made Stravinsky edgy and insecure. It was bad enough that Ramuz took a third of the *Renard* royalties whenever, as with the Ballets Russes in 1929, it was done in French translation (he would have taken them for *Les Noces* as well, but Stravinsky was by then routinely opposing its performance in French).[10] But it was doubly aggravating that the composer himself was still effectively stateless for copyright purposes, and dependent for his own percentages on the good offices of publishers like Chester whom he regarded as no better than bandits. He began to think seriously about changing his nationality. His French courtesy passport was coming up for renewal in 1930, and for some reason it crossed his mind to become Swiss. So Ramuz was enlisted as a secretarial go-between to establish the Berne conditions for naturalization and to arrange for the necessary personal approaches to be made to influential ministers. The fact that these approaches were indeed made seems to show that Stravinsky was prepared to bind himself in the event that they succeeded. As it happened, though, they merely demonstrated— as might perhaps have been expected—that the Swiss authorities insisted on a residential qualification which Stravinsky did not, and did not intend to, satisfy.[11]

Meanwhile, the composer's irritation with Monteux over the Salle Pleyel advertisement smoldered on, fanned by the OSP affair and the spectacle of Ansermet being outmaneuvered by the Parisian cabals. It had been clever of the French Gramophone Company to promote Monteux as the "authorized" conductor of *The Rite of Spring* while at the same time outrageously suggesting that it was only his subsequent advocacy that had saved it from oblivion, just when Stravinsky himself was (as they well knew) about to issue his own recording. But the composer's revenge, when it came, was exquisite. It took the form of an unblinking counterassertion, printed in the OSP's Salle Pleyel program for 6 December, that "the *Rite of Spring* which Columbia have just recorded under my direction is a true masterpiece of gramophone realization . . . a model of recording that renders a true service to all those who would like to know the tradition of performance (not interpretation) of my work."[12] It was precisely at this concert that Stravinsky gave the premiere of his Capriccio under Ansermet, while the program for the evening coolly reminded the audience that the artistic director of the OSP was Pierre Monteux, the very man whose

Rite of Spring had so recently been "the only model on which all conductors base their performances."

The tone of the advertisement was restrained. Stravinsky's real feelings boiled over in a vitriolic letter to Columbia's Paris director, Jean Bérard.

> If this poor Jew can find no other way of maintaining his prestige as an avant-garde musician with his admirers, I certainly shan't be the one to amuse myself by exposing this profiteer's intrigues. . . . This man of limited horizons, vain and small-spirited, something one often finds among orchestral musicians, was by a whim of fate the first to conduct *Petrushka* and *The Rite of Spring* at the Ballets Russes, since when he had dubbed himself the "creator" of *Petrushka* and the "creator" of *The Rite*.[13]

But when Monteux told him, in a tone of injured dignity, that he had turned down an offer to conduct a Stravinsky concert in Brussels, including the Capriccio played by the composer, "since you are no longer happy with my performances," the response was almost comically disingenuous: "I am highly astonished by what you tell me. Whoever told you that I am no longer happy with your performances of my works?" Monteux, of course, had not been told anything of the kind, but had merely deduced it from a combination of the advertisement and the fact that "you no longer entrust me with the first performance of any of your works." But now that Stravinsky had stated that he was *not* dissatisfied with Monteux's performances, he—Monteux—would show his goodwill by conducting *The Rite of Spring* at his next concert (on, as it happened, his fifty-fifth birthday) and by inviting Stravinsky to play his Capriccio again in an OSP concert a month later.[14]

The most striking thing about this whole exchange is its extraordinary lack of candor. Monteux's real reason for turning down the Brussels date was probably not the Stravinsky advertisement at all, but the fact that the composer had just approached the OSP with the suggestion of recording the Capriccio for Columbia under Ansermet.[15] Monteux now had effective power at the OSP, having rescued it from financial difficulties at his own risk. But he felt too insecure in his prestige either to allow his orchestra to record with so dangerous a rival or, alternatively, to refuse point blank. Instead he skirted the question, pretending that he was upset by Stravinsky's general failure to give him first performances, when it was this particular first performance that rankled, and offering the composer concert dates when what he was waiting for was a reply on the question of the recording.[16] At long last, under pressure from the OSP's own executive, Monteux was forced to admit that his pride was wounded by the suggestion that the OSP record without him, and that it was particularly disagreeable to him that his place should be taken by Ansermet. He would agree to release the orchestra, but only on condition that it not be named on the records.[17]

It was too late. Stravinsky and Ansermet had already taken the precaution of booking the rival Straram Orchestra for the sessions in early May. For one glorious moment they thought of taking advantage of the double booking to record the Piano Concerto as well as the Capriccio. But this idea was firmly scotched by Columbia, through their Paris representative Jean Couesnon, who pointed out that they had already, after barely a year, made two years' worth of Stravinsky recordings.[18] So the Capriccio alone was recorded, with the Straram Orchestra; and Monteux, apparently piqued at the rejection of his offer, sulkily withdrew the extra OSP concert on the excuse that the date was inconvenient and the fee too high. "It all points," Stravinsky told Ansermet, "to a desire to be frankly disagreeable to me. What a sad character, this Monteux!"[19]

The Benois affair, meanwhile, had not been helped by Diaghilev's death, which had prompted articles about the Ballets Russes, not all of which had seen the great days of the company in exactly the light Stravinsky would have wished. Young Nabokov, for instance, wrote a lengthy obituary in the Pleyel journal in the course of which he remarked incautiously that "Diaghilev seems to have provided the idea for *Petrushka*, and certainly provided the initial idea for *Liturgie*, that is, for what became *Les Noces*."[20] Poor Nabokov could hardly know how raw was the nerve he was touching. The film idea had now been reactivated, and the company in question, Albatross Films, had even come up with a scenario. In March 1930 Païchadze met Benois and managed to establish that he, Benois, would not insist on having a hand in the adaptation if—in Stravinsky's choice phrase—it was going to "shit up the negotiations."[21] Unfortunately Benois chose this precise moment to deliver a public lecture about *Petrushka* at the Russian Academy of Art in Paris, in which he claimed sole authorship of the original ballet scenario (though not, it should be emphasized, of the idea behind the subject). Stravinsky read the lecture text in *Posledniye novosti* and in a fury scrawled in the margin, "What an outrageous and barefaced lie!"[22] A few days later he let off steam to Païchadze: "Your conversation with this poor conceited Benois no longer has much importance, since I'm virtually sure our plan will never work out." But, significantly, he added pleadingly: "Write me one of your nice letters, soothe me, reassure me, send me your affection, I need it."[23]

Insecurity, the demon that lurked permanently in the inner regions of Stravinsky's consciousness, had suddenly poked out its head and was busy interfering with his life. His correspondence with his numerous concert agents bore stark witness to his growing inability to cope equably with the ups and downs of daily professional dealings. He was rowing with most of them, often on the slightest pretext, sometimes for no apparent reason at all. He would abuse them for their dilatoriness or inefficiency, as he saw it, or for their failure to secure him bookings or adequate fees. When his Berlin agent Wolff and Sachs had the temerity to question his manner, he informed them that "the often disagreeable tone of my letters to you comes from the fact that your agency's inexact replies and careless reading of my letters puts me into a state of nerves."[24] The trouble for them was that he still expected to command big fees for concert appearances in Germany, his most important source of income, at a time when money was becoming scarcer and the atmosphere turning against modern music. Willy Strecker (Ludwig's younger brother at Schott), whom he had met in London in June 1929, and who had promised to help promote him as a performer with German orchestras, told him frankly that his fee of five hundred dollars was too high and that resident conductors would oppose his engagement because they feared the competition.[25] Yet he still had so many German bookings in 1930 that he was living for months on end with Vera in hotel rooms and railway trains, his large income from playing and conducting a kind of hedge against the material vulnerability he continued to feel as a creative artist in exile. But the compensating home life was if anything growing more, not less, hollow: a haven of peace increasingly undermined by sickness, absence, and, one can hardly doubt, mistrust.

Not that his family was any less close to him when it came to their own needs. In Biarritz, the Belyankins had somehow struggled on at the Château Basque, with the help of frequent cash transfusions from Nice. But after so many disasters, the Wall Street crash of October 1929 seems to have been the final straw for a business so heavily dependent on an American clientele, and in 1930 Belyankin went bankrupt, with a total debt to the Stravinskys of almost 50,000 French francs (about 2,000 dollars, or four concert fees). Nothing of significance had ever come of poor Grisha's Polish dreams. It was true that Katya's cousin Dmitry Nosenko had been able to start gradually repaying his much larger debt in 1927 out of the compensation on his Volhynian property at Omelno. But the compensation was at a punitively low rate, and when Dmitry died early in 1929 he still owed the Stravinskys 150,000 French francs, and left his daughter Vera with the thankless (and ultimately vain) task of dealing personally with land agents and peasant squatters far away beyond the river Bug.[26]

Igor Stravinsky had grown impatient of his wife's relations, apart from the attractive, intelligent, and above all self-sufficient Ira, and perhaps also her epileptic brother, Ganya. Vera Nosenko's tongue may have been sharp and her sister Olga's heart loving when they were all young together in Ustilug. But in the late twenties they were just another pair of slightly boring expatriate Russians, to be avoided or endured when visiting Lausanne, where they lived and Igor sometimes gave concerts.[27] It never seems to have crossed his (or for that matter Katya's) mind to remit their debts, which by 1930 he certainly could have done without serious cost to himself, particularly in view of their extremely slim prospects of repayment. On the contrary, he continued to insist on meticulous accounting. He and Katya surprised the seventy-eight-year-old Dmitry in 1927 by requiring a formal statement that he had begun to repay his debt,[28] and the tale of his loans to the Belyankins is punctuated by receipts, promissory notes, and statements of account, up to the moment in 1930 when—whether from exasperation or sheer lack of time—he asked Païchadze to deal with Grisha on his behalf and then questioned the publisher's businesslike punctiliousness, which he feared might harm Grisha's situation.[29] At bottom, perhaps not surprisingly, he was contemptuous of the wretched Grisha, who seemed so incapable of running even a healthy business enterprise in an orderly fashion. But Katya must have wept for her poor sister, morally and physically weighed down by the burdens of exile, as surely as she herself was being slowly destroyed by disease and her husband's infidelity. "It's terrible to think," Lyudmila wrote, "that the years are passing, and less and less time remains for us to repay our debt to you, both materially and morally. I suppose that's why it becomes harder and harder to accept. It was easier before—it was as if today you extend a helping hand to us, but tomorrow it will be our turn to help you. But somehow fate has decreed that the whole burden falls on one side only."[30]

It was fear of just this situation that had long governed Igor's own attitude to money. What were the endless battles with Diaghilev but the squabbling of young birds thrown out of the nest into a garden of marauding cats? And now Diaghilev himself was gone, dead in a hotel room "like a vagabond," as Ansermet had put it with uncomfortable perspicacity.[31] Ansermet had realized at once that Diaghilev's death would be like a family bereavement for Stravinsky. Even he did not go so far as to suggest that the composer had, for the third time in his life, lost a father. Yet it was curious that, just as Lifar and Kochno had fought "like savage beasts" over Diaghilev's body in the Grand Hotel,[32] Stravinsky was now locked in a no less savage moral struggle with precisely those two artists—Benois and Monteux—who had contributed most intimately to his great early successes for the Ballets Russes.

And as if all this were not evidence enough of the uncertainty of emigrant life, he was now having to watch his own children go out into the world and do battle with problems which, if he was honest, he knew to be partly of his own making. Theodore had had real success as a painter and designer, had had commissions and Paris exhibitions. But there remained a question about his true autonomy as an artist. His *Oedipus Rex* designs had been little more than studio work for Cocteau. In 1930, in a *Cahiers de Belgique* article, Luc Bischoff identified Picasso and Auberjonois—two of the crucial painters in Theodore's father's life—as formative influences on the twenty-three-year-old artist.[33] Whether or not the article itself was the result of string-pulling (since it appeared in an issue otherwise mainly devoted to his father's music), Theodore had certainly been consulted about possible authors, and for some reason had suggested another close friend of his father's, Charles-Albert Cingria—to Cingria's intense irritation, since he understandably disliked being pestered for promotional copy on his friends' children.[34] Meanwhile Svetik, aged nineteen, had been packed off to Paris in October 1929 to study harmony and music history with Nadia Boulanger, who was also detailed to find him a piano teacher (she found him a certain Mme C. Chailley-Richez).

As a musician, Svetik faced an even greater challenge in trying to assert any kind of independence. That he was an able student seems beyond question. Like his father, he was an excellent keyboard sight-reader, and he was probably better grounded musically than Igor had been at the same age. He could make himself useful in musical tasks such as proofreading. But both brothers, however lively and intelligent,[35] were immature and unsophisticated. Home, for them, was a disturbing mixture of cultural and social tyranny on the one hand, and on the other an emotional atmosphere that was at once intense and provisional, absolute and partial. Dumped by their father in remote corners of southern France, they had to watch him come and go, imposing his demands on them and their ailing mother for one half of the year, abandoning them for the other half. For almost ten years, their life had been, for him, both essential and inadequate, and by the same token they may well have felt it both necessary and impossible either to live up to any extreme expectations he may have had of them or to escape from his preconceptions of what they could or could not be.

They were both soon regaling his Paris spies with unsuitable emotional attachments which Lourié, for one, in his anxiety neither to trivialize nor demonize these first careless raptures, managed to portray as worryingly complicated in his letters to the composer.[36] Vera entertained the two brothers and their girlfriends to tea—an interesting variant on the "meet my folks" theme.[37] By March Theodore was talking about marriage, and two months later Svetik, still only nineteen, seems to have been actually engaged to a girl called Diantha, and was begging Mlle Boulanger to intercede with his father.[38] Whether the composer responded to all this initially with sympathy, fury, or indifference we do not know; there survives only, from a few months later, a gently discouraging letter from Katya which doubtless reflects his views in substance if not tone.[39] But though these particular attachments faded away, the mood of intense transferred emotion, so indicative of thwarted childhood, had been set once and for all.

.   .   .

A MONTH OR SO before Svetik's arrival in Paris, his father had been sounded out by the Boston Symphony Orchestra on the question of a symphony for the orchestra's fiftieth-anniversary season, 1930–31. Four years had passed since he had abandoned the idea of writing a symphony, apparently under the force of the specifically religious inspiration which had produced both *Oedipus Rex* and his return to the Orthodox communion. This time, again, there was no mention of a sacred work, and in the contract which Stravinsky eventually signed on 12 December, six days after the premiere of the Capriccio, a purely orchestral score was still implied. But on Russian Christmas Eve (6 January), having spent a few days making expanded orchestral versions of the Three Little Songs *(Souvenirs de mon enfance)*, he jotted down part of the Latin text of Psalm 39 (verses 13–15, "Hear my prayer, O Lord, and with thine ears consider my calling"). And from that point on, the symphony had become, not merely choral, but severely, ritualistically sacred. Each of the outer movements would be studiously inscribed to a church festival: the finale, which he completed first, to the week after Easter (27 April), the first movement (completed last), to the Feast of the Assumption (15 August). Even the unavoidable dedication to the Boston Symphony is, somewhat incongruously, overridden by the assertion that the symphony is *"composée à la gloire de DIEU."*[40]

The commission from Koussevitzky's orchestra, with its handsome cachet of six thousand dollars, struck an ironic note in the offices of his Paris publishing house, which was in financial difficulties and not able, with any certainty, to meet the composer's stern demand for half that sum as an advance on the Capriccio.[41] Despite his occasional homely talk of ERM as "we," Stravinsky showed little inclination to soften his contractual demands on their account, and this could lead to tense negotiations and long, self-pitying letters from Païchadze. By contrast, he seems always to have been at home to Koussevitzky, despite the bloodlettings of the past, and despite the fact that, in private correspondence, he habitually referred to the great ex-contrabassist in terms of the most withering contempt. In fact, "Get Koussevitzky" was a common theme among emigrant Russian musicians, who tended to resent their financial and artistic subservience to a man they regarded as little better than a circus performer, and a Jewish one at that. Recently, Lourié had got himself into a particularly embarrassing spot in this respect, having been forced by sheer indigence to accept a commission from Koussevitzky to write his biography, a work he knew perfectly well would earn him bitter reproaches from Stravinsky.[42] Nor does Stravinsky seem to have been particularly sympathetic when, having written the book, Lourié was virtually dragged screaming to the Koussevitzkys' and forced to read it out loud while Natalie Koussevitzky stood over him and made him change anything that she considered insufficiently complimentary to her husband. Optimistically, he suggested to Stravinsky that "it has turned out to be a funny book. For those who know how to read it, it's full of malicious irony."[43] But in reality, he knew that the laugh was on him. "You were right," he admitted to Stravinsky a year or so later, "to try to stop me writing that book, and if I'd listened to you, I'd have been spared a very bitter time that I lived through. I yielded to the temptation of material necessity, and was forced to take the job for no other reason."[44] And Lourié did not forbear to bite the hand that had fed them both: "The one thing that is extremely unpleasant for me about this book is the linking of my name to Koussevitzky's," which may not have been an entirely tactful remark to the composer of the Symphony of Psalms.

As so often in the past, Stravinsky made a few sketches for the new work at the start of January, then had to put it aside because of concert tours. In Berlin, on the nineteenth, he and Vera heard Klemperer conduct *The Magic Flute*, and four days later he played the Capriccio on the stage of the Kroll, in a program that also included the Berlin premiere of *The Fairy's Kiss*, conducted by Klemperer. Later (on the twenty-sixth) he himself conducted *The Fairy's Kiss*, with *Apollo*, in an afternoon concert for the Berlin radio. Then they all set off for Leipzig, where (after sitting stoically through a performance of Wagner's *Rienzi* on the twenty-ninth), he and Klemperer repeated the Capriccio with the Gewandhaus Orchestra the following evening.

Not surprisingly, the serious-minded German critics expressed puzzlement at these latest, apparently soft-centered products of the great avant-gardist. In Berlin Heinrich Strobel talked about "a dangerous reaction," while the Leipzig critic Adolf Aber wrote condescendingly of the composer of Capriccio as no more than "a witty conversationalist."[45] But it is misleading to suggest, as Peter Heyworth does, that Stravinsky's neoclassical works were in general making little headway in Germany. On the contrary, the Capriccio was immediately in demand there, and bookings were restricted mainly by Stravinsky's fee, which was widely regarded as excessive, and by the fact that he usually refused to play and conduct in the same program because he found that rehearsing an orchestra left his hands and arms tired when it came to the concert. In his autumn tour of 1930, in fact, he played the new work in at least six German cities, including Berlin again (under Ansermet), as well as all over Switzerland, in Vienna, and in Brussels. Meanwhile, in Düsseldorf in early February, he conducted the Weisbach Orchestra in a program that included *Apollo*, and was so impressed by their playing that he wrote an appreciative letter about them to the city's Oberbürgermeister.[46]

Rather more exciting, if not on purely musical grounds, was the trip which immediately followed to the Romanian capital, Bucharest, a thirteen-hundred-mile train journey from the Rhineland. Here too he played the Capriccio (under the local conductor, Georges Georgescu, on 12 February), and four days later conducted an exceedingly cautious program of his own works, including the *Scherzo fantastique*, *Fireworks*, and the early Symphony in E-flat, with only the *Petrushka* Suite representing the proper, mature Stravinsky. But if Bucharest was provincial in its appreciation of modern music, it was the hub of the universe when it came to royal personages. It was on this visit (and not in 1925, as he suggests in *Memories and Commentaries*) that there took place the memorable audience with Queen Marie at which Stravinsky shocked the ladies-in-waiting by assuring them that the most interesting spot in Paris was the flea market.[47] He and Vera also had tea with two of Queen Marie's daughters, both of whom were queens in their own right: Elisabetha, the wife of the exiled king of Greece, and Mignon, wife of King Alexander of Yugoslavia. In his self-consciously downbeat reminiscences of royalty, Stravinsky seems to have forgotten about this particular, somewhat Gilbertian repast, superficially so unconnected with the economically ruinous conditions of life in the southeastern reaches of Europe at the start of the 1930s. To add to the sense of unreality, the couple also went to an Oscar Wilde play done in Romanian. Alas, Vera omitted to record (and perhaps simply did not know) which one.[48]

In Prague, on the way home, Stravinsky played the Capriccio under Václav Talich and dined with the quarter-tone composer Alois Hába, which did not prevent him from telling reporters that "I recognize only half-tones as the basis of music. Quarter-tones seem to me simply like glissandos between pairs of half-tones."[49] (Five years before, he had told an American interviewer that the work of composers like Hába sounded to him "like ordinary music just a little off. *Es klingt falsch.* That's all. They try to write the music of the future, strange unheard of combinations, and all they succeed in writing is quarter-tone Brahms.")[50] He also told the Czech reporters about the new work he was writing. It would, he said, be a concise, essentially concentrated composition. "One can't write large-scale movements anymore. . . . A century ago people had plenty of time. But we live today, and have to live our lives accordingly."[51]

This was, of course, supremely true of his own lifestyle. He had originally set aside March for composition, but had been unable to resist an invitation from Reinhart to play in Winterthur and stay at the Rychenberg, which meant three days out of the middle of the month.[52] Thereafter he could settle down for somewhat longer, so that the finale (as it was to be) was completed in draft form before the end of April. But May was then dismembered by the Paris recording sessions for the Capriccio and by recently arranged concerts in Brussels and Amsterdam (including a staged production of *The Soldier's Tale*). Only in June did the summer stretch away in an unbroken line to the autumn horizon, by which time the symphony had to be finished. For a few days he toyed with ideas for Psalm 39 (the eventual first movement), then turned instead to the fugal setting of Psalm 40, which he worked on for a month, so that, as with the Capriccio, the three movements were written in reverse order.[53]

Towards the end of June he went to Paris, where Pleyel had now set him up in a studio at their new Salle Pleyel headquarters at the far end of the rue du Faubourg-Saint Honoré. In the next-door studio Nicolas Nabokov was struggling to write a piece for the new Pleyel harpsichord, and was only too willing to be distracted by Stravinsky's vivid working methods and no less vivid style of relaxation. The row over Diaghilev seems to have been forgotten. They would go and drink café arosé, or eat lunch in the little Russian restaurant in the rue Daru, opposite the Orthodox church. Or they would sight-read Bach cantatas or Handel oratorios four-hands at the piano, to get Stravinsky into the mood for writing his choral symphony. One day, when the choir was rehearsing loudly in the nearby Russian church, Stravinsky was captivated by a mistake the sopranos kept making and hurried to his studio to incorporate it, in stylized form, in the symphony.[54]

Then, in mid-July, Stravinsky again left Paris with Vera. They went to Avignon and Marseilles, after which Stravinsky returned to Nice and bore his family off to a new summer retreat at Charavines-les-Bains, a little resort on the Lac de Paladru in the gentle hill country to the northwest of Grenoble.[55] Here, at the Villa Waddington, he completed the Symphony of Psalms, as he had now decided to call it.[56] Ten days later he went with Theodore and Svetik to the spa town of Plombières-les-Bains in the Vosges and played the symphony through to Koussevitzky and Païchadze "on a saucepan in B-flat [at the casino], since Koussevitzky had no piano in his house(!)";[57] and to Lourié, "who brought Koussevitzky his terrible book, commissioned from him by the latter in the belief that Lourié's pen could immortalise his 'genius.' "

When he commissioned the new symphony, Koussevitzky naturally also bought the world premiere. Stravinsky on his side imposed the condition that the performance must take place by late November 1930 (as he did not want European performances held up by procrastinations at a distance of three thousand miles). But meanwhile the pressure mounted from conductors eager to stage the European premiere. Klemperer wanted it for Berlin, Ansermet for Paris. Stravinsky might well have supported either project. Despite his well-advertised distaste for conductors in general, he had a huge admiration for Klemperer, who made no bones about his enthusiasm for Stravinsky's music, and performed it with attention to his wishes. Between playing his Sonata and Capriccio on Berlin radio on consecutive days in November, Stravinsky went to hear Klemperer conduct Schoenberg at the Kroll, including the world premiere of the Begleitmusik *zu einer Lichtspielszene,* on the very day (the sixth) that the Kroll's impend-ing closure was announced.[58] Then, with his own concerts out of the way, he put in an ostentatious appearance at Klemperer's *Soldier's Tale* and took a bow with him to tumultuous applause. In the next few days, several Berlin papers ran interviews in which Stravinsky expressed his astonish-ment at the Kroll's closure. "In no other city," he told *Tempo,* "have I and my works met with such interest and understanding as in Berlin. For that I have to thank above all Otto Klemperer and the Kroll Opera."[59] To the *Tagebuch* he protested that "I simply can't understand this closure, and don't want to believe it."[60]

But Klemperer missed getting the symphony premiere by a matter of two months, and so did Paris.[61] Monteux's concert in Brussels, which had for a time been a pawn in his gramophone war with Stravinsky, had mean-while devolved onto Ansermet. And with the Boston performance delayed till 19 December, it was here in the Palais des Beaux-Arts on the thirteenth that the composer played his Capriccio and Ansermet conducted what had by the accident of dates become the world premiere of the Symphony of Psalms.

THE AGE OF ANXIETY

WHAT WAS IT THAT INDUCED Stravinsky to turn the Boston commission for a secular symphonic work into a major choral setting of biblical texts? One might fill a chapter with possible answers, both general and specific. The year 1930 was not just the arithmetical terminus of the frivolous, care-free twenties, nor was the Wall Street crash a merely symbolic end to the bubble of optimism on which the developed world had apparently been floating since the end of the war. If a sudden rash of religious or quasi-religious choral works is in some imponderable way evidence of anxiety, then anxiety was in the air when Bartók composed his *Cantata profana* and Stravinsky his Symphony of Psalms in 1930, or Hindemith his oratorio *Das Unaufhörliche* in 1931. But with Stravinsky at least one hardly needs the Zeitgeist to help explain what was not just a predictable, but a pre-dicted, turn in his artistic evolution. Boris de Schloezer's remark that the logical successor to *Apollon musagète* would be a Mass[1] was largely, if not literally, vindicated by the symphony; and nobody who was on visiting terms with the Stravinskys in Nice had any business to be surprised at any-thing in general about the new work except, perhaps, that it had been so long in coming.

The anxiety which, for the world, was such a weighty consequence of the economic crash of October 1929 had been with Stravinsky almost ever since he could remember. For him and his family it was the inevitable companion of their exile. It was made worse by their own ill health, and by the misfortunes of those who were forever knocking on their door. The death of Diaghilev had left them more exposed, psychologically if not financially, than at any period since the Revolution. But something else had been gnawing at their existence for almost the whole of that time, the agonizing issue of the composer's divided emotional life. Craft implies, without quite stating, that it was a sense of guilt at his infidelity that pro-vided the soil for Stravinsky's growing need for religious consolation in the mid-twenties.[2] He also suggests that it was Katya as much as Igor who, in her ailing and abandoned state, turned fervently to the church for solace and reassurance. Certainly Katya became increasingly pious during the thirties. But the paraphernalia of religion also started to matter to him. By the late twenties he was becoming wedded to religious objects. Icons appeared on his piano alongside Katya's photograph, and it was in this context that he had asked Diaghilev to bring him back icons from Mount Athos in 1928.3 Four year later he compiled an inventory of fifty such objects which he had lent to the Russian church in Nice, and of which it seems the parish was claiming ownership.4 The parish priest, Father Nikolay Podosenov, whom Stravinsky later described as "practically a member of our household during a period of five years,"5 had been summarily suspended by the metropolitan, and Igor and Katya (by that time no longer living in Nice) were supporting him by insisting on the return of the objects unless Father Nikolay was reinstated. "I intended eventually," the composer claimed, "to build a chapel at my home, after which I would want these objects restored for my own use there. . . . I have not abandoned my project."6 No chapel was ever built. But the Stravinsky house remained a place of icons, votary candles, and sacred relics. And for a time at least, the family attended church regularly. On Russian Good Friday (10 April) 1931, Stravinsky wrote to Païchadze that he expected to be at church all day.

So far as his creative work was concerned, the impact of such things was surprisingly modest. Sketches might be dated by the church calendar. But of conventional piety there is barely a trace in the actual music, even in an unassuming liturgical piece like the Lord's Prayer, which was in fact his only setting of a sacred text before the Symphony of Psalms. The crucial point here is that while the family devotions were exclusively Orthodox in tone and content, artistically and intellectually Stravinsky was, from the moment he settled in France, under Catholic influences. There were several reasons for this. For a musician, an important one might be that since musical instruments were not allowed in the Orthodox Church, there was no Russian tradition of accompanied sacred music, though since the Lord's Prayer is unaccompanied and the symphony is not liturgical, this had apparently not yet been an issue for Stravinsky in 1930. What *had* been an issue, as we have seen, was the question of intellectual lineage. Reading Maritain in the early twenties, he had been reading into a theological tradition that stretched back in a continuous line to the Middle Ages and beyond, by implication, to Aristotle. And because Maritain's writing was both historically based and alert to the problems of modern sensibility, it seemed to offer solid, authoritative spiritual answers to contemporary aesthetic questions. *Art et scolastique* had argued that the instability in late-nineteenth-century Catholic thought and late-romantic art had common causes and a common antidote, which amounted to the deindividualization of personal expression and the return to a quasi-medieval ideal of humility and anonymity, and a divine concept of order.

Whatever the other sources of neoclassicism, and however ambiguously it may have fulfilled Maritain's aims, it thus had from the start a spiritual, even devotional, dimension which was only half-obscured by the cool objectivity of its typical early products. That Stravinsky's first public performance of his Piano Sonata should have taken place only by courtesy of a "miracle" cure showed, if nothing else, that clinical music did not necessarily imply mechanistic explanations. Soon, in *Oedipus Rex* and *Apollo*, neoclassicism was openly making its peace with the irrational, with passion and fear, and, at the end of *Apollo*, with a mysterious, otherworldly purity that Schloezer was quick to see as an intimation of the sacramental. No doubt the Symphony of Psalms was not quite what the critic had in mind when he predicted that Stravinsky would compose a Mass. He grasped the link between Stravinsky's "thirst for renunciation, his need of purity and serenity"[7] and the specifically religious impulse. But he failed to point out the connection in the composer's mind between that impulse and the concept of order which Stravinsky was now placing at the forefront of his creative code. "The more you cut yourself off from the canons of the Christian Church," he told a Belgian interviewer while at work on the symphony,

> the more you cut yourself off from the truth. These canons are as true for the composition of an orchestra as they are for the life of an individual. They are the only place where order is practiced to the full: not a speculative, artificial order, but the divine order which is given to us and which must reveal itself as much in the inner life as in its exteriorization in painting, music, etc. It's the struggle against anarchy, not so much disorder as the absence of order. I'm an advocate of architecture in art, since architecture is the embodiment of order; creative work is a protest against anarchy and nonexistence. Suicide is the greatest sin, because it despairs of order and returns to that nonexistence from which God has rescued us for the sake of and by means of form. The absence of order, and suicide, are a protest against God.[8]

The Symphony of Psalms, then, was his gesture of solidarity with the divine order: antique songs of praise cast into the grandest of modern classical forms.

In fact the symphony, scored for an orchestra without violins or violas, is hardly classical in actual design at all, but owes more to the organizing principles of the high baroque, and particularly Bach. This is most obvious in the superb double fugue of the second movement (the orchestra plays one fugue, the choir sings the other). But it also comes out in the thematic organization of the whole work, which is more concentrated than anything

Stravinsky had ever written before. Almost everything hinges on one or two melodic intervals and figures, reiterated over and over again in such unvarying patterns that a kind of sublime monotony emerges as the controlling idea of the symphony, reaching its climax in the final verses of Psalm 150, where a three-in-a-bar setting of the words swings along against a four-beat figure in the bass repeated more than thirty times without any variation. The music seems to float, in defiance of tonal and rhythmic gravity. As usual with Stravinsky, the whole effect has astonishing economy and precision. "Never have self-pity," he had told Nabokov that summer in Paris. "Never give in to any kind of self-indulgence when you compose. Approximations won't do in music. To compose is like shooting darts—one has to hit the O right in the middle. All the rest does not mean anything at all."9

Stravinsky arrived in Brussels for the first performance at the end of an exhausting autumn concert tour. It had begun in early October in Basle, where he appeared for the first time playing the Capriccio with the twenty-four-year-old Paul Sacher's Basle Chamber Orchestra. Later there had been a string of German concerts in Vera's company, including in Wiesbaden—the Streckers' hometown—and Frankfurt, where he played the Capriccio with Hans Rosbaud and talked about it in a radio interview. Rosbaud impressed him. "I led our final rehearsal with great satisfaction," he wrote to Katya. "The conductor here is very good and a good musician, and he has this not yet very solid orchestra, which has existed for only a year, well in hand."10 In Vienna, five days later, he gave the same work under Martin Spanjaard, who "evidently is no sort of conductor and, judging from the time I spent with him at lunch and at rehearsals, is the most uncultivated man I have ever met."11 Five days after that he played the Capriccio in Nuremberg, his eleventh performance on the tour, then finished it by conducting in Mannheim on 9 December.

The spa town of Wiesbaden in late October was as usual an island of repose in this lucrative but somewhat manic progress. Willy Strecker had had the idea that Stravinsky should write a violin concerto which Schott would publish, and he had invited Samuel Dushkin to dine with them all in Wiesbaden and discuss the idea. Dushkin was a bright, boyish-looking thirty-nine-year-old Polish-born Jew, more recently a pupil of Auer in New York, and now a naturalized American and the adopted son of the American composer Blair Fairchild. The two musicians hit it off at once, and the next day (the twenty-seventh) the composer made his first jottings for the new concerto. The idea, of course, was that Dushkin would advise Stravinsky, who was not a string player, on the technical aspects of writing for solo violin. He would be David to Stravinsky's Mendelssohn, Joachim to his Brahms.12 Strecker had promised that Dushkin was no idiot virtuoso, but a cultivated and dedicated musician of intelligence. And so Stravinsky found.[13] They all met again in Nuremberg and drew up a contract under which Stravinsky agreed, for 7,000 dollars and a ten percent royalty, to conduct the first eight performances of the concerto for no further fee, while Dushkin got 250 dollars for the premiere plus a two-year exclusivity. Strecker still had to square Païchadze, Stravinsky's contract publisher, whose finances, however, were becoming so precarious that it suited him to pass up the occasional work by this expensive and demanding genius. Meanwhile, the composer, accustomed as he was to dealing with a Paris-based publisher not well placed to fix performances of new works, blithely offered the concerto premiere to his friend Sam Bottenheim, Mengelberg's secretary at the Concertgebouw in Amsterdam, unaware that Strecker was no less blithely offering it to the Berlin radio. Berlin, Strecker insisted when he heard of the double booking, would make bigger waves on Stravinsky's behalf (perhaps he meant that they would make more trouble if jilted).[14] No doubt there was some national bias in this view. On the face of it, Stravinsky had more to lose at the Concertgebouw, whose committee was planning a Stravinsky festival of three concerts around the concerto premiere but who, when they heard they were losing the premiere, promptly cancelled the entire festival. But Strecker stuck to his guns, and Stravinsky had to content himself with squeezing an extra 250 dollars out of Berlin. As for Amsterdam, the only trace left by the concerto was a sketch on the composer's bill at Brack's Doelen Hotel.[15]

This incident did nothing to ease his growing sense of insecurity over the question of German concerts. After the Amsterdam cancellation in March 1931, he was soon grumbling to Strecker about the shortage of bookings in German cities.[16] Strecker, for his part, had been warning him against his habit of multiplying concert agents and setting them into competition with one another[17] (Stravinsky had even used a secondary Paris agent, Lola Bossan, for his Berlin concert bookings in 1930, after which he spent several months trying to extract her commission from her Berlin opposite number.) Strecker was also desperately anxious that he should moderate his fee, or at least accept it at a fixed rate of German marks, rather than in U.S. dollars, whose mark equivalent was constantly rising. Star performers from abroad could still, he admitted, command these high fees, but only to the detriment of native musicians, who were finding it harder and harder to get bookings at all.[18] Behind these anxieties, of course, loomed the calamitous situation of the German economy, which was close to bankruptcy when, in June 1931, the American president, Herbert Hoover, proposed his one-year moratorium on German war reparations. As yet the political consequences of economic collapse barely figured in Strecker's admonitions (beyond dark hints that they "would be impossible to assess"),[19] and it was enough that he managed to persuade

Stravinsky to appear in several German towns in the autumn and winter of 1931–32 for significantly reduced fees.[20] But Païchadze saw and reported the situation on the streets as well as behind the scenes:

> Virtually all life in Germany has come to a standstill, since nobody has any money. The shops are empty. . . . The theatres, restaurants, cinemas, and even the bars, are deserted. Traffic in the streets is a third of what it was last year. . . . In a word, the outward feeling is utterly cheerless. . . . The atmosphere there certainly isn't going to clear, and the next months are bound to be fraught with incident. I won't detail to you the vicious circle in which the German economy now finds itself. . . . The important thing is that the Germans themselves see no way out of it, and the other Powers won't make up their minds to give them effective aid. To my mind, this is the total downfall of Versailles. . . . The present situation in the German economy is the basis of an intense struggle among the political parties, complicated by the fact that there is no combination of programs that can produce a reasonable government majority. Now the nationalists are gaining strength in the country, and the struggle in the coming period will be between them and the social-democratic center, though who knows whether in the end they won't be split by the communists, who've so far kept to one side but are a significant force there. Pray God I'm wrong, but it seems to me that if present circumstances don't change, we must expect explosions there by the year's end.[21]

As for Stravinsky, he was left to brood on the expense of maintaining two grown-up but dependent sons in Paris, a by no means abstemious mistress on tour, and a lavish household in the south of France, with the whole basis of his income under threat.

The French capital, as it happened, was treating him comparatively well this year. Just before Christmas, he had performed his Piano Concerto for Robert Siohan's Association des Concerts Siohan (founded in 1929). Then in February he played the Capriccio in a Straram concert conducted by Ansermet, and four days later (on the twenty-fourth) himself conducted this same orchestra in the French premiere of the Symphony of Psalms in the Théâtre des Champs-Elysées. The symphony, which had been greeted with puzzled respect in Brussels and the usual benign condescension in America (one Boston reviewer suggested illuminatingly that "the music seems on a first hearing to have been written in the composer's own musical language, as the best musical expression he could contrive of the meaning of the text"),[22] made a powerful impression on Paris critics who had not always in the past been willing to respond to Stravinsky's flights of eschatology. "The Capriccio aroused our interest," wrote one, "the Psalms brought tears to our eyes."[23] The music's effect, suggested another (perhaps remembering an earlier Stravinsky premiere in the Champs-Elysées), "seems to work not only through its violent impact on the physique, but also on those more elevated regions of the being not much attended to by the music of our time."[24] Boris de Schloezer, apparently disturbed by the force of such an overtly religious yet dispassionate work, went home and tried laboriously to talk himself (and his readers) out of it. "I freely admit," he wrote,

> that I entirely shared the enthusiasm of the great majority of the audience and was at once subjugated by the power and splendor of this music. But when I began to study the piano score the next day, I not only could not rediscover my initial impression . . . but could not even explain to myself, or even remotely understand, how Stravinsky had managed to achieve the sublime, and make seem rich and generous a music that was in reality strangely dry and poverty-stricken. . . . We certainly have no right to doubt for an instant the sincerity of the feeling that prompted the Symphony of Psalms; but it must be said that Stravinsky is turning to religious music and devoting his art to God precisely at the moment when that art is becoming *decorative* and, in repudiation of what has hitherto constituted its real value, seeming to aim increasingly at external effect. There is here a truly tragic contradiction which no theory, no technique can conceal.[25]

But the contradiction, blatantly, was de Schloezer's own, in trying to conceal the music's admitted impact behind arguments that were, precisely, theoretical and technical. He simply could not believe that a religious impulse of such force could "express" itself so unemotionally—in a sense, so impersonally. Thirty years later, Ansermet himself would try to explain away a similar anxiety by suggesting that "the signification of the Symphony of Psalms . . . is the religiosity of others, that of the imaginary choir of which the choir which actually sings is the *analogon* . . . Such is Stravinsky's art and the sense he has of the expressivity of musical images, that he is capable of signifying religiosity without its expressing his own feeling."[26] But the composer himself had a simpler explanation, which he gave to a reporter in Trieste two months after the Paris performance. "Individualism in art, philosophy, and religion," he observed, "implies a state of revolt against God. Look at Nietzsche's Antichrist. The principle of individualism, and of atheism, is contrary to the principle of personality and subordination before God: in the former we find the supermen, in the latter we recognize men."[27]

Stravinsky had somehow let himself in for no fewer than four winter crossings of the English Channel, on the first of which, on 26 January, Vera was violently sick (her diary gratefully records a "good crossing" on the way back a week later).[28] Normally so careful about dates, Stravinsky had got himself caught between the bureaucratic inflexibility of the BBC, for whom he was booked to play the Piano Concerto at the end of January, and the patrician determination of Mrs. Samuel Courtauld, wife of the textiles tycoon, who wanted Stravinsky for her Courtauld-Sargent series in March and knew how, through a combination of charm and bossiness, to get her way. More than a year before, the composer had promised her the British premiere of the Capriccio, but he had also (or so she claimed) promised not to appear anywhere else in London that season before March. So when it reached her ears that he was playing for the BBC in January at a public concert in the Queen's Hall (where her own concerts took place), she made her distress so plain that the usually hard-nosed composer was forced into a, for him, positively abject apology and the consoling offer of the British premiere of the Symphony of Psalms (admittedly he offered it to the BBC as well; but Mrs. Courtauld was equal to that complication, and undertook to pull the necessary strings while also calmly accepting Stravinsky's counteroffer of the Violin Concerto). In fact she won every trick. She even overrode Stravinsky's routine objection to playing (the Capriccio) and conducting *(The Firebird)* in the same program, on two consecutive nights, and then swept away any possible rancor by inviting him and Theodore to stay in her house. By the time Igor and Vera left London after their January visit, he and Mrs. Courtauld were already, he told Strecker, firm friends.[29] A month later, just before his arrival back in London for her concerts, she wrote to assure him that she wouldn't forget "the diet and the Café Hag."[30]

There was still an old-fashioned grandeur about London hospitality. In January Igor and Vera dined with the Courtaulds at their house in Portman Square with Klemperer, who was conducting Beethoven's "Choral" Symphony in the Courtauld series a few nights later, as fellow guest. They went to tea with Margot Asquith. They lunched with Igor's old friend Lord Berners. But artistically London was starting to modernize itself. The January 28 concert was his first experience of the brilliant new BBC Symphony Orchestra, which Ansermet conducted in a full-blown Stravinsky program, including *Apollo, The Rite of Spring,* and the Four Studies, as well as the concerto. Edwin Evans, who had been irritating the composer with demands for program-note information in advance, thought the strings in *Apollo* "a truly wonderful body," while the performance of *The Rite* was "magnificent."[31]

London also now offered other, "alternative" musical experiences. Some months earlier, Stravinsky had been approached by the bandleader Jack Hylton with a general request for permission to arrange his music for jazz band, to which he had responded with the suggestion that *Mavra* might offer suitable material for the attentions of Hylton's arranger, Billy Ternent. Curiously enough, Hylton did not balk at this surprising (if not wholly illogical, in view of the work's jazz elements) idea, and the day after the BBC concert Stravinsky and Ansermet attended a session in which Hylton conducted, and probably recorded, the duet and quartet from the opera arranged for band without voices. What this performance can have been like one can only guess. The players were of top quality, but Hylton, though used to arrangements of classical music, had little or no experience of conducting music like Stravinsky's in variable meter, and according to one of the players could not in fact do so. Nonetheless, he included the *Mavra* items in a concert given by his band in the unlikely surroundings of the Paris Opéra three weeks after the London session, a concert Stravinsky attended. And perhaps a recording would have been issued if Columbia had not got wind of it and insisted that the composer not allow his name to be associated with it. Stravinsky duly dispatched a stern letter to the bandleader to that effect.[32]

Columbia may well have been influenced in their attitude by the fact that the maestro was at that moment about to record the Symphony of Psalms for them in Paris; in fact the recording was made in the Théâtre des Champs-Elysées in mid-February a week before the concert premiere there, and of course with the same performers. The day had not yet come when to be connected with popular commercial music could help promote a classical composer, particularly the composer of so quintessentially lofty and serious a masterpiece.

As for the recording of the symphony, it was the most important Stravinsky made in these early years, being uninhibited by technical limitations (unlike his early recordings of the ballets) and so supporting his claim that a composer's recording of his own work is an authoritative document of its performance style. Modern Western taste would perhaps now reject the swooping portamenti of the Alexis Vlassov Choir. But this is to some extent a measure of how far Stravinsky's neoclassical works have drifted away, in the modern perception, from their Russian origins (and been partly neutered, some would say, in the process). Quite apart from the Russianisms that, according to Stravinsky himself, lay behind the setting of the Latin text,[33] several aspects of the work's harmony and rhythm hark back almost nostalgically to a time when he was composing Russian texts and Russian scenarios. They are an artistic correlative of the choir rehearsing in the Orthodox church in the rue Daru, or even of the Russian lunches with Nabokov, with their *pirozhki* and *côtelettes Pozharski*, in the little restaurant opposite.[34]

In Paris, amid all this to-ing and fro-ing between the French and

English capitals, Stravinsky saw a lot of Dushkin and talked about the technical aspects of the new Violin Concerto. Here the emphasis must have been somewhat different. Dushkin's role, before all else, was to mediate between Stravinsky's strongly developed style and method and the needs and possibilities of a conservatory-trained violin virtuoso. "Stravinsky's music," he wrote later, "is so original and so personal that it constantly posed new problems of technique and sound for the violin. These problems often touched the very core of the composition itself and led to most of our discussions."35 Dushkin's story of the three-note violin chord which Stravinsky wanted as an opening gesture for each movement is emblematic of the relationship at this early stage.

> I had never a seen a chord with such an enormous stretch, from the "E" to the top "A," and I said, "No." Stravinsky said sadly, "Quel dommage." ("What a pity.") After I got home, I tried it, and, to my astonishment, I found that in that register the stretch of the eleventh was relatively easy to play, and the sound fascinated me. I telephoned Stravinsky at once to tell him that it could be done. When the concerto was finished, more than six months later, I understood his disappointment when I first said, "No." This chord, in a different dress, begins each of the four movements. Stravinsky himself calls it his "passport" to that concerto.36

Not till the second week of March did Stravinsky get back to Nice and begin serious work on the concerto. All the same, by the end of the month the first movement was complete, and the second would doubtless have followed quickly but for a conducting date in Trieste on 24 April, to which he saw fit to append a week-long holiday with Vera. From Trieste to Venice they went by seaplane (Vera's first flight, Igor's second or third). In Venice they visited Diaghilev's grave, then drifted back through northern Italy, reaching Nice only at the very end of April. Dushkin was staying at Antibes, visiting the composer to discuss the concerto as it was written, and even sometimes taking the violin part away for correction or revision in the light of the instrument's technical needs. His task was unenviable. He had to make effective bravura out of ideas that might lie awkwardly for the violin, but without compromising the ideas themselves. If Stravinsky accepted an alteration, he would insist on recomposing the passage in question. "He behaved like an architect who if asked to change a room on the third floor had to go down to the foundations to keep the proportions of his whole structure."37 If he rejected it, he would say, "You remind me of a salesman at the Galeries Lafayette. You say, 'Isn't this brilliant, isn't this exquisite, look at the beautiful colors, everybody's wearing it.' I say, 'Yes, it

is brilliant, it is beautiful, everyone is wearing it—I don't want it.' "
Dushkin soon noticed how incorruptible Stravinsky was where his musical ideas were concerned. He had a religious attitude to inspiration. Just as
he had warned Nabokov against self-indulgence and the temptation to
make do with approximations and quick solutions, so he talked to Dushkin about the need for patience and faith. "The waiting in anguish is the
price we must pay." And yet even so the divine solution might in the end
be a return to the original idea. "First ideas are very important. They come
from God. And if after working and working and working, I return to these
ideas, then I know they're good."[38]

In this way the first three movements were composed by the second
week of June, well on schedule for the Berlin premiere in late October. By
the twelfth he had started the finale. But he was restless and far from well.
He had a severe liver infection and had been on a ferocious diet for
months. As usual, he worried unduly about money: the German situation,
the boys in Paris, the Belyankins. In a crotchety moment, he had complained bitterly to Ira about her father's improvidence, a complaint that
she not unnaturally passed on.[39] And now, to add insult to injury, he was
being pressed for payment by his Volhynian lawyer to pursue a court
award on his old Rovno mortgage, which, in the unlikely event of its being
paid back in full, would be worth barely a tenth of the value of his property
in Nice.[40] A few days after starting the concerto finale, he took a train to
Grenoble, with the idea of looking for a house for the summer in the Charavines region they had liked so much the year before. What he found was a
miniature "château" called La Vironnière—really a large family house in a
two-acre park—on the outskirts of the little town of Voreppe, between
Grenoble and Charavines. Soon afterwards he went to Paris. On Bastille
Day (14 July), he and Vera celebrated their tenth "anniversary." They called
on Nadia Boulanger at Gargenville and presumably talked about Svetik—
his piano playing and his unfortunate engagement. Gradually the idea was
forming of selling up in Nice and moving to Paris. After settling the family
in at Voreppe, Stravinsky was soon back in the capital, having a heart-to-
heart ("explanations," her diary calls it)[41] with Vera; and the next day they
drove out of Paris to look at houses in the countryside there.

What was going on? Was he wavering between on the one hand bringing his entire family to Paris and settling them in the outskirts, and on the
other hand simply shifting his own base there? What was the heart-to-
heart about? It perhaps centered on Vera's future situation as the composer's part-time mistress, a situation which, for all the extended tours and
smiling photographs, must have made her deeply frustrated and miserable. But unfortunately her diary entries are too cursory and matter-of-fact
for the reader to do more than guess what lay behind this or that meeting,
this or that excursion. At Voreppe, Igor was rediscovering the joys of home

country life in summertime. He had his studio in the attic of La Vironnière, from where he could look down the broad valley of the Isère to Grenoble, nine miles to the southeast. The little walled park had broad gravel paths, a stone fountain with a recumbent greyhound on a plinth, and tall trees under which the family often took their meals. Behind, the woods rose precipitously to the Rocher de Chalves; in the slope on the upper edge of the park was an old orangery, and, among the trees beyond, a sinister grotto with an iron grille.[42] "I like this slightly wild landscape," he told Heinrich Strobel, who came to interview him in August. "Each morning I drink a glass of water and walk in the park. It is very healthy."[43] In fact he liked it so much—and felt so healthy—that he decided after all not to move to Paris but to stay put at Voreppe. So the rest of the family's belongings were summoned from Nice, and the Villa des Roses quietly ceased to be home after seven years, Igor's longest stay at a single address since the Kryukov Canal.

Early in September, he at last completed the Violin Concerto, "among half unpacked trunks and boxes and the coming and going of removers, upholsterers, electricians and plumbers."[44] Dushkin was again installed locally, working on what Stravinsky called his definitive version of the solo part.[45] Three days after completing the short score of the finale (on the twelfth), the composer suddenly decided to give the movements generic titles to help the audience grasp their essential character.[46] The Berlin premiere was now less than six weeks away, and they were both—composer and violinist alike—getting agitated: Dushkin, of course, because the time was short for him to prepare what would surely be the most important concert of his career so far; Stravinsky for less tangible reasons to do with lingering irritation at the loss of his Amsterdam concerts and the fact that the Symphony of Psalms, which was also to have figured in the Berlin program, was now looking doubtful because of problems with the chorus. He begged Strecker to try to rescue the symphony: "It was the one German concert this season whose program interested me," he complained. "It's really discouraging for me always to conduct the same things while seeing others conduct—'interpret'—my works." Yet the Berlin program remained enterprising, with the new concerto alongside *Apollo* and *Petrushka* (which, moreover, Stravinsky had insisted on keeping even though—or perhaps because—Furtwängler of all "interpreters" had conducted it in Berlin less than a fortnight before).[47]

But his temper was hardly improved by a letter from Païchadze ticking him off for his lack of candor, as Païchadze saw it, over the question of whether he wanted Edition Russe to continue publishing his music. This was presumably a response to Stravinsky's surely mischievous inquiry as to whether Païchadze could guarantee him (that is, pay him as a retainer) three thousand to five thousand dollars "for the purchase of a large-scale composition that I propose to work on after finishing the Violin Concerto."[48] He knew perfectly well that ERM, having just brought out the Symphony of Psalms, were in no position to underwrite a new work on such a scale, whatever it might be (a question he himself probably could not have answered); and perhaps he realized that his bluff had been called. At any rate, Païchadze's homily went unanswered for several weeks; and then poor Svetik was detailed to cover the paternal tracks. "My father's nerves," he wrote, "have been very tense lately. He's off to Germany not much reassured by the letters he's been getting from those parts and in a state of great unease which gives him not a day of respite."[49]

And yet there seem to have been no grounds for disquiet. Stravinsky was conducting first in Oslo, his first visit to the city. But when he got to Berlin, on the twentieth, everything was in good order, and three days later the broadcast concert, including the concerto premiere, went off with spectacular success in a jam-packed Philharmonie.[50] The critics rightly drew attention to the contrast in style between the concerto and the Symphony of Psalms, which Berlin had heard for the first time under Klemperer in February (two days after the Paris premiere). Klemperer had used the single word "Ravenna" to encapsulate the austere splendor of the symphony.[51] The concerto, by contrast, universally conjured up the name "Bach." It was a concertante work in which the solo part was not so much dominant as first among equals, and yet, paradoxically, it was rich in virtuosity and much more traditional violinistically than anything Stravinsky had written before (Dushkin's role in editing the solo part appears not to have been generally known). The violin would sometimes vanish into the structure, Alfred Einstein suggested, "even if the player had at his disposal a bigger, more cutting tone than the otherwise very musical and virtuoso-trained Samuel Dushkin."[52] This impression may partly have been due to problems of balance in the hall. Dushkin himself complained that he had been drowned by the trumpets,[53] and Ansermet later reported that while on the radio the violin had been if anything too prominent, friends who were at the concert had told him that it was too weak.[54] In general, though the Berlin critics mostly treated Stravinsky with implicit respect, there was a feeling that this was one of his lightweight pieces: "far from pure intellectualism . . . a small-scale, amusing, incredibly witty music of inspired refinement, music of a thousand touches, and scored as only Stravinsky knows how."[55] "Nobody but Stravinsky," Einstein agreed, "could write such a piece today." And, perhaps to his own surprise, he seems to have meant it as a compliment. But the xenophobic right-wing press was beginning to line up ominously against what it saw as Stravinsky's distortion of traditional German values. Fritz Stege called the concerto "a desecration of Bach . . . which, beneath the makeup of French civilization, reveals clearly enough the savagery of half-Asiatic instincts."[56]

The Berlin performance was swiftly followed by several more in north-ern Germany, with an excursion back to London for Mrs. Courtauld and a return to Paris in mid-December for the French premiere in the Salle Pleyel on the seventeenth.[57] On the day Stravinsky got to Paris, he went to hear Roger Désormière conduct *The Rite of Spring* at the Salle Gaveau, along with Satie's *Parade* and a new ballet score by Igor Markevitch called *Rébus*. With its Diaghilev thread, it was one of those modern concerts that attract a literary, arty audience. Cocteau arrived "bedecked in enormous, thick white gloves," Raïssa Maritain noted in her diary, adding melodra-matically that "death enters with him," in the person of Jean Desbordes, Cocteau's lover (detested by the Maritains), who has become "thin and scrawny, and looks as if he has been sicker than Cocteau."[58] Cocteau had recently embarked on a completely new career as a filmmaker, but his first and perhaps most remarkable film, *Le Sang d'un poète* (with Desbordes in a minor role), had been held up by the censor, apparently in retaliation against the anticlericalism of the recently shown Dali-Buñuel *L'Age d'or*, which had the same backer, Charles de Noailles. André Schaeffner, whose book on Stravinsky was just out, had told him in July that Cocteau had can-celled a private showing and withdrawn the film for revision for fear that its "scabrous passages . . . might offend your 'religion.' "[59] But Schaeffner had allowed himself to fall for one of Cocteau's canards. In fact the film had been withdrawn at the Noailles' insistence, because they themselves were shown in a stage box applauding a suicide, and were insisting that the scene be remade. It was eventually shown publicly in January 1932, a month or so after the Salle Gaveau concert. But whether or not Stravinsky saw it, nobody knows.[60]

Back in Voreppe at Christmas, he was already contemplating a new work for Dushkin, this time a recital piece with piano that they could play together without all the complications of booking and rehearsing an orchestra. Dushkin said later that the recital idea was Stravinsky's.[61] But it may equally have been suggested, after the early concerto performances, by agents who wanted to engage the two musicians together but could not provide an orchestra or make dates coincide. Their first recital appearance together was in Milan at the end of March, and at this point repertoire was a problem; they played the Violin Concerto with piano accompaniment and the old 1925 Kochanski suite (from *Pulcinella*), but to make a whole program Stravinsky had also to play his Piano Sonata and Dushkin a Bach sonata, the new duo being far from ready. For some reason, the suite must also have dissatisfied him, since he soon embarked on a new arrangement of movements from *Pulcinella* which was similar in content (with one brief extra movement), but noticeably different in technique—in fact, the tech-nical differences suggest that Dushkin may not have been well suited by, or may even have disliked, the violin writing in the old version. The new *Suite italienne,* as it was called, brings the violin farther forward as a melody instrument and generally makes less play with special string effects. Yet oddly enough, after making this arrangement in the summer of 1932, he then quickly composed a similar (though by no means identical) suite for the cellist Gregor Piatigorsky, in which the cello writing is once again more spectacular.[62] A comparison of these three *Pulcinella* suites lends strong support to Dushkin's remark that Stravinsky was uninterested in routine arranging but always wanted "to go back to the essence of the music and rewrite or recreate the music in the spirit of the new instrument."[63]

Composing a new violin-piano duo presented quite another set of problems. He had never written an original piece of any kind for a stringed instrument with piano, and in fact in his autobiography, written only two or three years later, he admits that he had never much liked the combination, and only came round to it as a result of working with Dushkin.[64] He also claims, more bizarrely, that Charles-Albert Cingria's study of Petrarch, "which had just appeared and which had greatly delighted me," was an important source of general ideas for the new duo. He quotes Cingria's concept of the relationship between lyricism and discipline, and adds that "my object was to create a lyrical composition, a work of musical versification, and I was more than ever experiencing the advantage of a rigorous discipline which gives a taste for the craft and the satisfaction of being able to apply it."[65] Critics have expressed puzzlement at this remark, since the Duo Concertant is only an intermittently lyrical work and not, by Stravinsky's standards, a particularly rigorous one. Even the usually loyal Eric Walter White admits that "it is best to put Stravinsky's various explanations on one side and accept the work at its musical face value."[66] In fact Cingria's *Pétrarque* was not even published by the time the Duo had its first performance, in October 1932, and Stravinsky received his inscribed copy only in December. The book undoubtedly influenced his work; but not yet and not this one.[67] More plausible and interesting is his remark to a Budapest press conference a few months later that the Duo was "created under the influence of Virgil's pastoral idylls."[68] Two of the eventual five movements are called Eglogue, while the finale, though a dithyrambe by name, is entirely gentle and reflective in character. Stravinsky even suggests, in his autobiography, that he thought of the whole work as a "musical parallel to the old pastoral poetry."[69] The link is doubly intriguing because of the very strong Greek-pastoral element in his next, much more ambitious score, a work whose subject was not his idea but the librettist's.

If a busy concert schedule had ever in the past had a disruptive effect on Stravinsky's creative style (which seems very doubtful), then one would certainly be entitled to adduce some such explanation for the remarkable stylistic diversity of the Duo Concertant. No sooner had he got going on the Cantilène first movement (a piece he years later described to Szigeti as "extrèmement travaillé")[70] than he was off again for concerts in Paris and London. For the first time ever, he conducted another pianist (Jacques Février) in one of his own piano concertos, the Capriccio (Salle Pleyel, 24 January), then three days later played this same work himself under Ansermet in a BBC concert in the Queen's Hall, his sixth appearance there in twelve months. Six weeks later he was in Antwerp and Brussels, from where he went direct to Italy and for the first time conducted in Venice (at La Fenice) and Florence, before going on to Milan for the Dushkin recital. As if all this were not enough, he then drove to Paris at the start of May to record the Suite from *The Soldier's Tale,* the Octet, and two movements from *Pulcinella,* returning to Voreppe in the middle of the month. On top of everything he had planned a trip to Buenos Aires in the summer, and even got so far as to consult Strecker on the most discreet way of travelling with Vera without causing gossip on the boat or outrage among the notoriously prim Argentines.[71] How he would have reconciled all this travel with writing the large-scale composition for which he had sought backing from Païchadze is a matter for speculation. But perhaps fortunately, in any case, the South American trip fell through, and he was able to spend the interstices of the summer finishing off the Duo (which surely was not that composition) and working with Dushkin on the *Suite italienne* and the other arrangements, from *Firebird, Petrushka,* and *The Nightingale,* which he needed to make up the whole program the two of them had been planning since the Milan début.[72]

In June he stayed at Voreppe long enough to celebrate his fiftieth birthday on the eighteenth with his family, and long enough for a visit of several days from Rosbaud to discuss a two-concert Stravinsky festival Rosbaud was conducting in Frankfurt in honor of that same event. On the actual birthday, photographs were taken in the park: Igor alone, Igor with his mother, Igor with his daughters, Igor with his sons, Igor with Katya (Igor, who liked gadgets, had an automatic shutter release for his camera, which it may have amused him to try out on an occasion like this).[73] But if the now famous composer expected or hoped for an inundation of birthday greetings, he was disappointed. Writing a month later to thank Ansermet for *his* telegram, he complained bitterly that he had had "plenty of letters and telegrams from Germany . . . but only two from Paris—Pleyel and Schaeffner!!! It's true, I'm forgetting that France is my second homeland."[74] In fact there were at least three from Paris, since Nadia Boulanger, the most indefatigable marker of dates, not only wrote but also promised a present of sufficiently embarrassing proportions for Stravinsky to write back imploring her "not to do anything silly to find me things I adore passionately but which, in these sinister times, are prohibitive for us musicians. Let's leave such things to the rich, if there are any."[75]

The day after his birthday, the supposedly poverty-stricken composer took a train to Chalon-sur-Saône, where he joined up with Vera and Nouvel for a celebratory trip to Frankfurt to hear the second Rosbaud concert on the twenty-third (*Mavra* and *Oedipus Rex*) with the radio orchestra, after which the three of them drove slowly back to Paris by way of Heidelberg and Alsace. Whether or not this was a gastronomic tour for Vera and Valechka, Igor was still on a diet and would have had to content himself with the physical grandeur of the Great Tun at Heidelberg, which he had first seen on his visit to the Rimsky-Korsakovs thirty years before, and the aesthetic riches of Grünewald and Schongauer in Colmar and the great cathedral in Strasbourg. When they got to Paris, he checked in for a colitis cure at Hérissy, near Fontainebleau,[76] and only got back to Voreppe a week later. He at last finished the Duo Concertant a week after that, on 15 July. Then within a month he was off again, this time taking four days to drive with Vera across the south of France to Biarritz, where he conducted a single concert in the casino on the twenty-fifth. Then they wended their way to Paris with Blaise Cendrars and his wife, in extremely leisurely fashion, and with numerous socializing calls on the way.[77] Not long afterwards, Cendrars transmitted an idea from his American agent, W. A. Bradley, that Stravinsky write his memoirs. "With Vera," Cendrars thought, "you could make a very beautiful book, telling all that's in your heart, your life, your creations, their four truths, to a mass of people."[78] Even Stravinsky must have been struck by the impossibility of having Vera Sudeykina ghost *his* autobiography at this particular moment in their lives. In any case, he replied with the idea of "a book of a polemical character," which, he said, he had been thinking about for some time, and which he would write in collaboration with a friend "with whom I am in complete spiritual sympathy."[79] The friend was certainly not Vera (since the word "ami" is masculine), nor Lourié, who was gradually fading out of Stravinsky's counsels, but surely Valechka Nouvel. They must all have discussed the project, at least in outline, on their German trip in June. One can imagine Stravinsky holding forth in the car about expression in music, about conductors, about Beethoven, about Diaghilev, and Valechka suggesting that it would all make an excellent, very marketable book. And yet, in the end, the book they wrote together two or three years later was not a polemic, though it does address issues of this kind. Instead it was, precisely, an extended memoir of the sort Bradley had proposed. But by then Bradley himself had vanished from the reckoning, and the book had become a specifically Gallic product, aimed at a specifically French readership.

Meanwhile, Stravinsky had little choice but to continue to direct his concert plans towards Germany and, to a lesser extent, Switzerland. Even in those countries things were far from easy. Since June he had been trying to set up a Swiss tour with Dushkin through Reinhart; but only Winterthur, backed by Reinhart himself, could afford their joint fee of two thousand Swiss francs. As for Germany, the market was so sluggish that as late as mid-September it looked as if the Duo Concertant would have its world premiere in remote Danzig.[80] Then Stravinsky's German agent came up with a Berlin radio premiere at the end of October. Other bookings were still hamstrung by the economic situation. Stravinsky insisted, for instance, that he would only appear in Budapest if he were allowed to export his fee.[81] The political news from Germany went from bad to worse. There, too, foreign artists were de facto discriminated against. But the discrimination was partly conscious as well. Strecker pointed out that even Rosbaud, as an Austrian, was in difficulties in Frankfurt and felt that "if he were at the present moment to engage you with Dushkin or [the young American pianist Beveridge] Webster, the result would be his immediate dismissal."[82] This explained (though Strecker did not say so) why Rosbaud had been unable to book Stravinsky for an autumn concert. The discrimination was not yet overwhelmingly anti-Semitic, though it often operated, and perhaps *a fortiori*, against Jews. When Dushkin risked what he must have known would be, with Stravinsky, an unwelcome expression of relief that they had few German concerts that winter, it was as a Jew contemplating a land where there were "too many Nazis and not enough money."[83] One wonders what he would have said if he had known that even his friendly Swiss hosts, though some of them still had money, privately nourished their own not so amiable prejudices. Reinhart himself, for instance. "I didn't realize," Stravinsky had written to his patron two or three years before, "that you were not indifferent to these Antichrists [the freemasons], and this with your disgust, as conscious as it is (I hope) natural, for universal Jewry (of which the freemasons are merely the lackeys): all this overwhelms me with joy!"[84] For that matter, one wonders how exact was Dushkin's awareness of his duo partner's own attitudes in this respect.

The Berlin recital, on 28 October in the studios of the Berlin Radio, was the first of many in which the two of them played what soon became the basis of a standard program. The Duo Concertant and the *Suite italienne* were heard for the first time, together with the duo version of the concerto. Later, in public recitals (the first in Danzig five days later), they would leaven it with a selection of the transcriptions they had made or would subsequently make: the little ballet or opera pieces; the "Pastorale," which Stravinsky arranged and expanded during 1933 from the early vocalise which he had already (in 1923) transcribed for wind quartet; and the Divertimento suite from *The Fairy's Kiss*, which followed at the end of 1934.[85] But even without these pieces, the Berlin critics—reviewing the concert over the air—were struck by the repertoire's dependence on music they knew already. Einstein had read over his notice of the Violin Concerto and had nothing to add on the version with piano, except the sarcastic comment that "this time the Berlin Radio Orchestra made a better showing and hit off the work's precision-based style more faithfully."[86] Dushkin's playing was praised, to some extent routinely—not in detail—as is the way of critics reviewing music they scarcely know.

But as for the composer, he was "perhaps for the first time standing still; repeating, copying himself. Where will he go from here? Will he find anywhere to go?" It was a question which Stravinsky was already—not for the first time—asking himself.

DESCENT AND REBIRTH

THE FIFTEENTH ANNIVERSARY of the Revolution, in early November 1932, found Stravinsky still nominally Russian but almost entirely cut off from contact with his native land. His situation was quite different from that of Prokofiev, who had been visiting the Soviet Union since 1927, and would shortly be in Moscow and Leningrad again to play his new Fifth Piano Concerto. Prokofiev was seriously considering a permanent return. From 1933 he had a flat in Moscow, and in 1936 he settled there definitively with his Spanish wife and their two small sons. Such a move was out of the question for Stravinsky. Not only had he consistently resisted Soviet invitations, but he had for some time been hinting quite openly to journalists that he had little faith in Soviet attitudes to his work. When a Viennese reporter had asked him as long ago as 1926 whether the Russians appreciated his music, his voice hardened as he replied that "in Russia the Soviets are in charge," and "one had the feeling that he didn't want to say any more about Russia."[1]

Stravinsky, a *dvoryanin* whose property had been sequestrated or even destroyed after the Revolution, had more to fear and less to expect from the Bolsheviks than Prokofiev, who had lost only a St. Petersburg flat and whose mother was descended from serfs. It may just be true, therefore, as Craft suggests, that he was afraid of being detained by the Soviet authorities if he ever set foot in the country.[2] But it probably is not true that he no longer felt sufficiently Russian to care whether he went home or not. His remark to a Swiss interviewer that "I don't consider myself particularly Russian. I am a cosmopolitan"[3] has to be read in the context of his current work, and in the context of what was still vulgarly understood as "Russian" in Western Europe in the late twenties. As a matter of aesthetic policy he had been in flight from that kind of Russianism ever since *Mavra*. Yet nobody who visited him at Nice or Voreppe, as Rosbaud had recently done, and noticed the "magnificent silver icons" which adorned his study, could have doubted for a moment that he still felt the pull of Russia as it had been in his childhood.[4] But this was above all a religious attachment. It simply was not in his nature to waste spiritual energy on vain regrets for a past or a concept which he no longer believed had any real hope of life. Whatever may have been his contacts with the Eurasians or Berdyayev in the mid-twenties, he had lost all interest in millennialist expatriate movements by 1930. "God preserve me," he exploded to Païchadze, "from getting mixed up with these activities of the Russian immigration!!!!!!"[5] As for visiting Russia, no doubt he feared what he would find there and detested in advance those he would have to meet; and as for settling there, with a chronically tubercular wife and daughter, an almost octogenarian mother, and a whole family of incurable hypochondriacs—quite apart from any political or artistic considerations—it was flatly out of the question.

Yet his situation in France was also growing more insecure by the month. Life in exile had been bearable for the seven fat years since his first American tour. But at the start of 1933 the outlook was darkening rapidly. The catastrophic situation in Germany came into menacing focus in Berlin at the end of January, with Hindenburg's appointment of Adolf Hitler as chancellor of the Reich. By a supreme irony, Stravinsky was in Wiesbaden on that day, discussing a new stage work with André Gide and lunching with Rosbaud, who was booking him to conduct *Oedipus Rex* and the Symphony of Psalms in Frankfurt that spring. Within weeks the invitation had been withdrawn, as the Nazis bore down on modern art and foreign performers. Rosbaud's own position in Frankfurt became increasingly precarious, and was, as we saw, certainly not proof against the indiscreet booking of suspect foreign artists. Meanwhile, Stravinsky had gone from Wiesbaden to Munich, where he gave a recital with Dushkin in the Odeon on 2 February. A day or two later, he and Vera were dining with a friend who had helped set up the Munich concert, the photographer Eric Schaal, when three Nazi officials came into the restaurant and began to direct loud anti-Semitic remarks at them. They left hurriedly, but the men followed them into the street and launched a vicious attack on Schaal, punching and kicking him, until Igor and Vera somehow managed to bundle him into a taxi and get him away.[6] From Stravinsky's point of view, not the least disturbing aspect of the incident was that the thugs seemed to identify him, too, as a Jew (while Schaal, by Stravinsky's own account, was attacked because he protested). Luckily Dushkin, who was Jewish both in appearance and in fact, was not with them that evening and only heard all about it later from Schaal.[7] The violinist had hastened back to Paris to be with his adoptive father, Blair Fairchild, who was mortally ill with tuberculosis and died at his home in Fontainebleau less than three months later.[8]

Whether or not he was Jewish, the outlook in Nazi Germany for a musician of such prominent modernist tendencies as Stravinsky's was bleak indeed. Willy Strecker reported on the atmosphere two months after Hitler's accession. The mood, he said, was excitable, and already a "Kultur

Kampfbund" (Fighting Front for Culture) had been formed "with the aim of promoting German art and suppressing Jewish and Bolshevik art." There were lists of undesirables, and Stravinsky's name was on the list of Jews. So Strecker asked him to send a statement of his ancestry, to be kept on file against any future need for "authentic, reliable proof."[9] Stravinsky's reply is disagreeable evidence of his willingness to acquiesce in the distinctions which made it necessary; it provided a detailed genealogy, bristling with particles of nobility (*de* Stravinsky, *de* Kholodovsky, *de* Nosenko), and calling down anathema on any political and intellectual system of which the Nazis might disapprove: "all communism, all Marxism, the execrable Soviet monster, but every kind of liberalism, democratism, atheism, etc."[10] "I take this opportunity," he concluded, apparently without irony, "to wish you and all yours a good and happy Easter."

The trouble was that in the new Germany, definite policies on art were slow to emerge, and when they did there were frequent contradictions, apparently due to the division of authority which was partly an aspect of Nazi administrative structures, partly the result of personal taste or on the other hand the fear of making a wrong move which might later be held against you. Strecker was encouraged by the fact that a recent Monteux concert in Berlin, including a work by Stravinsky, had been "ostentatiously attended by government people, a sign that those in leading positions have perfectly sensible views."[11] But he later reported a series of difficult and abrasive exchanges with unnamed bureaucrats on the subject of Stravinsky's "degenerate Bolshevik art."[12] Theatres and concert promoters were avoiding all foreign works for lack of clear official guidance, and since the Nazi takeover Stravinsky performances had died out almost completely. Yet Strecker, while affected commercially by the politics of the situation and no doubt busily engaged in diplomatic negotiations on behalf of Schott's publishing interests behind the scenes, was by no means hostile to the general objectives of the new regime. "The movement," he assured Stravinsky,

> has so much that is healthy and desirable about it that one can await the outcome, even in the arts, in an entirely calm frame of mind. The main battle is against the Communists, but then also against the Jews, whose influence is being fundamentally reduced. But in addition there's also to be a drive toward a good clean-up in every respect, so as to restore decency and order. There will doubtless be a temporary setback for non-German art, but the really worthwhile will still enjoy the position it deserves.[13]

It perhaps needs saying that, whatever we may now think of such sentiments, neither Strecker nor Stravinsky can have had any inkling of what this cleaning-up process would ultimately amount to. Strecker's anti-Semitism was as natural as the air he breathed, and could combine conde-scension and generosity with a calm acceptance of the grotesquely unfair that is like nothing so much as a Victorian factory owner's imperturbable regret at the high death rate from malnutrition among his employees. "Our friend Dushkin," the publisher remarked placidly, "will for the time being find himself in an unfavorable situation," and "he had better wait until early 1934 to visit Germany again."[14] These are not the attitudes of a Nazi; but Nazism would have made little progress without them.

Stravinsky's own behavior was motivated largely by artistic and finan-cial considerations, and there is only limited evidence that he took account of, or fully grasped, the nature of the regime with which he was so anxious to go on doing business. Once again he was "inside the whale," composing his music and occasionally firing off broadsides at anyone who put mate-rial difficulties in his way. So Hitler was a nuisance to be circumvented. Stravinsky's opportunism was nevertheless at times repellently calculat-ing. Just as he could imagine that antiliberalism was a useful credential for acceptance in Nazi Berlin (as if such a regime bothered itself with the worldview of those it chose to detest), so he could agonize about being associated with Jewish artists who were now personae non gratae there. "I adopt a cautious approach to Germany, which has banished these Jews (Klemperer and Walter)," he told Païchadze, "and to express solidarity with them is perhaps politically imprudent."[15] Taruskin cites this letter as illus-trating Stravinsky's political astuteness. But not only is the question not very astute, it is not even anti-Semitic. It only shows what even Craft has to admit is a "callous indifference to the fate of friends, Semitic or other-wise."[16] For Stravinsky had never shown any personal fastidiousness in his association with Jews like Steinberg, Bakst, Klemperer, Lourié, Dushkin, or even (until they crossed swords musically) Koussevitzky. The issue sim-ply did not arise. His anti-Semitism was almost entirely generalized, and surfaced only rarely in a personal context, such as in his patronizing description of Sam Bottenheim as "mon cher Hausjude" in another letter to Païchadze.[17] His apparent readiness to desert admired colleagues like Klemperer, whom he had so recently defended in the German press, merely reflects his observation that such people were not doing well in Hitler's Germany. In itself it shows neither distaste for Klemperer nor sympathy for the Nazis.[18]

His attitude to Mussolini, in Italy, was quite another matter. From Munich in February 1933 it so happened that he travelled to Milan, Turin, and eventually Rome, where he conducted a concert for Italian Radio on the twenty-third. That same day he was summoned by telegram to an audi-ence in the Palazzo Venezia. The Duce may have heard about Stravinsky's remark to the *Tribuna* music critic, Alberto Gasco, that nobody venerated Mussolini more than he did:

> To me, he is the *one man who counts* nowadays in the whole world. I have travelled a great deal: I know many exalted personages, and my artist's mind does not shrink from political and social issues. Well, after having seen so many events and so many more or less representative men, I have an overpowering urge to render homage to your Duce. He is the saviour of Italy and—let us hope—of Europe.[19]

Mussolini sat at a huge desk in his office "flanked by ugly modern lamps," and talked to Stravinsky about the violin, an instrument he himself played.[20] Indeed he prided himself on his knowledge of music and probably claimed acquaintance with Stravinsky's work. "Maestro," the composer reported him as saying, "I know you."[21] To Gasco, Stravinsky remarked that "the mental image I had formed of this formidable man was exactly right. The conversation I had with him has made an indelible impression on me. This pilgrimage to Rome will remain one of the happiest events of my life."[22] Eight months later, Stravinsky sent greetings to Mussolini on his fiftieth birthday, having first confirmed the date with his friend the Italian musicologist Domenico de Paoli. De Paoli wrote back that "you're right, but I had to ask a lot of people because all public festivity has been forbidden, along with any publicizing of the occasion."[23] Despite this access of modesty on the part of the great leader, his office graciously thanked the composer for his good wishes.[24]

At first glance this fulsome behavior towards a puffed-up petty despot and demagogue may seem as surprising as it is distasteful. Stravinsky knew something about the dark side of fascism, even though Mussolini had not yet embarked on the international adventures (starting with Ethiopia in 1935) which revealed him starkly as a ruthless mass murderer and dangerous political maneuverer. Over the Toscanini incident in 1926 the composer may reasonably have felt that the issue of the "Giovinezza" was at bottom no more than a battle of political will, rather than the moral crusade it was later painted.[25] But he also knew about Charles-Albert Cingria's summary arrest and incarceration in the Regina Coeli Prison in Rome in October of that same year on a trumped-up charge of subversion, and he knew how badly Cingria, one of his closest friends, had been treated and how ill served by the Italian legal system.[26]

But Stravinsky came to his thirties politics no longer from the point of view of social or moral equity, and certainly not from any consideration of the normal base political factors such as economics or the balance of power. His motives were partly atavistic, partly aesthetic, partly—as we have seen—pure self-preservation. In the days when leftism had meant siding with the intelligentsia against the decaying tyranny of the Romanovs, he, like most of his class, had longed for democracy and freedom. But now that leftism meant the Bolsheviks, and democracy apparently equalled unstable world markets and rigid protectionism, he wanted none of them. In their place he looked for order and stability, and if they could be found in a country which still welcomed him and his music and which also happened to be the historical focus of European art and culture, then that country could be sure of his favor. So it was Fascist Italy, with its imagined cult of efficiency and its apparent open-door treatment of art, including modern art, that gave Stravinsky the comfortable feeling of ordered progress which was, in a sense, his own spiritual world, bearing in mind that the return to order in Maritain and Cocteau, and in his own work of the early twenties, had been in social and political terms precisely a reactionary movement, exalting the worker, but only as long as he knew his place, kept to the rules, and avoided a disruptive individualism. Nazi Germany, by contrast, was not at all a comfortable place for a Russian musician like Stravinsky to contemplate. It was protectionist and turbulent; in principle it was hostile to work such as his, even if in practice it sometimes admitted it; and, perhaps worst of all, it had abandoned him as a working musician, as a performer. Stravinsky scarcely turned against Germany in or immediately after 1933. He seems to have been unconcerned at the Nazis' brutalization of daily life, as he had experienced it in Munich (an incident he apparently did not mention to Strecker), and he was hardly likely to take arms against their anti-Semitism. But he could not be at ease with them so long as they behaved equivocally towards him and his work.

AFTER FINISHING the Duo Concertant and the other violin-piano pieces in early August 1932, Stravinsky had—perhaps by way of escape—composed a liturgical four-part chant version of the Slavonic Creed, music unimaginably remote from the recital room and the problems of instrumental combination he was having to think about with Dushkin. Then, later, after autumn concerts in Berlin and Königsberg, he began sketching a large-scale work for two pianos. In mid-November he drafted several pages of music for this difficult but rewarding medium, then abandoned it, he tells us, "because I could not *hear* the second piano. All my life I have tried out my music as I have composed it, orchestral as well as any other kind, four hands at one keyboard. That way I am able to test it as I cannot when the other player is seated at another piano."[27] Two-piano music was particularly intractable because the "doubleness" was essential to the sound. It could not be simulated on a single instrument.

The new work was one way he had of helping Svetik, now twenty-two and on the lookout for concert dates, to get started as a solo pianist. For three years now, Svetik had been studying in Paris with Mme Chailley-Richez, and latterly, with Isidore Philipp, and giving the occasional recital, including one that Vera had attended (or at least written down to attend) at the Ecole Normale in May 1931.[28] But if his father was finding it harder and harder to get concert dates, what chance did he have, an unknown young Swiss-Russian pianist, however talented (and even this question had yet to be tested)? Igor Stravinsky had been chivvying his influential friends for some time to smooth Svetik's path. Reinhart, who was already, at the composer's request, pulling strings to get Theodore a Zurich exhibition, had more recently come under pressure to set up concerts there and in Winterthur for Theodore's younger brother. A year before, Stravinsky had sent him a heavily pumped-up leaflet about Soulima (as he planned to call himself) from his Paris agent, including Cortot and Alexander Nápravník among his piano teachers and claiming successful debuts already in Switzerland. "It goes without saying," the leaflet added, "that the work of his celebrated father finds in him an exceptional interpreter for the faithful rendition of the great musician's subtlest intentions."[29] Reinhart probably groaned inwardly at this new tax on his patronage, and did nothing. Meanwhile, by the end of 1932 he had managed to set up a private exhibition for Theodore in Basle, something he could arrange without his concert committee's approval.[30] But when Stravinsky returned to the attack on behalf of Svetik, in May 1933, Reinhart raised the matter with his committee but otherwise once again did nothing. Only when the composer unblinkingly copied his letter to Winterthur at the end of August was Reinhart at last obliged to act. But two handwritten words on the May original, *"Sitzung"* ("meeting," crossed out in blue crayon) and *"ablegen"* ("put on file"), show the true limits of his natural willingness to take exceptional steps in such cases.[31]

As for the two-piano concerto, Stravinsky may well have been having problems with the medium. But what actually forced him to put the sketches aside at the start of December was Paris: the French premiere of the Duo Concertant with Dushkin in the Salle Pleyel on the eighth, preceded on the seventh by a private performance at the princesse de Polignac's. It was a visit crowded with other concerts. There was a whole Prokofiev evening, at which the master unveiled his new Fifth Piano Concerto and Jeanne Gautier played the D major for violin; and a few days later Stravinsky went to see Prokofiev's new Lifar ballet, *On the Dnieper,* at the Opéra, and (according to Prokofiev himself) was one of the few who defended it.[32] The Noailles had meanwhile switched from Cocteau to Kurt Weill and had backed semistaged productions of the *Mahagonny Songspiel* and *Der Jasager* in the Salle Gaveau. Stravinsky was there and, by his own later testimony, admired both works and got to know their composer, whom he had first met in Berlin at *Die Dreigroschenoper* in June 1929.[33] It was a moment of nexus for the maligned Paris musical scene. Prokofiev was already wooing (or being wooed by) Moscow, and was recently back from there. Weill would soon be in flight from the Nazis, to whom he stood for almost everything that was most villainous in modern life: Jewishness, jazz, and—through Brecht—communism. But, whatever Stravinsky may have thought of these composers' music, theirs were not the kinds of fusion that released his creative juices. Instead he was soon opening the esoteric pages of Cingria's *Pétrarque*, which he found waiting for him in Voreppe when he got back there just before Christmas; and through them he entered a world as far removed from *Zeitoper* as fourteenth-century Arezzo was from the Kurfürstendamm or the Champs-Elysées.

Cingria's book, only in part biographical, is a rambling disquisition on Petrarch's work and his reputation as the reviver of classical letters and the father of the Renaissance. Its overarching theme is that Petrarch's neo-Romanism was a herald, not of a genuinely modern republicanism, but of the kind of nationalism which was, at that very moment, "shrouding Europe in darkness." Petrarch's classicism, Cingria says, was not in fact progressive at all, but traditionalist, even reactionary. It supported the Church against renegade schoolmen, and thus "had nothing to do with a supposed liberation by the Renaissance from the Middle Ages."[34] Classicism itself was merely a symptom of poetry having forgotten its true origins in music, to the point where, around 1600, composers like Caccini were actually arguing that music should be subordinated to speech patterns. But this, Cingria argues, is simply a case of the intellect taking over from the instincts; and he quotes with approval Nietzsche's remark that "tragedy emerged from song, and was originally choral and nothing but choral."[35] For Cingria, the essential Petrarch is not the great Ciceronian with his "eloquence, his erudition, his great sentiments, his moralizing . . . his nationalism, his irony, skepticism, and pretentiousness," but the lyric poet whom the Renaissance tended to regard with contempt. "A sequence by Notker," he insists, "is a thousand times more beautiful than a Latin eclogue by Petrarch."[36]

On the face of it, Stravinsky was an unlikely admirer of such a text. For one thing, he was more interested these days in Apollonian order and control than in Dionysian instinct; and while he might have agreed with Cingria (rather than Nietzsche) that the new fascist regimes were in some obscure way part of a tradition that had lost touch with feeling, he would no longer necessarily disapprove of them on those grounds, as he might have done twenty years before, when he advised Andrey Rimsky-Korsakov not to "stop yourself feeling."[37] But he was intrigued by certain technical aspects of the book's argument. He liked Cingria's corrective and paradoxical remark that "lyricism does not exist without rules, and they must be strict," and that "art . . . must be clever and difficult, otherwise everyone would be a poet." And he was sufficiently struck by one passage, a Petrarch dialogue between Joy and Reason given by Cingria in a contemporary French translation, to spend part of early January 1933 drafting a vocal setting of it.[38]

Joy speaks, here, for the spontaneity of the unreflective love of music (and, later, of dance). Reason is the intellectual killjoy. "I am softened and comforted by the sweetness of music," says Joy. "Naturalists tell us," says Reason, "that the spider softens its prey before biting it . . . and some men are never more terrible than when they seem most gentle." But if Cingria had somewhere in the back of his mind the music-loving Mussolini or the dog-loving Hitler, Stravinsky was more interested in the prosodic issue of setting medieval French to music. His only previous settings of French texts of any kind had been the Verlaine songs of 1910. Now, in the Petrarch dialogue, his imagination is caught by something schematic in the form, a certain quality of "litany" (most noticeable, admittedly, in the Latin original, which Cingria places alongside the translation). The French words are set in an incantatory, quasi-robotic style which almost overacknowledges the stylized character of the dialogue and the relatively accentless quality of the French language. At the same time, there is a distinct suggestion of the six-line sestina, with its rotating rhyme schemes, of which Cingria prints examples by Petrarch and (complete with music) the troubadour Arnaut Daniel.[39] One does not need an unduly vivid imagination to see some influence of the patterned sestina melody on Stravinsky's own singsong vocal lines.

But any projected complete setting of the Petrarch text was destined to go no farther than a few fragmentary notations (including rhythmic figures in the handwritten text) and a pair of drafts of one brief section. Once again he had to break off and leave Voreppe for Paris, this time at the start of the long tour of Germany and Italy which was to include the Munich incident and the meeting with Mussolini.[40] And in Paris word reached him, probably via Païchadze, of a new Ida Rubinstein commission, a stage work with a text by a leading French writer. He guessed, and perhaps hoped, that the writer was Valéry. But a few days later Païchadze wrote to him in Wiesbaden that it was André Gide, his old would-be collaborator in Ida's staging of *Antony and Cleopatra* fifteen years before, and since then a frequent visitor to the Pleyel studio, where he would come to discuss Russian literature.[41] No less delighted than if it had been Valéry, Stravinsky quickly invited Gide to meet him at the Hotel Rose in Wiesbaden; and they were together there, as we saw, on the day Hitler took power in Berlin.[42]

Gide's idea was, at first sight, as remote from contemporary events as Petrarch. Thirty years earlier, long before the war, he had written an extended poem based on the Homeric hymn about Demeter, the corn goddess, and her daughter Persephone, who, the legend runs, was playing innocently with her friends in the flowery meadows of Boeotia when she was abducted by Zeus's brother Hades and carried off to the Underworld. After wandering far and wide in search of her daughter, Demeter blackmailed Zeus into interceding with Hades, by placing a blight on all seed and all new growth for a whole year. Terrified that she would bring perpetual famine to the earth, Zeus persuaded his brother to give Persephone up. But Hades tricked the girl into eating the food of the dead, in the form of a pomegranate seed, and only after further threats from Demeter did he agree to share Persephone with the upper earth. From that day to this, Persephone has spent one of the three Greek seasons (winter) in the Underworld, and the other two (spring and summer) among men. Each summer's end she descends once more, like the seed which must lie in the ground in order to germinate the next spring, when Persephone returns again to the earth.

Gide had originally used this story as the basis for what he had called a "dramatic symphony in four tableaux," but with episodic digressions featuring various well-known ancient Greeks, including Hercules, Tantalus, Mercury, and Eurydice.[43] But Stravinsky convinced him in Wiesbaden that, however diverse the forces Ida wanted to deploy in staging the work (and they included chorus as well as vocal soloists, dancers, and herself in the part-mimed, part-spoken title role), the actual treatment needed to be severe and mythic. "I was very stirred," Gide wrote to the composer, "by what you told me in Wiesbaden: the interest that would attach to marking and enclosing the cycle of the seasons."[44] He in turn must have explained his idea of Persephone as a proto-Christ, whose descent is not forced but voluntary, prompted by compassion for "a people without hope, pale, unquiet and sorrowful," whom she glimpses as she gazes into a narcissus she has picked. When he received the finished libretto of the first scene at the end of February, Stravinsky assured Gide that "I love your work too seriously and deeply, and I am too seduced by the beauty of your magnificent text . . . not to aspire with all my power to erect a very substantial monument in sound to go with yours."[45] But the remark already reveals tension. Gide, while declaring his willingness to "listen to all of your criticisms, directions, suggestions,"[46] had given his collaborator grounds for fearing that their respective ideas about musical theatre might not exactly tally. "We must have a little tranquillity," Stravinsky suggested, "to see it (the 'libretto') as a whole from the theatrical point of view, and so that I can make you feel very clearly my conceptions and ideas about the role of music in the theatre in general, and in your work in particular." The work would have to be "an independent musical organism, serving neither to embellish the text (beautiful in itself), nor to color it, nor to guide the public (*Leitmusik*—Wagner) through the various evolutions of the drama."[47] Gide had clearly, if unconsciously, betrayed an attitude that Stravinsky felt needed refuting.

An enthusiastic amateur pianist, Gide entertained naive ideas about the musical setting of his libretto which he was indiscreet enough to pass on to Stravinsky. In particular the draft typescript, whose first installment he sent at the end of February, includes many indications of musical character which the composer not unnaturally regarded as encroaching on his territory.[48] Directions like "an unfamiliar disquiet has slipped into the orchestra, which was hitherto expressing a pure joy," or "the music becomes gradually more tender, less plaintive, and as if gently recovering its serenity," receive exclamation marks, underlinings, or bracketings. But eventually Stravinsky loses patience and decorates the typescript with exasperated comments in Russian, culminating in "what a mentality!" against Gide's "outburst of laughter in the orchestra." The trouble was that Gide had in general little interest in vocal music and little feeling for the relationship of words to music. "In the appreciation of music," he wrote, "I experience no need to filter it through literature or painting, and I concern myself very little with the 'meaning' of a piece. . . . And that's also why music without words pleases me above all."[49] If music was to be added to a text of his, its role was to be purely anecdotal, as in the old French genre of mélodrame, where music was used as humble accompaniment to speech. If his words were actually to be set to music, then "the musical purpose should be to imitate or underline the verbal pattern." The composer "would simply have to find pitches for the syllables, since he [Gide] considered he had already composed the rhythm."[50] Not surprisingly, Gide had little grasp of Stravinsky's own kind of purism, in which words were as much musical material as notes, and the "meaning," such as it might be, lay in the music of their combination.

There was another, less technical, disagreement which, if it never completely surfaced, must surely have hovered over their discussions. Two years earlier, Gide had openly declared his allegiance to communism, and one may feel that, behind the classical innocence of the Homeric legend, his *Persephone* was meant to convey a political message. Persephone descends to help the oppressed and later, back on earth, marries Triptolemus, the tiller of the soil.[51] For Stravinsky, such considerations would have been beyond the pale even if Gide's parable had been more to the liking of a self-confessed admirer of Mussolini, and even if he himself had not been at that very moment, in public and in private, loudly denouncing communism and even liberalism.[52] He simply did not see art as a vehicle for changing society, whether morally or politically. "His world," as Craft later pointed out specifically in connection with *Persephone*, was "one of order, form, rule, and the acceptance of impositions from above."[53] Any discrepancy, therefore, between the anecdotal and sentimental atmosphere of Gide's poem and the ceremonial form of Stravinsky's treatment was built in from the first.

The new work—"neither opera, nor ballet, but rather, if you insist on a label, melodrama"[54]—was slated for performance in December. But Stravinsky was not able to start composing until late April, and then only because Blair Fairchild's death on the twenty-third meant the cancellation of a French concert tour with Dushkin. March had already been the familiar muddle of concerts: a BBC recital with Dushkin, a Paris concert with the OSP, then Winterthur with Dushkin again, and finally a week with Vera in Budapest, where he conducted the American prodigy Rosalind Kaplan in his Piano Concerto.[55] He would have gone to Vienna as well, but the Viennese would not pay a fee for the relatively unknown Dushkin.[56] Instead they spent two days in Paris recording the Duo Concertant and part of the Suite italienne; and the composer dined with Mme Rubinstein and spent a day with Gide refining the Persephone text.[57] He returned to Voreppe only just before Easter; and it was on Good Friday (the fourteenth) that he penned his pro-Nazi genealogy for Strecker.

As he worked away on Persephone at La Vironnière during the summer of 1933, the poise and serenity of the music he was writing and the outward calm of his life were more than ever at odds with reality. This was not just a matter of politics or money. His children were almost grown up, and rural life was becoming an impediment to them. Even little Milène was nineteen now. Theodore and Svetik were themselves much in Paris. Poor Mika had inherited her mother's health, and neither they nor Igor's own aging mother were well placed in lowland Isère, with its damp, chilly winters, miles from specialist doctoring. In after years, when Stravinsky would tell Robert Craft that "I was very fond of this house . . . but the inconveniences of country life and the need to drive to Grenoble for provisions were too much for me and I eventually had to move,"[58] he was trivializing a turning point in his family's existence. Provisions were probably the one Stravinsky necessity that a typical large French village like Voreppe could supply. What it could not supply was proximity, that need, which at certain times of life becomes overriding, to be close to the center of things. Perhaps it was even some dawning stockade instinct which prompted him to ask his Russian friends—Païchadze and Vera, of course, but also (as if it were an extra term in the Persephone contract they had signed in late April) the stately Ida herself—to look out for a Paris flat for the whole family for the coming winter. This, he told Païchadze, would solve one of his biggest anxieties.[59] And it was Ida who, early in July, rang to say that she had found a suitable apartment in the rue Viète, in the seventeenth arrondissement not far from the Salle Pleyel.[60] It would be a trial. Voreppe could be kept on for the following summer; and meanwhile longer-term decisions could be taken in view of the family's (and especially Igor's) somewhat complicated circumstances.

Ida had telephoned to Voreppe. But she had not dared ask how her melodrama was coming on, and perhaps she would not have been entirely reassured had she done so. What with another fortnight in Paris in the first half of June (for more recordings with Dushkin, and a visit with Gide and Ida to hear a children's choir at Saint-Louis-les-Invalides), Stravinsky had still not finished the first of the three tableaux, and at this very moment Païchadze had for some reason decided to publish the Symphonies of Wind Instruments, which had been languishing in the ERM hire library, unconsidered and largely unperformed, for almost ten years. Fortunately Ansermet, so often in South America at this time of year, was for once on hand and willing to proofread a work which, in all probability, he now knew better than the composer (who had in fact never conducted it). But Stravinsky still had to cope with Ansermet's queries,[61] which, though not particularly numerous, were hard to resolve without some attempt at reinhabiting a style he had long since abandoned. Deep in what he called his "romance with Persephone,"[62] he was unwilling or unable to make the necessary leap. So despite Ansermet's best efforts, errors slipped through in the corrected proofs—errors due as much as anything to misreadings of this curious work's more bizarre details. In the end the ERM edition never came out, and when (in 1947) Stravinsky at last got round to revising his score, with only Ansermet's proof in front of him, he simply transferred its mistakes to the new version, where they remain to this day. Thus, consciously or unconsciously, "the true creator . . . draws profit from something unforeseen that a momentary lapse reveals to him."[63]

Meanwhile, Persephone had just descended to Hades, early in the second tableau, when Domenico de Paoli turned up at Voreppe in mid-August and enjoyed the rare privilege of being shown and played the score in its current state. "In this music," he reported, "there is a freshness, a happiness, a creative joy, an irresistible spring radiance. For a month I have been pursued by the singing of these delicious little choruses."[64] But after he left, the composer went down with what he called "bile poisoning," and by the second week of September the central, winter, tableau was still incomplete. Autumn was looming in the upper world, and with it Stravinsky's house move, which involved not just a trunk or two from Voreppe to Paris, but also the vacating of his Pleyel studio, which had practically lost its justification since the collapse of the piano-roll market at the end of the twenties. And after that he would have to prepare for November concerts in Barcelona, including his first-ever public appearance with Svetik (in the Capriccio).[65] It must have been at this point that the premiere was postponed from December to February; and even then, there was barely time to finish the score. By or soon after 24 January, the actual completion date, the first performance had been firmly put back to the end of April.[66]

The trouble was that *Persephone* promised to be as complicated to put on as it had been to plan. As with *Oedipus Rex*, Stravinsky had preferred in principle to hide away while writing the music, leaving others to organize such mundane matters as finance (not a problem in this case), performers, choreographers, and designers. But in practice, he was not willing to relinquish such decisions altogether. When Ida proposed engaging Fokine as choreographer, Stravinsky was stung into wiring back that "to collaborate with him would be extremely painful to me."[67] He would not consider any choreographer except either Massine or Balanchine, whose world-premiere production of Weill's *Seven Deadly Sins* he may have seen at the Théâtre des Champs-Elysées that June, in between recording sessions with Dushkin. But what he chiefly had in mind was an overall stage producer; and for this he envisaged Jacques Copeau, the founder of the Vieux-Colombier and the reader of the whole text of *The Soldier's Tale* in Stravinsky's Salle Pleyel performance back in March 1929. Copeau was on the editorial board of the *NRF*, so it seems likely that he was either proposed by Gide (the journal's co-founder, and still its éminence grise) or else chosen as being likely to work sympathetically with him. But Stravinsky also liked the idea. "For me," he wrote to Copeau, "it's a sure talisman of the success of our triple collaboration, I mean Rubinstein, you, and me. It's this working atmosphere that I need."[68]

What he had not bargained for was that Copeau would choose his own designer (and perhaps also the choreographer, Kurt Jooss) without further ado. Stravinsky had had some half-formed idea of getting the designer's job for Theodore, and when he heard early in January that Copeau had already engaged André Barsacq, an artist unknown to him, he got on his high horse. "To judge from this affair," he scolded, "my role as musician in *Persephone* was considered as secondary, from the moment when I was not consulted about the set and costume designer."[69] It was a wound that refused to heal. Stravinsky never had a good word to say about Barsacq's designs, and his name is not mentioned in the autobiography or conversations. As for Copeau, he stayed in the composer's bad books for several years. "My participation," Stravinsky recorded sulkily in his autobiography a year or so later, "was limited to conducting the music," but he admits that "it is all too recent for me to discuss it with the necessary detachment."[70] Alas for Copeau, the accidental slight against Theodore had come at a bad moment. A few months earlier, Stravinsky had at last persuaded Werner Reinhart to give Svetik an opening in the form of a private unpaid recital at the Rychenberg in January, as well as a soirée at his friends the Reiffs' (for which Svetik, perhaps too familiar with his father's methods, had rather uppishly demanded a fee).⁷¹ But now Svetik, after his Barcelona debut, had collapsed with exhaustion, and the doctor had ordered him to take three months off. After all the pressure and cajoling, Winterthur had to be cancelled. And the composer was left to wonder what he must do to launch his son's careers and to get them (naturally enough) off his own hands.

That he continued to work hard on his children's account cannot be doubted. But all four of them were a perpetual worry. Variously but unspectacularly talented, they suffered cruelly from their own expectations in their father's shadow. And perhaps his string pulling—in the most exalted quarters—was not always as helpful as he might have expected. Svetik, Ansermet observed, was in danger of burning out from the effort and worry of satisfying his own hopes.⁷² Theodore had been diagnosed as (mildly) tubercular. Even Milène had recently been ill. Paris might or might not alleviate these problems. At least it meant that Igor could keep a personal eye on his family, instead of relying—as he had done—on Vera, or close friends like Souvtchinsky or Nadia, to watch and report. His own situation, of course, would be radically altered. Had he been less autocratic, less candidly self-centered in the way he organized his life, he might have balked at having Katya and Vera in adjacent arrondissements. As it was, his main worry was that his mother, now almost eighty but perfectly lucid and in good health, would find out about Vera and in some way disrupt the mood of stoical acceptance which had long since cloaked the unhappy arrangement. It seems that in the six years of life that remained her she never did grasp what was going on. Or if she did, she assumed a severe and dignified ignorance of affairs that were beneath the notice of the daughter of a Russian State Councillor.

Her son, though, had at last made up his mind to become French, in fact as well as spirit, and this decision, too, drew him towards Paris. "Why," he later rhetorically asked a newspaper reporter "have I taken so long, since for so many years I have found in France . . . my intellectual climate? It is because I was responding to a kind of shame towards my motherland."⁷³ But being Russian no longer had anything to do with the reality of that country. He could not sympathize with—could scarcely even endure—those who were content to inhabit a Russia of the mind: the emigration with all its factions and fantasies. Perhaps working, however idiosyncratically, with the text of *Persephone* had made him feel more than ever Gallic, more than ever in tune with the relived classicism of Poussin and Claude. But in another sense the decision was not that new. It was four years since he had seriously thought of taking Swiss nationality; and that intention certainly had had nothing to do with aesthetics, everything to do with practicalities as he saw them at the time, including his obscure but generally unfavorable copyright status under the Berne Convention. The situation now, in 1933, was merely worse. The political conditions were peculiarly threatening to a stateless exile dependent for his livelihood on the free circulation but due protection of intellectual property. Even Paris, as 1934 dawned, caught a disagreeable glimpse of the fires that were flaring up farther east. Early in February, the growing tension between the Communists and the self-styled Royalists (the old Action Française), fuelled by the Stavisky banking scandal and the consequent resignation of Camille Chautemps' cabinet, exploded in violent riots in which nearly a thousand people were injured and some twenty killed, including a chambermaid at the Hôtel Crillon who was hit between the eyes by a stray bullet. But Stravinsky, if he thought about these troubles at all, doubtless saw them as no more than a passing reflection of the political uncertainties elsewhere.

Ten days after the riots, he played the Capriccio under Siohan in the Salle Pleyel, then set off with Dushkin on his first-ever tour of the English provinces, taking in Manchester, Liverpool, Cambridge, London, and Oxford. He was in Liverpool on the day Elgar died, 24 February, and found himself at a lunch paying tribute to a composer whose music he scarcely knew, and with whom he can hardly have felt great sympathy (though perhaps he recalled that Elgar's First Symphony had been on the same program as the premiere of his *Scherzo fantastique* in St. Petersburg almost exactly twenty-five years before). And there was another curious reminder of his Russian past a few weeks later in Riga, which he and Dushkin visited on a Baltic tour in the fourth week of March, and where they were entertained by the seventy-year-old Jaseps Vitols, Stravinsky's old adversary on the *St. Petersburger Zeitung*. No doubt Stravinsky omitted to remind this "jovial man, with round face and round hands like a cat's paws,"[74] of his former opinion of *Petrushka* as "a mixture of creative poverty and unbelievable impudence of sense, sound, and form," or his impression of *The Rite of Spring* as "a dismal nightmare [which] even the bright day could not erase."[75]

Persephone had been finished in January, and at the end of that month he had played it through at Ida's flat in the place des Etats-Unis, which was surely the occasion he described thirty years later as having taken place in the princesse de Polignac's salon: "myself groaning [the choruses] at the piano, Suvchinsky singing a loud and abrasive Eumolpus, Claudel glaring at me from the other side of the keyboard, Gide bridling more noticeably with each phrase."[76] Gide seems to have been disconcerted not so much by the musical idiom itself (which was far less forbidding than earlier Stravinsky works he knew perfectly well) as by the cavalier treatment of his text, which Stravinsky had deconstructed metrically and syllabically much as he had previously deconstructed Russian nonsense poems. Gide, not unnaturally, had looked for more respect, if not actual deference, in the setting of a language which, after all, was his and not the composer's. Stravinsky had even consulted him about prosody and accentuation, an excellent omen.77 And now here was the result: his beautiful lines broken up into a drunken parody with accents all over the place, rests in the middles of words, rhymes strangled at birth, and most of his careful suggestions of musical mood and pointing studiously ignored. For the sensitive poet it was altogether too much. He fled: fled not just from Ida's, but from Paris, from France, all the way to Sicily, where he could reestablish contact with the classical spirit so essential to his libretto and so crassly destroyed by Stravinsky's doubtless "very beautiful score."78 He did not attend any of the rehearsals, nor the preview performance at Nadia Boulanger's two or three days before the premiere, nor even the premiere itself, conducted by the composer at the Opéra on 30 April.

Stravinsky, of course, knew why Gide was absenting himself, and went so far as to publish a preemptive apologia, in which he asserted the primacy, in vocal music, of the syllable over the word.79 The word with its meanings and patterns, he argued, was "a cumbersome intermediary," whereas syllables were beautiful and strong, which is why he congratulated himself on the choice of Gide, "whose text, highly poetic, but free of jolts, was to provide me with an excellent syllabic structure." "Music is not thought," he added. "It . . . is given to us solely to bring order to things: to move from an anarchic and individualistic state to a regulated, perfectly conscious state, complete with guarantees of vitality and durability. . . . One does not criticize someone or something that is in working order. A nose is not manufactured—a nose *is*. Thus my art."80

Gide may not have been much comforted to learn that he had merely been contributing to somebody else's protuberance, and perhaps he would have been annoyed to read his friend Paul Valéry's delighted response to the interview and to the work: "I am only a layman, but the divine *detachment* of your work touched me. . . . It's a question of attaining purity through the will. . . . Long live your Nose!"81 "Valéry," Stravinsky noted, "continued conspicuously to support me by attending all the performances." And that was important, not as a thrust against Gide for "the absence of rapport which emerges so obviously from your attitude,"82 but because Valéry, as an Academician and the acknowledged torchbearer of *poésie pure*, lent status to Stravinsky's French aspirations by specifically rejecting the run-of-the-mill Gallic assumption of linguistic superiority. In general, this was an attitude more to be expected of musicians. Poulenc, for instance, told the composer that since he had written *Persephone* "with the heart of a Christian ascetic, how do you expect me to accept [Gide's] Calvinist preciosity?"83 But even here there was an unmistakable subtext, equating one reason for Gide's unpopularity in some quarters—his chilly, unsmiling Protestantism—with another, his recent association with communism. It would take a different kind of asceticism to understand fully what Stravinsky meant when he claimed that

> this score, as it was written and as it must remain in the musical annals of the era, forms an indissoluble whole. Many tendencies, affirmed in my preceding compositions—*Oedipus Rex,* Symphony of Psalms, Capriccio, the Violin Concerto, Duo Concertant—are renewed here. In short, *Persephone* belongs to and represents the present link in a continuum of works whose autonomy has in no way been diminished by my abstention from the spectacular.[84]

The patrons of the Ballets Ida Rubinstein could be forgiven for overlooking both the work's indissoluble wholeness and, for that matter, its abstention from the spectacular. The music, certainly, is physically restrained by Stravinsky's standards. The first tableau, with its smooth, tensionless harmonies, its genteel ladies' choruses, its saucy rhythmic discontinuities, may well have seemed both softer-centered and less elevated in tone than its "obvious" ancestor, *Apollo.* And if the later tableaux have a sharper edge, it is at least superficially achieved through disruption of style, rather as in *Oedipus Rex,* where neo-Verdi had rubbed shoulders with neo-Handel, neo-Puccini, and music hall. Here French and quasi-French influences—Gluck, Berlioz, even Liszt—mingle with offcuts from Stravinsky's own workshop: *Oedipus* itself, *Apollo,* and most notably a stunning reincarnation of the "Song of the Volga Boatmen" in the flower chorus of the last tableau, which Stravinsky called his "Russian Easter music."[85] The truth is that *Persephone* is a work that astonishes by its richness and variety more than by its unity, and one which incidentally makes nonsense of the popular theory that Stravinsky could not write tunes. A more melodious score hardly exists in the repertoire of modernism.

There was much, though, to distract the first-night audience from the marvels of the music. Ida herself, in the spoken title role, cut a bizarre figure. The fact that she was "not a dancer, not an actress," Boris de Schloezer noted, was "so evident that it would be bad taste to insist on it, and in any case futile."[86] Gide had told Harry Kessler that the tall, sensuous beauty of Diaghilev's *Scheherazade* had become "curiously shrivelled, like an old woman";[87] and he probably only refrained from grumbling about her Russian accent because he had not heard her speak his verses. She retained, nevertheless, something of her former stage presence and dignity: her playing was "hieratic and full of poise, and fearfully monotonous."[88] As for the real dancers, Schloezer's colleague Julie Sazonova praised Jooss's choreography of the ensembles but found the solos "nothing but conventional leaping and prancing" (though she was even ruder about Fokine's choreography for another Ida special, the Honegger/Valéry *Semiramis*, which the company danced for the first time eleven days later).[89] Then there was the grandiose basilica of Barsacq's set and the somewhat prim Empire classicism of his costume designs, which Stravinsky and Gide detested—for different reasons—more or less equally. Maria Van Rysselberghe thought the costumes "delicious, [but] too distinguished, terribly lacking in wind in the hair."[90]

René Maison sang Eumolpus, the only sung solo role, fluently enough. Souvtchinsky, who counted a strong tenor voice among his various gifts, had longed to sing the part ever since Stravinsky had shown him Eumolpus's opening solo the previous July. "It's wonderfully written for the voice," he had enthused. "One sings it as if it were *La forza del destino*. Marvellous!"[91] But later he worried about the possibility of doing Stravinsky harm "with the imperfections of my performance" and came to feel that Ida "doesn't trust me and won't have inward sympathy with my participation."[92] At this stage, Stravinsky seems actually to have been composing with Souvtchinsky in mind, whatever he may later have said about his abrasive singing at the run-through. He agreed, after all, that a *tenore di forza* was required, and will only have felt flattered by the comparison with Verdi. "I blame myself," he wrote back to Souvtchinsky, "especially since I treated my sincere inner wish to see you as Eumolpus as if it were a settled fact. . . . But you *must* sing the part, if not this season, then next autumn. I want this very much."[93] The wish was to remain unfulfilled.

The Paris press generally treated *Persephone* with respect, if not vast enthusiasm. But for some reason Boris de Schloezer savaged it in the *NRF,* scarcely pausing to describe it or even to explain clearly what it was about it he disliked, but instead attacking Stravinsky's whole concept of order as nothing but a

> theory forged *pro domo sua.* Being incapable of creating or, more simply, inventing, the composer now falls back on the notion of order. . . . [But] there is order and order: there is the order which transmutes and sublimates the flattest, meanest reality (and I'm thinking of any picture by an old Dutch master), and there is the external, mechanical order imposed by an armed force—or again, the sort that reigns at Père-Lachaise. Is not a well-kept cemetery a model of order?[94]

More curiously, de Schloezer accused Stravinsky of writing music completely at odds with the lyricism of Gide's text. At this point, it is hard to believe that the critic is unaware of Gide's own objections to the way his poetry has been treated. Gide, after all, was one of the founders of the *NRF* and remained the power behind its literary, if not its political, attitudes. Cingria, for one, had reason to feel that Gide's personal hostility towards him had worked to his disadvantage in the columns of the journal,[95] and it may have been at least partly for that reason that he took it upon himself to reply at length to de Schloezer's review, never mentioning him by name, but attacking as "an openly ill-intentioned criticism" the one article which had shown hostility to what he called "this great event of the epoch."[96] It was beyond question, Cingria averred, "that Stravinsky's current phase is the phase of his greatest mastery. Those who state the contrary affirm themselves as more sensitive to the picturesque or some folklore curio or else to a music adapted to some text they love, than to the pure art of music."

"Five or six years ago," de Schloezer replied in the same issue,

> M. Cingria and I could have agreed; but since then, I freely confess, my attitude to Stravinsky's art has completely changed . . . and what I reproach myself for today is not having detected at the time of the Octet, Oedipus, and Apollo that Stravinsky's classicism was sliding towards academicism, and that this "Hellene," to speak M. Cingria's language, was an Alexandrian and not an Athenian. . . . I am even ready to admit that "Stravinsky's current phase is the phase of his greatest mastery" and that Persephone is better made than The Rite or even than Les Noces. But the question is precisely whether the aesthetic value of a work, in a word its beauty, is solely a function of the composer's mastery. The whole problem lies here. The science, the skill of Stravinsky are not in question.
>
> I know that some were surprised, perhaps shocked, by the violence of my reaction to Persephone; that's because the Stravinsky case has a huge import and concerns something very much other than the failure or success of a great artist.[97]

JUST THREE DAYS after the appearance of de Schloezer's review, on 4 June, Stravinsky became a Frenchman. With typical insensitivity to his reasons for changing, L'Intransigeant announced the news alongside a ten-year-old photograph of the composer at the piano with Wilhelm Furtwängler. Three days after that, he was in hospital in Montmartre for an appendectomy. This was no emergency, no repetition of his desperate illness after The Rite of Spring, but a precaution, even perhaps a feeling that one clean slate deserved another. Three weeks before, there had been a serious panic when Theodore had burst his appendix and undergone an emergency operation for peritonitis. "The operation fascinated me," Stravinsky told Craft; and he went around afterwards recommending it to any of his other children and any of his friends who complained of the slightest stomach pain.[98]

When he came out of hospital, he put his name to the lease of a large apartment at the city end of the rue du Faubourg-Saint-Honoré, a mere stone's throw from the Madeleine and the place de la Concorde. It was the clinching gesture of the newly inscribed French celebrity. The apartment had fifteen rooms, including three salons, four maids' rooms, and a huge kitchen plus two cellars; it opened onto a *grand cour* which you entered through an archway from the rue du Faubourg, and it cost 22,500 francs a year to rent.

Meanwhile, in distant Lomonosov, the old wooden dacha of Khudintsev was being ripped apart to make way for an electricity substation which would, for a few years at least, supply the basic needs of the local citizenry in their bed-sitters and communal flats.

To Stravinsky, even if he had heard about it, this unconscious piece of symbolic vandalism would have meant little beyond a dissociation that he himself had cultivated, and which he now openly and officially recognized. For fifteen years his music had been ostentatiously detaching itself from its Russian roots. It may well be that, in the mirror of hindsight, *Persephone*—like the image of family life at Voreppe—still preserves more of the old Stravinsky than he might have cared to admit (and not just in candid Russianisms like the floral chorus, and certainly not just in the veiled Sovietisms of Gide's text). But this was not apparent at the time even to friendly critics like Cingria, who saw in this latest masterpiece welcome evidence that its composer had finally thrown off the shackles of folklorism and the picturesque, and entered into what Stravinsky himself later remembered Cingria calling, with only slightly misplaced irony, "the international style [of] the master of Oranienbaum."[99] However odd the setting, *Persephone*'s text was a kind of assurance that this international language would hereafter be spoken, as was only right and proper in the shadow of Versailles, with a French accent.

After signing his lease, Stravinsky lingered in Paris (and briefly London) for a few weeks of recording.[100] Then, early in August, he caught a train to Voreppe for the last time, and took up the manuscript of the two-piano concerto at the point in the first movement where he had left it twenty months before. If a dream had told him, at that moment, that he would never again make an accompanied setting of a French text, he would have been incredulous. If it had told him that in exactly six years' time, he would be seeking a new nationality in a new land, he would have been frankly appalled.

DATES

The Russian Empire continued to use the Julian calendar until 1 February 1918, so there is a discrepancy between Russian (Old Style) and Western (New Style) datings for the period of the present biography before that date. Throughout the nineteenth century Russia was twelve days behind the rest of Europe and America; then from 29 February/ 13 March 1900 the difference was thirteen days (because in the Western Gregorian calendar 1900 was not a leap year and there was no 29 February 1900 New Style). Since Stravinsky was partly resident in France and Switzerland from June 1910, and wholly so after July 1914, I have normally used double datings for this later period only where some exchange with Russia is involved. Before 1910, I have frequently used double datings (slashed, as above). However, single datings for events in Russia during that period are always Old Style. Single datings after 1910 are always New Style. In cases of possible ambiguity I have added "(OS)" or "(NS)" to the single date. This may seem unnecessarily complicated, but it is, I hope, always clear in practice. Note that Finland, which had already adopted the Gregorian calendar when it became a Russian province in 1809, retained the New Style.

The Russian Orthodox Church has never adopted the Gregorian calendar, which is why, throughout the twentieth century, Orthodox Russians have celebrated Christmas on 7 January (= 25 December OS). Russian Easter, which is determined—like its Western equivalent—by the full moon on or after 21 March, thus varies erratically in relation to Western Easter (but is always either the same or later).

TRANSLITERATIONS AND FORMS OF NAMES

The system adopted is that of the *New Grove Dictionary of Music and Musicians* (London: Macmillan, 1980), which is a strict, letter-for-letter (or group-for-group) system with the single general exception that the Russian genitive ending "ogo" ("ago") is transliterated according to its sound, as "ovo" ("avo"). In addition, proper names ending "sky"— including that of the subject himself—are rendered thus, and not "skiy," which would be correct under the system. Like the *New Grove*, I have nevertheless retained certain familiar spellings of personal and place names, even though they do not conform to the system (Tchaikovsky, Prokofiev, etc.), including some rejected by *Grove* (Rachmaninov, Scriabin). I have also been more lenient than *Grove* over accepted forms of names whose owners emigrated to the West and adopted standard forms of their own (Diaghilev, Koussevitzky, Tcherepnin, and even Massine—a spelling which seriously distorts the Russian name "Myasin"). There is no hope of consistency in such matters, and instead I have aimed at clarity and usability.

Consistency is also impossible in the matter of feminine endings of Russian surnames. Some of these forms (Karsavina, Pavlova, Slobodskaya) are standard in the West, and to change them would be a ridiculous and confusing pedantry. On the other hand, it seems no less pedantic to insist on feminine forms for every female Stravinsky (Stravinskaya) or Belyankin (Belyankina) resident in Switzerland or France after the Revolution. As a rule I have used these forms only in the full name with patronymic (Lyudmila Gavrilovna Belyankina, but Lyudmila Belyankin).

In the case of Stravinsky's own name, I have preserved variant spellings which occur in French and German texts quoted ("Strawinsky," "Strawinski"), and I have also respected the form which his elder son, Theodore Strawinsky (who settled in Geneva after his marriage), continued to prefer, even though this occasionally makes for bizarre conjunctions of father and son in the sentence or paragraph.

As regards place names, I have tried where possible (and significant) to indicate correspondences between old and new (Oranienbaum/Lomonosov, Ofitserskaya/ Dekabristov). But I have adopted the general principle that the name of the place is the name in contemporary use. So the city which became Leningrad is St. Petersburg until 1914 and Petrograd thereafter until 1924. For Ukrainian or Polish place names which have *not*, in essence, changed (Kiev, Vladimir-Volïnsky, Ustilug) I have normally transliterated the Russian form of the name which Stravinsky knew, at the risk of offending Polish ("Uscilug") or Ukrainian ("Kyïv") sensibilities.

Money

Any life of Stravinsky is bound to concern itself in some measure with money, and not only because he himself was so fond of the stuff. Brought up under the comparatively stable economic conditions of prewar Russia, he found himself, after the war, having to make ends meet as an international artist amid turbulent exchange rates, hyperinflation, protectionism, and in circumstances where Europe and America were being politically destabilized by uncertainty in the financial markets.

For the biographer (and a fortiori the reader), there are two distinct problems: (1) contemporary exchange and (2) the modern equivalence. Of these, the second is by far the more intractable.

(1) Although in practice exchange rates fluctuated before as well as after the First World War, the fluctuations were in the context of stable official rates. Before the war, the Russian rouble converted officially at just under 10 to the pound sterling, or just under 2 to the United States dollar (the dollar traded at about 5 to the pound). There were 25 French francs to the pound (5 to the dollar), and the rouble was worth about 2.7 francs (the Belgian, Swiss, and Italian francs were nominally at parity with the French).

After the war and the Russian Revolution, the rouble fell out of the reckoning, and meanwhile inflation in Western Europe undermined the old stabilities. Although the German mark recovered from the hyperinflation of 1923 with the help of tight monetary controls, the French franc slithered downwards, so that by the late twenties the former parity between the French and Swiss francs had become a conversion of 5 French francs to 1 Swiss (£1 = 125 French or 25 Swiss; $1 = 25 French or 5 Swiss), while the German Reichsmark was still quoted at its prewar rate of just over 20 to the pound or rather more than 4 to the dollar (which did not help Stravinsky, since growing German protectionism and xenophobia made it increasingly hard for him to earn money there in any case). In 1927 the new Italian lira was fixed at 92.46 to the pound and 19 to the dollar.

(2) Stravinsky's father retired from the Mariyinsky Opera in 1901 with a pension of 11,400 roubles per annum, a high if not astronomical figure (equivalent to about £1,200 or $6,000 in the values of the day) which reflected his great but essentially local fame. He was paying his eighteen-year-old son, Igor (in his last year at school), a monthly allowance of 4 roubles (£0.42; $2.10); a bottle of good-quality beer cost 30 kopeks (0.3 roubles: about 3 pence or 15 cents); a toothbrush 25 kopeks; a haircut 50 kopeks; and a night in a top-class St. Petersburg hotel about 10 roubles. It cost 10 kopeks to post a letter abroad.

54

Igor Stravinsky's post-1914 finances are harder to understand, partly because unlike his father he did not keep ordered records, partly because he was sometimes supporting, and always underwriting, a large extended family. But after 1924, his first year as a regular concert performer, his income soared. For concerts and recordings in the United States in 1925 he earned some 25,000 dollars, and he continued to earn on this scale through concert fees, commissions, royalties, and recording and piano-roll contracts, at a time when the average annual wage for a working man in France was about 15,000 francs (£120; $600). In the twenties and thirties a night in a first-class hotel in France, Italy, or Germany might cost at most £1 ($5); a 250-mile rail journey about £2 ($10) first-class (the equivalent by air, £5 or $25); a good restaurant meal about £0.30 ($1.50); a cup of coffee about £0.02 (8–10 cents); and a packet of twenty cigarettes up to about £0.08 (40 cents), according to quality. To post an overseas letter from any of these three countries cost just over £0.01 (6 cents). According to Eugen Weber (*The Hollow Years*, London: Sinclair-Stevenson, 1995, p. 66), in 1929 the new 6hp Peugeot 201 compact saloon went on the market for about 21,000 francs (£170; $850).

Tarantella, for piano, 1898 (incomplete). Unpublished.

Tucha (The storm cloud) (words: Pushkin), romance for voice and piano, 1902. Published: Sovetskiy Kompozitor, in *Igor' Stravinsky Vokal'naya Muzïka*, vol. 1, 1982; Faber, 1986.

Scherzo, for piano, 1902. Published: in V. Smirnov, *Tvorcheskoye Formirovaniye I. F. Stravinskovo*, Leningrad, 1970 (facsimile); Faber, 1975.

Sonata in F-sharp Minor, for piano, 1903–4. First performance: St. Petersburg, 9/22 February 1905 (private). Published: Faber, 1974.

[Cantata (for the sixtieth birthday of Rimsky-Korsakov), for chorus and piano (?), 1904; St. Petersburg, 6/19 March 1904. Unpublished (lost).]

How the mushrooms prepared for war *(Kak gribï na voynu sobiralis),* song for bass and piano, 1904. Published: Boosey and Hawkes, 1979.

[The driver and the tarantula *(Konduktor i tarantul)* (words: Koz'ma Prutkov), song or piano piece, 1906. First performance: St. Petersburg, 6/19 March 1906. Unpublished (lost).]

Symphony in E-flat Major, for orchestra, op. 1, 1905–7. First performance: St. Petersburg, 14/27 April 1907 (movements 2 and 3 only); 22 January/4 February 1908 (complete). Published: Jurgenson, 1914; Forberg.

The Faun and the Shepherdess *(Favn' i pastushka)* (words: Pushkin), suite for mezzo-soprano and orchestra, op. 2, 1906. First performance: St. Petersburg, 14/27 April 1907. Published: Belyayev, 1908 (vocal score), 1913 (full score).

Two Songs (words: Gorodetsky), for mezzo-soprano and piano, op. 6, 1907–8. First performance: St. Petersburg, 27 December 1907/9 January 1908 (no. 1); 10/23 April 1910 (complete). Published: Jurgenson, 1912 or 1913; Boosey and Hawkes.

Pastorale, vocalise for soprano and piano, 1907. First performance: St. Petersburg, 27 December 1907/9 January 1908. Published: Jurgenson, 1910; Schott.
    Arranged for soprano, oboe, English horn, clarinet, and bassoon, 1923. First performance: Antwerp, 7 January 1924. Published: Schott.
    Arranged for violin and piano, 1933. Published: Schott, 1934.
    Arranged for violin, oboe, English horn, clarinet, and bassoon, 1933. Published: Schott, 1934.

Scherzo fantastique, for orchestra, op. 3, 1907–8. First performance: St. Petersburg, 24 January/6 February 1909. Published: Jurgenson, 1909; Schott.

Fireworks, for orchestra, op. 4, 1908; revised 1909. First performance: St. Petersburg, 9/22 January 1910. Published: Schott, 1910.

[Funeral Song (Pogrebal'naya pesn'), for orchestra, op. 5, 1908. First performance: St. Petersburg, 17/30 January 1909. Unpublished (lost).]

Four Studies, for piano, op. 7, 1908. Published: Jurgenson, 1910; Benjamin.

The Firebird *(Zhar'-ptitsa; L'Oiseau de feu)*, fairy story ballet in 2 scenes, for orchestra, 1909–10. First performance: Paris, Opéra, 25 June 1910. Published: Jurgenson, 1912; Schott.

> Suite, for orchestra, 1910. First performance: St. Petersburg, 23 October/5 November 1910. Published: Jurgenson, 1912.
> Suite, for orchestra, 1919. First performance: Geneva, 12 April 1919. Published: Chester, 1920.
> Suite, for orchestra, 1945. First performance: New York, 24 October 1945. Published: Leeds, 1946; Schott.
> Prelude, Ronde, arranged for violin and piano, 1926. Published: Schott, 1929.
> Berceuse, for violin and piano, 1926. Published: Schott, 1929.
> Berceuse, for violin and piano, 1931–32. Published: Schott, 1932.
> Scherzo, for violin and piano, 1932. Published: Schott, 1933.

Two Poems of Verlaine, for baritone and piano, op. 9, 1910. First performance: St.Petersburg, 13/26 January 1911. Published: Jurgenson, 1911; Boosey and Hawkes.

> Arranged for baritone and chamber orchestra, 1910, 1951–52. Published: Boosey and Hawkes, 1952–53.

Petrushka, burlesque in 4 scenes, for orchestra, 1910–11. First performance: Paris, Châtelet, 13 June 1911. Published: Edition russe, 1912. Revised 1946. Published: Boosey and Hawkes, 1948.

> Three Movements from *Petrushka*, for piano, 1921. First performance: Paris, 26 December 1922. Published: Edition russe, 1922; Boosey and Hawkes.
> Danse russe, for violin and piano, 1932. Published: Edition russe, 1932; Boosey and Hawkes.

Two poems of Konstantin Balmont, for soprano or tenor and piano, 1911. First performance: St. Petersburg, 28 November/11 December 1912. Published: Edition russe, 1912; Boosey and Hawkes.

> Arranged for soprano or tenor, 2 flutes, 2 clarinets, piano, and string quartet, 1954. Published: Boosey and Hawkes, 1954.

Zvezdolikiy (The King of the Stars) (words: Balmont), for male chorus and orchestra, 1911–12. First performance: Brussels, 19 April 1939. Published: Jurgenson, 1913.

The Rite of Spring *(Vesna svyashchennaya; Le sacre du printemps)*, scenes of pagan Russia in 2 parts, for orchestra, 1911–13. First performance: Paris, Champs-Elysées, 29 May 1913. Published: Edition russe, 1913 (for piano duet), Edition russe, 1921 (full score); Boosey and Hawkes.

Three Japanese Lyrics (words from the Japanese, translated by A. Brandt), for soprano, 2 flutes, 2 clarinets, piano, and string quartet; or soprano and piano, 1912–13. First performance: Paris, 14 January 1914. Published: Edition russe, 1913; Boosey and Hawkes.

Three Little Songs *(Souvenirs de mon enfance)* (words: Russian folk poems), for voice and piano, c. 1906, revised 1913. First performance: Petrograd, 23 April/6 May 1915. Published: Edition russe, 1914; Boosey and Hawkes.
> Arranged for voice and small orchestra, 1929–30. Published: Edition russe, 1934; Boosey and Hawkes.

The Nightingale *(Solovey; Le rossignol)* (libretto: S. Mitusov, after Andersen), musical fairy tale (opera) in 3 acts, 1908–9, 1913–14. First performance: Paris, Opéra, 26 May 1914. Published: Edition russe, 1923; Boosey and Hawkes.
> Arrangements: *see Song of the Nightingale* (1917)

Three Pieces, for string quartet, 1914, revised 1918. First performance: Paris, c. 13 May 1915. Published: Edition russe, 1922. Boosey and Hawkes.
> Arranged for piano duet. Published: Paul Sacher Stiftung 1994.
> *see also* Four Studies (1928)

Pribaoutki (words: Afanasyev), for male voice and 8 instruments, 1914. First performance: London, 22 February 1918. Published: Henn, 1917; Chester.

Valse des fleurs, for piano duet, 1914. Published: Thames and Hudson, in R. Craft, *A Stravinsky Scrapbook 1940–1971* (London, 1983: facsimile).

Three Easy Pieces, for piano duet, 1914–15. First performance: Paris, 9 February 1918. Published: Henn, 1917; Chester.
> March, for 12 instruments, 1915. Unpublished.
> Polka, for cimbalom, 1915. Published: in *Feuilles musicales*, Lausanne, March-April 1962 (facsimile).
> *see also* Suite no. 2 (1921)

Souvenir d'une marche boche, for piano, 1915. Published: in E. Wharton, ed.: *The Book of the Homeless*, London, 1916.

Berceuses du chat (words: Russian folk poems), for contralto and 3 clarinets. First performance: Paris, 20 November 1918. Published: Henn, 1917; Chester.

Renard *(Bayka)* (libretto: Stravinsky, after Afanasyev), burlesque in song and dance, for 2 tenors, 2 basses, and small orchestra, 1915–16. First performance: Paris, Opéra, 18 May 1922. Published: Henn, 1917; Chester.

Four Russian Peasant Songs *(Podblyudnïye)* (words: Russian folk poems), female voices, 1914–17. Published: Schott, 1930; Chester.
> Arranged for female voices and 4 horns, 1954. First performance: Los Angeles, 11 October 1954. Published: Chester, 1958; Schott.

Valse pour les enfants, for piano, 1916 or 1917. Published: in *Le Figaro*, Paris, 21 May 1922.

Five Easy Pieces, for piano duet, 1917. First performance: Paris, 9 February 1918. Published: Henn, 1917; Chester.
> *see also* Suite no. 1 (1925), Suite no. 2 (1921)

Three Children's Tales *(Tri Detskiye pesenki)* (words: Russian folk poems), for voice and piano, 1916–17. Published: Chester, 1920.
> "Tilimbom," for voice and orchestra (extended version), 1923. First performance: Antwerp, 7 January 1924. Published: Chester, 1927.

[Canons, for 2 horns, 1917. Unpublished (lost).]

Les Noces *(Svadebka; The Wedding)* (words: Stravinsky, after Kireyevsky), Russian choreographic scenes, in 4 scenes: first draft for voices and large mixed ensemble, 1914–17; intermediate draft (scenes 1 and 2 only) for voices, harmonium, 2 cimbaloms, pianola, and percussion, 1919; final version for solo voices, chorus, 4 pianos, and percussion, 1921–23. First performance: Paris, Gaîté Lyrique, 13 June 1923. Published: Chester, 1922 (vocal score), c. 1923 (full score).

The Song of the Nightingale *(Le Chant du rossignol)*, symphonic poem and ballet in 1 act (arranged from *The Nightingale*, acts 2–3), for orchestra, 1917. First concert performance: Geneva, 6 December 1919; first stage performance: Paris, Opéra, 2 February 1920. Published: Edition russe, 1921; Boosey and Hawkes.

> Chants du rossignol and Marche chinoise, for violin and piano, 1932. Published: Edition russe, 1934; Boosey and Hawkes.

Study, for pianola, 1917. Published: piano roll, no. T967B (Aeolian), 1921; unpublished in score.

> *see also* Four Studies (1928)

Berceuse (words: Stravinsky), for voice and piano, 1917. Published: Faber, in British edition of *Expositions and Developments*, 1962.

Lied ohne Namen, for 2 bassoons, 1916–18. First performance: London, 30 October 1979. Published: Faber, in *SSCI*, 1982; title added in 1949.

The Soldier's Tale *(L'Histoire du soldat)* (libretto: C. F. Ramuz), to be read, played, and danced, in 2 parts, for 7 players, 1918. First performance: Lausanne, Théâtre Municipal, 28 September 1918. Published: Chester, 1924.

> Suite, for 7 players, 1920. First performance: London, 20 July 1920. Published: Chester, 1922.
>
> Suite, for violin, clarinet, and piano, 1918–19. First performance: Lausanne, 8 November 1919. Published: Chester, 1920.

Ragtime, for 11 instruments, 1917–18. First performance: London, 27 April 1920. Published: Editions de la Sirène, 1920; Chester.

> Arranged for piano, 1917–18. First performance: Lausanne, 8 November 1919. Published: Chester, 1920.

Three Pieces, for clarinet, 1918. First performance: Lausanne, 8 November 1919. Published: Chester, 1920.

Four Russian Songs (words: Russian folk poems), for voice and piano, 1918–19. First performance: Paris, 7 February 1920. Published: *La Revue Romande*, 15 September 1919 (nos. 3 and 4 only); Chester, 1920.

> "Sektantskaya" (no. 4), for voice, flute, and cimbalom, 1918–19. Published: Faber, in *SSCI*, 1982 (facsimile).

Piano Rag Music, for piano, 1919. First performance: Lausanne, 8 November 1919. Published: Chester, 1920.

Pulcinella, ballet in 1 act (music after Pergolesi and others), for solo voices and chamber orchestra, 1919–20. First performance: Paris, Opéra, 15 May 1920. Published: Chester, 1920 (vocal score), Edition russe, 1924 (full score); Boosey and Hawkes.

Suite, for chamber orchestra, 1922. First performance: Boston, 22 December 1922. Published: Edition russe, 1924; Boosey and Hawkes.

Suite, for violin and piano, 1925. First performance: Winterthur, 12 November 1925. Published: Edition russe,1926; Boosey and Hawkes.

Suite italienne, for cello and piano, 1932. Published: Edition russe, 1934; Boosey and Hawkes.

Suite italienne, for violin and piano, 1932. First performance: Berlin, 28 October 1932. Published: Edition russe, 1934; Boosey and Hawkes.

Concertino, for string quartet, 1920. First performance: New York, 23 November 1920. Published: Hansen, 1923.

Arranged for piano duet, 1920 (?). Published: Hansen, 1923.

Arranged for 12 instruments, 1952. First performance: Los Angeles, 11 November, 1952. Published: Hansen, 1953.

Symphonies of Wind Instruments, for 24 instruments, 1920. First performance: London, 10 June 1921. Published: Edition russe: 1926 (piano reduction only). Revised 1947 for 23 instruments. First performance: New York, 31 January 1948. Published: Boosey and Hawkes, 1952.

Chorale, for wind ensemble without clarinets, 1945. First performance: New York, 30 January 1946. Unpublished.

Suite no. 2 (arrangement of Three Easy Pieces, and Galop from Five Easy Pieces), for small orchestra, 1915–21. First performance: Frankfurt am Main, 25 November 1925. Published: Chester, 1925.

Les cinq doigts (The Five Fingers), for piano, 1921. First performance: Paris, 15 December 1921. Published: Chester, 1922.

Eight Instrumental Miniatures, for 15 instruments, 1962. First performance: Los Angeles, 26 March 1962 (1–4 only); Toronto, 29 April 1962 (complete). Published: Chester, 1963.

Mavra (libretto: B. Kochno after Pushkin), opéra bouffe in 1 act, 1921–22. First performance: Paris, Opéra, 3 June 1922. Published: Edition russe, 1925; Boosey and Hawkes.

Chanson de Paracha (Russian Maiden's Song), for soprano and orchestra, 1922–23. First performance: Paris, 7 November 1923. Published: Edition russe, 1925; Boosey and Hawkes.

Chanson russe, for violin and piano (also cello and piano), 1937. Published: Edition russe, 1938; Boosey and Hawkes.

Octet, for wind instruments, 1922–23. First performance: Paris, 18 October 1923. Published: Edition russe, 1924; Boosey and Hawkes.

Concerto, for piano and wind instruments, 1923–24. First performance: Paris, 22 May 1924. Published: Edition russe, 1924 (reduction for 2 pianos), 1936 (full score); Boosey and Hawkes.

Sonata, for piano, 1924. First public performance: Donaueschingen, 16 July 1925. Published: Edition russe, 1925; Boosey and Hawkes.

Serenade in A, for piano, 1925. First performance: Frankfurt am Main, 24 November 1925. Published: Edition russe, 1926; Boosey and Hawkes.

Suite no. 1 (arrangement of Five Easy Pieces nos. 1–4), for small orchestra, 1925. First performance: Haarlem, 2 March 1926. Published: Chester, 1926.

Our Father (Otche nash') (Slavonic text), SATB choir, 1926. First performance: Paris, 18 May 1934. Published: Edition russe, 1932; Boosey and Hawkes. Revised as Pater noster (Latin text), 1949. Published: Boosey and Hawkes, 1949.

Oedipus rex (libretto: Jean Cocteau, Jean Daniélou), opera-oratorio in 2 acts, 1926–27. First concert performance: Paris, Théâtre Sarah-Bernhardt, 30 May 1927; first stage performance: Vienna, Staatsoper, 23 February 1928. Published: Edition russe, 1927 (vocal score only); Boosey and Hawkes, 1949 (full score).

Apollon musagète *(Apollo)*, ballet in 2 scenes, for string orchestra, 1927–28. First performance: Washington, Library of Congress, 27 April 1928. Published: Edition russe, 1928; Boosey and Hawkes.

The Fairy's Kiss *(Le baiser de la fée)*, ballet in 4 scenes (music after Tchaikovsky), for orchestra, 1928. First performance: Paris, Opéra, 27 November 1928. Published: Edition russe, 1928; Boosey and Hawkes.
   Ballad, for violin and piano, 1933 (with S. Dushkin). Unpublished.
   Divertimento, for violin and piano, 1934. First performance: Strasbourg, 12 December 1934. Published: Edition russe, 1934; Boosey and Hawkes.
   Divertimento, for orchestra, 1934. First performance: Paris, 4 November 1934. Published: Edition russe, 1934; Boosey and Hawkes.
   Ballad, for violin and piano, 1947 (with J. Gautier). Published: Boosey and Hawkes, 1951.

Four Studies (arrangement of Three Pieces for string quartet and Study for pianola), for orchestra, 1928–29. First performance: Paris, 16 November 1928 (no. 4 only); Berlin, 7 November 1930 (complete). Published: Edition russe, 1930; Boosey and Hawkes.

Capriccio, for piano and orchestra, 1928–29. First performance: Paris, 6 December 1929. Published: Edition russe, 1930; Boosey and Hawkes.

Symphony of Psalms (words: Psalms 38: 13–14; 39: 2–4; 150; vulgate), for chorus and orchestra, 1930. First performance: Brussels, 13 December 1930. Published: Edition russe, 1930 (vocal score), 1931 (full score); Boosey and Hawkes.

Concerto in D, for violin and orchestra, 1931. First performance: Berlin, 23 October 1931. Published: Schott, 1931.

Duo Concertant, for violin and piano, 1931–32. First performance: Berlin radio, 28 October 1932. Published: Edition russe, 1933; Boosey and Hawkes.

Creed (Simvol' Verï) (Slavonic text), for SATB choir, 1932. First performance: Paris, 18 May 1934. Published: Edition russe, 1933; Boosey and Hawkes. Revised as Credo (Latin text), 1949. Published: Boosey and Hawkes, 1949.

Persephone (words: André Gide), melodrama in 3 scenes, for speaker, solo tenor, chorus, and orchestra, 1933–34. First performance: Paris, Opéra, 30 April 1934. Published: Edition russe, 1934; Boosey and Hawkes.

Ave Maria (Bogoroditse devo) (Slavonic text), for SATB choir, 1934. First performance:

Paris, 18 May 1934. Published: Edition russe, 1934; Boosey and Hawkes. Revised as Ave Maria (Latin text), 1949. Published: Boosey and Hawkes, 1949.

Concerto, for 2 pianos, 1932–35. First performance: Paris, 21 November 1935. Published: Schott, 1936.

ARRANGEMENTS

CHOPIN

Nocturne in A-flat, op. 32, no. 2; Grand Valse brillante in E-flat, op. 18, arranged for orchestra, for the ballet *Les Sylphides,* 1909. First performance: Paris, 2 June 1909. Published: Boosey and Hawkes, 1997 (Grand Valse); in press (Nocturne).

BEETHOVEN-MUSORGSKY

Song of the Flea *(Pesnya Mefistofelya o blokhe)* (words from Goethe's *Faust),* arranged for baritone or bass and orchestra, 1909. First performance: St. Petersburg, 28 November/ 11 December 1909. Published: Sovetskiy Kompozitor, in *Igor' Stravinsky Vokal' naya Muzïka,* vol. 2, 1928; Boosey and Hawkes.

GRIEG

[Kobold, op. 71, no. 3, arranged for orchestra, 1910. First performance: St. Petersburg, 20 February/5 March 1910. Unpublished (lost).]

MUSORGSKY

Khovanshchina: aria of Shaklovitiy and final chorus, realized and orchestrated, 1913. First performance: Paris, 16 (or 18) June 1913. Published: Bessel, 1914 (vocal score of final chorus only).

Song of the Volga Boatmen, arranged for wind and percussion, 1917. First performance: Rome, 9 April 1917. Published: Chester, 1920.

Boris Godunov: opening chorus, arranged for piano, 1918. Published: Boosey and Hawkes, 1997.

ROUGET DE LISLE

La Marseillaise, arranged for solo violin, 1919. First public performance: London, 13 November 1979. Published: Boosey and Hawkes, 1997.

TCHAIKOVSKY

The Sleeping Beauty: Variation d'Aurore and Entr'acte (act 2), arranged for orchestra, 1921. First performance: London, 2 November 1921. Published: Boosey and Hawkes, 1981.

Library Abbreviations

BN	Bibliothèque Nationale, Paris
GMMK	Gosudarstvennïy muzey muzikal'noy kul'turï imeni M. I. Glinki (State Glinka Museum of Musical Culture), Moscow
KA	Kochno Archive, Bibliothèque de l'Opéra, Paris
PSS	Paul Sacher Stiftung, Basle
RGALI	Rossiyskiy Gosudarstvennïy arkhiv literaturï i iskusstva (Russian State Archive of Literature and Art), Moscow
RIII	Rossiyskiy institut istorii iskusstv (Russian Institute of the History of the Arts), St. Petersburg
RM	Russkiy muzey (Russian Museum), St. Petersburg
RNB	Rossiyskaya natsional'naya biblioteka (Russian National Library), St. Petersburg

Introduction

1 R. Craft, "Stravinsky: Relevance and Problems of Biography," in *Prejudices in Disguise*, 273–4.
2 R. Craft, "Stravinsky: A Centenary View," in *Present Perspectives*, 227.
3 *Mem*, 26.

1 The Polish Singer

1 The date is in A. Burak, "Vïdayushchiysya pevets i reformator stsyenï," *Baltiyskiy luch*, 29 June 1974.
2 *Mem*, 19.
3 *PRK*, 25. The Stravinskys were staying this time in the dacha of General Svistovsky in Lesna Ulitsa (as they did again in 1885).
4 This and other information is from a leaflet produced by the Oranienbaum School of Music in connection with the town's Music Days for Stravinsky's Birthday (1994), and kindly supplied to me by the school's director, Olga Rïbakova, who also acted as my guide round the town.
5 Jay Leyda and Sergei Bertensson (eds.), *The Musorgsky Reader* (New York: Da Capo Press, 1970), 404.
6 *FSS*, 190. The other roles are listed by Burak, op. cit., who also states that the Stravinsky family spent seven summer seasons in Oranienbaum. This, however, is not supported by *FSS* or by the relevant extracts from Fyodor's account books in *PRK*.

7   *Expo*, 19. It was also Dyadya (Uncle) Vanya who disappointed the tiny Igor by telling him to "watch the birdie" when there was no birdie to watch. Ivan Ivanovich had two brothers: Mikhail (Dyadya Misha), a "realist" painter, and Nikolay (Dyadya Kolya), who was commandant of the island fortress of Kronstadt, opposite Oranienbaum, and later served as a general in the Far East during the Russo-Japanese War. See *PRK*, 421–2.

8   The account-book entry is reproduced in *SB*, 139, and the calendar page in *SRT*, 91, and in *CISFam* (plate 1). Tatyana Yakovlev received six roubles a month, plus room and board, for her services, until 1 June 1883, when Igor was weaned. In later years (at least until 1900), she would visit the family at Easter or New Year and receive a small cash present.

9   *SRT*, 90–2. Taruskin also points out that the martyr Igor was a prince of Chernigov, near which city Fyodor was born, but that Igor, though the saint's historical name, was not his hagiographic one, so that the naming-in-honor was at best irregular. Igor itself is a name of Scandinavian origin, related etymologically to Ingvar.

10 *Mem*, 21–2.

11 *Expo*, 73–4. Stravinsky gives the date as 29 June, but the account-book entry (*PRK*, 20) confirms the later date, which is recorded also on the torn-off calendar page for 5 June. 29 July was also his mother's birthday.

12 *Mem*, 26.

13 The Decembrist Andrey Furman was another ancestor. For exhaustive information on Stravinsky's family tree, see *PRK*, appendix 1, 403–40.

14 Anna Engel-Litke was thus Diaghilev's great-great-grandmother and Stravinsky's great-great-great-aunt, and they were fourth cousins. Diaghilev was also related, through marriage, to Tchaikovsky, whose first cousin, Amaliya Schobert, had married Anna Litke's son Fyodor, and it was Amaliya's sons, Alexander and Konstantin, who, as Stravinsky records in *Expo* (80), kept vigil by Tchaikovsky's deathbed in 1893. These teenage boys were thus also cousins of Stravinsky, but he had no blood connection with Tchaikovsky.

15 And needed none, since Maria Romanovna Furman, whom he married in the forties, was a rich woman who inherited a huge property in Belarus from her childless Engel great-uncle (who also happened to be her stepgrandfather).

16 Letter of 13/25 May 1874, *FSS*, 84–6. Anna and Fyodor married in Kiev on 24 May/5 June.

17 I am grateful to Stefan Strawinski, of Gdansk, for supplying me with a copy of the admirably detailed and thorough genealogy he compiled, and to Adam Zamoyski for explaining its significance to me.

18 See Ludwik Erhardt, *Igor Strawinski*, for this and much other information on the Polish Strawinscys. The Stanislaw Strawinscy referred to here is apparently not the same as the kidnapper of King Stanislaw August whom the composer mentions as a possible ancestor (*Expo*, 49). Stefan Strawinski includes this famous subversive in an inset of his genealogy but is unable to prove a family link. As for the Ignace Stravinsky who was a Lithuanian chamberlain in 1778 (ibid.), he was not the father of the Noviy Dvor leaseholder (the composer's grandfather) but a third cousin two or three times removed. This Lithuanian branch had preserved a certain dignity as minor gentry, but with a dissident tendency traceable, presumably, to the fact that they had lost land and title in remote eastern Polish Lithuania when the region reverted to Russia in the mid-seventeenth century. Chamberlain Ignace, for instance, seems to have sided with Catherine the Great in the Confederacy of Targowica in 1792, which led to the partition of Poland. Kidnapper Stanislaw may also have been a member of this branch of the family.

19 *Mem*, 18.

20 See K. Stravinskaya, "Shto ya slïshala o svoem dede—F. I. Stravinskom," in *FSS*, 79. According to Erhardt, 11, Fyodor's mother left Ignaty because she had had enough of their poor standard of living.

21 Handwritten inscription on a photograph of the house, in the possession of Xenya Stravinsky's daughter, Yelena, who showed me this and many other family photos at her flat in St. Petersburg. The Bragin photo was taken in 1877, and shows Fyodor and his wife standing in front of the house with his maternal grandfather, then aged 110.

22 *Dial*, 63. The interview was originally printed in the *New York Review of Books* in 1965. Stravinsky attributes this canard to "family tradition." But curiously enough, in a radio conversation at the time of his eightieth birthday, three years earlier, he had said that his great-grandfather, "a very religious man," died after climbing the garden hedge on his way home from church. Since, though, in the same broadcast he stated that his grandmother, Skorokhodov's daughter, died at the age of ninety-seven (when actually she died at eighty or eighty-one), it might on the whole be safer to discount this entire memoir as nothing more than a good story.

23 Letter of 7/19 November 1877, in *FSS*, 93.

24 *IVSPA*, 36, caption to plate 21.

25 Letter of 16/29 July 1903, in *PRK*, 133–4. Alexander Stravinsky fought in the Russo-Turkish War of 1877–78 as a lieutenant colonel. Ivan Skorokhodov's letter to Fyodor (see note 23) seems to suggest that by November 1877, Alexander had still not met his sister-in-law Anna Kirillovna, three and a half years after her marriage.

26 Quoted in *FSS*, 174. But the reminiscence was an obituary notice, perhaps colored by Fyodor's subsequent fame.

27 Alexandra Skorokhodov, Fyodor's mother, is said to have had a good voice, but we do not know what kind of music she sang. *FSS*, 79.

28 *FSS*, 174. This contradicts Igor Stravinsky's memory (*Mem*, 18) that Fyodor only discovered his good voice and ear as a law student at Nezhin, though it was certainly at Nezhin that singing began to take over. According to Edward Stark, who knew Fyodor personally, he sang in the cathedral choir at Mozïr': *Peterburgskaya opera i yeyo mastera*, 192.

29 It may be necessary to emphasize here that, though poor and landless, the Stravinskys were still, in tsarist terms, noblemen. "The traditional 'career' for urbanized members of this class was a civil service sinecure, for which position one trained in the juridical faculty of the university. . . . A *dvoryanin* in a civil service niche did not have to be particularly good at anything in order to earn a comfortable living." *SRT*, 94. Fyodor was not yet urbanized, but he soon would be.

30 He was probably supported there, however, by his eldest brother, Alexander. See *FSS*, 79.

31 Stark, 192.

32 *SRT*, 77. Taruskin notes that in 1902, the year Fyodor died, "the earliest Russian-made discs, featuring the tenor Nikolai Figner and his Italian-born wife, Medea Mei-Figner, were being offered for sale."

33 See *SRT*, 81, for a revealing account of Stravinsky's success in this work at its premiere in 1884. Tchaikovsky himself conducted, but Stravinsky—in what is by no means a leading part—received the lion's share of the applause.

34 *SRT*, 78, note 3.

35 Letter of 8 August 1964 to Mikhail Goldstein, in *Musik des Ostens*, 7 (1975), 280–3 (German translation only). English translation from the Russian original in *SRT*, 161–2.

36 *Chron*, 16. In the conversation books, however, Stravinsky says little or nothing about his father's singing as such.

37 *FSS*, 176.

38 Stark, 194. But Stark, like Igor Stravinsky himself, can only have heard Fyodor properly in the last decade or so of his career.

39 The best study of Fyodor Stravinsky's voice and career is in Stark, 190–226. An excellent survey in English is in *SRT*, 77 et seq. For a more detailed account of Fyodor as man, performer, and bibliophile, see *FSS*.

40 Stark, 192.
41 For much of this information I am indebted to *FSS*, passim, but especially 176–80. Another member of Setov's company was a seventeen-year-old Polish dancer called Eleonora Bereda, the future mother of Vaslav Nijinsky. Did Fyodor Stravinsky know her? See Bronislava Nijinska, *Early Memoirs*, 8.
42 Letter from Fyodor to Anna, 13/25 May 1874, in *FSS*, 84–6.
43 According to Yelena Stravinsky, Nosenko had been a general practitioner in the Belarus village of Khorval, which Stravinsky's grandmother had inherited from her great-uncle. By the 1870s, however, he was medical director of the Imperial prisons in Kiev. See T. and D. Strawinsky, *Au coeur du Foyer*, 81. The statement in *FSS*, 86, note 3, that he was a lawyer seems to be an error.
44 See her autobiographical notes, quoted in *SRT*, 429.
45 There was also a daughter, Yulia, who married an Austrian baron called Rosen and settled in Vienna.
46 Proskurov is now called Khmel'nitsky. Pavlovka is twenty-seven versts—about eighteen miles—from the town of Bugul'ma (still so-called).
47 *Expo*, 38. A photo survives which seems to prove that he was at Pechisky in 1906. But there is no other evidence for this visit. In any case, his memories of his aunt's house are essentially childhood ones.
48 Family tradition has it that before these live births she had had two still-births by Nosenko, and before that no fewer than seven still-births or infant deaths by Pushchin. She died, Denise Strawinsky suggests, of exhaustion. See T. and D. Strawinsky, *Au coeur du Foyer*, 81.
49 *SPD*, 39.
50 *FSS*, 180: "The Kiev police opened a *Dossier on the Public's Excessive Expressions of Approval for the Singer Stravinsky*."
51 *Sankt-Peterburgskiye vedomosti*, no. 109 (1976), quoted in ibid.
52 Ibid. In fact he sang in thirty-nine performances in the 1876–77 season, then promptly renewed his contract at a salary of four thousand roubles.
53 Renamed Ulitsa Dekabristov after the Revolution. Since the fall of communism in 1991, many Petersburg streets (like the city itself) have resumed their old names, but this one is an exception.
54 Quoted in *FSS*, 188. Vsevolozhsky is best known as the inspiration and scenarist of Tchaikovsky's ballet *The Sleeping Beauty*, which is dedicated to him and for whose first performance at the Mariyinsky in 1890 he himself designed the costumes. In June 1882 he was relatively new in the post of director, and perhaps as yet unversed in the theatre's dressing-room politics. An affectionate drawing of Vsevolozhsky by Fyodor Stravinsky, reproduced in *FSS*, between pp. 16 and 17, suggests a good subsequent relationship between them. But Fyodor only found out about the attempt to have him dismissed in 1897.

2 THE KRYUKOV CANAL

1 See *Expo*, 13 et seq., for Stravinsky's own vivid memoir of the Kryukov Canal flat, with a plan on p. 15; the Bridge of Kisses is now more prosaically called Dekabristov Bridge. Fifty years after he last visited the flat, Stravinsky understandably misremembered certain details—for instance, the exact number of windows. (More remarkable is his statement in *Mem* (24) that "the house no longer exists, thanks to a German bomb.") In 1891 Fyodor extended the flat, taking in rooms from the next flat along, and it was the extra front room thus acquired which became the bedroom shared by Igor and his younger brother, Gury. For the view from the apartment windows, see the painting by Yury Stravinsky's wife, Yelena Novoselov, reproduced in *SPD*, 43. The Litovsky Zamok was destroyed in the February 1917 revolution.
2 *Expo*, 16. To accept the composer's memory of such details is risky, but they are not

out of keeping with what we know of domestic life in late-nineteenth-century Petersburg. Even Tamara Karsavina's parents, who were relatively poor apartment-dwellers and sometimes had to request moratoria on the rent, kept one or two maids and the inevitable *nyanya*. See *Theatre Street*, 11–14. The density of about 1.6 people per room was only just below the Petersburg average of 1.7. See James Bater, *St. Petersburg: Industrialization and Change*, 327. Semyon Ivanovich's cubbyhole is no more.

3 For a detailed account of Fyodor's routine for studying a new part, see Stark, 197–200. It always began with an intensive and painstaking process of research.

4 *FSS*, 81. The story was told by Nikolay to Yury's daughter Xenia.

5 *Mem*, 19.

6 The Stravinskys employed a succession of French governesses, few for any length of time. How many of them taught Igor is impossible to say, but no impropriety is recorded. Agnes Richter, who certainly did teach him, is said simply to have "abandoned the lessons" in February 1890 (after three and a half months). The account books also reveal that Roman and Yury had a separate tutor, also at home. Gury joined Igor with his governess a year or two later. See *PRK*, 30–3.

7 *Expo*, 38.

8 *Expo*, 39.

9 See, for instance, *SPD*, 40. In 1899 Gury, aged fifteen, is already three or four inches taller than his seventeen-year-old brother.

10 *Mem*, 20. In a letter to Anna Stravinsky of 31 January/12 February 1888, Glinka's sister, Lyudmila Shestakova, describes the twelve-year-old Roman as *"krasavets"*—a good-looker. See *FSS*, 147, note 4. Perhaps the best photograph of Roman shows him sitting for his portrait to his Nosenko cousins Katya and Olga. See *CISFam*, plate 10. But the photo, apparently taken in 1895 or 1896, is wrongly dated 1902, by which time Roman was dead.

11 Her French passport from the 1920s and 1930s gives her height as 1.52 meters, which is fractionally below five feet.

12 *Expo*, 73. His formal baptism in the Nikolsky Sobor at the age of eight weeks had apparently been preceded by a kind of emergency treatment in Oranienbaum on the actual day of his birth. Early baptism was in fact common in St. Petersburg, because of the regular cholera and smallpox epidemics. But there is no mention of this first-day christening in the account books.

13 *Theatre Street*, 12. The advice was, of course, ignored. For instance, the children often used the frozen canals as shortcuts.

14 *Mem*, 24.

15 15/28 August 1903, in *PRK*, 139.

16 23 August/5 September 1900, in *PRK*, 87–8.

17 Letter of 6/19 August 1907 from Ustilug, in *PRK*, 177–9. The letter is also in *SM*, 443, but without the passage quoted.

18 *Mem*, 19; *Expo*, 52. The account books from late August 1893 to the end of 1896 are unfortunately lost.

19 *Mem*, 20.

20 Yury's daughter Tanya found her noticeably colder than the rest of Igor's family when she stayed with them in Nice in 1925. See *SB*, 37.

21 *SB*, 24. Fyodor died in November 1902 (OS); Yury married in January 1904. According to Yury's granddaughter (private communication), Anna kept a photograph of Fyodor in his coffin by her bed, as well as preserving his library as a shrine.

22 *Mem*, 24.

23 Respectively: Igor to his parents, 27 July/8 August 1899, *PRK*, 74–5; Igor to his mother, 6/19 June 1903, ibid., 128–9; Igor to his mother, 5/18 July 1903, ibid., 131–2; Igor to his mother and Gury, 9 May 1911 (NS), ibid., 275–6.

24 Alexandre Benois, *Reminiscences of the Russian Ballet*, 11. The Benois family, who were Catholics of Franco-Italian origin, lived on the corner of Glinka Ulitsa and the Yekateringovsky (now Rimsky-Korsakov) Prospect, opposite the Nikolsky Sobor.

56

25 Ibid., 8.

26 *Mem,* 24.

27 *Mem,* 19.

28 V. V. Yastrebtsev, *Reminiscences of Rimsky-Korsakov,* 132. Fyodor had just sung Panas in Rimsky-Korsakov's *Christmas Eve* (28 November/10 December 1895).

29 *FSS,* 10.

30 The account books are still in the possession of the composer's great-niece in St. Petersburg. Entries relating to Igor Stravinsky are in *PRK,* 19–123 passim.

31 Igor noted (*Mem,* 19) that Fyodor showed him affection only when he, Igor, was ill, "which seems to me an excellent excuse for any hypochondriac tendencies I might have."

32 A German nanny like Bertha would have been called a *bonna,* but the distinction is trivial.

33 See *CISFam,* plate 52.

34 Letter of 7/20 January 1911 to Andrey Rimsky-Korsakov, in *PRK,* 260–1. The *garmoshka* is the Russian peasant concertina, or squeeze box. "Bottle-boots" were leather boots shaped like bottles.

35 Benois, *Reminiscences of the Russian Ballet,* 18–19.

36 *Expo,* 28.

37 Andrei Bely, *Petersburg,* trans. Robert A. Maguire and John E. Malmstad (Harmondsworth: Penguin, 1983), 22.

38 G. Dobson, *St. Petersburg,* quoted in Bater, 343–4. I am indebted to Bater's fascinating study for much of the information in this section. Among other things, it shows that Tchaikovsky's supposed drinking of unboiled water in a Petersburg restaurant in 1893 would have been dangerous even without the cholera epidemic of that year.

39 *Expo,* 14; Karsavina, *Theatre Street,* 12.

40 *PRK,* 40.

41 *Expo,* 17. The Russian for a doorman is *shveytsar*—a Swiss.

42 The school is still in the same place, somewhat altered, at the corner of Kazanskaya (now Ulitsa Plekhanova) and the Demidov (now Grivtsova) Pere-ulok, near the site of the original Conservatoire building. The (unnumbered) illustrations in *PRK* include two photographs of the school, at the turn of the century and in the 1990s, respectively.

43 Quoted in Hugh Seton-Watson, *The Russian Empire 1801–1917,* 476. Fyodor's account book records a payment of thirty roubles for the first half-year of Igor's schooling.

44 *PRK,* 52.

45 *Expo,* 17. See also *Chron,* 19. As it happens, the headmaster was also called Smirnov. On the other hand, Igor seems to have been friendly with a boy called Boris Wahrlich (the son of the conductor of the Court Orchestra), who wrote to him in 1956 reminding him of their long discussions "at the tea table in the cellar at break, where our beloved porter Ivan provided us with tea for a rouble a month." See *PRK,* 52, for these and other details.

46 Letter of 13/26 March 1908, in *PRK,* 186–7; *SM,* 444.

47 Alexander Yakovlev, "Iz detskix i yunosheskix let," in *Muz Ak* 1992, 112–5.

48 Letter of 15/28 January 1901, in *PRK,* 92. The word "less" has been underlined, presumably by Fyodor. The letter shows, incidentally, that science was on the curriculum at least of the higher classes in private gymnasia, even if excluded in the state system. See also *Mem,* 26–7. Stravinsky's remark there that "I had already been reproached for [composing] by the school director" is perhaps a remote memory of this incident. Another may be his telling the American journalist Janet Flanner that "his schoolmaster wrote his parents they need expect nothing from such a son" ("Russian Firebird," 23–8). The same story had appeared in André Schaeffner, *Strawinsky,* 7.

49 *Chron,* 14; *Expo,* 42. In his March 1908 letter to Timofeyev (see note 46) he records that she was the daughter of a Mariyinsky Theatre violinist.

50 *PRK*, 38. Varunts speculates elsewhere that Petrova's successor, Y. M. Yanovich, also gave the children music lessons (in autumn 1892); but the account books as published do not explicitly say so; ibid., 17.

51 *Expo*, 42; *PRK*, 67.

52 *PRK*, 186. Roman had also studied the piano as a child, and Gury did so briefly (also with Snetkova). But Yury apparently did not.

53 "As for my inclinations and predilections for music, they regarded them as mere amateurism. . . . This now seems to me quite natural." *Chron*, 28.

54 *Mem*, 21–2. In his next volume of conversations he makes the absurd observation that "very little immediate tradition lies behind *Le Sacre du printemps*" (*Expo*, 147). See *SRT*, passim, for a conclusive demolition of this view.

55 Letter to Anna Stravinsky, 31 January/12 February 1888, in *FSS*, 147, note 4. This is the letter in which she compliments Roman on his good looks (see above, note 10).

56 *Expo*, 36.

57 We shall see later on that Stravinsky consistently misremembered places and dates. As for L'zy, he even forgot where it was. The "nearby" Valdye (Valday) Hills and the "railway terminal" at Balagoyeh (Bologoye) are a good hundred miles away, a long droshky ride even by Russian standards.

58 *Chron*, 14.

59 *Conv*, 37.

60 Ibid. See also *Chron*, 15.

61 *Mem*, 31. The world premiere was on 3/15 January.

62 Lieven, *Birth of the Ballets-Russes*, quoted in *SRT*, 535–6.

63 *Expo*, 86; see also *Chron*, 16–17. Both accounts mistakenly connect this gala with Tchaikovsky's death (in October 1893).

64 *Chron*, 16.

65 The remark in *Expo* (61) that *Falstaff* was not played in St. Petersburg in Igor's youth is mistaken. Fyodor took the role of Pistol at the Russian premiere in January 1894, less than a year after the world premiere in Milan. A year after that he was the first Andrey Dubrovsky in *Dubrovsky* by Nápravník, who was chief conductor at the Mariyinsky and a neighbor of the Stravinskys on the Kryukov Canal.

66 Valeriy Smirnov, *Tvorcheskoye formirovaniye I. F. Stravinskovo*, 20.

67 *Journal de Genève*, 15 November 1928; reprinted in F. Lesure (ed.), *Stravinsky: Etudes et témoignages*, 242–6.

68 See Stark, 5–16, for this and other information on the Mariyinsky repertory at the turn of the century. *Khovanshchina* had had an amateur production in St. Petersburg in 1886 and had later been produced in Kiev in 1892 and by Savva Mamontov's Russian Private Opera at the Solodovnikov Theatre in Moscow in 1897. See *SRT*, 495, and 1038, note 13.

69 Letter of 20 October/1 November 1875 to Vladimir Stasov, in Leyda and Bertensson, *The Musorgsky Reader*, 312.

70 *Conv*, 29.

71 See his open letter to Wolfgang Wagner, 11 April 1968, in *T&C*, 206–7.

72 *Mem*, 25. Nikolay Findeyzen included "your dear son—the Wagnerian musician" in his New Year greetings to Fyodor Stravinsky at the end of 1900: letter of 28 December 1900/10 January 1901, in *FSS*, 141.

73 Stark, 15. Compare this incident from about 1900 with the "reminiscence" in *Expo* (62) that "when I spoke admiringly of Verdi to Rimsky, he would look at me as Boulez might if I had suggested playing my *Scènes de ballet* at Darmstadt."

74 Respectively: marginal note of 5 March 1938, quoted in *SPD*, 605, note 49; "Dans le train avec Igor Stravinsky," *Comoedia*, 21 January 1924; Stravinsky, *Poetics of Music*, 62.

75 K. Stravinskaya, "Iz semeynovo arkhiva Stravinskikh," 154–6.

76 The photograph is reproduced in *SPD*, 41.

77 *Expo*, 60: "The classics of our concerts were the tone poems of Liszt, Raff, and

Smetana, the overtures of Litolff . . . Berlioz, Mendelssohn, Weber, Ambroise Thomas, the concertos of Chopin, Grieg, Bruch, Vieuxtemps, Wieniawski. Haydn, Mozart, and Beethoven were played, of course, but badly played, and always the same few pieces over and over again." Apart from the matter of performance quality, and with a few differences of detail, it looks like a case of *plus ça change.*

78   *Expo,* 60–1. But see *Chron,* 22–5, for a balanced and reasonably sympathetic memoir of the Belyayev enterprise.

79   It probably included Glazunov's dull Third Symphony, which was premiered under Lyadov at the first Belyayev concert of the 1892–93 season; see *Conv,* 37. Taruskin rightly chastises Stravinsky's ex post facto critique of this event, while assuming that it was the (much superior) Fourth Symphony that he heard. But he was eleven, not "nine or ten," when this was first played, on 21 January/2 February 1894. See *SRT,* 5.

3   Nests of Gentle Folk

1   *Chron,* 11–13; *Expo,* 36. Sadly, the old man makes no appearance in the conversation books, perhaps because he was too much of a conventional *yurodivy* (holy fool), like the Idiot in *Boris Godunov,* and reminded Stravinsky of those Russian stereotypes from which he was by then distancing himself.

2   *My Musical Life,* 344.

3   Yastrebtsev, *Reminiscences of Rimsky-Korsakov,* 82. In *Expo,* 35, Stravinsky makes no mention of Vechasha, but combines it in memory with L'zy, which is in fact some eight kilometers from Lake Pesno. He also gets the year of his own later visit wrong; it was 1904, not 1902.

4   *Mem,* 22. Again the date is wrong, and so is the statement that he next made the trip eighteen years later. But the thumbnail description of the journey is characteristically vivid. Igor and Yury had just recovered from scarlet fever, during which illness the other two boys had been sent away to the Yelachiches' St. Petersburg flat. See *PRK,* 28. For the factual data about the Volga trip, see K. Baedeker, *La Russie,* 301–9.

5   See the illustrations insert of this book. Another photo of the house at Pavlovka is on the back cover of the original Faber Music edition of Stravinsky's Piano Sonata in F-sharp Minor.

6   Letter of 19 June/2 July 1904, from Vladimir Rimsky-Korsakov to his mother, *PRK,* 143–4.

7   Letters of 6/19 and 16/29 June 1903, respectively; *PRK,* 128–31.

8   Paul Horgan, *Encounters with Stravinsky,* 184.

9   Letter of 5/18 July 1903, *PRK,* 131–2.

10   I. Ya. Vershinina, *Ranniye baletï Stravinskovo,* 11–12. Further information on Yelachich is in *PRK,* 434–6.

11   According to his great-grandson Michel Yelachich (private conversation), his work as an agronomist had particularly to do with the economic consequences of emancipation.

12   Guyau, *Les Problèmes de l'esthétique contemporaine,* 90. Igor Stravinsky read this book, presumably in the Russian translation by L. Chudinov, in 1899.

13   See, for example, *Chron,* 20–1. Uncle Alexander emerges better from the conversation books, but only in comparison with Stravinsky's scathing later memories of his family circle as a whole. Yet his great-grandson Michel Yelachich told me that when he visited Stravinsky in Los Angeles in July 1969, "Dyadya Alya" was the only one of his Yelachich relations the by then decrepit composer could remember at all. See also *PRK,* 435, note.

14   Letters to Vladimir Rimsky-Korsakov, 5/18 June 1906, *PRK,* 159–60; and to Yelena Stravinsky, 3/16 December 1906, *PRK,* 166, respectively: "Yesterday," he wrote to his sister-in-law, "Saturday 2/15 December, in St. Petersburg, a bomb was thrown at Dubasov—and he again remained in one piece. 'Lord, save your people.' "

15   Letter to Vladimir Rimsky-Korsakov, 15/28 July 1905, *PRK,* 151–2. "People here," he

explained, "are very liberal, advanced, and to me extraordinarily sympathetic." In fact just like Uncle Alexander, whose class "all prided themselves on their liberalism, extolled progress, and considered it the thing to profess so-called 'advanced' opinions in politics, art, and all branches of social life" (*Chron*, 20).

16 *Conv*, 43. But Stravinsky's antithesis—"Uncle Alexander was an admirer of Musorgsky and as such he had little use for Rimsky-Korsakov"—is pat and unconvincing (the implication that these two composers were mutually exclusive by the nineties is absurd).

17 Alexander and his brothers were Orthodox by upbringing, as required by Russian law in cases of mixed marriage: the Catholic Franz Leopold Yelachich had married an Orthodox wife. See *Chron*, 20, for the assertion that Uncle Alexander was an atheist. Michel Yelachich thinks not, calling him rather "a free-thinker and very tolerant" (private communication).

18 Smirnov, *Tvorcheskoye formirovaniye*, 18.

19 *Conv*, 43.

20 *Chron*, 21.

21 *Mem*, 58. Stravinsky kept the medal all his life, and there is a photograph in *SSCII*, 488.

22 Letter to Vladimir Rimsky-Korsakov, of 3/16 July 1904, *PRK*, 144–5. Was it Rachmaninov or Rimsky-Korsakov Stravinsky meant when he wrote to Mrs. Rimsky-Korsakov a fortnight later, looking forward to playing and discussing "that music for which I find little sympathy here"? Letter of 17/30 July 1904, *PRK*, 146.

23 See *Expo*, 47, for Igor's bittersweet memories of Nikolay's wedding in about 1893. Nikolay was a pianist who had been a private pupil of Rimsky-Korsakov in the late eighties prior to studying law at the university, and whom Igor recalled accompanying his father in Schumann lieder at a New Year's Eve party at the Yelachiches' in St. Petersburg at the end of 1899. He later aspired to play Igor's music, too, but by then the composer had his own weaponry (see chapter 26). Nikolay was the only one of the five brothers who stayed in Russia after the Revolution. Eventually he was arrested and shot by Stalin's secret police at Borovichi in 1938. See *PRK*, 436, for more on this.

24 *Expo*, 47–8.

25 Letter of 5/18 July 1903 from Pavlovka to his mother; *PRK*, 131–2.

26 Letter of 16/29 July 1903 to his mother; *PRK*, 133–4.

27 Letter of July 1899 to his mother, quoted in Anna Stravinsky's letter of 27 July 1899 (OS) to her husband. See *FSS*, 102. Gury's letter has not survived.

28 Letter of 10/23 July 1904, in *Muz Ak* 1992, 116; reprinted in *PRK*, 145–6. After the Bolshevik Revolution, Sergey Yelachich fled to China, where he died destitute in 1940 (*PRK*, 437). Mikhail fought in the White Army during the Civil War and died in Yugoslavia in 1922. Zhenya became a writer—a poet and author of children's books. He went to Belgrade and was murdered there by the Chetniks in 1944 (*PRK*, 437–8). Gavriyil, the youngest brother, also died in Belgrade, the victim of a German bomb the day after returning to the Orthodox Church in 1941. He, too, was a poet, a friend of Blok, and an habitué of the Stray Dog nightclub in St. Petersburg (*PRK*, 438). Stravinsky received several requests for funds from the Yelachiches: from Sergey in China in 1929; from Mikhail's widow, Elizabeth, in China in about 1946; and from a Mrs. Yelachich—perhaps also Elizabeth—in Belgrade in 1920. Stravinsky seems to have sent money on each occasion. See also *SSCII*, 263, note 4.

29 *Expo*, 37. The account books show that Igor was first taken to Yarmolintsï in June 1892, then went again, with the Pechisky estate manager Ivan Rïlik, in 1897 (*PRK*, 39, 49).

30 Letter of 5 July 1901 (OS) to P. A. Efremov, in *FSS*, 131–2. The year before, the graveside *panikhida* (funeral rite) in Roman's memory had had to be held in the church because of heavy rain: *PRK*, 84, entry for 10 June.

31 His memory of last seeing Pechisky in 1895 is, of course, an error, as is his remark

that he last spent a summer there in 1892. See *Expo,* 39. His last visit may have been in 1906 (as possibly evidenced by a photograph in the possession of his great-niece), but was otherwise in 1901. A drawing by Yury Stravinsky of the house at Pechisky, a typical long-fronted, single-storey edifice, is reproduced in *Muz Ak* 1992, 114.

32 *Expo,* 38.

33 Letter of 27 July 1899 (OS), in *FSS,* 103. The reference is of course to Roman's grave, in the village churchyard at Khodakovtsï, by the Pechisky estate. A *panikhida* (funeral rite) was arranged every year in the Nikolsky Sobor in St. Petersburg on the anniversary of Roman's birthday, 1 October, and the year after his death Fyodor set up a scholarship in his name in the law faculty at St. Petersburg University, where Roman had been studying, to be awarded to a student from Kiev, where he had been born.

34 Baedeker, *La Russie,* 328.

35 Letter of August 1893 from Pechisky to his parents in Germany, *PRK,* 43–4. Alyosha was Igor's aunt's grandson Alexey Kirillovich Yelachich, the child who, according to Stravinsky's memoirs, Aunt Yekaterina had "confiscated" from her daughter-in-law. See *Expo,* 38. Alyosha was about a year old at the time of this letter.

36 Letter of 28 July 1893 (OS) from Pechisky to his parents in Bad Homburg, *PRK,* 41–2.

37 *Expo,* 39.

38 Their true first meeting was in August 1883, when the Stravinskys visited the Nosenkos in Kiev (*PRK,* 23). Katya was two and a half years old, and Igor fourteen months.

39 At some time after 1901, a rail service was introduced between Kovel' and Vladimir, which reduced this part of the journey to two hours. Stravinsky's memory that Pechisky was four hundred miles from Ustilug was presumably a distorted reminiscence of this journey, which did in fact cover some such distance. See *Expo,* 37.

40 According to Baedeker (xvii), the average speed of express trains in turn-of-the-century Russia was about fifty versts (thirty-three miles) per hour.

41 *Expo,* 48, 54; Baedeker, xix. See also Nicolas Nabokov, *Bagazh,* 3–8, for a vivid description of his family's rail journey from Germany back to Russia in 1908.

42 Hostowiec, "Dom Strawinskiego w Uscilugu," 28; Stempowski, 66–7.

43 Private communication from Olena Ogneva, of the Volhynian Regional Museum in Lutsk. According to a booklet issued by the museum, at the turn of the century Ustilug had "two candle factories, an alcohol-purification plant, a distillery, a brickworks, a sawmill, and a peatery." It does not say whether Gavriyil Nosenko personally set up any of these operations, though he certainly owned the distillery. See O. D. Ogneva, *Muzey I. Stravinskovo v Ustiluzi;* also *Expo,* 52.

44 Mikhail Lobanov, however, calls the surviving house (now, much altered, the clerical wing of the local hospital) "as mean as a peasant's hut," adding that it must always have been so. See M. A. Lobanov, "Rasskazï starozhilov Ustiluga o Stravinskom i yevo okruzhenii," in V. P. Varunts (ed.), *I. F. Stravinsky, Sbornik statey,* 103–12. A photograph of the front of the house is included in the illustrations insert of this book.

45 After 1945 the Bug at this point formed the Soviet-Polish border. Between the wars, however, Volhynia was part of Poland.

46 Since Olga and Vera Nosenko played a significant part in Igor's early life, it should perhaps be emphasized here that they were not related to him. Lyudmila and Yekaterina Nosenko were, of course, his first cousins.

47 *Expo,* 39–40.

48 Letter of July 1899 to his parents: *PRK,* 73.

49 Ibid.

50 Letter of 8 July 1899 (OS) to his parents: *FSS,* 97–9, *PRK,* 69–71.

51 Letter of late July or early August 1899 to his parents: *PRK,* 76.

52 Letter of 22 June 1900 (OS) to his parents: *PRK,* 84–5.

53 Letter of 10 July 1900 (OS) to his parents: *FSS,* 106–7, *PRK,* 86.

54 Letter of 17 July 1901 (OS) to his parents: *FSS*, 107–9, *PRK*, 102–3.
55 Ibid.
56 Letter of 27 July 1901 (OS) to his parents: *FSS*, 109–10, *PRK*, 104–5.
57 *Expo*, 42.
58 Letter of 17 July.
59 Letter of 27 July. The composer's great-niece showed me a family photograph, probably taken at Ustilug in 1901, in which Igor has his arm round Katya: a gesture of intimacy that seems to echo the tone of this letter.
60 Letter of 16 June 1903 (OS): *PRK*, 130–1.
61 On 15 July 1901, Yury wrote to his parents from St. Petersburg, sympathizing with
them over what he calls "Igor's sudden departure [from Pechisky] for Ustilug," while
"perfectly well guessing the reasons" (*PRK*, 101–2). Viktor Varunts interprets these
reasons as Igor's "first stirrings of love for his cousin Katya." But the evidence for
such a decisive reading is slender. It seems just as likely that Igor had simply
expressed his distaste for the atmosphere at Pechisky and had left against his parents' wishes. Gury, by contrast, had stayed behind. "Igor," Sergey Yelachich had
remarked, "is an egoist, while Gury thinks of his parents and worries about them."
On 11 July Fyodor noted in his account book "Igor's departure for Ustilug (our Gur-
in'ka stayed with us. Thank you, dear son-friend!)": *PRK*, 100.
62 Or for that matter England: witness Jane Austen's *Mansfield Park*.
63 See Lynn Garafola, *Diaghilev's Ballets Russes*, especially chapter 5, for more detail on
this process and its consequences.
64 *PRK*, 72–3, note 11.
65 Letter of 27 July 1899 (OS) to his parents: *FSS*, 100–1. The performance had been on
the twenty-third.
66 Letter of 27 July 1899 (OS): *FSS*, 102. Gury's letter of 23 July to Anna Stravinsky is
lost.
67 Though Pierrot-type plays and masquerades might sometimes be encountered in
country-house settings. See Chloe Obolensky, *The Russian Empire: A Portrait in
Photographs*, plate 169, for a group photo of the cast for such a presentation at exactly
the period under discussion.
68 Letter of 8 July 1899 (OS) to his parents: *FSS*, 97–9, *PRK*, 69–71.
69 Letter of 10 July 1900 (OS) to his parents: *FSS*, 106–7, *PRK*, 86.
70 Letter of 23 August 1900 (OS) to his parents in Pechisky: *PRK*, 87–8.
71 Smirnov, *Tvorcheskoye formirovaniye*, 22.
72 The tarantella, which is still unpublished, was first described and quoted by Smirnov
(*Tvorcheskoye formirovaniye*, 26–7). See also Igor Stravinsky's letter of 22 April 1899
(OS) to M. E. Osten-Saken: *PRK*, 64–5. Osten-Saken was a classmate of Igor's at the
Gurevich school.
73 *Expo*, 52.
74 *FSS*, 198–9.
75 Ibid., 200.
76 In fact at least two photos were taken within a few minutes of each other, as can be
seen by comparing the version in *SPD*, 36, with the one in *Muz Ak* 1992, 113.
According to Fyodor's own annotation, they were taken at 8:30 a.m., which perhaps
accounts for the sixteen-year-old Yury's absence. An Ionic "temple" now stands on
the site of the near end of the colonnade. Not far away is the single-domed Russian
chapel, designed by Alexander Benois's uncle Louis, and erected in 1897, the year of
Igor's brief second visit.
77 *Dial*, 116, note 6. But the memoir is suspect. Craft reports merely that the Stravinskys caught a glimpse of Frau Schumann in the Kurpark at Homburg (but he
ascribes the incident to 1897—impossibly, as she died in 1896); see *SPD*, 38. Moreover, Fyodor himself was far from helpless in German. See *FSS*, 11, according to
which Fyodor spoke not only Russian and Ukrainian, but also French, German, Italian, and Polish.

78 *Expo*, 83.

79 *T&C*, 43.

80 See K. Y. Stravinskaya, "Iz semeynovo arkhiva Stravinskikh," for descriptions and reproductions of these drawings. See also *SNB*, 264, for a reproduction of an oil painting by Igor of a ruined castle, but dated 1900.

81 *Expo*, 39. Fyodor's account book shows, however, that the journey home was not via Vienna but via Breslau and Krakow: *PRK*, 49.

82 Stravinsky's later memoir of this accident (in *Mem*, 20) is supported by his letter of 19 July 1899 from Ustilug, where he asks "how Papochka feels after his horrible accident": *FSS*, 100, *PRK*, 73–4.

83 Letter of Fyodor Stravinsky to P. A. Yefremov, 29 June 1902 (OS), in *FSS*, 132–3.

84 Letter of 8/21 July 1902 to Vladimir Rimsky-Korsakov: *PRK*, 114.

85 *SPD*, 41–2, quoting a letter from Frau Marie Wilhelm to Igor Stravinsky, 14 November 1958. Frau Wilhelm seems to have muddled Igor with his brother Gury, and I have taken the liberty of reversing her reminiscence accordingly.

86 Letter to Nadezhda Rimsky-Korsakov (senior), 5/18 August 1902: *PRK*, 118. It seems that as late as October 1902, Fyodor's cancer remained unacknowledged, though surely not undiagnosed, notwithstanding Andrey Rimsky-Korsakov's letter to his parents of 25 October/7 November (*PRK*, 123), remarking that "it's incomprehensible that the doctors took so long to establish what was actually wrong with him." Fyodor had been operated on in March, and it is hard to believe that the cause of his pain was unknown.

4 A POLYPHONY OF TEACHERS

1 Letter of 19 August 1899 (OS): *PRK*, 78.

2 *PRK*, 57. Varunts considers that Igor had come into conflict with the gymnasium authorities and had been in effect invited to leave; see ibid., 52. The account books, however, contain no reference to such an incident.

3 *PRK*, 58–60.

4 *Expo*, 42. At the very least, she taught him from December 1896 to April 1899. But the first account-book mention of her name follows a break of three and a half years for which the books are lost. Stravinsky's autobiography tells us that "at that moment the question of my vocation had not been raised in any definite form either by my parents or by myself." *Chron*, 27. But this is plainly contradicted by his letter to Timofeyev of 13 March 1908 (OS) (*PRK*, 186–7).

5 Letter of 22 April 1899: *PRK*, 64–5. The idea may have come from the Yelachiches: Uncle Alexander, who was supporting Igor's musical ambitions; and cousin Nikolay, who knew Tcherepnin from his gymnasium days. See N. Tcherepnin, *Vospominaniya muzïkanta*, 20.

6 Letter to Timofeyev, op. cit. According to Fyodor's account book, the lessons with Akimenko did not begin until November 1901, by which time Igor was at the university. But according to Smirnov, there is in the Theatrical Institute in St. Petersburg a copy of Lyadov's Canons of 1898 inscribed "I. Stravinsky, 1900." See Smirnov, 28. This is presumably the "ordinary manual" which the composer tells us in his autobiography he began to study on his own when he was eighteen. *Chron*, 29–30.

7 Ibid. The letter was written in response to a request from Timofeyev for biographical information for an article on Stravinsky in the *Bol'shaya Entsiklopediya*, edited by S. N. Yuzhakov. A few weeks earlier, Stravinsky's E-flat Symphony and *The Faun and the Shepherdess* had had their public premieres in the Assembly of the Nobles.

8 *Mem*, 25–6. Kashperova, though not actually named, emerges with more credit from the autobiography: "Notwithstanding our differences of opinion, this excellent musician managed to give a new impetus to my piano-playing and to the development of my technique." *Chron*, 27.

9   The account books record the purchase of music by Chopin for Igor in November 1897: *PRK*, 51.

10 See *SRT*, 96–9, for these and other details on Kashperova.

11 Ibid., 98.

12 Letters of 13 and 17 July (OS): *PRK*, 100–1 and 102–3, respectively (17 July also in *FSS*, 107–9).

13 *Mem*, 26.

14 G. M. Yaron, quoted in *PRK*, 93, note 3.

15 V. A. Obolensky, in ibid. For a photograph of Gurevich at about the time that he taught Stravinsky, see ibid., plate 13.

16 For example to Andrey Rimsky-Korsakov, 7/20 January 1911: *PRK*, 260–1, *SM*, 453; also to Stepan Mitusov, 28 January/10 February 1912: *PRK*, 307–8, *Muz Ak* 1992, 147. The contexts suggest that Gurevich was a hard-nosed putter-down of youthful fantasies. According to Taruskin, Andrey was teaching in the school at the time of Igor's letter (*SRT*, 700, note 103). But Gurevich had died in 1906.

17 *Mem*, 26–7.

18 Ibid., 26.

19 *PRK*, 87. The fact is that Fyodor paid for the cab, as is confirmed by a series of unpublished account-book entries. Gury, who started at Gurevich's at the same time as Igor, naturally took the cab as well.

20 Ibid., 83; entry for 17 May 1900 (OS).

21 Letter of 23 August 1900 (OS) to his parents: ibid., 87–8.

22 *Mem*, 60; *Expo*, 43–4. The *Judith* gala was on 3/16 January 1901.

23 *Expo*, 50; letter of August 1893 to his parents: *PRK*, 43–5. Varunts has been unable to find any of the books Stravinsky said he was reading, but he quotes a review of one of them, a story about a sensitive, music-loving cabin boy who is so tormented by the captain and crew that he finally blows the whole ship up.

24 *PRK*, 39. Igor later told an interviewer in Vienna that Turgenev had been a personal friend of his father's: "Strawinsky unterwegs nach Wien," *Die Stunde*, 17 March 1926.

25 *Mem*, 28.

26 Letter to his parents of 8 July 1899 (OS): *PRK*, 69–71 (the same letter refers to the Guyau volume).

27 See Vladimir Seduro, *Dostoyevski in Russian Literary Criticism* (New York: Columbia University Press, 1957), 76–9, for a useful résumé.

28 *Conv*, 84.

29 *Expo*, 50.

30 See *FSS*, 21–33, for this and much other information on Fyodor Stravinsky's library and bibliophilia. Part of the library was sold by Yury Stravinsky before the Revolution, and part of it was appropriated and/or sold by temporary wartime occupants of the Stravinsky flat in the Second World War. A small part remains in the possession of the composer's great-niece in St. Petersburg.

31 Ibid., 73.

32 Letter of 15/28 July 1905 to Vladimir Rimsky-Korsakov: *PRK*, 151–2.

33 See Niklaus Röthlin, "Strawinskys juristische Ausbildung," 46, for a fine color fac-simile of the diploma (also reproduced in monochrome in *SPD*, 45). Igor left Ustilug on about 11 August (OS) to spend time at Pechisky with Gury, who was going to Vilnius on the seventeenth, and Yury, who was likewise off to Ustilug before returning to Kiev: letters of 27 July and 3 August (OS), respectively: *PRK*, 104–6 (27 July also in *FSS*, 109–10). The letters are revealing about Igor's family feeling and anxiety to be with his brothers, but oddly say nothing about his own impending matriculation.

34 *Mem*, 27.

35 *Expo*, 42; *PRK*, 109, 112.

36 A description which partly echoes Jaseps Vitols's "placid, good-hearted, pint-sized Greek": Ya. Vitol [sic], *Vospominaniya, stat'i, pis'ma*, 63. Kalafati and Akimenko

appear together in a group photograph of Rimsky-Korsakov's class of 1899, reproduced in S. L. Ginzburg (ed.), *N. A. Rimsky-Korsakov i muzïkal'noye obrazovaniye*, facing p. 16.

37 Undated note from, probably, winter 1903–4: "Dear Uncle Vasya, I would much appreciate it if you came to me today, as I myself can't go out—I've had an operation on my leg and have to lie down for a few days. I await an answer" (*PRK*, 139).

38 *Expo*, 43. This account may be taken as correcting, or at least supplementing, Stravinsky's suggestion in his autobiography that his counterpoint studies were entirely conducted on his own. See *Chron*, 29–30. Nicolas Slonimsky, who studied with Kalafati just before the First World War, gives an amusing picture of his amiable pedantry, in *Perfect Pitch*, 39. But Kalafati's remark to Slonimsky that "Stravinsky had had great difficulties in mastering elementary harmony" was no more than a malicious sideswipe at the composer of *Petrushka* and *The Rite of Spring*, whose Parisian success was so inexplicable to the pillars of Russian musical propriety.

39 *SRT*, 100. The grounds for this assumption include the fact that scherzos were prescribed by Balakirev as early composition training. But this is a questionable reason for arguing that Rimsky-Korsakov or his pupils would so prescribe, even if their role had been that of composition teacher.

40 *Expo*, 44–5; *SRT*, 103.

41 See Anatoly Kuznetsov, "Muzïka Stravinskovo na kontsertnoy estrade Rossii," in *Muz Ak* 1992, 119. To be exact, Kuznetsov quotes a newspaper announcement of the concert. That it did in fact take place is an assumption.

42 *Expo*, 26; see also *Chron*, 25–6 (probably helped by Walter Nouvel, the ghost writer of *Chron*, who must also have known Pokrovsky well).

43 Ginzburg, *N. A. Rimsky-Korsakov i muzïkal'noye obrazovaniye*, 266.

44 B. Yarustovsky, *Igor Stravinsky*, 17.

45 Smirnov, *Tvorcheskoye formirovaniye*, 25.

46 *SRT*, 308.

47 *Chron*, 25.

48 See *SRT*, 308 et seq., for a slightly different route to a similar conclusion. The mature Stravinsky's cult of Gounod and Chabrier seems to have begun, in fact, with Diaghilev's productions of a series of operas by these composers early in 1924.

49 He later studied with Auer; see *PRK*, 152, note 1.

50 *Expo*, 43–4. The account book records that all three boys were taken to *Sadko* (in the production by Savva Mamontov's Moscow company) on 23 February/7 March, which tallies with Stravinsky's memory that he was fifteen or sixteen at the time. Rimsky-Korsakov had composed the part of Duda for Fyodor, who, however, did not sing it until the Mariyinsky premiere in January 1901—his last new role, as it turned out.

51 *Journal de Genève*, 15 November 1928: in Lesure (ed.), *Stravinsky: Etudes et témoignages*, 243. Varunts speculates plausibly that the delay in arranging the visit may have been due to opposition from Volodya's father, who was heavily involved in the composition of his opera *Pan Voyevoda* and the orchestration of Dargomïzhsky's *The Stone Guest* but finally could not refuse to see the son of so highly respected a colleague. *PRK*, 115–6, note 1.

52 Not at Neckargemünd, as stated in *Expo*, 44, which also records the wrong year for the visit.

53 Letter of 8/21 July 1902, in Kiselyov (ed.), *N. A. Rimsky-Korsakov: Sbornik dokumentov*, 72–3. See also Rimsky-Korsakov, *My Musical Life*, 402.

54 Postcard of 14 August 1902 (NS): *PRK*, 117.

55 Even though the accounts in *Chron*, 30–3, and *Expo*, 44–5, contradict one another on several fundamental points. For instance, in *Chron* we read that Igor was "upset" and "somewhat downcast" by the great man's reaction to his works, whereas in *Expo* we find that he was "overjoyed"; in *Chron* he is "thoroughly bored" at his continuing studies with Kalafati and feels that he is "making scarcely any progress," but in *Expo* he is so excited that he applies himself to Kalafati's exercises and even fills "several

notebooks with them by the end of the summer." I have taken the view that the more detailed account in *Chron* is on the whole more consistent and probable. The meeting was never referred to in writing by Rimsky-Korsakov.

56 *Chron*, 31. Smirnov (*Tvorcheskoye formirovaniye*, 28) considers that the scherzo was composed after the visit to Rimsky-Korsakov.

57 See, for instance, Rimsky-Korsakov's letter of 20 January 1902 to Alfred Bruneau, in Kiselyov, *N. A. Rimsky-Korsakov: Sbornik dokumentov*, 65.

58 "Proyekt preobrazovaniya programmï teorii muziki i prakticheskovo sochineniya v konservatoriyakh" (1901), quoted in Ginzburg, 21.

59 *Chron*, 31–2. There is a striking parallel with Jean-François Le Sueur's advice to Berlioz eighty years earlier: "There is a great deal of warmth and dramatic movement here," Le Sueur told the nineteen-year-old Berlioz, "but you do not know yet how to write, and your harmonies are so spattered with mistakes that it would be pointless to indicate them to you. Gerono [a Le Sueur pupil] will be so kind as to make you conversant with our harmonic principles, and as soon as you know them sufficiently to understand me I shall be happy to have you as one of my pupils." Quoted in David Cairns, *Berlioz*, vol. 1 (London: André Deutsch, 1989), 120.

60 See Vitols, *Vospominaniya, stat'i, pis'ma*, 70, for a reminiscence of Stravinsky and the Rimsky-Korsakov brothers playing the fool at a Rimsky party after a Russian Symphony Concert in 1908. They "invented a new Franco-Russian language: 'Quelle nachalité vopiyante!,' 'Quelle charmante pogoda,' etc." Vitols dates this to early May, but it may have been the evening recorded by Yastrebtsev under 8 March: "a very gay evening with lots of laughter. The Stravinsky brothers made up a story based on the names of singers, composers, and conductors." See Yastrebtsev, *Reminiscences*, 446.

61 Galina Kopitova, commentary to the correspondence with the Rimsky-Korsakovs and Maximilian Steinberg, in *Muz Ak* 1992, 140. "Music," Andrey wrote to his father from Berlin in September 1902, "is more precious to me than philosophy."

62 The oldest Rimsky-Korsakov brother, Mikhail, and the elder sister, Soph'ya, were never apparently close to Stravinsky.

63 Letter of 17 September 1902 (NS): *PRK*, 120.

64 Letter of 28 September (NS): ibid., 121. Igor, however, had seen Weber's masterpiece at least once before, at the Mariyinsky the previous November: *PRK*, 109.

65 Quoted in *SRT*, 111. It is just possible that the Stravinsky referred to was Gury.

66 *Mem*, 20. Taruskin's suggestion (*SRT*, 377, note 18) that Igor took part in an Evenings of Contemporary Music concert on this date must be a mistake.

5 THE BELYAYEVTSÏ

1 The second-floor flat is now a beautifully arranged but little visited apartment museum. The house has to be sought out, since it stands in a large courtyard behind the main façade of the Zagorodnïy Prospect.

2 For instance, on 4 January 1906 there were thirty-five people, and on 1 February eighteen, in a salon roughly twenty-five feet by twenty. See Yastrebtsev, *Reminiscences of Rimsky-Korsakov*, 379, 383. The published diary of Rimsky-Korsakov's friend and admirer Vasiliy Vasilyevich Yastrebtsev is the main source of information about Rimsky-Korsakov's Wednesdays. Yastrebtsev acted as a self-appointed Boswell to the Master, assiduously reporting everything that happened at the fortnightly and other gatherings, and piously recording the great man's utterances and opinions. The diaries probably faithfully reflect the awe in which Rimsky-Korsakov was held in Petersburg musical circles between the 1870s and the First World War. For a description of the music room in the Rimsky-Korsakov flat, see Maximilian Steinberg's memoirs in Ginzburg, 204.

3 See *SRT*, 47–52 and passim for a comprehensive survey of the Belyayev question. Much of what follows is indebted to Taruskin.

4 *My Musical Life*, 288.

5 Letter of 28 September 1897, quoted in Ginzburg, 76.

6 Letter of 27 February 1904, Vladimir Stasov to his brother Dmitry, quoted in *SRT,* 70 (italics in original). Belyayev had died on 22 December 1903 (OS).

7 Yastrebtsev, 350, 419, 341. Mahler had previously conducted in St. Petersburg in March 1902, and "impressed me greatly, himself and his conducting" (*Conv*, 38). But this was before the Rimsky meeting, which may be why Stravinsky says the Master did not attend.

8 Ibid., 341.

9 Laloy, *La Musique retrouvée*, 72.

10 Rimsky-Korsakov's profound and genuine distaste for Strauss's *Salome*, which he also saw in Paris in 1907, is independently attested by Chaliapin: "How much suffering this music of Strauss's caused him! We went after the performance to the Café de la Paix—he was literally ill." See F. Chaliapin, *Ma Vie*, trans. André Pierre (Paris: Albin Michel, 1932), 170.

11 See *SRT,* 376–7, note 17. Stravinsky's own Rimsky-Korsakov/Scriabin story is also to the point: "He didn't like Scriabin's music at all, but to those people who were indignant about it his answer was: 'I like Scriabin's music very much' " (*Conv*, 39). The Stravinsky version of the Debussy story is on the same page, and previously in *Chron*, 35.

12 Ginzburg, 205. The best Stravinsky memoir is in "Chronological Progress in Musical Art," *The Etude*, August 1926, 559–60: "One thing [Rimsky-Korsakov's] pupils well remember and that is that he made no complimentary remarks. The pupil who expected pats on the back would have been disappointed with Rimsky-Korsakoff."

13 Laloy, *La Musique retrouvée*, 72.

14 Janet Flanner, "Russian Firebird," 23.

15 Yastrebtsev, *N. A. Rimsky-Korsakov: Vospominaniya 1886–1908*, vol. 2, 277 (the entry is omitted from the English edition). Yastrebtsev does not specifically say that he met Igor at the rehearsal, but that is the implication.

16 Yastrebtsev, *Reminiscences of Rimsky-Korsakov*, 327–8.

17 See his letter of 13 March 1908 (OS) to Timofeyev, in *PRK*, 186–7; also *SRT,* 111. Even the titles of Stravinsky's Prutkov pieces are lost, with the single exception of *Konduktor i tarantul* (The Driver and the Tarantula), which we know about because Yastrebtsev mentions that it was performed at Rimsky-Korsakov's birthday party three years later. Since he states that Stravinsky "played" the piece, it may have been a piano solo rather than a setting of the Prutkov poem. See Yastrebtsev, 386; also *Dial*, 134. Stravinsky's enthusiasm for the verbosities and posturings of Prutkov broke out again briefly in 1914: see chapter 17.

18 Richter, a rotund, slightly raffish figure with a black moustache, appears in a surviving photo of the Berlin days in the possession of Yelena Stravinsky. Two further photos, of him clean-shaven, are in *PRK*, plates 26–7. The manuscript of the piano Scherzo was discovered among Richter's papers in the Leningrad Public Library in the 1960s.

19 *T&C*, 201. The published fragments of Mitusov's memoirs are unclear on the question of his studies with Rimsky-Korsakov. See Larisa Kazanskaya, "Stepan Mitusov."

20 See Yastrebtsev, *Reminiscences*, 447 (8 March 1908), 308 (16 March 1902), 339 (17 February 1904), 387 (6 March 1906), respectively (all dates OS).

21 Ibid., 245 (25 December 1899).

22 *Chron*, 33.

23 *Expo*, 27.

24 *SRT,* 438.

25 For detailed information on the background, development, and aesthetics of the World of Art movement, see Bowlt, *The Silver Age*, especially 47–121; also Benois, *Reminiscences of the Russian Ballet*, passim.

26 *Chron*, 33.

27   Rimsky did nevertheless visit the exhibition, but "I knew almost no one there, and if I had, being by nature a confirmed Social Democrat, I wouldn't have liked them." See Yastrebtsev, *Reminiscences*, 364–5.

28   *Chron.*, 34. See *SRT*, 307–8, for a categorical refutation of Pokrovsky's founding role. But Taruskin fails to explain why Nouvel, who certainly was one of the founders, and who actually ghosted the *Chroniques*, made this mistake or allowed it to survive. Curiously enough, Taruskin seems to regard Nouvel's authorship as somehow explaining the error.

29   When Prokofiev auditioned for the Evenings in 1908, at least four of the panel were the same. Only Medem is not mentioned by name. See David H. Appel (ed.), *Prokofiev by Prokofiev*, 243–4; abridged edition, 133–4.

30   Smirnov, *Tvorcheskoye formirovaniye*, 51. He does not say what these connections were. Mitusov was a cousin of the wife of the future Ballets Russes designer Nikolay Roerich. But Roerich, though his work had appeared in *Mir iskusstva* by 1900, was not directly connected with the journal. As for Stravinsky's assertion that he first met Mitusov "as far back as my sixteenth year, for he was an intimate friend of the Rimsky-Korsakov family" (*Expo*, 26), this looks like a typical early-dating. Stravinsky was certainly not automatically meeting friends of the Rimsky-Korsakovs before 1902, his twenty-first year.

31   See Benois, *Memoirs*, vol. 1, 270. An excellently detailed picture of Nouvel can be built up from a selective reading of Benois's *Memoirs* and *Reminiscences* in general.

32   Benois, *Reminiscences*, 173, 224.

33   Ibid., 173–4.

34   *Mir iskusstva*, 1902, no. 2, quoted in *SRT*, 375.

35   Compare his memoirs in *Chron*, 36, and *Mem*, 28–9, with the analysis of the Evenings repertoire in *SRT*, 376–7. The Dukas sonata was played on 6 March 1903 (OS), the same evening as Rimsky-Korsakov's fifty-ninth birthday party, so Stravinsky may not have been at the concert.

36   *SRT*, 367–8. Taruskin says, for instance, that Montéclair was played not at the Evenings, but by Henri Casadesus's Société des instruments anciens; cf. *Mem*, 29.

37   See Kuznetsov, "Muzïka Stravinskovo na kontsertnoy estrade Rossii (1907–1917)," *Muz Ak* 1992, 119–27, for a complete listing of known public performances of Stravinsky's music in prerevolutionary Russia.

38   *Mem*, 28.

39   *Expo*, 45.

40   *SRT*, 377, note 18. Earlier (99), Taruskin states firmly that the performance in question took place during the 1902–03 season, but gives no source.

41   *Dial*, 41, note 2.

42   *Mem*, 82. That Stravinsky and Blok never met is stated by Craft in *SPD*, 638, note 149.

43   *Mem*, 29.

44   The provisional document is finely reproduced in Röthlin, "Strawinskys juristische Ausbildung," 41 (also, in monochrome, in *SPD*, 44, but wrongly dated to November); an English translation is in *SSCI*, 382. The document was issued in May 1903. In March 1908 Stravinsky "presented himself for military duty," but was permanently exempted as "completely unfit for military service," presumably on health grounds. See *SSCI*, 386, for an English translation.

45   Letter of 6 June 1903 (OS) to his mother: *PRK*, 128–9.

46   See Vladimir Rimsky-Korsakov's letter to his mother of 19 June 1904 (OS), *PRK*, 143–4. Unfortunately the account book for the time when Igor was thirteen is lost.

47   Letter of 16 June 1903 (OS) to his mother: *PRK*, 130–1.

48   *Chron*, 38–9.

49   Letter of 16 July 1903 (OS) to his mother: *PRK*, 133–4.

50   This is apparently the drift of an otherwise enigmatic postscript to the 16 June letter to his mother.

51 Letter of 16/29 July. Presumably the Mikhail ("Misha") in question was Uncle Alexander's son of that name, not his brother.

52 And did not do so, as far as is known, before his visit to the Soviet Union in 1962.

53 It was this region, rather than the twin villages of L'zy, that Stravinsky was remembering when he spoke of the "cool breezes from the nearby Valdye Hills" which made it a popular summer resort with Petersburgers (*Expo*, 35–6). The same confusion made him refer to Bologoye as the railhead for L'zy. It was actually the main junction for Okulovka on the Pskov-Rybinsk line. But the error may be significant, since while Stravinsky will certainly not have arrived at Bologoye on his way to L'zy after Rimsky-Korsakov's death in 1908, he would have changed there if he had taken a train from Rybinsk on his way from Pavlovka to Krapachukha in 1903. This is a somewhat tenuous argument against his having gone with Mikhail via Moscow. But why else should he remember Bologoye at all?

54 *Chron*, 38–9.

55 To his mother, 15 August 1903 (OS): *PRK*, 139.

56 *Chron*, 39–40. The opera in question was *Pan Voyevoda*. According to Taruskin (*SRT*, 166), this comparative work began at Vechasha the following summer, but there seems no reason to doubt Stravinsky's dating in this case, especially since he correctly recalled that *Pan Voyevoda* was a recently completed work. Rimsky had finished it at Krapachukha in July, and when Stravinsky arrived he had already begun sketching *The Legend of the Invisible City of Kitezh*. But the statement in a 1913 article that "Stravinsky made the pf arrangement of R-Korsakov's *Pan-Voyevoda* [sic]"— information which must have come from Stravinsky himself—is at best improbable. See B. Tyuneyev, "Igor Stravinsky," 71. The facts (though not the date) are correct in Emil Vuillermoz, "Igor Strawinsky," 16, which must also be based on interviews with the composer.

57 See M. K. Mikhailov, "N. A. Rimsky-Korsakov—vospitatel kompozitorov," in Ginzburg, 13–45. The article, like much of the book, is excessively general, but its Soviet bias, as such, comes out mainly in its sweeping overestimate of its subject's importance.

58 See especially chapter 3, "The Composition of Music," of *The Poetics of Music*. It is hard to agree with Taruskin, though, that that chapter owes a specific debt to Rimsky-Korsakov's belief that formulae helped a composer to keep going when the Muse had gone on strike. See *SRT*, 169. Stravinsky's advice to Isherwood to "find a model" is a very different matter from the use of formulae in place of inspiration, which Taruskin no doubt rightly discerns in the late Rimsky-Korsakov of *Pan Voyevoda*.

6 ACTS OF CREATION

1 Letter of early August 1903: *PRK*, 135–8.

2 *SB*, 24–5. Transport was something of a motif of this wedding, which took place in the private church of the Institute of Communications.

3 Letter of 21 June 1905: *PRK*, 50–1.

4 Now the Moskovsky (Moscow) Station. *SB*, 24.

5 *Mem*, 24.

6 *SB*, 25–7.

7 Letter of 13 March 1908 (OS): *PRK*, 186–7. The question of when actually his university course ended is considered below.

8 *SRT*, 113 et seq. See also Rimsky-Korsakov's letter of 20 January 1902 (OS) to Bruneau, in Kiselyov, 65; also in Ginzburg, 247–8; English translation in *SRT*, 172. One has to assume that the remark in *Chron*, 40, that regular lessons began in 1903 was a slip of memory. It does, nevertheless, suggest that lessons of a kind already took place that year, which is in any case what one would expect.

9   See Yastrebtsev, *Reminiscences*, 340; also *Vospominaniya 1886–1908*, vol. 2, 303 and 560, note 13. Neither Yastrebtsev nor Rimsky-Korsakov mentions a piano accompaniment, which is nevertheless given in the work list in the appendix to the Russian edition of the conversations (*Dialogi*, 375). Stravinsky himself had "no recollection of this *Tafelmusik*." *Dial*, 133.

10 *Conv*, 38. The hyperbolic "every day" idiom is Robert Craft's: cf. his remark to the author during a series of interviews in 1995 for BBC Radio 3 that "Stravinsky changed his pajamas four or five times every night of his life." But Craft may, of course, have caught this habit from Stravinsky.

11 Respectively: Kabalevsky, vol. 2, 16, and Yastrebtsev, *Reminiscences*, 341, entry for 23 April 1904. Stravinsky is not mentioned among those present on this occasion; but such views must have been frequently expressed. The *Estampes* were played by Felix Blumenfeld at the sixtieth birthday party.

12 *Mem*, 55.

13 Taruskin wrongly dates Volodya's visit to 1903: *SRT*, 114. As for the account of the events of this summer in *Expo*, 35, it is perhaps simplest to say that almost every verifiable fact there is wrong.

14 Letter of 19 June/2 July, Vladimir Rimsky-Korsakov to his mother: *PRK*, 143–4.

15 See Vladimir Rimsky-Korsakov's letter to his brother Andrey (no date given, but about 6/19 June 1904); also his and Stravinsky's postcard of 6/19 June to Vladimir's parents: *PRK*, 141–3.

16 Letter of 10/23 July: *PRK*, 145–6.

17 Letter of 3/16 July 1904: *PRK*, 144–5.

18 Letter of 19 July/1 August: *PRK*, 147.

19 *SRT*, 115. See also Walsh, *The Music of Stravinsky*, 6.

20 *SRT*, 114–5. He supports the argument by suggesting that "it was then and there that [Rimsky] began administering the orchestration exercises that have become so celebrated to readers of the Stravinsky literature." But, as we saw in chapter 5 (note 56), there seems no particular reason to dispute Stravinsky's own memory that the first such exercises were set the year before at Krapachukha.

21 Yastrebtsev, *Reminiscences*, 343: entry for 22 August 1904 (translation slightly modified).

22 Ibid., 344: 23 August.

23 See Steinberg's memoir, in Ginzburg, 207: "Need I say how proud I was to be given so responsible a commission by my beloved teacher?"

24 See *SRT*, 138–62, for an exhaustive study of the musical derivations of this insignificant piece, which Taruskin believes (on extremely circumstantial evidence) to have been composed in memory of Fyodor Stravinsky.

25 See Seton-Watson, *The Russian Empire 1801–1917*, 591–8; also Pipes, *Russia Under the Old Regime*, 169.

26 Letter of 15/28 July: *PRK*, 151–2.

27 Ibid., 159–60: letter of 5/18 June 1906.

28 Yastrebtsev, *Reminiscences*, 365.

29 Ibid., 351: entry of 19 January 1905.

30 For these and other relevant documents, see *My Musical Life*, appendixes 6–8, 474–80; also Yastrebtsev, *Reminiscences*, 352–7.

31 G. Abraham, *Rimsky-Korsakov*, 116–7.

32 Detailed accounts of the occasion are in Yastrebtsev, *Reminiscences*, 357–9; Steinberg's memoirs, in Ginzburg, 203; and Rimsky-Korsakov, *My Musical Life*, 413. All three contradict Röthlin's assertion ("Strawinskys juristische Ausbildung," 43) that "the police did not dare to intervene." No doubt Stravinsky was present.

33 *Mem*, 27. The Soviet critic Boris Yarustovsky maintains that Stravinsky was taking part in the demonstration and was held by the police for several days, though the Russian text of the conversations (published, however, two years after his monograph) tallies with the English at this point. Did Yarustovsky have some other source,

or was he merely claiming Stravinsky for the Glorious Revolution? See B. Yarustovsky, *Igor Stravinsky*, 18, and *Dialogi*, 31.

34 In *Chron*, 41, he states unequivocally that he finished his university course in the spring of 1905, which tallies with his remark to Timofeyev that he "attended all eight semesters." But his diploma, reproduced in Röthlin, 47 (*SPD*, 45), is dated 24 April 1906. Exactly what happened in the law faculty from month to month between January 1905 and mid-1906 is hard to establish from published sources, but that there was some considerable disruption to the normal academic routine is certain. See Ascher, *The Revolution of 1905*, for a meticulously detailed account of the whole episode.

35 *Expo*, 63. Rimsky-Korsakov had in fact been dead more than a year by the time his last opera was staged, in October 1909, and the performance took place, not at "a private theatre in the Nevsky Prospect [in St. Petersburg]," but at the Solodovnikov Private Theatre in Moscow. Stravinsky was certainly not present.

36 Rimsky had initiated his fortnightly *jours fixes* at the start of the year "following a suggestion by Byelsky," and the first two had taken place on 5 and 19 January. There was then a hiatus, with 9 February earmarked for a play-through of the just-finished *Kitezh*. For some reason this was postponed until the twenty-third, when Richter and Blumenfeld played the first two acts. See Yastrebtsev, *Reminiscences*, 350–4. Confusingly, he calls the twenty-third the "third" Wednesday.

37 Ibid., 353. There is no evidence that the sonata was ever played at the Evenings of Contemporary Music, as claimed in *Mem*, 28.

38 It was apparently this May that he and Gury took the Scandinavian holiday described in *Conv* (84–5), during which they caught sight of Henrik Ibsen in an Oslo street.

39 Letter of 21 June/4 July 1905, *PRK*, 150–1. Taruskin deduces a slightly earlier start on the symphony from the survival of early sketches for it on the same block as the draft of "How the Mushrooms Prepared for War." See *SRT*, 172, and the facsimile on 176.

40 "Today I finished the Scherzo of the symphony," he wrote to Volodya on 15/28 July (*PRK*, 152). Since the draft fair copy of the first movement, in the Bibliothèque Nationale in Paris, is dated 18 July, it must have been finished in rough before the Scherzo. The fair copy of the Scherzo second movement is dated 21 July.

41 Letters of 15/28 July and 21 June/4 July, respectively. I am assuming that the Yury Stravinskys had not meanwhile left.

42 Judging by a photo card signed by both Igor and Katya, the announcement was actually made at Dmitry Nosenko's estate at Omelno, Dmitry being de facto, if not de jure, Katya and Lyudmila's guardian. See *CISFam*, plate 16. But Dmitry was at Ustilug at some stage that summer, according to the evidence of a group photograph apparently taken there and now in the possession of Yelena Stravinsky. Igor's memory that the engagement was announced "at Ustilug in October" (*Expo*, 40) may therefore be only partly mistaken.

43 Letters of 4/17 and 16/29 June, respectively: *PRK*, 127–8, 130–1.

44 According to Theodore Strawinsky, at an establishment called the Académie Colarossi; see *CISFam*, n.p. Theodore also reproduces the photograph (plate 12).

45 *Expo*, 40. He says, though, that she studied, not drawing, but singing.

46 *Expo*, 26 and 41–2.

47 Letter of 15/28 July. The Belyankins had married in 1901.

48 *Chron*, 20.

49 Varunts identifies it as *Gosudarstvennïy stroy i politicheskiye partii v Zapadnoy Yevrope i Severo-Amerikanskikh shtatakh* (St. Petersburg, 1904). But he notes that only one of the volumes to which Stravinsky refers had actually appeared by 1905. See *PRK*, 153, note 5.

50 See Erhardt, *Igor Strawinski*, 16 and 364, note 12. The doctor is specifically identified in *Expo*, 52–3.

51 Letter of 15/28 July. A note in *PRK*, 153, note 9, further indicates the omission of an "unprintable word."

52   Ibid.

53   *SRT*, 186–7. See also Yastrebtsev, *Reminiscences*, 374–5, which refers to the work in its original published numbering (no. 1).

54   *My Musical Life*, 418, note 13; also Yastrebtsev, *Reminiscences*, 376–7.

55   Yastrebtsev, *Reminiscences*, 376. Yastrebtsev reports that the concert made a net profit of fifteen hundred roubles.

56   The original 1905 draft of the symphony, with heavy annotations and corrections by both Stravinsky and Rimsky-Korsakov, is in BN.

57   Yastrebtsev, *Reminiscences*, 382.

58   *Mem*, 55. According to Andrey Rimsky-Korsakov, Stravinsky's lessons were weekly and lasted two hours, from four till six. See his "Chronicle" in *My Musical Life*, 430, which refers, however, to the years 1907 and 1908. Yastrebtsev tells us that this particular dinner ended at eight o'clock sharp.

59   Yastrebtsev, *Reminiscences*, 378; see also *SRT*, 180–6.

60   As it happened, Rimsky was about to do more work on *Boris*, adding revisions of several items omitted from his 1896 score. Perhaps Stravinsky's symphony gave him the appetite. See *My Musical Life*, 421.

61   Yastrebtsev, *Reminiscences*, 377, 379–80. Stasov died the following October.

62   *Mem*, 21.

63   *Expo*, 41. A photograph of the church as it survives today is in *PRK*, plate 21. See also 154, note 3. The priest's name was Father Afanasy Popov.

64   *Expo*, 41.

65   *PRK*, 156–7. The date of sending must be OS, even though by this time Finland— still a "grand duchy" of the Russian Empire—had NS dating. The card to Andrey (*PRK*, 155) was sent on the fifteenth. The phrase "wonderful Imatra" is set to a tune which Igor calls "my autograph," and which bears an uncanny resemblance to the first phrase of the Ballerina's Dance in the third tableau of *Petrushka*.

66   Yastrebtsev, *Vospominaniya*, vol. 2, 374.

7   KATYA AND MAX

1   See the significantly titled "Sufferings and Humiliations of Catherine Stravinsky," in *Stravinsky: Glimpses of a Life*, 104–29, for the latest version of this material. Earlier versions were called "Igor, Catherine and God" (see, most recently, *SSCI*, 1–19).

2   *SB*, 27, 32. All the same, Tanya found in 1925 that "Aunt Katya looks very young: very well dressed, and with a touch of lipstick" (ibid., 36), which may, however, have been one of Katya's stratagems for concealing the extent of her illness from her family and others (ibid., 32).

3   *Expo*, 73–4. The account books show, however, that in 1892, for instance, Anna Stravinsky took communion with the three youngest boys, but Fyodor and the sixteen-year-old Roman apparently did not (*PRK*, 38).

4   Stravinsky himself states firmly that "my wife had founded a village clinic and appointed a doctor to direct it" (*Expo*, 52). This is supported by Ogneva, *Muzey I. Stravinskovo v Ustiluzi*, but it is unclear whether the source is local documentation or simply the composer's memoirs.

5   Ogneva, op. cit. See also Hostowiec, "Dom Strawinskiego w Uscilugu," 24; Stempowski, 59. The school and fire station are supposed to have been built by Lyudmila's husband, Grigory Belyankin, but surely with Nosenko money and on Nosenko land. Belyankin, who was an engineer, designed and supervised the building.

6   Quoted in Erhardt, *Igor Strawinski*, 364, note 12. Strzyzów, now in Poland, is five miles from Ustilug on the other side of the Bug.

7   See Igor's letters to his parents of 17/30 July and 27 July/9 August 1901: *FSS*, 107–10; *PRK*, 102–5.

8   Postcard of 15/28 January 1906: *PRK*, 154–5.

9   *Expo*, 41.

10 Letter of 5/18 June to Vladimir Rimsky-Korsakov: *PRK*, 159–60.

11 16/29 May: *PRK*, 158–9.

12 There is a problem of translation here due to the lack of the definite and indefinite article in Russian. It may be either "the" march (the one Volodya knew about) or "a" march (something new). But the parenthesis supports the former interpretation.

13 *PRK*, 160, note 3.

14 See *SRT*, 234–7, for a detailed examination of Pushkin's debt to Parny, of which, by the way, Stravinsky was apparently aware (see *Chron*, 42). Taruskin, however, exaggerates the work's significance as an *oeuvre à clef*, deciding, for example, that Yastrebtsev's report (27 February 1908: Russian edition only, vol. 2, 480) of a "heart-to-heart chat" with Stravinsky about the work implies that it had autobiographical significance: ibid., 236, note 77. The description of the work as an epithalamium is also Taruskin's. Another obvious prima-facie influence on the choice of subject might be Debussy's *Prélude à l'après-midi d'un faune*, which had had its Russian premiere at Pavlovsk only in the summer of 1904, and its Petersburg premiere the following January. But there is little or no perceptible musical influence.

15 Yastrebtsev, *Reminiscences*, 378: entry of 19 December 1905.

16 *SRT*, 233. Vocal writing was the final stage of the Conservatoire plan, after the writing of a symphony. But Taruskin's remark that *The Faun and the Shepherdess* was the first work Stravinsky wrote entirely under Rimsky-Korsakov's supervision is speculation on his part. There is no direct evidence that Rimsky supervised the work's composition at all.

17 *SB*, 27.

18 See the plan in *Expo*, 15.

19 We lack precise information about the couple's financial circumstances at this time. No doubt Anna retained control of any significant funds left by her husband. But, in any case, while Fyodor had a substantial income at the time of his last illness (including a pension of 11,400 roubles awarded him on his twenty-fifth jubilee in 1901) and was famously careful over expenditure, he never acquired land or property and is unlikely to have been in a position to leave a real cash competence to three grown-up sons. Katya, as heiress to half her father's Ustilug latifundia, was rich, but not necessarily liquid. Taruskin's remark (*SRT*, 381) that Stravinsky was financially independent as long as he stayed in Russia is probably an exaggeration. *PRK* (160, note 6) says that Anna Kirillovna settled 2,000 roubles a year on the couple, together with a percentage of securities left by Fyodor. This was certainly not a substantial family income.

20 *My Musical Life*, 419. Rimsky's letter of (purely formal) apology to the council is there reproduced as appendix 8, 479–80.

21 Yastrebtsev, *Vospominaniya*, vol. 2, 380.

22 Yastrebtsev, *Reminiscences*, 383, entry of 1 February 1906. *Kitezh* was premiered on 7 February 1907.

23 His formal apology to the council had gone off two days before. A week or so later he played host to a quasi-political meeting at which a friend of Andrey's gave a lecture "about the peasants of Vladimir Province" and there was a collection for the unemployed. Perhaps tongue-in-cheek, he invited Yastrebtsev. See ibid., entry for 9 February.

24 Ibid., 384, entry for 15 February.

25 Ibid., 385, entry for 26 February.

26 See chapter 5, note 17. It is not known if this was its first performance. Like all Stravinsky's Prutkov pieces, it is lost.

27 Vilna, now Vilnius, was one of the chief towns in the Pale of Settlement, the part of Imperial Russia in which it was permitted for Jews to live. Volhynia, the government in which Ustilug was situated, was also within the Pale. According to Steinberg himself, his first Wednesday was in the autumn of 1905, but his name first appears in

Yastrebtsev's published diary in the entry for 4 January 1906. See "Vospominaniya M. O. Shteynberga," in Ginzburg, 206; Yastrebtsev, *Vospominaniya*, vol. 2, 370.

28 See Ossovsky's memoirs in Ginzburg, 192; also Glazunov, letter of 24 May 1904, in Ganina, *A. Glazunov: Pis'ma, stat'i, vospominaniya*, 250. Ossovsky, like other Rimsky-Korsakov pupils, including Stravinsky (and indeed Steinberg), notes how rare such praise was coming from his lips. "The only composer I ever heard him refer to as talented was . . . Steinberg" (*Expo*, 45).

29 Originally founded by Alexander III as a palace orchestra of cavalry musicians, the Court Orchestra had started giving public concerts in 1902 on the initiative of their German-born conductor, Hugo Wahrlich. Performances were mounted, often in the morning, with only a single prior run-through to correct mistakes. Steinberg himself reported that Wahrlich was good at this error-spotting process, but an undistinguished conductor in other respects: see Ginzburg, 206. The run-through of Steinberg's Variations took place on 17 February. See *SRT*, 222–4, for more details about the orchestra and its concerts.

30 *Dial*, 99.

31 *SRT*, 369–72. Taruskin ridicules Stravinsky's memory of Gnesin as "a striking character [who] dressed as an Orthodox Hebrew," but unfortunately does not say why. The trouble is that Taruskin is so determined to establish that Stravinsky was deeply and systematically anti-Semitic that he tends to exaggerate the signs.

32 Glezer, *M. F. Gnesin: Stat'i, vospominaniya, materiali*, 146.

33 Varunts shows (*ISPS*, 10, note 2: *PRK*, 159, note 1) that Stravinsky never took his full degree exams, but only "audited" *("slushal")* the courses, and received a half-course *("polukursoviy")* diploma. By contrast, his fellow law student Vladimir Rimsky-Korsakov was still sitting his finals in May. See Stravinsky's letter to him of 16/29 May. In his next letter (5/18 June), Igor congratulates Volodya on passing his exams, "which gives you the possibility of working for money," but then tells him (in a new paragraph) that "I can't wait for the time when I shall be in a position to earn my bread." See *PRK*, 158–60; also Rimsky-Korsakov, *My Musical Life*, 422.

34 Letter of 16/29 May: *PRK*, 158.

35 He was beginning what turned out to be a serious and prolonged bout of tuberculosis. But Igor's description of it to their mother as a "nervous ailment," though it recalls the diagnosis of Fyodor's terminal illness, may not have been meant as strictly clinical.

36 Letter of Igor to his mother, late June or early July 1906: *PRK*, 163–4.

37 Letter to his mother, mid-July (OS) 1906: *SM*, 439–40, *PRK*, 164–5.

38 Ibid.

39 Letter to Vladimir Rimsky-Korsakov, 16/29 June: *PRK*, 161–2.

40 Letter to Vladimir Rimsky-Korsakov, 5/18 June: *PRK*, 159–60. The letter refers to a paper called *Izvestiya Krasnïkh deputatov* (Red Deputies News) and to "Katya's and my attitude" to it, but does not say what this was.

41 Letter of 16/29 June: *PRK*, 161–2.

42 Letter to his mother of mid-July 1906, loc. cit.

43 Letter of 16/29 June, Stravinsky to Vladimir Rimsky-Korsakov, loc. cit. Volodya's letter has not survived.

44 See, for instance, the letters of Nikolay Rimsky-Korsakov from Italy to Steinberg and Kruglikov, excerpted in *My Musical Life*, 423, note 27.

45 Letter of 16/29 June.

46 Yastrebtsev, *Reminiscences*, 393 (retranslated from *Vospominaniya*, vol. 2, 395). Vladimir Stasov had died on 10 October, and on the eleventh Rimsky and his circle, presumably including Steinberg and Stravinsky, went to a memorial service for him. His funeral was on the thirteenth.

47 *Vospominaniya*, 477 (*Reminiscences*, 441), entry of 16 February 1908.

48 *Mem*, 59.

49 Yastrebtsev, *Vospominaniya*, vol. 2, 414–5; entry of 27 February. The performance,

which Yastrebtsev had missed, was on the twenty-first. He says only that "Stravinsky's romances were done," but the Pushkin suite is the only candidate, unless we take it as a reference to the songs which became the *Three Little Songs* six years later, and which Stravinsky recalled having played to Rimsky-Korsakov in 1906 (*Expo*, 120, note 2). Neither the Gorodetsky songs nor the "Pastorale" had yet been composed, and Yastrebtsev would not report having missed trivia such as Koz'ma Prutkov settings, even if there had been "romances" among them.

50 See *Mem*, 56; *Expo*, 45; *Dial*, 99.

51 Taruskin's case is aired in *SRT*, 389 et seq. The supposition of an attachment between Igor and Nadya Rimsky-Korsakov is based on a casual observation by Robert Craft unsupported by any contemporary evidence.

52 Letter of 8/21 May 1910: *PRK*, 221. Varunts appends (in a footnote) the text of an unpublished article by Nadezhda Rimsky-Korsakov, written after the Russian premiere of excerpts from *Petrushka* in January 1913. The article is a sweeping attack on Stravinsky's music and a categorical denial of its true descent from or kinship with her husband's work. But both the circumstances and Stravinsky's music had changed radically in the nearly three intervening years, and Nadezhda had, as we shall see, new motives for her hostility.

8 First and Last Performances

1 *SRT*, 360: "It is the kind of chore traditionally done by pupils (especially nonpaying pupils) and disciples." Igor seems never to have paid Rimsky a kopek for his lessons: "Another of his wedding presents was the gift of his teaching—though, to be sure, he had never accepted money from me before my marriage" (*Expo*, 41).

2 Yastrebtsev, *Reminiscences*, 403.

3 *CISFam*, n.p. The album includes two photographs (plates 20 and 21) of Katya and Igor taken soon after the child's birth. For a photograph of a Russian wet nurse in "uniform" at the turn of the century, see Obolensky, *The Russian Empire*, plate 164.

4 *PRK*, 169. Stravinsky and Yastrebtsev had been together at Rimsky-Korsakov's only four days before, at a string-quartet evening at which works by Steinberg, Glazunov, and Schubert had been performed. See Yastrebtsev, *Reminiscences*, 407.

5 See chapter 3, note 21.

6 *Mem*, 58–9. Stravinsky reports this as a remark about the symphony, but it seems more likely to have referred to *The Faun*. Still later he recalled Glazunov's reaction to the symphony as "rather heavy scoring for such empty music," which—without the "empty"—rings true and was much remarked at the time. See his letter to the *Observer*, 27 November 1961, reprinted in *Dial*, 132.

7 For instance: Glazunov "was always rude to me but I think that was because my remark that he was only a Carl Philipp Emanuel Rimsky-Korsakov had been repeated to him." Ibid.

8 See, for instance, Nadezhda Rimsky-Korsakov's letter to her daughter Sonya, quoted in the last chapter. But even Steinberg soon overstepped the mark: "Glazunov seems to have given me up as a bad job," he told Igor in 1913 (letter of 4/17 April, PSS).

9 Letter of 11/24 August 1908: *SM*, 445–6; *PRK*, 195–6.

10 *Russkoye Slovo*, 10 June 1908, quoted in Ginzburg, 156. Rimsky had died two days before.

11 See Telyakovsky's diary entry for 29 December 1912, in Zilbershteyn and Samkov (eds.), *Sergey Diaghilev i russkoye iskusstvo*, vol. 2, 425, note 3; and cf. Glazunov's report to the pianist Konstantin Igumnov thirteen years later that "a good friend of mine has pointedly remarked that Stravinsky orchestrates first and then composes" (letter of 17 April 1926, in Ganina, 379). But in 1912 Glazunov knew *Petrushka* at best only from the published score.

12 Letter to his mother, 16/29 March 1912: *PRK*, 323–4.

13 Letter to his mother, 17 March 1912 (NS): *PRK*, 319–20. Varunts identifies Kahn as the German composer Robert Kahn (1865–1951). The two composers' later remarks about each other have a certain entertainment value. Glazunov is supposed to have told Artur Schnabel that "of all the two thousand pupils I taught at the Conservatory in St. Petersburg, Stravinsky had the worst ear" (though, as Stravinsky observed, "I was never Glazunov's pupil, never a student in the St. Petersburg Conservatory, and Glazunov's only opportunity to judge my ear was through my music, a test *he* failed." See his letter to the *Observer*, in *Dial*, 131.) "A good musician I never thought Stravinsky," Glazunov told Igumnov in 1926. "I've proof that he lacked a well-developed ear; this was mentioned to me by his teacher Rimsky-Korsakov, whom the pupil now renounces." (Letter of 12 April, in Ganina, 379.) But Stravinsky's memory (*Dial*, 132) of visiting Glazunov backstage at a Salle Pleyel concert in 1935 and being greeted with a dour look, a half-handshake, and silence (*Mem*, 29) should be read in conjunction with Glazunov's own more detailed account of the meeting, which actually took place in 1929: see chapter 30, p. 482.

14 See *SRT*, 6 for clarification of this point. Stravinsky was apparently anxious in later life to claim originality in his admiration for Tchaikovsky, while at the same time exaggerating the gap between the nationalist school from which he himself had descended and the cosmopolitan, or westernizing, tendency which he had rather pointedly espoused in the twenties.

15 *Conv*, 27 (note). But Debussy is hardly in evidence, especially bearing in mind that possible models included *L'après-midi d'un faune*. Stravinsky makes no serious attempt at a comparable sensuality of either harmony or sonority.

16 Yastrebtsev, *Reminiscences*, 408, entry for 18 April 1907. Yastrebtsev simply mentions "the orchestral score" (*"orkestrovuyu partituru"*: see *Vospominaniya*, vol. 2, 422), but the English translator agrees with Stravinsky (*Dial*, 134) that the score in question was the manuscript.

17 The assumption that the recommendation came from Ziloti is my interpretation of Stravinsky's remark in a letter to Rimsky-Korsakov that "since Ziloti asked me about it, I shall tell him, for he promised that in that case he would never again recommend any music to Zimmermann" (letter of 18 June/1 July 1907: *SM*, 440; *PRK*, 171–3). But the first approach may have come from Rimsky. Steinberg certainly knew of the proposal and had written from Paris congratulating Igor as early as mid-May. Igor wrote correcting the error and with some gratuitous abuse of Zimmermann: "I'll spit right in his face, and when I pass his shop I'll shit on his porch! That'll show him I'm not to be trifled with" (letter of 1/14 June 1907: *PRK*, 170).

18 Letter of 28 June/11 July 1907: *PRK*, 174.

19 Rimsky-Korsakov's correspondence with Artsïbushev makes it clear that Glazunov, another trustee, supported the recommendation (see *PRK*, 175–6; *SRT*, 251). But at the time, Stravinsky took it for granted that his mainstay on the board was the third trustee, Lyadov, "who is in sympathy with me, and I with him times four, and what's more I adore him" (letter to his mother, 6/19 August 1907: *SM*, 443–4; *PRK*, 177–9).

20 The performances duly took place, as we shall see. The work also came out in piano score, published by Belyayev, in 1908; but the orchestral score had to wait until 1913.

21 Letter of 18 June/1 July 1907: *SM*, 440, *PRK*, 171–3. According to Smirnov (*Tvorcheskoye formirovaniye*, 75), the *Bees* idea came from Lyadov, but he gives no source for the information. It will in any case be clear that everything Stravinsky says in *Conv* (40) about having written the *Scherzo fantastique* "as a piece of 'pure' symphonic music" is disproved by this letter. But the program was suppressed at an early stage. There is no mention of it in Stravinsky's autobiographical letter of 1908 to Timofeyev (*PRK*, 186–7), or in the reviews of the first performance, in 1909. "I have taken account of your remark about the program," Igor told Rimsky-Korsakov in a letter of 10/23 July 1907 (*PRK*, 174–5). But after her husband's death in 1908, Nadezhda claimed herself to have influenced Stravinsky against revealing the program (letter to Steinberg, 15 July/22 August 1910 [sic]: *PRK*, 232, note 1).

22 A fortnight earlier, however, he had told Steinberg that he was orchestrating. Letter of 1/14 June: *PRK*, 170.

23 See the account of this transaction in *Expo*, 53.

24 Letter of 18 June/1 July.

25 *Expo*, 52.

26 Letter of 10/23 July. What these ideas were we, alas, never discover. Beethoven quartets were frequently played at Zagorodnïy *jours fixes* the following winter, but Yastrebtsev records no discussion about them or their composer.

27 See Igor's letter to his mother of 6/19 August 1907: *PRK*, 177–9. Igor and Yury were destined never to meet again (unless Denise Strawinsky is correct in saying that Yury visited Igor's family in Brittany in 1920; see T. and D. Strawinsky, *Au coeur du Foyer*, 77). After two years in Davos, Yury and his family went to live in the Crimea, and only came back to St. Petersburg in 1923. Yury died there of a stroke in 1941. Although he was apparently a good architect and engineer, and his wife, Yelena, a skillful and versatile painter and craftswoman, they suffered atrocious hardship in the Crimea during the Revolution and the ensuing civil war, and were for a time reduced to living on dolphin fat. Conditions in St. Petersburg, particularly in the thirties and early forties, were probably not a great deal better. As we shall see, the two families were back in touch in the twenties. But the family closeness and intimacy of their early married years was never retrieved, and by the time Igor published his conversation books, it had apparently vanished altogether, from his memory at least. See *SB*, 28 and passim, for these and other details.

28 Letter to his mother of 6/19 August 1907.

29 Letter of early August (or late July) 1907: *SM*, 442, *PRK*, 176–7.

30 *SRT*, 318 et seq.

31 *Mem*, 58–9. Yastrebtsev notes Rimsky-Korsakov's view that "while the first movement contains some very beautiful harmonic and instrumental episodes, on the whole the orchestration is excessively heavy." Entry for 15 January 1908, p. 434.

32 Letter of 18 June/1 July 1907. For the complete program of the Evenings concert, which also included songs by Steinberg, Gnesin, and Karatïgin, see Yastrebtsev, *Reminiscences*, 534, note 45.

33 Yastrebtsev, *Reminiscences*, 419. The Russian word *izobrazil* may suggest that he gave an impression of the song rather than fully performing it.

34 Ibid., 426–7.

35 Ibid., 419.

36 Ibid., 427 (translation slightly modified). The closing quotation—"mglï i tumana"—is a reference to a phrase of the poem.

37 Ibid., 429.

38 The poem was from a recently published volume called *Yar'*, much of which is devoted to an imaginary folk mythology akin to the contemporary paintings of Roerich and Bilibin. According to Stravinsky, Gorodetsky heard the song—presumably at the Evenings concert in December—and complained to him that "the music is very pretty, but it really does not interpret my texts accurately, since I describe a time-to-time ringing of long, slow bells and your music is a kind of jingle bells" (*Mem*, 82).

39 *Rech'*, 29 December 1907, reprinted in *PRK*, 441–2. Apart from a bland report of the original Court Orchestra run-through of *The Faun and the Shepherdess* in the *Peterburgskiy listok* (15 April 1907, repr. in *PRK*, 441), this seems to have been the first review of a work by Stravinsky.

40 *SRT*, 366–8.

41 *Stolichnaya pochta*, 25 January 1908, repr. in *PRK*, 443–4. A fuller translation of Karatïgin's review is in *SRT*, 225.

42 A. Koptyayev, *Birzhevïye vedomosti*, 18 February 1908, repr. in *PRK*, 445.

43 *Russkaya muzïkal'naya gazeta*, nos. 8–9 (1908), column 213, repr. in ibid., 446–7.

44 Yastrebtsev, *Reminiscences*, 441. Scriabin's *Poem of Ecstasy* was to have received its premiere, but the parts were not ready in time.

45 Yastrebtsev, *Vospominaniya*, vol. 2, 477.

46 Yastrebtsev, *Reminiscences*, 449.

47 *My Musical Life*, 446.

48 Yastrebtsev, *Reminiscences*, 426: entry for 25 December 1907.

49 Ibid., 445: entry for 6 March 1908.

50 Ibid., 454. Max's engagement had been announced on 12 February and celebrated at a party at Zagorodnïy on 8 March (Max's First Symphony had had its premiere at a Russian Symphony Concert earlier that same evening). The *Scherzo fantastique*, as already noted, was completed on 30 March.

51 Postcard of 11/24 April 1908: *PRK*, 188.

52 Telegram of 22 April/5 May and letter of 24 April/7 May 1908: *PRK*, 189.

53 *Expo*, 35, with the now-familiar confusions of geography. That Stravinsky acted as a bearer in St. Petersburg is recorded by Findeyzen in his journal (RNB).

54 That he certainly attended the actual funeral is confirmed by a letter of 1/14 July 1908 from Steinberg to Gnesin: "I saw him [Stravinsky] at the funeral and after . . .": *PRK*, 191. Craft's remark in *Conv* (45) that "you do not mention in your autobiography whether you attended Rimsky-Korsakov's funeral" is an oversight, since Stravinsky explicitly states in *Chron* (44) that he was there. Rimsky's remains and monument were transferred to the Alexander Nevsky Cemetery, at the eastern extremity of the Nevsky Prospect, in 1936.

55 *Conv*, 45.

56 Letter of 29 June/12 July 1908 to S. N. Kruglikov, in Ganina, 340. Findeyzen noted in his journal that "I stood by Nadezhda Nikolayevna . . . and she and I wept bitterly. Poor, poor thing!" (RNB).

57 *Chron*, 44.

58 See his letter of 28 July/10 August to Nadezhda Rimsky-Korsakov: *SM*, 445; *PRK*, 193.

59 *PRK*, 191. This letter disproves Taruskin's contention (*SRT*, 333–4) that *Fireworks* was not completed until late 1908 or early 1909. A fragment of a letter survives from Igor to his mother with an anonymous pencil dating "Ustilug 1908" (late May or early June at the latest, since it refers to Igor's forthcoming birthday on 5 June) stating that "I have finished *Fireworks* and sent it off to Ziloti" (*PRK*, 206–7). This letter does in fact date from 1909, as is proved by a reference to "the proofs of my two songs, which I have received from Jurgenson" (in early June 1908 Igor had not yet made contact with Jurgenson, nor had he even completed the second Gorodetsky song). But the *Fireworks* score referred to must be the revision mentioned in Igor's letter to Max of 12/25 May 1909: "I have only just, these last few days, diligently sat down to orchestrate *Fireworks*, and I shall finish it any day now—a lot of changes" (*SM*, 446–7, *PRK*, 204). The original Steinberg letter indicates that this was a reorchestration.

60 Letter of 28 July/10 August.

61 Letter to Vladimir Rimsky-Korsakov, 1/14 August 1908: *PRK*, 193–4.

62 Postcard of late July 1908. The postcard has not survived, but is quoted in Stravinsky's reply of 1/14 August.

63 Letter of 11/24 August 1908 to Nadezhda Rimsky-Korsakov: *SM*, 445–6, *PRK*, 195–6. Taruskin includes a complete English translation in *SRT*, 399–400.

64 Letter to Vladimir Rimsky-Korsakov, 19 August/1 September 1908: *PRK*, 197–8. Glazunov, unable to finish his tribute in time for the Ziloti concert on 11 October, had passed the commission to Steinberg, whose *Prélude symphonique* was duly played at the concert.

65 Ibid.

66 Ibid.

9 THE IMPRESARIO AND THE NIGHTINGALE

1 Ogneva, "Muzey I. Stravinskovo v Ustiluzi," 3.

2 Hostowiec, "Dom Strawinskiego w Uscilugu," 30; Stempowski, 70 (Pawel Hostowiec was Stempowski's pseudonym). Stempowski suggests that this was simply the villagers' way of explaining the oddities of the house's Sezession style, since they knew that Belyankin had been a naval officer. The house is still standing, and supposedly in its original form, though in a very run-down state. When I visited it in 1994, it was a hospital. A photograph, as grim as the house itself, is in *Muz Ak* 1992, 143.

3 Hostowiec, 25; Stempowski, 60.

4 *Chron*, 97–8.

5 Hostowiec, 25–6; Stempowski, 61. Against this has to be set Theodore Strawinsky's description of his father's study at the Old Farm as a large downstairs room, with a grand piano "at which my father had lately composed *Fireworks*" (*CISFam*, n.p.). *Fireworks* must in fact have been composed in the old Nosenko house, but revised in the new one, when Theodore was still only two. Of course, Stravinsky may have had an upper sanctum as well, for serious composition. Photographs survive of the study, with its prints and portraits, its high ceiling, and its Bechstein grand, which Igor had transported from St. Petersburg.

6 Quoted in *PMP*, 500, note 3 to letter 140.

7 Erhardt, *Igor Strawinski*, 16. He gives no source for this information.

8 In *Expo*, 53, Stravinsky says that he wrote two of the Four Piano Studies, as well as *Fireworks*, in the new house, which would argue a move in early May (as well as an earlier dating for one of the last three studies). But it seems more likely that, like Theodore, he was thinking of the revision of *Fireworks*, and that the move took place at the end of August. Presumably the new house was financed by a land sale, enabling a division between the two sisters. But little is known of any such transaction, and for obvious reasons land sales and registrations in prerevolutionary Ukraine are now almost impossible to trace. Two letters survive (22 August and 3 September 1908 [OS]: *PRK*, 198–9) from Stravinsky to Yastrebtsev which suggest that a mortgage may have been involved. But whether the former Nosenko estate was itself actually sold is unknown.

9 See *SRT*, 359–60. The "marriage" in question is, by implication, to Christ, but with a hint of group sex as part of the ceremony, a point that Taruskin uncharacteristically overlooks.

10 The official Rimsky-Korsakov view had been that he was "a great talent, who, despite his unusual pungency, is an impeccable harmonist and, unlike Reger and Strauss, does not write rubbish." See Yastrebtsev, *Reminiscences*, 375 (entry for 23 November 1905). "Of course," the diarist adds pointedly, "he has strayed off somewhere and will never come back," a remark which the annotator of the English edition interprets geographically (since Scriabin was living abroad), but which obviously really has to do with harmonic language. Scriabin had remained the one important non-Petersburg composer in the Belyayev catalogue. But, in practice, there was increasing resistance to his newest works on the Belyayev board. See, for instance, *SRT*, 253, note 92.

11 See Charles Joseph, *Stravinsky and the Piano*, 44–54, for a detailed comparison and a facsimile of Stravinsky's autograph.

12 *SRT*, 380.

13 Ibid. Taruskin even finds an original for the out-of-phase meter of the final study in Scriabin's op. 42/8. Stravinsky was to remember this device again in his *Three Japanese Lyrics*, four or five years later.

14 Letter of 20 September/3 October: *PRK*, 199–200.

15 Letter of 14 June 1908 to G. P. Jurgenson: *PRK*, 190. The date is Old Style, even

though Ziloti was at Viborg, in the Grand Duchy of Finland, where New Style dating was in force.

16 Letters of 18 and 23 June 1908 (OS), respectively: *PRK*, 190–1.

17 Letter of 1/14 August 1908. The "odd way" was that the negotiations were conducted by Ziloti.

18 Letter of 19 August/1 September 1908 to Fyodor Gruss: *PRK*, 196. This history of Stravinsky's debut as a published composer corrects some erroneous speculation by Taruskin, who, in arguing that the completion of *Fireworks* was delayed, deduces that the package sent to Lyubensk must have contained the *Scherzo fantastique*. But that score was already in Ziloti's possession by early June 1908. Also mistaken is Taruskin's assertion that *The Faun* and *Fireworks* were Stravinsky's only published works before 1910, and that the connection with Jurgenson began in that year. This is important only because Taruskin uses the supposed lack of success with publishers to support his theory that Stravinsky was tortured by jealousy of Steinberg. See *SRT*, 390–1.

19 Letter of 1/14 August. A grivna was worth ten kopeks.

20 Anatoly Kuznetzov's note in *Muz Ak* 1992, 120, that "the *Scherzo fantastique* was originally slated for performance in the Ziloti concert of 11 October 1908 (in memory of Rimsky-Korsakov)" seems to be without foundation. As we have seen, it was down for January even before Rimsky's death. In any case it would have made a very odd funeral tribute.

21 The combination, that is, of primary triads separated by a tritone. This important discovery is as usual Taruskin's. See *SRT*, 402–6.

22 Letter of 30 December 1908/12 January 1909: *PRK*, 200. The letter proves, incidentally, that the work was for normal orchestra, wind and strings, not for wind only, as recalled by Stravinsky in *Mem*, 59, and repeated by everyone since except Taruskin, who perhaps deduced that it was for a normal combination from the fact that no reviewer commented otherwise.

23 Informed Russian opinion is, nevertheless, that the materials probably survive in the archives of the St. Petersburg Philharmonie, formerly the Assembly of the Nobles (see, for instance, *PRK*, 491). The Belyayev board was not normally quick to return materials, even when no decision had been taken to publish, and Stravinsky himself recalled that the score and parts had been left in the firm's St. Petersburg office. Taruskin's fear that they were at Ustilug when the First World War broke out may be unduly pessimistic. See *SRT*, 401.

24 G. N. Timofeyev, "Iz muzïkal'noy khroniki," *Vestnik Yevropï*, no. 10 (1909), 760: repr. in *PRK*, 448. A full English translation of the relevant text is in *SRT*, 406.

25 Respectively: "La-mi," *Rech'*, 19 January 1909; I. Krïzhanovsky, *Slovo*, 21 January 1909: repr. in *PRK*, 447–8.

26 *Chron*, 45.

27 *SRT*, 401.

28 Smirnov, *Tvorcheskoye formirovaniye*, 80.

29 *Novoye vremya*, 20 January 1909, quoted in *PRK*, 447–8.

30 See Mikhail Gnesin, "Vospominaniya o Skryabine," quoted in *SRT*, 793–4. According to Gnesin, Stravinsky played *The Faun and the Shepherdess*. Scriabin had been living abroad since 1904, so Stravinsky's memory (*Mem*, 64) of having met him often at Zagorodnïy is almost certainly at fault. Yastrebtsev in fact records no visit after 1901.

31 *Expo*, 15; *SB*, 27. A week after his daughter's birth Stravinsky probably attended an Evenings concert in the Reformatsky School at which the seventeen-year-old Prokofiev played a number of his own piano pieces. See Appel, *Prokofiev by Prokofiev*, 281; abridged edition, 159. It was after this concert, according to Craft, that the two young composers became friends (*SPD*, 310).

32 Letter of 19 August/1 September: *PRK*, 197–8.

33 Yastrebtsev, *Reminiscences*, 445: entry for 6 March 1908.

34 Ibid., 447: entry for 8 March. The Russian original (vol. 2, 487) means literally "[a toast] to the fact that only here, at the Rimsky-Korsakovs', and precisely thanks to Nikolay Andreyevich himself, could he (it was S. S. Mitusov speaking) year after year 'comb out' to satiety his spiritual thirst for such 'combing.' " No wonder they all laughed till they cried.

35 *Chron*, 43.

36 *Expo*, 36. Not, at any rate, those for the *Scherzo fantastique*, as stated in *Chron*. Rimsky must have seen the finished score of that.

37 *SSCII*, 432. A week earlier Igor had attended, with the rest of his family, the unveiling of the ornate memorial which still adorns his father's grave (now in the Nevsky cemetery, but at that time in the Novodevichy). A tribute by Nikolay Findeyzen, together with a photograph of the monument, surrounded by a sort of conservatory, appeared in the *Russkaya muzïkal'naya gazeta*, 15, no. 49 (7 December 1908), cols. 1122–3.

38 V. B[askin], *Rossiya*, 1 February 1909; repr. in *PRK*, 449.

39 *Russkaya muzïkal'naya gazeta*, no. 5 (1909), 146–8, repr. in ibid.

40 *Russkiye vedomosti*, 7 February 1909, repr. in *PRK*, 450. The attribution to Derzhanovsky is Varunts's; Taruskin (*SRT*, 410–11) credits the review to Yuliy Engel.

41 Letter of 25 January/7 February 1909: *PRK*, 201–2.

42 Letter of 6/19 February 1909: *PRK*, 202.

43 This was not the last time Stravinsky would have Elgar as a somewhat corpulent bedfellow in the Dvoryansky Sobraniye. Four years later the Russian premiere of music from *Petrushka* would be coupled with that of Elgar's Violin Concerto, played by Fritz Kreisler.

44 Pierre Souvtchinsky, quoted in White, *Stravinsky: The Composer and His Works*, 181. White's assertion that *Fireworks* was also played at this concert has been much repeated in the Stravinsky literature, including the present author's *The Music of Stravinsky*. But the Souvtchinsky story, though recorded under *Fireworks*, undoubtedly refers to the *Scherzo fantastique*.

45 Buckle, *Diaghilev*, 129.

46 Drummond, *Speaking of Diaghilev*, 21.

47 *SPD*, 23. Diaghilev told Misia Sert that he had first met Stravinsky at a concert of St. Petersburg Conservatoire students. See Sert, *Two or Three Muses*, 131.

48 Grigoriev, *The Diaghilev Ballet*, 28–9. Igor Blazhkov, the editor of the letters section in *SM*, makes a direct connection between the decision to rescore and a performance at the Conservatoire: see *SM*, 498, note 6.

49 Buckle, *Diaghilev*, 129.

50 *Revue de deux mondes*, 15 July 1909, quoted in *SRT*, 417. Benois complained that "our first-class composers, Liadov, Glazunov and Tcherepnine . . . made their orchestral version too complicated and modern, lacking simplicity and airiness" (*Reminiscences of the Russian Ballet*, 293). He seems to have forgotten about Stravinsky's contribution.

51 See Sotheby's sale catalogue, *Continental Printed Books, Manuscripts and Music*, 3–4 December 1992, lot 632, pp. 312–4. The catalogue includes facsimiles of pages 9, 14, and 15 of the manuscript. The autograph was acquired by PSS in 1997, and a further facsimile of page 8 is in F. Meyer (ed.) *Settling New Scores*, 7. The autograph of the transcription of the Grande Valse brillante was sold at auction by J. A. Stargardt, Marburg, West Germany, on 25 November 1981, and is now in the library of the University of Austin, Texas. A study score of the Waltz is published by Boosey and Hawkes, and the Nocturne is currently in press and due out in late 1999 or early 2000.

52 Letter of 12/25 May 1909: *SM*, 446–7, *PRK*, 204. "Do you know how the rehearsals of *Chopiniana* are going?" he asks in a postscript. "What about my bits?" *Les Sylphides* had its premiere at the Théâtre du Châtelet in Paris on 2 June (that is, 20 May OS). But Steinberg's reply, if any, is lost.

53 Letter of late May 1909 to his mother: *PRK*, 206–7. See chapter 8, note 59.

54 Letter of 9 June 1909 (NS). For details of this correspondence see the preface to the Eulenburg miniature score, no. 1396. The original materials are in the archives of Schott (Mainz); copies in PSS.

55 Letter of 19 June: ibid.

56 Letter of 21 July/3 August 1909: *PRK*, 214–5.

57 Ibid.

58 Letter of August (or early September) 1909: *PRK*, 217–8. The letter is misdated to 1913 in *SSCII*, 437–8. The book in question was Gorodetsky's *Yar'*.

59 Letter of 21 July/3 August 1909. The Mitusov quotations are from letters of (in my opinion) July and (the final quote) early August 1909, respectively (Mitusov seldom dated his letters, and Varunts disagrees with my dating of the "July" letter, excluding it from the first volume of *PRK*, which ends in 1912; the August 1909 letter is in *PRK*, 217–8). The bulk of Mitusov's surviving letters to Stravinsky are published in English translation in *SSCII*, appendix C (the "July" letter quoted here is an exception), but with a number of misdatings and often highly confusing translations.

60 Yastrebtsev, *Reminiscences*, 445. "*Vinograd zelyoniy*"—"green vine"—can also be "sour grapes."

61 *SRT*, 468.

62 *Mem*, 83.

63 Letter of 21 July/3 August 1909: *PRK*, 214–5. The footnote is Stravinsky's own.

64 Letter of (probably) late July 1913 (PSS); *SSCII*, 436 (my translation).

65 Letter of 7/20 June 1909: *PRK*, 209–12.

66 Letter of 21 July/3 August. But he himself rarely did it subsequently.

67 Ibid.

68 Letter of 17/30 August 1909: *PRK*, 216.

69 Zilbershteyn and Samkov, *Sergey Diaghilev*, vol. 2, 109–10.

10 Birds of a Feather

1 "The ballet is one of the most consistent and complete expressions of the idea of the *Gesamtkunstwerk*, the idea for which our circle was ready to give its soul. It was no accident that what was afterwards known as the *Ballets Russes* was originally conceived not by the professionals of the dance, but by a circle of artists, linked together by the idea of Art as an entity." Benois, *Reminiscences of the Russian Ballet*, 370–1.

2 O. Vasilyev, quoted in S. Lifar, *Serge Diaghilev*, 21–2.

3 Quoted in Haskell, *Diaghileff: His Artistic and Private Life*, 19. Haskell's own pen portrait of Diaghilev in 1890 is "this apple-cheeked young country bumpkin" (ibid., 17).

4 Benois, *Reminiscences of the Russian Ballet*, 163.

5 Ibid., 266. A fine color reproduction of the set design for the second scene is in Richard Shead, *Ballets Russes*, 24–5. But according to the journalist Robert Brussel, Diaghilev had mentioned the idea of showing the Imperial Ballet in Paris as much as a year before the *Armide* premiere. See Buckle, *Diaghilev*, 119 and 550, note 1.

6 See Grigoriev, *The Diaghilev Ballet*, 8. But Fokine probably got the idea for such medleys from Isadora Duncan, who routinely performed to the accompaniment of "classical" music, including, notably, Chopin.

7 *Cléopâtre* had originally had a complete score by Arensky when it was done at the Mariyinsky in March 1908 under the title *Une Nuit d'Egypte*, but Diaghilev had "considered the Arensky music very weak and felt that it would be impossible to present the ballet in Paris with such music." Fokine, *Memoirs of a Ballet Master*, 141–2.

8 *Mercure de France*, quoted in *SRT*, 551, note 170. My translation.

9 Letter of 12/25 June 1909, in Zilbershteyn and Samkov, vol. 2, 108–9.

10 Letter of 24 July 1908, in ibid., 181.

11 *SRT*, 525.

12 Letter of September 1909, in Zilbershteyn and Samkov, vol. 2, 110–1.

13 Ibid. The Debussy project came to nothing. See Lockspeiser, *Debussy: His Life and Mind*, vol. 2, 169–70 and 262–3.

14 See Donald Street, "A Forgotten Firebird." But the most decisive connection between Tcherepnin's music and Fokine's scenario is in the twelve-line poem which prefaces the score with a reference to the demon Kashchey. Taruskin shows that the connection between Kashchey and the Firebird is an idea of Fokine's and is not found in any previous tale about either character. See *SRT*, 575.

15 Benois, *Reminiscences of the Russian Ballet*, 304.

16 *SRT*, 575.

17 "Le mois," *Revue musical S.I.M.*, no. 5 (June 1909), quoted in *SRT*, 551.

18 Benois, *Reminiscences of the Russian Ballet*, 303–4. He names only Tcherepnin, Fokine, Stelletsky, Golovin, and himself. The folklorist Remizov and the painter Bilibin are also mentioned, but it is not clear that they attended group meetings. Grigoriev also states that the scenario was worked out after the Paris season, and claims to have had a hand in it: *The Diaghilev Ballet*, 28.

19 Letter of September 1909. Taruskin supposes that Diaghilev also approached another Rimsky-Korsakov pupil, Nikolay Sokolov, but ridicules Kochno's assertion that the Moscow composer Sergey Vasilenko was likewise considered. Such speculations can get out of hand. There is no serious evidence for either suggestion. See *SRT*, 579 and 575–6, note 44, respectively.

20 *Memoirs of a Ballet Master*, 159.

21 Street, op. cit., 675. Asafyev's memoir claiming to have suggested Stravinsky to Diaghilev is in Zilbershteyn and Samkov, vol. 2, 425, note 3; English translation in *SRT*, 578. Fokine also claims a share of the credit for the discovery of Stravinsky. See *Memoirs of a Ballet Master*, 161.

22 *Chron.*, 47. Both Asafyev and Stravinsky mention that Diaghilev had just returned to St. Petersburg when he approached them. This was probably at the beginning of September (OS), less than a fortnight after the Lyadov letter. Clearly he was not yet in a position to commission Stravinsky firmly.

23 *Expo*, 128.

24 Fokine, *Memoirs of a Ballet Master*, 161.

25 Ibid., 159. For a description of the sketches, see Savenko, "*L'Oiseau de feu*—zur Geschichte der ersten Fassung," which includes excellent monochrome reproductions of this and two other sketch pages of the five which survive in all. The title page is also reproduced, less clearly, in *SSCII*, 223, and the musical sketches are transcribed in *SRT*, 581–3.

26 *Expo*, 128.

27 The inscription is dated 5 December 1909. See *PRK*, 220, note 4.

28 *Expo*, 127. Diaghilev's phone calls were already as notorious as his telegrams. Fokine wrote that "my left ear would become swollen as the result of a four-hour continuous telephone conversation with Diaghilev." *Memoirs of a Ballet Master*, 142.

29 Benois, *Reminiscences of the Russian Ballet*, 304.

30 *SRT*, 557. The present discussion is heavily indebted to Taruskin's painstaking account of the sources of *The Firebird*.

31 Fokine represents himself as sole author in *Memoirs of a Ballet Master* (158–9). But he was a notorious claimer of intellectual copyright. Grigoriev (28) describes the collective piecing together of different episodes from Afanasyev. Taruskin traces the idea also to a poem by Yakov Polonsky, written as long ago as the 1840s: *SRT*, 556–7. But he also proves that certain details—like the episode of the princesses with the golden apples—must have come from Fokine: ibid., 569–70. Diaghilev gave it out that Fokine was the author of the libretto. See for instance his interview with the *Peterburgskaya gazeta* (11 February 1910), in Zilbershteyn and Samkov, vol. 1, 212–3. This may have been for tactical reasons. But Fokine is also credited as author on the title page of the published, though not the autograph, full score.

32 *Expo*, 129.

33 Fokine, *Memoirs of a Ballet Master*, 159, 171.

34 *Expo*, 128.

35 Fokine, *Memoirs of a Ballet Master*, 161.

36 *Expo*, 129. See also Karsavina, *Theatre Street*, 260–1, for an account of how Stravinsky and Fokine worked on the score at Diaghilev's flat, appealing to him "in every collision over the tempi."

37 See Savenko, op. cit., 32, and *SRT*, 580–3; also *SSCII*, 223.

38 *Expo*, 128, and note 2.

39 For instance, the glissando of string harmonics in the Introduction, six bars before curtain up, comes from Rimsky-Korsakov's opera *Christmas Eve*, notwithstanding Stravinsky's claim to have invented it (*Expo*, 132). As far as I know, Nikolay Tcherepnin was the first to point out this derivation: *Vospominaniya muzïkanta*, 46–7. Stravinsky's reference to "Richard Strauss's astonishment when he heard [this effect] two years later in Berlin" is thus somewhat poignant, since Strauss's attitude to *Christmas Eve* was dismissive: "This is all very well," he is said to have remarked, "but unfortunately we are no longer children." See Yastrebtsev, *Reminiscences*, 410.

40 *Expo*, 131.

41 Fokine, *Memoirs of a Ballet Master*, 160.

42 B. Tyuneyev, *Russkaya muzïkal'naya gazeta*, no. 3 (1910), col. 79; quoted in *PRK*, 451–2.

43 "Muzïkal'naya khronika: kontsertï Ziloti," *Apollon* no. 4 (1910), 74; quoted in *PRK*, 452.

44 *SRT*, 418.

45 See Louis Cyr, "The Autograph Manuscript of *The Firebird* (1910)," in *L'Oiseau de feu: Facsimile du manuscrit*, 194–5. The datings in the manuscript score contradict Stravinsky's memory that "the complete music was mailed to Paris by mid-April" (*Expo*, 128). Work continued steadily until 5 May.

46 Letter of 4 September 1909, Zilbershteyn and Samkov, *Sergey Diaghilev*, vol. 2, 109–10.

47 See Garafola, 386. Garafola also asserts that Stravinsky arranged a Sinding piece as well as the Grieg. But she gives no source. According to Buckle (*Nijinsky*, 147), Diaghilev's commission is recorded for February 1910 in his black notebook, with a fee of 75 roubles, but only for the Grieg. Neither score has resurfaced.

48 *Chron*, 55–6.

49 Letter of 2/15 December 1912: *SM*, 470–1, *PRK*, 386–8; English translation in *RiteSk*, appendix 2, 32–3. The list of works which Stravinsky attached to the letter is included only in *PRK*.

50 See, respectively, Roerich, *Iz literaturnovo naslediya*, 457 (typescript in the Lawrence Morton Archive of UCLA); and P. Belikov and V. Knyazeva, *Rerikh*, quoted in *SRT*, 864.

51 See, for instance, *Russkoye slovo*, 15 July 1910; and "Balet khudozhnika N. K. Rerikha," *Peterburgskaya gazeta*, 18 August 1910: both texts quoted in *SRT*, 863. In his letter to Vladimir Rimsky-Korsakov of 6–12 September 1910 (NS) (*PRK*, 236–8), he mentions "the ballet about which you probably know from the newspapers." Later, however, this changed. Two and a half years later he was writing to Steinberg: "I see that notices are appearing in the papers that Roerich has written a ballet called *Vesna Svyashchennaya*, that he is working out the scenario—and that I personally have been busy with it for a whole month. They'll soon be writing things like: '*Life for the Tsar*—opera by Baron Rosen with music by M. Glinka.'" Letter of 2 February 1913 (RIII).

52 *SRT*, 569.

53 "Avant la féerie," *Revue musicale* 11, no. 110 (December 1930), 40: translation from White, *Stravinsky: The Composer and His Works*, 184. Incidentally, Stravinsky himself remembered the "modest and dimly lit dwelling" for "the perversely large number of mirrors on [its] walls" (*Expo*, 24).

54 "Muzïkal'nïy vecher v 'Apollone,'" *Apollon*, no. 7 (1910), 54–5. The program also included the two Gorodetsky songs, op. 6, of which the second, "Rosyanka," was actually receiving its "public" premiere.

55 Tamara Karsavina, "A Recollection of Strawinsky."

56 Grigoriev, *The Diaghilev Ballet*, 32.

57 *Chron*, 50.

58 *Expo*, 24.

59 The full score was completed on 5/18 May.

11   THE PUPPETEERS

1 Jean-Jacques Eigeldinger, "The Firebird (1910): Genesis—Creation—Reception," in Cyr, *L'Oiseau de feu: Facsimile du manuscrit*, 180, gives 7 June as the date of his arrival, but provides no source. Stravinsky himself (*Expo*, 129) says it was "towards the end of May," but he may still have been thinking Old Style dating.

2 Letter of 8/21 January 1908 to S. P. Belanovsky, quoted in *My Musical Life*, 446–7.

3 Karsavina, *Theatre Street*, 219.

4 *Expo*, 129.

5 Karsavina, "A Recollection of Strawinsky," 8.

6 Grigoriev, *The Diaghilev Ballet*, 37. Stravinsky told Roerich that the orchestra found the music so hard that they needed the exceptional number of nine rehearsals to learn it. Letter of 19 June/2 July 1910: *PRK*, 224–6, English translation in *RiteSk*, appendix 2, 27–8.

7 *Early Memoirs*, 299.

8 Stravinsky to Roerich, 19 June/2 July 1910.

9 There seem only ever to have been two animals, for all Stravinsky's memory of "a procession of real horses," one of whom, "a better critic than an actor, left a malodorous calling card" (*Expo*, 130). The horses were in any case abandoned at an early stage, either after the dress rehearsal or after the first or second performance: see Fokine, *Memoirs of a Ballet Master*, 170–1, and Grigoriev, *The Diaghilev Ballet*, 38.

10 See Zilbershteyn and Samkov, vol. 1, 428, note 4.

11 *Expo*, 129. By contrast he said nothing about the musical performance, except that the offstage trumpets missed their cue at the Lever du jour. *Les Orientales*, with Stravinsky's Grieg arrangement, had its premiere on the same bill.

12 Karsavina, *Theatre Street*, 211.

13 *Expo*, 130–1. But Eigeldinger (op. cit., 187, note 27) doubts some of the others, and especially Claudel, who was French consul in Prague at the time.

14 Karsavina, *Theatre Street*, 198–9.

15 *Reminiscences of the Russian Ballet*, 306–7. Benois had severed an artery in his wrist after smashing a window in annoyance at Diaghilev's failure to arrange his visa to travel with the company to Paris. See his letter to Diaghilev of 27 June 1910 from Montagnola (Lugano), in Zilbershteyn and Samkov, vol. 2, 112–3.

16 Fokine, *Memoirs of a Ballet Master*, 166. Golovine's gouache of the main décor is in the State Tretyakov Gallery, Moscow.

17 Henri Ghéon, "Propos divers sur le ballet russe."

18 Calvocoressi, "A Russian Composer of To-day."

19 Benois, *Reminiscences of the Russian Ballet*, 304.

20 Letters of, respectively, 7 and 9 July (NS): *PRK*, 229–30. Varunts omits the remarks about *Scheherazade*, but they can be deduced from Volodya's reply of 1/14 July (ibid., 230).

21 *PRK*, 224–6; *RiteSk*, appendix 2, 27–8.

22 Letter of 17/ 30 June 1910: *SM*, 448, *PRK*, 224.

23 Letter of 19 June/2 July to Roerich.

24 Twenty-five years later she reminded Igor that "something was undoubtedly slightly

wrong after I had Mikusha [Lyudmila]" (letter of 18 August 1935, PSS), so perhaps Lausanne was simply a precaution.

25 Letter of 24 June/7 July: *PRK*, 229.

26 Letter of 2/15 August 1910: *PRK*, 232. Steinberg pointedly links the wintering abroad to the head turning, but adds a "partly for family reasons" to take the sting out of the complaint.

27 Letter of 28 December 1910 (OS) to A. P. Tretyakova-Botkina: *PRK*, 257.

28 Respectively: *CISFam*, n.p., and letter of 6–12 September 1910 (NS) to Vladimir Rimsky-Korsakov: *PRK*, 236–8.

29 *CISFam*, which also includes a family photo. But the composer remembered "a beach-side hotel" (*Expo*, 133). Perhaps he lived and worked apart from the ragtag and bobtail.

30 Letter of 19 June/2 July to Roerich. The letter was continued at La Baule on 29 June/12 July.

31 *CISFam*, italics Theodore's. Igor seems never to have been to the seaside before, except possibly on honeymoon at Helsinki, or on the Baltic holiday he took with Gury in May 1905. Oranienbaum is *by* the sea, but does not front onto it in any recreational sense. In any case, the water at the head of the Baltic is almost fresh.

32 Letter of 14/27 July to Roerich: *PRK*, 231–2.

33 Taruskin's assertion that he set the poems in Mitusov's syllabic Russian translation is disproved by a letter of 4/17 January 1911 from Jurgenson to Mitusov, reminding him that "on 13 December, at the wish of I. F. Stravinsky, I sent you two songs of his, in proof, for translation" (*PRK*, 260); cf. *SRT*, 655. The songs had their premiere at an Evenings of Contemporary Music concert in St. Petersburg nine days after Jurgenson's letter, sung by Gualtier Bossé.

34 *SRT*, 655–7; *Expo*, 131.

35 *Mem*, 21.

36 *Expo*, 67, 134. But why did they go to Vevey, which is several miles beyond Lausanne on the line from Paris?

37 Letter of 6–12 September 1910. On 15 July, *Russkoye slovo* had reported that "academician N. K. Roerich, Igor Stravinsky, the young composer of *The Firebird*, and ballet master M. M. Fokine are working on a ballet under the name *The Great Sacrifice*, devoted to old Slavic religious customs. Subject matter and staging are by N. K. Roerich." See also chapter 10, note 52.

38 *Chron*, 56.

39 Better known as Soulima, a name he only adopted, however, as part of his professional name, Soulima-Stravinsky, in the 1930s. For biographical purposes I shall preserve Sviatoslav, or its standard abbreviation, Svetik, or occasionally his nickname, Nini.

40 Stravinsky remembered moving from Lausanne to the Châtelard (*Expo*, 67). But letters of early November show that by that time he was living at Les Tilleuls. The Châtelard was pulled down long ago, but Les Tilleuls still stands, a tall apartment house rising above the northern exit from Clarens, on what is now the rue Sacre du Printemps but was then the rue Gambetta.

41 See Stravinsky's letters to Roerich of 2 and 27 July (NS), respectively.

42 So, at least, Stravinsky told his wife after meeting Diaghilev in Carlsbad in August 1911. The letter has not survived, but its contents are reported by Katya in a letter to her mother-in-law of 17/30 August 1911: *PRK*, 298.

43 Quoted in Vershinina, "Pis'ma I. Stravinskovo N. Rerikhu," 62, note 3.

44 See Stravinsky to Roerich, 2 July.

45 Letter of 6 September 1910 (NS): *SM*, 448, *PRK*, 235. Craft misinterprets this letter as indicating that Benois had visited Stravinsky at La Baule (*SSCI*, 408). Benois had sent some photos to (not of or from) La Baule, from where they were forwarded to Lausanne.

46 Benois tacitly admits in *Reminiscences of the Russian Ballet* (323–4) that Diaghilev

tried to get round him with the offer of various projects, but claims to have stood firm. This is apparently contradicted by Stravinsky's letter, which proves that Benois had mentioned a possible collaboration in his own letter to which that was a reply. But Benois probably *had* refused Diaghilev. Stravinsky's letter to him of 3 November 1910 (NS) includes an apology "for involving you in work which you turned down in Lugano." See *SM*, 449–50; *PRK*, 242–4.

47 Letter of 3 November.

48 Lieven, *Birth of the Ballets-Russes*, quoted in *SRT*, 670. The original has not survived, but its contents are confirmed in detail by Benois himself in *Reminiscences of the Russian Ballet*, 324.

49 *Chron*, 57.

50 *Les Nouvelles littéraires*, 8 December 1928; reprinted in Lesure, *Stravinsky: Etudes et témoignages*, 248.

51 Letter of 2/15 February 1911: in *SM*, 455–6, *PRK*, 266–7. The Marsovoye Pole, or Champs de Mars, is a huge parade ground, now a public park, in St. Petersburg near the river Neva. The Shrovetide fairs had moved there from Admiralty Square in the 1880s.

52 Benois, *Reminiscences of the Russian Ballet*, 28. The ice slide (or "switchback") was a double slide, constructed of timber, with a high tower and an ice-sliding channel. "The switchbacks usually stood in pairs, facing each other, so that, having come down the first, you could immediately climb up the other and slide down again."

53 "What is postponed is not lost." Letter of 9 October 1910, in Zilbershteyn and Samkov, vol. 2, 113–4.

54 Respectively, Igor Stravinsky to Benois, 3 November (NS); and Gury Stravinsky to Benois, 6/19 November: *PRK*, 246.

55 Benois to Igor Stravinsky, 9/22 December 1910: *PRK*, 252–4.

56 Letter of 2/15 August 1910: *PRK*, 232.

57 *Rech'*, 25 July 1910. The letter is substantially reprinted in Zilbershteyn and Samkov, vol. 1, 437–8.

58 *Rech'*, 10 September 1910: ibid., 220–2.

59 Letter of 22 October (NS): *PRK*, 240–1. He also inquires about a recent illness of Andrey's mother's.

60 This is the reason he gives in his letter to Benois of 3 November, as it had also been his pretext for not returning from La Baule to Paris for discussions with Diaghilev.

61 Letter of 6–12 September 1910. The contract with Diaghilev was worth 1,500 roubles, according to Buckle (*Diaghilev*, 176); but as we shall see, Diaghilev was an extremely erratic payer.

62 *CISFam*. The house was at 1 avenue des Anglais, their eighth or ninth address in just over six months.

63 Letter of 12/25 November 1910: *PRK*, 248.

64 Letter of 26 November 1910 to Andrey Rimsky-Korsakov: *SM*, 451, *PRK*, 248–9. The concert was on the afternoon of the twenty-sixth.

65 Undated cutting (probably December 1910) in PSS. Curiously enough, Alfred Bruneau also reviewed the concert, in *Le Matin* (28 November), but made no mention of any audience noise: "Performed with extreme verve, this curious musical fantasy amused me enormously." Robert Brussel, in *Le Figaro*, reported that the work enjoyed "a very great success."

66 Respectively: V. Valter, *Rech'*, 25 October 1910; N. Bernshteyn, *Sankt-Peterburgskiye vedomosti*, 26 October 1910; unsigned, *Novoye vremya*, 25 October 1910: all reprinted in *PRK*, 458–9.

67 V. G. Karatïgin, "Muzïka v Peterburge," *Apollon*, no. 12 (1910), reprinted in *PRK*, 460.

68 29 October 1910; reprinted in Vitol[s], *Vospominaniya, stat'i, pis'ma*, 226–9.

69 Letter of 26 November 1910.

70 Letter of 7/20 November 1910: *SM*, 450, *PRK*, 247.

71 Letter of 8 November 1910 (NS): *PRK*, 245. Gury's letter, of 4 November, has not survived, but is discussed in Igor's.

72 Letter of 7/20 January 1911: *SM*, 453, *PRK*, 260–1.

12 THE RIGHT MAN IN THE RIGHT PLACE

1 *Mem*, 96. But the trouble went back thirty years earlier, to a time in 1929 when Stravinsky had tried to alter his agreement with Benois so that the latter took a percentage only from stage performances. See *SPD*, 71, and the present volume, chapter 31. Since the autobiography was written after that date, its own attempt to write Benois out of the *Petrushka* discussions (*Chron*, 57–8) has also to be taken with a pinch of salt.

2 Benois was twelve years older than Stravinsky, and where the Shrovetide fairs were concerned that was a whole generation, since the fairs had died out rapidly after moving to the Marsovoye Pole in the 1880s.

3 *SM*, 449–50, *PRK*, 242–4.

4 Letter of 9/22 December 1910: *PRK*, 252–4. The letter shows that Diaghilev originally hoped to stage the new ballet as early as April 1911, when his newly established permanent company would be dancing its first season in its winter quarters in Monte Carlo. According to Grigoriev, 47, the date was put back—initially to May—because of the unavailability of the Mariyinsky dancer Alexander Orlov, whom Diaghilev wanted as the Moor.

5 Letter of 9 November 1910 (NS): *PRK*, 246.

6 Letter of 3 November, Stravinsky to Benois. The Russian name for this character is Fokusnik—Magician. In French, however, it is always given as Charlatan, which as in English has the sense of a trickster, someone whose magic is fake. As for Petrushka himself, Taruskin rightly observes that the Stravinsky-Benois character is really as much like the commedia loser-figure Pierrot as his nominal original, Pulcinella. See *SRT*, 667.

7 *Chron*, 57–8. Lieven maintains that the coachmen and the grooms in the fourth tableau were suggested by Diaghilev. See *Birth of the Ballets-Russes*, 139. But Grigoriev's claim (*The Diaghilev Ballet*, 46) that Diaghilev thought of the whole subject is demonstrably wrong.

8 Grigoriev, 46, says he did. But he does not mention the July visit, so he is probably misdating.

9 See Buckle, *Diaghilev*, 180. Diaghilev was in London on 10 October (having travelled from Venice, presumably via Clarens) and back in Paris on the twenty-seventh. Some datings in Buckle are too dependent on unreliable memoirs, but these particular ones are from correspondence. At the time of Stravinsky's letter of 22 November to Andrey Rimsky-Korsakov, Diaghilev was still—or again—in Paris.

10 *Reminiscences of the Russian Ballet*, 324–7.

11 Letter of 12/25 December 1910: *PRK*, 254–6.

12 But as yet apparently without the organ-grinder episode. See below.

13 Letter of 12/25 December.

14 The exact dates of the visit are not known. He was not yet there on 12/25 December (the date of Benois's letter) and had left by 28 December/10 January. See Vera Ziloti's letter to her sister of that date in *PRK*, 257.

15 *Reminiscences of the Russian Ballet*, 327. Benois describes a play-through in his own apartment, but it must also have been heard at Diaghilev's.

16 Not "Rake Vendor," as he is ludicrously called in the revised Boosey and Hawkes score. The character is an *"ykhar-kupets"*—a "rake merchant" only in the sense of a merchant who is also a rake.

17 *Reminiscences of the Russian Ballet*, 329. Taruskin suggests a source for this idea in Alexander Serov's opera *The Power of Evil*, in which Fyodor Stravinsky was famous

for his portrayal of the role of the blacksmith Yeryomka. *SRT*, 692–3. More interestingly still, he also points out musical derivations.

18   Letter of 7/20 January 1911 to Andrey Rimsky-Korsakov, in *PRK*, 260–1 (see also chapter 2, note 35). How different from his much later memory that "the city I had known only a few months before as the grandest in the world now seemed sadly small and provincial" (*Expo*, 135).

19   Letter of 13/26 January 1911: *SM*, 454, *PRK*, 262–3. Not all these details are now recognizable: the "drama" is presumably what became the "goat and pig charade" (fig. 239 in the revised score), and the "revelry" is the general dance which is interrupted by the final scene between Petrushka and the Moor. But the cripples seem not to have survived, unless the five-in-a-bar music at 240 was meant to represent some real or mimed physical handicap, of which, however, the stage directions preserve no record.

20   Letter of 2/15 January: *SM*, 452–3; *PRK*, 258–9.

21   Stravinsky to Benois, letter of 13/26 January.

22   Letter of 3/16 December 1910: *SM*, 451–2, *PRK*, 250–1.

23   *Expo*, 135.

24   The composer was Emile Spencer. According to Craft, approximately ten percent of *Petrushka* royalties went, and continue to go, to Spencer's estate (*SPD*, 609, note 98).

25   Letter of 7/20 January 1911.

26   *SRT*, 719.

27   *Reminiscences of the Russian Ballet*, 325. For more detail on this, and on the contemporary vogue for commedia stylizations and Petrushka plays in general, see *SRT*, 674 et seq.

28   *Reminiscences of the Russian Ballet*, 325.

29   The letter is referred to in Stravinsky's to Benois of 13/26 January 1911.

30   See ibid., and also, more fully, letter of 21 January/3 February 1911: *SM*, 455, *PRK*, 264–5.

31   Letter of 2/15 February 1911: *SM*, 455–6; *PRK*, 266–7. An editorial addition in the published text (both editions) has Stravinsky say "unfortunately you [do not] agree with me," which may seem logical in terms of the psychology of agreement, but makes no sense in terms of the letter's subsequent contents. If Benois had disagreed with Stravinsky, there would have been no musical problem. But Benois may momentarily have taken his eye off the ball. On 31 January (OS) he wrote to Diaghilev resigning from the project on financial grounds. Diaghilev must somehow have brought him round, apparently without word of the threat reaching Stravinsky: *PRK*, 265.

32   Letter of 1/14 March to Alexander Ossovsky: *PRK*, 271–2. Theodore Strawinsky describes his father composing "scenes of popular rejoicing . . . [while] under his windows the Beaulieu carnival masks passed backwards and forwards in the bright Mediterranean sunshine" (*CISFam*).

33   *Expo*, 135. As so often with him, the event is supposed to have been announced by a dream. "I thought I had become a hunchback, and I awoke in great pain to discover that I was unable to stand or even sit in an erect position."

34   *Chron*, 59. In 1924 he had told the Belgian musicologist Paul Collaer that the illness was a reaction to French tobacco, after the mild Russian cigarettes to which he was accustomed. See "Introduction à la vie et à l'oeuvre d'Igor Strawinsky."

35   *SM*, 456–7, *PRK*, 269–70.

36   Letter of 13/26 March 1911 to Nadezhda Rimsky-Korsakov: *PRK*, 273. According to Buckle, Stravinsky had just received a three-day visit (23–25 March) from Diaghilev and Nijinsky, who stayed at the Hotel Bristol in Beaulieu. See *Diaghilev*, 189 and 555, note 40.

37   Letter of 1/14 March.

38   Letter of 22 February/7 March.

39   The contract with Jurgenson for *The Firebird* is dated 25 January 1911 (presumably

OS): see *SSCII*, 219, note 2. At almost the same instant, the Gorodetsky songs, op. 6, and the "Pastorale" came out, and in mid-April the Moscow journal *Muzïka* announced the receipt of the Four Piano Studies and the *Two Poems of Verlaine*—all Jurgenson publications. The piano reduction of *Firebird* came out in June. It seems, though, that Jurgenson declined *Petrushka*, possibly disliking the composer's five-year exclusivity agreement with Diaghilev, which applied to *Petrushka* as well as to *Firebird*.

40 Postcard of about 27 April 1911: *PRK*, 273.

41 Letter of 8/21 July 1911: *SM*, 459–62, *PRK*, 290–4.

42 Grigoriev, 50–1.

43 Letter of 9 May 1911: *PRK*, 275–6.

44 Ibid.

45 *Reminiscences of the Russian Ballet*, 330. In an earlier article, written in 1930, Benois stated that a few bars of the ending were not composed until Paris, "almost the day before the performance" ("Petrushka," *Posledniye novosti*, 2 December 1930). But the full score is dated "Rome 13/26 May 1911," using Latin script for the first time, as Stravinsky later told an interviewer in Bologna in 1935, because he had so much fallen for Italy; see *SPD*, 209.

46 Letter of 12/25 December 1910: *PRK*, 254–6.

47 *Expo*, 137.

48 Grigoriev, *The Diaghilev Ballet*, 51.

49 Fokine, *Memoirs of a Ballet Master*, 185.

50 Karsavina, "A Recollection of Strawinsky," 8.

51 Buckle, *Diaghilev*, 195.

52 Fokine, *Memoirs of a Ballet Master*, 185–6.

53 Ibid., 188.

54 Karsavina, "A Recollection of Strawinsky," 8.

55 Letter of 28 May/10 June 1911, Gury Stravinsky to Vladimir Rimsky-Korsakov: *PRK*, 278.

56 Letter of 8/21 July 1911.

57 Lieven, *Birth of the Ballets-Russes*, 143.

58 *Expo*, 137.

59 Grigoriev, *The Diaghilev Ballet*, 54. This probably refers to the extra dress rehearsal Diaghilev called on the day of the official premiere, rather than the public "dress" on the evening of the twelfth (which was attended by the press).

60 Letter of 12 June: *PRK*, 278–9.

61 Gold and Fizdale, *Misia*, 141.

62 Benois, *Reminiscences of the Russian Ballet*, 338.

63 Letter of 16/29 June 1911: *PRK*, 282–3.

64 *Le Matin*, 14 June 1911.

65 *Comoedia*, 14 June 1911. Vuillemin's review occupied three whole columns of the front page and the top quarter of page 2, accompanied by several large photographs.

66 Letter of 14 June: *PRK*, 279–81.

67 Letter of 18 December 1911, in Lesure, *Claude Debussy: Correspondance 1884–1918*, 296–7.

68 Letter of 13 April 1912, in ibid., 306.

69 Letter of 28 January/10 February 1913, quoted in *SPD*, 57. Steinberg's copy of the score was a gift from the composer.

70 N. Y. Myaskovsky, "*Petrushka*, balet Ig. Stravinskavo," *Muzïka* no. 59 (14 January 1912), 72–5. See also his letter to the editor of *Muzïka*, Vladimir Derzhanovsky, 5/18 December 1911: "I'm carried away by Stravinsky's *Petrushka*, of which I've procured a proof score" (*PRK*, 304).

71 Letter of 26 January 1913 (OS), in *PMP*, 104.

72 Letter to Myaskovsky of 11/24 June 1913, in *PMP*, 107–8; Robinson (ed.), *Selected Letters of Sergei Prokofiev*, 235–6 (my translation). The "official" Petersburg view that

Petrushka could not survive away from the stage contrasts sharply with the dance critic Andrey Levinson's observation in *Ballet Old and New* that "*Petrushka*, a wonderful example of musical representationalism, renders the ballet itself superfluous." Quoted in *SRT*, 761.

73 Because these tunes are, respectively, about a betrothal ceremony and a midsummer festival, Taruskin (*SRT*, 707–9, 867) considers that the dance must have been based on an existing sketch for *The Great Sacrifice*. But Stravinsky's request to Volodya in early September 1910 for folk-song collections "except for Rimsky-Korsakov and Balakirev, which I've got" suggests that the second tune, which is in neither of these collections, was not yet incorporated (letter of 6–12 September [NS]: *PRK*, 238).

13 RUE SACRE DU PRINTEMPS

1 *CISFam.*
2 Letter to Anna Stravinsky of 15/28 August 1911: *PRK*, 297.
3 Letter of 2/15 July 1911: *PRK*, 289; *RiteSk*, appendix 2, 29–30. The letter implies that Roerich had queried the need for a meeting, but the earlier communications have not survived.
4 The letter or letters have not survived, but their contents can be more or less deduced from Gury's reply of 30 June 1911 (OS) and Igor's letter to Volodya of 16/29 June: *PRK*, 288 and 282–3, respectively. Gury had shown Igor Volodya's letter.
5 Letter of 30 June. Two months later, on his way to see Benois in Lugano, Igor ran into Gnesin in Munich and seriously advised him to move to Paris, offering to help him by pulling strings through his "grand contacts" (memoir by Gnesin, quoted in *PRK*, 191, note 1 to item 144).
6 Letter of 30 June/13 July: *SM*, 457–9, *PRK*, 285–7. The intention was still to settle in Paris after January, as is clear from Stravinsky's postcard of 7/20 July to Florent Schmitt; see F. Lesure (ed.), *Stravinsky: Etudes et témoignages*, 231.
7 Letter of 8/21 August 1911 to Andrey Rimsky-Korsakov: *SM*, 462–3; *PRK*, 295.
8 Gury to Volodya, letter of 30 June: *PRK*, 288.
9 Lieven, *The Birth of the Ballets-Russes*, 56.
10 Letter of 8/21 July 1911: *SM*, 459–62, *PRK*, 290–4. A complete English translation is in *SRT*, 972–4.
11 Letter of 24 September/7 October 1911: *SM*, 463–4, *PRK*, 300–1. The Russian text of Fuchs's essay is "Tanets," in *Fial' Strastey* (St. Petersburg: Venok, 1910), 59–96. I have failed to trace the German original.
12 Letter of 30 June/13 July 1911.
13 Letter of 28 January/10 February 1912: *PRK*, 307–8. It seems that he tinkered with the music before deciding to abandon it, at least to judge from the four pages of *Nightingale* (act 2) sketches of approximately this same date in the *Rite of Spring* sketchbook (42–5). The following autumn he told a newspaper reporter in St. Petersburg that the existing scene had come out as a self-contained concert piece: see *Peterburgskaya gazeta*, 27 September 1912, in *ISPS*, 11. But while RMV may have held the manuscript score for this purpose, it was not printed until after work had resumed on the later scenes in 1913, and probably no performance materials existed.
14 *Peterburgskaya gazeta*, 27 September 1912.
15 Postcard of 7/20 July 1911: Lesure (ed.), *Stravinsky: Etudes et témoignages*, 231.
16 See *SRT*, 780–91, for this and other information on Balmont and his position in Russian poetry at that time; also Irina Vershinina, "Balmont i Stravinsky," in *Muz Ak* 1992, 130–5.
17 *Mem*, 83.
18 Or so he told Vladimir Derzhanovsky (letter of 31 July/13 August 1912, *PRK*, 350–1). In fact the MS of the vocal score, reproduced in facsimile in Vershinina, "*Zvezdolikiy:*

Odin iz avtografov," Muz Ak 1992, 135–9, includes four bars of eight-part writing. See also Vershinina (ed.), *Igor Stravinsky: Vokal'naya muzïka,* vol. 3, 5.

19   RMV apparently declined after consulting Steinberg, a fact of which Stravinsky was presumably unaware. See Nadezhda Rimsky-Korsakov (senior) to Steinberg, letter of 13/26 October 1912: *PRK,* 367–8.

20   Stravinsky's correspondence with Jurgenson and Derzhanovsky reveals important new information about this strange and often maligned work. In simplifying the chorus parts, the composer also modified their harmonies, but without altering the basic harmonic structure, as represented by the piano reduction (see his letters to Derzhanovsky, note 18 above, and Jurgenson, 18 January 1913, unpublished, GMMK). The mottolike setting of the title was unquestionably meant to be performed, even though Stravinsky omitted to reduce it to four parts from six "Is Calvo-coressi doing the translation and when will it be ready? How is he translating the word *Zvezdolikiy?* This latter is particularly important because it will have to feature as a title, and besides it's to be sung, since the title is sung in the Russian" (to Jurgenson, 15/28 April 1913, GMMK; the motto was left untranslated). The orchestration was carried out in late July and early August 1912, and the score dispatched to Derzhanovsky on 8 August (NS). But after the performance on the twenty-second fell through, Stravinsky recalled the score and seems to have made more changes, to judge by his letter to Schmitt of 18 September, which mentions that he is at work on "the instrumentation of the chorus" (BN; also *SSCII,* 105).

21   See Roerich, "Vesna Svyashchennaya," *Iz literaturnogo naslediya;* quoted in *SRT,* 894.

22   See Stravinsky's letters to Roerich of, respectively, 19 June/2 July and 14/27 July 1910: *PRK,* 224–6 and 231–2; *RiteSk,* appendix 2, 27–9. Neither of these libretti has survived.

23   "Balet khudozhnika N. K. Rerikha," *Peterburgskaya gazeta,* 18 August 1910: quoted in *SRT,* 866.

24   N. K. Roerich, *Realm of Light,* quoted in *SRT,* 871.

25   *Expo,* 141.

26   7 September 1911; quoted in Y. Polyakova, *Rerikh: Zhizn' v iskusstve,* 170. Craft states that the section titles were contributed by Roerich, while the idea of a division into two parts, representing day and night, was Stravinsky's: see *"The Rite of Spring: Genesis of a Masterpiece,"* in *RiteSk,* xvii. The original title of the whole work, *Velikaya zhertva—The Great Sacrifice—* was retained for the second part.

27   As told in *Expo,* 140–1, this incident happened on the way to Talashkino. But André Schaeffner, who must have had the story from Stravinsky's mouth, and sooner after the event, says that it happened on the way back. See Schaeffner, *Strawinsky,* 39.

28   See his letter to Roerich of 2/15 July 1911.

29   A year later a note in Stravinsky's "Copie des lettres" folder records this subsidy of 100 Czech kronen, but wrongly dates the trip to July: see *SPD,* 83 and 613, note 146.

30   *SM,* 462–3; *PRK,* 295. Andrey's letter is lost, but we can deduce its drift from Igor's. "How wretched," he exclaims, "that we aren't together! I'm convinced we'd see eye to eye! . . . I have sent you *The Firebird.* But *Petrushka* doesn't greet you, as you've forgotten about him."

31   Much of this information about the Karlsbad meetings is contained in Katya Stravinsky's letters to her mother-in-law of 17/30 August and 21 August/3 September: *PRK,* 298–9. Clearly some changes were made to the scenario at Diaghilev's behest, since Igor later told Roerich that "I am burning with impatience to find out your opinion of this rearrangement" (letter of 13/26 September 1911: *PRK,* 300; *RiteSk,* appendix 2, 30). But we do not know what they were.

32   Letter of 21 August/3 September, Katya to Anna Stravinsky.

33   Ibid. On the fifth he sent the proofs of the first two tableaux of *Petrushka* to Benois for checking; see his letter to Benois of that date in *SM,* 463, *PRK,* 299.

34   Letter to Schmitt of 20 September 1911 (NS). This is apparently the first (near) refer-

ence to the new work's eventual French title, which may, however, have been an attempt to translate *Prazdnik vesnïy*.

35 Letter of 13/26 September 1911.
36 Letter of 24 September (OS): *SM*, 464; *PRK*, 300–1.
37 For a vivid description of this room—"exactly the sort of room . . . claustrophobic to me, that he loves, and not only loves but compulsively needs, to crowd still further with the objects and artifacts that to him signify order"—see Craft, *Stravinsky: Chronicle of a Friendship*, 404–6. Stravinsky revisited Les Tilleuls in 1965 and was filmed by CBS in conversation with his former landlady, Mme Louise Rambert. Craft's description is part of his account of this visit. A photograph of Stravinsky composing there in 1911 or 1912 is the frontispiece of *Expo*, with a caption claiming that he wallpapered the room himself.
38 Ibid., 405. The main railway line is a few hundred yards down the hill from Les Tilleuls.
39 Letter to Benois of 21 November 1911: *SM*, 464–5, *PRK*, 303–4.
40 *SPD*, 83, gives the amount received as 479 francs 80 centimes (the approximate equivalent of 200 roubles). But a naught must have been left off. The true amount should have been 2,000 roubles, or just under 5,000 francs.
41 Letter of 21 November.
42 *RiteSk*.
43 For further information, see Pasler, "Stravinsky and the Apaches."
44 Calvocoressi, "A Russian Composer of Today."
45 Letter of 2 February 1912 (BN); and *SSCII*, 104, where, however, it is wrongly dated 2 November 1911 (my translation). Stravinsky was responding to the work's dedication. The subsequent correspondence with Schmitt suggests that Stravinsky helped persuade Diaghilev to stage the work, though, according to Craft, Stravinsky later told Richard Buckle that the decision was political, "Schmitt being an important critic," adding that "it's terrible music" (*SPD*, 82). But this last opinion also needs to be treated with caution. Stravinsky never really forgave Schmitt for beating him to Dukas's vacant *fauteuil* at the Académie des Beaux-Arts in 1936.
46 Letter of 26 January 1912: *PRK*, 305–7 (wrongly dated 2 January in *SPD*, 84). However, Stravinsky was apparently not telling the exact truth. The Rondes printanières is dated 12 February in the autograph full score—that is, more than a fortnight after the letter to Benois.
47 Ibid. Stravinsky was probably referring to this trip when he recalled that he spent his fifth [sic] wedding anniversary in Genoa: *Dial*, 21.
48 *Expo*, 142. Nor can I find any primary evidence that Stravinsky went to Vienna for the company's opening on 19 February, even though most authorities state that he was there. See, for instance, *SPD*, 84; Buckle, *Diaghilev*, 216. Finally, Craft's remark that "Stravinsky spent most of February [1912] in London with the Ballet" is a good sample of the wholesale confusion that has bedevilled Stravinsky biography: neither Stravinsky nor any other member of the Ballets Russes spent a single minute in London in February 1912. See "Genesis of a Masterpiece," *RiteSk*, xviii.
49 Letter to Benois, 2/15 February 1912: *SM*, 465–6, *PRK*, 309–10.
50 *PRK*, 314, *RiteSk*, appendix 2, 31. The end of part 1 in the short-score draft is dated 11/24 February, while the date on the orchestral score is 16/29 February, which tends to confirm that at the end of the Danse de la terre the two stages of composition—the making of a finished draft from the sketches, and the final orchestration—were almost simultaneous. I am grateful to Louis Cyr for bringing this point to my attention.
51 Letter of 7 March 1912: *SM*, 466–7; *PRK*, 315–6.
52 Letter of 13/26 March 1912: *PRK*, 322. According to *SPD*, 84, Diaghilev paid Stravinsky 300 francs to make the journey.
53 See his letters of 17 and 29 March 1912 from Monte Carlo and Clarens, respectively: *PRK*, 319–20, 323–4.

54 Letters of 17 and 13/26 March, respectively.

55 Letter of 17/30 March: *PRK*, 324–5. They did not meet, but Steinberg apparently encountered some of the Apaches in Paris, including Calvocoressi, to whom Stravinsky wrote on 11 April: "Did you fall under the happy influence of our poor friend Steinberg, who seems to me to have plunged absolutely into academicism? In one of his last letters he declares that he understands nothing in my most recent compositions." PSS; *SSCII*, 98 (my translation). Steinberg may have expressed puzzlement at *Petrushka*, which had just come out and which Stravinsky had bought for him on account at RMV. But the tone of Stravinsky's reply makes one doubt that anything stronger was said. See his letters of 10/23 and 30 March 1912: *PRK*, 321, 324–5. Steinberg's letters of this period are lost.

56 Letter of 11 April 1912: *SSCII*, 98.

57 "Early Years," in Lederman, *Stravinsky in the Theatre*, 128–9. Obviously Stravinsky played only the first part of the ballet.

58 Nijinsky's sister claimed that the choreography for both *Faune* and the Danse sacrale in *Sacre* were worked out before the Hellerau visits. But this hardly seems possible in the case of the Stravinsky. See Bronislava Nijinska, *Early Memoirs*, 450.

59 Letter of K. A. Somov to M. G. Lukyanov, 18 April 1912, in Zilbershteyn and Samkov, vol. 2, 197–8. Somov dined with Stravinsky, Diaghilev, and Nijinsky after the dress rehearsal of *Petrushka* on the seventeenth.

60 *Diaghilev*, 225.

61 According to Craft in *SPD*, 87, presumably quoting Stravinsky's memory.

62 *Chron*, 65. According to Pasler, "Stravinsky and the Apaches," 405, note 21, Ravel played fragments of *Daphnis* to the Apaches as early as 1910.

63 Letter of 5 November 1912, in Lesure (ed.), *Correspondance*, 314–5. See *SPD*, 90, and *SSCIII*, 3–4, for two other very different translations of the relevant part of this letter. Laloy also left a memoir of a piano run-through (four hands) by Stravinsky and Debussy at his house "in the spring of 1913" (*La Musique retrouvée*, 213). All authorities simply assume a slip of dating on Laloy's part. But there may well have been two separate performances, the second one, as Laloy recalled, a few days before the premiere in May 1913. There is unlikely to have been a usable four-hand score as early as June 1912, and certainly Monteux does not mention one in his reminiscence of the Monte Carlo play-through a few weeks before. In "Genesis of a Masterpiece," xviii, note 9, Craft introduces a new confusion by suggesting that Debussy's letter referred to a run-through in Paris in early November 1912 (see chapter 14, note 10). But the Paris visit took place after Debussy's letter was written: Stravinsky was still in Clarens on the sixth, returning there on the twelfth.

64 Letter of 8/21 June 1912: *PRK*, 337–9.

65 See variously *SPD*, 99 and 614, note 171; *SSCI*, 23, note 4; *SSCII*, 276, note 9, for details of this first of Stravinsky's many litigations. Exactly why Stravinsky, himself short of money, should have been lending on such a scale to previously unknown musicians remains a mystery.

66 Letter to Benois, 21 June/4 July 1912: *PRK*, 339–40. "Do you remember the wonderful pear we shared that night on the way back from taking Argutinsky home?" Delage reminded Stravinsky in a letter of 23 October 1912: *SSCI*, 24 (my translation).

67 Benois, *Reminiscences of the Russian Ballet*, 343–5. The project was never realized.

68 Letter of 21 June/4 July to Benois.

69 Letter of 2/15 May 1912. The letter has not survived, but much of its content can be reconstructed from Stravinsky's detailed replies of 5/18 June (*SM*, 468–9; *PRK*, 335–6; *SSCI*, 43–4) and 22 June/5 July (*PRK*, 340–2).

70 Letter of 22 June/5 July.

71 See Stravinsky to Derzhanovsky, letter of 31 July/13 August, *PRK*, 350–1. Significantly, Koussevitzky himself conducted the Russian premiere of excerpts from *Petrushka* in St. Petersburg five months later.

72 Postcard of 26 July/8 August, *PRK*, 348. Six days before, the composer had told Derzhanovsky that "I am working day and night on the orchestration."

73 Letter of 28 July/10 August 1912, *PRK*, 348–9.

74 19 August (NS), *PRK*, 352.

75 Interview in the Nuremberg paper *8 Uhr-Blatt*, 3 December 1930, quoted in *SPD*, 88. He also recalled arriving in Nuremberg from Vienna, which is possible but unlikely, unless he had given Berlin a miss—which, in the circumstances, is even more unlikely.

76 *Chron*, 66–70. The anecdote is curiously like his childhood memories of the Mariyinsky in that it records in detail everything except the music.

77 Letter of 2 February 1913 (RIII); according to *SPD*, 94, the performance was on 26 January. The embargo on *Parsifal* expired at the end of 1913, but was infringed— openly or by subterfuge—in a number of places in the preceding months. Diaghilev, according to an art-collector friend, was thinking of staging the work when the embargo ran out: see I. S. Ostroukhov to A. P. Tretyakova-Botkina, letter of 16/29 August 1911, in *PRK*, 297–8. Guinsbourg was director of the Monte Carlo Opera.

78 See chapter 2, notes 73 and 76.

79 *SSCII*, 4. A letter Stravinsky wrote to Maeterlinck on 6 February 1917, after the scherzo had been used for a ballet about bees at the Paris Opéra, seems to prove that Maeterlinck had been party to the original proposal, and had even wanted the composer "to enlarge the frame and music . . . with a view to deriving a more or less substantial stage work from it" (PSS). Stravinsky was admittedly being threatened with legal action and may have been setting up a line of defense; but Maeterlinck seems not to have denied the claim.

80 Benois, *Reminiscences of the Russian Ballet*, 346–8.

81 Letter of 1 September 1912: *PRK*, 354. The letter corrects the faulty chronologies of Craft, in *SPD*, 88, and Buckle, in *Diaghilev*, 236–7.

82 "Stravinsky in His Own Words," in *Igor Stravinsky: The Recorded Legacy* (CBS/Sony Classical); see also *SPD*, 89. Buckle (*Diaghilev*, 237) sets this play-through, perhaps rightly, in the Grand Hôtel des Bains on the Lido. At all these play-throughs Stravinsky must have read from the particell, or short-score draft, which was always his main compositional record before writing up in full score, which in this case he seems to have done as he went along. There is no need to posit, as André Schaeffner does, the existence of a formal piano score or, alternatively, a habit of improvising play-throughs. See Schaeffner, "Au fil des esquisses du *Sacre*," 186.

83 See his letter to Schmitt of 18 September 1912 (NS), in *SSCII*, 104–5.

84 Figure 99 in the score; see *SPD*, 89.

85 Letter to Steinberg of 13/26 September 1912: *PRK*, 358. Steinberg's so-called musical-mime triptych had been written on a scenario by Bakst, obviously with a view to staging by the Ballets Russes.

86 *Birzhevïye vedomosti*, 25 September 1912; reprinted in *ISPS*, 9.

87 See Steinberg's letter to Stravinsky of 2/15 October 1912, which quotes the main chord of the Augurs of Spring with the forlorn postscript: "All that I could remember from the first time." Stravinsky later recalled that Steinberg "jerked his shoulders in mockery of the 'primitive' rhythms and this, as you see, has offended me until now" (Craft, "Genesis of a Masterpiece," *RiteSk*, xviii, note 6). This is supposed to have happened at a Paris run-through the following month. But Stravinsky's letter to Steinberg of 13 November (*PRK*, 373) proves that Steinberg was not in Paris on that occasion.

88 Benois was allocated one-sixth, on the basis of his half-share in the scenario. The correspondence shows that this was an amicable arrangement, actually proposed by Stravinsky, notwithstanding his bitter complaints about it in later years. See especially his letter of 8/21 June 1912: *PRK*, 337–9.

89 *SSCI*, plate following page 234.

14 PETRUSHKA MEETS PIERROT

1 Letter of Stravinsky to Nadezhda Rimsky-Korsakov of 2/15 October, *PRK*, 363.
2 Craft dates the sketch to July 1911, but Taruskin argues convincingly that it belongs to the autumn of 1912. See Craft, review of Allen Forte, *The Harmonic Organization of "The Rite of Spring,"* in *Musical Quarterly* 64 (1978), 534; also *SRT*, 858–9, note 26.
3 *SSCI*, 23.
4 *CISFam*. The book also includes a photograph (plate 30) demonstrating the point.
5 See Delage's letter to Stravinsky of 23 October 1912: "I owe you some Japanese prints, which are asleep in a drawer waiting for you," PSS; *SSCI*, 24 (my translation). In Berlin, Igor told Andrey Rimsky-Korsakov, "I bought some Japanese paper." Letter of 23 October/5 November 1912: *SM*, 469; *PRK*, 371.
6 *CISFam*. Theodore does not date this reminiscence, but it cannot have been before 1911, when Stravinsky became an RMV composer, or after 1913, the family's last summer in Ustilug; and insofar as (Theodore implies) it was an annual occurrence it presumably happened in 1912.
7 Ibid.
8 *Expo*, 141.
9 *Expo*, 148.
10 *La France*, 12 November 1912. See also André Schaeffner, "Au fil des esquisses du Sacre," 189, which shows that the run-through was on the tenth.
11 Letter of about 5 November 1912, in Lesure (ed.), *Claude Debussy: Correspondance*, 314–5. See chapter 13, note 62.
12 Letter of 13 November, *PRK*, 373.
13 Letter of 10/23 December 1912: *PRK*, 392–3. Stravinsky told Craft that "Debussy was in close contact with me during the composition of *Jeux* and he frequently consulted me about problems of orchestration" (*Conv*, 50, note 2). But since *Jeux* was composed in July–August 1912 (when Stravinsky was in Ustilug) and orchestrated in late August (when he was in Lugano) and March–April 1913 (when he was in Clarens), the claim seems farfetched as well as musically improbable. See Robert Orledge, *Debussy and the Theatre* (Cambridge: Cambridge University Press, 1982), 326.
14 Letter of 20 November 1912 (PSS). *SPD*, 137, refers also to an earlier letter of the twelfth, but there was in fact only one. The princess wrote again with details of scoring on 4, 5, and 12 December.
15 The princess's letters of 4, 5, and 12 December accept his idea that the work should be a concerto (his own letters are apparently lost). Her letter of reminder is dated 4 April 1913 (PSS).
16 *Chron*, 75. Strauss had followed his own advice in *Elektra*.
17 Letter of 2/15 December 1912: *PRK*, 384–5.
18 See letters to Andrey Rimsky-Korsakov, 23 October/5 November 1912, and Roerich, 1/14 December 1912: *PRK*, 383–4; *RiteSk*, appendix 2, 31.
19 Quoted in Beecham, *A Mingled Chime*, 113.
20 Letter to Derzhanovsky, 10/23 December 1912.
21 Grigoriev, *The Diaghilev Ballet*, 76. Grigoriev implies that neither Stravinsky ballet was on the opening bill, but this seems to be contradicted by the handbill for the first night, reproduced in *SPD*, 91.
22 Letter of Struve to Alexander Ossovsky, about 5 December 1912: *PRK*, 378 (dated "after 20 November").
23 See *Dial*, 104–5, for Stravinsky's main reminiscence of the Schoenberg meetings, which amplifies the account in *Conv*, 68–9.
24 Moldenhauer, *Anton von Webern*, 167; J. Brand, C. Hailey, and D. Harris (eds.),

The Berg-Schoenberg Correspondence (Basingstoke and London: Macmillan, 1987), 130–6.

25 "Stravinsky's *Oedipus*," in L. Stein, *Style and Idea*, 482–3.

26 Letter of 26 December 1912: *SM*, 518, note 4; *PRK*, 395. It will be recalled that Karatïgin was one of the organizers of the Evenings of Contemporary Music.

27 Letter of 22 January 1913: Lesure (ed.), *Stravinsky: Etudes et témoignages*, 232. The letter is translated in *SSCII*, 108, but with the phrase about Schoenberg unaccountably left out (cf. *SPD*, 94).

28 13 February 1913, quoted in White, "Stravinsky in Interview." According to Bakst, Diaghilev was no less excited about Schoenberg. See his letter of 8 March 1913 to Ziloti, in Ziloti, *Aleksander Il'ich Ziloti, 1863–1945*, 287.

29 *SPD*, 107. We have to take Craft's word for it that the original instrumentation was noted down at the same time as the composition sketch—that is, October 1912.

30 *Conv*, 69.

31 Letter to Robert Godet of 14 October 1915, in Lesure (ed.), *Claude Debussy: Correspondance*, 358.

32 *Dial*, 105.

33 Letter of 18 December 1912: *PRK*, 390.

34 Letter of 1/14 December 1912.

35 Buckle, *Diaghilev*, 238–9; see also Lynn Garafola, *Diaghilev's Ballets Russes*, 60–1, and Nijinska, *Early Memoirs*, passim, for various, partly conflicting, accounts of how Dalcrozian Eurhythmics affected Nijinsky's choreography for *Jeux* and *The Rite of Spring*. Soon after this visit, Dalcroze himself wrote Stravinsky a long letter urging him to acquaint himself with the Eurhythmic method, warning him against the limitations of the Russian dancers, and inviting him to spend a fortnight at Hellerau. Dalcroze seems to have taken fright at the idea of his method being balleticized with the help of his young pupil. Letter of 7 January 1913: *SSCII*, 77–9. Curiously, Millicent Hodson's detailed account of the background to Nijinsky's choreography in *Nijinsky's Crime Against Grace* virtually ignores Dalcroze.

36 In a letter of 28 November/11 December 1912 (*PRK*, 381–2), Jurgenson tried to establish a fixed scale of honoraria based on a number of conventional work classifications (symphony, symphonic poem, suite, etc.). Not surprisingly, Stravinsky, who was about to embark on a phase of unbroken innovation in musical genres, was utterly unwilling to be tied down in such ways.

37 Letter to Benois of 2/15 December 1912: *PRK*, 384–5.

38 Letter of 17 November 1912: *PRK*, 375–6.

39 Letter of 4 December 1912: *PRK*, 379–80. Roger-Ducasse's *Orphée* was in fact a Mariyinsky commission, and fragments of it were played in St. Petersburg under Ziloti in 1914. It was never staged by Diaghilev.

40 Letter of 3/16 December (PSS).

41 Letter of (probably) 20 November 1912: *SSCII*, 277–9.

42 Robert Craft, commentary in *SSCII*, 275.

43 *SSCII*, 278.

44 Telegram of 2 January 1913 (PSS); *SSCII*, 5 (my translation).

45 Bronislava Nijinska calls it "the completed orchestral score," but that did not yet exist. See *Early Memoirs*, 457.

46 As we can deduce from Monteux's reproachful letter of, presumably, the following morning, announcing that he has just tendered his resignation to Diaghilev: letter of 5 January 1913, in *SSCII*, 51. But the trouble soon blew over.

47 Letter to Steinberg, 20 January/2 February 1913 (RIII). In *Chron*, 77, Stravinsky says that the local ballet company resented the fact that the Ballets Russes had been engaged by the director of the Hofoper.

48 Letter to Schmitt, 16 January: *SSCII*, 106 (but misdated 17 January). Schmitt promptly incorporated an edited version of the letter in his column in *La France* of 21 January. For a report of the rehearsal, see "Intsident mezhdu russkim kompozi-

torom i venskim korolevskim orkestrom," in *Peterburgskaya gazeta*, no. 10 (11–24 January 1913); also Buckle, *Diaghilev*, 241.

49 Letter of 22 January 1913: *SSCII*, 108, but with "piano à queue" ("grand piano") translated, with perhaps unconscious wit, as "piano at bottom."

50 6 February 1913.

51 *Daily Mail*, 13 February 1913, quoted in White, "Stravinsky in Interview," 7.

52 Letter of 2 March 1913: *SM*, 471.

53 16 February 1913.

54 Buckle, *Diaghilev*, 233–4.

55 *Mem*, 86. Stravinsky misdates the meeting to 1912.

56 Letter to Stravinsky of 3 March 1913: *SSCI*, 28. The baffling word "indignant" in the translated text (describing an article "Scott Evans" had written about Stravinsky's music) should read "intelligent."

57 13 February 1913, quoted in White, "Stravinsky in Interview," 7.

58 "Simfonicheskiy kontsert S. Kusevitskavo," *Vechernyaya birzhevaya gazeta*, 24 January 1913 (OS). But when Monteux conducted concert performances of *Petrushka* in March 1914 he wrote to Stravinsky that "you can have no idea how much this music gains by being played in concert." Letter of 14 March 1914 PSS; *SSCII*, 58 (my translation). Not surprisingly, Stravinsky underlined the remark in red: see *SPD*, 511.

59 "7-y simfonicheskiy kontsert S. Kusevitskavo," *Russkaya molva*, 25 January 1913. See *SRT*, 764, for a substantial quotation in English of Andrey's review, which clearly shows, incidentally, that Max had already conveyed his impressions of *The Rite of Spring* to his brother-in-law.

60 Letter of 29 January (OS), in Shlifshteyn, *N. Ya. Myaskovsky: Stat'i, pis'ma, vospominaniya*, vol. 2, 320.

61 12 January 1913, quoted in Zilbershteyn and Samkov, vol. 1, 441.

62 See his "Otvet N. N. Rimskoy-Korsakovoy" (Reply to N. N. Rimsky-Korsakov), in *Rech'*, 10 September 1910, reprinted in Zilbershteyn and Samkov, vol. 1, 220–2.

63 *Birzhevïye vedomosti*, 22 January 1913. See *SRT*, 1042–4, for a translation of the main article and a good survey of the opinions elicited.

64 *SRT*, 1043.

65 Postcard of 28 January 1913 (OS), quoted in *SRT*, 1044.

66 "Pis'mo v redaktsiyu," *Birzhevïye vedomosti*, 4 February 1913, in Zilbershteyn and Samkov, vol. 1, 233; English text in *SRT*, 1044. The letter is dated "London, 12 February 1913" (NS), so no doubt Stravinsky knew Diaghilev was writing it.

67 Letter to Stravinsky, 25 January 1913 (PSS); partial Russian text in *Muz Ak* 1996/2, 157; *SSCII*, 46–7 (my translation). Stravinsky probably did not receive it before leaving for London, as it was addressed to Ustilug.

68 See *RiteSk*, appendix 3, "The Stravinsky-Nijinsky Choreography," 35–43.

69 Buckle, *Diaghilev*, 238.

70 Ibid., 247.

71 Letter of Lincoln Kirstein to Robert Craft, 21 October 1973, in *SPD*, 513, paraphrasing an account given to Kirstein by Dame Marie Rambert. The incident is supposed to have taken place in Berlin, but the documentary evidence, as we have seen, is that rehearsals did not begin there; moreover, Buckle (239) suggests that Rambert could not have arrived in the German capital before 19 December, more than a week after Stravinsky's departure.

72 This was not the world premiere, which had been given at the St. Petersburg Conservatoire by Alexandra Sandra-Belling on 28 November 1912 (OS).

73 Apart from a revised scoring of the four bars after 86, which I take to be the "four added measures" referred to in Monteux's letter of 15 April as having just been received from RMV in Berlin (see *SSCII*, 54). I am indebted to Louis Cyr for finally (as I think) resolving the detailed chronology of this completion, in an unpublished revision of his seminal article on *The Rite of Spring* in Lesure (ed.), *Stravinsky: Etudes*

et témoignages, 89–147. See also Walsh, "Review-Survey: Some Recent Stravinsky Literature," 206–7.

74   *CISFam*. Theodore was just six.

75   Stravinsky's chorus was published as a separate number, in vocal score, by Bessel in 1914. But the full score was never published, and at the time of writing it remains unavailable for study. The Deutsche Grammophon recording of *Khovanshchina* conducted by Claudio Abbado (recorded in 1989) concludes with Stravinsky's chorus, but in a speculative orchestration made by Michael Nagy on the basis of Stravinsky's surviving sketches (a fact which was not, however, acknowledged in the accompanying booklet). Information kindly supplied by Mr. Nagy. For details of Ravel's contribution and substantial chunks of his article in defense of the project, "O parizhskoy redaktsii 'Khovanshchinï' " (On the Paris version of "Khovanshchina"), which appeared in *Muzïka*, no. 129 (14 May 1913), 338–42, see *SRT*, 1041 et seq., including also excerpts from Andrey Rimsky-Korsakov's reply in *Comoedia illustré* of 20 August (original Russian text in *Muzïka*, no. 139, 473–5).

76   E. Ansermet, *Les Fondements de la musique dans la conscience humaine*, vol. 2, 267.

77   Letter of Ravel to Hélène Kahn-Casella, 2 April 1913, in H. H. Stuckenschmidt, *Maurice Ravel: Variations on His Life and Work*, trans. Samuel R. Rosenbaum (London: Calder and Boyars, 1969), 131. As we saw, Schmitt had already had this idea, as Ravel perhaps knew, since he later invited Schmitt to take part.

78   See the correspondence with Diaghilev in *SSCII*, 7–8; and with Monteux, in *SSCII*, 54.

79   Letter to Alexander Sanin, 6/19 March 1913, in Kinkulkina, "Pis'ma I. F. Stravinskovo i F. I. Shalyapina k A. A. Saninu," 93–4; an English translation, heavily cut and reconstructed, is in *SSCII*, 198–9.

80   See Sechiari's letters of 13 October and 28 November 1912 (PSS).

81   Letter of 3 May 1913; the letter is in *SM*, 473, but with the relevant postscript omitted. It explains the otherwise baffling references to "grattage de nez" and "l'augmentation de votre nez" in Ravel's letters of "Monday" (28 April 1913) and 5 May 1913, in White, *Stravinsky*, 594–5; English translations in *SSCIII*, 16–7.

82   Letter of 17 February/2 March 1913; *SSCII*, 197–8 (my translation). The *Muzïka* announcement, referring to the work in the diminutive form *Svadebka*, was made in the journal's "Khronika" (Chronicle) column, and since it included other Free Theatre program details (including the intriguing information that Scriabin was writing incidental music for a production of Maeterlinck's *La Princesse Maleine*), it was probably based on a press release from the theatre itself. See *Muzïka*, 16 March 1913, 207. Sanin and Stravinsky had presumably talked in Paris in November 1912.

83   See Sanin's letter of 17 February/2 March; also Stravinsky's reply of 6/19 March 1913, in Kinkulkina, op. cit., 93 (*SSCII*, 198).

84   See letter of Léon Bernstein to Stravinsky, 28 July 1913, in *SSCII*, 8–9, note 13.

85   Telegrams of 27 and 28 March and letter of 30 March 1913: Kinkulkina, "Pis'ma I. F. Stravinskovo i F. I. Shalyapina k A. A. Saninu," 96, note 2, 94–5; English précis in *SSCII*, 200–2. Datings are confused, partly because of the Old Style datings on telegrams received in Russia from the West. I believe the above sequence to be correct.

86   Telegram of 19 April 1913 (Moscow Arts Theatre Museum); Sanin's letter of acceptance-in-principle is undated, but must be a few days earlier than the telegram, unless Stravinsky's reply is to a prior telegram of the kind much used in this correspondence. See *SSCII*, 202–3, for additional materials, but again with somewhat obscure datings.

87   Telegrams of 27 April (PSS); see also *SSCII*, 203, for a slightly different version of Stravinsky's telegram. In fact two contradictory copies survive in PSS, but the above text is the one that fits the actual facts. The telegram as received in Moscow has not surfaced.

15   FISTICUFFS AND A BAD OYSTER

1   *Le Coq et l'arlequin*, 87–8: "Under this regime, you digest in a hammock, you doze: you brush away the really new like a fly; it annoys you."

2   For this and much other information in the present chapter I am indebted to Bullard, *The First Performance of Igor Stravinsky's "Sacre du Printemps."* See also Garafola, *Diaghilev's Ballets Russes,* especially 296–8, for an account of the democratization of Diaghilev's audience by 1913.

3   Letter of 5 May 1913, in White, *Stravinsky,* 595; *SSCIII,* 17 (my translation).

4   Letter of 9 June 1913, in Lesure (ed.), *Claude Debussy: Correspondance,* 320–1.

5   See Bullard, vol. 1, 96–7. Bullard gives a complete list of the ninety-seven players at appendix D, 236–8.

6   Doris Monteux, *It's All in the Music,* 91.

7   Memoir by Henri Girard (1970), in Bullard, vol. 1, 97–8. The "offending conglomeration" was presumably the passage after fig. 53 in the Spring Rounds.

8   *Chron,* 81–2.

9   Bullard, vol. 1, 102 et seq. On the intervening Thursday (22 May), subscribers saw Musorgsky's *Boris Godunov* with Chaliapin in the title role. The following Thursday, 5 June, they would see the same composer's *Khovanshchina* (postponed from 30 May); and two weeks later, on 12 June, it would be the new Schmitt ballet, *La Tragédie de Salomé.*

10   See Louis Vuillemin, in *Comoedia,* 31 May 1913, reprinted in Lesure (ed.), *Igor Stravinsky: "Le Sacre du printemps": Dossier de presse,* 20–1.

11   *La France,* 4 June 1913: in Lesure (ed.), *Dossier de presse,* 24.

12   G. de Pawlowski, in *Comoedia,* 31 May 1913: in Lesure (ed.), *Dossier de presse,* 19.

13   See Grigoriev, *The Diaghilev Ballet,* 83, confirmed by Stravinsky in his letter to Steinberg of 3 July: *SM,* 473–4.

14   *Expo,* 143.

15   The lights stratagem seems to have worked temporarily. "It amused me," Valentine Gross wrote, "to see how certain boxes whose occupants had been so noisy and vindictive in the dark quietened down when the lights went on" (quoted in Buckle, *Diaghilev,* 253). Bullard refutes Grigoriev's suggestion that the lights were to help the police identify troublemakers: see Bullard, vol. 1, 148–9, note 93; Grigoriev, 83–4.

16   Bullard, vol. 1, 149–50. But according to Grigoriev (83), "the shouting continued even during the change of scene"; and, as Bullard points out, nobody else seems to have noticed Astruc's speech.

17   Sokolova, *Dancing for Diaghilev,* 43–4.

18   Romola Nijinsky, *Nijinsky,* 200. Marie Rambert told Buckle that Piltz was only "a poor copy, a postcard reproduction" of Nijinsky's own dancing of the role in private (Buckle, *Diaghilev,* 246). But everyone paled beside Nijinsky, with whom, in any case, Rambert was in love in 1913.

19   Levinson, "Stravinsky and the Dance," quoted in Bullard, vol. 1, 152. For a discussion of Levinson's more immediate review of the performance in the St. Petersburg newspaper *Rech'* (3 June 1913), see *SRT,* 1012–3.

20   See Gustave Linor, *Comoedia,* 30 May 1913, quoted in Bullard, vol. 3, 23–5. Linor states, ambiguously, that Monteux received a personal ovation "at the end."

21   31 May 1913: in Lesure (ed.), *Dossier de presse,* 17–18.

22   Adolphe Boschot, *L'Echo de Paris,* 30 May 1913: ibid., 15–16. Italics in original.

23   Octave Maus, *L'Art moderne,* 1 June 1913: in Bullard, vol. 3, 61–5.

24   *La France,* 4 June 1913: in Lesure (ed.), *Dossier de presse,* 23–5.

25   *Comoedia,* 31 May 1913: in Lesure (ed.), *Dossier de presse,* 18–20. It seems to have been Pawlowski who coined the phrase "le massacre du printemps," to describe, not the music, but the way it had been treated. "Never was experiment more roundly mis-

understood. This wasn't the *Sacre*, but the *Massacre du printemps*, and the fact may seem at the very least scandalous."

26 *Comoedia illustré*, 5 June 1913: in Lesure (ed.), *Dossier de presse*, 25–7.

27 *Montjoie!*, nos. 9–10 (14/29 June 1913); in Bullard, vol. 3, 156–9. Roland-Manuel's real name was Roland Alexis Manuel Lévy.

28 *Le Coq et l'arlequin*, 89. Rivière's article appeared in the journal of which he himself later became director, the *Nouvelle Revue française*, 4 (November 1913), 706–30.

29 Letter to Roerich, 13/26 September 1911: *PRK*, 300.

30 Letter of 2/15 December 1912: *SM*, 470–1; *PRK*, 386–8 (including the "list of my works," omitted from *SM*). Findeyzen was editor of the *Russkaya muzïkal'naya gazeta* and had asked Stravinsky for information to go in an article about his work. The article, by Boris Tyuneyev, appeared in *RMG* 20, no. 3 (1913), 71–8, with much of Stravinsky's letter used verbatim.

31 A single photograph survives of Stravinsky taking down a song sung by a "blind" hurdy-gurdy player on the steps of the Old Farm at Ustilug (see *CISFam*, plate 23). But, as Taruskin points out, the photo is very much posed, and probably more significant for that reason than as a sample of the composer's working method.

32 The French text is reproduced in facsimile in Lesure (ed.), *Dossier de presse*, 13–5. An English translation, which appeared in the *Boston Evening Transcript* of 12 February 1916, is reprinted in *SPD*, 524–6.

33 See his letter of 20 September 1911 to Schmitt: "Yesterday I received an article by Ricciotto Canudo in *La Renaissance contemporaine* called 'Ballets russes et snobs latins'—not bad!" (BN).

34 See Canudo's letters to Stravinsky in PSS. The initial note is simply dated "Monday morning."

35 See *SPD*, 523, for Craft's account. But Craft bases himself on a faulty translation. Canudo wrote, "On m'a montré aujourd'hui le démenti que vous donnez à une annonce parue l'autre jour, et que j'ignorai," which Craft renders as "I was shown your refutation of the article that appeared the other day." But "annonce" (notice) could not refer to a substantial article, and Canudo's final phrase "and of which I was unaware"—applying to the *annonce*—makes no sense in Craft's context (which may be why he omits it). The *démenti* appeared in *Excelsior*, (Friday) 4 July 1913, and Canudo's reply, dated simply "Friday," was presumably written the same day. The envelope is postmarked 5 July.

36 Derzhanovsky acknowledged receipt of the journal in his letter of 19 July/1 August 1913: English text in *SSCI*, 54–5, together with Stravinsky's draft corrections of the *Muzïka* translation (original in PSS). The original text of the letter (PSS) is unpublished, but reveals that the published translation is crucially inaccurate. Derzhanovsky wrote: "Thank you for *Montjoie!* Interesting. You've indeed modified your principle, and actual attitude! ... And for us you didn't want to." The point is that Derzhanovsky had previously asked Stravinsky to supply explanatory and biographical material for an article in *Muzïka*, but he had declined, on the grounds that "I absolutely refuse this as I do interviews even by the most exalted people" (letter of 22 June/5 July 1912: *PRK*, 340–2). The published translation, by contrast, seems to support some assumed remark by Stravinsky that the article itself was evidence of bad faith on the part of *Montjoie!* The Russian text of the article appeared in *Muzïka*, 141 (1913), 489–91; reprinted in *ISPS*, 14–18, with an invaluable commentary by Viktor Varunts.

37 See, for instance, his letter of 12/25 August 1913, in *SM*, 476–7: "I'm very embarrassed at the style of this letter [sic], which was written for *Montjoie!* practically on the run; they asked me to give them at least two words about *The Rite*. For an event like the season premiere, and in French, everything came out more decently and coherently than this translation you published in *Muzïka*."

38 Taruskin suggests (*SRT*, 998) that this tone was specifically Canudo's; but it is by no means foreign to the atmosphere of the original conception. See, for instance, the three versions of the scenario in *SPD*, 75–7.

39 "Ce que j'ai voulu exprimer dans *Le Sacre du printemps*": Lesure (ed.), *Dossier de presse*, 14 (paragraphs elided).

40 For a brilliant and encyclopedic study of the ethnographic, musical, and literary sources of *The Rite of Spring*, see *SRT*, 849 et seq.

41 Letter of Katya Stravinsky to Steinberg, 8 June 1913 (RIII).

42 Letter of 13 June 1913 (RNB).

43 Letter of about 27 June to Mitusov (RNB).

44 Letters of 13 and 16 June to Boris Jurgenson (GMMK) and 8 June to Steinberg (RIII). Steinberg, who had been kept in St. Petersburg by examination duties, feared a wasted journey to London. In the end he did not go.

45 *Chron*, 85–6. In *Expo* (138), Stravinsky recalled that "Ravel came and wept, which frightened me." He also received a visit from Puccini, who had heard *The Rite* on the second and had written to Tito Ricordi that "the choreography is ridiculous, the music sheer cacophony. There is some originality, however, and a certain amount of talent. But taken together, it might be the creation of a madman" (quoted in Bullard, vol. 1, 157, note 110). Stravinsky had first met Casella in St. Petersburg in 1907 (or so Casella claims in *Music in My Time*, 78; in *Conv*, 38, Stravinsky denies that they met on that occasion).

46 Quoted in Gold and Fizdale, *Misia*, 151, but with the usual error as to the date of the four-hand reading.

47 Letter of 23 June, in Lesure (ed.), *Claude Debussy: Correspondance*, 322–3. Stravinsky had sent Debussy a copy of the four-hand score two weeks before. See *SSCIII*, 5, note 5; but the date of the inscription, 9 June, suggests that it can hardly be autograph, since Stravinsky was still at the height of his fever.

48 Debussy's pneu (Parisian express letter), dated 31 May, and Emma Debussy's follow-up note of 11 June are in *SSCIII*, 5.

49 Andrey Rimsky-Korsakov, who attended *The Rite* on the fourth, reported to his mother that "the third performance . . . was as rowdy as the first" (letter of 2/15 June, RIII). But he had not, of course, experienced the premiere. As for *Khovanshchina*, Diaghilev's huge cuts, including the whole of the dialogue-based second act, had turned the work into what Taruskin calls "a choral pageant with basso obbligato [Chaliapin]" (*SRT*, 1042).

50 *Comoedia*, 19 June 1913.

51 Unpublished MS in KA.

52 Letter of 25 August: *SM*, 476–7. But this looks like an invention on his part. For instance, Louis Vuillemin's notice in *Comoedia* (7 June, but apparently written beforehand and based on press releases or an advance program) mentions the contribution of Stravinsky and Ravel but without critical comment, while the paper's actual reviewer, Linor, does not refer to Stravinsky at all. It should be added that while Ravel's orchestrations were performed throughout the run, Stravinsky's scoring of Shaklovity's act 3 aria was never performed, since Chaliapin, who was supposed to sing it (in the role of Dosifey), in the end refused to do so.

53 *Chron*, 85–6.

54 Letter of about 16 June 1913 (RIII). Max wanted Igor to press Diaghilev on the question of the London consultation, so it is just possible that Katya was fending him off with a mild exaggeration.

55 *Expo*, 138. *SPD* (516), however, records that "Diaghilev left his calling cards and faithfully inquired about the recovery."

56 Letter of 30 July/12 August 1913: *SM*, 474–6. The collaborators did not include Benois himself, as he had not come to Paris at all that season.

57 Postcard of 3 July 1913: *SM*, 473–4.

58 Undated letter of mid-July 1913, quoted in Gold and Fizdale, *Misia*, 154–6.

59 Letter of 7 July: *SSCII*, 55–6. In *SPD*, 516, Craft suggests that Stravinsky's letter ("July 7 or 8") crossed with Monteux's. But this looks merely like an assumption based on Misia's account of the rehearsal incident.

60 Gold and Fizdale, *Misia*, 156.
61 Letter of 10 July, in ibid., 153–4.
62 Ibid., 154. Craft, as loyal to the composer as she to Diaghilev, represents this as Stravinsky "ignoring" Misia. But Misia must have hoped for a direct word to Diaghilev, which was the surest sign of her success.

16 THE NIGHTINGALE AND NOT THE LARK

1   22 June 1913, quoted in *SSCII*, 203.
2   Letter of Katya Stravinsky to Mitusov, 13 June 1913 (RNB).
3   Letter of 17/30 March 1913: N. Kinkulkina (ed.), "Pis'ma I. F. Stravinskovo i F. I. Shalyapina k A. A. Saninu," 94–5; *SSCII*, 200–2.
4   Mitusov was at Ustilug, staying with Grigory Belyankin, from 17 to 22 July, but a day was lost because of a bizarre and disturbing tragedy, which Styopa related in a letter to his wife (7/20 July: see L. Kazanskaya, "Stravinsky i Mitusov," *Muzïkal'naya zhizn,* 9–10 [1996], 33–4). A young Polish girl, with whom he and Gury had been chatting lightheartedly in the passage of Belyankin's house only an hour before, blew her brains out in Gury's room and with his gun. Curiously enough, this shattering and suggestive incident was apparently never referred to in subsequent correspondence by either Styopa or Igor.
5   Letters of (probably) mid-July (OS) and 24 July/6 August 1913. Russian texts unpublished (PSS); English equivalents are in *SSCII*, 437 and 440.
6   Letter of about 1 August 1913 (OS), Russian text in PSS. The translation in *SSCII*, 439–40, is hopelessly garbled, and in fact makes no sense at all.
7   Letter of 5/18 August 1913 (RNB). The first version was duly restored.
8   Letter of 24 July/6 August 1913. The Emperor is reacting to the Ghosts of his Past Deeds at the start of act 3.
9   Letter of 31 July/13 August 1913 (RNB).
10 Letter of 26 June/9 July (PSS).
11 Letter of 16/29 July: *SM*, 474. The proofs were those of the symphony, *Zvezdolikiy,* and *The Rite of Spring*. The piano reduction of *Zvezdolikiy* was out in July, and Debussy, the work's dedicatee, received his copy in August and wrote to Stravinsky acknowledging receipt of "this cantata for the 'spheres' " (letter of 18 August, in Lesure (ed.), *Claude Debussy: Correspondance,* 326–7). The full score was ready by November; Debussy again received a copy and again wrote (9 November, in ibid., 330–1). But this time, he failed to name the "very beautiful thing, which time will render still more beautiful," and it has been otherwise identified as the *Three Japanese Lyrics* (by Lesure, ibid., note 55) and the (piano) score of *The Rite of Spring (Conv,* 52).
12 Letter of 30 July (presumably OS), quoted in Gold and Fizdale, *Misia*, 157.
13 Letter to Mitusov, 31 July/13 August 1913 (RNB).
14 Letter of 12 May 1913 (NS), Benois to Stravinsky (PSS).
15 Ibid. The brilliant caricature by Sem of Astruc dining with Nijinsky (reproduced in Buckle, *Diaghilev,* 203) somehow captures all these features except the top hat, and even manages to suggest the accent.
16 Letter of 30 July/12 August 1913: *SM*, 474–6.
17 Letter of 17/30 September 1913 (PSS); *Mem,* 134 (my translation).
18 Diaghilev cabled in mid-August to ask when *Nightingale* would be finished, almost certainly because he wanted to know when Stravinsky would be free to start composing *Svadebka*. Telegram of 14 August, in *SSCII*, 8.
19 Letter of 20 September/3 October 1913, Stravinsky to Benois: *SM*, 477–8.
20 Sert, *Two or Three Muses,* 120–1.
21 Letter of 20 September/3 October.
22 *SPD*, 105, 605, note 51.

23 Letter of 30 October 1913 (NS) (GMMK).

24 Benois, *Reminiscences of the Russian Ballet*, 302.

25 See his letter to Scriabin of 17/30 September 1913: *SM*, 510.

26 Letter of 30 October to Derzhanovsky. See also Stravinsky's letter of 29 September/12 October 1913 to Steinberg, in *SM*, 478–9. Stravinsky told Jurgenson that "Scriabin promised to send me his three latest sonatas, which I only set eyes on at his house in Lausanne some two months ago, but he has not sent them. I should like to have them. Please remind him of his promise, if you see him." Letter of 16 December 1913 (NS) (GMMK).

27 Benois's letter of the thirtieth, retailing a garbled account of the disaster, arrived at Clarens on the third.

28 *Mem*, 135, note 2. Stravinsky recalls, wrongly, that this was the occasion when Diaghilev himself first heard the news.

29 Letter to Benois of 20 September/3 October. The letter, though quite long, makes no direct reference to Diaghilev's misery, though it speaks of "a very heavy impression and . . . a serious decline in my [i.e., Stravinsky's] spiritual energies."

30 Letter of 3 July 1913, in *SM*, 40.

31 See Igor Stravinsky's letter to Benois of 18/31 March 1913 (*SM*, 471–2), in which he asks Benois to use his influence to get Gury a job with the new enterprise.

32 Letter of 22 September/5 October 1913 (PSS); *Mem*, 135–6 (my translation).

33 Letter of 4/17 November 1913 (PSS); fragment in *SSCII*, 204, but very misleadingly translated.

34 Letter of 21 October/3 November 1913 (PSS); *SSCI*, 59–61 (my translation).

35 Letter of 3/16 November (PSS); *SSCI*, 62–3 (my translation).

36 Letter of 1 November; in Kinkulkina, 95–6. Diaghilev had visited Clarens again at the end of October, but his decision had already been communicated in a telegram of 20 October (see *SSCII*, 9).

37 Letter of 14/27 November: *SSCII*, 205–6.

38 See Struve's letters to Stravinsky of 1 and 4 December 1913 (NS), respectively: excerpted in *SSCII*, 205–6 (where, however, the earlier letter is implicitly dated in Old Style).

39 The autograph, now in BN, is inscribed with a request to return it by 14 August (OS) and not to show it to anyone but Derzhanovsky, and also with the autograph note that "this manuscript is a copy of my manuscript made *before* the performance." The correspondence makes it clear that Stravinsky sent the score in response to Derzhanovsky's request for review materials, not, as Craft suggests in *SPD* (105), to be checked for errors.

40 Letter of 8/21 September 1913, in Shlifshteyn, *N. Ya. Myaskovsky: Stat'i, pis'ma, vospominaniya*, vol. 2, 521, note 125. There is no evidence that Steinberg ever read proofs for Stravinsky, but the rumor itself is suggestive.

41 *SRT*, 983.

42 27 June and 8 June 1913, respectively. Both reviews are presented in extenso, in English, by Taruskin, in *SRT*, 1013–7.

43 Letter to Stravinsky of 8/21 July 1913 (PSS); *SSCI*, 51–3, but wrongly dated (my translation). Stravinsky got his own back on Sabaneyev, perhaps unwittingly, when he wrote to Derzhanovsky denouncing Sabaneyev's article on Debussy, which had appeared in *Muzïka* at the time of Debussy's Russian visit. Derzhanovsky later told Stravinsky that he had spoken to Sabaneyev and "we decided that he would write only about theoretical questions and Scriabin. This is the direct result of your letter and I must now thank you for it." See Stravinsky to Derzhanovsky, 26 December 1913 (NS) (*SM*, 480–1; *SSCI*, 64–5), and Derzhanovsky to Stravinsky, 2/15 May 1914 (PSS); *SSCI*, 65–9 (my translation).

44 3 June (OS), in *PMP*, 106–7.

45 Letter of 12/25 September 1913, in Shlifshteyn, vol. 2, 328.

46 Letter of 26 August/8 September 1914 (RGALI).

47 Letter of 1 November, Stravinsky to Sanin.

48 White, *Stravinsky*, 220; see also *Chron*, 86, and *Expo*, 120, note 2. The tune of the third song, "Chicher-Yacher," had also turned up in the finale of the E-flat Symphony, which both supports the dating and suggests that Stravinsky may have been reminded of the tunes by his proof work on the symphony in the late summer of 1913 (even though the finale itself was eventually checked by Karagichev). Alexander Ossovsky, a Zagorodniy regular, also recalled Stravinsky improvising a song on the text of the second of the "souvenirs," "Vorona" (The Crow), at one of Rimsky-Korsakov's *jours fixes:* see *PRK*, 140, note 1.

49 Letter of 15 December 1913, in Lesure (ed.), *Stravinsky: Etudes et témoignages*, 233–4.

50 In *Ecrits sur la musique*, 17, Ansermet implies that he met Stravinsky at one of his Thursday-afternoon Montreux concerts during his first season there, that is, 1911–12. But Stravinsky recalled that "Ansermet introduced himself to me in a street in Clarens one day in 1911 and invited me to his home for dinner. . . . His appearance—the beard—startled me: he was like an apparition of the Charlatan in *Petrushka*" (*T&C*, 229).

51 14/27 November 1913: *SSCII*, 205–6.

52 *Teatr*, 27 November 1913, reprinted in Zilbershteyn and Samkov, vol. 1, 234–5. Although it would seem likely that Benois's name figured in the October discussions with Diaghilev, there is no evidence of an active collaboration before January.

53 Letter of 1/14 January 1914 (PSS); *Mem*, 136–7 (my translation).

54 Letter of 20 February 1914. The letter is in *SM*, 481–5, but without the longish paragraph relating to Katya's illness.

55 Ibid. Taruskin (*SRT*, 642, note 124) refers to a concert supposedly conducted by Stravinsky in Bordeaux on 8 February. But the concert, which included the first performance of the Berceuse from *The Firebird* in Stravinsky's reduced orchestration, was in fact conducted by Florent Schmitt. Stravinsky's letter of 28 March/10 April 1912 to Jurgenson (*PRK*, 329–30) reveals, incidentally, that he had already made the arrangement by that date.

56 Igor had written to her on 20 December asking her to bring a selection of four-hand piano arrangements of works by Lyadov, Glinka, and Rimsky-Korsakov, "for teaching purposes," as well as his own Verlaine and Gorodetsky songs. He also asked her to report by telegram on Koussevitzky's St. Petersburg concert on 24 December (NS), which was to have included *The Rite of Spring*. "Don't be afraid if they whistle at *The Rite*," he told her, "it's quite natural." But the performance was postponed until February. See *SM*, 479–80.

57 Respectively: letter of 14 January, Delage to Stravinsky (*SSCI*, 33–4); and 16 January, Calvocoressi to Stravinsky (*SSCII*, 102). Stravinsky reported a "sensational success" to Struve (letter of 26 January, PSS), by which time he had spoken personally to some of those present, including Delage and Misia Edwards.

58 *La France*, 26 January 1914. Schmitt himself had a piece in the program, a four-hand piano suite called *Une Semaine du petit elfe Ferme-l'Oeil*.

59 *S.I.M. Revue musicale*, 1 February 1914, 56–7. This was the monthly bulletin of the Société Internationale de Musique, and had no connection with the S.M.I.

60 Letter of Calvocoressi to Stravinsky, 16 January. Within three weeks (on the twenty-third OS) the songs were done in Moscow, at one of Derzhanovsky's Evenings of Contemporary Music, sung by his wife, Yekaterina Koposova. Struve grumbled to the composer that the parts had not been hired from the publisher but copied from the score, a technical infringement of an (in fact) unenforceable copyright (letter to Stravinsky of 25 February 1914, PSS).

61 Letter of 22 January 1914 to Katya (PSS).

62 1 December 1913, in *SSCII*, 47–8; fragment in *Muz Ak* 1996/2, 158. Misia Edwards had alerted Stravinsky by telegram (27 December) to the new understanding with Fokine. See *SPD*, 518.

63 Stravinsky reported this to Benois in his letter of 20 February: *SM*, 481–5.

64   See Stravinsky's letter to Struve, 26 January 1914. According to Tom Gordon, *Stravinsky and the New Classicism*, 46, the *NRF* play-through was on the twenty-second.

65   Letter of 12 February 1914: *SSCI*, 76.

66   Letter of 9 March 1914: *SM*, 485–6.

67   On 28 March Stravinsky sent the final seven pages of the score to Ansermet with a request that he have them copied ready for collection on 30 March. See *CASI*, 11; *SSCI*, 129.

68   Steegmuller, *Cocteau*, 99.

69   *SSCI*, 77. Steegmuller (97) suggests that Diaghilev put him up to this. But, as we have already seen, Stravinsky did not need prompting when it came to stating his terms.

70   Other translations in *SSCI*, 77, and Steegmuller, 97. I have referred back to the original (PSS).

71   Steegmuller, 103.

72   See his letter of 15 March to Copeau, in *SSCI*, 82. The story that Diaghilev himself turned up at Leysin and greeted Stravinsky with "Bonjour, Monsieur David" appears to be apocryphal.

73   Letter of 21 February 1914, in Ziloti, *Aleksandr Il'ich Ziloti 1863–1945: Vospominaniya i pis'ma*, 287–9; précised in *SSCII*, 208.

74   PSS; *SSCI*, 81–2 (my translation).

75   Undated letter, quoted in Steegmuller, 102–3.

76   Letter of 12 March, in Cocteau, *Lettres à sa mère*, vol. 1, 140.

77   Undated letter, Cocteau to Gide, March 1914, quoted in Steegmuller, 103.

78   Letters of 16, 17, and 19 March, in Cocteau, *Lettres à sa mère*, 144, 146. Thévenaz "working with Igor" may simply have meant painting his portrait.

79   Ibid., 150.

80   See Sanin's letter to Stravinsky, 14/27 March 1913: *SSCII*, 200.

81   Undated letter in Cocteau, *Lettres à sa mère*, 476. The letter seems to have been sent as from both Cocteau and Stravinsky.

82   Letter to Stravinsky, 26 May 1914 (PSS); *SSCI*, 84 (my translation).

83   Gold and Fizdale, *Misia*, 168.

84   See Monteux's letter to him of 14 March 1914, in *SSCII*, 58; also Tom Gordon, "Streichquartett-Komponist 'wider Willen,' " in Danuser (ed.), *Igor Strawinsky: Trois Pièces pour quatuor à cordes: Skizzen, Fassungen, Dokumente, Essays*, 29–38.

85   See Stravinsky's letter to Misia of 24 July 1916: "this poor quartet (which was composed for you . . . to be played in your Chinese salon; do you remember?)": in Gold and Fizdale, *Misia*, 176.

86   Undated draft of a letter to Misia Edwards, March 1914, quoted in Gordon, "Streichquartett-Komponist 'wider Willen,' " 33.

87   See ibid., 29–38, for more on the possible connection between *David* and the Three Pieces.

88   Letter of 9 March 1914: *SM*, 485–6.

89   *Mem*, 132.

90   Undated letter of, probably, January 1914, in Kuznetsov (ed.), *Emil Cooper: Stat'i, vospominaniya, materialï*, 211–2.

91   Benois, *Reminiscences of the Russian Ballet*, 359. Benois's detailed account of the staging is almost as vivid as his letters to Stravinsky on the subject.

92   Letter of 14–17 February 1914 (OS); another, very free, translation is in *Mem*, 139–41.

93   Letter to Myaskovsky, 9/22 February 1914 (GMMK).

94   Letter to Derzhanovsky, 16 February/1 March 1914 (GMMK).

95   See Stravinsky's postcard to Cocteau, 26 February 1914: "Go on Sunday and hear Pierre Monteux's concert at the Casino de Paris—*Petrushka*. He's playing it complete in concert for the first time." Original in the Pierpont Morgan Library, New York. The confused translation in *SSCI*, 80, seems unfortunately to have been based on Steegmuller (*Cocteau*, 100).

96 Letter of 14 March 1914 (PSS); *SSCII*, 58 (my translation).

97 *SSCII*, 60, note 11. Stravinsky had of course heard the undisturbed public dress rehearsal on 28 May 1913, as well as the at least relatively audible second scheduled performance on 2 June.

98 *S.I.M. Revue musicale*, 1 May 1914.

99 *Le Temps*, 21 April 1914.

100 *Comoedia*, 6 April 1914.

101 *Expo*, 144. The only contemporary account of this incident seems to be in Jean Chantevoine's review in *Excelsior* (6 April 1914): "M. Stravinsky, recognized by a group from the audience, was the object of a tumultuous demonstration, continuing out into the street." The group included his future biographer André Schaeffner: see Schaeffner's letter to Stravinsky of 22 June 1929 (PSS).

102 See Gordon, "Streichquartett-Komponist 'wider Willen,' " 34–5, for a photograph of the manuscript, which itself apparently no longer survives.

103 "This artist possesses a clear and sober gift for conducting, sometimes even a little cold," wrote the critic of the *Messager de Montreux* (17 April 1914).

104 Craft several times states categorically that Stravinsky did not attend the concert on the twenty-sixth, but his ticket stub survives to prove that he did. Moreover, he wrote to Jurgenson on the fifteenth announcing his intention to go to Paris on the twenty-fifth, and Cocteau's telegram from Paris to Clarens on the twenty-seventh ("was unable to say good-bye properly"—PSS; *SSCI*, 83: my translation)—obviously relates to a meeting in the previous day or so. Delage wrote, probably on the twenty-ninth, that he was "again deeply moved by your great triumph in Paris" (*SSCI*, 35). As for the Kiev trip, both Cocteau and Delage refer to it as certain and immediate.

105 These and other problems are the gist of Benois's letter to Stravinsky of 31 March/13 April 1914 (draft in RM). On the Beecham rescue, see Garafola, *Diaghilev's Ballets Russes*, 184–6.

106 Benois, *Reminiscences of the Russian Ballet*, 361.

107 Undated and unidentified cutting (late May or early June 1914) in PSS.

108 *Comoedia*, 28 May 1914.

109 *Gil Blas*, 30 May 1914, quoted in *SSCII*, 60–1. Stravinsky had attended the two performances, on 26 and 28 May, which were all that were given in Paris.

110 Benois, *Reminiscences of the Russian Ballet*, 364–5. In its context—Benois's rapturous account of *The Nightingale*—this is indeed the faintest of faint praise.

111 For details of Steinberg's Paris stay I have drawn on his "Notebooks," and on his almost daily letters of late May 1914 to his wife, Nadezhda (all in RIII). I am grateful to Viktor Varunts for drawing my attention to these documents and supplying me with transcripts.

112 18 February/3 March 1914 (PSS): "I say nothing about *The Rite of Spring*, as we need to talk about it, and talk a lot."

113 Letter of G. Kozlovsky (Stravinsky's Ustilug gardener) to Stravinsky, 6/19 February 1914 (PSS).

114 *Expo*, 68.

115 *CISFam*. The album includes (plate 49) a charming drawing made at Salvan by the seven-year-old Theodore, captioned "General mobilisation of the Swiss army."

116 Osbert Sitwell, *Great Morning*, 244. Sitwell comments on the apathy of progressive British artists and musicians towards the Russian ballet.

117 Program details quoted in *SPD*, 616, note 201.

118 *Conv*, 94.

119 See *Mem*, 95. Tom Gordon, wishing to date the first sketches for the second piece to the spring of 1914, speculates that Stravinsky saw Little Tich on his earlier London visit in February 1913 (or, he suggests, June 1912; but Stravinsky was not in London on that occasion). But the whole argument is somewhat strained, and it seems that for once one can accept Stravinsky's own account as broadly accurate. See "Streichquartett-Komponist 'wider Willen,' " 33.

120 Rex Lawson, "Stravinsky and the Pianola," in Pasler, *Confronting Stravinsky,* 284–301. There is no evidence that Stravinsky was personally involved in the production of these rolls.
121 Evans, *Music and the Dance,* 89–90. The date was probably 21 June.
122 T&C, 36.
123 Letter of 15/28 January 1914 (PSS). Andrey had written to announce his marriage a few months before.
124 Letter of 4/17 June 1914 (RIII).
125 Letter of 3 February 1914; in *Muz Ak,* 142. The letter was dated in error "3 January" by Stravinsky.

17 FRAGMENTS OF OLD RUSSIA

1 Letter of 19 June 1914: Niklaus Röthlin "Dokumente zur Entstehungs- und Rezeptionsgeschichte," in Danuser, *Igor Strawinsky: Trois Pièces pour quatuor à cordes,* 75.
2 Letter of 26 July 1914, in ibid., 76.
3 Telayakovsky did, in the end, agree to pay 6000 roubles, which—added to the 2000 Stravinsky had received as an advance from the Free Theatre—made a total of 8000, of which ten percent would go to Mitusov, and more would be lost in the currency exchange. See especially Stravinsky's letter to Ziloti, 24 March/6 April 1915, in Ziloti, *Aleksandr Il'ich Ziloti, 1863–1945; Vospominaniya i pis'ma,* 290–1.
4 See *SSCII,* 276–82 for a miscellany of documents relating to Stravinsky's prewar Ukrainian finances. Eighty thousand roubles was worth about nine thousand pounds in the money of the day.
5 Letter of 14 July 1914: *SM,* 486–7 (my translation); a partial English translation is in *SPD,* 133.
6 Wordsworth, *The Prelude,* book 1, 77–9.
7 Letter to Benois of 14 July. On Koz'ma Prutkov, see chapter 5, note 17.
8 Barbara Heldt Monter, *Koz'ma Prutkov: The Art of Parody* (The Hague: Mouton, 1972), 120.
9 Letter of 23 July 1914 (PSS, my translation): other translations in *Mem,* 142–3, and *SPD,* 133–4.
10 Letter of 24 July 1914 (RM).
11 Letter of 23 July. Both this and Stravinsky's earlier letter are wrongly dated in *SPD,* 133–4.
12 *SPD,* 133. I have been unable to identify the sketches in question.
13 *Mem,* 142, note 1.
14 Letter of 24 July.
15 Letter to Zingel, 26 July 1914, in Röthlin, "Dokumente zur Entstehungs- und Rezeptionsgeschichte," 76; *SSCI,* 407.
16 See Stravinsky's letter to Jurgenson of 11/24 July 1914 (GMMK) and Jurgenson's reply of 16/29 July (PSS). Although Stravinsky states that the arrangement has already been made, the manuscript is actually dated the twenty-seventh, three days after the letter. But ten days before that, on 4 July Old Style, Gury Stravinsky had performed the songs with orchestra in a Moscow concert conducted by Nikolay Malko. No doubt the orchestral version had always existed, and the July 1914 version was simply either a revision or redone from memory. Jurgenson did not publish it, however, and the published Boosey and Hawkes arrangement, for a smaller orchestra, was not made until 1951.
17 Ibid. The concert was cancelled because of the war, but Stravinsky still made the arrangement, which is dated 31 March 1915 (see *SPD,* 59).
18 For this and much other information on the sources of Stravinsky's Russian songs and theatre pieces, I am indebted to Taruskin: *SRT,* 1136 et seq. For a detailed discussion of Stravinsky's debt to Tereshchenko in *Svadebka,* see *SRT,* 1324 et seq.

19 *Expo*, 121.

20 *SRT*, 1217.

21 *SRT*, 1154–5, quoting Sakharov. See also Simon Karlinsky, "Igor Stravinsky and Russian Preliterate Theater," in Pasler, *Confronting Stravinsky*, 14–15, note 23. Taruskin and Karlinsky show conclusively that Stravinsky's own account of the *Podblyudnïye* choruses, in *Expo* 118–9, is wildly confused.

22 Stravinsky's letter inviting her to Clarens, a draft of which is reproduced in *SPD*, 134, mentions no duties beyond that of giving pleasure to the children. But the photographs of Bertha in Switzerland in *CISFam* suggest that she was not allowed simply to retire.

23 Letter of 20 September 1914: *SM*, 487. By the following April his anti-Germanism had grown to the point of describing Beethoven as "that most pernicious German idol" and advocating the exclusion of Wagner from the repertoire. Letter of 10 April 1915 to Benois (RM).

24 Romain Rolland, *Journal des années de guerre*, 59–61, entry for 26 September 1914, including the text of Stravinsky's letter. Stravinsky remembered his first meeting with Rolland as having taken place on a pleasure steamer on Lake Lucerne (*Mem*, 79). But this meeting was in July 1916, as recorded by Rolland in ibid., 852–3. See also *SRT*, 1126 et seq., for an interpretation of Stravinsky's remarks in relation to the postwar Russian émigré movement known as Eurasianism, with which, as we shall see, Stravinsky developed contacts.

25 Telegram of 5 September 1914, in *SSCII*, 12.

26 See Buckle, *Diaghilev*, 283 et seq., for an account of the origins of *Liturgie*, with details of the scenario.

27 Essentially because Stravinsky asked too high a fee. The same thing happened a year later when Count San Martino, the president of the Accademia di Santa Cecilia, again tried to negotiate a Stravinsky concert for the autumn. Not only the high fee, but Stravinsky's complicated instructions over part rental and copying, seem to have been too much for San Martino. See *SSCII*, 136–7, note 6, and compare Stravinsky's letter of 13 October 1916 to Gerald Tyrwhitt, in ibid., 138–9.

28 Letter of 25 November 1914, in *Muz Ak* 1996/2, 160–1. As usual, the English translation in *SSCII*, 15–6, is excessively free.

29 Letter to Percy Scholes, 19 August 1915; quoted in *SRT*, 1379, note 64.

30 See Ansermet's letter to Stravinsky of 1 June 1919, in *CASI*, 109; also *Mem*, 48, note 1.

31 Letter of 6 June 1919, in *CASI*, 111; *SSCI*, 138 (my translation).

32 *Dial*, 40. In the summer of 1915 Misia Edwards wrote to Cocteau that Serge was "fatter and fatter, his clothes tighter and his hat smaller, rather 'circus director,' as Igor says." Quoted in Gold and Fizdale, *Misia*, 173.

33 The "Valse des fleurs" was published for the first time only in 1983, in the form of a photographic facsimile of the manuscript fair copy, in Craft, *A Stravinsky Scrapbook*, 146–7.

34 Postcard of 10 January 1915, in Orenstein, *Maurice Ravel: Lettres, écrits, entretiens*, 147.

35 Rolland, 236–7. Also present at this concert were Bakst and Dalcroze, a conjunction somewhat typical of wartime Switzerland in the twentieth century.

36 Yvonne Rácz-Barblan, "Igor Stravinsky vu par le cymbaliste Aladár Rácz." The memoir by Rácz is a transcription of a Hungarian radio broadcast (1956).

37 Letter of 28 January 1915 (PSS). Published accounts of this episode—including the Rácz memoirs; White, *Stravinsky*, 55–6; and *SPD*, 152 and 620, note 246—differ considerably in detail and chronology. *SPD* is the most reliable, but misdates Bovy's letter and also the original encounter with Rácz.

38 Buckle, *Diaghilev*, 288. See also Casella, *Music in My Time*, 123–4. Casella also recalls Stravinsky attending a pair of piano recitals he gave during this time in Rome, at the

second of which "a notoriously Germanophile professor had words with some young men," there was a scuffle, and Casella had to play the Royal March to establish order (ibid., 125).

39 Letter of 18 February 1915: *SM*, 487.

40 Quoted in Garafola, *Diaghilev's Ballets Russes*, 77–8.

41 Letter of 8 March 1915, in *Muz Ak* 1996/3–4, 181–2; also Zilbershteyn and Samkov, vol. 2, 124–5; and *SSCII*, 19–20 (my translation). A facsimile of the first page of the draft he may have used is in *SPD*, 144, and there is another facsimile page in *SNB*, 86.

42 Stravinsky remembered playing the Polka (only) to Diaghilev and Casella in Milan, and that "Casella was so genuinely enthusiastic about the Polka that I promised to write a little piece for him too" (*Dial*, 41). But Casella was not in Milan in early April, when Stravinsky and Diaghilev met there. The play-through must have been in Rome, and if, as seems likely, it included the March, what Casella probably craved was the dedication. See *SNB*, 62, for a facsimile sketch of the first page, with a graphic dedication to Casella being fired from a cannon.

43 Stravinsky's dandyism was often remarked by those hostile to him. See, for instance, Romola Nijinsky's description from 1915, of Stravinsky "dressed like a dandy, with the most indescribable taste" (*Nijinsky*, 306). Debussy called his fellow composer "a young savage who wears tumultuous ties, and kisses women's hands while stepping on their feet" (letter to Robert Godet, 4 January 1916, in Lesure [ed.], *Claude Debussy: Correspondance*, 365).

44 C.-F. Ramuz, *Souvenirs sur Igor Strawinksy*, 67. The "wheeled instrument" was the so-called Stravigor—a several-sized wheeled stavewriter (rastrum), which Stravinsky had invented in about 1911 and had tried to patent through Nikolay Struve before the war. It figures first in his sketches for *The Rite of Spring*. Thereafter he usually drew his own staves on blank paper, filling in gaps at all angles to avoid waste.

45 *Expo*, 114.

46 See *SRT*, 1337 et seq., for details of this text and a discussion of its relation to the definitive version.

47 *Muzïka*, no. 219 (18 April 1915 [OS]), 262–3; English translation in *SRT*, 1319–20. But Taruskin is mistaken, as we have seen, in calling this the first public notice of the work (see chapter 14, note 82). Prokofiev's role as messenger is confirmed by his letter to Stravinsky of 3/16 June 1915 (*SM*, 517; Brown, "Prokofiev's Correspondence with Stravinsky and Shostakovich," 273–4), replying to the latter's inquiry whether he was responsible (12 May 1915, ibid., 487–8). But a year before that Prokofiev had already known about *Svadba* [sic], which he mentions in a letter of 25 June 1914 to Myaskovsky, as forming part of Diaghilev's plans for "next season." See *PMP*, 116; Robinson (ed.), *Selected Letters of Sergei Prokofiev*, 237.

48 Respectively: *Expo*, 118; *Muzïka*, 18 April 1915.

49 Letter of 19 August 1915, Wise to Scholes.

50 *Chron*, 97–8.

51 Postcards to Ravel, 10 January 1915, in Orenstein, *Maurice Ravel: Lettres, écrits, entretiens*, 147; and to Schmitt, 21 January 1915 (BN). Stravinsky uses the phrase "jusqu'à ce qu'il fait beau" ("until the weather is good"), but this must be an error of language.

52 Letter of 8 March 1915, in *Muz Ak* 1996/3–4, 181–2, also Zilbershteyn and Samkov, vol. 2, 124–5; and *SSCII*, 19–20 (my translation).

53 This and the preceding quotations are from Cangiullo, *Le serate futuriste*, 245–51. Cangiullo was a painter and the portraitist of the group.

54 Letter of 3 April 1915, in *PMP*, 132; Robinson (ed.), *Selected Letters of Sergei Prokofiev*, 244 (my translation).

55 Letter of 3 March 1915, *Muz Ak* 1996/3–4, 180; *SSCII*, 18 (my translation).

56 Ramuz, *Souvenirs*, 81.

57 CISFam.
58 Undated letter (July 1915), in Gold and Fizdale, *Misia*, 172–3.
59 Sokolova, *Dancing for Diaghilev*, 69.
60 Letter to Cocteau, *Misia*, 172–3.
61 Letter of 28 June 1915 (OS), in *PMP*, 137–8.
62 *Russkaya muzïkal'naya gazeta*, no. 37–8 (September 1915), 565; quoted in *PMP*, 500 (note 3 to letter 140).
63 Letter of 27 August 1964, Igor Blazhkov to Stravinsky, quoted in *SRT*, 401, note 76; also Stravinsky to Blazhkov, 20 March 1962, in *SM*, 497, note 1 to letter 7.
64 Interview with Moshe Burland (a native of Ustilug), quoted in *SRT*, 401, note 76. Moshe remembered the liquid as whisky, but in fact it was either vodka or, more likely, pure alcohol.

18   A Fox Among the Vines

1   Louis Lavanchy, "L'Oeuvre des *Cahiers vaudois*," in *Essais critiques 1925–1935*, 19, 17.
2   Ibid., 39. The Felibrige was the nineteenth-century Provençal "Académie," dedicated to the preservation of the *langue d'oc*.
3   C.-F. Ramuz, *Souvenirs sur Igor Strawinsky*, 13.
4   Pierre-Paul Clément, preface to Ramuz, *Souvenirs sur Igor Strawinsky* (Pully: Editions de l'Aire, 1978).
5   *Souvenirs*, 56.
6   *SPD*, 171–4. See also *Expo*, 96, where Stravinsky pointedly remembers "our work together preparing the French versions of my Russian texts" as "one of the most enjoyable literary associations of my life," leaving the reader to understand that the *artistic* collaboration on *The Soldier's Tale*, for which Ramuz wrote an original text, was neither particularly enjoyable nor particularly significant as such.
7   Letter of mid-March 1916 to Florian Delhorbe, in Guisan, *Du Côté des "Cahiers vaudois*," 43–5.
8   Ibid. Jouy-en-Josas is a remote southwestern suburb of Paris, not far from Versailles. The princesse de Polignac had a house there.
9   *Expo*, 95.
10 *Souvenirs*, 45, 49.
11 The drawing adorns the cover of Claude Tappolet (ed.), *Correspondance Ansermet-Ramuz (1906–1941)* (Geneva: Georg, 1989).
12 *Souvenirs*, 38.
13 Ramuz, *Raison d'être* (cahier 1, March 1914), quoted in Lavanchy, "L'Oeuvre des *Cahiers vaudois*," 34–5.
14 *Souvenirs*, 100.
15 Letter of 11/24 July 1914; see chapter 17, notes 11 and 15.
16 Letter of Wise to Percy Scholes, 19 August 1915, quoted in *SRT*, 1379, note 64.
17 *SRT*, 1246. Taruskin's discussion of *Renard* in general is a masterpiece of tightly argued analytical source-study.
18 Taruskin takes issue with the other main authority on the background to Stravinsky's "Russian" stage works, Simon Karlinsky, on the question of whether *Renard* adheres to an authentic street-theatre tradition which Stravinsky was in some sense co-opting, or was rather the product of his own well-tuned imaginative antennae. See ibid., and also Karlinsky, "Igor Stravinsky and Russian Preliterate Theater," in Pasler, *Confronting Stravinsky*, 10–1.
19 *Souvenirs*, 35–6.
20 *Expo*, 120.
21 Postcard of 9 June 1919 to Alban Berg, quoted in Moldenhauer, *Anton von Webern*, 229 (translation slightly modified). The two Stravinsky sets had been performed at

a concert of the Verein für musikalische Privataufführung in Vienna a few days earlier.

22 The song is dated 30 December 1915 (OS), but Craft (*SPD*, 138) considers that it was probably composed in November.

23 His essay of that title is a study of the work of Henry Miller, who had compared his lover Anaïs Nin's diaries to Jonah in the whale's belly because of their complete lack of connection with the everyday world.

24 See Joseph, *Stravinsky and the Piano*, 60. For Edith Wharton's letter and other details, see *SPD*, 610, note 122.

25 *The Nightingale* was eventually staged at the Mariyinsky on 30 May 1918, in a production by Vsevolod Meyerhold. But *Petrushka* received its Russian stage premiere only on 20 November 1920.

26 The programs of these two performances, reproduced in *CASI*, 36–8, reveal that whereas Ansermet conducted the regular 1912 Jurgenson suite, Stravinsky took out the concluding Ronde des princesses and Danse infernale and in their place conducted the Berceuse and Finale in their new reduced scorings—apparently the first time the latter arrangement (completed in March 1915) had been played in public.

27 *CISFam*. Theodore had naturally heard his father's stories about his own first visit to the Mariyinsky.

28 *CASI*, 35.

29 Letter of 11 February 1916, in Ziloti, *Aleksandr Ziloti*, 294.

30 Blanche, *Cahiers d'un artiste*, 4th series, 61–3.

31 Ibid., 55–8.

32 See her memorandum of 4 January 1916 to an unspecified "Cher Prince," and her letter of 12 January to Stravinsky (PSS).

33 See Stravinsky's letter to Diaghilev of 17 April 1916, in *Muz Ak* 1996/3–4, 183; and *SSCII*, 24–5, for details of the financial arrangements, which eventually also involved the more intractable (because RMV played tougher than Jurgenson) matter of the *Petrushka* exclusivity renewable that spring. Craft, however, muddles the arithmetic, and mistranslates one crucial sentence: not "they advise that it would be to my advantage to renew the *Petrushka* contract for one year only," but "they will permit me to renew," etc.

34 See Stravinsky's letter to Boris Jurgenson of 10 February 1916, in *Muz Ak* 1992, 148: "Diaghilev is the only Russian making propaganda, cleverly and on a big scale, for Russian art abroad, and not for his own enrichment, but exclusively out of boundless love for the art itself." This must have been cold commercial comfort for Jurgenson, particularly in view of Diaghilev's extreme dilatoriness in paying hire fees. But it was probably sincere.

35 Polignac, "Memoirs of the Late Princesse Edmond de Polignac," 134–5.

36 *SPD*, 138. Stravinsky wrote to Goncharova on 16 February that the princess had agreed to Laryonov's fee of 3,000 francs. See Lesure (ed.), *Igor Stravinsky: La Carrière européenne*, 47, item 141.

37 Romola Nijinsky, *Nijinsky*, 306–7.

38 The relevant correspondence is in *SSCII*, 23–4, and *SPD*, 606, note 59. As usual, the translations have to be treated with caution, but the gist is accurate. The point about the Russian exemption is that Nijinsky was afraid of being arrested as a deserter by the French.

39 See his telegram of 26 March 1916 to Diaghilev, in *SSCII*, 24. Two weeks later, however, he referred, in a postcard to Prince Argutinsky, to "that *most intolerable* Nijinsky couple. God, what a relief they've gone!" (9 April 1916).

40 *Chron*, 103.

41 *Nijinksy*, 308–9.

42 Nijinski [sic], *Cahiers*, 125.

43 See Ansermet's telegram of 10 February 1916, and Stravinsky's letter of 14 February,

in *CASI*, 41–2. In a postcard of 17 May from Cadiz, Ansermet bluntly described Stravinsky's price as "trop fort" (ibid., 50).

44 *Music After the Great War*, 87–8. The first American performance of the Three Pieces for String Quartet was on 8 November 1915 in Chicago, but they had previously been played at the Salle des Agriculteurs in Paris on (probably) 13 May 1915, by Yvonne Astruc, Darius Milhaud, Felix Delgrange, and a viola player called Jurgensen. See Gordon, "Streichquartett-Komponist 'wider Willen,' " in Danuser, 37, note 32.

45 Letter of 31 March–7 April 1916, in *CASI*, 45–9.

46 See her letter to Cocteau of June 1916, in Gold and Fizdale, *Misia*, 188. The new ballet was *Parade*.

47 "Les Espagnols aux Ballets russes," *Comoedia*, 15 May 1921, in Lesure (ed.), *Stravinsky: Etudes et témoignages*, 238.

48 *Chron*, 105.

49 *SPD*, 141. Buckle pictures Alfonso's Spain as "a serene paradise garden undisturbed by the baying of the dogs of war" (*Diaghilev*, 313).

50 *Chron*, 107.

51 Rolland, *Journal des années de guerre*, 852. Stravinsky had bumped into Rolland on a boat on the Thünersee and had antagonized him by lecturing him nonstop about Spain, Italy, and the war.

52 *SPD*, 141–2. Buckle calls it a "flirtation," and names the composer's second wife, Vera, as his source. *Diaghilev*, 313.

53 *SRT*, 678.

54 Letter to Stravinsky, 7 April 1916, in *CASI*, 47.

55 Haskell, *Diaghileff: His Artistic and Private Life*, 244–5. But Haskell is vague in his chronology, and Barocchi's exact whereabouts during the summer are not known.

56 Buckle, *Diaghilev*, 357. See also Ansermet's letter to Stravinsky, 11 July 1919, in *CASI*, 130–1. Many years later, Falla recalled "our strolls in Madrid and Segovia . . . which would have continued in Granada but for your sudden change of route." Undated letter of 1929 (PSS); *SSCII*, 169 (my translation).

57 Buckle, *Diaghilev*, 312 and 565, note 165. For a good pen portrait of her, a reproduction of Jacques-Emile Blanche's 1890 pastel portrait, and an account of her relations with Picasso, see Richardson, *A Life of Picasso*, vol. 2 (1907–1917), 390–2.

58 Letter of 21 February 1917 (PSS).

59 Letter of 17 March 1917 (PSS).

60 Letter of 2 July 1916, Princesse de Polignac to Stravinsky (PSS). Stravinsky's letter to her has not surfaced, but its contents can be deduced from her reply and his own next letter (11 July), of which a draft is preserved in PSS.

61 This is admittedly a calligraphic copy. But Stravinsky was in the habit of dating his fair copies according to the actual date of completion, without regard to the date of copying. The march was added and sent by the first week of October. See Stravinsky's letter to the princess of 5 October 1916 (but the relevant sentence is unfortunately omitted from the translation of this letter in *SSCIII*, 29, note 11).

62 See her letter of 2 September 1916, in PSS. In fact only three thousand francs was credited, which suggests that she may after all previously have taken pity on Stravinsky to the tune of the odd thousand.

63 Letter of 20 July 1916 (PSS); *SSCIII*, 28–9 (my translation).

64 Letter of 5 October 1916, partially translated in *SSCIII*, 29, note 11, but with the revised fee wrongly printed as one thousand francs (copy of original in PSS).

65 *Souvenirs*, 45–7.

66 Letter of 24 July 1916, in Gold and Fizdale, *Misia*, 175–6. On the same day Stravinsky wired Diaghilev a reminder that he owed him two thousand francs on his *Firebird-Petrushka* installments. See *SSCII*, 26.

67 Letter of 12 August 1916, in *CASI*, 52–3. But the letter was never finished, and Ansermet only sent it, incomplete, with his next one (probably 15 September, though dated "1/8 September" in *CASI*, 54–5).

68   *Conv*, 99.
69   Letter of 24 July.
70   Letter of (probably) 19 July 1916, in Gold and Fizdale, *Misia*, 174–5. The concert, in Poiret's art gallery on 18 July, was also attended by Cocteau, who sent the composer a lively account of the smart Parisian ladies who were still arranging their dresses when the pieces ended and, "finally ready to *hear*, heard *nothing*. Even good *[brave]* Misia *heard nothing*. She shrinks from the era and judges impressionistically, with brio but without form, as Bonnard and Vuillard paint" (letter of 11 August 1916: PSS; the translation in *SSCI*, 86–8 is to be treated with caution).
71   Sokolova, *Dancing for Diaghilev*, 86.
72   Postcard of 9 or 10 September 1916: *SM*, 488.
73   Stravinsky mentions this exclusivity in another letter to his mother, written from Paris on the eleventh on his way back to Morges (*SM*, 489). But it left him free, as he told her, to promote the work in Russia, and he wanted her to place a newspaper announcement to that effect. "This '*tale*,'" he wrote, "is played by dancers or marionettes," an idea which suggests recent discussions with Massine, who was interested in a choreography derived from the loose-limbed movements of puppets.
74   Telegram from Diaghilev to Stravinsky, 3 November 1916, in *SSCII*, 28. In *Chron* (110–11), Stravinsky says that Diaghilev's ballet idea happened to coincide with his own intention to extract a symphonic poem from the opera. But he wrongly dates the initial talks to a time after the Italian trip.
75   Letter of mid-November 1916. See *Muz Ak* 1996/3–4, 184, also *SSCII*, 28–9 (for a slightly freer translation than mine). Craft dates the letter firmly to the sixteenth.
76   Letter of 21 November 1916, Stravinsky to Diaghilev, in *Muz Ak* 1996/3–4, 185–6; *SSCII*, 30–2 (my translation).
77   Rolland, *Journal des années de guerre*, 852.
78   Letter of 21 November 1916, Stravinsky to Khvoshchinsky (PSS).
79   Letter of about 15 November 1916 (PSS); *SSCII*, 30, note 39 (my translation).
80   Letter of 21 November.
81   Letter of about 20 November 1916, Diaghilev to Stravinsky; *Muz Ak* 1996/3–4, 185; *SSCII*, 29–30. The Toscanini concert, on the nineteenth, had been brought to a premature close by the demonstrations. A few months later Gerald Tyrwhitt wrote from Rome that "what you predicted about Khvoshchinsky came true, and now, as I was the only person with whom he had not quarrelled, he quarrelled with me too!" Letter of 15 September 1917 (PSS); *SSCII*, 146 (my translation).
82   Most interestingly, in 1916 she acted as Tyrwhitt's intermediary in his attempts to get Stravinsky's advice about his ambition to be a full-time composer. See the Khvoshchinsky correspondence in PSS. The *Podblyudnïye* choruses, the last two of which were written a few weeks after the Rome incident, are dedicated to her.

19   NEVER MORE GO HOME

1   Letter of 21 November 1916 to Diaghilev, in *Muz Ak* 1996/3–4, 185–6; *SSCII*, 30–2. Debussy died in March 1918.
2   Morand, *Journal d'un attaché d'ambassade*, 77–8.
3   Letter of 17 November 1916 (PSS); *SSCII*, 89 (my translation).
4   Undated draft letter (probably of late November 1916) in Ramuz's hand (PSS, catalogued in the Polignac file). This is the earliest reference to the *Berceuses* and *Pribaoutki* as such. The quartet pieces had been sold to RMV, who eventually (as Edition Russe de Musique) brought them out in Paris in 1922.
5   Stravinsky's contract with Henn is dated 1 June 1917 and includes the Five Easy Pieces, which Stravinsky had composed between January and early April. The works were all published towards the end of that year.

6   Undated letter of about March 1917 (PSS).

7   Letter of 26 February 1916 (PSS).

8   Letter of 12 October 1916, Stravinsky to the princesse de Polignac (PSS).

9   Letter of 2 September 1916 (PSS). This particular invitation had been to stay with her in her house at Versailles.

10   Stravinsky was invited by Prince Murat (letter of 25 December 1916, in PSS) to donate his royalty for the opening night to an army benevolent fund, but his reply has not survived.

11   Letters of 22 January 1917, Maeterlinck to Stravinsky, and 6 February 1917, Stravinsky to Maeterlinck; both in PSS. See also *SRT*, 316–8, and the present volume, chapter 13, note 78.

12   PSS.

13   *Conv*, 40.

14   *Chron*, 110.

15   Letter of 17 December 1916 to Katya Stravinsky, in *Muz Ak* 1996/3–4, 187–8 (but with errors of transcription); *SSCII*, 33–4 (my translation from autograph in PSS).

16   In this second set the "right hand" (that is, the primo, or upper, part) is the easy one, written "as music lessons for my children Theodore and Mika" (*Dial*, 41); in the earlier pieces it was the secondo.

17   Letter of 14 February 1916, in *CASI*, 42; *SSCI*, 130. See also *SPD*, 176, and *Dial*, 41–2.

18   *SSCII*, 425–6. One of the admirers was the future dada painter Alice Bailly, whom Stravinsky knew through Ramuz's wife, Cécile. The day after the concert, he sent her an apologetic note in the form of a graphic musical depiction of "Les Cris de Pétrouchka," which Craft reproduces in facsimile from Lesure (ed.), *Igor Stravinsky: La Carrière européenne*, 53–4.

19   Ramuz, *Souvenirs sur Igor Strawinsky*, 107–8. The rue du Petit-Chêne is one of the steep streets of Lausanne.

20   Ibid., 108–9.

21   Received by her on 24 May 1917. But Stravinsky's handwritten draft is dated, plausibly enough, 20 March. In other words, the cable took more than two months—long enough for Igor to have walked from Morges to Petrograd. See *SM*, 489, for the French text as transmitted.

22   Letter of 17 December 1916.

23   Undated telegram of, probably, 26 March, in *SSCII*, 34. After the Naples excursion, Diaghilev again went to Paris, returning to Rome on the twenty-sixth, as is revealed by Ansermet's letter to Stravinsky of that date, in *CASI*, 60.

24   Garafola, *Diaghilev's Ballets Russes*, 79.

25   Ibid. See Graff, *Stravinsky and the Dance*, 20, plate 2, for a reproduction of what is presumably the design Garafola is describing.

26   Graff, *Stravinsky and the Dance*, 44.

27   A detail from Balla's decor is in ibid., 22, plate 1. This was not the stage premiere of *Fireworks*, which had been danced, also in conjunction with a light show, by Loie Fuller at the Châtelet in May 1914.

28   Letter of 26 March 1917, Ansermet to Stravinsky, in *CASI*, 60. See also Morand, *Journal d'un attaché d'ambassade*, 228.

29   *Chron*, 112.

30   *SRT*, 1183–4, quoting Rimsky-Korsakov's article of 21 March 1917.

31   *Chron*, 112. Taruskin's view that Stravinsky was commissioned by Petrograd seems to be based on a translation of Morand's phrase "on commande à Strawinski" to mean "they [the people who have asked Diaghilev to return] have ordered from Stravinsky." But "Stravinsky has been commissioned" is as likely, leaving doubt about the agency.

32   *SRT*, 1188.

33   Postcard to Stravinsky of 14 April, reproduced in *CASI*, 61. The French text is loosely

615

attached to a popular tune taken down, presumably, from the mechanical street piano of which Ansermet added a drawing to the picture of the Hotel Victoria.

34 *Conv*, 104–5.

35 Letter of 11 August 1916 (PSS); *SSCI*, 88 (my translation).

36 Letter of 25 April, Tyrwhitt to Stravinsky, in *SSCII*, 142; see also *SPD*, 182.

37 *Chron*, 114–5; *Mem*, 83–4.

38 Letters of 18 May and 6 June; in *SSCII*, 142–3.

39 *CISFam*; *Mem*, 20.

40 Telegram of 29 May, Ziloti to Stravinsky; letter of 9/22 June. See *SSCII*, 216.

41 Letter of 23 June/6 July (PSS); *SPD*, 550 (with the date 5/18 July) (my translation).

42 Collected as the *Trois Histoires pour enfants (Detskiye pesenki)*. "Tilim-bom" was completed on 22 May, "Gusi-Lebedi" on 28 June.

43 Letter to Stravinsky, undated but certainly 1917 (PSS); an incomplete translation is in *SSCIII*, 111–2. I am assuming a spring outing, but an autumn one is also possible. Stravinsky had met Kibalchich in Geneva in 1915.

44 *Expo*, 69. Neuchâtel is about fifty miles by road from Morges, so presumably they went home by train.

45 *Expo*, 96.

46 See the postscript to Ansermet's letter of (probably) 19 January 1917, in *CASI*, 57: "Tell me what the doctor says about Mika."

47 See the correspondence with Bakst, who acted as Rubinstein's agent, in *SSCII*, 89–97. Bakst's first letter, of 10 June 1917, is there wrongly dated 12 June. A few musical sketches survive dating probably from early November, some of which were used in *The Soldier's Tale* (see *SSCIII*, 466–9). The music for *Antony and Cleopatra* was eventually written by Florent Schmitt.

48 *CISFam*. His description of the workbench is supported by a photograph later in the album (plate 66). When I visited Les Diablerets in 1985, the story was still remembered locally of the Russian composer arriving with his piano on a cart.

49 For all the precise details which Buckle (taking a hint from Romola Nijinsky) gives of Stravinsky's supposed Spanish trip this summer, it seems likely that he did not go. See *Diaghilev*, 332–3; Romola Nijinsky, *Nijinsky*, 359. Nor was he in Paris on 11 May to see *Firebird* with, in the final scene, a muzhik in red waving an enormous red flag.

50 See Stravinsky's letter to Ansermet of 26 May 1919, in *CASI*, 103–6 (*SSCI*, 133–6), for a detailed summary of the discussions. They had been so rushed that in the train back up to Les Diablerets, Stravinsky noticed mistakes, and had to send a correcting letter (25 July) with Tyrwhitt to Italy.

51 Meylan, *Une Amitié célèbre*, 14–15. See *SPD*, 162, for the list of pieces. Gide had come to Switzerland partly to visit Jacques Rivière, who was in a clinic in the Engadin, having recently been released from a German POW camp because of ill health. See Gordon, *Stravinsky and the New Classicism*, 48.

52 See his note of 13 August, apparently hand-delivered by Theodore, in *SSCIII*, 184. The "nephews" were of course a fiction, like Gide's alter-ego travelling companion, Fabrice, in the *Journals*. Whether or not Stravinsky was aware of the true relationship between Gide and Marc (Michel in the *Journals*) is unclear. See André Gide, *Journal 1887–1925*, ed. Eric Marty (Paris: Gallimard, 1996), 1035–8, 1666–7.

53 *CISFam*. Meylan's remark (*Une Amitié célèbre*, 15) that this visit "was the first milestone in a sympathy which bore fruit later in *Perséphone*" shows only that he knew nothing about that later collaboration. Theodore's "two such fundamentally different personalities could never really become close to each other" is nearer the mark.

54 See Gury's obituary in *Russkoye slovo*, 30 July 1917 (OS). The obituary contradicts Igor Stravinsky's later assertion (*Mem*, 21) that Gury had been conscripted.

55 Letter of late July 1917, in *Muz Ak* 1992, 117–8.

56 Letter of 16 August 1917 (PSS); in *SSCIII*, 31–2 (my translation). Since this is a reply to a reply to his of the fourteenth, Stravinsky's was presumably written on the fifteenth.

57 Letter of 20 August 1917 (PSS). This is a rare direct reference to Ramuz's family. Presumably Stravinsky had not replied to the previous letter.

58 See Tyrwhitt's letters to Stravinsky of 13 and 28 August 1917, respectively, in *SSCII*, 145. Stravinsky's letter to Orchestrelle is apparently lost, and we can only guess its contents from Orchestrelle's reply to Tyrwhitt of 23 August (PSS).

59 *Chron*, 116–7. But Stravinsky may be mistaken in saying that the piece was written "expressly for the Pianola." The first sketches seem to indicate an orchestral work, and there are then workings for a mixed ensemble including Pianola before the eventual draft, dated 10 September 1917, which is largely for Pianola, but still has indications for other instruments, including oboe, bassoon, and harpsichord. See *SPD*, 163, and the manuscript material in PSS. For two facsimile pages of this draft, see *SNB*, 70–1. There is also evidence that Naples, not Madrid, may have supplied the material, which closely resembles the tune on Ansermet's postcard of 14 April 1917 from that city (see note 33, above). I am grateful to Rex Lawson for pointing this out.

60 The dedication to Eugenia Errazuriz was probably added in December, when Stravinsky sent her the manuscript together with a sketchbook for the Five Easy Pieces. See Stravinsky's letter of 18 December 1917 to Alfred Cortot, and Cortot's reply of 27 December, in *SSCII*, 182–3, note 4.

61 See Orchestrelle's letter of 24 August 1917 to Dunant (PSS), which reveals that the composer had offered a "suite of studies," but on impossible terms; also Evans's letters of 17 November and 11 December 1917, excerpted in *SSCII*, 119–20. But Evans's letter of 15 October, urging the composer to moderate his demands in order to keep Orchestrelle interested, is not in *SSCII*. Stravinsky's letter of 28 October setting out his conditions (ibid., 118) is a reply to this. See Sotheby's catalogue *Music, Continental Manuscripts and Printed Books, Science and Medicine*, 17–18 November 1988, lot 466 (p. 197), for a partial facsimile and other quotations from the original French text.

62 Letter to Ansermet, 6 June 1919, in *CASI*, 110–1; *SSCI*, 138 (my translation). See also Ansermet's letter of 1 June 1919, in *CASI*, 109–10, and Evans's letter to Stravinsky of 22 September 1917, in *SSCII*, 117.

63 See Auberjonois's letter of 5 September to Hans Graber, in Hugo Wagner, "Igor Strawinsky und René Auberjonois," *SNB*, 312–3. A drawing of Stravinsky is dated "Morges, August 1917," but that is unlikely unless the portrait was done from memory.

64 The earliest surviving communication is a letter of 22 December 1916 from Auberjonois, expressing regret at Stravinsky's illness. On 14 February, Auberjonois wrote from Sierre that "I was at the station at 5:02—nobody! I returned home cursing you" (PSS).

65 Fernand Auberjonois, "The Swiss Years of Igor Stravinsky," 73–80. It is purely my speculation that the question of accommodation came up at the same time as that of the sale of the *Firebird* manuscript.

66 Ramuz, *Souvenirs*, 81–2.

67 F. Auberjonois, "The Swiss Years of Igor Stravinsky," 76.

68 Ramuz, *Souvenirs*, 82–3.

69 In a letter to Edwin Evans of 6 March 1918, he described his *Ragtime* as "written for an ensemble such as one finds in American bars" (unidentified sale catalogue, with facsimile, in PSS). Evans was detailed to find the work a London publisher.

70 *Expo*, 92.

71 Craft, "The Composer and the Phonograph," 35.

72 C. Stanley Wise, " 'American Music Is True Art' Says Stravinsky," *New York Tribune*, 16 January 1916.

73 See his letter of 31 March–7 April 1916 to Stravinsky, in *CASI*, 48; also *Dial*, 54, where, however, Ansermet's trip is significantly misdated 1918. For the suggestion that Ansermet brought back records as well as sheet music, see Craft, "Stravinsky et

le gramophone"; also Hudry, *Ernest Ansermet, pionnier de la musique*, 58 (whose source, however, may simply be Craft).

74 See Edwin Evans's letter to Stravinsky of 14 March 1918, requesting the dedication of *Ragtime*, and claiming to have discussed the piece with the composer in Paris. At that time, Stravinsky's most recent visit to Paris had been in November 1916.

75 Letter of 31 October 1917, in *SSCII*, 94.

76 See Bakst's letter of 25 October, in ibid., 94–7, with accompanying footnotes. The implication is that Stravinsky received this letter only after writing his own.

77 Stravinsky seems originally to have intended to publish this piece with the three songs which became the *Three Tales for Children* as *Four Russian Songs for Children*. See his letter of 19 November 1918 to Edwin Evans, in *SSCII*, 120–1. It was eventually published in *Expo*, 149–51.

78 Letter to Edwin Evans, 6 March 1918. Tyrwhitt's letter dated 8 January in *SSCII*, 149, which seems to suggest that *Ragtime* was already complete by then, was actually written on 8 March. I am grateful to Rex Lawson for pointing this out.

79 See Gide's letter of 8 March and Stravinsky's reply of 7 April, in *SSCIII*, 184–6. That Gide blamed Stravinsky for the breakdown in the collaboration is proved by his later remark that Cocteau's *Antigone* responded to "the same sentiment as made Stravinsky say he would willingly collaborate on *Antony and Cleopatra*, but only if Antony was given the uniform of an Italian *bersagliere*"; *Journal 1887–1925* (ed. Marty), 1205, entry for 16 January 1923.

80 "A subsequent film of the event caused more casualties than the capture of the Winter Palace had done." Norman Stone, *Europe Transformed, 1878–1919* (London: Fontana, 1983), 380.

81 *Dial*, 54. The score is in fact dated: "Jour de la délivrance. Messieurs les Allemands ont capitulé. Dimanche 10 Novembre 1918 Morges"—that is, the day of the surrender, not of the actual Armistice. See *SRT*, 1307.

82 Letters of 8 and 29 January 1918, in Gold and Fizdale, *Misia*, 178–9.

83 It was also at this time that Stravinsky was approached (probably at Falla's suggestion: see his letter to Stravinsky of 1 May 1918, in *SSCIII*, 162) by the Cercle des Beaux-Arts in Madrid, with the proposal that he conduct a series of concerts in Spain and Madrid for a fee of six thousand francs. This would have been his first experience of conducting whole concerts. But the proposal fell through. See *SSCIII*, 34, note 19 (where, however, the fee is startlingly given as six million).

84 Pahissa, *Manuel de Falla: His Life and Works*, 106. Ansermet surmised that three of the five thousand were actually from Mme Errazuriz, but added that "as regards the 5,000 francs, R[ubinstein] leaves you completely free to decide how you will take them." See his letter of "[13 June 1918]" (actually probably 2 May 1918) in *CASI*, 65–7.

85 Telegram to Eugenia Errazuriz, 23 March 1918; *SSCII*, 183 (my translation). Presumably Mme Errazuriz had notified Stravinsky of the pianist's intention. But Falla only sent the actual letter of credit on 1 May. In his memoirs Rubinstein makes no mention of any donation to Stravinsky in 1918, referring only to a contribution to the American support group the following year (which is confirmed by Mrs. D. G. Mason's letter to the composer of 16 June 1919). See *My Many Years*, 59–60. But it looks as if he has confused two distinct episodes.

86 See *Expo*, 89–96. The errors include the statements that the pasodoble was suggested by a visit to Seville in Holy Week, a visit which actually took place in 1921; that Denges and Denezy are imaginary place names; and that the Narrator's intrusion into the action was "an idea borrowed from Pirandello," whose first play involving disrupted reality neither Stravinsky nor Ramuz is likely to have seen by 1919, when the device was incorporated in the revised text.

87 Letter of 28 February, in Ramuz, *Lettres 1900–1918*, 353; another, somewhat inexact, English translation is in *SSCIII*, 33. In fact Ramuz had already, on this same day, completed a first draft of the text. See Hugo Wagner, "Igor Strawinsky und René

Auberjonois," in *SNB*, 313. For a detailed study of the libretto in its various stages of growth and revision, see Jacquot, "*Histoire du soldat:* La Genèse du texte et la représentation de 1918."

88 *Souvenirs*, 97–8, 100. According to Ansermet, these first discussions took place at his house in Lausanne. See Ansermet, "La Naissance de *L'Histoire du soldat*," in Ramuz, *Lettres 1900–1918*, 35–7.

89 *Souvenirs*, 99–100. See *SRT*, 1295–7, for a nearly complete translation of the original story, with a concordance of the musical numbers in Stravinsky's score. A French translation of the tale is in Jacquot, 140–2. The joint nature of the project is confirmed by Ansermet in "La Naissance de *L'Histoire du soldat*."

90 The letter of approach to Reinhart, signed by Ramuz and dated 2 March, is in *10 Komp*, vol. 3, 20–1. In his letter to Stravinsky of 10 March, Ramuz mentions the sum of three thousand francs. See *Lettres 1900–1918*, 353–4; *SSCIII*, 34.

91 Steven-Paul Robert, who was one of them, told Jacquot that Ramuz talent-spotted at a student production of Claudel's *Protée*. See Jacquot, 105, note 49 bis.

92 At least two actors (Gaston Bridel and a certain Demiéville) were earmarked for this role before it was absorbed into the narration in mid-July.

93 Ramuz, *Souvenirs*, 100.

94 See *SSCIII*, 466–9. But the opening of the march, which Stravinsky recalled (*Expo*, 92) as the first thematic idea for the work, was new. Ramuz's letter of 28 February contains the suggestion that the march should be repeated at the end of the work (as in *Renard*).

95 *Conv*, 17. Stravinsky says that he "joyfully included this motive in the music of the *Petit Concert*" (where it does indeed also figure). But that piece was a later idea, as is proved by Ramuz's letter of 21 April, where the linkage between the recovery of the violin and the dances for the sick Princess is described in quite different terms. See *Lettres 1900–1918*, 354–5; *SSCIII*, 35–6 (but a very confused translation). The Little Concerto is dated 10 August in the sketches.

96 Ansermet, "La Naissance de *L'Histoire du soldat*," 36–7. See also Meylan, *Une Amitié célèbre*, 16. Meylan rightly points out the economic *dis*advantages of the heterogeneous *Soldier's Tale* ensemble of violin, double bass, clarinet, bassoon, cornet, trombone, and percussion, especially in wartime Lausanne.

97 *Expo*, 91–2.

98 *Souvenirs*, 44.

99 Pitoëff, "Souvenirs intimes de *L'Histoire du soldat*," 167.

100 Not, though, the world premiere, it seems. PSS holds a copy of a program for a concert in Paris, 6 rue Huyghens, on 9 February 1918, in which both sets were played by Juliette Meerovitch and Alfredo Casella.

101 Letter of 8 June 1918, in Wagner, "Igor Strawinsky and René Auberjonois," *SNB*, 316.

102 Letter of 5 July, in ibid., 316–7.

103 Letter of 1 August, in Ramuz, *Lettres 1900–1918*, 360; the translation in *SSCIII*, 39, interprets (without comment) the initial "R" as "Rosset," the actor who played the Soldier, but it in fact clearly refers to Reinhart. Ramuz presumably meant how much the players were going to cost as well as what other money would be forthcoming.

104 See his letter of 13 August to Stravinsky, in *CASI*, 72.

105 See *SPD*, 170–1, for an abstract of these accounts, but without the cash entries.

106 See Ramuz's letters to Stravinsky of 15 and 20 July, in *Lettres 1900–1918*, 357–9; *SSCIII*, 37–8.

107 Letter to Stravinsky of 2 August, in Wagner, "Igor Strawinsky und René Auberjonois," *SNB*, 318.

108 Letter of 25 August, Auberjonois to Stravinsky, in ibid., 319.

109 Fernand Auberjonois, "The Swiss Years of Igor Stravinsky," 78.

110 Letter of 5 September, in Ramuz, *Lettres 1900–1918*, 363–4. Two or three weeks before, Ramuz had shown Stravinsky a draft letter of rejection to Robert (*SSCIII*,

39–40). But it cannot have been sent, since Ramuz told Auberjonois on 8 September that it had only just been finally decided to replace Robert with Gagnebin, who in turn wrote Ramuz a long letter protesting his reluctance to switch roles (he did not do so). A mere three weeks before the opening, the production was floundering in a sea of amateurism. See Ramuz and Auberjonois, "Autour de *L'Histoire du soldat*."

111 Rosset had ambitions as a film actor, which may give some clue as to the intended style of mime in the *Tale*, since Ramuz took it as a recommendation (but Craft's "he would play it with an eye to the cinema" is an overinformed mistranslation of the purely factual "il va jouer pour des cinémas." See Ramuz's letter of 15 July, in *SSCIII*, 37; cf. *Lettres 1900–1918*, 357).

112 See Ramuz's undated letter of (probably) 5 September to Stravinsky, in Ramuz, *Lettres 1900–1918*, 367; and *SSCIII*, 42–3 (with "vivrez" mistranslated as "liven"). See also his letter of this date to Auberjonois.

113 See Wagner, "Igor Strawinsky und René Auberjonois," *SNB*, 323, for a reproduction, with a catalogue description at 321–2.

114 Jean Villard-Gilles, *Mon Demi-siècle*, quoted in ibid., 322. See Jacquot, 105, for a somewhat different version of this memoir, in which Stravinsky's "paroxysms of enthusiasm, invention, joy, indignation, and migraine" are contrasted with Ramuz's almost shamefaced but imperturbable patience in "putting himself in our place, seeking with us . . . while following with a malicious joy Stravinsky's inspired cavortings."

115 Letter of 5 September, in Ramuz, *Lettres 1900–1918*, 363.

116 See especially his marginalia to Ramuz's letter of (probably) 1 September, about the masks, quoted in *SSCIII*, 42, note 36. It should be noted that the annotations are not in the positions Craft implies, though his interpretation seems correct enough. There also remains the faintest suspicion that they may not be contemporary with the date of receipt.

117 Jacquot, 98.

118 *Expo*, 94. The eleven-year-old Theodore Strawinsky, who was at the performance with his brother Soulima, painted a vivid watercolor which clearly shows both the smartness of the audience, and the actual stage setup, with the band to the left of the interior stage, the "irrelevant" front drop, with its Arctic seascape, whale, and icebergs, the Narrator's table to the right, and the Devil (Jean Villard) in his disguise as a cattle dealer, dangling his legs over the front of the main stage. See Schouvaloff and Borovsky, *Stravinsky on Stage*, 85, for an excellent reproduction. Soulima, who was just eight, also painted the first night. See Jacquot, 109, for a monochrome reproduction.

119 Letter of 9 October, in *SSCIII*, 45–6.

120 Letter of 7 October (PSS).

121 *CISFam*. On 8 October, Ramuz wrote to the Zurich Lesezirkel that "Stravinsky still has a violent fever, after eight days" (quoted in *SPD*, 166), and there is a hint in letters from Ansermet (15 October, *CASI*, 76) and Ramuz (probably 19 October, *SSCIII*, 47–8) that the flu may have temporarily reactivated Katya's tuberculosis.

122 *Expo*, 94. He himself probably went down on the thirtieth—an uncanny echo of his typhoid after *The Rite of Spring*.

123 Letter of 16 October, Auberjonois to Graber, in Wagner, "Igor Strawinsky und René Auberjonois," *SNB*, 326.

124 *SSCIII*, 44, note 42.

125 Letters of 9 and 20 October to Stravinsky, in *CASI*, 75, 77.

126 Letter of 15 October: ibid., 76.

127 *Expo*, 93.

128 *Chron*, 129–30. The third piece was completed on 15 November, four days after the Armistice.

129 Letter of 19 October, in *SSCIII*, 45, note 44. See also Ramuz's letter to Stravinsky of 2 February 1919, in *SSCIII*, 48.

130 Letter of 16 October to Graber, in Wagner, "Igor Strawinsky und René Auberjonois," *SNB*, 326.

131 Letter of 29 May 1954 to Jean Villard, quoted in ibid., 327. The letter was a response to the publication of Villard's *Mon Demi-siècle*. But according to Auberjonois's son Fernand, the designer scribbled on a program that "the play owed its success to Stravinsky and to him alone" ("The Swiss Years of Igor Stravinsky," 78).

20 WHO OWES THE PIPER CALLS THE TUNE

1 *Dial*, 54.

2 Kling, a French Swiss born in Geneva, had been London manager of Breitkopf & Härtel before the war, and was suspected in some quarters of pro-German sympathies. In 1916 he published a detailed disclaimer in the Chester house journal, complete with birth certificate and a formal affidavit. See "A Personal Explanation," *The Chesterian*, no. 5 (November 1916), 67–71. I am grateful to Paul Griffiths for bringing this article to my attention.

3 29 April 1918 (PSS); *SSCII*, 184, where, however, the letter is wrongly dated 1917 (my translation).

4 Hugo, *Avant d'oublier, 1918–1931*, 245.

5 See *SPD*, 174, and *SSCII*, 262–3, for these and other details. But Craft misidentifies the grandmother as Lyudmila's mother, Maria Nosenko, who had died in 1882. Ansermet told Diaghilev that the Belyankins had brought money for Stravinsky, but whether this was his money or their contribution is not clear. Letter of 6 August 1919 (KA).

6 Anne Ansermet, *Ernest Ansermet, mon père*, 46.

7 See *SPD*, 623–4, note 288. *CASI*, 65, note 3, mentions that Bartholoni was a board member of the new Orchestre de la Suisse Romande. But the note should be treated with caution, since it contains four demonstrable factual errors in eight lines of text.

8 Beecham had given Stravinsky two thousand five hundred francs at the start of the war and another ten thousand at Christmas 1915. Curiously enough, Stravinsky had tried to maintain that the first sum was a payment on account for the London performances of *The Nightingale* (with the implication that more was owing). So the second payment, ex gratia, was doubly generous. See *Mem*, 133, and *T&C*, 230; *SSCII*, 216–7, note 15; also a letter of 22 March 1915 from Donald Baylis to Cyril Scott, asserting the voluntary character of the donation (PSS).

9 Although Stravinsky announced his intention to make this arrangement in a letter to Kling of 17 January 1919 (*SSCIII*, 48, note 46), some of it had existed since the time when he had been revising the main score in the autumn. See *SPD*, 175, for relevant dates. A letter from Reinhart of 10 March conveys regret at being unable "to reply exactly to your request" (*SSCIII*, 144), which may have been a proposition about the trio suite.

10 *SSCII*, 261–2. Many of the items listed by Craft as income were nothing of the kind: for instance, royalties, Diaghilev's performance rights, publishers' advances. None of these were paid even where due. As for the donations Stravinsky undoubtedly received, they of course tend to demonstrate that a need existed.

11 See "Stravinsky: A Centenary View," in *Present Perspectives*, 215.

12 Letter of 14 August 1920, in *SSCII*, 228. See also *Chron*, 132.

13 Letter of 21 December 1918, in *CASI*, 79.

14 That the suite was materially commissioned by the OSR is uncertain but likely, in view of the fulsome dedication "to the Orchestre Romande, its conductor Ernest Ansermet and its committee" on the title page of the MS full score, now in BN. The OSR did at least agree to pay for Stravinsky's copyist, Jules Piotton. See Ansermet's letter to Stravinsky of 11 March 1919, in *CASI*, 79–80.

15 In Ansermet's letter to Stravinsky of 10 June 1919, *CASI*, 112.

16   Both Tyrwhitt (by now Lord Berners), in a letter of 15 February (*SSCII*, 153), and Kling, in a letter of 26 February (PSS), refer to Mika's illness, and Kling mentions an operation. But the rest is speculation.

17   See Ansermet's letter to Stravinsky of 18 July 1919, in *CASI*, 135. In fact, seven players are needed for the 1919 version of *Les Noces*, including three percussionists.

18   Letter of 26 March 1919 (PSS).

19   See Stravinsky's letter of 6 April and Struve's reply of 15 April 1919 (PSS).

20   Letter of 8 June 1919, Struve to Stravinsky (PSS).

21   Letter of 1 March 1919, filed under "Polignac" in PSS, and with a very faint copy of the letter to Kahn attached. Stravinsky's most shameless outbursts of anti-Semitism were usually provoked by questions of money.

22   See Stravinsky's letter to Ansermet of 23 July 1919, in *CASI*, 140; *SSCI*, 142 (my translation). Struve had reported in his letter of 8 June that there were six performances.

23   See Struve's letter of 26 November and Stravinsky's reply of 11 December 1919 (PSS); a partial translation of Stravinsky's letter is in *SSCI*, 401.

24   Letter of 18 April 1919; see Sotheby's sale catalogue *Collection Boris Kochno*, 11–12 October 1991, lot 398, for a summary with quotation, including a still more vicious diatribe against the "three Israelites—Otto Kahn, Adolph Bolm, and Pierre Monteux."

25   Letter of 6 April 1919 (PSS), quoted in *SPD*, 154.

26   Telegram of 1 May 1919, in *CASI*, 84.

27   Letter of 4 May, in *CASI*, 87–8.

28   Letter of 7 May, in *CASI*, 90–1. Ansermet later attributed this apparent change of heart to Massine's influence. See his letter of 17 May, in *CASI*, 95–6.

29   Letter of 26 May 1919, in *CASI*, 103–6; *SSCI*, 133–6 (my translation).

30   See Ramuz's letter to Ansermet of 5 June 1919, in Tappolet (ed.), *Correspondance Ansermet–Ramuz*, 77.

31   Letter of 30 May, in *CASI*, 107–8; *SSCI*, 136–8. Stravinsky claimed that he had had offers from America for *Les Noces* and *The Song of the Nightingale*. See the letter of Mrs. Brooks's daughter Noémi Pernessin Raymond to him of 21 October 1919 (PSS).

32   On 5 June. See Ansermet's letter of 10 June, in *CASI*, 112–3. This is not quite the first reference to a Pergolesi ballet (there is a more oblique hint in Ansermet's letter of 25 May; see *CASI*, 100), but his slighting tone proves that there was as yet no talk of Stravinsky's being involved. At this stage, Diaghilev seems to have wanted Falla to do it. See Pahissa, *Manuel de Falla*, 111–2.

33   Letter of 29 May 1919, in Tappolet (ed.), *Correspondance Ansermet–Ramuz*, 75.

34   Telegram of 18 June 1919 (PSS).

35   As reported by Ansermet in his letter to Stravinsky of 10 June 1919, in *CASI*, 112.

36   Letter of 16 May 1919, in *CASI*, 94.

37   Letter of 29 June 1919, Nouvel to Bakst (KA). A note from Bakst indicates that he passed the letter on to Diaghilev.

38   Letter of 20 June, in *CASI*, 119–20.

39   Letter of 7 July, Ansermet to Stravinsky, *CASI*, 127–9.

40   Letter of 18 July, *CASI*, 134–6.

41   Ansermet to Diaghilev, letter of 6 August (KA). But the revision is already referred to by Ramuz in a letter to Ansermet of 5 June, in Tappolet, *Correspondance Ansermet–Ramuz*, 77.

42   Letter to Ansermet, 23 July 1919, in *CASI*, 141; *SSCI*, 144. This confirms Stravinsky's reminiscence in *Expo*, 117–8.

43   Letter of 6 August to Diaghilev.

44   Ansermet had been investigating the whole pianola question on Stravinsky's behalf, and had had technical discussions with Edwin Evans and the Aeolian Company in London in June. His letter of 12 June (in *CASI*, 115–7) details his findings. But, for all Taruskin's claim that the letter called into question the feasibility of the project (*SRT,*

1501), its tone is generally encouraging, and there is no mention of problems of coordination.

45 Diaghilev's telegram and Stravinsky's reply are both lost. Ansermet refers to the incident in his letter to Diaghilev of 21 August (KA), and notes that Igor would be sending another wire "expressing his thought more exactly." This I take to be the telegram of 18 August, in *SSCII*, 35. Unfortunately Craft's translation is from a handwritten draft or copy in the Paul Sacher Stiftung, the text of which differs radically from what was actually sent: "ai fait nécessaire auprès consul Italien encore aucune réponse de lui ni de toi serait infiniment plus commode se voir suisse lors votre retour" ("have taken necessary steps with Italian consul still no response from him or you would be infinitely more convenient to meet Switzerland on your return") (KA).

46 The literature contains references to more than one previous postwar trip. Craft states firmly that Stravinsky was in Paris in December 1918 (*SPD*, 624, note 296); he is also supposed to have attended the premiere of Satie's *Socrate* at Monnier's on 21 March 1919 (see de Cossart, *The Food of Love*, 137); and Stravinsky himself says in *Chron* (132) that "I went to Paris in the early spring [of 1919] on a short visit." But I can find no corroborative evidence for these trips, and there is some counterevidence; for instance, the *Chron* account includes a meeting with Diaghilev. But the evidence of the Ansermet and Misia correspondence is that Stravinsky did not see Diaghilev between July 1917 and September 1919.

47 Letter of 24 April 1919. Stravinsky sent his Three Pieces for String Quartet, but they were not performed (his letter of 27 May is in Röthlin, "Dokumente zur Entstehungs- und Rezeptionsgeschichte," in Danuser, 87). Meanwhile, Schoenberg's society included the *Berceuses du chat* and *Pribaoutki* in its concert of 6 June. See *SPD*, 136 and 637, note 123.

48 Letter of 17 August (PSS).

49 One sketch is for violin, two violas, and cello. Pochon wrote on 18 October 1919 (PSS) insisting on a conventional string quartet, but suggesting a scordatura (tuning-down) of the second violin's G string to F or even E.

50 Pahissa, *Manuel de Falla*, 111–2. Ansermet's letter to Stravinsky of 10 June (*CASI*, 113) shows that Picasso was already included in the package, whether or not he himself had been informed.

51 *Expo*, 111. Stravinsky, as we saw, wrongly assigned this encounter to the spring.

52 For Massine's account see *My Life in Ballet*, 92, 145–5. But Massine is almost certainly mistaken in remembering researching in Naples in 1919. He and Diaghilev probably got no farther than Stresa and Venice that summer.

53 *Comoedia*, 31 January 1920.

54 *Expo*, 111–2. Stravinsky is politer about Pergolesi in *Chron*, but the Ansermet correspondence for once supports the later reminiscence.

55 The most up-to-date and fully referenced list of *Pulcinella* sources is in *SRT*, 1464–5. Diaghilev's Naples material seems to have consisted of manuscript copies of works in the Conservatorio library, bought in the Casa Musicale Metronomo of a certain Professor A. Ricci, while the trio sonatas (actually by Domenico Gallo) were in copies Diaghilev had had made in the British Museum in September 1918. All or most of these copies were in fact, contrary to Massine's belief, of published material.

56 *Chron*, facing 224. Stravinsky formally agreed to compose *Pulcinella* at the end of September. See *SSCI*, 135, note 15.

57 At least he and Ravel did not meet. Ravel wrote on the day Stravinsky left Paris, "I am upset not to have been able to see you" (letter of 16 September [PSS]; *SSCIII*, 21 [my translation]). Schmitt's letter of 28 November (in *SSCII*, 113) makes it clear that no recent meeting had taken place.

58 See Hugo, *Avant d'oublier*, 31. Hugo seems to imply that the soirée took place in late 1918 (which would mean that the work played was the piano version of *Ragtime*), but the later date is clinched by Poulenc's letter to Stravinsky of 26 September 1919 and

Stravinsky's reply of 1 October: Chimènes, *Francis Poulenc: Correspondance*, 100–1; *SSCII*, 199.

59 Telegram of 18 October. The items of correspondence in *SSCII*, 37, need to be supplemented by Stravinsky's telegram of 5 October, which is unfortunately misquoted in *SPD*, 185 (it is not lost time but lost money that is bothering him), and by his unpublished correspondence with Kling, particularly his letter of 14 November (PSS).

60 See Kling's letter of 3 November and Stravinsky's of 14 November (PSS). Stravinsky sent sets of pages to Kling on various dates, and on 23 November instructed Kling to pass this material on to Diaghilev.

61 *Expo*, 113.

62 The program is reproduced in *SPD*, 173. The concert was repeated in the Zurich Tonhalle on November 20 and in the Salle d'Athénée, Geneva, on 17 December.

63 The concert was unfortunately not reported or reviewed in the Lausanne papers. See Pierre Meylan, "Igor Stravinsky donna trois concerts de ses oeuvres," *Revue musicale de Suisse Romande* (June 1964), 9–12.

64 Letter of 24 November 1919 to Kling (PSS); *SSCIII*, 51, note 52 (my translation). The letter includes a detailed breakdown of the performance costs.

65 See his letter of 3 March 1920, in *SSCII*, 227, for a formal statement of the problem.

66 The contract is dated 7 December 1919.

67 The exclusivity in *Pulcinella* was from 1 January 1920, and in *Les Noces* from 1 August 1920.

68 See Stravinsky's letter of 16 December 1919, in *SSCIII*, 52, note 53.

69 See Stravinsky's letters to Kling of 5 December and 7 December, respectively (PSS). Eight weeks later he told *Comoedia* (31 January 1920) that the performance had been impeccable.

70 *SPD*, 123.

71 Letter of 11 December, Stravinsky to Kling. According to Paul Piguet, in the *Droit du peuple* of that same date, the work was greeted with laughter in Lausanne, but at the end "the acclamations of the crowd" opposed "the whistle blasts which rent the air."

72 *Tagblatt Prag*, 7 December 1919.

73 *Courrier musical*, 15 February 1920, 66.

74 *My Life in Ballet*, 148.

75 Boris Kochno, *Diaghilev and the Ballets Russes*, 138. But Stravinsky claimed that it was the orchestra that was underrehearsed, so that "there was a lack of coordination between pit and stage, and the result was unworthy of the best standards of the company" (*Mem*, 42).

76 Tenroc must have been aware of Stravinsky's remark in his *Comoedia* interview of 31 January that he had completely rewritten the original score to make it suitable for dancing.

77 9 February 1920.

78 *Comoedia*, 4 February 1920, quoted in *SPD*, 124–5.

79 *Conv*, 105. See Christian Geelhaar, "Strawinsky und Picasso: Zwei ebenbürtige Genies," in *SNB*, 292–304, for more detail on Picasso's work on *Pulcinella*, including several color reproductions. In *Conv*, Stravinsky observes that "Diaghilev did succeed in getting him to do a Commedia dell'Arte *Pulcinella*," but Massine states that Diaghilev chose Picasso in the first place because "he wanted a completely abstract décor." See *My Life in Ballet*, 148.

80 See Kling's letter to Stravinsky, 23 March (PSS).

81 Ramuz, *Souvenirs*, 100.

82 See his letter to Stravinsky of 27 February 1920, in Ramuz, *Lettres 1919–1947*, 70–1. The omission of this (and many other) Ramuz letters from *SSCIII* may well have no more sinister explanation than the disorder in Stravinsky's files at the time of his death. But it remains true that its inclusion would have made it harder for Craft to suggest that Ramuz objected to Stravinsky's use of the music in concert suites, which he could not reasonably have done and there is actually no evidence that he

ever did. See *SSCIII*, 56–7, and note 60. The phrase "withdraw your music and use it elsewhere" ("repreniez en quelque sorte votre musique pour l'utiliser autrement"—that is, not "elsewhere" but "in another way") in Ramuz's letter of 27 August 1920 obviously refers to its reuse in the theatre, since at the time to which Ramuz refers (spring 1920) the concert suites had already existed, either had been or were about to be performed, and can have come as no surprise to him.

83 Letter of 23 August 1920, in Guisan, *C.-F. Ramuz, ses amis et son temps*, vol. 6, 48–9.
84 *Mem*, 43–4.
85 See Ansermet's letter to Stravinsky of 2 May 1920, in *CASI*, 147–8.
86 See Kling's letter to Stravinsky of 5 March 1920, and Stravinsky's reply dated 22 March (though it was in fact sent on 14 August), in *SSCII*, 227–8.
87 The evidence for Stravinsky's visit is Grigoriev, 154. But if anything Ansermet's letter to Stravinsky of 5 May (in *CASI*, 147–8) implies that he did not go.
88 Letter of 25 February (PSS). This was before the agreement with Kling over the *Firebird* Suite.
89 André Rigaud, "M. Igor Stravinsky nous parle de la musique de *Pulcinella*," *Comoedia*, 15 May 1920.
90 *Comoedia*, 17 May 1920.
91 *Excelsior*, 17 May 1920. "People who had never heard of, or cared about, the originals cried 'sacrilege': 'The classics are ours. Leave the classics alone.' To them all my answer was and is the same: You 'respect,' but I love," Stravinsky wrote in *Expo*, 113–4. But he had already made the remark his own by October 1925, when it was attributed to him by Cocteau in *Lettre à Jacques Maritain*, 23.
92 The party, given by Prince Farouz of Persia, is described by Jean Hugo in *Avant d'oublier*, 67, and—minus the pillow fight—by Raymond Radiguet (who was there with Cocteau) in his novel *Le Bal du comte d'Orgel*.

21 CHERCHEZ LA FEMME

1 To judge from a telegram of 24 May 1920 from Claudel, inviting him to dinner on the twenty-seventh (PSS).
2 *SPD*, 626, note 5.
3 *CISFam*. Theodore implies that Ernest Ansermet was there too, but Ansermet was already in London with the Ballets Russes. See his letter to Stravinsky (undated, but 12 June) in *CASI*, 154, where, however, it is wrongly dated 2 July. Ansermet is writing on the Saturday after the London opening of *Pulcinella* on the tenth.
4 Letter of 23 August 1920, in Guisan, *C.-F. Ramuz, ses amis et son temps*, 49, my translation; another, partial, translation is in *SSCIII*, 56.
5 Letter of 21 June 1920 (PSS).
6 See Ansermet's telegram of 23 June 1920, in *CASI*, 152. Stravinsky declined by telegram ("letter follows") on the twenty-fifth. Tappolet cross-refers to subsequent letters of 28 June and 1 July, but this is manifestly wrong.
7 *Chron*, 148, misleadingly implies that the musical ideas in the chorale were born with the commission. The sketchbooks prove this was not the case. The chorale duly appeared in the music supplement of *La Revue musicale* 1, no. 2 (1 December 1920), 22–3.
8 For a full account of the textual history of the Symphonies of Wind Instruments, see Walsh, "Stravinsky's Symphonies: Accident or Design?"
9 Letter of 10 July 1920 in *CASI*, 158–9.
10 Letter of 25 July 1920, in *CASI*, 163–6. The article's actual concluding words were: "Amid all the theories (so far rather incompletely presented) supporting the new music, the observer can grasp at the right it arrogates to do all things even to the

point of excruciation, save to be pretentious and boring. Plainly this is a home thrust at much of the most adulated music, both symphonic and dramatic, of the past 100 years." "Turning Tides in New Music," *Daily Mail*, 22 July 1920.

11 Letter of 25 July.

12 Ibid. Subsequent events suggest that it was not only Ansermet's absences that she had to endure.

13 See Ansermet's postcard to Stravinsky of 28 July 1920, in *CASI*, 167. According to Craft (*SPD*, 222), Ansermet brought money from Diaghilev. But his date for the meeting, 3 August, looks doubtful.

14 Charles-Roux, *Chanel*, 185.

15 Another was Felix Yusupov, whose brother Nikolay is supposed to have connived at an examination swap with Stravinsky at St. Petersburg University. See *Mem*, 28.

16 *IVSPA*, 7. Craft's informant was Vera Stravinsky.

17 See Morand, *L'Allure de Chanel*, 121–4.

18 Suzanne Gaudin's reminiscence is in the original French edition of Charles-Roux, *L'Irrégulière*, 307, but was for some reason omitted from *Chanel*. Apart from Morand's obviously suspect account from the Chanel side (including her claim that the composer told Katya he was in love even before he told Chanel), the only other informed reminiscence of the "affair" is Misia's remark that, after meeting Chanel at her house in 1920, "Stravinsky in particular fell desperately in love with her"— which might or might not refer to an affair (Gold and Fizdale, *Misia*, 199). Artur Rubinstein recalled rumors of a "great flirtation" and was at a party thrown by Chanel at the Ritz when "she asked for a glass of water and Stravinsky, in a playful mood, or maybe in a fit of jealousy, filled a large glass with vodka and brought it to her. . . . She had to be carried up to her bedroom" (*My Many Years*, 151).

19 The Concertino was completed on 24 September. Pochon wrote from America acknowledging receipt of the score on 28 October, and the Flonzaley Quartet gave the work its premiere in New York on 23 November.

20 *SPD*, 527; *SSCII*, 400–1.

21 Kochno, *Diaghilev and the Ballets Russes*, 89. Years later Chanel told Paul Morand that she had given Diaghilev 300,000 francs; see Buckle, *Diaghilev*, 571–2, note 122. Kochno reports that Chanel's gesture was a result of hearing Diaghilev and Misia discuss his problems in Venice that summer. But if there had been another, less innocent motive, Kochno would certainly have been discreet about it, Coco having originally demanded secrecy of Diaghilev.

22 Massine, *My Life in Ballet*, 151–2. But Massine is surely himself mistaken in recalling that he visited Stravinsky in Switzerland at the end of the Ballets Russes' spring season. Stravinsky moved to France at the end of the first week in June, and Massine could hardly have got to Morges before the London season opened on the tenth.

23 "Les deux *Sacre du Printemps*," *Comoedia*, 14 December 1920, reprinted in Lesure (ed.), *"Le Sacre du printemps": Dossier de presse*, 53. Roerich's original sets and costumes were reused, above all, of course, for financial reasons, and in the end Diaghilev did away with the set for the first scene and played the whole ballet in the original set for scene 2.

24 Sokolova, *Dancing for Diaghilev*, 162.

25 Ibid., 164–7. But the "twelve minutes" may be either an exaggeration or evidence of slow tempos. Assuming the curtain rose at the end of the Introduction, an average modern timing from there to the start of the Danse sacrale would be something under ten minutes, from which have to be subtracted the preliminary actions for the corps de ballet as described by Sokolova. This is not, of course, to belittle her achievement, which was obviously prodigious.

26 *L'Eclair*, 20 December 1920, reproduced in Lesure (ed.), *"Le Sacre du printemps": Dossier de presse*, 54–5.

27 *La Revue musicale*, 1 February 1921, reproduced in ibid., 58–60.

28 Buckle, *Diaghilev*, 370–2.

29 Specifically to Semyon Katzental, a minister in the Commisariat of Popular Education, and Arthur Lourié, head of the music division (MUZO) in the same commissariat (letters of 2 and 9 September 1920, in PSS). Stravinsky may or may not yet have been aware that Kryukov Canal no. 66 had been turned into a state archive, with his mother as titular archivist, or that Lourié had himself gone to live there for a time the previous winter, because of the lack of heating in his own flat. (Information kindly supplied by Viktor Varunts, from Nikolay Findeyzen's journal in RNB.)

30 *SPD*, 210.

31 Pochon had tried to sell Schirmer the *Concertino*, but the publisher wanted only songs and piano pieces, preferably based on Russian folk themes. Stravinsky told Pochon that "I don't do that sort of thing to commission." But in fact *The Five Fingers* is to some extent based on folk song, and even so Schirmer did not buy it. The pieces were published by Chester, and first performed publicly by Jean Wiéner in the Salle des Agriculteurs, Paris, on 15 December 1921.

32 Stravinsky had taken the studio by 19 February, at the latest, as is proved by his letter to Otto Kling of that date (PSS). Whether or not he paid rent for the studio is not clear; the item is not mentioned in his Pleyel contracts, though he himself recalled being paid "3000 francs a month and the use of one of their Paris studios" (*Expo*, 69). His contract of 1 May actually provides for a payment to him of 72,000 francs in monthly installments over five years: that is 1,200 francs a month. Pleyel also provided a musical assistant in the shape of the composer Jacques Larmanjat.

33 Letter to Ansermet, 22 February 1921, in *CASI*, 179–80; *SSCI*, 153 (wrongly dated "November") (my translation).

34 Letter of 6 March, in ibid., 180–1.

35 See Kling's letter to Stravinsky of 3 March 1921 (PSS).

36 Letter of Stravinsky to Kling, 26 May 1921 (PSS).

37 *Chron*, 172.

38 For this and much other information, see Lawson, "Stravinsky and the Pianola," in Pasler, *Confronting Stravinsky*, 284–301.

39 For details of the early history of the Letuchaya Mïsh (to give it its original Russian name), see Harold B. Segel, *Turn-of-the-Century Cabaret*, 255–69; also Lawrence Sullivan, "Nikita Baliev's Le Théâtre de la Chauve-Souris: An Avant-Garde Theater." For a description of the Paris show, including much information about its musical and literary aspects, see *SRT*, 1539–49. Stravinsky had already seen a dress rehearsal of the show on 4 February; see Sullivan, note 82, quoting *Comoedia*.

40 *SPD*, 240. "Moody" is to be understood as "in a bad mood."

41 For these and other details see Bowlt, *The Salon Album of Vera Sudeikin-Stravinsky*, passim; *SPD*, 239–40; *IVSPA*, 7, 45–6. None of the Sudeykin couple's previous marriages were ever legally dissolved (see below, chapter 22). On Yury Stravinsky's life in the Crimea, see *SB*, 28. By coincidence, Yury's wife, Yelena, had eight items in a Yalta exhibition of October 1918 called "Art in the Crimea," which also included work by both Sergey and Vera Sudeykin. See Bowlt, *Salon Album*, xix.

42 Livshits, *The One and a Half-Eyed Archer*, 173.

43 Mayakovsky, *Parizhskiye ocherki*, 229.

44 See Bowlt, *Salon Album*, xiii–xiv.

45 Theatre program for the Chauve-Souris United States tour of 1925, quoted in *SRT*, 1545. Taruskin was the first to note the influence of the Chauve-Souris on Stravinsky's work, and I have made no attempt to disguise my debt to him.

46 Rubinstein, *My Many Years*, 106.

47 See *SPD*, 627, note 11; *SRT*, 1546–8. Stravinsky recalled orchestrating all four pieces of what became his Suite no. 2 for "a Paris music-hall" (i.e., the Chauve-Souris) (*Chron*, 154). In fact the Three Easy Pieces already existed in a version for chamber

ensemble. Stravinsky simply expanded the orchestration of the March and Polka and added the Galop from the Five Easy Pieces. The Waltz remained in its original chamber scoring.

48 *Chron*, 154.

49 *DB*, 13, note 2.

50 Rubinstein, *My Many Years*, 104. For Kochno's first meeting with Diaghilev, I have conflated the accounts in Kochno, *Diaghilev and the Ballets Russes*, 152–5; Buckle, *Diaghilev*, 376–7; and *DB*, 13, note 2. Where they contradict each other, however, I have preferred Kochno himself and Buckle, whose information came directly from Kochno.

51 *SPD*, 618, note 232.

52 Morand, *L'Allure de Chanel*, 123–4 (paragraphs elided).

53 Ibid. For Craft's disclaimer, see *SPD*, 210.

54 Letter of 29 March 1921, in *CASI*, 183–4.

55 Buckle, *Diaghilev*, 378; Kochno, *Diaghilev and the Ballets Russes*, 184.

56 Cochran, *The Secrets of a Showman*, 362.

57 *Comoedia*, 15 May 1921; reprinted in Lesure (ed.), *Stravinsky: Etudes et témoignages*, 238. Diaghilev's ballet *Cuadro flamenco* opened on the seventeenth, with designs by Picasso.

58 According to Craft (*SPD*, 143), he conducted *Petrushka* in Madrid, a command performance for King Alfonso, on the eighteenth. But he wrote to Falla from Paris on the fourteenth at the latest; see *SSCII*, 163.

59 Letter of 18 August 1921, in Guisan, *C.-F. Ramuz, ses amis et son temps*, 54–6.

60 *Expo*, 69.

61 Goossens, *Overture and Beginners*, 158.

62 Or so Evans reported in his review in the *Sunday Evening Telegram*, 12 June 1921. Goossens noted (op. cit., 161) that Diaghilev was with Massine, which must be an error, though curiously enough Buckle (*Diaghilev*, 384 and 572–3, note 39) repeats it without comment.

63 Christopher St. John, *Time and Tide*, 17 June 1921; reproduced in Lesure (ed.), *"Le Sacre du printemps": Dossier de presse*, 68–9. Half a century later Paul Horgan wrote that "Goossens was the only conductor out of the great many whom I had discussed with Stravinsky about whom he had never said an adversely critical word." *Encounters with Stravinsky*, 161–2.

64 *Manchester Guardian*, 16 June 1921; reprinted in Baltensperger and Meyer, *Igor Strawinsky: Symphonies d'instruments à vent*, 42.

65 "Misunderstood! Stravinsky Says Audience Did Not Hiss Enough," *Weekly Dispatch*, 12 June 1921 (some paragraphs elided). An added problem was that Koussevitzky did not reseat his wind players, who remained in their orchestral places, with neither visual nor aural focus; see *Chron*, 157–8. See also Leigh Henry, "London Letter," in *The Chesterian*, new series no. 16 (June 1921), 498–9, for an attack on the performance so cogent that one suspects it had profited from conversation with the composer.

66 *Manchester Guardian*, 16 June 1921; in Baltensperger and Meyer, 42.

67 *Daily Telegraph*, 18 June 1921.

68 "The End of a Chapter," *Sunday Times*, 3 July 1921; reproduced in Lesure (ed.), *"Le Sacre du printemps": Dossier de presse*, 74–5.

69 *Sunday Times*, 10 July 1921; in Baltensperger and Meyer, 42.

70 Letter to the editor, *Sunday Times*, 24 July 1921; partly reprinted in Baltensperger and Meyer, 42–3. The claim that Stravinsky had pressed Koussevitzky to program the work is contradicted in the composer's autobiography, which has the conductor asking Stravinsky "to entrust him with the first performance" (*Chron*, 156). But the book studiously avoids blaming Koussevitzky for the work's failure.

71 Undated letter, about 25 July 1921; see *Muz Ak* 1996/3–4, 189; *SSCII*, 39–40 (my translation).

72 Letter of 27 July 1921, *Muz Ak* 1996/3–4, 190.

73 See Ansermet's letter of 7 September 1921 and Stravinsky's reply of 12 September, in *CASI*, 191–3. Stravinsky's letter is also in *SSCI*, 149–50, dated the "end of July."

74 *Chron*, 156.

75 See his telegram of 25 June from Biarritz to Diaghilev in London, announcing his arrival on Monday evening (the twenty-seventh) (KA).

76 André Rigaud, *Mavra* à l'Opéra," *Comoedia*, 3 June 1922. This bears out Kochno's memory of the origins of *Mavra*, as reported by Buckle (*Diaghilev*, 379). Kochno's own published account is less precise, stating only that *Mavra* was to be a curtain raiser, without specifying what to. See *Diaghilev and the Ballets Russes*, 182–4. Taruskin (*SRT*, 1538) offers some rather unconvincing circumstantial arguments against all this.

77 Diaghilev's copy of this volume, which he presented to Boris after the premiere of *Mavra*, is now in KA.

78 *SPD*, 618, note 231.

79 Robert Craft has recently claimed that the affair with Zhenya Nikitina antedated the Chauve-Souris visit in mid-February, which in fact effectively brought it to an end, since "Stravinsky's *billets-doux* to Mme Sudeikina during the following weeks confirm that he had experienced a *coup de foudre.*" See his review of *SRT* in the *Times Literary Supplement*, 13 September 1996. Unfortunately, the *billets-doux* have not resurfaced.

22 GUISES AND DISGUISES

1 See for instance the series of early photos in *IVSPA*, 33–5; also *SPD*, 234–5; Bowlt, *Salon Album*, x.

2 For these and other details, see *SPD*, 233–6; *IVSPA*, 32–5 and 40–2; *DB*, 5–6; and Bowlt, *Salon Album*, 15 and passim. It should be noted that Craft's various memoirs of Vera Stravinsky are not always mutually consistent in detail. Moreover, Craft's obvious affection for his subject, though very attractive in itself, leaves no room for the slightest coloring of her actions. Needless to say, a very different portrait emerges from conversation with any relation of Katya's.

3 *Harper's and Queen*, October 1979, quoted in *IVSPA*, 42.

4 *SPD*, 288–9. See Bowlt, *Salon Album*, 13–14, 87, who, however, believes that Vera's elopement may have been in 1914.

5 "Vsyo mï brazhniki zdes," from *Chotki* (Rosary).

6 "Zolotistovo myoda struya iz butïlki tekla" (*Tristia*, no. 3) (my translation). See Bowlt, *Salon Album*, 38–9 and plate 51a, for a facsimile of the manuscript, another English translation, and a detailed account of the circumstances.

7 *DB*, 6.

8 Undated letter in *DB*, 13.

9 Letters respectively: undated (mid-July), 27 July, and 8 August, in *DB*, 13–14.

10 Letters of 27 July and 21 August, respectively, in *DB*, 14.

11 Letter of 19 September 1921, in *DB*, 14. The Picabia collaboration came to nothing, though the artist sent his scenario the following May, and Stravinsky seems to have been sufficiently interested to accept a dinner date at which it was to be discussed. The scenario is printed in translation in *SSCII*, 193–4.

12 Letter of 19 September.

13 *Muz Ak* 1996/3–4, 191 (dated "second half of 1921").

14 KA. Diaghilev was still in London, it being the final day of the ballet season there.

15 *My Many Years*, 138–41. Rubinstein, as usual, makes himself the pivot of the whole project. But though, as a Westernized Pole, he understandably makes fun of this fat, bearded Russian whose worldly wealth consisted of land that was now part of Poland, it contains too much accurate detail that Rubinstein could not have known except by remembering it to be discounted as pure pantomime. For instance, his

memory that Belyankin (actually his father-in-law) had bought his Ustilug estate after its owner, "a Polish revolutionary [Lubomirski] . . . had been sent to Siberia and his property confiscated," seems to be broadly correct, and as far as I know there is no other Western source for the information.

16 Letter of 18 August 1921, in Guisan, *C.-F. Ramuz, ses amis et son temps*, 56; *SSCIII*, 62 (my translation). The final monthly installment on his 1919 contract with Chester had been paid a fortnight before, and Stravinsky was soon pestering Diaghilev for *his* August payment.

17 Stravinsky to Diaghilev, letter of 11 January 1922 (KA).

18 Letter of 18 August 1921, RMV to Stravinsky, quoted in *SPD* 635, note 83. Stravinsky's original letter has not surfaced.

19 Letter of 18 August 1921, in Guisan, *C.-F. Ramuz, ses amis et son temps*, 56; *SSCIII*, 62.

20 Letter of 11 September 1921, in *CASI*, 192–3; *SSCI*, 150 (dated 10 September), italics his (my translation).

21 Rubinstein, *My Many Years*, 101–2.

22 Ibid., 135.

23 *Expo*, 69.

24 *My Many Years*, 148. In fact the first documented performance was given by Jean Wiéner at the Théâtre des Champs-Elysées on 26 December 1922.

25 Ibid., 138.

26 *Expo*, 139. Neither in *Chron* (162) nor in his lengthy discussion of the piece in "Quelques confidences sur la musique" (reprinted in White, *Stravinsky*, 581–5) does the composer so much as breathe Rubinstein's name.

27 Letter of 8 October 1921, quoted in *SPD*, 629–30, note 37.

28 *Expo* (81) misidentifies the entr'acte, confusing it with the Entr'acte symphonique which follows, and which, as Taruskin points out, could hardly be cut since it accompanies the awakening kiss. *SRT*, 1521, note 41.

29 Igor Stravinsky, "The Genius of Tchaikovsky," open letter to Sergey Diaghilev, *Times* (London), 18 October 1921; reprinted in White, *Stravinsky*, 573–4.

30 Ibid. It was presumably on this visit that the young Aaron Copland glimpsed Stravinsky in the rue Saint-Honoré and followed him "as if drawn by a magnet." They met for the first time soon afterwards at one of Nadia Boulanger's Wednesday-afternoon classes. See Aaron Copland and Vivian Perlis, *Copland*, vol. 1, 72.

31 Letter of 18 August 1921, in Guisan, *C.-F. Ramuz, ses amis et son temps*, 55; punctuation regularized. Theodore's murals were in the Biarritz house of Mme Errazuriz (see T. and D. Strawinsky, *Au coeur du Foyer*, 93–4).

32 Letter of 15 October 1921, in ibid., 56–7. The production did not materialize, partly because Stravinsky made difficulties about letting Hébertot borrow the sets without charge.

33 Letter of 19 September, in *DB*, 16.

34 According to a letter he wrote to Diaghilev in December, he himself had signed Vera's contract, but "never thought that it would last more than two months." Undated letter of (probably) early December 1921 (KA).

35 Letter of 4 October (KA). According to Haskell, Bakst blackmailed Diaghilev by refusing to deliver his Tchaikovsky drawings until Diaghilev agreed to his designing *Mavra* as well. *Diaghileff: His Artistic and Private Life*, 296–7.

36 Igor Stravinsky, "The Diaghilev I Knew," 35.

37 *Times* (London), 3 November 1921.

38 Stravinsky, "The Genius of Tchaikovsky," reprinted in White, *Stravinsky*, 573–4.

39 As observed by the balletomane Cyril Beaumont (though his physical description of Stravinsky is curiously inaccurate). See Beaumont, *The Diaghilev Ballet in London*, 193.

40 Letter of 9 October, in *CASI*, 194–5.

41 Letter of 20 December, in *CASI*, 205–6. The concert was on the twelfth, and also

included *The Rite of Spring*, Goossens's third performance of that work in just over six months. Ansermet himself had conducted the Symphonies for the first time in Geneva on 26 November.

42 Unfortunately, in his commentary to the *Salon Album*, John Bowlt seems to contradict himself, stating in the introduction (xxv) that while Vera was in London for *The Sleeping Beauty*, Sudeykin "languished in Paris, waiting for a major theatrical commission that never came," but in the commentary (37) that "Sudeikin and Kochno were again in London in October–November 1921." The painter was certainly in Paris on 19 November, when he sent Diaghilev an anxious telegram about Vera's well-being (quoted in Buckle, *Diaghilev*, 573, note 99). His two surviving letters, also from Paris, are undated but must be later than the telegram.

43 Translation from *DB*, 16, note 2. The original Russian, dated 27 October 1921, remains unpublished.

44 The poem is reproduced in facsimile in Bowlt, *Salon Album*, plates 48–9, with an English translation and commentary on 36–8.

45 Telegram of 15 November, part of an unsold lot (399) in the auction by Sotheby's of the Boris Kochno Collection, Monaco, 11–12 October 1991, but not specifically itemized in the catalogue.

46 Letter of 17 November 1921, in ibid., lot 401, also unsold: translation mine. The catalogue includes a facsimile of the first page of the letter. Vera's November letters to Stravinsky have not surfaced.

47 Ibid. Translation partly mine from the facsimile, partly quoted from the catalogue entry, which includes text not reproduced in the facsimile while excluding some of the reproduced text.

48 Letter of 19 November, in ibid., lot 403 (sold). The lot description suggests that the composer implicitly ruled out the possibility of leaving his wife, but this cannot be confirmed from the passage quoted.

49 Letter of 19 November, in ibid., lot 404 (sold); translation mine.

50 Undated letter of (probably) late November 1921 (KA).

51 Sudeykin's second letter is also undated but probably from early December (KA). Diaghilev had noted on the back of the first letter that "the second actress may be Burakovskaya; she is the same size but lacks an attractive appearance."

52 Letter of 28 December 1921 (KA).

53 Letter of about 30 November 1921, also quoting Vera's letter of 28 November. Sotheby's catalogue, op. cit., lot 400 (sold), with facsimile page. The letter is dated "Wednesday," but internal evidence suggests it was written late on Tuesday (the twenty-ninth). As before, the text given here includes my own translation of the facsimile passages alongside direct quotation of the catalogue translation of other passages.

54 *SRT*, 1549.

55 *Expo*, 113.

56 Letter of 2 December, in *CASI*, 204; *SSCI*, 154 (my translation).

57 Letter of 11 January 1922 (KA).

58 Undated letter fragment quoted in Sotheby's catalogue, op. cit., lot 399 (unsold).

59 Ibid.

60 See, mainly, his letter of 27 November 1921, in *CASI*, 201–2; but the remark quoted is from his letter of 5 December, in ibid., 204.

61 *Expo*, 118. But Stravinsky's memory that he thought of the definitive instrumentation while living at Garches is mistaken. The first reference to it is in a telegram to Ansermet of 18 April 1922, in *CASII*, 8; and *SSCI*, 155 (where it is dated "end of February"). The text in *CAS* is from a copy (apparently handwritten) in the Bibliothèque cantonale et universitaire, Lausanne, while the *SSC* translation seems to be based on a separate draft. Both texts are confused. The original telegram, now in KA, reads:

"Diaghilew accepte conditions vous prie conduire Sacre et Noces dont instrumenta- tion contiendra seulement 4 pianos et percussion stop jouant pas Tchaikowsky étais forcé céder Renard Fitelberg Strawinsky" (Diaghilev accepts conditions I beg you to conduct Sacre and Noces whose scoring will include only 4 pianos and percussion stop not playing Tchaikovsky I was forced to give Fitelberg Renard Stravinsky).

62 Nijinska, "Creation of *Les Noces*," 59.

63 Ibid. The drawings Bronya saw were presumably those of the "Northern spring" ver- sion, as described and illustrated by Goncharova in her article "The Metamorphoses of the Ballet *Les Noces*." Goncharova avoids crediting Bronya with the subsequent abandonment of these designs, but she admits that the prompting came from out- side (Laryonov or Diaghilev) and that she was at first disconcerted by the idea.

64 Buckle, *Diaghilev*, 401.

65 Telegrams of 23 April, Diaghilev to Stravinsky, and 24 April, Stravinsky to Diaghilev (PSS); *SSCII*, 40 (my translation).

66 See variously: Buckle, 400–2; *Chron*, 168; Nijinska, "Creation of *Les Noces*," 59. The telegrams themselves are confusingly worded, but the interpretation given here seems the most likely.

67 Haskell, *Diaghileff*, 299.

68 Buckle, *Diaghilev*, 401. But Buckle's suggestion that Diaghilev wished to compensate Sudeykin for the loss of Vera is almost ghoulishly perverse. If he had wanted to rub his face in the dirt, he could hardly have found a better way.

69 *Excelsior*, 20 May 1922.

70 *La Revue musicale*, 3, no. 8 (June 1922), 264.

71 *Comoedia*, 20 May 1922.

72 "Une Lettre de Stravinsky sur Tchaïkovsky," *Le Figaro*, 18 May 1922.

73 Clive Bell, *Old Friends*, 179–80. James Joyce—lover of Italian opera—was also pres- ent but held his peace.

74 Haskell, *Diaghileff*, 297.

75 Letter of 26 April 1922 (KA).

76 Letter to Ansermet, 9 September 1923, in *CASII*, 68; *SSCI*, 173.

77 KA. The note to Diaghilev is simply dated "Friday" (possibly 9 June), while the Kochno note is undated. Yankel is the name of the wily money-lender and landlord in Gogol's *Taras Bulba*, one of the most malignant portraits of a Jew in Russian lit- erature. When the Cossack Bulba asks for Yankel's help in rescuing his son from the Poles, the Jew's first image is "of the two thousand gold ducats that had been placed on Bulba's head; but he at once repented of his avarice and endeavoured to suppress within him that everlasting obsession with money which winds like a worm around the soul of every Jew" (trans. Christopher English [Oxford: Oxford University Press, 1994], 344–5).

78 *SPD*, 232.

79 Pneu in KA.

80 *IVSPA*, 54.

81 *DB*, 16. But the entry for the third is omitted from *DB*.

82 It seems that *Renard*, which is usually said to have been on the same bill, was only added at the second performance on the sixth.

83 *Expo*, 82.

84 Ibid.; see also *Mem*, 40–1.

85 See Charles Tenroc's review of the "interprétation," also in *Comoedia*, 5 June 1922, on the same page as Laloy's account of the work.

86 *L'Eclair*, 5 June 1922.

87 De Schloezer attended the concert preview in the Hôtel Continental and, by his own account, was the only member of the audience who did not go and congratulate the composer at the end of the performance. See his interview with André Boucourech-

liev, in the *Nouvelle Revue française* for March 1959, quoted in *Boris de Schloezer* (Paris: Cahiers "Pour un temps," Pandora Editions, 1981), 21. Schloezer's first review of a Stravinsky work seems to have been his somewhat neutral notice of the Flonzaley Quartet's Paris premiere of the Concertino in October 1921: *La Revue musicale*, 3, no. 1 (1 November 1921), 59–60.

88 See de Schloezer's review in the Paris Russian-language paper, *Posledniya novosti*, 22 June 1922.

89 Ibid.; see also *Nouvelle Revue française*, 19 (July 1922), 115–20.

90 Letter of 6 June 1922, quoted in unidentified sale catalogue, lot 102. I can find no evidence for Craft's assertion that Roland-Manuel wrote to Stravinsky before *Mavra* was performed "bravely dissenting from his views about the merits of Tchaikovsky." His earliest surviving letter to the composer, dated 18 June 1922, refers to an earlier conversation and remarks that, while still not fully converted to Tchaikovsky, he now understands his importance to Stravinsky. His subsequent reference (quoted by Craft) to a letter of 6 January 1922 is an error for 6 June. See *SSCII*, 504.

91 Undated draft reply to de Schloezer's letter of 27 June 1922, quoted in *SSCI*, 157, note 87. At this stage, Stravinsky had read the *Posledniya novosti* review, but not the one in the *NRF*, as is indicated by his letter to Ansermet of 11 August (*CASII*, 14–15; *SSCI*, 156–8). In his *NRF* review, de Schloezer claims to have heard *Mavra* five or six times, "trying to discover the reasons for some people's enthusiasm and my disappointment: you have to be prudent with Stravinsky; might this not be some new revelation?"

23   FOUR PIANOS AND A WEDDING

1 Compare *Dial*, 39, with *Chron*, 170–1, where the composer tells us that "I began to write this music without knowing what its sound medium would be."

2 "Some Ideas About My Octuor," *The Arts*, Brooklyn (January 1924), 4–6; reprinted in White, *Stravinsky*, 574–7.

3 *DB*, 14, note 1; the description was apparently Stravinsky's own, in a "lost or destroyed" letter to Vera. Craft told me that he personally destroyed Igor's letters to Vera after the composer's death, and on his instructions.

4 Bowlt, *Salon Album*, xxvi.

5 *Philadelphia Inquirer*, 29 March 1925, reproduced in facsimile in *IVSPA*, 63. The paper's own explanation of this surprising communication was that it had "reached New York from Paris through intimate friends of Mme Soudeikine." The intimate friends had evidently forgotten her Christian name, and the article called her Sonya throughout.

6 Letter of 22 July 1922, in *CASII*, 10; *SSCI*, 155–6.

7 Hammond was also, however, a board member of the Franco-American Music Society, which may have had hopes of a technical way round the copyright problem. At any rate, Hammond told Craft many years later that "for some technical reason the matter couldn't go through." See *SSCI*, 155, note 78.

8 Letter of 28 March 1922 (PSS).

9 Letter of 25 June 1922 (PSS). The Jurgenson firm had of course been nationalized along with all imperial publishing enterprises, and its former proprietors reduced to subordinate managerial roles.

10 See their rapid exchange of letters during August 1922, in *CASII*, 12–25 (*SSCI*, 156–61: Stravinsky's side only); also Stravinsky's correspondence with RMV (PSS).

11 See Ansermet's letter of 29 August and Stravinsky's reply of 2 September, in *CASII*, 25 and 27 (Stravinsky's letter also in *SSCI*, 162).

12 Letter of 13 February 1923, in *CASII*, 45.

13 See his letter of 27 August 1922 to Ansermet, in *CASII*, 23; *SSCI*, 161.

14 Letter of 9 September 1922, in Chimènes, *Francis Poulenc: Correspondance*, 177; *SSCIII*, 202 (my translation).

15 George Antheil asserts that Stravinsky "remained in Berlin for exactly two months" (*Bad Boy of Music*, 30). Pierre Souvtchinsky told Prince Trubetskoy that the composer "was here for a couple of weeks" (letter of 25 November 1922; information supplied by Viktor Varunts). But this is certainly an understatement.

16 *SPD*, 242–3.

17 Berdyayev, *Dream and Reality*, 244. Presumably the acceptance of forced emigrants was arranged at high level.

18 Kryukov, *Materiali k biografii B. Asafyeva*, 30. For details of this episode and an excerpt from the Asafyev article, see *SRT*, 1119–26.

19 P. N. Savitsky, "A Turn to the East," in *Iskhod k Vostoku*, quoted in Riasanovsky, "The Emergence of Eurasianism," 39–40; cf. Rolland, *Journal des années de guerre*, 59–60. The first writer to point out and develop this connection was Richard Taruskin, in *SRT*, 1126–9.

20 The material in quotation marks is Souvtchinsky, "The Strength of the Weak," quoted in Riasanovsky, op. cit., 40. The material in extract is a paraphrase of Souvtchinsky, "The Age of Faith," in ibid., 41.

21 Rolland, op. cit., 59.

22 Antheil, *Bad Boy of Music*, 31–2.

23 Ibid., 38.

24 Antheil's much-embroidered account of this episode is in essence corroborated by a letter Stravinsky wrote Souvtchinsky on 1 January 1923 (PSS), after the American had failed to turn up in Paris for the planned concert in Christmas week. Antheil had been otherwise occupied trying to impress the Socialist girl of his dreams with his Polish peasant ancestry. See *Bad Boy of Music*, 62–70.

25 Letter of 1 January 1923. Souvtchinsky's telegram is lost.

26 Ansermet wrote him a detailed account of this meeting, including a sharp character sketch of Antheil: "He is in the process of betraying his sponsors by his exorbitant expenditure, the upheaval he has created in Berlin with Russian or Hungarian women, and the preposterous music he is writing." Letter of 16 March 1923, in *CASII*, 52–4.

27 *Bad Boy of Music*, 86–8.

28 Ibid., 36–7; italics his.

29 Letter of 20 November 1922 (PSS), paraphrased (and wrongly dated) in *SPD*, 658, note 53.

30 See Ansermet's letter of 14 August 1922, together with Stravinsky's marginal notes, in *CASII*, 17–20.

31 See *SPD*, 243, for a photograph of the flier for this concert.

32 Mayakovsky, *Parizhskiye ocherki*, 228–9.

33 *Conv*, 88.

34 Buckle, *Diaghilev*, 408.

35 According to unpublished autobiographical notes quoted in Irina Graham, "Arthur Sergeevic Lourié—Biographische Notizen," 196.

36 In a letter to Stravinsky of 14 February 1924 (PSS), Lourié says that he "did not seek meetings," which might mean that they met but he did not pursue the acquaintance.

37 Ramuz grumbled about Stravinsky's "bad atheist habit of giving your concerts on Christmas Day." Letter of 11 December 1922: PSS; *SSCIII*, 69–70 (my translation). But the Stravinskys, of course, observed Russian Christmas, on 25 December Old Style, or 7 January.

38 According to Stravinsky's letter of 15 August to Ansermet, in *CASII*, 21–2; *SSCI*, 159–60. The details are confirmed by Poulenc's letter of 16 August to Milhaud, in Chimènes, *Francis Poulenc: Correspondance*, 169–71.

39 Letter of 11 August 1922, in *CASII*, 14–5; *SSCI*, 157.

40 Letter to Ansermet, 15 August 1922; punctuation regularized.

41 *Les Nouvelles littéraires*, 6 January 1923.

42 Letter of 1 January 1923, in Chimènes, *Francis Poulenc: Correspondance*, 183; *SSCIII*, 202 (my translation).

43 Letter to Stravinsky, 9 January 1923, in *CASII*, 36 (with the date 2 January). The letter, in reply to Stravinsky's of 31 December, is dated only "Tuesday," but since it opens "I've been meaning to reply to your letter for several days," the later Tuesday seems probable.

44 *DB*, 18.

45 Letter of 7 October 1923, in *CASII*, 79–80; *SSCI*, 166 (dated 11 February). Stravinsky seems to have seen the Gounod again in the autumn, probably with Benois, who was by that time designing it for Diaghilev.

46 See also *Chron*, 181–2.

47 *DB*, 18, note 1.

48 Vera's diary, cf. ibid., 18. The last two words have run into the space for January 21 (and are so presented in *DB*), which can suggest a more exalted interpretation of the whole entry (especially with the gastronomic reference omitted, as it is).

49 Letter of 23 January 1923; also Stravinsky's letter of "about 15 January" (in fact, probably the twenty-first): *CASII*, 38–41; *SSCI*, 162–3 (Stravinsky's letter only).

50 See Rex Lawson, "Stravinsky and the Pianola," in Pasler, *Confronting Stravinsky*, 284–301, for an expert survey and a catalogue of Stravinsky's known piano roll transcriptions.

51 Garafola, *Diaghilev's Ballets Russes*, 435, note 66.

52 Letter to Ansermet of 15 March, in *CASII*, 51.

53 According to Craft, Vera was to have played the role of the Bride, but withdrew because of illness (see *IVSPA*, 56–7). This is frankly hard to credit, considering that Nijinska's staging was technically complicated (it was danced on point), and Vera was not a fully trained dancer. Perhaps Stravinsky had wanted her in the role. Or perhaps her bridal status was no more than symbolic.

54 Nijinska, "Creation of *Les Noces*," 59.

55 *Zveno*, 25 June 1923.

56 The exact disposition of the pianos at the first performance is a matter of some doubt. Goncharova's final designs include pairs of grand pianos, not always in the same position, but clearly incorporated in the design scheme (see for instance Schouvaloff and Borovsky, *Stravinsky on Stage*, 123; and "Stravinsky's *Les Noces*," translated and with introductions by Roberta Reeder and Arthur Comegno, *Dance Research Journal* 18, no. 2 [winter 1986–87], 37, for contrasting designs of the final tableau). Goncharova herself recalled that "Diaghilev replaced the four pianos with two 'Pleyela' placed in the orchestra pit" ("The Creation of *Les Noces*," *Ballet and Opera* [September 1949], 23–6); and Gustav Linor, reviewing the performance in *Comoedia* (16 June 1923), refers to the "tiresome placing of the double Pleyels . . . at the opposite two extremities of the pit." The composer himself remembered (*Expo*, 117) that "the four pianos [sic] filled the corners of the scene, thus being separated from the percussion ensemble and the chorus and solo singers in the pit." Linor added that "the use of the double piano, with its twinned mechanisms, can only be regarded, in my opinion, as a compromise or a necessary evil." Essentially the double Pleyel is a large rectangular box with a keyboard at each end, two complete mechanisms inside, but a single large soundboard. So Linor is implying that the tone was inferior to that of two separate pianos. In the London performances of 1926, four grand pianos were used, but when the production was revived at Covent Garden in 1966, the pianos vanished into the pit.

57 "*Noces*—Igor Strawinsky," *La Revue musicale*, 4, no. 10 (August 1923), 69–72; *Excelsior*, 18 June 1923.

58 *Nouvelle Revue française*, 21 (1923), 247, quoted in D. Bancroft, "Stravinsky and the 'NRF' (1920–29)," 265. See also *Zveno*, 25 June 1923.

59 Bancroft, "Stravinsky and the 'NRF' (1920–29)," 264.

60 Privately printed leaflet (1926), reprinted in White, *Stravinsky,* 260–1. See also Chapter 27.

61 *Zveno,* 25 June 1923.

62 "Stravinsky, Stokowski, and Madame Incognito," in *SSCI,* 430–5.

63 Letter of 24 November 1923 (PSS), quoted (rather inaccurately) in *SSCI,* 432; original in English.

64 Letter of 14 May 1923, in *CASII,* 55; *SSCI,* 167–8.

65 Letter of 4 June 1923, in *10 Komp,* vol. 1, 28.

66 Letter to Stravinsky, 22 May 1923, in *CASII,* 56–7.

67 Letter of 25 May 1923, in *SSCIII,* 145–6.

68 Letter of 22 May 1923, Ansermet to Stravinsky, in *CASII,* 56. For detailed information about the Frankfurt production, see *10 Komp,* vol. 1, 31–5.

69 Postcard of 26 May 1923, in *10 Komp,* vol. 3, 48.

70 See *10 Komp,* vol. 1, 29, and *SSCIII,* 146–7, whither, however, a substantial part of the text of Reinhart's later letter (10 August) has been transferred in error. For the relevant part of the 6 June letter, see the last two main paragraphs of the letter printed as "10 August" in ibid., 149–50.

71 See Tomkins, *Living Well Is the Best Revenge,* 30–3, for a name-dropping and factually unreliable account of the Murphys' party. According to Craft (*SPD,* 158), Tomkins even gets its date (1 July) wrong by a whole fortnight—a nice thrust in the old battle between the pot and the kettle.

72 According to Pahissa, *Manuel de Falla,* 120–1, the performers refused to repeat the work because they had not been invited to the dinner.

73 Buckle, *Diaghilev,* 412–3. Stravinsky's own account of the occasion is in "The Diaghilev I Knew."

74 *Chron,* 177–8. See also *DB,* 18. The Africans were probably Senegalese troops in the French occupation force.

75 Letter of 5 August 1923, in Antony Beaumont (ed.), *Ferruccio Busoni: Selected Letters* (London: Faber, 1987), 369. Le Boeuf sur le toit—the ox on the roof—was a Paris bar (named after the ballet by Cocteau and Milhaud) which opened in January 1922 and quickly became a byword for Parisian frivolity. The swine in the cellar are presumably the suffering Germans, trodden into the dirt by the fun-loving French (Philipp was Hungarian).

76 Letter of 9 September 1923, in *CASII,* 67–9; *SSCI,* 170–3 (my translation).

77 Quoted in Edward J. Dent, *Ferruccio Busoni* (London: Oxford University Press, 1933), 283.

78 According to Vera's diary, she and Stravinsky spent the evening after the performance with Kandinsky and his wife and the conductor, Scherchen: *DB,* 18. Stravinsky seems to have forgotten this meeting in *Conv* (89), and his claim never to have met Klee is directly contradicted by an unsourced footnote to the diary entry. Kandinsky was for a time supposed to be designing the production; see Scherchen's letter to Stravinsky quoted in *SSCIII,* 148, note 12.

79 Letter of 9 September 1923, in *CASII,* 67–9; *SSCI,* 170–3 (my translation).

80 Letter of 14 August 1922, in *CASII,* 19.

81 Antony Beaumont, *Busoni the Composer* (London and Boston: Faber, 1985), 302.

82 She did so the following month; see *DB,* 18.

83 Benois, *Reminiscences of the Russian Ballet,* 380–1. Benois designed two Gounod operas: *Le Médecin malgré lui* and *Philémon et Baucis.*

84 *SPD,* 224.

85 Letter-card of 29 July 1921, in *Muz Ak* 1996/3–4, 190.

86 ERM, as I shall call it from now on, had been in existence since 1921. The Berlin office (RMV) was retained, but gradually assumed lesser importance.

87 The plan is referred to in Stravinsky's letter to Ansermet of 9 September 1923, in *CASII,* 67–9; *SSCI,* 170–3.

88 See Wiéner's furious letter of 6 October 1923 (PSS); also Stravinsky's letter to Anser-

met of 29 July 1923, in *CASII*, 60–2 (*SSCI*, 169–70), where various possible programs for Wiéner are set out, all of them containing the Octet. In fact the piece had originally been announced for a Wiéner concert in early June.

89 Letter of 21 September, in *CASII*, 76–7; *SSCI*, 175–6 (but a faulty translation).

90 In *Chron*, 185, Stravinsky recalls that Koussevitzky made this suggestion when the concerto was nearing completion (that is, in April 1924); but there is no evidence that Koussevitzky was in Biarritz then, and in any case Stravinsky had already accepted to play the premiere by the end of February at the latest, as a letter of the twenty-seventh to Falla proves (*SSCII*, 164–5).

91 See his letter to Stokowski of 30 November 1923, quoted in *SSCI*, 432.

92 Letter of 29 July 1921. Koussevitzky would, Stravinsky had meant, know how to capitalize like a Jew on any reply Diaghilev might make.

93 *Dial*, 40.

94 Cocteau, "Stravinsky dernière heure," *La Revue musicale*, 5, no. 2 (1 December 1923), 142–4; reprinted in *Le Coq et l'Arlequin*, 110–1.

95 *Courrier musical* (1 November 1923), 340–1.

96 *La Revue musicale*, 5, no. 1 (1 November 1923), 66–7.

97 See Philip Stuart, *Igor Stravinsky: The Composer in the Recording Studio*, 4–5, 26, for such details of this recording as are known. The following February, Berners wrote to the composer asking where he could get the discs (letter of 24 February 1924: *SSCII*, 155 and note 33).

98 Letter of 15 November 1923, in *CASII*, 81; *SSCI*, 176–7 (my translation).

99 *La Revue musicale*, 5, no. 2 (December 1923), 170–1.

100 *DB*, 18. But the dating is suspect. On 22 October, Stravinsky was in Paris and had been for a fortnight. So why should Vera suddenly refer to his "writing constantly"? Moreover, there were as yet no known plans for the (three-week) Spanish trip which Igor made (with Vera) in March 1924. Alexander Kahn sent the draft agreement for Barcelona only on 27 November. The separate sheet is no longer with the diaries (in PSS).

24 Words Speak Loud, Actions Louder

1 *The Arts*, January 1924, 4–6 (including an autograph facsimile of the first seven bars of the Allegro moderato); reprinted, without the facsimile and the brief editorial note, in White, *Stravinsky*, 574–7. Gaby's involvement is confirmed by her letter to Stravinsky of 5 December 1923, enclosing his fee (PSS).

2 Michel Georges-Michel, "Les deux *Sacre du printemps*," *Comoedia*, 14 December 1920, reproduced in Lesure (ed.), *Dossier de presse*, 53; also "Ce que j'ai voulu exprimer dans *Le Sacre du printemps*," in ibid., 13–5.

3 See his undated agreement with Gaby Picabia, quoted in *SSCIII*, 78, note 74. Remarkably, this private arrangement reserved to her the right to alter the text, a right that was not, presumably, Stravinsky's to concede.

4 Alexey Kruchenikh, quoted in Erlich, *Russian Formalism*, 44–5.

5 Rivière, "*Le Sacre du printemps*," 706.

6 "L'oeuvre d'Igor Strawinsky," *La Revue musicale*, 2, no. 9 (1 July 1921), 1–27. Stravinsky had himself recommended Ansermet to the journal's editor, Henry Prunières. *SPD*, 243; also Gordon, *Stravinsky and the New Classicism*, 240.

7 "La Musique," *Revue contemporaine* (1923), 245–8.

8 *Nouvelle Revue française*, 21 (1923), 247, quoted in D. Bancroft, "Stravinsky and the 'NRF' (1920–29)," 265. Perhaps significantly, the same points are made but in a much less loaded way in de Schloezer's Russian-language review in *Zveno* (25 June 1923).

9 *Art et scolastique*, 3.

10 *Art et scolastique*, 9, 18–19. The internal quotation is from St. Thomas Aquinas. The idea of Stravinsky as preeminently an artisan is already put forward by Ansermet in

his 1921 article, "L'oeuvre d'Igor Strawinsky," 2–3, 16, where he refers specifically to Maritain and quotes him.

11 Steegmuller, *Cocteau*, 314.

12 *Le Coq et l'Arlequin*, 80–1.

13 Letter of 16 July 1917 (PSS); *SSCI*, 90 (my translation).

14 *Le Coq et l'Arlequin*, 80–1. Cocteau has already remarked (79) that "all music to be listened to head in hands is suspect." And he cites Debussy's *Pelléas et Mélisande* and Wagner in general as cases in point.

15 Letter of 11 August 1922, in *CASII*, 14–15; *SSCI*, 157 (my translation).

16 12 June 1922. See also *La Revue musicale*, 3, no. 8 (June 1922), 264; and "Revues et la presse," ibid., 3, no. 10 (August 1922), 188.

17 "Critics and the Common Spirit," *Vanity Fair* (September 1922); reprinted in Corle, *Igor Stravinsky*, 21–4.

18 "A propos de *Mavra* de Igor Strawinsky." Poulenc had sent a copy with his letter of 31 July; see *SSCIII*, 201.

19 A *normalien* is a student of the Ecole Normale, the name given to the French network of teacher training colleges; used pejoratively, the term might suggest a didactic, overintellectualized mentality.

20 *SRT*, 1598–9. Milhaud, however, was—at least privately—unenthusiastic: "Pity about *Mavra*," he wrote to Paul Collaer from the Camargue. "I prefer my horse and my evenings with the local fishermen and bull breeders" (letter of 1 June 1922, in Wangermée, *Paul Collaer: Correspondance avec des amis musiciens*, 101).

21 Letter of 9 August 1922, in *SSCIII*, 11. Stravinsky had written in reply to a request from Satie for biographical details to go in an article he was writing. But the reply has not surfaced.

22 20 December 1922, at the Théâtre de l'Atelier in Montmartre.

23 Letters of 24 July and 2 August, respectively; Steegmuller, *Cocteau*, 308.

24 R. Maritain, *Journal de Raïssa*, 152.

25 Letter of 30 November 1923 (PSS).

26 In 1924 he demanded four thousand French francs (the equivalent of one thousand Swiss francs) per conducting appearance.

27 Janacopoulos had sung "Tilimbom" accompanied by a Pleyel piano roll in a concert in the Salle des Agriculteurs on 29 May 1923. For the Antwerp concert she was preparing the (tenor) Fisherman's song from *The Nightingale* as well as the soprano music.

28 Letter to Stravinsky of 10 December 1919 (PSS); Brown, "Prokofiev's Correspondence with Stravinsky and Shostakovich," 275; also *SPD*, 132 (my translation).

29 See the letter of 29 December 1923 from (probably) Constantin Piron to Stravinsky, inviting him and the "friend" to dinner (PSS).

30 Postcard of 26 December 1923, to Stravinsky, in *CASII*, 86.

31 Vera's diary: "nemnogo moux," a characteristic Esperanto of Russian and French (*DB*, 18, suggests "too soft"). Arthur Prévost was the brother of Germain Prévost, the viola player of the Pro Arte Quartet.

32 Wangermée, *Paul Collaer: Correspondance avec des amis musiciens*, 32. Collaer's *Strawinsky* eventually came out in 1930, but without the biographical chapter. Collaer had sent the composer a nearly complete manuscript in 1925 and was pained and surprised by his negative response. Stravinsky complained (with good reason) of factual errors; but there must have been more to it than that, to judge from Collaer's final, despairing "Ne parlons plus de cette affaire" (letter of 14 November 1925, PSS). The chapter was published separately immediately after Stravinsky's death, as "Introduction à la vie et l'oeuvre d'Igor Strawinsky."

33 *DB*, 20.

34 E. Closson, in *L'Indépendance belge*, 17 January 1924.

35 Quoted (accurately) in *SPD*, 290. But this should be compared with the same entry in *DB*, 20: "Lourié is very happy to see and to talk with Igor."

36 Letters of 14 February and 10 April, respectively (PSS).

37 Letter of 6 February 1923 to Myaskovsky, in *PMP*, 152–3; Robinson (ed.), *Selected Letters of Sergei Prokofiev*, 248 (my translation).

38 For Lourié's refusal to renounce "his own youthful Communist ideals," see Gojowy, "Arthur Lourié der Futurist," 147.

39 Letter of 7 September 1924 to Stravinsky (PSS).

40 Stravinsky to Falla, 18 January 1924, in *SSCII*, 164; and Ansermet to Stravinsky, 21 February 1924, in *CASII*, 88.

41 Letter of 23 February, in *CASII*, 89–90; *SSCI*, 177–8 (my translation).

42 As he informed Falla in a letter of 27 February, in *SSCII*, 164–5.

43 Letter of 1 February 1924, in *SSCII*, 64–5. The only previous U.S. performance had been by Stokowski in Philadelphia in March 1922.

44 Letter of 26 February (PSS), quoted in *SSCI*, 433. The performance was on the fifth.

45 Undated letter of about 10 February (PSS).

46 Letter of 24 February 1924 (PSS).

47 Letter to Lyon, 28 March 1924 (PSS).

48 Letter of 24 March from Madrid; in *CASII*, 91; *SSCI*, 178–9 (my translation).

49 Letter of 14 February from Joaquim Pena, secretary of the Orquestra Pau Casals (PSS).

50 *DB*, 20.

51 *ABC*, 25 March 1924.

52 Letter of 29 November 1923, in *SSCIII*, 73–4 and passim.

53 See his letter to Stravinsky of 21 February 1924, in *CASII*, 88, and the advertisement reproduced in *10 Komp*, vol. 3, 52.

54 Letter of 13 February 1924, G. Picabia to Stravinsky (PSS). See also her letter of 11 March to Ramuz, in *SSCIII*, 77, note 74.

55 Buckle, *Diaghilev*, 425.

56 Letter of 21 February to Stravinsky, in *CASII*, 89.

57 Letter of 19 March to Stravinsky (PSS). The previous month she had even had to go to London in order to negotiate, with Lord Berners's help, a contract with Chester.

58 *SSCIII*, 78, note 74. PSS contains various undated notes and letters relevant to this private deal, for which Vera Sudeykina, Gabrielle's flatmate, acted as go-between.

59 Letter of 25 March 1924, quoted in Jacquot, "*Histoire du soldat:* La Genèse du texte," 106.

60 Letter of 27 March 1924, in Wagner, "Igor Strawinsky und René Auberjonois," *SNB*, 329.

61 Quoted in Jacquot, op. cit., 106.

62 Letter of 26 April, quoted in ibid. The supporting actors were M. A. Penay (Soldier) and Jim Geralds (Devil). See *CASII*, 97, for a facsimile of the program handout at the public dress rehearsal on 24 April. The work was the final item on a triple bill with Berners's *Le Carrosse du Saint-Sacrement* and the twenty-two-year-old Henri Sauguet's *Le Plumet du colonel*.

63 *Les Nouvelles littéraires*, 3 May 1924.

64 Letter of 30 April 1924, quoted in *10 Komp*, vol. 1, 47.

65 Marcelle Meyer had written to Stravinsky on 18 April expressing regret that he would not let her play the concerto. But two undated letters from 1926 suggest that he later allowed her to break the embargo (PSS).

66 *SPD*, 629, note 29.

67 I rely on Vera's diaries (cf. *DB*, 20) for the Polignac date. *SPD*, 218, gives the fifteenth as the date of the Salle Gaveau performance, with the Polignac preview that same evening; but it seems more likely that the Polignac performance came first.

68 Letter of 23 May, in Guisan, *C.-F. Ramuz, ses amis et son temps*, 98; a somewhat free English translation is in *SSCIII*, 79.

69 Letter of 1 June 1924, in *PMP*, 195; Robinson (ed.), *Selected Letters of Sergei Prokofiev*, 252–3 (my translation). The Stravinsky anecdote is in *Chron*, 187.

70 *La Revue musicale,* 5, no. 9 (July 1924), 68–9.
71 Undated letter of May 1924 (PSS); *SCII,* 156 (my translation).
72 Asafyev, *A Book About Stravinsky,* 242.
73 Doris Monteux, *It's All in the Music,* 132–4.
74 Buckle, *Diaghilev,* 428–9.
75 Letter of 3 February 1924, in Chimènes, *Francis Poulenc: Correspondance,* 223–4; *SSCIII,* 206.
76 Letter of 1 June 1924.
77 Duke, *Passport to Paris,* 119. Duke and Dukelsky are of course one and the same.
78 See his letters to his mother of 4/17 March and 16/29 March 1912: *PRK,* 319–20, 323–4.
79 Duke, *Passport to Paris,* 114–5.
80 Letter of 16 June, in Guisan, *C.-F. Ramuz, ses amis et son temps,* vol. 6, 101–2; *SSCIII,* 80–1, under the date 26 June (my translation). The Cigale was the mildly seedy home of Beaumont's "Soirées de Paris"—hence Stravinsky's pun on the Gaumont Palace (original phrase in English, but perversely translated by Craft into French).
81 *Chron,* 188.
82 18 July. The concert was originally scheduled for earlier in the month, but Stravinsky wrote on 27 June requesting a postponement because he had flu.
83 Letter of 23 July 1924 (PSS); *SSCIII,* 83 (my translation). Soon after this the French authorities gave him (and his family) French courtesy passports. Vera continued to travel on a Nansen (stateless) passport.
84 Letter of 6 August 1924 (PSS); in *SSCII,* 84–5 (my translation).
85 The agreement, with Sam Bottenheim, committed him to being in the United States from 7 January to 11 March, in return for which Bottenheim guaranteed him a minimum of ten concerts underwritten by Clarence Mackay of the New York Philharmonic Orchestra at twelve hundred dollars each.
86 Undated letter (early September) to Peter Sirota (PSS).
87 *SB,* 62–3.
88 Letter of 22 October 1924 to Ansermet, in *CASII,* 107. He left Nice for Paris on the night of the twenty-eighth.

25   "O MY AMERICA! MY NEW-FOUND LAND"

1   Letter of 2 November 1924, in *SSCII,* 282–3.
2   Quoted in Erhardt, *Igor Strawiński,* 17. But Szymanowski was not in Warsaw during Stravinsky's visit, and wired his apologies from Lwów. See *SPD,* 616–7, note 206.
3   *Wiadomosci Literackie,* 16 November 1924, quoted in Erhardt, 220; a more complete text in Russian translation is in *ISPS,* 47–9. A color photograph of the watch and red morocco case, with a medallion of Alexander III, is in *SPD,* plate 1 (facing 144).
4   See *IVSPA,* 61, for a photograph of this occasion, with identifications of those present. The unidentified figure on the right-hand edge of the picture is presumably Iwaszkiewicz.
5   *ISPS,* 48–9.
6   *Muzyka,* no. 1 (1924), in *ISPS,* 43–5.
7   Ibid.
8   "Igor Strawiński o muzyce nowoczesnej," *Almanach nowej sztuki,* no. 1 (1925), quoted in Erhardt, 221; fuller Russian translation in *ISPS,* 46–7.
9   Ibid. In his *Muzyka* interview, he had called harmony "a fluid and unstable substance." But it would be unfair to make too much of a passing image.
10 Joseph Szigeti, *With Strings Attached,* 124. Szigeti dates the incident to 1923.
11 Asafyev, *A Book About Stravinsky,* 255. Asafyev is referring also to Stravinsky's next work, the Serenade in A, also for solo piano.
12 *Rul'* (Berlin), 18 November 1924, quoted in *ISPS,* 52, note 1. According to *DB,* 26,

there were four thousand in the audience—mainly Germans, *Rul'* reported, because Stravinsky's agent was German. Five years later, when he next visited Prague, Stravinsky recalled that he had conducted this concert with a high temperature (*Prager Presse*, 23 February 1930).

13 *Auftakt*, November 1924, 280–1; Russian translation in *ISPS*, 49–50.

14 *Prager Presse*, 13 November 1924; original in German, but translated here from the Russian text in *ISPS*, 50–2. The interview also appeared in English in the *New York Times*, 7 December 1924, under the headline "Igor Stravinsky Surveys His Own and Others' Music."

15 *Rul'*, 11 December 1924, in *ISPS*, 52–3.

16 11 December 1924, in *ISPS*, 52–3: the Mengelberg concerts were in Amsterdam on 20 November and The Hague on the twenty-second. Stravinsky later radically altered his opinion of Mengelberg; see *T&C*, 226–7.

17 *SSCIII*, 86.

18 *DB*, 26 and ibid., note 4. The actual diary entries look like an outline of plans; for instance, *DB*'s "Igor goes to Lausanne and I go directly to Leipzig" is a considerable gloss on the diary's "(to Lausanne?)."

19 26 November 1924. See Reinhart's letter of 7 October 1925 (*SSCIII*, 162), reminding him that the previous year's piano had been too soft-toned, and advising him to take steps to ensure a better one for that autumn.

20 *DB*, 26. This at least is my reading of the diary.

21 *T&C*, 226.

22 *B.Z. am Mittag*, 8 December 1924.

23 Count Harry Kessler, *Tagebücher*, 395. Stravinsky reported the cut to Henry Kling of Chester in a letter of 14 April 1925 (see *SSCIII*, 464; Otto Kling had died in May 1924); but the review of the concert in *Rul'* (17 December 1924) clearly implies that the Triumphal March was played.

24 Letter of 28 December 1924, in *DB*, 26. Lyon had intended to sail with Igor, but had been prevented by work in connection with Pleyel's impending move to new headquarters.

25 *Prejudices in Disguise*, 73; the remark (if not the sentiment) was expunged from the equivalent passage in *SPD*, 241. The telegram, dated 1 March 1925, is quoted in *DB*, 26.

26 Letter of 28 December 1925 to Mr. and Mrs. Paul Kochanski, quoted in Sotheby's sale catalogue, *Fine Printed and Manuscript Music* (London, 21 November 1990), lot 294.

27 "Igor Stravinsky not a 'Modernist,'" *New York Times*, 6 January 1925; also H. O. Osgood, "Stravinsky Conducts an Interview and a Concert," *Musical Courier*, 15 January 1925.

28 Osgood, op. cit.

29 Ibid. In view of these remarks' consequences, it should be reemphasized that Stravinsky spoke no English, and there is evidence that his words were understood differently by different reporters. For instance, the *New York Herald Tribune* reported him as saying that " 'modern music, at bottom, is not of today.' The term has become a formula"—which reads like a random precis of the *Courier* report. The *Tribune* subeditors also concocted a pair of incomprehensible headlines out of supposed remarks by the composer: "Stravinsky Aids Modern Music But Detests It" and " 'Composer of Today' Says Interpretation Can Become 'Portrait, not Lithograph,' in Proper Hands." The *Courier* report is the more convincing, but a slight doubt remains.

30 See *SPD*, 658–9, note 54. Mackay's note (PSS) is dated 6 January.

31 *Musical Courier*, 15 January. Osgood says that *Pulcinella* was also a novelty, but in fact Monteux had conducted a partial suite in New York early in 1923.

32 *New York Herald Tribune*, 9 January 1925.

33 *New York Times*, 9 January.

34 Ibid. It did; after the first concert he attended a reception at the East Sixty-ninth Street apartment of Arthur Sachs, the banker and patron of the New York Philharmonic Orchestra. It must have been at this party that Stravinsky and the twenty-six-year-old George Gershwin were dragged to the (presumably electric) piano and only rescued from a very public mismatch when John Jay Hammond switched the instrument off. See Joan Peyser, *The Memory of All That* (New York: Billboard, 1998), 96–7.

35 The description is Stravinsky's niece Tanya's, as is the story about the pianos. See *SB*, 53. The composer took home a magnificent photograph of the dinner (see *IVSPA*, 27). "Unfortunately," Tanya laments, "the cake was gobbled up there and then."

36 *New York Herald Tribune*, 26 January 1925.

37 *New York Times*, 26 January.

38 *New York Herald Tribune*, 9 January 1925.

39 Totality was at 9:17 a.m. on the 24th.

40 Leibowitz, *Musical Impressions*, 146.

41 Ibid.

42 In the Duo-Art system the rolls were cut automatically from the pianist's playing, so the recordings probably took less time than they would have done at Pleyel. See above, chapter 21, and Lawson, "Stravinsky and the Pianola," in Pasler, *Confronting Stravinsky*, 284–301.

43 18 and 19 January, respectively.

44 Or so I deduce from the fact that Stravinsky would not release the work in question, the Suite for Violin and Piano on Themes from *Pulcinella*, for Alma Moodie to premiere it until he had obtained Kochanski's permission. He had apparently been planning the suite since 1921, the date on the manuscript of the Gavotte, which is already dedicated to Kochanski. See *SSCII*, 293, notes 1–2.

45 Interview with *La Noche* (Barcelona), 25 March 1925, quoted in *IVSPA*, 15–6.

46 5 and 6 February.

47 *New York Times*, 6 February 1925.

48 *Chron*, 200. But writing three days after the concert, Stravinsky gives the rehearsal time as one hour and twenty minutes: see his letter to Sam Bottenheim, 18 February 1925, abstracted (and misdated) in Sotheby's sale catalogue, *Continental Printed Books, Manuscripts and Music* (London, 1–2 December 1993), lot 520. Reiner also conducted the overture to Berlioz's *Benvenuto Cellini*, Bartók's Suite no. 1, and Strauss's *Till Eulenspiegel*. Perhaps because of this initial experience, he was one of the few conductors for whom Stravinsky never lost respect, describing him at the end of his life as "a salutary antidote to the windmill school of conducting" (*T&C*, 225).

49 For this and other information on Enescu's *Oedipe*, see Noel Malcolm, *George Enescu: His Life and Music* (London: Toccata Press, 1990), 139–59. It was presumably also at this dinner that Stravinsky suffered the theft of the Cartier cigarette holder given him by the princesse de Polignac (letter to Bottenheim, 18 February 1925, loc. cit.).

50 See his remarks about Stock's conducting to an interviewer in Copenhagen the following November, quoted in *IVSPA*, 16. The implication there is that Stock conducted items in Stravinsky's actual concerts with the Chicago Symphony Orchestra on 20 and 21 February, but this seems not to have been the case.

51 "Igor Stravinsky Appears Tuesday," *Detroit News*, about 28 February (undated cutting in PSS). Stravinsky always later claimed that rehearsing as a conductor tired his arms for piano playing.

52 Charles Ludwig, " 'I Love America,' Composer Declares," unidentified Cincinnati paper, early March 1925 (cutting in PSS). This article is also the source of the Carpenter and Ford anecdotes.

53 Samuel T. Wilson, "Stravinsky a Sensation at Concert . . . ," unidentified Cincinnati paper, 7 March 1925 (cutting in PSS).

54 Stuart, *Igor Stravinsky: The Composer in the Recording Studio*, 9, 26.

55 Stravinsky later recalled wrongly that the Brunswick recordings were electrical. See Craft, "The Composer and the Phonograph," 35.

56 See *IVSPA*, 62–3. It was a fortnight after this that the *Philadelphia Inquirer* ran its scurrilous whole-page spread on the Stravinsky-Sudeykin triangle. See ibid., and above, chapter 23. But on 15 August 1924 Stravinsky had written to Sudeykin expressing pleasure at his designing the New York *Petrushka* (RGALI). An equally friendly reply from Sudeykin, undated, is in PSS.

57 *New York Herald Tribune*, 14 March 1925.

58 Ludwig, " 'I Love America,' Composer Declares." Praise of his hosts was admittedly a standard Stravinsky interview technique for deflecting awkward requests for his opinion about the work of local musicians.

59 "Chronological Progress in Musical Art," *Etude* (August 1926), 559–60.

60 Glenn Dillard Gunn, "Igor Stravinsky Leads Chicago Symphony," unidentified Chicago paper, 21 February 1925 (cutting in PSS).

61 Warren Storey Smith, "Stravinsky Captivates at Concert," *Boston Post*, 25 January 1925.

62 *New York Herald Tribune*, 9 January 1925.

63 *SPD*, 254. Craft attributes Varèse's standoffishness to Stravinsky's failure to respond helpfully to the idea of a New York performance of *Les Noces*. Stravinsky certainly knew about Varèse's music from the harpist and composer Carlos Salzedo, who played in the Aeolian Hall concert and was also involved in the *Noces* plan. See Leibowitz, *Musical Impressions*, 149.

64 Nadia played the first performance of Copland's Organ Symphony in the Aeolian Hall under Walter Damrosch on 11 January, the night of the Steinway dinner. See Aaron Copland and Vivian Perlis, *Copland*, vol. 1, 101 et seq.

65 *SB*, 52–3.

26 THE GIRL FROM LENINGRAD

1 *SB*, 30.

2 Letter of 25 July 1925, in *SB*, 64. Yury had written on 16 July. Igor Stravinsky nevertheless subsequently sent money to his elder brother, certainly on two or three occasions in 1928, and no doubt at other times as well.

3 Letters of 29 June and 1 July, in *SB*, 58–9.

4 Letter of 6 February 1926, in *SB*, 76–7.

5 *SB*, 35–7, from Tanya's first letter home, 24–29 March 1925.

6 Letter of 6 April, in *SB*, 40.

7 *SB*, 37, 48: letters of 24–29 March, 25–27 April.

8 Letter of 6 April, in *SB*, 40.

9 Letter of 22–23 August 1925, in *SB*, 67.

10 Letter of 19 April, in *SB*, 45.

11 The first sketches for the Cadenza-Finale, the first movement Stravinsky composed, are dated 11 April. The "latest system" was not yet electrical; the first electromagnetic gramophone, made—ironically enough—by Brunswick, came on the market only at the end of 1925.

12 Letters of 6 April and 7 August, in *SB*, 40, 65.

13 Letter of 7 August, ibid.

14 Letter of 20–21 July, in *SB*, 61. Tanya had heard her uncle "play" *Petrushka, Firebird, Pulcinella, Nightingale*, the Concertino, *Les Noces*, the Octet, Parasha's song from *Mavra*, and "a mass of small pieces."

15 Letter of 16–18 June, in *SB*, 56.

16 Letter of 19 June, in *SB*, 57. But either this or the previous letter must be misdated. Yury Stravinsky's intervening letter has apparently not survived.

17 Letter of 3 May, in *SB*, 48–9.

18 Concerts on 19 and 25 April, respectively. The vocal items were sung by Vera Janacopoulos.

19 Letter of 2 May 1925, in *10 Komp*, vol. 3, 62–3; emphasis his. The Pirandello production, under the auspices of Casella's New Music Association in the Teatro Odescalchi, opened on 27 April after a series of delays which Scherchen only put a stop to by announcing his imminent departure from Rome. His letter implies, however, that Stravinsky attended on the twenty-eighth, the day of Katya's operation. Benito Mussolini was also at this performance, but whether or not he met the composer is unknown.

20 Letter of 27 May 1925 to Reinhart, in ibid., 64–5.

21 Letter of 10 May, in *SB*, 49–50; see also T. and D. Stravinsky, *Au coeur du Foyer*, 111–12. Igor and Vera probably visited Count Guy de Matharel and his wife at their villa at Cap Brun. See *DB*, 31, note 1.

22 The photo is reproduced in *SSCIII*, following p. 242. Robert Craft told me that Stravinsky also kept nude photos of Vera.

23 Letter of 14 May, in *SB*, 50. But presumably Katya was opting out of the gymnastics for the time being.

24 *SB*, 52.

25 *SB*, 54. The Cadenza-Finale was completed on 20 May, and they left Nice on about the twenty-fourth.

26 See Lourié's letter to Stravinsky, 14 April 1925 (PSS).

27 See Forberg's letter of 27 May 1925 (copy in PSS). But the rolls were not issued until August 1926. See Lawson, "Stravinsky and the Pianola," in Pasler, *Confronting Stravinsky*, 300.

28 Letter to Myaskovsky of 20 October 1925, in *PMP*, 222–3. Diaghilev was at this performance, and as a result commissioned Prokofiev to write a ballet. Yet curiously enough, in listing the Russian connoisseurs who heard his symphony and who either did or did not understand it, Prokofiev does not mention Diaghilev.

29 Information kindly supplied by Sylvia Kahan.

30 Letter of 4 August 1925, in *PMP*, 216–8; Robinson (ed.), *Selected Letters of Sergei Prokofiev*, 258–60 (my translation).

31 Quoted in *10 Komp*, vol. 1, 56. A telegram survives in PSS inviting Stravinsky to play the sonata on 20 July, but the Petyrek performance was on the sixteenth.

32 *La Revue musicale*, 6, no. 11 (October 1925), 250. Stravinsky did not attempt to impose an embargo on the sonata. The music went on sale, and it was soon being played by other pianists, including his friend Marcelle Meyer. As early as 13 April he had written to Marcelle regretting his need to enforce his exclusivity in the Piano Concerto, but consoling her with the remark that "Vera tells me you play the sonata beautifully" (PSS).

33 See Bernard Taper, *Balanchine*, 67.

34 Solomon Volkov, *Balanchine's Tchaikovsky* (London and Boston: Faber and Faber, 1993), 123–4.

35 Taper, *Balanchine*, 78.

36 Letter of 16–18 June 1925 (but probably misdated), in *SB*, 56. Katya, however, was subsequently more assiduous in keeping up with their Yelachich relations.

37 Letter of 14 May 1925, in *SB*, 54.

38 Myaskovsky, for one, took it for granted that Stravinsky's reluctance to visit Russia in the twenties was due to the fact that Russians were more aware of his musical sources than Western Europeans. See his letter to Prokofiev of 10 August 1927, in *PMP*, 263–4, where he lists what he regards as the more obvious borrowings from Russian music in *Oedipus Rex*.

39 These and other details are in Steinberg's letters to his wife of 7, 13, 15, and 21 June 1925 (RIII). See also his letter of 16 June to Stravinsky (PSS).

40 *Mem*, 56. Stravinsky implies wrongly that Steinberg heard the 1924 premiere.

41 Steinberg had been going on to his pupil Dmitry Shostakovich about "the inviolable

foundations of the Mighty Handful, the sacred traditions of Nikolai Andreevich [Rimsky-Korsakov] and other such pompous phrases." See Elizabeth Wilson, *Shostakovich: A Life Remembered* (London: Faber, 1994), 45–6.

42 Letter of 25 July 1925, Tanya to Yury Stravinsky, in *SB*, 63.

43 Letter of 14 August, in *SB*, 65–7.

44 See his letter to Wolff of 23 August 1925 (PSS).

45 Letter of 4 May 1925 (PSS). Styopa omitted to mention that he, like Lourié, had held an influential post after the Revolution, in the music division of the Commisariat of Popular Education. Seven years later, and without her husband's knowledge, Yekaterina Mitusov wrote to Stravinsky asking after outstanding royalties on *The Nightingale*. Finding that Styopa had never been registered with SACD, the relevant copyright agency, Stravinsky paid her out of his own pocket. See her letters of 27 April and 28 September 1932 to Stravinsky, and SACD's to him of 11 July (PSS).

46 Letter of 5 June, in *SSCII*, 265. The next item there is an IOU in respect of the loan, dated 15 June.

47 For a secondhand report of these events, see Tanya's letter to her parents of 20–21 July, in *SB*, 59; also *IVSPA*, 65.

48 Letters of 25 July and 22–23 August 1925, in *SB*, 64, 67.

49 Letter of 29 July 1925 (PSS); *SSCIII*, 89 (my translation).

50 Letter of 25 July 1925, in *SB*, 64.

51 Letter of 29 July 1925.

52 *ABC* (Madrid), 25 March 1924, quoted in *IVSPA*, 15 (my translation).

53 Letter of 1 August 1925, in *SSCIII*, 156–7.

54 See Reinhart's letter of 29 July, and Stravinsky's of 1 August, in ibid., 154–7.

55 See *SSCII*, 474–81, for the entire surviving correspondence relating to this affair. But there is a significant error of sequence. Sabline's letter dated "July 24, 1925" is in fact a reply to Katya's of 6 August and was written on the eleventh.

56 Stravinsky's own account of this incident, in *Dial*, 26, is supported by Tanya's report to her parents (letter of 20 September, in *SB*, 69) and by Dukelsky's (hostile) description of a dinner at the Villa des Roses soon afterwards (*Passport to Paris*, 200). According to Denise Strawinsky, the composer had prayed long and hard in the pilgrimage church of Notre-Dame-de-Laghet before leaving for Venice. See T. and D. Strawinsky, *Au coeur du Foyer*, 108.

57 *Dial*, 21.

58 Letter of 31 August 1925, in *SSCIII*, 132–3.

59 Quoted in *10 Komp*, vol. 1, 55.

60 Dent, "Looking Backward," 21.

61 Quoted in Stuckenschmidt, *Arnold Schoenberg: His Life, World and Work*, 309.

62 Apart from certain obvious resemblances, the fact that Roerig claims to have interviewed Stravinsky in Carnegie Hall during a rehearsal of *Ragtime* (which was played in the Aeolian Hall) is a fairly clear indication of the fake. In fact, if the interview was genuine, it was based on the composer's first press conference, in the Hotel Langdon.

63 The article appeared in the *Beilage der Berliner Börsen-Courier*, 5 July 1925; but Schoenberg's cutting (of a slightly edited version) is from another, unidentified source, presumably of about the same date. The commentary, labelled "Der Restaurateur," is dated July 1926, while the marginalia nearly all carry the date 1932, so it is possible—though unlikely—that Schoenberg came across the article some time after Venice. See Leonard Stein, "Schoenberg and 'Kleine Modernsky,'" in Pasler, *Confronting Stravinsky*, 310–24, for a facsimile and translations of the cutting and marginalia, together with an English text of "Der Restaurateur."

64 Translation from ibid., 312.

65 Letter to Gavriyil Païchadze, 23 September 1925, quoted in *SSCI*, 4, note 5. Craft may be right that it was his concert tours which decided him to limit the number of movements to four.

66 See Stravinsky's letters of 25 July and 1 August 1925, and Reinhart's of 29 July 1925, respectively; *SSCIII*, 154–7 (my translation).

67 Letter of 1 August and following correspondence, in ibid., 156 et seq. The French text of Stravinsky's letter of 12 August is in *10 Komp*, vol. 3, 66.

68 Steegmuller, *Cocteau*, 344. My paragraph is more or less a precis of information in Steegmuller.

69 Ibid., 348.

70 *Dial*, 97–8.

71 Letter of 9 September 1925, quoted in Steegmuller, *Cocteau*, 356, note. The letter also notes that "tomorrow night I read my play to Igor S." But Stravinsky was still in Italy on the tenth.

72 Letter of 11 October; original French text in *Dial*, 135. See *SSCI*, 94–5, for another translation. The letter was in effect a contract to make sure that the fickle poet did not hawk his libretto around.

73 *Dial*, 22. Cocteau later published what is presumably this first version as a play, with the end date 27 October 1925.

74 Zurich was on 8 November, Winterthur on the twelfth, and Basle on the fourteenth.

75 Heyworth, *Conversations with Klemperer*, 61. The Wiesbaden concert was on 17 November.

76 Hanns Gutman, in *Anbruch* (December 1925), quoted in *10 Komp*, vol. 1, 59.

77 The Frankfurt festival was on 24 and 25 November 1925.

78 2 December. The photograph was originally reproduced in *SPD*, 261, but with Nielsen wrongly identified. The later reproduction in *DB*, 30, includes Stravinsky's own marginal identifications, and shows how the mistake arose. A Haakon Nilson is identified, but Carl Nielsen is not: so it seems that Stravinsky may not have known whom he was sitting next to.

79 Thorvald Nielsen, "Some Personal Reminiscences," in Jürgen Balzer (ed.), *Carl Nielsen Centenary Essays* (London: Dennis Dobson, 1965), 17.

80 Letter of 20 December, in *CASII*, 114–6; *SSCI*, 183–4 (my translation).

81 See Tanya's letters to her parents of 12 and 25 December 1925, in *SB*, 74. The accident to Matharel is also described in *SPD*, 454.

82 Letter of December 1925.

27 THE PRIEST AND THE ORACLE

1 Published as Suite no. 1.

2 Steegmuller, *Cocteau*, 358.

3 Letter of 19 January, quoted in *SSCI*, 95, note 39.

4 Cocteau, *Paris Album*, 101.

5 Letter to his mother of 19 January. See *Dial*, 23, for Stravinsky's assertion that the idea was Cocteau's, and ibid., 29–30, for his criticism of it.

6 For more extensive discussion of these and other aspects of the work's dramaturgy, see Walsh, *Stravinsky: Oedipus Rex*; also the entry in Holden (ed.), *The Viking Opera Guide*, 1048–50.

7 Fowlie, *Journals of Jean Cocteau*, 162.

8 Letter of 6 March 1926 (PSS); *SSCI*, 96 (my translation). But Cocteau's generosity was in character. "This same Jean," Theodore recalled, "light and frivolous to some, is there at your side, in the silence, when unhappiness strikes you." T. and D. Stravinsky, *Au coeur du Foyer*, 115.

9 23 January 1926. The event is mentioned in Robert Lyon's letter of 21 January (PSS). Lyon himself performed a series of piano rolls. But the letter went to Nice, and Stravinsky would not have read it until he got back there on the twenty-fourth.

10 Letter of 28 January, partially quoted in *SSCI*, 198–9, note 220. The concert, on the twenty-seventh, was promoted by the *Revue musicale*.

11   Letter to Ansermet, 30 January 1926, *CASII*, 119–20; *SSCI*, 185 (my translation).

12   This was the world premiere of the Suite no. 1. *The Algemeen Handelsblad* (1 March) praised the "calm assurance" of Stravinsky's conducting of *The Rite*, but said nothing else about his performance.

13   Unidentified newspaper cutting, quoted in *SPD*, 302.

14   The reception was reported in several newspapers on 18 March 1926. The guests also included Egon Wellesz, Guido Adler, and Franz Schalk.

15   *DB*, 31. But see also *IVSPA*, 68: "On this concert trip to the Austrian capital, Stravinsky spent an afternoon with, among other musicians, Alban Berg and Anton Webern." A caption to the entry in *DB* modifies this to "Alban Berg and Anton Webern came to see Stravinsky at one of the receptions," but confirms that the meeting is not mentioned in the diary.

16   "Strawinsky unterwegs nach Wien," *Die Stunde*, 17 March 1926.

17   Letter to Oeberg of 23 September 1925, quoted in *SPD*, 634, note 80. See also "Strawinski e il suo Arlecchino," *Corriere della sera*, 7 May 1926.

18   *Chron*, 211–4.

19   *Mem*, 132; cf. also 111–2.

20   26 April 1926, quoted in Sachs, *Music in Fascist Italy*, 211.

21   See Charles-Albert's letter to his brother of (probably) June 1926, in Cingria, *Correspondance générale*, vol. 2, 69 and note 3; also the following correspondence. The letter, which includes an account of a conversation with Stravinsky, is undated, but can be assigned to June or early July on internal grounds.

22   See chapter 33.

23   *ABC* (Madrid), 25 March 1924.

24   *Corriere della sera*, 10 February 1933. See also *Expo*, 137–8; *SPD*, 102.

25   "Strawinski e il suo Arlecchino," *Corriere della sera*, 7 May 1926.

26   Letter of 6 April 1926, Stravinsky to Diaghilev, *Muz Ak* 1996/3–4, 193–4; for another, slightly garbled, English translation, see *SSCII*, 40. No doubt, as he suggests, Stravinsky wrote several such letters.

27   Letter of 7 April, *Muz Ak* 1996/3–4, 194; *SSCII*, 41 (my translation).

28   Quoted in Alexander Dru, "Catholic Humanism," in John Cruickshank (ed.), *French Literature and Its Background* (London: Oxford University Press, 1970), 129.

29   *Le Coq et l'Arlequin*, 61.

30   For instance, "[Musical] sensations only find their objective and living expression in the form which, so to speak, determines their nature" (quoted in White, *Stravinsky*, 576); cf. Maritain's "Beauty is form shining on the proportioned parts of the material" (*Art et scolastique*, 34, quoting St. Thomas Aquinas). But neither Maritain's aestheticism nor his ethics play any part in Stravinsky's thinking.

31   See Maritain's letter to Stravinsky of 11 June (PSS).

32   Lourié, "La Sonate pour piano de Strawinsky."

33   Lourié, "Muzïka Stravinskovo," 119–20. The editor of the new journal was Souvtchinsky.

34   See, for instance, his claim that "I follow in my art an instinctive logic and . . . do not formulate its theory in any other way than *ex post facto*" ("Some Ideas About My Octuor," in White, *Stravinsky*, 577).

35   The principal author of the view that Lourié exerted an overriding intellectual influence on Stravinsky is Robert Craft. See chapter 29.

36   Maritain and his wife had been received in 1906, Lourié (according to his own biographical notes) in 1908, when he was fourteen. See Graham, "Arthur Sergeevic Lourié—Biographische Notizen," 186. But in "Arthur Lourié der Futurist," ibid., 152, Gojowy gives the date of Lourié's conversion as 1913.

37   P. N. Savitsky, quoted in Zernov, *The Russian Religious Renaissance of the Twentieth Century*, 222. Stravinsky also read the Orthodox theologian Viktor Nesmelov's *Nauka o cheloveke* (The Science of Man), an investigation of the links between faith and scientific positivism which exerted a profound influence on Berdyayev and other

64

Orthodox thinkers of his generation. Stravinsky's heavily annotated copy is of the 1905/7 edition, but alas for the theory that it was an early influence on him, the annotations are largely in another hand. A few notes in the second volume are his. It seems likely that he bought the book secondhand in the late twenties or early thirties and read it, in whole or part, then.

38 See Cingria's letter of June or July 1926 to his brother, Alexandre. For Berdyayev's own vigorous account of the interconfessional gatherings, see *Dream and Reality*, 258 et seq.

39 *SPD*, 212; cf. the sketches in PSS. Craft's remark (*SPD*, 628, note 17) that Stravinsky had a confessor in Biarritz is also misleading. Abbé Touya, the (Catholic) priest in question, was in fact tutor to the composer's sons. See T. and D. Strawinsky, *Au coeur du Foyer*, 90.

40 *Expo*, 75–6.

41 Cingria refers to this piece in the letter of June or July 1926 already quoted.

42 Father Nikolay wrote to the Stravinskys on 26 August thanking them for their hospitality (PSS).

43 Letter of 6 September 1926 (PSS). Lourié had copied out a "remarkable" Russian prayer and enclosed it with the letter.

44 Letters of 10 and 24 November and 21 December 1926 (PSS). The quotation is from II Corinthians 10:5.

45 See *SB*, 80–2, letters of 10 and 19 May and 2 June 1926, respectively. Tanya nevertheless stayed in Paris for another two months; but no subsequent letters appear to have survived.

46 *SSCII*, 266–9.

47 *SB*, 82; letter of 2 June 1926.

48 Duke, *Passport to Paris*, 185.

49 *Daily Telegraph*, 15 June 1926.

50 *Sunday Times*, 20 June 1926.

51 *Times* (London), 16 June 1923, quoted in Beaumont, *Complete Book of Ballets*, 804.

52 Open letter to the press, 18 June 1926; reprinted in White, *Stravinsky*, 260–1. The letter was reprinted as a flier and slipped into the programs for subsequent performances.

53 Duke, *Passport to Paris*, 185–6.

54 *SPD*, 303–5, letter of 12 September 1954. An interview with the *Daily Sketch* (9 July) is quoted in *SSCII*, 41, note 51.

55 The word is Cocteau's, in his letter to Stravinsky of Christmas 1926 (*SSCI*, 100). But Diaghilev surely knew already that something was in the wind, since Cocteau was notoriously unable to keep a secret. "No one in the world suspects *Oedipus*," he had written to Stravinsky on 1 May. "The funny thing is that the Comédie-Française has [also] asked me for one." (PSS; other translations in Steegmuller, *Cocteau*, 361; *SSCI*, 100.)

56 The contract is dated 14 June 1926, and gave him an advance of 5,000 dollars, paid as 1,000 down and eight monthly installments of 500. At some stage the delivery date was extended to June 1927.

57 Letter of 1 September 1926, quoted in *SPD*, 265.

58 Letter of 29 July 1923, in *CASII*, 62; *SSCI*, 170.

59 *ABC* (Madrid), 24 March 1924; *IVSPA*, 15.

60 Buckle, *Diaghilev*, 473–4. These costumes can be seen in front of the final-act backcloth in a photograph of a later revival, in Schouvaloff and Borovsky, *Stravinsky on Stage*, 43, below a reproduction of Goncharova's colored design for the backcloth.

61 Telegram of 29 October 1926. See "*Firebird*: A Publishing History in Correspondence," in *SSCII*, 219–58, for much of the relevant documentation; also *SPD*, 503–5.

62 English translation in *SSCII*, 228.

63 Letter to Stravinsky of 31 May 1922, in ibid., 228–9.

64 Letter of 25 June 1922; partial translation in ibid., 229.

65   Letter of 20 April 1925, in ibid., 230.
66   The complaint was filed on 2 December 1926; *SSCII*, 231–3.
67   On 21 December, Lourié wrote that he was "sorry that your Paris trip was so unsuccessful and that we saw so little of you" (PSS).
68   Letter of about 22 December 1926 (PSS). The translation in *SSCI*, 100–1, is unfortunately badly confused.

28   A VERY MACABRE PRESENT

1   Letter of 10 February 1927 (PSS); *SSCI*, 102 (my translation).
2   Letter of 8 February 1927 (PSS); wrongly dated to 19 January in *SSCI*, 101.
3   Letter of 10 February, loc. cit.
4   Letter of 3 March 1927, in *CASII*, 130. Stravinsky's letter, evidently accusing him of gossiping to Diaghilev's new young composer Nicolas Nabokov, is lost. How the supposed indiscretion had got back to Stravinsky is likewise not clear.
5   Letter of 31 January 1927 (KA).
6   Letter of 10 February 1927, loc. cit.
7   *DB*, 36.
8   Another was Roussadana Mdivani, the young sculptress (actually the daughter of a Georgian general) who was busy enticing Sert away from Misia. See Gold and Fizdale, *Misia*, 249–50.
9   Letter to Stravinsky of 20 March 1927, in *SSCI*, 105, note 48.
10   See Cocteau's letter to Stravinsky of 2 April 1927, in PSS; a very unreliable translation is in *SSCI*, 106. It may be emphasized here that the Cocteau correspondence in *SSCI* is at times so inaccurately translated as to be grossly misleading. For instance, in the letter quoted here, the French text "De toute façon elle trouverait sage d'établir des devis exacts. Si tu étais là tout se passait comme sur des roulettes" (Anyway she would deem it wise to establish the exact estimates. If you were here everything would go like clockwork) comes out as: "Anyway, she will have Serge establish the exact amount. If you had been there, it would have been like a game of roulette." In an earlier telegram from Stravinsky, the phrase "Suis reconnaissant Chanel" (Am grateful to Chanel) is rendered as "Am wary of Chanel," and the following phrase "pas prêter attention potins" (pay no attention to gossip) is simply omitted (ibid., 104). These are only a few examples among many.
11   Letter of 20 March 1927 (PSS); *SSCI*, 105, note 48 (my translation).
12   See the telegram (probably early April) discussed in footnote 10.
13   Letter of 11 April 1927 (PSS); *SSCI*, 108–9 (my translation).
14   Letter to Stravinsky [of 22 April?], in ibid., 109–10. For more on Cocteau's dependence on Chanel at this period, see Steegmuller, *Cocteau*, 388–90.
15   Grigoriev claimed to have convinced Diaghilev that to stage a work for only three or four performances would make economic nonsense, while Kochno later told Richard Buckle that Diaghilev decided against staging because if the curtain rose on scenery, the audience would expect a ballet. But neither claim is convincing. Diaghilev had staged opera often enough before, and as for money, there was either none available for staging anyway, or it would be paid by someone else. See Grigoriev, *The Diaghilev Ballet*, 233–4; Buckle, *Diaghilev*, 486.
16   Stravinsky reported this increase in a letter to Diaghilev of 21 April (Kochno Archive). The princess had already indicated to Diaghilev that she would increase her contribution to this amount, but was still careful to insist that the outstanding sum (which had meanwhile also risen) had to be guaranteed as well. See Païchadze's letter of 7 April to Stravinsky (PSS). Since this offer seems to have been made just as Coco left Paris, one naturally assumes that Mme de Polignac knew her offer would not be matched in time, and had calculated that it would leave her as sole sponsor of a concert performance.

17 See Cocteau's letter to his mother of 19 January 1926, in *SSCI*, 95, note 39.

18 See his letter to Cocteau of 11 April 1927.

19 *Dial*, 25.

20 Letter of 11 April 1927.

21 Letter of 26 April 1927 (PSS); *SSCI*, 111 (my translation). Cocteau had been helping set up an exhibition of Theodore's paintings at the Galérie des Quatre Chemins.

22 Letter of 28 April 1927 (PSS); *SSCI*, 111–12 (my translation). Nevertheless nearly half a century later Kochno told Buckle that Diaghilev disliked Theodore's "conventional Greek temple-palace"; *Diaghilev*, 486.

23 Letter (undated) of about 30 April 1927 (PSS); *SSCI*, 112 (my translation).

24 Letter of 21 April 1927, in *MuzAk* 1996/3–4, 195. Diaghilev, who was still in Monte Carlo, did in fact make a donation.

25 Georges Lanskoy doubled the roles of Creon and the Messenger. Otto Klemperer's recollection (in Heyworth, *Conversations with Klemperer*, 60) that the accompaniment was played four-hands by Stravinsky and Prokofiev is not borne out by any other source. In fact, no authentic four-hand score of *Oedipus* exists.

26 For a good description and two photographs of the Polignac salon, see Brooks, "Nadia Boulanger and the Salon of the Princesse de Polignac," 422–5. Brooks is surely mistaken, though, in including *Renard* among the works that had their first performances there. I am grateful to Sylvia Kahan for confirming this point.

27 Nabokov, *Bagazh*, 166. For further details of the performance, see Walsh, *Stravinsky: Oedipus Rex*, 70.

28 *Dial*, 25.

29 Heyworth, *Conversations with Klemperer*, 60.

30 Charles Tenroc, in *Courrier musical*, 15 June 1927.

31 "Chronique musicale," *Nouvelle Revue française*, 29 (1 August 1927), 244–8.

32 *Dial*, 29–30.

33 Lourié, "Oedipus-Rex." The Russian version of the article appeared in *Vyörsti* several months later as part of the longer piece called "Dve operï Stravinskovo." For a view on the actual function of the Speaker, see Walsh, *Stravinsky: Oedipus Rex*, 30–1.

34 *Dial*, 25.

35 Beaumont, *Complete Book of Ballets*, 975.

36 *Dial*, 24–5.

37 "Beseda so Stravinskim," *Zhisn' iskusstva* (Leningrad), 14 June 1927, reprinted in *ISPS*, 74–7. The interview seems to have taken place before the first night of *Oedipus*. Was it the mood of tragedy, or memories of Sabaneyev's treachery, that prompted Stravinsky to allude in a roundabout way to Claudius in *Hamlet* (act 3, scene 3)?

> *My words fly up, my thoughts remain below:*
> *Words without thoughts never to heaven go.*

38 Letter of 10 August 1927, in *PMP*, 263–4.

39 Letter to Myaskovsky, 9 July 1928, in ibid., 281–2; Robinson (ed.), *Selected Letters of Sergei Prokofiev*, 274–5 (my translation).

40 See, for instance, the *Evening Standard*, 18 June. The BBC program consisted of the *Mavra* Overture, the Suite no. 1 for small orchestra, the 1919 *Firebird* Suite, and the Piano Concerto with Edward Clark conducting.

41 *Observer*, 19 June and 3 July 1927, respectively.

42 28 June 1927.

43 Goossens, *Overture and Beginners*, 246–7.

44 Letter of 6 April 1927, quoted in *SPD*, 275.

45 This took place only on 25 March 1928 at the Jolson Theatre, New York, in a production by Michio Ito for the League of Composers.

46 The additional information about the size of the room is in Engel's letter of 11 July, quoted in *SPD*, 275. Stravinsky had not been in touch with Bolm since the New York *Petrushka* of 1918–19.

47 *Chron*, 218–20, which also borrows the account of the opening scene from the sketch.
48 Letter of 15 July 1927, quoted in *SPD*, 300.
49 Letter of 29 June, in *SSCII*, 244.
50 Telegram and letter of 27 September (KA); the letter is in *MuzAk* 1996/3–4, 195. Stravinsky was leaving for Paris at teatime on the twenty-eighth.
51 Letter of 23 September 1927, in *PMP*, 264–6.
52 Lifar, *Serge Diaghilev*, 452–3 (and note); cf. *Chron*, 218–9.
53 Letter of 30 September 1927, quoted in Lifar, 452–3.
54 *Dial*, 32.
55 *Excelsior*, 27 October 1927. Lifar refers to the "anathema of Christ" remark as having been made in a letter to Diaghilev, but this may be a mistake of memory. See *Serge Diaghilev*, 237.
56 Letter to Ansermet of about 15 December 1927, in *CASII*, 140–1; *SSCI*, 188–9 (my translation).
57 *L'Intransigeant*, 2 December 1927.
58 Only the *Firebird* rolls were ever issued, but a letter of 21 February 1928 from G. W. Reed, Aeolian's deputy managing director in London, to Stravinsky refers to both works as being almost ready (PSS).
59 P. J. Petridis, *Musical Times*, 68 (1 December 1927), 1134.
60 See Stravinsky's letter to Ansermet of 31 July 1928, in *CASII*, 286 (wrongly dated to 1927 in *SSCI*, 188). The Pleyel fire, apparently caused by an electrical short-circuit, was on 19 July 1928.
61 *DB*, 38, entry for 24 November: "Igor arrives unexpectedly."
62 The final page of the draft score is reproduced in *SPD*, 274.
63 Letter of 9 July 1928, in *PMP*, 281; Robinson (ed.), *Selected Letters of Sergei Prokofiev*, 274–5 (my translation).
64 Probably on 23 January. See Stravinsky's telegram to Diaghilev of either the twenty-first (*SSCII*, 43, note 55) or twenty-second (Buckle, *Diaghilev*, 495).
65 *SSCII*, 43, note 55.

29 APOLLO IN THE LIBRARY

1 On 8 December, Schoenberg conducted the Colonne Orchestra in his *Pelleas und Melisande*, excerpts from *Gurrelieder*, a pair of Bach arrangements, and *Pierrot lunaire* (with Marya Freund and, presumably, members of the orchestra); on the fifteenth, *Pierrot* formed the centerpiece of a chamber program, with the Suite, the op. 6 songs, and a group of piano pieces played by Eduard Steuermann.
2 Letter of 9 December 1927 (PSS). Both Prunières and Schoenberg were Jews, like Lourié himself, and Lourié may have been unaware that Schoenberg was (also like himself) a Christian convert, albeit to Lutheranism.
3 *SRT*, 1587. See also *SPD*, 219–21, 288–91, and 632, note 52.
4 "Influence or Assistance," *Stravinsky: Glimpses of a Life*, 44, italics his. Craft does argue, nevertheless, that in his case the difference in age increased Stravinsky's dependence.
5 Nabokov, *Bagazh*, 166; Gojowy, *Arthur Lourié und der russische Futurismus*, 174–5.
6 Tamara was his second wife; according to Gojowy, his first wife, Jadwiga Cybulska, by whom he had a daughter, had died: ibid., 172. But as late as 1930 Lourié told Stravinsky that "I have had a distressing letter from my first wife in Moscow—she has heart disease and needs help" (letter of 7 October [PSS]).
7 8 May 1926 (PSS). He and Stravinsky always preserved the polite "vï" form of the second-person pronoun.
8 Letter of 5 September 1935 (PSS).
9 See bibliography. Lourié later wrote a polemic on the Capriccio for Piano and

65

Orchestra, which, he told Stravinsky, had come out "extremely venomous" (letter of 8 March 1930). Stravinsky told Ansermet that "I didn't much like Lourié's article this time" (letter of 20 April 1930, *CASII*, 232; *SSCI*, 212, my translation). Lourié's "Strawinsky à Bruxelles" is a brief introduction to the Symphony of Psalms.

10 *Muzyka* (Warsaw), no. 1 (1924), 15–17. Original in Polish; translated here from the Russian text in *ISPS*, 43–5.

11 *Almanach Nowej Sztuki* (Warsaw), no. 1 (1925), 43–4: *ISPS* 46–7.

12 Lourié, "La Sonate pour piano de Strawinsky," 100–1.

13 Lourié, "Muzïka Stravinskovo," 120; italics his.

14 Ibid., 133.

15 Ibid., 126.

16 Ibid., 130.

17 Lourié, "Muzïka Stravinskovo," 121.

18 Lourié, "Oedipus-Rex," 243.

19 Lourié, "Neogothic and Neoclassic," 6.

20 *Prager Presse,* 13 November 1924. Russian text in *ISPS*, 50–2.

21 Lourié, "Neogothic and Neoclassic," 7.

22 "A propos de l'*Apollon* d'Igor Strawinsky," 118.

23 Letter of 12 December 1927 (PSS); *SSCI*, 172, note 134 (my translation).

24 Unidentified cuttings in PSS. Coeuroy's piece is a review of the second concert. Schaeffner's apparent overfamiliarity seems to be a misprint.

25 *SSCIII*, 519.

26 A drawing and plan of the set are reproduced in Schouvaloff and Borovsky, *Stravinsky on Stage*, 128–9, and there is what looks like a photograph of the actual set in Heyworth, *Otto Klemperer*, vol. 1, 265.

27 *Zeitschrift für Musik*, 95 (April 1928), 216–7. Stravinsky later recalled that the Speaker wore a "black Pierrot costume" because, as the director told him, "in our country only the *Kapellmeister* is allowed to wear a *Frack*" (*Dial*, 25).

28 Adorno, "Berliner Memorial," *Neue Musik Zeitung*, 49 (1928), 419–20.

29 *Dial*, 25.

30 *Rul'*, 29 February 1928, reprinted in *ISPS*, 81–2; *Chron*, 225. An edited version of the *Rul'* interview appeared four weeks later in the Paris paper *Comoedia* (25 March); this French text is reprinted in Lesure (ed.), *Stravinsky: Etudes et témoignages*, 240–2.

31 Letter of 3 March 1928 (PSS); another, partial translation in *SSCI*, 190, note 193. See also Stravinsky's letter of 6 March to Bottenheim (PSS).

32 Adorno, "Berliner Memorial," 419.

33 "Stravinsky's *Oedipus—1928*," in Stein, *Style and Idea*, 482–3. The note is dated 24 February.

34 Heyworth, *Otto Klemperer*, vol. 1, 266.

35 Letter to Stravinsky of 15 March 1928 (PSS).

36 See Heyworth, op. cit., 266–7. Païchadze had been in Berlin with Stravinsky, as is indicated by a photograph in *IVSPA*, 72.

37 *Chron*, 232.

38 Letter of 8 April 1928 (PSS); *SSCII*, 42, note 53 (my translation).

39 Olin Downes, "Stravinsky Ballet in World Premiere," *New York Times*, 28 April 1928.

40 J.M. (presumably the paper's dance critic, John Martin), *New York Times*, 6 May 1928.

41 "New Stravinsky Ballet Brilliantly Performed," *Washington Post*, 28 April 1928.

42 *New York Times*, 6 May 1928.

43 The United States (concert) premiere, by the Boston Symphony Orchestra under Koussevitzky, was on 24 February 1928.

44 Nabokov, *Bagazh*, 165. "How Nabokov has wounded me by his complete indifference to *Apollo*," Stravinsky wrote to Souvtchinsky: letter of 13 June 1928 (PSS).

45 See Stravinsky's letter of 13 March 1928 to Païchadze: "I insist on *Apollon musagète* (and I guess that it's with Diaghilev that you've had this conversation)" (PSS). This

should be set against Craft's remark that *Apollo* was "the name that Stravinsky continued to prefer until the end of his life" (*SPD*, 275).

46 Nabokov, *Bagazh*, 162.

47 Lifar notes his "arrival" for rehearsals, as if he had come, like Nabokov, from a distance and for a lengthy stay (*Serge Diaghilev*, 466).

48 Letter to Balanchine of 22 November 1935, quoted in *SPD*, 275. Curiously enough, Craft quotes a (different) letter of 25 November 1935 in *SSCII* (313–4) as being Stravinsky's first to the choreographer since 1928.

49 Kochno claimed, however, that Bauchant never actually produced any drawings, and both the sets and the costumes were in the event adapted from existing Bauchant paintings. *Diaghilev and the Ballets Russes*, 266.

50 P.-B. Gheusi, in *Le Figaro*, 19 June 1928.

51 *Chron*, 233.

52 Lifar, *Serge Diaghilev*, 467.

53 *Dial*, 33.

54 Lifar, *Serge Diaghilev*, 468.

55 Henry Malherbe, *Le Temps*, 20 June 1928.

56 *Le Figaro*, 19 June 1928.

57 *Revue musicale* (1 July 1928), 287–8.

58 De Schloezer, "Chronique musicale," *Nouvelle Revue française*, 31 (1 July 1928), 104–8. The same remarks, slightly rephrased, conclude de Schloezer's book *Igor Stravinsky*.

59 Buckle, *Diaghilev*, 502.

60 14 June 1928. In *Dial*, 32, Stravinsky says that the cut was made "on tour," and this is apparently confirmed by his letter to Ansermet of 11 June 1929: *CASII*, 183, 187; *SSCI*, 196–7.

30 DEATH OF A SHOWMAN

1 Casella, full of himself as usual, reported that *The Nightingale* was "not too successful," while *La Giara*, which he conducted, "had a very gratifying success." See *Music in My Time*, 179. As for the Bellini evening, assuming the program order was as on the poster reproduced in *SPD* (280), the performance started at a quarter to nine with *Sonnambula*, and Stravinsky must have stepped onto the rostrum at about midnight.

2 Letter of 20 April, in *CASII*, 147. Craft misreads the words "quel morceau de musique" as "quel [sic] horreur de musique" (*SPD*, 605, note 50; *SSCI*, 191). But his sense is probably not far wrong.

3 Letter of 10 April 1928, in *CASII*, 145–6.

4 Letter of 20 April, ibid., 147.

5 Published under the pseudonym Igor Glebov (Leningrad: Muzgiz, 1929). Stravinsky's copy of the original Soviet edition is in PSS.

6 Asafyev, *A Book About Stravinsky*, 152; *Kniga o Stravinskom*, 213. For a brief commentary on the marginalia and a facsimile page, see V. Varunts, "Strawinsky protestiert . . ."; see also Craft's introduction to *A Book About Stravinsky*, vii–xvii.

7 Asafyev, *A Book About Stravinsky*, 161; *Kniga o Stravinskom*, 226.

8 He nevertheless told Prokofiev in 1934 that Asafyev's was the best book on his music. See Prokofiev's letter of 6 September 1934 to Asafyev, in Harlow Robinson (ed.), *Selected Letters of Sergei Prokofiev*, 137.

9 "The World of Music: *Oedipus Rex*," *Sunday Times*, 20 May 1928. The second performance seems to have come about because Stravinsky would not go to London for a single concert fee, so Païchadze himself subsidized the second fifty-guinea fee, initially without his knowledge, though the presence in PSS of a copy of his letter of 17 February 1928 to the BBC's head of music, Percy Pitt, suggests otherwise.

10 T&C, 227.

11 For a full account of this convoluted lawsuit, see SSCII, 471–4.

12 The orchestra for Petrushka is not credited. Louis Cyr suggests that it was the London Symphony Orchestra, which could not be named as it was under contract to HMV (see the insert booklet with the CD reissue by Pearl, GEMM CD 9329). For the Firebird recording, the Walter Straram Concerts Orchestra was used (see Stuart, Igor Stravinsky: The Composer in the Recording Studio, 27). Two days later, Stravinsky also recorded two sides of excerpts from Pulcinella.

13 Les Nouvelles littéraires, 8 December 1928; reprinted in Lesure (ed.), Stravinsky: Etudes et témoignages, 247–50. Stravinsky seems to be explaining why the necessary timings could not be achieved by slowing down or speeding up the machinery.

14 The new Pleyel contract, dated 30 June 1928 (PSS), included a monthly advance of thirty thousand francs.

15 Chron, 235–7.

16 Letter to Ansermet of 11 August 1928, in CASII, 154; SSCI, 192.

17 Letter of 25 August 1928 (PSS).

18 Letter to Ramuz, 11 August 1928, in SSCIII, 93.

19 Letter to Ansermet, 7 August 1928, in CASII, 151; SSCI, 192 (my translation).

20 Letter of 12 July 1928, quoted in SPD, 284–5 (where it is misdated 12 August). Denise Strawinsky has recently claimed that Andersen's story was suggested by Svetik. See T. and D. Strawinsky, Au coeur du Foyer, 117.

21 Chron, 239–40.

22 See Stravinsky's letter of 24 July 1928 to Païchadze, acknowledging receipt of the songs and complaining of the anxiety the delay had cost him (PSS).

23 Chron, 241.

24 According to a telegram of 30 August 1928 from Païchadze (PSS).

25 Letter of 18 October 1928 (PSS). The piano score was finished on the sixteenth.

26 Ibid.

27 Letter of 6 October, Sviatoslav Stravinsky to Païchadze (PSS). Svetik was also acting as copyist for the new ballet.

28 Letter of 17 October 1928, quoted in SPD, 285.

29 Letter of 20 October 1928 (PSS).

30 Letter of 22 November 1928 to Souvtchinsky (PSS).

31 Revue musicale, 10, no. 3 (January 1929), 242–3.

32 Letter of 28 November 1928 to Lifar; quoted in Lifar, Serge Diaghilev, 476–7.

33 Letter of 10 August 1928, in MuzAk 1996/3–4, 196; SSCII, 43 (my translation).

34 Letter of 15 August 1928 to Diaghilev; MuzAk 1996/3–4, 196–7; SSCII, 44–5 (my translation).

35 Letter of 15 August.

36 Boris Kochno, unpublished memoir (Preface) (KA).

37 Vozrozhdeniya, 18 December 1928, reprinted in Zilbershteyn and Samkov, vol. 1, 250–2; also Stravinsky's letter to Païchadze of 20 December 1928 (PSS). A cutting of the article, with the composer's marginalia, is in PSS.

38 Letter of 11 January 1929 to Païchadze (PSS). Stravinsky's particular complaint was that Ida was giving only a single performance of The Fairy's Kiss in Monte Carlo. A few weeks earlier in Brussels she had effectively sabotaged the piece with scene-changing breaks of several minutes between the tableaux of what is, musically, a continuous score.

39 See Stravinsky's letter to Ansermet, 11 June 1929, in CASII, 183; SSCI, 196–7.

40 Letter to Ansermet, 19 June 1929, CASII, 187–8; SSCI, 197–8 (my translation).

41 Letter of 8 [or probably 9] August 1928, in CASII, 152–3.

42 Letter of 19 February [1929], in ibid., 172.

43 Letter of 11 October 1928 (PSS).

44 See Stravinsky's letter of 14 October 1928 to Pellier (PSS) and his telegram of 15 October to Ansermet, in CASII, 161.

45 It also included Mozart's "Linz" Symphony and Prokofiev's D Major Violin Concerto played by Szigeti.

46 See Ansermet's letter of 23 September 1928 to Stravinsky, in *CASII*, 157–8.

47 Letter of 3 March 1929 to Stravinsky, in ibid., 175–6.

48 See his review of the inaugural concerts in *Nouvelle Revue française*, 16, no. 183 (1 December 1928), 883–6. Other points in this paragraph are also indebted to de Schloezer's review.

49 Letter of 1 January 1929; also Stravinsky's reply of 4 January; *CASII*, 163–7; *SSCI*, 195 (Stravinsky's letter only).

50 Letter of 27 December 1928; see also Lourié's earlier letter of 22 December (both PSS). The concerts were on the twenty-first and the twenty-third.

51 Letter to Ansermet of 16 February 1929, in *CASII*, 171; *SSCI*, 202–3 misdates the letter to November.

52 Heyworth, *Otto Klemperer*, vol. 1, 307.

53 *Weltstadt*, 24 June 1929.

54 Rolland, *Journal des années de guerre*, 61.

55 He conducted *The Soldier's Tale* and played the Piano Sonata and Serenade.

56 See *Serge Diaghilev*, 492–504, for Lifar's remarkably self-advertising account of the first night and the events leading up to it. Sylvia Kahan, the leading authority on the princesse de Polignac, told me that *Renard* was possibly, but not certainly, also played at the Polignac soirée the previous evening, along with Prokofiev's *The Prodigal Son*.

57 Buckle, *Diaghilev*, 518.

58 The concert was given twice, on 31 May and 1 June. See Monteux's letter of 31 March 1930 (*SSCII*, 67) for the suggestion that Stravinsky did not attend.

59 *Mem*, 29, note 1; *Dial*, 132.

60 Quoted in *SRT*, 393.

61 Letter to Stravinsky of 8 February 1931 (PSS).

62 Letter of 11 June 1929, in *CASII*, 183–6; *SSCI*, 197 (my translation).

63 Letter of 19 June, in *CASII*; *SSCI*, 197–8.

64 *Expo*, 85.

65 Buckle, *Diaghilev*, 525.

66 Letter to Ansermet of 16 July 1929, in *CASII*, 190–1; *SSCI*, 198–9.

67 Letter of 26 August; partial facsimile in Sotheby's sale catalogue "Ballet Material and Manuscripts from the Serge Lifar Collection," London, 9 May 1984, lot 225. Stravinsky says that he had only heard about the death two days after it happened. But since he also calls "today" (the twenty-sixth) the "ninth day of his death," it looks as if he may have thought that Diaghilev had died on the seventeenth.

68 Letter of 30 August 1929, in *Mem*, 47.

69 Zilbershteyn and Samkov, vol. 1, 259.

70 Letter of 23 July 1929, quoted in Markevitch, *Etre et avoir été*, 184–5.

31 A PASSAGE OF RIGHTS

1 Letter of 11 September 1929, in *PMP*, 319–20. See also letter of 21 January 1929, ibid., 290–1. English translations in Robinson (ed.), *Selected Letters of Sergei Prokofiev*, 284–5, 278.

2 Letter of 25 September 1929 to Georg Kugel (PSS).

3 Lausanne: Mermod, 1929. Ramuz and Mermod were among Stravinsky's visitors this summer at Echarvines.

4 *SPD*, 172.

5 Letter of 16 December 1928; see ibid., also *SSCIII*, 96–7. French text in Guisan, *C.-F. Ramuz, ses amis et son temps*, 191.

6 *L'Instrumental*, January 1929. The extensive account includes transcripts of reports

from other newspapers, among whom there is disagreement over whether Stravinsky conducted *Firebird* or *Petrushka,* and some consequent ambiguity as to whether he was actually present directing a live demonstration in addition to the film clip. The gala was on 15 December.

7 Letter of 25 March 1929 (PSS). The passage about *The Firebird* is quoted in *SPD,* 58, but misdated.

8 Letter of 21 June 1929, quoted briefly in *SPD,* 71. Stravinsky's letter to Benois of 21 November 1911 makes the actual position (though not the eventual percentages) crystal clear. "The author of the music of a ballet usually gets three-quarters, and the author of the libretto one-quarter, but since we were half-and-half authors of this, each of us gets half of that quarter." It goes on, significantly: "As regards *Firebird,* the author of the libretto is considered to be Fokine, who will receive the whole quarter. I beg you to sign everything where marked in pencil, and also do me a favor and ask Fokine to do the same—or better, to avoid error, have him do it in your presence. I count on you for this and thank you in advance." *SM,* 464–5.

9 Letter from J. Raulet ("Avocat à la Cour") to Païchadze, 4 July 1929 (PSS). Taruskin asserts that there was a lawsuit over the *Petrushka* rights (*SRT,* 671). But Païchadze was simply taking counsel's opinion.

10 For instance, he told the Barcelona concert agent Clemente Lozano not to program *Les Noces* in French, because the text had too many wrong accentuations (letter of 6 August 1929, quoted in *SPD,* 145). Stravinsky's own recordings of both works are all in English.

11 See Ramuz's letters of 18 and 30 September and 31 October 1929, in *SSCIII,* 98–9.

12 ". . . la tradition de l'exécution (non de l'interprétation) de mon oeuvre," expressly refuting the terms of the Monteux advertisement. The same statement appeared in Columbia brochures of the time.

13 Letter of 15 January 1930 (PSS). In French the "creator" of a work is the musician who gives its first performance *(création).*

14 See the relevant correspondence (February to April 1930), in PSS; *SSCII,* 66–9 (my translation).

15 See Vera's letter of 23 January 1930 to Ansermet, quoted in *SSCI,* 201, note 231; and Ansermet's telegram of 24 January to Stravinsky: "Barring bankruptcy OSP Paris plan certain to happen" (*CASII,* 205). Monteux's first letter, about his Brussels refusal, is dated 3 February.

16 Telegram of 11 April 1930, in *SSCII,* 68.

17 Letter of 17 April 1930, in ibid., 69. André Schaeffner, the OSP's artistic secretary, had written to Stravinsky on the twelfth, hinting that Monteux was in a jealous and insecure frame of mind but might be open to persuasion. See also Stravinsky's letter of 14 April to Ansermet, in *CASII,* 216–7 (wrongly dated 14 March); *SSCI,* 209.

18 Telegram of 22 April 1930, quoted by Stravinsky in his letter of that date to Ansermet, *CASII,* 234; *SSCI,* 212–3. See also Stuart, *Igor Stravinsky: The Composer in the Recording Studio,* 7.

19 Letter of 24 April, in *CASII,* 235; *SSCI,* 213–4 (my translation). The Capriccio recording was made on 8, 9, and 10 May.

20 Nabokov, "La Vie et l'oeuvre de Serge de Diaghilew." Stravinsky's sharp correction appeared in the following issue. For the subsequent exchange, see *SSCII,* 368, and *SPD,* 293, which quotes a letter from Maritain to Stravinsky interceding on Nabokov's behalf.

21 The phrase is from his letter of 14 July 1929 to Païchadze (PSS).

22 Benois, "Maslyanitsa." Stravinsky's copy (of the first part only of the two-part article) is in PSS.

23 Letter of 5 April 1930 (PSS). Stravinsky was right in predicting that the Albatross negotiations would come to nothing.

24 Letter of 17 May 1930 (PSS).

25 Letter of 17 August 1929 (PSS). See also Stravinsky's letter of 10 August to Strecker, in *SSCIII*, 220–1.

26 See *SSCII*, 270–4 and 284–92, for the relevant correspondence.

27 See, for instance, his letter of 25 October 1928 to Ramuz, in *SSCIII*, 94.

28 See Dmitry's letter of 8 December to Katya, in *SSCII*, 285–6.

29 See especially Païchadze's letter of 28 October 1930, in ibid., 274. Païchadze had learnt of Stravinsky's anxiety from Vera, so the possibility cannot be ruled out that the anxiety was actually hers (since Ira Belline was one of her closest friends).

30 Letter of 5 January 1931 to Igor Stravinsky, in ibid., 275.

31 Letter of 21 August 1929 to Stravinsky, in *CASII*, 193.

32 Misia Sert, *Two or Three Muses*, 163.

33 Bischoff, "Le Peintre Théodore Strawinsky."

34 See Cingria's letter of 2 [July?] 1930 to his brother Alexandre, in *Correspondance générale*, vol. 2, 116.

35 Ramuz's letters to the composer often include compliments to or about Theodore: for instance, "He seems to me to be turning out very well. . . . He is lively, he is bright; he is perhaps a little too intelligent!" (letter of 13 July 1925, PSS). In general, as in this case, such remarks about Stravinsky's children are omitted from *SSC*.

36 Letters of 8, 13, and 15 March 1930 (PSS). At this time, Lourié was, he said, seeing Theodore almost every day.

37 *DB*, 44; entry for 16 March 1930.

38 Letter of 9 May 1930 (BN, Boulanger Archive).

39 Letter of 8 April 1931 to Nadia Boulanger (BN, Boulanger Archive).

40 For much of this information, see *SPD*, 296, where, however, "Ascension" (*Vozneseniye*) must be a misreading of *Voskreseniye* ("Resurrection"). In 1930 Russian Easter fell on the same day as its Western equivalent, 20 April.

41 See Stravinsky's letter of 14 September 1929 to Païchadze (PSS), partially quoted in *SPD*, 294.

42 See his letter of 23 August 1929, excusing himself in advance (PSS).

43 Letter of 20 August 1930 (PSS). Lourié described the scene at the Koussevitzky's in hilarious detail in a letter of 25 September. Both letters are extensively quoted in *SSCI*, 216–7, note 275 (with the August letter quoted here wrongly dated to September).

44 Letter of 21 April 1932 (PSS).

45 Quoted in Heyworth, *Otto Klemperer*, vol. 1, 308.

46 Letter of 6 February 1930 (PSS). The concert had taken place that evening and also included the two early ballet suites and the suites for small orchestra.

47 *Mem*, 87.

48 *DB*, 44.

49 *Prager Presse*, 23 February 1930. See also *IVSPA*, 77.

50 *Musical America*, 10 January 1925.

51 *Prager Presse*, 23 February 1930.

52 The concert, conducted by Ansermet, was on the nineteenth.

53 *SPD*, 296.

54 Nabokov, *Bagazh*, 166–70. It must be said that Nabokov's account of the "choir" incident (which he says inspired the ending of the whole work) is hard to reconcile with the sketches, which show that it was the second movement which Stravinsky worked on and finished at this time (17 July). The finale, written first, had been completed at Easter. But in any case the memoir (if not a wholesale fabrication) refutes Craft's claim in *SSCII*, 371, that Nabokov and Stravinsky did not meet between 1928 and 1942.

55 In *Expo* (70–1), and again in *Dial* (44), Stravinsky perhaps understandably confuses Charavines with Echarvines, and Craft makes the same mistake in *SPD*, 296.

56 In an interview for *L'Etoile belge* (22 May 1930), he had referred to the symphony of psalms he was writing, but with small letters—as it were, descriptively rather than in the sense of a title.

57   Letter of 3 September 1930 to Ansermet, in *CASII*, 245–6; *SSCI*, 216–7 (my transla-
       tion). The exclamation mark implies "What do you expect of a conductor who can't
       play the piano?"
58   His attendance at the Schoenberg concert is recorded in *DB*, 51, though Vera does
       not mention the *Begleitmusik*, referring only to Schoenberg's Bach (sic in the original
       diary; that is, the "St. Anne" Prelude and Fugue). See Heyworth, *Otto Klemperer*,
       vol. 1, 333.
59   12 November 1930, quoted in Heyworth, op. cit., 349.
60   15 November 1930. Stravinsky's protest was accompanied by others in the same
       issue, notably from Hindemith, Weill, and Thomas Mann.
61   The Berlin premiere was on 19 February; the Paris premiere, conducted by Stravin-
       sky in the Théâtre des Champs-Elysées, on the twenty-fourth.

32   THE AGE OF ANXIETY

1   De Schloezer, "Chronique musicale," *Nouvelle Revue française*, 31 (1 July 1928), 106;
       Igor Stravinsky, 175.
2   *SPD*, 211.
3   Letter of 15 August 1928, in *Muz Ak* 1996/3–4, 196–7; *SSCII*, 44–5.
4   The inventory is reproduced in *SSCI*, 386–8.
5   *Expo*, 76. But Craft is unduly optimistic when he suggests that Father Nikolay's let-
       ters are "the principal source for the study of the composer's religious life at the
       time" (*SSCII*, 42, note 54). In fact they are mainly concerned with local church
       matters.
6   Letter of 6 December 1931 to Archbishop Serafim; quoted in *SSCI*, 388, note 8. The
       draft in PSS is in Vera's hand.
7   De Schloezer, "Chronique musicale," 106.
8   "Igor Strawinsky: Compositeur chrétien," *Le Vingtième Siècle*, 27 May 1930.
9   Nabokov, *Bagazh*, 168.
10   Letter of 22 November 1930 (PSS). The concert was on the twenty-fourth.
11   Letter of 28 November 1930 (PSS).
12   Dushkin, "Working with Stravinsky," in Corle, *Igor Stravinsky*, 180.
13   *Chron*, 268–70.
14   Letter of 22 December 1930 (PSS).
15   *SSCIII*, 222, note 11. Craft dates this to November, but Stravinsky was not in Holland
       at any time that month. He went to Amsterdam after the second Brussels perfor-
       mance of the Symphony of Psalms on 14 December.
16   See for instance his letter of 30 March 1931 (PSS).
17   Letter of 13 February 1931 (PSS).
18   Letter of 30 September 1931 (PSS).
19   Letter of 13 July 1931 (PSS).
20   For instance, he conducted in Darmstadt in November for 250 dollars, about half his
       usual fee.
21   Letter of 24 August 1931 to Stravinsky (PSS); *SSCIII*, 219 (my translation).
22   L. A. Soper, "Stravinsky Returns to Himself," *Christian Science Monitor*, 20 Decem-
       ber 1930.
23   Guy Bernard de La Pierre, *La Revue nouvelle*, 66 (March 1931), 108–11.
24   Robert Brussel, *Le Figaro*, 2 March 1931.
25   De Schloezer, "Chronique musicale," *Nouvelle Revue française*, 36 (1 April 1931),
       623–5.
26   Ansermet, *Les Fondements de la musique dans la conscience humaine*, vol. 1, 498.
27   *Il Piccolo di Trieste*, 23 April 1931; quoted in *IVSPA*, 21.
28   *DB*, 51. On the way to London, Stravinsky had come straight from concerts in Berlin,
       Winterthur, and Lausanne.

29 See Stravinsky's letter of 7 February 1931, in *SSCIII*, 224. The relevant correspondence with Mrs. Courtauld, and with Pedro Tillett and Edward Clark of the BBC, is in PSS.

30 Undated letter of late February 1931 (PSS).

31 *Musical Times*, 72 (1 March 1931), 262. See also Evans's letter of 30 December 1930 to Stravinsky, in *SSCII*, 123; also Stravinsky's letter of 2 January 1931 to Ansermet, grumbling about Evans, in *CASIII*, 1; *SSCI*, 219.

32 See *SSCII*, 123, note 6, for details of this short-lived collaboration. I am grateful to Peter Faint for additional information. Stravinsky's own account of the episode, which refers to the concert but not the recording session, is in *Expo*, 82, note 1. No copy of the recording—if indeed one was made—appears to have survived.

33 *Dial*, 46.

34 Nabokov, *Bagazh*, 167.

35 Dushkin, "Working with Stravinsky," in Corle, 186–7.

36 Ibid., 182.

37 Ibid., 186.

38 Ibid., 185.

39 See Grigory Belyankin's letter to Stravinsky of 23 May 1931, in *SSCII*, 275.

40 Ibid., 288–9.

41 *DB*, 53. The Russian word is *razgovorï* (talks).

42 At least, it has an iron grille today, and much graffiti on the walls. The house is now a "media" library—the Médiathèque Stravinski—with a rather incongruous modern extension, and the lane outside is the rue Igor Stravinski.

43 *Berliner Börsen-Courier*, quoted in *SPD*, 300. Strobel was at La Vironnière on the twenty-third.

44 *Chron*, 274.

45 Letter to Strecker of 15 September 1931, in *SSCIII*, 228.

46 Ibid.

47 See Stravinsky's letters of 3 October 1931 to Strecker (PSS; *SSCIII*, 228, my translation) and the Berlin Radio (PSS), respectively. Seven months earlier Stravinsky had told ERM's Berlin director F. V. Weber: "The fact that Furtwängler will play *Petrushka* on his German tour is good news for you but not for me, as I am not an admirer of this conductor." Letter of 2 March 1931 (PSS); quoted in *SSCI*, 396, note 7.

48 Païchadze's letter is dated 5 September 1931; Stravinsky's, undated, belongs to the first weeks in Voreppe (PSS: Stravinsky's letter is located after Païchadze's on film 83, frames 0068–9).

49 Letter of 3 October (PSS), a day on which Stravinsky was perfectly well enough to write in person to Strecker and the Berlin Radio, as we have seen.

50 For a superb photograph of the auditorium during the performance of *Apollo*, see *DB*, 56. The apparent lack of any gangways would give a modern safety officer apoplexy. It is also worth noting that some wind players of the Radio Orchestra appear to be already in their seats for the strings-only ballet score, which opened the program.

51 Heyworth, *Otto Klemperer*, vol. 1, 355.

52 *Berliner Tageblatt*, 24 October 1931.

53 Letter to Stravinsky of 2 November 1931, quoted in *SSCII*, 297, note 20.

54 Letter of 1 January 1932, in *CASIII*, 13–14. Stravinsky wrote in the margin: "I can well believe it with this orchestra which gets itself insulted by everyone!" In *Mem*, 152, he recalled that Hindemith "bravely chastised the Berlin Radio Orchestra for its bad playing of my new violin concerto."

55 A.W., *Vorwärts*, 26 October 1931.

56 *Zeitschrift für Musik* (December 1931); quoted in Joan Evans, "Die Rezeption der Musik Igor Strawinskys in Hitlerdeutschland."

57 Stravinsky gave two Courtauld-Sargent concerts in the Queen's Hall, on 16 and 17 November, conducting the Violin Concerto and the Symphony of Psalms in both.

Only six weeks later, Stravinsky heard from Dushkin that Mrs. Courtauld had died suddenly.

58 R. Maritain, *Journal de Raïssa*, 198.

59 Letter of 8 July 1931, quoted in *SPD*, 272.

60 See Steegmuller, *Cocteau*, 405 et seq., for these and other details on *Le Sang d'un poète*.

61 Dushkin, "Working with Stravinsky," 189.

62 The violin *Suite italienne* is dated 18 July, while the cello suite, which has the same title, was completed by 1 August, when Stravinsky announced its dispatch to Païchadze.

63 Dushkin, "Working with Stravinsky," 188.

64 *Chron*, 275.

65 Ibid., 277.

66 White, *Stravinsky: The Composer and His Works*, 373.

67 See the relevant correspondence in *SSCIII*, 113–4, including Cingria's remarks about the Duo, and his description of the trouble he had had writing the book the previous summer, i.e., 1932. Cingria also wrote to his brother Alexandre on Christmas Day 1932 announcing that "the book is out" and adding that "the Stravinskys—but especially Igor—are taking an enormous interest in this book" (*Correspondance générale*, vol. 2, 145–8).

68 *Pesti Hirlap*, about 29 March 1933, in *IVSPA*, 23.

69 *Chron*, 278.

70 Szigeti, *With Strings Attached*, 124. He told Prokofiev, at the time, that the thinking was "compressed and concentrated 'like a diamond.' " See Prokofiev's letter to Boris Asafyev of 8 June 1932, in Harlow Robinson (ed.), *Selected Letters of Sergei Prokofiev*, 127–8.

71 See his letter to Strecker of 20 February and Strecker's handwritten reply of the twenty-third (PSS). Stravinsky's letter (much abridged) is in *SSCIII*, 231.

72 As early as 18 April 1932, he had written to Strecker that he and Dushkin were working on "un joli Kammerabend," including the Duo, the new suite, the Danse russe from *Petrushka*, the Berceuse from *The Firebird*, and the duo version of the concerto. The *Firebird* scherzo (The Princesses' Game with the Golden Apples) and the two *Nightingale* pieces (a portmanteau version of the songs of the Nightingale and the Chinese March) followed in the late summer.

73 Strecker, whom Stravinsky often sent on shopping errands, had written on 6 April that "I still have a little automatic shutter release belonging to your camera, and I will personally send it to you in Paris at the next opportunity" (PSS); *SSCIII*, 232, note 23 (my translation).

74 See Ansermet's telegram of 17 June and Stravinsky's reply of 14 July, in *CASIII*, 21–2; another translation of Stravinsky's letter is in *SSCI*, 221.

75 Letter of 5/18 June [sic] 1932 (BN: Boulanger Archive); Nadia's letter has not survived. The form of the date seems to indicate that Stravinsky now firmly accepted the eighteenth as the NS equivalent of his birthday, even though Ansermet's telegram suggests that the seventeenth was also still, so to speak, in circulation. Stravinsky would have celebrated on the seventeenth in Berlin with his parents in 1897, but presumably on the eighteenth when he arrived in Paris in 1910.

76 *SPD*, 299.

77 For their full itinerary, see *SSCII*, 191–2, note 14. In Biarritz, they renewed acquaintance with Eugenia Errazuriz, who was living there and was evidently a patron of the concert.

78 Letter of 18 September 1932 (PSS); *SSCII*, 190 (my translation).

79 Letter to W. A. Bradley, 24 September 1932 (PSS); *SSCII*, 491 (my translation).

80 See Stravinsky's letter to Strecker of 14 September 1932, in *SSCIII*, 234.

81 Letter to Detmar Walther of 19 September 1932 (PSS).

82 Letter of 19 September 1932 (PSS); *SSCIII*, 234–5, note 28 (my translation).

83 Letter of August or September 1932, quoted in *SSCII*, 298.

84 Letter of 27 March 1930, in *10 Komp*, vol. 3, 74–6. The letter is translated in *SSCIII*, 168, but with this passage omitted.

85 Craft says this transcription was made at Fontainebleau in autumn 1933. But as it was not programmed until the French tour of December 1934 (starting at Strasbourg on the twelfth), and they would certainly have played it if it had been ready, the assumption must be either that it was not finished until 1934, or that Dushkin was taking time to prepare it. The first performance of the orchestral version that I can trace was in an OSP concert which Stravinsky conducted in the Salle Pleyel on 4 November 1934, when it was simply called "Fragments from the ballet *Le Baiser de la fée.*"

86 *Berliner Tageblatt*, 1 November 1932.

33   DESCENT AND REBIRTH

1   "Strawinsky unterwegs nach Wien," *Die Stunde*, 17 March 1926.

2   *SPD*, 551. No doubt the fear was unjustified, at least before 1934.

3   *Journal de Genève*, 15 November 1928; reprinted in Lesure (ed.), *Stravinsky: Etudes et témoignages*, 242–6.

4   Joan Evans, *Hans Rosbaud: A Bio-Bibliography*, 17.

5   Letter of 10 February 1931 (PSS).

6   *Dial*, 51.

7   So he reported to Stravinsky in a letter of (probably) 10 February 1933, quoted in *SSCII*, 300. Schaal wrote to Stravinsky (15 April 1933) that because of a new amnesty law promulgated after the incident, the police were not proceeding against the assailants, even though the identity of at least one of them was known. But on 9 December he sent a newspaper cutting which revealed that this individual, one Werner von Alvensleben, had been arrested for trying to blow up the security chief of the Austrian Tyrol. So, he concluded, they had got off fairly lightly. See Schaal's correspondence with Stravinsky in PSS.

8   A year later, in April 1934, Stravinsky composed an unaccompanied setting of the Slavonic Ave Maria—"Bogoroditse devo"—in Fairchild's memory, and he conducted it, together with his Lord's Prayer and Creed settings, at a memorial concert in the Salle Gaveau on 18 May.

9   Letter of 29 March 1933 (PSS); *SSCIII*, 236, note 29 (my translation).

10 Letter of 14 April 1933 (PSS); *SSCIII*, 235–6 (my translation).

11 Letter of 18 April 1933 (PSS); ibid., 236–7, note 29 (my translation).

12 Letter of 20 July 1933, in ibid., 237, note 30.

13 Letter of 18 April 1933 (PSS); ibid., 218 (my translation).

14 Letters of 18 April and 20 July (passage not in *SSCIII*). Dushkin told Craft that Willy Strecker was neither a member nor a sympathizer of the Nazi Party, but that his brother Ludwig was both; see *SSCIII*, 218.

15 Letter of 7 September 1933, quoted in Taruskin, "The Dark Side of Modern Music" (but misdated "April") (my translation).

16 Craft, "Jews and Geniuses," 276. The letter's continuation is admittedly another matter. "I don't know," Stravinsky remarks, "if mine will be the last name on the list of signatories to this appeal [on behalf of Klemperer, Walter, and others], which is very important as I don't want to risk seeing myself later alongside such gentry as Milhaud, or other trash building careers on other people's backs."

17 25 August 1928 (PSS). Craft may be special-pleading when he claims that "anti-Semitic remarks between White Russians, like anti-*goy* remarks between Jews, are not invariably, or even usually . . . expressions of deep hatred" ("Jews and Geniuses," 275). They remain, after all, anti-Semitic, but in an inert, incantatory sense, like tales of sexual prowess exchanged by pub drunks.

18 According to Craft: "He loathed the Nazis, and filled scrapbooks with newspaper photographs of Himmler and Goering in ridiculous poses, adding captions such as *'cons'* and *'derrières'* " (*SPD*, 553). But this may, of course, have been at a later date.

19 Quoted in Sachs, *Music in Fascist Italy*, 168.

20 *Expo*, 88–9.

21 Milton Widder, "Igor Stravinsky—Small Body but a Giant Brain," *Cleveland Press*, 20 February 1937 (cutting in PSS).

22 Sachs, op. cit., 168.

23 Letter of 30 August 1933 (PSS). De Paoli was also advising Stravinsky on the best time to visit Turin for the exposition of the Holy Shroud that year. But it seems he did not go.

24 Letter of 5 October 1933 from the Italian vice-consul in Grenoble (PSS).

25 See Taruskin, "The Dark Side of Modern Music," 30, for a detailed discussion of this incident not as "an inspiring saga of political courage in the face of despotism, but [as] a rather less edifying spectacle of two Duci engaged in a protracted battle of wills."

26 See above, chapter 27.

27 *Dial*, 42. Stravinsky recalled starting the Concerto for Two Solo Pianos in 1931, after finishing the Violin Concerto. But the sketches support the later dating. According to Denise Strawinsky, the idea for the work came from Svetik himself. See T. and D. Strawinsky, *Au coeur du Foyer*, 133.

28 *DB*, 53.

29 The leaflet was enclosed with Stravinsky's letter of 9 October 1931 (Stadtbibliothek Winterthur), which also reveals that Reinhart was already working on the idea of a show for Theodore.

30 See his letter to Stravinsky of 18 November 1932.

31 Stravinsky repeated his letter of 26 May 1933 on 25 August. Both copies are in the Stadtbibliothek Winterthur.

32 See Prokofiev's letter to Myaskovsky of 18 February 1933, in *PMP*, 395–6; Robinson (ed.), *Selected Letters of Sergei Prokofiev*, 307. The Prokofiev concert was on 10 December, and *On the Dnieper* opened on the sixteenth.

33 *Expo*, 66. The Salle Gaveau concert was on 11 December 1932.

34 Cingria, *Pétrarque*, 160.

35 Ibid., 121, quoting Nietzsche's *The Birth of Tragedy*.

36 Ibid., 41–3. A sequence was originally a wordless melodic extension of a sung "Alleluia" in the church liturgy. Later, rhyming texts were added to such melodies, and this is the origin of liturgical sequences like the Dies Irae.

37 Letter of 24 September 1911 (OS): *SM*, 464; *PRK*, 300–1.

38 Cingria, *Pétrarque*, 46, 71–3. An autograph copy of Stravinsky's draft is reproduced in facsimile, with a note by Robert Craft (to whom Stravinsky presented the copy in 1949), in *SSCI*, 370–8.

39 Cingria, *Pétrarque*, 47–54. The book also prints part of an organ canzona by Banchieri (65) and a recitative from Gluck's *Orphée* (124–5), but *pace* Craft (*SSCI*, 370) nothing by Bardi or Caccini.

40 As well as a brief excursion with Vera to the Czech city of Ostrava, where he played the Capriccio under Jaroslav Vogel on 26 January.

41 Letter of 24 January 1933, in *SPD*, 314. Gide had lectured on Dostoyevsky at Copeau's Vieux-Colombier in 1922.

42 Stravinsky is supposed to have told Gide: "I can get on completely with you, but I could never collaborate with that atheist Valéry" (Van Rysselberghe, *Les Cahiers de la petite dame: 1929–1937*, quoted in Pollard, "*Sit Tityrus Orpheus:* Gide et la musique," 51–2). But it is hard to believe that Stravinsky was unaware of Gide's communism, however ignorant he may have been of his revolt against his childhood Calvinism.

43 The Roman forms match the Latin name of the heroine in this early version: Proserpina. Gide had offered the text to Dukas in 1904. But Dukas, who was writing his

Maeterlinck opera, *Ariane et Barbe-bleu*, declined. Later, in the spring of 1913, Gide tried to interest Diaghilev in the piece; but a planned reading for some reason did not take place. See Pollard, introduction to *André Gide: "Proserpine" (drame), "Perséphone" (mélodrame)*, 27–8; also Moutote, "Gide, Valéry et la musique."

44 Letter of 8 February 1933 (PSS); *SSCIII*, 187 (my translation).

45 Letter of 5 March 1933, in *SSCIII*, 189.

46 Letter of 24 February 1933 (PSS); *SSCIII*, 188 (my translation).

47 Letter of 5 March 1933.

48 The typescript is reproduced in facsimile, with annotations by Craft, in *SSCIII*, 490–507.

49 Gide, *Notes sur Chopin*, 53.

50 *Mem*, 75. After reading the prepublished text, then hearing the performance, André Schaeffner enquired caustically: "Why doesn't he also ask for the music to do pee-pee on command?" (letter to Stravinsky, 13 May 1934 [PSS]).

51 But "do we have to believe," Pollard asks somewhat wearily, "that its humanitarian concerns make the piece a 'communist allegory'? . . . If we must invoke communism, let us rather speak of that 'Gidean communism' which sums up his faith in humanity." Introduction to *André Gide: "Proserpine" (drame), "Perséphone" (mélodrame)*, 45. Nevertheless for Stravinsky, at the time, the mere suspicion would have been disturbing enough.

52 The day after meeting Gide in Wiesbaden, he told a Munich interviewer that "I was never a Communist, materialist, atheist, or Bolshevik, as is frequently said of me." *Münchner Telegramm Zeitung und Sport-Telegraf*, 2 February 1933, translation in *IVSPA*, 22.

53 *SSCIII*, 476.

54 *Pesti Hirlap*, about 29 March 1933; in *IVSPA*, 23.

55 Stravinsky had refused to take part in a Salle Pleyel concert of works commissioned by the princesse de Polignac on 21 March, two days after his OSP concert, possibly because he had been led to believe that he was expected to appear without fee. See her letter of 9 January and the OSP's of 19 January (PSS).

56 See, for example, the letter of 19 December 1932 from the Viennese agency ITHMA to Stravinsky (PSS).

57 If Ida's invitation of 1 April worked out, Debussy's widow (Emma Bardac) and Nadia Boulanger were also at the dinner.

58 *Dial*, 47.

59 Letter of 7 July, quoted in *SPD*, 316.

60 Ibid. But the assumption that it was the rue Viète flat Ida had found is mine.

61 See Ansermet's letters of 27 and 30 June 1933, with Stravinsky's handwritten replies in the margins, printed in facsimile in *CASIII*, 31–4.

62 Letter to Strecker of about 31 July 1933. The letter, which is in fact undated, is included under this date in *SSCIII*, 237, but without the phrase quoted, which figures instead in ibid., 191, note 13.

63 *Poetics of Music*, 54–5. For a detailed history of this aspect of the Symphonies, see Walsh, "Stravinsky's Symphonies: Accident or Design?"

64 "Neue Werke von Malipiero und Strawinsky," *Schweizerische Musikzeitung und Sängerblatt*, Heft 20 (15 October 1933), 651–2. Stravinsky later recalled writing the lullaby, "Sur ce lit elle repose," for Vera during a Paris heat wave (*Dial*, 38). But a note in *SPD*, plate 31, shows that it was written in Voreppe in August in memory of such an occasion, and sent to Vera with a Russian text.

65 Stravinsky moved into the rue Viète apartment on 15 October. The Barcelona concert with Svetik was on 16 November.

66 See Strecker's letter to Stravinsky of 23 November and Stravinsky's to him of 9 February 1934, quoted in *SSCIII*, 191, note 13.

67 Telegram of 1 September 1933, quoted in *SSCIII*, 480, note 4.

68 Letter of 24 October 1933, quoted in *SSCIII*, 480, note 5.

69 Letter of 6 January 1934, rough draft in PSS; a free translation is in *SSCIII*, 481, note 5.

70 *Chron*, 281.

71 Letter to Reinhart of 1 September 1933 (Stadtbibliothek Winterthur). The tone as well as the content of Svetik's letters is noticeably Stravinskyish, perhaps because he sometimes also dealt with his father's business correspondence.

72 Letter to Igor Stravinsky of 13 January 1934, in *CASIII*, 41–3.

73 Interview in *Le Journal*, 4 June 1934.

74 *Mem*, 63–4.

75 *St. Petersburger Zeitung*, 13 December 1913 and 15 February 1914, respectively (originals in German). Reprinted in Russian in Vitol[s], *Vospominaniya, stat'i, pis'ma*, 250, 254. Stravinsky seems to have forgotten all about Vitols's reviews and remembered him only as a teacher at the St. Petersburg Conservatory.

76 *Dial*, 36. This first run-through is located at Ida's by Goubault, surely correctly (see Goubault, *Igor Stravinsky*, 75). The Polignac performance, of excerpts only, took place on 17 May, more than two weeks after the stage premiere, and with René Maison singing Eumolpus. Gide was certainly absent, but his friend the novelist Julien Green was there, and noted "the cyclopean power of the rhythms" while finding that "the intervening sections very often drift, [and] the parts seemed to me feebly connected to one another" (*Journals*, 165).

77 Letter of 29 July 1933, in *SSCIII*, 190–1.

78 "Ainsi soit-it," in André Gide, *Journal 1939–1949—Souvenirs* (Paris: Gallimard, 1954), 1167. He arrived at Syracuse on 1 February 1934, which suggests that the run-through had been on the 30th. See Gide, *Journal 1889–1939*, 1193, entry for 6 February.

79 All the same, Gide seems by this time to have been more indifferent than alienated. He considered taking a friend to the third performance on 5 May, but in the end went to a Communist Party meeting instead. See Van Rysselberghe, *Les Cahiers de la petite dame: 1929–1937*, 379.

80 *Excelsior*, 29 April 1934, but repeated on 1 May owing to the omission of part of the text. Reprinted in White, *Stravinsky*, 579–81. Cingria had helped write the article, as his letter of 30 April (*SSCIII*, 117) shows.

81 Letter of 2 May 1934 (PSS); *Mem*, 76 (my translation).

82 Letter of 26 May 1934, Stravinsky to Gide (PSS); *SSCIII*, 192 (my translation).

83 Letter of 11 May 1934, in Chimènes, *Francis Poulenc: Correspondance*, 394.

84 *Excelsior*, 29 April and 1 May 1934.

85 *Dial*, 38.

86 "Les Spectacles Ida Rubinstein," *Nouvelle Revue française* 42 (1 June 1934), 1027–30.

87 Kessler, *Tagebücher*, 713, entry for 19 March 1933.

88 Van Rysselberghe, *Les Cahiers de la petite dame: 1929–1937*, 377.

89 *Nouvelle Revue française*, 42 (1 June 1934), 1030–1.

90 Van Rysselberghe, *Les Cahiers de la petite dame: 1929–1937*, 377. The set and several costume designs are reproduced in Schouvaloff and Borovsky, *Stravinsky on Stage*, 151–2. Before Barsacq's involvement, Gide noted, "there were to have been three scenes: one by the sea, one in the Elysian Fields, and a third on a hill at the birth of spring. Now everything will take place in a temple with different carpets to indicate the changes of mood; mon vieux, they're going to say Mass! and not in a Greek temple!!!" (*Les Cahiers de la petite dame*, 335).

91 Letter of 31 July 1933 (PSS).

92 Letter of 11 November 1933 (PSS).

93 Pneu of 12 November 1933 (PSS).

94 "Les Spectacles Ida Rubinstein," loc. cit., 1029.

95 Nearly a year before he had tried to find out from Claudel why his reviews were not appearing in the journal, and Claudel had replied that you have the redoubtable hostility of Gide and [Jean] Schlumberger" (letter of late August 1933, in Cingria, *Correspondance générale*, vol. 4, 50–1). Cingria sensed that politics lay behind all this.

Though an admirer of Gide's work, he had (he told his brother Alexandre) "been openly anticommunist since Gide converted to Moscow" (letter of 12 June 1933, in ibid., vol. 2, 154). However, after a sparkling review of his *Pétrarque* in the April 1933 issue, Cingria's own reviews eventually began to appear more frequently.

96 Cingria, "*Perséphone* et la critique."

97 Ibid., 301–3.

98 *Dial*, 43.

99 Cingria, "*Perséphone* et la critique," *Mem*, 19.

100 On 5 and 6 July he recorded the *Piano Rag Music* and the Serenade, then flew to London, where on the tenth he conducted the first-ever recording of *Les Noces* (in English). Back in Paris, he then recorded *Ragtime*, with ensemble, on the thirteenth.

Principal Sources

10 Komp	Peter Sulzer (ed.), *Zehn Komponisten um Werner Reinhart*, 3 vols. (Zurich: Stadtbibliothek Winterthur, Atlantis Musikbuch-Verlag, 1979, 1980, 1983).
CASI, CASII, CASIII	Claude Tappolet (ed.), *Correspondance Ansermet–Strawinsky (1914–1967)*, 3 vols. (Geneva: Georg, 1990, 1991, 1992).
Chron	Igor Stravinsky, *Chronicle of My Life* (London: Victor Gollancz, 1936).
CISFam	Theodore Stravinsky, *Catherine & Igor Stravinsky: A Family Album* (London: Boosey and Hawkes, 1973).
Conv	Igor Stravinsky and Robert Craft, *Conversations with Igor Stravinsky* (London: Faber and Faber, 1959).
DB	Robert Craft (ed.), *Dearest Bubushkin: The Correspondence of Vera and Igor Stravinsky, 1921–1954, with Excerpts from Vera Stravinsky's Diaries, 1922–1971*, trans. Lucia Davidova (London: Thames and Hudson, 1985).
Dial	Igor Stravinsky and Robert Craft, *Dialogues and a Diary* (London: Faber and Faber, 1968).
Expo	Igor Stravinsky and Robert Craft, *Expositions and Developments* (London: Faber and Faber, 1962).
FSS	L. Kutateladze and A. Gozenpud (eds.), *F. Stravinsky: Stat'i, pis'ma, vospominaniya* (Leningrad: Muzïka, 1972).
ISPS	Viktor Varunts (ed.), *I. Stravinsky: Publitsist i sobesednik* (Moscow: Sovetskiy Kompozitor, 1988).
IVSPA	Vera Stravinsky, Rita McCaffrey, and Robert Craft, *Igor and Vera Stravinsky: A Photograph Album, 1921 to 1971* (London: Thames and Hudson, 1982).
Mem	Igor Stravinsky and Robert Craft, *Memories and Commentaries* (London: Faber and Faber, 1960).
Muz Ak 1992	*Muzïkal'naya Akademiya* (Moscow), no. 4 (1992), Stravinsky issue.
Muz Ak 1996/2	*Muzïkal 'naya Akademiya* (Moscow), no. 2 (1996).
Muz Ak 1996/3–4	*Muzïkal 'naya Akademiya* (Moscow), no. 3–4 (1996).
PMP	M. G. Kozlova and N. R. Yatsenko (eds.), *S. S. Prokof'yev i N. Ya. Myaskovsky: Perepiska* (Moscow: Sovetskiy Kompozitor, 1977).
PRK	Viktor Varunts (ed.), *I. F. Stravinsky: Perepiska s russkimi korrespondentami. Materialï k biographi*, vol. 1 (Moscow: Kompozitor, 1997).
RiteSk	Igor Stravinsky, *"The Rite of Spring": Sketches, 1911–1913*.

Facsimile Reproductions from the Autographs (London: Boosey and Hawkes, 1969).

SB   K. Yu. Stravinskaya, *O I. F. Stravinskom i evo blizkikh* (Leningrad: Muzïka, 1978).

SM   L. S. Dyachkova (ed.), *I. F. Stravinsky: Stat'i i materialï* (Moscow: Sovetskiy Kompozitor, 1973).

SNB   *Strawinsky: Sein Nachlass. Sein Bild* (Basle: Kunstmuseum Basel in Zusammenarbeit mit der Paul Sacher Stiftung, 1984).

SPD   Vera Stravinsky and Robert Craft, *Stravinsky in Pictures and Documents* (New York: Simon and Schuster, 1978).

SRT   Richard Taruskin, *Stravinsky and the Russian Traditions: A Biography of the Works Through "Mavra"* (Oxford: Oxford University Press, 1996).

SSCI, SSCII, SSCIII   Robert Craft (ed.), *Stravinsky: Selected Correspondence*, 3 vol. (London: Faber and Faber, 1982, 1984, 1985).

T&C   Igor Stravinsky, *Themes and Conclusions* (London: Faber and Faber, 1972).

SECONDARY SOURCES

Abraham, G. *Rimsky-Korsakov: A Short Biography* (London: Duckworth, 1945).

Adorno, T. W. *Philosophy of Modern Music*, trans. A. Mitchell and W. Bloomster (London: Sheed and Ward, 1973).

Albright, D. *The Music Box and the Nightingale* (New York: Gordon and Breach, 1989).

Alfeyevskaya, G., and I. Vershinina (eds.). *I. F. Stravinsky: Stat'i, vospominaniya* (Moscow: Sovetskiy Kompozitor, 1985).

Andriessen, L., and E. Schönberger. *The Apollonian Clockwork: On Stravinsky*, trans. J. Hamburg (Oxford and New York: Oxford University Press, 1989).

Ansermet, A. *Ernest Ansermet, mon père* (Lausanne: Payot, 1983)

Ansermet, E. *Ecrits sur la musique* (Neuchâtel: A la Baconnière, 1971).

———. *Les Fondements de la musique dans la conscience humaine* (Neuchâtel: A la Baconnière, 1961).

———. "*L'Histoire du Soldat*," The Chesterian, 10 (1920), 289–95.

———. "L'Oeuvre d'Igor Strawinsky," *La Revue musicale*, 2, no. 9 (1 July 1921), 1–27.

Ansermet, E., and J. C. Piguet. *Entretiens sur la musique* (Neuchâtel: A la Baconnière, 1963).

Antheil, G. *Bad Boy of Music* (London: Hutchinson, 1949).

Appel, D. H. (ed.). *Prokofiev by Prokofiev: A Composer's Memoir* (New York: Doubleday, 1979).

Asafyev, B. *A Book About Stravinsky*, trans. Richard F. French (Ann Arbor: UMI Research Press, 1982).

Ascher, A. *The Revolution of 1905*, 2 vols. (Stanford: Stanford University Press, 1988, 1992).

Auberjonois, F. "The Swiss Years of Igor Stravinsky," *Adam International Review*, 39 (1973–74), 73–80.

Auric, G. "Du *Sacre du printemps* à *Mavra*," *Nouvelles littéraires*, 6 January 1923.

Baedeker, K. *La Russie* (3rd ed.; Leipzig: Karl Baedeker, 1902).

Baltensperger, A., and F. Meyer (eds.). *Igor Strawinsky: Symphonies d'instruments à vent: Faksimileausgabe des Particells und der Partitur der Erstfassung (1920)* (Winterthur: Amadeus, 1991).

Bancroft, D. "Stravinsky and the 'NRF' (1910–20)," *Music and Letters*, 53 (1972), 274–93; "Stravinsky and the 'NRF' (1920–29)," *Music and Letters*, 55 (1974), 261–80.

Bater, J. *St. Petersburg: Industrialization and Change* (London: Edward Arnold, 1976).

Beaumont, C. *Complete Book of Ballets* (rev. ed.; London: Putnam, 1949).

——. *The Diaghilev Ballet in London* (London: Putnam, 1945).

Beecham, T. *A Mingled Chime* (London: Hutchinson, 1944).

Bell, C. *Old Friends* (London: Chatto and Windus, 1956).

Benois, A. "Khudozhestvennïye pis'ma: Russkiye spektakli v Parizhe: *Zhar-ptitsa*," *Rech'*, 18 July 1910.

——. "Khudozhestvennïye pis'ma," *Rech'*, 4 August 1911; repr. as "*Petrushka* Igorya Stravinskavo," *Muzïka*, no. 89, (27 August 1911) 796–804.

——. "Maslyanitsa," *Posledniye novosti*, 21–22 March 1930.

——. "*Petrushka*," *Posledniye novosti*, 2 December 1930.

——. *Reminiscences of the Russian Ballet* (London: Putnam, 1941).

——. *Memoirs*, trans. Moura Budberg, vol. 1 (London: Columbus Books, 1988).

Berdyayev, N. *Dream and Reality: An Essay in Autobiography*, trans. Katharine Lampert (London: Geoffrey Bles, 1950).

Bischoff, L. "Le Peintre Théodore Strawinsky," *Cahiers de Belgique*, 3, no. 10 (December 1930), 339–43.

Blanche, J.-E. *Cahiers d'un artiste*, 4th series (Paris: Emile-Paul Frères, 1917).

Boucourechliev, A. *Stravinsky*, trans. M. Cooper (London: Victor Gollancz, 1987).

Boulanger, N. *Lectures on Modern Music* (Houston: Rice Institute, 1926).

Bowlt, J. E. (ed.). *The Salon Album of Vera Sudeikin-Stravinsky* (Princeton: Princeton University Press, 1995).

——. *The Silver Age* (Newtonville, Mass.: Oriental Research Partners, 1979).

Brooks, J. "Nadia Boulanger and the Salon of the Princesse de Polignac," *Journal of the American Musicological Society*, 46 (1993), 415–68.

Brown, M. H. "Prokofiev's Correspondence with Stravinsky and Shostakovich," in Brown (ed.), *Slavonic and Western Music: Essays for Gerald Abraham* (Ann Arbor and Oxford: UMI Research Press and Oxford University Press, 1985).

Buckle, R. *Diaghilev* (London: Weidenfeld and Nicolson, 1979).

——. *Nijinsky* (Harmondsworth: Penguin, 1975).

Bullard, T. *The First Performance of Igor Stravinsky's Sacre du pintemps*, Ph.D. thesis, 3 vols. (Rochester, New York: Eastman School, 1971).

Burak, A. "Vïdayushchiysya pevets i reformator stsyenï," *Baltiyskiy Luch*, 29 June 1974.

Calvocoressi, M. D. "A Russian Composer of To-day: Igor Stravinsky," *Musical Times*, 52 (1911), 511–12.

Campbell, S. "The *Mavras* of Pushkin, Kochno, and Stravinsky," *Music and Letters*, 58 (1977), 304–21.

Cangiullo, F. *Le serate futuriste* (Milan: Ceschina, 1961).

Casella, A. *Music in My Time*, trans. Spencer Norton (Norman: University of Oklahoma Press, 1955).

——. *Igor Strawinski* (Rome: Formiggini, 1926).

Charles-Roux, E. *L'Irrégulière* (Paris: Grasset, 1974); English trans. by Nancy Amphoux, as *Chanel* (London: Jonathan Cape, 1976).

Chimènes, M. (ed.). *Francis Poulenc: Correspondance, 1910–1963* (Paris: Fayard, 1994); English trans. (of an earlier, less full edition) by Sidney Buckland, as *Francis Poulenc: Echo and Source* (London: Gollancz, 1991).

Cingria, C.-A. "*Perséphone* et la critique," *Nouvelle Revue française*, 43 (August 1934), 297–301.

——. *Correspondance générale*, vols. 2, 4, and 5 (Lausanne: Editions L'Age d'Homme, 1975, 1979, 1980).

——. *Pétrarque* (Lausanne: Librairie Payot, 1932).

——. *Portraits* (Lausanne: L'Age d'Homme, 1994).

Claude, J. "Autour de *Perséphone*," *Bulletin des amis d'André Gide*, 15 (1987), 23–55.

Cochran, C. B. *The Secrets of a Showman* (London: William Heinemann, 1925).

Cocteau, J. *Le Coq et l'Arlequin* (Paris: Stock, 1979).

——. *Lettre à Jacques Maritain* (Paris: Stock, 1926).

——. *Lettres à sa mère*, vol. 1 (Paris: Gallimard, 1989).

————. *Paris Album, 1900–1914*, trans. Margaret Crosland (London: W. H. Allen, 1956).

Collaer, P. "Introduction à la vie et à l'oeuvre d'Igor Strawinsky," *Revue générale* (May 1971), 21–37.

————. *Strawinsky* (Brussels: Equilibres, 1930).

Copland, A., and V. Perlis. *Copland*, vol. 1 (London and Boston: Faber, 1984).

Corle, E. (ed.). *Igor Stravinsky* (New York: Duell, Sloan & Pearce, 1949).

Craft, R. (ed.). *Avec Stravinsky* (Monaco: Editions du Rocher, 1958).

————. "Jews and Geniuses," *Small Craft Advisories* (New York: Thames and Hudson, 1989), 274–81.

————. "Prince Igor's Dance," *Times Literary Supplement*, 13 September 1996.

————. "The Composer and the Phonograph," *High Fidelity*, 7 (June 1957), 34–5, 99–100.

————. *A Stravinsky Scrapbook 1940–1971* (London: Thames and Hudson, 1983).

————. *Prejudices in Disguise* (New York: Alfred A. Knopf, 1974).

————. *Present Perspectives* (New York: Alfred A. Knopf, 1984).

————. *Stravinsky: Glimpses of a Life* (London: Lime Tree, 1992; New York: St. Martin's Press, 1993).

————. *Stravinsky: Chronicle of a Friendship* (rev. and expanded ed.; Nashville and London: Vanderbilt University Press, 1994).

Cyr, L. (ed.). *L'Oiseau de feu: Facsimile du manuscrit* (Geneva: Minkoff, 1985).

Danuser, H. (ed.). *Igor Stravinsky: Trois pièces pour quatuor à cordes: Skizzen, Fassungen, Dokumente, Essays* (Winterthur: Amadeus, 1994).

de Cossart, M. *The Food of Love: Princesse Edmond de Polignac and Her Salon* (London: Hamish Hamilton, 1978).

Dent, E. J. "Looking Backward," *Music Today*, 1 (1949), 6–22.

Dorati, A., et al. "Remembering Igor Stravinsky," *Hungarian Book Review* (May–August 1972), 44–5.

Drummond, J. *Speaking of Diaghilev* (London and Boston: Faber and Faber, 1997).

Druskin, M. *Igor Stravinsky: His Life, Works and Views*, trans. M. Cooper (Cambridge: Cambridge University Press, 1983).

Duke, V. *Passport to Paris* (Boston and Toronto: Little, Brown, 1955).

Erhardt, L. *Igor Strawinski* (Warsaw: Panstwowy Instytut Wydawniczy, 1978).

Erlich, V. *Russian Formalism: History—Doctrine* (New Haven and London: Yale University Press, 1981).

Evans, E. *Music and the Dance* (London: Jenkins, 1948).

————. "The Stravinsky Debate," *Music Student*, no. 13 (December 1920), 139–45.

Evans, J. " 'Diabolus triumphans': Stravinsky's *Histoire du soldat* in Weimar and Nazi Germany," in J. Daverio and J. Ogasapian (eds.): *Varieties of Musicology: Essays for Murray Lefkowitz* (Warren, Mich.: Harmonie Park Press, 1999), 179–89.

————. "Die Rezeption der Musik Igor Strawinskys in Hitlerdeutschland," *Archiv für Musikwissenschaft*, 55, no. 2 (1998), 91–109.

————. *Hans Rosbaud: A Bio-Bibliography* (New York, Westport, and London: Greenwood Press, 1992).

Flanner, J. "Russian Firebird," *New Yorker* (5 January 1935), 23–8.

Fokine, M. *Memoirs of a Ballet Master*, trans. Vitale Fokine, ed. Anatole Chujoy (London: Constable, 1961).

Fowlie, W. (ed.). *Journals of Jean Cocteau* (London: Museum Press, 1957).

Ganina, M. (ed.). *A. Glazunov: Pis'ma, stat'i, vospominaniya* (Moscow: Gosudarstvennoye Muzïkal'noye Izdatel'stvo, 1958).

Garafola, L. *Diaghilev's Ballets Russes* (New York and Oxford: Oxford University Press, 1989).

Ghéon, H. "Propos divers sur le ballet russe," *Nouvelle Revue française*, 4 (1910), 210–11.

Gide, A. *Journal, 1887–1925*, ed. Eric Marty (Paris: Gallimard, 1996).

————. *Journal, 1889–1939* (Paris: Gallimard, 1948).

————. *Notes sur Chopin* (Paris: L'Arche, 1948).

Ginzburg, S. L. (ed.). *N. A. Rimsky-Korsakov i muzīkal'noye obrazovaniye* (Leningrad: Muzgiz, 1959).

Glezer, R. V. (ed.). *M. F. Gnesin: Stat'i, vospominaniya, materialī* (Moscow: Sovetskiy Kompozitor, 1961).

Gnesin, M. F. *Mīsli i vospominaniya o N. A. Rimskom-Korsakove* (Moscow: Muzgiz, 1956).

Gojowy, D. "Arthur Lourié der Futurist," *Hindemith-Jahrbuch*, 8 (1979), 147–85.

———. *Arthur Lourié und der russische Futurismus* (Laaber: Laaber Verlag, 1993).

Gold, A., and R. Fizdale. *Misia* (New York: Alfred A. Knopf, 1980).

Goldstein, M. "Zwei Briefe von Igor Stravinskij (Erstveröffentlichung)," *Musik des Ostens*, 7 (1975), 280–3.

Goncharova, N. "The Metamorphoses of the Ballet *Les Noces*," *Leonardo*, 12 (1979), 137–43.

———. "The Creation of *Les Noces*," *Ballet and Opera* (September 1949), 23–6.

Goossens, E. *Overture and Beginners* (London: Methuen, 1951).

Gordon, T. *Stravinsky and the New Classicism*, Ph.D. thesis (Toronto: University of Toronto, 1983).

Goubault, C. *Igor Stravinsky* (Paris: Champion, 1991).

Graff, M. *Stravinsky and the Dance: A Survey of Ballet Productions, 1910–1962* (New York: Dance Collection of the New York Public Library, 1962).

Graham, I. "Arthur Sergeevic Lourié—Biographische Notizen," *Hindemith-Jahrbuch*, 8 (1979), 186–207.

Green, J. *Journals, 1928–1958* (Paris: Plon, 1961).

Griffiths, P. *Stravinsky* (London: Master Musicians, Dent, 1992).

Grigoriev, S. *The Diaghilev Ballet, 1909–1929* (London: Constable, 1953).

Guisan, G. (ed.). *C.-F. Ramuz, ses amis et son temps*, vol. 6 (Lausanne and Paris: La Bibliothèque des Arts, 1970).

——— (ed.). *Du Côté des Cahiers vaudois, 1914–1916* (Lausanne: Payot, 1964).

Guyau, M.-J. *Les Problèmes de l'esthétique contemporaine* (2nd ed.; Paris: Alcan, 1891).

Hamm, C. (ed.). *Petrushka* (New York: Norton Critical Scores, W. W. Norton, 1967).

Haskell, A., and W. Nouvel. *Diaghileff: His Artistic and Private Life* (New York: Simon and Schuster, 1935).

Heyman, B. "Stravinsky and Ragtime," *Musical Quarterly*, 68 (1982), 543–62.

Heyworth, P. (ed.). *Conversations with Klemperer* (London: Gollancz, 1973).

———. *Otto Klemperer: His Life and Times*, vol. 1 (Cambridge: Cambridge University Press, 1983).

Hodson, M. *Nijinsky's Crime Against Grace* (Stuyvesant, N.Y.: Pendragon Press, 1996).

Holden, A. (ed.). *The Viking Opera Guide* (London: Viking Penguin, 1993).

Holloway, R. "Customised Goods," *Musical Times*, 138 (October 1997), 21–5; (November 1997), 25–8; (December 1997), 21–5.

Horgan, P. *Encounters with Stravinsky* (rev. ed.; Middletown, Conn.: Wesleyan University Press, 1989).

Hostowiec, P. (pseudonym of J. Stempowski). "Dom Strawinskiego w Uscilugu," in *Kultura* (Paris, 1949), 19–34; reprinted in J. Stempowski, *W dolinie Dniestru i inne eseje ukrainskie* (Warsaw: LNB, 1993), 49–77.

Hudry, F. *Ernest Ansermet, pionnier de la musique* (Lausanne: L'Aire Musicale, 1983).

Hugo, J. *Avant d'oublier 1918–1931* (Paris: Fayard, 1976).

Jacquot, J. "*Histoire du Soldat*: La genèse du texte et la représentation de 1918," in *Les Voies de la création théâtrale*, vol. 6 (Paris: Editions du Centre national de la recherche scientifique, 1978).

Joseph, C. *Stravinsky and the Piano* (Ann Arbor: UMI Research Press, 1983).

———. "Stravinsky on Film," *Mitteilungen der Paul Sacher Stiftung*, no. 6 (1993), 30–4.

Kabalevsky, D. (ed.). *Rimsky-Korsakov: Issledovaniya, materialī, pis'ma*, vol. 2 (Moscow: Izdatelstvo Akademii Nauk SSSR, 1954).

Karlinsky, S. "A pocket full of buttered figs," *Times Literary Supplement*, 5 July 1985.

Bibliography

———. "Igor Stravinsky and Russian Preliterate Theater," in J. Pasler (ed.), *Confronting Stravinsky*, 3–15.

Karsavina, T. *Theatre Street: The Reminiscences of Tamara Karsavina* (rev. ed.; London: Constable, 1948).

———. "A Recollection of Strawinsky," *Tempo*, no. 8 (summer 1948), 7–9.

Kazanskaya, L. "Stepan Mitusov," *Sovetskaya muzïka*, no. 12 (1990), 82–8.

Kessler, Count H. *Tagebücher (1918–1937)* (Frankfurt-am-Main: Insel Verlag, 1961).

Keynes, M. (ed.). *Lydia Lopokova* (New York: St. Martin's Press, 1982).

Kinkulkina, N. (ed.). "Pis'ma I. F. Stravinskovo i F. I. Shalyapina k A. A. Saninu," *Sovetskaya Muzïka*, no. 6 (1978), 92–6.

Kiselyov, V. (ed.). *N. A. Rimsky-Korsakov: Sbornik dokumentov* (Moscow and Leningrad: Muzgiz, 1951).

Klimovitsky, A. "Dve 'Pesni o Blokhe'—Betkhovena i Musorgskovo—v instrumentovke Stravinskovo," *Pamyatniki kul'turï: novïye otkrïtiya, 1984* (Leningrad: Nauka, 1986), 196–216.

Kling, O. "A Personal Explanation," *The Chesterian*, no. 5 (November 1916), 67–71.

Kochno, B. *Diaghilev and the Ballets Russes*, trans. Adrienne Foulke (New York: Harper and Row, 1970).

Kryukov, A. (ed.). *Materialï k biographii B. Asafyeva* (Leningrad: Muzïka, 1981).

Kurchenko, A. "Stravinsky i Dostoyevsky," *Sovetskaya muzïka*, no. 3 (March 1990), 103–12.

Kuznetsov, A. (ed.). *Emil Cooper: Stat'i, vospominaniya, materialï* (Moscow: Sovetskiy Kompozitor, 1988).

Laloy, L. *La Musique retrouvée* (Paris: Plon, 1928).

Lavanchy, L. *Essais critiques, 1925–1935* (Lausanne: Éditions des Trois Collines, 1939).

Lawson, R. "Stravinsky and the Pianola," in J. Pasler (ed.), *Confronting Stravinsky*, 284–301.

Lederman, M. (ed.). *Stravinsky in the Theatre* (New York: Da Capo, 1975).

Leibowitz, H. A. (ed.). *Musical Impressions: Selections from Paul Rosenfeld's Criticism* (New York: Hill and Wang, 1969).

Lessem, A. "Schoenberg, Stravinsky and Neo-Classicism: The Issues Reexamined," *Musical Quarterly*, 68 (1982), 527–42.

Lesure, F. (ed.). *Claude Debussy: Correspondance, 1884–1918* (Paris: Hermann, 1993).

——— (ed.). *Igor Stravinsky: La Carrière européenne* (Paris: exhibition catalogue, Musée d'Art Moderne, 1980).

——— (ed.). *Igor Stravinsky: "Le Sacre du printemps": Dossier de presse* (Geneva: Editions Minkoff, 1980).

——— (ed.). *Stravinsky: Etudes et témoignages* (Paris: J. C. Lattès, 1982).

Levi, E. *Music in the Third Reich* (London: Macmillan, 1994).

Levinson, A. "Stravinsky and the Dance," *Theatre Arts Monthly*, 8 (1924), 741–54.

Lieven, P. *Birth of the Ballets-Russes* (London: George Allen and Unwin, 1936).

Lifar, S. *Serge Diaghilev: His Life, His Work, His Legend* (London and New York: Putnam, 1940).

Livshits, B. *The One and a Half-Eyed Archer*, trans. John E. Bowlt (Newtonville, Mass.: Oriental Research Partners, 1977).

Lockspeiser, E. *Debussy: His Life and Mind*, vol. 2 (London: Cassell, 1965).

Lourié, A. "A propos de l'*Apollon* d'Igor Strawinsky," *Musique*, 1 (1928), 117–9.

———. "Dve operï Stravinskovo," *Vyorstï*, no. 3 (1928), 109–26.

———. "La Sonate pour piano de Strawinsky," *La Revue musicale*, 6 (1925), 100–4.

———. "Le Capriccio de Strawinsky," *La Revue musicale*, 103 (1 April 1930), 353–5.

———. "Muzïka Stravinskovo," *Vyorstï*, no. 1 (1926), 119–35.

———. "Neogothic and Neoclassic," *Modern Music*, 5 (1928), 3–8.

———. "*Oedipus-Rex*," *La Revue musicale*, 8 (1 August 1927), 240–53.

———. "Strawinsky à Bruxelles," *Cahiers de Belgique*, 3, no. 10 (December 1930), 330–2.

Maritain, J. *Art et scolastique* (Paris: Art Catholique, 1920).

Maritain, R. *Journal de Raïssa* (Paris: Desclée de Brouwer, 1963).

Markevitch, I. *Etre et avoir été* (Paris: Gallimard, 1980).

Massine, L. *My Life in Ballet*, ed. Phyllis Hartnoll and Robert Rubens (London: Macmillan, 1968).

Mayakovsky, V. *Parizhskiye Ocherki*, in *Polnoye Sobraniye Sochineniy*, vol. 4 (Moscow: Gosudarstvennoye Izdatelstvo Khudozhestvennoy Literaturï, 1957).

Mazo, M. "Stravinsky's *Les Noces* and Russian Village Wedding Ritual," *Journal of the American Musicological Society*, 43 (1990), 99–142.

Messing, S. *Neoclassicism in Music* (Ann Arbor: UMI Research Press, 1988).

Meyer, F. (ed.). *Settling New Scores: Music Manuscripts from the Paul Sacher Foundation* (Mainz: Schott, 1998).

Meylan, P. *Une Amitié célèbre* (Lausanne: Editions du Cervin, 1961).

Moldenhauer, H. *Anton von Webern: A Chronicle of His Life and Work* (London: Victor Gollancz, 1978).

Monsaingeon, B. *Mademoiselle: Entretiens avec Nadia Boulanger* (Van de Velde, 1981); eng. trans. by R. Marsack, as *Mademoiselle: Conversations with Nadia Boulanger* (Manchester: Carcanet, 1985).

Monteux, D. *It's All in the Music* (London: William Kimber, 1966).

Morand, P. *Journal d'un attaché d'ambassade, 1916–17* (Paris: La Table Ronde, 1949).

———. *L'Allure de Chanel* (Paris: Hermann, 1976).

Moutote, D. "Gide, Valéry et la musique," *Bulletin des Amis d'André Gide*, 19ᵉ année, 24 (October 1996), 392–410.

Myaskovsky, N. "*Petrushka*, balet lg. Stravinskavo," *Muzïka*, no. 59 (14 January 1912), 72–5.

Nabokov, N. "La vie et l'oeuvre de Serge de Diaghilew," *Musique*, 3, no. 2 (15 November 1929), 54–68; "Une lettre d'Igor Strawinsky," *Musique*, 3, no. 3 (15 December 1929), 119.

———. *Bagazh* (New York: Atheneum, 1975).

Nijinska, B. "Creation of *Les Noces*," *Dance Magazine* (December 1974), 58–61.

———. *Early Memoirs*, trans. and ed. Irina Nijinska and Jean Rawlinson (New York: Holt, Rinehart and Winston, 1981).

Nijinski [sic], V. *Cahiers*, version non expurgée, trans. Christian Dumais-Lvowski and Galina Pogojeva (Arles: Actes Sud, 1995).

Nijinsky, R. *Nijinsky* (London: Victor Gollancz, 1933).

Noble, J. "Debussy and Stravinsky," *Musical Times*, 108 (1967), 22–4.

Obolensky, C. *The Russian Empire: A Portrait in Photographs* (London: Jonathan Cape, 1980).

Ogneva, O. D. *Muzey I. Stravinskovo v Ustiluzi* (Lutsk: Volhynian Regional Museum, 1994).

Oja, C. (ed.). *Stravinsky in Modern Music (1926–1946)* (New York: Da Capo, 1982).

Orenstein, A. (ed.). *Maurice Ravel: Lettres, écrits, entretiens* (Paris: Flammarion, 1989).

Pahissa, J. *Manuel de Falla: His Life and Works*, trans. Jean Wagstaff (Westport, Conn.: Hyperion Press, 1979).

Pasler, J. (ed.). *Confronting Stravinsky* (Berkeley: University of California Press, 1986).

———. "Stravinsky and the Apaches," *Musical Times*, 123 (1982), 403–7.

Piatigorsky, G. *Cellist* (New York: Doubleday, 1965).

Pipes, R. *Russia Under the Old Regime* (New York: Charles Scribner, 1974).

Pitoëff, L. "Souvenirs intimes de *L'Histoire du soldat*," *Le Quartier Latin* (Montreal), 23 March 1945, 167.

Polignac, Princesse E. de. "Memoirs of the Late Princesse Edmond de Polignac," *Horizon* (August 1945), 110–41.

Pollard, P. (ed.). *André Gide: "Proserpine" (drame), "Perséphone" (mélodrame): Edition critique* (Lyon: Université de Lyon, Centre d'études gidiennes, 1977), 27–8.

———. "*Sit Tityrus Orpheus*: Gide et la musique," *Bulletin des Amis d'André Gide*, 23ᵉ année, no. 85, 18 (1990), 17–64.

Polyakova, Ye. *Rerikh: Zhizn' v iskusstve* (Moscow: Iskusstvo, 1973).

Poulenc, F. "A propos de *Mavra* de Igor Strawinsky," *Les Feuilles libres* (June–July 1922), 222–4.

———. *My Friends and Myself (Conversations with Stéphane Audel)*, trans. J. Harding (London: Dennis Dobson, 1978).

Rácz-Barblan, Y. "Igor Stravinsky vu par le cymbaliste Aladár Rácz," *Feuilles musicales* (Lausanne) (March–April 1962), 35–9.

Rambert, M. *Quicksilver* (London: Macmillan, 1972).

Ramuz, C.-F., and R. Auberjonois. "Autour de *L'Histoire du soldat*," in *Etudes de lettres*, no. 4, (1978), 87–93.

———. *Lettres, 1900–1918* (Lausanne: Editions Clairefontaine, 1956).

———. *Lettres, 1919–1947* (Etoy, Vaud: Grasset, 1959).

———. *Souvenirs sur Igor Strawinsky* (Lausanne: Mermod, 1952).

Ravel, M. "O parizhskoy redaktsii *Khovanshchina*," *Muzïka* (Moscow), no. 129, 14 May 1913, 338–42.

Reeder, R., and A. Comegno. "Stravinsky's *Les Noces*," translated and with introductions, *Dance Research Journal*, 18, no. 2 (winter 1986–87), 31–53.

Riasanovsky, N. "The Emergence of Eurasianism," *California Slavic Studies*, 4 (1967), 39–72.

Richardson, J. *A Life of Picasso*, vol. 2 (1907–1917) (London: Jonathan Cape, 1996).

Rimsky-Korsakov, A. N. "Baletï Igorya Stravinskavo," *Apollon*, no. 1 (1915), 46–57.

———. *N. A. Rimsky-Korsakov: Zhizn' i tvorchestvo*, vols. 3–5 (Moscow: Muzgiz, 1936–46).

Rimsky-Korsakov, A. N., et al. (eds.). *V. G. Karatïgin: zhizn', deyatel'nost, stat'i i materialï* (Leningrad: Academia, 1927).

Rimsky-Korsakov, N. A. *My Musical Life*, trans. Judah A. Joffe (London: Eulenburg, 1974).

Rivière, J. "*Le Sacre du printemps*," *Nouvelle Revue française*, 4 (November 1913), 706–30.

Robinson, H. *Sergei Prokofiev* (London: Robert Hale, 1987).

——— (ed.). *Selected Letters of Sergei Prokofiev* (Boston: Northeastern University Press, 1998).

Roerich [Rerikh], N. K. "Novïy balet—*Vesna svyashchennaya*," *Rech'* (St. Petersburg), 22 November 1912.

Roland-Manuel. "Stravinsky et la critique," *Revue Pleyel*, 9 (1924), 17–18.

Rolland, R. *Journal des années de guerre (1914–1919)* (Paris: Éditions Albin Michel, 1952).

Rosenstiel, L. *Nadia Boulanger: A Life in Music* (New York and London: Norton, 1982).

Röthlin, N. "Strawinskys juristische Ausbildung," in H. Oesch (ed.), *Quellenstudien I* (Winterthur: Amadeus, 1991).

Rubinstein, A. *My Many Years* (New York: Alfred A. Knopf, 1980).

Sabaneyev, L. "Dawn or Dusk? Stravinsky's New Ballets," *Musical Times*, 70 (1929), 403–6.

———. *Modern Russian Composers*, trans. Judah A. Joffe (New York: Da Capo, 1975).

———. "The Stravinsky Legends," *Musical Times*, 69 (1928), 785–7.

Sachs, H. *Music in Fascist Italy* (London: Weidenfeld and Nicolson, 1987).

Savenko, S. "*L'Oiseau de feu*: Zur Geschichte der ersten Fassung," *Mitteilungen der Paul Sacher Stiftung*, no. 8 (March 1995), 31–5.

Schaeffner, A. *Strawinsky* (Paris: Les Editions Rieder, 1931).

———. "Au fil des esquisses du *Sacre*," *Revue de musicologie*, 57 (1971), 179–90.

———. "Variations Schoenberg," *Contrepoints*, 7 (1950), 110–29.

Scherliess, V. *Igor Strawinsky und seine Zeit* (Laaber: Laaber Verlag, 1983).

Schloezer, B. de. "A propos de la Sonate de Strawinsky," *Revue Pleyel*, 26 (1925), 18–20.

———. "Igor Stravinsky," *La Revue musicale*, 5, no. 2 (1 December 1923), 97–141.

———. "Igor Stravinsky," *The Dial*, 85 (1928), 271–83; 86 (1929), 105–15, 298–303, 463–74.

———. "Les Spectacles Ida Rubinstein," *Nouvelle Revue française*, 42 (1 June 1934), 1027–30.

———. *Igor Stravinsky* (Paris: Editions Claude Aveline, 1929).

Schouvaloff, A., and V. Borovsky. *Stravinsky on Stage* (London: Stainer and Bell, 1982).

Segel, H. B. *Turn-of-the-Century Cabaret* (New York: Columbia University Press, 1987).

Sert, M. *Two or Three Muses: The Memoirs of Misia Sert*, trans. Moura Budberg (London: Museum Press, 1953).

Seton-Watson, H. *The Russian Empire, 1801–1917* (Oxford: Oxford University Press, 1967).

Shead, R. *Ballets Russes* (London: Apple Press, 1989).

———. *Music in the 1920s* (New York: St. Martin's Press, 1976).

Shlifshteyn, S. (ed.). *N. Ya. Myaskovsky: Stat'i, pis'ma, vospominaniya*, 2 vols. (Moscow: Sovetskiy Kompozitor, 1960).

Siohan, R. *Stravinsky*, trans. E. W. White (London: Calder and Boyars, 1965).

Sitwell, O. *Great Morning* (London: Reprint Society, 1949).

Slonimsky, N. *Perfect Pitch* (Oxford and New York: Oxford University Press, 1988).

Smirnov, V. *Tvorcheskoye formirovaniye I. F. Stravinskovo* (Leningrad: Muzïka, 1970).

———. "Tvorcheskaya vesna Igorya Stravinskovo," in M. G. Aranovsky (ed.), *Rasskazï o muzïke i muzïkantakh* (Leningrad and Moscow: Sovetskiy Kompozitor, 1973), 55–79.

Sokolova, L. *Dancing for Diaghilev* (London: John Murray, 1960).

Stark, E. *Peterburgskaya opera i yeyo mastera* (Leningrad and Moscow: Iskusstvo, 1940).

Steegmuller, F. *Cocteau* (London: Macmillan, 1970).

Stein, L. (ed.). *Style and Idea: Selected Writings of Arnold Schoenberg* (London: Faber, 1975), 482–3.

Stempowski, J. (see Hostowiec)

Stone, E. and K. *The Writings of Elliott Carter* (Bloomington and London: Indiana University Press, 1977).

Stravinskaya, K. "Iz semeynovo arkhiva Stravinskix," *Sovetskaya muzïka*, 34 (September 1970), 154–6.

Stravinsky, I. "Ce que j'ai voulu exprimer dans *Le Sacre du printemps*," *Montjoie!*, no. 8 (29 May 1913), reprinted in Lesure (ed.), *Igor Stravinsky: "Le Sacre du printemps": Dossier de presse*, 13–15. Eng. trans. (by Edward Burlingame Hill) as "What I Wished to Express in *The Rite of Spring*," *Boston Evening Transcript*, 12 February 1916.

———. "Les Espagnols aux Ballets Russes," *Comoedia*, 15 May 1921; reprinted in Lesure (ed.), *Stravinsky: Etudes et témoignages*, 238.

———. "The Genius of Tchaikovsky" (Open Letter to Serge Diaghilev), *The Times* (London), 18 October 1921; reprinted in White, *Stravinsky: The Composer and His Works*, 573–4.

———. "Une lettre de Stravinsky sur Tchaikovsky," *Le Figaro*, 18 May 1922; reprinted in *La Revue musicale*, 3, no. 9 (July 1922).

———. "Some Ideas About My Octuor," *The Arts* (Brooklyn), January 1924, 4–6; reprinted in White, *Stravinsky: The Composer and His Works*, 574–7.

———. "Avertissement . . . A Warning," *The Dominant* (London), December 1927, 13–14; reprinted in White, *Stravinsky: The Composer and His Works*, 577–8.

———. *Poetics of Music in the Form of Six Lessons*, trans. A. Knodel and I. Dahl (Cambridge, Mass.: Harvard University Press, 1947).

———. "The Diaghilev I Knew," trans. Mercedes de Acosta, *Atlantic Monthly* (November 1953), 33–6.

———. *Dialogi*, Russian omnibus edition of the Stravinsky-Craft conversation books, trans. V. Linnik (Leningrad: Muzïka, 1971).

———. "Igor Strawinsky nous parle de *Perséphone*," *Excelsior*, 29 April 1934 (repeated with corrections, 1 May 1934); reprinted in White, *Stravinsky: The Composer and His Works*, 579–81.

———. "Quelques Confidences sur la musique," *Conferencia*, 15 December 1935; reprinted in White, *Stravinsky: The Composer and His Works*, 581–5.

Strawinsky, T. *Le Message d'Igor Strawinsky* (Lausanne: Librairie F. Rouge, 1948); Eng. trans. by R. Craft and A. Marion, as *The Message of Igor Strawinsky* (London: Boosey and Hawkes, 1953).

Strawinsky, T. and D. *Au coeur du Foyer* (Bourg-la-Reine: ZurfluH, 1998).

Street, D. "A Forgotten Firebird," *Musical Times*, 119 (1978), 674–6.

Strobel, H. "Strawinsky privat," *Melos*, 10 (1931), 315–8.

Stuart, P. *Igor Stravinsky: The Composer in the Recording Studio* (New York, Westport, and London: Greenwood Press, 1991).

Stuckenschmidt, H. H. *Arnold Schoenberg: His Life, World and Work*, trans. Humphrey Searle (London: John Calder, 1977).

Sullivan, L. "Nikita Baliev's Le Théâtre de la Chauve-Souris: An Avant-Garde Theater," *Dance Research Journal*, 18, no. 2 (winter 1986–87), 17–29.

Szigeti, J. *With Strings Attached* (London: Cassell, 1949).

Taper, B. *Balanchine* (Berkeley, Los Angeles, and London: University of California Press, 1984).

Tappolet, C. (ed.). *Correspondance Ansermet–Ramuz (1906–1941)* (Geneva: Georg, 1989).

Tappolet, W. "Strawinsky en Suisse romande," *La Revue musicale suisse* (May 1942), 145–8, 172–7.

Taruskin, R. "The Dark Side of Modern Music," *New Republic* (5 September 1988), 28–34.

———. *Defining Russia Musically* (Princeton: Princeton University Press, 1997).

Taruskin, R., and R. Craft. "Jews and Geniuses: An Exchange," *New York Review of Books*, 15 June 1989, 57–8.

Tcherepnin, N. *Vospominaniya muzïkanta* (Leningrad: Muzïka, 1976).

Threlfall, R. "The Stravinsky Version of *Khovanshchina*," *Studies in Music*, 15 (1981), 106–15.

Tomkins, C. *Living Well Is the Best Revenge* (New York: Viking Press, 1971).

Tyuneyev, B. "Igor Stravinsky," *Russkaya muzïkal'naya gazeta*, 20, no. 3 (20 January 1913), 72–8.

Van Rysselberghe, M. (ed.). *Les Cahiers de la petite dame*, vol. 1 (1918–1929); vol. 2 (1929–1937) (Paris: Gallimard, 1973, 1974).

Van Vechten, C. *Music After the Great War and Other Studies* (New York: Schirmer, 1915).

Varunts, V. (ed.). *I. F. Stravinsky: Sbornik statey* (Moscow: Moscow State Conservatory, 1997).

———. "Strawinsky protestiert . . . ," *Mitteilungen der Paul Sacher Stiftung*, no. 6 (March 1993), 35–7.

Vershinina, I. *Ranniye baletï Stravinskovo* (Moscow: Nauka, 1967).

———. "Pis'ma I. Stravinskovo N. Rerikhu," *Sovetskaya muzïka*, no. 8 (1966), 57–63.

———. "Musorgsky i Stravinsky," in *M. P. Musorgsky i muzïka XX veka* (Moscow: Muzïka, 1990).

Vitol [Vitols], J. *Vospominaniya, stat'i, pis'ma* (Leningrad: Muzïka, 1969).

Vlad, R. *Stravinsky* (2nd ed.; London: Oxford University Press, 1967).

Vuillermoz, E. "Igor Strawinsky," *S.I.M. Monthly Bulletin* (15 May 1912), 15–21.

Walsh, S. "Review-Survey: Some Recent Stravinsky Literature," *Music Analysis*, 3, no. 2 (July 1984).

———. "Stravinsky and the Vicious Circle," in W. Thomas (ed.), *Composition—Performance—Reception* (Aldershot: Ashgate, 1998), 132–44.

———. "Stravinsky's Symphonies: Accident or Design?" in Craig Ayrey and Mark Everist (eds.), *Analytical Strategies and Musical Interpretation* (Cambridge: Cambridge University Press, 1996), 35–71.

———. *Stravinsky: Oedipus Rex* (Cambridge: Cambridge University Press, 1993).

———. *The Music of Stravinsky* (Oxford: Oxford University Press, 1993).

Wangermée, R. (ed.). *Paul Collaer: Correspondance avec des amis musiciens* (Sprimont: Mardaga, 1996).

White, E. W. "Stravinsky in Interview," *Tempo*, no. 97 (1971), 6–9.

———. *Stravinsky's Sacrifice to Apollo* (London: Hogarth Press, 1930).

———. *Stravinsky: The Composer and His Works* (2nd ed.; London and Boston: Faber and Faber, 1979).

Wise, C. S. "Impressions of Igor Stravinsky," *Musical Quarterly*, 2 (1916), 249–56.

Yarustovsky, B. *Igor Stravinsky* (Moscow: Sovetskiy Kompozitor, 1969).

Yastrebtsev, V. N. A. *Rimsky-Korsakov: Vospominaniya, 1886–1908*, ed. A. V. Ossovsky, 2 vols. (Leningrad: Muzgiz, 1959–60); abridged English trans. by F. Jonas, as *Reminiscences of Rimsky-Korsakov* (New York: Columbia University Press, 1985).

Zernov, N. *The Russian Religious Renaissance of the Twentieth Century* (London: Darton, Longman & Todd, 1963).

Zilbershteyn, I., and V. Samkov (eds.). *Sergey Diaghilev i russkoye iskusstvo* (Moscow: Izobraziteľnoye iskusstvo, 1982).

Ziloti, A. *Aleksandr Iľich Ziloti, 1863–1945: Vospominaniya i pis'ma* (Leningrad: Gosudarstvennoye Muzïkaľnoye Izdateľstvo, 1963).

PERMISSIONS ACKNOWLEDGMENTS

Grateful acknowledgment is made to the following for permission to reprint previously published and unpublished material:

Truman C. Bullard: Excerpts from his thesis, "The First Performance of Igor Stravinsky's *Sacre du Printemps,*" by Truman C. Bullard (1971). Reprinted by permission of Truman C. Bullard.

Dance Magazine: Excerpt from "Creation of 'Les Noces' " by Bronislava Nijinska, copyright © 1999 by *Dance Magazine.* Reprinted by permission of *Dance Magazine.*

Editions Albin Michel: Excerpts translated from *Le Journal des Annees de Guerre 1914–1918* by Romain Rolland (Paris: Editions Albin Michel, 1953). Reprinted by permission of Editions Albin Michel.

Faber and Faber Limited: Excerpts from *Conversations with Igor Stravinsky* by Igor Stravinsky and Robert Craft. Reprinted by permission of Faber and Faber Limited, London.

Farrar, Straus & Giroux, Inc.: Excerpt from "Early Years" by Pierre Monteux from *Stravinsky in the Theatre,* edited by Minna Lederman, copyright © 1949 by Dance Index–Ballet Caravan, Inc. Reprinted by permission of Farrar, Straus & Giroux, Inc.

Alfred A. Knopf: Excerpts from *Prejudices in Disguise: Articles, Essays, Reviews* by Robert Craft, copyright © 1974 by Robert Craft; excerpts from *Present Perspectives* by Robert Craft, copyright © 1984 by Robert Craft. Reprinted by permission of Alfred A. Knopf, a division of Random House, Inc.

Alfred A. Knopf and *Faber and Faber Limited:* Excerpted material from *Stravinsky: Selected Correspondence,* vols. I, II, III, edited by Robert Craft, copyright © 1982 by Robert Craft. Rights outside the United States administered by Faber and Faber Limited, London. Reprinted by permission of Alfred A. Knopf, a division of Random House, Inc., and Faber and Faber Limited.

Marianne Olivieri-Ramuz: Excerpts translated by Stephen Walsh from *Souvenirs sur Igor Strawinsky* by C. F. Ramuz. Reprinted by permission of Marianne Olivieri-Ramuz, Pully, Switzerland.

Permissions Acknowledgments

Random House UK Ltd.: Excerpts from *Reminiscences of the Russian Ballet* by Alexandre Benois, translated by Mary Britnieva (London: Putnam, 1941). Reprinted by permission of Random House UK Ltd., London.

Simon & Schuster, Inc.: Excerpts from *Stravinsky in Pictures and Documents* by Vera Stravinsky and Robert Craft, copyright © 1978 by Vera Stravinsky, Trapezoid, Inc., and Robert Craft. Reprinted by permission of Simon & Schuster, Inc.

The Paul Sacher Stiftung: Excerpts from various documents. Reprinted by permission of The Paul Sacher Stiftung.

John Stravinsky: Excerpts from *Chroniques de ma vie* by Igor Stravinsky. Reprinted by permission of John Stravinsky on behalf of the Stravinsky Estate.

Mme. Theodore Strawinsky and *Mr. John Stravinsky:* Excerpts from the letters of Igor and Catherine Stravinsky. Reprinted by permission of Mme. Theodore Strawinsky and Mr. John Stravinsky on behalf of the Stravinsky Estate.

Richard Taruskin: Excerpts from *Stravinsky and the Russian Traditions* by Richard Taruskin (Berkeley: University of California Press, 1996). Reprinted by permission of Professor Richard Taruskin.

Thames and Hudson International Ltd.: Excerpts from *Dearest Bubushkin* edited by Robert Craft, translated by Lucia Davidova (London: Thames and Hudson, 1985), copyright © 1985 by Robert Craft; excerpts from *Igor and Vera Stravinsky: A Photograph Album* by Vera Stravinsky, Rita McCaffrey, and Robert Craft (London: Thames and Hudson, 1982), copyright © 1982 by Robert Craft. Reprinted by permission of Thames and Hudson International Ltd.

University of California Press: Excerpts from "The Emergence of Eurasianism by N. V. Riasonovsky from *California Slavic Studies,* vol. 4, copyright © 1967 by The Regents of the University of California. Reprinted by permission of University of California Press.

University of California Press and *Faber and Faber Ltd:* Excerpt from "Stravinsky's Oedipus" by Arnold Schoenberg from *Style and Idea: Selected Writings,* edited by Leonard Stein and Arnold Schoenberg, translated by Leo Black, copyright © 1975 by Belmont Music Publishers. Rights outside the United States administered by Faber and Faber Limited, London. Reprinted by permission of University of California Press and Faber and Faber Limited.

Excerpts from *Dialogues* by Igor Stravinsky and Robert Craft, copyright © 1982 by Igor Stravinsky; excerpts from *Expositions and Developments* by Igor Stravinsky and Robert Craft, copyright © 1959, 1960, 1961, 1962 by Igor Stravinsky; excerpts from *Memories and Commentaries* by Igor Stravinsky and Robert Craft, copyright © 1960 by Igor Stravinsky. Rights in the United Kingdom administered by Faber and Faber Limited, London. Reprinted by permission of University of California Press and Faber and Faber Limited.

A. P. Watt Ltd.: Article on "Les Noces" by H. G. Wells. Reprinted by permission of A. P. Watt Ltd., London, on behalf of the Literary Executors of the Estate of H. G. Wells.

ILLUSTRATION CREDITS

Paul Sacher Stiftung, Basel: Sammlung Igor Strawinsky: Fyodor Stravinsky in 1885; Igor at 15 months, Kiev; the Nosenko girls with Gavriyil Nosenko; Igor Stravinsky's house at Ustilug; Igor and Katya Stravinsky at Zagorodniy Prospect 28 with Rimsky-Korsakov; Igor and Katya Stravinsky, St. Petersburg, 1906; Debussy and Stravinsky; Massine, Goncharova, Larionov, Stravinsky, and Bakst at Ouchy; with Ramuz and the family of the painter Albert Muret; with Lydia Lopukhova at Anglet; Katya Stravinsky with her children; Stravinsky with his two daughters; Tanya Stravinsky; with Vera in her Paris flat; with Pierre Monteux, Barcelona; Stravinsky conducting; Arthur Lourie; rehearsing with Samuel Duschkin; at dinner with Gavriyil Paichadze; Svetik (Soulima) and Igor Stravinsky with Dushkin; rehearsing his *Capriccio* under Eugen Pabst; coaching Svetik (Soulima) in the mid-thirties

Yelena Stravinsky: Fyodor and Anna Stravinsky with Alexander and Sophie Yelachich; Kryukov Canal; Khudintsev's dacha in Oranienbaum; Stravinsky and Yelachich families at Pavlovka, 1896; Igor and Gury Stravinsky with their mother

Denise Strawinsky: the Stravinsky family at tea; with his mother at Echarvines

Central State Archive of Cinema and Photo Documents, St. Petersburg: the Gostiny Dvor, Nevsky Prospect, St. Petersburg, 1898

State Museum of Theatre and Music, St. Petersburg: Mikhail Fokine directing a rehearsal of *The Firebird*

Bibliothèque Nationale, Paris: Fokine and Karsavina in *The Firebird;* Ansermet, Diaghilev, Stravinsky, and Prokofiev

Corbis-Bettman: Stravinsky with Vaclav Nijinsky

Boosey and Hawkes Music Publishers Ltd.: a page from the *Rite of Spring* sketchbook

No credit: Stravinsky with Alexander Benois at Tivoli; Vera Sudeikin at the Café Gaillac, Paris

A NOTE ABOUT THE AUTHOR

Stephen Walsh is a critic and musicologist who has written
and broadcast extensively on Stravinsky and other aspects of
twentieth-century music. He was for some years a music critic
with *The Observer*, and has also reviewed regularly for the
London *Times*, the *Daily Telegraph*, *The Listener*, and most
recently, *The Independent*. He is currently Reader in Music at
Cardiff University, Wales.

A NOTE ON THE TYPE

This book was set in Scala, a typeface designed in 1988 by
Martin Majoor and published in 1991 as the first serious text
face by FontFont, a digital type foundry.

Composed by Creative Graphics, Allentown, Pennsylvania
Printed and bound by Quebecor Printing,
Fairfield, Pennsylvania
Designed by Anthea Lingeman

\